# THE OXFORD HANDBOOK OF CRIMINOLOGY

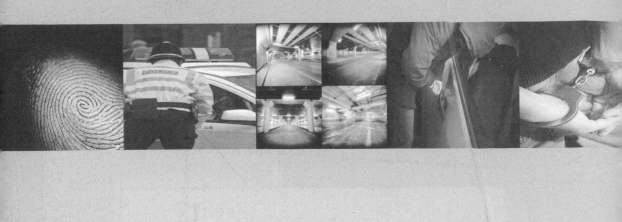

# THE OXFORD HANDBOOK OF CRIMINOLOGY

*Fifth Edition*

EDITED BY

## MIKE MAGUIRE
## ROD MORGAN
AND
## ROBERT REINER

OXFORD

UNIVERSITY PRESS

**OXFORD**
UNIVERSITY PRESS

Great Clarendon Street, Oxford, OX2 6DP,
United Kingdom

Oxford University Press is a department of the University of Oxford.
It furthers the University's objective of excellence in research, scholarship,
and education by publishing worldwide. Oxford is a registered trade mark of
Oxford University Press in the UK and in certain other countries

© Oxford University Press 2012

The moral rights of the authors have been asserted

Second edition 1997
Third edition 2002
Fourth edition 2007

Impression: 1

Public sector information reproduced under Open Government Licence v1.0
(http://www.nationalarchives.gov.uk/doc/open-government-licence/open-government-licence.htm)

Crown Copyright material reproduced with the permission of the
Controller, HMSO (under the terms of the Click Use licence)

British Library Cataloguing in Publication Data
Data available

Library of Congress Cataloging in Publication Data
Library of Congress Control Number: 2012932749

ISBN 978-0-19-959027-8

Printed in Italy by
L.E.G.O. S.p.A. – Lavis TN

# OUTLINE CONTENTS

## PART I  CRIMINOLOGY: HISTORY AND THEORY

## PART II  SOCIAL CONSTRUCTIONS OF CRIME AND CRIME CONTROL

## PART III  DIMENSIONS OF CRIME

## PART IV  FORMS OF CRIME

## PART V  REACTIONS TO CRIME

# DETAILED CONTENTS

## PART I  CRIMINOLOGY: HISTORY AND THEORY

## PART II  SOCIAL CONSTRUCTIONS OF CRIME AND CRIME CONTROL

## PART III  DIMENSIONS OF CRIME

## PART IV  FORMS OF CRIME

## PART V    REACTIONS TO CRIME

# NOTES ON CONTRIBUTORS

ANDREW ASHWORTH is Vinerian Professor of English Law and a member of the Centre of Criminology, University of Oxford.

SIR ANTHONY BOTTOMS is Emeritus Wolfson Professor of Criminology at the University of Cambridge and Honorary Professor of Criminology at the University of Sheffield.

BEN BOWLING is Professor of Criminology and Criminal Justice and Director of Criminological Studies in the School of Law, King's College, London.

FIONA BROOKMAN is a Reader in Criminology and Criminal Justice and Deputy Director of the Centre for Criminology at the University of Glamorgan.

ADAM CRAWFORD is Professor of Criminology and Criminal Justice and Director of the Security and Justice Research Group in the School of Law, University of Leeds.

BEN CREWE is Deputy Director of the Cambridge Institute of Criminology's Prisons Research Centre, University of Cambridge.

DAVID DOWNES is Professor Emeritus of Social Administration at the London School of Economics.

KAREN EVANS is a Senior Lecturer in the Department of Sociology, Social Policy and Criminology at the University of Liverpool.

PENNY GREEN is Professor of Law, Head of Research and Director of the Research Degree Programme, School of Law, King's College, London.

CHRIS GREER is Senior Lecturer in Sociology and Criminology, Department of Sociology, City University, London.

KEITH HAYWARD is Professor of Criminology, School of Social Policy, Sociology and Social Research, University of Kent.

FRANCES HEIDENSOHN is Visiting Professor, Sociology Department, LSE; Emeritus Professor of Social Policy, University of London; General Editor of the *British Journal of Sociology*.

CLIVE HOLLIN is Professor of Criminological Psychology in the School of Psychology at The University of Leicester.

MIKE HOUGH is Professor of Criminal Policy and Co Director of the Institute for Criminal Policy Research at Birkbeck, University of London.

CAROLYN HOYLE is Professor of Criminology at the Centre for Criminology, University of Oxford and a Fellow of Green Templaton College, Oxford.

MARTIN INNES is Director of the Universities' Police Science Institute and Professor in the School of Social Sciences at Cardiff University.

TREVOR JONES is Reader in Criminology at the Centre for Crime, Law and Justice, School of Social Sciences, Cardiff University.

NICOLA LACEY is Senior Research Fellow, All Souls College, Oxford.

MICHAEL LEVI is Professor of Criminology at the Centre for Crime, Law and Justice, Cardiff School of Social Sciences, Cardiff University.

ALISON LIEBLING is Professor of Criminology and Criminal Justice at the University of Cambridge and Director of Cambridge Institute of Criminology's Prisons Research Centre.

IAN LOADER is Professor of Criminology, Director of the Centre of Criminology at the University of Oxford and Fellow of All Souls College, Oxford.

FRIEDRICH LÖSEL is Director of the Institute of Criminology at the University of Cambridge and Professor of Psychology at the University of Erlangen-Nuremberg, Germany.

LESLEY McARA is Professor of Penology and Head of the School of Law at the University of Edinburgh.

SUSAN McVIE is Professor of Quantitative Criminology in the School of Law at the University of Edinburgh.

MIKE MAGUIRE is Professor of Criminology and Criminal Justice at the University of Glamorgan, Emeritus Professor at Cardiff University, and Director of the Welsh Centre for Crime and Social Justice.

FIONA MEASHAM is Senior Lecturer in Criminology, Dept. of Applied Social Science, Lancaster University.

ROD MORGAN is Professor Emeritus of Criminal Justice, University of Bristol and Visiting Professor, Universities' Police Science Institute at Cardiff University.

DAVID NELKEN is Distinguished Professor of Sociology, University of Macerata; Visiting Professor of Criminology, Law Faculty, Oxford University; Distinguished Research Professor of Law, Cardiff University; Visiting Professor, Mannheim Centre of Criminology, LSE.

TIM NEWBURN is Professor of Criminology and Social Policy, London School of Economics and Political Science.

NICOLA PADFIELD is Lecturer in Law and Fellow of Fitzwilliam College, Cambridge, and a Recorder in the Crown Court.

JILL PEAY is Professor of Law, Law Department, LSE.

CORETTA PHILLIPS is Senior Lecturer in Social Policy, Social Policy Department, LSE.

PETER RAYNOR is Professor of Criminology and Criminal Justice in the Law School at Swansea University, and a former probation officer.

ROBERT REINER is Emeritus Professor of Criminology, Law Department, LSE.

JULIAN ROBERTS is Professor of Criminology at the University of Oxford and Fellow of Worcester College.

AMANDA ROBINSON is a Senior Lecturer in Criminology in the School of Social Sciences at Cardiff University.

PAUL ROCK is Emeritus Professor of Sociology, Sociology Department, LSE.

ANDREW SANDERS is Professor of Criminal Law and Criminology and Head of the Birmingham Law School at the University of Birmingham.

MARISA SILVESTRI is Senior Lecturer in Criminology, Department of Social Sciences, London South Bank University.

NIGEL SOUTH is Professor of Sociology, and Pro-Vice Chancellor (Academic Partnerships) and Faculty of Law and Management, Essex University.

RICHARD SPARKS is Professor of Criminology at the University of Edinburgh and Co-Director of the Scottish Centre for Crime and Justice Research.

TONY WARD is Reader in Law at Hull University.

JOCK YOUNG is Distinguished Professor of Criminal Justice, The Graduate Center, John Jay College of Criminal Justice, City University of New York; Professor of Sociology, School of Social Policy, Sociology and Social Research, University of Kent.

RICHARD YOUNG is Professor of Law and Policy Research, School of Law, University of Bristol.

LUCIA ZEDNER is Professor of Criminal Justice, Law Faculty; Fellow of Corpus Christi College, University of Oxford; and Conjoint Professor, Faculty of Law, University of New South Wales, Sydney

# INTRODUCTION TO THE FIFTH EDITION

## Robert Reiner, Mike Maguire, and Rod Morgan

The first edition of *The Oxford Handbook of Criminology* was published in 1994. It was launched just as criminology was beginning to expand as a graduate subject in Britain. This was of course one of our reasons for producing it. However, we certainly did not anticipate the subsequent boom in the subject, particularly at undergraduate level (CSI inspired perhaps?). This also coincided with what Rod Morgan and David Downes, in their successive chapters on the politics of law and order, identified as a new consensus on crime control that emerged after 1992/3, predicated on the legendary 'tough on crime, tough on the causes of crime' formulation, and an ensuing party political competition to be tougher than thou. The appearance of *The Oxford Handbook of Criminology* also came just before crime rates began a record fall that has been sustained until recently, although sadly we cannot claim credit for this. Altogether the *Handbook* providentially hit a widening student and practitioner market for criminology. The current economic travails raise question marks about the continuation of the benign trends in crime levels as well as the academic future for criminology and other humanities subjects, but we hope that there will continue to be an audience and a need for well-grounded and responsible analysis of crime and criminal justice.

Our basic aim (as set out in detail in the long 'Introduction to the First Edition') was to provide a reliable review of theoretical and policy debate and research in British criminology, commissioning chapters that were intended to be definitive, state of the art analyses of their particular areas. We thought this was only possible by bringing together the different leading authorities on the diverse topics, as we believed no single author or small team could know enough about them all.

We made it very clear that we were *not* seeking to impose a particular political or theoretical view on what the boundaries or nature of the subject should be. This does not mean we claimed an unattainable objectivity in our choices: we recognized that our interpretation would be challenged, as indeed it has been. Nonetheless we were seeking something like what John Rawls in *Political Liberalism* called an 'overlapping consensus' about the field. Our selection of topics was and remains neither our own personal preferences, nor a pretence to know what is important in some absolute Olympian sense. Rather it was a hypothesis about what most colleagues and students would most want to see in such a handbook. Getting to the 5th edition suggests we may not have been too far off the mark in this. One reader's comments on the Amazon website sums up our aim, and gratifyingly she suggests it worked for her. The *Handbook* is, she says, a 'one-stop shop' for essays and assignments, and several other reviewers testify to its value in getting them through their degrees.

# NEW TO THE FIFTH EDITION

As in previous editions all chapters have been thoroughly updated and revised by authors who are leading specialist experts on their topics. In addition we have added new chapters on public views about crime and justice; terrorism; state crime; out-of-court penalties; and 'what works'. We believe this continues the *Handbook*'s tradition of providing an authoritative and up-to-date guide to the major issues in crime and criminal justice.

# GUIDED TOUR OF THE ONLINE RESOURCE CENTRE

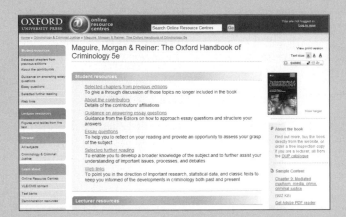

www.oxfordtextbooks.co.uk/orc/maguire5e/

The Online Resource Centre that accompanies this book provides students and lecturers with ready-to-use teaching and learning materials. These resources are free of charge and are designed to maximize the learning experience.

## STUDENT RESOURCES

### SELECTED CHAPTERS FROM PREVIOUS EDITIONS

In-depth material on topics, including the development of criminology as a discipline, and key issues such as punishment and control, and crime reduction, have been taken from the previous two editions of this text and provided in electronic format for those interested in a more thorough discussion of these topics.

This resource is password protected. The login details to enter this part of the Online Resource Centre are:

Username: maguire5e
Password: chapters

## WEB LINKS

A selection of annotated web links, chosen by the Editors, has been provided to point you in the direction of important research, statistical data, and classic texts to keep you informed of the developments in criminology both past and present.

## SELECTED FURTHER READING

Each chapter contains a list of selected further reading to enable you to develop a broader knowledge of the subject and to assist further your understanding of important issues, processes, and debates.

## ESSAY QUESTIONS

To encourage you to fully consider the key criminological issues, the Editors have written essay questions to accompany each chapter. These essay questions will help you to reflect on your reading and provide an opportunity to assess your understanding of the subject.

## ADVICE ON ANSWERING ESSAY QUESTIONS

Advice from the Editors has been included on how to approach essay questions and to structure your answers to ensure you are successful in demonstrating your knowledge and critical understanding of criminology.

# LECTURER RESOURCES

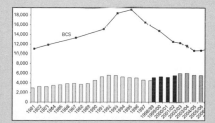

## FIGURES AND TABLES FROM THE TEXT

A selection of figures and tables from the text has been provided in high resolution format for downloading into presentation software for use in assignments and exam material.

PART I

# CRIMINOLOGY: HISTORY AND TIIEORY

# SITUATING CRIMINOLOGY: ON THE PRODUCTION AND CONSUMPTION OF KNOWLEDGE ABOUT CRIME AND JUSTICE

*Ian Loader and Richard Sparks*

## INTRODUCTION: MORE 'FOOTPRINTS IN THE SAND'

The development of social scientific theory and knowledge takes place not simply within the heads of individuals, but within particular institutional domains. These domains are, in turn, shaped by their surroundings: how academic institutions are organized, how disciplines are divided and subdivided, how disputes emerge, how research is funded, and how findings are published and used. In criminology, an understanding of these institutional domains is especially important for knowledge is situated not just, or even primarily, in the 'pure' academic world, but in the applied domain of the state's crime control apparatus. (Cohen 1988: 67)

Three decades ago, in 1981, Stanley Cohen published a report on the current state of criminology and the sociology of deviance in Britain.[1] The paper, entitled *Footprints in the Sand*, outlined the visions and divisions of the field of social scientific research and teaching on crime as Cohen observed them at the time. Cohen described the institutional locations, disciplinary affiliations, and guiding preoccupations of what he termed 'mainstream British criminology', and charted some of the key changes that occurred during the 1970s. He also mapped the formation and fractious development of the National Deviancy Conference and set out the ideas that were challenging, and seeking to transcend, the parochialism of conventional

---

[1] The report was published as one of a set of readings produced for a third-level Open University course on 'Issues in Crime and Society' (Fitzgerald *et al.* 1981). It was later reprinted in a collection of Cohen's essays (Cohen 1988). All citations are from the reprint.

criminology. His conclusion was that while at the edges of the academic field new ideas were being absorbed and accommodations made, little was happening to dent the collective self-confidence of the mainstream. 'At the centre of the criminological enterprise', Cohen remarked, 'it is business as usual' (Cohen 1988: 84).

Business was not to remain 'as usual' for much longer. Revisiting Cohen's analysis today one is struck by two things. It is clear, first of all, that Cohen was writing on the cusp of significant change—inside criminology and in the social institutions and practices within which it is enmeshed and that it strives to understand and explain. In 1981 academic criminology in Britain remained a smallish cottage industry, albeit one that had recently been given impetus by the expansion of higher education in the 1960s. It comprised a few dozen active researchers. There was no annual criminology conference. Criminological education was limited to a handful of masters' programmes and a smattering of final year options on law and sociology degrees. The idea that one could teach entire criminology degrees to undergraduates had yet to capture the imagination of any would-be course director or entrepreneurial vice-chancellor. The field had two dedicated journals—*The British Journal of Criminology* and *The Howard Journal of Criminal Justice*—and each year generated a relatively small, and manageable, number of books, articles, and reports. It was possible to read *everything* that was produced. In the intervening period criminology has boomed, in Britain and in several other jurisdictions around the world (Kerner 1998). There has, as we shall see, been a dramatic increase in the number of researchers, teachers, courses, students, conferences, books, and journals. As a result, criminology has— somewhat to the dismay of Cohen and many of his contemporaries—taken on the institutional paraphernalia of an autonomous discipline (Garland 2011). The publication and contents of this weighty *Handbook* (first published in 1994, and now in its fifth edition) are testament to this transformed state of affairs![2]

This expansion has occurred in part because the objects of criminological enquiry—crime, policing, justice, punishment, fear, victims, control, order, security—have since the 1980s come to occupy a much more prominent and disputed place in the lives and consciousness of citizens and the talk and actions of governing authorities, in Britain and in many other Western democracies (Garland 2001; Simon 2007). At the time of Cohen's essay the early sightings of this 'heating up' of the crime question were already discernable, and indeed had been astutely dissected by Cohen (1980). Rising crime rates, panics and mobilizations around youth subcultures and the 'black mugger', and police clashes with protestors and strikers had made the 1979 General Election the first in which 'law and order' figured loudly and swayed voters (Downes and Morgan 1994)—even if the institutions and settled assumptions of 'liberal elitism' and 'penal welfarism' remained largely in place (Loader 2006). But in the intervening three decades the landscapes of crime, order, and control shifted decisively (Loader and Sparks 2007). The growth of mass imprisonment, private security, and surveillance technology; the rise of penal populism and the victims' movement; the globalization of crime and development of transnational crime control networks; 9/11 and 7/7; and the advent of the internet, wall-to-wall news and new social media—all this attests to the prominent and emotive place that crime and crime control have come to assume

---

[2]  For a review of the first edition situating the *Handbook* in terms of what is says about, and what it might do to, the expanding field of criminology, see Loader and Worrall (1995).

in contemporary social relations and political culture. This prominence is plainly and intimately connected to the expansion of criminology. In our view, these altered contexts also call for fresh thinking about the field's boundaries, focus, and ambition.

The second striking—and still valuable—thing about Cohen's essay is that it has a spirit and orientation that can assist us in this task. *Footprints in the Sand* is an early exemplar of an activity that has since become more common across the social sciences—namely, the attempt to think *sociologically* about the production and consumption of knowledge, in this case criminological knowledge. To think about—and hence 'situate'—criminology in this manner is to ask where this activity is located, what its boundaries are, and what relations exist between criminology and the institutions which support it. It means attending not only to the questions, approaches, and knowledge claims that constitute the activity, but also to the conditions of possibility for different kinds of knowledge production, and to the circulation and effects of the knowledge produced. It is to study criminology not as a discipline (we do not, as will become clear, think that this is the most helpful way of thinking about it) but as a 'field', not just in its commonplace sense but also in Pierre Bourdieu's more particular application of this term. This orients enquiry towards where and how criminology is constituted, to its lines of vision and division, and to its relations to other fields—academic, legal, political, bureaucratic, journalistic, and so forth (Bourdieu 2004).

To suggest that this approach has become more common in the years since Cohen's essay was written is to point to a thriving—if rarely uncontroversial—body of work in 'science and technology studies' which has examined, *inter alia*, the laboratory practices of scientists, the politics of scientific claims-making, and the role and power of science in democratic societies (e.g. Latour 1987; Collins and Pinch 1998; Irwin and Michael 2003). To date, little of this work—and its questions and concepts—has been turned 'back' on the social sciences themselves; there is nothing like a *social* science studies of equivalent empirical depth and theoretical sophistication.[3] Such an orientation has thus only sporadically found expression in studies of criminology. There are, to be sure, several important historical accounts of the origins and development of 'the science of the criminal' which emphasize that criminology was constituted in prisons and reformatories before establishing itself as an academic subject inside universities (e.g. Garland 1988, 2002; Rafter 2009). The work of the late Richard Ericson returned time and again to the question of how criminological knowledge is produced and communicated within circuits of power (Ericson 2003). Other writers have investigated the often tense relations that exist between criminological researchers and the sponsors and users of their knowledge (Zedner 2003; Walters 2003), and one can point to a notable recent collection of reflections on the condition, borders, and futures of the field (Bosworth and Hoyle 2011). The question of criminological engagement with politics and public life has also been the subject of our own recent work (Loader and Sparks 2010). Yet research and writing about criminology as a field of enquiry remains a sporadic and unsystematic activity, lacking much historical depth. It is, moreover, often dismissed as 'navel-gazing'. Even Cohen ended his report on criminology with a warning about 'the dangers of obsessive self-reflection' (Cohen 1988: 89).

---

[3] There are, it should be said, some notable exceptions (e.g. Abbott 2001; Haney 2008; Lamont 2009; Savage 2010).

There are some obvious reasons for this impatient and sometimes dismissive attitude towards reflection on criminology. They have to do with the social and political import, and the sociological interest, of criminology's organizing questions. Cohen says that there are just three: 'Why are laws made?', 'Why are they broken?', and 'What do we do or what should we do about this?' (Cohen 1988: 9; see also Sutherland *et al.* 1992: 3). How one answers these questions has major practical and policy implications. They are also intimately entangled with individual subjectivity and well-being; the texture of collective life, and the scope, power, legitimacy, and accountability of the state and other governing authorities. These are questions that lie close to the heart of social science's abiding concern with the 'problem of order' and are inseparable from political contests regarding the nature of the good society. Given this, the sceptic asks, why would anyone trouble themselves with something as trivial as the study of *criminology* or as tedious as the activities and self-understandings of *criminologists*? We have some sympathy with this view and well understand, indeed share, an impatience to get back to more substantive questions. Yet it is precisely *because* of the close proximity of criminology's subject matter to the lives and preoccupations of citizens, and the powers and interests of governing authorities, that those who produce and consume knowledge about crime and justice ought to cultivate and sustain a reflexive awareness about the conditions under which such knowledge is (or is not) produced and the contexts in which it is used, abused, championed, derided, or ignored. Reflexivity in this sense is not a distraction from the real business of trying to answer any one of Cohen's three questions. It is a vital constituent of good social science research in respect of each of them.

These, at any rate, are the thoughts that animate our attempt in this chapter to provide a sketch—and it can only really be a sketch—of the contours of contemporary criminology.[4] We begin by focusing on the conditions and settings of criminological *production*. We describe the ways in which criminology has expanded in the years since *Footprints in the Sand* appeared and analyse the institutional arrangements and relations that condition the production of knowledge about crime and justice today. Our concern here is in thinking through some of the benefits and dangers of criminology's emergence as an autonomous 'discipline'. We turn next to the *object(s)* of criminology. We outline some of the lines of vision and division that shape the field in respect of competing accounts of what it means to produce knowledge of the social world. The range of issues that are selected for criminological scrutiny today is very wide; and the new modes and topics of enquiry that are attracting attention in today's globalized and insecure world extend from genetics to genocide. We then examine the *consumption* of criminological knowledge. Our concern here is with the audiences, forms of engagement, and visions of governance

---

[4] Much of the focus of this institutional analysis will be on criminology in Britain though we will make comparison with other jurisdictions when it seems valuable to do so. Having said this, we are aware that one of the criticisms made of earlier editions of the *Oxford Handbook* is that they were about criminology and criminal justice in Britain, or even something called 'British criminology'. We hope to make it clear that, under conditions in which justice ideas and programmes flow back and forth across borders, it makes little sense to speak of British or any other national criminology, as if they were discrete entities. There is no 'methodological nationalism' here (Wimmer and Glick Schiller 2002). Nevertheless the criminologies practised in different places around the world are significantly shaped by distinct sets of institutional locations and disciplinary traditions, as also needs to be acknowledged.

that are postulated by producers of criminological research as they go about their work. We note some of the ways in which criminology is received in the wider circuits of culture and politics, and the contests that occur between criminology and other claims to know about crime and justice, and the demands for action which flow from them. In conclusion, we suggest that this inescapably raises the question of how criminological projects are entangled with competing conceptions of the good society—and hence with politics. We argue that certain visions of politics lie buried within different conceptions of criminology and that there is merit in making these more explicit, before setting out the case for a research agenda that takes as its object of enquiry the relationship between crime, punishment, and democratic politics.

## THE FIELD OF CRIMINOLOGY

Knowledge about crime and justice doesn't just happen. Nor is it located solely in the heads and activities of the individuals who produce it. The question of what comes to be known, from what theoretical perspectives, by what methods, about what crimes, and ways of responding to crime, in what forms, and with what effects is conditioned by a whole range of institutions. These institutions employ researchers (permanently or temporarily); fund (or do not fund) research projects and programmes; permit (or refuse) access to data, research subjects and sites; offer outlets for publication; and use, abuse, champion, or ignore the products of that research. Each of these institutions— universities, research councils, charities, think tanks, consultancy firms, publishing houses, newspapers, broadcasters and new social media, campaign groups and lobbyists, political parties, prisons, police forces, government departments, and so on—are themselves situated in economic, social, and political contexts that shape how each of them think and can act. To study criminology as a 'field' is to explore how power relations and struggles between actors in these different institutional sites structure the knowledge that is (and is not) produced.[5]

One great virtue of Stanley Cohen's essay is that it sought, back in 1981, to map the field of criminology with these issues very much in mind. Cohen noted the importance to criminology in Britain since 1945 of a small number of key academic institutions, notably the Cambridge Institute of Criminology (founded with government backing in 1960—Butler 1974; Radzinowicz 1988), but also the London School of Economics and small clusters of criminological activity in Edinburgh, Oxford, and Sheffield. He also registered the size and significance of criminological research conducted within or funded by government—most importantly by the Home Office Research and Planning Unit (established in 1959—Lodge 1974) but also in research branches of the prisons department and the Metropolitan Police. Cohen further signalled the role played by 'quasi-academic bodies' (1988: 83) with reformist ambitions

---

[5] In a recent extension of Bourdieu's field theory to the sociology of punishment, Page usefully defines this field as a 'semi-autonomous, relatively bounded sphere of action in which people, groups, and organizations struggle with and against each other' (2012).

and close links to criminal justice and psychiatric practitioners. The Institute for the Study and Treatment of Delinquency, which founded and owned the *British Journal of Criminology*, was foremost among these, though mention should also be made of the Howard League for Penal Reform, a pressure group which housed the field's other key journal, the *Howard Journal of Criminal Justice*. Cohen's point was that this institutional assemblage structured the main contours of post-war British criminology. First, its 'pragmatic frame of reference' (1988: 69) and distaste for theory— its self–understanding as 'realistic', 'empirical', and 'moderate' (Radzinowicz 1999). Second, the shape of its inter-disciplinary eclecticism—Sir Leon Radzinowicz, founding Director of the Cambridge Institute and the towering figure of mid-twentieth century British criminology, viewed inter-disciplinary criminology in the following terms: 'A psychiatrist, a social psychologist, a penologist, a lawyer, a statistician joining together on a combined research operation' (1961: 177). Third, criminology's orientation to the task of producing what it saw as an effective and humane—in short, a 'civilized'—justice system. Finally, its remote and mutually suspicious relation to sociology.

Cohen also set out, however, to describe the intellectual and political challenges that were beginning to emerge to this conception of criminology and its relation to the world. A new generation of sociologists, embarking on academic careers in the new universities of the 1960s, and embroiled in the political and cultural tumult of that decade, brought new objects of enquiry to the fore: deviance, social control, political conflict and state violence, police power, ideology and the manufacture of news, not to mention the reflexive and intentionally subversive re-examination of the claims and effects of criminology itself which were so much at issue in Cohen's essay and in other writing of the period. New theoretical perspectives and concepts were imported (from the US and from elsewhere in the social sciences) and put to use: appreciation, labelling, moral panics, symbolic interactionism, anti-psychiatry, Marxism, and feminism. New institutions were assembled to provide a platform for these perspectives and to build alliances with radical social workers and lawyers, anti-psychiatrists, students, prisoners' organizations and campaigns against state violence. Foremost among them were the aforementioned National Deviancy Conference (1968–79) and the European Group for the Study of Deviance and Social Control (founded in 1973 and still in existence). The then smallish social world of British criminology had become one of conflict and schism.[6]

What though has happened in the years since Cohen's essay was written? What does the field of criminology look like today if we try to understand it in Cohen's terms? The big theme is one of expansion across a number of dimensions. The platform for growth has been the embedding of criminology within mass higher education. The first undergraduate programme in criminology in Britain was launched at Keele University in 1991. Twenty years on, 87 UK universities teach criminology and criminal justice in single and joint degrees that number well into the hundreds. Sixty three British universities run postgraduate programmes. This development sparked a two-decade long explosion of academic posts in the field. This has in turn—in part under pressure of a governmental research assessment regime—led to a burgeoning

---

[6]  Key publications from the period include Cohen (1971), Taylor, Walton, and Young (1973, 1975), Taylor and Taylor (1975), Pearson (1975), Smart (1977), Hall *et al.* (1978), and Downes and Rock (1979).

number of textbooks, handbooks, monographs, edited volumes, and journal articles. We ourselves, and all our peers of whatever political and theoretical orientation, have been beneficiaries of and participants in the resulting boom. In Britain, much of the increasing flow of books was brought into existence by criminology's own specialist academic publisher—Willan.[7] New journals proliferated and now include (mentioning only the most prominent): *Policing and Society* (founded in 1990), *Theoretical Criminology* (1997), *Global Crime* (1999), *Punishment and Society* (1999), *Criminology and Criminal Justice* (2001), *Youth Justice* (2001), *Crime, Media, Culture* (2005), and *Feminist Criminology* (2006). The rejuvenated British Society of Criminology has over 700 members, awards numerous prizes, and runs an annual conference that reliably attracts around 500 participants. Specialist conferences are an almost weekly occurrence. However one measures it, this is a tale of rapid and remarkable growth in what was once a small and relatively obscure corner of the social sciences. One of the central ironies of this story of course is that in Britain at least it was precisely the radical, sceptical, and critical versions of criminology, those most apt to question its disciplinary pretensions, that played a leading role in stimulating its growth and institutionalization within the teaching and research programmes of the expanded university system. In this regard the boundaries, though often invested with no little emotive importance from either flank, between 'mainstream' and 'critical' versions of criminology seem increasingly blurred and confused (cf. Carlen 2011: 98). Stanley Cohen himself had perhaps the sharpest eye for the resulting ironies:

> The more successful our attack on the old regime, the more we received PhDs, tenure, publishers' contracts and research funds, appeared on booklists and examination questions, and even became directors of institutes of criminology (Cohen 1988: 8).

The expansion of criminology in Britain has been especially striking. But it is by no means uniquely a British phenomenon. Rapid growth in criminology and criminal justice programmes has also occurred in the United States, especially in the form of professional criminal justice education at state universities and colleges sponsored by the Justice Department's Law Enforcement Assistance Agency (Akers 1995; Savelsberg *et al.* 2002). Criminology and criminal justice majors now far outstrip those enrolled on sociology programmes. The annual meetings of the American Society of Criminology and the more applied Academy of Criminal Justice Sciences regularly attract over 3,000 participants. The field comprises numerous dedicated journals.[8] Across Europe, a more diverse picture can be found. In certain instances criminology has recently undergone rapid expansion, somewhat in the British manner (The Netherlands). Elsewhere, one encounters places where criminology has little autonomous institutional existence (Germany and Italy) and where its niche in respect of its 'parent' disciplines—principally law and sociology—seems relatively precarious. Certain societies have small but active and influential criminological traditions (Finland, Norway, and Sweden). In some places criminology remains a fledgling activity striving to

---

[7] In 2010, Willan was sold to the Taylor and Francis Group.

[8] Including, *Criminology* and *Criminology and Public Policy* (run by ASC), *Justice Quarterly*, (run by ACJS), *Crime and Delinquency*, *Criminal Justice and Behavior*, *Journal of Criminal Law and Criminology*, *Journal of Research in Crime and Delinquency*, *Journal of Quantitative Criminology*, and the *Journal of Interpersonal Violence*.

establish itself—whether in countries such as the Republic of Ireland and Spain, or in post-communist societies such as Estonia and Poland. Yet for all this unevenness, an overall trend towards expansion can nonetheless be discerned. The European Society of Criminology (founded in 2000) has been a key organizational conduit for this: it currently has around 850 members from some 50 countries; hosts an annual conference attracting in the region of 700 participants, and publishes the *European Journal of Criminology*.[9] One should note, finally, that criminology departments and programmes have spread across Canada, Australia, New Zealand, and South Africa, and have begun to develop in India, China, and throughout Asia (Braithwaite 2011; Smith *et al.* 2011: pt. III).

A second key theme has been that of growing autonomy: as criminology has assumed the institutional properties associated with scientific disciplines it has found a more established and discrete place inside the academic field (Garland 2011). Part of this story has to do with internal specialization. As the field of criminology has expanded so too has the effort of handling the resulting diversity (in theoretical orientations, methods, questions posed, disciplines drawn upon, commitments expressed, audiences supposed) by institutionalizing the salient differences of focus and purpose. We have discussed these multiple divisions and differentiations elsewhere, and noted the dangers of so many contending *criminologies* frequently claiming to be much more than simple subject specialisms and instead casting doubt on one another's intellectual or political credibility (Loader and Sparks 2010: ch. 1). But related risks also attach to the second aspect of criminology's growing autonomy—its separation from fields of social enquiry that have historically nourished criminological theory and research. Throughout its history, many of its leading exponents have been careful to deny that criminology is a discipline—they have indeed, like us, been attracted by its disciplinary impurity and recidivist transgression of boundaries (Braithwaite 2011: 133). For example, Savelsberg and Sampson (2002: 101) argue that criminology is a multi-disciplinary field that 'has a subject matter but no unique methodological commitment or paradigmatic theoretical framework'. Moreover, they argue, 'there are no common assumptions or guiding insights. There is no intellectual idea that animates criminology'. David Downes (1988) has, in a similar vein, famously described criminology as a 'rendezvous subject'—a field organized around a social problem which serves as a crossroads for exchange between researchers trained in more basic disciplines (sociology, psychology, law, philosophy, history, economics, political science), and is repeatedly animated and rejuvenated by ideas and concepts imported from outside.

Yet, despite these protestations, criminology's expansion has seen it assume the *organizational* properties of a discipline—separate departments, degrees, journals, conferences, and prizes as well as, over time, hiring researchers whose entire higher education has been in criminology. In this context, it is worth recalling Andrew Abbott's (2001) analysis of the cultural functions of disciplines. Disciplines, Abbott argues, have what one might call existential and epistemic purposes. In the former case, '[d]isciplines provide dreams and models both of reality and of learning. They give images of coherent discourse. They create modes of knowledge that seem, to the

---

[9] This brief overview draws heavily on the invaluable 'country surveys' that the *European Journal of Criminology* has routinely commissioned since its inception in 2004.

participants, uniquely real. Every academic knows the experience of reading work from outside of his or her discipline and knows the unsettling feeling it induces. Disciplines in fact provide the core of identity for the vast majority of intellectuals.' In the latter case:

> A cultural function of disciplines is that of preventing knowledge from becoming too abstract or overwhelming. Disciplines legitimate our necessarily partial knowledge. They define what it is permissible not to know and thereby limit the body of books one must have read. They provide a specific tradition and lineage. They provide common sets of research practices that unify groups with diverse substantive interests. Often...these various limits are quite arbitrary. (Abbott 2001: 130–1)

Abbott's point is that the organization of disciplines matters: it has material effects on knowledge production. Steve Fuller comments on these dynamics pointedly. Disciplinary boundaries, he suggests, are 'artificial barriers to the transaction of knowledge claims. Such boundaries are necessary evils that become more evil the more they are perceived as necessary' (1993: 36). Viewed in this light, the risks of criminology morphing into an autonomous 'discipline' are several. There is a risk that the field will lose connection with basic disciplines (Garland 2011: 300) in a manner that narrows intellectual horizons, insulates criminology from key ideas and debates in the social and political sciences, and generates work which lacks ambition and wider scholarly interest—or indeed which simply mis states its intellectual origins and resources and disclaims all interest in its own history (Rock 2005). This disconnection would leave criminology ill-equipped to respond to the challenges of living in globalizing, fretful, and insecure times—a point made a decade ago by Garland and Sparks (2000). There is a risk of criminological research and teaching programmes becoming more vulnerable to external influence and control in ways that orient the field towards policy-directed problem-solving and away from curiosity-driven problem-raising.[10] As Andrew Abbott reminds us: 'There is ample evidence that problem-oriented empirical work does not create enduring, self-producing communities like disciplines except in areas with stable and strongly institutionalized external clienteles like criminology' (Abbott 2001: 134). There is a risk, finally, of criminology predominantly adopting a contractor-style relationship with the most powerful of these clienteles, while losing connection with fields of social and professional practice (some of which have played significant roles in its historical development— social work, most obviously, but also public health) and with oppositional and counter-publics such as the women's movement, prisoners' rights campaigns, and civil liberties groups. Under such conditions the *policy* relevance of criminology may appear at least to be established (though we shall have more to say about this later), but its *civic* role and functions may become attenuated and obscure (see Hope 2011: 167).

The existence of 'institutionalized external clienteles' is, in fact, a key dimension of the tale we have just recounted about academic criminology. The expansion and expanded autonomy of criminology cannot be explained by internal reference to activities within the field, or even by taking account of the condition and incentive

---

[10] In an important sociological study of US criminology, Savelsberg and his colleagues have demonstrated empirically this very effect (Savelsberg *et al.* 2002, 2004; Savelsberg and Flood 2004).

structures of universities. The dramatic rise of criminology has been coincident with—and may be an effect of—what we have elsewhere described as the 'heating up' of the criminal question (Loader and Sparks 2010: ch. 3). For much of the twentieth century in Britain crime and punishment were not routinely issues of major public concern, nor did they figure prominently in contests for political office. The criminal question was for the most part managed 'off-stage' by a network of senior government officials, strategic criminal justice practitioners, and concerned but 'respectable' reform groups (Ryan 1978). These elites understood their responsibilities to be administering an effective and humane penal system (an activity in which the rehabilitative ideal played a crucial legitimating role); forging expert consensus on what were taken to be difficult—even intractable—social problems, and managing always potentially volatile 'public opinion' (Loader 2006; see also Ryan 2003). The world of 'mainstream criminology' described by Stanley Cohen in 1981 was closely aligned—ideologically and institutionally—with those circuits of elite liberal governance. As we have intimated, however, Cohen was writing on the cusp of the fall from grace of those elites and their preferred mode of governing crime.

The last three decades have seen some far-reaching changes in the place that the criminal question occupies in everyday social relations and political cultures of Britain and many other Western liberal democracies. The effort to make sense of these changes has given rise to some of the most important work and significant debate in contemporary criminology, whether in respect of the 'culture of control' (Garland 2001), 'governing through crime' (Simon 2007), or the penal effects of neo-liberalism (Reiner 2007; Wacquant 2009a). We do not have space to describe the relevant shifts in any detail. Nor can we analyse the vectors of disagreement, beyond noting that the developments these terms denote are unevenly encountered within and between states (Tonry 2007; Lacey 2008; Barker 2009); that one needs to emphasize continuities and contingency rather than epochs and catastrophes (Loader and Sparks 2004; O'Malley 2000), and that aspects of them remain actively disputed (Matthews 2005). Nevertheless, this altered landscape of governance is of great pertinence to the question of situating criminology, as we shall see. A brief—and necessarily crude—summary of key developments is therefore in order:

- *Politicization of crime.* Crime is no longer managed 'off-stage' by experts but has become the subject of political dispute and contest. As crime becomes a token of political competition governmental reactions to it are heavily swayed by short-term calculation and expediency. In this climate, crime policy comes increasingly under the influence of mass media and 'public opinion' and at the mercy of sometimes actively whipped-up popular emotion. Victims emerge as influential political actors and representatives of the public interest. The result is a policy environment that is hyperactive, volatile, and unstable, one in which it becomes difficult to make reason and evidence the drivers of what is said and done. All this is underpinned, and to some extent driven, by a heightened crime consciousness among citizens, as anxieties about crime assume a more prominent place in shaping everyday routines and social institutions.

- *Re-centring of the penal state.* In the face of rising insecurities and demands for order (generated by socio-economic precariousness and the partial retraction of social welfare) the criminal justice state becomes materially and symbolically central to the management of order and control of marginal populations. Prison 'returns' as the modal institution of social regulation and is accompanied by an era of mass penal supervision. New powers and orders proliferate to control anti-social behaviour, violent and sex offenders, and terrorism. Policing becomes more visible and pivotal to efforts to manage conflicts and assuage social anxieties. This is accompanied by a public framing of the criminal question which privileges public protection against the criminal Other.

- *A 'silent revolution' in crime control.* The reassertion of sovereign authority is accompanied by what David Garland (2001) calls 'adaptive strategies' for managing crime risk. Situational crime prevention schemes manipulate the environment to reduce opportunities for offending. Local multi-agency partnerships proliferate, as does problem-solving policing. Government makes greater efforts—through targets, inspection, and audit—to micro-manage criminal justice bureaucracies and shape outcomes. New techniques and discourses of risk management are used to predict future crime, target offenders, and address the behaviour of those under penal supervision. This is often accompanied by systemic demands for new knowledge and a greater orientation to locating crime control in an evidence base.

- *Pluralization of policing and security.* The state has become but one of a number of actors engaged in the delivery of punishment and the governance of security. Responsibility for crime prevention spreads 'downwards' to private citizens and to businesses, schools, hospitals, planners, and so on. Involvement in crime control spreads 'outwards' to the private sector whose personnel and hardware play a greater role in policing and protection and the building and management of prisons. Responsibility and capacity also spreads 'upwards' to new international and transnational bodies, including the European Union (which assumes a vital new place in cross-border policing and the control of migration), the Council of Europe, and the International Criminal Court.

- *Global flows of crime and crime policies.* Under conditions of globalization, there is acceleration in the intensity and extensity in the flow of capital, ideas, people, and goods across borders. The world becomes one of networks and flows rather than places and borders, and the conditions exist for criminal activity to be organized and take place across frontiers. But the same holds for circulation and exchange between institutional actors and policy prescriptions. We inhabit an age of transnational policy elites, mobile entrepreneurs, and global think tanks which play key roles in the international circulation of such crime control innovations as zero-tolerance, community policing, three-strikes sentencing, and penal privatization. One needs now to attend to the 'travels of the criminal question' (Melossi *et al.* 2011a). This means investigating not only the agents of diffusion, but also the forms and meanings that policies assume in different local contexts, and the reasons why some crime control techniques find it difficult, or even fail more or less completely, to travel.

What though is the impact of these socio-political transformations on the production of knowledge about crime and justice and the shape of academic criminology?

The most direct of these changes concern the relation between government and criminological knowledge production (Newburn 2011). There are of course institutional reasons why this relation is tense and prone to conflict—as, indeed, it long has since been (Zedner 2003). But the altered climate of crime governance we have just described has tended to make governments more demanding, less loyal, and, arguably, less pivotal sponsors of criminological knowledge. On the one hand, the politicized policy environment has intensified the long-standing tendency of government to directly and indirectly support research with short time horizons that answer pressing policy concerns, while also giving rise to micro-management of the research process and heightened wariness about potentially scandal-creating findings. Some who have been scarred by this new climate have used their experience to expose government's claim to be doing evidence-based policy as a fiction and to call for a boycott of official research conducted under these conditions (Hope and Walters 2008). Those on the other side of the commissioning fence routinely claim that criminology is today lacking in the required skills and appropriate disposition (Wiles 2001). On the other hand, government has increasingly resorted to other—less demanding and risky—knowledge producers, such as consultancy firms, social research companies, and a thriving 'public opinion' industry, to supply the information it requires.

Some actors in this market are attractive to the users of research simply because they deliver the product on time, in a technically competent manner, with fewer overheads and less self-regard than university-based academics. Others can exercise appeal—and persuasive, even sometimes decisive, political influence—precisely because they have a *line*, a known and readily communicated position, which, moreover, happens to align with the political preferences and prevailing rationality of governments, or aspirants to govern. The periods of ascendancy enjoyed by the inventors of certain well-known policy diagnoses (Murray 1984), recipes and interventions (Wilson and Kelling 1982; Kelling and Coles 1998), and techniques or methods (Bratton 1998) need to be understood in something like these terms (Jones and Newburn 2006; Wacquant 2009b). These innovators are no mere technicians, still less disinterested scholars. They become political players in their own right, entrepreneurs of packaged programmes and solutions, and the court philosophers to powerful policy actors. In this regard the more focal crime and punishment have become to the programmes of political parties and the decision-making of institutions (Simon 2007), and the more salient in the wider circuits of political discourse and popular culture, the more the production and exchange of knowledge about crime has seeped out from the universities and in-house government research units and become the stock-in-trade on one hand of consultants, analysts, and various more or less technical experts, and on the other of think tanks, lobbyists, campaigners, pundits, and sales-persons.

One outcome of this more contested and plural crime complex is that, even while the criminal question has become more politically charged, government—or as we might say, sometimes contentiously, 'the state'—is arguably displaced from its once pre-eminent place as the primary sponsor and recipient of criminological research. In this altered climate, police and penal professionals, private security firms, non-governmental organizations (NGOs), and pressure groups also become producers, mediators, and users of knowledge about crime and justice, as well as a source of new modes of engagement and collaboration.[11] There are dangers of 'capture' at many points in these developments, and many instances of criminology making itself all-too-readily available as a docile and un-questioning producer of serviceable knowledge for rationalizing the operations of the already powerful. Or, as John Braithwaite more polemically puts it: 'For the moment, criminology is too comfortable with itself to see the potential to leave a great intellectual legacy. It is too much a creature of capitalism to turn around and bite it the way capitalism needs to be bitten' (Braithwaite 2011: 142). But there may also be a possibility of liberation into less constrained, more democratically involved and accessible, creative, and imaginative roles as we have tried to indicate elsewhere (Garland and Sparks 2000; Loader 2010; Loader and Sparks 2010). We take up these issues in more detail in the section on the consumption of criminology below.

Let us take stock. What lessons can be taken from our brief overview of the field of criminology and its conditions of possibility? We think there are three. First, that only the most un-reflexive exponents of the criminological craft, and incurious among its students, will regard the growth and autonomy of criminology as a self-evident good. In our view, there are in fact sound reasons to pay careful attention to its potentially damaging effects, if only so one is better equipped to guard against them. Second, we have shown that the production of knowledge about crime and justice is structured by institutional contexts, not only inside the academic field, but also in terms of the relation of knowledge producers to political, bureaucratic, and journalistic fields, and their preferred forms of capital and operative rules. Institutional arrangements matter. But this should not, thirdly, lead us to an analytical stance which reduces *disposition* to *position,* closes down the space for agency, and detracts attention from debating the substantive claims of the criminology that is produced. People make their own knowledge about crime and justice. But, as Marx (1852: 15) reminds us: 'They do not make it as they please; they do not make it under self-selected circumstances, but under circumstances existing already, given and transmitted from the past.' One needs to remain mindful of this as we turn to the stuff itself.

## THE OBJECT(S) OF CRIMINOLOGY

The doubts about criminology set in early. In a brilliantly premonitory article of 1933 entitled 'Some basic problems of criminology' Jerome Hall looked across dubiously from the ostensibly higher ground of criminal law theory. In its current state of development, he said, social science looks like little more than 'social policy more or less disguised' (1933: 119). Criminology, in particular, contains 'expressions of approbation or displeasure' masquerading as objective judgements. It struck Hall as unlikely that criminology would advance beyond this condition any time soon for the primary

---

[11] Mention might be made in this context of the proliferation of quasi-academic journals which aim to straddle the worlds of knowledge production and practice. These include, *inter alia*, *Probation Journal*, *Policing, Police Practice and Research, Crime Prevention and Community Safety*, and *The Security Journal*.

reason that rather than taking a discrete scientific object of investigation it moved in a world in which 'our frames of reference have been constructed for us' (ibid.). Hall could see no necessary relation between 'wise policy' and 'the endless refinement of scientific precision' (1933: 128). The prospects for criminology were limited in that it was composed of 'several fields that overlap and intersect at so many points that it is impossible to detect any common characteristics' (1933: 132).

Much has changed in the intervening almost 80 years—but not everything. Some at least of Hall's concerns have distinct contemporary echoes, even if he wrote before almost all that we now pass on to students as the canonical (if not indeed clichéd) account of the succession of landmarks in criminological theory remained to be written. Two kinds of question resound down the decades. The first regards whether criminology ever can have or should aspire towards some form of paradigmatic unity or consensus. The second concerns the uncertain relationship between criminological knowledge and social and political action in the world.

Since Hall wrote, most serious considerations of the question of paradigmatic unity in criminology have concluded that this is at best unlikely, if not indeed actually dangerous. In what we might now view as a companion piece to Cohen's classic 1981 essay, appearing in the same volume, Jock Young precisely and formally set down a number of 'models' of criminology. Those that concerned him then were: classicism, positivism, conservatism, strain theory, new deviancy theory, and Marxism. Young compared and contrasted these positions in terms of their assumptions on a series of dichotomous dimensions—human nature (voluntarism or determinism); social order (consensus or coercion); the definition of crime (legal or social); the extent and distribution of crime (limited or extensive); the causes of crime (the individual versus society) and policy (punishment or treatment). Others have subsequently undertaken similar 'mapping' exercises—see, for example, Einstadter and Henry (2006) for one of the more stimulating recent examples.

Young was of course acutely aware that most of these models were not uniquely *criminological* theories; nor indeed were they theories of quite the same kind (Young 1981: 250). Classicism is the name given by criminologists to a certain version of social contract theory as applied to crime and punishment. Positivism is in the first instance a position in the philosophy of (social) science. Conservatism is a body of political beliefs and sensibilities. Strain theory is a sociological hypothesis with a bearing on the explanation of crime in certain kinds of social structure. New deviancy theory is self-consciously a challenge to what it construes as conventional criminology. Marxism is a materialist theory of historical development via dynamic change in the means and social relations of production and exchange. As Young observes, it is not just criminologists who think seriously about crime. Moreover, part of the point is that these disparate and uneasy bedfellows both converge and, ultimately, diverge, in some cases irreconcilably. Their disagreement is permanent, but not entirely chaotic. There will be, Young correctly predicts, no unilinear development, no single dominant theory (despite various takeover bids). There will also be, he argues even more acutely, a high degree of historical forgetfulness and naïve rediscovery (1981: 306–7). This is finally because 'the study of crime is not a marginal concern to the citizen but plunges us immediately into fundamental questions of order and morality in society and to the examination of the very basis of the civilization we live in' (1981: 307).

Rather than attempt another typology or formal exposition of positions or paradigms, we intend to follow Young's precept where we think it takes us. This means picking up the second strand of unresolved questioning echoing down the decades from Jerome Hall onwards and focusing upon the relationships between criminological theory and various forms of social action in respect of the changing world to which that theory responds. One source of guidance here is again provided by Young, writing a bit over a decade later in the first edition of this very *Handbook*. By this time, in 1994, the sample of theoretical positions that engage Young's attention have changed. The criminologies of relevance in the 1980s and 1990s are for him all ways of addressing (or denying) the conjoined crises of *aetiology* and *policy*—he terms these Left idealism/radical social constructionism; New administrative criminology; Right realism and Left realism. The substance of this particular bit of cartography is not our main concern here—seen from other vantage points in the world the mapping would have been done on a different projection, just as things look different again another 15 years on. Young's points include that these positions are themselves mainly versions of the earlier ones, a reiteration made possible by historical amnesia and seeming 'rediscovery' (cf. Rock 2005). He goes on to argue that disciplines have both an 'interior' and an 'exterior' history. The interior history involves many of the topics we have already addressed above—the nature of academic exchange, the institutional settings in which research is conducted, its funding, publishing, and so on—and hence its constitution as a viable *field*. The exterior history, meanwhile, involves the extent to which the 'interior dialogue is propelled by the exterior world'; scholars of different conviction 'clash on a terrain determined by the specificity of their society' (Young 1994: 71; see also Melossi 2008). Theory, for Young, 'emerges out of a certain social and political conjuncture' and has different uses and applications in diverse contexts around the world. Generalizations are not altogether impossible, but they do not all travel as well as their producers sometimes imagine (see Melossi *et al.* 2011a).

It is apparent nevertheless that the various criminologies, while not all by any means expressly affiliated to one or other political ideology, and by no means only conducted by overtly political people, involve distinct theories of action, depictions of institutions, assumptions regarding the feasibility of various forms of policy, visions of smaller or grander forms of 'moral invention' (O'Malley 1992), management and intervention. They claim certain kinds of social or political change—small or large—as possible and desirable and dismiss or preclude others as either unattainable or unacceptable. They feature different notions of the viability of intervention through the institutions of the criminal justice system as conventionally understood, and distinct premises regarding the effectiveness or otherwise of various modes of punishment or other species of social regulation. They envisage different kinds of relationship between the role of states in coercive social control and their activities in educational, health, or family policies and attribute different weights and significance to these. They project different and in some cases ultimately mutually exclusive images of the proper roles of government agencies and other loci of collective action, commercial or associational. They magnify some problems and dispute the relative significance of others. In other words, criminological theories may not all *be* political theories (they may be, and very frequently are, all too ignorant of the claims of political theory properly so-called— Loader and Sparks 2010: ch. 5), but they all, without exception, find their uses and applications in circumstances that are shaped and conditioned by the realm of politics and they carry implications from and for that world.

There are two primary kinds of challenge with which criminology has to come to terms today, and these are both acutely *contemporary* forms of the same challenges that Jerome Hall noted in 1933. The first, which is in some degree the *leitmotif* of this chapter, concerns the various ways in which criminology deals with its inherently *trans*-disciplinary character, at the same time as coping intelligently and productively with a range of contingent pressures and incentives towards disciplinary consolidation. The second has to do with the ways in which its practitioners estimate the relative urgency and importance of a range of substantive topics and questions, some more or less familiar but others entirely novel, and find compelling ways to speak to these before a variety of possible audiences. The latter point also by extension returns us to the vexed issue of how, by whom and with what effects, criminology is consumed and put to use, and the chances criminologists have of influencing those uses. We address these questions separately in the next section.

Every now and again somebody comes up with a more or less prescriptive view on what criminology is or should be really all about. Really it is all about variations in self-control. Really it is all about criminal events, not criminal dispositions. Really it is all about psycho-social development. Really it is all about the appropriation by states of the power to criminalize human action. Conversely, every now and again someone states that really and truly criminology has failed, or indeed cannot exist. We have discussed a number of such moves and why we think they are all implausible, at some length elsewhere (Loader and Sparks 2010: 17–26) and do not intend to rehearse that argument again now. More commonly, criminologists tend to affirm (some would say 'pay lip-service to') the principle that criminology is indeed a multi- or inter- or trans-disciplinary enterprise. Sometimes these statements are themselves disguised attempts at closure—really criminology is just a species of something else, be it psychology or sociology, to take only the most common. We ourselves are at times tempted to say that really criminology is a species of the genus 'Politics', but we know this would be reductive and over-simplify our own point and so, mostly, manage to refrain.

Criminology, we suggest, not very originally, has strong reasons to acknowledge its hybrid and cross-disciplinary status and in various ways and degrees has long done so. Since it stands at the confluence between, and seeks to engage with, a series of fields and streams of influence that constitute its subject-matter, and since these fields are of (at least) political, legal, philosophical, economic, cultural, institutional, policy, professional, practical, and personal characters, it can scarcely do otherwise. While the particular configuration of streams that are arranged around the criminal question may be unique, the dilemmas of disciplinarity arise certainly across the social sciences and in all likelihood everywhere. For this reason the question of how disciplines are constituted—how they come into being, develop, consolidate, and disperse—is itself the topic of increasing attention (Repko 2008). In the case of criminology certain terms crop up frequently. Sometimes criminology is thought of as a kind of scavenger or gleaner—it 'raids' other disciplines for what it can get out of them (e.g. Zedner 2007). Its relationship with them is somewhat opportunist, if not actually parasitic. On other occasions criminology is depicted more peaceably as having a 'bridging' function between other more separate, but more fundamental, subjects (Garland 2011: 293). As Repko (2008: 22–4) points out, such metaphors arise frequently wherever disciplinary boundaries are placed in question, or a need is sensed to transcend or subvert them.

What should we deduce from this little excursus? First, we have argued repeatedly that while criminologists continue to teach and to debate some version (but evolving and shifting versions) of a canon of known, 'classic' positions we should also cultivate a conception of criminology as a field with open, porous borders, receptive to new inputs, perhaps from unexpected quarters (Loader and Sparks 2010: ch. 5). Second, criminological theories are evaluated just like others in terms of coherence and explanatory power, evidentiary weight, accountability, originality, and so on, and not by any special or uniquely 'criminological' characteristic. None of this means, however, that debate in or about criminology is either merely chaotic or unnecessary. Criminology shares its provisional and contingent quasi-disciplinary character with many other fields of study. For these reasons we think it makes most sense to think about criminology socially and institutionally, rather than deductively or prescriptively. Richard Jones has argued that we think of 'it' as an aggregation of communities, or following Etienne Wenger, of 'communities of practice' (Wenger 1998) with certain shared, disputed, or 'brokered' 'boundary objects'.[12]

If we cannot seal the borders we cannot seal them *a priori* on any side, choosing to engage only with those forms of knowledge we find most congenial. Many students of criminology—ourselves very much included—continue to insist on seeing criminology as among 'the more social of the social sciences', to borrow a phrase Mary Douglas (1992: 12) once used in another context. That is, its disputatious and contested character is intrinsic, given that its objects of inquiry themselves belong in the domains of strife and disorder, and are characterized by conflicts over their meaning and interpretation, as much as over the practical measures undertaken towards them by way of control or redress. Crime, criminalization, sanctioning, and social control have always been socially and politically constituted at their very core. As Garland points out (2011: 307), with reference to Kitsuse and Cicourel (1963) and Hindess (1973), students of crime and its control have known this for a very long time, implying that there are few excuses for behaving as if it were either not known, or was merely of tangential relevance. Yet this in no way precludes the pursuit of more 'primary', etiological and explanatory questions about how and why people come to act in violation of law. Those questions have always had a central place among the *raisons d'être* of the field, and criminology cannot simply shrug off the legitimate expectation from various quarters that it has something to contribute to addressing them. To disclaim any such interest is to cede the relevant ground to others who may be, as Garland puts it in a slightly different context, 'innocent of all criminological theory' (2011: 302).[13] The point, rather, is to insist that such explanatory projects meet the requirements imposed in studying such a complex object, in terms of definitional precision, awareness of cultural and jurisdictional variation and contingency, of coherent connections between relevant

---

[12] Jones made this point in oral presentation at the launch of Bosworth and Hoyle's *What is Criminology?*, All Souls College, Oxford, 3 February 2011.

[13] Garland refers here to the growth of terrorism and security studies, largely in ignorance of the potential contribution of analogous themes and insights from criminology.

levels of explanation and so on. All of these considerations necessarily stand among the facts that a theory of crime has to fit.

No doubt there are criminologists—they may even be quite numerous—who would sooner carry on doing the old work in the old way. Nevertheless it seems clear that some of those who are currently conducting the more creative and original explanatory work are well aware of these conceptual problems, and take pains to address them. Recent work by investigators such as Sampson and Laub (1993, 2003), Wikström (2010a and b) and others demonstrates an enhanced awareness of, *inter alia*, the dimensions of time and space in all human action, and of the knotty and inherently contingent connections between individuals, situations, settings, communities, and actions (see generally Wikström and Sampson 2006). In this regard some of the more intriguing and potentially fruitful developments from within the heartlands of the field flow from the increasing availability of data from maturing longitudinal studies (inherently costly and demanding many years of investment and committed work).

Moreover, the world we now inhabit is one that is being re-made at every moment by scientific and technical developments. Our relations with the world of things, our communicative capacities, our social relationships, our relations with our own very bodies and identities are all in change for these reasons. Indeed much of the most sophisticated current work in the social sciences is directed towards precisely this intersection (Barnes 2000; Yearley 2005). Now more than ever, it is fruitless to attempt to defend the *social* in social science merely by building defensive walls against the natural sciences on grounds of their imputed taint of 'positivism'. We have little option but to address an environment in which knowledge drawn from genetics, neuroscience, evolutionary psychology, and other such newer socio-technical fields *will* claim application to questions of crime and punishment. One foreseeable outcome of such developments is a new set of boundary disputes in which criminologists become drawn into a series of arguments over what Ericson (2003: 43) called their disciplinary 'jurisdiction'. Another, perhaps more fruitful, response is to proceed not by reflex rejection but rather by participating in conversations that subject these developments to rigorous ethical, conceptual, and indeed sociological inquiry, the better to estimate not just the validity of their substantive claims but also their ideological effects and their potentially far-reaching roles in reconstructing the governance of crime. As Garland points out, it is criminology's fate to have as its object of study 'a state-defined social problem and the set of state and non-state practices through which [it] is managed' (2011: 305). If this makes criminology necessarily 'governmental' it seems to follow that it is compelled to track, analyse, comprehend, and critique the changing modes of knowledge and technique that bear upon the governance of crime.

One set of questions about such new scientific knowledges could be that several of them might be seen to have in common the tendency to direct attention onto the characteristics of *individuals*. In this respect, if not in all, they might appear to reproduce characteristics long associated with biological positivism, and social critiques thereof. One of the tasks fulfilled by the intellectual histories of those earlier movements (Melossi 2008; Rafter 2009) is to remind us, paraphrasing E. P. Thompson's celebrated expression, that 'the mind has walked these cliffs before', even as we struggle to accommodate to the new landscapes of knowledge that confront us now. It would indeed be regrettable if criminology were allowed to succumb to a new individualism when so many of the emergent problems and questions that currently confront the social sciences precisely demand attention to new configurations in economy, culture, technology, and social organization that circulate globally and which pose distinct and testing questions about governance, policy, institutional design at multiple levels, including the supranational. We noted above that the environment that current criminology addresses—and which constitutes what Young termed its 'exterior' history—changes continually and in dynamic ways. We identified new forms of politicization and the intensification in penal politics in many countries, the advent of new modes and techniques of management and ordering, the pluralization of policing and security, and the increasingly global flow of both crime and crime policies as prominent features of the terrain that criminology now confronts. Here we can only pick out a small number of what seem to us to be the most salient points, in terms of their implications for the production and circulation of criminological knowledge.

We have argued previously (Loader and Sparks 2007) and continue to hold that, as Bauman (2001: 11) has it, the advent of 'global figuration' is 'by far the most prominent and seminal feature of our times'. Without rehearsing our own and others' arguments in ways that space forbids, and which would in any case be redundant, we took a lead from David Held and his colleagues who conceptualize globalization in the following terms:

> A process (or set of processes) which embodies a transformation in the spatial organization of social relations and transactions—assessed in terms of their extensity, intensity, velocity and impact—generating transcontinental or interregional flows and networks of activity, interaction, and the exercise of power (Held *et al.* 1999: 16).

As numerous analysts have noted, this poses problems for the examination of 'socio ties' as distinct entities with clear boundaries and instead brings to the fore the issue of networks and flows—movements of capital, goods, people, symbols, and information across formerly separate national contexts (Castells 1996). We also took it to suggest that local social relations, and the fate of particular places, are being reconfigured in ways that contemporary social   and criminological—enquiry is only beginning to get to grips with, and that sovereign authority is no longer merely territorial, the sole prerogative of nation states, but instead also inhabits new sites of power beyond the state. Such developments certainly affect and frequently intensify social cleavages, insecurities, and inequalities (of affluence and destitution, access and exclusion, mobility and fixity). By extension we live in a time of contradictory political responses that globality has ushered forth—old fundamentalisms and violent protectionism on the one hand, new international social movements and cosmopolitan possibilities on the other.

Certain of the effects of these altered mobilities and relationships in terms both of 'transnational organized crime' and of transnational developments in policing and security are now becoming more fully registered in a range of scholarly and policy literatures, even if the scale of what is at stake in these fields can baffle and deter. As Castells (1998: 166) has aptly suggested, these are new phenomena that 'profoundly affect international and national economies, politics, security, and, ultimately, societies at large'. Certain key substantive issues thus posed—notably that of trafficking in people for purposes of sexual and economic exploitation—have latterly begun to receive more intense attention as topics of both research and intervention (e.g. Munro 2006; Lee 2007, 2011). Topics of this magnitude necessarily breach disciplinary and sectoral boundaries. They reach across national and international law and policy, development economics, gender relations, and a variety of other bodies of work; and contributions to knowledge on them arises from groups and individuals ranging from local activists and NGOs, to journalists, to some of the most powerful governmental organizations in the world. A host of similar points might be made, *inter alia*, about debates on drugs, environmental harm, migration and the criminalization of mobile populations, and terrorism and security policies.

Our point here is not to try to stipulate what criminologists or others must or should do: we have gone to some lengths elsewhere to dispute the value of such 'legislative' utterances (Loader and Sparks 2010: 20–2). Our claim is simply that while it has long been true that criminology inhabits a range of distinct sites and registers—it is as Ericson (2003: 43) put it 'a multi-disciplinary, multi-professional, multi-institutional field'—the scope, reach, and complexity of the problems that it might legitimately bear upon today is very great. This is not to presuppose, still less to try to impose, some kind of humanly unfeasible omni-competence on the part of criminologists. But it is to raise questions about their professional formation, the curricula they study and teach, their openness to multiple perspectives, and the ways in which we debate and discuss the priority that we accord to different possible topics and objects of inquiry. What, properly speaking, might be said to be the *criminological* contribution to discussions of genocide and other crimes against humanity (Hagan and Rymond-Richmond 2009; Savelsberg 2011)—and does this question still make sense?

At least three implications stand out as worthy of further brief mention. First, there is scope for criminologists to give renewed attention to the sense in which their subject is a *legal* as well as a policy field (Lacey and Zedner, this volume; Zedner 2011). This concerns not just the obvious yet somehow all-too-often neglected point that criminology has an internal relationship to problems in the definition and application of criminal sanctions—in short to criminalization and its alternatives (Simester and von Hirsch 2011). It also, in the context of the developments sketched above, suggests a need for more intense attention to a series of constitutional and jurisdictional questions, such as those raised in respect of questions of multi-level governance, international treaties and convention-compliance, and so on. This point has been well-made by Murphy and Whitty (2007) with specific regard to studies of contemporary prisons by criminologists and other social scientists, but it has wider application. They remark on what they see as the existence of a curious disciplinary divergence in which social scientists make scant reference (or none at all) to human rights, notwithstanding their increasing salience in the vocabulary of prison administration and their role in restructuring prison governance. This omission, they argue, results from some combination of disciplinary closure and over-dependence by researchers on officially-defined pragmatic and managerial considerations (ibid.: 800). The irony here is that social scientists, in failing to engage with legal scholarship, miss key aspects of what is going on.

These factors go some way towards explaining why [British] criminologists have not engaged in a sustained and informed way with human rights. That said, it remains hard to understand why the 1990s criminological turn towards the rise in *punishment* did not prompt a companion interest in the growth of *rights*-based legal constitutionalism in the United Kingdom or, more specifically, in the impact of the European Court of Human Rights on UK law in relation to matters such as prisoner release dates, disciplinary hearings, or prisoner access to legal advice and the courts (cf. Lazarus 2004).

Conversely, Murphy and Whitty suggest, while there has been some development in doctrinal and substantive discussion among lawyers of human rights, with respect to prisons as in other fields, there is still 'very little empirical literature within law on the impact of human rights [in the United Kingdom], in terms of both the initiation of rights claims and the implementation of rights norms' (2007: 801). In similar vein, but on a broader European canvas, van Zyl Smit and Snacken (2009) advert in the sub-title of their book to a concern to connect 'Penology and Human Rights'. They argue that the 'growing recognition of the human rights of prisoners in Europe, including the principle of the use of imprisonment as a last resort' (2009: xvii) is in part attributable to empirical research on the characteristics of prisons as institutions, and the effects of imprisonment, as well as to wider reflections on theories of punishment and the aims of imprisonment. These seem strong arguments for mutual learning.

Secondly, it no longer seems good enough for criminologists to focus the overwhelming bulk of their attention on the domestic concerns of a handful of the world's wealthiest nations. For all that criminologists have a long and in many cases honourable record of concern for the effects of inequalities within those nations, the field's track-record of genuine curiosity in, or concern with, the majority of the world's countries or people is limited at best. In light of the foregoing this is no longer sustainable. As Agozino (2010) sharply remarks 'Western' 'modernist' criminology has for too long 'buried its head in the snows' of Europe and North America. This has resulted, notwithstanding the efforts of a number of pioneers (e.g. Sumner 1992; Cain 2000; Agozino 2005), in a selective ignorance concerning the effects that Western policy and intervention have had, and continue to have, around the world. It distracts from the sense in which the experiences of African or Latin-American societies might temper or correct the purportedly generalizing claims of 'Anglo-Saxon' criminologies. In other words, the world ushered into being by the successive historical effects of colonialism and latterly of capitalist globalization is as connected as it is unequal—a 'multiplicity without unity', as Beck puts it (2000. 11). As one of us has noted elsewhere (Melossi et al. 2011b: 6) these concerns continue to pose as crucial the embeddedness and particularity of the criminal question in each national, historical configuration (the traditional domain, that is to say, of *comparative* criminology—Nelken, Chapter 5, this volume), at the same time as drawing attention to the ways in which various forms of *savoir* travel along lines of historical, economic, political, and linguistic influence or affinity.

One version of the latter argument has recently been canvassed eloquently and influentially by Loïc Wacquant. In Wacquant's view convergences between the language and practice of criminal justice systems round the world do not result simply from common responses to similar problems, nor yet from the pragmatic adoption or emulation of lessons or techniques. Rather, Wacquant detects the dominance of a certain set of models and slogans—'broken windows', 'zero tolerance', 'no-frills prisons', and so on—that are, in his view, integral to the ways in which 'hegemonic neoliberalism' (2009b: 5) superintends the insecurities and fears that it itself engenders.

These developments, on this account, come as a package and are actively and energetically exported by think tanks, consultants, and other evangelists for neo-liberalism and for its penological and policing solutions. In these ways, Wacquant argues, 'the dissemination of 'zero tolerance' partakes of a broader international traffic in policy formulae that binds together market rule, social retrenchment, and penal enlargement' (Wacquant 2009b: 171).

Melossi *et al.* (2011b: 9) suggest that some versions of a 'strong, diffusionist' thesis need to pay greater attention to the ways in which 'translation and translocation raise obdurate and challenging conceptual issues'. How are discourses and practices changed in the process of their movement between cultural contexts? As well as such questions of reception, however, there is an increasing requirement on Western criminologists to attend much more carefully to voices from the Global South as *producers* of criminological knowledge. The criminology of the post-colonial world (Cuneen 2011) necessarily concerns not just assimilating the often disturbing implications and effects of history but also why certain 'generic' solutions fail to apply when lifted out of context, as well as why other more contextually appropriate ones may. In these respects the discoveries and implications of African, Asian, and Latin-American scholarship, as well as studies of indigenous peoples within 'Western' countries, are likely to be among the leading and most provocative themes of the next few decades.

Thirdly, and finally for now, we need to demonstrate awareness that the world of globalization is not 'flat'. A concern with the implications of macro-level developments for criminological theory and research is not now (any more than at any other time) simply a licence for preferring the novel, the fashionable, and the sweeping over the grounded, the empirical, and the local, nor for disengaging from intricate and detailed problems of policy and politics wherever we happen to encounter them. In the midst of some potentially far-reaching transformations in the world we inhabit, there remains much to be said for research strategies that continue to attend to such things as experience, beliefs, values, sensibilities, and feeling. There is, furthermore, much to be gained from seeking to grasp aspects of global social and political change *microscopically*—through ethnography, and observation, and talking to people about the lived texture of their everyday lives. Those dimensions of social life denoted by the idea of 'culture' continue, in short, to matter and ought properly to command criminological attention.

They matter because macro-level social change of the kind we have been concerned with here filters into the lives, experiences and dispositions, of individuals and social groups (become, as it were, features of mundane culture) in ways that are uneven and never entirely predictable, and which cannot simply be 'read off' from the texts and tenets of social theory—they stand, in other words, in need of patient empirical investigation. In part, this points to the renewed significance of that rich body of enquiry concerned with how crime, order, justice, and punishment are represented through print and an increasingly bewildering and diverse array of electronic media; this being one of the principal routes through which the profane meanings of notions such as security, risk, and danger and encoded and passed into cultural circulation. The criminological gaze might also fruitfully turn (further) here towards the ways in which crime and social order figure in the lived, and always in some part local, social relations of differently-situated persons in a wide, surprising, and frequently vastly under-explored variety of places and circumstances. There remains a powerful need for what Daly, following Christie (1997), calls 'near data research' (2011: 117–19), and for an ethnographic imagination that is committed to capturing the passion and particularity of the ways in which the criminal question is lived, transacted, and fought out around the world.

## THE CONSUMPTION OF CRIMINOLOGY

Among the ways in which criminologies differ is their conception of their relation to audiences, impacts, and influences—for who and for what purposes are they written? What modes or models of influencing are envisaged by them and how successful are they in realizing these? As the field has expanded and diversified, in the ways we outline above, so the explicit or implied answers offered to these questions by different schools and practitioners have become more various and arguably more contested.

Cohen's implicit sociology of knowledge in *Footprints in the Sand* was sophisticated and appreciative, but the world it addressed seemed both smaller and in some respects less complex than the one that criminology confronts today. In its formative periods most versions of the map of possibilities of the ways in which criminology might be put to use in the world envisaged the criminologist as being on fairly intimate terms with their intended audiences. For those in the 'mainstream'—of whom, in Britain at least, Radzinowicz was the dominant and emblematic figure—this meant civil servants and senior professionals. If criminology produced knowledge-for-policy it did so in a milieu whose locale was rather more the senior common room than the laboratory. Indeed at least one alert social critic of the period, Raymond Williams (1983), argued that the informality and casual amiability of these exchanges was a key aspect of the ways in which members of the dominant intellectual and political groups maintained their dominance and reproduced a shared picture of the world. In Britain, Radzinowicz was a serial member of Royal Commissions and other august bodies, such as the Advisory Council on the Penal System (Radzinowicz 1999). Nigel Walker, Radzinowicz's successor as Director of the Cambridge Institute of Criminology, was a civil servant before he was an academic. Some analyses of the lost world of elite liberalism of the 1950s and 1960s, from the vantage point of the harder and hotter 1990s (Windlesham 1997) are sometimes also in part expression of regret for the social worlds that sustained those postures, and the easy circuits of communication that were a feature of their mode of operation.

For the radicals and critics from the 1970s onwards there were also interlocutors and reference groups, but these were of different temper— many of them previously un-represented and un-heard in academic discourse. They included prisoners, the families of people who had died in custody, and a number of less privileged practitioner groups such as youth workers. Aspirationally at least, and sometimes genuinely and effectively, the new oppositional accounts of criminology saw themselves as related to various fields of social struggle. Of these, feminism has clearly been the most durable and the one that has fundamentally affected the field, as it has most fields of research across the humanities and social sciences. There has also however been a gradually increasing acknowledgement of intersectionality vis-à-vis race and class (Sokoloff and Burgess-Proctor 2011).

In sum, the space of positions for policy and political engagement in the world that Cohen addressed in 1981 seemed somewhat simpler. There was 'mainstream' criminology directed principally towards government; and there were the radical criminologies assembled within the NDC oriented to new social movements and radicalized professionals. This distinction is arguably of limited utility in a world in which criminology has expanded and diversified and in which the politics of the criminal question have heated up. To think about these matters today raises a number of questions. For example: Who are the postulated audiences for criminological research? If criminological knowledge today circulates in a more contested space, what other discourses and interests surround and intersect with it? How does criminological work engage with the worlds of politics, policy, and the media? Are there beneficial by-products of the hotter climate, for example because things become more explicit and more clearly problematized? In the remainder of this section we take up these questions and the issues at stake in answering them. In so doing, we use the evidence-based policy movement (EBP) in criminology, and the claims, presuppositions, and visions of politics and good governance mobilized by some key actors, as our case in point.

In our earlier discussion of the various modes of engagement of criminologists with social action and policy debates (Loader and Sparks 2010) we note that students of crime and punishment of all 'sides', factions, schools, and convictions have taken seriously the contributions of the knowledge that they produce to policy, to public discourse more broadly, to decision-making, and to professional practices of various kinds. As several thoughtful commentators have observed something of this kind is more or less foundational for the field (Ericson 2003; Garland 2011), just as it is among the originating concerns of the social sciences more generally. The positions concerned vary in their epistemological self-confidence, and in their expectations of direct influence, but they are all versions of knowledge/policy or knowledge/practice relations.

Most of the positions currently in play, in criminology as elsewhere, have an affinity with—may even be seen as versions of—one or more 'classic' attempts to resolve the problem of knowledge/policy relations that have been attempted at earlier points in the history of social science. For example, many of the current arguments of evidence-based and experimental criminology (Sherman 2009) are reminiscent of the view of the 'sciences of democracy' associated with Harold Lasswell (1951) —one which understands 'the policy analyst's operational task as focusing the attention of all those involved in policymaking so as to bring about their maximum rationality' (Hoppe 2005: 202). These views contrast somewhat with the no less celebrated accounts of Lindblom (1959) and Schön (1983). Lindblom's famous paper offers a modest vision of the capabilities of social science in an environment of 'incrementalism' and 'polyarchic competition'. Schön takes us further again in the direction of a sceptical and provisional understanding of the capabilities of knowledge to inform policy. In a famous statement he suggests that:

There is a high, hard ground where practitioners can make effective use of research-based theory and technique, and there is a swampy lowland where situations are confusing 'messes' incapable of technical solution. The difficulty is that the problems of the high ground, however great their technical interest, are often relatively unimportant to clients or to the large society, while in the swamp are the problems of greatest human concern. Shall the practitioner stay on the high, hard ground where he can practice rigorously, as he understands rigor, but where he is constrained to deal with problems of relatively little social importance? Or shall he descend to the swamp where he can engage the most important and challenging problems if he is willing to forsake technical rigor? [ ... ] There are those who choose the swampy lowland. They deliberately involve themselves in messy but crucially important problems and, when asked to describe their methods of inquiry, they speak of experience, trial and error, intuition, and muddling through. (Schön 1983: 42–3)

These utterances remind us of the need to acknowledge a spectrum of positions on the feasibility of scientific support for decisions. The most ebullient versions of this support envisage what Hoppe (2005: 202) calls the 'scientization of the knowledge system', characterized by the 'instrumental use or research as data', in direct support of decision-making. Most knowledge utilization, in crime policy or anywhere else, has not historically looked much like this, although advocates of EBP in criminal justice have in recent years come close to claiming that it should.

In the UK a high water-mark of the latter view came in a speech by then Labour Cabinet Minister David Blunkett in 2000. 'Tell us what works and why', the Minister enjoined. For Blunkett it is 'self-evident that decisions on Government policy ought to be informed by sound evidence' (Blunkett 2000, cited by Parsons 2002: 43). What policy-makers require is 'to be able to measure the size of the effect of A on B. This is genuine social science and reliable answers can only be reached if the best social scientists are willing to engage in this endeavour' (ibid.). This is plainly a direct governmental demand for explicit, instrumentally applicable knowledge—what one sceptical commentator called a view of evidence as things that can be 'added up, joined up and wired up' (Parsons 2002: 48). Blunkett's invitation certainly found a number of willing and conscientious takers. Nevertheless, many subsequent observations have been less sanguine than he might have hoped. There have been at least two very distinct lines of critical response to EBP in criminal justice in Britain. The first suggests that it never really happened; 'they' were not serious, or at best they were intensely (and ideologically) selective. EBP is, on this view, more rhetoric than practice, a scientific cloak for a series of thinly disguised political preferences (Hope and Walters 2008). The second says: 'it' did happen but its instrumentalism, and its association with the proliferation of governmental surveillance systems (audit trails, performance units, 'delivery' metrics, etc.) make EBP inherently tied to a command-and-control logic of knowledge production and use (Parsons 2002). Conversely, of course, there are social scientists for whom EBP is not a managerialist convenience, but an item of deeply held conviction and as-yet unrealized aspiration. On this view, the task of evidence-based or experimental criminology is to use 'the highest quality scientific research evidence available to encourage more efficacious and just public policy' (Farrington and Welsh 2007: ix), and to make it a top priority of government to cast aside 'political rhetoric and the need to satisfy a "mythical" punitive public in favour of research evidence' (ibid.). This may, as Farrington and Welsh concede, be a 'tall order'. But it is the task that evidence-based criminology has set itself.

We have argued elsewhere (Loader and Sparks 2010: ch. 2) that students of *natural* science (not just the sociologists of science, but scientists themselves) have grasped more completely than many crime and justice researchers that knowledge and politics necessarily travel together. One does not have to assume a relativist stance on the character of that knowledge in order to see this. Indeed the primary reason why the relationship between science and politics is so intense is that science really *is* transformative, creating new socio-technical possibilities and new ethical dilemmas at every moment. However if, as Zedner (2003) argues, we take sufficiently seriously the range of effects on policy and practice that criminological knowledge can and does exercise then we can see more clearly that something similar is true for it too. In that criminology relates to controversial subjects, decided politically, its role in framing those decisions, however, is neither entirely transparent nor necessarily innocent.

The question of controversy/contestability is thus of major significance in respect of the circulation and use of knowledge about crime and punishment. As Boswell points out (referring to the uses of expertise in regard to another area of intense controversy, immigration policy), under conditions of high contestation 'organizations facing opposition to their policy preferences may find it expedient to draw on additional resources to lend credibility to their views' (2008: 474). What Boswell calls 'technocratic modes of settlement' prevail when scientific evidence and analysis are accepted as legitimate criteria for adjudicating preferences. These are the conditions that the more literal versions of EBP think can or should prevail most of the time, but which Boswell and others argue are in fact rather rare (cf. Hope 2004). By contrast, 'democratic' modes prevail in policy areas in which popular support is considered decisive. Typically, these are areas in which conflict revolves around differences of values or interests, rather than competing knowledge claims (Radaelli 1999).

Boswell makes a related distinction between 'action-oriented organizations' and 'political organizations'—the former seek 'instrumental knowledge' and favour a technocratic mode of settlement. There, in principle, the question of who offers the best advice ought to be comparatively straightforward even if often technically very complicated. But many organizations breach these boundaries, and their relation to expert knowledge is more varied and ambiguous. Thus, we might suggest, a prison system is in many senses an action organization with pronounced technical needs. Policing is an action function of government in many respects and has many requirements for strictly instrumental kinds of knowledge. But these are both also political organizations, and their relation to expert knowledges is correspondingly complex. They also confront major controversies, serious normative disagreements, deploy power over other citizens, and operate in environments where public support, comprehension, and legitimation are critical problems. There is promise and risk in this. Boswell's concern is that the realities of these modes of operation dictate that expertise is commonly deployed in justification of preferences, or as Ericson put it, as rhetoric.

This is not a counsel of despair. Indeed it is not bad news at all, necessarily. Students of knowledge utilization just tell a more modulated story about the real conditions under which knowledge 'transfers' or 'is exchanged'. It is a story about differing ways of drawing and defining boundaries between the spheres of production and use, and hence differing conceptions of the 'inter-institutional contract' (not necessarily a formal contract—often a relatively informal agreement) between different kinds of actors whose work requires them to operate *across* the boundaries (Hoppe 2005). On this account, the hard, physical, masculine language of 'impact' gives way to a set of more fluid, liquid metaphors: knowledge filters, seeps, creeps, flows, and trickles. Thus Meagher *et al.* (2008: 171) argue, with reference to the increasingly obligatory vocabulary of 'impact', that:

> Impacts are most likely to arise as a result of two-way interactions, characterised by mutual respect, iterative dialogue, long-term relationships and reciprocal benefits to users and researchers. Early interactions can help to frame research questions that are both academically sound and potentially of interest to users; later iterations can help to test preliminary findings; continuing interactions as a body of work accrues can make it more likely that research understanding will make its way into policy or practice.

In our view, these reflections offer the opportunity of mediation between otherwise rather dogmatic-looking positions. There is much more to thinking about knowledge and policy (or about 'public criminology?') than simply sticking up for advocacy research in lieu of science, or vice versa. Some of the arguments ranged on either side don't stand up, especially when they try to depict the field in a binary fashion. It is mistaken to suggest that criminologists of various stripes are uninterested in public purposes. It would equally be wrong to hold that people working with a range of methods and in diverse traditions are somehow indifferent to evidence. Conversely, taking up arms against 'evidence-based policy' *as such* (because of its current local associations and rhetorical appropriations) seems an odd thing to do. Much more interesting is the argument to be had about what it means to *base* one's policies in evidence, or to enact a policy consistent with evidence etc. —and those arguments have developed further in other areas, for example in medicine but also to some extent in education, than they have so far done in criminology. We need a wider, more lateral sense of perspective. We also need a better historical perspective. It is not as if the questions of how social science 'applies', how it might be rendered democratically accountable, and which purposes it can and cannot feasibly be asked to serve, have not already been intensively debated. We might benefit, finally, from a more cosmopolitan orientation towards these questions—one that encourages us to think more systematically in a comparative way about the institutional relationships between research production and policy utilization in different countries. There is much conceptual and empirical work still to do.

## CRIMINOLOGY AND BEYOND: CRIME, PUNISHMENT, AND DEMOCRATIC POLITICS

How then should criminology respond to the landscapes of knowledge production and circulation that we have described in this chapter and the predicaments that they throw up? We have been engaged by this broad question for some time now (e.g. Loader and Sparks 2007). In recent work we argued that criminology can most coherently engage with its altered conditions of possibility and utilization—what we termed the 'heating up' of the criminal question—by interpreting its role to be that of a *democratic under-labourer* (Loader and Sparks 2010: ch. 5). We do not want to repeat the details of this argument here, nor seek to correct misreadings of our position (see, further, Loader and Sparks 2011). However, given that our efforts at 'situating criminology' in the present chapter build upon the argument made in *Public Criminology?* we want to conclude by picking up the thread of that argument and considering its implications for future work.

The first key claim is a commitment to an intellectually capacious conception of the field of criminology—to making a virtue out of the necessity of criminological pluralism. On this view, criminology needs to sustain three distinct but necessary 'moments' or dimensions, none of which can be neglected or jettisoned without cost to the field's vibrancy and purchase. We termed these the moment of *discovery* (where the primary task is the production of reliable knowledge about such matters as crime causes, patterns, and trends etc.); the *institutional-critical* moment (which seeks, *inter alia*, to explain why criminal justice stubbornly refuses to make much room for criminological reason, or why penal questions have heated up in recent years and with what effects); and the *normative* moment (which requires disciplined reflection on criminalization, the meanings of justice, proportionate punishment etc., and teasing out and articulating what is fully at stake in criminological and public debate about crime). This is not to argue that every criminological researcher, or student, or knowledge user, should be proficient across all of these dimensions. Rather, it is that there are compelling reasons to collectively organize the field in a manner that seeks to ensure that each dimension flourishes and that mutual debate and learning can take place between them. Our arguments in this chapter have been orientated to underscoring this basic point.

The second key claim pertains to criminology's long-standing, and arguably constitutive, connection to the world of practice. The argument here is that one can best give coherence to criminology's engagements with public life if one thinks of its task as that of contributing to a *better politics of crime and its regulation*. What though does this entail? It means, first, bringing criminological knowledge to bear on matters of public concern about crime and justice with the aim of 'raising the quality of political argument' about crime (Swift and White 2008: 54). In contexts where crime has become an emotive, mass-mediated and politically-charged topic, and penal practices are 'unmoored' from the 'accumulated store of criminological knowledge' (Currie 2011: 4), this is no easy task. While that task may benefit from political skills and nous, it does not mean simply becoming a politician or a lobbyist for this or that cause. Engagement in public life requires criminologists to retain an academic 'formative intention' (Collins and Evans 2007) oriented to knowledge production and to deploy that knowledge to clarify and inform, to provoke and unsettle, and to generally question the categories, assumptions, and self-understandings that make up 'common-sense' about crime. Often, in emotive, highly-charged contexts, this will require a sceptical and defensive posture—problem-raising, illusion-bursting, pouring cold-water on ill-informed punitive enthusiasms. To engage in public life as a *democratic* under-labourer means, however, that one strives to generate and extend debate, not silence the claims of others, close down argument, or play the trump card of expertise. It further requires that criminology cultivates a more cogent understanding than has been developed hitherto of the institutional contexts in which knowledge is taken-up, used, and abused—an analysis, in other words, of the condition, dynamics, and pathologies of actually existing politics and their impact upon the crime question. Our purpose in this chapter has been to further such understanding.

But we can also apprehend criminology's relation to politics in a less defensive—more forward-looking and reconstructive—sense which is oriented to redeeming the unfulfilled promise of modern democracy (Stears 2011). This entails seeking to 'make and imagine' (Unger 1987) a *better* politics of crime and its regulation. It means theorizing, researching, and experimenting with the kinds of social and political institutions that can give effect to more inclusive and deliberative democratic practices—whether in national, sub-national, or emergent transnational spaces. Given the pathologies of contemporary politics, and their deleterious impact on the governance of crime, this too is a legitimate, exciting, and urgent criminological task. It is also one that calls for a closer, more fruitful encounter than has been evident up till now between criminology and the resources of political analysis and theory.[14] Such an encounter would seek to explicate and develop the relationship between criminology's issues, problems, theories, and research, and re-thinking and renewing the institutional arrangements that govern and determine the conduct of crime control and criminal justice.

It is not our intention to make inflated claims on behalf of criminology's contribution to the better politics that we would like to encourage. Indeed we think that in certain respects a more sober evaluation of the role of social science knowledge in policy-making and politics serves to moderate (and complicate) some of the more eager hopes of the evidence-based policy movement. Yet we also argue that in our kind of society the relationship between knowledge and policy, and hence between politics and evidence, is a crucial and unavoidable one. In this regard what is at stake cannot be allowed to be reduced, corralled, or over-managed. As Parsons remarks (Parsons 2002: 56; see also Dzur 2008), contrasting the version of evidence for policy promoted in Britain by New Labour with the earlier, and grander, aspirations of Lasswell's 'sciences of democracy', the latter:

> focused on the fact that policy making took place in conditions of power inequalities and recognised that knowledge is utterly embedded in power and value contexts and relationships. The task of policy analysis was not to produce 'evidence' to drive policy, but to facilitate the clarification of values and contexts. This involved democratisation, rather than simply modernisation.

We are scarcely the first to notice the connection between crime and politics, or to pinpoint the tensions between intellectual scepticism and political commitment that arise when one practices criminology at the interface between them. Stanley Cohen—on whose shoulders we have sought to stand in this chapter—was and is an astute and

---

[14] Some important recent studies of the kind we have in mind have begun to examine empirically the effects of different political institutions and cultures on the framing of, and responses to, crime issues—e.g. Lacey (2008), Barker (2009), and Miller (2009).

engaged analyst of these issues (Cohen 1985: ch. 7; 1990; 1996). The wider intellectual project of which Cohen has long been a leading exponent can best be seen as an effort to 'politicize' crime and deviance, to remind us that the key issues at stake in their definition and control are never managerial and technical ones (Taylor *et al.* 1973). In this light, it is possible to identify, or where necessary tease out, the relations that exist between competing visions of politics and various projects of criminological theory and research. Criminological work invariably accords meaning and significance to terms such as order, justice, rights, liberty, authority, and legitimacy; or assumes a position on the powers and limits of the state and other governing authorities, or posits a view on the role of markets or citizens in crime control. In these and other ways criminology mobilizes some conception of the good—or at least a better—society. Often the relevant connections lie buried, scarcely articulated, and undefended.[15] Yet one can also find many examples of criminological work where these wider political questions are clearly in play and at issue.

Cohen once remarked that all serious thought about crime 'touches on the nature of liberalism' (1988: 14) and one can find plenty of crime and justice researchers who more or less explicitly labour in—and seek to elaborate and defend—this political tradition (von Hirsch 1996; Ashworth and Zedner 2008). But the same holds for conservatism— think of the work of James Q. Wilson (1985) and John Dilulio (1990); for socialism and social democracy (e.g. Currie 1985; Reiner 2006); in respect of the influence of feminist politics on criminology (Heidensohn 2000); in the traces of anarchism found in abolitionism and cultural criminology; in those of the environmental movement on green criminology, and of republican or communitarian political thought on the work of John Braithwaite and many other restorative justice advocates (Braithwaite and Pettit 1990). Moreover, one can find examples of criminologists becoming practically engaged in promoting various institutional 'experiments' in security and justice (O'Malley 2008). In recent years, in response to the illiberal heating up of the crime question, some authors have advocated institutions that can 'insulate' crime and punishment *from* politics (Pettit 1990; Zimring and Johnson 2006; Lacey 2008: ch. 4; Sherman 2009)—a project whose feasibility and desirability we have questioned elsewhere (Loader and Sparks 2010: ch. 4; Loader 2010). Others, however, have sought to give practical effect to alternative ways of politically framing and governing crime— notably, Clifford Shearing and his colleagues in their work on community capacity-building and John Braithwaite and many others on restorative justice (Braithwaite 2002; Shearing and Wood 2007).

Yet this open, reconstructive orientation to crime and justice remains relatively rare in the field, as O'Malley (2010) has recently noted. Criminological work is much more typically to be found problem-raising than in thinking creatively about new democratic institutions and practices. Criminologists appear to be more comfortable trading in negations than in positing goods. In part, this is a product of criminology's

---

[15] See, to take but one example, the idea of 'an evidence-based society' (Welsh and Farrington 2001: 166–9) which informs recent work in experimental criminology. One seldom, if ever, finds experimental criminologists elaborating on what such a society would look like, how it would differ from actual existing societies, or why an evidence-based society is either feasible or desirable.

focus on a contestable, state-defined social 'bad'—crime. It is partly an effect of the fact that the instruments conventionally used to respond to crime—police, courts, prisons, etc. —are themselves morally problematic; repositories of coercive power that simultaneously guarantee and threaten the liberty and security of citizens. It also flows from criminology's responsibility as a social science to pinpoint and explain unintended consequences, and highlight the capture and distortion of radical ideas and the malign outcomes of progressive reformist intentions—something for which crime control supplies plentiful historical and contemporary examples.[16] There are good reasons why criminology is a dismal science.

We do not want to devalue this sceptical, problem-raising disposition—it is a vital part of what criminology has to offer to a democratic polity. But it might usefully be supplemented by a forward-looking and imaginative 'criminology of possibilities' (O'Malley 2010: 39) capable of thinking about how to fashion a better democratic politics of crime and its regulation—a criminology that is equipped with the range of intellectual resources required to understand the shifting landscapes of crime and its control in a globalized modernity, and the imaginative capacity to think and act beyond them. This means thinking creatively about the promise, risks, and limits of democratizing crime control; about the ways in which a better democratic politics is prefigured in the present; about the social movements which might articulate it, and about the institutional design questions that must be tackled before a more equitable and deliberative democratic politics of crime can take practical shape. Criminology, in short, needs to be in the business of envisioning 'real utopias' (Olin Wright 2010).

The effort we have made in this chapter to situate criminology, and think about its changing conditions of possibility and utilization, has in the end been about supplying some background and resources for this wider undertaking. We have wanted to post a reminder to all those who produce or consume knowledge about crime and justice that criminology deals with a subject matter whose connection to politics is inescapable—and valuable. Part of what it means to live in a democracy is that we attend to matters of crime and its regulation in these terms, that we see politics as a site not only of competing interests and struggles, but of resource distribution, conflict resolution, and recursive dialogue over the terms of collective existence. Given this, there is much to be said for making these connections explicit and serious reflection and debate about them part of the criminological and wider public argument. It also gives value, legitimacy, even urgency to the idea that one does committed theoretical and empirical work on problems of crime and justice from *within* political traditions.

With all this in mind, let us conclude by revisiting Sir Leon Radzinowicz's famous portrayal of the ideal criminological research team that we cited earlier. Radzinowicz picked his team—'a psychiatrist, a social psychologist, a penologist, a lawyer, a statistician joining together on a combined research operation' back in 1961, during the heyday of modern Fabian criminology. What half a century on, in the altered social and political conditions we have described, would such an ideal criminological research outfit look like? Given what we have said about the diversity of the

---

[16] To evidence this fully would require a *very* long footnote. On one infamous case—that of 'net-widening'—see Cohen (1985).

field, it is likely that readers will pick very different teams. A serious answer to the question would, of course, also depend upon the research question at hand—as any 'Criminology 101' student knows. But if pressed to choose a team equipped for the challenges that face criminology today ours would look something like this: a political theorist, an international human rights lawyer, an urban ethnographer, an analyst of media and communications, a development economist, an international relations scholar and...

### ■ SELECTED FURTHER READING

Readers will know by now that we think Stanley Cohen's essay 'Footprints in the Sand' still repays careful reading— and the same goes for the rest of his impressive body of work. The collection of Cohen's essays, entitled *Against Criminology* (1988), is a good place to start.

Jock Young's companion essay on 'Thinking Seriously about Crime' (1981) also remains an invaluable attempt to identify what is at stake in explaining crime; Einstadter and Henry's *Criminological Theory: An Analysis of its Underlying Assumptions* extends and applies a similar framework to a larger canvass of criminological theory.

Readers interested in the historical formation of the subject can usefully start with Nicole Rafter's (2009) reader on *The Origins of Criminology*.

Dario Melossi's (2008) *Controlling Crime, Controlling Society* is a simply brilliant contextual account of the formation and development of sociological thought on crime in Europe and America close in spirit to the approach to criminology we have adopted in this essay.

Sir Leon Radzinowicz's (1999) autobiography, *Adventures in Criminology*, is a stimulating portrait of the life, work and worldly engagements of a big figure in twentieth century criminology.

Readers who want to know what the 'radicals' who assembled around the National Deviancy Conference objected to in 'mainstream' criminology, and sought to research and write about in its place, can take a look at the two collections of essays that emerged from the early conferences: *Images of Deviance* (edited by Stanley Cohen, 1971) and *Politics and Deviance* (edited by Ian Taylor and Laurie Taylor, 1975).

The social and political transformations in the governance of crime in subsequent decades are described and analysed in David Garland's *The Culture of Control* (2001), Jonathan Simon's *Governing Through Crime* (2007), and—more polemically—in Loïc Wacquant's *Punishing the Poor* (2009). The challenges that these transformations throw up for the study of crime and justice have been discussed in a number of places of late. Mary Bosworth and Carolyn Hoyle's edited collection *What is Criminology?* (2011) brings together a diverse range of scholars to discuss the condition and futures of the field. John Braithwaite's recent essay 'Opportunities and Dangers of Capitalist Criminology' (2011) treats the same issues in a characteristically insightful and trenchant way. Our own efforts to get to grips with the challenges that criminology confronts today, and to think about how crime and justice researchers can coherently engage with public life, can be found in our little book on *Public Criminology?* (2010).

As ever, the best advice for anyone who wishes to keep abreast of developments in the field is to keep a keen eye on the journals we have mentioned in the text.

# ■ REFERENCES

ABBOTT, A. (2001), *Chaos of Disciplines*, Chicago: University of Chicago Press.

AGOZINO, B. (2005), 'Crime, Criminology and Post-colonial Theory: Criminological Reflections on West Africa', in J. Sheptycki (ed.), *Transnational and Comparative Criminology*, London: Glasshouse Press.

—— (2010), 'What is Criminology?: A Control-Freak Discipline!', *African Journal of Criminology and Justice Studies* 4/1: i–xx.

AKERS, R. (1995), 'Linking Sociology and its Specialties: The Case of Criminology', *Social Forces*, 71: 1–16.

ASHWORTH, A. and ZEDNER, L. (2008), 'Defending the Criminal Law: Reflections on the Changing Character of Crime, Procedure and Sanctions', *Criminal Law and Philosophy*, 2: 21–51.

BARKER, V. (2009), *The Politics of Imprisonment*, Oxford: Oxford University Press.

BARNES, B. (2000), *Understanding Agency*, London: Sage.

BAUMAN, Z. (2001), 'Wars of the Globalization Era', *European Journal of Social Theory*, 4(1): 11–28.

BECK, U. (2000), *What is Globalization?*, Cambridge: Polity.

BLUNKETT, D. (2000), 'Influence or Irrelevance: Can Social Science Improve Government', speech to Economic and Social Research Council, 2 February.

BOSWELL, C. (2008), 'The Political Functions of Expert Knowledge: Knowledge and Legitimation in European Union Immigration Policy', *Journal of European Public Policy*, 15(4). 471–00.

BOSWORTH, M and HOYLE, C. (eds) (2011), *What is Criminology?*, Oxford: Oxford University Press.

BOURDIEU, P. (2004), *Science of Science and Reflexivity*, Cambridge: Polity.

BRAITHWAITE, J. (2002), *Restorative Justice and Responsive Regulation*, Oxford: Oxford University Press.

—— (2011), 'Opportunities and Dangers of Capitalist Criminology', in S. Parmentier, I. Aertson, J. Maesschalck, L. Paoli, and L. Walgrave (eds), *The Sparking Discipline of Criminology: John Braithwaite and the Construction of Critical Social Science and Social Justice*, Leuven: Leuven University Press.

—— and PETTIT, P. (1990), *Not Just Deserts: A Republican Theory of Criminal Justice*, Oxford: Oxford University Press.

BRATTON, W. (1998), *Turnaround: How America's Top Cop Reversed the Crime Epidemic*, New York: Random House.

BUTLER, R. (1974), 'The Foundation of the Institute of Criminology in Cambridge', in R. Hood (ed.), *Crime, Criminology and Public Policy*, London: Heinemann.

CAIN, M. (2000), 'Orientalism, Occidentalism and the Sociology of Crime', in D. Garland and R. Sparks (eds), *Criminology and Social Theory*, Oxford: Oxford University Press.

CARLEN, P. (2011), 'Against Evangelism in Academic Criminology: For Criminology as a Scientific Art', in M. Bosworth and C. Hoyle (eds), *What is Criminology?*, Oxford: Oxford University Press.

CASTELLS, M. (1996), *The Information Age: Economy, Society and Culture: Vol. I—The Rise of the Network Society*, Oxford: Basil Blackwell.

—— (1998), *The Information Age: Economy, Society and Culture: Vol. III—End of Millennium*, Oxford: Basil Blackwell.

CHRISTIE, N. (1997), 'Four Blocks Against Insight: Notes on the Over-socialization of Criminologists', *Theoretical Criminology*, 1(1): 13–23.

COHEN, S. (ed.) (1971), *Images of Deviance*, Harmondsworth: Penguin.

—— (1980), *Folk Devils and Moral Panics*, London: Paladin.

—— (1985), *Visions of Social Control*, Cambridge: Polity.

—— (1988), *Against Criminology*, New Brunswick, NJ: Transaction.

—— (1990), *Intellectual Scepticism and Political Commitment: The Case of Radical Criminology*, University of Amsterdam: Bonger Institute of Criminology.

—— (1996), 'Crime and Politics: Spot the Difference', *British Journal of Sociology*, 47(1): 1–21.

COLLINS, H. and EVANS, R. (2007), *Rethinking Expertise*, Chicago: University of Chicago Press.

COLLINS, H. and PINCH, T. (1998), *The Golem: What you Should Know about Science*, Cambridge: Cambridge University Press.

CUNEEN, C. (2011), 'Postcolonial Perspectives for Criminology', in M. Bosworth and C. Hoyle (eds), *What is Criminology?* Oxford: Oxford University Press.

CURRIE, E. (1985), *Confronting Crime: An American Challenge*, New York: Pantheon.

—— (2011), 'Thinking about Criminology', *British Journal of Criminology*, 51(4): 710–13.

DALY, K. (2011), 'Shake it up Baby: Practising Rock 'n' Roll Criminology', in M Bosworth and C. Hoyle (eds), *What is Criminology?*, Oxford: Oxford University Press.

DILULIO, J. (1990), *Governing Prisons*, New York: Simon and Schuster.

DOUGLAS, M. (1992), *Risk and Blame*, London: Routledge.

DOWNES, D. (1988), 'The Sociology of Crime and Social Control in Britain, 1960–87', in P. Rock (ed.), *A History of British Criminology*, Oxford: Oxford University Press.

—— and ROCK, P. (eds) (1979), *Deviant Interpretations*, London: Martin Robertson.

—— and MORGAN, R. (1994), ' "Hostages to Fortune": The Politics of Law and Order in Post-war Britain', in M. Maguire, R. Morgan, and R. Reiner (eds), *The*

*Oxford Handbook of Criminology*, 1st edn, Oxford: Oxford University Press.

DZUR, A. (2008), *Democratic Professionalism: Citizen Participation and the Reconstruction of Professional Ethics, Identity, and Practice*, University Park, PA: Penn State Press.

EINSTADTER, W. and HENRY, S. (2006), *Criminological Theory: An Analysis of its Underlying Assumptions*, Lanham, Maryland: Rowman & Littlefield.

ERICSON, R. (2003), 'The Culture and Power of Criminological Research', in L. Zedner and A. Ashworth (eds), *The Criminological Foundations of Penal Policy*, Oxford: Oxford University Press.

FARRINGTON, D. and WELSH, B. (2007), *Saving Children from a Life of Crime*, Oxford: Oxford University Press.

FITZGERALD, M., McLENNAN, G., and PAWSON, J. (eds) (1981), *Crime and Society: Readings in History and Theory*, Milton Keynes: Open University Press.

FULLER, S. (1993), *Philosophy of Science and Its Discontents*, London: Guilford Press.

GARLAND, D. (1988), 'British Criminology before 1935', *British Journal of Criminology*, 28(2): 1–17.

—— (2001), *The Culture of Control: Crime and Social Order in Contemporary Society*, Oxford: Oxford University Press.

—— (2002), 'Of Crimes and Criminals: The Development of Criminology in Britain', in M. Maguire, R. Morgan, and R. Reiner (eds), *The Oxford Handbook of Criminology*, 3rd edn, Oxford: Oxford University Press.

—— (2011), 'Criminology's Place in the Academic Field', in M. Bosworth and C. Hoyle (eds), *What is Criminology?*, Oxford: Oxford University Press.

—— and SPARKS, R. (2000), 'Criminology, Social Theory and the Challenge of Our Times', in D. Garland and R. Sparks (eds), *Criminology and Social Theory*, Oxford: Oxford University Press.

HAGAN, J. and RYMOND-RICHMOND, W. (2009), *Darfur and the Crime of Genocide*, Cambridge: Cambridge University Press.

HALL, J. (1933), 'Some Basic Problems of Criminology', *The ANNALS of the American Academy of Political and Social Science*, 169: 119–34.

HALL, S., CRITCHER, C., JEFFERSON, T., CLARKE, J., and ROBERTS, B. (1978), *Policing the Crisis*, London: Macmillan.

HANEY, P. (2008), *The Americanization of Social Science: Intellectuals and Public Responsibility in the Postwar United States*, Philadelphia: Temple University Press.

HEIDENSOHN, F. (2000), *Sexual Politics and Social Control*, Buckingham: Open University Press.

HELD, D., McGREW, A., GOLDBLATT, D., and PERRATON, J. (1999), *Global Transformations: Politics, Economics and Culture*, Cambridge: Polity.

HINDESS, B. (1973), *The Uses of Official Statistics in Sociology*, London: Macmillan.

HIRSCH, A. Von (1996), *Censure and Sanctions*, Oxford: Oxford University Press.

HOPE, T. (2004), 'Pretend it Works: Evidence and Governance in the Evaluation of the Reducing Burglary Initiative', *Criminology & Criminal Justice*, 4/3: 287–308.

—— (2011), 'Official Criminology and the New Crime Sciences', in M. Bosworth and C. Hoyle (eds), *What is Criminology?*, Oxford: Oxford University Press.

—— and Walters, R. (2008), *Critical Thinking about the Uses of Research*, London: Centre for Crime and Justice Studies.

HOPPE, R. (2005), 'Rethinking the Science-Policy Nexus: From Knowledge Utilization and Science Technology Studies to Types of Boundary Arrangements', *Poiesis and Praxis*, 3(3): 199–215.

IRWIN, A. and MICHAEL, M. (2003), *Science, Social Theory and Public Knowledge*, Buckingham: Open University Press.

JONES, T. and NEWBURN, T. (2006), *Policy Transfer and Criminal Justice*, Buckingham: Open University Press.

KELLING, G. and COLES, C. (1998), *Fixing Broken Windows*, New York: Free Press.

KERNER, H.-J. (1998), 'The Global Growth of Criminology', *International Annals of Criminology*, 36(1): 27–42.

KITSUSE, J. and CICOUREL, A. (1963), ' A Note on the Uses of Official Statistics', *Social Problems*, 11: 131–9.

LACEY, N. (2008), *The Prisoners' Dilemma: The Political Economy of Punishment in Comparative Perspective*, Cambridge: Cambridge University Press.

LAMONT, M. (2009), *How Professors Think: Inside the Curious World of Academic Judgement*, Camb., Mass.: Harvard University Press.

LASSWELL, H. (1951), 'The Policy Orientation', in D. Lerner and H. Lasswell (eds), *The Policy Sciences of Democracy*, Palo Alto: Stanford University Press.

LATOUR, B. (1987), *Science in Action*, Camb., Mass.: Harvard University Press.

LAZARUS, L. (2004), *Contrasting Prisoners' Rights*, Oxford: Oxford University Press.

LEE, M. (ed.) (2007), *Human Trafficking*, Cullompton: Willan.

—— (2011), *Trafficking and Global Crime Control*, London: Sage.

LINDBLOM, C. (1959), 'The Science of "Muddling Through"', *Public Administration Review*, 19(2): 79–88.

LOADER, I. (2006), 'Fall of the "Platonic Guardians": Liberalism, Criminology and Political Responses to Crime in England and Wales', *British Journal of Criminology*, 46(4): 561–86.

—— (2010), 'Is it NICE? The Appeal, Limits and Promise of Translating a Health Innovation into Criminal Justice, *Current Legal Problems*, 63: 72–91.

—— (2011), 'Playing with Fire? Democracy and the Emotions of Crime and Punishment', in S. Karstedt, I. Loader, and H. Strang (eds), *Emotions, Crime and Justice*, Oxford: Hart.

—— and WORRALL, A. (1995), 'Identikit Picture of a Subject', *Times Higher Education Supplement*. Available at: www.timeshighereducation.co.uk/story.asp?storyCode=161812&sectioncode=7.

LOADER, I. and SPARKS, R. (2004), 'For an Historical Sociology of Crime Policy in England and Wales since 1968', *Critical Review of International Social and Political Philosophy*, 7(2): 5–32.

—— and —— (2007), 'Contemporary Landscapes of Crime, Order and Control: Governance, Risk and Globalization', in M. Maguire, R. Morgan, and R. Reiner (eds), *The Oxford Handbook of Criminology*, 4th edn, Oxford: Oxford University Press.

—— and —— (2010) *Public Criminology?* London: Routledge.

—— and —— (2011), 'Criminology and Democratic Politics: A Reply to Critics', *British Journal of Criminology*, 51/4: 734–8.

LODGE, T. (1974), 'The Founding of the Home Office Research Unit', in R. Hood (ed.), *Crime, Criminology and Public Policy*, London: Heinemann.

MARX, K. (1852/2001), *The Eighteenth Brumaire of Louis Bonaparte*, Berlin: Mondial.

MATTHEWS, R. (2005), 'The Myth of Punitiveness', *Theoretical Criminology*, 9(2): 175–201.

MEAGHER, L., LYALL, C. and NUTLEY, S. (2008), 'Flows of Knowledge, Expertise and Influence: A Method for Assessing Policy and Practice Impacts from Social Science Research', *Research Evaluation* 17/3: 163–73.

MELOSSI, D. (2008), *Controlling Crime, Controlling Society*, Cambridge: Polity Press.

——, SOZZO, M., and SPARKS, R. (eds) (2011a), *The Travels of the Criminal Question*, Oxford: Hart.

——, ——, and —— (2011b), 'Introduction: Criminal Questions—Cultural Embeddedness and Global Mobilities', in D. Melossi, M. Sozzo, and R. Sparks (eds), *The Travels of the Criminal Question*, Oxford: Hart.

MILLER, L. (2009), *The Perils of Federalism: Race, Poverty, and the Politics of Crime Control*. Oxford: Oxford University Press.

MUNRO, V. (2006), 'Stopping Traffic? A Comparative Study of Responses to the Trafficking in Women for Prostitution' *British Journal of Criminology*, 46(2): 318–33.

MURPHY, T. and WHITTY, N. (2007), 'Risk and Human Rights in UK Prison Governance', *British Journal of Criminology*, 47(5): 798–816.

MURRAY, C. (1984), *Losing Ground: American Social Policy 1950–1980*, New York: Basic Books.

NEWBURN, T. (2011), 'Criminology and Government: Some Reflections on Recent Developments in England', in M. Bosworth and C. Hoyle (eds), *What is Criminology?*, Oxford: Oxford University Press.

OLIN WRIGHT, E. (2010), *Envisioning Real Utopias*, London: Verso.

O'MALLEY, P. (2000), 'Criminologies of Catastrophe? Understanding Criminal Justice on the Edge of the New Millennium', *The Australian and New Zealand Journal of Criminology*, 33: 153–67.

—— (2008), 'Experiments in Criminal Justice', *Theoretical Criminology*, 12(4): 451–69.

—— (2010) *Crime and Risk*, London: Sage.

PAGE, J. (2012), 'Punishment and the Penal Field', in J. Simon and R. Sparks (eds), *The Sage Handbook of Punishment and Society*, London: Sage.

PARSONS, W. (2002), 'From Muddling Through to Muddling Up—Evidence Based Policy Making and the Modernisation of British Government', *Public Policy and Administration*, 17(3): 43–60.

PEARSON, G. (1975), *The Deviant Imagination*, London: Macmillan.

PETTIT, P. (2001), 'Is Criminal Justice Politically Feasible?', *Buffalo Criminal Law Review* 5: 427–50.

RADAELLI, C. (1999), *Technocracy and the European Policy Process*, London: Longman.

RADINOWICZ, L. (1961), *In Search of Criminology*, London: Heinemann.

—— (1988), *The Cambridge Institute of Criminology*, London: Home Office.

—— (1999), *Adventures in Criminology*, London: Routledge.

RAFTER, N. (ed.) (2009), *The Origins of Criminology*, London: Routledge.

REINER, R. (2006), 'Beyond Risk: A Lament for Social Democratic Criminology', in T. Newburn (ed.), *The Politics of Crime Control*, Oxford: Oxford University Press.

—— (2007), *Law and Order: An Honest Citizen's Guide to Crime and Control*, Cambridge: Polity.

REPKO, A. (2008), *Interdisciplinary Research: Process and Theory*, London: Sage.

ROCK, P. (2005), 'Chronocentrism and British Criminology', *British Journal of Sociology*, 56(3). 473–791.

RYAN, M. (1978), *The Acceptable Pressure Group: A Case Study of Radical Alternatives to Prison and the Howard League*, Farnborough: Saxon House.

—— (2003), *Penal Policy and Political Culture in England and Wales*, London: Waterside Press.

SAMPSON, R and LAUB, J. (1993), *Crime in the Making: Pathways and Turning Points Through Life*, Cambridge. Mass.: Harvard University Press.

—— and —— (2003), *Shared Beginnings, Divergent Lives*, Cambridge, Mass.: Harvard University Press.

SAVAGE, M. (2010), *Identities and Change in Britain since 1940*, Oxford. Oxford University Press.

SAVELSBERG, J. (2011), *Crime and Human Rights*, London: Sage.

—— and SAMPSON, R. (2002), 'Mutual Engagement. Criminology and Sociology?', *Crime, Law and Social Change*, 37: 99–105.

—— and FLOOD, S. (2004), 'Criminological Knowledge: Period and Cohort Effects in Scholarship', *Criminology*, 42(4): 1009–41.

——, CLEVELAND, L., and KING, R. (2004), 'Institutional Environments and Scholarly Work: American Criminology, 1951–1993', *Social Forces*, 82/4: 1275–302.

——, KING, R., and CLEVELAND, L. (2002), 'Politicized Scholarship?: Science on Crime and the State', *Social Problems*, 49(3): 327–48.

SCHÖN, D. (1983), *The Reflective Practitioner. How Professionals Think in Action*, London: Temple Smith.

SHEARING, C. and WOOD, J. (2007), *Imagining Security*. Cullompton: Willan.

SHERMAN, L. (2009), 'Evidence and Liberty: The Promise of Experimental Criminology', *Criminology & Criminal Justice*, 9(1): 5–28.

SIMESTER, A. and VON HIRSCH, A. (2011), *Crimes, Harms and Wrongs*, Oxford: Hart.

SIMON, J. (2007), *Governing Through Crime: How the War on Crime Transformed American Democracy and Created a Culture of Fear*, New York: Oxford University Press.

SMART, C. (1977), *Women, Crime and Criminology*, London: RKP.

SMITH, C., ZHANG, S., and BARBALET, R. (eds) (2011), *The Routledge Handbook of International Criminology*, London: Routledge.

SOKOLOFF, N. and BURGESS-PROCTOR, A. (2011), 'Remembering Criminology's "Forgotten Theme": Seeking Justice in US Crime Policy Using an Intersectional Approach', in M. Bosworth and C. Hoyle (eds), *What is Criminology?*, Oxford: Oxford University Press.

STEARS, M. (2011), *Demanding Democracy: American Radicals in Search of a New Politics*, Princeton: Princeton University Press.

SUMNER, C. (ed.) (1982), *Crime, Justice and Underdevelopment*, London: Heinemann.

SUTHERLAND, E., CRESSEY, D., and LUCKENBILL, D. (1992), *Principles of Criminology*, 11th edn, Dix Hills, NY: General Hall.

SWIFT, A. and WHITE, S. (2008), 'Political Theory, Social Science, and Real Politics', in D. Leopold and M. Stears (eds), *Political Theory: Methods and Approaches*, Oxford: Oxford University Press.

TAYLOR, I. and TAYLOR, L. (eds) (1975), *Politics and Deviance*, Harmondsworth: Penguin.

——, WALTON, P., and YOUNG, J. (1973), *The New Criminology*, London: Routledge & Kegan Paul.

——, ——, and —— (eds) (1975), *Critical Criminology*. London: Routledge & Kegan Paul.

TONRY, M. (ed.) (2007), *Crime, Punishment and Politics in Comparative Perspective*, Chicago: University of Chicago Press.

UNGER, R. M. (1987), *Social Theory: Its Situation and Its Task*, Cambridge: Cambridge University Press.

WACQUANT, L. (2009a), *Punishing the Poor*, Durham, NC: Duke University Press.

—— (2009b), *Prisons of Poverty*, Minneapolis: University of Minnesota Press.

WALTERS, R. (2003), *Deviant Knowledge: Criminology, Politics and Policy*, Cullompton: Willan.

WELSH, B. and FARRINGTON, D. (2001), 'Toward an Evidence-Based Approach to Preventing Crime',

*The ANNALS of the American Academy of Social and Political Science*, 578: 158–73.

WENGER, E. (1998), *Communities of Practice: Learning, Meaning and Identity*, Cambridge: Cambridge University Press.

WIKSTRÖM, P.-O. (2010), 'Explaining Crime as Moral Actions', in S. Hitlin and S. Vaisey (eds), *Handbook of the Sociology of Morality*, New York: Springer.

—— (2010), 'Situational Action Theory', in B. Fisher and S. Lab (eds), *Encyclopaedia of Victimology and Crime Prevention*, Beverly Hills: Sage.

—— and SAMPSON, R. (eds), (2006) *The Explanation of Crime: Context, Mechanisms and Development*, Cambridge: Cambridge University Press.

WILES, P. (2002), 'Criminology in the 21st Century: Public Good or Private Interest?', *The Australian and New Zealand Journal of Criminology*, 35(2): 238–52.

WILLIAMS, R. (1983), *Towards 2000*, London: Chatto and Windus.

WILSON, J. Q. (1985), *Thinking About Crime* (rev edn), New York: Basic Books.

—— and KELLING, G. (1982), 'Broken Windows: The Police and Neighbourhood Safety', *Atlantic Monthly*, 249(3): 29–38.

WIMMER, A. and GLICK SCHILLER, N. (2002), 'Methodological Nationalism and Beyond', *Global Networks*, 2(4): 301–34.

WINDLESHAM, L. (1996), *Responses to Crime—Volume 3: Legislating with the Tide*, Oxford: Clarendon.

YEARLEY, S. (2005), *Making Sense of Science*, London: Sage.

YOUNG, J. (1981), 'Thinking Seriously about Crime: Some Models of Criminology', in M. Fitzgerald, G. McLennan, and J. Pawson (eds), *Crime and Society: Readings in History and Theory*, London: Routledge/Open University.

—— (1994), 'Incessant Chatter: Recent Paradigms in Criminology', in M. Maguire, R. Morgan, and R. Reiner (eds), *The Oxford Handbook of Criminology*, 1st edn, Oxford: Oxford University Press.

ZEDNER, L. (2003), 'Useful Knowledge? Debating the Role of Criminology in Post-war Britain', in L. Zedner and A. Ashworth (eds), *The Criminological Foundations of Penal Policy*, Oxford: Oxford University Press.

—— (2007), 'Pre-crime and Post-criminology', *Theoretical Criminology*, 11(2): 261–81.

—— (2011), 'Putting Crime Back on the Criminological Agenda', in M. Bosworth and C. Hoyle (eds), *What is Criminology?*, Oxford: Oxford University Press.

ZIMRING, F. and JOHNSON, D. (2006), 'Public Opinion and the Governance of Punishment in Democratic Political Systems', *The ANNALS of the American Academy of Social and Political Science* 605(1): 265–80.

ZYL SMIT, D. VAN and SNACKEN, S. (2009), *Principles of European Prison Law and Policy: Penology and Human Rights*, Oxford: Oxford University Press.

# 2

# SOCIOLOGICAL THEORIES OF CRIME

*Paul Rock*[1]

## INTRODUCTION: THE DEVELOPMENT OF CRIMINOLOGY IN BRITAIN

Criminology emerged so fitfully, discontinuously, and indecisively in Britain that its history does not lend itself easily to a coherent narrative (Rock 2011). Although it is now some 40 years old, Hermann Mannheim's account of its loosely connected stages remains as serviceable as any (1965: Vol. 1, 79). First, he said, there were private individuals working alone, and he cited as examples John Howard and Jeremy Bentham. Piers Beirne and others would call them part of an Enlightenment phase of thinking about crime and control (1994: xii) (although Garland (2002) would demur a little). One might also add that Howard, Bentham, and others were men working in a newly established tradition of social, juridical, and political improvement, often lawyers by training and Nonconformists or utilitarians by inclination, who believed in the possibility of reform through the application of reason to a welter of confusing and apparently illogical laws, institutions, and practices that composed an English and Welsh *ancien régime.* Jeremy Bentham, said John Stuart Mill, 'found the philosophy of law a chaos, he left it a science...'' (1838, republished 1950: 75).

It was a group that was tenuously united at the end of the eighteenth and the beginning of the nineteenth centuries by a copious correspondence; an independence of thought; an independence of wealth; the holding of pivotal positions as magistrates, sheriffs, and Members of Parliament; and a common membership of philanthropic societies and religious organizations (see Whitten 2002). They learned at first or second hand about conditions in Britain and elsewhere, and they cultivated in their turn the beginnings of a systematic, comparative, and investigative stance towards problems of crime, policing, and punishment. John Howard's *The State of the Prisons* of 1784, Colquhoun's *A Treatise on the Police of the Metropolis* of 1797, and Samuel Romilly's *Observations on the Criminal Law of England* of 1811 are prime examples of

[1] I am grateful to Robert Reiner for his very helpful comments on an earlier draft of this chapter.

their method. But, being largely independent individuals, they did not lay much of a foundation for an enduring tradition of research and teaching.

Second and third in Mannheim's chronology was what he described as the work of public officials acting first in a private and then in a public capacity, and he cited as examples A. M. Guerry and Cesare Lombroso (Beirne and others would call that the Positivist phase). One might again add that that second era was marked by the activity of embryonic criminologists who made use of the copious data and institutions that the newly reformed, expanding, interventionist, and increasingly wealthy state of the nineteenth century—the state that the Enlightenment reformers had built—furnished in the service of public administration. The very word 'statistic' refers to a fact bearing on the condition of the state, and it first came into use in the late 1780s, to be joined by the word 'statistician' in 1825, and they heralded the arrival of a new kind of blue book knowledge. The first population census in Britain was conducted in 1801; the new police, judicial, and penal authorities began to produce their own statistical returns after the 1830s; and a great mass of numerical data began to flood into the public realm. Chevalier remarked of that period in France that there was 'a determination to obtain figures for everything, to measure everything, to know everything, but to know it by numbers, [it was an] encyclopedic hunger' (1973: 43). The new statistics were eagerly explored by those who sought to discover patterns, commonalities, and trends in the social world: Fletcher (1850), Guerry (1864), and Quetelet (1848), above all, sought to devise a new social physics that could reveal law-like regularities of behaviour in space and time. One of the three, the Belgian, Quetelet, boldly claimed in 1846, for instance, that 'we can count in advance how many individuals will soil their hands with the blood of their fellows, how many will be swindlers, how many poisoners, almost as we can number in advance the births and deaths that will take place' (in Radzinowicz and Hood 1990: 51).

A second concomitant of the emergence of the new penitentiaries, police forces, and asylums (see Scull 1979) was the creation of a new stratum of penal administrators who managed, diagnosed, and ministered to their inmates, and claimed new mandates and fostered new intellectual disciplines to shore up their infant and somewhat fragile professional authority. There was W. D. Morrison, a prison chaplain and pioneering criminologist, the author of *Crime and its Causes*, published in 1891, and *Juvenile Offenders*, published in 1896, and the editor of the criminology series in which Lombroso's *The Criminal Woman* first appeared in English translation in 1895. There was S. A. Strahan, a doctor and lawyer, a physician at the Northampton County Asylum, and author of writings on 'instinctive criminality', criminal insanity, suicide, and morphine habituation. There was Henry Maudsley, the co-founder of the eponymous hospital, who wrote about homicidal insanity, insanity, and criminal responsibility, and other matters in the first stirrings of the new science (1888). These men established new professional associations to promote and defend their expertise—for instance, the Association of Medical Officers of Asylums and Hospitals for the Insane that was founded in 1841; and the Medico-Legal Association that was founded in 1901. And the new associations founded new journals and new stocks of knowledge (the first issue of *The Asylum Journal of Mental Science* appeared in 1853 and the first issue of the *Transactions of the Medico-Legal Society* appeared a year after the Medico-Legal Association in 1902).

The very word 'professional' appeared for the first time in 1848, to be followed by 'professionalism' eight years later, and these words signify the emergence of a new kind of expert. The new disciplines of criminal anthropology, criminal psychiatry, criminology, and medico-legal science gave them a capacity to control and speak about new problems, and it conferred a tenuous legitimacy, but they had few examples to follow, and it was to be medicine, the established science of bodily pathology, that became the principal template for their fledgling science of social pathology. British criminology took much of its form at that time, remaining for a long while a statistically driven, administratively-bent form of knowledge copying the forms of applied medicine, practised in the service of the state (see Sim 1990: 9) and adopting the language of diagnosis, prognosis, epidemiology, treatment, and rehabilitation. And, Garland would argue, it was a project that came to embody ensuing contradictions which have yet fully to be resolved: the quest, on the one hand, for a criminology as the science of the causes of crime and, on the other, for a discipline subordinate to the practical administrative demands of the state (2002).

The penultimate phase was identified by Mannheim as work undertaken by university departments or individual teachers (and by Beirne, an Englishman teaching in America, and rather parochially one might think, as the growth of criminology in the United States). By the end of the nineteenth century, enough had been accomplished by the pioneers to invite people to view a newly born criminology as a discrete perspective that could be detached from its anchorage in the applied, working practices of state institutions to be pursued as an intellectual object in its own right. The word 'criminology' was devised first in the 1850s and came into more general currency in the 1890s when it began to be taught in universities in Italy, Austria, Germany, and France. It was to be associated with a cluster of European thinkers, and particularly, and not always usefully, with Lombroso and his followers. Lombroso tended to be too fanciful, too extravagant in his mannerisms, to warrant serious consideration by the largely pragmatic and empirical scholars of the United Kingdom. His theories, said Kenny, which had been 'disseminated so quickly amongst the younger jurists of the Latin lands, did not find equally rapid acceptance in the countries of Teutonic speech. . . in the cooler latitudes of Leipzig or London or Boston, there is less reluctance to test the brilliant Italian theories by the results of old experience, and to discount their sweeping generalisations by patient analysis' (1910: 220). British criminology is not and never has been significantly Lombrosian in its affections, and when criminology did come eventually and tentatively to establish itself in Britain in the early 1920s, it was not as an offshoot of the new criminal anthropology (see Rock 2007). A university post in the discipline was created first at Birmingham University in 1921 for Maurice Hamblin Smith, and he was a Freudian-leaning psychologist (see Garland 1988: 8; Valiér 1995).

What came in time decisively to spur British criminology's growth was the flight of intellectuals from Nazi Europe in the 1930s (see Morris 1988: 24–6). Three legally trained *emigré* criminologists implanted the discipline in three universities: Leon Radzinowicz at the University of Cambridge in 1941; Max Grünhut, first at the London School of Economics in 1934, and thence in the University of Oxford in 1940, where he was appointed to the university's first lectureship in 1947; and Hermann Mannheim at the London School of Economics in 1935—and it was in that year of

1935, said Garland, that criminology was instituted as a professional academic discipline in Britain (1988: 1). Injected into English universities, virtually at a stroke, was the criminology which had been maturing apart in the universities of western Europe, but neither did it receive a ready acceptance (see Hood 2004) nor was it injected into an intellectual framework that yielded easily.

Mannheim's course on the Principles of Criminology at the LSE in the 1930s is indicative of what then passed as criminology. It was eclectic, comprehensive, and multi-disciplinary, embracing:

> I. The use of Criminal Statistics. History and present character of crime in England and abroad. II. The criminal types and the causes of crime: (1) Physical factors. The anthropological theory (Lombroso). The biological theory. The significance of physical defects. (2) Psychological and pathological factors: The intelligence of the criminal. Insanity and mental deficiency. The psychoanalytical explanation... (3) Alcoholism. Climate. Race and Religion. (4) The age factor... (5) The sex factor: Female delinquency and prostitution. (6) Social and economic factors: Family, broken homes, housing, delinquency areas... The gang. Profession and unemployment. Poverty. Economic and political crises.

What followed showed the same stamp. Thus the editorial of the first issue of the new *British Journal of Delinquency*, published in July 1950, about to become the chief vehicle of the newly institutionalized discipline, and later to be re-baptized the *British Journal of Criminology*, proclaimed:

> it is perhaps unnecessary to add that the *British Journal of Delinquency* is not in the customary sense a clinical journal. Clinical contributions will of course receive special consideration, but it is hoped to publish articles, both theoretical and practical, from trained workers in the various departments of criminology; namely, medical psychology, psychiatry, psychoanalysis, organic medicine, educational psychology, sociology, economics, anthropology, psycho-biology and statistics; also from social workers, probation officers, prison and other institutional personnel, and from forensic specialists whose work brings them into intimate contact with problems of delinquency.

That was the vein in which British criminology long remained: catholic, multi-causal, averse to a reliance on single theories and disciplines; grounded in medicine and medical metaphor; reformist, applied, and tied to the penal politics of the day. But its very eclecticism brought it about that successive generations of students were able routinely to receive instruction and conduct research across a very broad terrain. Sociologists like Terence Morris and Roger Hood could study under Hermann Mannheim or Leon Radzinowicz, and their students, like Bridget Hutter, David Downes, Stan Cohen, Paul Wiles, and Jock Young, and their students' students, like Dick Hobbs, Nigel Fielding, Ken Plummer, and Ian Taylor, could advance, refine, extend, widen, and revise criminology along a great chain of begats—and there were other centres and other lineages besides. When the great wave of university expansion was launched in England and Wales in the 1960s, when the number of universities grew from 30 to 52 in twenty years, the number of students from 130,000 to 600,000, and the number of academic staff from 19,000 to 46,000, criminology could come freely into its own, blossoming with the rest of the academy, and colonizing departments of psychology, law, social policy, and, above all, sociology. The 1970s were especially propitious: a survey conducted in

1986 revealed that nearly 60 per cent of the criminologists teaching in British universities had been appointed in that decade, and 30 per cent in the years between 1973 and 1976 alone (Rock 1988). In that take-off phase, urged on by publishers, made discontinuous with the past by a thrusting generation of newly appointed young Turks, criminology became striving, expansive, quarrelsome, factious, and open, its practitioners jostling with one another for a place in the sun (see Taylor, Walton, and Young 1973). Some established the National Deviancy Symposium in 1968 in open confrontation with what was conceived to be the old orthodoxies represented by the Institute of Criminology at the University of Cambridge and the Home Office Research Unit (S. Cohen 1971; Downes 1988). They splintered along the theoretical and political faultlines of sociology proper, refracting the larger arguments of Marxist and post-Marxist theory then in vogue, the new phenomenologies of social life, and feminism. And then, after a while and inevitably—in the 1980s and beyond—most, but not all (see Hillyard *et al.* 2004; Sumner 1994, 2004) were to become progressively reconciled to one another as new facts became available through instruments such as crime surveys, battle fatigue set in, scholars mellowed with age, and the pragmatics of having to work together continually in departments, committees, and journals began to supersede the earlier, heady pleasures of intellectual struggle. Yet what the young Turks had succeeded in constructing was an inchoate, exciting, and ambitious discipline that bore all the marks of its diverse origins, earlier quarrels, and competing aspirations, a discipline memorably described by David Downes as a 'rendezvous' subject that was shaped by the confluence of many ideas and schools around an empirical area rather than a single orthodoxy.

## SOCIOLOGICAL CRIMINOLOGY

*The Oxford English Dictionary* defined sociology as 'the study of social organization and institutions and of collective behaviour and interaction, including the individual's relationship to the group'. That is a catholic definition which encompasses almost every situation in which individuals or groups can influence one another. Sociological theories of crime are themselves correspondingly wide-reaching: they extend, for example, from an examination of the smallest detail of street encounters between adolescents and the police to comparative analyses of very large movements in nations' aggregate rates of crime over centuries (see Eisner 2003 and Spierenburg 2008), and it is sometimes difficult to determine where their boundaries should be drawn. Two of the sociological criminologists most influential in the development of the discipline once defined it in the most catholic terms as 'the body of knowledge regarding crime as a social phenomenon. It includes within its scope the processes of making laws, of breaking laws, and of reacting towards the breaking of laws' (Sutherland and Cressey 1955: 3).

There is no one, royal way to lay out the sociology of crime. In an empirically driven subdiscipline where formally different theories often contend with the same problems in very much the same way, as useful a procedure as any is to identify and describe a number of broad families of theories that share some big idea or ideas in common. The organization of the remainder of this chapter will therefore dwell on a group of intellectual themes which convey some part of the present preoccupations and environment of sociological criminology.

I shall, in particular, attend to the key issues of control, signification, and order. Crime, after all, is centrally bound up with the state's attempts to impose its will through law; with the meanings of those attempts to lawbreaker, law-enforcer, observer, and victim (Condry 2010); and with concomitant patterns of order and disorder. Criminologists differ about the weights and meanings that should be attached to those attributes: some, and control theorists in particular, would wish to be what David Matza once called 'correctionalist', that is, to use knowledge about crime to suppress it. Others would look upon the exercise of control more critically. Some are more hostile to interpretive sociology than others (see Clarke 1980). But they all feed off one another's ideas even if their practices and politics diverge. The themes I shall cover are visible features of the discipline's landscape, and I shall employ them to steer a more or less straight route through Durkheimian and Mertonian theories of anomie; control theories; rational choice theory; routine activities theory; the work of the 'Chicago School'; studies of the relations between control and space, including Newman's 'defensible space', and more recent ideas of risk and the marshalling of dangerous populations; radical criminology and Left Realism; functionalist criminology; and 'labelling theory' and cultural and subcultural analyses of crime as meaningful behaviour. I shall take it that such a grand tour should encompass most of the major landmarks which criminologists would now consider central to their field.

What this chapter cannot do, of course, is provide substantial context, history, criticism, and detail. That would be impossible in a relatively short piece, although the rest of this *Handbook* may be read as its frame. Neither is this chapter concerned with theories of penology or governance. I can hope at best to select only a few illustrative ideas that are of current or recent interest in criminology, as well as discussing some of the older arguments that informed them.

Further, like any scheme of classification, this chapter will inevitably face some problems of anomaly and overlap, not only internally but also with other chapters. If the study of crime cannot be severed from the analysis of control, the state, or gender, there will always be such problems at the margins. But this chapter should both furnish the larger contours of an introductory map of contemporary sociological theories of crime and serve as a complement to those other chapters.

# CRIME AND CONTROL

## ANOMIE AND THE CONTRADICTIONS OF SOCIAL ORDER

I shall begin by describing anomie theory, one of the most enduring and, for a while, hard-researched of all the ideas of criminological theory, and one that still persists in disguised form.

At heart, many theories take it that crime is a consequence of defective social regulation. People are said to deviate because the disciplines and authority of society are so flawed that they offer few restraints or moral direction. The idea is a very old one, antedating the emergence of sociology itself, but its formal birth into theory is linked indissolubly with anomie and the French sociologist, Émile Durkheim.

Durkheim awarded two rather different meanings to anomie, or normlessness. In *The Division of Labour in Society*, published in 1893, and in *Suicide*, published in 1897, he asserted that French society was in uneasy transition from one state of solidarity or social integration to another. A society without an elaborate division of labour rested on what he called (perhaps misleadingly) the mechanical solidarity of people who not only reacted much alike to problems, but also saw that everyone about them reacted alike to those problems, thereby lending objectivity, scale, unanimity, and solidity to moral response, and bringing a potential for massive disapproval and repression to bear down on the deviant. Such a social order was conceived to lie in the simpler past of a less differentiated pre-industrial society. The future of industrial society would be distinguished by a state of organic solidarity, the solidarity appropriate to a complex division of labour. People would then be allocated by merit and effort to very diverse positions, and they would not only recognize the legitimacy of the manner in which rewards were distributed, but also acknowledge the indispensability of what each did in his or her work for the other and for the common good. Organic solidarity would thus have controls peculiar to itself: 'Sheerly economic regulation is not enough ... there should be moral regulation, moral rules which specify the rights and obligations of individuals in a given occupation in relation to those in other occupations' (Giddens 1972: 11). People might no longer think wholly in unison, their moral response might not be substantial and undivided, but they should be able to compose their differences peaceably by means of a system of restitutive justice that made amends for losses suffered.

Durkheim's distinction between the two forms of solidarity and their accompanying modes of control was anthropologically suspect (see Llewellyn and Hoebel 1941), but it was in his analysis of the liminal state between them that criminologists were most interested. In that transition, where capitalism was thought to impose a 'forced division of labour', people acquiesced neither in the apportionment of rewards nor in the moral authority of the economy or state. They were obliged to work and act in a society that not only enjoyed little legitimacy but also exercised an incomplete control over their desires. In such a setting, it was held, 'man's nature [was to be] eternally dissatisfied, constantly to advance, without relief or rest, towards an indefinite goal' (Durkheim 1952: 256). Moral regulation was relatively deficient and people were correspondingly free to deviate, perhaps in a manner defiant towards the existing political and social arrangements (Sherman 2010). That is the first meaning Durkheim gave to anomie. His second will be visited below.

Given another, distinctively American, complexion by Robert Merton, anomie became a socially fostered state of discontent and deregulation that generated crime and deviance as part of the routine functioning of a society which promised much to everyone but actually denied them equal access to its attainment (Merton 1938). People might have been motivated to achieve success in the United States, the society on which Merton focused, but they confronted class, race, and other social differences, that manifestly contradicted the myth of openness. It was not easy for a poor, inner-city adolescent to receive sponsorship for jobs, achieve academic awards, or acquire capital. In a society where failure was interpreted as a sign of personal rather than social weakness, where failure tended to lead to individual guilt rather than to political or collective anger (Newman 2006), the pressure to succeed could be so powerful that it impelled people thus disadvantaged to bypass legitimate careers and take to illegitimate careers instead: 'the culture makes incompatible demands ... In this setting, a cardinal American virtue—"ambition"—promotes a cardinal American vice—"deviant behavior"' (Merton 1957: 145). Merton laid out a famous typology of deviant types whose critical features were allegiance to collective goals and to collective means of attaining success: chief amongst them were the innovator (who could be a criminal or an enterprising but law-observing individual); the retreatist (who might take to drugs or drink); the rebel; and the ritualist.

Merton's anomie theory was to be modified progressively for some 30 years. In the work of Richard Cloward and Lloyd Ohlin, for example, his model was elaborated to include *illegitimate* routes to success. Their *Delinquency and Opportunity* (1960) described the consequences of young American men (in the 1950s and 1960s the criminological gaze was almost wholly on the doings of young American *men*) not only being pushed into crime by the difficulties of acquiring money and position in conventional ways, but also being pulled by the lure of lucrative and unconventional criminal careers. There would be those who were offered an unorthodox path in professional or organized crime, and they could become thieves, robbers, or racketeers. There would be those for whom no path was available, and they could become members of conflict gangs. And there were those who failed to attain admission to either a law-abiding or a law-violating group, the 'double failures', who would, it was conjectured, give up and become drug-users and hustlers. Each of those modes of adaptation was, in effect, a way of life, supported by a system of meanings or a subculture, and Cloward and Ohlin provided one of the bridges between the structural and the interpretive models of crime which will be discussed towards the end of this chapter. The modes should probably not, moreover, be treated as exclusive of one another: for example, Murphy and Robinson (2008) talk about the 'maximizer' who may adopt a combination of legitimate and illegitimate routes to success.

In the work of Albert Cohen (1957), anomie was to be synthesized with the Freudian idea of 'reaction formation' in an attempt to explain the manifestly expressive and 'non-rational' nature of much delinquency. The prospect of failure was depicted as bringing about a major psychological rejection of what had formerly been sought, so that the once-aspiring working-class adolescent emphatically turned his back on the middle-class world that spurned him and adopted a style of behaviour that was its systematic inversion. The practical and utilitarian in middle-class life was transformed into non-utilitarian delinquency; respectability became malicious negativism; and the deferment of gratification became short-run hedonism. Again, in the work of David Downes, conducted in London in the early 1960s to explore how far beyond America anomie theory might be generalized, the ambitions of English adolescents were found to be so modulated by the presence of relatively abundant, albeit low-paid, jobs and what was then a stable and legitimated system of social stratification that working-class youth did not seem to undergo a taxing guilt, shame, or frustration in their failure to accomplish middle-class goals. They neither hankered after the middle-class world nor repudiated it. Rather, their response was 'dissociation'. Where they *did* experience a strong dissatisfaction, however, was in their thwarted attempts to enjoy leisure, and their delinquencies were principally hedonistic, focused on drinking, fighting, and malicious damage to property, rather than instrumentally turned towards the accumulation of wealth. And that theme—of the part played by the adolescent 'manufacture of excitement' and the courting of risk—was to be echoed repeatedly in the empirical and theoretical work of criminologists. Making 'something happen' in a world without significant cultural or material resources could easily bring about a drift into delinquency (see Matza 1964; Corrigan 1979; Cusson 1983; Katz 1988; Presdee 2000). Indeed, it was to be distinctive of much delinquency. Ferrell, Hayward, and Young, for example, talk about how many young people 'push themselves to "the edge", and engage there in "edgework", in search of "the adrenalin rush", authentic identity, and existential certainty; they lose control to take control' (2008: 72).

An incarnation of anomie theory is thus to be found in muted form in 'Left Realism' and its successor, 'cultural criminology', where the idea of structural tension is integrated with that of the social meanings of the act to produce a conception of delinquency as a motivated response to the inequalities of capitalism. 'The Mertonian notion of contradiction between culture and structure', wrote Jock Young, himself the father of 'Left Realism' turned father of 'cultural criminology', 'has run throughout all my work, from *The Drugtakers* onwards' (2004: 553). I shall return to Left Realism below. Another twist was added by Messner and Rosenfeld who claimed that different institutional configurations in society may encourage or discourage anomie of the form described by Merton. 'Institutional anomie' is, they argue, a possible outcome of a society dominated by the economy and economic pressures at the expense of other modes of behaviour and control (Messner and Rosenfeld 2009).

## ANOMIE AND SOCIAL DISORGANIZATION

The second reading of anomie stemming from Durkheim touched on moral regulation that was not so much flawed as in a critical or chronic state of near collapse. People, he argued, are not endowed at birth with fixed appetites and ambitions. On the contrary, their purposes and aspirations are shaped by the generalized opinions and reactions of others, by a collective conscience, that can appear through social ritual and routine to be externally derived, solid, and objective. When society is disturbed by rapid change or major disorder, however, that semblance of solidity, authority, and objectivity can itself founder, and people may no longer find their ambitions subject to effective social discipline. It is hard to live outside the reassuring structures of social life, and the condition of anomie was experienced as a 'malady of infinite aspiration' that was accompanied by 'weariness', 'disillusionment', 'disturbance, agitation and discontent'. In extreme cases, Lukes observed, 'this condition would lead a man to commit suicide and homicide' (1967: 139).

Durkheim conceived such anomic deregulation to be a matter of crisis, innately unstable and short-lived. Disorganization could not be tolerated for very long before a society collapsed or order of a sort was restored. Indeed, sociologists are generally ill-disposed towards the term, believing that it connotes a want of understanding and perception on the part of the observer (see Anderson 1976; Katz 1997; and Whyte 1942). It is evident that informal control can survive in even the most perverse circumstances (see Walklate and Evans 1999) and, even in Afghanistan, Iraq, the Congo, Sierra Leone, or Uganda at their most devastated, people are able to sustain a measure of organization within disorganization. Yet, on both the small and the large scale, there are also clear examples of people living in conditions where informal control and cooperativeness are only vestigial; where formal control is either absent or erratic; where others are, or are seen to be, predatory and dangerous; where life is unpredictable; and where, as cause and consequence, there is little personal safety, much anxiety, and abundant crime. Take William Julius Wilson's description of life in the poorest areas of the American city: 'broken families, antisocial behavior, social networks that do not extend beyond the ghetto environment, and a lack of informal social control over the behavior and activities of children and adults in the neighborhood' (1996: xvi). On some housing estates in Paris (Wacquant 2008), London (see Genn 1988), Nottingham (Davies 1998), and St Louis (Rainwater 1970), social groupings have been portrayed as so lacking in cohesion that they enjoyed no shared trust, neighbour preyed on neighbour, and joint defensive action was virtually impossible. John Hagan would add the anomie sometimes experienced by the very successful who have no constraints imposed on them (1977). One might think of the spiralling collapse of Enron or Lehman Brothers as cases in point.

Rampant anomie has been well documented. The neo-Durkheimian, Kai Erikson (1994), for example, laid out a number of graphic case studies of anomic societies where cohesion was impaired and informal social control eroded by natural or social disaster. People in those instances were free to deviate in a way that had been hitherto difficult. Consider, too, Davis's half-prophetic description of MacArthur Park, one of the poorest areas of Los Angeles, as 'feral' and dangerous, 'a free-fire zone where crack dealers and street gangs settle their scores with shotguns and Uzis' (1992a: 6). Consider Turnbull's description of the condition of the Ik of northern Uganda, a tribe that had been moved to a mountainous area after their traditional hunting grounds had been designated a national park. They could no longer live, cooperate, and work as they had done before; familiar patterns of social organization had become obsolete; and the Ik were portrayed as having become beset by 'acrimony, envy and suspicion' (1973: 239), 'excessive individualism, coupled with solitude and boredom' (ibid.: 238), and the victimization of the weak: 'without killing, it is difficult to get closer to disposal than by taking the food out of an old person's mouth, and this was primarily an adjacent-generation occupation, as were tripping and pushing off balance' (ibid.: 252).

A number of criminologists and others prophesy a new apocalypse in which anomie will flourish on such a massive scale that entire societies will dissolve into chaos and lawlessness. There are parts of the world, commonly called 'failed states', whose political structures are so radically disordered that it becomes difficult to talk about legitimate governments operating effectively within secure national boundaries at all (see Bayart, Ellis, and Hibou 1999). So it was that Kaplan wrote graphically about the road-warrior culture of Somalia, the anarchic implosion of criminal violence in the Ivory Coast, and Sierra Leone, which he depicted at the time as a lawless state that had lost control over its cities at night, whose national army was a 'rabble', and which was reverting to tribalism. The future for many, he luridly predicted, would be a 'rundown, crowded planet of skinhead Cossacks and *juju* warriors, influenced by the worst refuse of Western pop culture and ancient tribal hatreds, and battling over scraps of overused earth in guerilla conflicts' (1994: 62–3). So, too, Martin van Creveld analysed what he called the ubiquitous growth of 'low-intensity conflict' waged by guerrillas and terrorists who threatened the state's conventional monopoly of violence: 'Should present trends continue, then the kind of war that is based on the division between government, army, and people, seems to be on its way out ... . A degree of violent activity that even as late as the 1960s would have been considered outrageous is now accepted as an inevitable hazard of modern life' (1991: 192, 194). If Kaplan and van Creveld are even partially gifted with foresight (and much of their argument is quite stark), the trends they foretell will be of major consequence to criminology. Without a viable state legislature, laws, and law enforcement, without adequate state control over the distribution of violence, how can one manage to write intelligently about a discrete realm of crime at all? Crime, after all, is contingent on a state's ability clearly to define, ratify, and execute the law. When the police of a state are massively and routinely corrupt (as they appear to be in Mexico); when, for example, the Colombian president's aeroplane was found to be carrying large quantities of cocaine in September 1996 (see the *New York Times*, 22 September 1996); when the Taleban vie with a weak state and weak occupiers to impose control; and when a President of Liberia was accused of cannibalism (*The Times*, 2 November 1999); it is not difficult to recognize what Aldana-Pindell somewhat paradoxically called 'institutional *anomie*' (2002). Neither is it difficult to acknowledge the disarray to which Stan Cohen pointed when he asked whether it was possible any longer to distinguish firmly between crime and politics. There has been, he asserted, a widespread decline of the myth that the sovereign state can provide security, law, and order; a decline in the legitimacy of the state through corruption scandals; a growth of international crime and a rise of criminal states such as Chechnya; and, in Africa particularly, the emergence of barbarism, horror, and atrocity. In some settings, he remarked, 'lawlessness and crime have so destroyed the social fabric that the state itself has withdrawn' (1996: 9). Peter Godwin, for instance, has documented through a combination of journalism and autobiography the collapse of Zimbabwe into a state ravaged by gangs of 'war veterans' and political elites subject to no apparent formal, legal control (2006).

## CONTROL THEORY

A second, large, and linked cluster of theories centres loosely around the contention that people—almost all people—seek to commit crime because it is profitable, useful, or enjoyable for them to do so, and that they will almost certainly break the law if they can. This is certainly one theme in the explanation of the August 2011 urban riots in England (see http://www.guardian.co.uk/uk/series/reading-the-riots). Even if that contention, with its covert imagery of feral man (and woman), is not strictly 'valid', control theorists would argue that it certainly directs enquiry in a helpful direction. They profess to be interested less in the fidelity of description than in its yield for policy intervention and prediction in concrete situations. Theirs is a theory of practical rather than of empirical truths, and the practical is thought to suggest that more will be learned by exploring a few, uncomplicated factors that seem to *prevent* people from offending than by investigating all the complicated motives, meanings, and anteced-ents of their actions. Travis Hirschi put the issue baldly: 'The question "Why do they do it?" is simply not the question the theory is designed to answer. The question is, "Why don't we do it?"' (1969: 34). Such a doctrine is a recognizably close neighbour of anomie theories in its focus on the regulation of potentially unbridled appetites; and, indeed, it is occasionally very difficult to distinguish one set of ideas from the other. Earlier variants of control theory, compiled in the 1960s and 1970s, proceeded by drafting lists of the constraints which could check the would-be offender, an offender who, it was assumed for analytic purposes, could be much like you, me, or anyone. Thus, arguing against subcultural theory, and grounded in a Freudian conception of human impulses that required taming, Hirschi claimed that 'delinquent acts result when the individual's bond to society is weak or broken' (1969: 16).

Four chief elements were held by Hirschi to induce people to comply with rules: attachment, commitment, involvement, and belief. Attachment reflected a person's sensitivity to the opinions of others; commitment flowed from an investment of time, energy, and reputation in conformity; involvement stemmed from engrossment in conventional activity; and belief mirrored a person's conviction that he or she should obey legal rules. There is tautology and repetition in that formulation, but he never-theless usefully directed the criminological mind towards answering his one big ques-tion, 'Why *don't* we do it?'.

Later, with Gottfredson, Hirschi developed control theory by turning to self-control and impulsivity. Crime, they claimed, flows from low self-control: it provides a direct and simple gratification of desires that is attractive to those who cannot or will not postpone pleasure. In the main, it requires little skill or planning. It can be intrinsi-cally enjoyable because it involves the exercise of cunning, agility, deception, or power. It requires a lack of sympathy for the victim. But it does not provide medium- or long-term benefits equivalent to those that can flow from more orthodox careers. In short, it is, they say, likely to be committed by those who are 'impulsive, insensitive, physi-cal ... Risk-taking, short-sighted, and non-verbal' (1990: 90).

David Matza almost certainly would not have called himself a control theorist, but in *Delinquency and Drift* (1964) he did effectively straddle theories of control, anomie, and signification, and he did portray delinquents and delinquency in a manner that control theorists would find apposite. Delinquents are not very different from us, he argued. Most of the time they are conventional enough in belief and conduct, and it is difficult to predict who will conform and who will not. But there are occasions when the grip of control loosens, adolescents fatalistically experience themselves (perhaps for oppor-tunistic or rhetorical reasons) as if they were object and effect rather than as subject and cause, as if they were no longer morally responsible for their actions, and they will then find themselves released to drift in and out of delinquency. What eases that proc-ess of disengagement are widely-circulating accounts or 'techniques of neutralization' (a massively influential idea that he had developed earlier with Gresham Sykes (Sykes and Matza 1957)) which enable people methodically to counter the guilt and offset the censure they might experience when offending. Matza claimed that delinquents could be fortified in their resolve by their ability to condemn their condemners (by asserting that police and judges were themselves corrupt and invalid critics, for instance); to deny injury (by asserting that no significant harm was done); to deny the victim (by asserting that the victim was of no consequence, or deserved what happened); or to appeal to higher loyalties (a noble motive could be cited for an ignoble deed).

Steven Box attempted to take analysis yet further by reconciling Hirschi's emphasis on social bonds with Matza's conception of drift. He compiled his own new alliterative list of variables that were held to affect control: secrecy (the delinquent's chances of concealment); skills (a mastery of knowledge and techniques needed for the deviant act); supply (access to appropriate equipment); social support (the endorsement offered by peers and others); and symbolic support (the endorsement offered by accounts available in the wider culture) (1971: 150). The greater the access to requisite skills, secrecy, supplies, and social and symbolic support, he argued, the greater would be the likelihood of offending.

Perhaps one of the most telling and economical contributions to control theory was supplied by Harriet Wilson. Examining 'socially deprived' families in Birmingham, England, she was to conclude that what most sharply differentiated families with delinquent children from those with none was simply what she called the exercise of 'chaperonage' (1980). Parents who acted as chaperons effectively prevented their children from offending: they were so convinced that the neighbourhood in which they lived was dangerous and contaminating that they sought to protect their children by keeping them indoors or under close supervision, escorting them to school, and prohibiting them from playing with others defined as undesirable (and see Reckless 1957).

Control theory has also been applied with effect to the problem of gender differences in offending. Apart from age, no other demographic feature at present so powerfully discriminates between offenders and non-offenders. At one time, however, scant criminological attention was paid to female crime because there was so very little of it (see Innes 2003: 54). As Lemert once said, like Custer's men, criminologists rode to the sound of the guns, and there were few female guns indeed firing. By contrast, what made male offending appear so interesting was its sheer seriousness and scale.

Feminist criminologists and others adopting a control perspective retorted that that was precisely what made women so important analytically (Heidensohn 1968), and they inverted the problem by asking Travis Hirschi's central question (without actually citing Hirschi himself) about why women did *not* offend. There was the academically new and intriguing riddle of the conforming woman, and the riddle was answered, in part, by reference to the effects of differentials in control. John Hagan and his colleagues put it that deviation as a form of fun and excitement in public space was more commonly open to males than to females because daughters are more frequently risk-averse and more frequently subject to intense, continual, and diffuse family control in the private, domestic sphere. That control, by extension, not only removed girls from the purview of agents of formal social control, the criminal justice system, and the possibility of public identification as criminal; it also worked more effectively because it rested on the manipulation of emotional sanctions rather than the imposition of physical or custodial controls. Shaming strategies and the withdrawal of affection are seemingly more potent than fines, probation, or prison. It followed that the more firmly structured and hierarchical the family, the sharper the distinction drawn between male and female roles, the more women were confined to private space, the greater would be the disparity between rates of male and female offending (see Hagan *et al.* 1979, 1985, and 1988). Pat Carlen gave that analysis yet another twist by noting that female criminals were most likely to emerge when domestic family controls were eroded or removed altogether, when what she called the 'gender deal' was broken, young women left home or were taken into the care of the state, and were thereby exposed to controls characteristically experienced by men (1988). The answer to the 'crime problem', Frances Heidensohn once concluded, tongue in cheek, would have to lie in the feminization of control.

Control theory is now greatly in vogue, particularly in the United States, where it is linked with theories of 'life-course' in the work of authors such as Sampson and Laub, whose *Crime in the Making* of 1993 was to be succeeded by Laub and Sampson's *Shared Beginnings, Divergent Lives* of 2003. Both works explored the genesis of, and desistance from, delinquency in the lives of men studied over decades: and they devoted especial attention to the manner in which the social bonds of family, friends, employment, and military service work as informal controls that filter influences emanating from the wider social structure. Marriage, the onset of work, and military service, they argue, may act as critical turning points which induce discontinuities in a life history; create new sets of social relations, dependencies, and responsibilities; introduce new disciplines into social life; and invite stock-taking and reflection. Conversely, involvement with the criminal justice system and imprisonment may interrupt or undermine participation in stabilizing social environments; stigmatize the offender and prevent re-entry into the 'straight' world; encourage cynicism about criminal justice through a close acquaintance with its game-like and seedier features; and introduce the offender to other lawbreakers who help to amplify deviance through differential association. And, throughout, and following Matza, Katz, and others, Laub and Sampson portray the process not as a grim and ineluctable progression into criminality, but as a sequence of events and actions which is influenced always by the capacity of people to interpret and *choose* how they will respond. The part played by human agency and contingency is repeatedly underscored, leading them to observe how impossible it is to predict future criminality from present circumstances.

## RATIONAL CHOICE THEORY

An increasingly important, but not indispensable, foundation for control theories is 'rational choice theory', a resuscitation of old utilitarian theories that preceded sociology and were once linked with Adam Smith, Jeremy Bentham, Cesare Beccaria, and James Mill. Rational choice theory was reintroduced to criminology through the medium of a revived economics of crime, and it brought with it the convenient fiction of economic man (see Becker 1968), a fiction which has an immediate affinity with the criminal man (or woman) of control theory. Economic man, deemed to be continually looking about him for opportunities, making amoral and asocial choices to maximize his personal utility, may not be an empirically grounded or well-documented entity, but, it is argued, he does help to simplify model-making, strip away what rational choice theorists conceive to be unessential theoretical and descriptive clutter, and aim directly at what are conceived to be practically useful policy questions (see Clarke and Cornish 1985). Economic man in his (or her) criminal guise does not have a past, complex motives, rich social life, or, indeed, a recognizable social identity (a 'disposition' is how Ron Clarke put it (1992)). He or she does not need to have any of those attributes.

Indeed, he or she may not be perfectly rational, muddling through or 'satisficing', as we all do, on the basis of imperfect information and in the presence of risks and uncertainty. He or she is very much like any one of us or, better still, like some Everyman who stands abstractly and plainly for all of us. He or she needs no such complexity, because what weighs in control theory is the piecemeal theoretical analysis of discrete episodes of disembodied offending behaviour conducted by people making decisions around the issues of risk, effort, and reward (Clarke and Cornish 2000: 7) in the settings in which they take place (see introduction to Clarke and Felson 1993).

In Ron Clarke's particularly influential formulation, the rate of crime was held to vary in response to three broad configurations of factors. The first grouping revolved around increasing the effort Everyman would have to expend in committing a crime, and that entailed what was called 'target hardening' (by defending objects and people by shields and other devices); 'access control' (and that involved making it difficult for predators to approach targets); deflecting offenders (by encouraging them, for example, to act in a legitimate rather than an illegitimate manner through the provision of graffiti boards, litter bins, and spittoons); and 'controlling facilitators' (through gun control or checks on the sales of spray cans, for instance). The second revolved around increasing the risks of offending through the screening of people (by means of border searches, for example); formal surveillance by police, security guards, and others; surveillance by employees such as bus conductors, train guards, concierges, and janitors; and 'natural surveillance' (aided by lowering or removing obstacles such as hedges and shrubs around private dwellings (see Bennett and Wright 1984), installing closed circuit television cameras, lighting the interiors of stores, and enhanced street lighting). The final grouping was 'reducing the rewards' of crime, itself composed of 'target removal' (using electronic transactions and bus and 'oyster' cards to reduce the number of cash payments, and thus the accumulation of cash in single places, for instance); property identification; removal of inducements (by the rapid cleaning of graffiti or repair of vandalized property); and rule-setting (through income tax returns, customs declarations, and the like) (taken from Clarke 1992: 13). A pursuit of those common-sense, sometimes indistinguishable, but nevertheless practical ideas allowed research officers at the Home Office in the 1970s and early 1980s to undertake a succession of illustrative studies, discovering, for example, that compact, old school buildings on small urban sites were a third as likely to be burgled as large, sprawling, modern buildings with their many points of access and weak possibilities of surveillance (see Hope 1982); or that there was some 20 times as much malicious damage on the upper than on the lower decks of 'one man', double-decker buses whose drivers' powers of surveillance were confined to one level only (Mayhew et al. 1976: 26).

None of those variables touched on conventional sociological questions about who offenders might be, how they reason, and how they act (and for that rational choice theorists have been criticized (see Wright and Decker 1997; Fukuyama 2004; and Haggerty, who remarked a little astringently that control theorists are more akin to 'Wal-Mart security consultants than research criminologists' (2004: 218)). Control theorists concentrated instead on the imagined impact of different forms of control on Everyman or Everywoman abroad in space, and from that it was but a short step to extend control theory to an analysis of the disciplines that are built into everyday social practices, on the one hand, and into the social uses of space, on the other.

## ROUTINE ACTIVITIES THEORY

Ron Clarke, the situational control theorist, and Marcus Felson, the theorist of crime and routine activities, agreed that they shared ideas in common (see Clarke and Felson 1993) as well as ideas apart (thus situational control theory is microscopic, routine activities theory largely macroscopic in its application (Clarke and Cornish undated: 25)). Clarke and his colleagues had asked what prevented specific criminal incidents from occurring in specific situations. Felson asked how such incidents originate or are checked in the routine activities of mundane social life (1994). Just as Clarke and others had emphasized how, for explanatory purposes, it was convenient to assume that offenders were little different from anyone else, so Felson and his colleagues argued that most criminals are unremarkable, unskilled, petty, and non-violent people much like us. Just as control theorists made use of a tacit version of original sin, so routine activities theory adopted a series of presuppositions about basic human frailty, the importance of temptation and provocation, and the part played by idleness ('We are all born weak, but ... we are taught self-control', Felson claimed (1994: 20)).

The routine activities criminologist would argue that the analysis of predatory crime does not necessarily require weighty causes. Neither does it demand that the theorist commit the 'like-causes-like' fallacy which tacitly insists that a 'pathological' phenomenon such as crime must be explained by a pathological condition such as alienation, poverty, family dysfunction, or class or racial oppression. Crime was taken to be inscribed in the very architecture of everyday life. More precisely, it was to be found in the convergence in space and time of what were called motivated offenders, suitable targets, and capable guardians (see Cohen and Felson 1979): being affected by such matters as the weight, value, incidence, and distribution of stealable goods (the growth in the quantity of portable, high-cost goods such as lap-top computers, DVD-recorders, and mobile (or 'cell') telephones will encourage more theft, for instance); the impact of motor cars (they aid rapid flight, permit the discreet transportation of objects, and give rise to a geographical dispersal of the population which dilutes surveillance); habits of leisure (adolescents now have larger swathes of empty time than did their predecessors, time in which they can get up to mischief); habits of work (when all members of a household are in employment, there will be no capable guardians to protect a home); habits of residence (single people are less effective guardians of property than are larger households); the growth of technology (modern mobile telephones, for instance, amplify the public's ability to report and record crime); and so on. It is an uncomplicated enough theory but again, like its near neighbour, control theory, it does ask empirically productive questions.

# CRIME, CONTROL, AND SPACE

## THE CHICAGO SCHOOL

Routine activities theory and control theory both talk about convergence in space, and space has always been analytically to the fore in criminology. Indeed, one of the earliest and most productive of the research traditions laid down in criminology was the social ecology and urban mapping practised by the sociology department of the University of Chicago in the 1920s and beyond (see Park 1925; Thrasher 1927; and Landesco 1968).

As cities grow, it was held, so there would be a progressive, 'organic', and largely spontaneous differentiation of space, population, and function that concentrated different groupings in different areas. The main organizing structure was the *zone*, and the Chicago sociologists discerned five principal concentric zones shaping the city: the central business district around the 'Loop' at the very core; the 'zone in transition' about that centre; an area of stable working-class housing; middle-class housing; and outer suburbia.

The zone in transition was marked by the greatest volatility of its residents. It was an area of comparatively cheap rents, weak social control, internal social differentiation, and rapid physical change. It was to the zone in transition that new immigrant groupings most frequently came, and it was there that they settled into what were called 'natural areas', small, 'spontaneously'-generated, communal enclaves that were said to be relatively homogeneous in composition and culture. Chicago sociologists plotted the incidence of social problems on to census maps of the city, and it was the zone in transition that was found repeatedly to house the largest visible proportions of the poor, the illegitimate, the illiterate, the mentally ill (see Faris and Dunham 1939), juvenile delinquents (Shaw and McKay 1942), and prostitutes (Reckless 1933). The zone in transition was, in effect, virtually coextensive with what was then described as social pathology. Not only were formal social controls held to be at their weakest there (the zone in transition was, as it were, socially dislocated from the formal institutions and main body of American society (see Whyte 1942) ); but informal social controls were eroded by moral and social diversity, rapid population movement, and a lack of strong and pervasive local institutions: 'contacts are extended, heterogeneous groups mingle, neighborhoods disappear, and people, deprived of local and family ties, are forced to live under … loose, transient and impersonal relations' (Wirth 1964: 236).

A number of the early Chicago sociologists united social ecology, the study of the patterns formed by different groups living together in the same space, with the fieldwork methods of social anthropology, to explore the traditions, customs, and practices of the residents of natural areas. They found that, while there may well have been a measure of social and moral dislocation between the zone in transition and the wider society, as well as within the zone in transition itself, those natural areas could also manifest a remarkable inner coherence and persistence of culture and behaviour that were reproduced from generation to generation and from immigrant group to immigrant group within the same terrain over time. Delinquency was, in effect, not disorganized at all, but a stable attribute of social life, an example of continuity in change: 'to a very great extent … traditions of delinquency are preserved and transmitted through the medium of social contact with the unsupervised play group and the more highly organized delinquent and criminal gangs' (Shaw and McKay 1971: 260). Cultural transmission was to be the focus of the work pursued by a small group of second-generation Chicago sociologists. Sometimes under the name of 'differential association', it was studied as a normal process of learning motives, skills, and meanings in the company of others who bore criminal traditions (see Sutherland and Cressey 1955).

That urban research was to prepare a diverse legacy for criminology: the spatial analysis of crime; the study of subcultures (which I shall touch on below); the epidemiology of crime; crime as an interpretive practice (which I shall also touch on); and much else. Let me turn first to some examples of spatial analysis.

## CONTROL AND SPACE: BEYOND THE CHICAGO SCHOOL

The Chicago sociologists' preoccupation with the cultural and symbolic correlates of spatial congregations of people was to be steadily elaborated by criminologists. For instance, Wiles, Bottoms, and their colleagues, then working at the University of Sheffield, added two important observations. They argued first that, in a then more tightly regulated Britain, social segregation did not emerge, as it were, organically with unplanned city growth (although Chicago itself was never quite as unplanned as some of the early social ecologists had alleged (see Suttles 1972)), but with the intended and unintended consequences of policy decisions taken by local government departments responsible for housing a large proportion of the population in municipal rented accommodation. Housing allocation was an indirect and sometimes unintended reflection of moral judgements about tenants that resulted, or were assumed to result, in the concentration of criminal populations (see Bottoms *et al.* 1989). Further, and partly in accord with that argument, the reputations of natural areas themselves became a criminological issue: how was it, these criminologists asked, that the moral meanings attached to space by residents and outsiders affected people's reputations, choices, and action? One's very address could become a constraining moral fact that affected not only how one would be treated by others in and about the criminal justice system (see Damer 1974), but also how one would come to rate oneself as a potential deviant or conformist (see Gill 1977).

Secondly, Bottoms and his colleagues argued, while the Chicago sociologists may have examined the geographical distribution of offenders, it was instructive also to scrutinize how *offending* itself could be plotted, because the two measures need not correspond (Baldwin and Bottoms 1976 and see Morris 1957). Offending has its maps. Indeed, it appears to be densely concentrated, clustered around offenders' homes, areas of work and recreation, and the pathways in between (Brantingham and Brantingham 1981–2; Wikstrőm 2007). So it was that, pursuing routine activities theory, Sherman and his colleagues surveyed all calls made to the police in Minneapolis in one year; and they discovered that a few 'hot spots' had exceptional densities of crime: only 3 per cent of all places produced 50 per cent of the calls; all robberies took place in only 2.2 per cent of places, all rapes in 1.2 per cent of places, and all car thefts in 2.7 per cent of places (Sherman *et al.* 1989; see also Roncek and Maier 1991).

## DEFENSIBLE SPACE

If offending has its maps, so does social control; and criminologists and others have become ever more interested in the fashion in which space, conduct, and control intersect. One forerunner was Jane Jacobs, who speculated about the relations between city landscapes and informal controls, arguing, for example, that dense, busy thoroughfares with their *habitués* have many more 'eyes on the street' and opportunities for witness reporting and bystander intervention, than sterile pedestrian zones, 'confused' mixed space or streets without stores and other lures (Jacobs 1965).

The idea of 'defensible space', in particular, has been borrowed from anthropology and architecture, coupled with the concept of surveillance, and put to work in analysing formal and informal responses to different kinds of terrain. 'Defensible space' itself leans on the psychological notion of 'territoriality', the sense of attachment and symbolic investment that people can acquire in a place or places. Territoriality is held by some to be a human universal, an imperative that leads people to wish to guard what is their own. Those who have a stake in a physical area, it is argued, will care for it, police it, and report strangers and others who have no apparent good purpose to be there.

What is quite critical is how space is marked out and bounded. The prime author of this formulation of the idea of defensible space, Oscar Newman (1972), claimed that, other things being equal, what induces territorial sentiments is a clear demarcation between private and public areas, even if the demarcations are only token. The private will be protected in ways that the public is not, and the fault of many domestic and institutional buildings is that separations and segregations are not clearly enough inscribed in design. The geographer, Alice Coleman, and others took it that improvements to the physical structures of built space could then achieve a significant impact on crime: above all, she insisted on restricting access to sites; reducing the interconnections or 'walkways' between buildings; and emphasizing the distinction between public and private space and minimizing what Oscar Newman called 'confused space', the space that was neither one nor the other (Coleman 1985, 1986). She has been roundly faulted, both methodologically and analytically, for her neglect of dimensions other than the physical (see Hillier 1973, 1986), but she and Newman have succeeded in introducing an analytic focus on the interrelations between space and informal control that was largely absent before. Only rarely have criminologists such as Campbell (1993), Duneier (2001), Power (1997), and Shapland and Vagg (1988) enquired into the informal controlling practices of people as they observe, interpret, and respond to the ambiguous, deviant, and non-deviant conduct in the spaces around them.

It was Shapland and Vagg's contention, for instance, that there is a continuous, active, and often informed process of surveillance transacted by people on the ground; a process which is so discreet that it has escaped much formal notice, and which meshes only haphazardly with the work of the police. And very similarly Duneier laid bare the complex webs of informal control practised by homeless entrepreneurs selling books and magazines from stalls on New York's streets. Far from being a problem of deregulation, they acted as palpable but subtle agents of order, looking after and protecting one another, and preserving public stability.

## CRIME, POWER, AND SPACE

Surveillance has not always been construed as neutral or benign, and there are current debates about what its newer forms might portend. Even its sponsors in government departments and criminal justice agencies have spoken informally and privately about their anxiety that people are being encouraged to become unduly fearful of crime and to retreat into private fastnesses. It began to be argued, especially by those who followed Michel Foucault, that a 'punitive city' was in the making, that, in Stan Cohen's words, there was 'a deeper penetration of social control into the social body' (1979a: 356) (and, Cohen would add privately, sociologists do not in the main look on social control with a favourable eye).

Some came to claim not only that there has been a move progressively to differentiate and elaborate the distribution of controls in space, but also that there has been a proliferating surveillance of dangerous areas, often conducted obliquely and with an increasingly advanced technology. Michel Foucault's (1977) dramatic simile of Jeremy Bentham's model prison, the Panopticon, was to be put to massive use in criminology. Just as the Panopticon, or inspection house, was supposed to have permitted the unobserved observation of many inmates around the bright, illuminated rim of a circular prison by the few guards in its obscured centre, just as the uncertainty of unobserved observation worked to make the controlled control themselves, so, Foucault and those who followed him wished to argue, modern society is coming to exemplify the perfection of the automatic exercise of power through generalized surveillance. The carceral society was a machine in which everyone was supposed to be caught (even, it seems, the police, who may survey one another as well as the wider population (see *The Times*, 4 November 1999): it relied on diffuse control through unseen monitoring and the individualization and 'interiorization' of control (Gordon 1972)). Public space, it has been said, was becoming exposed to ever more perfunctory, distant, and technologically driven policing by formal state agencies; while control in private and semi-private space (the space of the shopping malls, university campus, and theme park) was itself becoming more dense, privatized, and widespread, placed in the private hands of security guards and store detectives, and reliant on a new electronic surveillance (Davis 1992b: 233; but see Welsh and Farrington 2002 which concluded that the introduction of CCTV appears to affect only the commission of motor thefts. All other forms of crime are untouched).

A paradigmatic case study of oblique regulation has been provided by Shearing and Stenning's ethnography of Disney World as a 'private, quasi-feudal domain of control' (Shearing and Stenning 1985: 347) that was comprehensively, discreetly, and adeptly controlled by employees, extensive surveillance, the encouragement of self-discipline, and the very configuration of physical space. The nature of crime and deviance itself can undergo change in such a transformed environment: they are no longer always and everywhere so markedly affronts to deep values but are, instead, very often breaches of what appear to be impersonal, morally neutral, technical controls (see Lianos and Douglas 2000: 270–1).

What also underlies much of that vision is a companion stress on the sociology of risk, a focus linked importantly with the work of Ulrich Beck (although he has not himself written about crime (1992)). It has been argued that people and groups are becoming significantly stratified by their exposure to risk and their power to neutralize harm (but see O'Malley 2010, who argues that risk has always been with us. It is the way in which it is regarded that has principally changed). The rich can afford private protection, the poor cannot, and a new ecology emerges (Simon 1987). Phrased only slightly differently, and merged with the newly burgeoning ideas about the pervasiveness of surveillance by machine and person (Gordon 1986–7 and Lyon 1994), those theories of risk suggest that controls are being applied by state and private organizations, not on the basis of some moralistic conception of individual wrong-doing, but on a foundation of the identification, classification, and management of groups categorized by their perceived dangerousness (Feeley and Simon 1992; Simon and Feeley 1995; Simon 2007). Groups are becoming ever more rigidly segregated in space: some (members of the new dangerous classes or underclass) being confined to prison, semi-freedom under surveillance, or parole in the community; others (the more affluent) retreating into their locked and gated communities, secure zones, private and 'mass private' spaces. There are new bifurcations of city space into a relatively uncontrolled 'badlands' occupied by the poor and highly controlled 'security bubbles' inhabited by the rich. Geographical and social exclusion thereby conspires to corral together populations of the unprotected, victimized, and victimizing—the mentally disordered, the young, and the homeless—reinforcing both their vulnerability and their propensities to offend (Carlen 1996; Hagan and McCarthy 1998).

The latest twist in the analysis of the links between crime, control, and space has been introduced by a revitalized political economy associated, for example, with the work of Loïc Wacquant (2008) who has examined through comparative analysis the links between patterns of exclusion, signification, and control in the urban ghettos of France and the United States. His argument in the instance of the United States is that areas of the city are the outcome of a combination of political inaction, racial exclusion, population filtration, and an application of the moralizing language of 'the underclass' which engenders 'hyperghettos' in which economic and social marginali-zation, welfare dependency, and crime are intermingled. Others have discussed how, in such places, where the allurements of a capitalist society still percolate, a rampant consumerism unchecked by informal social controls can lead to a vertiginous devi-ance of material acquisition (see Hallsworth 2005).

## RADICAL CRIMINOLOGY

So far, control has been treated without much direct allusion to the power, politics, and inequalities that are its bedfellows. There was to be a relatively short-lived but active challenge to such quiescence from the radical, new, or critical criminologies of the late 1960s and 1970s, criminologies that claimed their mandate in Marxism (Taylor, Walton, and Young 1973), libertarianism (Douglas 1971), anarchism (Kittrie 1971; Cohen 1985), or American populism (Quinney 1970), and whose ambitions pointed to the need for political activism or praxis (Mathiesen 1974).

Crime control was said to be an oppressive and mystifying process that worked through legislation, law enforcement, and ideological stereotyping to preserve une-qual class relations (Chambliss 1976; Box 1983). The radical political economy of crime sought chiefly to expose the hegemonic ideologies that masked the 'real' nature of crime and repression in capitalist society. Most mundane offending, it was argued, was actu-ally less politically or socially consequential than other social evils such as alienation, exploitation, or racism which received far too little attention (Scraton 1987). Much proletarian crime should actually be redefined as a form of redistributive class justice, or as a sign of the possessive individualism which resided in the core values of capitalist society. Criminal justice itself was engineered to create visible crowds of working-class and black scapegoats who could attract the public gaze away from the more serious delicts of the rich and the more serious ills of a capitalism that was usually said to be in terminal crisis. If the working class reacted in hostile fashion to the crime in their midst then they were, in effect, little more than the victims of a false consciousness which turned proletarian against proletarian, black against black, inflated the importance of petty problems, and concealed the true nature of bourgeois society.

So construed, signification, the act of giving meaning, was either manipulative or misconceived, a matter of giving and receiving incorrect and deformed interpretations of reality. Indeed, it was in the very nature of subordination in a capitalist society that most people must be politically unenlightened about crime, control, and much else, and the task of the radical criminologist was to expose, denounce, and demystify. It was concluded variously that crime was not a problem which the poor and their allies should actually address (there were more important matters for Marxists to think about: Hirst 1975); that the crime which *should* be analysed was the wrongdoing of the powerful (the wrong crimes and criminals were being observed: Chapman 1967; Reiman 1990; Pearce and Tombs 1998); or that crime and its problems would shrivel into insignificance as a criminogenic capitalism gave way to the tolerant diversity of socialism (Taylor, Walton, and Young 1973). The crime and criminals that chiefly warranted attention were the crimes of the powerful (Slapper and Tombs 1999) or those exceptional examples of law-breaking that seemed to represent an incipient revolt against the state, and they demanded cultivation as subjects of study, understanding, and possible politicization. Black prisoners, in particular, were sometimes depicted, and depicted themselves, as prisoners of class or race wars (Cleaver 1969). Prisons were the point of greatest state repression, and prison riots a possible spearhead of revolution (Fitzgerald 1977).

In its early guise, radical criminology withered somewhat under a quadruple-barrelled assault. In some places, and in America especially (where it had never been firmly implanted), it ran foul of university politics, and some criminology departments, such as that of the University of California at Berkeley, were actually closed down. More often, radical criminology did not lend itself to the government-funded, policy-driven, 'soft money', empiricist research that began to dominate schools of criminology in North America in the 1970s and 1980s.

Second was the effect of the publication of mass victim surveys in the 1970s and 1980s (Hough and Mayhew 1983) which disclosed both the extent of working-class victimization and the manner in which it revolved around intra-class, rather than inter-class, criminality. It was evident that crime *was* a manifest problem for the poor, adding immeasurably to their burdens, and difficult to dismiss as an ideological distraction (David Downes called it a regressive tax on the poor). Two prominent radical criminologists came frankly to concede that they had believed that 'property offences [were] directed solely against the bourgeoisie and that violence against the person [was] carried out by amateur Robin Hoods in the course of their righteous attempts to redistribute wealth. All of this [was], alas, untrue' (Lea and Young 1984: 262).

Third was the critique launched from within the left by a new generation of feminist scholars, who asserted that the victimization of women was no slight affair or ideological diversion, and that rape, sexual assault, child abuse, and domestic violence should be taken very seriously indeed (Smart 1977). Not only had the female criminal been neglected, they said, but so had the female victim, and it would not do to wait until the revolution for matters to be put right. Once more, a number of radical criminologists gave ground. There had been, Jones, Maclean, and Young observed, 'a general tendency in radical thought to idealize their historical subject (in this case the working class) and to play down intra-group conflict, blemishes and social disorganization. But the power of the feminist case resulted in a sort of cognitive schizophrenia amongst radicals' (Jones *et al.* 1986: 3). The revitalized criminology of women is one of the subjects of Chapter 13, the chapter that deals with gender and crime, in this volume.

Fourthly, there was a critique launched belatedly from non-feminist criminologists who resisted the imperious claims of radical criminology to be *the* sole fully social theory of crime (Downes and Rock 1979; Inciardi 1980). Marxist and radical theories of crime, it was argued, lacked a comparative emphasis: they neglected crime in 'non-capitalist' and 'pre-capitalist' societies and crime in 'socialist' societies. There was a naivety about the expectation that crime would wither away as the state itself disappeared after the revolution. There was a trust in socialist justice which could actually be very repressive indeed (socialist legality, Stan Cohen mused, tends to mean a 'model of social control in which offenders wearing sandwich-boards listing their crimes before a crowd which shouts "Down with the counter-revolutionaries!" and are then led away to be publicly shot' (1979b: 44)). And there was an irresponsibility about radical arguments that 'reformism' would only strengthen the grip of the capitalist system.

The radicals gave ground and 'Left Realism' was to be the outcome, represented by Jock Young, one of its revisionist parents, as a novel fusion of analyses of crime in the vein of anomie theory and symbolic interactionist analyses of the reactions which crime evokes (Young 1997: 484). It was 'realist' because, newly refusing to accept the so-called 'left idealists' dismissal of crime as an ideological trick, it acknowledged the practical force of crime in society and its especially heavy impact on the poor, minority ethnic people, and women. It was 'left' because it focused descriptively and politically on the structural inequalities of class, race, and gender. Its project was to examine patterns of crime and control as they emerged out of what Young came to call the 'square of crime', a field of forces dominated by the state, the victim, the offender, and the public.

Left Realism was to follow the earlier radical criminologists' injunction to act, but action was now as much in the service of more effective and practical policing and crime reduction strategies as in the cause of radical social change (if not more so). Left Realists joined the formerly disparaged 'administrative criminologists' working in and for the (usually local) state to work on situationally-based projects to prevent crime and the fear of crime (see Matthews and Young 1992). They designed new and confusing configurations of streets to make it more difficult for 'kerb-crawlers' to cruise in search of prostitutes. They explored the impact of improved street lighting on the fear of crime. They assisted in the rehabilitation of dilapidated housing estates. Were it not for their theoretical preambles, it was at times difficult to distinguish between the programmes of the Home Office or other state criminal justice ministries, on the one hand, and of Left Realism, on the other.

If Left Realism was radical criminology's *praxis*, its more scholarly current continued to evolve, and it evolved in diverse directions. A number of criminologists began to turn away from analyses of causation towards studies of current (Cohen 1985; Simon 1993 and 2007) and historical forms of social control (see Scull 1979), originally under the influence of E. P. Thompson and Eric Hobsbawm and then under that of Michel Foucault, Anthony Giddens, and Ulrich Beck. Others responded to the wider theories that began to dominate sociology proper in the 1980s and 1990s, incorporating them to write about crime, postmodernism (or late modernity), risk and globalization, and producing what were, in effect, examples of the 'fully social theory' promised by the new criminologists back in 1973. Above all, that promise was fulfilled by books published in 1999 by two of the original troika of new criminologists: Ian Taylor's *Crime in Context* and Jock Young's *The Exclusive Society*; and one in 2007 by Jock Young, *The Vertigo of Late Modernity*.

*Crime in Context* catalogues a series of crises flowing from transitions in the political and economic structures of society, and the manner in which they impinge upon poverty, class, gender, race, and the family to affect the national and transnational environments of crime and control. *The Exclusive Society* is subtitled 'Social Exclusion, Crime and Difference in Late Modernity', and its focus is more narrow but nevertheless effective, concentrating upon the social and political consequences of what then seemed to be the inexorable and vast increases in crime in the West. Crime was held by Young to be no longer regarded as abnormal, the property of a pathological few who can be restored therapeutically to the security of a moral community at one with itself, but *normal*, the actions of a significant, obdurate minority of Others who are impatiently excluded and demonized in a world newly insecure, fractured, and preoccupied with problems of risk and danger. More recently, late modernity was portrayed in *The Vertigo of Late Modernity* as an epoch of flux, mobility, and shifting boundaries; where selves, careers, and histories are unstable, marked by hybridization and a constant traffic of ideas across the frontiers of groups; an epoch where reward appears arbitrary and chaotic, community is weakened, class identity and biographical narratives are fractured; and where the prosperity of a seemingly contented middle class is dependent on the work of a largely unacknowledged, undervalued, humiliated, and underpaid service class labouring at home and overseas to form a new 'underclass', an underclass which becomes publicly visible only through a stigmatizing process of 'othering' and demonization as deviant, shiftless, and dependent. Crime itself is then presented, not so much as the work of a reasoning criminal, but as an angry, expressive *riposte* launched by the impoverished, dishonoured, powerless, and dispossessed, and it works through an answering language of control, selfhood, and violence, an 'othering', Jock Young says, of the 'otherers' who so devalue the poor. Crime's new companion, terrorism, is but a radical extension of such a project of existential affirmation. What perhaps these accounts do not accommodate with any success is the steady decline in crime rates across the Western world between the mid-1990s and 2008. (The above passage is borrowed from a review I published in what had been *The British Journal of Sociology*.) One wonders whether 'othering', 'hybridity', 'globalization', and the 'vertigo' of late modernity itself had moved into reverse, and, if they had, what the reason might be. No-one seems able to say (see Zimring 2007).

In other hands, what had once been a politically radical criminology became yoked to the analysis of what is called postmodernity, and it began to lose its connection to an analysis of the brute facts of power, structure, and stratification, becoming instead an epistemologically radical approach that concentrated on the consequences of a babble of contending interpretations (see Henry and Milovanovic 1996). Arrigo and Bernard came to declare of such a postmodern criminology that it now 'identifies the conflict over which various segments of society struggles to be about languaging [*sic*] reality/ existence through multiple voices and ways of knowing' (2002: 8).

## FUNCTIONALIST CRIMINOLOGY

Another, apparently dissimilar but substantially complementary, theory presented deviance and control as forces that worked discreetly to maintain social order. Functionalism was a theory of social systems or wholes, developed at the beginning of the twentieth century within a social anthropology grown tired of speculative accounts of the origins and evolution of societies which lacked the written history to support them, and dedicated to what was seen to be the scientific pursuit of intellectual problems. It was argued that the business of a social science necessitated moving enquiry beyond the reach of common sense or lay knowledge to an examination of the unintended, objective consequences of action that were visible only to the trained eye.

There were three clear implications. First, what ordinary people thought they were doing could be very different from what they actually achieved. The functionalist was preoccupied only with what were thought to be objective outcomes, and people's own accounts of action held little interest. Secondly, the functionalist looked at the impact made by institution upon institution, structure upon structure, in societies that were remarkable for their capacity to persist over time and beyond the lives of the individuals who composed them. Thirdly, those consequences, viewed as a totality, constituted a system in which, it was thought, not only did the parts affect one another and the whole, but also, the whole affected them in return. To be sure, some institutions were relatively detached, but functionalists would have argued that the alternative proposition—that social phenomena lack all influence upon one another, that there was no functional reciprocity between them—was conceptually insupportable. Systemic interrelations were an analytic *a priori*, a matter of self-evidence so compelling that Kingsley Davis could argue at one point that 'we are all functionalists now' (Davis 1959).

There have been very few dedicated functionalist criminologists (see Gottfredson and Hirschi 1990: 78). Functionalists tend to deal with the properties of whole systems rather than with empirical fragments such as crime. But crime and deviance did supply a particularly intriguing laboratory for thought-experiments about social order. It was easy enough to contend that religion or education shaped social cohesion, but how much harder it would be to show that *crime* succeeded in doing so. After all, 'everyone knew' that crime undermined social structures. It followed that functionalists occasionally found it tempting to try to confound that lay knowledge by showing that, to the contrary, the seemingly recalcitrant case of crime could be shown scientifically to contribute to the working of the social system. From time to time, therefore, they wrote about crime to demonstrate the potency of their theory. Only one functionalist, its grand master, Talcott Parsons, ever made the obvious, and therefore intellectually unsatisfying, point that crime could be what was called 'dysfunctional' or injurious to the social system as it was then constituted (Parsons 1951). Everyone else asserted that crime actually worked mysteriously to support it.

The outcome was a somewhat heterogeneous collection of papers documenting the multiple functions of deviance: Kingsley Davis showed that prostitution bolstered monogamy by providing an unemotional, impersonal, and unthreatening release for the sexual energy of the promiscuous married male (Davis 1937) (Mary McIntosh once wondered what the promiscuous married female was supposed to do about *her* sexual energy); Ned Polsky made much the same claim for pornography (Polsky 1967); Daniel Bell showed that racketeering provided 'queer ladders of success' and political and social stability in the New York dockside (1960); Émile Durkheim (1964) and George Herbert Mead (1918) contended that the formal rituals of trial and punishment enhanced social solidarity and consolidated moral boundaries; and, more complexly, Mary Douglas (1966), Kai Erikson (1966), Robert Scott (1972), and others argued that deviance offered social systems a dialectical or educational tool for the clarification and management of threats, ambiguities, and anomalies in classification systems. The list could be extended, but all the arguments tended to one end: what appeared, on the surface, to undermine social order accomplished the very reverse. A sociological counterpart of the invisible hand transmuted deviance into a force for the cohesion and permanence of community.

Functionalism was to be discarded by many criminologists in time: it smacked too much of teleology (the doctrine that effects can work retrospectively to act as the causes of events); it defied rigorous empirical investigation (see Cotterrell 1999: 75); and, for some, more politically driven criminologists, it represented a form of Panglossian conservatism that championed the status quo. But its ghost lingers on. Any who would argue that, contrary to appearances, crime and deviance buttress social order; any who argue for the study of seamless systems; any who argue that the sociologist should mistrust people's own accounts of their actions; any who insist that social science is the study of unintended consequences; must share something of the functionalist's standpoint. Anomie theories that represented crime as the system-stabilizing, unintended consequence of strains in the social order are one quite explicit example (see Merton 1995): deviance in that guise becomes the patterned adjustments that defuse an otherwise disruptive conflict and reconcile people to disadvantage (although, as I have argued, the theories can also envisage conditions in which crime becomes 'system-threatening'). And anomie theories were the direct offspring of functionalism, Merton himself being Parson's heir. But, less explicitly, some versions of radical criminology provide another example. More than one criminologist has argued that crime, deviance, and control were necessary for the survival of capitalism (Stinchcombe 1968). Again, although they did not talk explicitly of '*function*', the neo-Marxists, Hall *et al.* (1978), Pearce (1976), and Reiman (1990), *were* recognizably functionalist in their treatment of the criminal justice system's production of visible and scapegoated roles for the proletarian criminal, roles that attracted public anxiety and outrage, diverted anger away from the state, emasculated political opposition, and preserved capitalism (Pearce and Tombs 1998). Consider, for example, Ferrell and Sanders's observation that 'the simplistic criminogenic models at the core of … constructed moral panics … deflect attention from larger and more complex political problems like economic and ethnic inequality, and the alienation of young people and creative workers from confining institutions' (1995: 10). What could be more transparently functionalist than that?

## SIGNIFICATION

### LABELLING THEORY

Perhaps the only other outstanding big criminological idea is signification, the interpretive practice that orders social life. There has been an enduring strain of analysis, linked most particularly to symbolic interactionism and phenomenology, which insists that people do not, and cannot, respond immediately, uncritically, and passively to the world 'as it is'. Rather they necessarily respond to their *ideas* of the world, and the business of sociology is to capture, understand, and reproduce those ideas; examine their interaction with one another; and analyse the processes and structures that generated them. Sociology becomes the study of people, relations, and practices as symbolic and symbolizing processes.

Central to that idea is reflectivity, the capacity of consciousness to turn back on and translate itself into its own object. People are able to think about themselves, define themselves in various ways, toy with different identities, and project themselves imaginatively into any manner of contrived situation. They can view themselves vicariously by inferring the reactions of 'significant others', and, in so 'taking the role of the other', move symbolically to a distance outside themselves to inspect how they might appear. Elaborating action through 'significant gestures', the symbolic projection of acts and identities, they can anticipate the likely responses of others, and tailor their own prospective acts to accommodate them (Mead 1934). In all this, social worlds are compacted symbolically into the phrasing of action, and the medium that makes that possible is language.

Language is held to objectify, stabilize, and extend meaning. Used conversationally in the anticipation of an act, it permits people to be both their own subject and object, speaker and thing spoken about, 'I' and 'me', opening up the mind to reflective action. Conferring names, it enables people to impart moral and social meanings to their own and others' motives (Mills 1940; Sykes and Matza 1957; Scott and Lyman 1970), intentions, and identities. It will matter a great deal if someone is defined as eccentric, erratic, or mad; a drinker, a drunk, or an alcoholic; a lovelorn admirer or a stalker; a freedom fighter or a terrorist; a 'bit of a lad' or a delinquent. Consequences will flow from naming, consequences that affect not only how one regards oneself and one's position in the world, but also how one may be treated by others. Naming can create a self.

Transposed to the study of crime and deviance, symbolic interactionism and phenomenology gave prominence to the processes by which deviant acts and identities are constructed, interpreted, judged, and controlled (Katz 1988). A core pair of articles was Howard Becker's 'Becoming a Marihuana User' and 'Marihuana Use and Social Control', both reprinted in *Outsiders* (1963), and both describing the patterned sequence of steps that could shape the experience, moral character, and fate of one who began to smoke marihuana. Becoming a marihuana user was a tentative process, developing stage by stage, which required the user satisfactorily to learn, master, and interpret techniques, neutralize forbidding moral images of use and users, and succeed in disguising signs of use in the presence of those who might disapprove. It became paradigmatic.

Deviance itself was to become more generally likened to a moral career consisting of interlocking phases, each of which fed into and shaped the next; each of which presented different existential problems and opportunities; each of which was populated by different constellations of significant others; and each of which could distinctively mould the self of the deviant. But the process was not inexorable but contingent. Not every phase was inevitable or irreversible, and deviants could often choose to change direction. Luckenbill and Best (1981: 201) provide a graphic description:

> Riding escalators between floors may be an effective metaphor for respectable organizational careers, but it fails to capture the character of deviant careers. A more appropriate image is a walk in the woods. Here, some people take the pathways marked by their predecessors, while others strike out on their own. Some walk slowly, exploring before moving on, but others run, caught up in the action. Some have a destination in mind and proceed purposively; others view the trip and enjoy it for its own sake. Even those intent on reaching a destination may stray from the path; they may try to shortcut or they may lose sight of familiar landmarks, get lost, and find it necessary to backtrack.

What punctuates such a career is acts of naming, the deployment of language to confer and fix the meanings of behaviour, and symbolic interactionism and phenomenology became known within criminology as 'labelling theory'. One of the most frequently cited of all passages in sociological criminology was Becker's dictum that 'deviance is not a quality of the act the person commits, but rather a consequence of the application by others of rules and sanctions to an "offender". The deviant is one to whom that label has successfully been applied; deviant behavior is behavior that people so label' (1963: 9).

Labelling itself is contingent. Many deviant acts are not witnessed and most are not reported. Reporting may not lead to action. People may well be able to resist or modify deviant designations when attempts *are* made to apply them: after all, we are continually bombarded by attempts to label us in different ways and few succeed. But there are special occasions when the ability of the self to resist definition is circumscribed; and most fateful of all may be an encounter with agents of the criminal justice system, because they can work with the often seemingly irresistible power, force, and authority of the state. In such meetings, criminals and deviants are obliged to confront not only their own and others' possibly defensive, fleeting, and insubstantial reactions to what they have done, their 'primary deviation', but also contend publicly with the formal reactions of others, and their deviation can then become a response to responses, 'secondary deviation': 'When a person begins to employ his deviant behavior or a role based upon it as a means of defense, attack, or adjustment to the overt and covert problems created by the consequent societal reaction to him, his deviation is secondary' (Lemert 1951: 76).

What is significant about secondary deviation is that it may be a symbolic synthesis of more than just the meanings and activities of primary deviation. It may also incorporate the myths, professional knowledge, stereotypes, experience, and working assumptions of lay people, police officers, judges, medical practitioners, prison officers, prisoners, policy-makers, and politicians. Drug-users (see Schur 1963), mental patients (Goffman 1968; Scheff 1966), homosexuals (Hooker 1963), and others may be obliged to organize their significant gestures and character around the public symbols and interpretations of their behaviour. Who they are and what they do may then be explained as much by the symbolic incorporation of a public response as by any set of original conditions, and control will be written into the very fabric of their selves.

Secondary deviation may also entail confrontations with new obstacles that foreclose future choice. Thus, Gary Marx listed a number of the ironic consequences that can flow from forms of covert social control such as undercover policing and the work of *agents provocateurs*: they include generating a market for illegal goods; the provision of motives and meanings for illegal action; entrapping people in offences they might not otherwise have committed; the supply of false or misleading records; retaliatory action against informers, and the like (Marx 1988: 126–7). Once a person is publicly identified as a deviant, moreover, it may become difficult for him or her to slip back into the conventional world, and measures are being taken with increasing frequency to enlarge the visibility of the rule-breaker. In the United States, for instance, 'Megan's Law' makes it mandatory in certain jurisdictions for the names of sex offenders to be publicly advertised, possibly reducing risk to some but certainly freezing the criminal as a secondary deviant. Sheriffs have been known to shame prisoners by making them wear pink clothing or carry placards in public.

Quite deliberately in response to such dangerously amplified problems of the outlawed deviant is the increasing adoption by states of strategies of restorative justice, based largely on the work of Braithwaite (1989), which attempt to unite the informal control of shaming by significant others with rituals of reintegration that work against the alienating consequences of secondary deviation.

Borrowing its ideas from Durkheim and labelling theory and its procedures from a number of forms of dispute resolution, but from Maori and Japanese practice in particular, shaming is for Braithwaite at its most effective when it is practised by those whose opinions matter to the deviant—his or her 'significant others'; and that it would work only to exclude and estrange the deviant unless it was accompanied by rituals of reparation and restoration, effected, perhaps, by the tendering and acceptance of a public apology. Reintegrative shaming is currently one of the 'big ideas' underpinning the ideas (if not always the practice) of criminal justice policy across the Western world, but also in South Africa and elsewhere, where it is seen to be a return to the procedures of aboriginal justice. And it sits remarkably well with an interesting study of reoffending after prison that argues that the critical variable in desistance from crime is the capacity of a former inmate to construct a new narrative about his or her life which frames a new self now going 'straight' (Maruna 2001).

The most recent twist in the evolution of interactionist criminology has been the work of Randall Collins, a student of Erving Goffman, who adapted it to analyse the detail of violent transactions. Violence, he observes, is actually difficult to accomplish: most people—even soldiers and police who are professionally engaged to deploy force—are reluctant to attack or harm others. A mixture of tension and fear holds them back. It is the overwhelming passion of what he calls a 'forward panic' that can overcome that mix, and it may in part be facilitated by the obvious weakness of a potential victim who retreats or succumbs—making the violent act easier to perform—in part by the egging-on of spectators. It is then that 'the tension of the struggle [can] turn[] into…hot rush and vicious overkill' (2008: 135). Collins describes how victims themselves may enter into what he calls, following Goffman, interaction ritual chains of 'emotional entrainment', choreographed sequences in which their assailants are also embroiled, whereby both become progressively swept up in one another's actions and reactions, the offender overcoming his or her inhibitions and the victim dominated, steered, and incapacitated by the offender. Looking, say, at episodes of domestic violence or crowd disturbance, he is then able to relate how, step-by-step, people come collaboratively and almost collusively to engage in violent acts.

## CULTURE AND SUBCULTURE

Meanings and motives are not established and confirmed by the self in isolation. They are a social accomplishment, and criminology has paid sustained attention to signification as a collaborative, subcultural process. Subcultures themselves are taken to be exaggerations, accentuations, or editings of cultural themes prevalent in the wider society. Any social group which has permanence, a common pursuit, and, perhaps, common problems is likely to engender, inherit, or modify a subculture; but the criminologist's particular interest is in those subcultures that condone, promote, or otherwise make possible the commission of delinquent acts. A subculture was not conceived to be utterly distinct from the beliefs held by people at large. Neither was it necessarily oppositional. It was a *sub*culture, not a discrete culture or a counterculture, and the analytic stress has tended to be on dependency, 'hybridization', and synthesis rather than on conflict or symbolic autonomy.

The materials for subcultural theory are to be found across the broad range of criminology, and they could be combined in various proportions. Anomie theory supplied the supposition that social inequalities generate problems that may have delinquent solutions, and that those solutions, in their turn, could be shared and transmitted by people thrown together by their common disadvantage. Albert Cohen, the man who invented the phrase 'delinquent subculture', argued: 'The crucial condition for the emergence of new cultural forms is the existence, in effective interaction with one another, of a number of actors with similar problems of adjustment' (1957: 59). The social anthropology of the Chicago School, channelled for a while into differential association theory, supplied an emphasis upon the enduring, intelligible, and locally adapted cultural traditions shared both by professional criminals and by boys living, working, and playing together on the crowded streets of morally differentiated areas. Retaining the idea of a 'subculture of delinquency', David Matza and a number of control theorists pointed to the manner in which moral proscriptions could be neutralized by invoking commonly available and culturally transmitted extenuating accounts. And symbolic interactionism supplied a focus on the negotiated, collective, and processual character of meaning. In all this, an argument ran that young men (it was almost always young men), growing up in the city, banded together in groups or 'near-groups' (Yablonsky 1962) in the crowded and dangerous public life of the streets encountering common problems, exposed to common stereotypes and stigmas, subject to similar formal controls, flirting with transgressive excitement, and setting themselves against common Others who might 'disrespect' or attack them (Anderson 1990, 1999)—Others who are used oppositionally to define who they are—are likely to form joint interpretations that are sporadically favourable to delinquency. Subcultural theory and research were to dominate explanations of delinquency until they exhausted themselves for a while in the 1960s, only to be revived in a new guise a decade later.

Subcultural theory lent itself to amalgamation with radical criminology, and particularly that criminology which was preoccupied with the reproduction of class inequalities through the workings of ideology. In Britain, there was to be a renaissance of anomie-derived subcultural theory as a group of sociologists centred around Stuart Hall at the Centre for Contemporary Cultural Studies at the University of Birmingham gave special attention to the existential plight of young working-class men about to enter the labour market. The prototype for that work was Phil Cohen's analysis of proletarian cultures in London: young men responded to the post-war decline of community, loss of class cohesion, and economic insecurity by resurrecting in subcultural form an idealized and exaggerated version of working-class masculinity that 'express[ed] and resolve[d], albeit "magically", the contradictions which remain hidden or unresolved in the parent culture' (1972: 23). Deviance became a form of symbolic resistance to tensions perceived through the mists of false consciousness. It was doomed to disappoint because it did not address the root causes of discontent, but it *did* offer a fleeting release. There was a contradiction within that version of subcultural theory because it was not easy to reconcile a structural Marxism which depicted adolescent culture as illusory with a commitment to understanding meaning (Willis 1977). But it was a spirited and vivid revival of a theory that had gone into the doldrums in the 1960s, and it continues to influence theorizing (see Ferrell 1993). Indeed, interestingly, there are currently strong signs of a *rapprochement* between critical cultural studies, symbolic interactionism (see Becker and McCall 1990) and radical criminology, that has led to the creation of the new theoretical hybrid to which I have already alluded, cultural criminology (see Ferrell *et al.* 2004), which re-emphasizes how transgression attains meaning in what is called a fluid, pluralistic, contested, hedonistic, 'edgy', and 'media-saturated world'. It proclaims, a little brashly perhaps, that '[c]ultural criminology actively seeks to dissolve conventional understandings and accepted boundaries, whether they confine specific criminological theories or the institutionalized discipline of criminology itself... [Our] strategy of reinvigoration is as much historical as theoretical; if we are to engage critically with the present crisis in crime and control, intellectual revivification is essential' (Ferrell *et al.* 2008: 5—6). In its more recent variants, delinquency has become a celebration of a kind of fetishized, hedonistic consumerism which has become an end in itself (Hallsworth 2005).

## CRIMINOLOGY AS AN ECLECTIC DISCIPLINE

It would be misleading from my description so far to conclude that criminology can easily be laid out as an array of discrete clusters of theory. On the contrary, it has continually borrowed ideas from other disciplines, and has compared, contrasted, amalgamated, reworked, and experimented with them to furnish an eclectic discipline marked by an abundance of *ad hoc* theoretical overlaps, syntheses, and confusions (see Rock 2011).

There are exchanges and combinations of criminological ideas *within* disciplines. For instance, sociological criminologists have been exposed continually to changes in intellectual fashion in their parent discipline, and the result has been that almost every major theory in sociology has been fed in some form into criminology at some time, undergoing adaptation and editing in the process, and occasionally becoming very distant from its roots. Indeed, one of the distinctive properties of that process is that criminology can sometimes so extensively rework imported ideas that they will develop well beyond their original limits in sociology, becoming significant contributions to sociological theory in their own right. Anomie, the symbolic interactionist conception of the self and its others, and feminism are examples of arguments that have grown appreciably in scale and sophistication within the special environment of criminology.

There are exchanges and combinations *between* disciplines. Criminology is defined principally by its attachment to an empirical area: it is the study of *crime* that gives unity and order to the enterprise, not adherence to any particular theory or social science. It is in the examination of *crime* that psychologists, statisticians, lawyers, economists, social anthropologists, sociologists, social policy analysts, and psychiatrists meet and call themselves criminologists, and in that encounter, their attachments to the conventions and boundaries of their parent disciplines may weaken. So it is that sociological criminologists have confronted arguments born and applied in other disciplines and, from time to time, they have domesticated them to cultivate new intellectual hybrids. Stan Cohen (1972) and Jock Young (1971) did so in the early 1970s when they married the symbolic interactionism of Edwin Lemert (1951) and Howard Becker (1963) to the statistical and cybernetics theory of Leslie Wilkins (1964). Wilkins had argued that deviant events fall at the poles of normal distribution curves, that knowledge about those events will be distorted by the ensuing social distance, and that patterns of control and deviant responses are likely to become ever more exaggerated as they are affected by those distortions. That concept of deviance amplification married well with interactionist ideas of secondary deviation.

Thus constituted, the development of sociological criminology over the last few decades is at once marked by discontinuities and continuities. It may be represented as a staggered succession of interchanges with different schools and disciplines which do not always meld well together. It is evident, for instance, that the feminist may entertain a conception of theory and the theorist very unlike that of the functionalist or rational choice theorist. Yet there are also unities of a kind. All competent criminologists may be presumed to have a rough working knowledge of the wide range of theory in their discipline; theory once mastered is seldom forgotten or neglected entirely, and there is a propensity for scholars overtly and covertly to weave disparate ideas together as problems and needs arise. Quite typical was an observation offered in the author's introduction to a work on the lives of urban street criminals in Seattle, Washington: 'I link ... ethnographic data to criminological perspectives as a *bricoleur* seeking numerous sources of interpretation. Had I selected just one criminological perspective to complement these ethnographic data, the value of these firsthand accounts would be constrained' (Fleisher 1995: 5). Scholars thus tend frequently to be more accommodating in practice than in principle, and if there *is* an ensuing gap between a professed purity of theory and an active pragmatism of procedure, it may well be masked by the obliteration of sources or the renaming of ideas. Seemingly distinct sociological theories are open to continual merging and blurring as the practical work of criminology unfolds, and in that process may be found opportunities for theoretical innovation.

## PROSPECTS FOR THE FUTURE

What is uncertain, and what has always been uncertain, is how those criminological theories may be expected to evolve in the future. Very few would have predicted the rapid demise of radical criminology, a brand of theorizing that once seemed so strong that it would sweep all before it, at least in large parts of Europe, Canada, and Australasia. Few would have predicted the resurgence of utilitarian theories of rational choice—they seemed to have been superseded forever by a sociology that pointed to the part played by social and moral contexts in the shaping of meaning and action. Yet one criminologist felt himself constrained to lament that 'it seems that the hey-days of creative criminological (sociological) theory development in the US are long gone' (Marshall 2002: 21).

What may certainly be anticipated is a continuation of the semi-detached relations between criminology and its parent disciplines, and with sociology above all. The half-life of sociological theories is brief, often bound up with the duration of intellectual generations, and sociological theory is itself emergent, a compound of the familiar and the unfamiliar. It is to be assumed that there will always be something new out of sociology, and that criminology will almost always respond and innovate in its turn.

What has certainly made an appearance recently is a return in some important works to a larger political economy of crime and control. If Marxism is dead or dormant, a critically-informed analysis has re-emerged, and re-emerged, one might imagine, in sympathy with changes in the political and financial landscape of Europe and North America. It is here that criminology and penology merge. I have already alluded to the work of Loïc Wacquant as one instance. But others have displayed a renewed interest in crime and the economy, prompted, perhaps, by the vicissitudes of the first decade of the twenty-first century. A prime example is to be found in an interesting book, written by health epidemiologists, not by criminologists, and only sporadically related to crime, which suggests that rates of social mistrust, imprisonment, mental illness, and violence, including homicide, are all seemingly correlated with levels of financial inequality within rather than between societies (Wilkinson and Pickett 2009). Despite overall levels of wealth, the more unequal a society, they argue, the greater is its abundance of social problems, and the tempting conclusion is that a lack of moral and political authority, apparent injustice, and inequity of social arrangements conduce to strain (which they call stress) and criminality.

Extensions of that argument are to be found in the work of Simon (2007), Lacey (2008), and Reiner (2007), three authors whose ideas complement one another remarkably well. Jonathan Simon talked of how criminalization and incarceration have become the routine, default posture of governance in dealing with a multitude of social problems in the United States of America. What may formerly have been managed by the provision of welfare and of medical or psychiatric treatment has become swept up promiscuously into the criminal justice system and 'governed through crime'. Prisons now do the work that social assistance programmes, mental hospitals, and medicine once used to do.

So too, Nicola Lacey claims that there is an emerging spectrum of societies differentiated by their willingness to resort either to welfare or to criminal justice in the mitigation of social and economic problems. The more egalitarian societies of Scandinavia turn (or used to turn) to progressive taxation and substantial support in money and kind for those who are relatively poor or vulnerable, whilst the less equal societies of the United States and the United Kingdom rely more heavily on penal remedies for coping with all manner of problematic populations. The result is the manufacture of markedly different groupings: criminals and prisoners in the laissez-faire countries adopting what the French call the Anglo-Saxon route; and citizens diffusely supported in the welfarist regimes.

And finally, in a remarkably prescient book, written and published before the economic crisis of 2008, Reiner surveys the impact of neo-liberal political economy on crime and control. He argues that a rampant market system, prone to cycles of boom and depression, promotes anomic strains, erodes communality, exacerbates inequalities, generates increases in offending, and then proceeds to engender a concomitant political drive not only towards so-called wars on crime but also towards mass incarceration. To complete the trend, he says, there has been an accompanying move towards what David Garland and Pat O'Malley called 'responsibilization'—the devolution of much of the work of crime prevention on to the citizen who is expected to exercise prudence and take precautions in guarding his or her own person and property, purchasing security, and thereby reinforcing exclusions and social segregation. Of course, and despite popular and sociological expectations, the drift between 1994 and 2010 in the developed world was towards a continuous *decrease* in crime recorded by officials and reported by victims. For example, British Crime Survey figures show that those who were interviewed claimed to have suffered some 350,000 fewer crimes in 2008–9 than in 1981, and 'recorded crime increased during most of the 1980s, reaching a peak in 1992, and then fell each year until 1998/99 when the changes in the Counting Rules resulted in an increase in recorded offences' and then, when adjusted, fell again thereafter (http://rds.homeoffice.gov.uk/rds/crimeew0809.html). Prison populations may also start to fall under the pressure of the so-called 'fiscal crisis of the State', predicted some 30 years ago by Andrew Scull (1977) and long deferred. But much of the analysis of Simon, Lacey, and Reiner is fruitful, provocative, and plausible.

What else may be anticipated of the development of the discipline? First, criminology is, and will remain, a substantively defined discipline which tends not to detain the intellectual system-builders. Those who would be the sociological Newtons, the men and women who seek to explain the great clockwork of society, are often impatient with the limitations imposed by analysing the mere parts and fragments of larger totalities. At first or second hand, almost all the grand theorists have made something of a mark on criminology in the past, but they, or their disciples, have rarely stayed long. Their concern is with the wider systemic properties of society, not the surface features of empirical areas. Thus the phenomenologist, Phillipson, long ago remarked that '[we should] turn away from constitutive and arbitrary judgements of public rule breaking as deviance towards the concept of rule itself and the dialectical tension that ruling is, a subject more central to the fundamental practice of sociology' (1974: 5). And Marxists (Bankowski *et al.* 1977) and feminists (Smart 1989) have said much the same about the relations between their theories and the subdiscipline of criminology.

Secondly, criminology will probably persist in challenging economics as a contender for the title of the dismal science. Criminologists are not professionally optimistic. A prolonged exposure to the pain of crime, rates of offending that (until fairly recently at least) had seemed prone inexorably to rise, frequent abuses of authority, misconceived policies, and 'nothing' or very little appearing to work, seems to have fostered a propensity amongst thinkers to infuse their writing with gloom and to argue, in effect, that all is really not for the best in the best of all possible worlds Stan Cohen once confessed that 'most of us—consciously or not—probably hold a rather bleak view of social change'. Things must be getting worse' (1979a: 360). It certainly took criminologists a long time to accept the possibility that crime rates may actually have started to decline after 1994. Some have still failed to accept it. Prophecies of a criminological future may then still be tinged at the margins with the iconography of Mad Max, Neuromancer, and Blade Runner.

Thirdly, there is the growing influence of government and government money in shaping criminological work, particularly in North America, and that has shaped the form, mode, and content of the discipline. Formally, policy-makers and politicians have a liking for argument phrased in numbers: it lends itself to an appearance of exactitude and control. One commentator, Bernard, remarked that 'The past 20 years have seen a vast expansion of quantitative research in criminology. Twenty years ago there were fewer journals and they published a greater variety of articles, including quantitative and qualitative research, theoretical and policy arguments, and even polemical pieces. Today, there are more journals and they mainly publish quantitative research' (1990: 325). In some American universities, students of criminology are enjoined only to write for quantitative journals if they are to have a future as academics. And, substantively, policies and politics have conspired to make certain kinds of applied reasoning, such as restorative justice and rational choice theory, the criminological anti-theory, particularly attractive to criminal justice agencies. Restorative justice is quite new, and modest in its reach, and it seems to 'work'. Rational choice and control theories lay out a series of neat, inexpensive, small-scale, practicable, and non-controversial steps that may be taken to 'do something' about crime. Moreover, as theories that are tied to the apron strings of economics, they can borrow something of the powerful intellectual authority that economics used to wield in the social sciences.

A name has been given to this new face: public criminology, a criminology that is more self-consciously serviceable and responsive to the needs of community, society, and the state (Clear 2010; Loader and Sparks 2010; Rock 2010).

Fourth is the persistence of a feminist influence. Crime is clearly gendered, the intellectual yield of analysing the connections between gender and crime is still being explored, and women are entering the body of sociological criminology in ever greater numbers (although, to be sure, some feminists, like Carol Smart, have also emigrated and absolute numbers remain small). Twenty years ago, Valverde could observe that 'it is now no longer true that women's issues are being ignored, for there are whole shelves of work on women as victims of male violence, women offenders and women police officers. The more extreme examples of sexism found in criminological theory have been discredited—at least in the eyes of those who read feminist works' (1991: 241).

Criminological feminisms and feminist criminologies (Gelsthorpe and Morris 1988) will undoubtedly sustain work on gender, control, and deviance and, increasingly, on masculinity. After all, if crime is largely a male preserve, criminology must ask what it is about masculinity that seems to have such an affinity with offending. Connell (1987), not himself a criminologist, has sketched the possibilities of an answer in his writing on 'hegemonic masculinity'—the overriding ideology of male power, wealth, and physical strength—that lends itself to exploit, risk-taking, and aggression. Messerschmidt (1997), Bourgois (1995), and Polk (1994) have pursued that model of masculine behaviour into criminology, Bourgois exploring the work done to maintain 'respect' by cocaine-dealing Latin Americans on the streets of New York, and Polk describing how the defence of masculine conceptions of honour and face can precipitate homicide.

A role will continue to be played by the sociological criminology that attaches importance to the ethnographic study of signifying practices. Symbolic interactionism and phenomenology have supplied an enduring reminder of the importance of reflectivity; the symbolically mediated character of all social reality; and the sheer complexity, density, and intricacy of the social world. And, lastly, one would hope that criminology will continue to contribute its own distinct analysis of the wider social world, an analysis that can take it beyond the confines of a tightly defined nexus of relations between criminals, legislators, lawyers, and enforcement agents. A criminology without a wider vision of social process would be deformed. A sociology without a conception of rule-breaking and control would be an odd discipline indeed.

### ■ SELECTED FURTHER READING

There is no substitute for the original works, some of the more important of which are Howard Becker's *Outsiders* (1963); John Braithwaite's *Crime, Shame and Reintegration* (1989); Richard Cloward and Lloyd Ohlin's *Delinquency and Opportunity* (1960); David Matza's *Delinquency and Drift* (1964); Ian Taylor, Paul Walton, and Jock Young's *The New Criminology* (1973); and Jock Young's *The Exclusive Society* (1999). Among the secondary texts are David Downes and Paul Rock's *Understanding Deviance* (2011), John Tierney's *Criminology: Theory and Context* (1996 and 2005), and Tim Newburn's *Criminology*, Cullompton: Willan, 2007.

# ■ REFERENCES

AKERLOF, G. and YELLEN, J. (1994), 'Gang Behavior, Law Enforcement, and Community Values', in H. Aaron et al. (eds), Values and Public Policy, Washington DC: Brookings Institute.

AI DANA-PINDELL, R. (2002), 'In Vindication of Justiciable Victims' Rights to Truth and Justice for State-Sponsored Crimes', Vanderbilt Journal of Transnational Law, November, 35: 5.

ANDERSON, E. (1976), A Place on the Corner, Chicago: University of Chicago Press.

—— (1990), Streetwise, Chicago: University of Chicago Press.

—— (1999), Code of the Street, New York: W.W Norton.

ARRIGO, B. and BERNARD, T. (2002), 'Postmodern Criminology in Relation to Radical and Conflict Criminology', in S. Cote (ed.), Criminological Theories: Bridging the Past to the Future, Thousand Oaks: Sage.

BALDWIN, J. and BOTTOMS, A. (1976), The Urban Criminal, London: Tavistock.

BANKOWSKI, Z., MUNGHAM, G., and YOUNG, P. (1977), 'Radical Criminology or Radical Criminologist?', Contemporary Crises, 1(1): 37–51.

BAUMAN, Z. (1989), Modernity and the Holocaust, Cambridge: Polity Press.

BAYART, J.-F., ELLIS, S., and HIBOU, B. (1999), The Criminalization of the State in Africa, Bloomington: Indiana University Press.

BECK, U. (1992), Risk Society, London: Sage.

BECKER, G. (1968), 'Crime and Punishment: An Economic Approach', The Journal of Political Economy, 76.

BECKER, H. (1963), Outsiders, New York: Free Press.

—— and McCALL, M. (eds) (1990), Symbolic Interaction and Cultural Studies, Chicago: University of Chicago Press.

BEIRNE, P. (ed.) (1994), Introduction to The Origins and Growth of Criminology, Aldershot: Dartmouth.

BELL, D. (1960), 'The Racket-Ridden Longshoremen', in The End of Ideology, New York: Collier.

BENNETT, T. and WRIGHT, R. (1984), Burglars on Burglary: Prevention and the Offender, Aldershot: Gower.

BERNARD, T. (1990), 'Twenty Years of Testing Theories', Journal of Research in Crime and Delinquency, 27.

BOTTOMS, A. et al. (1989), 'A Tale of Two Estates', in D. Downes (ed.), Crime and the City, Macmillan: Basingstoke.

—— and WILES, P. (1996), 'Crime and Insecurity in the City', in C. Fijnaut et al. (eds), Changes in Society, Crime and Criminal Justice in Europe, The Hague: Kluwer.

BOURGOIS, P. (1995), In Search of Respect, Cambridge: Cambridge University Press.

BOX, S. (1971), Deviance, Reality and Society, London: Holt, Rinehart, and Winston.

—— (1983), Power, Crime and Mystification, London: Tavistock.

BRAITHWAITE, J. (1989), Crime, Shame and Reintegration, Cambridge: Cambridge University Press.

BRANTINGHAM, P. and BRANTINGHAM, P. (1981–2), 'Mobility, Notoriety, and Crime', Journal of Environmental Systems, 11(1).

CAMPBELL, B. (1993), Goliath: Britain's Dangerous Places, London: Methuen.

CARLEN, P. (1988), Women, Crime and Poverty, Milton Keynes: Open University Press.

—— (1996), Jigsaw: A Political Criminology of Youth Homelessness, Buckingham: Open University Press.

CHAMBLISS, W. (1976), 'The State and Criminal Law', in W. Chambliss and M. Mankoff (eds), Whose Law, What Order?, New York: Wiley

CHAPMAN, D. (1967), Sociology and the Storentype of the Criminal, London: Tavistock.

CHEVALIER, L. (1973), Labouring Classes and Dangerous Classes in Paris During the First Half of the Nineteenth Century, London: Routledge & Kegan Paul.

CLARKE, R. (1980), 'Situational Crime Prevention: Theory and Practice', British Journal of Criminology, 20.

—— (1992), Situational Crime Prevention, New York: Harrow and Heston.

—— (1999), 'Situational Prevention', paper delivered at the Cambridge Workshop on Situational Crime Prevention—Ethics and Social Context, 14–16 October.

—— and CORNISH, D. (undated), 'Rational Choice', unpublished.

—— and —— (1985), 'Modeling Offenders' Decisions', in M. Tonry and N. Morris (eds) Crime and Justice, 6, Chicago: University of Chicago Press.

—— and —— (2000), 'Analyzing Organized Crime', unpublished.

—— and FELSON, M. (eds) (1993), Routine Activity and Rational Choice, New Brunswick: Transaction.

CLEAR, T. (2010), 'Policy and Evidence: The Challenge to the American Society of Criminology: 2009 Presidential Address the American Society of Criminology', Criminology, 48: 701–25.

CLEAVER, E (1969), Post-Prison Writings and Speeches, London: Cape.

CLOWARD, R., and OHLIN, L. (1960), Delinquency and Opportunity, New York: Free Press.

COHEN, A. (1957), Delinquent Boys, Glencoe: Free Press.

COHEN, L., and FELSON, M. (1979), 'Social Change and Crime Rate Trends', American Sociological Review, 44.

COHEN, P. (1972), 'Working-Class Youth Cultures in East London', Working Papers in Cultural Studies, Birmingham, 2.

COHEN, S. (1971), Images of Deviance, London: Penguin.

—— (1972), *Folk Devils and Moral Panics*, London: Paladin.

—— (1979a), 'The Punitive City: Notes on the Dispersal of Social Control', *Contemporary Crises*, 3.

—— (1979b) 'Guilt, Justice and Tolerance', in D. Downes and P. Rock (eds), *Deviant Interpretations*, Oxford: Martin Robertson.

—— (1985), *Visions of Social Control*, Cambridge: Polity.

—— (1996), 'Crime and Politics: Spot the Difference', *British Journal of Sociology*, 47.

COLEMAN, A. (1985), *Utopia on Trial*, London: Hilary Shipman.

—— (1986), 'Dangerous Dreams', *Landscape Design*, 163.

COLLINS, R. (2008), *Violence: A Micro-Sociological Theory*, Princeton: Princeton University Press.

COLQUHOUN, P. (1797), *A Treatise on the Police of the Metropolis*, London: H. Fry.

CONDRY, R. (2010), 'Appreciating the Broad Reach of Serious Crime and the Interpretive Power of Claims to Secondary Victimization', in D. Downes, D. Hobbs, and T. Newburn (eds), *The Eternal Recurrence of Crime and Control*, Oxford: Oxford University Press.

CONNELL, R. (1987), *Gender and Power*, Cambridge: Polity.

CORRIGAN, P. (1979), *Schooling the Smash Street Kids*, London: Macmillan.

COTTERRELL, R. (1999), *Émile Durkheim: Law in a Moral Domain*, Stanford: Stanford University Press.

CUSSON, M. (1983), *Why Delinquency?*, Toronto: University of Toronto Press.

DAMER, S. (1974), 'Wine Alley: The Sociology of a Dreadful Enclosure', *Sociological Review*, 22.

DAVIES, N. (1998), *Dark Heart: The Shocking Truth about Hidden Britain*, London: Vintage.

DAVIS, K. (1937), 'The Sociology of Prostitution', *American Sociological Review*, 2.

—— (1959), 'The Myth of Functional Analysis as a Special Method in Sociology and Anthropology', *American Sociological Review*, 24.

DAVIS, M. (1992a), 'Beyond Blade Runner', *Open Magazine Pamphlet*, New Jersey.

—— (1992b), *City of Quartz*, New York: Vintage.

DOUGLAS, J. (1971), *American Social Order*, London: Collier-Macmillan.

DOUGLAS, M. (1966), *Purity and Danger*, London: Pelican.

DOWNES, D. (1966), *The Delinquent Solution*, London: Routledge & Kegan Paul.

—— (1988), 'The Sociology of Crime and Social Control in Britain, 1960–1987', in P. Rock (ed.), *A History of British Criminology*, Oxford: Clarendon Press.

—— and ROCK, P. (eds) (1979), *Deviant Interpretations*, Oxford: Martin Robertson.

—— and —— (2011), *Understanding Deviance*, Oxford: Oxford University Press.

DUNEIER, M. (2001), *Sidewalk*, New York: Farrar, Straus and Giroux.

DURKHEIM, É. (1952), *Suicide*, London: Routledge & Kegan Paul.

—— (1964), *The Division of Labour in Society*, New York: Free Press.

EISNER, M. (2003), 'Long-Term Historical Trends in Violent Crime', in M. Tonry (ed.), *Crime and Justice*, University of Chicago Press: Chicago.

ERIKSON, K. (1966), *Wayward Puritans*, New York: Wiley.

—— (1994), *A New Species of Trouble*, New York: Norton.

FARIS, R. and DUNHAM, H. (1939), *Mental Disorders in Urban Areas*, Chicago: University of Chicago Press.

FEELEY, M. (1996), 'The Decline of Women in the Criminal Process', in *Criminal Justice History*, 15, Westport, Ct.: Greenwood Press.

—— and SIMON, J. (1992), 'The New Penology', *Criminology*, 30.

FELSON, M. (1994), *Crime and Everyday Life*, California: Pine Forge.

—— and CLARKE, R. (1998), *Opportunity Makes the Thief*, Police Research Series Paper, London: Home Office.

FERRELL, J. (1993), *Crimes of Style*, Boston, Mass.: Northeastern University Press.

—— and SANDERS, C. (1995), *Cultural Criminology*, Boston, Mass.: Northeastern University Press.

—— , HAYWARD, K., MORRISON, W., and PRESDEE, M. (eds) (2004), *Cultural Criminology Unleashed*, London: Glasshouse.

—— , HAYWARD, K., and YOUNG, J. (2008), *Cultural Criminology*, London: Sage.

FITZGERALD, M. (1977), *Prisoners in Revolt*, Harmondsworth: Penguin.

FLEISHER, M. (1995), *Beggars and Thieves*, Madison, Wis.: University of Wisconsin Press.

FLETCHER, J. (1850), *Summary of the Moral (and Educational) Statistics of England and Wales*, London: privately printed.

FOUCAULT, M. (1977), *Discipline and Punish*, Harmondsworth: Penguin.

FUKUYAMA, F. (2004), *State Building*, London: Profile Books.

GARLAND, D. (1988), 'British Criminology before 1935', in P. Rock (ed.), *A History of British Criminology*, Oxford: Clarendon Press.

—— (2002), 'Of Crimes and Criminals: The Development of Criminology in Britain', in M. Maguire, R. Morgan, and R. Reiner (eds), *The Oxford Handbook of Criminology*, 3rd edn, Oxford: Oxford University Press.

GELSTHORPE, L. and MORRIS, A. (1988), 'Feminism and Criminology in Britain', *British Journal of Criminology*, 28.

GENN, H. (1988), 'Multiple Victimisation', in M. Maguire and J. Pointing (eds), *Victims of Crime: a New Deal?*, Milton Keynes: Open University Press.

GIDDENS, A. (1972), *Émile Durkheim: Selected Writings*, Cambridge: Cambridge University Press.

—— (1991), *Modernity and Self-Identity*, Cambridge: Polity Press.

GILL, O. (1977), *Luke Street: Housing Policy, Conflict and the Creation of the Delinquent Area*, London: Macmillan.

GLUCKMAN, M. (1955), *The Judicial Process Among the Barotse of Northern Rhodesia*, Manchester: Manchester University Press.

GODWIN, P. (2006), *When a Crocodile Eats the Sun*, New York: Back Bay Books.

GOFFMAN, E. (1968), *Asylums*, Harmondsworth: Penguin.

GORDON, C. (ed.) (1972), *Power/Knowledge*, Brighton: Harvester Press.

GORDON, D. (1986–7), 'The Electronic Panopticon', *Politics and Society*, 15.

GOTTFREDSON, M. and HIRSCHI, T. (1990), *A General Theory of Crime*, Stanford, Cal.: Stanford University Press.

GUERRY, A. (1864), *Statistique morale de l'Angleterre comparée avec la statistique morale de la France*, Paris: J. B. Bailliere et Fils.

HAGAN, J. (1985), 'The Class Structure of Gender and Delinquency: Toward a Power-Control Theory of Common Delinquent Behavior', *American Journal of Sociology*, 90.

—— (1988), *Structural Criminology*, Cambridge: Polity Press.

—— (1977), *The Disreputable Pleasures*, New York: McGraw-Hill Ryerson.

—— and McCARTHY, B. (1998), *Mean Streets: Youth Crime and Homelessness*, Cambridge: Cambridge University Press.

——, SIMPSON, J. H., and GILLIS, A. R. (1979), 'The Sexual Stratification of Social Control', *British Journal of Sociology*, 30.

HAGGERTY, K. (2004), 'Displaced Expertise', *Theoretical Criminology*, 8, 2.

HALL, S., CRITCHER, C., JEFFERSON, T., CLARKE, J., and ROBERTS, B. (1978), *Policing the Crisis*, London: Macmillan.

HALLSWORTH, S. (2005), *Street Crime*, Cullompton: Willan.

HEIDENSOHN, F. (1968), 'The Deviance of Women: A Critique and an Enquiry', *British Journal of Sociology*, 19.

HENRY, S. and MILOVANOVIĆ, D. (1006), *Constitutive Criminology: Beyond Postmodernism*, London: Sage.

HILLIER, W. (1973), 'In Defence of Space', *RIBA Journal*, November.

—— (1986), 'City of Alice's Dreams', *Architecture Journal*, 9.

HILLYARD, P., SIM, J., TOMBS, S., and WHYTE, D. (2004), 'Leaving a "Stain upon the Silence": Contemporary Criminology and the Politics of Dissent', *British Journal of Criminology*, 44: 369–90.

HIRSCHI, T. (1969), *The Causes of Delinquency*, Berkeley, Cal.: University of California Press.

HIRST, P. (1975), 'Marx and Engels on Law, Crime and Morality', in I. Taylor *et al.* (eds), *Critical Criminology*, London: Routledge & Kegan Paul.

HOOD, R. (2004), 'Hermann Mannheim and Max Grünhut: Criminological Pioneers in London and Oxford', *British Journal of Criminology*, July, 44(4): 469–95.

HOOKER, E. (1963), 'Male Homosexuality', in N. Farberow (ed.), *Taboo Topics*, New York: Prentice-Hall.

HOPE, T. (1982), *Burglary in Schools*, London: Home Office.

HOUGH, M. and MAYHEW, P. (1983), *The British Crime Survey*, London: HMSO.

HOWARD, J. (1784), *The State of the Prisons*, London: Cadell, Johnson, and Dilly.

INCIARDI, J. (ed.) (1980), *Radical Criminology: the Coming Crises*, Beverly Hills, Cal.: Sage.

INNES, M. (2003), *Understanding Social Control: Deviance, Crime And Social Order*, Maidenhead: Open University Press.

JACOBS, J. (1965), *The Death and Life of Great American Cities*, Harmondsworth: Penguin.

JONES, T., MACLEAN, B., and YOUNG, J. (1986), *The Islington Crime Survey*, Aldershot: Gower.

KAPLAN, R. (1994), 'The Coming Anarchy', *The Atlantic Monthly*, February.

KATZ, J. (1988), *Seductions of Crime*, New York: Basic Books.

—— (1997), 'Ethnography's Warrants', *Sociological Methods and Research*, 25: 4.

KENNY, C. (1910), untitled piece in *Journal of the Society of Comparative Legislation*, 10: 2.

KITTRIE, N. (1971), *The Right to be Different*, Baltimore, Md.: Johns Hopkins Press.

KORNHAUSER, R. (1978), *Social Sources of Delinquency: An Appraisal of Analytic Models*, Chicago: University of Chicago Press.

KUMAR, R. (1993), *The History of Doing*, New Delhi: Kali for Women.

LACEY, N., *The Prisoners' Dilemma: Political Economy and Punishment in Contemporary Societies*, Cambridge: Cambridge University Press.

LANDESCO, J. (rep. 1968), *Organized Crime in Chicago*, Chicago: University of Chicago Press.

LAUB, J. and SAMPSON, R. (2003), *Shared Beginnings: Divergent Lives: Delinquent Boys to Age 70*, Cambridge, Mass.: Harvard University Press.

LEA, J. and YOUNG, J. (1984), *What is to be Done about Law and Order?*, London: Penguin Books.

LEMERT, E. (1951), *Social Pathology*, New York: McGraw-Hill.

LIANOS, M. with DOUGLAS, M. (2000), 'Dangerisation and the End of Deviance: The Institutional Environment', *British Journal of Criminology*, Spring, 40: 2.

LLEWELLYN, K. and HOEBEL, A. (1941), *The Cheyenne Way: Conflict and Case Law in Primitive Jurisprudence*, Norman, Okla.: University of Oklahoma Press.

LOADER, I. and SPARKS, R. (2010), *Public Criminology?*, London: Routledge.

LOMBROSO, C. (1895), *The Female Offender*, London: T. Fisher Unwin.

LUCKENBILL, D. and BEST, J. (1981), 'Careers in Deviance and Respectability', *Social Problems*, 29.

LUKES, S. (1967), 'Alienation and Anomie', in P. Laslett and W. Runciman (eds), *Philosophy, Politics and Society*, Oxford: Blackwell.

LYON, D. (1994), *The Electronic Eye*, Cambridge: Polity Press.

McROBBIE, A. and GARBER, J. (1976), 'Girls and Subcultures', in S. Hall and T. Jefferson (eds), *Resistance through Ritual*, London: Hutchinson.

MANNHEIM, H. (1965), *Comparative Criminology*, London: Routledge and Kegan Paul.

MARSHALL, I. (2002), 'The Criminological Enterprise in Europe and America', in S. Cote (ed.), *Criminological Theories: Bridging the Past to the Future*, Thousand Oaks, Cal.: Sage.

MARTINSON, R. (1974), 'What Works? Questions and Answers about Penal Reform', *Public Interest*, 35.

MARUNA, S. (2001), *Making Good: How Ex-Convicts Reform and Rebuild their Lives*, Washington DC: American Psychological Association.

MARX, G. (1988), *Under Cover*, Berkeley, Cal.: University of California Press.

MATHIESEN, T. (1974), *The Politics of Abolition*, London: Martin Robertson.

MATTHEWS, R. and YOUNG, J. (eds) (1992), *Rethinking Criminology: The Realist Debate*, London: Sage.

MATZA, D. (1964), *Delinquency and Drift*, New York: Wiley.

—— (1969), *Becoming Deviant*, New Jersey: Prentice-Hall.

MAUDSLEY, H. (1888), 'Remarks on Crime and Criminals,' *Journal of Mental Science*, July.

MAYHEW, P., CLARKE, R. V. G., SHURMAN, A., and HOUGH, J. M. (1976), *Crime as Opportunity*, Home Office Research Study No. 34, London: Home Office.

MEAD, G. (1918), 'The Psychology of Punitive Justice', *American Journal of Sociology*, 23.

—— (1934), *Mind Self and Society*, Chicago: University of Chicago Press.

MERTON, R. (1938), 'Social Structure and Anomie', *American Sociological Review*, 3.

—— (1957), *Social Theory and Social Structure*, Glencoe, Ill.: Free Press.

—— (1995), 'Opportunity Structure: The Emergence, Diffusion and Differentiation of a Sociological Concept, 1930s–1950s', in F. Adler and W. Laufer (eds), *The Legacy of Anomie Theory*, New Brunswick: Transaction.

MESSERSCHMIDT, J. (1997), *Crime as Structured Action: Gender, Race, Class, and Crime in the Making*, Thousand Oaks, Cal.: Sage.

MESSNER, S. and ROSENFELD, R. (2009), 'Institutional Anomie Theory: A Macro-sociological Explanation of Crime', in M. Krohn, A. Lizotte, and G. Hall (eds), *Handbook on Crime and Deviance*, New York: Springer.

MILL, J. (originally published 1838, republished 1950), *Bentham and Coleridge*, London: Chatto and Windus.

MILLS, C. (1940), 'Situated Actions and Vocabularies of Motive', *American Sociological Review*, 5.

MORRIS, T. (1957), *The Criminal Area*, London: Routledge & Kegan Paul.

—— (1988), 'British Criminology: 1935–48', in P. Rock (ed.), *A History of British Criminology*, Oxford: Clarendon Press.

MORRISON, W. (1891), *Crime and its Causes*, London: Swan Sonnenschein.

—— (1896), *Juvenile Offenders*, London: Swan Sonnenschein.

MURPHY, D. and ROBINSON, M. (2008), ''The Maximizer: Clarifying Merton's Theories of Anomie and Strain', *Theoretical Criminology*, November, 12.

NEWBURN, T. and STANKO, E. (eds) (1994), *Just Boys Doing Business: Masculinity and Crime*, London: Routledge.

NEWMAN, K. (2006), *Chutes and Ladders: Navigating the Low-Wage Labor Market*, New York: Russell Sage Foundation.

NEWMAN, O. (1972), *Defensible Space: People and Design in the Violent City*, London: Architectural Press.

NORRIS, C. and ARMSTRONG, G. (1999), *The Maximum Surveillance Society*, Oxford: Berg.

O'MALLEY, P. (1992), 'Risk, Power and Crime Prevention', *Economy and Society*, August, 21.

—— (2010), *Crime and Risk*, London: Sage.

PARK, R. (1915), 'The City: Suggestions for the Investigation of Human Behavior in the City Environment', *American Journal of Sociology*, 20.

—— (1925), 'Community Organization and Juvenile Delinquency', in R. Park and R. Burgess (eds), *The City*, Chicago: University of Chicago Press.

PARSONS, T. (1951), *The Social System*, London: Routledge & Kegan Paul.

PEARCE, F. (1976), *Crimes of the Powerful*, London: Pluto.

—— and TOMBS, S. (1998), *Toxic Capitalism: Corporate Crime and the Chemical Industry*, Aldershot: Dartmouth.

PHILLIPSON, M. (1974), 'Thinking Out of Deviance', unpublished paper.

POLK, K. (1994), *When Men Kill*, Cambridge: Cambridge University Press.

POLSKY, N. (1967), *Hustlers, Beats and Others*, Chicago: Aldine.

POWER, A. (1997), *Estates on the Edge: The Social Consequences of Mass Housing in Northern Europe*, New York: St. Martin's Press.

PRESDEE, M. (2000), *Cultural Criminology and the Carnival of Crime*, London: Routledge.

QUETELET, L. (1848), *Du système social et des lois qui le régissent*, Paris: np.

QUINNEY, R. (1970), *The Social Reality of Crime*, Boston, Mass.: Little Brown.

RADZINOWICZ, L. and HOOD, R. (1990), *The Emergence of Penal Policy in Victorian and Edwardian England*, Oxford: Clarendon Press.

RAINWATER, L. (1970), *Behind Ghetto Walls*, Chicago: Aldine.

RECKLESS, W. (1933), *Vice in Chicago*, Chicago: University of Chicago Press.

—— *et al.* (1957), 'The Good Boy in a High Delinquency Area', *Journal of Criminal Law, Criminology, and Police Science*, 48.

REIMAN, J. (1990), *The Rich Get Richer and the Poor Get Prison*, New York: Macmillan.

REINER, R. (2007), *Law and Order: An Honest Citizen's Guide to Crime and Control*, Cambridge: Polity Press.

ROCK, P. (1988), 'The Present State of British Criminology', in P. Rock (ed.), *A History of British Criminology*, Oxford: Clarendon Press.

—— (2007), 'Caesare Lombroso as a Signal Criminologist', *Criminology and Criminal Justice*, 7.

—— 'Comment', *Criminology & Policy*, November 2010.

—— (2011), 'What have we done?', *Acta Criminologica*, 24(1): 19-43.

ROMILLY, S. (1811), *Observations on the Criminal Law of England*, London.

RONCEK, D. and MAIER, P. (1991), 'Bars, Blocks, and Crimes Revisited: Linking the Theory of Routine Activities to the Empiricism of "Hot Spots"', *Criminology*, 29.

RORTY, R. (1991), *Objectivity, Relativism, and Truth*, Cambridge: Cambridge University Press.

SAMPSON, R. and LAUB, J. (1993), *Crime in the Making: Pathways and Turning Points Through Life*, Cambridge, Mass.: Harvard University Press.

SCHEFF, T. (1966), *Being Mentally Ill*, London: Weidenfeld & Nicolson.

SCHUR, E. (1963), *Narcotic Addiction in Britain and America*, London: Tavistock.

SCOTT, M. and LYMAN, S. (1970), 'Accounts, Deviance and Social Order', in J. Douglas (ed.), *Deviance and Respectability*, New York: Basic Books.

SCOTT, R. (1972), 'A Proposed Framework for Analyzing Deviance as a Property of Social Order', in R. Scott and J. Douglas (eds), *Theoretical Perspectives on Deviance*, New York: Basic Books.

SCOTTISH CENTRAL RESEARCH UNIT (1999), 'The Effect of Closed Circuit Television on Recorded Crime Rates and Public Concern about Crime in Glasgow', Edinburgh: The Scottish Office.

SCRATON, P. (ed.) (1987), *Law, Order, and the Authoritarian State: Readings in Critical Criminology*, Milton Keynes: Open University Press.

SCULL, A. (1977), *Decarceration: Community Treatment and the Deviant*, Englewood Cliffs: Prentice-Hall.

—— (1979), *Museums of Madness: The Social Organization of Insanity in Nineteenth-Century England*, New York: Allen Lane.

SEMPLE, J. (1993), *Bentham's Prison: A Study of the Panopticon Penitentiary*, Oxford: Clarendon Press.

SHAPLAND, J. and VAGG, J. (1988), *Policing by the Public*, Oxford: Clarendon Press.

SHAW, C. (1971), 'Male Juvenile Delinquency and Group Behavior', in J. Short (ed.), *The Social Fabric of the Metropolis*, Chicago: University of Chicago Press.

—— and MCKAY, H. (1942), *Juvenile Delinquency and Urban Areas*, Chicago: University of Chicago Press.

SHEARING, C. and STENNING, P. (1985), 'From the Panopticon to Disney World: The Development of Discipline', in A. Doob and E. Greenspan (eds), *Perspectives in Criminal Law*, Aurora: Canada Law Book.

SHERMAN, L. (2010), 'Defiance, Compliance and Consilience: A General Theory of Criminology', in E. McLaughlin and T. Newburn (eds), *Sage Handbook of Criminological Theory*, London: Sage.

——, GARTIN, P., and BUERGER, M. (1989), 'Hot Spots of Predatory Crime: Routine Activities and the Criminology of Place', *Criminology*, 27.

SHORT, E. and DITTON, J. (1998), 'Seen and Now Heard: Talking to the Targets of Open Street CCTV', *British Journal of Criminology*, 38: 3.

SHORT, J. and STRODBECK, F. (1967), *Group Process and Gang Delinquency*, Chicago: University of Chicago Press.

SIM, J. (1990), *Medical Power in Prisons: The Prison Medical Service in England 1774-1989*, Milton Keynes: Open University Press.

SIMON, J. (1987), 'The Emergence of a Risk Society', *Socialist Review*.

—— (1993), *Poor Discipline: Parole and the Social Control of the Underclass*, Chicago: University of Chicago Press.

—— (2007), *Governing Through Crime: How the War on Crime Transformed American Democracy and Created a Culture of Fear*, New York: Oxford University Press.

—— and FEELEY, M. (1995), 'True Crime: The New Penology and Public Discourse on Crime', in T. Blomberg and S. Cohen (eds), *Punishment and Social Control*, New York: Aldine de Gruyter.

SLAPPER, G. and TOMBS, S. (1999), *Corporate Crime*, London: Longman.

SMART, C. (1977), *Women, Crime and Criminology*, London: Routledge & Kegan Paul.

—— (1989), *Feminism and the Power of Law*, London: Routledge.

SMITH, D. (2000), 'Changing Situations and Changing People', in A. von Hirsh, D. Garland, and A. Wakefield (eds), *Ethical and Social Perspectives on Situational Crime Prevention*, Oxford: Hart Publishing.

SPIERENBURG, P. (2008), *A History of Murder*, Cambridge: Polity.

STEPHENS, J. (1976), *Loners, Losers and Lovers*, Seattle: University of Washington Press.

STINCHCOMBE, A. (1968), *Constructing Social Theories*, New York: Harcourt Brace and World.

SUMNER, C. (1994), *The Sociology of Deviance: An Obituary*, Buckingham: Open University Press.

—— (ed.) (2004), Introduction to *The Blackwell Companion to Criminology*, Oxford: Blackwell.

SUTHERLAND, E. and CRESSEY, D. (1955), *Principles of Criminology*, Chicago: Lippincott.

SUTTLES, G. (1972), *The Social Construction of Communities*, Chicago: University of Chicago Press.

SYKES, G. and MATZA, D. (1957), 'Techniques of Neutralization', *American Sociological Review*, 22.

TAYLOR, I. (1999), *Crime in Context: A Critical Criminology of Market Societies*, Cambridge: Polity Press.

TAYLOR, I., WALTON, P., and YOUNG, J. (1973), *The New Criminology*, London: Routledge & Kegan Paul.

THRASHER, F. (1927), *The Gang*, Chicago: University of Chicago Press.

TIERNEY, J. (1996), *Criminology: Theory and Context*, 2nd edn 2005, London: Prentice-Hall.

TURNBULL, C. (1973), *The Mountain People*, London: Paladin.

VALIÉR, C. (1995), 'Psychoanalysis and crime in Britain During the Inter-War Years', The British Criminology Conferences: *Selected Proceedings. Volume 1: Emerging Themes in Criminology. Papers from the British Criminology Conference*, Loughborough University, 18–21 July.

VALVERDE, M. (1991), 'Feminist Perspectives on Criminology', in J. Gladstone, R. Ericson, and C. Shearing (eds.), *Criminology: A Reader's Guide*, Toronto: Centre of Criminology, University of Toronto.

VAN CREVELD, M. (1991), *The Transformation of War*, New York: Free Press.

WACQUANT, L. (2008), *Urban Outcasts: A Comparative Sociology of Advanced Marginality*, Cambridge; Polity.

WALKLATE, S. and EVANS, K. (1999), Zero Tolerance or Community Tolerance, Aldershot: Ashgate.

WELSH, B. and FARRINGTON, D. (2002), *Crime Prevention Effects of Closed Circuit Television: A Systematic Review*, London: Home Office.

WHITTEN, M. (2002), 'Protection, Prevention, Reformation: A History of the Philanthropic Society', PhD dissertation, London School of Economics.

WHYTE, W. (1942), *Street Corner Society*, Chicago: University of Chicago Press.

WIKSTRÖM, P-O. (2007), 'The Social Ecology of Crime: The Role of the Environment in Crime Causation', in H. Schneider (ed.), *Internationales Handbuch der Kriminologie*, Berlin: De Gruyter,

Wilkins, L. (1964), Social Deviance, London: Tavistock.

WILKINSON, R. and PICKETT, K., (2009), The Spirit Level: Why More Equal Societies Almost Always do Better, London: Allen Lane.

WILLIS, P. (1977), *Learning to Labour*, Farnborough, Hants: Gower.

WILSON, H. (1980), 'Parental Supervision: A Neglected Aspect of Delinquency', *British Journal of Criminology*, 20.

WILSON, W. (1996), *When Work Disappears: The World of the New Urban Poor*, New York: Alfred Knopf.

WIRTH, L. (1964), 'Culture Conflict and Misconduct', in *On Cities and Social Life*, Chicago: University of Chicago Press.

WRIGHT, R. and DECKER, S. (1997), *Armed Robbers in Action: Stickups and Street Culture*, Boston: Northeastern University Press.

YABLONSKY, L. (1962), *The Violent Gang*, London: Pelican.

YOUNG, J. (1971), *The Drugtakers*, London: Paladin.

—— (1997), 'Left Realist Criminology', in M. Maguire, R. Morgan, and R. Reiner (eds), *The Oxford Handbook of Criminology*, 2nd edn, Oxford: Oxford University Press.

—— (1998), 'From Inclusive to Exclusive Society: Nightmares in the European Dream', in V. Ruggiero, N. South, and I. Taylor (eds), *The New European Criminology*, London: Routledge.

—— (1999), *The Exclusive Society*, London: Sage.

—— (2004), 'Crime and the Dialectics of Inclusion/Exclusion', *British Journal of Criminology*, July, 44: 44.

—— (2007), *The Vertigo of Late Modernity*, London: Sage.

ZIMRING, F. (2007), *The Great American Crime Decline*, New York: Oxford University Press.

# 3

# CRIMINOLOGICAL PSYCHOLOGY

*Clive R. Hollin*

## INTRODUCTION

The vogue in Britain is to use the term 'forensic psychology' when referring to any topic even remotely connected with crime. Blackburn has commented on this etymological inaccuracy, noting of the word *forensic* that '[i]ts established English meaning is hence "pertaining to or used in courts of law", and that is how it has been understood by the public in general and lawyers in particular' (1996: 4). Indeed, this sense of psychology applied to legal decision-making is the way in which forensic psychology is properly understood elsewhere (Hess 2006). It is difficult, however, to find a term that accurately describes the application of psychological theory and research to antisocial conduct, criminal behaviour, and law. For many years The British Psychological Society (the professional body for psychologists in Britain) used the term 'Criminological and Legal Psychology' rather than 'Forensic Psychology' to describe this specialist area of psychological knowledge and practice. The British Psychological Society maintains this terminology in the title of its academic journal, *Legal and Criminological Psychology*.

The topic of legal psychology, the application of psychological knowledge and methods to the process of law has its own history with figures such as G. F. Arnold (Bornestein and Penrod 2008) and Hugo Münsterberg (Hale 1980) who were active in the early 1900s. Indeed, legal psychology has become a specialty in its own right (e.g. Bartol and Bartol 2008; Goldstein 2007; Kapardis 2010). However, the focus of this chapter is on *criminological* psychology: that is, the application of psychological theory and investigation to understanding (and attempting to change) criminal behaviour.

The chapter will be structured around the changing relationship over time between the disciplines of psychology and criminology. It will show how this relationship moved from early concord to conflict and a parting of the ways but more recently to something approaching a reconciliation. It begins by briefly tracing the early history of psychology as an academic discipline, noting differences between Europe and North America, and its relationship to the emerging discipline of criminology. The historical lineage to be discussed begins with the early psychological theories, drawing on Freud's ideas, which were used to attempt to understand juvenile offending. The growth of the behaviourist tradition is particularly important given its significance in the study of crime, as seen in several criminological theories. As we move to more recent times so the advent of personality theory gave rise to another level of explanation of criminal behaviour. The highly influential social learning theory, influenced by cognitive and social psychology, is very close to some criminological theories. The trend is now towards more complex 'multimodal' models and examples of this approach will be discussed.

It is important at the outset to emphasize the point that criminological psychology is concerned with the use of psychology to help explain criminal behaviour. It follows, therefore, that criminological psychology represents a meeting of psychology and criminology. The juxtaposition of psychology and criminology has been a constant issue for both disciplines. One way to understand the interplay between the disciplines, and hence the aetiology and changing emphases of criminological psychology, is to consider the historical highs and lows of this cross-discipline relationship. Adopting an historical perspective allows a picture to emerge of the theoretical points of contact and departure of the two disciplines. Based on this approach, Hayward (2005) offers a criminologist's perspective of psychology: as this chapter is concerned with psychology, the perspective here is from a psychological viewpoint.

## THE GROWTH OF PSYCHOLOGY AS AN ACADEMIC DISCIPLINE

Criminological psychology is a specialist branch of mainstream psychology, that is the assembly of knowledge and theory about human functioning. To understand the evolution of criminological psychology it is instructive to set this against the development of psychology as an academic discipline and a profession.

There is a long, long history of a search for an explanation of the human condition, from Greek philosophers to modern day geneticists and there is a myriad of accounts of why we are what we are. In some accounts it is an inner force—spiritual, biological, or psychological in nature—that is seen as the cause of an individual's behaviour. This tradition is evident in the history of psychology as an academic discipline, particularly in the style initially developed in the late nineteenth century in Continental Europe, heavily influenced by philosophy and intellectual analysis, as seen for example in Freud's psychoanalysis and in Gestalt Psychology (Brown 1961). However, pioneering work of a different kind saw the birth of psychology as a scientific, experimental discipline. This development is often linked to the founding of the first psychological laboratory at Leipzig in 1879 by Wilhelm Wundt (1832–1920), although another school of thought gives that particular credit to William James (1842–1940) at Harvard, and the contribution of James Rowland Angell (1899–1949) at the University of Chicago is perhaps often overlooked. Nonetheless, after the 1870s the spread of experimental psychology (with the attendant growth in sophisticated statistical techniques) was evident in universities in both Europe and the United States so that by the early 1900s psychology had become an established academic discipline (Schultz and Schultz 2008). The empirical, scientific approach adopted by the first experimental psychologists stood in marked contrast to the 'European' style of psychology dependent upon philosophy and intellectual analysis. In Britain the new discipline of psychology, influenced by figures such as Charles Darwin (1809–82) and Sir Francis Galton (1822–1911), was concerned with the study of individual differences. Thus the research of the early British psychologists, such as Sir Cyril Burt (1883–1971), was concerned with psychological constructs such as intelligence and personality combining biological as well as psychological variables.

## THE BEHAVIOURAL TRADITION

One of the most important aspects of early American psychology was a shift of focus away from the 'inner world' towards *overt behaviour* as the proper subject matter for psychological investigation. This focus was seen most clearly in the writings of John B. Watson (1878–1958), whose 1913 paper, 'Psychology as the Behaviorist Views It', is a manifesto for the development of behavioural psychology. The two trademarks of this emergent behavioural approach were: first, an implicit assumption that behaviour and biological structures are related; second a belief in the scientific legitimacy of the use of animals in experimental research intended to further understanding of humans. Willard Stanton Small (1870–1943) at Clarke University is credited as the first experimental psychologist to study the behaviour of rats in mazes to measure learning; while the learning theorist Edward L. Thorndike (1874–1949) at Columbia University was the first researcher to be awarded a psychology doctorate for research based on experiments with animals. In the rise of behaviourism the influence of the major physiologists of the time, including the Nobel Prizewinner Ivan Pavlov (1849–1936), is clearly discernible.

From the 1930s onwards, the focus on behaviour saw a profusion of theoretical positions under the general theme of 'behavioural' (O'Donohue and Kitchener 1999). The work of B. F. Skinner (1904–90) is undoubtedly the most influential within the behavioural tradition (Skinner 1938, 1974). Skinner was concerned to show empirically the relationship between behaviour, its environmental setting and its consequences. A body of experimental evidence accrued to show that the environment provides settings for particular behaviours to occur that are likely to produce predictable environmental effects. The environment is said to *operate* on the individual to increase or decrease the frequency of a given behaviour. Thus, the concept of *operant* learning was developed, with an attendant growth in understanding of how behaviour is acquired and maintained through the force of the environment on behaviour. The interaction between the environment and the individual is termed a *contingency*, of which there are several types.

In brief, behaviour that produces consequences that the individual finds rewarding is likely to be repeated, this is a *positive reinforcement* contingency; behaviour that produces the consequence of avoiding an outcome that the individual finds aversive is, similarly, likely to be repeated, which is a *negative reinforcement* contingency. On the other hand, behaviour that produces directly aversive consequences is likely to decrease in frequency, a *positive punishment* contingency; while behaviour with the consequence of losing something of value is also likely to decrease in frequency, a *negative punishment* contingency. (In operant theory the term 'punishment' is used in a technical sense: behaviour that is decreasing in frequency is said to be punished. Punishment in this sense is not value-laden, nor about physical chastisement, it simply refers to the nature of the relationship between a behaviour and its consequences.) Finally, behaviour is not random: an environmental signal indicates that if it takes place a specific behaviour will be rewarded (or punished). This relationship between Antecedent conditions, Behaviour, and Consequences is the A:B:C of behavioural theory and is correctly called a *three-term contingency*. The force of the behavioural approach lay in its emphasis on the role of the environment, so challenging the orthodoxy that the origins of behaviour are to be found inside the person.

Before returning to behaviourism and its significance in the development of criminological psychology we go back a little in time to explore the relations between the emerging disciplines of psychology and criminology, suggesting that during the late nineteenth and early twentieth centuries the two were closer than they would be for decades afterwards.

## PSYCHOLOGY AND CRIMINOLOGY: EARLY ACCORD

### THEORY AND CRIME

With their concern primarily on the individual, the first psychological theories of criminal behaviour variously applied what was known of genetics, intelligence, and psychic functioning. It is difficult at times to distinguish the concerns of early psychology and those of the similarly emergent discipline of criminology. For example, the study of genetics and individual differences was of interest to psychologists, as seen in the first empirical studies of intelligence (e.g. Spearman 1927) and there are similar interests in early criminology. Famously, Cesare Lombroso (1835–1909) advanced theories of criminal behaviour based primarily on the heritability of criminogenic traits (Lombroso 1876). Charles Goring (1870–1919) studied large numbers of prisoners, using anthropological methods and measures, and arrived at the view that criminals were characterized by defects in intelligence (Goring 1913). This concern with the interplay between genetic influences and physical and psychological conditions in explaining criminal behaviour occupied notable criminologists such as Raffaele Garofalo (1852–1934) and Enrico Ferri (1856–1929). Garland (2002) provides further discussion of the development of criminology in Britain.

Freud himself had remarkably little to say about criminal behaviour, although his theories were applied to explain criminal behaviour by several of the post-Freudians. For example, Aichhorn (1925/1955) developed a view of delinquency that saw juvenile crime as a consequence of a psychological disposition termed 'latent delinquency'. Based on the Freudian notion of a 'pleasure principle'—the hedonistic basis of behaviour—Aichhorn argued that a failure of socialization and emotional development allowed the latent delinquency to become overt behaviour. Similarly, Healy and Bronner (1936) used the psychoanalytic concept of *sublimation* (the channelling of unsatisfied psychological impulses into action) to explain anti-social behaviour. John Bowlby (1907–90) developed perhaps the most influential of the psychodynamic theories (e.g. Bowlby 1944, 1951; Bowlby and Slater-Ainsworth 1965). Bowlby's notion of 'maternal deprivation' was developed on the basis of clinical study. This still influential theory holds that the emotional impact on the child of separation from and rejection by his or her mother can provide a means by which to explain problems during childhood, including persistent delinquency, and later development.

## APPLYING THEORY

As practitioners, the early applied psychologists followed theory and so naturally gravitated towards a focus on the individual. Thus, the emerging areas of professional psychological practice became the selection of personnel, including military personnel during wartime (Capshew 1999), and an allegiance with the psychiatric profession in the treatment of individual distress and dysfunction. The early practitioners in psychology approached the task of working with offenders with an implicit understanding of criminal behaviour as a result of an individual failing or dysfunction. As early psychological theories, particularly the psychodynamic theories, were concerned with abnormal development, so explanations for criminal behaviour were couched in terms of psychopathology (Long and Midgely 1992). The answer to criminal behaviour favoured by practitioners, naturally, was to 'put right' the dysfunction 'causing' the criminal behaviour by the application of psychological methods of bringing about change. The methods employed to bring about such change were steeped in a quasimedical, clinical tradition as with psychotherapy, counselling, and group therapy. The thesis underpinning this approach is straightforward: criminal behaviour is a consequence of individual dysfunction; correct the dysfunction and the individual will no longer be criminal—thus the treatment ideal was conceived (Hollin 2012).

The notion of treating offenders found its place alongside the liberal reforms of the early twentieth century when the broader notion of rehabilitation of offenders had taken hold. The rehabilitative movement held that various measures, encompassing social welfare and educational improvements, were required to reduce crime. The association between criminology and psychology was evident. as Tierney (1996; 55) notes: 'By the late 1930s, mainstream criminology was linking criminal behaviour to a range of psychological and social factors, against the backdrop of a continuing debate about the relative importance of genetic endowment'. Tierney continues, 'by the time we reach World War Two psychology was clearly in pole position within criminological discourses' (ibid.). This discourse was primarily concerned with the interplay between heredity and environment, with criminal behaviour the product of a predisposition to crime interacting with inadequate social conditions.

The early attempts to understand and treat criminal behaviour, as Jeffery (1960) notes, hold implicit the three assumptions of *determinism*, *differentiation*, and *pathology*. Determinism in that factors outside the individual's control—be they biological, psychological, social, or some combination of these three—directly cause criminal behaviour. Differentiation because treatment implies that criminals are in some way (biologically, psychologically, or socially) different to non-criminals. Pathological, with clear medical overtones, because the difference between criminals and non-criminals, evinced by the criminal behaviour, necessitates a cure and so to treatment.

These assumptions form the basis of criticisms of psychological theory by some contemporary criminologists. As Siegal (1986: 175–6) comments: 'Psychological theories are useful as explanations of the behaviour of deeply disturbed, impulsive, or destructive people. However, they are limited as general explanations of criminality. For one thing, the phenomenon of crime and delinquency is so widespread that to claim that all criminals are psychologically disturbed is to make that claim against a vast majority of people'. Hopkins Burke (2001: 94–95) also comments that the implication of psychological theories 'is that there is such a thing as the criminal mind or personality . . . the causes are dysfunctional, abnormal emotional adjustment or deviant personality traits formed in early socialisation and childhood development'.

The accuracy of these statements from a contemporary perspective will be discussed in due course. However, as we move through the 1930s and beyond so tensions begin to appear in the relationship between psychology and criminology.

## PSYCHOLOGY AND CRIMINOLOGY: THE PARTING OF THE WAYS

### THE CHICAGO SCHOOL

The beginnings of the split between criminology and psychology are often traced back to the influence of the Chicago School of Criminology, particularly reflected in the work of Ernest Burgess, Clifford Shaw, and Henry McKay (see Rock, this volume). The Chicago School's research shifted the study of crime away from the individual (i.e., psychology) and towards social structure (i.e., sociology) so moving away from the notion that the study of criminal behaviour entailed the study of the individual. Instead, a richer understanding of criminal behaviour could be found in the study of the social structures that shaped, influenced, and defined the social ecology. Lilly, Cullen, and Ball (1995: 39) capture the essence of the Chicago School's position; 'It was only a short leap for them to believe that growing up in the city, particularly the slums, made a difference in people's lives. In this context crime could not be seen simply as an individual pathology, but made more sense when viewed as a social problem.'

In a series of seminal studies, Shaw and McKay illustrated how the development and persistence of delinquent behaviour is associated with social deprivation, disorganization, and disadvantage (e.g. Shaw and McKay 1942). Further, Shaw and McKay ventured that the process by which delinquency was transmitted across generations was via the loosening of social controls. If the societal and institutional forces that bind society—the church, the family, the educational system—are starved of resources then their influence weakens, leaving young people free to act in a delinquent way. Further, if weak social bonds create the conditions for delinquency, then ready association with delinquent peers provides the stimulus for persistent offending.

If social conditions create the setting for crime then environmental not individual change is required to reduce crime. Social policies to alleviate poverty and disadvantage were required, a message with a ready audience during the Progressive era of American political thought.

## DIFFERENTIAL ASSOCIATION THEORY

The environmental focus in criminology (particularly in America) during the 1930s and 1940s is seen in the formulation of Differential Association Theory by the American criminologist Edwin H. Sutherland (1853–1950). Influenced by the Chicago group, of which he was briefly a member, Sutherland placed a sociological emphasis on the forces that define crime and the types of environment in which crime most frequently occurs. In formulating the principles of Differential Association Theory, Sutherland advanced nine propositions (Sutherland 1947). The key principles, in which Sutherland demonstrated a keen anticipation of contemporary behavioural research, were hinged around the proposition that against a social backdrop, criminal behaviour is a *learned* behaviour. This approach immediately raises a number of questions. First, how does learning occur: what are the processes by which behaviour is acquired? Second, what exactly is learned? Third, what is the substance of learned behaviour? Sutherland's answers to these questions, bounded by the knowledge of his time, speculated that learning occurs in close social groups (not necessarily delinquent groups), and that behaviour is acquired through such contacts. The product of learning is not only the skills needed to commit a crime but also the attitudes favourable to delinquency and law-breaking. While not articulating the exact mechanisms by which behaviour is acquired, Sutherland made the critical statement that as a learned behaviour, criminal behaviour is no different in nature to any other learned behaviour.

From a psychological perspective there is nothing startling about the ideas expressed by the Chicago School. As American psychology was setting itself for the paradigm shift of behaviourism, in which the clear focus would be the power of the environment in shaping behaviour, a parallel stream of theorizing in another discipline could have been seen as an opportunity for collaboration. Ironically, Sutherland's theory failed to attract any substantial attention from psychologists, particularly behavioural psychologists, interested in explanations of crime. Psychological research maintained a focus on the individual offender, with studies of the relationship between physical physique and crime (Sheldon, Hartl, and McDermott 1949). Thus, at a key point psychology and criminology failed to connect and the opportunity for an alliance slipped away.

Criminology continued to move away from the individual and towards the environment, particularly in terms of social process and social structure. Nonetheless, it is possible to see obvious points of contact between the two disciplines and where fruitful connections could have been made. For example, the concept of drift draws on cognitive processes ('techniques of neutralization' such as denial of harm or responsibility) and suggests that in daring to become delinquent the individual has *learned* to play a social role (Matza 1964, 1969).

## DIFFERENTIAL REINFORCEMENT THEORY

The most overtly psychological theory of criminal behaviour of the period, again formulated by a criminologist, which clearly draws on the theoretical advances in behavioural psychology, is to be found in Differential Reinforcement Theory (Jeffery 1965). As with Sutherland's Differential Association Theory, Jeffery also suggested that learning plays a fundamental part in understanding criminal behaviour and refined the principles inherent in Differential Association Theory by importing theoretical constructs from operant learning theory. Jeffery suggested, following Sutherland's criminological lead and Skinner's behavioural research, that criminal behaviour is operant behaviour: in other words, criminal behaviour is a function of the consequences it produces for the individual concerned. An understanding of criminal behaviour therefore relies on a comprehension of the consequences of the act for the individual concerned. A substantial number of crimes produce material and financial gain: these gains are, in learning theory terms, positively reinforcing the offending. Alternatively, if the gains from theft help to avoid the effects of poverty then (again in learning theory terms) the criminal behaviour is negatively reinforced. The rewards from crime can be social as well as material, as with gains in social approval and status following offending. The aversive consequences of criminal behaviour—including prison, a probation order, family problems—can have a punishing effect (in the sense of decreasing the frequency of the behaviour).

As Jeffery (ibid.: 295) notes:

> The theory of differential reinforcement states that a criminal act occurs in an environment in which in the past the actor has been reinforced for behaving in this manner, and the aversive consequences attached to the behaviour have been of such a nature that they do not control or prevent the response.

Thus, the individual's history of reinforcement and punishment can be used to explain their criminal behaviour. The defining characteristic of this approach is that each person *must* be considered as an individual: depending on their social environment, some individuals will have gained rewards for criminal behaviour, others will have suffered aversive consequences. The patterns of reinforcement and punishment are unlikely to be constant either between individuals or for the same person over time. Within even similar social and cultural groups, individuals will differ in their experience of peer group interactions, family functioning, education, and so on. It is axiomatic that, even for individuals living within comparable environments, some people become criminal while others do not. Individuals have complex learning histories, leading to intricate theoretical accounts of the development and maintenance of criminal behaviour (Gresswell and Hollin 1992).

As we move through the 1950s and into the 1960s, behaviourism continues to be the main paradigm in mainstream psychological research. Advances in learning theory were utilized by criminologists but, somewhat ironically, criminological psychology failed to make the connection. At this time any common ground between criminology and psychology slipped away as the next phase unfolded in the aetiology of the two disciplines.

# PSYCHOLOGY AND CRIMINOLOGY: LITTLE COMMON GROUND

## PERSONALITY AND CRIME

The study of personality has a long tradition in psychology, particularly in Britain, and the use of increasingly sophisticated methodological and statistical techniques gave an impetus to its scientific study (Cattell 1965). Drawing on his own theory of personality, Hans Eysenck (1916–90) developed during the 1960s what is perhaps to date the most complete *psychological* theory of crime (Eysenck 1964), a theory which he continued to refine (Eysenck 1977, 1996; Eysenck and Gudjonsson 1989). As Eysenck's theory is a widely cited example of what psychological theory has to offer in explaining crime it is worth considering in some detail. However, as discussed below, its later dissection by the most influential criminology text of the time provides a perfect example of how the disciplines moved so far apart as to have little to say to each other.

Eysenck's theory is expansive in that it seeks to offer an explanation of crime based on an interaction of biological, social, and individual factors. The foundation of the theory is that through genetic inheritance there are individual differences in the functioning of the cortical and autonomic nervous systems and that these physiological differences are associated with individual differences in the ability to learn from, or more properly to *condition* to, environmental stimuli. In his early research, Eysenck (1959) defined two dimensions of personality, *extraversion* (E) and *neuroticism* (N). In later research (Eysenck and Eysenck 1968) a third personality dimension, *psychoticism* (P), was described. Eysenck conceives these three personality dimensions (E, N, and P) in terms of a continuum: most people fall at the centre of the continuum with, it follows, fewer individuals at the extremes. Extraversion runs from high (extravert) to low (introvert); similarly, neuroticism runs from high (neurotic) to low (stable); as also does psychoticism.

The interrelationship between extraversion and neuroticism is shown in Figure 3.1. It can be seen that there are four combinations of the two personality dimensions (P adds another dimension across all the quadrants), and the physiological differences between those at the extreme corners of quadrants forms the basis of Eysenck's theory. In terms of physiological functioning, Eysenck describes the extravert as cortically *under*-aroused, and therefore he or she seeks stimulation to increase cortical arousal to an optimal level: the extravert personality is characterized by impulsivity, risk-taking, and thrill-seeking. On the other hand, the introvert is cortically *over*-aroused and so avoids stimulation to hold arousal at a comfortable, optimal level: the introvert personality is characterized by a quiet, reserved demeanour, avoiding excitement and high levels of stimulation. In terms of conditioning, that is learning by Pavlovian conditioning or association (i.e., classical conditioning rather than operant learning), Eysenck's theory maintains that extraverts condition less efficiently than introverts.

Neuroticism, or emotionality, is held to be related to the functioning of the autonomic nervous system (ANS). Individuals at the high end of the N continuum are characterized by a highly labile ANS, so experiencing strong reactions to any unpleasant or painful stimuli. High N individuals are characterized by irritable, anxious behaviour, while those at the lower end of the neuroticism continuum have a highly stable ANS, showing calm, even-tempered behaviour even when under stress. As with E, N is also related to conditionability: High N is associated with poor conditioning given the disruptive effects of anxiety; Low N leads to efficient conditioning. As conditionability is related to levels of *both* E and N (see Figure 3.1 for the four combinations), it is further suggested that stable introverts (Low N–Low E) will condition best; stable extraverts (Low N–High E) and neurotic introverts (High N–Low E) will be at some mid-level; while neurotic extraverts (High N–High E) will condition least well.

These individual differences in conditionability lead to varying levels of socialization. An individual's stable patterns of behaviour, influenced by both biological and social factors, flow from that person's *personality*. Through the development of psychometric tests such as the Eysenck Personality Inventory, Eysenck provided a simple and straightforward means by which to measure personality. The standard psychometric tests typically give each individual a score on both E and N which can be used in research, say to look at the relationship between personality and some other form of behaviour.

The third personality dimension, psychoticism (P), is not so well formulated as E and N and its biological basis has not been described in detail (Eysenck and Eysenck 1976). Initially intended to differentiate the personality traits underlying psychosis, as opposed to neurosis, the proposal was later made that P might better denote psychopathy rather than psychoticism (Eysenck and Eysenck 1972). The P scale is concerned with aspects of behaviour such as a preference for solitude, a lack of feeling for others, the need for sensation-seeking, tough-mindedness, and aggressiveness (Eysenck, Eysenck, and Barrett 1985).

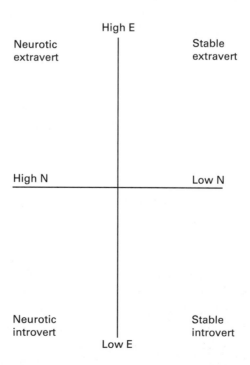

**Figure 3.1** Representation of the relationship between E and N

The application of Eysenck's theory of personality to explaining criminal behaviour incorporates the key proposition that as they grow older so children learn to control their antisocial behaviour as they develop a 'conscience'. The conscience, Eysenck maintains, is a set of conditioned emotional responses to the environmental events associated with anti-social behaviour. For example, if a child misbehaves and is chastised by his or her parents, the unpleasantness of the reprimand is associated with the anti-social behaviour: over time this process of conditioning determines the child's level of socialization which, in turn, mainly depends upon their personality. Now, as the High E–High N combination produces poor conditionability, so individuals with this particular combination of personality traits will condition poorly, have weak control over their behaviour and, the theory predicts, will be over-represented in offender populations. Conversely, the Low E–Low N personality configuration leads to effective socialization, so that this personality type would be predicted to be under-represented among offender groups. The remaining two combinations, High E–Low N and Low E–High N, would be at a mid-level and so would be found in both offender and non-offender groups. Psychoticism (P) is also seen to be related to criminal behaviour, particularly with regard to offences that involve aggression. In other words, as Eysenck (1977: 58) suggests 'in general terms, we would expect persons with strong antisocial inclinations to have high P, high E, and high N scores'.

## TESTING EYSENCK'S THEORY

Given the testability of its predictions and the ease of measuring personality, Eysenck's theory has generated a substantial body of empirical research. The reviews of the literature up to 1980 (e.g. Bartol 1980; Feldman 1977) suggest that there is strong support for the prediction that offenders, both young and adult, will score highly on P and on N. However, the findings are varied for E: some studies support the theory (i.e., high E scores in offenders); other studies report no difference in offender and non-offender samples; while a small number of studies report *lower* E scores in offender groups.

To explain the variation in findings for E, Eysenck and Eysenck (1971) suggested that E might be divided into two components, sociability and impulsiveness, with only the latter related to criminal behaviour. A study by Eysenck and McGurk (1980) provided evidence in support of this hypothesis, showing that an offender sample scored higher than a non-offender sample on impulsiveness but not sociability.

One of the criticisms of the pre-1980 studies is that they looked at the personality traits singly, rather than in combination as originally suggested by the theory. McGurk and McDougall (1981) used cluster analysis to look at the patterns of P, E, and N scores in delinquent and non-delinquent samples and found four personality clusters in each sample: both samples contained the Low E–High N and High E–Low N combinations, but the combinations predicted to be related to criminal behaviour—High E–High N and High P–High E–High N—were found only in the delinquent sample. The highly socialized Low E–Low N combination was, as predicted, found only in the non-delinquent group. Several subsequent studies attempted to replicate the McGurk and McDougall study, with varying degrees of exactness of match with the original theory (McEwan 1983; McEwan and Knowles 1984). While some research continues to test Eysenck's theory (e.g. Kirkcaldy and Brown 2000), personality theory has waned generally in mainstream psychology, as has enthusiasm for further testing of Eysenck's theory, although the 'Big Five' personality dimensions have been considered in the context of offending (Heaven 1995).

Overall, there is empirical evidence in favour of Eysenck's theory, leading one influential criminological psychologist to state that the 'Eysenckian personality dimensions are likely to make a useful contribution to the explanation of criminal behaviour' (Feldman 1977: 161). Nonetheless, there are reservations, as Eysenck acknowledges, such as the need firmly to establish the relationship between classical conditioning and socialization. Further, Eysenck's theory is specifically a trait theory of personality, an approach that is not without its critics in mainstream psychology (Mischel 1968). However, these points are mere quibbles when set against the criticism delivered by the new criminologists.

## NEW CRIMINOLOGY AND PERSONALITY

The text that heralded a sea change in criminology, certainly in Britain, was *The New Criminology* by Taylor, Walton, and Young (1973). Tierney (1986: 157) suggests that this text represented 'an ambitious attempt to develop a Marxist theory of deviance...Whatever the merits of *The New Criminology*, it stands as a supreme example of criminological work nurtured by the twin influences of the New Left and the counter culture'.

Eysenck is heavily cited in the first part of *The New Criminology* and there is intensive criticism of his theory. These criticisms decisively reject Eysenck's approach to understanding criminal behaviour. To appreciate the differences between Taylor *et al.* and Eysenck, is to understand how that at that time there could be no point of contact between the new criminology and psychology (of which Eysenck was a leading figure).

The first point of departure is to be seen in Taylor *et al.*'s analysis of positivism which, they suggest, characterizes Eysenck's work (as well as that of other researchers, including some criminologists). The key attribute of positivism 'is its insistence on the unity of scientific method' (Taylor *et al.* 1973: 11): certainly this is one characterization of positivism, although Halfpenny (1982/1992) identifies no fewer than 12 positivisms, not all of which would concord with the centrality of the scientific method. Thus, Taylor *et al.* continue, to promote a positivistic approach is implicitly to seek to measure and quantify behaviour, to proclaim the objectivity of the scientist, and to see human action as determinate and law-governed. A positivistic approach is to be found in the work of the early criminologists but it is Eysenck as a *biological* positivist who is placed in the critical spotlight.

Eysenck is clear in his understanding of human nature: through conditioning, influenced by biological factors (and hence personality), we become socialized in the sense that we learn to control our impulses and actions. Taylor *et al.* are forthright in their views on Eysenck's model of human functioning:

> Therefore man's voluntary, rational activity comes to be seen as being solely concerned with the satisfaction of his individual and pre-social ideas...The model of learning is Darwinian in its mindlessness...The conscience is a passive reflex which unthinkingly checks those hedonistic impulses by virtue of autonomic distress [1973: 49].

Thus, on the one hand there is the basic philosophical stance, exemplified by Eysenck, of a world in which behaviour is determinate: once the basic science is complete the intellectual problem will be solved (and practical solutions may well follow). On the other hand, Taylor *et al.* express an altogether different perspective. They do not deny the role of biological factors in understanding human behaviour: 'The central and autonomic nervous systems are undoubtedly involved in the learning process—to deny this would be to deny that man has a body' (ibid.: 51). However, Taylor *et al.* view the interaction between the biological individual and society not as something which is fixed and measurable, but as a dynamic, shifting process: 'His definitions of himself evolve not as a determinate result of the addition of social factors on to a biological substratum but rather as a *praxis*, as the meaningful attempt by the actor to construct and develop his own self-conception' (ibid.: 56).

Taylor *et al.* repeatedly make the point with respect to the centrality of meaning in their understanding of human nature. Thus, the reactions of society to criminal behaviour are not an automatic delivery of positive or negative consequences but 'are meaningful attempts of the powerful to maintain and justify the status quo' (ibid.: 52). Again, the different behaviour of extraverts and introverts is not a product of poor conditionability and socialization but represents 'meaningful behaviour by individuals which is judged by others, in this case the psychological testers, to be undesirable' (ibid.: 56). Yet further, Taylor *et al.* note that even if it were true that behaviour was biologically driven, this would not explain deviant behaviour: 'To explain social phenomena demands social analysis involving the meaning that behaviour has to the actor' (ibid.: 60).

The point made by Taylor *et al.* with regard to meaning is fundamental and, in truth, is a basic philosophical issue: is human behaviour determined (by whatever means), or are we active, rational agents shaping and interpreting our own destiny? This is an issue that has been played out in debate within the recent history of criminology, as seen with classical criminology (Roshier 1989), and in psychology with the notion of consciousness (Dennett 1991). On an altogether grander historical stage, the issue of free will versus determinism has been contemplated by philosophers through the ages (Honderich 1993; Russell 1961). It is a solid academic wager that the issue is not about to be resolved.

Taylor *et al.* turn next to the matter of the scientist as the objective recorder of human behaviour. The matter they raise is not one of technicalities, as with the finer points of Eysenck's use of psychometrics and statistics (although others have criticized Eysenck in this regard), rather they ask a bigger question: if Eysenck sees all behaviour as the product of mindless learning, how can understanding of the process of learning be put to work for the common good?

> Who are to be the far-seeing, 'unnatural' men who are able to transcend utilitarian natures and act rationally for society in general? Presumably the psychologists —but, if this is true, it would demand that Eysenck's paradigm of behaviour does not apply to all men [Taylor *et al.* 1973: 54].

This point is well made by Taylor *et al.*: in the human sciences, can the scientist ever be objective and detached? The issue here hinges around the idea of measurement, another of the basic issues Taylor *et al.* raised regarding this style of psychological research and theory. Is it possible to measure intangible constructs such as personality in a way that is value free and valid? As Richards (1996: 110) notes: 'For Psychology, quantifying the phenomena that it studies has been a perennial problem. For many thinkers, like Kant, it was the apparent impossibility of doing so that excluded Psychology from natural science'. Taylor *et al.* move on to perform a similar critical analysis of the work of Gordon Trasler, whose theories are perhaps more all-encompassing than Eysenck's in terms of an inclusion of a wide range of psychological and social factors (e.g. Trasler 1962).

A line was drawn and there could be no point of contact between the criminologist and the psychologist because 'the positivist conception of science as exemplified in the work of Eysenck, is a conception of science which denies any meaning to the action taken outside the consensus and thereby the established social order itself ' (Taylor *et al.* 1973: 61).

## PSYCHOLOGY AND CRIMINOLOGY: NOT ON SPEAKING TERMS

Eysenck's research is a reasonably representative example of mainstream academic psychology during the 1960s, 1970s, and into the 1980s: not all psychological research was of this nature but the predominant approach was empirical and experimental. There were a minority of psychologists engaged in research on criminal behaviour who were working in a style which would have meshed with Taylor *et al.*, but this work was the exception rather than the norm. In particular, the early work of Kevin Howells, influenced by Kelly's (1955) personal construct theory, sought to understand criminal acts in terms of the meaning they held for the individual (Howells 1978, 1979). Within the field of psychology and crime there are examples of work that continue this tradition (e.g. Houston 1998), although it is also the case that biological research continues apace with a focus on genetic transmission (Moffitt 2005) and neurodevelopmental factors (Eme 2010).

As we move out of the 1970s and into the 1980s, mainstream criminology developed further its political ideas with the advent of Left Realist Criminology (Young 1997) and became increasingly occupied with a feminist critique of criminology (Gelsthorpe 2002). Critical criminology offered an alternative political stance, while postmodernism made an impact (Hopkins Burke 2001). However, as psychology began to enter its next theoretical phase its focus did not follow criminology in moving outwards to look for social accounts of behaviour, but turned inwards to search for cognitive and biological explanations for human action. It becomes increasingly difficult to find any point of contact between psychology and criminology.

### COGNITION AND CRIME

As reflected in the title of Baars's (1986) text, *The Cognitive Revolution in Psychology*, the shift from a behavioural to a cognitive perspective in mainstream psychology seemed to happen almost overnight. Of course, psychologists have always been interested in cognition: for example, there is a long history of psychological research into intelligence, mathematical problem-solving, and the strategies used by high-level chess players. The cognitive revolution saw a resurgence of interest not only in these traditional topics, but also in what came to be called social cognition. Ross and Fabiano (1985) helpfully draw the distinction between *im*personal cognition, such as solving mathematical puzzles, and *inter*personal cognition that is concerned with the style and content of our thinking about ourselves and our relationships with other people. During the 1980s and into the 1990s, a clutch of studies appeared which were concerned with various aspects of cognition, but primarily interpersonal cognition, in offender groups. The contribution made by this cognitive slant was to reframe some existing theoretical concepts in cognitive terms and to introduce some fresh ideas. Some examples from the cognitive literature are given below.

A lack of *self-control*, at times leading to impulsive behaviour, has a long history in explanations of crime (Wilson and Hernstein 1985) and figures in at least one major theory of crime (Gottfredson and Hirschi 1990). Brownfield and Sorenson (1993) have suggested several different ways by which low levels of self-control may be related to criminal behaviour, including inability to defer gratification, a lack of concern about other people, and impulsivity. In keeping with the mood of the times, Ross and Fabiano (1985: 37) offered a cognitive perspective on impulsivity, which they view 'as a failure to insert between impulse and action a stage of reflection, a cognitive analysis of the situation'. Current thinking blends the social and the biological in developing an understanding of self-control (Ratchford and Beaver 2009).

The notion of *locus of control* refers to the degree to which an individual believes that his or her behaviour is under their personal control. Individuals high on *internal* control believe that what happens to them is under their own control; while individuals high on *external* control believe that forces such as luck or authority figures influence their behaviour (Rotter 1966). A number of studies have found that offenders tend to external control: that is, they explain their behaviour as controlled by outside influences beyond their personal control (e.g. Hollin and Wheeler 1981).

As we mature as individuals we develop the ability, variously termed *empathy*, or *perspective-taking*, or *role-taking*, to 'see things from the other person's point of view'. The cognitive processes underpinning empathy probably have two related components: first, the thinking skills that allow comprehension of the other person's situation; second, an emotional capacity to 'feel for' the other person. As empathy develops across the life-span, so we learn to adjust our own behaviour to account for how we judge our actions will affect others. Several studies have suggested that some offenders tend to view life principally from their own perspective, not taking the other person into account, as seen in low scores by offenders as compared to non-offenders on measures of empathy and perspective-taking ability (e.g. Ellis 1982; Feshbach 1989; Kaplan and Arbuthnot 1985).

*Moral reasoning* is another aspect of social cognition associated with criminal behaviour (Palmer 2003). The process of socialization is related to moral development in the theories of both Piaget (1932) and Kohlberg (1964, 1978). Kohlberg, like Piaget, takes the view that as the individual attains maturity so moral reasoning develops in

---

**Box 3.1** LEVELS AND STAGES OF MORAL JUDGEMENT IN KOHLBERG'S THEORY

**Level 1: Pre-Morality**

*Stage 1.* Punishment and obedience: moral behaviour is concerned with deferring to authority and avoiding punishment.

*Stage 2.* Hedonism: the concern is with one's own needs irrespective of others' concerns.

**Level 2: Conventional Conformity**

*Stage 3.* Interpersonal concordance: moral reasoning concerned with general conformity and gaining social approval.

*Stage 4.* Law and order: commitment to social order for its own sake, and hence deference to social and religious authorities.

**Level 3: Autonomous Principles**

*Stage 5.* Social contract: acknowledgement of individual rights and the role of the democratic process in deriving laws.

*Stage 6.* Universal ethical principles: moral judgement determined by justice, respect, and trust, and may transcend legal dictates.

---

a sequential manner. Kohlberg describes three levels of moral development, with two stages at each level. As shown in Box 3.1, at the lower stages moral reasoning is concrete in orientation, becoming more abstract as the stages progress to involve abstract ideas such as 'justice', 'rights', and 'principles'.

Offending, Kohlberg argues, is associated with a delay in the development of moral reasoning: when the opportunity for offending presents itself, the individual does not have the reasoning to allow them to control and resist temptation. A number of reviews have examined this basic premise and the generally accepted position is that offenders are typically more likely to show levels of reasoning commensurate with Kohlberg's immature stages (1 and 2) than non-offenders (e.g. Blasi 1980; Nelson, Smith, and Dodd 1990).

*Social problem-solving skills* are the complex cognitions we use to deal effectively with the interpersonal struggles that are part of life, including those circumstances that are associated with offending (McMurran and McGuire 2005). Social problem-solving skills require the ability first to understand the situation, then to envisage potential courses of action, then to consider and evaluate the outcomes that might follow the various actions, and finally to decide on a course of action and plan its execution to achieve a desired outcome. As compared to non-delinquents, male and female offenders give responses to social problems that are less socially competent than non-offenders (e.g. Antonowicz and Ross 2005; Palmer and Hollin 1996).

### Cognitive connections?

There are two points that arise from this body of research: first, how, if at all, do the various aspects of cognition connect to each other?; second, what is the overall model that explains the dynamics of cognition?

The search for an answer to the first point brings us to more recent concerns in psychological research. For example, the evidence suggests an association between antisocial behaviour and moral development as seen in immature, hedonistic, self-centred, moral judgements. However, as Gibbs (1993) notes, moral reasoning does not function in a vacuum arguing that the relationship between moral development and cognitive distortions provides a more complete theoretical picture (ibid.; Goldstein, Glick, and Gibbs 1998). In this context, the term 'cognitive distortions' is used to mean 'nonveridical attitudes or beliefs pertaining to the self or one's social behaviour' (Gibbs 1993: 165).

Gibbs suggests that cognitive distortions can function directly to support the attitudes consistent with sociomoral developmental delay, and can also act to reduce any dissonance. An example of self-centred moral reasoning is seen in the view that 'if I want it, I take it': Gibbs terms this type of reasoning a *primary distortion*. The distorted secondary cognitions associated with such a primary distortion serve to rationalize or mislabel the behaviour. To follow the example, the primary cognitive distortion evident in the reasoning 'I want it, I take it', might be rationalized (secondary cognitive distortion) by blaming other people: if car owners leave their cars unlocked then they 'deserve to have them stolen'; or victims of physical assault got what they deserved because 'they were asking for it'. Similarly, the secondary cognitive distortion seen in mislabelling is evident in a biased view of one's behaviour: for example, car theft is 'just a laugh', or 'nothing serious'; victims of assault 'could have had it worse' and 'no real damage was done' (Gibbs 1996). This distorted thinking may be socially supported and reinforced by the offender's peer group. Some of the recent work in this area looks for complex relationships between aspects of cognition such as sociomoral reasoning, perception of own parenting, and attribution of intent (Palmer and Hollin 2001); and the interplay between moral and social reasoning with social information processing (Harvey 2005).

## Social information processing

While appreciation of the content of some aspects of cognition may provide some understanding of offending, a model of cognitive functioning is required and criminological psychologists have borrowed the notion of *social information processing* from mainstream cognitive psychology. There are several models of social information processing but one of the most influential in criminological psychology has been developed by Nicki Crick and Kenneth Dodge (e.g. Crick and Dodge 1994, 1996). As shown in Box 3.2, Crick and Dodge's model of social information processing—which is not a model of abnormal or deviant behaviour but a general model of human functioning—has six related stages.

The first two stages are concerned with the encoding and interpretation of social cues: the way the individual actively perceives and attends to the words and actions of other people, and seeks to make sense of a given social interaction within its situational context. At the third stage the person attempts to set a desired endpoint for the situation. At the fourth stage the individual judges how best to respond to the situation, in the main by relying on previous experience, although novel situations may necessitate a new way of acting. The fifth stage, response decision, requires a range of cognitive skills, including generating a range of alternative responses, considering

BOX 3.2  SIX STAGES OF SOCIAL INFORMATION PROCESSING

1. Encoding of Social Cues.
2. Interpretation of Social Cues.
3. Clarification of Goals.
4. Response Access or Construction.
5. Response Decision.
6. Behavioural Enactment.

the consequences of different courses of action, and planning what to do to achieve the desired outcome. This type of cognitive activity overlaps closely with social problem-solving. Finally, the individual needs the social skills, both verbal and non-verbal, to perform the actions they have decided are best suited to gaining the outcome they want from the social interaction.

In summary, the model proposed by Crick and Dodge encompasses three questions central to human psychology: (1) How do we perceive and make sense of our social world?; (2) How do we effectively solve the problems our social world sets?; (3) What social skills do we need to respond to social situations and achieve the goals we value? These are basic psychological questions but the issue in criminological psychology is whether there is anything characteristic about the social information processing of offenders who behave in an anti-social manner towards others (typically in the form of aggression or violence).

### Applying the model

In the first part of the sequence the individual perceives and interprets situational cues. There is some evidence to suggest that aggressive individuals search for and perceive fewer social cues than non-violent people (e.g. Dodge and Newman 1981) and are more likely to interpret interpersonal cues in a hostile fashion (Slaby and Guerra 1988). In the next part of the model, social problem-solving, the aggressive person will make decisions on how to respond to the situation according to their perception of the situation. Thus, against the backdrop of a restricted perception of the situation and a hostile interpretation of events, the individual judges what outcome they want and what actions to take to gain this outcome. There is some evidence to suggest that violent people generate fewer solutions to interpersonal conflicts—remembering that the violent person may be perceiving hostility when others may not—and hence consider fewer consequences of their actions (Slaby and Guerra 1988). Finally, the individual must respond to the situation and there are two points to consider with regard to violent acts. The first point is that the individual may see their violent behaviour as an acceptable form of conduct, a legitimate behaviour in a hostile world (Slaby and Guerra 1988). The second point is that the violent person may not have learned the interpersonal skills to behave in a less aggressive manner, so that rather than being assertive, violence is used to solve interpersonal problems (Howells 1986).

## The role of emotion

The social psychologist Raymond Novaco has developed a model of violent behaviour which includes reciprocal relationships between environmental events (physical and social), cognitive processes, and the emotion of anger (e.g. Novaco 1975, 1994; Novaco and Welsh 1989). Novaco suggests that situational events can trigger angry thoughts and these angry thoughts heighten emotional (including physiological) arousal, in turn intensifying the hostile, angry thoughts. This reciprocity between cognition and emotional arousal increases the likelihood of violent behaviour. This model has much in common with Crick and Dodge in that, for example, Novaco and Welsh (1989) identified several information-processing biases in individuals prone to anger: these biases are all concerned with the cognitive encoding of external and internal cues, and the interpretation and cognitive representation of those cues. For example, Novaco and Welsh (ibid.) explain that the process of *attentional cueing* refers to the tendency of individuals who are prone to anger to see hostility and provocation in the words and actions of other people (cf. Dodge *et al.* 1990).

As the cognitive revolution gathered momentum, so the associated research base grew and the theoretical models became increasingly complex. Could there ultimately be a cognitive model of criminal behaviour? With regard to this question, Andrews and Bonta (1998: 190) are clear where they stand:

> Moral reasoning, egocentrism and empathy are just some of the cognitive factors that play a role in the development of delinquency. They are, however, not *necessary* factors: simply being unempathic, self-centered and functioning at Stage 2 of moral reasoning does not automatically result in antisocial behaviour. Sometimes other personal characteristics such as sensation-seeking and negative family socialization experiences are needed. Nevertheless, these cognitive abilities appear to be mild risk factors for delinquency.

The point here is that psychologists are beginning to develop complex models which, while incorporating psychological variables, seek to locate these variables within both biological confines and a broader social context. For example, Nietzel, Hasemann, and Lynam (1999) have provided a model of violence based on four sequential stages across the life span. First, there are distal antecedents to violence: Nietzel *et al.* suggest that these are *biological precursors*, including genetic transmission and ANS liability; psychological predispositions, including impulsivity and deficient problem-solving; and environmental factors, such as family functioning and the social fabric of the neighbourhood. Second, there are early indicators of violence in childhood including conduct disorder and poor emotional regulation. Third, as the child matures through adolescence so developmental processes, such as school failure, delinquent peers, and substance abuse, associated with the escalation of violent behaviour are evident. Finally, as the adolescent moves into adulthood, so maintenance variables come into force including continued reinforcement for violent conduct, association with criminal peers, and social conditions.

In summary, the cognitive revolution that swept through mainstream psychology also shifted the focus of psychological research into criminal behaviour. Nonetheless, there was an awareness that cognitive factors were not, in and of themselves, going to offer a full explanation for offending (cf. Andrews and Bonta 1998). However, before moving to the current concerns in criminological psychology, there is a detour to take within the cognition and crime literature.

## THE REASONING CRIMINAL

In terms of style of explanation, it is evident that most psychological (and some criminological) research takes a 'dispositional' approach to criminal behaviour. Thus, with varying degrees of emphasis, criminal behaviour is seen as the consequence of an interaction between individual, social, cultural, and legal variables which act to dispose the person towards an offence. A contrary approach, with overtones of classical theory (Roshier 1989), took shape during the 1970s and 1980s.

The beginnings of this approach are seen in research concerned with the environmental conditions in the parts of cities that attract crime. The link between specific environmental conditions and patterns of crime was seen, for example, in the rise in frequency of burglary and more empty houses as increasing numbers of family members leave to go to work, or a greater incidence of street violence in poorly lit areas of towns and cities. Cohen and Felson's (1979) routine activities theory drew this research together, suggesting that a crime will occur when three elements combine: these three elements are a specific situation (i.e., a time and a place), a target, and the absence of effective guardians (Crawford and Evans, this volume). The combination of these elements gives the *opportunity* for successful offending and the idea of 'crime as opportunity' took hold. Thus, a crime occurs when the environmental circumstances present the opportunity; the criminal is the individual who seizes the chance. While one line of work looked more closely at aspects of this approach such as the distinctiveness of a target (Bottoms; Crawford and Evans, this volume), another line focused on the individual.

Closer to economic rather than psychological theory (Banton 1995), the view was advanced that, motivated by self-interest, the basis of human action lies in the 'expected utility' from a criminal act. Van Den Haag (1982: 1,026–1,027) provides an example of this approach:

> I do not see any relevant difference between dentistry and prostitution or car theft, except that the latter do not require a license… The frequency of rape, or of mugging, is essentially determined by the expected comparative net advantage, just as is the rate of dentistry and burglary. The comparative net advantage consists in the satisfaction (produced by the money or by the violative act itself) expected from the crime, less the expected cost of achieving it, compared to the net satisfaction expected from other activities in which the offender has the opportunity to engage. Cost in the main equals the expected penalty divided by the risk of suffering it.

So, like an accountant with a balance sheet, the individual reckons his or her likely net gains and losses and enters the criminal market place intending to make a profit. Lilly *et al.* (1995) have dryly described this approach as offering a model of the criminal as a calculator. However, it is implicit within this approach that the offender does not act in a random or in a disorganized manner: rather, the individual makes rational choices about whether to obey or break the law so that the offender is a rational decision-maker, a 'reasoning criminal'.

A key text in the further development of this rational decision-making approach was *The Reasoning Criminal: Rational Choice Perspectives on Offending*, edited by Cornish and Clarke (1986). The thesis underpinning this approach, as articulated by Cornish and Clarke, is that personal benefit is the prime motivation for crime. In pursuit of personal gain, individuals make decisions and choices that, to a greater or lesser degree, are rational in nature. Social factors, including family and peer group, play a background role in an individual's development in growing up with an association with crime. However, the rational 'event decision' at the point of committing the offence is predominant in understanding the specific offence. For example, an entrance hidden from view, an open window, or sight of expensive goods may influence the offender's decision-making with respect to committing a burglary. The rational choice model has been applied to other offences including shoplifting, robbery, and drug use (Clarke 1992; Cornish and Clarke 1986).

Akers (1990) argues that it is questionable whether development of the idea of rational choice is a radical new development in criminology. Nonetheless, the point was made that the frequency of crime is associated with increased opportunity and, when confronted with the opportunity, offenders do make rational choices about their behaviour.

## PSYCHOLOGY AND CRIMINOLOGY: RETURN TO CORDIALITY?

As the 1980s became the 1990s and into the new millennium, criminological psychologists became sufficiently confident in their subject to produce a string of textbooks on psychology and crime (e.g. Ainsworth 2000; Andrews and Bonta 1994; Bartol and Bartol 2005; Blackburn 1993; Hollin 1989, 1992). As part of this growing confidence, some psychologists challenged directly what they perceived to be a criminological bias against psychology. For example, Andrews (1990) chastised the report of the Canadian Sentencing Commission for the criminological bias that led to its failure to utilize psychological research in setting its policies. Andrews and Wormith (1989) coined the term 'knowledge destruction' to describe what they saw as the spurious dismissal of psychological research and theory by criminologists. Andrews (1989) called on knowledge destruction to account for the tactics used by critics to discount evidence on the effectiveness of correctional treatment.

However, as Lilly *et al.* (2002) suggest, during the 1990s criminology itself was revisiting theories of crime with a focus on the individual offender.

### CRIMINOLOGY REDISCOVERS THE INDIVIDUAL

Lilly *et al.* (2002) suggest several strands of thinking, and a supporting weight of psychological research (including Eysenck), within American conservative criminology that have led criminologists to resurrect the study of the individual offender. The first reason is the return to popularity of biological theories, due partly to technological developments that allow improved observation and measurement, and partly to the growing weight of empirical data (some psychological). Second, the popularity of texts such as *Crime and Human Nature* (Wilson and Herrnstein 1985) which seek to explain crime primarily by recourse to constitutional and other biosocial factors. Third, a cluster of developments within criminology that placed the individual at centre stage, including the primacy of psychological factors such as intelligence (Herrnstein and Murray 1994), the spate of publications concerning a 'criminal mind' (Samenow 1984), the research into the 'reasoning criminal' (see above), and explanations for crime framed in terms of the offender's 'moral poverty' (Bennett *et al.* 1996).

While there is some overlap between American and British developments, there are another two lines of research which suggest increased harmony between criminologists and psychologists in Britain. The first unifying theme stems from Life-Course Criminology (Moffitt 1993; McAra and McVie, this volume) which shows empirically that complex models of behaviour, involving a wide range of individual and social factors, must be developed to have any degree of explanatory power.

The second area of research to stimulate discussion between criminologists and psychologists comes from the research on the effect of treatment on offenders. This particular line of enquiry will be considered in detail.

## 'WHAT'S WORKING'?

As documented in a string of publications (e.g. Gendreau 1996; Gendreau and Andrews 1990; Hollin 1994, 1999; Lipsey 1995; Lösel 1996), a reasonable consensus has developed regarding the characteristics of interventions that are effective in reducing offending. In Britain this initiative has coalesced around the theme of 'What Works' (McGuire 1995), a phrase borrowed from the title of Martinson's (1974) paper which essentially argues that 'nothing works'. The broader details of the 'What Works' initiative and offender treatment are discussed elsewhere in this text (Raynor; Lösel, this volume), but the theoretical issues it raises are germane to the current discussion.

Alongside treatment management (Hollin *et al.* 1995), the 'What Works' literature has given rise to the Risk-Needs-Responsivity (RNR) model. The RNR model suggests that effective interventions will target aspects of the offender's functioning related to their offending ('criminogenic needs') in order to reduce the risk of offending: the interventions should be responsive to the offender's capabilities. Effective interventions address the offender's behaviour and 'attitudes, values, and beliefs that support anti-social behaviour' (Gendreau and Andrews 1990: 182). The interweaving of behaviour and cognition in interventions is the hallmark of cognitive-behavioural treatment and, indeed, this particular approach to treatment has been identified as having the greatest likelihood of success (see also Lipsey *et al.* 2001).

### COGNITIVE-BEHAVIOURAL THEORY

The focus on cognitive-behavioural treatment has led to an upsurge in interest in cognitive-behavioural explanations for criminal behaviour. At face value cognitive-behavioural theory, alongside social learning theory (Akers 1985, 1999), provides a ready meeting point for criminology and psychology. There is a history of criminological

theories that include learning, behaviour, and cognition (e.g. differential association theory and differential reinforcement theory), and these concepts are central to
behavioural learning theories (e.g. operant theory) and cognitive theories (e.g. social
information-processing). However, a difficulty comes about when we look for a common understanding of the term 'cognitive-behavioural theory'.

In its traditional form, as with Skinner (see above), behavioural theory concentrated
on the relationship between the environment and observable behaviour. However,
the development of social learning theory, while maintaining its behavioural origins,
incorporated cognition and emotion into an account of human behaviour (Bandura
1977, 1986). As social learning theory precipitated interest in the role of cognition
within an overarching behavioural framework, the term cognitive-behavioural slipped
into popular usage. In particular, the term became increasingly used by practitioners,
and cognitive-behavioural treatment became popular for a range of groups, including
offenders (Hollin 1990). However, given its varied usage it is difficult to give a definition of the 'cognitive-behavioural' and it is preferable to see a cognitive behavioural
approach to practice as a general perspective rather than as a single theory (Kendall
and Bacon 1988; McGuire 2000).

Nonetheless, cognitive-behavioural theory and social learning theory, blending
cognitive, behavioural, and environmental factors, and drawing on principles of learning does provide common ground for criminology and psychology. Indeed, psychologists and criminologists are making essentially the same points regarding theory and
practice in light of 'What Works'. Hollin (1999: 369) observes:

> It is important that 'what works' develops as practice evolves, as the research base
> increases, and as other complementary models of effective practice unfold. Clearly,
> treatment will never eliminate crime, but if effective work with offenders can reduce the
> human and financial costs of victimization then the effort is surely worthwhile.

While from a criminological perspective, Crow (2001: 78–79) notes:

> Programmes for the individual offender need to be seen as part of a broader attack on
> the conditions that give rise to crime. Programmes for offenders rightly take many
> forms and include economic and social provision, including education, training, jobs
> and housing. However, unless programmes take place in circumstances which favour
> good educational, training and job prospects their impact may be no greater than that of
> Sisyphus rolling a rock uphill.

There are similar points made in these two quotations: first, there are no grandiose
claims for the benefits of treatment; second, that the 'What Works' style of treatment
needs to be connected to other styles of effective practice; third, this must all be set
against a backdrop that includes victims, financial costs, and social conditions.

## DOES 'WHAT WORKS' WORK?

The studies evaluating the effects of offending behaviour programmes show that when
offenders *complete* a programme there is a demonstrable and consistent treatment
effect on re-offending (Hanson & Bussière 1998; Hollin & Palmer 2006; McGuire
2008; McGuire, Bilby, Hatcher, Hollin, Hounsome, and Palmer 2008; Van Voorhis,
Spruance, Ritchey, Listwan, and Seabrook 2004). In accounting for this 'completion

effect' Debidin and Lovbakke (2005) assert that completion, '[s]imply served to sort those who would do well anyway from those who would not, regardless of the treatment' (p. 47); and that '[c]ompletion rates are strongly linked to motivation' (p. 50): dismissing any effects of treatment as explicable by an offender's motivation to change behaviour and stop offending. Merrington and Stanley (2004) have also argued that offenders who begin and complete a programme are strongly motivated before they enter a programme to change their behaviour in order to stop offending, hence it is the motivation not the treatment that is reducing re-offending.

Can the effect of treatment be dismissed (shades of knowledge destruction) by the offender's motivation? The evidence for this view is limited and sometimes contrary (Hanson & Bussière 1998; Wormith & Olver 2002), suggesting that the 'completion effect' is not to be explained away by recourse to motivation. The concept of motivation is one that is seen elsewhere in the criminological literature. For example, in commenting on offenders giving up crime, Farrell (2004) suggests that, '[h]aving the motivation to avoid further offending is perhaps one of the key factors in explaining desistance' (p. 195). Similarly, there are popular techniques, such as motivational interviewing (Mann, Ginsburg, and Weekes 2002), that are used with offenders (McMurran 2009).

Thus, the concept of motivation is used in two ways within the criminological literature: first as an explanation for why an intervention may have worked (regardless of the intervention itself); second as a vehicle by which positive changes in behaviour may be brought about. There is a long history of psychological research on motivation with current advances that clearly impact on its use within a criminological context.

## MOTIVATION, 'READINESS FOR CHANGE', AND RELAPSE PREVENTION: MODELS AND PROBLEMS

Across numerous areas, from stopping smoking to dieting, there is interest in motivation to change and how this influences peoples' engagement with interventions intended to bring about behavioural change. The Transtheoretical Model (TTM; Prochaska and DiClemente 1984) is a widely cited motivational model, used to inform attempts to change a range of behaviours, including offending (e.g. Tierney and McCabe 2001). The TTM holds that motivation to change moves through six discrete stages beginning with pre-contemplation, then through various phases of action, and culminating in complete behaviour change. Casey, Day, and Howells (2005) have considered the application of the TTM to offender populations and suggest that it has two main problems. First, there is a critical theoretical debate about the validity of stage models of motivation; second, for offender populations the process of behaviour change is particularly difficult to understand. Following the second point, offending has a relatively low frequency, compared say to problem drinking or smoking, so that changes are difficult to measure. There are also many pressures on offenders, such as eligibility for parole, to demonstrate behavioural change which have little to do with motivation. Casey *et al.* reach the view that, '[t]he conclusion to be drawn from this review of application of the TTM to offenders and offending is that the stages of change construct is, by itself, unlikely to adequately explain the process by which offenders desist from offending' (p. 167). West (2005) presents a thorough critical examination of the Stages of Change Model in which he lists four fundamental problems with the model: (i) the model is flawed in the way in which it uses the concept of a 'stage'; (ii) a stage classification wrongly assumes that individuals make coherent and stable plans that are consistent with the stages; (iii) the construct of a stage is muddled and has no relation to 'preparedness' or 'readiness' to change; (iv) with a concentration on conscious planning and making decisions the model neglects the role of learned habits of behaviour which operate outside awareness. West shows that empirical support for the model is weak and argues that it should be abandoned but that it remains attractive because of its apparent scientific standing: West suggests that, '[t]he model has been little more than a security blanket for researchers and clinicians' (p. 1038).

Drieschner, Lammers, and Staak (2004) review the literature and suggest that the widespread interest in the idea of treatment motivation '[s]harply contrasts with the almost chronic ambiguity of the concept' (p. 1116). This conceptual vagueness and lack of precision in meaning has led to several attempts to refine the notion of motivation (e.g. Viets, Walker, and Miller 2002), and to the development of alternative conceptualizations of motivation such as 'readiness for change' (Howells and Day 2003). The notion of readiness to change is interesting as it includes intrinsic motivation alongside other individual and situational factors that can influence engagement in behaviour change programmes (Howells and Day 2002). As Ward, Day, Howells, and Birgden (2004) note, readiness for change encompasses the person's motivation or willingness to change, their ability to respond appropriately, whether they find the process relevant and meaningful, and that they have the capacities to enter the programme.

The idea of readiness for change may offer an explanation of the supposed selection effect regarding programme entry and completion. Some offenders who enter programmes are ready to change, in the sense that they are ready to *try* to stop offending: their completion of the programme and reduced offending therefore flows from both their readiness to change *and* the effects of the programme. Clarke, Simmonds, and Wydall (2004) note that the desisting programme completers in their sample emphasized that readiness for change was critical in their completing and benefiting from a programme. Thus, it can be argued that the 'selection' effect is in fact a naturally occurring distinction in practice between offenders ready to seize the opportunity to change and those who reject the opportunity. The treatment programme, rather than some abstract notion of 'motivation', is therefore the vehicle by which readiness for change translates into real changes in behaviour.

A major problem with the use of psychological terms such as motivation is the implication that the force for change is *within* the offender. An alternative is to consider the *interaction* between the individual and the treatment environment. as Wormith and Olver (2002) suggest, to consider *responsivity* in terms of situational and individual factors. It is plain that situational factors are strongly associated with programme completion rates and hence treatment effects. Van Voorhis *et al.* (2004) noted an overall completion rate of 60 per cent for the *R & R* programme with parolees in 16 parole districts. However, the programme completion rates varied considerably across parole districts, from a low of 42 per cent completion to a high of 80 per cent. Similarly, across 20 prisons, Pelissier, Camp, and Motivans (2003) showed that both individual- and treatment-level variables predicted treatment non-completion among prisoners participating in drug treatment. Understanding more about readiness to change, programme completion and dropout, and desistance from offending is a pressing issue, both theoretically and practically, in crime reduction.

## GOOD LIVES MODEL (GLM)

The rise of the GLM as an influence in offender treatment represents s a triumph of faith over evidence. The GLM offers an alternative to the RNR model based on positive psychology, with an emphasis on strengths rather than risks, and has the aim of enabling offenders to lead, well, a good life (Ward and Brown 2004). Andrews, Bonta, and Wormith (2011) have provided a highly critical review of the GLM when set against the RNR model. There are, I feel, two further points to note: first, in an era of evidence-based practice, the evidence in support of the effectiveness interventions based on the GLM is scarce; second, in the *realpolitik* of bidding for resources within offender services aimed at crime reduction, an intervention that promises good lives for offenders is starting a long way behind the competition.

## CONCLUDING COMMENT

The time has come to put to rest the question of pathology, that psychological theories are only fit for explanation of abnormal states. Of course, there are mentally disordered offenders and a substantial theoretical and practical literature has accumulated in this specialist field (e.g. Blumenthal and Lavender 2000), although a meta-analysis of prediction of recidivism in mentally disordered offenders suggested that 'criminological predictors' such as offence history out-performed 'mental disorder' predictors such as diagnosis (Bonta *et al.* 1998). Psychological theories such as operant learning, social information-processing, and social learning theory, have been developed in mainstream psychology to generate theories of human behaviour in general, not abnormal or pathological behaviour. These psychological theories may be applied to abnormal states, but are not restricted to that context. (For discussion in relation to violent crime, see Brookman and Robinson, this volume.) If that point is taken and a connection can be made between criminological theory and psychological theory then, with informed collaboration, significant theoretical advances will be possible. A strong criminology-psychology theory that provides a solid platform for a coordinated multi-component crime prevention programme would be progress of the highest order.

### ■ SELECTED FURTHER READING

The texts listed below have been selected as giving reviews and informed commentary across the broad field of psychology and criminal behaviour. Inevitably, some stray into legal psychology, although it is useful to see the two topics together to appreciate their similarities and differences.

Curt and Anne Bartol's (2010) text, *Criminal Behaviour: A Psychosocial Approach* (Upper Saddle River, NJ: Prentice-Hall) is now in its ninth edition and offers a considered view of the field, as does the same authors' (2008) *Introduction to Forensic Psychology* (2nd edn, Thousand Oaks: Sage, 2008). A more assertive view of the role of psychology in explaining crime can be found in the fifth edition of *The Psychology of Criminal Conduct* (2010) by Don Andrews and James Bonta (Cincinnati, OH: Anderson Publishing). Clive Hollin's books *Psychology and Crime: An Introduction to Criminological Psychology* (London: Routledge, 1989) and *Criminal Behaviour: A Psychological Approach to Explanation and Prevention* (London: Falmer Press, 1992) were written primarily for an undergraduate audience, as was Graham Davies, Clive Hollin, and Ray Bull (eds) (2008), *Forensic Psychology* (Chichester: Wiley); Ron Blackburn's (1993) text *The Psychology of Criminal Conduct: Theory, Research and Practice* (Chichester: Wiley) reaches a more advanced readership. James McGuire provides an excellent text with *Understanding Psychology and Crime: Perspectives on Theory and Action* (Berkshire: Open University Press, 2004). A comprehensive overview of theory and practice with regard to treatment issues can be found in Clive Hollin's edited book, *Handbook of Offender Assessment and Treatment* (Chichester: John Wiley, 2001), or the more concise *Essential Handbook of Offender Assessment and Treatment* (Chichester: John Wiley, 2004).

# ■ REFERENCES

AICHHORN, A. (1955), *Wayward Youth* (trans.), New York: Meridian Books. Original work published 1925.

AKERS, R. L. (1985), *Deviant Behavior: A Social Learning Approach*, 3rd edn, Belmont, Ca.: Wadsworth.

—— (1990), 'Rational Choice, Deterrence, and Social Learning Theory in Criminology: The Path Not Taken', *Journal of Criminal Law and Criminology*, 81: 653–76.

—— (1999), *Social Learning and Social Structure: A General Theory of Crime and Deviance*, Boston, Mass.: Northeastern University Press.

ANDREWS, D. A. (1989), 'Recidivism is Predictable and Can Be Influenced: Using Risk Assessments to Reduce Recidivism', *Forum on Corrections Research*, 1: 11–18.

—— (1990), 'Some Criminological Sources of Anti-Rehabilitation Bias in the Report of The Canadian Sentencing Commission', *Canadian Journal of Criminology*, 32: 511–24.

—— and BONTA, J. (1994), *The Psychology of Criminal Conduct*, Cincinnati, OH: Anderson Publishing.

—— and —— (1998), *The Psychology of Criminal Conduct*, 2nd edn, Cincinnati, OH: Anderson Publishing.

—— and WORMITH, J. S. (1989), 'Personality and Crime: Knowledge Destruction and Construction in Criminology', *Justice Quarterly*, 6: 289–309.

—— and —— (2011), The Risk-Need-Responsivity (RNR) Model: Does adding the Good Lives Model contribute to effective crime prevention? *Criminal Justice and Behavior*, 38: 735–55.

ANTONOWICZ, D. H., and ROSS, R. R. (2005), 'Social Problem-Solving Deficits in Offenders', in M. McMurran and J. McGuire (eds), *Social Problem Solving and Offending: Evidence, Evaluation and Evolution*, Chichester: John Wiley.

BAARS, B. J. (1986), *The Cognitive Revolution in Psychology*, New York: Guilford Press.

BANDURA, A. (1977), *Social Learning Theory*, Englewood Cliffs, NJ: Prentice Hall.

—— (1986), *Social Foundations of Thought and Action: A Social-cognitive Theory*, Englewood Cliffs, NJ: Prentice Hall.

BANTON, M. (1995), 'Rational Choice Theories', *American Behavioral Scientist*, 38: 476–97.

BARTOL, C. R. (1980), *Criminal Behavior: A Psychological Approach*, Englewood Cliffs, NJ: Prentice Hall.

—— and BARTOL, A. (2005), *Criminal Behavior: A Psychological Approach*, 7th edn, Upper Saddle River, NJ: Prentice Hall.

—— and BARTOL, A. M. (2008), *Introduction to Forensic Psychology: Research and Application*, 2nd edn, Thousand Oaks, Cal.: Sage.

BENNETT, W. J., DILULIO, J. J. Jr, and WALTERS, J. P. (1996), *Body Count: Moral Poverty and How to Win America's War Against Crime and Drugs*, New York: Simon and Schuster.

BLACKBURN, R. (1993), *The Psychology of Criminal Conduct: Theory, Research and Practice*, Chichester: Wiley.

—— (1996), 'What *is* Forensic Psychology?', *Legal and Criminological Psychology*, 1: 3–16.

BLASI, A. (1980), 'Bridging Moral Cognition and Moral Action: A Critical Review', *Psychological Bulletin*, 88: 1–45.

BLUMENTHAL, S. and LAVENDER, T. (2000), *Violence and Mental Disorder: A Critical Aid to the Assessment and Management of Risk*, London: Jessica Kingsley Publishers.

BONTA, J., LAW, M., and HANSON, R. K. (1998), 'The Prediction of Criminal and Violent Recidivism Among Mentally Disordered Offenders: A Meta-analysis', *Psychological Bulletin*, 123: 123–42.

BORNSTEIN, B. H. and PENROD, S. D. (2008), 'Hugo Who? G. F. Arnold's Alternative Early Approach to Psychology and Law', *Applied Cognitive Psychology*, 22: 759–68.

BOWLBY, J. (1944), 'Forty-four Juvenile Thieves', *International Journal of Psychoanalysis*, 25: 1–57.

—— (1951), *Maternal Care and Mental Health*, Geneva: World Health Organisation.

—— and SALTER-AINSWORTH, M. D. (1965), *Child Care and the Growth of Love*, Harmondsworth: Penguin.

BROWN, W. C. (1961), *Freud and the Post-Freudians*, Harmondsworth: Penguin.

BROWNFIELD, D. and SORENSON, A. M. (1993), 'Self-control and Juvenile Delinquency: Theoretical Issues and an Empirical Assessment of Selected Elements of a General Theory of Crime', *Deviant Behavior*, 14: 243–64.

CAPSHEW, J. H. (1999), *Psychologists on the March: Science, Practice, and Professional Identity in America 1929–1969*, Cambridge: Cambridge University Press.

CASEY, S., DAY, A., and HOWELLS, K. (2005), 'The Application of the Transtheoretical Model to Offender Populations: Some Critical Issues', *Legal and Criminological Psychology*, 10: 157–71.

CATTELL, R. B. (1965), *The Scientific Analysis of Personality*, Harmondsworth: Penguin.

CLARKE, A., SIMMONDS, R., and WYDALL, S. (2004), *Delivering Cognitive Skills Programmes in Prison: A Qualitative Study*, Home Office Online Report 27/0, London: Home Office.

CLARKE, R. V. (ed.) (1992), *Situational Crime Prevention: Successful Case Studies*, New York: Harrow and Heston.

COHEN, L. E. and FELSON, M. (1979), 'Social Change and Crime Rate Trends: A Routine Activities Approach', *American Sociological Review*, 44: 588–608.

CORNISH, D. B. and CLARKE, R. V. G. (eds) (1986), *The Reasoning Criminal: Rational Choice Perspectives on Offending*, New York: Springer-Verlag.

CRICK, N. R. and DODGE, K. A. (1994), 'A Review and Reformulation of Social Information-processing Mechanisms in Children's Social Adjustment', *Psychological Bulletin*, 115: 74–101.

—— and —— (1996), 'Social Information-processing Mechanisms in Reactive and Proactive Aggression', *Child Development*, 67: 993–1002.

CROW, I. (2001), *The Treatment and Rehabilitation of Offenders*, London: Sage Publications.

DEBIDIN, M. and LOVBAKKE, J. (2005), 'Offending behaviour programmes in prison and probation', in G. Harper and C. Chitty (eds), *The Impact of Corrections on Re-offending: A Review of 'What Works'*, Home Office Research Study 291, 2nd edn, London: Home Office.

DENNETT, D. C. (1991), *Consciousness Explained*, London: Allen Lane.

DODGE, K. A. and NEWMAN, J. P. (1981), 'Biased Decision-making Processes in Aggressive Boys', *Journal of Abnormal Psychology*, 90: 375–9.

——, PRICE, J. M., BACHOROWSKI, J.-A., and NEWMAN, J. P. (1990), 'Hostile Attributional Biases in Severely Aggressive Adolescents', *Journal of Abnormal Psychology*, 99: 385–92.

DRIESCHNER, K. H., LAMMERS, S. M. M., and STAAK, C. P. F. van der (2004), 'Treatment Motivation: An Attempt for Clarification of an Ambiguous Concept', *Clinical Psychology Review*: 23: 1115–37.

ELLIS, P. L. (1982), 'Empathy: A Factor in Antisocial Behavior', *Journal of Abnormal Child Psychology*, 2: 123–33.

EME, R. (2009), 'Male life-course persistent antisocial behaviour: A review of neurodevelopmental factors', *Aggression and Violent Behavior*, 14: 348–58.

EYSENCK, H. J. (1959), *Manual of the Maudsley Personality Inventory*, London: University of London Press.

—— (1964), *Crime and Personality*, London: Routledge & Kegan Paul.

—— (1977), *Crime and Personality*, 3rd edn, London: Routledge & Kegan Paul.

—— (1996), 'Personality and Crime: Where Do We Stand?', *Psychology Crime & Law*, 2: 143–52.

—— and EYSENCK, S. B. G. (1968), 'A Factorial Study of Psychoticism as a Dimension of Personality', Special issue of *Multivariate Behavioural Research*: 15–31.

—— and —— (1976), *Psychoticism as a Dimension of Personality*, London: Hodder & Stoughton.

—— and GUDJONSSON, G. H. (1989), *The Causes and Cures of Criminality*, New York: Plenum Press.

EYSENCK, S. B. G. and EYSENCK, H. J. (1971), 'Crime and Personality: Item Analysis of Questionnaire Responses', *British Journal of Criminology*, 11: 49–62.

—— and —— (1972), 'The Questionnaire Measurement of Psychoticism', *Psychological Medicine*, 2: 50–55.

——, ——, and BARRETT, P. (1985), 'A Revised Version of the Psychoticism Scale', *Personality and Individual Differences*, 6: 21–29.

—— and McGURK, B. J. (1980), 'Impulsiveness and Venturesomeness in a Detention Centre Population', *Psychological Reports*, 47: 1299–306.

FARRALL, S. (2004), 'Supervision, Motivation and Social Context: What Matters Most When Probationers Desist?', in G. Mair (ed.), *What Matters in Probation*, 187–209, Cullompton: Willan Publishing.

FELDMAN, M. P. (1977), *Criminal Behaviour: A Psychological Analysis*, Chichester: Wiley.

FESHBACH, N. D. (1984), 'Empathy, Empathy Training and the Regulation of Aggression in Elementary

School Children', in R. M. Kaplan, V. J. Konecni, and R. W. Novaco (eds), *Aggression in Children and Youth*, The Hague: Martinus Nijhoff.

GARLAND, D. (2002). 'Of crimes and criminals: The development of criminology in Britain', in M. Maguire, R. Morgan, and R. Reiner (eds), *The Oxford Handbook of Criminology*, 3rd edn, Oxford: Oxford University Press.

GELSTHORPE, L. (2002). 'Feminism and criminology', in M. Maguire, R. Morgan, and R. Reiner (eds), *The Oxford Handbook of Criminology*, 3rd edn, 112–43, Oxford: Oxford University Press.

GENDREAU, P. (1996), 'Offender Rehabilitation: What We Know and What Needs to be Done', *Criminal Justice and Behavior*, 23: 144–61.

—— and ANDREWS, D. A. (1990), 'What the Meta-analyses of the Offender Treatment Literature Tells Us About "What Works"', *Canadian Journal of Criminology*, 32: 173–84.

GIBBS, J. C. (1993), 'Moral-cognitive Interventions', in A. P. Goldstein and C. R. Huff (eds), *The Gang Intervention Handbook*, Champaign, Ill.: Research Press.

—— (1996), 'Sociomoral Group Treatment for Young Offenders', in C. R. Hollin and K. Howells (eds), *Clinical Approaches to Working with Young Offenders*, Chichester: Wiley.

GOLDSTEIN, A. P., GLICK, B., and GIBBS, J. C. (1998), *Aggression Replacement Training* (rev. edn), Champaign, Ill.: Research Press.

GORING, C. (1913), *The English Convict*, London: Methuen.

GOTTFREDSON, M. R. and HIRSCHI, T. (1990), *A General Theory of Crime*, Paulo Alto, Cal.: Stanford University Press.

GRESSWELL, D. M. and HOLLIN, C. R. (1992), 'Towards a New Methodology for Making Sense of Case Material: An Illustrative Case Involving Attempted Multiple Murder', *Criminal Behaviour and Mental Health*, 2: 329–41.

HALE, M. (1980), *Human Science and Social Order: Hugo Münsterberg and the Origins of Applied Psychology*, Philadelphia, PA: Temple University Press.

HALFPENNY, P. (1982/1992), *Positivism and Sociology: Explaining Social Life*, London: George Allen & Unwin/Aldershot, Hants: Gregg Revivals.

HANSON, R. K. and BUSSIÈRE, M. T. (1998). 'Predicting Relapse: A Meta-Analysis of Sexual Offender Recidivism Studies', *Journal of Consulting and Clinical Psychology*, 66: 348–62.

HARVEY, R. (2005), 'Moral Reasoning', in M. McMurran and J. McGuire (eds), *Social Problem Solving and Offending: Evidence, Evaluation and Evolution*, Chichester: John Wiley.

HAYWARD, K. (2005), 'Psychology and Crime: Understanding the Interface', in C. Hale, K. Hayward, A. Wahidin, and E. Wincup (eds), *Criminology*, Oxford: Oxford University Press.

HEALY, W., and BRONNER, A. F. (1936), *New Light on Delinquency and Its Treatment*, New Haven, Conn.: Yale University Press.

HEAVEN. P. C. L. (1995), 'Personality and Self-reported Delinquency: Analysis of the "Big Five" Personality Dimensions', *Personality and Individual Differences*, 20: 47–54.

HERRNSTEIN, R. J. and MURRAY, C. (1994), *The Bell Curve: Intelligence and Class Structure in American Life*, New York: Free Press.

HESS, A. K. (2006), 'Defining Forensic Psychology', in I. B. Weiner and A. K. Hess (eds), *The Handbook of Forensic Psychology*, 3rd edn, 28–58, New York: Wiley.

—— and WEINER, I. B. (eds) (1999), *The Handbook of Forensic Psychology*, New York: Wiley.

HOLLIN, C. R. (1989), *Psychology and Crime: An Introduction to Criminological Psychology*, London: Routledge.

—— (1990), *Cognitive-behavioral Interventions With Young Offenders*, Elmsford, NY: Pergamon Press.

—— (1992), *Criminal Behaviour: A Psychological Approach to Explanation and Prevention*, London: Falmer Press.

—— (1994), 'Designing Effective Rehabilitation Programmes for Young Offenders', *Psychology, Crime, & Law*, 1: 193–99.

—— (1999), 'Treatment Programmes for Offenders: Meta-analysis, "What Works", and Beyond', *International Journal of Law and Psychiatry*, 22: 361–72.

—— (ed.) (2001), *Handbook of Offender Assessment and Treatment*, Chichester: Wiley.

—— (2006), 'Offending Behaviour Programmes and Contention: Evidence-based Practice, Manuals, and Programme Evaluation', in C. R. Hollin and E. J. Palmer (eds), *Offending Behaviour Programmes: Development, Application, and Controversies*, Chichester: John Wiley & Sons.

—— (2012), 'A Short History of Corrections: The Rise, Fall, and Resurrection of Rehabilitation Through Treatment', in J. Dvoskin, J. Skeem, R. Novaco, and K. Douglas (eds), *Applying Social Science to Reduce Reoffending*, Oxford: Oxford University Press.

——, EPPS, K., and KENDRICK, D. (1995), *Managing Behavioural Treatment: Policy and Practice With Delinquent Adolescents*, London: Routledge.

—— and Palmer, E. J. (eds), *Offending Behaviour Programmes: Development, Application, and Controversies*, Chichester: John Wiley & Sons.

—— and WHEELER, H. M. (1982), 'The Violent Young Offender: A Small Group Study of a Borstal Population', *Journal of Adolescence*, 5: 247–57.

HONDERICH, T. (1993), *How Free Are You? The Determinism Problem*, Oxford: Oxford University Press.

HOPKINS BURKE, R. (2001), *An Introduction to Criminological Theory*, Cullompton, Devon: Willan Publishing.

HOUSTON, J. (1998), *Making Sense with Offenders: Personal Constructs, Therapy and Change*, Chichester: Wiley.

HOWELLS, K. (1978), 'The Meaning of Poisoning to a Person Diagnosed as a Psychopath', *Medicine, Science and the Law*, 18: 179–84.

—— (1979), 'Some Meanings of Children for Pedophiles', in M. Cook and G. Wilson (eds), *Love and Attraction*, Oxford: Pergamon Press.

—— (1986), 'Social Skills Training and Criminal and Antisocial Behaviour in Adults', in C. R. Hollin and P. Trower (eds), *Handbook of Social Skills Training, Volume 1: Applications Across the Life Span*, 185–210, Oxford: Pergamon Press.

—— and DAY, A. (2003), 'Readiness for Anger Management: Clinical and Theoretical Issues', *Clinical Psychology Review*, 23: 319–37.

JEFFERY, C. R. (1960), 'The Historical Development of Criminology', in H. Mannheim (ed.), *Pioneers in Criminology*, London: Stevens.

—— (1965), 'Criminal Behavior and Learning Theory', *Journal of Criminal Law, Criminology and Police Science*, 56: 294–300.

KAPARDIS, A. (2010), *Psychology and Law: A Critical Introduction*, 3rd edn, Cambridge: Cambridge University Press.

KAPLAN, P. J. and ARBUTHNOT, J. (1985), 'Affective Empathy and Cognitive Role-taking in Delinquent and Non-delinquent Youth', *Adolescence*, 20: 323–33.

KELLY, G. A. (1955), *The Psychology of Personal Constructs*, New York: Norton.

KENDALL, P. C. and BACON, S. F. (1988), 'Cognitive Behavior Therapy', in D. B. Fishman, F. Rotgers, and C.M. Franks (eds), *Paradigms in Behavior Therapy: Present and Promise*, New York: Springer.

KIRKCALDY, B. D. and BROWN, J. M. (2000), 'Personality, Socioeconomics and Crime: An International Comparison', *Psychology, Crime, & Law*, 6: 113–25.

KOHLBERG, L. (1964), 'Development of Moral Character and Moral Ideology', in M. Hoffman and L. Hoffman (eds), *Review of Child Development Research*, Vol. 1, 383–431, New York: Russell Sage Foundation.

—— (1978), 'Revisions in the Theory and Practice of Mental Development', in W. Damon (ed.), *New Directions in Child Development: Moral Development*, San Francisco, Cal.: Jossey-Bass.

LILLY, J. R., CULLEN, F. T., and BALL, R. A. (1995), *Criminological Theory: Context and Consequences*, 2nd edn, Thousand Oaks, Cal.: Sage.

——, ——, and —— (2002), *Criminological Theory: Context and Consequences*, 3rd edn, Thousand Oaks, Cal.: Sage.

LIPSEY, M. W. (1995), 'What Do We Learn From 400 Studies on the Effectiveness of Treatment With Juvenile Delinquents?', in J. McGuire (ed.), *What Works: Reducing Reoffending*, 63–78, Chichester: Wiley.

——, CHAPMAN, G.L., and LANDENBERGER, N.A. (2001), 'Cognitive-behavioral Programs for Offenders', *Annals of The American Academy of Political and Social Science*, 578: 144–57.

LOMBROSO, C. (1876), *L'Uomo Delinquente*, 5th edn, Turin: Bocca, First pub. Milan: Hoepli.

LONG, C. G. and MIDGELY, M. (1992), 'On the Closeness of the Concepts of the Criminal and the Mentally Ill in the Nineteenth Century: Yesterday's Professional and Public Opinions Reflected Today', *Journal of Forensic Psychiatry*, 3: 63–79.

LÖSEL, F. (1996), 'Working With Young Offenders: The Impact of the Meta-analyses', in C.R. Hollin and K. Howells (eds), *Clinical Approaches to Working With Young Offenders*, 57–82, Chichester: Wiley.

MANN, R. E., GINSBURG, J. I. D., and WEEKES, J. R. (2002), 'Motivational Interviewing with Offenders', in M. McMurran (ed.), *Motivating Offenders to Change: A Guide to Enhancing Engagement in Therapy*, 87–102, Chichester: John Wiley.

MARTINSON, R. (1974), 'What Works? Questions and Answers About Prison Reform', *The Public Interest* 35: 22–54.

MATZA, D. (1964), *Delinquency and Drift*, New York: Wiley.

—— (1969), *Becoming Deviant*, Englewood Cliffs, NJ: Prentice Hall.

McEWAN, A. W. (1983), 'Eysenck's Theory of Criminality and the Personality Types and Offences of Young Delinquents', *Personality and Individual Differences*, 4: 201–4.

—— and KNOWLES, C. (1984), 'Delinquent Personality Types and the Situational Contexts of Their Crimes', *Personality and Individual Differences*, 5: 339–44.

McGUIRE, J. (ed.) (1995), *What Works: Reducing Reoffending*, Chichester: Wiley.

—— (2000), *Cognitive-behavioural Approaches: An Introduction to Theory and Research*, London: Home Office.

—— (2008), A Review of Effective Interventions for Reducing Aggression and Violence, *Philosophical Transactions of the Royal Society B*, 363: 2577–97.

——, Bilby, C. A. L., Hatcher, R. M., Hollin, C. R., Hounsome, J., and Palmer, E. J. (2008), 'Evaluation of Structured Cognitive-behavioural Treatment Programmes in Reducing Criminal Recidivism', *Journal of Experimental Criminology*, 4: 21–40.

——, MASON, T., and O'KANE, A. (2000) (eds), *Behaviour, Crime and Legal Processes: A Guide for Forensic Practitioners*, Chichester: John Wiley.

McGURK, B. J. and McDOUGALL, C. (1981), 'A New Approach to Eysenck's Theory of Criminality', *Personality and Individual Differences*, 2: 338–40.

McMURRAN, M. (2009), 'Motivational interviewing with offenders: A systematic review', *Legal and Criminological Psychology*, 14: 83–100.

—— and McGUIRE, J. (eds) (2005), *Social Problem Solving and Offending: Evidence, Evaluation and Evolution*, Chichester: John Wiley.

MERRINGTON, S. and STANLEY, S. (2004). '"What works?": Revisiting the evidence in England and Wales', *Probation Journal*, 2: 7–20.

MISCHEL, W. (1968), *Personality and Assessment*, New York: Wiley.

MOFFITT, T. E. (1993), 'Adolescence-Limited and Life-Course-Persistent Antisocial Behavior: A Developmental Taxonomy', *Psychological Review*, 100: 674–701.

—— (1993), 'The new look of behavioral genetics in developmental psychopathology: Gene-environment interplay in antisocial behaviors', *Psychological Bulletin*, 131: 533–54.

NELSON, J. R., SMITH, D. J., and DODD, J. (1990), 'The Moral Reasoning of Juvenile Delinquents: A Meta-analysis', *Journal of Abnormal Child Psychology*, 18: 709–27.

NIETZEL, M. T., HASEMANN, D. M., and LYNAM, D. R. (1999), 'Behavioral Perspective on Violent Behavior', in V. B. Van Hasselt and M. Hersen (eds), *Handbook of Psychological Approaches with Violent Offenders: Contemporary Strategies and Issues*, 39–66, New York: Kluwer Academic/Plenum.

NOVACO, R. W. (1975), *Anger Control: The Development and Evaluation of an Experimental Treatment*, Lexington, Mass.: D.C. Heath.

—— (1994), 'Anger as a Risk Factor for Violence Among the Mentally Disordered', in J. Monahan and H. Steadman (eds), *Violence and Mental Disorder: Developments in Risk Assessment*, 21–59, Chicago, Ill.: University of Chicago Press.

—— and WELSH, W. N. (1989), 'Anger Disturbances: Cognitive Mediation and Clinical Prescriptions', in K. Howells and C. R. Hollin (eds), *Clinical Approaches to Violence*, 39–60, Chichester: Wiley.

O'DONOHUE, W. and KITCHENER, R. (1999) (eds), *Handbook of Behaviorism*, San Diego, Cal.: Academic Press.

PALMER, E. J. (2003), *Offending Behaviour: Moral Reasoning, Criminal conduct and the Rehabilitation of Offenders*, Cullompton, Devon: Willan Publishing.

—— and HOLLIN, C. R. (1996), 'Assessing Adolescent Problems: An Overview of the Adolescent Problems Inventory', *Journal of Adolescence*, 19: 347–54.

—— and —— (2001), 'Sociomoral Reasoning, Perceptions of Parenting and Self-reported Delinquency in Adolescents', *Applied Cognitive Psychology*, 15: 85–100.

PELISSIER, B., CAMP, S. D., and MOTIVANS, M. (2003), 'Staying in Treatment: How Much Difference is There From Prison to Prison?', *Psychology of Addictive Behaviors*, 17: 134–41.

PIAGET, J. (1932), *The Moral Judgement of the Child*, London: Kegan Paul.

PROCHASKA, J. O. and DICLEMENTE, C. C. (1984), *The Transtheoretical Approach: Crossing Traditional Boundaries of Therapy*, Homewood, IL: Dow Jones-Irwin.

RATCHFORD, M. and BEAVER, K. M. (2009), 'Neuropsychological deficits, self-control, and delinquent involvement: Towards a biosocial explanation of delinquency', *Criminal Justice and Behavior*, 36: 147–62.

RICHARDS, G. (1996), *Putting Psychology in its Place: An Introduction from a Critical Historical Perspective*, London: Routledge.

ROSHIER, B. (1989), *Controlling Crime: The Classical Perspective in Criminology*, Milton Keynes: Open University Press.

ROSS, R. R. and FABIANO, E. A. (1985), *Time to Think: A Cognitive Model of Delinquency Prevention and Offender Rehabilitation*, Johnson City, Tenn.: Institute of Social Sciences and Arts.

ROTTER, J. B. (1966), 'Generalized Expectancies for Internal Versus External Control of Reinforcement', *Psychological Monographs*, 80 (Whole No. 609).

RUSSELL, B. (1961), *A History of Western Philosophy*, 2nd edn, London: George Allen & Unwin.

SAMENOW, S. E. (1984), *Inside the Criminal Mind*, New York: Times Books.

SCHULTZ, D. P. and SCHULTZ, S. E. (2008), *A History of Modern Psychology*, 3rd edn, Belmont, Cal.: Wadsworth.

SHAW, C.R. and MCKAY, H.D. (1942), *Juvenile Delinquency in Urban Areas*, Chicago, Ill.: Chicago University Press.

SHELDON, W. H., HARTL, E. M., and MCDERMOTT, E. (1949), *Varieties of Delinquent Youth: An Introduction to Constitutional Psychiatry*, New York: Harper.

SIEGAL, L.J. (1986), *Criminology*, 2nd edn, St Paul, Minn.: West Publishing.

SKINNER, B.F. (1938), *The Behavior of Organisms: An Experimental Analysis*, New York: Appleton-Century-Crofts.

—— (1974), *About Behaviorism*, London: Jonathon Cape.

SLABY, R.G. and GUERRA, N.G. (1988), 'Cognitive Mediators of Aggression in Adolescent Offenders: 1. Assessment', *Developmental Psychology*, 24: 580–88.

SPEARMAN, C. (1927), *The Nature of Intelligence and the Principles of Cognition*, London: Macmillan.

SUTHERLAND, E. H. (1947), *Principles of Criminology*, 4th edn, Philadelphia, Pa: Lippincott.

TAYLOR, I., WALTON, P., and YOUNG, J. (1973), *The New Criminology: For a Social Theory of Deviancy*, London: Routledge & Kegan Paul.

TIERNEY, D. W. and MCCABE, M. P. (2001), 'The validity of the transtheoretical model of behaviour change to investigate motivation to change among offenders', *Clinical Psychology and Psychotherapy*, 8: 176–90.

TIERNEY, J. (1996), *Criminology: Theory & Context*, London: Prentice Hall.

TRASLER, G. (1962), *The Explanation of Criminality*, London: Routledge & Kegan Paul.

VAN DEN HAAG, E. (1982), 'Could Successful Rehabilitation Reduce the Crime Rate?', *Journal of Criminal Law and Criminology*, 73: 1,02235.

VAN VOORHIS, P., SPRUANCE, L. M., RITCHEY, P. N., LISTWAN, S. J., and SEABROOK, R. (2004), 'The Georgia Cognitive Skills Experiment: A Replication of Reasoning and Rehabilitation, *Criminal Justice and Behavior*, 31: 282–305.

VIETS, V. L., WALKER, D. D., and MILLER, W.R. (2002), 'What is Motivation to Change? A Scientific Analysis', in M. McMurran (ed.), *Motivating Offenders to Change: A Guide to Enhancing Engagement in Therapy*, Chichester: John Wiley.

WARD, T. and BROWN, M. (2004), The good lives model and conceptual issues in offender rehabilitation, *Psychology, Crime, and Law*, 10: 243–57.

WARD, T., DAY, A., HOWELLS, K., and BIRGDEN, A. (2004), 'The Multifactor Offender Readiness Model', *Aggression and Violent Behavior*, 9: 645–73.

WATSON, J. B. (1913), 'Psychology as the Behaviourist Views It', *Psychological Review*, 20: 158–77.

WILSON, J. Q. and HERRNSTEIN, R. J. (1985), *Crime and Human Nature*, New York: Simon and Schuster.

WORMITH, J. S. and OLVER, M. E. (2002), 'Offender Treatment Attrition and its Relationship with Risk, Responsivity, and Recidivism', *Criminal Justice and Behavior*, 29: 447–71.

YOUNG, J. (1997), 'Left Realist Criminology: Radical in its Analysis, Realist in its Policy', in M. Maguire, R. Morgan, and R. Reiner (eds), *The Oxford Handbook of Criminology*, 2nd edn, Oxford: Oxford University Press.

# 4

# CULTURAL CRIMINOLOGY

*Keith Hayward and Jock Young*

## INTRODUCTION

What is cultural criminology? Above all else, it is the placing of crime and its control in the context of culture; that is, viewing both crime and the agencies of control as cultural products—as creative constructs. As such they must be read in terms of the meanings they carry. Furthermore, cultural criminology seeks to highlight how power affects the upwards and downwards constructions of criminological phenomena: rules created, rules broken, the constant interplay of moral entrepreneurship, moral innovation, and transgression. From the view of cultural criminology, then, the subject matter of criminology must include not only 'crime' and 'criminal justice' as narrowly conceived, but related and diverse phenomena such as media representations of crime, the uncriminalized deviance of political and financial elites, and public displays of emotion by crime victims. In these and other cases, the experience of crime and crime control is shaped by the meanings that are assigned to it, and by the cultural stockpile of historical references, established and evolving vectors of power, and common everyday perceptions from which these meanings are drawn.

## FOR A SOCIOLOGICALLY INSPIRED CRIMINOLOGY

Most fundamentally, cultural criminology seeks to *bring back sociological theory to criminology*; that is to continue to (re)integrate the role of culture, social construction, human meaning, creativity, class, and power relations into the criminological project. No doubt for some, this aim will seem redundant in that such key foci have always featured on the landscape of theoretical criminology (e.g. Downes 2005: 320; relatedly Rock 2005). However, recently there has been a growing tendency amongst some criminologists, particularly those who espouse a positivist viewpoint, to portray crime as the result of a *lack* of culture, to have little meaning and to be unrelated to the wider social structure and systems of power. Furthermore cultural criminology would seek to relate this return to sociology to also reflect the peculiarities and particularities of the late modern socio-cultural milieu. But what especially makes cultural criminology late modern? We suggest it is (at least) a twofold process.

First, there is the extraordinary emphasis on creativity, individualism, and generation of lifestyle in the present period, coupled with mass media which have expanded and proliferated so as to transform human subjectivity. From this perspective, the virtual community becomes as real as the community outside one's door—reference groups, vocabularies of motive, and identities become global in their demesne. Cultural criminology offers a powerful theoretical framework for analysing the relationship between these conditions and crime. With its mix of intellectual influences, it sets out to develop theories of crime that merge a 'phenomenology of transgression' (Katz 1988; Lyng 1990; Henry and Milovanovic 1996; Van Hoorebeeck 1997) with a sociological analysis of late modern culture to create what O'Malley and Mugford (1994) refer to as a 'historically contextualized phenomenology' (of which more later). In this reconstruction of aetiology, cultural criminology, arguably, returns to the original concerns of mainstream criminology. However, for us, it returns with fresh eyes, offering new and exciting ways in which to reinvigorate the study of crime and deviance through an ongoing engagement with debates on the transition into late capitalism.

Secondly, the antecedents of cultural criminology emerged at the beginning of the late modern period. We refer here to the intellectual energy that occurred in the sociology of deviance, which, lest we forget, was inherently cultural in its focus and postmodern in its sensibility. As Stan Cohen famously put it: 'After the mid 1960's—well before Foucault made these subjects intellectually respectable and a long way from the Left Bank—our little corner of the human sciences was seized by a deconstructionist impulse' (1997: 101). In Britain, there were two major influences on this process of deconstruction: phenomenology and subcultural theory. The radical phenomenological tradition of Becker, Kitsuse, and Lemert, supplemented by the social constructionist work of writers such as Peter Berger and Thomas Luckmann, was extraordinarily influential, particularly in so far as it involved a stress upon the existential freedoms of those 'curtailed' and 'oppressed' by the labels and essentialism(s) of the powerful. This was never truer than in David Matza's book, *Becoming Deviant* (1969), with its concepts of 'naturalism', 'drift', pluralism, ambiguity, and irony, on the one hand, and crime as transgression on the other. The synthesis of such an approach with subcultural theory commenced in the late 1960s at the London School of Economics with David Downes's book *The Delinquent Solution* (1966). Here an emphasis on both subcultures as 'problem solvers' and the expressive rather than the instrumental nature of much juvenile delinquency began to neutralize the more wooden American subcultural theory of the Mertonian tradition. Culture was not a thing out there to be learned and enacted, rather, lifestyles were something which constantly evolved. This line of inquiry was further developed in the work of PhD students at the LSE, including Mike Brake (1980), Stan Cohen (1972), and Jock Young (1971), all of whom focused on how deviant subcultures were both created by the actors involved and mediated and constructed by the impact of the mass media and the interventions of the powerful. It gathered further theoretical traction at the National Deviancy Conference; the work of Phil Cohen, Ian Taylor, and Geoff Pearson all stressing the need for a humanistic sociology of deviance that had at its core a sensitive ethnographic method. Finally, it came of age at the Birmingham Centre for Contemporary Cultural Studies, most notably in the various analyses of youth culture undertaken by Stuart Hall, John Clarke, Dick Hebdige, Tony Jefferson, Angela McRobbie, and Paul Willis. In this body of work, youth culture is seen as a hive of creativity, an arena of magical solutions where symbols are bricollaged into lifestyles, a place of identity and discovery, and, above all, a site of resistance.

This re-working of American sociology replaced a narrow subcultural theorization with notions of expressivity and style, relocating transgression as a source of meaning and 'leisure'. It evoked a rich narrative of symbolism and an awareness of mediated reality. By the mid-1980s such a humanistic sociology, buttressed by strong critiques of positivistic methods, was a major force within criminology. Since then, however, there has been a palpable lurch back to positivism. It is in this context that cultural criminology seeks to retrace its roots and move on into the twenty-first century.

## CRIMINOLOGY AND CULTURE

Crucial to the understanding of cultural criminology is its interpretation of the 'cultural', itself a subject of controversy and contest. First of all, it is not positivism in the sense that it does not see culture as a function of material situations or structural positions. Culture is *not* a dependent variable of structure. Yet, and here we have differences with the 'new American cultural sociology' (see Smith 1998; Alexander and Smith 2002), it does not see culture as an independent variable: It certainly is not autonomous of the patterns of inequality and power or the material predicaments of the actors. Witness, for example, the Gramscian concern with class and power in the work of the Birmingham School (e.g. Hall and Jefferson 1975; Hall *et al.* 1978; Willis 1977) which, incidentally, the cultural sociologists dismiss as a 'presuppositional commitment to a power-based frame of analysis' which is 'unduly restrictive' (Smith 1998; Sherwood *et al.* 1993). Of course, both the cultural hegemony of the powerful and the subcultures of acquiescence and resistance of the less powerful are scarcely independent of class and power. And as for the immediate material predicament of social actors, the very early subcultural work on 'the pains of imprisonment' demonstrated the dialectical relationship between conditions and culture. Namely, although all inmates experienced 'the pains of imprisonment', the extent and the nature of these pains are dependent on the culture they bring to the prison (e.g. in terms of class and gender) just as the pains in turn shape the particular inmate culture that arises in the attempt to surmount the privations of prison life (Young 1999: 89–90).

Secondly, and related to the first, cultural criminology is not a cultural positivism where crime or deviance is ascribed to the simple acting out of the static culture of a group. Thus it would take issue with the tradition of cultural conflict theory commencing with the work of Thorsten Sellin (1938) and highlighted in the well-known subcultural formulation of Walter Miller (1958), where crime is simply the enactment of lower-working-class values. Such a position originally formulated by Sellin in terms of the justification for vengeance and vendetta amongst Sicilian immigrants, which in turn led inevitably to conflicts with wider American values, has clear echoes today in the supposition that multiculturalism generates a sense of ineluctable collisions of norms, most particularly that between Muslim and Western values. Cultures are not static, they are not an essence waiting to be enacted, rather they are heterogeneous, they blur, cross boundaries, and hybridize. To talk, for example, of ahistorical and context free proclivities to crime in relationship to ethnic cultures—say Jewish or Jamaican—is a pointless essentialism, stereotypical in its notion of fixity and stasis and of no explanatory value.

In *Culture as Praxis*, Zygmunt Bauman distinguishes two discourses about culture, long-standing and seemingly diametrically opposed. The first conceptualizes 'culture as the activity of the free roaming spirit, the site of creativity, invention, self-critique and self-transcendence', suggesting 'the courage to break well-drawn horizons, to step beyond closely-guarded boundaries'. The second sees culture as 'a tool of routinization and continuity—a handmaiden of social order', here 'culture' stood for regularity and pattern—with freedom cast under the rubric of 'norm-breaking' and 'deviation' (1999: xvi–xvii).

Culture of the second sort is the province of orthodox social anthropology, of Parsonian Functionalism, of post-Parsonian cultural sociology. Culture is the stuff of cohesion, the glue of society, the preservative of predictability, the *soi-disant* support of social structure. Culture of the first sort fits much more readily within the subcultural tradition; it is culture as praxis, the culture of transgression, of resistance, of human creativity. And if for this first discourse, transgression signals creativity, with culture of the second sort, transgression signifies the very opposite: the absence of culture. Yet the two discourses are not irreconcilable, they both suggest an ongoing and contested negotiation of meaning and identity. Of course, the notion of culture as somehow outside of human creation, as an unreflexive prop of social structure, as a mysterious functional creation of the social organism, is preposterous. But the *belief* in tradition, the embracing of stasis and conformity, the mobilization of rigid stereotype and fundamental values is, of course, a fact in itself and a fact of considerable impact and reality.

Thus a sociology which foregrounds human creativity does not entail the ignoring of those cultures and actions which involve its renunciation. Human beings, as Matza (1969) famously pointed out, have always the feasibility, the capacity to transcend even the most dire circumstances but they have also the possibility of acting 'as if' they were a cultural puppet or an inanimate artifice. Thus, if we are, in Dwight Conquergood's (1991) wonderful phrase, to view culture as a verb rather than as a noun, then we must remember that this verb is cast both in a passive and an active tense. Culture may well be a performance, but it can be as much an act of acquiescence as of rebellion.

Criminology and the sociology of deviance by the very nature of their subject matter occupy a privileged cultural vantage point in sociology. Their focus is at precisely that point where norms are imposed and threatened, enacted and broken. They are borderline subjects which foreground the processes of cultural generation and are, of course intrinsically dyadic, that is, they involve the social constructions 'downwards' of the agencies of social control (the culture of control) and 'upwards' of the deviant individuals and groups (the culture of deviance). Here two of the various traditions which prefigure cultural criminology, labelling and subcultural theory, contribute immensely. The notion of a 'label' carries the stereotype of deviance (very frequently, of course, carrying implications of a lack of socialization and culture), whilst 'subculture' carries the motivations and justifications for deviance: both contribute to a narrative which involves creativity, negotiation, and change on behalf of both controllers and controlled. For control and deviance are cultural products, products of human creativity, an interplay of constructions which necessitate that the sociology of crime and the sociology of punishment frequently constituted as separate discourses come together within the rubric of cultural criminology.

In all these ways, then, cultural criminology seeks to develop a criminology which incorporates a notion of culture which is constantly in flux, which has always the potentiality for creativity and transcendence. And, of course, although such an analysis has always applied to the human condition, it is (as we stated earlier) all the more transparently applicable today. For in late modernity the insistent stress on expressivity and personal development, in a world where the narratives of work, family, and community no longer provide a constancy of identity, places a high emphasis on cultural change and personal reinvention. Couple this with an ever-present pluralism of values presented in terms of mass immigration and tourism and the vast plethora of factual and fictional cultural referents carried by the media as part of the process of globalization, and the role of cultural negotiation becomes dramatically heightened. In terms of criminality, the reference points which give rise to relative deprivation and discontent, the vocabularies of motives and techniques of neutralization available off the peg, so to speak, to justify crime, the *modus operandus* of the criminal act itself are manifold, plural, and global. And precisely the same is true of the other aspects of crime: the experience of victimization, images and justifications for punitiveness, modes of policing, political responses to crime are all heavily mediated and widely available. Yet although the moorings of social action are loosened in time and in space, this is not to suggest that vocabularies of motive circulate outside of the political economy of daily life, or without reference to material setting and applicability. Culture may no longer be so fixed in space and time, but the very act of creating culture, of making action meaningful, necessitates an appropriate fit between culture and predicament.

## CULTURAL CRIMINOLOGY: DOES IT HAVE ANY POLICY IMPLICATIONS?

It is often suggested that cultural criminology has an inherent romanticism towards its objects of study and that because of this it is unable to formulate any policy other than non-interventionism—leaving things alone. In this we have a clear echo of Alvin Gouldner's (1968) famous critique of Howard Becker and the labelling theorists over forty years ago; namely that they were simply 'zoo keepers of deviance' unwilling or unable to look objectively at their chosen transgressors. As the story goes, by prioritizing the micro and middle levels over and above the macro-level (the nature of late modern capitalism itself), this approach was incapable of a genuinely transformative politics. History, it is assumed, is now simply repeating itself.

In all of this cultural criminology is seen as the very antithesis of the realist criminology which preceded it—which was policy driven, interventionist, realistic about
the problems of crime, and (at least at a perfunctory level) attempted to place the micro
within the context of the total society and was committed to transformative politics
(Young 1992). We wish to argue that any truth in this is largely a question of emphasis
rather than incompatibility; that there is much that cultural criminology and realism
can learn from each other and that the major differences spring paradoxically from
the fact that both critical theories share the same theoretical roots. In particular, that
both embody a shared epistemology based on David Matza's concept of naturalism. In
*Becoming Deviant* (1969) Matza argued that such a naturalism should be faithful to the
human condition and to the form *and* substance of the social world. The tendency has
been for realism to concentrate on the form of social interaction and cultural criminology the substance. Yet what is actually required is a criminology that does *both*.

But first of all let us concentrate on the frequent criticism that cultural criminology
has little potentiality in the area of praxis and public policy. It is in Matza's terms an
'appreciative' approach which eschews 'correctionalism'. But to be appreciative does
not inevitably mean to romanticize or valorize, nor does a disdain for the correctionalism of conventional criminology and the criminal justice system necessitate a
hands-off approach to crime. Cultural criminologists are not oblivious of the problem
of crime. They are as capable of studying domestic burglars as they are urban graffiti
artists. Likewise there are plenty of activities which need to be controlled: domestic
violence, hate crimes, sexual violence, safety crimes at work, corporate malfeasance,
war crimes, genocide, predatory street crimes, police criminality to name but a few.
The priorities would however be somewhat different from those of establishment
criminology: they would tend to reflect the gravity of the offence rather than incorporate a miscellany of the genuinely serious, the merely worrisome, and actions that
simply disturb the tranquility of the powerful.

But, most importantly, if you do not understand the cultural meanings of crime and
the responses to it you have little chance of a successful intervention. Firstly, without
understanding the social predicament that is the source of the cultural response that
involves some element of criminality you have no chance of an appropriate response
to it. There is, as David Matza and Jack Katz after him (e.g. Katz and Jackson-Jacobs
2004), have pointed out, a whole research tradition in establishment criminology that
simply does not attempt to describe let alone understand a phenomenon. Too many
criminologists, for example, will happily, and wistfully, attempt to count the number
of gang members but will not describe the gang itself, or its meaning for gang members. They write books on homicide that do not describe a single murder. They are all
background and no foreground, all 'factors' and no meaning. And if the positivist
tradition has this as a customary blind spot, the classicist school with its administrative contemporaries, substitutes abstraction for *verstehen*. Here peculiar rational
actors, legal fictions, economic robots, are evoked, devoid of social context and human
emotion (Hayward 2007, 2012). But if you lose meaning, all that is left for policy are
the blunt instruments of force and containment, of punishment and prevention, the
concomitants of deterrence theory or rational choice logic.

Secondly, if you do not understand that the conventional responses to crime are
cultural then you have no ability to assess what are the forces that set the crime control

agenda, fix the human targets, energize the police, the courts, the media, and the public. You have a culture of crime but not a culture of control. You are left with assessing social responses to crime as if they were merely technical matters, not normative responses. But as scholars such as Dario Melossi (2001) have pointed out conceptions of penality and justice are deeply embedded in the culture of a nation. Thirdly, if you do not understand the cultural interpretation of the criminal justice response you have no ability to comprehend the likely impact of the intervention. The same measure of punishment can be seen, for example, as a matter of shame and social embarrassment, a badge of honour, a weighty deterrent, or an inducement to continue and perhaps escalate a life of transgression. It all depends on the culture of the group being punished (see for example Harcourt 2007 on the complexity of elasticities associated with certain forms of racial profiling). Let us note that all of this is underscored by the fact that orthodox criminology or positivism has been a complete failure at explaining either the extraordinary rise in crime in advanced industrial countries in the years from the 1960s onwards or the subsequent and, even more surprising, fall in crime in countries such as the US, England and Wales, and Canada, post 1995 (see, e.g., Zimring 2007, for such an admission on both counts).

Even dyed in the wool positivists note that the ability of orthodox theory to explain crime is low and seemingly falling over time. Thus a study of articles in the top American journal *Criminology* between 1968 and 2005 points to the fact that the average predictive power of the multivariate models used is in the region of 40 per cent, with 60 per cent of the crime remaining unexplained; furthermore there has actually been an acknowledged decline in predictive power over the period examined (Weisburd and Piquero 2008). This is combined with entirely inadequate attempts at measurement that results in poor and sometimes toxic data. As one of us has recently argued in *The Criminological Imagination* (Young 2011) this is due to the complete neglect of the cultural nature of crime. With this in mind the question becomes not whether cultural criminology is capable of policy interventions but rather whether much of the current funding directed at positivistic intervention is simply a waste of money?

## THE SQUARE OF CRIME AND THE POSSIBILITY OF A CULTURAL REALISM

Let us now return to the relationship between realism and cultural criminology and the possibility of a cultural realism. Realist Criminology emerged theoretically out of the fusion of the two strands of American new deviancy theory: subcultural theory and the labelling perspective. Such a synthesis was a central theme of the British new criminology and the subsequent core of the realism which followed it, which in policy terms was a response to the demands of radical Labour councils for progressive crime control policies (Mooney 2011). The immediate theoretical impact of such politics was the development of the dyad of crime (action and reaction) inherited from the new deviancy theorists, and the emergence of the key realist concept of the square of crime (Young 1987). The injunction 'to take crime seriously' necessitated a consideration of victimization, it shifted attention away from the sole focus on the offender to the notion that crime consisted fundamentally of an offender and a victim and the relationship between them. *Action* was thus rewritten. Secondly, the reaction (social control) side of the dyad was reconceived. For the social democratic critique of the criminal justice system as ineffective and frequently counterproductive gave rise to the consideration of the other agencies of the state and of civil society which affected the crime rate. That is the various institutions of the welfare state, education, the mass media, work, living conditions, and public opinion, etc. Thus the emphasis moved away from the criminal justice system as the central axis of control whilst the criminal justice system itself was seen as needing fundamental reform. All of this resulted in the notion of *multiagency social intervention* (Lea *et al.* 1989). Thus *reaction* was reconceived. In this fashion, the conventional dyad of criminal justice, system and offender, the old syllogism of 'police and thieves', became recast as a square of crime.

The square of crime suggests that all explanations of crime logically necessitate each of the four vertices and the relationship between them; it provides a critique of previous theories of crime as suffering from partiality—of focusing in on only one of the necessary components. In contrast, it suggests four points of social intervention. In this sense, it has much in common with the formal sociology of George Simmel in that it suggests the reality of deviance has this fourfold structure which necessitates such an explanatory agenda whatever the cultural context.

There is a certain serendipity to the synthesis between realism and cultural criminology because both fit together like pieces of a jigsaw puzzle: one depicts the form of the social interaction which we call crime, whilst the second breathes human life into it. If realism stresses that crime is a relationship between offender and victim and between actors and reactors, cultural criminology reminds us that such relationships are imbued with energy and meaning. They are cultural products not simple technical targets constituted by opportunity or pragmatic calculations of harm. The victims are rarely chosen randomly (and if so only by virtue of a conscious and perverse decision to randomly transgress); the act of victimization involves a stereotype of the deserving target. This is evidenced most explicitly in acts of violence which are greatly facilitated by a process of dehumanization; that is a cultural assessment that the transgressors lack culture. Physical violence demands in Bourdieu's (1991) terms *symbolic violence*; most violence is, as Iris Young (1990) points out, coterminous with hate crime(s). It is not simply the manifestation of individualistic anger but something which is culturally shaped, stereotypically targeted involving issues of appropriate and inappropriate behaviour, backed by questions of social worth and status. Furthermore the wide range of possible harms present within society are culturally filtered to focus minutely, in the vast majority of cases, upon the crimes of the poor, who are constituted as such as a culturally distinctive group within the confinement of our prisons. Thus all sorts of intense and exclusionary cultural sorting occurs, both in the act of crime and in the process of criminalization. Such processes involve the binaries of othering, of appropriate and inappropriate behaviour, of casual or essential deviance. Both for the offender and the labeller, cultural statements are being made as to their worthiness; transgression and intervention are both made on cultural grounds.

Thus cultural criminology brings to the square of crime meaning, energy, and emotion: it turns its formal structure into a lived reality.

# IS CULTURAL CRIMINOLOGY NECESSARILY IDIOGRAPHIC?

The nomothetic approach to comparative research looks for universal, social behaviour, whilst the idiographic looks at the unique cultural circumstances and forgoes generalization (Sztompka 1990; Edwards and Hughes 2005). With this distinction in mind criminological positivism is a nomothetic discipline *par excellence* in that it seeks to generalize from certain material variables wherever they are in the world to the incidence of criminal behaviour. Cultural criminology, on the other hand, with its insistence on cultural interpretation would seem to be a prime candidate for the idiographic. Is cultural criminology, then, condemned to the idiographic, to describe each social event within the parameters of a unique and particular cultural configuration? Is the world of nomothetic generalization alien to it?

In fact cultural criminology has consistently dismissed the notion of human behaviour as independent of material circumstances or existing social structures and institutions (see Ferrell 1992). In many ways it follows the cultural turn of the 1970s and '80s which swept through the social sciences albeit transposing the debates to fit the hyperpluralism and multimediated nature of late modernity. In the early seventies the eminent labour historian Edward Thompson, was one of the most significant writers involved in this movement. He famously argued that class could not be reduced to a reflex of economic conditions, that the experience of class and the emergence (or lack of) class consciousness was shaped by culture: religion, nationalist, and ethnic traditions, gender and age differences, political settings. Yet he was adamant about retaining a material base. Thus he wrote:

> Any theory of culture must include the concept of the dialectical interaction between culture and something that is not culture. We must suppose the raw material of life – experience be at one pole and all the infinitely-complex human disciplines and systems, articulate and inarticulate, formalised in institutions or dispersed in the least formal ways, which 'handle', transmit or distort this raw material to be at the other. It is in the active process – which is at the same time the process through which men make their history that I am insisting on. (1981: 398)

Adding later:

> What we see – and study – in our work are repeated events within 'social being' – such events being indeed often consequent upon material causes, which go behind the back of consciousness or intention – which inevitably do and give rise to lived experience, which do not instantly break through as 'reflections' into experience but whose pressure on the whole field of consciousness cannot be indefinitely diverted, postponed, falsified or suppressed. (Ibid.: 406)

If positivists place all of the explanation of human action in terms of background material determinants whether biological, psychological or social, phenomenologists, such as Jack Katz, stress the foreground, subjective aspects and disdain this materialism. Cultural criminology will have none of either and would echo Thompson's demand that a theory of culture must incorporate both 'culture and something that it is not'. The material changes, say in income distribution, the chances of unemployment, the movement from manufacturing to service jobs, the reduction in possibilities of immigration, the extent and type of jobs available for women, the amount of disposable income in the hands of youth, create possibilities or barriers for people, avenues for reshaping their lives, dead ends or seeming freeways, influencing everything from social mobility to mortality rates. But they do not *determine*; for 'objective' determinants are turned into subjective courses of action, factors become motives, influences are transformed into narratives by cultural interpretation. Each of these material changes is surrounded—particularly in late modernity—by an array of alternative and conflicting narratives. Some of these are narratives of the powerful, cynically propagated to mislead or, more frequently, really believed in by those whom fortune has smiled upon. Thus many of these narratives will suggest that we are actually living in a meritocratic society (the American Dream), that class divisions have disappeared, that women's equality has actually been achieved, or that unemployment is a function of individual failure. Some, on the other hand, are narratives of resistance and of hope and some are narratives of acquiescence: all of them have effects on the wide array of human behaviour: crime is one of them.

## TRANSGRESSIVE SUBJECTS: UNCOVERING THE MEANINGS AND EMOTIONS OF CRIME

Crime is an act of rule-breaking. It involves an attitude to rules, an assessment of their justness and appropriateness, and a motivation to break them whether by outright transgression or by neutralization. It is not, as in positivism, a situation where the actor is mechanistically propelled towards desiderata and on the way happens to cross the rules; it is not, as in rational choice theory, a scenario where the actor merely seeks the holes in the net of social control and ducks and dives his or her way through them. Rather, in cultural criminology, the act of transgression itself has attractions—it is through rule-breaking that subcultural problems attempt solution.

Cultural criminology strives to re-energize aetiological questions of crime by replacing the current bias towards rational choice and sociological determinism with an emphasis on—as suggested above—the 'lived experience' of everyday life and existential parameters of choice within a 'winner-loser' consumer society. Its aim is to introduce notions of passion, anger, joy, and amusement as well as tedium, boredom, repression, and elective conformity to the overly cognitive account of human action and rationality (see de Haan and Vos 2003; Hayward 2007). Put simply, cultural criminology seeks to emphasize the emotional and interpretative qualities of crime and deviance. Important here is the stress placed by cultural criminology on the foreground of experience and the existential psychodynamics of the actor, rather than on the background factors of traditional positivism (e.g. unemployment, poverty, poor neighbourhoods, lack of education, etc.). In this sense cultural criminology can be seen as following the framework set out by Jack Katz (1988) but, at the same moment, it is also critical of his position for the way it dismisses any focus on social background as irretrievably positivistic or as a mistaken materialism. Thus Jeff Ferrell, in his review of Katz's *Seductions of Crime*, where he writes that, despite Katz's critique, 'the disjunctions between Katz's criminology and certain aspects of left criminology are not insurmountable'. Understanding 'social and economic inequality to be a cause, or at least a primary context, for crime, we can also understand that this inequality is mediated and expressed through the situational dynamics, the symbolism and style, of criminal events'. And so, 'while we cannot make sense of crime without analyzing structures of inequality, we cannot make sense of crime by *only* analyzing these structures, either. The aesthetics of criminal events interlocks with the political economy of criminality' (Ferrell 1992: 118–19; see also Young 2003; Hayward 2004: 152–7; Hayward and Hobbs 2007). By melding Katz's ideas with the cultural tradition within criminology, a cultural criminology has emerged that seeks to reinterpret criminal behaviour (in terms of meaning) as a technique for resolving certain psychic conflicts—conflicts that in many instances are indelibly linked with various features of contemporary life/culture.

For example, cultural criminology would point to the way poverty is perceived in an affluent society as an act of exclusion—the ultimate humiliation in a consumer society. It is an *intense* experience, not merely of material deprivation, but of a sense of injustice and of ontological insecurity. But to go even further than this, that late modernity, as described earlier, represents a *shift in consciousness*, so that individualism, expressivity, and identity become paramount and material deprivation, however important, is powerfully supplemented by a widespread sense of ontological deprivation. In other words, what we are witnessing today is a *crisis of being* in a society where self-fulfilment, expression, and immediacy are paramount values, yet the possibilities of realizing such dreams are strictly curtailed by the increasing bureaucratization of work (its so-called McDonaldization) and the commodification of leisure. Crime and transgression in this new context can be seen as the breaking through of restraints, a realization of immediacy, and a reassertion of identity and ontology. In this sense, identity becomes woven into rule-breaking.

An extraordinary example of this line of thinking within cultural criminology is the work of Stephen Lyng (1990) and his associates on edgework. Here cultural criminologists study the way in which individuals engaging in acts of extreme risk-taking (base-jumping, joyriding, sky-diving, motorbike racing, etc.), push themselves to the edge of danger in search of both excitement and certainty. Like a metaphor for reality, they lose control only to take control.

At this point it is essential to stress that cultural criminology's focus on the dynamic nature of experience takes many forms. It is not, as certain critics have erroneously suggested (O'Brien 2005: 610; Ruggiero 2005: 499; Howe 2003: 279), simply a criminology of 'thrills and risks'.[1] Many cultural criminologists have been drawn to the

---

[1] Edgework's focus on prototypically masculine, high-risk pursuits has been criticized by a number of feminist criminologists. However, recent works by the likes of Rajah (2007), Franko-Aas (2005), Gailey (2007), and Lois (2005) suggest that edgework can be applied to an array of variously gendered settings. Likewise cultural criminologist Alison Young's corpus of work on 'affect' shifts the focus away from rudimentary notions of edgework to factor in more complex and nuanced notions of emotionality (see e.g. Young 2009).

'pursuit of passions' and the exciting and violent feelings which crime often induces both in offenders and victims, producing—*à la* Katz—a series of phenomenologically inspired accounts of various forms of expressive criminality (see Cottee and Hayward 2011 for a recent example). It is wrong to suggest, though, that cultural criminology's analytical framework is blind to the more mundane aspects of criminality (see, e.g., Ferrell 2004; Yar 2005). Cultural criminology's focus on meaning, representation, and subcultural milieu ensures that it is equally at home explaining the monotonous tasks and dull rhythms associated with DVD piracy or the illegal trade in counterfeit 'grey' automotive components, as it is unravelling the *sub rosa* world of illegal graffiti artists. Moreover, it is obvious that the formal components of an adequate criminological analysis must be covered, namely the actor, the control agencies—both informal and formal—and the victim. Here, we urge the continued development of a cultural criminology of the state (e.g. Wender 2001; Hamm 2004, 2007; Morrison 2006; Hayward 2011). Thus as stated above there would be no contradiction with the realist 'square of crime': rather, that realism, by being overly and simplistically rationalistic in its conception of agency, is not realistic enough. The substantive requirements of a fully social theory of crime and deviance must incorporate a notion of agency which involves energy, tension, and alternative rationalities.

## INSIDE THE 'HALL OF MIRRORS': MEDIA, REPRESENTATION, AND THE COMMODIFICATION OF CRIME

A defining feature of the last two decades has been the rise of the 'Mediascape' (Appaduarai 1996)—that tangle of media which manufactures information and disseminates images via an ever expanding array of digital technologies. In this enveloping world of media festival and digital spectacle, the logic of speed accelerates the liquidity of form as images bleed from one medium to the next. Uploaded and downloaded, copied and cross-posted, Flickr-ed, Facebook-ed, and PhotoShop-ped, the image today is as much about porosity and transmutation as it is about visual fixity and representation. This fluidity of representation is never more apparent than in the contemporary construction of crime's image. From criminals who post their crimes on YouTube, to the grainy CCTV footage that drives the slurry of primetime 'cops and robbers' compilation shows, from unreal 'reality TV' moments that shape moral values and social norms to stylized representations of crime in comic books and on criminology textbook covers, ours is a world 'where the screen scripts the street and the street scripts the screen' (Hayward and Young 2004: 259). It is one of the primary goals of cultural criminology, then, to attempt to understand the ways in which mediated processes of cultural reproduction and exchange 'constitute' the experience of crime, self, and society under conditions of late modernity.

Some critics will no doubt dismiss cultural criminology's focus on representation, image, style, and spectacle simply as a decorative or 'aesthetic' criminology—but this would be to mistake method for meaning. In a world where power is increasingly exercised through mediated representation and symbolic production, battles over image, meaning, and cultural representation emerge as essential moments in the contested negotiation of late modern reality. Other critics meanwhile will counter that criminology is already well placed to interpret 'the visual'; after all, phrases like 'images of' and 'media constructions of' are now common, and commonly accepted, prefixes to conventional criminological categories such as policing and prison studies. However, as we have stated elsewhere, '[t]his disciplinary drift into the realm of the image hardly constitutes an adequate visual criminology... Simply importing images into a discipline defined by words and numbers is in fact likely to *retard* the development of a visual criminology, since it will leave in place the ugly notion that written or numeric analysis can somehow penetrate the obfuscation, conquer the opaqueness, of the image' (Ferrell *et al.* 2008: 184–6). Instead of simply studying 'images' cultural criminology advocates a new methodological orientation towards the visual that is capable of encompassing meaning, affect, situation, and symbolic power and efficiency in the same 'frame'.[2] Some of the particular visual methods used by cultural criminologists are discussed briefly later in the chapter. For now, let us proceed with some select examples of just one aspect of cultural criminology's approach to the crime-media nexus: 'the commodification of crime'.

It is a notable irony that the more the British government attempts to control the youth crime problem by imposing a series of dominant and seemingly logical controls—everything from curfews to exclusion orders, from benefit reform to Public Disorder Acts—the more it fails in its attempt to engender compliant rationality and creates instead heightened emotionality. Hence a sort of mutating double helix in which the 'irrational responses' of young people provoke ever-more punitive measures from the state (Presdee 2000). Youth culture thus becomes at once the site of excitement and social contestation, of experimentation and dissonance. That this is the case is not surprising. The transgressive nature of youth (sub)cultural practices has long provoked indignation among politicians keen to curry favour with the 'moral majority' by vilifying the perceived 'immorality of contemporary youth'. Whether lowering the age and harm threshold of imprisonment for children or siding with schools that ban snowball fights, the government is turning the screw on the young, subjecting not only their 'oppositional forms of popular and personal pleasure', but also their legitimate cultural practices and even, in many instances, their everyday round to increasing political arbitration and state agency sanction. However, rather than dwell on the obvious (Foucauldian) point about repression/control proliferating rather than suppressing its object of alteration, we are here interested in how that other great agent of social reaction—*the market*—is reacting and contributing to this social dynamic.

The family board game *Monopoly* has been around for generations. Recently, however, it experienced a number of thematic makeovers. In the United States, *Ghettopoly* is a *Monopoly*-style game in which 'playas' move around from 'Tyron's Gun Shop' to 'Ling Ling's Massage Parlour', building crack houses, 'pimping', and selling guns as they go. Meanwhile in the UK, one games manufacturer recently courted controversy

---

[2] See, e.g., Young (2009); Hayward and Presdee (2010); Jewkes (2010); Greer (2012).

with their *Chavopoly* variant, where properties include 'Dealer's flat' and 'Vandalised bus stop', and where the 'community chest' has become a 'community pest'! To the untrained criminological eye, the development of such games might not mean much. However, to cultural criminologists, it exemplifies a more widespread tendency. Not only is the relationship between criminality and consumer lifestyle a dominant theme within these games, but they also illustrate the extent to which crime, criminality, and punishment now feature as popular forms of entertainment and amusement.

In recent years, corporations have increasingly come to rely on images of crime and deviance as prime marketing tools for selling products in the youth market. At one level, there is nothing inherently new about this. The compelling and salacious nature of certain criminal acts ensures a ready audience for crime and it has remained an enduring theme in popular culture throughout the twentieth century. What has changed, however, is both the force and range of the message and the speed at which it loops and reverberates. 'Crime has been seized upon: it is being packaged and marketed to young people as a romantic, exciting, cool, and fashionable cultural symbol. It is in this cultural context that transgression becomes a desirable consumer choice' (Fenwick and Hayward 2000: 44) (consider, for example, the British fashion labels *Criminal* and *Section 60*; the latter named after the police power to stop and search). Here, within consumer culture, crime becomes an aesthetic, a style, a fashion. This is not to suggest any deterministic link between images of violence and crime in consumer culture and contemporary youth crime; it is simply to suggest that the distinction between representations of criminality and the pursuit of excitement, especially in the area of youth culture, is becoming extremely blurred.

One very obvious example is the way 'gangster' rap combines images of criminality with street gang iconography and designer chic to create a product that is immediately seductive to youth audiences (Miller 1995; Kubrin 2005). However, it is no longer simply a question of identifying whether gangsta rap imagery and styling are affecting 'the code of the street' or vice versa. Now, the market has decided to plug into the rap scene and use the aural backdrop of urban hip hop to peddle luxury products to young people desperate for some ontological stability within social environments often stripped of traditional avenues of advancement and self-expression. While brands have always been an intrinsic element of rap culture, in recent years the stakes have increased. Once hardcore artists like IceT or Ice Cube rapped about $60 Nike trainers and 40oz bottles of Colt 45 beer; today the giants of corporate hip-hop like P.Diddy and Jay-Z extol the virtues of (and gratuitously product place) Louis Vuitton luggage, Cristal champagne, and the new Chrysler 300 C sedan. In the 2004 video for the Snoop Dogg and Pharell Williams hit *Drop it Like It's Hot*, for example, luxury cars and jewel-encrusted accoutrement seem intended to function as signifiers of both consumerist success and the street 'hustla' lifestyle (De Jong and Schuilenburg 2006), with transgressive stance and self-worth now conflated in simple commodity codes, as interpretable as a Nike 'swoosh' or a Gucci monogram (Hayward 2004: 181).

With its long association with criminality, rap is an obvious place for the selling of crime (see Ilan 2012 for an interesting counter reading). More remarkable and revealing is the way violent transgression is now emerging within more mainstream areas of consumerist cultural production (Muzzatti 2010). Car stereo ads now feature images of street riots (Kenwood)—with car commercials referencing 'joyriding' (Nissan

*Shogun*), terrorist suicide bombing (Volkswagen *Polo*), graffiti (Plymouth *Neon*), and even pyromania (Audi *A3*). Even Prince Charles has got in on the act. A recent poster advertisement for the Prince's Trust Volunteers used a manipulated marijuana leaf image and posed the question 'How high can you get?' Meanwhile, the fashion industry, when it's not trading on edgy notions of the forbidden (*Opium*, *Poison*, *Obsession*), Lolita-like sexuality, 'heroin chic', or allusions to sex and sadomasochism, is increasingly relying on a stylized tableau of female violence and victimization. Recently, the fashion house Dolce and Gabbana were forced to withdraw newspaper ads following a public outcry over their violently sexist content. In Spain, an advertisement showing a woman held to the ground by a group of half-dressed men was condemned by Labour Ministry officials as an offence to women's dignity and an 'incitement' to sexual violence. Meanwhile on the British high street, the clothing chain FCUK commodify transgression twice over; first 'branded' into the very identity of the retailer, then in a national shop window campaign featuring young women in bikinis provocatively fighting each other. With fashionistas like Dolce and Gabbana ignoring the larger meaning of their advertisements, with companies making deals to place their consumer products in misogynistic rap videos, a particular interplay of crime, media, and profit is made manifest: the willingness of mainstream corporations and their advertisers to commodify crime in a bid to sell products.

Even forms of subversive resistance and counter-cultural expression are now packaged and sold within the economics of entertainment (Hall *et al.* 2008: ch. 5). The cultural criminologist Heitor Alvelos, for example, has carefully documented the appropriation of street graffiti by multi-national corporations and their advertisers through a 'guerrilla marketing' technique known as 'brandalism'. Indeed, as the illicit visual marker of urban hipness, graffiti is now incorporated into everything from corporate theme parks, to automobile adverts, and video games. Similarly, as McRobbie and Thornton (1995) make clear, even 'moral panics' have become, literally, incorporated, as companies actively use moral and political opprobrium (in the form of 'a bit of controversy—the threat of censorship, the suggestion of sexual scandal or subversive activity') for their own profitable ends.

In a bid to explain and unravel the processes associated with the commodification of crime and other implications of the media-saturated nature of late modernity, cultural criminologists have developed a theory of *media loops and spirals* (Manning 1998; Ferrell *et al* 2008: 129–37)—conceptual processes designed to catch and elucidate the circulating cultural fluidity that overwhelms any certain distinction between an event and its representation, a mediated image and its effects, a criminal moment and its social construction. In place of the traditional positivist distinction between a phenomenon and its depiction, this approach suggests that representation now constitutes in many cases the phenomenon itself; as photographic and televisual images 'bounce endlessly one off the other' in a mediated 'hall of mirrors' (Ferrell 1999: 97). Violent gang assaults and inter school fights are not just caught on camera, but staged for the camera and later packaged together in 'underground fight videos' such as *Beatdowns*, *Felony Fights*, and *Urban Warfare: Gangs Caught on Tape*. Police dashboard-mounted car cameras not only capture the police at work, but alter the way in which they work, with TV shows like *C.O.P.S* and *L.A.P.D: Life on the Street* used by certain US police forces as both a visual recruiting sergeant and as a form of 'image management'—30 minute media friendly police promo videos. In this light, even the most basic of criminological subjects—street crime, everyday policing, court procedures—take shape not as objectively measurable phenomena but as entanglements of emerging images.

But let us conclude this section with one final criminological observation about the commodification of crime—this time about the way in which designer labels and brand logos are now contributing to new regimes of control and management of youth in public space. In a cruel irony, overt displays of designer clothing have inspired a whole new raft of bizarre micro social control mechanisms, including everything from town centre pubs and night clubs refusing entry to individuals wearing certain brands on their premises, to the recent 'zero tolerance' policy imposed on 'designer hoodies' and baseball caps by major shopping centres such as Bluewater in Kent. Bizarrely we have a situation in which many of the labels and monograms so valued by young people as badges of identity now function also as symbols of deviance (Hayward and Yar 2006). As such they become tools of classification and identification by which agencies of social control construct profiles of potential criminal protagonists. For example, in many towns in the UK local bars and the police collaborate to compile lists of branded clothing that they perceive to be 'socially problematic'.

While the state responds to the reconfigurations and transformations associated with the late modern condition by imposing what it believes to be more 'rational' forms of control and authority, the market takes a very different approach. Rather than attempt to curtail the excitement and emotionality that, for many individuals, is the preferred antidote to ontological precariousness, the market chooses instead to exacerbate, celebrate, and, very importantly, commodify these same sensations. Whether experiencing the vicarious thrill of the violent visual imagery associated with the 'digital crime environment' of shoot-em-up games like *Manhunt* or *Grand Theft Auto IV,* or attempting to subvert mainstream cultural values by sporting a 'goggle hoodie' (Treadwell 2008), looped and spiralled images of criminality are now firmly tied into the production of youth culture/identity and inscribed in numerous forms of related entertainment and stylistic performance.

# DANGEROUS KNOWLEDGE AND THE METHOD(S) OF CULTURAL CRIMINOLOGY

In his remarkable *Geographies of Exclusion*, David Sibley talks not only of spatial and social exclusion—the exclusion of the dangerous classes—but the exclusion of *dangerous knowledge*, in that knowledge is:

> conditioned by power relations which determine the boundaries of 'knowledge' and exclude dangerous or threatening ideas and authors. It follows that any prescriptions for a better integrated and more egalitarian society must also include proposals for change in the way academic knowledge is produced [Sibley 1995: xvi].

In fact the traditional positivism of sociologists and psychologists, or the private applications associated with 'crime science', have exceptional interest in *maintaining* rigid definitions and demarcations between science and non-science, between crime and 'normality', between the expert and the criminal, between criminology and more humanistic academic disciplines—and even between the individuals studied themselves as isolated atoms incapable of collective activity. It is the nature of cultural criminology that it questions all these distinctions and is thus an anathema to the project of criminology as a 'science' of crime. It seeks not to add to the 'state-serving' noise that Foucault famously dismissed as the 'garrulous discourse' of criminological knowledge, but actively to identify and challenge the external, material forces that are transforming criminology. Two (closely interrelated) current tendencies are perhaps most notable, both of which bring with them their own corrosive set of methodological, theoretical, ideological, and substantive constraints.

First, the rapid growth of punitive criminal justice systems in the United States, and the ongoing roll-out of neo-liberal forms of governance and control and associated culture(s) of risk and resource management in the United Kingdom, are increasingly bringing about the replacement of a critically inspired sociological criminology with 'administrative' forms of 'criminal justice management'. This seemingly unchecked development involves massive expenditure on prisons, police, and a growing array of dubious, unsubstantiated treatment regimes and crime prevention devices, from CCTV to electronic 'tagging'. It is a process accompanied and augmented by the 'war' against drugs and, more recently, 'the war against terrorism'. Such developments have ensured, of course, that the demand for consultancy and evaluative research has rocketed. These transformations are clearly reflected in the way criminology is now taught and delivered in western universities, as departments respond to new demands to train criminal justice personnel, both practitioners and researchers. Indeed, the exponential growth in criminal justice studies has ensured that this subdiscipline is now the largest sector of social science teaching. In the United States, for example, students, who once would have studied social policy and public administration, now routinely study criminal justice—a clear consequence of the movement from welfare to 'justice system' interventions as the leading edge of social policy. Further, the restricted funding available for higher education has led to considerable pressure on faculties to bring in external funding from research (see Robinson 2001; Walters 2003; Hillyard et al. 2004). The crime control industry has, therefore, come to exert a hegemonic influence upon academic criminology. The subsequent 'wars' against crime, drugs, terrorism, and now 'antisocial behaviour', demand facts, numbers, quantitative incomes, and outcomes (of which, more later)—they do not demand debates as to the very nature of these battles. Nor for that matter do they want to question definition, rather they want 'hard' facts and 'concrete' evidence; disciplinary imperatives that ensure the social basis for positivism is firmly established.

The response in the academy has been substantial and far-reaching. Research has begun to be dominated by statistical testing, theory has been downplayed, and 'soft' data eschewed (Ferrell 2004; Young 2004). It takes little reflection to realize that the now dominant journal format—ill-developed theory, regression analysis, usually followed by rather inconclusive results—is, in fact, a relatively recent genre. Data that are in fact technically weak (because of the well-known difficulties inherent in the collection of statistics whether by the police, victimization studies, or self-report studies) and, by their very nature, contested, blurred, ambiguous, and unsuited for quantification, are mindlessly churned through personal computers.[3] The journals and the articles become myriad yet their conclusions and pontification become more and more obscure—lost in a mess of figures, techno-speak, and methodological obfuscation (see relatedly, Waters 2004). Meanwhile the ramifications within the academy involve a form of quasi-professionalization or bureaucratization. This is most blatantly apparent in current PhD programmes. Here, induction into quantitative methodological techniques becomes a central part of academic training. Qualitative methods, meanwhile, take a more lowly position—and even here bizarre attempts are made to produce software that will enable the researcher to quantify the qualitative. The distance between the world out there—the place, you will remember, where Robert Park famously admonished his students to: stop 'grubbing in the library' and to go get the 'seat of your pants dirty in real research' (Park quoted in McKinney 1966: 71)—and the academy becomes wider and wider, fenced in by numbers and sanitized by computer printouts. On top of this, the bureaucratization of the research process by overseeing academic committees has stultified the possible range and type of research. As Patricia and Peter Adler put it, with the proliferation of institutional review boards, codes of ethics, and subject benchmarks, we risk losing

> any ethnographic research involving a covert role for the investigator (thus removing hidden populations further from view), any ethnographic research on minors that does not obtain parental consent (obviously problematic for youth involved in deviance or crime or who are victims of parental abuse), and any ethnographic research on vulnerable populations or sensitive (including criminal) issues without signed consent forms that explicitly indicate the researchers' inability to protect subjects' confidentiality. This approach puts governmental and institutional bureaucratic mandates ahead of the research bargains and confidences previously forged by fieldworkers, denigrating the impact of critical dimensions of fieldwork techniques such as reciprocity, trust, evolving relationships, depth, shifting roles, and the relative weighting of research loyalty (subjects versus society) [1998: xiv–xv].

Between the iron cage of the institutional review board and the gentle pulling and pushing of government funding, the discipline inevitably changes its form, its critical edge, and its direction.

The second point stems directly from the ascendance of neo-liberal thinking in the economic and political spheres, and the inexorable rise of the 'market society' wherein corporate values and consumerist subjectivities are now the dominant ethos. One of the baselines within cultural criminology has been a fundamental concern with the cultural conditions of late capitalism and the ways in which global economies now run on the endless creation of hyper-consumptive panic, on the symbolic construction of insatiable wants and desires. Cultural criminology's assault on consumerism continues, but it must now be extended to include the impact of the market on intellectual and university life, for developments in this area are directly affecting criminology's long-term ability to function as a sociologically and critically inspired discipline.

---

[3] On this point see Nils Christie's (1997) notion of 'the compelling archive'.

In 1961 the Robbins Committee on British higher education declared that 'the essential function of the institutions of higher education' should be the 'search for truth'. However, the policies of successive UK governments have severely compromised this edict. The belief that universities are institutions where ideas are fostered and critical thinking (in all its various forms) is encouraged is fast being replaced by the view that seats of learning must now be 'relevant' and 'in tune' with 'the perceived needs of commerce and industry'. At the level of education provision, this will only exacerbate the situation documented by Hall and Winlow who found that, for most young people, 'education is [now] simply another site of atomized instrumental competition over the acquisition of the symbolic and cultural capital necessary for favourable selection in the labour market and upgraded participation in social life loosely structured by various modes of conspicuous consumption' (2006: 314; and Hayes and Wynward 2002).[4] More worrying, however, is the way this commercial ethos pushes open the door to what Reece Walters (2003) describes as 'market-led criminology'. Under this rubric, the increasing commercialization of the university sector within neo-liberal political and economic discourses 'continues to colonise research agendas with critical voices demarcated to an increasingly marginalised periphery'—all the time ensuring that academics are forced to act as 'service providers to paying clients' (often signing away their entitlements to publish in the process) (ibid.: 146–8).

It is against this backdrop that cultural criminology seeks to re-create a sociologically inspired criminology that is more critical, not less—a criminology capable of understanding the full implications of this fundamental shift to the 'consumer society' and which is thus fully equipped with the analytic tools that can unpick (and thereby expose) the representations and structures through which market discourses and subsequent power relations are exercised.

So what specific methodological approaches do cultural criminologists employ in their alternative attempts to frame problems of crime, inequality, and criminal justice? In its early years, cultural criminologists typically utilized either one of two main research methods (Ferrell 1999): ethnographic and qualitative fieldwork techniques[5] or the scholarly deconstruction of media images and cultural texts (Altheide 1996). However, as cultural criminology gathered momentum, its mélange of intellectual and interdisciplinary influences impacted on the range and type of research methods employed. As a consequence, cultural criminologists are today as likely to employ research methods like participative action research (Whyte 1989, O'Neill et al. 2004), netnography (Kozinets 2010), or 'narrative criminology' (Sandberg 2010) as they are more established tools of ethnography or media discourse/content analysis. Indeed,

---

[4] One could also point to the intensified regulation and standardization of higher education facilitated by the practices introduced in the name of 'quality assurance'. As Beckmann and Cooper (2004) suggest, these centrally defined statements introduce prescription, instrumentalism, uniformity and compliance within nationally-determined objectives, resulting in the increasing production of 'raw material' or 'uncritical thinkers, compliant to the needs of the market'.

[5] See especially Ferrell (1997) for an early statement on the importance of the ethnographic 'moment' in cultural criminology; Ferrell and Hamm (1998) for a classic collection of ethnographic cultural criminology essays; and relatedly Miller and Tewkesbury (2000).

even these two original cultural criminological methods have undergone considerable augmentation.

While long-term ethnography remains a key method of cultural criminology, we also recognize, of course, that due to the publication pressures associated with (in the UK) bureaucratic strictures like the Research Assessment Framework, or the ethical governance exerted (in the US) by university Institutional Review Boards, deep ethnographic immersion is becoming harder to undertake. However, this does not mean that cultural criminology cannot be avowedly defined by an *ethnographic sensibility*:

> [P]ut into play, this ethnographic sensibility orients cultural criminology to particular practices: It opens research to the meaningful worlds of others, and seeks to understand the symbolic processes through which these worlds are made...Thought of in this way, 'ethnography' is not a method that excludes all but the most committed researchers, but an invitation to all researchers, all criminologists, to engage an attitude of attentiveness and respect. Thought of as a sensibility, ethnography can endure for months or for a moment, and can be brought to bear on social situations, mediated communications, or global processes (Ferrell *et al.* 2008: 179).

Hence cultural criminologists have developed techniques known as 'instant ethnography' and 'liquid ethnography' (ibid.: 179–84): the former concerned with single 'decisive moments' of phenomenological serendipity—whether unpredictable or predictable, unexceptional or exceptional—that illustrate or embrace something of cultural criminology's progressive mandate; the latter a research strategy perfectly attuned to the permutations of late modernity and thus sensitive to the ambiguities and uncertainties of, *inter alia*, destabilized or diasporic communities, the interplay of images discussed above, or even the shifting boundaries between research, research subjects, and cultural activism.

Likewise cultural criminology's long-standing interest in media analysis has also been the subject of an ongoing methodological overhaul. Cultural criminologists no longer limit themselves to the traditional techniques associated with media/content analysis. Instead they transcend simple analyses of the static image/picture and employ visual research methods attuned to the way individual and collective behaviour are now increasingly affected by a culture in which the image is truly ascendant (see Hayward 2010). As a result cultural criminologists now regularly employ the techniques of documentary and auto-ethnographic diary photography, semiotics, and iconology, image signification systems and other indexical film studies techniques, video film-making, participatory digital cartography, and other forms of video-recorded social activism.

That said, in terms of their methodological framework some constants remain central to the cultural criminological enterprise and its particular position vis-à-vis what they describe as 'orthodox criminological research': see Young (2004) for a classic statement on cultural criminology's rejection of abstracted empiricism, Parnell and Kane (2003) on how the techniques of cultural anthropology can be applied to the study of deviance; and Katz (2002) for a statement on how to commence phenomenological fieldwork. For a general overview of cultural criminology's often controversial position regarding traditional criminological method, see chapter 6 ('Dangerous Knowledge') in Ferrell *et al.*'s *Cultural Criminology: an Invitation*, and relatedly Manning (1995).

# CONCLUSION

Cultural criminology seeks to reconnect to the roots of sociological criminology, to its origins in phenomenological sociology and in subcultural theory, to critically appraise these earlier positions, and to develop a theory which can fully comprehend the conditions of late modernity in which we now find ourselves. It has its basis in the discourse on culture which stresses the potentiality of human reflexivity and transcendence, but which is only too fully aware that much cultural activity is ritualistic and essentialist, seeking to escape the privations and tribulations of modern life. It spans the compass from acquiescence to rebellion, although it stresses that resistance and resilience are frequently found in groups which are conventionally scorned and pathologized (Brotherton and Barrios 2004). It is concerned with the phenomenology both of excitement and of tedium, it is a sociology neither solely of thrills nor of thrall. Culture is placed at the centre of the analysis but it is a culture rooted in the material predicament of the actors concerned. It eschews both a social positivism of material conditions and a cultural positivism of stasis and of essence. In contrast cultural criminology puts great stress on fluidity and change: a loosening of moorings, particularly in this period of cultural globalization and manifest pluralism of values. And lastly, in terms of method, it must seek to rescue the human actors who form the focus of our subject, whether offenders, victims, police officers, or members of the public, from the condescension both of inappropriate quantification and of deterministic methods which diminish and obfuscate the underlying creativity of social action.

## ■ SELECTED FURTHER READING

Many of the ideas and themes covered in this chapter are explored in greater detail in *Cultural Criminology: an Invitation* (Ferrell *et al.* 2008, a second edition is in development). Aimed at undergraduate students, and replete with numerous examples and illustrations– even a filmography—this is the most accessible and comprehensive introduction to the field to date, and provides an excellent starting point for future research. Another useful overview is Ferrell and Hayward's *Cultural Criminology: Theories of Crime* (2011, Farnham: Ashgate); a collection that consolidates classic precursor works with key examples of contemporary cultural criminology. An alternative starting point is the annotated bibliography of around 100 cultural criminology references in the 2012 *Oxford Bibliographies Online*.

A number of edited compilations exist. The first collection of essays entitled *Cultural Criminology* was compiled by Ferrell and Sanders in 1995. In this work (and in subsequent early review articles such as Ferrell 1999), we see cultural criminology in its original US manifestation, i.e. tending to focus on illicit subcultures, labelling theory, and various criminalized forms of music and style. A more recent 24-chapter collection that focuses on crime and culture across a variety of local, regional, and national settings is Ferrell *et al.*'s (2004) *Cultural Criminology Unleashed*. Although more suitable for postgraduate students, the 2004 Special Edition of the international journal *Theoretical Criminology* (Vol. 8 No. 3) is also of interest.

If early cultural criminology was preoccupied with meaning, subculture, and media representation, more recent work has sought to add a more materialist dimension. See for example Hayward's *City Limits: Crime, Consumer Culture and the Urban Experience* (2004) on the relationship between consumerism and expressive criminality; Young's (2003) article 'Merton with energy, Katz with structure: the sociology of vindictiveness and the criminology of transgression', which attempts to ground transgression in a structural context; Presdee's *Cultural Criminology and the Carnival of Crime* (2000) on the commodification of crime and punishment; Hayward and Yar's (2006) work on 'Chavs' and how consumerism is now a locus around which exclusion is configured and the excluded identified and surveyed; and the intentionally polemical dialogic exchange about crime, culture, and capitalism between Jeff Ferrell and Steve Hall and Simon Winlow in the journal *Crime, Media, Culture* (Vol. 3 No. 1). See also Morrison (2006), Hamm (2007), and Hayward (2011) for examples of an emerging cultural criminology of the state.

A primary feature of cultural criminology is its interest in the emotions and existential realities associated with the commission of much crime. The foundational work in this reconstruction of experiential aetiology is Jack Katz's *The Seductions of Crime* (1988); a text that serves as a touchstone for subsequent cultural criminological analyses on crime and emotionality such as O'Malley and Mugford (1994), Morrison (1995: ch. 15), and Fenwick and Hayward (2000). The dialectic between excitement and control is also a major interest of cultural criminology; as evidenced by Stephen Lyng's seminal concept of 'Edgework' (1990, 2005; see also Rajah 2007), and Hayward's critique of rational choice theories of crime (2007, 2012).

For student-friendly introductions to cultural criminology's interest in the way crime is woven into the fabric of everyday life, see the chapters by Ferrell (2009), Presdee (2009), and Ferrell and Ilan (2003) in the second and third editions of the Oxford University Press textbook *Criminology* (edited by C. Hale *et al.*). For book-length (ethnographic) examples of how cultural criminologists attempt to communicate the criminological, political, gendered, and theoretical importance of the everyday, see Dunier (1999), Ferrell (2006), Miller (2008), and Garot (2010).

For examples of cultural criminological research on crime and the media see *Framing Crime: Cultural Criminology and the Image* (Hayward and Presdee 2010); Frankie Bailey and Donna Hale's (1998) book *Popular Culture, Crime and Justice*; Alison Young's *The Scene of Violence* (2009); Chris Greer's *Crime News* (2012), and the international journal *Crime, Media, Culture* (London: Sage), a periodical dedicated to exploring the relationships between crime, criminal justice, and the media.

Finally, in terms of research methodology, see Young's *The Criminological Imagination* (2011) and chapter 6 ('Dangerous Knowledge') of *Cultural Criminology: an Invitation* for covering statements. On the ethnographic aspect of cultural criminology, see Ferrell and Hamm's *Ethnography at the Edge* (1998); Ferrell's (1997) account of criminological *verstehen*; and Stephanie Kane's article, 'The unconventional methods in cultural criminology', in the aforementioned Special Edition of *Theoretical Criminology*.

For further examples of cultural criminological research, readers are advised to explore the references listed in the present chapter. Finally, to access a number of key papers and to keep up to date with news about conferences and publications in the area of cultural criminology log on to www.culturalcriminology.org.

## ■ REFERENCES

ADLER, P. and ADLER, P. (1998), 'Moving Backwards', in J. Ferrell and M. Hamm (eds), *Ethnography on the Edge*, Boston: Northeastern University Press.

ALEXANDER, J. and SMITH, P. (2002), 'The Strong Program in Cultural Theory', in J. Turner (ed.), *Handbook of Sociological Theory*, New York: Plenum.

ALTHEIDE, D. (1996), *Qualitative Media Analysis*, Thousand Oaks, CA: Sage.

ALVELOS, H. (2004), 'The desert of imagination in the city of signs', in J. Ferrell *et al.* (eds), *Cultural Criminology Unleashed*, London: GlassHouse.

APPADURAI, A. (1996), *Modernity at Large*, Minneapolis: University of Minnesota Press.

BAILEY, F. and HALE, D. (1998), *Popular Culture, Crime and Justice*, Belmont, Cal.: Wadsworth.

BANKS, C. (2000), *Developing Cultural Criminology: Theory and Practice in Papua New Guinea*, Sydney: University of Sydney Press.

BAUMAN, Z. (1998), *Consumerism, Work and the New Poor*, Buckingham: Open University Press.

—— (1999), *Culture as Praxis*, London: Sage.

BECKMANN, A. and COOPER, C. (2004), '"Globalisation", the new managerialism and education: rethinking the purpose of education in Britain', *Journal for Critical Education Policy Studies*, 2: 2.

BOURDIEU, P. (1991), *Language and Symbolic Power*, Cambridge: Polity.

BRAKE, M. (1980), *The Sociology of Youth Culture*, London: Routledge & Kegan Paul.

BROTHERTON, D. (2009), 'Proceedings from the Transnational/Street Organization Seminar', *Crime Media Culture*, 3(2): 72–81.

—— and BARRIOS, L. (2004), *The Almighty Latin King and Queen Nation*, New York: Columbia University Press.

CHRISTIE, N. (1997), 'Four blocks against insight: notes on the oversocialization of criminologists', *Theoretical Criminology*, 1(1): 3–23.

COHEN, S. (1972), *Folk Devils and Moral Panics*, London: McGibbon and Kee.

—— (1997), 'Intellectual Scepticism and Political Commitment', in P. Walton and J. Young (eds), *The New Criminology Revisited*, London: Macmillan

CONQUERGOOD, D. (1991), 'On Rethinking Ethnography', *Communications Monographs*, 58: 335–59.

COTTEE, S. and HAYWARD, K. J. (2011), 'Terrorist (E) motives: the existential attractions of terrorism', *Studies in Conflict and Terrorism*, 34(12): 963–86.

DE HAAN, W. and VOS, J. (2003), 'A crying shame: the over-rationalized conception of man in the rational choice perspective', *Theoretical Criminology*, 7(1): 29–54.

DE JONG, A. and SCHUILENBURG, M. (2006), *Mediapolis*, Rotterdam: 010 Publishers.

DOWNES, D. (1966), *The Delinquent Solution*, London: Routledge & Kegan Paul.

—— (2005), 'Book Review. *City Limits, Crime, Consumerism and the Urban Experience*', *Criminal Justice*, 5(3): 319–21.

DUNIER, M. (1999), *Sidewalk*, New York: Farrar, Straus and Giroux.

EDWARDS, A. and HUGHES, G. (2005), 'Comparing the Governance of Safety in Europe', *Theoretical Criminology*, 9(3): 345–63.

FENWICK, M. and HAYWARD, K. J. (2000), 'Youth Crime, Excitement and Consumer Culture: The Reconstruction of Aetiology in Contemporary Theoretical Criminology', in J. Pickford (ed.), *Youth Justice: Theory and Practice*. London: Cavendish.

FERRELL, J. (1992), 'Making Sense of Crime: Review Essay on Jack Katz's *Seductions of Crime*', *Social Justice*, 19(3): 111–23.

—— (1997), 'Criminological *Verstehen*: Inside the Immediacy of Crime', *Justice Quarterly*, 14(1): 3–23.

—— (1999), 'Cultural Criminology', *Annual Review of Sociology*, 25: 395–418.

—— (2004), 'Boredom, crime and criminology', *Theoretical Criminology*, 8(3): 287–302.

—— (2006), *Empire of Scrounge*, New York: New York University Press.

—— and HAMM, M. (1998), *Ethnography at the Edge*, Boston: Northeastern University Press.

—— and SANDERS, C. (eds) (1995), *Cultural Criminology*, Boston: Northeastern University Press.

——, HAYWARD, K., MORRISON, W., and PRESDEE, M. (2004), *Cultural Criminology Unleashed*, London: Glasshouse.

GAILEY, J. (2007), 'The Pro-Ana Culture as Edgework', Paper presented at the American Society of Criminology Annual Meetings.

GAROT, R. (2010), *Who You Claim*, New York: New York University Press.

GOFFMAN, E. (1980), *Asylums*, Harmondsworth: Penguin.

GOULDNER, A. (1968), 'The Sociologist as Partisan', *American Sociologist*, 3: 103–16.

GREER, C. (2012), *Crime News*, London: Routledge.

*GUARDIAN, THE* (2003), 'Hodge stands firm over research funding', 30 April.

HALL, S., WINLOW, S., and ANCRUM, C. (2009), *Criminal Identities and Consumer Culture*, Cullompton: Willan.

HALL, S. and JEFFERSON, T. (eds) (1975), *Resistance Through Ritual*, London: Hutchinson,

—— and WINLOW, S. (2006), *Violent Night*, Oxford: Berg.

——, CRITCHER, C., JEFFERSON, T., CLARKE, J., and ROBERTS, B. (eds) (1978), *Policing the Crisis: Mugging, the State and Law 'n' Order*, London: Macmillan.

HAMM, M. (2004), 'The US Patriot Act and the politics of fear', in J. Ferrell, K. Hayward, W. Morrison, and M. Presdee (2004), *Cultural Criminology, Unleashed*. London: Glasshouse.

—— (2007), 'High crimes and misdemeanours: George W Bush and the sins of Abu Ghraib', *Crime, Media, Culture*, 3(3): 259–84.

HARCOURT, B. (2007), *Against Prediction: Profiling, Policing, and Punishment in an Actuarial Age*, Chicago: Chicago University Press.

HAYES, D. and WYNWARD, R. (2002), *The McDonaldization of Higher Education*, Westport, Conn.: Greenwood Press.

HAYWARD, K. J. (2003), 'Consumer Culture and Crime in late Modernity', in C. Sumner (ed.), *The Blackwell Companion to Criminology*, Oxford: Blackwell.

—— (2004), *City Limits: Crime, Consumer Culture and the Urban Experience*, London: Routledge-Glasshouse.

—— (2007), 'Situational crime prevention and its discontents: rational choice theory versus the "culture of now"', *Social Policy and Administration*, 41(3): 232–50.

—— (2010), 'Opening the lens: cultural criminology and the image', in K. J. Hayward and M. Presdee, *Framing Crime: Cultural Criminology and the Image*, London: Routledge.

—— (2011), 'The critical terrorism studies-cultural criminology nexus: some thoughts on how to "toughen up" the critical studies approach', *Critical Studies on Terrorism*, 4(1): 57–73.

—— (2012), 'A response to Farrell', *Social Policy and Administration*, 46(1).

—— and HOBBS, D. (2007), 'Beyond the binge in Booze Britain: market-led liminalization and the spectacle of binge drinking', *British Journal of Sociology*, 58(3): 437–56.

—— and PRESDEE, M. (2010), *Framing Crime: Cultural Criminology and the Image*, London: Routledge.

—— and YAR, M. (2006), 'The "Chav" phenomenon: consumption, media and the construction of a new underclass', *Crime, Media, Culture*, 2(1): 9–28.

—— and YOUNG, J. (eds) (2004), Special Edition on Cultural Criminology, *Theoretical Criminology*, 8(3).

HENRY, S. and MILOVANOVIC, D. (1996), *Constitutive Criminology: Beyond Postmodernism*, London: Sage.

HILLYARD, P., SIM, J., TOMBS, S., and WHYTE, D. (2004), 'Leaving "a stain upon the silence": contemporary criminology and the politics of dissent', *British Journal of Criminology*, 44(3): 369–90.

HOWE, A. (2003), 'Managing men's violence in the criminological arena', in C. Sumner (ed.), *The Blackwell Companion to Criminology*, Oxford: Blackwell.

ILAN, J. (2012), '"The industry's the new road": crime, commodification and street cultural tropes in UK urban music', *Crime, Media, Culture*, Forthcoming.

JEWKES, Y. (2010), *Media and Crime*, London: Sage.

KATZ, J. (1988), *Seductions of Crime*, New York: Basic Books.

—— and JACKSON-JACOBS, C. (2004), 'The Criminologists' Gang', in C. Sumner (ed.), *Blackwell Companion to Criminology*, Oxford: Blackwells.

KOZINETS, R. V. (2010), *Netnography*, London: Sage.

KUBRIN, C. (2005), 'Gangstas, Thugs and Hustlas: identity and the code of the street in Rap music', *Social Problems*, 52(3): 360–78.

LEA, J., MATTHEWS, R., and YOUNG J. (1989), *The State, Multiagency Approaches and Crime Control*, London: Middlesex University, Centre for Criminology.

LOIS, J. (2005), 'Gender and emotion management in the stages of edgework', in S. Lyng (ed.), *Edgework*, New York: Routledge.

LYNG, S. (1990), 'Edgework: A Social Psychological Analysis of Voluntary Risk-Taking', *American Journal of Sociology*, 95(4): 876–921.

—— (ed.) (2005), *Edgework*, New York: Routledge.

McKINNEY, J. C. (1966), *Constructive Typology and Social Theory*, New York: Appleton-Century-Crofts.

McROBBIE, A. and THORNTON, S. (1995), 'Rethinking "moral panic" for multi-mediated social worlds', *British Journal of Sociology*, 46(4): 245–59.

MANNING, P. (1998), 'Media loops', in F. Bailey and D. Hale (eds), *Popular Culture, Crime and Justice*, Belmont, CA: Wadsworth.

MATZA, D. (1969), *Becoming Deviant*, Englewood Cliffs, NJ: Prentice Hall.

MELOSSI, D. (2001), 'The Cultural Embeddness of Social Control', *Theoretical Criminology*, 5(4): 403–24.

MILLER, J. (1995), 'Struggles over the symbolic: gang style and the meanings of social control', in J. Ferrell and C. R. Sanders (eds), *Cultural Criminology*, Boston: Northeastern University Press.

—— (2008), *Getting Played: African American Girls, Urban Inequality, and Gendered Violence*, New York: New York University Press.

MILLER, W. (1958), 'Lower Class Culture as a Generating Milieu of Gang Delinquency', *Journal of Social Issues*, 14: 5–19.

MILLS WRIGHT, C. (1959), *The Sociological Imagination*, London: Penguin.

MOONEY, J. (2011), 'Finding a Political Voice: The Emergence of Critical Criminology in Britain', in W. DeKeresedy and M. Dragiewicz (eds), *Critical Criminology*, London: Routledge.

MORRISON, W. (2005), *Theoretical Criminology*, London: Cavendish.

—— (2006), *Criminology, Civilization and the New World Order*, London: GlassHouse.

MUZZATTI, S. (2010), '"Drive it like you stole it": a cultural criminology of car commercials', in K. J. Hayward and M. Presdee (eds), *Framing Crime: Cultural Criminology and the Image*, London: Routledge.

O'BRIEN, M. (2005), 'What is *cultural* about cultural criminology?', *British Journal of Criminology*, 45(5): 599–612.

O'MALLEY, P. and MUGFORD, S. (1994), 'Crime, excitement and modernity', in G. Barak (ed.), *Varieties of Criminology*, Westport, Conn.: Praeger.

O'NEILL, M. WOODS, P., and WEBSTER, M. (2004), 'New Arrivals: participatory action research, imagined communities and "visions" of social justice', *Social Justice*, 32(1): 75–89.

PEARSON, I. (2002), *Universities and Innovation: Meeting the Challenge*, London: Social Market Foundation, March.

PRESDEE, M. (2000), *Cultural Criminology and the Carnival of Crime*, London: Routledge.

RAJAH, V. (2007), 'Resistance as edgework in violent intimate relationships of drug-involved women', *British Journal of Criminology*, 47(2): 196–213.

ROBINSON, M. (2001), 'Whither Criminal Justice?', *Critical Criminology*, 10(2): 97–106.

ROCK, P. (2005), 'Chronocentrism and British criminology', *British Journal of Sociology*, 56(3): 473–91.

RUGGIERO, V. (2005), 'Review: *City Limits: Crime, Consumer Culture and the Urban Experience*', *Theoretical Criminology*, 9(4): 497–9.

SANDBERG, S. (2010), 'What can "lies" tell us about life? Notes towards a framework of narrative criminology', *Journal of Criminal Justice Education*, 21(4): 447–65.

SELLIN, T. (1938), *Culture Conflict and Crime*, New York: Social Science Research Council.

SHERWOOD, S., SMITH, P., and ALEXANDER, J. (1993), 'The British are Coming...Again! The Hidden Agenda of Cultural Studies', *Contemporary Sociology*, 22(2): 370–5.

SIBLEY, D. (1995), *Geographies of Exclusion*, London: Routledge.

SMITH, P. (1998), 'Introduction', in P. Smith (ed.), *The New American Cultural Sociology*, Cambridge: Cambridge University Press.

SYKES, G. (1958), *Society of Captives*, Princeton NJ: University of Princeton Press.

SZTOMPKA, P. (1990), 'Conceptual Frameworks in Comparative Research: Divergent and Convergent', in M. Albrow and E. King (eds), *Globalization, Knowledge and Society*, London: Sage.

THOMPSON, E. P. (1981), 'The Politics of Theory', in R. Samuel (ed.), *People's History and Socialist Theory*, London: Routledge.

TREADWELL, J. (2008), 'Call the (fashion) police: how fashion becomes criminalised', *Papers from the British Criminology Conference*, Vol. 8: 117–33.

VAN HOOREBEECK, B. (1997), 'Prospects of reconstructing aetiology', *Theoretical Criminology*, 1(4): 501–18.

WALTERS, R. (2003), *Deviant Knowledge*, Cullompton, Devon: Willan.

—— (2004), 'Deviant Knowledge: reclaiming the critical voice' posted at www.theorynetwork.org.

WATERS, L. (2004), *Enemies of Promise: Publishing, Perishing, and the Eclipse of Scholarship*, Chicago: Prickly Paradigm Press.

WEISBURD, D. and PIQUERO, A. (2008), 'Taking Stock of How Well Criminologists Explain Crime', *Crime and Justice*, Vol. 37, 453–50, Chicago: Chicago University Press.

WENDER, J. (2001), 'The eye of the painter and the eye of the police: what criminology and law enforcement can learn from Manet', Paper presented at the Annual Conference of the American Society of Criminology, Atlanta.

WHYTE, W. F. (1989), 'Advancing Scientific Knowledge Through Participating Action Research', *Sociological Forum*, 4(3): 367–85.

WILLIS, P. (1977), *Learning to Labour*, Aldershot: Gower.

YAR, M. (2005), 'The Global "Epidemic" of Movie "Piracy": Crime-Wave or Social Construction?', *Media, Culture & Society*, 27(5): 677–96.

YOUNG, A. (2009), *The Scene of Violence: Crime, Cinema and Affect*, London: Routledge.

YOUNG, I. (1990), *Justice and the Politics of Difference*, Princeton: Princeton University Press.

YOUNG, J. (1971), *The Drugtakers*, London: Paladin.

—— (1987), 'The Tasks Facing a Realist Criminology', *Contemporary Crises*, 11(4): 337–56.

—— (1992), 'Ten Points of Realism', in R. Matthews and J. Young (eds), *Rethinking Criminology*, London: Sage.

—— (1999), *The Exclusive Society*, London: Sage.

—— (2003), 'Merton with Energy, Katz with Structure', *Theoretical Criminology*, 7(3): 389–414.

—— (2004), 'Voodoo criminology and the numbers game', in J. Ferrell, K. Hayward, W. Morrison, and M. Presdee (eds), *Cultural Criminology Unleashed*, London: Glasshouse.

—— (2011), *The Criminological Imagination*, Oxford: Polity.

ZIMRING, F. (2007), *The Great American Crime Decline*, New York: Oxford University Press.

# 5

# COMPARING CRIMINAL JUSTICE

*David Nelken*

In the few years since the last edition of this *Handbook* was published the literature relevant to this chapter has developed significantly. A number of valuable textbooks and collections have been published as well as a host of important books and articles examining specific systems in a comparative perspective (see the note on selected further reading).

In addition, there is also a growing literature on the crucial question of the globalization of crime and criminal justice and the way this affects how ideas and practices of criminal justice are shaped internationally or 'transferred' from one place to another. Comparative research now figures in some of the most debated issues on the criminological mainstream. Information from international comparative victim surveys has helped demonstrate how little changes in crime levels could explain patterns of punishment over time and space. David Garland's famous thesis about the rising culture of control set out to describe the trends in growing punitiveness in the USA and the UK (Garland 2000). But in implying that these countries could be seen as exemplars of widely shared late-modern conditions he prompted many other authors to see whether (and how) his claims applied elsewhere (see, e.g., Cavadino and Dignan 2006; Lacey 2008). Comparison is also central for those who seek to explain why the death penalty is retained in some places rather than others (Zimring and Johnson 2008)—and even Garland now seeks to explain what makes the USA specific in this respect rather than what makes it an illustration of wider trends (Garland 2010).

Given the space constraints it is not possible to do justice to all the new work that has been published. I have added something about the challenge that globalization poses to comparative criminal justice and the ways that global trends affect the nation state or other more locally-based justice practices. But the chapter continues to concentrate on general issues concerning the rationales, methods, and approaches to comparative research on criminal justice. Why do we do such research? What types of theoretical approaches should we draw on in comparing criminal justice systems? What methods can we use to gather our data? Even if comparative research is increasingly seen as offering a contribution to answering criminology's basic questions about the causes of crime and the way it is sanctioned, it still faces special problems in its search to find ways to understand difference—and make the familiar unfamiliar.

# WHY STUDY CRIMINAL JUSTICE COMPARATIVELY?

Interest in learning more about different systems of criminal justice can be shaped by a variety of goals of explanation, understanding, and reform. For many scholars the major contribution of comparative work lies in the way it could advance the agenda of a scientific criminology aimed at identifying the correlates of crime as antisocial behaviour. These writers use cross-national data so as to test claims about the link between crime and age, crime and social structure, crime and modernization, and so on. Much the same could be done in constructing arguments about variations between types of crime and social reaction (Black 1997).

By contrast, evidence of differences in the relationship between crime and criminal justice may be sought in order to excavate the positivist worm at the core of criminology. When 'crime' is treated as a social construct, a product of contrasting social and political censures, criminology is obliged to open out to larger debates in moral philosophy and the humanities as well as in the social sciences themselves. By posing fundamental problems of understanding the 'other' it challenges scholars to overcome ethnocentrism without denying difference or resorting to stereotypes. Engaging in comparative criminology thus has the potential to make criminologists become more reflexive (Nelken 1994a), for example learning to avoid the common error of treating the modern Anglo-American type of 'pragmatic instrumental' approach to law as if it were universal. Setting out to describe other countries' systems of criminal justice in fact often leads to rival accounts proposed by criminologists of the countries concerned (see, e.g., Downes 1988, 1990; Franke 1990; Clinard 1978; Balvig 1988; Killias 1989). The debates that follow, painful and replete with misunderstanding as they sometimes tend to be, are fundamentally healthy for limiting the pretensions of a discipline that too often studies the powerless.

One result of studying the way crime is defined and handled in different jurisdictions by legislatures, criminal justice agencies, and the media (and others) is to discover—yet again—the crucial need to relate the study of crime to that of criminal justice. But it also demonstrates the difficulty of distinguishing criminal justice from social control more broadly. The proportionally low crime rates in Switzerland and Japan, for example, can only be understood in terms of such interrelationships. Likewise, if Italian courts send to prison only one-fifth of the youngsters who end up there, in England and Wales this may in part be explained by differences in the type and level of offences carried out by young people. But it will also have to do with the way Italian juvenile court judges and social workers feel they can (and should) defer to family social controls—given that children generally live at home at least until their late twenties, and often rely on family help to find work. On the other hand, cross-national data may on occasion also show that criminal behaviour is relatively uninfluenced by legal and social responses. There is evidence that even when different nation states change their drug laws at different times and in different directions, the patterns of national drug use (and drug overdose) seem to be less affected by this than by international developments in supply and demand.

But we should not limit our interest in comparative criminal justice only to its effects on levels of crime. We can also study it in its own right. This sort of comparative enquiry has as one of its chief concerns the effort to identify the way a country's types of crime control resonate with other aspects of its culture. Why is it that countries like the UK and Denmark, who complain most about the imposition of European Union law, also maintain the best records of implementation? What does this tell us about the centrality of enforcement as an aspect of law in different societies? Why, in the United States and the UK, does it often take a sex scandal to create official interest in doing something about corruption, whereas in Latin countries it takes a major corruption scandal to excite interest in marital unfaithfulness? What does this suggest about the way culture conditions the boundaries of law and the way criminal law helps shape those self-same boundaries (Nelken 2002a)?

It can be important to investigate how far particular methods of crime control are conditioned by these sorts of cultural factors. Much British writing on the police, for example, takes it for granted that nothing could be more ill-advised than for the police to risk losing touch with the public by relying too much on military, technological, or other impersonal methods of crime control. The results of this, it is claimed, could only be a spiral of alienation that would spell the end of 'policing by consent'. In Italy, however, two of the main police forces are still part of the military, and this insulation from the pressures of local people is actually what inspires public confidence. Britain, like most English-speaking countries, adopts a preventive style of responding to many white-collar offences which is sufficiently different to be characterized as a system of 'compliance' as compared to 'punishment' (Nelken, this volume). This is often justified as the only logical way of proceeding given the nature of the crimes and offenders involved. But in Italy such a contrast is much less noticeable. Enforcement is guided by the judiciary, who do their best to combat pollution, the neglect of safety at work, etc. using the normal techniques of criminal law and punishment.

As these examples illustrate, the interest in how criminal justice is organized elsewhere is often (some would say predominantly) guided by practical and policy goals. Perceived differences, such as the continued use of the death penalty in the United States, as well as its relatively high rate of imprisonment, may be used to reassure us about the superiority of our own institutions. But, more commonly, scholars cite evidence from abroad in an attempt to challenge and improve the way we do things at home. The concern for reform is manifest for example in the long-standing search by Anglo-American authors to see whether anything can be learned from Continental European countries about better ways of controlling police discretion (Frase 1990; Hodgson 2005). Many descriptive or explanatory cross-cultural exercises are often shaped by a more or less hidden normative agenda, or finish by making policy recommendations. Even cross-national victim surveys can be deployed as much as a tool for change as in a search for understanding variability (Van Dijk 2000).

The search for patterned differences in law and practice also raises the question of what it could mean to affirm (either as a sociological or a normative claim) that a country has the system it 'requires'. What price might a society have to pay to introduce 'reintegrative shaming'? What are the costs of pursuing 'zero tolerance'? If the Italian criminal process can effectively decriminalize most cases involving juvenile delinquency (with the important exceptions of cases involving young immigrants or Gypsies), could we and should we do the same (Nelken 2006a)? If prosecutors in Japan succeed in keeping down the level of cases sent to court, could we and should we follow their example (Johnson 2000)? Policy-led research can itself produce interesting descriptive and explanatory findings. But cultural variability in ideas and values means that it can also be tricky. Is it safe, for example, to assume that 'all criminal justice systems have to handle the "built-in-conflict" of how to maximise convictions of the guilty at the same time as maximising the acquittal of the innocent' (Feest and Murayama 2000)? What would it mean to shift our focus from 'taking or leaving' single elements of other systems in favour of a broader effort to re-think practices as a whole in the light of how things are done elsewhere (Hodgson 2000)?

The search to find convincing, plausible interpretations of systems of criminal justice at the level of the nation state, as in accounts of 'Japanese criminal justice' or descriptions of 'French criminal procedure', continues to be an ambition of comparative researchers. But, in an era of globalization, there is increasing recognition of the difficulties of drawing boundaries between systems of criminal justice. Attempts to deal with a host of perceived international or transnational threats such as (amongst others) organized crime, terrorism, human trafficking, corruption, illegal dumping of waste, computer crime, money-laundering, and tax evasion raise the problem of how far it is possible or advisable to harmonize different systems of criminal justice (Nelken 1997b).

As noted in the previous edition, however, globalization is a name for complex and contradictory developments. At a minimum, however, we could think of it as referring to the consequence of the greater mobility of capital (sometimes, but not always, willingly embraced by states as a political neo-liberal choice) and new forms of international interconnections that have grown at the expense of national ones as nation states are incorporated into the global economy and informational cyberspace. State sovereignty is challenged by international courts, human rights conventions, multinational private security enterprises, cross-border policing, policy networks and flows, and technologies of global surveillance. Key crime initiatives now link regional or local centres of power (Edwards and Hughes 2005) or are delegated to the private sector. War making, peace-keeping, and criminal justice come to overlap and even war is privatized. At the same time the use of cyberspace requires and generates a variety of forms of control and resistance, as it points to unprecedented (not necessarily utopian) forms of social ordering.

On the other hand, nation state boundaries still often coincide with language and cultural differences, and represent the source of criminal law and criminal statistics. The imposition of a common legal code and the common training of legal officials form part of attempts to achieve and consolidate national identity and 'borders' continue to play important instrumental and symbolic roles, not least in responding to immigration. Nation states use neo-liberal strategies to (re)assert national boundaries and priorities and the criminal law continues to be a powerful icon of sovereign statehood. And the nation state remains a key site where the insecurities and uncertainties brought about by (economic) globalization are expected to be 'resolved'. These tensions need to be born in mind when studying the work of international bodies such as non-governmental organizations and intergovernmental organizations and the influential think tanks who formulate and spread what have been called 'global prescriptions'—including ideas about what to do about crime.

According to Savelsberg, globalization occurs along three paths: norms and practices, including those on punishment, change as a consequence of global shifts in social structure, and culture, there is a nation-specific processing of global scripts and nation-specific responses to the arrival of (late) modernity, and a new type of international criminal law has been gaining strength at the global level (Savelsberg 2011). For him, as for many other commentators, globalization should be seen as a *process*—one in which the role of agents is crucial. As Muncie puts it:

> the argument that criminal justice is becoming a standardised global product can be sustained only at the very highest level of generality. Economic forces are not uncontrollable, do meet resistance and have effects that are neither uniform nor consistent. Nor should we expect that policy transfer be direct or complete or exact or successful. Rather, it is mediated through national and local cultures, which are themselves changing at the same time (Muncie 2011: 100).

In examining the spread of such blueprints we need to study *what* it is that is being spread—scripts, norms, institutions, technologies, fears, ways of seeing, problems, solutions—new forms of policing, punitiveness, or conceptual legal innovations such as 'the law of the enemy', mediation, restitutive or therapeutic justice? We can also ask *where* it is being spread, e.g. from or to national, sub-national and supranational levels in Europe, or more widely? How is agreement achieved amongst signatories to conventions or those subject to regulatory networks? We also need to take quite a broad view of *who* is involved. The key actors include politicians, inter-governmental and non-governmental organizations or pressure groups, regulatory bodies, journalists, and even academics themselves and not only judges, lawyers, police, probation officers, or prison officers. They may also be representatives of businesses such as security providers or those who build and run private prisons. Attention needs to be given to the role of institutions, singly, collectively, or in competition. In Europe—but also beyond—European Union institutions, the Council of Europe, and the Human Rights Court system are important players. The same crime threat may call forth responses from a variety of inter-Governmental and non-Governmental organizations, such as the UN commissioner for rights etc., the international labour organization, or the international organization for migration, Human Rights Watch, Amnesty etc. (Nelken 2011).

The questions of 'success' and its implications for diversity are complex ones. When assessing the effects of globalizing, authors sometimes confuse explaining whether a certain model has spread successfully and whether this is a good thing. On the one hand, we may be told that 'zero tolerance' ideas have not changed practices on the ground and are merely 'symbolic' (Jones and Newburn 2006). On the other, if human rights ideas do begin to change the local discourse, as in the case of conventions dealing with violence against women, this may be counted as success even if they do not change (other) practice on the ground (Merry 2006). Globalization itself also blurs the line between the normative and the descriptive. As pressures for global conformity rise there is often confusion between what is 'normal' in the sense of not falling below a standard and the somewhat different meaning of what is normal or average.

Comparative criminal justice involves not only comparing objects of inquiry but also differences in the ways of constructing such objects. Hence the discourses of national and globalizing criminologies must also be brought within the frame of comparison (Nelken 2010a). 'Second order comparison' (comparing how others compare) is called for as increasing interaction at the transnational level affects the ideas that people have about criminal justice elsewhere and the desire to be similar to or be different from them. Prison rates (or decisions about keeping the death penalty) for example, need to be understood not only as measures describing the operations of local criminal justice systems but as results of choices to come into line with what others are doing (Von Hofer 2003). They not (only) reflect policy differences in the way states choose to deal with marginal citizens but differential ways of responding to a similar transnational trend, or even the results of the marketing and imitation of an American model of penalty (Waquant 2009). This does not mean of course that those doing the comparison have got it 'right'. Typically, places or groups construct other societies in terms that reflect their own concerns and assumptions—even when they are seeking to collaborate with them. Ross, for example has shown the considerable difficulties faced by those working in the US criminal justice system when seeking to bring their own working practices into alignment with those belonging to other systems of criminal justice (see, e.g., Ross 2004).

Although there is nothing new about the borrowing and imposition of law from elsewhere (Nelken and Feest 2001) in the many ways it blurs the differences between 'units', globalization is changing the meaning of place and the location and significance of boundaries. And students of comparative criminal justice are still uncertain about how best to integrate its effects into their traditional classificatory and descriptive schemes. Material that fits awkwardly into the normal comparative paradigm is relegated to a separate book (Reichel 2007), to an early chapter (Reichel 2008), or a closing one (Dammer, Fairchild, and Albanese 2005). Sheptycki and Wardak in their edited collection distinguish 'area studies', 'transnational crime issues', and 'transnational control responses' (Sheptycki and Wardak 2005). But they admit that more needs to be said about when an account of a country's criminal justice system should focus more on internal factors or on external influences. Larsen and Smandych argue that 'the effects of rapid globalisation have changed social, political, and legal realities in such a way that comparative and international approaches to crime and justice are inadequate to capture the full complexity of these issues on a global scale' (Larsen and Smandych 2008: xi). Aas insists that 'one can no longer study, for example, Italy by simply looking at what happens inside its territory, but rather need to acknowledge the effects that distant conflicts and developments have on national crime and security concerns and vice versa' (Aas 2007: 286). And Pakes too worries that 'diffuse interrelations and complications brought about by globalisation are ignored or understated' (Pakes 2010b: 17). He suggests that the comparative approach could be seen as just a matter of methodology whereas globalization is an 'object of study' (Pakes 2010b: 18–19). But he also recognizes the need to move away from 'methodological nationalism'.

## APPROACHES TO COMPARISON

Within the social sciences, some argue that *all* sociological research is inherently comparative: the aim is always the same: the explanation of 'variation' (Feeley 1997). But explicitly comparative work does have to face special difficulties. These range from the technical, conceptual, and linguistic problems posed by the unreliability of statistics, lack of appropriate data, meaning of foreign terms, etc., to the complications of understanding the differences in other languages, practices, and world views which make it difficult to know whether we are comparing like with like. Indeed often it is that which becomes the research task. Others claim that for these and other reasons comparative work is near impossible. Legrand, for example, argues that what he calls 'legal epistemes' are incommensurable and certainly never the same matter for those who have been socialized in the culture being studied and those who are merely researching into it (Legrand 2001; but see Nelken 2002a). Cain, who prefers a form of active collaboration with the subjects of her research, insists that comparison faces the allegedly unavoidable dangers of 'Occidentalism'—thinking that other societies are necessarily like ours—or 'Orientalism'—assuming that they are inherently different from us. Her advice is to 'avoid comparison, for it implies a lurking occidentalist standard and user, and focuses on static and dyadic rather than dynamic and complex relations' (Cain 2000: 258).

These reservations about comparison are given added point by the current processes of globalization. In a globalized world there is no Archimedean point of comparison from which to understand distinct nations or traditions. Within anthropology the process of producing accounts of other cultures has become increasingly contested (Clifford and Marcus 1986). The very idea of 'culture' becomes highly problematic, no more than a label to be manipulated by elements within the culture concerned or by outside observers (Kuper 1999). Cultures are influenced by global flows and trends; the purported uniformity, coherence, or stability of given national cultures will often be no more than ideological projection or rhetorical device. The links between societies and individuals have been so extended and transformed that it makes little sense to look for independent legal cultures. Hence 'all totalising accounts of society, tradition and culture are exclusionary and enact a social violence by suppressing contingent and continually emergent differences' (Coombe 2000). For all this, however, at any given time there continue to be important and systematic differences in criminal justice, whether this be regarding the relationship between law and politics, the role of legal and lay actors, levels of leniency, degrees of delay, and so on (Nelken 2002a).

In exploring such differences some studies set out:

1. to test and validate explanatory theories of crime or social control (which we may, at some risk of oversimplification, call the approach of 'behavioural science' or 'positivist sociology');

2. to show how the meaning of crime and criminal justice is embedded within changing, local and international, historical and cultural contexts (an approach which we will call 'interpretivist');

3. to classify and learn from the rules, ideals, and practice of criminal justice in other jurisdictions (which we can call the approach followed by 'legal comparativists' and 'policy researchers').

The behavioural science approach itself includes a wide range of different points of view about the role of comparative work. For some writers, taking the model of science seriously means that comparative work must show that cultural variability is as *irrelevant* to social laws as it is to physical laws. Gottfredson and Hirschi argue that failure to recognize this has meant that up until now 'cross national research has literally not known what it was looking for and its contributions have rightfully been more or less ignored' (Gottfredson and Hirschi 1990: 179). Some of the most influential American explanations of crime, such as Merton's anomie theory and Cohen's subcultural theory of delinquency, on the other hand, seem almost deliberately ethnocentric in the sense that the explanation is designed to fit variables found in American society. Yet anomie theory was first developed in France, and only afterwards was it reworked in the United States with particular reference to the American dream of egalitarianism and the cultural emphasis on success as measured in money. It has since been applied with advantage in very different cultural contexts; for example, in Italy to explain the growth of political corruption in the 1980s (Magatti 1996), and in Japan to account for the relative lack of crime there (Miyazawa 1997). Is the same theory being employed? How and why does this matter?

Gottfredson and Hirschi argue that Cohen's account of the frustrations of American lower-class children is hardly likely to be applicable to the genesis of delinquency in an African or Indian slum, and this spells its doom. Rather than assume that every culture will have its own crime with its own unique causes, which need to be sought in all their specificity, the object of criminological theorizing must be to transcend cultural diversity in order to arrive at genuine scientific statements (Gottfredson and Hirschi 1990: 172–3). In this search for a universal criminology Gottfredson and Hirschi define crimes as 'acts of force or fraud undertaken in pursuit of self interest'. For them, different cultural settings cannot influence the causes of crime except by affecting the opportunities and the ease with which crimes can occur. They are therefore comforted by apparent cross-cultural consistency in correlations between crime involvement and age and sex differences, urban–rural differences, and indices of family stability. A similar approach is—or could be—followed by those scholars who seek to establish general laws about judicial institutions. Shapiro's classic study of appeal courts sets out to demonstrate that higher courts always function primarily as agents of social control, whatever other political and legal differences may characterize the systems in which they are found, and whatever other legitimating ideologies they may themselves employ (Shapiro 1981). Gottfredson and Hirschi, however, just *assume* that the agencies that apply the criminal law have the universal task of reminding people both of their own long-term interests and of those of other people.

Most behavioural scientists are less concerned than Gottfredson and Hirschi with finding cultural universals. What matters is the *implicit* generalizability of the variables, not whether they actually do apply universally. For theories which link crime and industrialization, for example, it is strategically important to investigate apparent counter-instances such as Switzerland (Clinard 1978) or Japan (Miyazawa 1997), both so as to test existing hypotheses and so as to uncover new ones. Similarly, we can ask about variations in the patterns of policing, courts, or prisons in terms of the patterns found in different cultures or historical periods. If the Dutch prison rate could, at least until recently, be kept so much lower than that of other countries in Europe, this is important not only because it shows that there is no inevitable connection between crime rates and prison rates but also because it challenges us to look for the particular variables that explain the Dutch case (Downes 1988).

On the other hand, many scholars of comparative criminal justice are more fascinated by difference than by similarity. Yet the point of compiling differences, apart from its value as description or in correcting ethnocentrism, is not always made as clear as it might be. Certainly, the assumption that all economically advanced countries would be expected to have exactly similar ideas and practices for dealing with crime seems far-fetched. Why study difference? The interpretivist approach seeks to uncover the inner meaning of the facts that positivist social scientists take as the starting or finishing points of their comparisons. Even the technical definition of crime varies between legal systems, so that in Japan, for example, assaults that result in death are classified as assault, not murder; and in Greece the definition of 'rape' includes lewdness, sodomy, seduction of a child, incest, prostitution, and procuring (Kalish 1988). Less obviously, there is considerable variation in the importance that legislatures, justice agencies, or the media put on responding to different sorts of behaviour as crime. Until very recently, in Germany or Italy the police and the mass media kept a remarkably low profile regarding most street crime or burglary, at least by British or American standards (Zedner 1995; Nelken 2000b).

The prosecution or prison statistics that constitute the data of behavioural science explanations are here treated as cultural products. But it would be wrong to take too extreme a stand on the idea of crime as a cultural construction. This could lead to a relativism by which comparative criminology would become implausible (Beirne 1983), and this could be simply countered by the argument that if understanding 'the other' was really so difficult then even social science research into different social worlds at home would be impossible (Leavitt 1990). As noted, criminal justice cultures are in any case less and less sealed off from each other for them not to have some common language in which to express their concerns. Far from being either cognitively or morally relativist, the interpretivist approach in fact actually presupposes the possibility of producing and learning from cross-cultural comparisons, even if it does seek to display difference more than demonstrate similarity. It may be used, for example, to compare different societies in terms of their levels of 'punitiveness' (Nelken 2005) or 'tolerance' (Nelken 2006a), taking care to distinguish the external observers' judgement from the way such practices are experienced by members of the societies concerned. It is unfortunate that some scholars continue to insist that the interpretivist approach is necessarily relativist and non-evaluative (Pakes 2004: 13 ff.; cf Nelken 1994b).

The search for difference only really becomes interesting when the attempt is made to show how differences in the punitiveness or any other aspect of criminal justice are linked to other differences (e.g. in types of political culture). If the positivist approach operationalizes 'culture' (or deliberately simplified aspects of it) to explain variation in levels and types of crime and social control, this second approach tends more to use crime and criminal justice as themselves an 'index' of culture. Grasping the 'other' requires the willingness to put our assumptions in question: the more so the greater the cultural distance. Some of the most exciting work in comparative criminal justice sets out to interpret what is distinctive in the practice and discourse of a given system of criminal justice by drawing an explicit or implicit contrast with another system, usually that of the scholar's culture of origin (Zedner 1995). In an important study,

Whitman seeks to explain the relative harshness of the treatment of criminals in the USA in comparison to that reserved for them in the countries of Continental Europe. His argument is that whereas France and Germany 'levelled up' their treatment of criminals, on the basis of long-standing more respectful treatment for higher-status prisoners, in America criminals suffered from a general levelling-down process that presupposed status equality (Whitman 2003; Nelken 2006b).

This said, interpretative approaches do face their own problems (Nelken 1995). One difficulty is that of knowing who or what can speak for the culture (especially when matters are controversial). Very different results will be obtained by analysing texts and documents, testing public attitudes, or relying on selected informants such as criminologists or public officials: the drawbacks of exclusive reliance on these last sources have already been discussed. Because the interpretative approach is so labour intensive it does not allow for large-scale, cross-cultural comparison. Much therefore depends on which other system is taken as the yardstick of comparison—and how this is to be justified. Taking criminal justice discourse in England as our starting point may reveal that France works with one model of 'mediation' whereas we have several (Crawford 2000). If we compare England with Germany, on the other hand, we may find that Germany seems to have several ideas of 'community' where we have just one (Lacey and Zedner 1995, 1998). But what exactly is the significance of such findings?

Care also needs to be taken in assuming that a given feature of the practice or discourse of criminal justice necessarily indexes, or 'resonates' with, the rest of a culture. Specific ideals and values of criminal justice may not always be widely diffused in the culture. In many societies there is a wide gulf between legal and general culture, as where the criminal law purports to maintain principles of impersonal equality before the law in polities where clientilistic and other particularistic practices are widespread. It is also not easy to get the balance right between identifying relatively enduring features as compared to contingent aspects of other cultures. Relying on ideas of national character would make it difficult to reconcile the defiance of law in Weimar Germany as compared to the over-deference to law of the Fascist period. What are taken to be entrenched cultural practices in the sphere of criminal justice can be overturned with remarkable rapidity. The Dutch penal system was rightly celebrated for its 'tolerance', from the 1960s on, keeping its proportionate prison population well below that of its European neighbours (Downes 1988). But shortly after gaining such praise, the criminal justice elite who pioneered the 'Utrecht' approach was sidelined by the pressures of gaining popular political consensus in the face of Holland's growing drug problem (Downes 1996). Holland engaged in a massive programme of prison-building that took it back towards the levels of the 1950s, a period when its relative level of incarceration was comparable to the rest of Europe.

The third approach, followed by students of procedure and comparative lawyers, highlights the role of criminal procedure. This is important in order to see how criminal justice outcomes reflected in indicators of prison or other rates is actually produced. Understanding how and why different systems try to achieve 'autonomy' from pressures from government and the public provides a crucial key to understanding differences in punitiveness (Nelken 2009: Montana and Nelken 2011). Another advantage of this focus lies in the way its language and concerns connect directly to those used by many of the legal actors themselves whose behaviour is being interpreted. It must be relevant to pay attention to rules and ideals to which actors are obliged at least to pay lip-service but which they may well take as guides for much of the time. The evolution of the discourse used by criminal justice actors may also be better understood, even for sociological purposes, when related to its own forms rather than simply translated into sociological language.

Research carried out by comparative lawyers is sufficiently different from comparative social science for both to have something to gain from the other's approach. Although comparative lawyers rely mainly on historical, philosophical, and juridical analyses they are well aware that legal and other rules are not always applied in practice, and that legal outcomes do not necessarily turn out as planned. But the sociological significance of such evidence is usually ignored in favour of processing it normatively, as an example of deviance or 'failure', to which the solution is typically a (further) change in the law. The weaknesses of this approach, which are the converse of its strengths, thus come from its tendency to share rather than understand or criticize the self-understanding of the legal perspective. Because the terms it uses are legal and normative it will not capture many of the organizational or personal sources of action which shape what actors are trying to do, still less the influences of which actors are not aware.

Social scientists, on the other hand, are more interested in what does happen than in what should happen, looking beyond written rules and documents to the structures which shape the repeated patterns of everyday action. Their approach has the opposite drawbacks. The determination to take practice more seriously than protestations of ideals can sometimes lead to an underestimation of the role law plays in many cultures as a representation of values, including 'counterfactual' values (Van Swaaningen 1998, 1999), which are all the more important for not being tied to existing practice. And the importance given to the present, rather than to the past or future of law, can block an appreciation of law's character as a bearer of tradition that makes 'the past live in the present'.

Each of these three approaches to comparison tends to be associated, in its pure form, with a distinctive epistemology, respectively (predictive) explanation, 'understanding by translation', and categorization-evaluation. The standard way of deciding which approach to choose is to ask: are we trying to contribute to the development of explanatory social science, or to improve existing penal practice? Combining such different enterprises, it is said, will only produce confusion (Feeley 1997). But, on the other hand, social scientists cannot afford to lose touch with those nuances of legal culture that bring the comparative exercise to life. Effective comparison is as much a matter of good translation as of successful explanation. We may need, for example, to understand how and why 'diversion' from criminal justice is treated as intrinsic to the criminal process in Holland, but as somehow extrinsic to it in the UK (Brants and Field 2000). And this will require considerable historical, juridical, and linguistic analysis.

In practice these three approaches are rarely found in their pure form. Sociologists—especially those interested in legal culture and ideology—need to know about law and legal procedures (and sometimes get it wrong); comparative lawyers often make sociologically questionable assumptions about what a system is trying to do and how it actually operates. Debates within, as well as between, comparative law and sociological criminology turn on mixed questions of explanation and evaluation, so that it is not the choice of one or other of these aims which guarantees either insight or confusion. Within the field of comparative law, Goldstein and Marcus, who reported that there was little America could learn from Europe in order to reform its pre-trial procedures, used sociological-type arguments based on the attempt to see how the rules actually worked in practice (Goldstein and Marcus 1977). But those who claimed that this understanding of Continental procedure was superficial were able to show how the very desire for generalizable explanation reinforced American ethnocentrism (Langbein and Weinreb 1978). On the other hand, Downes's sociological study of the role of prosecutors in keeping down prison rates in Holland clearly had a practical purpose aimed at changing the situation in Britain, but it was not (or at least not for that reason) unsuccessful in illuminating the Dutch situation.

Key conceptual building blocks for comparing criminal justice, such as the term 'legal culture' (Nelken 1997a), figure in each of the three approaches even if they are often employed with competing meanings. Another heuristic idea, used both by social scientists and by comparative lawyers, is that of 'functional equivalence'. One comparative law textbook tells us to assume that other societies will often meet a given legal 'problem' by using unfamiliar types of law and legal techniques (Zweigert and Kotz 1987). Likewise, Feest and Murayama, in their study of criminal justice in Spain, Germany, and Japan, demonstrate that each jurisdiction has some (but not necessarily the same) crucial pre-trial and post-trial filters to distinguish the innocent from the guilty, while others are more formalistic and typically presuppose that the required critical attention has or will be given at another stage. They come close to suggesting that there are 'functional equivalents' in each system for legitimizing even unsound cases of police arrests, and that systems 'self-correct' to reach rather similar outcomes (Feest and Murayama 2000).

But assumptions of functional equivalence can also be misleading. At a minimum we shall also need to extend our analysis to the role of non-legal institutions, alternatives to law, and competing professional expertises as well as to other groupings within civil society such as the family or patron-client networks. Moreover, in some cultures, some problems may simply find no 'solution'—especially, but not only, if the 'problem' is not perceived as such. Cultures have the power to produce relatively circular definitions of what is worth fighting for and against, and their institutions and practices can express genuinely different histories and distinct priorities (Nelken 1996). Often matters are 'problematized' only when a society is exposed to the definition used elsewhere. In the 1980s, for example, the appearance of league tables of relative levels of incarceration induced Finland to move towards the norm by reducing its prison population—and were used in Holland to justify doing the opposite!

## METHODS OF COMPARATIVE RESEARCH

With some exceptions, most texts about comparative criminal justice contain little about the actual process of doing cross-cultural research in criminal justice. At best this question is addressed by the editors rather than by the contributors themselves (e.g. Cole *et al.* 1987; Fields and Moore 1996; Heiland, Shelley, and Katoh 1992). Admittedly, there is never only one ideal research method, and choice of method is inseparably linked to the objectives being pursued. But the questions posed in comparative work are often more ambitious than the methodologies which comparative lawyers usually adopt. For example, Fennell *et al.* ask, 'could there be a relationship between the mildness or severity of a penal climate and an inquisitorial or an accusatorial system of justice?' (Fennell *et al.* 1995: xvi). But they then add immediately afterwards, 'or is the question absurd?'. Methodological issues loom still larger when comparative enquiries seek to tackle fundamental problems such as, 'how do different societies conceive "disorder"?', how do 'differences in social, political, and legal culture inform perceptions of crime and the role of criminal agencies in responding to it?', or 'what factors underlie the salience of law and order as a political issue?' (Zedner 1996). Only long and intimate familiarity with a society could even begin to unravel such complex puzzles.

How, then, are we to acquire sufficient knowledge of another culture for such purposes? Either we can rely mainly on cooperation with foreign experts, or we can go abroad to interview legal officials and others, or we can draw on our direct experience of living and working in the country concerned. These three possible strategies I have elsewhere dubbed as 'virtually there', 'researching there', or 'living there' (see Nelken 2000a, 2010a; Heidensohn 2006).

The first of these methods allows for a variety of focused forms of international collaboration in comparative research. Feest and Murayama, for example, describe the result of a 'thought experiment' which starts from a careful description of the actual case of an American student arrested and tried in Spain on a false charge of participating in an illegal squatting demonstration. The authors then discuss what would have been the likely outcome given the same sequence of events in Germany and Japan, the countries whose criminal justice systems they know best (Feest and Murayama 2000). Other scholars set out to explain past and possible future trajectories in various aspects of the work of police, courts, or prisons. Thus Brants and Field ask how different jurisdictions have responded to the rise of covert and proactive policing—and why (Brants and Field 2000). These authors are constantly worried about the dangers of not comparing like with like, and they draw attention to the continuing difficulties of reaching shared meanings between experts in different legal cultures even after long experience of cooperation. Such collaboration, they say, requires a high degree of mutual trust and involves 'negotiating' mutually acceptable descriptions of legal practice in each of their home countries. The lesson they seek to drive home is that correct interpretation of even the smallest detail of criminal justice organization requires sensitivity to 'broader institutional and ideological contexts'.

Given these difficulties it is not surprising to find that many scholars advocate going to the research site in person. Immersion in another social context gives the researcher invaluable opportunities to become more directly involved in the experience of cultural translation. On the basis of his regular visits to France, Crawford, for example, offers a sophisticated reading of the contrasting meanings of mediation in two different settings (Crawford 2000). In France the move to introduce mediation can be seen as part of a project of 'bringing law to the people' both by making the criminal justice response more immediate in time and also by subtly transforming its referent. But it is not about involving the 'community' in the actual delivery of criminal justice. For this conception of the 'community' has a meaning and appeal which is strongly tied to the Anglo-American type of political and social order. In France it has historically been the role of the state to represent the larger community, and its social institutions have it as their fundamental task to lead those who are not yet part of the *polis* into becoming bona fide French citizens. 'Researching there' also provides the chance for 'open-ended' enquiry that can lead to the discovery of new questions and new findings about the 'law in action'. Some things are never written down because they belong to 'craft rules of thumb'. Other matters are considered secrets that should not be written down, for example, because theory and practice do not coincide, and so on (Hodgson 2000).

Short research visits, however, usually involve considerable reliance on local experts and practitioners. Indeed obtaining their views is very often the whole point of the exercise. But care must be taken in drawing on such insiders as the direct or indirect source of claims about other cultures. Who count as experts, and how do *they* know? What are the similarities and differences between academics and practitioners? If experts and practitioners are in agreement, could this be because experts themselves get their information from practitioners? In all cultures descriptions of social and legal ideas carry political implications, in some cases even issuing directly from particular political or social philosophies. When we think of experts in our own culture we will normally, without much difficulty, be able to associate them with 'standing' for given political or policy positions. But what about this factor when we rely on experts from abroad? In much of the comparative criminal justice literature there seems to be little recognition, and less discussion, of the extent to which those describing the aims or results of local legal practices or reforms are themselves *part* of the context they are describing, in the sense of being partial to one position rather than another. In France some commentators are strongly against importing ideas from the common law world, others are less antagonistic; in Italy, some academics are notoriously pro-judges, others are anti-judges. It can be misleading to rely on the opinions or work of members of different camps without making allowance for this fact.

Moreover, cultural variability means that the problem faced here is not always the same. There are some cultures (Italy and Latin America, for example) where many consider it quite appropriate for academics—and even for judges and prosecutors—to identify and to be identified as members of a faction. In playing the role of what Gramsci called an 'organic intellectual', your prime duty is understood, both by your allies and by your opponents, to be the furtherance of a specific group ideal. In consequence, in such societies the question of social and political affiliation is one of the first questions raised (even if not always openly) in considering the point and validity of academic criticisms of current practices and of corresponding proposals for reform. In other cultures, however, the approved practice is to do one's best to avoid such identification. In some cases this just makes the process of establishing affiliation more elusive. Alternatively, the extent of political consensus, or of admiration for allegedly neutral criteria based on 'results' or 'efficiency', may be such that academics are indeed less pressed to take sides. Or intellectuals may simply count for less politically! The point again is that without knowledge about their affiliations, and an understanding of the responsibilities attached to different roles in the culture under investigation, it can be hard to know what credit to give to the arguments of any expert about criminal justice.

Even if we assume that our sources are not 'partial' (or, better still, if we try to make proper allowance for this) there still remains the problem that experts and practitioners are undoubtedly part of their own culture. This is after all why we consult them. But this also means that they do not necessarily ask or answer questions based on where the researcher is 'coming from' (and may not even have the basis for understanding such questions). In a multitude of ways both their descriptions and their criticisms will also belong to their culture. In Italy, local commentators regularly attack a principled but inefficient system on grounds of principle; in England and Wales, a system highly influenced by managerial considerations, sometimes at the expense of principle, will tend to be criticized for its remaining inefficiencies.

Longer-term involvement in another culture offers, amongst other advantages, a better route to grasping the intellectual and political affiliations of insiders. Through everyday experience of another culture, 'observant participation' (Nelken 2000a), rather than merely 'participation observation' in a given research site, the researcher can begin to fill in the 'taken-for-granted' background to natives' views and actions. Direct experience and involvement with what is being studied can also help give the researcher's accounts the credibility that comes from 'being there' (Nelken 2004). But actually moving to a research site—for shorter or longer periods—does not mean that the researcher necessarily comes to see things as a native. Our 'starting points' (Nelken 2000b) play a vital role in what we set out to discover. Our own cultural assumptions continue to shape the questions we ask or the answers we find convincing. Much of the voluminous American research on the specificity of Japanese criminal justice, for example, can be criticized for seeking to explain what is distinctive about Japanese legal culture in contrast to familiar American models without recognizing how much it derived from the civil law systems of Continental Europe from which Japan borrowed.

Similarities and differences come to life for an observer when they are exemplified by 'significant absences' in relation to past experience. A good example is provided by Lacey and Zedner's discussion of the lack of any reference to 'community' in discourse about crime prevention in Germany (Lacey and Zedner 1995, 1998). But the vital question of starting points is often left begging, especially in research based on short visits, because of the implicit collusion between the writer and his or her audience which *privileges what the audience wants to know as if it is what it should want to know.* The long-stay researcher, by contrast, is engaged in a process of being slowly resocialized. He or she will increasingly want to reformulate the questions others back home wish to address to the foreign setting. As important, he or she may even begin to doubt whether they ever really understood their own culture of origin. Sometimes the researcher will try to see things like a native insider, at other times he or she will try to do 'better' than the natives. The ability to look at a culture with new eyes is, after all, the great strength of any outsider.

This said, the heavy investment required by 'observant participation', or by sustained ethnography, may not always be necessary or feasible. The choice to follow any particular approach to data gathering is linked to the many considerations which influence the feasibility of a given research project; not least the time available, whether one is able to visit the country concerned, and with what sort of commitment. Depending on its purposes, collaboration with experts or a limited period of interviewing abroad may even have some advantages as compared with living and working in a country. There are the usual trade-offs amongst methodologies. It is possible to cover a large number of cases with questionnaires or interviews only by dispensing with in-depth observation. And the short-termer can also pretend to a useful naivety that the long-term researcher must abandon, since that is part of what it means to become an insider/outsider. In practice, even the insider/outsider or 'observant participant' cannot possibly experience everything at first hand. So all three approaches have to face, to some extent, similar problems in knowing who to trust, and then conveying credibility. However findings are (re)presented, they are always in large part the result of interviews and consultation of experts and practitioners, and the resident scholar may often obtain these in ways which are less systematic than those followed by the other approaches. The main advantage of 'full immersion' in another society for this purpose is that enquiry becomes more fruitful when you have enough cultural background to identify the right questions to ask. Beyond this, method is also more than a means to an end insofar as it poses the problem of how to engage with 'the other', and when and why it is justifiable to speak 'for them' rather than let them speak for themselves.

## ■ SELECTED FURTHER READING

For examples of recent textbooks, collections and readers see Crawford (ed.) (2011); Dammer, Fairchild, and Albanese (2006); Drake, Muncie, and Westmarland (eds) (2009); Larsen and Smandych (2008); Muncie, Talbot, and Walters (eds) (2009); Nelken (2010a); Pakes (2010a); Reichel (2008); Shoptycki and Wardak (eds) (2005); Tonry (ed.) (2007); Winterdyk, and Cao (eds.) (2004); and Winterdyk, Reichel, and Dammer (2009). For a recent bibliography see Winterdyk, Reichel, and Dammer (2009).

Illustrations of cross- national perspectives on crime and criminal justice may be found in Newman (ed.) (1999), Tonry (ed.) (2007), Van Dijk (2007), and Van Dijk, Van Kesteren, and Smit (2007). For discussions of blueprints, convergence, and cross-national borrowing see Melossi, Sozzo, and Sparks (eds) (2011); Newburn, and Sparks (2004); Jones and Newburn (2006); and Nolan (2009).

For good studies of specific societies see, for example, Downes (1988) or Johnson (2001). Works inspired by the comparative law or interpretative approaches to comparative criminal justice still do not usually communicate much with debates in the criminological mainstream (e.g. Vogler 2005, but see Whitman 2003). Depending on the topic in hand the student of comparative criminal will need to sample literatures that touch on a variety of disciplines. For example, a lot of the running in anything to do with judges is made by political scientists. On the other hand, information on governmental and official websites on criminal justice systems in specific countries should be treated more as presentational data in need of explanation rather than as a solid basis for cross-cultural comparison. Similar caution should be exercised when using the sites of inter-governmental and non-governmental organizations.

# ■ REFERENCES

AASK, F. (2007), *Globalization and Crime*, London: Sage.

BALVIG, F. (1988), *The Snow White Image: The Hidden Reality of Crime in Switzerland*, Scandinavian Studies in Criminology, 17, Oslo: Norwegian University Press, Scandinavian Research Council for Criminology.

BEIRNE, P. (1983), 'Cultural Relativism and Comparative Criminology', *Contemporary Crises*, 7: 371–91.

BLACK, D. (1997), *The Social Structure of Right and Wrong*, New York: Academic Press.

BRANTS, C. and FIELD, S. (2000), 'Legal Culture, Political Cultures and Procedural Traditions: Towards a Comparative Interpretation of Covert and Proactive Policing in England and Wales and the Netherlands', in D. Nelken (ed.), *Contrasting Criminal Justice*, 77–116, Aldershot: Dartmouth.

CAIN, M. (2000), 'Orientalism, Occidentalism and the Sociology of Crime', *British Journal of Criminology*, 40: 239–60.

CAVADINO, M. and DIGNAN, J. (2006), *Penal Systems: A Comparative Approach*, London: Sage.

CLIFFORD, J. and MARCUS, G. (1986), *Writing Culture: The Poetics and Politics of Ethnography*, Berkeley, Cal.: University of California Press.

CLINARD, M. B. (1978), *Cities with Little Crime*, Cambridge: Cambridge University Press.

COLE, G. F., FRANKOWSKI, S. J., and GERTZ, M. G. (eds) (1987), *Major Criminal Justice Systems: A Comparative Survey*, 2nd edn, Beverly Hills, Cal.: Sage.

COOMBE, R. J. (2000), 'Contingent Articulations: Critical Studies of Law', in A. Sarat and T. Kearns (eds), *Law in the Domains of Culture*, Ann Arbor: University of Michigan Press.

CRAWFORD, A. (2000), 'Contrasts in Victim/Offender Mediation and Appeals to Community in Comparative Cultural Contexts: France and England and Wales', in D. Nelken (ed.), *Contrasting Criminal Justice*, Aldershot: Dartmouth.

—— (ed.) (2011), *International and Comparative Criminal Justice and Urban Governance*. Cambridge: Cambridge University Press.

DAMMER, H., FAIRCHILD, E., and ALBANESE, J. (2005), *Comparative Criminal Justice*, Belmont, CA: Thomson.

DOWNES, D. (1988), *Contrasts in Tolerance*, Oxford: Clarendon Press.

—— (1990), 'Response to H. Franke', *British Journal of Criminology*, 30(1): 94–6.

—— (1996), 'The Buckling of the Shields: Dutch Penal Policy 1985–1995', unpublished paper presented at the Onati Workshop on Comparing Legal Cultures, April.

DRAKE, D., MUNCIE, J., and WESTMARLAND, L. (eds) (2009), *Criminal Justice, Local and Global*, Collumpton: Willan.

EDWARDS, A. and HUGHES, G. (2005), 'Comparing the governance of safety in Europe', *Theoretical Criminology*, 9(3): 345–63.

FAVELL, A. (1998), *Philosophies of Integration, Immigration and the Idea of Citizenship in France and England*, Basingstoke: Macmillan.

FEELEY, M. (1997), 'Comparative Law for Criminologists: Comparing for what?', in D. Nelken (ed.), *Comparing Legal Cultures*, Aldershot: Dartmouth.

FEEST, J. and MURAYAMA, M. (2000), 'Protecting the Innocent through Criminal Justice: A Case Study from Spain, Virtually compared to Germany and Japan', in D. Nelken (ed.), *Contrasting Criminal Justice*, Aldershot: Dartmouth.

FENNELL, P., SWART, B., JORG, N., and HARDING, A. (1995), 'Introduction', in C. Harding, P. Fennell, N. Jorg, and B. Swart (eds), *Criminal Justice in Europe: A Comparative Study*, xv–xix, Oxford: Clarendon Press.

FIELDS, C. B. and MOORE, R. H. (eds) (1996), *Comparative Criminal Justice*, Prospect Heights, Ill.: Waveland Press.

FRANKE, H. (1990), 'Dutch Tolerance: Facts and Fallacies', *British Journal of Criminology*, 30(1): 81–93.

FRASE, R. S. (1990), 'Comparative Criminal Justice as a Guide to American Law Reform', *California Law Review*: 79: 539.

GARLAND, D. ( 2001), *The culture of Control*, Oxford: Oxford University Press.

—— (2010), *Peculiar Institution. America's Death Penalty in an age of Abolition*, Cambridge: Harvard University Press.

GOLDSTEIN, A. and MARCUS, M. (1977), 'The Myth of Judicial Supervision in Three Inquisitorial Systems: France, Italy and Germany', *Yale Law Journal*, 87: 240.

GOTTFREDSON, M. and HIRSCHI, T. (1990), *A General Theory of Crime*, Stanford, Cal.: Stanford University Press.

HEILAND, H. G., SHELLEY, L. I., and KATOH, H. (eds) (1992), *Crime and Control in Comparative Perspectives*, Berlin: de Gruyter.

HODGSON, J. (2000), 'Comparing Legal Cultures: The Comparativist as Participant Observer', in D. Nelken (ed.), *Contrasting Criminal Justice*, Aldershot: Dartmouth.

—— (2005), *French Criminal Justice*, Oxford: Hart.

JOHNSON, D. (2000), 'Prosecutor Culture in Japan and USA', in D. Nelken (ed.), *Contrasting Criminal Justice*, Aldershot: Dartmouth.

—— (2001), *The Japanese Way of Justice*, Oxford: Oxford University Press.

—— and ZIMRING, F. (2009), *The Next Frontier: National Development, Political Change, and the Death Penalty in Asia*, Oxford, Oxford University Press.

JONES, T. and NEWBURN, T. (2006), *Policy Transfer and Criminal Justice*, Milton Keynes, Open University Press.

KALISH, C. (1988), *International Crime Rates*, Washington DC: Bureau of Justice Statistics, US Department of Justice.

KILLIAS, M. (1989), book review (of Balvig), *British Journal of Criminology*, 29: 300–5.

KUPER, A. (1999), *Culture: The Anthropologist's Account*, Cambridge, Mass.: Harvard University Press.

LACEY, N. (2008), *The Prisoners'Dilemma: Political Economy and Punishment in Contemporary Democracies*, Cambridge: Cambridge University Press.

—— and ZEDNER, L. (1995), 'Discourses of Community in Criminal Justice', *Journal of Law and Society*, 22(1): 301–20.

—— and —— (1998), 'Community in German Criminal Justice: A Significant Absence?', *Social and Legal Studies*, 7: 7–25.

LANGBEIN, J. and WEINREB, L. (1978), 'Continental Criminal Procedure: Myth and Reality', *Yale Law Journal*, 87. 1549.

LARSEN, N. and SMANDYCH, R. (eds) (2008), *Global Criminology and Criminal Justice: Current Issues and Perspectives*, Buffalo NY, Broadview Press.

LEAVITT, G. (1990), 'Relativism and Cross-Cultural Criminology', *Journal of Crime and Delinquency*, 27(1): 5–29.

LEGRAND, P. (2001), 'What "Legal Transplants?"', in D. Nelken and J. Feest (eds), *Adapting Legal Cultures*, Oxford: Hart.

MAGATTI, M. (1996), *Corruzione Politica e Società Italiana*, Bologna: Il Mulino.

MELOSSI, D, SOZZO, M., and SPARKS, R. (eds) (2011), *Travels of the Criminal Question: Cultural Embeddedness and Diffusion*, Oxford: Hart

MIYAZAWA, S. (1997), 'The Enigma of Japan as a Testing Ground for Cross Cultural Criminological Studies', in D. Nelken (ed.), *Comparing Legal Cultures*, Aldershot: Dartmouth.

MONTANA, R. and NELKEN, D. (2011), 'The ambivalent role of Italian Prosecutors and their resistance to "moral panics" about crime', in C. Smith, S. Smith, Sholdon X. Zhang, and R. Barberet (eds), *Routledge Handbook of International Criminology*, London: Taylor and Francis.

MUNCIE, J. (2011), 'On Globalization and exceptionalism', in D. Nelken (ed.)*Comparative Criminal Justice and Globalization*, Aldershot: Ashgate.

——, Talbot, D., and Walters, R (eds) (2009),*Crime: Local and Global*, Cullompton: Willan Publishing.

NELKEN, D., (1994a), 'Reflexive criminology', in D. Nelken (ed.), *The Futures of Criminology*, London: Sage.

—— (1994b), 'Whom can you trust? The future of comparative criminology', in D. Nelken (ed.), *The Futures of Criminology*, London: Sage.

—— (1995), 'Disclosing/Invoking Legal Culture', in D. Nelken (ed.), *Legal Culture, Diversity and Globalization*, special issue of *Social and Legal Studies*, 4(4): 435–52.

—— (1996), 'Law without Order: A letter from Italy', in V. Gessner, A. Hoeland, and C. Varga (eds), *European Legal Cultures*, Aldershot: Dartmouth.

—— (ed.) (1997a), *Comparing Legal Cultures*, Aldershot: Dartmouth.

—— (1997b), 'The Globalisation of Crime and Criminal Justice: Prospects and Problems', in M. Freeman (ed.), *Law at the Turn of the Century*, Oxford: Oxford University Press.

—— (ed.) (2000a), *Contrasting Criminal Justice*, Aldershot: Dartmouth.

——(2000b), 'Telling Difference: Of Crime and Criminal Justice in Italy', in D. Nelken (ed.), *Contrasting Criminal Justice*, Aldershot: Dartmouth.

—— (2002a), 'Comparative Sociology of Law', in M. Travers and R. Benakar (eds), *Introduction to Law and Social Theory*, Oxford: Hart.

—— (2004), 'Being there', in L. Chao and J. Winterdyk (eds), *Lessons from International/Comparative Criminology*, Toronto: De Sitter publications.

—— (2005), 'When is a Society non-punitive? A case study of Italy', in J. Pratt, D. Brown, S. Hallsworth, M. Brown, and W. Morrison, (eds), *The New Punitiveness: Current Trends, Theories, Perspectives*, Cullompton, Devon: Willan.

—— (2006a), 'Italy: A lesson in tolerance?', in J. Muncie and B. Goldson (eds), *Comparative Youth Justice: Critical Issues*, London: Sage.

—— (2006b), 'Patterns of Punishment', *Modern Law Review*, 69: 262–77.

—— (2009) 'Comparative Criminal Justice: Beyond Ethnocentricism and Relativism', *European Journal of Criminology*, 6(4) 2009: 291–311.

—— (2010a), *Comparative Criminal Justice: Making Sense of Difference*, London: Sage.

—— (2011a), 'Human Trafficking and Legal Culture', 43, *Israel Law Review*.

—— (ed.) (2011b), *Comparative Criminal Justice and Globalization*, Aldershot: Ashgate.

—— and Feest, J. (eds) (2001c), *Adapting Legal Cultures*, Oxford: Hart.

NEWBURN, T. and SPARKS, R (eds) (2004), *Criminal Justice and Political Cultures: National and International Dimensions of Crime Control*, Cullompton, Devon: Willan.

NEWMAN, G. (ed.) (1999), *Global Report on Crime and Justice*, Oxford: Oxford University Press.

NOLAN, J. (2009), *Legal Accents, Legal Borrowing: The International Problem-Solving Court Movement*, Princeton: Princeton University Press.

PAKES, F. (2004), *Comparative Criminal Justice*, Cullompton, Devon. Willan.

—— (2010a), *Comparative Criminal Justice*, 2nd edn, Cullompton, Willan.

—— (2010b), 'The Comparative method in Globalised Criminology', *43 Australian and New Zealand Journal of Criminology*, 17–34.

REICHEL, P. (2007), *Handbook of Transnational Crime and Justice*, 4th edn, New York: Sage.

—— (2008), 5th edn, *Comparative Criminal Justice Systems*, Upper Saddle River, NJ: Prentice Hall.

SAVELSBERG, J. (2011), 'Globalization and States of Punishment', in D. Nelken (ed.), *Comparative Criminal Justice and Globalization*, Aldershot: Ashgate.

SHAPIRO, M. (1981), *Courts*, Chicago: Chicago University Press.

SHEPTYCKI, J. and WARDAK, A. (2005), *Transnational and Comparative Criminology*, London: Glasshouse Press.

TONRY, M. (ed.) (2007),*Crime and Justice vol 36: Crime, Punishment and Politics in Comparative Perspective*, Chicago: University of Chicago.

VAGG, J. (1994), *Prison Systems*, Oxford: Oxford University Press.

VANDIJK, J. (2000), 'Implications of the International Crime Victims survey for a victim perspective', in A. Crawford and J. Goodey (eds), *Integrating a Victim Perspective within Criminal Justice: International Debates*, Aldershot: Dartmouth.

—— (2007), *The World of Crime*, London: Sage.

——, VAN KESTEREN, J., SMIT, P. (2007),*Criminal Victimisation in International Perspective: Key Findings from the 2004–2005 ICVS and EU,* Vienna: UN office on Drugs and Crime.

VAN SWAANINGEN, R. (1998), *Critical Criminology in Europe*, London: Sage.

—— (1999), 'Reclaiming Critical Criminology: Social Justice and the European Tradition', *Theoretical Criminology*, 3(1): 5–29.

VOGLER, R. (2005), *A World View of Criminal Justice*, Aldershot: Ashgate.

VON HOFER, H. (2003), 'Prison populations as political Constructs: the Case of Finland, Holland and Sweden', *Journal of Scandinavian Studies in Criminology and Crime Prevention*, 4(1): 21–38.

WAQUANT, L. (2009), *Prisons of Poverty*, Minneappolis: University of Minnesota Press.

WHITMAN, J. (2003), *Harsh Justice*, Oxford: Oxford University Press.

WINTERDYK, J. and CAO, L. (2004), *Lessons from International/ Comparative Criminology/Criminal Justice*, Toronto: De Sitter.

——, REICHEL, P., and DAMMER, H. (2009), *A Guided Reader to Research In Comparative Criminology/ Criminal Justice*, Bochum: Brockmeyer Verlag.

ZENDER, L. (1995), 'In Pursuit of the Vernacular: Comparing Law and Order Discourse in Britain and Germany', in *Social and Legal Studies*, 4(4): 517–35.

—— (1996), 'German Criminal Justice Culture', unpublished paper presented at the Onati Workshop on Changing Legal Cultures, 13–14 July.

ZWEIGERT, K. and KOTZ, H. (1987), *An Introduction to Comparative Law*, Oxford: Oxford University Press.

# PART II

# SOCIAL CONSTRUCTIONS OF CRIME AND CRIME CONTROL

# 6

# LEGAL CONSTRUCTIONS OF CRIME

*Nicola Lacey and Lucia Zedner*[1]

The concept of crime is so familiar that it is taken for granted: by lawyers, by criminal justice practitioners and scholars, and by the general public. Yet when we try to subject it to analysis, it defies neat characterization. It might seem natural for the criminologist to turn to criminal law for help here. Criminal law, surely, plays a key role in defining the subject matter of criminology as a discipline, and hence promises to identify the scope and limits of criminal liability. The idea that the intellectual concerns of criminology are connected in this way with those of criminal law seems obvious. Yet both the professional autonomy of legal scholarship and the technical nature of contemporary legal argumentation have lent themselves to the construction of relatively rigid disciplinary boundaries. And although the status of criminology as a discrete discipline has always been contested and criminological research is inevitably informed by the methods and insights of the wider social sciences, criminological interest in and interaction with criminal law is much more limited. It is almost as rare to find a criminology text which concerns itself with the scope and nature of criminal law as it is to find a criminal law text which addresses criminological questions about crime (though see Lacey, Wells, and Quick 2010; Bronitt and McSherry 2010).

In this chapter, we examine the relationship between legal constructions of crime (criminal law) on the one hand and social constructions of crime and criminality (the subject matter of criminology and criminal justice studies) on the other. The chapter falls into five main sections. In the first section, we sketch a conceptual framework—that of criminalization—in the context of which the relationship between legal and social constructions of crime may be understood (Lacey 1995, 2010). Criminalization keeps the close relationship between criminal legal and criminal justice practices in view, while avoiding a synthesis which would lose sight of their specific contributions. In the second section, we use that framework to consider the way in which the boundaries between legal and social constructions of crime are contingent on the environment in which they are formed, illustrating this by analysis of their development in the English system over the last 300 years. The third section sketches the principal

[1] The authors are grateful to Carolyn Hoyle and to Mike Maguire, Rod Morgan, and Robert Reiner for comments on previous drafts of this chapter.

distinguishing features of the ways in which law formally constructs crime in England and Wales today, and teases out the normative vision of criminal law implicit in that formal structure. In the fourth section, we consider some of the most important substantive changes in the legal construction of crime in England and Wales over the last two decades. And in the final section, we consider what contribution criminology might make to our understanding of the proper scope of, and limits on, criminalization. On the basis of this analysis, we illuminate what criminologists need to know about criminal law and what they might learn from criminal law scholarship.

## CRIMINAL LAW, CRIMINOLOGY, AND CRIMINALIZATION

In the United Kingdom, the study of the various social practices associated with 'criminal justice' is currently divided into two main areas marked by a combination of disciplinary tools and institutional objects. Let us call these two areas the social and legal construction of crime (while accepting that legal constructions of crime are, evidently, themselves social phenomena). Study of the social construction of crime divides into two broad fields—criminology and criminal justice—brought together in this volume. Criminology concerns itself with social and individual antecedents of crime and with the nature of crime as a social phenomenon. Its disciplinary resources come mainly from sociology, social theory, psychology, history and, more rarely, economics and political science. Criminologists address a variety of questions about patterns of criminality and its social construction, along with their historical, economic, political, and social conditions of existence. Criminal justice studies, informed by history, sociology, and socio-legal scholarship, deal specifically with the institutional aspects of the social construction of crime: with criminal processes such as policing, prosecution, plea bargaining (McConville and Mirsky 2005), trial (Duff *et al.* 2004b, 2005, 2007), sentencing and punishment (Ashworth 2010), and with normative questions about the principles around which a criminal justice system worth the name ought to be organized (Ashworth and Redmayne 2010; Lacey 2006; Zedner 2004).

Criminal law, by contrast, concerns itself with the formally established norms according to which individuals or groups are adjudged guilty or innocent of criminal offences. Criminal law encompasses substantive rules of conduct addressed to citizens and also rules determining how liability should be attributed and how breaches of criminal norms should be graded—rules which are addressed primarily to officials rather than to potential offenders (Robinson 1997). Contemporary criminal lawyers tend to be concerned not so much with the development and scope of these norms—matters which would be of obvious interest to the criminologist—as with their conceptual structure, doctrinal content, and judicial interpretation in particular cases. And they are concerned with the framework of principles within which interpretive legal practice and legislative development purportedly proceed (Ashworth 2009; Williams 1953, 1983). The rules of evidence and procedure find only a small place in criminal law studies in Britain, and are often dealt with in specialist courses or relegated to interstitial treatment in criminal justice or legal methods courses. While the organization of research conforms less rigidly to this division, it nonetheless bears a close relationship to the different areas of expertise claimed by scholars within their respective fields. This partitioning of the intellectual terrain is both historically and culturally specific. Although a superficially similar division has characterized the English approach for much of the twentieth century, criminal law treatise writers of the nineteenth century saw offence definitions, procedure, and punishment as equally central to their terrain (Stephen 1893). And from the perspective of countries like France and Germany, where the very language of *droit penal* and *Strafrecht* make clear the close relationship between criminal law and punishment and where sentencing decisions are closely integrated with decisions about criminal liability, the Anglo-American separation of criminal law and criminal procedure, and of criminal law and sentencing, appears extraordinary (Fletcher 1978).

The contemporary division of labour between lawyers and criminologists is based on their respective expertise and the distinctive roles of legal and social factors in the construction of crime. Yet, this division may also obscure certain crucially important issues. The practices of legislation and of legal interpretation take place within a social context and in relation to criminal laws which are themselves the product of a political process relevant to their application and enforcement (Reiner 2006). Moreover the boundaries of criminalization as a discrete object of inquiry are porous: criminal justice practices exist alongside and relate intimately to other political, economic, moral, psychiatric, religious, educational, familial, normative, labelling, and sanctioning practices (Lacey, Wells, and Quick 2010: ch. 1). Nonetheless, in defining offences and constituting the key institutions (the police, criminal process, courts, and so on) through which criminalization takes place, legal rules set the formal boundaries of criminalizing power. Understanding how these boundaries are set, where they lie, and how they shape that power therefore seems important for the criminologist.

That said, statutes and law reports can be forbiddingly technical documents to non-lawyers. So it may be more useful for the criminologist to think in terms of a broad social process of criminalization, to which legislative and judicial decisions provide one interpretive key. Within this broad concept of criminalization, we need to make three distinctions.

First, we can draw a distinction between criminalization as an outcome or a pattern and criminalization as a practice. Criminalization as an outcome refers to the *results* of legislative, judicial, prosecutorial, or other processes; as in, 'the new terrorism legislation has expanded the scope of criminalization'. Criminalization as a practice, on the other hand, directs our attention to the creative, interpretive, or enforcement activities of specific actors such as legislators, judges, police officers, and members of the public. Official practices of criminalization are nested within particular institutions and shaped by the norms peculiar to particular roles and professions: they coalesce over time to constitute the outcomes to which criminalization in the first sense refers. Thinking about criminalization as outcome and as practice cuts across the distinction between legal and social constructions of crime: both outcomes and practices are shaped by law and broader social dynamics. But while the legal contribution to patterns of criminalization is made primarily by criminal law, practices of criminalization are structured primarily by rules of criminal procedure, constitutional law, and a range of constitutional and administrative law rules defining the responsibilities and powers of officials (police, judges, magistrates, and lawyers).

Second, we need to distinguish between formal and substantive criminalization. When terrorism legislation expands the boundaries of criminal law by creating a new offence proscribing acts preparatory to terrorist offences, this marks a shift in formal criminalization: but substantive criminalization remains unchanged until police, prosecutors, and courts act on that new law. This distinction between formal and substantive criminalization is much more than merely a matter of conceptual integrity. Heightened anxiety about terrorism might prompt an increase in terrorist prosecutions and convictions irrespective of changes in law (or levels of terrorist activity). Conversely, expanded formal criminalization of terrorism will not necessarily lead to greater substantive criminalization unless certain other conditions—notably an increase in the resources available to enforcement agencies, or a change in their incentives—are met. Formal criminalization sets, in principle if not always in practice, parameters within which substantive criminalization proceeds; but the development of substantive criminalization depends on many factors beyond law. This is where criminology comes in to explain why criminalization occurs as it does. Factors such as penal politics, media coverage, and the extensive discretion exercised by criminal justice officials have a powerful impact on the scope of what is in practice criminalized (Stuntz 2001).

The distinction between formal and substantive criminalization also applies to criminalization as a social practice. Constitutionally, the various practices which combine to produce patterns of criminalization—legislation, policing, prosecution, trial, and adjudication—are the responsibility of different actors. Legislators are not supposed to pre-empt prosecutorial, let alone judicial, decisions; police and prosecutors are supposed to exercise their distinctive enforcement roles within the contours of legal norms; and while the distinction between judicial interpretation and judicial creativity is notoriously contested, judges are certainly not entitled to create new criminal offences. But when we move from formal to substantive practices of criminalization, we find that the boundaries between law-creation, interpretation, and enforcement are notoriously fluid, with the reporting decisions of ordinary citizens influencing how official practices of criminalization are invoked. Practices like plea-bargaining accord prosecutors quasi-adjudicative and judges quasi-legislative power—an influence which makes itself felt in the ultimate patterns of criminalization. The ASBO, for example, permits the judge to determine the individualized conditions of the order, breach of which can result in a criminal sanction of up to five years' imprisonment. In so doing it effectively delegates legislative power to criminalize to the civil court (Ashworth and Zedner 2010: 84). Moreover criminal justice officials on occasion exceed or abuse their legal powers—for example by using undue pressure to elicit confessions. Where such abuses go undetected, substantive criminalization may stray far beyond its formal boundaries.

Note that, unlike the distinction between criminalization as outcome and as practice, the distinction between formal and substantive criminalization tracks that between legal and social constructions of crime. Criminal law, the law of evidence and procedure, constitutional law, public law, and human rights law combine to define the boundaries of formal patterns and practices of criminalization, while substantive patterns and practices can only be understood on the basis of a combined appreciation of legal and social processes. A focus on formal criminalization would not satisfy the criminologist curious about the legal construction of crime, however, because it says nothing about the relationship between legal and social constructions of crime. The changing contours of criminal law over time and space, and the changing balance between different kinds of legal regulation and between legal and informal social modes of governance are all essential to a full understanding of criminalization.

A further distinction pertains not to the meaning of criminalization itself, but to the different approaches to criminalization in criminological and legal scholarship. This is the distinction between descriptive, analytical, or explanatory approaches on the one hand and normative or prescriptive approaches on the other. Just as much legal scholarship—a standard criminal law textbook for example—is devoted to tracking the boundaries of formal criminalization, much criminological scholarship tracks the boundaries of substantive criminalization. Legal scholarship, similarly, describes the technical powers and responsibilities of the different actors whose decision-making constitutes the practice of criminalization, while much criminology and criminal justice scholarship seeks to explain how these powers are exercised and how these roles are understood and fulfilled in practice, and in a broader social and institutional context. A rather different project is that of delineating and advocating legitimate or even ideal patterns or practices of criminalization. The project of normative theorizing—of designing and seeking to justify an ideal conception of criminalization—is more often to be found in legal and philosophical than in criminological scholarship (Feinberg 1984–88, Duff et al. 2010; Husak 2007; Simester and von Hirsch 2011). Yet the more politicized traditions in criminological scholarship—abolitionism to name only the most obvious (Mathiesen 1974; Hillyard et al. 2004)—also engage in normative theorizing about criminalization, broadly understood, while criminal justice studies and penal theory have long featured prescriptive accounts (Packer 1968; Ashworth and Redmayne 2010; Hart 1968; Lacey 1988). However, there has been relatively little interaction between the normative theorizing undertaken by lawyers in respect of criminalization and that undertaken in critical criminology and criminal justice studies.

Although the distinction between normative/prescriptive and descriptive, analytical, or explanatory approaches to criminalization may be clear in principle, it is often blurred in practice. This is not simply a product of intellectual confusion. For the characterization or analysis of formal criminalization also entails detailing the values and aspirations which purportedly underlie formal norms and practices, render them a coherent whole, and distinguish criminalization from state violence (Ashworth 2009: ch. 3). If values are internal to systems of formal criminalization, even a descriptive characterization, explanation, or analysis of criminal law must engage with and incorporate normative arguments.

In what follows, we shall continue to draw distinctions between formal and substantive criminalization in the sense of patterns or practices, while considering the contribution of different scholarly approaches to our understanding of legal constructions of crime and their significance for criminology. How is formal criminalization organized? What is its content? How does it influence substantive criminalization? What values does it purport to embody or respect, and how far does it do so? Are those values coherent or otherwise appealing? Do the answers to these questions change over time, and if so, why?

# CRIMINALIZATION IN HISTORICAL PERSPECTIVE: DESCRIPTIVE, ANALYTICAL, AND EXPLANATORY APPROACHES

For answers to these questions, an obvious starting point for the criminologist would be to seek an overall conception of just what criminal law 'is': a conception not only of the formal features of criminal law, but of its distinctive aims and functions. She might expect that this conception would be nested within an account which explains why the legal order deals with certain kinds of conduct as a criminal rather than as a civil or private matter; as calling for state prosecution and punishment rather than privately initiated resolution. Why are some social harms dealt with by criminal law while others—equally costly or damaging—are not? (Hillyard *et al.* 2004). But when turning to a criminal law text, the criminologist will find that lawyers' definitions of crime are framed—unhelpfully—almost exclusively in procedural terms (Farmer 1996a): criminal laws are simply those which are tried in criminal courts; in which the prosecution bears a burden of proof beyond reasonable doubt; in which the principle of legality and presumption of innocence, now enshrined in English law by the Human Rights Act 1998, apply; and which are backed up by penal sanctions. For a substantive account of criminal law, she will probably find herself referred by the lawyer to the work of political theorists and philosophers (of whose arguments we shall hear more below).

Why do legal texts typically lack a substantive account of the rationale of criminal law (Katz 2002)? The answer is highly significant for the criminologist. In a system in which criminal law is regarded as a regulatory tool of government and in which (in England and Wales) there are very weak constitutional constraints on what kinds of conduct can be criminally proscribed—everything from homicide and serious fraud through dumping litter to licensing infractions and 'raves' can be criminalized—it seems impossible to distinguish criminal law by reference to its substance. This is, however, a contingent matter. If we look back to the legal commentaries of the mid-eighteenth century we find a rich, confident assertion of a substantive rationale for criminal law: of the interests and values which criminal law sets out to express and protect. In Blackstone's *Commentaries on the Laws of England* (Blackstone 1765–9), for example, the exposition of the law is framed by a vigorously asserted notion of crime as public wrong, organized in terms of groups of offences threatening distinctively public or shared interests: offences against God and religion; offences against the state; offences against the person; and offences against property. It is this nature of crime as public wrong which also shapes the precepts of criminal procedure in Blackstone's account (Farmer 1996b; Lacey 2001a). Nothing could be further from the question-begging propositions with which mid-twentieth century legal texts define criminal law as that body of legal rules to which criminal procedure applies. It is as if there is an inverse relationship between the growing conceptual sophistication and formal complexity of criminal law over time and the diminishing plausibility of a coherent substantive account of its nature.

This shift is indicative of some fundamental changes in the nature and intensity of law's involvement in criminalization over the course of modern English history, themselves premised on radical changes in the form and content of criminal law, the structure of the criminal trial, and the composition of the agencies invested with the power to interpret and enforce the law. At the time of Blackstone's *Commentaries*, while statutory offences were already numerous, criminal law was still seen primarily as a creature of the judge-made doctrines of the common law which had evolved slowly over centuries (Simon 2004: 1323). In this context, the idea of a core of offences grounded in a widely shared conception of public wrong was still credible. Moreover the trial and enforcement process looked distinctly less formalized—indeed less fully legally prescribed—than it did a century later. Let us review the most important changes in the framework for formal criminalization since the seventeenth century.

First, the categories of criminal offence are contingent upon time and place, prevailing social mores, cultural sensibilities, and religious and moral precepts (Lacey 1995). Reiner notes the 'huge cultural variation across space and time in what is counted by the law as criminal' (Reiner 2007: 25) and observes how many seventeenth century offences no longer exist today, including: witchcraft, failing to attend church, adultery, fornication, bridal pregnancy, scolding, disrupting the Sabbath, and 'wearing felt hats' (ibid.). Property-related offences predominated historically, as they do today, and in the period before the establishment of the formal police, 'thief-taking' was a private enterprise pursued for profit and driven by a complex system of rewards and protection arrangements (McMullen 1996). Until the mid-eighteenth century the office of constable was held voluntarily by members of the community backed up by the ancient institutions of 'hue and cry' and the Posse Comitatus that required able men to join in pursuit of a felon (Zedner 2006: 88). However, voluntary systems of policing came to work less well in growing towns and cities whose larger populations were more mobile and social relations consequently weaker. Those unwilling to serve voluntarily as constables often paid deputies instead, creating a profitable market in private policing and protection. The better-off formed mutually beneficial 'prosecution associations' to share the financial burden of bringing offenders to trial by private prosecution (King 2000: 53–7). The protection of interests ostensibly provided by the criminal law was far from universally enjoyed since prosecution was at least partially dependent on financial means. The claim that eighteenth century criminal law was a product of the English class system or tool of ruling class oppression (Hay 1975: 52) has, however, been challenged by evidence of widespread recourse to the criminal law by non-elite groups and the labouring poor to protect their interests (Langbein 1983; King 2000).

In the second half of the eighteenth century the growing pressures of industrialization and urbanization necessitated a criminal law capable of effective deterrence. A growing sense of the ungovernability of urban society, spawned by riots in London in the 1780s, resulted in propertied citizens forming 'Voluntary Associations for Defence' which undertook detection and apprehension as well as prosecution (Radzinowicz 1956: 100). The development of new economic relations and changes in wealth production resulted in the rapid growth of capital sentences, particularly for property crimes and offences involving the exploitation of trust, such as forgery. There was no general police force under government control in London until 1829; similar systematization in the rest of the country came even later. The form of the modern adversarial criminal trial emerged only during the close of the eighteenth and early nineteenth century.

Lawyers came to dominate trial argumentation only gradually: felony defendants did not gain the right to full legal representation until 1836. Prosecutions were initiated by private individuals, who might or might not have legal representation at trial: cases were selected for trial by a grand jury composed of local landowners sitting as justices of the peace (precursors to modern day magistrates). These justices or magistrates also heard the vast majority of criminal cases, with a mere dozen judges travelling the assize circuit even in the latter part of the eighteenth century. Even assize hearings were relatively speedy and non-technical affairs: it has been estimated that the average length of a criminal trial in the late eighteenth century was between 20 and 30 minutes (Langbein 2003: 16–18, 21–5; Beattie 1986: 378; 1991: 222; 2001: 260). Other than in exceptional cases such as treason, and very serious cases such as homicide, the criminal trial up to the early nineteenth century (and, of course, all the way up to the present day, in the forum of lay magistrates' courts) was usually a lay-dominated rather than a lawyer-dominated affair. The institutional conditions favourable to a gradual development, refinement, and systematic application of general legal doctrines—legal representation, rules of evidence, systematic reporting of criminal cases, legal education, and, finally at the end of the nineteenth century, a system of appeals—were gradually constructed over a period of almost 200 years. The process of criminalization operated more or less on the basis of a presumption of guilt which the trial gave the defendant an opportunity to rebut, generally on the basis of character evidence (Langbein 2003: 263; Lacey 2007; see also King 2000; Beattie 1986, 1991; Emsley 2007). The law of evidence was developed gradually through the entire eighteenth and nineteenth centuries; matters such as law reporting, a framework for the regular testing of points of law via criminal appeals, and legal education developed over this period, fostering the decisive formalization and professionalization of criminal law. The abolition of many of the capital statutes in the 1820s and the expansion of the penitentiary system replaced an *ancien régime* criminal law organized around draconian threats tempered by extensive discretion and exercise of mercy (King 2000) with a system of calibrated and regularly administered penalties (Hay 1975; Wiener 1990). These changes can be ascribed partly to civilizing processes that fed a growing revulsion against public execution and partly to the development of modern police and prisons which reduced the need for spectacular deterrent penalties.

What explains these changes over time, and what can they tell the criminologist about the nature of criminal law? Like any system of social norms, criminal law has to specify the practical conditions for its own operation and to legitimate its activities *vis à vis* those who are subject to them. Let us call these the tasks of coordination and of legitimation. In facing these tasks, criminal law enjoys resources and confronts challenges which are shaped by the broader features of its environment. Fundamental social, political, and economic changes transformed this environment, underpinning a decisive change in the relationship between legal and social constructions of crime over the eighteenth and nineteenth centuries. The extension of the franchise gradually changed the legitimation conditions for criminal law, with the decisive expansion of suffrage in the Reform Act of 1867 strengthening the popular mandate for formal criminalization. The development of the police, and the emergence of medical science and psychology and other forms of specialist knowledge and technology posed further challenges—and possibilities—for legitimation, as well as fundamentally altering the criminal justice system's powers to coordinate the knowledge base from which its judgements could be made. At the same time, urbanization, greater mobility, and social anonymity deprived the criminal justice system of reliable sources of local knowledge on which the eighteenth century criminal process—decentralized, dominated by lay justice, and far less professionalized—had been able to rely. The expansion of criminal law's role in the regulatory field, in the hands of an increasingly ambitious government, along with increasing social diversity and moral pluralism, particularly in the growing urban areas, further complicated criminal law's core tasks.

Already by the mid-nineteenth century, new ambiguities were emerging in the very concept of crime: a long-standing split between a moralized notion of crime as wrong or even evil (*mala in se*) and a legalized notion of crime as infraction (*mala prohibita*), already reflected in the great modern commentaries, intensified in the wake of the expansion of statutory offences, many of them regulating new urban and industrial activities. Later in the century, the position was further complicated by the emergence of new scientific notions of crime as pathology or atavism, reflected in statutes instituting distinctive criminalization regimes for particular categories of offender such as the 'habitual criminal' and the 'feeble-minded' (Radzinowicz and Hood 1990; Zedner 1991). These generated disagreements about the proper division of labour in defining crime as between judge, doctor, jury, and (increasingly active) legislature (Smith 1981).

Blackstone's notion of crime as public wrong had worked well enough for a circumscribed, common law-dominated system of criminal law. But as the scope and functions of criminal law increased dramatically, it could no longer bear the weight placed upon it. Many continental European countries avoided such an expansion through the creation of a separate legal edifice of regulatory law, assisted by a set of second order constraints on criminal law deriving from an entrenched constitutional structure which was entirely absent in England (Whitman 2003: ch. 4). But in England expansion was the order of the day; and this entailed a fragmentation of criminal law's rationale and an intensification of focus, in legal commentaries, on criminal procedure as the defining feature of criminal law.

## NORMATIVE ACCOUNTS: RATIONALIZING AND LEGITIMATING CRIMINAL THROUGH 'GENERAL PRINCIPLES'

Let us review the argument so far. 300 years ago, English criminal law was far less extensive than it is today, and was more readily rationalized in terms of a set of core interests and values. Of course, this does not mean that there was no social or value conflict or that criminal law was not already being used for 'regulatory' purposes. But with rapid urbanization and industrialization and the growth of the nation state's governmental capacities and ambitions, the conditions under which criminal law operated changed markedly (Lacey 2001a, 2008). Social mobility also had direct implications for the extent of social reliance on criminal law, as opposed to informal or private ordering and dispute resolution. The first institutional responses to these developments were the reforms of the policing, prosecution, trial, and penal processes of the nineteenth century (Langbein 2003; Lacey 2001b, 2008), with the professionalization of enforcement and legal practice, the spectacular reduction in capital offences, the rapid expansion of the prison system, and a regularization of penal practice consonant with an emerging, rationalist, modern, and, potentially, liberal conception of criminal law (Dubber 2005). While full-scale codification never materialized, the effort to modernize the substance of criminal law resulted in the consolidating legislation of the mid-nineteenth century (for example, the Offences Against the Person Act 1861 which still defines crimes of interpersonal violence today). But these legislative reforms left criminal law diverse, extensive, and divided between a vaguely differentiated terrain of 'real crime' and 'regulatory offences' that made substantive rationalization problematic.

Yet the impulse to rationalize criminal law, and make general statements about its aims, functions, underlying values, and *modus operandi,* has never ceased to make itself felt. In texts and commentaries of the first half of the twentieth century, we see the gradual construction of a 'general part' of criminal law, consisting of principles governing the conditions of liability across the offences (Kenny 1902; Radzinowicz and Turner 1945); a development which culminated in Glanville Williams' magisterial *Criminal Law: The General Part,* first published in 1953. But these 'general principles' have little bearing on the substance of criminal offences: the 'special part' of criminal law. The fact that Williams never followed up his original plan to publish a second volume on the 'special part' is significant. For it implies that it had now become unnecessary—as well as difficult—to rationalize criminal law in anything like the terms which had come naturally to Blackstone (Blackstone 1765–9) 200 years earlier, or indeed to James Fitzjames Stephen (1893) 100 years before: the substance of the offences themselves, and in particular the wrongs or interests which they articulate.

In English texts today, two rather different visions of the substantive defining features of criminal law—visions which have competed for dominance since the explosion of formal criminalization and the fragmentation of criminal law's scope attendant on the growth of the regulatory state in the nineteenth century (Ashworth 2009; Lacey, Wells, and Quick 2010)— still predominate. On the one hand, criminal law is understood—as distinct from civil law—as being concerned with *wrongdoing* in a quasi-moral sense. On this view, crime is conduct judged to be a sufficiently seriously violation of core social interests or shared values that it is appropriate for the state to proscribe and punish it. This is a view which sits naturally with a retributive approach to punishment and an emphasis on the expressive dimensions of criminal justice (Duff 2001). On the other hand, criminal law is understood in more neutrally instrumental terms as a regulatory system: attaching costs, through sanctions, to certain kinds of conduct which it is in the public interest to reduce. This second view sits naturally with a deterrent or otherwise utilitarian view of punishment. The obvious question arises as to how these competing views are to be reconciled as rationalizations of criminal law.

It is hardly surprising that in the twentieth century the most influential approaches attempted to incorporate both quasi-moral and regulatory aspects of criminal law. For example, H.L.A. Hart's account, which builds on the liberal utilitarianism of J.S. Mill (Hart 1963, 1968; Mill 1859), argues that, while the general justifying aim of criminal law is a utilitarian one of crime reduction through deterrence, the state is only justified in invoking its coercive criminalizing power as against conduct for which an individual is responsible and which is harmful to others or (in Hart's modified, social-democratic version of Mill's 'harm principle'), under certain conditions, to oneself. This is a less moralistic account of the nature of crime than is the quasi-moral, retributive conception, while nonetheless explaining why criminal law is of special moral significance. It has difficulty, however, in generating an adequately specified concept of harm: for example, does the offence felt by people who disapprove of behaviour such as homosexual conduct or public nudity count as 'harm' (Feinberg 1984–8)? If not, should the offence potentially created constitute an independent basis for criminalization? This approach fails to ask an obvious—and, for any social scientist, crucially important—question: if the concept of 'harm' is neither fixed nor analytically robust, how are socio-cultural notions of 'harm' constructed, and how do they influence criminal/legal constructions of harm? (Harcourt 1999; Hillyard *et al.* 2004).

In legal scholarship, the most common approach to making sense of these different aspects divides the terrain of criminal law between the 'moral core' of 'real crime'—theft, homicide, assault, rape and so on—and the 'quasi-criminal' 'regulatory offences'—health and safety, licensing offences, driving offences, tax offences, pollution offences, and so on (Quirk *et al.* 2010). This approach accepts that criminal law has not one, but two rationales: to define and punish wrongdoing; and to regulate social life. Their co-existence is enabled by a functional differentiation between offences. This functional differentiation is then, so the argument goes, mapped onto legal doctrine. However, this pragmatic reconciliation leaves many questions of interest to the social scientist unaddressed. How is the division between 'quasi-moral' and 'regulatory' crimes defined, and is the boundary a clear one, in practice as well as in law? How does it change over time? Under what conditions does such a criminal law system emerge, and what broader governmental roles, if any, does it pursue? These are questions, however, in which contemporary criminal lawyers are relatively uninterested, for their rationalization of criminal law moves on quickly from the substantive conceptions mentioned above to a more elaborated, technical account of the specific form which criminal liability must take (Simester and von Hirsch 2011).

This shift to a formal conception of criminal law was itself a function of the modernization process already described (Norrie 2001): the successive attempts at codification, along with modernization of the trial process, produced a more sophisticated institutional basis for working out a conceptual framework within which offence definitions and legal argumentation could proceed (Williams 1953; Smith 1998). In a world in which the substance of criminal law is fragmented, diverse, and hence hard to rationalize in a coherent way, it has become tempting for lawyers to regard the identity of criminal law as residing in formal features such as the presumption of innocence, the principle of legality, and the principles of conduct and responsibility which apply irrespective of the content of the offences. These doctrinal developments helped to address the changing problems of gathering and validating knowledge—the facts on the basis of which a criminal conviction is arrived at via the application of legal norms—in an increasingly centralized system in which reliance on the local knowledge of jurors and justices of the peace, characteristic of the early modern criminal law, was no longer feasible.

Today contemporary codes and commentaries on criminal law in both the common law and the civilian traditions tend to be organized around a core framework which sets out the general conditions under which liability may be established. This framework—often known as the 'general part' or 'general principles' of criminal law—consists of the set of rules and doctrines which apply across the whole terrain of criminal law rather than to specific offences (Gardner 1998; Ashworth 2009: chs 4–6). In the criminal law of England and Wales, this framework consists of four main elements: capacity, conduct, responsibility and (absence of) defence. One striking feature is the gradual formalization of principles of criminal responsibility around mental concepts such as intention, knowledge, belief, and recklessness, as opposed to the overtly evaluative concepts such as malice and wilfulness which had characterized the common law for centuries (Binder 2002; Horder 1997). This shift from older ideas of 'fault' to a more empirically based conception of 'responsibility' was made possible by the growth of psychology and psychiatry, premised on a certain understanding of the mind–body distinction and of mental capacity as a discrete object of social knowledge. But the legal development could not have occurred had it not been for the further belief that the factual question of what is going on in someone's mind can be an object of investigation and proof in a criminal court (Smith 1981). This in turn depended on developments such as the professionalization of the trial process and the development of the law of evidence already considered (Lacey 2001b).

Today, the foundations of criminal liability are generally thought to consist in four clusters of normative elements: elements relating to capacity, to conduct, to responsibility or fault, and to defence. We deal with each of these in turn:

1. *Capacity*: only those who share certain basic cognitive and volitional capacities are regarded as legitimate subjects of criminal law. One might regard defences such as insanity as defining certain kinds of people as simply outwith the system of communication embodied by criminal law. Since law operates in terms of general standards, the line between criminal capacity and criminal incapacity is a relatively crude one. For example, almost every criminal law system exempts from criminal liability people under a certain age, whatever their actual capacities: but—yet again underlining the interplay between legal and social constructions of crime—the age at which the line between capacity and incapacity is drawn, varies significantly by country and over time. In England and Wales, the abolition of the presumption of incapacity for 10–14 year olds has in effect reduced the age of criminal liability to 10, while it stands at 13 in France and at 15 in the Nordic countries. Since it cannot plausibly be claimed that children mature at such widely differing rates in neighbouring countries, capacity must be understood as a legal construct contingent on local legal culture and politics.

2. *Conduct*: criminal conviction is founded on conduct specified in the offence definition: appropriating another person's property in the case of theft; causing a person's death in the case of homicide; having sexual intercourse with a person without their consent in the case of rape; driving with a certain level of alcohol in one's blood in the case of driving while intoxicated. Though there are exceptions in English criminal law doctrine, it is generally asserted that mere thoughts; being of a certain status rather than doing an act; and (in the absence of a specific duty to act) omitting to do something, are insufficient to found criminal liability. To take some illustrative examples: if I simply fantasize about committing a sophisticated fraud, without taking any steps towards it, I am

guilty of no crime; and my failure to rescue a drowning child will only attract criminal liability if my relationship with the child or my professional responsibility imposes a special duty to act. This last example is a further reminder of the contingency of legal constructions of crime: in France a relatively wide-ranging duty of rescue is enshrined in statute so that failing to rescue a drowning child could render me criminally liable.

3. *Responsibility/fault*: criminal liability is generally said to depend on a person with capacity being responsible for or at fault in committing the conduct specified in the offence definition. To put it crudely, we do not hold people liable for accidents. Responsibility or fault conditions generally consist of mental states or attitudes such as intention, recklessness, knowledge, belief, dishonesty, or negligence. In the examples above, the relevant conditions consist in a dishonest intention permanently to deprive in the case of theft; an intention to kill or cause serious bodily harm or gross negligence in homicide; recklessness or negligence as to the victim's lack of consent in respect of rape. The fourth example—driving while intoxicated—is an exception to the general principle that a discrete responsibility element must be proven by the prosecution: only the driving and the blood alcohol level need be established by the prosecution. Notwithstanding their 'exceptional' status, however, these offences of 'strict' liability probably outnumber offences requiring a mental element or *mens rea* in English criminal law today by a substantial margin (though it is difficult to count). Ashworth and Blake estimated (1996: 309) that even of the more serious criminal offences about half featured either 'strict' no-fault liability or only a partial fault requirement, and 40 per cent a reverse burden of proof, placing the burden on the defendant to disprove liability. This division between offences of strict liability and offences requiring proof of fault maps on to the 'instrumental/regulatory' and 'quasi-moral' terrains of criminal law doctrine: that is, most strict liability offences are said to be regulatory rather than condemnatory. However, as the example of driving while intoxicated illustrates, this line is neither clear nor static: 30 years ago 'drunk driving' was regarded as a quintessentially regulatory offence; today it carries a marked moral stigma. Changing moral and social values influence the meaning, as well as the practice, of the criminal law and point to the importance of criminological and sociological knowledge in understanding how crime is defined.

4. *Defences*: Even where a person with criminal capacity has committed the relevant conduct with the requisite degree of fault, a range of defences may preclude or mitigate his or her liability (Duff 2007: ch. 11). For example, if the defendant has committed a theft while under a threat of violence, she may plead a defence of duress. If a person kills, intentionally, in order to defend himself against an immediate attack, he may plead self-defence. 'General defences' apply not only to crimes which require proof of responsibility but also to those of strict liability. Hence, for example, a person who drives while intoxicated because under duress, by threat, or in highly compelling circumstances, may escape liability. So, for example, if you threaten to shoot me if I fail to drive you home, I may be exonerated even if I do so while intoxicated.

Defences are often thought to fall into three main groups—exemptions, justifications and excuses—each relating to the other three components of liability already mentioned. The defence of insanity, for example, arguably operates to recognize that the defendant's incapacity *exempts* her from the communications of criminal law. If for example I kill while suffering a mental illness which causes me to misunderstand entirely the nature of my own action, I am considered to be beyond the reach of criminal law as a system of rational communication. Even before trial I may be deemed unfit to plead; or I may be found not guilty by reason of insanity. If on the other hand I kill while defending myself from attack, my plea of self-defence may be seen as amounting to a claim that my conduct was, in the circumstances, *justified* and hence not the sort of conduct which criminal law sets out to proscribe. And if I plead that I assaulted someone because a third party had threatened me or my family with violence if I did not do so, my defence of duress may be viewed as *excusing* me on the basis that the conditions under which I formed the relevant fault condition mitigate my guilt. The defences may thus be seen as fine-tuning, along contextualized and morally sensitive lines, the presumptive inferences of liability produced by the first three elements (capacity, conduct, and fault).

This conceptual framework is analytic: it provides building blocks with which legislators and lawyers construct criminal liability. At the same time, as the reference to 'general principles' suggests, it contains an implicit set of assumptions about what makes the imposition of criminal liability legitimate. The idea, for example, that there should be no punishment for mere thoughts, or under circumstances in which some internal capacity or external circumstance deprived a defendant of a fair opportunity to conform to the law, or that a defendant should not be convicted unless they were in some sense responsible for their conduct, expresses a normative view of criminal law as not merely an institutionalized system of coercion but as a system which addresses its subjects in a particular way and which is structured around certain broadly liberal principles of justice or morality (Ashworth and Zedner 2008). This normative aspect of the 'general part' of criminal law becomes yet clearer in the light of two broad procedural standards which characterize most modern systems. The first is the *principle of legality*: namely that there should be no penalty without law and that criminal law must be announced clearly to citizens in advance of its imposition so that they have a fair opportunity to conform to it. Principles such as clarity, certainty, and non-retroactivity are therefore central tenets of the liberal ideal of the rule of law. The second procedural doctrine is the *presumption of innocence*: a crime must be proven by the prosecution (generally the state and hence far more powerful than the individual defendant) beyond all reasonable doubt (Ashworth and Blake 1996; Tadros and Tierney 2004). Criminal law is therefore implicitly justified not only in terms of its role in proscribing, condemning and, perhaps, reducing conduct which causes or risks a variety of harms, but also in treating its subjects with respect, as beings whose conduct is (normally) under their control, and who must be assessed in terms of their degree of responsible agency and not merely in terms of the effects they create.

Furthermore, acknowledging the individual as independent, rational, and free-willed requires that those who commit wrongdoing are identified, held to account, and punished proportionately. To do otherwise, it is argued, would constitute a failure to acknowledge individuals as moral agents who can justly be held responsible for their actions and instead would treat wrongdoers as 'tigers might be treated in a circus, as beings that have to be restrained, intimidated, or conditioned into compliance because they are incapable of understanding why biting people (or other tigers) is wrong' (von Hirsch 1993: 11). Individual autonomy and dignity are also protected, in theory at least, by the requirement of adherence to procedural safeguards relating to investigation, prosecution, and the criminal trial intended to protect individuals against unwarranted state interference and uphold fundamental human rights (enshrined in the European Convention of Human Rights). This paradigmatic liberal account of criminal law emphasizes respect for the rights and dignity of the individual in the criminal process (Roberts 2006). This said, formal protections are often ignored, subverted, or breached. Some suggest that the rhetoric of respect for the individual espoused by legal liberalism masks or even makes possible a legal process that has more to do with crime control than due process (McBarnet 1981: 156).

The various assumptions underlying the conceptual framework within which criminal liability is constructed are of real significance for criminologists and criminal justice scholars. For they give us insight into the processes of interpretation in the court room—one key site in the process of criminalization. They also provide some interesting points of contrast and similarity when compared with the assumptions underpinning other practices within the criminal process. Are the assumptions of rationality, understanding, and self-control which lie at the heart of criminal law's understanding of (normal) defendants the same as, or even consistent with, those that underpin the development of policing strategy, sentencing decision-making, probation practice or prison regimes? If not, does it matter? How consistently are they observed in either formal or substantive criminalization in England and Wales today? And are the assumptions of moral autonomy, free will, and rationality consistent with criminological knowledge about factors closely associated with offending such as drug and alcohol abuse, mental disorder, and social and economic deprivation (Delgado 1985; Peay, this volume; Rock, this volume; South and Measham, this volume)?

## THE SHIFTING BOUNDARIES OF CONTEMPORARY CRIMINAL LAW

It is estimated that over 3,200 new offences were added to the statute books in the decade following 1997.[2] Some of these result from new legislation against particular areas of activity such as serious and organized crime, immigration, and terrorism. Some are caused by the increasing number of regulatory agencies to which the government grants powers to introduce the secondary legislation which generated about two-thirds of the new crimes. Aside from the powers already held by local authorities

---

[2]  1,169 in primary legislation and 1,854 in subordinate legislation. Halsbury's Statutes of England and Wales has four volumes devoted to criminal laws: strikingly, more than two and a half times as many pages were needed in Halsbury's Statutes to cover offences created in the 19 years between 1989 and 2008 than were needed to cover the offences created in the preceding 637 years (The Law Commission 2010: 5).

and trading standards authorities, there are now over 60 national regulatory bodies with the power to create criminal law in support of their regulatory functions. By way of example, in 2008 the Department for the Environment, Food and Rural Affairs (DEFRA) introduced the Transmissible Spongiform Encephalopathies (No 2) (Amendment) Regulations 2008 which created no less than 103 new criminal offences aimed at reducing the risk posed by the spread of BSE.

Untrammelled expansion of the criminal law is a cause for concern not least because it has the potential to limit individual autonomy and expand the power of the state to exercise its most coercive powers over more and more aspects of daily life. Recent developments have seen liability extend downwards (regulatory offences), back in time (inchoate offences, preparatory offences, possession, risk-creation, and other precursor offences), and outwards (associative crimes—especially in respect of fraud, organized crime, and terrorism), adding considerably to the discretionary powers of prosecutors and the police. Yet many new criminal offences, especially those created by regulatory agencies, are rarely used. For example, section 8 of the Asylum and Immigration Act 1996, which prohibits the employment of illegal migrant workers, resulted in, on average, only one prosecution a year between 1998 and 2004. Nor has the steep increase in numbers of criminal offences since 1997 led to a corresponding increase in prosecutions and convictions. Prosecutions in magistrates' courts fell from 2 million in 1997 to 1.6 million in 2008 and, although there was a small increase in prosecutions in the Crown Court, the total number of people found guilty in both magistrates' and Crown Courts fell from 1.49 million to 1.36 million over the same period. Thus the expansion of criminal law appears to have coincided with a growing gap between formal and substantive criminalization.

Part of the explanation lies in a growing sense that the criminal trial is often unduly expensive, time-consuming, ineffective, inappropriate, or even simply unnecessary as a means of dealing with low-level offending (Ashworth and Zedner 2010: 23). Part lies in a focus on low-level offensive behaviour, consistent with Wilson and Kelling's broken windows thesis (1982), as an appropriate object of early intervention (Crawford 2009: 816). This has led to greater recourse to mechanisms for diversion; use of fixed penalties (for example the Penalty Notice for Disorder or PND) (Padfield, Morgan, and Maguire, this volume); and of a growing range of civil and hybrid civil–criminal measures (of which the Anti-Social Behaviour Order or ASBO is only the best known) that reduce reliance upon the criminal law. Criminalization becomes just one tool in a growing array of administrative and regulatory measures (Zedner 2010: 396). It would be a mistake, however, to assume that these measures are necessarily less intrusive or less burdensome than the criminal law. The Penalty Notice for Disorder imposes a fixed penalty that may be significantly more onerous than a court fine (which must be set in accordance with the offender's means). Similarly, the ASBO may target low levels of nuisance well below the normal threshold of the criminal law. The minimum term for an ASBO is two years and conduct in breach may result in a much more severe sentence (up to five years' imprisonment) than would have been possible for a criminal offence itself (Simester and von Hirsch 2006). Rather than limiting the scope of the criminal law, resort to hybrid civil-criminal measures can be seen both as 'a form of criminalization: an ex ante prohibition not ex post criminal verdict' (Simester and von Hirsch 2006: 178) and as an individuation of the criminal law, in that ASBOs create a personal penal code for the person subject to the order.

Whether the response to low-level or regulatory offences ought properly to lie within the ambit of the criminal law, or be replaced by administrative measures (as has occurred in Germany in the guise of *Ordnungswidrigkeiten*), or with civil orders of the sort just described is a matter of lively debate. On the one hand it is suggested that where appropriate levels of punishment or deterrence can be secured by lesser civil means these should be preferred over stigmatizing and potentially overly punitive criminalization (Law Commission 2010). On the other hand it can be argued that to the extent that civil measures impose burdens equivalent to punishment, placing these measures within civil procedure denies individuals subject to them the protections that adhere to the criminal process and constitute an instance of under-criminalization (Ashworth and Zedner 2010). And yet as Crawford observes, '[i]t is a supreme irony that whilst many of the new technologies of control have sought to circumvent criminal procedures due to their apparent ineffectiveness, this has not diminished the appetite for more criminal laws' (2009: 826).[3]

It can be seen that two dominant and divergent trends characterize practices of criminalization over the past two decades. On the one hand there has been recourse to diversion (for example through fixed penalties and civil–criminal preventive measures) and downgrading, through greater use of summary trials, stronger incentives to plead guilty, and an increase in offences of strict liability (mostly, though not all, carrying low penalties). On the other hand there has been a steep increase in the number of criminal offences and in the severity of penal measures, notably in the use of imprisonment (the prison population is now at its highest ever level at nearly 87,000).[4] As a consequence, and notwithstanding the fall in recorded crime across many offence categories since the mid-1990s, there is well documented growing public concern about the scale and extent of crime. No surprise then that determining the proper limits of criminalization has become a matter of academic and political interest to criminal lawyers anxious to restrain the tendency to 'over-criminalization' that is such a defining feature of contemporary life in countries such as England and the United States (Husak 2008; Stuntz 2011). Interestingly, although it is precisely the sociological phenomena of popular anxiety, media hype, and political attention to crime which in turn result in a 'new punitiveness' and over-criminalization that have prompted legal interest in criminalization and the appropriate boundaries of the criminal law (Duff *et al.* 2010), that interest has hardly been shared by criminology. While lawyers are alert to the sociological drivers of over-criminalization (Husak 2008: ch.1), criminological focus on penal politics and popular punitivism prioritizes penal parsimony (*Theoretical Criminology Special Issue* 2010) and does not address criminalization *per se*. As a result, lawyers, philosophers, and political theorists seek to determine the proper limits of criminalization unaided by criminology, despite

---

[3] In a bid to cap the proliferation of new criminal offences the Ministry of Justice announced in 2010 the creation of a 'Gateway' designed to scrutinize all new proposals for legislation containing criminal offences 'to ensure that they are justified and proportionate', www.justice.gov.uk/news/announcement300710b.htm.

[4] The World Prison Brief recorded the prison population in England and Wales in September 2011 as 86,751, www.prisonstudies.org/info/worldbrief/wpb_country.php?country=169.

the obvious contribution that criminology might make to a fully social and political account of why and to what ends conduct is criminalized (Zedner 2011).

## LIMITS ON CRIMINALIZATION: THE CONTRIBUTION OF CRIMINOLOGY

Prevailing theories of criminal law are closely tied to theories of the state and the dominant political order (Duff *et al.* 2004a; Brudner 2009): the liberal legal account of crime as a means of holding individuals to account for wrongful conduct has come to prevail as the dominant model of criminal law. Yet this account has been subject to severe criticism from many quarters. Christie famously characterized crimes as disputes between private individuals whose proprietorial interests were consequently 'stolen' by the state (Christie 1977). Understanding crime not as an infraction of the law deserving of punishment but as a matter to be resolved by those party to it gave rise to the development of Restorative Justice, an alternative to the criminal justice paradigm, that proposed dialogue in place of prosecution, dispute resolution in place of the trial, and 'reintegrative shaming' in place of punishment (Braithwaite 1989, see also Hoyle; Lösel, this volume). Such has been the power and influence of this advocacy that liberal legal theorists have been moved to take up the challenge of trying to determine how the claims of Restorative Justice might be reconciled with more conventional accounts of crime and criminal justice (von Hirsch *et al.* 2003).

Perhaps the most trenchant criticism of liberal accounts of criminal liability has come from communitarian thinkers who argue that they are premised on an atomized view of the individual that overplays autonomy and fails to recognize that we are social beings inseparable from our personal and social relations (Lacey 1988: ch. 8). Recognizing the importance of community to the individual and the choices they make has profound implications for our thinking about wrongdoing and places in question the very assumption of individual responsibility upon which the criminal law is predicated. Significant efforts have been made to combine the insights of the liberal and communitarian traditions, balancing the liberal strengths of respect for human agency and rights with a textured account of the ways in which the social antecedents of crime should feed into the construction of defences and of responsibility more generally (Braithwaite and Pettit 1990; Duff 2001, 2007).

A more radical critique still comes from the attempt by some criminologists to move 'beyond crime' (Hillyard *et al.* 2004) on the grounds that crime is said to be too restrictive a concept to capture the full extent of harmful behaviours which cause most loss and suffering. Hillyard and colleagues claim that crime relies on a dubious relationship to reality, that criminal liability is attributed by questionable means, and that placing the liability of the individual at the heart of the criminal law fails to address serious social harms inflicted by groups, organizations, and states (Hillyard *et al.* 2004). Zemiology—as this approach is called—suggests that 'a disciplinary approach organized around a notion of social harm may prove to be more productive' (Hillyard and Tombs 2007: 9). It is striking that this attack on the very category of crime is motivated partly by the observation that 'criminology has largely failed to be self-reflective regarding the dominant, state defined notion of "crime".... The issue of what crime is, is rarely stated, but rather simply assumed' (Hillyard and Tombs 2007: 11). If this is true, it might equally suggest that criminology ought to make good this failure by engaging with the scope and nature of crime, the principles upon which it is defined, and the legal structures in which it is inscribed (Zedner 2011).

Although this chapter has as its focus legal constructions of crime, it should not be concluded that criminology has nothing to contribute to the ongoing and often heated debates around criminalization. Quite the contrary, criminology has a vital role to play in ensuring that the normative questions are neither framed nor answered as purely normative or legal issues. These questions cannot be divorced from the messy social realities underpinning the ways that offences are identified as criminal wrongs (rather than matters subject to other kinds of legal or social regulation) and that criminal categories are defined, framed, and structured. It is commonly asserted that there is a core of offences universally accepted as criminal wrongs around which exists a penumbra of lesser, disputed categories. Yet even the most serious of offences pose challenges. For example, the 'core' offence of murder poses interpretive difficulty in cases such as mercy killing. And even the most serious offences may escape criminalization if they do not easily supply the paradigmatic individual offender who can be held to account. Take two examples from either end of the scale of criminalization as currently constructed: crimes of the state often appear to be above or too big for criminalization (Cohen 2001; Green and Ward, this volume), while workplace injuries are often dealt with as regulatory matters by Health and Safety authorities rather than resulting in the prosecution of employers and factory owners (Hawkins 2002). Identifying the contextual and structural conditions of and impediments to criminalization is a task that has long eluded criminal lawyers but one which criminology with its social scientific expertise is well equipped to tackle.

As we have seen, for lawyers the construction of crime proceeds by reference to concepts of culpability, wrongfulness, harm, and offence; by delineating the boundary between civil and criminal liability; by seeking to determine which harms are too remote and which offences too trivial to merit criminalization. But lawyerly attention to these normative questions risks overlooking practical, structural, and policy considerations that criminologists are arguably better placed to address. What, for example, is or should be the relevance of the prevalence of conduct in a particular area or at a given time and the level of public concern about it? What consideration should be given to the enforceability of a prohibition or the costs of enforcement? Should the financial burdens of policing an activity or the intrusions entailed by enforcement measures be a consideration in determining what is and what is not criminalized? What role should public opinion play? Should public consensus play any part in determining what is criminalized—given the difficulty of ensuring compliance if there is widespread dissent—and, if so, in what circumstances? Should the danger that a law will be widely flouted or otherwise prove impossible to enforce (as was the case in respect of the much derided ban on fox-hunting) be considered a valid policy consideration or not?

To these policy questions one might add research into the ways in which political processes, and not least party political interests, influence the construction and application of legal categories. Consider too the administrative pressures and constraints upon the implementation of laws, the training of criminal justice officials and the influence of professional culture. These extra-legal factors play an important part in determining how crime is actually policed and prosecuted through the criminal justice process. Criminological knowledge is no less central to understanding how, in practice, legal categories are applied, to whom, in what circumstances, and with what consequences. It opens up to view the relations of class, race, and gender, the cultural assumptions and prejudices, and the political considerations that inform and influence the practice of law. And it explains how and why the formal equality and universality of the criminal law may be undermined by the partial, targeted, and often discriminatory ways in which it is applied. No less important is the larger *Realpolitik* of inter-governmental and international politics that frames the construction and implementation of international criminal law, of supranational offences like organized crime, the smuggling of peoples and of drugs, and terrorism.

Criminology is alert to the volatile and contradictory character of modern penal politics (O'Malley 1999; Garland 2001). On the one hand it has observed an ever greater willingness to resort to the criminal law, and to deploy its powers coercively. This authoritarian tendency has its roots in the rise of penal populism fed by demands for greater public protection, in media constructions of crime, and in a punitive cross-party penal politics. On the other hand it has observed the normalization of crime as a fact of everyday life (Felson 2002) to be managed and regulated. This routinization of crime licenses 'defining deviance down', the removal of lesser offences from the criminal process to the less onerous channels of civil and administrative law, and resort to other regulatory mechanisms, not least the 'contractual governance' of deviance (Crawford 2003). Yet it is far from clear that these managerial, regulatory, and contractual developments have resulted in less commitment to the control of crime through the criminal law. Indeed, as we have seen, recent decades have witnessed an extraordinary and unprecedented programme of criminalization. Yet the legal construction of crime is one part of the picture of contemporary penal politics that criminology has yet to engage with in any sustained fashion. It should by now be clear that criminalization is not just a matter of legal principle but 'a politically charged set of decisions that result in a complex set of individual laws by which the state seeks to govern its subjects' (Ashworth and Zedner 2008: 44). Recognizing that criminal law is an engine of governance renders it impossible to separate its study not only from that of political theory and political economy but also, and not least, from criminology.

### ■ SELECTED FURTHER READING

The relationship between questions of criminal law and criminal justice is explored extensively in Lacey, Wells, and Quick, *Reconstructing Criminal Law* (2010), 4th edn, edited by Celia Wells and Oliver Quick, Cambridge: Cambridge University Press. For interesting reflections by a criminal lawyer on his own discipline see Lindsay Farmer (1996a), 'The Obsession with Definition', 5 *Social and Legal Studies*, 57. For an assessment of the relationship between developments in political culture, criminal justice institutions and criminal law doctrine see Nicola Lacey (2001a) 'In Search of the Responsible Subject', 64 *Modern Law Review*, 350–71.

On recent developments and on the changing scope, exercise, and aims of the criminal law see Andrew Ashworth and Lucia Zedner (2008), 'Defending the Criminal Law', *Criminal Law and Philosophy*, 21–51 and also Hannah Quirk, Toby Seddon, and Graham Smith (eds) (2010),*Regulation and Criminal Justice*, Cambridge: Cambridge University Press. For a legal-philosophical treatment of criminalization see Antony Duff and Stuart Green (eds) (2011), *Philosophical Foundations of the Criminal Law*, Oxford University Press and Andrew Simester and Andreas von Hirsch (2011), *Crimes, Harms, and Wrongs: on the principles of criminalisation*, Oxford: Hart Publishing. Finally, Antony Duff *et al.* (eds) (2010), *The Boundaries of the Criminal Law*, Oxford: Oxford University Press and Anthony Duff *et al.* (eds) (2011), *The Structures of the Criminal Law*, Oxford: Oxford University Press are the first of several volumes due to appear as part of a larger project on criminalization involving criminal lawyers, philosophers, and criminologists which begins to breach the gulf between disciplines described in this chapter.

## ■ REFERENCES

ASHWORTH, A. (2009), *Principles of Criminal Law*, 6th edn, Oxford: Clarendon Press.

ASHWORTH, A. (2010), *Sentencing and Criminal Justice*, 5th edn, Cambridge: Cambridge University Press.

ASHWORTH, A, and ZEDNER, L. (2008), 'Defending the Criminal Law', *Criminal Law and Philosophy*, 21 51

—— and —— (2010), 'Preventive Orders: a case of undercriminalization', in R. A. Duff, L. Farmer, S. Marshall, M. Renzo, and V. Tadros (eds), *The Boundaries of the Criminal Law*, Oxford: Oxford University Press.

—— and BLAKE, M. (1996), 'The Presumption of Innocence in English Criminal Law', *Criminal Law Review*, 306

—— and REDMAYNE, M. (2010), *The Criminal Process: An Evaluative Study*, 4th edn, Oxford: Oxford University Press.

BEATTIE, J. M. (1986), *Crime and the Courts in England 1660–1800*, Princeton: Princeton University Press.

—— (1991), 'Scales of Justice', 9 *Law and History Review*, 221.

—— (2001), *Policing and Punishment in London 1660–1750: Urban Crime and the Limits of Terror*, Oxford: Oxford University Press.

BLACKSTONE, W. (1765–9), *Commentaries on the Laws of England* (1979), Chicago: University of Chicago Press.

BINDER, G. (2002), 'The Rhetoric of Motive and Intent', *Buffalo Criminal Law Review*, 1–96.

BRAITHWAITE, J. (1989), *Crime, Shame and Reintegration*, Cambridge: Cambridge University Press.

—— and PETTIT, P. (1990), *Not Just Deserts? A Republican Theory of Criminal Justice*, Oxford: Oxford University Press.

BRONITT, S. and McSHERRY, B. (2010), *Principles of Criminal Law*, 3rd edn, Pyrmont, N.S.W.: Law Book Company.

BRUDNER, A. (2009), *Punishment and Freedom*, Oxford: Oxford University Press.

CHRISTIE, N. (1977), 'Conflicts as Property', *British Journal of Criminology*, 17: 1–15.

COHEN, S. (2001), *States of Denial: Knowing about Atrocities and Suffering*, Cambridge Polity Press.

CRAWFORD, A. (2003), '"Contractual Governance" of Deviant Behaviour', *Journal of Law and Society*, 30(4): 479–505.

—— (2009), 'Governing through Anti-Social Behaviour: Regulatory Challenges to Criminal Justice', *British Journal of Criminology*, 49: 810-831.

DELGADO, R. (1985), '"Rotten Social Background": Should the Criminal Law Recognize a Defence of Severe Environmental Deprivation?', *Law and Inequality*, 3: 9–90.

DUBBER, M. D. (2005), *The Police Power*, New York: Columbia University Press.

DUFF, R.A. (2001), *Punishment, Communication and Community*, Oxford: Oxford University Press.

—— (2007), *Answering for Crime: Responsibility and Liability in the Criminal Law*, Oxford: Hart Publishing.

—— *et al.* (2004a), 'Introduction: Towards a Normative Theory of the Criminal Trial', in R. A. Duff, L. Farmer, S. E. Marshall, and V. Tadros (eds),*The Trial on Trial, Volume 1* Oxford: Hart Publishing.

—— *et al.* (2011), *The Structures of the Criminal Law*, Oxford: Oxford University Press.

——, FARMER, L.,MARSHALL,S.E.,and TADROS,V. (eds) (2004b, 2005, 2007), *The Trial on Trial: Volumes I: Truth and Due Process; II: Judgment and Calling to Account; III: Towards a Normative Theory of the Criminal Trial*, Oxford: Hart Publishing.

——, FARMER, L., MARSHALL, S. E., RENZO, M., and TADROS, V. (eds) (2010), *The Boundaries of the Criminal Law*, Oxford: Oxford University Press.

EMSLEY, C. (2007), 'Historical Perspectives on Crime', in M. Maguire, R. Morgan, and R. Reiner (eds), *The Oxford Handbook of Criminology*, 4th edn, Oxford: Oxford University Press.

FARMER, L. (1996a), 'The Obsession with Definition', 5 *Social and Legal Studies*, 57.

—— (1996b), *Criminal Law, Tradition and Legal Order*, Cambridge: Cambridge University Press.

FEINBERG, J. (1984–8), *The Moral Limits of the Criminal Law*, Oxford and New York: Oxford University Press.

FELSON, M. (2002), *Crime and Everyday Life*, London: Sage.

FLETCHER, G. (1978), *Rethinking Criminal Law*, Boston and Toronto: Little, Brown & Co.

GARDNER, J. (1998), 'On the General Part of the Criminal Law', in R.A. Duff (ed.), *Philosophy and the Criminal Law: Principle and Critique*, Cambridge: Cambridge University Press.

GARLAND, D. (2001), *The Culture of Control: Crime and Social Order in Contemporary Society*, Oxford, Oxford University Press.

HARCOURT, B. (1999), 'The Collapse of the Harm Principle', 90 *Journal of Criminal Law and Criminology*, 109.

HART, H.L.A. (1963), *Law, Liberty and Morality*, Oxford: Oxford University Press.

—— (1968), *Punishment and Responsibility*, Oxford: Clarendon Press.

HAWKINS, K. (2002), *Law as Last Resort: Prosecution Decision-Making in a Regulatory Agency*, Oxford, Oxford University Press.

HAY, D. (1975), 'Property, Authority and Criminal Law', in D. Hay, P. Linebaugh, and E.P. Thompson (eds), *Albion's Fatal Tree*, Harmondsworth: Penguin.

HILLYARD, P., PANTAZIS, C.,TOMBS,S., and GORDON,D. (eds) (2004), *Beyond Criminology: Taking Harm Seriously*, London: Pluto Press.

—— and S. TOMBS (2007), 'From "crime" to social harm?', *Crime, Law and Social Change*, 48: 9–25.

HORDER, J. (1997), 'Two Histories and Four Hidden Principles of Mens Rea', 113, *Law Quarterly Review*, 95.

HUSAK, D. N. (2007) *Overcriminalization*, New York: Oxford University Press.

KATZ, L. (2002), 'Villainy and Felony: A Problem Concerning Criminalization', 6, *Buffalo Criminal Law Review*, 451.

KENNY, C.S. (1902), *Outlines of Criminal Law*, 1st edn, Cambridge: Cambridge University Press.

KING, P. (2000), *Crime, Justice and Discretion in England 1740–1820*, Oxford: Oxford University Press.

LACEY, N. (1988), *State Punishment*, Oxford: Oxford University Press.

—— (1995), 'Contingency and Criminalization', in I. Loveland (ed.), *Frontiers of Criminality*, London: Sweet and Maxwell.

—— (2001a), 'In Search of the Responsible Subject', 64 *Modern Law Review*, 350–71.

—— (2001b), 'Responsibility and Modernity in Criminal Law', 9 *Journal of Political Philosophy*, 249–77.

—— (2004), 'Criminalization as Regulation', in C.Parker, C.Scott, N. Lacey, and J. Braithwaite (eds) *Regulating Law*, Oxford: Oxford University Press.

—— (2006), 'Criminal Justice' in R. E. Goodin, P. Pettit, and T. Pogge (eds), *Companion to Contemporary Political Philosophy*, Oxford: Blackwells.

—— (2007), 'Character, Capacity, Outcome: Towards a framework for assessing the shifting pattern of criminal responsibility in modern English law', in M. Dubber and L. Farmer (eds), *Modern Histories of Crime and Punishment*, Stanford: Stanford University Press.

—— (2008), *Women, Crime and Character: from Moll Flanders to Tess of the d'Urbervilles*, Oxford: Oxford University Press.

—— (2009), 'Historicising Criminalization: Conceptual and Empirical Issues', 72(6), *Modern Law Review*, 936–61.

——, WELLS, C., and QUICK, O. (2010), *Reconstructing Criminal Law: Critical Perspectives on Crime and the Criminal Process*, 4th edn, Cambridge: Cambridge University Press.

LANGBEIN, J. (1983), 'Albion's Fatal Flaws', *Past and Present*, 98: 96–120.

—— (2003), *The Origins of Adversary Criminal Trial*, Oxford: Oxford University Press.

THE LAW COMMISSION (2010), *Criminal Liability in Regulatory Contexts. Consultation Paper No 195* London: Law Commission.

MCBARNET, D. (1982), *Conviction: Law, the State and the Construction of Justice*, London: Macmillan.

MCCONVILLE, M. and MIRSKY, C. L. (2005), *Jury Trials and Plea-Bargaining*, Oxford: Hart Publishing.

MCMULLEN, J. (1996), 'The New Improved Monied Police: Reform, Crime Control, and the Commodification of Policing in London', *British Journal of Criminology*, 36/1: 85–108.

MATHIESEN, T. (1974), *The Politics of Abolition*, London: Martin Robertson.

MILL, J.S. (1859), *On Liberty*, Harmondsworth: Penguin 1974.

NORRIE, A. (2001), *Crime, Reason and History*, 2nd edn, London: Butterworths.

O'MALLEY, P. (1999), 'Volatile and Contradictory Punishment', *Theoretical Criminology*, 3: 175–96.

PACKER, H. (1968), *The Limits of the Criminal Sanction*, Stanford University Press.

QUIRK, H, SEDDON, T., and SMITH, G. (eds) (2010), *Regulation and Criminal Justice*, Cambridge: Cambridge University Press.

RADZINOWICZ, L. (1956), *A History of English Criminal Law and its Administration from 1750*. Vol. 3, London: Steven & Sons Limited.

—— and HOOD, R. (1990), *The Emergence of Penal Policy in Victorian and Edwardian England*, Oxford: Oxford University Press.

—— and TURNER, J. W. C. (1945), *The Modern Approach to Criminal Law*, London: Macmillan.

REINER, R. (2006), *Beyond Risk: A Lament for a Social Democratic Criminology*, in T. Newburn and P. Rock (eds), *The Politics of Crime Control*, Oxford: Oxford University Press.

—— (2007), *Law and Order: An Honest Citizen's Guide to Crime and Control*, Cambridge: Polity Press.

ROBERTS, P. (2006), 'Theorising Procedural Tradition: Subjects, Objects and Values in Criminal Adjudication', in R. A. Duff *et al.* (eds),*The Trial on Trial, Volume 2*, Oxford: Hart Publishing.

ROBINSON, P.H. (1997), *Structure and Function in Criminal Law*, Oxford: Clarendon Press.

SIMESTER, A. P. and VON HIRSCH, A. (2006), 'Regulating offensive conduct through two-step prohibitions', in von Hirsch and Simester (eds), *Incivilities: Regulating offensive behaviour*, Oxford: Hart Publishing.

—— and —— (2011), *Crimes, Harms, and Wrongs: on the principles of criminalisation*, Oxford: Hart Publishing.

SIMON, J. (2004), 'Teaching Criminal Law in an Era of Governing through Crime', 48, *St. Louis University Law Journal*, 1313–45.

SMITH, K.J.M. (1998), *Lawyers, Legislators and Theorists*, Oxford: Clarendon Press.

SMITH, R. (1981), *Trial by Medicine*, Edinburgh: Edinburgh University Press 1981.

STEPHEN, J.F. (1893), *A History of the Criminal Law of England*, London: Macmillan.

STUNTZ, W.J. (2001), 'The Pathological Politics of Criminal Law', *Michigan Law Review*, 100, 505–600.

—— (2011), *The Collapse of American Criminal Justice*, Cambridge: Harvard University Press.

TADROS, V. and TIERNEY, S (2004), 'The Presumption of Innocence and the Human Rights Act', 67 *Modern Law Review*, 402–34.

THEORETICAL CRIMINOLOGY (2010), *Special Issue—Penal Parsimony*, 14(3).

VON HIRSCH, A. (1993), *Censure and Sanctions*, Oxford: Oxford University Press.

—— *et al.* (eds) (2003), *Restorative Justice and Criminal Justice*, Oxford: Hart Publishing.

WHITMAN, J. (2003), *Harsh Justice: Criminal Punishment and the Widening Divide between America and Europe*, New York: Oxford University Press.

WIENER, M. (1990), *Reconstructing the Criminal: Culture, Law and Policy in England,1830–1914*, Cambridge: Cambridge University Press.

WILLIAMS, G. (1953, (2nd edn, 1961)), *Criminal Law: The General Part*, London: Stevens.

—— (1983, 2nd edn), *A Textbook of Criminal Law*, London: Stevens.

WILSON, J. Q. and KELLING, G. L. (1982), 'Broken Windows: the police and neighbourhood safety', *Atlantic Monthly*, 29–38.

ZEDNER, L. (1991), *Women, Crime and Custody in Victorian England*, Oxford: Oxford University Press.

—— (2004), *Criminal Justice*, Oxford: Oxford University Press.

—— (2006), 'Policing before and after the Police: the historical antecedents of contemporary crime control', 40 *British Journal of Criminology*, 78–96.

—— (2010), 'Security, the State and the Citizen: the changing architecture of crime control', *New Criminal Law Review*, 13(2): 379–403.

—— (2011), 'Putting Crime back on the Criminological Agenda', in M. Bosworth and C. Hoyle (eds), *What is Criminology?*, Oxford: Oxford University Press.

# 7

# OVERTAKING ON THE LEFT? THE POLITICS OF LAW AND ORDER IN THE 'BIG SOCIETY'

*David Downes and Rod Morgan*

## INTRODUCTION

This chapter, like its predecessors in previous editions of this *Handbook*, concerns the public contestation of crime and disorder—debates about which phenomena should be defined as such, how crime and disorder events are interpreted, and, above all, how they are reacted to. Our key players are: the major political parties; ministers in the Home Office and the Ministry of Justice and their Opposition teams; senior civil servants who, despite their non-political role, bear crucial advisory responsibilities; criminal justice pressure and interest groups; and the mass media. What follows is necessarily a highly abbreviated account. Perfect comprehension cannot be achieved even when key players' words are quoted. We have not space to consider the detail of timing, context, and much else. Our purpose is limited: to demonstrate a point or change of direction rather than to convey some total reality.

We have always emphasized that compared with the contested party politics of the economy, foreign affairs, health, education, etc., those of 'law and order' are of relatively recent origin: they emerged in the mid-1960s, and came decisively to the fore in the 1979 General Election which heralded the decade of Thatcherism. This absence from party political discourse seems now to be surprising. We tend to think of law and order as emotive, fundamentally political issues: we have become used to the fact that they arouse passionate political debate. But it was not always so. The fact that it was not for so long testifies perhaps to the strength of belief that crime, like the weather, is beyond political influence; and that the operation of the law and criminal justice should be above it. This is not to deny that criminal law reform has long been regarded as the prerogative of Parliament. But once laws are enacted, the liberal doctrine of the separation of powers holds that their enforcement is the preserve of the police and the judiciary. Hence, bipartisanship regarding criminal justice issues was the rule rather than the exception for most of the 20th century. Even at the fringes of political life, few challenges were made to this profound consensus.

This bipartisan approach was largely abandoned in the 1970s and 1980s though we may in the twenty-first century be witnessing a return to some underlying agreement. Party political squabbles today are largely about relative levels of expenditure on law and order services, police numbers, and the like. Moreover, contemporary campaigns typically involve one or more competitively expressive gestures about what should be done with some particular group of deviants—predatory psychopaths, grave young offenders, or suspected terrorists, for example—recently the high-profile subject of concern. But closer analysis of party statements generally reveals that this sound and fury masks substantial agreement that the incidence of volume crime—common property crime and public disorder—is not easily reduced by legislation or the manner in which the law is applied, and that responsibility for reasserting control must be more widely dispersed.

The reasons for the change from a broadly bipartisan, to a sharply contested, and now a more twin-track, politics of law and order, are central to our concerns. The prelude to the change was significant because the nature of the bipartisanship was both complex and far from apolitical. But this was a politics more of nuance and inflection than of explicit difference. The politics of law-breaking are not necessarily those of order-defiance and the latter has a far more developed history, particularly in the realm of industrial conflict. Friction over public order legislation and its enforcement has throughout the period been far more evident than that concerning straightforward criminality. It was the achievement of 'Thatcherism' to blur the difference between the two and even to fuse them symbolically to political effect. And the consequences of the change have been more than a simple matter of the major parties taking up starkly opposing stances across the range of relevant issues. Despite new, overt differences, a species of second-order consensus has emerged to replace former orthodoxies. Moreover, the politics of law and order are not confined to the party sphere. Extra-parliamentary processes have often been more vigorous than those at Westminster, and developments at local government level, or formulations by pressure groups and lobbies, have frequently been the stimulus for national attention. Finally, the eruption of particular scandals and concerns, via a rapidly changing media framework, have consistently proved catalysts for changing policies. We shall address these topics in turn.

## BRITISH GENERAL ELECTIONS AND 'LAW AND ORDER' 1945–2010

Earlier versions of this chapter (Downes and Morgan 1992, 1997, 2002, 2007) examined in some detail how law and order issues figured in the 19 General Elections from 1945 to 2005 inclusive. Those of our readers interested in that detail should refer to those earlier versions. For present purposes it is necessary only to summarize what those analyses demonstrated as a prelude to a close examination of the 2010 Election when New Labour lost after 13 years in power and the Conservative-Liberal Democrat Coalition was formed.

## FROM ATTLEE TO THATCHER TO BLAIR AND BROWN: THE POST-WAR MANIFESTOS AND CAMPAIGNS 1945–2005

In 1945 the huge task of post-war reconstruction led the three main political parties to contend overwhelmingly about the priorities of rebuilding the economy and constructing the 'welfare state'. A form of consensus prevailed, usually known as 'Butskellism', which limited political conflict. Full employment, core entitlements to receive mainstream public services, a mixed economy and economic growth based on Keynesian assumptions, were broadly accepted as shared goals. Issues relating to crime, policing, and criminal justice were minor, taken-for-granted aspects of this consensus and did not significantly figure in the five post-war elections from 1945–1959. During the 1960s 'law and order' issues began to creep into manifesto statements. Recorded crime rates had begun steeply to rise and all three parties began to indicate how they would pursue policies more effectively to combat crime. But they did not suggest that crime was attributable to the policies of the party in government.

All that changed in the 1970s. The Conservatives began to argue that Labour in government was responsible for aspects of the worsening crime figures. By 1979, the incoming Thatcher Government claimed a much stronger connection, both during their victorious 1979 Election campaign and subsequently, between crime, protest, and the industrial disputes during the time of the preceding Labour administration. This set the tone for the 1980s and the following 18 years of continuous Conservative rule. The Conservatives fused the issues of law-breaking and order-defiance. They attacked not just the policies but the integrity of Labour. They refashioned their traditional claim to be the natural party of government, representing the order of established authority. They successfully pinned to Labour responsibility for the alleged 'ungovernability' of Britain. They capitalized on widespread public fears about: national decline; loss of economic competitiveness and bad industrial relations; the growth of permissiveness and declining public morals; fear of crime, inner city decay and the extravagances of youth fashion and street protests. They made restoring the 'rule of law', which they claimed Labour had undermined, one of their five major tasks. They undertook to do so by implementing a whole raft of specific law and order policies and spending more on law and order services (police, courts, and prisons) while economising elsewhere. They dispelled the last vestiges of the bipartisan consensus on law and order.

Neither Labour nor the Liberals initially made much of a response to the gradually raised law and order stakes. But they abandoned their self-restraint in 1979. They also began to devote space to these issues in their manifestos and campaigns. But Labour stuck to its traditional objective of creating 'one nation' by attacking 'the social deprivation which allows crime to flourish' and continued to put its faith in the welfare state. Most of Labour's law and order policy was implicitly to be found elsewhere in its manifesto, in its social and economic policies.

The evidence suggests that the stance developed by the Conservatives during the 1970s was greatly to the detriment of Labour. Opinion polls showed that 'maintaining law and order' grew in importance and in 1979 *no* policy placed the Conservatives so far ahead of Labour (Butler and Kavanagh 1980: 163). Yet Thatcherite rhetoric ran well ahead of Thatcherite policies: it was only under the post-Thatcher premiership of John Major, and in the context of New Labour's rebranding as 'tough on crime', that characteristically 'Thatcherite' policies matched her rhetoric on law and order and criminal justice reform (Farrall and Hay 2010).

Hence the Conservatives' tough stance in the early '80s was the prelude to a *bravura* performance, given that the decade witnessed a continued rise in recorded crime, a rash of ferocious inner-city disorders, and the bitter, year-long Miners' Strike of 1984–5. Labour initially stuck to their 'one nation' position, focusing on 'healing the wounds' brought about by unemployment and the Conservative cuts in public expenditure. They also promised to repeal some of the police powers granted by the Police and Criminal Evidence Act 1984. By contrast the Liberals (and subsequently the Liberal Democrats) took a more radically reformist position, arguing for incorporation into domestic law of the European Convention of Human Rights, the creation of a Ministry of Justice, and local authority crime prevention units. In the 1987 and 1992 elections, however, all the main parties began to adjust their positions, displaying more realism and restraint. The Conservatives no longer claimed that their policies would straightforwardly reduce the incidence of crime: crime prevention was now a task for everyone because the origins of crime lie 'deep in society'. Meanwhile Labour abandoned its opposition to the new police powers and assured voters, vis à vis the governance of the police, that they would not tamper with police responsibility for operational matters. Labour also began playing the Conservatives at their own law and order game. In the 1987 election they attributed to Conservative policies the continued steady rise in recorded crime and in 1992 called for greater police numbers. But they failed to press home this attack. The Conservatives accused them of being 'soft and flabby on crime' and unveiled a poster depicting a policeman with one hand tied behind his back. The opinion poll evidence suggested that the Conservatives still inspired greater confidence on this issue, though the gap had narrowed somewhat due to a steepening rise in the crime rate in the context of high unemployment. By September 1993, however, Labour were neck-and-neck on crime, law and order, and by May 1994 moved into the lead they held more or less continuously for a decade (Ipsos MORI, 2010).

By the early 1990s law and order issues were less prominent than a decade earlier. A new second-order consensus had emerged. No party could any longer afford to cede the law and order ground to the opposition: all parties felt obliged to address it in some way. They all: asserted their support for the police and the need to increase their effectiveness; agreed that crime prevention and victim support were priorities; and accepted the logic of 'bifurcation' (Bottoms 1977), according to which longer custodial sentences for serious, repeat and dangerous offenders, but an enhanced range of non-custodial measures for minor, occasional offenders, were considered appropriate. Following the 1992 election, however, Labour began systematically to fashion a more resolutely critical law and order stance skilfully summarized in Tony Blair's borrowed American slogan 'tough on crime, tough on the causes of crime'.

Law and order issues were not prominent in the election campaigns of 1997, 2001, or 2005. In their manifestos all three major political parties devoted what has in recent years become the required high proportion of space to community safety, policing, and criminal justice issues. In 2001, and even more so in 2005, coverage of immigration and political asylum questions was added to this mix. New Labour displayed their 'law and order' laurels (crime down, the time taken to bring persistent young offenders to court halved, and so on) but were careful not to rest on them. Much remained to be done. However, none of these detailed messages attracted much press comment or inspired high-profile inter-party argument during the campaigns. In all three elections it was: the management of the economy; the future shape of taxation; Britain's place in Europe; constitutional issues; and the general quality of public services; which assumed the greatest importance (Butler and Kavanagh 1997). It was 'the economy, stupid' and everything else—including the effective management of crime—appeared derivative.

Through an assiduous programme of modernization, New Labour had established themselves as a credible party to take up the reins of government and after two terms in government claimed now to be *the* party of 'law and order'. By their failure to criticize Conservative proposals while in Opposition, and by their legislation and other initiatives while in Government, it was the 'tough on crime' part of their slogan that they emphasized. It was not that they were unable in 2001 and 2005 to point to policy initiatives which addressed the 'causes of crime' and diminished 'social exclusion', but the latter policies were noticeably less hard-hitting than the ones being pursued against criminals. After eight years in office Labour were convincingly able to claim to be managing crime. The Conservatives fired their best shots but were unable effectively to resurrect the old adage that Labour were 'soft': it was manifestly not the case; in fact New Labour were by now attracting considerable criticism for carelessness with civil liberties.

## THE 2010 GENERAL ELECTION AND FORMATION OF THE CONSERVATIVE–LIBERAL DEMOCRAT COALITION

The 2010 Election seems likely to be accorded an historical significance similar to that of 1945 and 1979: one of seismic change. It followed the deepest economic recession since the 1920s, a recession involving a banking crisis so serious that it called into question the regulatory capacity of the state, the economic competence of the Government, and the critical faculties of the Opposition. All three major political parties were led by new leaders whose fitness to be Prime Minister was widely doubted, albeit for different reasons. In the case of Labour, the succession of Gordon Brown from Tony Blair in 2008 was clouded by long-lasting, fratricidal, party in-fighting, the reputational pall resulting from the decision to invade Iraq and military engagement in Afghanistan judged likely by many commentators to result in ignominy and many more pointless deaths. MPs generally were tainted by a parliamentary expenses scandal in which both sides of the House of Commons were mired (see below). For the first time in a British General Election all three parties agreed that their leaders, Gordon Brown, David Cameron, and Nicholas Clegg, would participate in a series of television debates during which, it was generally agreed, no decisive knockout blows were landed. The opinion polls throughout the campaign suggested that the outcome of the election would not be decisive. In this feverish, highly charged, political debate, 'law and order' issues scarcely figured. There were the customary, by now obligatory, references in the manifestos, but none of the party leaders chose an aspect of 'law and order' to belabour their opponents in the television debates or elsewhere.

The Labour Party devoted one of ten manifesto chapters to 'crime and immigration'. It summarized achievements during 13 years in government combined with undertakings to consolidate existing policies. The record high number of police and police community support officers, would in future be where the public wanted them, visible, on the beat. Crime was down but for the '50,000 most dysfunctional families who cause misery to their neighbours, we will provide Family Intervention Projects—proven to tackle anti-social behaviour—a no-nonsense regime of one-to-one support with tough sanctions for non-compliance' (Labour Party 2010: 5.3). Likewise with persistent young offenders, gun and knife crime, binge drinking, and anti-social behaviour generally, the Government had introduced tough, effective measures that were working, but the measures would now be targeted and applied more intensively. 'Community payback', Labour's brand-name for the unpaid work community sanction, had been toughened: offenders were now to be seen doing hard work, in public, in orange jackets. An additional 26,000 prison places had been provided since 1997, offenders were going to prison for longer and there would be provided yet more places, 96,000 overall, by 2014. Finally immigration was now being effectively controlled with an entry points system.

The Conservative Manifesto set out very similar law and order targets and solutions but did so from a different starting point. 'Broken Britain' was to be repaired by means of the 'Big Society'. Boldly stated in large graphics on a red background was the proclamation 'There is such a thing as society: But it's not the same thing as the state'. The 'Big Society' was not to be 'Big Government', the tag attached to Labour. Cameron's team sought explicitly to distance the Conservative Party from what had become, in the popular imagination at least, a key aspect of Thatcherism, the lauding of individualist over social solutions. In the same way that Blair successfully established New Labour in the mid-1990s as a party that could be trusted to deliver 'law and order' by distancing itself from some radically law and order-challenging aspects of the Old Labour record (Downes and Morgan 2007: 208–22) so the Conservatives sought the high, electoral, middle ground by emphasizing that they believed in 'society' and proposed overtaking New Labour on what, in key symbolic terms, constitutes the left.

This meant an end to Labour's top-down approach to policy and micro-management of services. The Conservatives would:

> give the people much more say about the things that affect their daily lives. We will make government, politics and public services much more open and transparent... and... give the people who work in our public services much greater responsibility. But, in return, they will have to answer to the people. All these measures will help restore trust in our broken political system. (Conservative Party 2010: *ix*)

The keywords were devolution, localism, restored discretion, partnership working, responsibility. Labour's interpretation of the criminal statistics was rejected: violent crime had risen and instead of crime fighting the police had been deluged with bureaucratic 'form filling' and 'box-ticking'. The police would have discretion restored to them: the *quid pro quo* was that they would be made more accountable to local people through the creation of directly elected police commissioners who would have the power to set local policing priorities (a proposal which harked back to Labour Party plans in the early 1980s to empower local police authorities—see Lustgarten 1986). A raft of measures was promised to curb binge drinking and the 'blunt instrument' of the ASBO would be replaced by earlier and more focused sanctions. Knife crime would be tackled more vigorously and victims looked after better. A Border Police Force would be created. Sentencing would be reformed so that the courts could fix minimum and maximum periods of imprisonment. Prisons would be made more purposeful by creating Prison and Rehabilitation Trusts and a system of payment by results. Most telling, however, was the Conservative's promise to restore civil liberties which under New Labour had been subject to 'unprecedented attack'. 'Huge databases' had been compiled to 'track the activities of millions of perfectly innocent people, giving public bodies extraordinary powers to intervene in the way we live our lives' (ibid.: 79). Labour's plans for ID cards would be scrapped, the Human Rights Act would be replaced with a UK Bill of Rights, the Information Commissioner would be given increased powers to penalize any public body mismanaging data about citizens, the ability of local authorities to use anti-terrorism powers to spy on people would be curbed, and the police would no longer be allowed to retain DNA samples of people not subsequently convicted.

The Liberal Democrats covered very similar law and order ground. They would introduce directly elected police authorities (rather than individual commissioners) and cut police bureaucracy, but also promised to appoint 3,000 extra beat officers. They also would appoint a Border Police Force. Regarding sentencing they proposed that Neighbourhood Justice Panels be established so that residents could themselves decide how minor offences and offenders were dealt with, They wanted to see wider use of restorative justice measures, would make prisoners contribute earned money to a victim compensation fund, and introduce a presumption against use of short-term prison sentences. They also would restore civil liberties.

Not only did 'law and order' not figure as a major election issue in 2010 but close examination of the parties' specific proposals reveals that the policies they undertook to pursue if elected were very similar. The clear water that the Conservatives sought to open up between themselves and Labour was less blue than pink. The Big Idea they promulgated was strategic, cultural, about the nature of governance itself. Labour was painted as Big Government, high spending, statist, authoritarian, and managerialist. The Conservatives would remove from both citizens and practitioners working in the major public services, including criminal justice, the hampering, bureaucratic reins installed by Labour, restoring to practitioners their traditional liberties and lost professional discretion. In this the Conservative manifesto pitch was ideologically closer to the traditional values of the Liberal than to the Labour Party and it was therefore not surprising that in the jockeying that took place after the inconclusive election results were announced it was a Conservative–Lib Dem and not a Labour-Lib Dem Coalition Government that emerged.

The opinion polls proved accurate: the election results were close. With 306 seats the Conservatives gained heavily, but were 20 seats short of an outright majority. With 258 seats Labour lost heavily, but not as badly as some had feared. And despite the positive prominence gained by Nick Clegg as a result of his performance in the TV debates, the Liberal Democrats, with 57 seats, failed to make their hoped-for breakthrough: indeed they lost five seats. No party won the unalloyed confidence of the electorate. There followed an unprecedented five days of negotiation between the parties, most of it between the Conservatives and the Liberal Democrats. On the fourth day Gordon Brown resigned as Labour leader and on the fifth David Cameron was invited to form a coalition government. The Conservative-Liberal Democrat Agreement, published a week later (HM Government 2010), achieved competitive status with the manifestos on which the electorate had voted. Out went the Liberal Democrat undertaking to provide more beat police officers. In went the Conservative plan for directly elected police commissioners. Sentencing policy and the case for a bill of rights was to be reviewed. ID cards were immediately scrapped. Civil liberties in various guises were to be restored. The Agreement was almost entirely about specific policy propositions rather than policy values. Thus the Big Society was not mentioned. But the foreword spoke of redistributing power 'from Westminster and Whitehall to councils communities and homes' so that 'wherever possible' people could 'call the shots over the decisions that affect their lives' (ibid.: 7). Four months later, however, in the anxiously awaited Comprehensive Spending Review White Paper which announced how the Coalition would deal with the national deficit through public expenditure cuts, the Conservative Big Idea was restated. The spending priorities and departmental budgetary settlements were underpinned by the aim of radically reforming public services to build the *Big Society* 'where everyone plays their part.... shifting power away from central government to the local level, as well as getting the best possible value for taxpayers' money' (HM Treasury 2010: 6).

## CRIME AND THE 'BIG SOCIETY': A NEW CONSERVATISM?

By 2010 the Conservative Party had substantially lost what used to be said to be its principal strength—its oneness with traditional British sovereignty (Parkin 1967; Honderich 1990) and its status as the natural party of government. It was now a party with an identity problem. It had lost three elections in a row, was led by its fourth leader, David Cameron, since John Major's resignation after the General Election of 1997 and its parliamentary leadership was largely without ministerial experience. The Labour Party, meanwhile, had morphed into what appeared, until the banking crisis of 2008, to be a managerially successful version of 'Thatcherism' and, even when the crisis broke, its leader, Gordon Brown, appeared to have a better grasp of what should be done than other international leaders.

New Labour had enthusiastically embraced policies and principles associated with neo-liberalism rather than social democracy. It had eschewed increases in direct taxation, adopting in 2009 a 50 pence top rate only as an emergency measure on earnings over £150,000 per year. It had pursued public-private partnerships in the capital renewal and management of public services ranging from public transport to schools and hospitals. Though the Party still derived a substantial proportion of its income from the trade unions it had also attracted the largesse of wealthy figures in the City. It had shaken off its identification with the underdog and radical challenge. It had been 'tough on crime'. It had had no hesitation in vigorously wielding the stick rather than the carrot to deal with offenders, young and old, whom focus groups and the British Crime Survey identified as a source of public concern. The rhetoric of 'zero tolerance' had been deployed (Jones and Newburn 2006) and the logic of 'prison works' effectively bought into (Downes 2001). Tony Blair had proclaimed 'the end of the 1960s liberal consensus on law and order': 'the rules of the game', he said, 'had been changed', 'law-abiding citizens' were now the Party's 'boss' (Morgan 2006). There were many more offenders in prison and many more had been criminalized (see Lösel, this volume).

Whether New Labour had truly introduced during 13 years in government more than 50 criminal justice-related bills and created over 4,400 new criminal offences (*Sunday Times*, 14 March 2010) depends on how one does the calculation. But at least one Labour ex-Home Secretary was prepared to admit *mea culpa* in this regard (Clarke 2009). There had been waves of new statutes and huge change: police and court powers had been greatly increased. In response to the terrorist threat, for example, when Labour came to power the longest period a suspect could be held in police detention without charge was four days, a provision of more than a decade's standing. In 2000 Labour raised the limit to seven days, in 2003 to 14 days and in 2006 to 28 days. In 2008 the Government then attempted to raise it to 90 days, was defeated in the Commons, and then went for 42 days, only to be defeated in the Lords. As a former Lord Chief Justice, quoting Benjamin Franklin, put it in response to Tony Blair's claim that it was a 'dangerous misjudgement' to give priority to civil liberties or Gordon Brown's assertion that he put 'security' first, 'he who would put security before liberty deserves neither' (Bingham 2010: 136). It was an excoriating judicial judgement on New Labour's record.

Whether Britain was in 2010 a safer country as a result of Labour's 'law and order' policies is open to doubt. Volume crime had undoubtedly declined substantially since the mid-1990s, though the Government's claim that this decline was to a large extent the consequence of tougher sentencing was accepted by few analysts. Further there was no shortage of voices suggesting that Labour's civil liberties record, combined with the Government's invasion and occupation of Iraq, was putting at risk the security of the nation, a charge given substance by the appearance of home-grown Islamic terrorism in 2005 and 2007. The evidence from the British Crime Survey (BCS) indicated that though people generally thought their risk of being victimized by crime or anti-social behaviour locally had significantly reduced, their concerns about crime nationally remained largely unaltered (Flatley *et al.* 2010, ch. 5). The fact that people did not feel safer (Reiner 2007: chs 3 and 5) may be one reason for the Labour Government not benefiting more electorally from the overall fall in the crime rate during their 13 years in office.

Given its position as the traditional party of 'law and order' the Conservatives were thus faced with a dilemma. On what basis was Labour to be criticized? How was the Conservative Party to re-establish its appeal? The answer lay in its re-working of the One Nation Conservativism of Benjamin Disraeli and David Cameron's insistence, almost a year after attaining office and in the face of growing media cynicism, including that expressed in sections of the normally supportive Tory press, that the Big Society was his 'personal mission' and represented the Party's 'fundamental political philosophy' (Cameron—speech at Somerset House, 14 February 2011). Support for this proposition was to be found in a burgeoning Conservative or otherwise supportive literature (Blond 2010; Norman 2010; Halpern 2010).

The 2010 Conservative Manifesto emphasized Britain's divided state after 13 years of Labour Government. The country was 'broken', riven by inequality, split north and south, lacking in social mobility, mired in debt, blighted by unemployment. The Labour Party was responsible for much of this division. Despite massive state spending, the root cause of the huge national debt, social inequality stood at a record high and the number of people living in poverty had risen in recent years (Conservative Party 2010: 35). The British economy was unbalanced. The Conservative Party would promote fairness, togetherness, partnership, and personal responsibility. Their invitation to the people was 'to join' a 'Government of Britain' which would be more devolved and transparent.

The Conservative leadership faced obvious difficulties getting these messages across, not least because when in opposition they had pressed the Government continually for ever-lighter regulation of corporate and investment finance. But Gordon Brown's jibe that Conservative policy had been 'dreamt up on the playing fields of Eton' did not go well either. Labour had been conspicuously at war with itself. It had alienated large sections of trade union opinion and working-class voters. Its outposts in Scotland and Wales remained substantially Old Labour. It had split the country over its foreign policy. Its public service reforms were the source of widespread disquiet among middle-class floating voters as well as on the left.

In the event the Conservative invitation to join the government was taken up to a greater extent than bargained for. But the coalition with the Liberal Democrats became an expressive opportunity for the Conservative One Nation–Big Society image. The compromise between the two parties was spelt out (HM Government 2010). Though the *Coalition Agreement* dealt mostly with specific policy propositions rather than policy values, its foreword spoke of redistributing power 'from Westminster and Whitehall to councils communities and homes' (ibid.: 7). Likewise the long-awaited *Comprehensive Spending Review* published in October 2010 emphasized that the Government's spending priorities and departmental budgetary settlements were underpinned by the aim of radically reforming public services to build the *Big Society* (HM Treasury 2010: 6). This meant, *inter alia*:

- 'localizing power and funding', the removal of resourcing ring-fences, and 'extending use of personal budgets for service users;'
- 'cutting the burdens on frontline staff, including policing';
- 'increased diversity of provision in public services through further use of payment by results, removing barriers to greater independent provision, and supporting communities, citizens and volunteers to play a greater role in shaping and providing services'; and
- 'improving the transparency, efficiency and accountability of public services' (ibid.: 8).

The Home Office spelt out what this meant specifically for the police. The Coalition partners had by now agreed what to do about the governance of the police (on which issue the *Coalition Agreement* had been silent). There would be directly elected Police and Crime Commissioners able to determine policing priorities, the police would be obliged to publish monthly local crime statistics, and there would be regular neighbourhood beat meetings. There would be an end to 'bureaucratic accountability'—meaning no more national targets and institutional structures 'simplified' (Home Office 2010: 54). All this would be in the context of a 23 per cent reduction in real terms in the overall Home Office budget over four years.

In December 2010 a Green Paper, *Breaking the Cycle*, on penal policy spelt out the direction ahead (Ministry of Justice 2010). Alongside the traditionally tough sounding phrases (ensuring 'hard', 'challenging' work in prisons, tougher curfew requirements, more 'demanding' community payback schemes, the deportation of foreign offenders, and no resort to early prison release schemes) was substantial evidence of intended restraint. Pathfinder projects designed to reduce the number of young offenders in custody were to be launched. Proposals significantly to reduce resort to indeterminate sentences and ease the release of the dramatically increased number of prisoners already serving indeterminate sentences for public protection (IPPs—see Jacobson and Hough 2010) (ibid.: 55) were outlined. An undertaking was given to restore to the police, youth justice workers, probation officers, and sentencers, decision-making discretion. Greater resort to restorative justice procedures, a proposition earlier commended by an independent inquiry into youth justice (Independent Commission 2010; see also Lösel, this volume), was promised. Moreover, all of these proposals were robustly defended, in the face of considerable scepticism from within the Conservative Party and the media, by Kenneth Clarke, a Minister for Justice noted for his independence and self-confidence. Here, conspicuously, was an experienced minister with no political ambitions for preferment. He appeared to mean it, even if his motivation proves largely to save money. Whether even so formidable a politician can carry it off, in the face of growing Tory backbench unease, remains to be seen.

The intervention by the Prime Minister in June 2011 ruling out larger sentencing discounts for early guilty pleas (a proposition canvassed in the Green Paper) was a clear sign of nervousness (Ministry of Justice 2011) and the decision to replace the public sector management of an existing prison, Winson Green in Birmingham, by a private company suggests a background motive of a more traditional kind for the Conservative Party. In the past, only new prisons have been open to private as well as public tenders, so this broke new ground at a time when the main emphasis is meant to be on reducing the prison population and evaluating modes of assessing reoffending rates.

The penal pressure groups, long critical of New Labour's emphasis on 'governing through crime' (Garland 2001; Simon 2007)—that is, applying criminal justice measures to social problems arguably more effectively addressed by other means (Halpern 2010: 64–5)—cautiously welcomed the Coalition's indicated direction of travel. Trends already heading downwards—the number of young offenders in custody and entering the youth justice system—were being pushed further downwards, the adult prison population stabilized, and the Ministry of Justice announced that several new prison building projects had been scrapped and three existing prisons were to close. Their caution, however, arose out of their difficulty deciding whether the glass was half full or empty. For there were good reasons also to sound alarums.

First, if the party political, law and order 'arms race' was to be abandoned or cooled at Westminster, might it not be resurrected, possibly more intensively, locally with the election of Police and Crime Commissioners? Who would stand for these posts, on what issues would they campaign, and who would vote for them? Would this not likely act as a powerful pressure on the police—particularly at a time of sharply rising youth unemployment and possibly increased social disaffection—to make increased use of the anti-social behaviour and criminal sanctions the parsimonious use of which the criminal justice expenditure cuts suggested would now be sensible? Possibly not if the 'Big Society' became a reality. But was that likely? Most of the voluntary sector partners providing support services to offenders in the community—mentoring organizations, drugs and alcohol services, employment and training advice, debt counsellors, housing providers, etc.—did so on the basis of central or local state contracts or grants. Yet during late winter 2010–11 it became apparent that local government expenditure cuts were as severe, if not severer, than anything being faced by the police, the courts, and the penal services. Nor do the proposed reforms return to local authorities the freedom to set their own levels of local taxation: the 'cap' brought in by the Thatcher Government in the 1980s still applies. Localism is in effect a Do-It-Yourself society, lacking the essential powers to raise money, and expecting community groups to supply funding streams, all at a time of economic retrenchment.

The signs were that the size and quality of the voluntary sector was under threat. The small charities that would now have to bid for contracts of formidable complexity lacked the infrastructure to do so. Would this sector not be likely swallowed up by the big commercial players, Serco, Capita, etc. Moreover, it was all very well talking about citizens volunteering to provide services—the evidence was that a considerable proportion did so already—but volunteers were not a free good. They might not be paid. But they had to be recruited, trained, organized, and professionally backed up. This was as true in the sphere of criminal justice as anywhere else (on volunteers in the criminal justice system see Gill and Mawby 1990: on the cost of voluntary lay magistrates compared to that of professional district judges see Morgan and Russell 2000: ch. 6).

Coalition ministers were keen to argue in spring 2011 that the Big Society was about more than the use of volunteers or even partnerships to deliver services. It was about delivering services differently. So, for example, Home Office ministers, drawing on inspection reports, argued that the costs of various policing functions differed markedly between police forces. If all forces were to do as well, that is, as cost-effectively as the best, then substantial savings could be achieved without negatively affecting the quality of front-line services (see Herbert 2011, drawing on HMIC 2010). Similar messages were being delivered to probation trusts and youth offending teams. 'Back office' (HR and finance) and 'middle office' (training, custody, control room staffing, and criminal justice administration) police functions could be merged with those of other forces or outsourced. In the field of probation, the organization and management of unpaid work could be outsourced. Indeed in all the criminal justice services analysis needed to be done to determine which functions *had* to be undertaken by, for example, sworn police officers or qualified probation officers with a view to employing civilians to perform those functions which could equally be done, probably at lower cost, by them. The big agenda item, however—no longer the elephant in the room because it was being encouraged to trumpet—was the outsourcing of services to the commercial or voluntary sectors. That is, the Coalition was pursuing even more vigorously the mixed economy, public sector reforms embarked on by New Labour. Behind the Big Society lurks the 'Big Market'.

The fate of criminal justice services in the 'Big Society' may possibly be gauged from experience to date with the Coalition's health service reforms. The health service, the Conservative Manifesto assured, was to be spared the expenditure cuts imposed on other public services and, the Coalition Agreement declared: 'We will stop the top-down reorganisations of the NHS that have got in the way of patient care' (2010: 24). Yet in autumn 2010 the Government announced radical top-down reorganization plans. NHS Trusts were to be replaced by locally-based GP consortia dispensing 80 billion pounds worth of health-care. Coalition politics did not legitimize so radical a reversal, justified by the Minister of Health, Andrew Lansley, as more cost-effective and sensitive to local needs. This defence was assailed by practically all the health service professional groups and individual politicians, including leading Conservatives and Liberal Democrats, across the political spectrum. The result was rapid intervention by No 10, a 10-week 'listening exercise' resulting in an announcement in June 2011 that the health service reform bill was to be fundamentally amended. The role of competition—opening up the NHS to 'every willing provider'—was to be watered down, GPs would have to share their commissioning responsibilities with other health service professionals, and the 2013 deadline for change was dropped: the new commissioning consortia would now be phased in as and when local plans were developed.

One commentator's policy incoherence, confusion, and humiliating U-turn is of course another's wise response to intelligent consultation, a sign of strength rather than weakness. Coalition politics, moreover, necessarily involve a more complex trajectory for policy development than characterizes single party governments with clear majorities. The best one can say after a year of Coalition Government is that there are clear indications of policy travel, but the speed and extent of change remains uncertain. U-turns or major rethinks may be the order of the day but certain underlying objectives and mechanisms are unlikely to be dispensed with.

Thus, for example, the well-documented disaster of the Private Finance Initiatives (PFIs) under New Labour is the model: long-term, unbreakable, and costly contracts to build what public finances could have built far cheaper, given the political will. But the public finances will still have to foot the bill. Moreover, Labour's embrace of PFIs was ultimately to enable the NHS to begin to bring its provision closer to the levels of Western Europe, where countries like France had spent 2–3 per cent more of their GDP on health services. The Tory motive may be more radical: to open up the NHS to the market and transform local authorities into predominantly commissioning agencies rather than providers.

All of which implies that criminal justice services will be similarly contracted out. Some police forces have already contracted out 'back' and 'middle' office functions to commercial security company consortia and the Ministry of Justice is at the time of writing commissioning private/voluntary sector consortia to supervise the supervision of unpaid work, a community sentence previously managed directly by the probation service. The 2010 Green Paper's 'rehabilitation revolution' will hinge on commercial and charitable agencies being refunded for success in reducing rates of reoffending by those ex-offenders and ex-prisoners consigned to their care. The processes of evaluation and audit have yet to be spelt out, but the precedents are none too encouraging. The pursuit of targets holds great delusional potential. Stan Cohen's classic metaphor of 'visions of social control' (1985) as applied to crime control—net-widening, mesh thinning, blurring and penetration—also apply only too well to the new mixed political economy: the market's net over service provision is ever wider; its mesh is increasingly dense; the lines between public and private provision are blurring fast; and the market penetrates ever more deeply into the public sector. In short, the very basis for Social Democracy to survive, let alone flourish, faces systematic erosion, as state intervention into the market for key service provision is not only rolled back, but camouflaged and rebranded.

Moreover, deep and sudden cuts to key services, combined with rising unemployment, is a likely catalyst for rises in the crime rate to recur, despite the immense investment in crime prevention technology over the past two decades. If so, one truly welcome aspect of the Coalition's programme—to reduce the prison population from its unprecedented level of 85,000 in 2010—will be vulnerable to the same fate as the last significant fall in prison numbers. In 1993, the 'Prison Works' mantra of Michael Howard was coined in the wake of an over 40 per cent rise in the crime rate between 1988 and 1992, the result in part of the long and deep recession over that period, and the prelude to a doubling of the prison population over the next decade and a half. And, right on cue, as it were, the August 2011 riots (see below) have led to a prison population of over 86,000.

## FROM PRESSURE GROUPS TO POLICY-MAKING: RECENT DEVELOPMENTS

In the previous edition of this *Handbook*, we gave a more extensive analysis than space now allows of the following:

- The changing landscape of pressure group and interest group activity. The rise, proliferation, and professionalization of penal pressure and reform groups from the mid 1960s was related to the rise in crime and prison population rates from the mid-1950s onwards, and the problems such trends generated for established traditions of policy-making.

- The emergence of reform consortia from the late 1970s culminated in the Woolf Inquiry and Report into Prison Disturbances 1990–1, which set a new standard for more democratic participation in consultative procedures in the inquiry stage. By contrast, ministerial policy initiatives all too often ignored such processes, seeing them as tiresome constraints on bold leadership. Perhaps the outstanding example of the damage wreaked by such means is the 2003 Imprisonment for Public Protection Act, a product of David Blunkett's term of office as Home Secretary, which led to the unwarranted rise in the prison population of several thousand prisoners (Hough 2010). A consequence is that key issues lack adequate public and parliamentary debate. For example, police tactics of 'kettling'—the confinement of demonstrators to an unduly limited public space for several hours—has been no more a matter of debate than the Special Patrol Groups three decades ago, whose activities sparked the Brixton Riots and brought about the death of Blair Peach in Southall.

- So-called think tanks were a new trend in the recent past, rivals to single-issue pressure groups, which they displaced to some extent as influences on the early stages of policy-making. They are now somewhat less prominent, needing a flow of new initiatives to maintain momentum and appeal that is difficult to sustain.

- The mass media were for a time in the 1980s and 1990s open to the voices of reform groups, whose grasp of the criminal justice and penal fields was often more authoritative than those of party or official spokesmen. However, so great is the jostling for air time that the trend is for penal reform groups to act as background support for celebrity dissenters, such as Lord Woolf and Lord Ramsbotham, on specific issues.

The past few years have added little that is new to this panorama. Pressure groups with a research base have continued to proliferate. Recent additions to make an impact on the scene have been Skills for Justice, Make Justice Work, and the Restorative Justice Council. The Centre for the Study of Crime and Justice has produced a stream of reports relevant to criminal justice reform. The International Prison Study Centre challenges the UK's disproportionately high prison population in constant comparative perspective. The key contribution of such pressure groups is perhaps not so much to spark change off as to provide informed support for government when it moves policy in their preferred direction. The current Green Paper, *Breaking the Cycle*, on penal policy has offered just such an opportunity, espousing the need to reduce the prison population with community alternatives, including restorative justice in various forms as an alternative to short prison sentences in particular.

After 17 years of almost incessant rises in the prison population, despite a declining crime rate and a more or less stable number of convictions, the trend is entirely in line with successive governments' involvement in the so-called 'arms race' of 'tough on crime' policies, it is undeniably difficult to account for the embrace of reductionist policies by Kenneth Clarke, the current Minister of Justice. Twenty years ago, it was Clarke who instigated the move away from the key clauses in the 1991 Criminal Justice Act which were designed to produce that same effect. As things stand, the aim is modest: to reduce the prison population from 86,000 to 83,000 by 2014. It remains to be seen whether or not he can succeed: but the very attempt is notable, given the bipartisan acceptance of the logic of 'Prison Works' for the past two decades.

In the British context, it is worth noting that no penal pressure group is in favour of penal expansion, not even interest groups such as the Prison Governors Association and the Prison Officers Association. Contrast this with the situation in the USA, where think tanks such as the Manhattan Institute have proved potent backers of mass imprisonment. Loïc Wacquant (2009) has argued that right wing think tanks in the USA have played a momentous role in promoting mass imprisonment in America and penal expansion globally, especially in Western Europe. As Cohen remarks in criticizing this line of analysis, this turns them into 'carriers of much too massive a load. And whilst American think-tanks may well have their French counterparts, it is doubtful whether they have British counterparts' (Cohen 2010: 388; see also Newburn 2010). Arguably far more influential have been the electoral successes of, first, Republican and then, with Clinton, Democrat Parties wielding the 'tough on crime' banner, imported into Britain by Blair, Brown, and Straw following the electioneering oracle, Philip Gould. However, Cohen is too sweeping in his dismissal of 'broken windows', 'zero tolerance', and 'Prison Works' as 'Mickey Mouse ideas'. They *do* have theoretical as well as popular resonance, and cannot be lightly discounted.

What seems to have happened in Britain instead is not so much the rise of punitive think tanks—though the persistence of the case for penal expansion is evident in the more extreme right wing analyses of Civitas and the Adam Smith Institute—as the ebbing of the influence of the better informed pressure groups. The bases for mounting authoritative 'Truth to Power' challenges have also been eroded from within government, by the shackling of such research bodies as the Home Office Research Unit, and independently of government by its hyperactive policy-making. The key event in that regard is the dismissal in 2009 of Professor David Nutt, as Chairman of the main governmental advisory body on drugs, the Drugs Advisory Council. The Council had long advised government to downgrade the categorization of cannabis from B to C, the least dangerous class of illegal drug. David Blunkett as Home Secretary, *contra* his impetuosity in introducing indeterminate sentencing for 'dangerous' prisoners, had listened to their advice and gone some way to acting on it. In 2008 his successor, Jacqui Smith reversed that decision against the Committee's advice, on what appeared to be the instruction of the tabloid press. Nutt then adopted a more high-profile role to get his case across, at one point asserting, on the evidence, that horse riding was more lethally dangerous than consuming the drug ecstasy. He was dismissed from his position by the then Home Secretary, Alan Johnson. It has nevertheless still proved possible for highly informed and energetic lobbying to carry the day against over-hasty and misconceived legislation, as in the successful campaign in 2008 undertaken by *Liberty* to oppose the attempt by Gordon Brown, on assuming the Premiership, to push through an extension of the length of detention without trial in the case of terrorism suspects from 28 to 42 days.

## MATTERS OF SCANDAL AND CONCERN

The remaining variable is the unpredictable realm of scandal and concern. Both parliamentary and extra-parliamentary groupings can be utterly outpaced by events which explode in such a way that unusual responses are called for by 'public opinion'—a phenomenon for which media attention is often taken as proxy. In the law and order realm, four types of events seemingly dwarf all others in their dramatic impact on politics and policy: prison escapes; high-profile crimes; miscarriages of justice; and riotous assemblies. Examples are legion, and in previous editions we have singled out:

- prison escapes in 1965–6 and 1994–5, and the prison occupations in 1990;
- the murder of James Bulger in 1993;
- the murder of Stephen Lawrence in 1993, the bungled police response, the campaign for a re-trial by his parents, and the subsequent inquiry and report chaired by Lord Macpherson, with its key conclusion on 'institutional racism';
- the paedophile murder of Sarah Payne by Roy Whiting in 2000;
- the murder of Zahid Mubarek in Feltham Young Offenders Institution in 2000; the release of the Guildford Four, the Birmingham Six, and the Maguire Seven, all Irish suspects convicted of multiple homicides by verdicts declared 'unsafe' as long as 15–17 years later;
- the miasma of debate surrounding immigration, both legal and illegal; refugees and asylum-seeking; migrant labour; host/migrant community tensions; and majority/ethnic minority tensions, erupting in several towns and cities into riotous conflicts (e.g. Bradford 2001, Birmingham 2005);
- the response to domestic Islamic terrorism in 2005 and 2007 in the wake of 9/11, the invasion of Iraq and the war in Afghanistan;
- post-millennium scandals, concerns, and tensions arising out of our dependence on and exploitation of migrant labour from Eastern Europe and elsewhere.

Responses to such 'events' are highly variable. Governments at times act promptly and decisively, as with the establishment of the Mountbatten Inquiry into the prison escapes of the mid-1960s, and the Woolf Inquiry into the occupation of Strangeways Prison and other prison disturbances in 1990. Their recommendations are at times followed, at times not; sometimes they are acted on initially and then abandoned, or the reverse. There is no clear tariff of response or policy process. Three examples of events in the last four years knocking policy-makers off course, the consequences of which at the time writing remain highly speculative, are the parliamentary expenses and phone-hacking scandals and the five-day spree of violence, destruction, and looting of August 2011.

## THE PARLIAMENTARY EXPENSES SCANDAL

The most unanticipated scandal over the past four years has been the exposure of, and subsequent effort to reformulate control over, parliamentary expenses claimed by Members of Parliament in the House of Commons and, to a far lesser extent, the House of Lords. 'A High Court judgment [in 2008] had finally quashed attempts by MPs to prevent exposure of their expense claims, a conspiracy to keep them hidden in which both Labour and the Tories were complicit.' (Rawnsley 2010: 639) The original demand for the release of expenses data had been made early in 2008 by three journalists under Freedom of Information legislation introduced by Labour in 1998, but had been rejected by the Speaker as 'unlawfully intrusive'. The High Court judgment led the Commons to promise a full version of expenses would be published but in the event it was heavily 'redacted'. Before that could occur, however, the entire body of data was leaked to the *Daily Telegraph* who published them in a string of exclusives after 8 May 2009. The resulting scandal eclipsed even the earlier saga of the 'cash for honours' investigation of New Labour fundraisers by Scotland Yard, which lasted 15 months in 2007–8 and involved the arrest, without subsequent charge, of Lord Levy, a close personal friend and advisor of Prime Minister Blair.

MPs and Lords had long been allowed to claim allowances and expenses incurred as essential for the pursuance of their parliamentary duties, and a few disturbing cases of MPs claiming incomes for family members doing 'research' which turned out to be spurious had already aroused adverse and bitter comment. But it still came as a nasty revelation to the British public that such bizarre claims had been allowed as—most notoriously—for an ornamental 'duck house' for the pond of a Conservative MP. The scope and scale of the claims for such items as chocolate bars and carrier bags 'made MPs look pathetically money-grubbing... Luxury items—massage chairs, champagne flutes, silk cushions, whirlpool baths, plasma TV screens—suggested the funding of sybaritic life-styles on the taxpayer... The most lucrative racket was the practice of "flipping". MPs played the property market at the taxpayers' expense by making claims for mortgage interest and refurbishment on one house and then changing the desig-nation of their "second home" to start claiming on another.' (Rawnsley: 646) Both ministers as well as backbenchers were seen to be involved, and the sense of public out-rage mounted as the examples of widespread malfeasance multiplied. Compounding the resulting cynicism about the 'political class' as a whole was the evident incompe-tence with which the system had been operated by the Commons authorities, and the attempts to block any real exposé of what was occurring. Sadly, even MPs who had remained utterly virtuous became subject to blanket condemnation.

Resignations, standing down as a candidate in the 2010 election, and in a few cases prosecution, conviction, and imprisonment have followed. The whole system of par-liamentary expenses has been overhauled. But the major fallout from the expenses scandal fell disproportionately on the New Labour Government, whose handling of the affair fell well short of competence. Nor has the experience proved a fillip to the better understanding of and sympathy for those labelled criminal more generally. The recent attempt to enact voting for prisoners, following a European Court of Human Rights directive, was thrown out after a series of venomous attacks on the very notion of the right of prisoners to be enfranchised, especially by the former Home Secretary and Minister of Justice, Jack Straw, who has expressed pride in his human rights record, and the Prime Minister, David Cameron, who pronounced himself 'sickened' by the very idea.

## PHONE-HACKING AND THE INTRUSION OF PRIVACY

On 22 January 2011 Andy Coulson resigned as director of communications for David Cameron's office. His resignation was forced by what he called the 'wave of allegations' about his involvement in illegal phone hacking during his editorship of the *News of the World* (NoW). He had resigned as editor in January 2007, when the 'royal editor' of that Sunday paper, Clive Goodman, along with a private investigator, Glenn Mulcaire, were jailed for hacking into the phones of members of the royal household. Coulson insisted he had had no knowledge of what the paper claimed had been the actions of 'one rogue reporter', and on that basis the police wound up their investigation of the entire case. A few months later Cameron appointed Coulson as communications director for the then Conservative Opposition.

Nevertheless, the suspicion persisted that a great deal more illegality was being covered up, along with concerns as to why the police had terminated their investigations so swiftly. The whole issue was revived by the pursuit of further demands by civil litigants ranging from the actor Sienna Miller, who accepted an out-of-court settlement to Lord Prescott, the former Deputy Prime Minister, who sought no cash settlement at all but pressed for confirmation that their phones had been tapped on the basis of leaks from the earlier investigation. Payouts by way of out-of-court settlements running into two million pounds had been made to several litigants, fuelling suspicion that the paper had a great deal to hide. As the *News of the Screws*, as it has traditionally been known, was a key part of the Murdoch empire, along with the *Sun*, the *Times*, and the *Sunday Times*, and as Rupert Murdoch was in the course of a highly controversial bid to extend his ownership of *BSkyB* media, pressure on the police mounted to reopen the investigation. The story as a whole had long been pursued by the *Guardian* newspaper, whose leading investigative reporter, Nick Davies, saw such developments as far more prevalent than the misdeeds of one reporter on one newspaper (Davies 2008). The likelihood was that changing technology coinciding with dwindling circulations was fuelling a search for scandal by frankly illegal means.

At stake was the increasing anxiety that key institutions of the state, the police, the Crown Prosecution Service, and Parliament itself, are unable effectively to withstand the power of the Murdoch empire, a trans-national media corporation whose writ has purportedly played a major role in deciding elections since that of Margaret Thatcher in 1979. Attempts to elicit more information by the Select Committee on Media and Culture had been brushed aside by Coulson and Rebekah Brooks, his editorial predecessor, then Head of News International. However, under pressure from those who felt they had been victims of illegal phone hacking, which now included the former Prime Minister, Gordon Brown, the police reopened their enquiries. It remained to be seen how much further they would dare to go, especially as alleged police corruption is part of the story, in that media payments to some officers even at senior levels for information on newsworthy cases had long been taken for granted as part of what Davies terms the 'dark arts' culture. The feeling was still rife that it would all 'blow over' and—after a few minor changes to press regulation—it would be back to 'business as usual'.

On Tuesday 5 July 2011, the *Guardian* led with the report that transformed a matter of major concern into a full-blown national scandal. In 2002, NoW journalists had hacked into the mobile phone of Milly Dowler, a 13-year-old murder victim, in such a way, before her body was found, as to have misled her family into hoping she was still alive. Overnight, a sleazy way of assembling gossip about the hidden lives of 'celebrities' became an odious intrusion wantonly inflicted on the 'ordinary' families of victims of lethal violence: not only the Dowler family but also those of the victims of the Soham murders, of the 7/7 bombings in 2005 and of soldiers killed in Afghanistan. News Corp's interests in the USA were reportedly under scrutiny for similar practices there. The Murdochs and Rebekah Brooks were suddenly at bay, pressured into reappearing before the Select Committee on Culture, Media and Sport. Though contrite, they contrived unconvincingly to present themselves as victims of the corporation they had created and run. In what looked like a 'scorched earth' policy rather than an act of contrition, Rupert Murdoch closed the NoW down, with over 200 employees cast out of a job. The sense of public outrage triggered the resignations of top Metropolitan police officers, Sir Paul Stephenson, its Chief, for hiring a former NoW editor as a consultant, and John Yates, an Assistant Commissioner, who had ruled against any reopening of the hacking investigation in 2009. The scandal came close to enveloping David Cameron, for his encounters with News International numbering 26 meetings in 15 months, and raising questions about his role in the BSkyB takeover bid, which Murdoch had to withdraw pending the outcome of a judicial inquiry. Forced to react to demands, not least from a suddenly revived Opposition leader, Ed Miliband, Cameron set up two inquiries into the scandal: the first, to be chaired by Lord Justice Leveson, is to be into both the scale and character of the phone illegalities and its ramifications into the media and the police—though including the BBC in its remit was seen by some as at best an irrelevance, at worst a wrecking tactic—and into how to improve its regulation; the second to report on the 'culture, practices and ethics' of the British press. These responses were interpreted as a welcome reassertion of authority by Parliament over a media empire which had appeared all too successful at suborning key figures in core institutions. The outcomes will take years to materialize, but perhaps the best verdict is that of Nick Davies, who did most to maintain scrutiny of what Boris Johnson, Mayor of London, had dismissed as 'a load of codswallop':

> The truth is that what was once the occasional indulgence of a few shifty crime correspondents has become the regular habit of most news organisations. The hypocrisy is wonderful to behold. These organisations exist to tell the truth and yet routinely they lie about themselves. Many of these organisations have been the loudest voices in the law-and-order lobby, calling for tougher penalties against villains, tougher action against antisocial behaviour, even while they themselves indulge in bribery, corruption and the theft of confidential information. (Davies 2008: 286)

## THE 'SHOPPING SPREE WITH VIOLENCE' DISORDERS OF AUGUST 2011

It is generally unwise to focus in a text which will be read for several years on events that are literally unfolding as one goes to press. But it seems virtually certain that the unprecedented disorders of 6–10 August 2011 will have a major impact on the 'law and order' debate in Britain for some time.

On 6 August a peaceful protest took place in Tottenham, North London about the fatal police shooting of a suspect, Mark Duggan. Such protests are not without precedent and sometimes have escalated into disorders involving battles with the police. But on this occasion the protest seems to have sparked a chain reaction lasting five days of major disorders comprising massive destruction, violence, and looting in many locations across the country (other London boroughs, Birmingham, Bristol, Gloucester, Manchester, Liverpool, etc.). The participants appear to have been drawn, depending on the location, from all racial groups and though the early evidence suggests that the initial perpetrators were overwhelmingly older adolescents and young adults, the profile of the hundreds of persons arrested and charged in the immediate aftermath suggests that older adults and very young children were drawn into what the media dubbed a 'shopping spree with violence', that is the targeted looting of shops selling fashionable clothing and electrical goods that are emblematic of consumerist society. Property and vehicles were set ablaze. Violence was used against people defending their property as well as the police and the emergency services. At least four people died as a direct result: many more were injured.

The response of the police to these events triggered a constitutional conflict the reverberations of which will almost certainly make an impact on the Coalition Government's policy programme discussed earlier in this chapter. The police response to the initial events in Tottenham was to treat them as the police would normally respond to a limited and focused public protest. But a combination of text messaging and BMX bikes set off fast moving, sporadic, hit and run attacks in many places to which the police were ill-equipped and slow to respond. They were literally outpaced and out-manoeuvred. Voices were soon raised that the rioters were acting with impunity with the police apparently impotent. Politicians, notably Prime Minister Cameron, Home Secretary Theresa May, and London Mayor Boris Johnson soon became aware that these were no minor disorders. They returned hotfoot from their summer holiday locations and immediately convened Cobra, the government's civil contingency emergency forum, following which statements were made about the policing of the disorders which subsequently gave rise to angry responses from senior chief constables. The Prime Minister gave the impression that it was the return and intervention of ministers that prompted the police taking more vigorous measures. Theresa May stated that she had 'ordered' chief constables to cancel all leave, an instruction which Sir Hugh Orde, President of the Association of Chief Police Officers bluntly reminded everyone that she had not the constitutional power to do. The return of ministers, Orde said, had been 'irrelevant': the police had made all the operational decisions which led to a more appropriate response to the events and after five days to their cessation.

Criminal justice processes were then levered into an unprecedented, higher gear. Within a week almost 2,000 suspects had been arrested for disturbance-related offences with scores already convicted and sentenced. Some courts sat throughout the night. The early evidence suggested that bail was denied in the majority of cases and that custodial sentences of a severe, exemplary nature way above the sentencing guideline tariffs were being imposed. Public arguments soon arose about the appropriateness of these responses. Meanwhile police representatives were not slow to argue that were the Government to carry through its plans to cut police budgets, with the implication of reduced police numbers, then the public would be put at risk of further disorders which the police would be less capable to contain, a proposition to which Boris Johnson gave some support. British police pride was further dented by Cameron's decision to employ a celebrity American police chief, Bill Bratton, as a police advisor.

The Government's programme for slimming police budgets, restraining the use of custody, and introducing directly elected police and crime commissioners will in the light of August 2011 now be contentious to a degree which few commentators anticipated. Its plans may be knocked off course. On the other hand several commentators noted that the disturbances demonstrated, with the exception of the Mayor of London, a signal lack of civic leadership in contemporary British governance. This may enhance the Coalition's proposals that there be directly elected local government leaders, mayors, and police and crime commissioners, in England's major cities.

## CONCLUSION

How has all this changed the politics of law and order? In previous editions, we have sought to analyse how New Labour had forfeited its long-standing commitment to civil liberties, among other 'hostages to fortune' which it defined as electorally damaging. Despite introducing human rights legislation and the Freedom of Information Act, such policies as the extension of remand in custody to 28 days (having failed to achieve 90 and then 42 days) for terrorism suspects, the ill-drafted Imprisonment for Public Protection Act, and a swathe of 'tough on crime' measures such as ASBOs and the proposed Titan prisons, meant that the erosion of civil liberties became in itself a 'hostage to fortune' for Labour. Ironically, by their coalition with the Liberal Democrats, and the unexpected advocacy of the case for reducing the prison population by Kenneth Clarke as Minister of Justice, the Conservatives could claim to have overtaken Labour as the party of liberal reform in criminal justice and penal policy. The fact that they have launched a programme of unprecedented cuts to the public sector will, however, in all probability soon begin to offset and undermine their potential changes on this front.

In other respects, the very fact that so high-profile a minister as Clarke has embraced the case for decarceration, however limited, and the 'rehabilitation revolution', however difficult to achieve, is the first sign for almost 20 years that the 'governing through crime' agenda, with its imperative to promote ever tougher punitive policies, may have become debased currency. There are signs that this is the case also with the media coverage of serious offences which, in the recent past, would have triggered 'heart of darkness' imagery. Examples include the case of two young boys (at Edlington, near Doncaster, South Yorkshire in April 2009) who assaulted and even tortured a boy to the point where his death could easily have resulted; and the revelation at an inquest in April 2009 of the mother (Fiona Pilkington) of a disabled child (18-year-old Francesca Hardwick) whose harassment by local youths (at Barwell, Leicestershire in April 2007) led, despite repeated calls to the police and local social services, to no prosecutions and their joint suicide . Reportage of these cases was certainly dramatic but fell short of the intense demonization of those responsible for the child on-child homicide of James Bulger (see David Green 2007 for a cross-national analysis). Compared with the bipartisan rivalries in claiming supremacy in the 'tough on crime' stakes over the past two decades, however, these may simply prove to be straws in the wind, and all too ephemeral in the event of a recurrence of rising crime rates and a spate of high-profile crimes. Parsimony in the advocacy and use of criminal justice solutions for Britain's social ills will certainly not have been made easier to deliver in the wake of the August 2011 urban disturbances.

## ■ SELECTED FURTHER READING

There have been few studies of the part played by 'law and order' in British political life. Philip Norton's (1984), *Law and Order and British Politics* and Mike Brake and Chris Hale's (1992), *Public Order and Private Lives: the Politics of Law and Order,* the latter a highly critical account of the Thatcher years, are exceptions. David Downes' (1992) edited collection, *Unravelling Criminal Justice,* contains relevant essays, particularly those by Bottoms and Stevenson on the extent and difficulties of the liberal consensus, and McBarnet on the burgeoning field of tax avoidance and evasion. Roger Hood's (1974) collection, *Crime, Criminology and Public Policy: Essays in Honour of Leon Radzinowicz,* provides detailed scrutiny of the public policy issues of the mid-period, and Terence Morris' (1989), *Crime and Criminal Justice in Britain since 1945* covers a longer period with shrewd political insight. The criminal justice record in government of New Labour since 1997 is the subject of critical scrutiny by Michael Tonry (2003) in *Confronting Crime* and David Green's (2008), *When Children Kill Children: Penal Populism and Political Culture* and Nicola Lacey's (2008), *The Prisoners' Dilemma: Political Economy and Punishment on Contemporary Democracies* provide incisive analyses of the politics of particular penal policy binds. The collections of essays edited by Kevin Stenson and Richard Sullivan, *Crime, Risk and Justice: The politics of crime control in liberal democracies* (Willan, 2001) and Tim Newburn and Richard Sparks, *Criminal Justice and Political Cultures – National and international dimensions of crime control* (Willan 2004), together with Trevor Jones and Tim Newburn's monograph, *Policy Transfer and Criminal Justice* (Open University Press 2006), place British developments in a broader, international, comparative dimension, in particular tracing American influence. Regarding the latter Jonathan Simon's (2007), *Governing Through Crime* is indispensable. Michael Cavadino and James Dignan's (2006), *Penal Systems: A Comparative Approach* does the same specifically for penal policy. Finally, Mick Ryan (*Penal Policy and Political Culture in England and Wales,* 2003) is a political scientist in criminology who over many years has documented the micro-politics of penal reform in the wider political economy of Britain.

## ■ REFERENCES

ASHWORTH, A. (2011), 'Avoiding criminal justice: diversion and sentencing', in A. Silvestri (ed.), *Lessons for the Coalition: an end of term report on New Labour and criminal justice,* London: Centre for Crime and Justice Studies.

BINGHAM, T. (2010), *The Rule of Law,* London: Allen Lane.

BLOND, P. (2010), *Red Tory: How Left and Right have broken Britain and how we can fix it,* London: Faber and Faber.

BOTTOMS, A. E. (1974), 'Reflections on the Renaissance of Dangerousness', *Howard Journal,* 16: 70–96.

BRAKE, M. and HALE, C. (1992), *Public Order and Private Lives: the Politics of Law and Order,* London: Routledge.

BUTLER, D. and KAVANAGH, D. (1980), *The British General Election 1979,* Basingstoke: Macmillan.

—— and KAVANAGH, D. (1997), *The British General Election 1997,* Basingstoke: Macmillan.

CAVADINO, M. and DIGNAN, J. (2006), *Penal Systems: A Comparative Approach,* London: Sage.

CENTRE FOR SOCIAL JUSTICE (2009a), *'A Force to be Reckoned With': A Policy Report by the Police Reform Working Group,* London: CSJ.

—— (2009b), *'Locked Up Potential': A Strategy for Reforming Prisons and Rehabilitating Prisoners,* London: CSJ.

—— (2010), *The Centre for Social Justice Green Paper on Criminal Justice and Addiction,* London: CSJ.

CLARKE, C. (2009), 'Labour can Unify Liberty and Security', *Guardian,* 21 October 2009.

COHEN, S. (2010), 'Ideology? What ideology?', *Criminology and Criminal Justice,* 10(4): 387–92 (November).

CONSERVATIVE PARTY (2010), *Invitation to Join the Government of Britain: the Conservative Manifesto 2010,* London: Conservative Party.

DAVIES, N. (2008), *Flat Earth News: An Award-Winning Reporter Exposes Falsehood, Distortion and Propaganda in the Global Media,* London: Chatto & Windus.

DOWNES, D. (2001), 'The macho penal economy', *Punishment and Society,* 3(1): 61–80.

—— (ed) (1992), *Unravelling Criminal Justice,* London: Macmillan.

—— and MORGAN, R. (1994), ' "Hostages to Fortune"?: The Politics of Law and Order in Post-War Britain', in M. Maguire, R. Morgan, and R. Reiner (eds), *The Oxford Handbook of Criminology,* 1st edn, Oxford: Oxford University Press.

—— and —— (1997), 'Dumping the "Hostages to Fortune"?: The Politics of Law and Order in Post-War Britain', in M. Maguire, R. Morgan R, and R. Reiner (eds), *The Oxford Handbook of Criminology*, 2nd edn, Oxford: Oxford University Press.

—— and —— (2002), 'The Skeletons in the Cupboard. The Politics of Law and Order at the Turn of the Millennium', in M. Maguire, R. Morgan, and R. Reiner (eds), *The Oxford Handbook of Criminology*, 3rd edn, Oxford: Oxford University Press.

—— and —— (2007), 'No Turning Back: The Politics of Law and Order into the Millennium', in M. Maguire, R. Morgan, and R. Reiner (eds), *The Oxford Handbook of Criminology*, 4th edn, Oxford: Oxford University Press.

FARRALL, S. and HAY, C. (2010), 'Not so Tough on Crime?: Why Weren't the Thatcher Governments More Radical in Reforming the Criminal Justice System?', *British Journal of Criminology*, 50(3), 550–69.

FLATLEY, J., KERSHAW, C., SMITH, K., CHAPLIN, R., and MOON, D. (2010), *Crime in England and Wales 2009/2010: Findings from the British Crime Survey and police recorded crime*, London: Home Office.

GARLAND, D. (2001), *The Culture of Control: Crime and Social Order in Contemporary Society*, Oxford: Oxford University Press.

GILL, M. and MAWBY, R. I. (1990), *Volunteers in the Criminal Justice System: A comparative study of probation, police and victim support*, Buckingham: Open University Press.

GREEN, D. (2008), *When Children Kill Children: Penal Populism and Political Culture*, Oxford: Clarendon.

HALPERN, D. (2010), *The Hidden Wealth of Nations*, Cambridge: Polity.

HM GOVERNMENT (2010), *The Coalition: our programme for government*, London: HM Government.

HER MAJESTY'S INSPECTORATE OF CONSTABULARY (2010), *Police Governance in Austerity*, London: HMIC.

HM TREASURY (2010), *Spending Review 2010*, Cm 7492, London: Stationery Office.

HONDERICH, T. (1990), *Conservatism*, London: Hamish Hamilton.

HOOD, R. (ed) (1974), *Crime, Criminology and Public Policy: Essays in Honour of Leon Radzinowicz*, London: Heinemann.

INDEPENDENT COMMISSION (2010), *Time for a Fresh Start: The report of the Independent Commission on Youth Crime and Antisocial Behaviour*, London: Police Foundation/Nuffield Foundation.

IPSOS-MORI (24 March 2010), *Best Party on Key Issues. Crime/Law and Order*.

JACOBSON, J. and HOUGH, M. (2010), *Unjust Deserts: imprisonment for public protection*, London: Prison Reform Trust.

JONES, T. and NEWBURN, T. (2006), *Policy Transfer and Criminal Justice*, Buckingham: Open University Press.

JUDT, T. (2007), *Postwar: A History of Europe since 1945*, London: Pimlico.

LABOUR PARTY (2010), *Manifesto: a Future Fair For All*, London: Labour Party.

LACEY, N. (2008), *The Prisoners' Dilemma: Political Economy and Punishment on Contemporary Democracies* (The Hamlyn Lectures 2007), Cambridge: Cambridge University Press.

LIBERAL DEMOCRATIC PARTY (2010), *The Liberal Democrat Manifesto 2010*, London: Liberal Democratic Party.

LUSTGARTEN, L. (1986), *The Governance of the Police*, London: Sweet and Maxwell.

MINISTRY OF JUSTICE (2010), *Breaking the Cycle: Effective Punishment, Rehabilitation and Sentencing of Offenders*, London: The Stationery Office.

—— (2011), *Breaking the Cycle: Government response*, London: Ministry of Justice.

MORGAN, R. (2006), 'With Respect to Order, the Rules of the Game Have Changed: New Labour's Dominance of the "Law and Order" Agenda', in T. Newburn and P. Rock (2006) (eds), *The Politics of Crime Control. Essays in Honour of David Downes*, Oxford: Clarendon.

—— and RUSSELL, N. (2006), *The Judiciary in the Magistrates Courts*, London: LCD/Home Office.

MORRIS, T. (1989), *Crime and Criminal Justice in Britain since 1945*, Oxford: Blackwell.

NEWBURN, T. (2010), 'Diffusion, differentiation and resistance in comparative penality', *Criminology and Criminal Justice*, 10 (4): 341–52 (November).

—— and SPARKS, R. (eds) (2004), *Criminal Justice and Political Cultures – National and international dimensions of crime control*, Cullompton, Devon: Willan.

NORMAN, J. (2010), *The Big Society: the anatomy of the new politics*, Buckingham: University of Buckingham Press.

NORTON, P. (1984), *Law and Order and British Politics*, Aldershot: Gower.

PARKIN, F. (1967), 'Working-Class Conservatives: A Theory of Political Deviance', *British Journal of Sociology*, 18(3). 270–00.

RAWNSLEY, A. (2010), *The End of the Party: The Rise and Fall of New Labour*, London: Viking.

REINER, R. (2007), *Law and Order: An Honest Citizen's Guide to Crime and Control*, Cambridge: Polity.

RYAN, M. (2003), *Penal Policy and Political Culture in England and Wales*, Shorfield-on-Loddon, Hants.: Waterside.

SILVESTRI, A. (ed.) (2011), *Lessons for the Coalition: an end of term report on New Labour and criminal justice*, London: Centre for Crime and Justice Studies.

SIMON, J. (2007), *Governing Through Crime: How the War on Crime Transformed American Democracy and Created a Culture of Fear*, Oxford: Oxford University Press.

STENSON, K. and SULLIVAN, R. (eds) (2001), *Crime, Risk and Justice: The politics of crime control in liberal democracies*, Cullompton, Devon: Willan.

TONRY, M. (2003), *Confronting Crime*, Cullompton, Devon: Willan.

TOYNBEE, P. and WALKER, D. (2010), *The Verdict: Did Labour Change Britain?*, London: Granta.

WACQUANT, L. (2009), *Prisons of Poverty*, expanded edn, Minneapolis: University of Minnesota Press.

# 8

# CRIMINAL STATISTICS AND THE CONSTRUCTION OF CRIME

*Mike Maguire*

## INTRODUCTION

This chapter explores a number of interrelated questions about 'crime levels', 'crime patterns', and 'crime trends' and how they are measured. These range from what may sound like (but are not) straightforward empirical and methodological questions, such as 'how much crime is there?', 'how is it changing?', and 'how do we know?', to more sociological and political questions about the relationships between, on the one hand, the kinds of crime data which are collected and published and, on the other, changing perceptions of the nature of 'the crime problem' and developments in criminal justice policy and the politics of crime control.

As elsewhere in the *Handbook*, the main focus will be on England and Wales, though examples from elsewhere will be drawn upon where appropriate. The discussion will centre around what are colloquially known as the 'official crime statistics': figures published on a regular basis by or on behalf of government to produce a national picture of the level of crime and to map trends over time. In England and Wales, these date back over 150 years. Until 2002, they consisted of compilations of offences recorded by the police, but since then have also included figures from the British Crime Survey (BCS). While for most of their history the status of the official statistics as a national 'barometer' of crime was rarely challenged, in the last 30 years (and especially over the last decade), they have come under increasingly critical scrutiny from academics, policy-makers, politicians, and the media. They have been criticized as 'unfit for purpose' in terms of new data needs, and the general picture they paint of the scale and changing contours of the 'crime problem' has been challenged as misleading and incomplete. There is also evidence of a decline in public trust in the published figures, reflecting a mismatch with commonly held perceptions of the 'true' state of crime as well as a growing reluctance to believe government statistics of any kind. The chapter will explore the reasons behind this shift in thinking and will examine some of the responses and recommended changes it has provoked.

The chapter is divided into three main sections. The first outlines the processes by which the official statistics are produced from their two main sources, police records and the BCS. It also looks at what the data from each appear to tell us about the scale of crime and trends over time, and to what extent they give similar, complementary, or contradictory messages. The second section examines, and explores the reasons behind, a rapid growth in demand for new kinds of information about crime which has been evident since the 1970s, fuelling (and being fuelled by) a massive expansion in data collection and analysis, and a 'pluralization' of sources, methodologies, and providers. Particular attention is paid to types of crime that are especially difficult to 'count', such as domestic violence, crimes within closed institutions, corporate fraud, cross-border and organized crime, and crimes by governments. While noting that the growth in information in these areas has served to highlight the limitations of the official statistics, it is argued that the overall state of knowledge about them remains patchy and contradictory, owing to the serious methodological challenges they present. The final section looks at recent proposals about the future of the official statistics, which have been prompted by continuing concerns about comprehensibility, coverage, integrity, and 'relevance'. These reveal basic dilemmas inherent in the concept of a single set of national statistics, such as whether it should strive for 'comprehensiveness' (in the metaphor used by the National Statistician, continually fill in missing pieces of a jigsaw) or for relevance to current policy needs, or whether it should simply aim to provide a stable and easily understood 'index' of more serious offences to allow reliable measurement of trends over time.

# THE 'OFFICIAL STATISTICS'

## HISTORICAL BACKGROUND

The idea of 'measuring' crime in a systematic way—for example, attempting to count the numbers of offences committed, or to determine where and when they most often occur—first came to prominence in France in the 1830s, where it was promoted by the so-called 'moral statisticians', Quetelet and Guerry, as part of a scientific vision of discovering laws and regularities in the social world akin to those that had been identified in the natural world (see, e.g., Beirne 1993). However, the idea was also highly compatible with the aims and practices of the centralized bureaucracies that were expanding across Europe in support of the emerging nation states. As theorists such as Foucault (1977) have argued, the compilation of detailed information about many aspects of social life was a crucial factor in the development of modernity, and closely tied up with the consolidation of governments' control over their populations. It was unsurprising, therefore, that the collection and analysis of crime data soon became predominantly the province of government employees, rather than academic scientists.

In England and Wales, particular value came to be attached to regular statistical series based on annual returns to the Home Office from the police and the courts in local areas, which were checked and aggregated by government statisticians. The first set of these national crime statistics was compiled in 1857 and soon settled into a published format which, despite periodic changes in terminology and coverage, remained remarkably similar until 2002. This took the form of an annual Command Paper under the title *Criminal Statistics, England and Wales*. The publication was divided into two main sections, one covering offences recorded by the police and the other 'offenders cautioned or found guilty'. Most of the tables on recorded crime comprised counts of specific types of offence, classified by legal categories and broken down by, for example, police force area. They also showed trends in the various totals over both the long and short term. The offender-based tables were mainly concerned with the types and lengths of sentence given for different categories of offence, broken down variously by age, sex, and area. Innovation in presentation or analysis was rare, as the statisticians (who over time became to some extent distanced from the policy-making world) attached higher priority to the accurate measurement of trends through consistent statistical series than to producing data or analysis geared to immediate practical needs.

The production of annual criminal statistics of these kinds has a number of potential purposes and uses, the prominence and value of which can change over time. Their introduction in England and Wales initially provided an important new window for central administrators on to what was going on in different areas of the country, and the statistics were increasingly used to assist them in allocating resources and monitoring court and police activities. At a more abstract level, they came to be seen as providing something akin to an official barometer of the 'moral health of the nation', paralleling the use of mortality statistics to assess its physical health. To some extent, too, they were taken as a measure of the success or failure of government policies in protecting the public from crime. However, until the late 1950s official crime rates generally remained low and there were few rapid upward trends to generate serious concern. There was also something of a tacit agreement among politicians that the power of governments to influence crime rates over the short term is limited, and it was not until much later that crime control began to be regarded as a major issue in General Elections (see Downes and Morgan, this volume). Thus while the publication of the annual volume of *Criminal Statistics* usually attracted some political debate and media attention, this was usually fairly muted and short-lived. Moreover, although (a) the police, as sole providers of crime data and (b) the Home Office, as the agency which determined how they should be recorded and presented, together had almost total control over how the shape and scale of the 'crime problem' were portrayed to the country, surprisingly few challenges were mounted against the validity of the data or the 'truth' of the picture they painted. As we shall see, this situation has since changed substantially. First, however, let us look more closely at the official statistics themselves.

## CRIMES RECORDED BY THE POLICE

### Raw totals

Let us begin by looking at what the traditional 'official statistics', based on crimes recorded by the police, would appear to tell us *if we were to take them entirely at face value.* These figures, it should first be noted, are misleadingly precise. The latest statistics available at the time of writing indicate that the total number of crimes recorded by the police in England and Wales in the financial year 2010/11[1] was 4,150,097 (Chaplin *et al.* 2011).

As the records date back over a very long period, it is interesting to look at long term trends in such figures. Figure 8.1 presents a graphical representation of the raw 'official totals' for the 135-year period 1876–2011. What immediately leaps out from this histogram is that, while there was relatively little change for the first 80 years, the period from the mid-1950s to the early 1990s saw an unprecedented sustained increase in recorded crime. It is also worth noting that a similar pattern is discernible in the recorded crime statistics of most other Western democracies. Trends since the early 1990s, which have been less clear (and have been obscured by major changes in recording practice), will be discussed later.

In addition to overall totals, the official crime statistics break recorded crimes down into separate offence groups. Table 8.1 shows in simplified form the contributions of the main such groups to the total number of offences recorded in 2010/11. The picture of the current 'crime problem' which emerges is one in which, as one might expect, the theft of property looms quite large: theft and handling offences (including those involving vehicles) together with burglaries constitute close to half of the total. However, the relative sizes of the different offence groups have changed markedly over time, and despite increasing in absolute numbers, thefts and burglaries now make up a smaller proportion of the total than they used to. By contrast, two offence groups in particular—criminal damage and violence against the person—have become much more prominent. The number of offences of criminal damage recorded is over 140 times higher than in the early 1950s, when it was an almost negligible category.[2] Likewise, the raw numbers of recorded offences of violence against the person have risen over the same period from under 7,000 to 822,000, and now make up 20 per cent of all recorded crime, compared with 2 per cent then.

### Interpreting the data: key issues to consider

Of course, none of the above figures should be taken at face value. If they are to be used to say anything sensible about the size and shape of the 'crime problem' or about trends over time, they have to be carefully interpreted. This necessitates at least a basic understanding of what kinds of data are collected and how, as well as consideration of the possibility that some, or even all, of a particular change in offence totals does not reflect a change in criminal behaviour, but is an artefact of changes in rules or behaviour involved in the production of the statistics—a comment, as we shall see, particularly pertinent to the period since 1998. Box 8.1 outlines some of the key factors which should be borne in mind when interpreting statistics derived from police records. These are discussed in a little more detail below.

---

[1] Before 1997, criminal statistics were presented on the basis of calendar years, but have since moved to the financial year (April to March).

[2] Between 1950 and 1954, the average annual recorded total of 'malicious injuries to property' was just over 5,000.

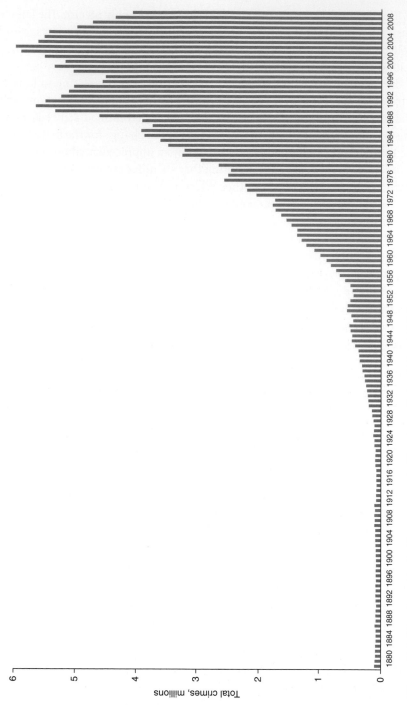

**Figure 8.1** 'Raw' totals of offences recorded by the police, 1876-2010/11

**Table 8.1** Offences recorded by the police, 2010/11

| Offence group | Number (to the nearest 1,000) | Per cent |
| --- | --- | --- |
| Theft/handling | 1,079,000 | 26 |
| Violence against the person | 822,000 | 20 |
| Criminal damage | 701,000 | 17 |
| Burglary | 522,000 | 13 |
| Theft of/from vehicles | 450,000 | 11 |
| Drugs | 232,000 | 6 |
| Fraud and forgery | 146,000 | 4 |
| Robbery | 76,000 | 2 |
| Sexual offences | 55,000 | 1 |
| Other | 67,000 | 2 |
| Total | 4,150,000 | 100 |

*Note:* percentages do not sum to 100 due to rounding.
*Source:* Adapted from Chaplin *et al.* (2011) *Crime in England and Wales 2010/11.* London: Home Office.

**BOX 8.1** KEY FACTORS AFFECTING RECORDED CRIME FIGURES

**1. The Notifiable Offence List**

The 'Notifiable Offence List' determines which offence categories are included when recorded crime figures are compiled; additions to, or removals from, the list can artificially raise or lower the overall total.

Legislation may create new offences or legalize behaviour that was previously defined as criminal; definitions of offences may also be significantly changed.

**2. Rules on the Counting and Classification of Offences**

The Home Office's 'counting rules' provide guidance on how many individual offences should be recorded when, for example, an offender repeats the same type of criminal behaviour many times within a short period; similarly, guidance is produced on the type of offence that should be recorded in different situations. The rules and guidance change over time.

**3. Police Recording Behaviour and the NCRS**

Despite increasingly prescriptive rules to limit it, the police inevitably retain some discretion as to which of the incidents observed by or reported to them are deemed to be crimes and recorded as such. How this discretion is exercised or constrained can be influenced by a wide variety of social, political, and institutional factors, and may change over time.

The key development in this context in recent years has been the introduction of the National Crime Recording Standard (NCRS), which has significantly increased the proportion of incidents reported to the police which end up as recorded offences.

**4. The Reporting Behaviour of the Public**

The propensity of the public to report crimes to the police may be affected by a range of factors, including views of the seriousness of particular forms of behaviour, degree of faith in the police, and more pragmatic considerations such as the need to report offences to support insurance claims; again, such factors can change over time.

## WHAT OFFICIALLY COUNTS AS CRIME AND WHAT DOES NOT? THE NOTIFIABLE OFFENCE LIST

The first point to stress is that the overall recorded crime totals do not include all types of offence. The statistical returns submitted by the police, on which they are based, include only those categories of crime that appear on the 'Notifiable Offence List'. This consists of all 'indictable' and 'triable either way' offences (i.e. those which must or may be tried in a Crown Court), as well as a relatively small selection of summary offences (i.e. offences triable only in magistrates' courts). As a result, large numbers of criminal offences processed by the police, not to mention those dealt with by other agencies, are by definition excluded from the published figures. The full totals of such offences are not known, as most of the available statistics refer only to those which result in a court conviction or other formal penalty, but they are clearly substantial. For example, in 2010/11, there were about 1,153,000 magistrates' court convictions and 49,000 Penalty Notices for Disorder for non-notifiable criminal offences (Chaplin *et al.* 2011: 23; on PNDs, see Padfield, Morgan, and Maguire, this volume). Again, numerous cases of tax and benefit fraud are known to HM Revenue & Customs or to benefits agencies, but remain uncounted because, although many would be classified as notifiable offences if recorded by the police, such agencies often use their administrative powers to levy financial penalties rather than take offenders to court (Levi 1993). The published figures also exclude over 10 million traffic and parking offences annually, dealt with by fixed penalty notices issued by the police or local authorities—although many would argue that these should not be regarded as 'crime'.

Traditionally, the main reason given for restricting the official figures largely to indictable offences (apart from a wish to avoid excessive bureaucratic burdens on the police) has been that the aim should be to provide a clear picture of the extent of, and trends in, crime above a certain level of seriousness, rather than one dominated by a multitude of minor infractions. However, the boundary between 'serious' and 'minor' forms of crime is both blurred and variable over time, and debates about the logic of including (or not) particular categories of offence in the recorded crime totals have periodically led the Home Office to change its instructions to police forces on how to complete their annual statistical returns. Such changes have in some cases produced significant 'artificial' rises or falls in the official figures. For example, a decision in 1977 to include offences of criminal damage of £20 or less, which had previously not been counted, immediately raised the 'total volume of crime' by about 7 per cent. More recently, in 1998/9, on the grounds of producing a more accurate and comprehensive picture of violent crime, it was decided to add to the Notifiable Offence List the summary offences of common assault, harassment, and assault on a constable. Between them, these added over 250,000 extra offences of 'violence against the person' to the total. While in such situations government statisticians make appropriate adjustments to tables or warn that direct year-on-year comparisons cannot be made, these caveats are often ignored in public (and particularly political and media) debates, and in the latter case a widespread impression was created of a major 'rise in violent crime'— ironically, as will be discussed later, at a time when the British Crime Survey was indicating a sizeable fall.

The Notifiable Offences List can also from time to time be affected by legislation which creates new criminal offences and redefines others, thus causing further problems for the measurement of trends. For example, under the Theft Act 1968 the definition of burglary, which had previously been restricted to 'breaking and entering' at night, was extended to include 'entering as a trespasser with intent' at any time, while offences such as 'housebreaking' and 'shopbreaking' disappeared (Maguire and Bennett 1982: 8–9). This necessitated several changes to the offence categories shown in *Criminal Statistics*, making it difficult to make meaningful comparisons pre- and post-1968 across a broad range of property crime. Other examples include the Public Order Act 1986, which created several new offences including 'violent disorder'; and the Fraud Act 2006, which changed and added offences relating especially to cheque fraud.

## RECORDING RULES: CLASSIFICATION AND COUNTING

In addition to the issue of which categories of offence are included, there are important points to consider about how individual crimes are both *classified* and *counted*. In many reported incidents it is not immediately obvious what kinds of offence, if any, have been committed. For example, if a thief steals items from close to a house without entering it, a decision may have to be made between recording an attempted burglary or a theft; similarly, there may be a fine line between a robbery and a theft from the person. Decisions in such cases can have a cumulative impact on the overall picture of crime produced, as burglaries and robberies are considerably more serious offences. Indeed, before 1998 (when common assault became a notifiable offence), decisions about the classification of minor acts of violence had a substantial effect on the overall scale of recorded crime, in that choices to record them as common assault (as opposed to, say, assault occasioning actual bodily harm) meant that they were excluded from the official statistics. Generally speaking, there was little central oversight of such decisions. However, over the last decade, the Home Office has adopted a much more prescriptive and interventionist approach, frequently issuing detailed instructions about how to classify different kinds of incident.

Similar comments apply to decisions about how many offences to record in complex or closely linked incidents. Some kinds of offence tend to be repeated many times within a short period, so that, though there may be several separate actions or people involved, they could be considered to form part of one concerted criminal incident. For example, a thief may go through 20 trouser pockets in a changing-room, or steal a cheque card and use it many times to obtain goods or cash. Equally, a large affray—for example, at a demonstration or football match—may involve numerous assaults by many people on many others; or a man may assault his partner virtually every night for a period of months or years. Until the late 1960s, little attention was paid to discrepancies between police forces in the numbers of separate offences recorded in such situations. However, following the Perks Committee in 1967, clearer 'counting rules' were established (Home Office 1971). These were significantly revised in 1998, partly to align them more closely with the counting rules used in the British Crime Survey. The basic rule is now that, wherever possible, the statistics should reflect the *number of victims*, rather than the number of criminal acts. This principle was previously applied in relation to violent offences, but was new for property offences. In the above examples, then, the changing room thief and the cheque fraudster, who might previously have produced only one offence each, would now produce several (depending upon how many victims can be identified). As under the previous rules, the spouse abuser is likely to be credited with only one offence, and the affray may produce a large number. Overall, it has been estimated that the joint impact of the inclusion of more summary offences and the changes in counting rules was to elevate the total number of recorded offences between 1997/8 and 1998/9 by about 14 per cent (Home Office 2001: 28).

In short, statisticians involved in the compilation and presentation of criminal statistics—and especially in the measurement of trends—have had to take account of a confusing array of changes in legislation, the Notifiable Offences List, and recording and counting rules, all of which have taken place within a relatively short period. Some idea of the complexity of their task can be gleaned from a glance at the notes to Table 2.04 in Chaplin *et al.* (2011), which shows recorded crime by offence type, from 1997 to 2010/11. There are no fewer than 41 notes, most of them explaining changes and discontinuities in particular rows of data. Again, while experts may be able to make informed judgements about the extent to which each of these changes affects any conclusions that might be drawn about trends over time, it is hardly to be expected that readers such as politicians or journalists will read the notes in detail or apply appropriate caution.

## POLICE RECORDING PRACTICE AND THE EFFECT OF THE NATIONAL CRIME RECORDING STANDARD

Of course, Home Office rules provide only the formal framework for the recording of crime. It is equally important to consider the extent to which these are followed in practice. Concerns about both the consistency and the integrity of police recording practices were frequently cited in the 1980s and 1990s as reason to doubt the validity of official crime statistics. Studies like those of Farrington and Dowds (1985), which explored the puzzle of why Nottinghamshire consistently produced exceptionally high crime rates, clearly demonstrated the existence of major differences between police forces in approaches to crime recording. Other researchers found evidence of dubious practices including, on the one hand, the 'cuffing' (hiding) of offences for reasons ranging from work avoidance to a wish to improve the overall clear up rate (Bottomley and Coleman 1981; Young 1991) and on the other, the recording (amounting to the 'creation') of large numbers of minor offences in order to elevate the crime rate, for example with a view to supporting a case for more resources.[3]

Partly in response to such concerns—but also to allow fairer comparisons to be made between police force areas when measuring their 'performance' in relation to

---

[3] One particularly strong critic in this regard, Hal Pepinsky, showed how significant increases in crime could be created simply by recording every trivial offence that comes to light: for example, in a small unpublished study in one subdivision of a British city he claimed that almost half the year's 'increase in crime' had been produced by the police recording every admission by one offender who stole milk bottles from doorsteps. On a wider scale, Selke and Pepinsky (1984) claimed that rises and falls in crime figures in Indiana could be shown to coincide closely with shifts in the political aims of the police.

crime reduction targets—new policy initiatives have during the last decade brought about some remarkable changes in recording practice. In 2002, a new National Crime Recording Standard (NCRS) was introduced. The NCRS was consciously designed to increase recording rates—in particular, to bring about closer correspondence between the numbers of 'crime incidents' logged and the number of 'crimes' recorded. It stipulated a basic rule that any incident log containing a report of a crime—most commonly, the result of a telephone call from a member of the public—should be taken at face value and *automatically* recorded as a crime. Thereafter, it could be removed from the crime records, with a supervisor's agreement (and subject to later audit), only if there was clear evidence that no offence had actually taken place.[4] This approach has been described as applying a *prima facie* principle, in contrast to the previously used 'evidential' approach, whereby crime reports tended to be included in the official records only if officers decided that there was clear evidence that an offence had actually been committed (Simmons 2000).

The available evidence suggests that the NCRS has had a significant effect on police recording behaviour. Calculations from BCS data indicated that the recording rate (i.e. the percentage of personal and household 'crimes' reported to the police that end up as recorded offences) rose from 62 per cent in 2000/1 to 75 per cent in 2003/4. The greatest impact was seen in figures on violence against the person, where there was an estimated 'NCRS effect' of 23 per cent in the first year of implementation (Simmons *et al.* 2003). As it took a number of years to establish the NCRS fully, it continued to have an 'inflationary' effect on crime statistics for quite a long period: as late as 2007, the Audit Commission was still reporting improvements in compliance as the slowest forces to change adapted to its requirements.[5] While this signals a success story in some respects, the implementation of the NCRS, like the changes to the Notifiable Offence List described earlier, made year-on-year comparisons of crime figures highly problematic, thus adding to the problem of identifying trends. It should also not be forgotten that there is a limit to how far discretion can be constrained and how closely practices can be monitored, and it remains to be seen to what extent the changes described will be maintained over the long term.

Finally, in this context, it should be noted that changes in the numbers of offences 'discovered' by the police themselves—for example during patrols, or through admissions by arrested offenders—as opposed to being reported by the public, can have an impact on recorded crime levels. The NCRS has less 'teeth' in such cases, where individual officers retain a high degree of individual discretion. The chances of officers observing relevant incidents are also affected by changes in police operational

---

[4] To give the NCRS more teeth, a national audit system was implemented, whereby files were regularly sampled to check whether the rules were being followed. Although this lasted only a few years, each police force still retains a Force Crime Registrar, who monitors the application of the counting rules and has a final say in any disputed recording decisions. There is also a high-level National Crime Recording Steering Group, which oversees efforts to promote consistency in recording practice, and Home Office statisticians are encouraged to investigate and report any unusual trends or patterns they notice which might signal deviation from the rules (Home Office 2011). Importantly, too, Her Majesty's Inspectorate of Constabulary takes a close interest in forces' compliance with guidelines, and at the time of writing is conducting a full review of crime data quality assurance systems in every force.

[5] In that year it assessed 38 of the 43 police forces in England as 'good' or 'excellent' for crime data quality, compared with 12 in 2003/4 (Audit Commission 2007).

priorities, the extent and nature of patrolling, or external pressures to 'do something' about particular kinds of behaviour. At local level, planned operations or 'crackdowns' will often result in an increase in arrests and the recording of many new offences; for example, strong policing of a pop festival is almost guaranteed to generate a boost in an area's recorded drug offences, while current concern about alcohol-related violence has led to greater police presence and more arrests around city centre pubs and clubs. Conversely, numbers may fall owing to reduced police interest in a particular type of crime, as in the early 1960s when, anticipating legislation to legalize homosexuality, most forces turned a blind eye to 'indecency between males' and the recorded total of such offences declined to half the previous level (Walker 1971). The introduction in Amsterdam of the well-known liberal policies towards the possession of drugs for personal consumption presumably had a similar effect on recorded drugs offences in the city.

## THE REPORTING BEHAVIOUR OF THE PUBLIC

Important as 'police-generated' offences are, it remains the case that the bulk of recorded crimes first come to official notice through reports from members of the public.[6] Decisions on whether to report possible offences to the police are influenced by a variety of factors, including views about the police and expectations of their response, the ease with which reports can be made (to which, for example, the spread of mobile phones has made a difference), the number of victims with insurance policies, and levels of public tolerance of particular kinds of behaviour—all of which can change markedly within a few years and hence have a significant 'artificial' effect on recorded crime trends. An often quoted example is a rise during the 1980s in victims' willingness to report rape, leading to a significant increase in recorded offences of this kind: this was partly explained by well publicized improvements in the treatment of victims such as the design of special facilities in police stations and a greater willingness on the part of police officers to believe their accounts (Blair 1984). Over the longer term, too, major social changes such as the gradual erosion of traditional communities and the increasing anonymity of life in urban areas may have made people more inclined to call in the police rather than 'sort the problem out' by themselves or with neighbours: this applies particularly to minor criminal behaviour by local children.

## OTHER CONSIDERATIONS AND POTENTIAL PITFALLS

In addition to the key factors discussed above, it is worth briefly mentioning three other potential pitfalls which should be borne in mind when interpreting police recorded statistics.

### Short-term 'trends'

One of the most common kinds of statistic featuring in newspaper headlines is references to apparent trends in crime (e.g. 'Burglary up 20 per cent') which turn out to be

---

[6] McCabe and Sutcliffe (1978) calculated this from samples of records at about 85%.

based only on a rise or fall relative to the previous year, paying no attention to earlier years. This tells us nothing about genuine trends in that offence—for example, the figures might have been moving in the opposite direction for the previous five years. Sometimes, too—a practice which, if used deliberately, borders on dishonesty—commentators refer to a percentage fall or increase since a particular year, selecting as their baseline year one out of line with the underlying trend. To take a concrete example, if one had stated at the end of 1992 that, 'recorded burglaries have risen by 65 per cent since 1988', this would have been factually correct, but it would be misleading not to point out that 1988 had produced one of the lowest recorded totals of burglary for many years and that, for example, the figure had risen by only 45 per cent since 1986. To represent trends properly, it is necessary at least to use figures produced at regular intervals over a sufficient period of time.

## Populations and property 'at risk'

It is important when comparing crime figures over time or between areas, to consider differences in the size and composition of the populations. For example, the population of a town may double over 20 years, creating many more potential victims and offenders. To make some allowance for such differences (especially when looking at long-term trends or comparing police force areas) government statisticians often express recorded crime rates in the form of 'offences per 100,000 population'. However, this is by no means the end of the story, as the social characteristics of the population (e.g. the proportion of young or old people, or the average income level) may be more important than its overall size, in determining the numbers of people 'at risk'. Similarly, a major increase in, say, the numbers of cars on the road, or the numbers of people using cheque cards or internet banking, means more potential targets for thieves and fraudsters, and is clearly a factor to consider in any analysis, but even then it cannot be simply assumed that they are all equally at risk.

## Context

Finally, it is important not to jump to conclusions about the reality behind a rise in the incidence of a particular legal category of offence. A long-standing criticism of the recorded crime figures (see, e.g., McLintock and Avison 1968) has been that they do not give a clear enough picture of the social or situational context of crimes. For example, 'robbery' includes actions as diverse as an organized bank raid, the theft at knifepoint of the contents of a shopkeeper's till, or a drunken attempt to snatch a handbag. Over the years, the use of subcategories has increased considerably, but even now the official robbery figures are divided simply into 'robbery of business property' and 'robbery of personal property' Knowing that 68,452 of the latter were recorded in 2010/11, or that this represented a reduction of 6 per cent over the previous year, does not tell us whether specific modes of robbery are declining or becoming more prevalent. Increases in recorded robbery in the late 1990s and early 2000s led to considerable political argument (at one point the term 'national emergency' being used) and the setting up at short notice of the high-profile Street Crime Initiative, directed from central government and involving the deployment of 2,000 officers across 10 cities in England and Wales. However, it emerged later that much of the increase was accounted for by schoolchildren taking mobile phones from their peers, particularly in London (Curran *et al.* 2005). While undoubtedly a problem that should be taken seriously, whether this warranted such a dramatic, government-coordinated response is highly debatable.

## THE NEW ORTHODOXY? THE BRITISH CRIME SURVEY

It has already been mentioned that the 'official crime statistics' no longer contain only offences recorded by the police. Since 2002, the main annual statistical publication (renamed *Crime in England and Wales*) has also included large amounts of data from the British Crime Survey. This decision was not taken lightly: the BCS had been running for over 20 years before the change occurred. However, over that period it had established itself as a well-respected alternative source of information about crime levels and trends, and for the Home Office to continue to publish its results separately from the police figures risked it taking on the appearance of a 'rival' set of official statistics. By bringing them together, it was hoped to show that the two datasets were complementary rather than in competition, and jointly provided a richer and more 'complete' picture of crime than previously. In the section, we look briefly at the origins of the BCS and its development over time, then explore similarities and differences vis-à-vis police recorded crime. We also look at some of the limitations of the BCS and the critiques that have been made of it.

The first BCS was conducted in 1982 and its results published the following year (Hough and Mayhew 1983). It was not a new concept: victimization surveys had been conducted in the United States since the late 1960s, and Sparks, Genn, and Dodd (1977) had already undertaken an experimental survey in London. Like these earlier surveys, the BCS was born out of curiosity about the size of the 'dark figure' of crime—i.e. unreported and/or unrecorded offences. The main rationale was that, by asking representative samples of members of the public to describe crimes committed against them within the past 12 months, the vagaries of reporting and recording behaviour are neatly avoided, and the responses can be grossed up to produce a 'fuller' (and arguably more reliable) picture than the recorded crime statistics of the incidence of certain types of offence (Mayhew and Hough 1988). It was also timely in that it was introduced in a period of rising concern about crime victims, and provided valuable data about their experiences. Over the years, it has grown steadily in prominence and status, being repeated bi-annually from 1991 and annually from 2000/1. Since 2000/1 it has also been sufficiently large (now 46,000 interviews a year) to allow analysis at police force as well as national level.

The basic format of the survey, and the framework for presenting the results, have changed little over the years. One person over 16 from each household in the sample is randomly selected to answer the questions. Using the core Victimization Module, the interviewer first establishes whether this person, or anyone else in the household, has been the victim of any of a specified list of vehicle or property-related crimes (described to them in ordinary language) within the past 12 months; and secondly, whether the respondent him/herself has been the victim of a 'personal crime' (mainly assault) over the same period. If any positive answers are received, further details of each incident are recorded—up to a maximum of five for any type of offence—on a 'victim form'.[7] The results are analysed and grossed up to produce estimated national totals of both broad types of incident—described as 'household' and 'personal' crimes—based on calculations using, respectively, the total number of households and the total adult population of England and Wales.[8]

In addition to being asked about offences to which they have fallen victim, various subsets of respondents answer questions from a range of other modules. These include sets of questions to elicit their views on a range of crime-related topics (which vary from year to year) as well as 'self-completion' questionnaires in which respondents enter their answers directly on to a computer screen (which is not seen by the interviewer). These usually concern sensitive topics, such as their knowledge about and use of illicit drugs, or their experiences of sexual attacks or 'stalking'.[9] Since 2009, too, separate victimization surveys have been conducted with substantial samples of 10–15 year olds (Chaplin *et al.* 2011). However, the results of these exercises do not (as yet) form part of the core estimates of crime numbers and trends.

## A fuller picture of crime?

Table 8.2 shows the estimates of the extent of 'BCS crime' that were calculated from the results of the survey in 2010/11. If one compares the overall picture painted by these

**Table 8.2** Estimated totals of offences in England and Wales, 2010/11, as derived from the British Crime Survey

|  | Number (to the nearest 1,000) | Per cent |
|---|---|---|
| *Broadly comparable with police figures:* |  |  |
| Violence | 2,203,000 | 23 |
| Vandalism | 2,156,000 | 22 |
| Vehicle related theft | 1,189,000 | 12 |
| Burglary | 745,000 | 8 |
| Theft from person | 563,000 | 6 |
| Bicycle theft | 526,000 | 5 |
| *Not comparable:* |  |  |
| Other household theft | 1,244,000 | 13 |
| Other theft personal property | 993,000 | 10 |
| **Total** | **9,618,000** | **100** |

*Source:* Adapted from Chaplin et al. (2011) *Crime in England and Wales 2010/1.* London: Home Office.

[7] However, if the respondent reports a number of similar events involving the same offender, these may be treated as one 'series incident'.

[8] As the total interview sample deliberately includes an over-representation of households from denser urban areas (to maximize the chances of finding 'victims' to interview), the calculated victimization rates are weighted to take account of this (Home Office 2010; TNS-BMRB 2010).

[9] In 2009/10, for example, there were modules on, *inter alia*, 'experiences of the police', 'attitudes to the criminal justice system', 'crime prevention and security', 'plastic card fraud', 'identity fraud', and 'anti-social behaviour', and self-completion modules on 'drug use and drinking' and 'inter-personal violence' (TNS-BMRB 2010).

figures with that derived from police records (Table 8.1, earlier) the two most obvious differences are that (i) the crime categories included are different; and (ii) the overall estimated total of 'BCS crime' (9,180,000 offences) is more than double that of police-recorded crime.

Neither of these differences is surprising, but their implications need some discussion. The first point to emphasize is that the BCS has never set out to cover all kinds of crime recorded by the police. As its designers pointed out at the outset (Hough and Mayhew 1985: ch. 1), public surveys are more suited to gleaning information about some types of incident than others. What it has always aimed to produce first and foremost is a measure of *household and personal crimes against adults* (and, indeed, not all types of these). Thus the annual estimate of 'BCS crime' does not include crimes against commercial or corporate victims, fraudulent offences,[10] sexual offences, or 'consensual' crimes such as the possession of or dealing in drugs, nor does it (at the time of writing) include crimes against children under 16. As will be discussed later, quite a lot of data is available on these 'missing' categories (for example, the BCS interview data now gathered on crimes against 11–15-year-olds, data from BCS self-completion modules on sexual assault, and data on crime against businesses collected in other surveys) and consideration is being given to including some of it in the annual publication (Matheson 2011). However, to date 'BCS crime' continues to be based only on the core Victimization Module, which has changed little since the 1980s. This is partly because some of the other available data are considered less reliable, but mainly because (like the long-term 'series' produced from police statistics) one of the aims of the BCS has been to make reliable year-on-year comparisons and track long-term trends in victimization levels.

It is also clear, vice versa, that not all 'crimes' included in the BCS estimates would have been identified and recorded as criminal offences if they had been reported to the police. The survey gathers information on large numbers of (overwhelmingly minor) personal and household thefts which do not map sufficiently well on to police definitions of crime for any direct comparisons to be made.

The above differences mean that one cannot simply compare the two overall totals (9.6 million BCS crimes, 4.2 million police-recorded crimes) and conclude that the BCS shows that there is 'a little over twice as much crime' as the official records suggest: this would not be comparing like with like. There are, however, some specific offence categories where meaningful comparisons are possible, once some statistical adjustments have been made. Combined together, these form what is known as the *comparable subset* (see Home Office 2011: 17–18). Although the fit is not perfect, this allows fair comparisons between about three-quarters of the estimated total of BCS crimes and just under half of all crimes recorded by the police. Most of the BCS crimes in the first five categories shown in Table 8.2 are included in the comparable subset, while 'other household thefts' and 'other thefts of personal property' are excluded. *Within this subset*, the BCS clearly does provide a 'fuller' picture than the equivalent police figures. Since the BCS was first conducted, the results have consistently indicated that

---

[10] The BCS has included some questions on 'plastic fraud' since 2006/7, though they measure prevalence rather than incidence, and are not included in the main 'BCS crime' count. The latest results indicate that just over 5% of plastic card users were victims of such fraud in 2010/11 (Chaplin *et al.* 2011: 81).

*victims are aware of between three and four times more offences of these particular kinds than appear in the police recorded statistics.* It is interesting to contrast this ratio with the estimate by Sparks *et al.* (1977) from their pioneering victim survey in London, that the volume of unrecorded crime (the so-called 'dark figure') was *11* times higher than the police figure. The discrepancy is partly explained by differences in the nature of the areas surveyed and in the methodologies used, but also by the rather different spread of offences covered: the London survey, carried out mainly in deprived areas, included more minor offences with low reporting rates, which served to increase the ratio.[11] These comments are pertinent to debates about major differences in findings between national and local surveys, which will be discussed later.

In short, 'BCS crime', like 'recorded crime', is to some extent an arbitrarily constructed aggregation of disparate types of offence: both include some offences in the count, and omit others. It is therefore a serious misunderstanding to regard the BCS as offering a full picture of 'crime in England and Wales'. Indeed, looked at as a whole, it does not necessarily present a fuller—or indeed, 'truer'— picture than that provided by the recorded crime statistics, simply a different one: it is fuller in some important respects (notably the inclusion of unrecorded and unreported offences), but less full in others (notably the exclusion of consensual crimes, crimes against organizations, and crimes against children under 16). It is only in relation to certain well-defined individual offence types, or to the 'comparable subset', that it can safely be said to provide a fuller picture than the police figures—though even then, questions remain about how accurately it reflects the nature and scale of the behaviour in question (see later).

### Comparisons of trends

For much of the 1980s and 1990s, the basic shapes of the trends displayed by both BCS and official crime statistics were fairly similar. Between 1982 and 1997, both showed an increase to a peak in the early to mid-1990s, followed by the beginnings of a downward trend. Indeed, a statistical analysis by Farrington and Langan (1998) of the relationship between the two sets of data from 1981–96, found that they were closely correlated in relation to all four categories of crime examined (vehicle theft, burglary, robbery, and assault). The main difference was that, as with surveys in the USA, the rise in BCS crime was less steep than police figures suggested. Between 1981 and 1991 recorded crime rose by 78 per cent, while the BCS estimated totals rose by 37 per cent. In addition, while recorded crime peaked in 1992, the BCS totals peaked in 1995.

However, since 1998 the picture has become much less clear, and apparent differences in trends have caused confusion and sparked debate. Estimated BCS crime totals began to fall steeply after their peak of 19.1 million in 1995, and although the decreasing trend flattened out considerably from the mid-2000s, by 2010/11 the total

---

[11] Victim surveys have consistently shown wide variations between offence types in reporting and recording rates. For example, in the 2010/11 BCS, 79% of respondents whose home had been burgled with entry, but only 39% of victims of bicycle theft and 34 per cent of victims of 'vandalism', said that they had reported the incident to the police. The gap is widened by subsequent differences in police recording behaviour. In broad terms, BCS findings indicate that just under half of all house burglaries (with entry) known to residents end up in the official police statistics, whereas the equivalent ratio for bicycle thefts is around one in five. Offences such as shoplifting are known to be under-reported and under-recorded to a higher degree still (Martin 1962).

had fallen to 9.6 million—a figure lower than that calculated from the first BCS in 1982. By contrast, the raw police-recorded crime totals rose for some of this same period, peaking in 2003/4 at 6.0 million, before decreasing quite rapidly to 4.2 million by 2010/11 (see Figure 8.2).

Clearly, much of the substantial increase in police figures between 1999 and 2004 was artificial, being accounted for by additions to the types of offence counted, other changes in counting rules, and the introduction of the NCRS. Nevertheless, there have remained some puzzles, particularly around crimes of violence, where differences in trends between the two sources have been most visible. Home Office researchers conceded that rises in police recorded violence over this period (when 'BCS violence' was falling sharply) were not entirely explained by technical changes (Walker *et al.* 2006: 66; see also Maguire 2007 and Brookman and Robinson, this volume). Moreover, if one looks at year-on-year figures since 2002/3 for violent offences resulting in injury— which should be less subject to variations in recording practice than violence without injury—it is apparent that, in every year except one, the BCS estimates and police figures have moved in a different direction (see Table 8.3).

In many cases, the differences between successive years were not statistically significant, while apparent divergences in overall trends have been much smaller than often claimed. Nevertheless, their visibility to commentators—and hence their media and political profile—has been heightened since 2002 by the publication of both BCS and recorded crime figures in the same annual research bulletin, *Crime in England and Wales*. When these appear to contradict each other, disputes break out about which should be 'believed'.

### More similar than different?

How, then, can we summarize the similarities and differences between the pictures of crime that have emerged from the BCS and the recorded crime figures? First, the

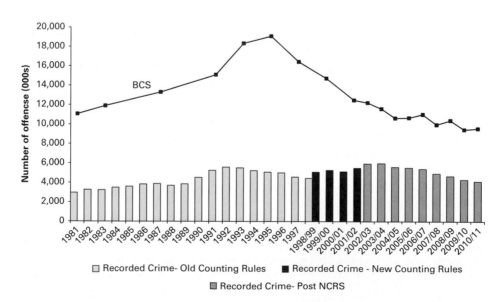

**Figure 8.2** Trends in recorded crime and BCS, 1981–2010/11

**Table 8.3** Violence with injury: BCS estimates and police-recorded offences, 2003/4–2010/11

|  | Recorded violence against the person with injury | | BCS violence with injury | |
|  | 000s | +/- 000s | 000s | +/- 000s |
| --- | --- | --- | --- | --- |
| 2002/3 | 372 |  | 1441 |  |
| 2003/4 | 457 | +85 | 1366 | -75 |
| 2004/5 | 515 | +58 | 1301 | -65 |
| 2005/6 | 543 | +32 | 1228 | -73 |
| 2006/7 | 505 | -38 | 1271 | +43 |
| 2007/8 | 453 | -52 | 1063 | -218 |
| 2008/9 | 421 | -32 | 1116 | +73 |
| 2009/10 | 402 | -19 | 1063 | -53 |
| 2010/11 | 387 | -15 | 1211 | +148 |

central message sent out by the authors of the BCS in its early years was, in essence: the bad news is that there is a lot more crime than we thought, the good news is that most of it is not very serious. Their remark about 'the petty nature of most law-breaking' (Hough and Mayhew 1983:33) was designed to deflect a possible moral panic in reaction to the huge amount of 'new' crime revealed by the survey, but it also reflected the key finding—supported by all surveys conducted since—that unreported crimes generally involve much lower levels of financial loss, damage, and injury than those reported to the police.

Second, aside from the much larger totals of offences, the BCS produces a basic picture of crime not wildly dissimilar to that projected by police records: for example, 'autocrime' (theft of or from vehicles) is prominent in both sets of figures, and property crime is more frequent than violence.

Finally, the overall shape of trends in crime between the early 1980s and the late 1990s emerges as similar in each case—a long-term rise followed by a fall—although the BCS suggests a steeper rise and a later beginning to the fall. The two sets of data also give similar messages about continuing falls in certain offences since the mid-1990s—notably burglary between 1995 and 2005, and vehicle theft between 1995 and 2011. However, since 1999 it has become much more difficult to compare overall trends, owing to major changes in the rules governing police crime recording, and confusion has been sown by some contradictory short-term movements in the figures, particularly in relation to violent crime.

### Critiques of the BCS

The BCS has undoubtedly had a major impact on criminology, as well as criminal justice policy and practice. In addition to its core contribution to the measurement of unreported crime, it has in effect replaced police crime statistics as the most reliable tool for measuring trends in crime. It has also gathered huge amounts of data over the years about public attitudes to crime, victims' experiences, risks of victimization, and so on (see, respectively, chapters by Hough and Roberts, Hoyle, and Brookman and

Robinson, this volume). However, it is all too easy to slip from recognition of its value into uncritical acceptance of its findings as 'the truth about crime'. Like all public surveys, it has weaknesses in terms of sampling errors, non-response, inaccurate recall of events by respondents, weighting procedures, classification of responses, and so on, which all affect the reliability of the results (such issues are addressed honestly in the technical reports and user guides published alongside the results: see Home Office 2011; TNS-BMRB 2010). More fundamentally, it focuses on a relatively narrow range of criminal behaviour which, critics have argued, creates a somewhat distorted picture of crime and patterns of victimization—a picture reinforced by the strong reputation and high profile of the BCS.

Like police statistics, 'BCS crime' is dominated by offences committed by *strangers*: for example, as with police figures, the BCS uncovers many fewer cases of domestic violence than of stranger or acquaintance violence. Equally, it tells us little more about 'serial' offences against the same victim. Most incidents reported to the survey consist of discrete events in which individuals suddenly and unexpectedly suffer an assault, theft, damage to their property, or illegal entry into their house. Crime in this mode takes on an appearance in many ways akin to an accident, or an 'act of God'—an almost random event which can strike anyone at any time, but which is fairly infrequent in the life of any individual.

In the 1980s, criminologists writing from a Left Realist and/or a feminist perspective also argued that the BCS did not sufficiently reflect the experiences either of women or of the very poor (see, e.g., Matthews and Young 1986; Young 1988a; Stanko 1988; Genn 1988; Dobash and Dobash 1992). It was pointed out that a large proportion of assaults on women are likely to be committed by people known to them, including their partners, and that they are unlikely to report these in response to brief questions from an interviewer on the doorstep. Moreover, many members of marginalized groups—the homeless, the mentally ill, those who drift from bed-sitter to bed-sitter, and so on—are relatively unlikely to have contact with interviewers in a survey based on samples of households; such people may also be subject to exceptionally high levels of victimization.

To correct this imbalance, some academics conducted rather different kinds of crime surveys. These were local surveys, funded mainly by left-leaning local authorities in inner city areas, which aimed to uncover areas of criminal behaviour not seriously touched by the BCS and to explore their distribution among the population (see, e.g., Kinsey 1984; Jones *et al.* 1986, 1987; Crawford *et al.* 1990). By focusing chiefly on inner city areas, such surveys (unlike the BCS) showed that victimization is heavily concentrated in some small areas—predominantly those blighted by poverty. For example, the first Islington Crime Survey (Jones *et al.* 1986) indicated that a third of local households had been touched by burglary, robbery, or assault within the previous 12 months: a situation quite different from that of the notional 'statistically average' person referred to in the first BCS.[12]

---

[12] In the first BCS report, it was calculated that a 'statistically average' person aged 16 or over could expect to fall victim to:

- a robbery once every five centuries (excluding attempts);
- an assault resulting in injury (even if slight) once every century;

In addition, efforts were made to find ways of obtaining more information about sexual and other assaults on women. These included less restrictive wording of questions and emphasis on sensitive approaches to these topics in the training and selection of interviewers. Again, the results stood in considerable contrast to the BCS findings: in the Islington survey, significantly higher levels of sexual assault were found, while over one-fifth of reported assaults were classified as 'domestic'—more than twice the BCS proportion at that time. Moreover, questions were asked about incidents which would not necessarily be classified by the police as 'crime', but may be experienced as serious by victims, namely sexual and racial 'harassment'. It was found, for example, that over two-thirds of women under the age of 24 had been 'upset by harassment' in the previous 12 months.

One of the most important general insights that emerged from the local surveys was that, while there are differences in risks of victimization between broad social groups (male and female, old and young, etc.), such differences can be massive when one looks at very specific subgroups. A striking finding in the Islington survey, for example, was that young, black females in the area were 29 times more likely to be assaulted than white females over 45. As Young (1988b:171) observed, such findings illustrate 'the fallacy of talking of the problem of women as a whole, or of men, blacks, whites, youths, etc'. Rather, he insisted, criminological analysis should 'start from the actual subgroups in which people live their lives'.

A graphic illustration of this point is the early exploration by Hazel Genn (1988) of the problem of 'multiple victimization'. Genn, a co-author of the first large-scale victim survey in London (Sparks *et al.* 1977) revisited—and temporarily lived with—some of the female respondents who had claimed to have been victimized many times. She gives an eye-opening account of the way that the lives of these women were blighted by frequent sexual and physical assaults, thefts, burglaries, and other forms of mistreatment, often by people with whom they had a continuing relationship. Yet this kind of crime, she notes, is lost from view in most surveys, partly because they tend to impose artificial limits on the number of crimes that can be counted for any one victim, and partly because such victims may be less likely than others to respond to the survey or to admit their victimization to interviewers. At the same time, Genn raises fundamental questions about how meaningful it is to 'count' certain crimes at all. She writes:

> In asking respondents about their experiences of crime, victim surveys have tended to use an approach which Skogan has termed 'the events orientation': that which conceptualises crime as discrete incidents. This can be traced back to one of the original primary objectives of victim surveys: the estimation of the 'dark figure' of unrecorded crime for direct comparison with police statistics. In order to accomplish this,.. information obtained from victims had to be accommodated within a rigid 'counting' frame of reference. Although isolated incidents of burglary, car theft or stranger attacks may present few measurement problems, for certain categories of violent crime and for certain types

- a family car stolen or taken by joyriders once every 60 years;
- a burglary in the home once every 40 years.

The authors added that '[t]hese risks can be compared with the likelihood of encountering other sorts of mishaps: the chances of burglary are slightly less than the chances...of a fire in the home; the chances a household runs of car theft are smaller than the chances.. of having one of its members injured in a car accident.' (Hough and Mayhew 1983: 15) of crime victim, the 'counting' procedure leads to difficulties. *It is clear that violent victimization may often be better conceptualized as a process rather than as a series of discrete events.* This is most evident in cases of prolonged and habitual domestic violence, but there are also other situations in which violence, abuse and petty theft are an integral part of victims' day-to-day existence. (Genn 1988: 91) [emphasis added]

Finally, an important related point is that while it is informative to examine differential risks of victimization between social groups, this should be complemented with an understanding of the differential *impact* of crime on these groups. A debate about this arose from the prominence given in the first BCS reports to findings that younger males, and people who frequently went out drinking, faced the highest risks of being assaulted. From these findings the Home Office authors concluded that the fears of street violence expressed by both women and the elderly (which were greater than those of young men) were to some extent 'irrational' (Hough and Mayhew 1983). Young (1988b:173–5) responded that such a conclusion, like their argument that fears are exaggerated because much crime is 'trivial' in terms of loss or injury, obscures the fact that what are 'objectively' similar events can have enormously different meanings and consequences for different people:

> People differ greatly in their ability to withstand crime. The 'same' punch can mean totally different things in different circumstances.. Violence, like all kinds of crime, is a social relationship. It is rarely random: it inevitably involves particular social meanings and occurs in particular hierarchies of power. Its impact, likewise, is predicated on the relationship within which it occurs…The relatively powerless situation of women—economically, socially and physically—makes them more unequal victims than men.

Later BCS 'sweeps' and reports benefited from the above kinds of criticism, and more attention has since been paid to differential patterns of victimization. For example, 'booster' samples have been interviewed to explore the victimization of ethnic minorities (Clancy *et al.* 2001); separate analysis has been undertaken of crime against older people (Chivite-Matthews and Maggs 2002); computer-aided self-interviewing has been used to produce more reliable data on domestic violence as well as to explore offences like sexual assault and 'stalking' (Percy and Mayhew 1997; Mirrlees-Black 1999; Budd and Mattinson 2000; Walby and Allen 2004); and more recently, the survey has included a sample of 11–15-year-olds (Chaplin *et al.* 2011).

## THE EXPANSION AND 'PLURALIZATION' OF CRIME DATA

While the BCS has played a big part over the last 30 years in the move away from over-reliance on police recorded statistics and the opening up of new windows on crime, it has by no means been the only important contributor. In this section we outline a much broader process of expansion and 'pluralization' that has taken place over this period in the production of knowledge about crime levels, patterns, and trends. This has included a wide range of innovative and creative efforts, by a variety of individuals and organizations for a variety of purposes, to find out more about the nature and scale of previously under-explored kinds of criminal activity, and especially those which were largely hidden from external scrutiny. As many such offences are seriously under-represented in recorded crime statistics, one of the effects of this work has been to highlight the limitations of the official statistics and hence to undermine the credibility of claims that they provide a realistic picture of the 'national state of crime'.

## NEW THINKING AND NEW DATA DEMANDS

Before the 1970s, apart from the regular statistical returns from criminal justice agencies, the crime data cupboard was largely bare—or, at least, stocked with a very limited range of products. A large proportion of criminological research was aimed at understanding why some individuals engage in crime and how to 'treat' them, and hence data collection focused mainly on the characteristics of offenders. By contrast, little attention was paid to the physical and social circumstances or geographical distribution of offences. Analysis or discussion of crime patterns was based on limited sources and carried out within a narrow frame of reference. It had a low public profile and was largely left to government statisticians, occasionally assisted by academics who rarely looked beyond the official figures or questioned the assumptions behind their production.

However, all this has since changed. There now appears to be an almost unquenchable thirst for information about crime. Crime has become a major focus of public concern and a critical issue in party politics (Downes and Morgan, this volume). Governments have increasingly set out to 'manage' crime problems, and the crime prevention and control industry, in the broadest sense of the term, has expanded rapidly (Garland 2001). Rather than relying predominantly on traditional criminal justice responses such as punishment and rehabilitation, this has involved a range of new theoretical and practical approaches, many of them based around detailed assessment and management of the risk of future offences, and around measuring and improving the effectiveness of crime reduction initiatives.[13] Of course, this process has been greatly facilitated and encouraged by advances in information technology, including the capacity to collect, store, and analyse massive electronic datasets. However, in trying to make sense of what has happened, it is important to look not just at technological change, but at changes in ways of thinking about and responding to crime. These stand in a dynamic relationship with the production of crime data, both driving demands for new kinds of information and in turn being influenced by the new knowledge they generate. Over the period, key developments have included:

- Policies based on identifying and targeting aspects of the environment which facilitate criminal activity, and altering them (for example, through new designs of buildings or vehicles) to reduce the opportunities for crime and their attractiveness to potential offenders. This is encapsulated in the 'situational crime prevention' approach developed in the 1980s (Clarke 1980; Crawford and Evans this

---

[13] Earlier versions of this chapter in previous editions of the *Handbook* contained more detailed accounts of these changes and the reasons behind them (see Maguire 2007—available online at http://www.oup.com/uk/orc/bin/9780199205431/maguire_chap10.pdf). This time, there is space only for a brief summary.

volume) and later underpinned by 'rational choice' and 'routine activities' theories (Clarke and Felson 1993; Rock, this volume).

- Intelligence-led and problem-oriented forms of policing (Bullock and Tilley 2003; Maguire and Hopkins 2003; Maguire 2000, 2008), latterly underpinned by the National Intelligence Model (Maguire and John 2006). Such approaches aim to identify, analyse, and prioritize existing or emerging crime problems and then deploy appropriate resources to deal with them.

- The direct involvement in crime control activities, including joint working and data sharing, of agencies outside the criminal justice field, particularly through their incorporation into formal partnerships (notably the statutory Community Safety Partnerships: see Crawford and Evans, this volume).

- The promotion of an 'evidence-based' or 'What Works' philosophy, based on systematically evaluating a range of interventions and adopting those that emerge as most effective—encapsulated in the ambitious Crime Reduction Programme in the early 2000s (see Hough 2004; and chapters by Raynor and Lösel, this volume).

- The growth of managerialism, including the setting of 'performance targets' aimed at improving the effectiveness of crime control agencies, and measurement of their progress through baskets of statistical 'indicators' (see Hough 2007 and Senior *et al.* 2007 for critical accounts of these practices).

All of the above factors have contributed to the continuing demand for more and 'better' statistical and other kinds of information about crime, including detailed analysis of patterns in specific types of offence that can directly inform policy-making and operational practice, and data that can be processed and disseminated much more quickly than in the past. They have also fuelled the development of increasingly sophisticated methodologies for analysing data (including mapping techniques, 'hot spot' analysis, and criminal market profiles), as well as intelligence products such as the 'strategic assessments' and 'problem profiles' built into the National Intelligence Model (John and Maguire 2007).

In addition, the field of concern has extended far beyond the 'conventional' forms of crime (such as theft, burglary, and criminal damage) which make up the bulk of recorded offences, to many kinds of criminal behaviour (such as domestic violence and child sexual abuse) that previously remained largely hidden from official view. This has been strongly influenced by campaigns to get particular forms of behaviour taken more seriously by the police and justice agencies, notably the pioneering efforts of feminist groups in the 1970s in relation to domestic violence and sexual assault, and the persistent demands of organizations such as Childline (set up in 1986) for more government and police action in relation to child sexual abuse. Recently, too, attention has grown to new and often highly organized forms of crime with international dimensions (such as Internet fraud, people trafficking, and money laundering) made possible by rapid technological change and globalization (Brookman *et al.* 2010; Levi, this volume) —and of course, especially since '9/11' in 2001, to international terrorism (Innes and Levi, this volume). Again, all these developments have created major new data needs at local, national, and international level.

The overall response to this continuing surge in demand for crime-related information, combined with the emergence of crime as one of the top issues on the national political agenda (which has persuaded government ministers to supply much of the necessary funding), has been a huge increase in the range and numbers of people engaged in data collection and research, and in the volume of information available to them, as well as the opening up of numerous new fields of inquiry—in short, a veritable 'data explosion' in the field. This has been evident within government itself, where the Home Office and Ministry of Justice (despite recent cutbacks) both retain large research teams which have played major roles in the development of new ways of measuring crime and analysing re-offending. At the same time, criminology in universities has grown from a minor subsidiary subject to a flourishing specialist discipline employing several hundred academics, many of them engaged in empirical research (Loader and Sparks, this volume). Many public, private, and voluntary sector organizations with a role in crime reduction or security now employ their own researchers to analyse records or conduct surveys to produce new data (at national, regional, or local level) about specific types of crime. Organizations outside the criminal justice system have also been persuaded to collect and share crime data for the general good—as seen, for example, in the use of records of assault victims attending Accident and Emergency departments to measure trends in violence (Estrada 2006; Maxwell *et al.* 2007; Sivarajasingam *et al.* 2009).

## NEW KNOWLEDGE: ACHIEVEMENTS AND CHALLENGES

In essence, then, we have moved from a situation in which there was only one 'official picture' of crime, to one in which not only are the official crime statistics themselves based on more than one kind of data (BCS results as well as police records), but data from many other sources provide a kaleidoscope of windows on to a much broader range of criminal activity.

Although the volume of work devoted to the production of new information about crime has increased enormously, this should not be taken to suggest that the picture it has collectively created is a clear one. On the contrary, it consists of many different overlapping, and in some cases competing, images. Some important areas of criminal activity remain relatively unexplored, while others are characterized by conflicting findings. To put a little more flesh on the bones, some brief illustrative examples are given below of attempts that have been made to produce new knowledge about the prevalence and incidence of specific types of criminal activity, together with comments on the strengths and limitations of some of the methodologies that have been used—and hence on the reliability of the conclusions.

### Domestic violence and sexual abuse

Because much domestic violence (or 'abuse') involves a continuing series of aggressive acts in particular households, it makes little sense to attempt to count the overall number of individual 'offences' which have been committed. Estimates of the extent of such crime are therefore most often expressed in terms of prevalence: i.e. the proportion of a given population experiencing it over a given period. However, this too can be misleading, especially in 'lifetime prevalence' studies, for example if no effort is made to distinguish those who have been assaulted only once from those who have been victimized repeatedly over many years. Moreover, definitions of what is being measured can make a critical difference to the results. For example, in the 1970s the designers of the feasibility study for the first National Incidence Study of Child Abuse and Neglect, a major survey of health service and other professionals across the USA, initially defined 'child maltreatment' simply in terms of harmful parental conduct, leading to an estimate that 30 per cent of all children in the USA had been victims of maltreatment over the previous year. When the definition was restricted to conduct resulting in a minimum degree of demonstrable harm (e.g. marks on the skin lasting at least 48 hours), the estimate dropped to only 1 per cent (see Besharov 1981). The survey has since been repeated three times, the latest figures indicating a national prevalence rate of 1.7 per cent in 2005/6 (Sedlak *et al.* 2010).

Similar caveats apply to estimates of the incidence of all kinds of domestic abuse. In the UK, domestic violence against adult women was afforded special attention in the local crime surveys pioneered in the 1980s, as discussed above. The topic was also explored around the same period through surveys of women, mainly conducted by feminist researchers. For example, Hanmer and Saunders (1984) found that 59 per cent of 129 women surveyed in Leeds had suffered some form of threat, violence, or sexual harassment within the previous year, and Hall (1985) and Radford (1987) produced even more startling figures. A survey by Painter (1991), based on a representative sample of over 1,000 married women, suggested that 14 per cent had been raped by their husbands at some time during their marriage—over 40 per cent of them perceiving the incident as 'rape' at the time. Other work has since been carried out to investigate the extent of domestic violence against men (Grady 2002; Dobash and Dobash 2004; see also Saunders 2002) and between same-sex partners (Henderson 2003). Generally speaking, these independent studies have produced much higher estimates of domestic violence than the BCS, even after its introduction of self-completion modules (Walby and Allen 2004), and most commentators believe that the BCS significantly under-estimates the prevalence of this kind of crime (see Robinson 2010). However, it should not automatically be assumed that one set of findings is 'right' and another 'wrong': they may be counting different things. Results vary widely depending on the offence definitions used, the kind of population sampled, the time period referred to, the wording of the questions, the situation in which they are put, and so on. The crucial point is that the methodologies have to be closely examined and 'headline' figures should never be taken at face value.

While it is feasible to ask adults in surveys about physical or even sexual violence by intimates, this presents major practical and ethical difficulties in relation to children. Some evidence on the incidence of physical abuse of children has been gleaned from hospital data on 'non-accidental injuries', although what is recorded of course depends on whether children are seriously enough injured to go to hospital and whether hospital staff recognize their injuries as the result of violence. Until recently, most evidence about the prevalence of child abuse, including sexual abuse, came from surveys of adults asked to recall events from their own childhoods, with predictably conflicting results arising from varying methodologies (see Straus, Gelles, and Steinmetz 1980;

Baker and Duncan 1985; Finkelhor and Araji 1986; Morgan and Zedner 1992; Hoyle, this volume). However, important new findings have emerged from an innovative UK survey by Radford *et al.* (2011), based on over 6,000 interviews with random probability samples of parents or guardians of children under 11, young people aged 11–17, and young adults aged 18–24 years. These indicate that between 5 and 14.5 per cent of the groups of young people referred to had experienced 'severe maltreatment' by a parent or guardian at some point during their childhood (predominantly 'severe neglect' and to a lesser extent severe physical violence—contact sexual abuse was revealed in under 1 per cent of replies from any of the groups). The research also indicates that 2.5 per cent of under 11s and 6 per cent of 11–17s had experienced one or more of these types of abuse *in the past year.* All the above terms are carefully defined in the study, and repetitive abuse is distinguished from one-off incidents.

## Crimes against businesses

Crimes against businesses may be committed by members of the public (for example, through shoplifting or cheque frauds), by employees (though workplace theft or embezzlement), or by other businesses (for example, through 'long firm fraud'—see Levi 2008). Such crimes all pose considerable difficulties for measurement. First, in many cases they never come to light: for example, losses through low-level employee theft may be not be distinguishable from legitimate forms of 'shrinkage' (such as goods being damaged at warehouses), and embezzlement by people responsible for preparing the firm's accounts can be very difficult to detect. Secondly, it may not be clear when losses through theft are detected (often a considerable time after they have occurred) whether they have been committed by, say, shoplifters or counter staff. Thirdly, it may be unclear whether losses are the result of a small number of sizeable crimes by relatively few people or a large number of minor thefts by a large number of people (or indeed, repeated minor thefts over a long period by the same person). Fraud, in particular, causes major problems of definition and measurement. The *Fraud Review* (Attorney General's Office 2006) noted that, although recorded crime statistics show reductions in cheque and credit card fraud since 2000, only an estimated 5 per cent of fraudulent credit card transactions are reported to the police, so one can have little confidence in such figures. As with domestic violence, attempting to 'count crimes' is often unproductive in this field, so it is usually considered more useful to measure the scale of business-related crime either in terms of the prevalence of victimization or as (gu)estimates of the total amount stolen in various ways over defined periods (Levi *et al.* 2007).

A number of sources of information are available which, despite their individual limitations, together provide a useful window into this neglected area. A few large-scale surveys have been undertaken, including the national *Commercial Victimisation Survey* (Shury *et al.* 2005) and the *Business Crime Survey* (British Chambers of Commerce 2008), in both of which more than 50 per cent of businesses surveyed reported having experienced crime in the previous year. Most of the offences reported were by 'outsiders' rather than staff, with burglary, vandalism, and damage to vehicles prominent. The former survey also found 'theft by customers' (43 per cent) and 'fraud by outsiders' (18 per cent—mainly cheque fraud) most common among retailers.

On fraud specifically, some public sector organizations make estimates of losses based on samples of transactions in a given area of spend (e.g. income support) which are assessed to determine whether the claim was genuine (Attorney General's Office 2006: 31). More recently, statisticians have been exploring the potential for measuring fraud through reports from banks, financial institutions, and individual victims to the National Fraud Authority (Matheson 2011).

Despite all this activity, the overall picture remains very unclear, and many of the estimates of losses to organizations through theft and fraud—especially when one gets into the realm of global costs to international companies (e.g. Pricewaterhouse Coopers 2005; see also Levi 2001) —remain highly speculative. It is also worth considering that a sense of the scale of theft within various types of workplace may be best achieved through qualitative research, such as that undertaken many years ago by Ditton (1977) and Mars (1982), who spent time with people working in warehouses and docks, and came to understand the informal cultural rules among employees about pilfering.

### Crime in closed institutions

Despite the vulnerability of many of their 'inmates', criminal activity which takes place in closed institutions such as prisons, army barracks, mental institutions, children's homes, old people's homes, and boarding schools rarely comes to police notice, and often goes unrecorded internally. Cultures of secrecy and sometimes intimidation make collection of reliable data very difficult. Although some surveys have been conducted, this is another area that may be better researched through qualitative methodologies such as in-depth interviews with ex-residents or participant observation. Innovative examples include studies of bullying among prisoners (Ireland 2005) and in children's homes (Barter *et al.* 2005; see also Evans 2010). Research on the other institutions mentioned is less well developed, despite recent high-profile cases involving deaths in army barracks and maltreatment of old people.

### Corporate crime

Crime *by* organizations is even harder to 'measure' in any meaningful way. It may include crimes against an organization's own employees (such as neglect of health and safety rules leading to death or injury), against other organizations (including failures to pay for orders, and the operation of illegal cartels), or against customers or the general public (e.g. the sale of sub-standard or stolen goods, deliberate frauds and 'scams', and pollution of the environment). The topic of corporate crime is covered by Nelken in this volume (see also Minkes 2010; Tombs 2010), so it will not be considered further here. However, it is worth making the point that some of the best insights into such offences—which can involve millions of pounds—have come from reconstructions of large-scale cases through analysis of investigation files, court records, or newspaper stories (see, e.g., Passas and Groskin 2001 on the BCCI swindle). There have been some attempts to gather data on corporate criminal behaviour that has not yet come to light, for example by investigative journalists, or to explore the problem through interviews with businesspeople or auditors, but systematic studies are rare and the overall level of knowledge in the field remains low.

## INTERNATIONAL, ORGANIZED, AND CROSS-BORDER CRIME

The growing need for crime data on an international scale has been recognized through the development of major surveys which collect information in a consistent way across several different countries at once. Most notable among these are the *International Crime Victim Survey* (Alvazzi del Frate and Van Kesteren 2004; van Dijk *et al.* 2010; see also Hoyle, this volume) and the *International Crime Business Survey* (Alvazzi Del Frate 2005). Both suffer from methodological problems and shortages of resources, but offer rich sets of data for analysis.

By contrast, there is very little strong evidence available about the scale of crime that crosses international borders (such as EU subsidy fraud, money laundering, smuggling, and drug or people trafficking), and especially about crime of this kind committed by highly organized groups. Owing to the rapidly changing and well-concealed nature of the activities, this is an area in which conventional methods of gathering data are plainly inadequate. At present, among the most systematic attempts to summarize what is known in a UK and Europe context are regular 'threat assessments' produced by the National Criminal Intelligence Service, Border Agency, Europol and others. These are based on wide variety of data from both closed and open sources, and are published in sanitized form (e.g. SOCA 2009). Otherwise, much of the available information is based on newspaper reports, court cases, police or secret service agencies' investigation files, and interviews with convicted organized criminals: getting closer to the 'field' clearly entails considerable dangers to researchers and informants. Generally speaking, empirical investigations have tended to focus on charting the numbers, size, and ethnic connections of organized criminal groups, rather than attempting to measure the scale of 'organized crime' in terms of offences committed. The latter, indeed, comes up against the problem that some kinds of offence are committed as much by individuals as by 'organized' criminal groups (see Levi, this volume, and Levi and Maguire 2004, for further discussion).

## CRIMES BY GOVERNMENTS AND IN WAR

Finally, Green and Ward (this volume) draw attention to a plethora of horrific state-sanctioned crimes, including crimes against humanity, that have to a large extent remained off the radar of most criminological work (see also Cohen 2001). Unsurprisingly, figures on war crimes, torture, or killings sanctioned by governments are not usually gathered or published by state officials, but by external bodies such as Amnesty International and Human Rights Watch. Such data are gradually being used in analysis by small numbers of criminologists (for good examples, see the Special Issue of the *British Journal of Criminology* edited by Green and Ward 2005) but are still too rarely thought of as 'criminal statistics'—which, of course, they are.

## CONCLUDING COMMENTS

To sum up this section, over the past 30 or so years a process of expansion and pluralization has taken place in relation to the sources of data that are used to 'measure' crime, the ownership and control of systems of data collection and analysis, and the messages about the shape of the 'crime problem' that are conveyed to the outside world through publication of the results. The counting of offences officially recorded by the police has thereby been relegated to only one of a variety of alternative ways of exploring the nature and scale of crime, and the somewhat static, monochrome picture it produces has been challenged by a shifting—and often contradictory and confusing—kaleidoscope of new pictures produced by a wide range of individuals and organizations. This is not to deny the continuing importance of the traditional recorded crime figures, especially at the level of symbolic politics: on the contrary, the salience of crime in current political and media discourse ensures that even a small percentage rise in one category of recorded offences can set off tabloid headlines and heated political debates. However, with the change in status accorded to the BCS, they no longer have even the field of 'official crime statistics' entirely to themselves. Similarly, while the Home Office remains the major player in the field, it no longer has anything like a 'monopoly on truth' where statements about the extent of crime are concerned. Crime figures now occupy a contested—and increasingly politicized—area, in which knowledge claims are often challenged, public and media mistrust of 'official statistics' have grown, and the achievement of legitimacy is becoming as important as the quality of the data.

## THE UNCERTAIN FUTURE OF THE 'OFFICIAL STATISTICS'

We turn in this last section to questions about the current status and the future of the 'official' crime statistics. Recent years have seen a series of inquiries, reports, and policy recommendations on this topic, reflecting a sense of uncertainty about both their legitimacy and their core purposes—even something of an 'identity crisis'—that has surrounded them for some time. The most recent report at the time of writing (Matheson 2011) confirms that there are likely to be further shifts in the three main directions of travel that have already begun: the pursuit of 'relevance', the search for 'comprehensiveness', and the transfer of responsibility and control away from the Home Office into more independent hands. Proposals of this kind are being driven, it is suggested, by a combination of changing data demands from policy-makers and practitioners, new thinking about the purpose of official statistics, and concerns about public mistrust. However, they also come up against some fundamental dilemmas and contradictions inherent in the very concept of a single set of national ('official') statistics.

### 'MODERNIZATION', 'RELEVANCE', AND THE SEARCH FOR THE 'FULL JIGSAW'

The case for relevance and comprehensiveness was made forcefully in 2000 in a radical report by a senior civil servant which advocated no less than '[a revision of] the philosophy underlying the production of statistics', in which '19th century aims and practices' would be replaced by

> a more flexible view of information—one where we first define the problems requiring solution and then develop the information needed to better understand those problems,.. rather than rely on the routine statistics supplied in summary form by the police. (Simmons 2000:ii)

His recommendations included the replacement of the traditional *Criminal Statistics* with an annual 'Picture of Crime in England and Wales' incorporating not just police crime records, but information from a range of other sources including the BCS, police incident data, research studies, other kinds of survey, and administrative data from other agencies and institutions. If information was to be useful, he argued, it had to be as comprehensive—and as timely, reliable, and context-rich—as possible. Thus, for example, the author looked forward to a system of data collection in which a common incident record format would be used by every police force, and part-records of individual cases (as opposed to simply counts of offence types) could be transferred electronically to the Home Office, hence allowing more collation and analysis to be undertaken centrally. Policies should also be introduced to encourage or compel police officers to

> ensure that *every* incident relating to crimes, allegations of crimes and also disorder that is brought to their attention is recorded as an incident (or 'call for service'). (Simmons 2000: 19, original emphasis)

Further recommendations included a relaxation of the traditional focus on legally defined offences, with greater use being made of social definitions of crime (such as 'knife crime' or 'cheque card fraud') and even of measures of non-crime events (especially 'anti-social behaviour') which cause concern to the public.

This report provides a good illustration of the theme explored in the early part of this chapter, that decisions about how to collect and present crime data do not occur in a vacuum: they respond to the changing demands of the 'consumers' of the information and to the dominant preoccupations of the day. It argues, in essence, that there is no longer a strong case for the annual production of a crude single measure of the level of crime, constructed from simple counts of recorded offences: the needs of modern government are for more malleable and contextualized forms of information with which to assess and respond quickly to the highly specific and fast-changing 'crime problems' which emerge at frequent intervals to preoccupy the public, politicians, and media.

The changes which actually took place in the early 2000s fell well short of Simmons' ambitions, but both the publication of BCS results alongside police data in the annual publication *Crime in England and Wales* (which in effect awarded the survey results equal status with police figures as an 'official' measure of crime) and the introduction of the National Crime Recording Standard, (based on a '*prima facie*' approach to crime recording, as discussed earlier), were clearly in line with his thinking. Moreover, many of the themes in his report have re-emerged in subsequent reviews of statistics. For example, the independent review commissioned by the Home Secretary and chaired by Professor Adrian Smith recognized the need for reliable data of relevance to the needs of policy-makers and practitioners, and also identified 'serious and growing gaps in the national figures', accepting the need to 'extend the coverage of national statistics' (Smith 2006: 7–11). More recently, Simmons' recommendations for an even more 'comprehensive' approach have been revived by the National Statistician, who uses the analogy of a jigsaw with missing pieces to make the case for the gradual incorporation of a much wider range of data sources into published presentations of the national statistics. She writes:

> This overall picture of crime could be conceived as a 'jigsaw puzzle'. The BCS and police recorded crime represent major pieces of this jigsaw. The publication of additional data (for example on ASB incidents) as more contextual information could form further pieces of the jigsaw. With the inclusion of appropriate explanations about overlaps and remaining gaps, this could provide users and the public with more transparency and a better understanding of the overall picture. As gaps are filled, for example as new data streams become available from the National Fraud Authority, these estimates could be added to the jigsaw. (Matheson 2011: 13)

She lists the following as suitable 'pieces' to be added to the jigsaw as part of an 'overall published framework', though it is not fully clear which would be included in the main annual statistical bulletin (or 'headline release') and which in supplementary reports:

- BCS findings on crimes against children aged 10–15;
- counts of non-notifiable summary offences (based on Ministry of Justice records of penalties imposed through magistrates' court sentences, cautions, penalty notices for disorder, etc.); and
- police records of incidents of 'anti-social behaviour',

and the following as areas for future development:

- fraud data (especially from reports to the National Fraud Authority);
- crimes against business (from a proposed national survey of such crimes, conducted every two years);
- estimates of the extent of cybercrime.

### THE PROBLEM OF TRUST

The other major issue that has emerged in recent years is that of public distrust of the official statistics. The Smith Report summed up the problem as follows:

> Public trust in crime statistics can be undermined by any or all of the following: presentations of statistics that are perceived to be in conflict with—or of no relevance to—the direct individual experiences of members of the public; presentations of statistics using categories or definitions that do not accord with public commonsense interpretations; presentation of conflicting statistics apparently open to widely differing interpretations; lack of coverage of significant areas of criminal activity and victims; perceived potential for police or ministerial interference in the production and presentation of the statistics. (Smith 2006: p. iii)

Ironically, this suggests that some of the changes discussed earlier, that were introduced ostensibly to improve the reliability and 'truth' of the official statistics (such as the inclusion of common assault in the Notifiable Offence List, the NCRS, and the publication of BCS findings alongside police figures), have actually had the perverse effect of *increasing* distrust. They have made the statistics more difficult for casual observers to interpret and have opened up more opportunities for politicians to exploit contradictions in the data and 'cherry pick' figures to their party's advantage, or to sow general mistrust of the integrity of the data. Media responses to the release of statistics tend to look no further than the raw figures, and show little interest in 'technical' arguments that there have 'actually' been falls, not rises.

Concerns have also been expressed that the presentation and publication of the national statistics have been increasingly caught up in political 'spin'.[14] Undoubtedly, as the political climate around crime has heated up, the pressure on civil servants involved in this process has increased. The old *Criminal Statistics* consisted mainly of standard tables with little comment, but the new statistical bulletins require analysis and interpretation—for example, in explaining possible reasons for differences in trends in police and BCS figures. There is an inevitable temptation for them, consciously or unconsciously, to offer the most favourable interpretation from the Government's point of view (and even if they do not, they will be accused of it). The process of releasing the publication, too, has come under critical scrutiny. For example, the Statistics Commission (2005: 4) stated:

> [O]ur impression is that, faced with a sceptical and at times antagonistic press, the Home Office and other official bodies have sought to contain the flow of statistical messages—prescribing the frequency and form in which statistics are released, and making sure that policy responses are issued at the earliest possible moment, sometimes ahead of the figures themselves. Whilst there is inevitably an element of conjecture in this 'outsider's analysis', we believe that any such control is almost always counterproductive in terms of public confidence. It creates an environment in which the media and public assume that they are receiving a filtered, government friendly, version of the truth—even though the statistical message may not be either of those things.

Finally, a rather different reason for declining faith in criminal statistics has been an increasing mismatch between what the general public tend to think of as 'crime' (influenced by their own experiences, images in the media, and so on) and what is measured in the official crime statistics. Most people tend to make little distinction between 'crime' and 'anti-social behaviour'. As the general impression seems to be that levels of, for example, aggressive behaviour in the street by groups of youths, or late night disorder in town centres—much of which is not counted as crime in the published statistics—have increased significantly in recent years, it is therefore not surprising that there is widespread reluctance to believe the official message that crime rates have been falling. In every sweep of the BCS since 1996—a period in which both BCS and police-recorded crime totals have fallen quite sharply—it has been found that between 58 and 75 per cent of respondents believed that over the previous two years, there had

---

[14] This is of course not unique to crime statistics: disbelief of government figures and concerns about 'spin' are widespread in many other areas of policy (Duffy *et al.* 2005). However, it has been one of the most prominent themes in recent discussions about the future of crime statistics.

been 'a little more' or 'a lot more' crime in the country as a whole: see Chaplin *et al.* 2011: 82.

Most of the recent inquiries into the future of criminal statistics have concluded that overcoming the problem of public mistrust requires greater transparency and more independent oversight and control of the process of collecting, analysing, and presenting data (Statistics Commission 2006; UK Statistics Authority 2010). In 2010 the Home Secretary decided that the main responsibility for management of the process and publication of the results would be transferred to an independent body. The body selected is the Office for National Statistics, the current plan being for the ONS to take on contract management of the BCS and the compilation of police-recorded crime estimates, while leaving responsibility for the collection and validation of recorded crime data with the Home Office (Matheson 2011). By placing control over the interpretation and presentation of the data in independent hands, it is hoped that the main causes of mistrust will be removed.


BACK TO BASICS?

While the transfer of the official criminal statistics into independent hands may impact upon public trust, it will not in itself solve some of the fundamental dilemmas surrounding the concept of a regularly updated national 'picture' of crime. Many of the recent developments and proposed changes discussed in this chapter raise basic questions about the purposes of such a set of statistics, and what it should or should not contain.

As stated at the beginning of the chapter, although it has always had other uses as well, the main justification for the continued existence of the official statistics is the need for a national 'barometer' of the level of crime. This is seen as part of the democratic accountability of the government for the welfare of its citizens. An important element of this is the capacity to track change over time, as represented by both long- and short-term 'trends' in the figures produced. Another desirable element is simplicity—at the extreme the production of a *single measure* (such as a total number of recorded crimes) that can be compared year-on-year.

For many years, the annual statistical series based on police-recorded crime served this purpose and met these criteria well enough in most people's eyes. However, as modes of offending grew in complexity and knowledge about a variety of previously 'hidden' crime increased, it became increasingly difficult to argue that these figures—and particularly the incongruously precise single total of recorded offences (4,150,097 in 2010/11)—represented anything like the 'true state of crime' in the country. Moreover, attempts to produce a fuller and more realistic picture (through changes in counting rules, the NCRS, and so on) had the serious drawback of undermining the comparability of data year-on-year, so that measurement of trends became difficult, complex, and confusing. This basic dilemma—between the constant pursuit of 'comprehensiveness' and the need for comparability over time—can still be seen in the recent debates about the future of the official statistics. For example, the Smith Review recommended extending their coverage (to include under-16s and non-household residents in the BCS figures, as well as new sources of data on crimes currently inadequately covered), yet at the same time urged caution about the pace of change, recommending that, 'when significant changes are made, a period of relative stability should be planned while they are absorbed' (Smith 2006: 17).

Similar points can be made about the demand for 'relevance'. If the national statistics are frequently tinkered with to produce data of a kind and in a form that policy-makers find useful at that particular point in time (for example, by replacing legal classifications of offences with new categories and datasets reflecting socially constructed 'crime problems' of the day), year-on-year comparison becomes highly problematic.

A more fundamental question is whether, even leaving aside the problem of measuring trends, it makes any sense to aim to produce an 'overall' or 'total' measure of crime—to use the National Statistician's analogy, to try to complete the full jigsaw. Clearly, if this was understood in terms of adding together every 'crime' known (through any reliable source available) to have been committed in a given year, and coming up with a total figure, the task would be made almost impossibly difficult by problems of definition, double counting, serial victimization, and so on. More importantly, one would have to question whether the resulting figure would have any sensible meaning, having been arrived at by adding together a range of very different types of behaviour, (the proverbial 'apples and pears'), some of them inherently more 'countable' than others. They would inevitably be dominated, too, by a vast number of minor offences, many of them on the very fuzzy borderline between criminal and anti-social (but non-criminal) behaviour. In the words of Smith (2006: 9):

> We are also clear that there can never be a measure of 'overall' or 'total' crime. There will always be crimes not adequately captured in the statistics and a single total number would bring together a very wide range of acts and degrees of seriousness in a not very meaningful way. What matters—and is attainable—is to develop national crime statistics series that have clearly understood strengths and weaknesses and are consistent enough over time to provide trend data for whatever area of crime each measures.

Given these arguments, the logical conclusion seems to be that any attempt to present the 'national state of crime' through a single statistical measure (both in any given year, and as a trend over time) should focus on *more serious and more reliably measurable offences*. Some consideration has been given to the production of a 'crime index' based around a 'basket' of selected offences of these kinds, whose contents would change little from year to year, allowing relatively robust measurement of trends. Rather like the FTSE index in relation to all company shares, it would act as a reasonably sound proxy for the overall state of crime.[15] The core argument for such an index is put by the National Statistician (Matheson 2011: 49) as follows:

> The user need is to provide the general population, politicians and decision makers with a clear understanding what is happening over time with crime in England and Wales which is not heavily influenced or dominated by changes in reporting or recording practices or dominated by high volume low severity offences.

---

[15] It could be argued that this is not far off what the recorded crime statistics have always done: by including only notifiable offences they focus on the more serious end of the crime spectrum, and—apart from periods of upheaval—roughly the same 'basket' has been measured in a similar way each year. However, the difference is that notifiable offences have not been selected in any logical fashion to represent 'crime': they are accidental products of a long history of legislation and contain a mixture of the very serious and the almost trivial, and of offences more and less susceptible to the vagaries of reporting and recording behaviour.

Objections to such a move—which, paradoxically, seems to go against the current trend towards *extending* statistical coverage, rather than limiting it—include the concern that it might be interpreted as a message that the Government does not care about 'minor' crimes, and it is partly for this reason that the idea has so far been shelved. However, Smith (2006) suggests that this objection can be met by developing ways of measuring, mapping, and sharing information with the public about minor crime and anti-social behaviour at a *local* level:

> At local level we believe that we should no longer be thinking about crime statistics in the traditional static sense of tables of numbers and graphs published as a record, but rather as a dynamic exchange of potentially useful information between the police and the public. For that reason, considerations about the level and form of information and its mode of communication are quite different from those applied to national crime statistics.

This clear distinction between the purposes of national and local crime statistics—the one filling the traditional role of a 'barometer' of the 'national state of crime' and the other flexible enough to respond to emerging crime problems and the fast-changing data requirements of practitioners—seems to offer a promising way forward out of the contradictory situation in which policies around criminal statistics have found themselves. Whether the 'barometer' is provided by a single measure like a crime index or by some other means (for example, through separate analyses of trends in specific offences based on data from different sources) is a secondary issue: the key point is that in recent years the 'official' (national) statistics have been expected to serve too many purposes at once, and that it may be time for a return to basics and a renewed focus on their traditional role.

### ■ SELECTED FURTHER READING

There are relatively few recent textbooks on criminal statistics, especially in the UK. Although obviously out of date in some respects, *Understanding Crime Data*, by Clive Coleman and Jenny Moynihan (Open University Press 1996) is still one of the best British textbooks on the subject, and covers in more depth several of the main issues discussed in this chapter. It has the added advantage of accessibility and a light and humorous touch.

The annual statistical bulletin, *Crime in England and Wales* (the most recent at the time of writing authored by R. Chaplin, J. Flatley, and K. Smith (Home Office 2011), though responsibility will eventually pass to the Office of National Statistics) is highly recommended both as the key source of national statistics and for its clarity of style and presentation. For those interested in methodological issues in relation to recorded crime and the British Crime Survey, the *User Guide to Home Office Crime Statistics* (Home Office 2011) is informative and readily comprehensible. Both can be downloaded from the Home Office website, whose research and statistics pages (www.homeoffice.gov.uk/publications/science-research-statistics/research-statistics/crime-research/) should be the first port of call for anyone wishing to explore the subject. The site contains other statistical bulletins and analyses of data from police and other agency records, the BCS, and other crime-related surveys. Among those most relevant to discussions in this chapter are Shury et al. (2005), *Crime against retail and manufacturing premises: Findings from the 2002 Commercial Victimisation Survey*, and Millard, B. and Flatley, J. (eds) (2010), *Experimental statistics on victimisation of children aged 10 to 15: Findings from the British Crime Survey for the year ending December 2009*.

Older research reports can be found in the National Archive (webarchive.nationalarchives. gov.uk/20110218135832/http://rds.homeoffice.gov.uk/rds/pubsintro1.html).

There are also several compilations of data and statistics providing international comparisons of crime rates and patterns. Among the most comprehensive is the *European Sourcebook of Crime and Criminal Justice Statistics* (2010), 4th edn (The Hague: Ministry of Justice, Research and Documentation Centre). Interesting cross-national surveys include the *International Crime Victim Survey* (Alvazzi del Frate and Van Kesteren 2004; van Dijke *et al.* 2010) and the *International Crime Business Survey* (see Alvazzi Del Frate 2005).

Statistical and other kinds of research data on the nature and extent of over 40 separate types of crime (together with data on their history and social context) are presented and analysed in the comprehensive *Handbook on Crime*, edited by Brookman *et al.* (2010).

Finally, two thoughtful reviews of the future of crime statistics are provided by Adrian Smith's (2006) *Crime Statistics: An Independent Review* (Home Office) and Jil Matheson's (2011) *National Statistician's Review of Crime Statistics: England and Wales* (Government Statistical Service).

# ■ REFERENCES

ALVAZZI DEL FRATE, A. (2005), 'The International Crime Business Survey: Findings from Nine Central–Eastern European Cities', *European Journal on Criminal Policy and Research*, Vol. 10, 2(3): 137–61.

—— and VAN KESTEREN, J. N. (2004), *Criminal Victimisation in Urban Europe. Key Findings of the 2000 International Crime Victims Survey*, Turin: UNICRI.

ATTORNEY GENERAL'S OFFICE (2006), *Fraud Review: Final Report*, London: Attorney General's Office.

AUDIT COMMISSION (2004), *Improving the Quality of Crime Records in Police Authorities and Forces in England and Wales*, London: Audit Commission.

—— and the WALES AUDIT OFFICE (2006), *Crime Recording 2005: Improving the Quality of Crime Records In Police Authorities and Forces in England and Wales*, London: Audit Commission.

BAKER, A. and DUNCAN, S. (1985), 'Child Sexual Abuse: A Study of Prevalence in Great Britain', *Child Abuse and Neglect*, 9: 457–67.

BARTER, C., RENOLD, E., BERRIDGE, D., and CAWSON, P. (2004), *Peer Violence in Children's Residential Care*, Basingstoke: Palgrave Macmillan.

BEIRNE, P. (1993), *Inventing Criminology: Essays on the Rise of 'Homo Criminalis'*, Albany, NY: State University of New York Press.

BESCHAROV, D. (1981), 'Toward better research on child abuse and neglect: Making definitional issues an explicit methodological concern', *Child Abuse and Neglect*, 5: 383–90.

BLAIR, I. (1984), *Investigating Rape: A New Approach for the Police*, London: Croom Helm.

BOTTOMLEY, A. K. and COLEMAN, C. A. (1981), *Understanding Crime Rates*, Farnborough: Saxon House.

BOTTOMS, A. E. (1995), 'The Philosophy and Politics of Punishment and Sentencing', in C. Clarkson and R.

Morgan (eds), *The Politics of Sentencing Reform*, Oxford: Clarendon Press.

BRAITHWAITE, J. (1979), *Inequality, Crime and Public Policy*, London: Routledge & Kegan Paul.

BRITISH CHAMBERS OF COMMERCE (2008), *The Invisible Crime: A Business Crime Survey*, London: British Chambers of Commerce.

BROOKMAN, F., MAGUIRE, M., PIERPOINT, H., and BENNETT, T. (eds) (2010), *Handbook on Crime*, Devon: Willan.

BUDD, T. and MATTINSON, J. (2000), *The Extent and Nature of Stalking: Finding from the 1998 British Crime Survey*, Research Study No. 210, London: Home Office.

BULLOCK, K. and TILLEY, N. (ed.) (2003), *Crime Reduction and Problem-oriented Policing*, Devon: Willan.

CHAPLIN, R., FLATLEY, J., and SMITH, K. (2011), *Crime in England and Wales, 2010/11*, Statistical Bulletin 10/11, London: Home Office. www.homeoffice. gov.uk/publications/science-research-statistics/research-statistics/crime-research/hosb1011/.

CHIVITE-MATTHEWS, N. and MAGGS, P. (2002), *Crime, Policing and Justice: The Experience of Older People. Findings from the British Crime Survey, England and Wales*, Online Report 08/02, London: Home Office.

CLANCY, A., HOUGH, M., AUST, R., and KERSHAW, C. (2001), *Crime, Policing and Justice: The Experience of Ethnic Minorities. Findings from the 2000 British Crime Survey*, Home Office Research Study No. 223, London: Home Office.

CLARKE, R. V. G. (1980), 'Situational Crime Prevention: Theory and Practice', *British Journal of Criminology*, 20: 136–47.

—— and FELSON, M. (eds) (1993), *Routine Activity and Rational Choice. Advances in Criminological Theory, Vol 5*, New Brunswick, NJ: Transaction Books.

COHEN, S. (2001), *States of Denial: Knowing about Atrocities and Suffering*, Cambridge: Polity Press.

COLEMAN, C. and MOYNIHAN, J. (1996), *Understanding Crime Data*, Buckingham and Philadelphia, Penn.: Open University Press.

CRAWFORD, A., JONES, T., WOODHOUSE, T., and YOUNG, J. (1990), *Second Islington Crime Survey*, London: Middlesex Polytechnic.

CURRAN, C., DALE, M., EDMUNDS, M., HOUGH, M., MILLIE, A., and WAGSTAFF, M. (2005), 'Street Crime in London: Deterrence, Disruption and Displacement', London: Government Office for London.

DITTON, J. (1977), *Part-time Crime*, London: Macmillan.

DOBASH, R. E. and DOBASH, R. P. (1992), *Women, Violence and Social Change*, London: Routledge.

—— and —— (2004), 'Women's Violence to Men in Intimate Relationships', *British Journal of Criminology*, 44(3): 324–49.

DUFFY, B., HALL, S., and WILLIAMS, M. (2005), *Who do you Believe? Trust in Government Information*, London: MORI.

ESTRADA, F. (2006), 'Violence in Scandinavia According to Different Indicators: An Exemplification of the Value of Swedish Hospital Data', *British Journal of Criminology*, 46(3): 486–504.

EVANS, J. (2010), 'Institutional abuse and children's homes', in F. Brookman, M. Maguire, H. Pierpoint, and T. Bennett (eds) (2010), *Handbook on Crime*, Devon: Willan.

FARRINGTON, D. P. and DOWDS, E. A. (1985), 'Disentangling Criminal Behaviour and Police Reaction', in D. P. Farrington and J. Gunn (eds), *Reaction to Crime: The Public, The Police, Courts and Prisons*, Chichester: John Wiley.

—— and LANGAN, P. (1998), *Crime and Justice in the United States and in England and Wales 1981–96*, Washington DC: Bureau of Justice.

FINKELHOR, D. and ARAJI, S. (1986), *A Sourcebook on Child Sexual Abuse*, Newbury Park: Sage.

FOUCAULT, M. (1977), *Discipline and Punish: The Birth of the Prison*, London: Allen Lane.

GARLAND, D. (2001), *The Culture of Control*, Oxford: Oxford University Press.

GENN, H. (1988), 'Multiple Victimization', in M. Maguire and J. Pointing (eds), *Victims of Crime: A New Deal?*, Milton Keynes: Open University Press.

GRADY, A. (2002), 'Female-on-Male Domestic Abuse: Uncommon or Ignored?', in C. Hoyle and R. Young (eds), *New Visions of Crime Victims*, Oxford: Hart Publishing.

GREEN, P. and WARD, T. (2005), 'Introduction', Special Issue, *British Journal of Criminology*, Vol. 45(4): 431–3.

HALL, R. (1985), *Ask Any Woman: A London Enquiry into Rape and Sexual Assault*, Bristol: Falling Wall Press.

HANMER, J. and SAUNDERS, S. (1984), *Well-founded Fear*, London: Hutchinson.

HENDERSON, L. (2003), *Prevalence of Domestic Violence among Lesbians and Gay Men: Data report to Flame TV*, London: Sigma Research.

HOME OFFICE (1971), *Instructions for the Preparation of Statistics Relating to Crime*, London: HMSO.

—— (2001), *Criminal Statistics, England and Wales 2000*, Cmnd. 5312, London: Home Office.

—— (2011), *User Guide to Home Office Crime Statistics*, London: Home Office. www.home-office.gov.uk/publications/science-research-statistics/research-statistics/crime-research/user-guide-crime-statistics/.

HOUGH, M. (ed.) (2004), *Evaluating the Crime Reduction Programme*, Special Issue of *Criminal Justice*, 3(3): 211–25.

—— (2007), 'Policing, New Public Management and Legitimacy', in T. Tyler (ed.), *Legitimacy and Criminal Justice*, New York: Russell Sage Foundation.

—— and MAYHEW, P. (1983), *The British Crime Survey*, Home Office Research Study No. 76, London: HMSO.

—— and —— (1985), *Taking Account of Crime: Key Findings from the Second British Crime Survey*, Home Office Research Study No. 85, London: HMSO.

IRELAND, J. (ed.) (2005), *Bullying Among Prisoners: Innovations in Research and Theory*, Devon: Willan.

JOHN. T. and MAGUIRE, M. (2007), 'Criminal Intelligence and the National Intelligence Model', in T. Newburn (ed.), *Handbook of Criminal Investigation*, Devon: Willan.

JONES, T., MACLEAN, B., and YOUNG, J. (1986), The *Islington Crime Survey: Crime, Victimization and Policing in Inner City London*, Aldershot: Gower.

—— LEA, J., and YOUNG, J. (1987), *Saving the Inner City: The First Report of the Broadwater Farm Survey*, London: Middlesex Polytechnic.

KINSEY, R. (1984), *Merseyside Crime Survey: First Report*, Liverpool: Merseyside Metropolitan Council.

LEVI, M. (1985), *The Investigation, Prosecution and Trial of Serious Fraud*. Research Report No. 14, London: Royal Commission on Criminal Justice.

—— (2001), 'The costs of transnational and other financial crime: making sense of worldwide data', *International Journal of Comparative Criminology*, 1(2): 8–26.

—— (2008), *The Phantom Capitalists: The Organization and Control of Long-Firm Fraud*, 2nd edn, Andover: Ashgate.

—— and BURROWS, J. (2008), 'Measuring the Impact of Fraud in the UK: A Conceptual and Empirical Journey', *British Journal of Criminology*, 48(3): 293–318.

—— and MAGUIRE, M. (2004), 'Reducing and preventing organised crime: an evidence-based critique', *Crime, Law and Social Change*, 41(5): 397–469.

McCABE, S. and SUTCLIFFE, F. (1978), *Defining Crime: A Study of Police Decisions*, Oxford: Blackwell.

McLINTOCK, F., and AVISON, N. H. (1968), *Crime in England and Wales*, London: Heinemann.

MAGUIRE, M. (2000), 'Policing by risks and targets: Some dimensions and implications of intelligence-led crime control', *Policing and Society*, Vol 9: 1–22.

—— (2007), 'Crime data and statistics', in M Maguire, R. Morgan, and R. Reiner (eds), *The Oxford*

*Handbook of Criminology*, 4th edn, Oxford: Oxford University Press. http://www.oup.com/uk/orc/bin/9780199205431/maguire_chap10.pdf.

—— (2008), 'Criminal Investigation and Crime Control', in T. Newburn (ed.), *Handbook of Policing*, 2nd edn, Devon: Willan.

—— in collaboration with BENNETT, T. (1982), *Burglary in a Dwelling: The Offence, the Offender and the Victim*, London: Heinemann Educational Books.

—— and HOPKINS, M. (2003), 'Data and analysis for problem-solving: alcohol-related crime in pubs, clubs and the street', in K. Bullock and N. Tilley (eds), *Crime Reduction and Problem-oriented Policing*, Devon: Willan.

—— and JOHN, T. (2006), 'Intelligence Led Policing, Managerialism and Community Engagement: Competing Priorities and the Role of the National Intelligence Model in the UK', *Policing and Society*, 16(1): 67–85.

MARS, G. (1982), *Cheats at Work*, London: Allen and Unwin.

MARTIN, J. P. (1962), *Offenders as Employees*, London: Macmillan.

MATHESON, J. (2011), *National Statistician's Review of Crime Statistics: England and Wales*, London: Government Statistical Service.

MATTHEWS, R. and YOUNG, J. (eds) (1986), *Confronting Crime*, London: Sage.

MAXWELL, R., TROTTER, C., BROWN, P., and GUNNELL, D., 'Trends in admissions to hospital involving an assault using a knife or other sharp instrument, England, 1997–2005', *Journal of Public Health*, 29(2): 186–90.

—— and HOUGH, J. M. (1988), 'The British Crime Survey: Origins and Impact', in M. Maguire and J. Pointing (eds), *Victims of Crime: A New Deal?*, Milton Keynes: Open University Press.

MINKES, J. (2010), 'Corporate financial crimes', in F. Brookman, M. Maguire, H. Pierpoint, and T. Bennett (eds), *Handbook on Crime*, Devon: Willan.

MIRRLEES-BLACK, C. (1999), *Domestic Violence: Findings from a new British Crime Survey Self-Completion Questionnaire*, Home Office Research Study No. 191. London: Home Office.

—— and ZEDNER, L. (1992), *Child Victims: Crime, Impact and Criminal Justice*, Oxford: Oxford University Press.

PAINTER, K. (1991), *Wife Rape, Marriage and the Law: Survey Report*, Manchester: Faculty of Economic and Social Science, University of Manchester.

PASSAS, N. and GROSKIN, R. (2001), 'Overseeing and overlooking: The US federal authorities' response to money laundering and other misconduct at BCCI', *Crime Law and Social Change*, 35(1–2): 141–75.

PERCY, A. and MAYHEW, P. (1997), 'Estimating sexual victimisation in a national crime survey: a new approach', *Studies in Crime and Crime Prevention* 6(2): 125–50.

PRICEWATERHOUSE COOPERS (2005), 'Global Economic Crime Survey 2005'. www.econcrime.uni-halle.de, www.pwcglobal.com.

RADFORD, J. (1987), 'Policing Male Violence', in J. Hanmer and M. Maynard (eds), *Women, Violence and Social Control*, London: Macmillan.

RADFORD, L., CORRAL, S., BRADLEY, C., FISHER, H., BASSETT, C., HOWAT, N., and COLLISHAW, S. (2011), *Child abuse and neglect in the UK today*, London: NSPCC.

ROBINSON, A. L. (2010), 'Domestic violence', in F. Brookman, M. Maguire, H. Pierpoint, and T. Bennett (eds), *Handbook of Crime*, Devon: Willan.

SAUNDERS, D. (2002), 'Are Physical Assaults by Wives and Girlfriends a Major Social Problem? A Review of the Literature', *Violence Against Women*, 8(12): 1424–48.

SEDLAK, A. J., METTENBURG, J., BASENA, M., PETTA, I., McPHERSON, K., GREENE, A., and LI, S. (2010), *Fourth National Incidence Study of Child Abuse and Neglect (NIS–4): Report to Congress*, Washington, DC: US Department of Health and Human Services, Administration for Children and Families.

SELKE, W. and PEPINSKY, H. (1984), 'The Politics of Police Reporting in Indianapolis 1948–78', in W. J. Chambliss (ed.), *Criminal Law in Action*, New York: Wiley.

SENIOR, P. CROWTHER-DOVEY, C., and LONG, M. (2007), *Understanding the Modernisation of Criminal Justice*, Milton Keynes: Open University Press.

SHURY, J., SPEED, M., VIVIAN, D., KUECHEL, A., and NICHOLAS, S. (2005), *Crime against retail and manufacturing premises: Findings from the 2002 Commercial Victimisation Survey, Online report 37/05*, London: Home Office.

SIMMONS, J. (2000), *Review of Crime Statistics: A Discussion Document*, London: Home Office.

——, LEGG, C., and HOSKING, R. (2003), *National Crime Recording Standard (NCRS): an Analysis of the Impact on Recorded Crime*, Home Office Online Report 31/03, London: Home Office. http://webarchive.nationalarchives.gov.uk/20110218135832/http://rds.homeoffice.gov.uk/rds/pdfs2/rdsolr3103.pdf.

SIVARAJASINGAM, V., MORGAN, P., MATTHEWS, K., SHEPHER, J., and WALKER, R. (2009), 'Trends in violence in England and Wales 2000–2004: an accident and emergency perspective', *Injury*, 40(8): 820–5.

SMITH, A. (2006), *Crime Statistics: An Independent Review*, London: Home Office.

SERIOUS ORGANISED CRIME AGENCY (2009), *The United Kingdom Threat Assessment of Organised Crime 2009/10*, London: Serious Organised Crime Agency.

SPARKS, R., GENN, H., and DODD, D. (1977), *Surveying Victims*, Chichester: John Wiley.

STANKO, E. (1988), 'Hidden Violence against Women', in M. Maguire and J. Pointing (eds), *Victims of Crime: A New Deal?*, Milton Keynes: Open University Press.

STATISTICS COMMISSION (2005), *Crime Statistics: User Perspectives*, Interim Report, London: Statistics Commission.

—— (2006), *Crime Statistics: User Perspectives*, Report No. 30, London: Statistics Commission.

STRAUS, M., GELLES, R., and STEINMETZ, S. (1980), *Behind Closed Doors*, New York: Anchor Press.

TNS-BRMB (2010), *British Crime Survey 2009–10 Technical report*, London: Home Office. www.homeoffice.gov.uk/publications/science-research-statistics/research-statistics/crime-research/bcs0910tech1.

TOMBS, S. (2010), 'Corporate Violence and Harm', in F. Brookman, M. Maguire, H. Pierpoint, and T. Bennett (eds), *Handbook on Crime*, Devon: Willan.

UK STATISTICS AUTHORITY (2010), *Overcoming Barriers to Trust in Crime Statistics: England and Wales*, Monitoring Report 5, London: UK Statistics Authority.

VAN DIJK, J., VAN KESTFREN, J. and SMIT, P. (2010), Criminal Victimisation in International Perspective, Den Haag: WODC. http://62.50.10.34/icvs/Products/Archive/ICVS_5_2004_5.

WALBY, S. and ALLEN, J. (2004), *Domestic violence, sexual assault and stalking: Findings from the British Crime Survey*, Home Office Research Study 276, London: Home Office Development and Statistics Directorate.

WALKER, N. D. (1971), *Crimes, Courts and Figures: An Introduction to Criminal Statistics*, Harmondsworth: Penguin.

YOUNG, J. (1988a), 'Radical Criminology in Britain: The Emergence of a Competing Paradigm', *British Journal of Criminology*, 28(2): 289–313.

—— (1988b), 'Risk of Crime and Fear of Crime: a Realist Critique of Survey-based Assumptions', in M. Maguire and J. Pointing (eds), *Victims of Crime: A New Deal?*, Milton Keynes: Open University Press.

YOUNG, M. (1991), *An Inside Job*, Oxford: Clarendon Press.

# 9

# MEDIATED MAYHEM: MEDIA, CRIME, CRIMINAL JUSTICE

*Chris Greer and Robert Reiner*

## INTRODUCTION: COPS, CROOKS, AND CULTURE— THE REACH OF MEDIATED IMAGES

A key feature of contemporary societies is the omnipresence of mass media of communication, in rapidly proliferating new forms. A significant part of each day is devoted by most people to media consumption of various kinds. In 2010, on average people watched 4.03 hours of television daily (BARB: *Trends in Television Viewing 2010*, February 2011).

There is much controversy about the significance and effects of this media consumption, in particular for crime and criminal justice (see Hayward and Young, this volume, on 'Cultural Criminology' and Hough and Roberts, this volume, about public views on crime and justice). The salience of the media as perceived by people themselves is huge. A 2002 survey of Londoners found for example that their 'knowledge' of the police was overwhelmingly drawn from the media. 80 per cent of those interviewed said their main source of information about policing was the news media (four times as many as cited direct experience). Perhaps even more surprising is that 29 per cent saw 'media fiction' as a crucial source—9 per cent more than 'direct experience'. It is fascinating to ponder whether this is mainly the more 'realistic' fictional representations, such as *The Bill* (described by former Met Commissioner Ian Blair as a permanent NVQ on policing) or *The Wire*, or *Midsomer Murders*, the rural idyll shattered by more killings than Al Capone's Chicago (and where it was a deliberate choice to exclude ethnic minority characters—'Midsomer Murders producer suspended over diversity remarks', *The Guardian*, 15 March 2011; McCaw 2011: ch. 7).

The ubiquity and the widely perceived influence of media representations of crime and criminal justice have stimulated various concerns about mass media representations of crime, deviance, and disorder that have accompanied their development. It has long been feared, in particular by more conservative opinion, that the media are a significant cause of offending, and are fundamentally subversive. This has been a perennially recurring aspect of the 'history of respectable fears' that Geoffrey Pearson has traced back through the last few centuries (Pearson 1983).

A contrasting concern about media representations of crime has worried liberals and radicals (Wykes 2001). To them the media are the cause not of crime itself but of exaggerated public alarm about law and order, generating support for repressive solutions (Gerbner 1970, 1995). In their ideal-typical form these perspectives are polar opposites, sharing in common only their demonization of the media. Each has generated huge research industries conducting empirical studies of media content, production, and effects (for critical analytic reviews see Brown 2003; Carrabine 2008; Marsh 2008; Greer 2009; Jewkes 2010).

The difficulties in rigorously establishing straightforward causal relationships between images and effects have evoked the canard that media researchers are blinkered by libertarian prejudices. For example, Melanie Phillips has claimed that 'for years, media academics have pooh-poohed any link between violence on screen and in real life', because 'media images . . . merely provide "chewing gum for the eyes"' (Phillips 1996). This is a caricature of the media research on effects. A more sophisticated criticism of the effects research is that 'repeated failures to find anything much out would . . . suggest that the wrong question was being asked' (Brown 2003: 28). But the pervasiveness and prominence of media in contemporary life mean that 'the effects debate refuses to go away' (ibid.).

The purpose of this chapter is to offer an analytic overview of the extensive empirical research and theoretical debates about how media represent crime and criminal justice. What patterns and trends are there in these representations, what is their impact, and how are they shaped and developed? In short, it will examine the *content*, *consequences*, and *causes* of media representations of crime and criminal justice, and how these have changed and are changing.

In previous editions of *The Oxford Handbook of Criminology* a long chapter described in some detail the findings of the huge volume of empirical research, mainly within a positivist paradigm, on the content and consequences of media representations. This will only be briefly summarized here, partly because of the severe methodological and theoretical limitations of such research (the more detailed account found in earlier volumes will still be available on the website). Instead the focus here will be on theoretical analyses of media production and impact, and the dramatically changing character of these in contemporary culture.

The next section will provide a brief summary and critique of the empirical research on content, consequences, and causes of media representations of crime and justice. The second part will then give an overview of the theoretical debates about media, crime, criminalization, and control. The final section offers an analysis of the heightened significance of media representations of criminality and deviance in contemporary political-economic and cultural conditions.

# THE CONTENT AND CONSEQUENCES OF MEDIA REPRESENTATIONS OF CRIME: A BRIEF REVIEW OF EMPIRICAL RESEARCH

## CONTENT ANALYSIS: SOME METHODOLOGICAL HEALTH WARNINGS

'Content analysis' usually refers to a specific methodology for analysing the content of media, deploying quantitative techniques within a positivist theoretical paradigm. As defined by one leading practitioner, 'content analysis is a method of studying and analyzing communications in a systematic, objective, and quantitative manner for the purpose of measuring certain message variables, . . . free of the subjective bias of the reviewer' (Dominick 1978: 106–7).

There are major problems with the claim that content analysis is 'objective'. While the categories used to quantify 'certain message attributes' may be free of 'subjective bias' they are not randomly plucked out of thin air, and cannot miraculously reflect a structure of meaning objectively inherent in the texts. They necessarily embody theoretical presuppositions by the researcher about criteria of significance. Moreover, the categories selected for quantification usually presuppose some theory about likely consequences. Meticulously counting units of 'violence' is not a form of train-spotting for sadists but motivated by concern that exposure to these images carries risks such as desensitization, or heightened anxiety (Sparks 1992: 79–80).

There is a further fundamental problem with traditional content analyses. What the researcher codifies as instances of the 'same' image may have very different meanings within particular narratives and contexts of reception. How viewers interpret images of 'violence', for example, is not just a function of the amount of blood seen or number of screams heard. The same physical behaviour, for instance a shooting, means different things in different genres, say a Western, a war film, a contemporary cop show, or news bulletins. It will be interpreted differently if the violence is perpetrated on or by a character constructed in the narrative as sympathetic. How audiences construe violence will vary according to how they see their own position vis-à-vis the narrative characters, quite apart from any preferred reading intended by the creators or supposedly inscribed in the narrative. For example, to black audiences, Rodney King, whose beating by Los Angeles police officers was captured on an amateur videotape, was a victim of police racism, while to many white police officers he appeared to be a threatening deviant who invited the beating (Lawrence 2000: 70–3).

These problems do not mean that quantification can or should be avoided, but they refute the claims of positivist content analysis to quantify a supposed objective structure in texts. Counting features of texts should be self consciously seen as based on the observer's frame of reference, according to explicit criteria. Results must be interpreted reflexively and tentatively as one possible reading. As such, they can yield valuable insights and questions about the significance of trends and patterns.

## CONTENT ANALYSIS: A ROUND-UP OF RESULTS

### Crime 'fact', crime 'fiction': blurring the boundaries

Crime and criminal justice have long been sources of popular spectacle and entertainment, even before the rise of the mass media. This is illustrated by the genre of
criminal biography and pre-execution confessions and apologias, of various degrees
of authenticity, which flourished in the seventeenth and eighteenth centuries (Faller
1987; Rawlings 1992; Durston 1997). Similar accounts continue to the present day, filling the 'true crime' shelves of bookshops (Rawlings 1998; Peay 1998; Wilson 2000: ch.
4; Biressi 2001), and they have been joined by the many volumes retelling the exploits
of legendary cops as if they were fictional sleuths (e.g. Fabian 1950, 1954). In overtly
fictional crime narratives, ultra-realism (often a quasi-documentary style of presentation) has been the predominant style (Potter and Marshall 2010; Brunsdon 2010).

The fact/fiction distinction has become ever more fluid, with the emergence of what
is usually referred to as 'reality' television or 'infotainment' (Fishman and Cavender
1998; Leishman and Mason 2002: ch. 7). There has been the growth of programming
such as *Crimewatch UK* that re-creates current cases, often with an avowed purpose of
solving them (Jewkes 2010: ch. 6). Fly-on-the-wall footage of actual incidents has proliferated in documentaries like Roger Graef's pioneering 1982 Thames Valley Police
series, and entertainment programming based on real cops in action, for example *Cops*
(Doyle 2003). Live newscasts of particular occurrences are increasingly common, such
as the O. J. Simpson car chase and subsequent trial (Brown 2003: 56–60). Film footage of criminal events in process is frequently used in news broadcasts, perhaps most
influentially in the CCTV shots of Jamie Bulger being led away by his killers (Green
2008). Police deviance has been caught increasingly often on citizens' cameras since
the amateur video capturing the 1991 beating by Los Angeles police of Rodney King.
The video footage that showed newspaper seller Ian Tomlinson had been struck and
pushed to the ground by a police officer shortly before he died during the 2009 London
G20 demonstration is a recent dramatic example, leading to a coroner's verdict of
unlawful killing (Greer and McLaughlin 2011). Such challenging of official accounts
by the proliferation of citizen media, dubbed 'synopticon' (Mathiesen 1997) or 'sous-
veillance' (Mann *et al.* 2003) is a hugely significant factor making contemporary
media representations more complex and multi-faceted (Greer 2009: pt. 6). The police
for their part have increasingly resorted to the media as a part of criminal investigations (Innes 1999, 2003), as well as to cultivate support more generally (Mawby 1999,
2002, 2003, 2010a). The media and criminal justice systems are penetrating each other
increasingly, making a firm distinction between 'factual' and 'fictional' programming
tenuous (Manning 1998). The implications will be explored further in the conclusions,
but we will turn next to a consideration of the results of content analyses.

### Deviant news: extent

Crime narratives and representations are, and have always been, a prominent part of
the content of all mass media. The proportion of media content that is constituted by
crime items clearly will depend on the definitions of 'crime' used.

Richard Ericson and his colleagues adopted an exceptionally broad definition of
deviance for their study of news-making in Toronto (Ericson *et al.* 1987, 1989, 1991):

'the behaviour of a thing or person that strays from the normal . . . not only . . . criminal acts' (Ericson *et al.* 1987: 4). When defined so widely deviance is the essence of news, '*the* defining characteristic of what journalists regard as newsworthy' (ibid.). Unsurprisingly, given their broad definition, Ericson *et al.* found that a remarkably high proportion of news was about 'deviance and control', ranging from 45.3 per cent in a quality newspaper to 71.5 per cent on a quality radio station (Ericson *et al.* 1991: 239–42). Contrary to most other studies, they found that 'quality' broadcasting outlets had *more* deviance stories (both about violence and economic malpractice), because of 'their particular emphasis on deviance and control in public bureaucracies' (ibid.). Stories about crime in the narrower sense of violations of criminal law are a more limited but nonetheless generally high proportion of news, varying somewhat according to medium (e.g. radio, television, or print journalism), market (e.g. 'quality' or 'popular' journalism), and methodology (e.g. do we only consider stories about specific criminal incidents or include reports, articles, or also include editorials about the state of crime and criminal justice generally).

The proportion of crime news varies over time, and has generally increased in recent decades (albeit with persisting variations according to 'market'). The first study of crime news in Britain looked at crime news reporting in September 1938, 1955, and 1967 (Roshier 1973), and found that on average 4 per cent of stories in the three newspapers sampled were about crime. More recent studies have found higher percentages of crime news, for example a study of six Scottish newspapers in 1981 found that an average of 6.5 per cent of space was given to crime news (Ditton and Duffy 1983: 161; see also Smith 1984; Schlesinger *et al.* 1991: 411–15). This rise was confirmed by a later study comparing coverage of crime in 10 national daily newspapers for four weeks from 19 June 1989 (Williams and Dickinson 1993). 'On average, 12.7% of event-oriented news reports were about crime' (ibid.: 40). The proportion of space devoted to crime was greater the more 'downmarket' the newspaper. The smallest proportion of crime news was 5.1 per cent in the *Guardian*; the largest was 30.4 per cent in the *Sun* (ibid.: 41). The reporting of white-collar crime tends to be concentrated in 'quality' newspapers and is often restricted to specialist financial pages, sections, or newspapers (Stephenson-Burton 1995: 137–44), framed in ways that mark it off from 'real' crime unless they are sensational celebrity-style stories that are treated as a form of 'infotainment' (Tombs and Whyte 2001; Levi 2006).

A long-term historical study examined a random sample of issues of *The Times* and the *Mirror* for each year between 1945 and 1991 (Reiner *et al.* 2003). It found a generally upward (albeit fluctuating) trend in the proportion of stories focused on crime in both newspapers (from under 10 per cent in the 1940s to over 20 per cent in the 1990s). The sharpest increase occurred during the late 1960s, when the average annual proportion of crime stories almost doubled, from around 10 per cent to around 20 per cent in both papers. In both papers the proportion of stories about the criminal justice system, as distinct from the commission of criminal offences, has clearly increased since the Second World War. Criminal justice stories were on average 2 per cent of all stories in the *Mirror* between 1945 and 1951, and 3 per cent in *The Times*. By 1985–91 the average had increased to 6 per cent in the *Mirror*, and 9 per cent in *The Times*.

In conclusion, deviance and control in a broad sense are the very stuff of news. However, stories about the commission of particular offences are more common in 'popular' news outlets (although for official or corporate crime the reverse is true). The proportion of news devoted to crime and criminal justice has increased over the last half-century.

### Deviant news: patterns

Crime news exhibits remarkably similar patterns in studies conducted at many different times and places. From the earliest studies onwards, analyses of news reports have found that crimes of violence are featured disproportionately compared to their incidence in official crime statistics. In the USA 'the ratio of violent-to-property crime stories appearing in the surveyed newspapers was 8 to 2; however, official statistics reflected a property-to-violent crime ratio of more than 9 to 1 during the survey period' (Marsh 1991: 73). A similar pattern was found in 14 other countries (ibid.: 74–6). Indeed a general finding has been the lack of relationship between patterns and trends in crime news and crime statistics (Beckett 1997).

The previously cited historical study of two British newspapers since the Second World War found that homicide was by far the most common type of crime reported, accounting for about one-third of all crime news stories throughout the period (Reiner *et al.* 2000, 2001, 2003). Other violent crimes were the next most common. However, there were significant shifts in the proportion of stories featuring other sorts of crime. In particular there was a marked decline in the proportion of stories featuring 'volume' property crimes such as burglary in which no violence occurred (these are of course the overwhelming majority of crimes according to official statistics and crime surveys, cf. Maguire, this volume). During the 1940s and 1950s property crimes featured frequently in news stories, but after the mid-1960s they were hardly ever reported unless there was some celebrity angle. On the other hand, some offences began to feature prominently in news stories only after the mid-1960s, notably drug offences, which by the 1990s accounted for about 10 per cent of all crime stories.

Several studies confirm the pattern of increasing over-representation of violent and interpersonal (especially sex) crimes. Between 1951 and 1985 the number of rape trials in Britain increased nearly four times, from 119 to 450. In the same period, the number of rape cases reported in the press increased more than five times, from 28 to 154. The percentage of rape cases reported jumped from 23.5 per cent in 1951 to 34.2 per cent in 1985 (Soothill and Walby 1991: 20–2). In Northern Ireland, press reporting of sex cases tripled during the 1980s and 1990s (Greer 2003).

The proportion of news devoted to crime of different types, and the prominence with which it is presented, varies according to market and medium. In one month of 1989, 64.5 per cent of British newspaper crime stories featured violence, while the British Crime Survey found that only 6 per cent of crimes reported by victims were violent (Williams and Dickinson 1993: 40). The percentage of stories dealing with crimes involving personal violence, and the salience they were given, was considerably greater in more downmarket newspapers (ibid.: 40–3).

In Britain, the proportion of violent crimes reported in television news broadcasts is closer to the tabloid figure than the quality press, especially for local rather than national bulletins. One study found that the proportion of crime stories reporting non-sexual violence against the person in 'quality', 'mid-market', and 'tabloid' newspapers respectively was 24.7 per cent, 38.8 per cent, and 45.9 per cent. On national news bulletins it was 40 per cent; on local bulletins violent crime stories were 63.2 per cent of all crime news (Schlesinger *et al.* 1991: 412–15).

Homicide in general is the most prominent crime in news stories, but the likelihood of particular cases being reported varies systematically. A recent study analysed the reporting of homicide in three British newspapers between 1993 and 1997 (Peelo *et al.* 2004). Of the 2,685 police-recorded homicides in this period, just under 40 per cent were reported in at least one of the papers studied (ibid.: 261). 'Sexual homicides were most likely to be reported in all three newspapers, as were homicides where there was a clear motive for monetary gain, or a jealousy or revenge motive' (ibid.: 272). Least likely to be reported were the most common homicides, those arising out of 'rage or quarrel' (ibid.: 269). Victim characteristics were also important determinants of the likelihood of reporting. Homicides where the victim was a child (but not an infant), female, or of higher status were more likely to be reported (ibid.: 262–7).

An indirect consequence of the pattern of offences reported by news stories is an exaggeration of police success in clearing-up crime, 'because the police are more successful in solving violent crimes than property crimes' (Marsh 1991: 73). However, the representation of police success is declining: the 'clear-up' rate in news stories fell from 73 per cent in 1945–64 to 51 per cent in 1981–91 (Reiner *et al.* 2003: 23).

Most studies find that offenders and victims featuring in news reports are typically older and of higher status than those officially processed by the criminal justice system (Roshier 1973: 43–6; Reiner *et al.* 2003: 19–21). There is contradictory evidence about whether news reports disproportionately feature ethnic minority offenders (Graber 1980; Marsh 1991: 74; Sacco 1995: 143; Barlow 1998). Crime reports in local newspapers or broadcasting clearly focus more on ethnic minority and lower-status group suspects (Garofalo 1981: 324; Beckett and Sasson 2000: 79). 'Reality' television programmes also present a marked variation to national news reports in terms of the demography of the offenders portrayed, concentrating on stories with young, ethnic minority suspects (Oliver and Armstrong 1998). The one demographic characteristic of offenders which is overwhelmingly congruent in news stories and in all other data sources on crime is their gender: 'both crime statistics and crime news portray offending as predominantly a male activity' (Sacco 1995: 143).

Studies assessing the profile of victims in news stories are fewer in number than analyses of the representation of offenders. There is, however, a clear trend for victims to become the pivotal focus of news stories in the last three decades (Reiner *et al.* 2003), paralleling the increasing centrality of victims in criminal justice and criminology (see Hoyle, this volume) and crime fiction (Reiner *et al.* 2000 and 2001). News stories exaggerate the crime risks faced by higher status white people, as well as disproportionately representing women, children, or older people as victims (Mawby and Brown 1983; Chermak 1995; Chiricos *et al.* 1997; Beckett and Sasson 2000: 79–80; Greer 2003: 70–2; Reiner *et al.* 2003: 21–2; Peelo *et al.* 2004: 262–7).

Another consistent finding is the predominance of stories about criminal incidents, rather than analyses of crime patterns or the possible causes of crime (Garofalo 1981: 325; Marsh 1991: 76; Sasson 1995; Barlow 1998; Beckett and Sasson 2000: 80–1; Greer 2003: 66–70). Although an aspect of the more general event-orientation that is part of the 'eternal recurrence' of news (Rock 1973), the 'mass media provide citizens with a public awareness of crime . . . based upon an information-rich and knowledge-poor foundation' (Sherizen 1978: 204). An important example is the reporting of rape and other sex crimes, where issues of power and gender disappear in the fascination with the demonization of individual offenders or victims (Soothill and Walby 1991; Lees 1995; Greer 2003). Stories with child homicide victims and/or perpetrators are particularly likely to be featured so prominently that they become long-running stories with a familiar cast of characters, regularly invoked as symbols of wider issues or the state of the nation, illustrated by the Moors murders, and the Jamie Bulger and Soham cases (Jones and Wardle 2007; Green 2008).

The tendency to exclude analysis of broader structural processes or explanations is also evident in stories about political disorder (Halloran *et al.* 1970; Hall 1973: 232–43; Sumner 1982; Tumber 1982; Cottle 1993; De Luca and Peeples 2006). The portrayal of political conflict such as riot or terrorism is often in terms of sheer criminality (Clarke and Taylor 1980; Hillyard 1982; Iyengar 1991: 24–46; Hutchinson and Lester 2006).

There is a tendency in recent years for critical and campaigning groups to have more access to the media, partly because of the increasing politicization of law and order (Schlesinger and Tumber 1994; Reiner 2007: ch. 5; Downes and Morgan, this volume; Cottle 2008). Although critical stories exposing malpractice by the police or other criminal justice officials are regularly published, this 'watchdog' function has not served historically to undermine the legitimacy of criminal justice institutions. Corruption and other police deviance stories have tended to be situated within the 'one bad apple' framework, whereby the exposure of individual wrongdoing is interpreted as a testimony to the integrity of the system which dealt with it (Chibnall 1977: ch. 5). As the volume of police deviance stories has increased in recent years (Reiner *et al.* 2003: 22–4), the 'one bad apple' story becomes harder to recycle. An alternative damage-limitation narrative is to present scandals as stories of institutional reform. This acknowledges previous malpractice, but safeguards the legitimacy of the institution as it is portrayed as putting things right (Schlesinger and Tumber 1994: ch. 7).

Recently, this narrative has been complicated by a shift in media emphasis from 'institutional reform' as a means of re-legitimation to 'institutional failure' as a systemic characteristic of publicly funded bodies and a key determinant of newsworthiness (Greer and McLaughlin 2010). In a context of increased market competition, shrinking readerships, and a decline in deference to authority, newspapers in particular have gone on the offensive. The press now routinely engage in 'attack journalism', questioning the integrity of institutional power and seeking, often via 'trial by media', to hound senior public figures out of office (Greer and McLaughlin 2011).

## The content of crime fiction

Although there are some quantitative content analyses of film and television crime fiction,[1] a variety of qualitative techniques and theoretical perspectives drawn from literary, film, and social theory have more frequently been used.[2] The pattern of representation of crime in fictional stories, in all media, resembles the content analyses of crime news.

---

[1]  Pandiani 1978; Carlson 1985; Lichter *et al.* 1994; Powers *et al.* 1996; Allen *et al.* 1998.

[2]  Chibnall and Murphy 1999; Leishman and Mason 2002; Rafter 2006; Reiner 2008, 2010: ch.6; Rafter and Brown 2011 are just some of the most recent analyses of crime fiction.

Crime and detection have always been staples of modern literature, as Defoe, Fielding, Poe, and Dickens illustrate (Ousby 1976). Some authors have postulated an ancient ancestry for the detective story. 'We find sporadic examples of it in Oriental folk-tales, in the Apocryphal Books of the Old Testament, in the play-scene in *Hamlet*; while Aristotle in his *Poetics* puts forward observations about dramatic plot-construction which are applicable today to the construction of a detective mystery' (Sayers 1936: vii). This was clearly an attempt to emphasize the 'snobbery' rather than the 'violence' of the classic ratiocinative detective story (Watson 1971). The dominant style of crime fiction has varied from the classic puzzle mystery exemplified by Dorothy Sayers and Agatha Christie, to the tougher private eye stories pioneered by Dashiell Hammett and Raymond Chandler, and the police procedurals of Ed McBain, Joseph Wambaugh, and others. One estimate suggests that 'between a quarter and a third of total paperback output could probably be put into the category of "thriller" of one kind or another . . . since 1945, at least 10,000 million copies of crime stories have been sold world-wide' (Mandel 1984: 66–7).

Crime stories have also been a prominent genre in the cinema, the dominant mass medium of the first half of the twentieth century. As with its successors, television, video, and now digital media, the cinema has been haunted by respectable fears about its portrayal of crime and violence (Barker and Petley 2001). The proportion of films about crime has fluctuated cyclically since the Second World War, but there is no long-term increase or decrease (Allen *et al.* 1997). In most years, around 20 per cent of all films are crime movies, and around half of all films have significant crime content.

Radio was the main broadcasting medium of the first half of the twentieth century. Stories about crime and law enforcement were a popular part of radio drama, in Britain and North America, although never as dominant as they subsequently became on television (Shale 1996).

Stories about crime and law enforcement have saturated television ever since it became the leading broadcasting medium in the 1950s. By 1959 over one-third of American prime-time television was crime shows (Dominick 1978: 114). Crime shows are just as much a staple of British television. Since 1955 around 25 per cent of the most popular television shows in Britain in most years have been crime or police series. While there are sharp cyclical fluctuations, there is no long-term trend (Reiner *et al.* 2000 and 2001), but there have been changes in *how* crime and criminal justice are represented.

## The pattern of crime in fiction

The pattern of fictional representations of crime is similar to that in news stories—and shows similar discrepancies from the picture conveyed by official crime statistics. Murder and other violent crimes feature vastly more frequently than the property offences that predominate in official statistics. A historical analysis of the crime films that have done best at the British box office since the Second World War (Allen *et al.* 1998; Reiner *et al.* 2000 and 2001) found that murder was the primary crime (the McGuffin of the plot, in Hitchcock's terminology) in the overwhelming majority of films throughout the period. However, property offences provided the McGuffin in a significant minority of films up to the late 1960s, though seldom thereafter. Sex and drug offences began to appear as central aspects of narratives only after the late 1960s.

Since then crime is represented increasingly as an all-pervasive threat, not an abnormal, one-off intrusion into a stable order. Linked to this is the increasing prevalence in films of police heroes, signifying that crime has become sufficiently routine to provide employment for a large bureaucracy, not just a diversion for enthusiastic amateurs at country house weekends.

The representation of violence has become increasingly graphic throughout the period since the Second World War. Up to the early 1970s hardly any films showed more than a minor degree of pain or suffering by victims—even if they were murdered! Since then an increasing proportion of films depict victims in severe torment (Reiner *et al.* 2001: 184; Rafter and Brown 2011).

On television too, fictional narratives have always featured violent crimes most prominently, but are focusing on them even more. Studies of American television suggest that about two-thirds of crime on prime-time shows consists of murder, assault, or armed robbery (Lichter *et al.* 1994; Beckett and Sasson 2000: ch. 6). Ironically, in relation to property crime risks, television has become safer than the world presented in official statistics. Between 1955 and 1984, the average annual rate for serious property offences in the USA increased from 10 to 50 incidents per 1,000 people according to FBI data. However, on television 'the rate for serious property crimes has remained steady at 20 incidents per 1,000 characters over the thirty years of our study' (ibid.: 284). Thus between 1955 and 1964 the television property crime rate exceeded the official statistics, but since then it has fallen far behind them. There is also a trend for the cinema (and newspapers) to increasingly *understate* the risks of property crime (Allen *et al.* 1998: 65; Reiner *et al.* 2003: 18–19).

The character of crimes depicted in fiction is also vastly different from the officially recorded pattern. While most 'real' murders are extensions of brawls between young men (Dorling 2004), or domestic disputes, in fiction murder is usually motivated by greed and calculation (Allen *et al.* 1998: 69). Rape and other sex crimes are also presented in opposite ways in fiction (or news) and criminal justice statistics (Greer 2003: ch. 7). Most rapes are perpetrated by intimates or acquaintances, but on television and other fiction (and in news stories), rape is usually committed by psychopathic strangers and involves extreme brutality, often torture and murder.

While crime fiction presents property crime less frequently than the reality suggested by crime statistics, those it does portray are far more serious. Official statistics and victim surveys concur in calculating that the overwhelming majority of property crimes involve little or no loss or damage, and no physical threat or harm to the victim—indeed, there is usually no contact at all with the perpetrator. In fiction, however, most property crimes involve tightly planned, high-value, project thefts, and are frequently accompanied by violence.

Related to the disproportionate emphasis on the most serious end of the crime spectrum is the portrayal of the demographic characteristics of offenders and victims. Offenders in fiction are primarily higher-status, white, middle-aged males (Pandiani 1978: 442–7; Garofalo 1981: 326; Lichter *et al.* 1994: 290–5; Reiner *et al.* 2000 and 2001). Interestingly, the new genre of 'reality' infotainment cop shows such as *Cops* differs from this pattern, primarily presenting offenders as non-white, underclass youth (Fishman and Cavender 1998; Valverde 2006). The social characteristics of fictional victims are similar, but a higher proportion are female. The demographic profile of offenders and victims in fiction is the polar opposite of criminal justice statistics, apart from the maleness of most offenders (Surette 2010 calls this 'the law of opposites').

A final important feature of fictional crime is the high clear-up rate: media cops usually get their man in 50 minutes with commercial breaks. In a representative sample of movies since 1945, there was no film before 1952 in which criminals escaped capture, and hardly any up to the early 1970s. Thereafter, offenders get away with their crimes in an increasing number of films, albeit still a minority (Allen *et al.* 1998: 185; Reiner *et al.* 2000 and 2001). Trends on television are similar, with the overwhelming majority of crimes cleared up by the police, but an increasing minority where they fail (Lichter *et al.* 1994: ch. 9.).

The police and the criminal justice system are thus overwhelmingly portrayed in a positive light in popular fiction, as the successful protectors of victims against serious harm and violence. This continues to be so, although with increasing questioning of police success and integrity (Leishman and Mason 2003; Brown 2007; Cavender and Deutsch 2007; Reiner 2008). Although the majority of police characters in films and television shows are represented as sympathetic, honest, and just, there is an increasing portrayal of police deviance. Corrupt, brutal, and discriminatory police officers have become more common since the mid-1960s in films (Powers *et al.* 1996: 113–16; Allen *et al.* 1998: 185–6) and television (Lichter *et al.* 1994: ch. 9), as has acceptance of routine police violation of legal restraints.

Victims have moved from a shadowy and purely functional role in crime narratives to a pivotal position. Film and television stories focus increasingly on the plight of victims, whose suffering is portrayed more graphically and often constitutes the driving force of the story (Allen *et al.* 1998; Reiner *et al.* 2000 and 2001). Support for law enforcement and criminal justice is increasingly constructed in narratives by presenting them as defenders or avengers of victims with whose suffering the audience is invited to identify.

## Media representation of crime: a summary

1. News and fiction stories about crime are prominent in all media. While there is evidence of increasing attention to crime in some parts of the media, overall this fascination has been constant throughout media history.

2. News and fiction concentrate overwhelmingly on serious violent crimes against individuals, albeit with some variation according to medium and market. The proportion of different crimes represented is the inverse of official statistics.

3. The demographic profile of offenders and victims in the media is older and higher status than those processed by the criminal justice system. Child victims and perpetrators are also represented disproportionately.

4. The risks of crime as portrayed by the media are both quantitatively and qualitatively more serious than the official statistically recorded picture, although the media underplay the current probabilities of victimization by property crimes.

5. The media generally present a very positive image of the success and integrity of the police, and criminal justice more generally. However, in both news and fiction there is a clear trend to criticism of law enforcement, in terms of both its effectiveness and its justice and honesty. While in the past the unbroken media

picture was that *Crime Does Not Pay* (the title of a series of short films produced by MGM between 1935 and 1947), this is increasingly called into question in contemporary news and fiction.

6. Individual victims and their suffering increasingly provide the motive force of crime stories.

### THE CONSEQUENCES OF MEDIA IMAGES OF CRIME

A vast body of (mainly positivistic) research has sought to measure two possible consequences of media representations (which are not mutually exclusive): criminal behaviour (especially violence); and fear of crime (for a detailed critical survey see Howitt 1998: chs 1, 5–8, 10–11).

There are many possible links in criminological theory between media representations and crime. The media may impact on how crimes are labelled; the motives, means, and opportunities for offending; and the formal and informal controls militating against crime.

### Labelling

For an act to be 'criminal' (as distinct from harmful, immoral, anti-social, etc.) it has to be labelled as such. This involves the creation of a legal category. A recorded crime also requires the labelling of the act as criminal by citizens and/or law-enforcement officers.

The role of the media in developing new (and eroding old) categories of crime has been emphasized in most of the classic studies of the emergence of criminal law within the 'labelling' tradition. Becker's seminal *Outsiders* analysed the 1937 passage of the US Marijuana Tax Act, showing the use of the media as a tool of the Federal Bureau of Narcotics' moral entrepreneurship (Becker 1963: ch. 7). Jock Young analysed how media representations amplified the deviance of drug-takers (Young 1971). Stan Cohen coined the influential concept of 'moral panic' in his study of how the media together with the police developed a spiral of respectable fear about 'mods' and 'rockers' (Cohen 1972). Hall *et al*.'s analysis of the 1973 moral panic about a supposedly new type of robbery, 'mugging', emphasized the crucial part played by the media. Newspapers stimulated public anxiety, producing changes in policing and criminal justice that became a self-fulfilling spiral of deviancy amplification (Hall *et al*. 1978).

Many subsequent studies have illustrated the role of the media in shaping the boundaries of criminality by creating new categories of offence, or by changing perceptions and sensitivities, leading to fluctuations in apparent crime. For example, Roger Graef's celebrated 1982 fly-on-the-wall documentary about the Thames Valley Police was a key impetus to reform of police treatment of rape victims. This also contributed, however, to a rise in the proportion of victims reporting rape, and thus an increase in the recorded rate. Many other studies have documented media-amplified 'crime waves' and 'moral panics' about law and order.[3]

---

[3]  e.g. recent overviews include: Critcher 2003, 2006; Carrabine 2008: ch.8; Greer 2009: pt.5; Goode and Ben-Yehuda 2009; Special Issue of *British Journal of Criminology* 49/1 2009; Jewkes 2010: ch.3; Special Issue of *Crime, Media, Culture: An International Journal* (2011: 7/3).

## Motive

A crime will not occur unless someone is tempted, driven, or otherwise motivated to carry out the 'labelled' act. The media feature in many of the most commonly offered social and psychological theories of the formation of criminal dispositions. Probably the most influential sociological theory of how criminal motives are formed is Merton's version of anomie theory (Merton 1938; Messner and Rosenfeld 2006; Reiner 2007: 9, 14–5, 84–5; Special Issue of *Theoretical Criminology*, 11 January 2007; Rock, in this volume). The media present universal emulation images of affluent lifestyles and a consumerist culture, accentuating relative deprivation and generating pressures to acquire ever higher levels of material success regardless of the legitimacy of the means used. Psychological theories of the formation of motives to commit offences also often feature media effects as part of the process. It has been claimed that the images of crime and violence presented by the media are a form of social learning, and may encourage crime by imitation or arousal effects (Livingstone 1996: 308).

## Means

It has often been alleged that the media act as an open university of crime, spreading knowledge of criminal techniques. This is frequently claimed in relation to particular *causes célèbres* or horrific crimes. A notorious case was the allegation that the murderers of Jamie Bulger had been influenced by the video *Child's Play 3* in the manner in which they killed the unfortunate toddler (Jewkes 2010. 16). Video games such as *Grand Theft Auto* have been accused of being an especially potent source of learning about crime, as the player is placed in the subject position of a criminal (Hayward 2004: 172–3, 193–4). Despite much discussion, the evidence that these are major sources of crime is weak (Young 2004; Hargrave and Livingstone 2006).

New forms of media have sometimes been seen as creating new means to commit crime. This concern has been particularly stimulated by the Internet, which is feared as facilitating all sorts of offences, from fraud, identity theft, child pornography, and grooming children for sex, to organizing transnational crime and terrorism (Wall 2001, 2007; Jewkes 2003, 2006; Yar 2006; Jewkes and Yar 2009).

## Opportunity

The media may increase opportunities to commit offences by contributing to the development of a consumerist ethos, in which the availability of tempting targets of theft proliferates (Hayward 2004; Hallsworth 2005: 62–3, ch. 7; Hall, Winlow, and Ancrum 2008). They can also alter 'routine activities', especially in relation to the use of leisure time, which structure opportunities for offending (Cohen and Felson 1979). The domestic hardware and software of mass media use—TVs, videos, radios, CDs, personal computers, mobile phones—are the common currency of routine property crime, and their proliferation has been an important aspect of the spread of criminal opportunities.

## Absence of controls

Motivated potential offenders, with the means and opportunities to commit offences, may still not carry out these crimes if effective social controls are in place. These might be *external*—the deterrent threat of sanctions represented in the first place by the police—or *internal*—the still, small voice of conscience—what Eysenck has called the 'inner policeman'.

A regularly recurring theme of respectable anxieties about the criminogenic consequences of media images of crime is that they erode the efficacy of both external and internal controls. They may undermine external controls by derogatory representations of criminal justice, for example ridiculing its agents, a key complaint at least since the days of Shakespeare's Dogberry, with the perennial popularity of comic cops and constables. Serious representations of criminal justice might undermine its legitimacy by questioning the integrity and fairness, or the efficiency and effectiveness of the police. Negative representations of criminal justice could lessen public cooperation with the system, or potential offenders' perception of the probability of sanctions, with the consequence of increasing crime.

Probably the most frequently suggested line of causation between media representations and criminal behaviour is the allegation that the media undermine internalized controls, by regularly presenting sympathetic or glamorous images of offending. In academic form this is found in psychological theories of disinhibition and desensitization (Wartella 1995: 309–12).

## CRIMINOGENIC MEDIA? THE RESEARCH EVIDENCE

In a comprehensive review of the research literature, Sonia Livingstone noted that 'since the 1920s thousands of studies of mass media effects have been conducted' (Livingstone 1996: 306). She added that even listing the references to research in the previous decade would exhaust the space allocated to her article (some 20 pages). Reviews of the literature regularly recycle the apotheosis of agnosticism represented by the conclusion of one major study from the 1960s: 'for some children, under some conditions, some television is harmful. For some children under the same conditions, or for the same children under other conditions, it may be beneficial. For most children, under most conditions, most television is probably neither particularly harmful nor particularly beneficial' (Schramm *et al.* 1961: 11).

This meagre conclusion from the expenditure of countless research hours and dollars is primarily a testimony to the limitations and difficulties of empirical social science. The armoury of possible research techniques for assessing directly the effects of media images on crime is sparse, and suffers from evident and long-recognized limitations.

The archetypal technique has been some version of the classic experiment: a group of subjects are exposed to a media stimulus—say a film—and the response is measured, by comparing behaviour or attitudes before and after. In a characteristic example, children of four to five were shown a five-minute film in the researcher's office, and then taken to a room with toys and observed for 20 minutes through a one-way mirror (Bandura *et al.* 1961, 1963). The children were randomly assigned to watch one of three films, enacting scenarios in which a boy who attacked another boy and took some toys was depicted as being rewarded, or punished, or neither. The children (especially the boys) who saw the film about the boy rewarded for his attack by getting all the toys, were observed to carry out twice as much imitative aggression as the other groups, but no more non-imitative aggression.

This example shows all the problems of inferring conclusions about links between media and violence from laboratory-style experiments. Are the results a Hawthorn effect arising from the experimental situation itself? For instance, were the more aggressive children who saw a film in which aggression was rewarded influenced by their perception that the experimenter approved of such behaviour? How far can results from one context of viewing be extrapolated to others? Do experimental results exaggerate the links in the everyday world by picking up short-term effects of media exposure that rapidly evaporate? Or do they under-estimate the long-term cumulative effects of regular, repeated exposures by measuring only one-off results?

Given the huge number of such experimental studies (using different forms of stimuli and different types of measures of response, for different sorts of subjects, at many different times and places) it is hardly surprising that there are variations in the extent of effect shown, if any. However, most studies do show *some* effect, and the few that conducted follow-ups over time found that while effects diminished by about 25 per cent over the fortnight or so after an experiment, they do not disappear (Livingstone 1996: 309–10). There are many suggestions in the experimental literature about what determines the degree of effect caused by media exposures. These include the perceived realism of the representation, whether violence or deviance was seen as justified, punished, or rewarded, whether the viewers identified with the perpetrator, the variable vulnerability or susceptibility of the viewer, and so on (ibid.).

Typically, however, the effects of exposure to media stimuli in experimental situations are small. Interestingly, most of the research has looked at supposed negative effects of media, such as violence. The few studies that have examined the effects of 'pro-social' images suggest that these are much larger (Livingstone 1996: 309).

Given the limitations of laboratory experiments, some studies have tried to assess the effects of media exposure in 'natural' everyday situations. One method has been by looking at the introduction of some form of medium (usually television) in an area where it did not exist before. This was most frequently done in the 1950s, when the spread of television ownership, first in the USA, then in the UK, provided the opportunity of a once-and-for-all natural experiment. One study of matched sets of 34 US cities in the early 1950s found that larceny increased by about 5 per cent in those cities where television was introduced for the first time, compared to cities without TV or those that had been receiving it for some time (Hennigan *et al.* 1982). However, British research in the same period does not find similar effects on deviance (Livingstone 1996: 312–13). Since the virtually universal availability of television, such natural experiments are seldom possible. One rare example found that children's verbal and physical aggression increased in a Northern Canadian town after television was introduced, compared to two towns with established television (Williams 1986). While such natural experiments do not suffer from the artificiality of their laboratory counterparts, they are of course less completely controlled: the possibility can never be ruled out that differences between areas (even if roughly matched) were due to factors other than television.

Several studies have compared the viewing patterns of known offenders and (supposed) non-offenders. Some have concluded that more exposure to television is related to greater aggressiveness (Wartella 1995: 307–9); others that the viewing preferences of delinquents are remarkably similar to the general pattern for their age (Hagell and

Newburn 1994). Neither conclusion is free from the possibility of other, unmeasured factors explaining either the association or the lack of it.

There is also evidence that abuses of power by police and other criminal justice agents may be affected by media representations. One study of 'reality' television programmes such as *Cops* suggested that the police may adopt forms of entrapment or illicit punishment of offenders to ensure good video footage for such shows (Doyle 1998: 110–12, 2003).

Conversely, the influence of reality and fictional forensic and crime science programmes—*CSI: Crime Scene Investigation* being the prime example—on public expectations of criminal justice has been the subject of much speculation, and some research. The key concern is that jurors who see the high-quality forensic evidence presented on *CSI* have increased expectations in real trials, where the actual available evidence tends to be much more uncertain. Though evidence of a *CSI* effect on trial juries is at best equivocal (Tyler 2006), research does indicate some impact on public expectations of the police, leading to unrealistic requests for hi-tech investigative miracles at crime scenes (Huey 2010).

## THE BIG FIX: THE MEDIA-CRIME CONNECTION

Reviews of the research literature generally 'conclude that there is a correlation between violence viewing and aggressive behaviour, a relationship that holds even when a variety of controls are imposed' (Wartella 1995: 306). However, the overall negative effects of media exposure seem to be small compared to other features in the social experience of offenders. Thus 'the question that remains is not whether media violence has an effect, but rather how important that effect has been, in comparison with other factors, in bringing about major social changes such as the post-war rise in crime' (ibid.: 312).

One problem with most of the effects debate and research is that it has often been directed at a rather implausible notion (Brown 2003: 27–9). What has been at issue is the will-o'-the-wisp of a 'pure' media effect. The implicit model was of the media as hypodermic syringe, injecting ideas and values into a passive public of cultural dopes. Audiences are not passive recipients, however, but active interpreters, in a complex process of interaction with other cultural and social practices (Livingstone *et al.* 2001). Changes in media representations do not come fully formed from another planet and affect behaviour patterns *ex nihilo*, but reflect ongoing changes in social perceptions and practices. Changing media images are interpreted by different audiences in various ways, which may reinforce or alter emerging social patterns. The relationship between developments in the media and in the wider society is a dialectical one. While this makes the isolation and measurement of pure media effects chimerical, it certainly does not imply that media representations have no significant consequences. 'Most media researchers believe that the media have significant effects, even though they are hard to demonstrate, and most would agree that the media make a significant contribution to the social construction of reality. The problem is to move beyond this platitude . . . The study of enculturation processes, which work over long time periods, and which are integral to rather than separate from other forms of social determination, would not ask how the media make us act or think, but rather how the media contribute to making us who we are' (Livingstone 1996: 31–2).

A further limitation of the effects literature is that it has been almost exclusively concerned with the consequences of violent and other representations of deviance. The theoretical connections examined earlier suggest that media representations of non-law-breaking behaviour, for example advertising and other images of consumerist lifestyles, may increase anomie and hence offending. The most plausible criminogenic implications of media representations concern how they impact on material aspirations and conceptions of legitimate means of achievement, not how they depict crime or violence directly.

## THE MEDIA AND FEAR OF CRIME

In recent years policy debates have identified fear of crime as an issue potentially as serious as crime itself (Ditton and Farrell 2000; Hope and Sparks 2000; Jackson 2004; Ditton *et al.* 2004; Chadee and Ditton 2005). Concern is not just about the unnecessary pain of excessive anxiety, nor even the damage done to trust and social relations by fear and the prevention strategies it encourages.

In the 'cultivation analysis' tradition which Gerbner and his associates have been developing for 30 years, media images of crime and violence are a threat to democracy (Gerbner 1970, 1995). Fearful people are more dependent, more easily manipulated and controlled, more susceptible to deceptively simple, strong, tough measures and hard-line postures—both political and religious. They may accept and even welcome repression if it promises to relieve their insecurities and other anxieties (Signorielli 1990: 102). When reel-world violence is compared to real-world crime as measured by official statistics, it appears that the media images exaggerate the probability and severity of danger. This is said to 'cultivate' a misleading view of the world based on unnecessary anxiety about levels of risk from violent crime (ibid.: 96–102).

There has been extensive criticism of the empirical and theoretical validity of these claims (Howitt 1998: ch. 4; Greer 2009: pt. 5). How much of the association between measures of exposure to the media and of fearfulness survives the introduction of other control variables such as class, race, gender, place of residence, and actual experience of crime (Doob and MacDonald 1979; Chadee 2001; Roberts 2001)? Could any association between viewing and fearfulness result from the opposite causal process, that is, do more fearful viewers watch more television rather than vice versa? More generally, it appears that 'cultivation' does not export well. British attempts to replicate the Gerbner findings have failed to do so (Wober 1978; Gunter 1985).

Although the debate about the empirical validity of the cultivation hypothesis continues, there is only limited evidence from other studies to confirm the plausible idea that exposure to media images is associated with fear of crime. An extensive multivariate analysis concluded that there was a significant relationship between reading newspapers with more emphasis on violent crime and measures of fearfulness expressed in a survey (Williams and Dickinson 1993). This association survived control by a number of demographic variables, such as socio-economic status, gender, and age. However, this association was not found with behavioural concomitants of fear, such as going out after dark. Neither could the study rule out the possibility that fear led to heavier readership of newspapers with more crime, rather than vice versa. On the empirical issue, while it remains a reasonable hypothesis that much public fear of crime is created or accentuated by media exposure, the research evidence remains equivocal about the strength, or even existence, of such a causal relationship (Ditton *et al.* 2004; Chadee and Ditton 2005). Most studies have not examined how frequently people experience fear, as opposed to their responses to particular surveys (Farrall and Gadd 2004).

Much of this inconclusiveness is rooted in the theoretical limitations of positivist content analysis (Sparks 1992: ch. 4). Items of violence are collated according to operational definitions used by observers, without reference to the narrative contexts within which they are embedded. Most stories have conclusions concurring with Miss Prism's celebrated definition of fiction: 'The good ended happily, and the bad unhappily' (Oscar Wilde, *The Importance of Being Earnest*, Act II). Although there is a trend towards greater ambivalence and ambiguity, most crime stories still have an underlying emphasis on just resolutions of conflict and violence (Zillman and Wakshlag 1987; Reiner *et al.* 2000 and 2001). It is not obvious that exposure to high degrees of violence en route to a happy ending has a fear-enhancing effect. 'When suspenseful drama featuring victimisation is known to contain a satisfying resolution, apprehensive individuals should anticipate pleasure and enjoyment' (Wakshlag *et al.* 1983: 238).

Quantitative assessments of the relationship between 'objectively' measured units of media content and survey responses cannot begin to understand the complex and dynamic interdependence of the differential experiences of crime, violence, and risk of different social groups and their subjective interpretations of the meaning of texts. The subtle intertwinings of differential social positions and life experiences with the reception of media texts is only beginning to be addressed by studies of content and interpretation. These use qualitative methods and ways of reading that seek to be sensitive to the complexities of analysing meaning (Sparks 1992, 2000, 2001; Schlesinger *et al.* 1992; Livingstone *et al.* 2001; Ditton *et al.* 2004). As with the issue of the effects of media images on criminality, so too with fear, the issue is not whether media representations have consequences. Hardly anyone would deny this. The agenda is the unravelling of the complex interrelationship of media content and other dimensions of social structure and experience in shaping offending behaviour, fear of crime, and the politics of law and order (Sasson 1995; Beckett 1997; Girling *et al.* 2000; Cavender 2004; Reiner 2007: 141–51).

## THE CAUSES OF MEDIA REPRESENTATIONS OF CRIME

Theoretical perspectives come and go, and drift in and out of academic favour. Theoretical concepts, in contrast, exist independently of the various perspectives within which they may be situated. One concept utilized by almost all crime news studies, regardless of other methodological and theoretical differences, is that of 'newsworthiness'. This concept, therefore, provides a useful starting point for understanding the causes of media representations of crime.

## CRIME NEWSWORTHINESS

News content is generated and filtered primarily through reporters' sense of 'news-worthiness'——what makes a good story that their audience wants to know about. The first academic exploration of newsworthiness was conducted by Norwegian media researchers Galtung and Ruge (1965), and resulted in the identification of 12 'news values' that work collectively to inform the selection and production of events as news. Core values include immediacy, dramatization, personalization, titillation, and novelty (see also Chibnall 1977: 22–45; Jewkes 2010: ch. 2 offers an elaborated set). The primacy of these news values explains the predominant emphasis on violent and sex offences, and the concentration on higher status offenders and victims, especially celebrities. It also accounts for the tendency to avoid stories about crime trends and patterns. These news values also encourage the presentation of political violence or disorder in terms of individual pathology rather than ideological opposition; as discrete criminal events, not manifestations of structural conflict (Halloran *et al.* 1970; Hall 1973; Lawrence 2000: ch. 3).

'Whatever the influences on new organizations that affect their selection and rejection of particular stories, daily newsreaders have an independent fascination with the stories that are published' (Katz 1987: 48). An alternative reading of crime newsworthiness focuses on the symbolic relevance and psycho-social utility of crime news for media consumers. From this perspective, crime is not newsworthy because it shocks, frightens, or titillates. Rather, its reporting offers consumers the opportunity to engage in daily ritual moral workouts to test their own moral fortitude. Crime news 'speaks dramatically to issues that are of direct relevance to readers' existential challenges, whether or not readers are preoccupied with the possible personal misfortune of becoming victims to crime' (Katz 1987: 68).

While a grasp of newsworthiness is crucial to understanding the reporting of crime, it is insufficient on its own to explain the content of crime news. For a deeper understanding of the processes and priorities that produce the pattern of representation of crime, researchers have turned to analysing the news production process.

## CRIME NEWS AS HEGEMONY IN ACTION

Most of the early studies of crime news production supported a version of the hegemonic or control model. Control approaches are influenced by Marxist and critical theory, and stress the unequal distribution of economic and cultural power throughout society. From this perspective, the role of news media is to reproduce dominant ideology, legitimate the capitalist system, and promote the interests of the ruling elite to the extent that their ways of seeing the world become 'hegemonic'. In addition to the important role of news values, the key drivers of news production are seen as: the political ideology of the press, and; the structural-cultural determinants of news-making.

### The political ideology of the press

The majority of newspapers have a more or less overtly C/conservative political ideology, and individual reporters are aware of this whatever their personal leanings. The

broadcasting media, especially the BBC, are characterized by an ethic of political neutrality and professional objectivity in performing a public service of providing news
information. In practice, however, this becomes a viewpoint which takes for granted
certain broad beliefs and values, those of moderate, middle-of-the-road majority
opinion—what Stuart Hall succinctly called a 'world at one with itself' (Hall 1970).
The master concepts of this worldview include such notions as the 'national interest',
the 'British way of life', and the 'democratic process' as epitomized by Westminster.

The implications of this prevailing worldview informed critical research in the
1970s which sought to demonstrate how broadcast and press reporting of crime, deviance, and control marginalizes dissenting voices and reinforces ruling class interests. Halloran, Elliott, and Murdock (1970: 315, emphasis in original) analysed press
and television reporting of the 1968 Vietnam demonstrations in London's Grosvenor
Square to illustrate the media's role in 'defining the situation and in cultivating the
assumption that *this is the way it is*'. The demonstrations were defined early on as likely
to involve violence between the forces of law and order (the police) and the forces of
anarchy (the demonstrators). Though the protests turned out to be largely peaceful,
the event was still reported in line within the 'framework of violence', and thus it was
the issue of violence, minimal though it was, that provided 'the news'. In their analyses of television news coverage of industrial disputes, The Glasgow University Media
Group (1976, 1980; see also Eldridge 2006) found a dearth of alternative viewpoints
and concluded that journalists 'actively embrace' the dominant ideological viewpoint
'in a way that would be hard to justify as impartial'. Their activities include 'not only
the agenda-setting functions we have described, but also a systematic partiality in the
reporting and interpretive use of government statistics' (1980: 401). Hall *et al.* (1978)
explored the generation of a 'moral panic' (see also Cohen 1972/2002) around 'mugging' in the midst of deep economic recession and an emergent crisis in state hegemony. They show how sensational media coverage simultaneously tapped into existing
fears around law and order, race, and social decline, and created a 'folk devil'—the
young black street criminal—against whom all 'respectable' people could unite. These
exceptional times called for exceptional measures. The moral panic created the right
conditions for the state to step in while simultaneously stepping up its authoritarianism, relegitimating itself, and re-establishing hegemonic control by cracking down
hard on the perceived crime problem (*Crime Media Culture*, Special Issue 2008).

These early studies demonstrated that crime reporting is not only highly selective,
but also politically oriented toward the reproduction of dominant ideology. The 'manufacture of news' (Cohen and Young 1973/1981; Sherizan 1978) for a mass audience
involves a simultaneous narrowing of otherwise distinct behaviours and practices into
a simplified category of crime. Political and industrial conflict tend to be viewed as
being perpetrated by 'mindless militants' manipulated by extremist minorities seeking 'anarchy' and subversion, with only the 'thin blue line' to save the day for law and
order (Chibnall 1977: 21; see also Greer and McLaughlin 2010). Politically subversive
behaviours are depoliticized and assimilated to routine crime: both are portrayed as
pathological conditions unrelated to wider social structures (Clarke and Taylor 1980;
Hillyard 1982; Iyengar 1991; Lawrence 2000: 57–60).

Furthermore, traditional crime reporters explicitly saw it as their responsibility to
present the police and the criminal justice system in as favourable a light as possible.

As one put it: 'If I've got to come down on one side or the other, either the goodies or the baddies, then obviously I'd come down on the side of the goodies, in the interests of law and order' (Chibnall 1977: 145). Of course even the most pro-police crime reporter would pursue stories of police malpractice as assiduously as possible. But this sense of responsibility nevertheless generated a tendency to present these within a 'one bad apple' framework (ibid.: ch. 5).

## Structural-cultural determinants of news-making

The reporting of crime, deviance, and control is further influenced by a variety of concrete organizational pressures that have unintended consequences, bolstering the law and order stance of most crime news stories. For example, concentrating personnel at institutional settings like courts, where newsworthy events can be expected to recur regularly, is an economic use of reporting resources. But it has the unintended consequence of concentrating on cleared-up cases, creating a misleading sense of police effectiveness (Ericson *et al.* 1991; Leishman and Mason 2003).

The police and the criminal justice system control much of the information on which crime reporters rely, and this gives them a degree of power as essential accredited sources. News production is structurally oriented, in the name of journalistic 'objectivity' and 'impartiality', to appeal first to accredited experts who command cultural and institutional power. This places powerful groups in the position to establish 'an initial definition or *primary interpretation* of the topic in question' (Hall *et al.* 1978: 58; Lawrence 2000: ch. 8). Once the primary definition has been established it is extremely difficult to override, and future debate is contained within a forum of 'controlled discourse', governed by the primary definers. Crime reporters tend to develop a symbiotic relationship with the contacts and organizations they use regularly, especially the police (Chibnall 1977: chs 3 and 6), as the recent revelations about the Murdoch newspapers have underlined. But 'the journalist is always in an inferior negotiating position—the journalist who cannot get information is out of a job, whereas the policeman who retains it is not' (Chibnall 1977: 155).

The need to produce reports to fit the time schedules of news production contributes to their event-orientation, the concentration on specific crimes at the expense of analysis of causal processes or policies (Rock 1973: 76–9; Lawrence 2000: ch. 8). Considerations of personal safety and convenience lead cameramen covering riots typically to film from behind police lines, which unintentionally structures an image of the police as vulnerable 'us' threatened by menacing 'them' (Murdock 1982: 108–9; Schlesinger *et al.* 1993).

In sum, the control model sees news content as the largely unintended but determined consequence of the structure, culture and political economy of news production. 'Journalists are not *necessarily* biased towards the powerful—but their routine assumptions make them willing conduits of that power' (McNair 2009: 59).

## CRIME NEWS AS NEGOTIATED CONTROL

### Organizational interdependence and contingency

From the 1980s researchers sought to develop a deeper and more nuanced appreciation of the news production process. Empirical studies were based on interviews with reporters and other creative personnel, or the police (e.g. Fishman 1981; Ross 1998; Mawby 1998, 1999, 2001, 2002; Innes 1999, 2001; Greer 2003), and/or observation (Ericson *et al*. 1987, 1989, 1991; Schlesinger *et al*. 1991; Schlesinger and Tumber 1992, 1993, 1994; Chermak 1995, 1998; Skidmore 1996; Doyle 1998, 2003). This research suggests that the deterministic implications of the hegemonic model require qualification. The underpinning idea that, in the last instance, the news media operate as a 'largely uncritical conduit for official views' (Schlesinger *et al*. 1983: 166) has been a particular point of contention.

Earlier research consistently reaffirmed the asymmetrical relations between journalists and powerful sources because it was 'grounded in the perspective of journalists' (Ericson *et al*. 1987: 125), thus overlooking the important levels of 'convergence' between media and source organizations. Consideration of source perspectives reveals that the police, for example, are constrained by news discourses just as journalists are constrained by police discourses: 'police-reporter transactions entail controls from both sides, and interdependency' (Ericson *et al*. 1989: 125). Whilst the police 'controlled the primary definitions of the subject of address (crime, criminality and its control by the police), they sensed a loss of control over the specific terms of the communication process' (Ericson *et al*. 1989: 123).

There is also greater diversity, negotiation, and contingency in the use of sources. These range far beyond the accredited agencies of the formal criminal justice institutions (Schlesinger and Tumber 1994; Greer 2003: 32–3). Groups critical of the establishment (such as penal reform or civil liberties groups) *are* given a voice, depending in part on their organizational and presentational skills, their hold on interesting knowledge, and on medium and market differences.

News stories vary in character. Many are routine fillers, where a clearly established paradigm is followed, albeit with new names, dates, and details each time. But there are also systematic variations between news stories in different media and markets. This is partly because they have different variants of political and professional journalistic ideology according to patterns of ownership (state versus private, for example) and perceived audience (business or policy elites, other opinion leaders, liberal professionals, or a mass public seeking entertainment; local or national). These are interconnected with differences in technological resources, budgetary limitations, and the different 'grammars' of written and spoken language, still and moving pictures.

There is always a tension between two contradictory pressures. The highest journalistic accolade is the 'scoop', reporting a high-news-value story that has not yet been reported. This exerts pressure to be ahead of the pack, to seek out sources that no rivals have yet found. However, the worst possible scenario is to miss important information that everybody else has. This generates a tendency to hunt with the pack, mining the same sources as rivals. The fear of failure usually prevails over the lure of the scoop, on minimax principles, which is why front pages tend to be so similar.

In recent years the production of crime news (like news in general) has been transformed by a decline in the use of specialist reporters, including court and crime correspondents. This is due to the increasing news emphasis on celebrities, and the increasingly commercial orientation of the multimedia conglomerates that own most news outlets, which has restricted editorial budgets severely. Many crime and criminal justice stories, cases, and issues now fail to get aired prominently or perhaps at all, even in the sensationalist manner that used to be a core news staple (Davies 1999). Crime news increasingly shares in the dominant celebrity culture. Stories with famous victims or perpetrators are the acme of news value. Some crime victims achieve celebrity through media coverage of their cases. The global phenomenon that has been the disappearance of Madeleine McCann is one case in point.

There is thus scope for flexibility and judgement in the selection and production of crime news; the newsroom is not characterized by normative consensus but by negotiation and conflict between reporters, editors, and sources. In this context, the dominance of any ideological position should be considered an 'achievement rather than a wholly structurally determined outcome' (Schlesinger, 1989: 79).

While empirical analyses of news production emphasize its contingency and fluidity, they do not fundamentally challenge the hegemonic model. They confirm the structuring of newsgathering and presentation around a sense of news values and other criteria leading to the selection of particular types of stories and perspectives. These constitute a 'vocabulary of precedents': not hard-and-fast rules, but 'what previous exemplars tell them should be done in the present instance' (Ericson *et al.* 1987: 348). Journalists and sources engage in 'legitimation work' in the representation of crime and justice. News contributes to the formation of a stable 'symbolic canopy', based on but not restricted to dominant ideology, that helps to reinforce the 'consensual paradigm' for society as a whole (Ericson *et al.* 1987: 27–43). News may be a competitive arena of conflicting viewpoints, but it is also culturally and structurally loaded. For all the fluidity and contingency observed in the process of production, in the final analysis 'the news media are as much an agency of *policing* as the law enforcement agencies whose activities and classifications are reported on' (Ericson *et al.* 1991: 74). They reproduce order in the process of representing it.

## CRIME NEWS, SOCIAL DIVISION, AND RISK

The control model has been diversified to explore the ideological legitimation of inequalities not only in terms of class, but also gender, race, and other social divisions.

With the development of critical feminist research on crime reporting the control model underwent some conceptual reconfiguration. Here, dominant ideology is no less important, but it is framed primarily in terms of gender, and relates to the tendency of news reports to reinforce gender stereotypes that maintain unequal power relations in a patriarchal society (Cameron and Fraser 1987; Kitzinger and Skidmore 1995; Soothill and Walby 1991; Chancer 2003). Given the cultural saturation of myths about gender, sex and rape, women in sex crime cases can be polarized into 'virgins' or 'whores' by even the most well-meaning journalists (Benedict 1992: 26). Reporting of everyday, non-celebrity violence against women, when deemed newsworthy, is informed by 'traditional notions of appropriate gender roles' that institutionalize women's inequality and subjugation (Meyers 1997: 3). In stark contrast, the demonic nature of criminal women can be amplified by, for example, the disproportionate use of visual images and sensational headlines, even when they are not the main protagonists in crime cases (Jones and Wardle 2008; Humphries 2009; Seal 2009, 2010).

Research on the news construction of race, ethnicity, and crime have evidenced similarly reductive reporting habits. The criminalization in the news media of visible minorities has been evidenced in myriad studies (Barlow 1998; Chiricos and Eschholz 2002; Law 2002; Cottle 2005; Dixon and Linz 2006; Stabile 2006; Gannon 2008; Brotherton and Barrios 2009), though few have looked in depth at production processes. Prevailing stereotypes regarding race and ethnicity make it more difficult for visible minority crime victims to secure media attention, public sympathy, and legitimate victim status. Indeed, given the high levels of racialization in the news, black and minority ethnic crime victims may need to be 'deracialized'—that is, represented in a way that obscures 'race' to the point of writing it 'out of the script'—to become 'legitimate' victims worthy of widespread public sympathy (McLaughlin 2005a). As with gendered crime reporting, the racialization of crime news cannot adequately be understood through blanket accusations of institutionalized media prejudice (Greer 2007). It is more often, though no less problematically, the product of structurally and culturally embedded myths and newsroom practices that promote the marginalization of certain values and interest and the promotion of others.

For 'risk society' theorists, the transition from modernity to late modernity has been characterized by a shift away from the focus on economic inequality and toward the nature, patterning, and control of 'risk' (Beck 1992). In this context, the control paradigm's focus on the class-based interests of a ruling elite and the media reproduction of dominant ideology loses purchase. Reiner *et al.* (2000, 2001) adopt a 'risk society' framework in their research on media representations of crime and justice in the post-war era. They find that over time news reports of criminal offending include less acknowledgement of possible structural causation and more condemnation of what is presented as individual evil. Portrayals of criminal justice remain broadly supportive, but are increasingly complex and critical, focusing more, for example, on police ineffectiveness, systemic corruption, and conflict between official institutions. And, in the most significant change, crime victims shift from being incidental characters to becoming the central focus for highly emotionalized news stories built around their experiences of suffering (Reiner *et al.* 2000: 187). The risk society thesis provides a useful theoretical framework for exploring media representations of crime and justice, and the changing political and cultural sensibilities that shape the late modern condition.

## THE PRODUCTION OF CRIME FICTION

Although there have been many studies of the production of crime news, there has been little comparable research on fiction. All we have is memoirs of writers, directors, and other creators of crime fiction, and fan-oriented biographies or accounts of the making of particular films or programmes (see, e.g., Bennett 2006; McLaughlin 2005b). The sole exception is an interview study of Hollywood writers, directors, and producers of television shows and cinema films (Lichter *et al.* 1994: pt. IV; Powers *et al.* 1996: ch. 3). This depicts them as former 1960s radicals on a 'long march' through the institutions. Their ideology combines acceptance of the economic and political institutions of America, to which they owe their status and privileges, with a libertarian stance on issues of personal and sexual morality that they have carried since their youth. They feel a mission to put as much of this into their work as is compatible with the overriding priority of keeping the audience ratings high and the networks happy.

How this expressed ideology translates into actual creative and production practices has not been studied, however, in any body of research analogous to that on crime news. A recent ethnographic study of the long-running series *The Bill* does demonstrate the significance of shifting political-economic pressures and the related cultural changes amongst productive personnel for developments in storylines and representations of policing (Colbran 2007, 2009a, and b).

## OBSERVERS OR PLAYERS? THE MEDIA AND CRIME IN POSTMODERNITY

In the introduction to this chapter two competing concerns about media representations of crime were outlined: the 'respectable fear' that they were subversive and desubordinating; and the radical anxiety that they were a means of social control and discipline. The review of research suggests that there is a complex interplay between media representations of crime, criminal behaviour, and criminal justice.

With variations according to medium and market, mass media news and entertainment are saturated with stories about crime. These disproportionately feature the most serious and violent crimes, but strip them from any analytic framework. The emphasis is on crime as the product of individual choice and free-floating evil, diverting attention from any links to social structure or culture (Sasson 1995; Reiner *et al.* 2001; Greer 2007). There is strong evidence that media images *can* influence criminal behaviour, but overall their direct effect is small relative to other factors. This is largely because people vary in their interpretation of representations according to demographic, generational, and other life course factors. There is a variety of ways theoretically in which media representations could influence crime rates and patterns. For example, the overall volume of property crime is likely to be affected by media portrayals of material success as the acme of the good life in a context of structural inequalities of opportunity, as Mertonian strain theories suggest. It is unlikely to be an accident that the remorseless rise of volume property crime after the mid-1950s in Britain coincided with the advent of commercial television. Research on media effects has mainly assessed the consequences of representations of crime, using rather inadequate models and methods, not the theoretically more plausible criminogenic implications of other aspects of the media, for example the celebration of consumerism.

The disciplinary role of media stories about crime, reproducing as well as representing order, is supported more clearly by the research. This is partly because media representations exaggerate the threat of crime and in the main promote policing and punishment as the antidote. Because of organizational exigencies as much as ideological reasons, the media present viewpoints on crime and criminal justice policy which—though not monolithic—are loaded towards official definitions. They tend to frame crime issues increasingly in a 'law and order' perspective so other approaches become marginalized (Beckett 1997; Altheide 2002; Cavender 2004; Reiner 2007).

The present trends indicate a growing symbiosis between media images, criminality, and criminal justice. In Simon Lee's words, '[t]he media are no longer, if they ever were, observers of the scene, they are players in the game' (cited in Peay 1998: 8). This accentuates past patterns to an extent amounting to a qualitatively new stage. The insecure borderline between purportedly factual and fictional narratives is eroding. A growing variety of criminal justice lobbies and pressure groups seek to influence, if not construct, the news. At the same time technological developments interact with cultural changes to produce more 'reality' broadcasting (Fishman and Cavender 1998).

The current stage of development reflects the impact of the more general features of 'postmodernity' on the relationship between media, crime, and criminal justice (Brown 2003). The space–time distanciation between criminal cases and their reporting in the media, and the reciprocal feedback of images on practice, are eroding rapidly (Giddens 1984; Thompson 1995). 'We live in a dramatised world' (Ericson 1991: 235), where the media are participants in the processes they represent. An ever-wider range of participants in the criminal justice process are not only seeking to influence representations but are creating 'spectacles' specifically for the media (Greer and McLaughlin 2012). Events such as the 1992 Los Angeles riots or the O. J. Simpson case are broadcast around the world literally as they are happening. The tragedy of 11 September 2001 is simply the most vivid and dramatic example of these developments to date, when thousands of people were murdered in front of the eyes of television audiences around the globe, in a way calculated to achieve the maximum possible media impact (Castells, 2004; Young 2007).

The mass media are important not only because of their ideological significance. Media technology plays an increasingly direct role in social control, above all through the growth of CCTV and other forms of surveillance (Norris and Armstrong 1999; McCahill 2003; Jewkes 2010: ch. 7; Coleman 2005; Norris and McCahill 2006; Lyon 2009; Lippert and Wilkinson 2010; Koskela 2011). Media technology can also be used to control the controllers, to make authorities more accountable, as the use of CCTV and other recording devices in police stations shows (Newburn and Hayman 2001).

Criminal justice agencies thus seek to tailor their activities in a public relations-friendly way that plays well in the news. Police investigate (sometimes instigate) all the crimes fit to print. Crimes and legal processes are not only reflected in reporting with greater rapidity, they may be created for news stories. Offences have been incited by law-enforcement agencies in order to have the successful investigation televised (as in the Azscam entrapment case analysed by Altheide 1993). Since the 1960s, protesters and police act with self-conscious awareness that 'the whole world is watching' (Gitlin 1980). In the hi-tech, high surveillance context of contemporary public order events, accusations of police violence can no longer simply be denied away. The routine, real-time filming of policing activities by citizen and professional journalists is subjecting the institution to unprecedented levels of media and public scrutiny, and transforming how the police manage public order situations (Greer and McLaughlin 2010; HMIC 2009).

Mass media technologies make the model of contemporary social control a Synopticon (Mathiesen 1997): they provide the means for the many to see the few, offsetting the Benthamite paradigm of the few observing the many. However, this reciprocal process of surveillance between elites and masses remains highly unbalanced (Lyon 2003). The greater vulnerability of the powerful to exposure and scandal does not fundamentally change structures of power and advantage. Indeed Mathiesen argues plausibly that the illusion of intimacy with elites, provided by contemporary media surveillance of their activities, gives people a misleading sense of empowerment which acts as a more complex process of discipline than traditional forms of legitimation. It is possible, he argues, 'that the control and discipline of the "soul", that is, the creation of human beings who control themselves through self-control and thus fit neatly into a so-called democratic capitalist society, is a task which is actually fulfilled by a modern Synopticon' (Mathiesen 1997: 215).

The growing interdependence of media representation and social 'reality' raises the spectre of 'a media spiral in which the representations of crime and the fear of crime precisely constitute…the hyperreal' (Osborne 1996: 36; Ferrell *et al.* 2008). Certainly these developments vastly complicate the vexed question of how images and narratives that are felt to be undesirable can be regulated or influenced. Perhaps hope lies precisely in the greater openness of the media to a diversity of inputs and influences. Past experience, however, suggests the more pessimistic prediction that although contemporary mass communications present 'an appreciably open terrain for struggles for justice' (Ericson 1991: 242), the dice are loaded in favour of dominant interests—even if they have to struggle harder for their hegemony.

## ■ SELECTED FURTHER READING

Chris Greer (ed.) (2009), *Crime and Media: A Reader* (London: Routledge) is an annotated collection of key contributions covering all the issues discussed in this chapter. Richard Sparks's (1992) *Television and the Drama of Crime* (Buckingham: Open University Press) offers a theoretically sophisticated critique of content analyses of crime fiction, and their relationship to fear of crime. Illuminating studies of the production of crime news are the trilogy by R. Ericson, P. Baranek, and J. Chan, *Visualising Deviance, Negotiating Control, and Representing Order* (Milton Keynes: Open University Press, 1987, 1989, 1991 respectively); P. Schlesinger and H. Tumber's (1994) *Reporting Crime* (Oxford: Oxford University Press); C. Greer's (2004), *Sex Crime and the Media* (Cullompton, Devon: Willan) and (2010) 'News-Making Criminology', in E.McLaughlin and T.Newburn (eds), *The Sage Handbook of Criminological Theory* (London: Sage). Useful reviews of the research on media effects can be found in: S. Livingstone (1996), 'On the Continuing Problem of Media Effects', in J. Curran and M. Gurevitch (eds), *Mass Media and Society* (London: Arnold); D. Howitt (1998), *Crime, The Media and the Law* (London: Wiley); and from a fundamentally critical perspective, M. Barker and J. Petley (eds) (2001), *Ill Effects*, 2nd edn (London: Routledge). Excellent recent texts on crime and media are S. Brown (2003), *Crime and Law in Media Culture* (Buckingham: Open University Press); E. Carrabine (2008),*Crime, Culture, and the Media* (Cambridge: Polity); Y. Jewkes (2010), *Media and Crime*, 2nd edn (London: Sage). Useful edited volumes offering a rich diversity of research papers on media and crime are: R. Ericson (ed.) (1995), *Crime and the Media* (Aldershot: Dartmouth); D. Kidd-Hewitt and R. Osborne (eds) (1996), *Crime and the Media: The Post-Modern Spectacle* (London: Pluto); P. Mason (ed.) (2003), *Criminal Visions* (Cullompton, Devon: Willan). The journal *Crime, Media, Culture: An International Journal* (London: Sage) is the key source for current articles.

# ■ REFERENCES

ALLEN, J., LIVINGSTONE, S., and REINER, R. (1997), 'The Changing Generic Location of Crime in Film', *Journal of Communication*, 47(4): 1–13.

——, ——, and —— (1998), 'True Lies: Changing Images of Crime in British Postwar Cinema', *European Journal of Communication*, 13(1): 53–75.

ALTHEIDE, D. (1993), 'Electronic Media and State Control: The Case of Azscam', *The Sociological Quarterly*, 34(1): 53–69.

—— (2002),*Creating Fear: News and the Construction of Crisis*, New York: Aldine de Gruyter.

BAILEY, F. and HALE, D. (eds) (1998), *Popular Culture, Crime and Justice*, Belmont, Cal.: Wadsworth.

BANDURA, A., ROSS, D., and ROSS, S.A. (1961), 'Transmission of Aggression Through Imitation of Aggressive Models', *Journal of Abnormal and Social Psychology*, 63(3): 575–82.

BARAK, G. (ed.) (1994), *Media, Process, and the Social Construction of Crime*, New York: Garland.

BARCLAY, G. and TAVARES, C. (1999), *Information on the Criminal Justice System in England and Wales: Digest 4*, London: Home Office.

BARKER, M. (1984a), *A Haunt of Fears*, London: Pluto.

—— (1984b), *The Video Nasties: Freedom and Censorship in the Media*, London: Pluto.

—— and PETLEY, J. (eds) (2001), *Ill Effects: The Media/ Violence Debate*, 2nd edn, London: Routledge.

BARLOW, M. H. (1998), 'Race and the Problem of Crime in Time and Newsweek Cover Stories, 1946–1995', *Social Justice*, 25: 149–83.

BECKER, H. (1963), *Outsiders*, New York: Free Press.

BECKETT, K. (1997), *Making Crime Pay*, New York: Oxford University Press.

—— and SASSON, T. (2000), *The Politics of Injustice*, Thousand Oaks, Cal.: Pine Forge Press.

BELL, I. A. and DALDRY, G. (eds) (1990), *Watching the Detectives*, London: Macmillan.

BELSON, W. (1978), *Television Violence and the Adolescent Boy*, Westmead: Saxon House.

Bennett, J. (2006),''We might be Locked up, but we're not Thick": Rex Bloomstein's Kids Behind Bars', *Crime Media, Culture: An International Journal*, 2(3): 268–85.

BINYON, T. J. (1989), *Murder Will Out: The Detective in Fiction*, Oxford: Oxford University Press.

BIRESSI, A. (2001), *Crime, Fear and the Law in True Crime Stories*, London: Palgrave.

BROTHERTON, D. and BARRIOS, L. (2009), 'Displacement and Stigma: The Social-Psychological Crisis of the Deportee', *Crime, Media, Culture: An International Journal*, 5(1): 29–55.

BROWN, M. (2007), 'Mapping Discursive Closings in the War on Drugs', *Crime, Media, Culture*, 3(1): 11–29.

BROWN, S. (2003), *Crime and Law in Media Culture*, Buckingham: Open University Press.

BROWNSTEIN, H. (1995), 'The Media and the Construction of Random Drug Violence', in J. Ferrell and C.R. Sanders (eds), *Cultural Criminology*, 45–65, Boston, Mass.: Northeastern University Press.

BUXTON, D. (1990), *From The Avengers to Miami Vice: Form and Ideology in Television Series*, Manchester: Manchester University Press.

CAREY, S. (1993), 'Mass Media Violence and Aggressive Behaviour', *Criminal Justice Matters*, 11 (Spring): 8–9.

CARLSON, J. M. (1985), *Prime-Time Law Enforcement: Crime Show Viewing and Attitudes to the Criminal Justice System*, New York: Praeger.

CARRABINE, E., COX, P., LEE, M., and SOUTH, N. (eds), (2002), *Crime in Modern Britain*, Oxford: Oxford University Press.

——, IGANSKI, P., LEE, M., PLUMME R, K., and SOUTH, M. (2004), *Criminology*, London: Routledge.

CASTELLS, M. (2004), *The Power of Identity*, 2nd edn, Oxford: Blackwell.

CAVENDER, G. (2004), 'Media and Crime Policy', *Punishment and Society*, 6(3): 335–48.

—— and DEUTSCH, S. (2007), 'CSI and Moral Authority: The Police and Science', in *Crime, Media, Culture: An International Journal*, 3, 1: 67–81.

CAWELTI, J. G. (1976), *Adventure, Mystery and Romance*, Chicago: Chicago University Press.

CHADEE, D. (2001), 'Fear of Crime and the Media: From Perceptions to Reality', *Criminal Justice Matters*, 43: 10–11.

—— and DITTON, J. (2005), 'Fear of Crime and the Media: Assessing the Lack of Relationship', *Crime, Media, Culture*, 1(3): 322–32.

CHERMAK, S. M. (1995), *Victims in the News: Crime in American News Media*, Boulder Cal.: Westview.

—— (1998), 'Police, Courts, and Corrections in the Media', in F.Bailey and D. Hale (eds), *Popular Culture, Crime and Justice*, Belmont, Cal.: Wadsworth.

CHIBNALL, S. (1977), *Law-and-Order News*, London: Tavistock.

—— and MURPHY, R. (eds) (1999), *British Crime Cinema*, London: Routledge.

CHIRICOS, T and ESCHHOLZ, S. (2002), 'The Racial and Ethnic Typification of Crime and The Criminal Typification of Race and Ethnicity in Local Television News', *Journal of Research in Crime and Delinquency*, 39(4): 400–20.

——, ——, and GERTZ, M. (1997), 'Crime, News and Fear of Crime', *Social Problems*, 44(3): 342–57.

CHRISTENSEN, J., SCHMIDT, J., and HENDERSON, J. (1982). 'The Selling of the Police: Media Ideology and Crime Control', *Contemporary Crises*, 6(3): 227–39.

CLARENS, C. (1997), *Crime Movies*, New York: Da Capo.

CLARKE, A. (1982), *Television Police Series and Law and Order* (Popular Culture Course Unit 22), Milton Keynes: Open University.

—— (1983), 'Holding the Blue Lamp: Television and the Police in Britain', *Crime and Social Justice*, 19: 44–51.

—— (1986), 'This is Not the Boy Scouts: Television Police Series and Definitions of Law and Order', in T.Bennett, C. Mercer, and J.Woollacott (eds), *Popular Culture and Social Relations*, Milton Keynes: Open University Press.

—— (1992), '"You're Nicked!" Television Police Series and the Fictional Representation of Law and Order', in D. Strinati and S. Wagg (eds), *Come On Down? Popular Media Culture in Post-War Britain*, London: Routledge.

—— and TAYLOR, I. (1980), 'Vandals, Pickets and Muggers: Television Coverage of Law and Order in the 1979 Election', *Screen Education*, 36: 99–112.

CLARKE, J. (2001), 'The Pleasures of Crime: Interrogating the Detective Story', in J. Muncie and E.McLaughlin (eds), *The Problem of Crime*, 2nd edn, 71–106, London: Sage.

COHEN, L. and FELSON, S. (1979), 'Social Change and Crime Rate Trends: A Routine Activities Approach', *American Sociological Review*, 44: 588–608.

COHEN, S. (1972), *Folk Devils and Moral Panics*, London: Paladin.

—— and YOUNG, J. (eds) (1973), *The Manufacture of News*, London: Constable.

COLEMAN, R. (2005), 'Surveillance in the City: Primary Definition and Urban Spatial Order', *Crime, Media, Culture: An International Journal*, 1(2): 131–48.

COTTLE, S. (2011), 'Media and the Arab uprisings of 2011: Research notes', *Journalism* 12, 5: 647–59.

—— (2008), 'Reporting demonstrations: the changing media politics of dissent', *Media, Culture and Society*, 30(6): 853–72.

—— (1993), *TV News, Urban Conflict and the Inner City*, Leicester: Leicester University Press.

CRITCHLEY, C. (2003), *Moral Panics and the Media*, Buckingham: Open University Press.

CUMBERBATCH, G. (1989), *A Measure of Uncertainty: The Effects of Mass Media*, Broadcasting Standards Council Research Monograph 1, London: John Libbey.

——, WOODS, S., and MAGUIRE, A. (1995), *Crime in the News: Television, Radio and Newspapers: A Report for BBC Broadcasting Research*, Birmingham: Aston University, Communications Research Group.

DAHLGREN, P. (1988), 'Crime News: The Fascination of the Mundane', *European Journal of Communication*, 3(1): 189–206.

DAVIES, N. (1999), 'Getting away with murder', *The Guardian* (*Media Section*): 4–5, 11 January.

DAVIS, J. (1952), 'Crime News in Colorado Newspapers', *American Journal of Sociology*, 57: 325–30.

DE LUCA, K. and PEEPLES, J. (2002), 'From Public Sphere to Public Screen: Democracy, Activism and the "Violence" of Seattle', *Critical Studies in Media Communication*, 19(2): 125–51.

DEUTSCHMANN, P. (1959), *News Page Content of Twelve Metropolitan Dailies*, Cincinnati, Ohio: Scripps-Howard Research Centre.

DITTON, J. and DUFFY, J. (1983), 'Bias in the Newspaper Reporting of Crime News', *British Journal of Criminology*, 23(2): 159–65.

—— and FARRALL, S. (eds) (2000), *The Fear of Crime*, Aldershot: Dartmouth.

——, CHADEE, D., FARRALL, S., GILCHRIST, E., and BANNISTER, J. (2004), 'From Imitation to Intimidation: A Note on the Curious and Changing Relationship Between the Media, Crime and Fear of Crime', *British Journal of Criminology*, 44(4): 595–610.

DIXON, T. and LINZ, D. (2006), 'Overrepresentation and underrepresentation of African Americans and Latinos as lawbreakers on television news', *Journal of Communication*, 50(2): 131–54.

DOMINICK, J. (1978), 'Crime and Law Enforcement in the Mass Media', in C. Winick (ed.), *Deviance and Mass Media*, 105–28, Beverly Hills, Cal.: Sage.

DOOB, A. and MACDONALD, G. (1979), 'Television Viewing and the Fear of Victimisation: Is the Relationship Causal?', *Journal of Personality and Social Psychology*, 37(1): 170–9.

DORLING, D. (2004), 'Prime Suspect: Murder in Britain', in P. Hillyard, C. Pantazis, S. Tombs, and D. Gordon (eds), *Beyond Criminology*, 178–91, London: Pluto.

DOVE, G. (1982), *The Police Procedural*, Bowling Green, Ohio: Bowling Green Popular Press.

—— and BARGAINNIER, E. (eds) (1986), *Cops and Constables: American and British Fictional Policemen*, Bowling Green, Ohio: Bowling Green Popular Press.

DOYLE, A. (1998), '"Cops": Television Policing As Policing Reality', in M. Fishman and G. Cavender (eds), *Entertaining Crime*, New York: Aldine De Gruyter.

—— (2003), *Arresting Images*, Toronto: University of Toronto Press.

DURSTON, G. (1997), *Moll Flanders: Analysis of 18th Century Criminal Biography*, Chichester: Barry Rose.

EATON, M. (1996), 'A Fair Cop? Viewing the Effects of the Canteen Culture in *Prime Suspect* and *Between the Lines*', in D. Kidd-Hewitt and R. Osborne (eds), *Crime and the Media: The Post-Modern Spectacle*, London: Pluto.

ELTON, B. (1996), *Popcorn*, London: Simon & Schuster.

ERICSON, R. (1991), 'Mass Media, Crime, Law, and Justice', *British Journal of Criminology*, 31(3): 219–49.

—— (ed.) (1995), *Crime and the Media*, Aldershot: Dartmouth.

——, BARANEK, P., and CHAN, J. (1987), *Visualising Deviance*, Milton Keynes: Open University Press.

——, ——, and —— (1989), *Negotiating Control*, Milton Keynes: Open University Press.

——, ——, and —— (1991), *Representing Order*, Milton Keynes: Open University Press.

EVERSON, W. (1972), *The Detective in Film*, New York: Citadel.

FABIAN, R. (1950), *Fabian of the Yard*, London: Naldrett.

—— (1954), *London After Dark*, London: Naldrett.

FALLER, L. (1987), *Turned to Account: The Forms and Functions of Criminal Biography in Late Seventeenth and Early Eighteenth Century England*, Cambridge: Cambridge University Press.

FARRALL, S. and GADD, D. (2004), 'The Frequency of the Fear of Crime', *British Journal of Criminology*, 44(1): 127–32.

FERRELL, J. and SANDERS, C. R. (eds) (1995), *Cultural Criminology*, Boston, Mass.: Northeastern University Press.

——, HAYWARD, K. and YOUNG, J. (2008), *Cultural Criminology: An Invitation*, London: Sage.

FISHMAN, M. (1981), 'Police News: Constructing An Image of Crime', *Urban Life*, 9(4): 371–94.

—— and CAVENDER, G. (eds) (1998), *Entertaining Crime: Television Reality Programs*, New York: Aldine De Gruyter.

GALTUNG, J. and RUGE, M. (1965), 'The Structure of Foreign News: The Presentation of the Congo, Cuba and Cyprus Crises in Four Norwegian Newspapers', *Journal of Peace Research*, 2(1): 64–91.

GANNON, S. (2008), 'Crime's family tree: Conflating race, criminality and family in New Zealand', *Crime, Media, Culture: An International Journal*, 4(3): 411–19.

GARLAND, D. (2001), *The Culture of Control*, Oxford: Oxford University Press.

GAROFALO, J. (1981), 'Crime and the Mass Media: A Selective Review of Research', *Journal of Research in Crime and Delinquency*, 18(2): 319–50.

GERBNER, G. (1970), 'Cultural Indicators: The Case of Violence in Television Drama', *Annals of the American Academy of Political and Social Science*, 338(1): 69–81.

—— (1995), 'Television Violence: The Power and the Peril', in G. Dines and J. Humez (eds), *Gender, Race and Class in the Media*, Thousand Oaks, Cal.: Sage.

—— and GROSS, L. (1976), 'Living With Television: The Violence Profile', *Journal of Communication*, 26(1): 173–99.

GIDDENS, A. (1984), *The Constitution of Society*, Cambridge: Polity Press.

GIRLING, E., LOADER, I., and SPARKS, R. (2000), *Crime and Social Change in Middle England*, London: Routledge.

GITLIN, T. (1980), *The Whole World Is Watching*, Berkeley, Cal.: University of California Press.

—— (2000), *Inside Prime Time*, revised edn, Berkeley, Cal.: University of California Press.

GRABER, D. (1980), *Crime News and the Public*, New York: Praeger.

GREEN, P. (2000), 'American Television, Crime and the Risk Society', in K. Stenson and R. Sullivan (eds), *Crime, Risk and Justice*, Cullompton, Devon: Willan.

GREER, C. (2003), *Sex Crime and the Media*, Cullompton, Devon: Willan.

—— (ed.) (2009), *Crime and Media: A Reader*, London: Routledge.

—— (2007), 'News Media, Victims and Crime', in P. Davies, P. Francis, C. Greer (eds), *Victims, Crime and Society*, London: Sage.

—— (2010), 'Crime and Media', in C. Hale, K. Hayward, A. Wahidin, and E. Wincup (eds), *Criminology*, 2nd edn, Oxford: Oxford University Press.

—— and McLAUGHLIN, E. (2010), 'We Predict a Riot: Public Order Policing, New Media Environments and the Rise of the Citizen Journalist', *British Journal of Criminology*, 50(6): 1041–59.

—— and McLAUGHLIN, E. (2011), 'Trial by Media: Policing, the 24-7 News Mediasphere, and the Politics of Outrage', *Theoretical Criminology*, 15(1): 23–46.

—— and —— (2012), 'This is not Justice: Ian Tomlinson, Institutional Failure and the Press Politics of Outrage, *British Journal of Criminology*, 52(6): forthcoming.

GREVE, W. (2004), 'Fear of Crime Among Older and Younger Adults: Paradoxes and Misconceptions', in H.-J. Albrecht, T. Serassis, and H. Kania (eds), *Images of Crime II*, Freiburg: Max Planck Institute.

GUNTER, B. (1981), 'Measuring Television Violence: A Review and Suggestions for a New Analytic Perspective', *Current Psychological Research*, 1(1): 91–112.

—— (1985), *Dimensions of Television Violence*, Aldershot: Gower.

HAGELL, A. and NEWBURN, T. (1994), *Young Offenders and the Media*, London: Policy Studies Institute.

HALE, D. C. (1998), 'Keeping Women in their Place: An Analysis of Policewomen in Videos, 1972–1996', in F. Bailey and D. Hale (eds), *Popular Culture, Crime and Justice*, Belmont, Cal.: Wadsworth.

HALL, S. (1970), 'A World At One With Itself', *New Society*, 18 June: 1056–8.

—— (1973), 'The Determination of News Photographs', in S. Cohen and J. Young (eds), *The Manufacture of News*, 226–43, London: Constable.

—— (1979), *Drifting Into A Law and Order Society*, London: Cobden Trust.

——, CRITCHLEY, C., JEFFERSON, T., CLARKE, J., and ROBERTS, B. (1978), *Policing the Crisis*, London: Macmillan.

HALLORAN, J., ELLIOTT, L., and MURDOCK, G. (1970), *Demonstrations and Communication*, London: Penguin.

HALLSWORTH, S. (2005), *Street Crime*, Cullompton, Devon: Willan.

HARDY, P. (1997), *The BFI Companion to Crime*, London: Cassell.

—— (1998), *Gangsters*, London: Aurum.

HARGRAVE, A. M. and LIVINGSTONE, S. (2006), *Harm and Offence in Media Content: A Review of the Evidence*, Bristol: Intellect.

HAYCRAFT, H. (1941), *Murder For Pleasure*, New York: Appleton Century.

HAYWARD, K. (2004), *City Limits*, London: Glasshouse.

HEAROLD, S. (1986), 'A Synthesis of 1043 Effects of Television on Social Behaviour', in G. Comstock (ed.), *Public Communications and Behaviour Vol. 1*, 65–133, New York: Academic Press.

HENNIGAN, K. M., DELROSARIO, M. L., HEATH, L., COOK, J. D. and CALDER, B. J. (1982), 'Impact of the Introduction of Television Crime in the United States: Empirical Findings and Theoretical Implications', *Journal of Personality and Social Psychology*, 42(3): 461–77.

HILLYARD, P. (1982), 'The Media Coverage of Crime and Justice in Northern Ireland', in C. Sumner (ed.), *Crime, Justice and the Mass Media*, 36–54 (Cropwood Papers 14), Cambridge: Institute of Criminology.

HIMMELWEIT, H., OPPENHEIM, A. N., and VINCE, P. (1958), *Television and the Child*, London: Oxford University Press.

HMIC (2009), *Adapting to Protest*, London: HMIC.

HOPE, T. and SPARKS, R. (eds) (2000), *Crime, Risk and Insecurity*, London: Routledge.

HOWITT, D. (1998), *Crime, The Media and The Law*, London: Wiley

HUEY, L. (2010), '"I've Seen This on *CSI*": Criminal Investigators' Perceptions About the Management of Public Expectations in the Field', in *Crime, Media, Culture: An International Journal*, 6(1): 49–68.

HUMPHRIES, D. (ed.) (2009), *Women, Violence and the Media*, Lebanon, NE: Northeastern University Press.

HURD, G. (1979), 'The Television Presentation of the Police', in S. Holdaway (ed.), *The British Police*, London: Edward Arnold.

HUTCHINSON, B. and LESTER, L. (2006), 'Environmental Protest and Tap-dancing with the Media in the Information Age', *Media, Culture & Society*, 28(2): 433–51.

INCIARDI, J., and DEE, J. L. (1987), 'From the Keystone Cops to Miami Vice: Images of Policing in American Popular Culture', *Journal of Popular Culture*, 21(2): 84–102.

INNES, M. (1999), 'The Media as an Investigative Resource in Murder Enquiries', *British Journal of Criminology*, 39(2): 268–85.

—— (2001), '"Crimewatching": Homicide Investigations in the Age of Information', *Criminal Justice Matters*, 43: 42–3.

—— (2003), '"Signal Crimes": Detective Work, Mass Media and Constructing Collective Memory', in P. Mason (ed.), *Criminal Visions*, 51–69, Cullompton, Devon: Willan.

IYENGAR, S. (1991), *Is Anyone Responsible? How Television Frames Political Issues*, Chicago, Ill.: Chicago University Press.

JACKSON, J. (2004), 'An Analysis of a Construct and Debate: The Fear of Crime', in H-J. Albrecht, T. Serassis and H. Kania (eds), *Images of Crime II*, 35–64, Freiburg: Max Planck Institute.

JEWKES, Y. (ed.) (2003), *Dot.Cons: Crime, Deviance and Identity on the Internet*, Cullompton, Devon: Willan.

—— (2010), *Media and Crime*, 2nd edn, London: Sage.

JONES, P. and WARDLE, C. (2008), 'No Emotion, No Sympathy': The Visual Construction of Maxine Carr, *Crime Media Culture: An International Journal*, 4(1): 53–71.

KATZ, J. (1987), 'What Makes Crime "News"?', *Media, Culture and Society*, 9(1): 47–75.

KERR, P. (1981), 'Watching the Detectives: American Television Crime Series 1949–81', *Prime-Time*, 1(1): 2–6.

KIDD-HEWITT, D. and OSBORNE, R. (eds) (1996), *Crime and the Media: The Post-modern Spectacle*, London: Pluto.

KING, N. (1999), *Heroes in Hard Times: Cop Action Movies in the US*, Philadelphia: Temple University Press.

KOSKELA, H. (2011), 'Don't mess with Texas! Texas Virtual Border Watch Program and the (botched) politics of responsibilization', *Crime, Media, Culture: An International Journal*, 7(1): 49–65.

KNIGHT, S. (1980), *Form and Ideology in Crime Fiction*, London: Macmillan.

LAING, S. (1991), 'Banging in Some Reality: The Original "Z-Cars"', in J. Corner (ed.), *Popular Television In Britain: Studies in Cultural History*, 125–43, London: British Film Institute.

LAWRENCE, R. G. (2000), *The Politics of Force: Media and the Construction of Police Brutality*, Berkeley, Cal.: University of California Press.

LEES, S. (1995), 'Media Reporting of Rape: The 1993 British "Date Rape" Controversy', in D. Kidd-Hewitt and R. Osborne (eds), *Crime and the Media*, 107–30, London: Pluto.

LEISHMAN, F. and MASON, P. (2002), *Policing and the Media: Facts, Fictions and Factions*, Cullompton, Devon: Willan

LEVI, M. (2001), 'White-Collar Crime in the News', *Criminal Justice Matters*, 43: 24–5.

—— (2006), 'The Media Construction of Financial and White Collar Crimes', *British Journal of Criminology* (forthcoming).

LICHTER, S. R., LICHTER, L. S., and ROTHMAN, S. (1994), *Prime Time: How TV Portrays American Culture*, Washington: Regnery.

LIPPERT, R. AND WILKINSON, B. (2010), 'Capturing Crime, Criminals and the Public's Imagination: Assembling Crime Stoppers and CCTV Surveillance', *Crime, Media, Culture: An International Journal*, 6(2):131–52.

LIVINGSTONE, S. (1996), 'On the Continuing Problem of Media Effects', in J. Curran and M. Gurevitch (eds), *Mass Media and Society*, London: Arnold.

——, ALLEN, J., and REINER, R. (2001), 'Audiences for Crime Media 1946–91: A Historical Approach to Reception Studies', *Communication Review*, 4(2): 165–92.

LYON, D, (2003), *Surveillance as Social Sorting: Privacy, Risk and Digital Discrimination*, London: Routledge.

—— (2009), *Identifying Citizens: ID Cards as Surveillance*, Cambridge: Polity.

MCARTHUR, C. (1972), *Underworld USA*, London: Secker and Warburg.

MCCAHILL, M. (2003), 'Media Representations of Visual Surveillance', in P. Mason (ed.), *Criminal Visions*, Cullompton, Devon: Willan.

McCARTY, J. (1993), *Hollywood Gangland*, New York: St Martin's Press.

McLAUGHLIN, E. (2005a), 'Recovering Blackness—Repudiating Whiteness: The Daily Mail's Construction of the Five White Suspects Accused of the Racist Murder of Stephen Lawrence', in K. Murji and J. Solomos (eds), *Racialization: Studies in Theory and Practice*, Oxford: Oxford University Press.

—— (2005b), 'From Reel to Ideal: The Blue Lamp and the Popular Cultural Construction of the English "Bobby", *Crime Media, Culture: An International Journal*, 1(1): 11–30.

McNAIR, B. (2009), *News and Journalism in the UK*, 5th edn, London: Routledge.

MANDEL, E. (1984), *Delightful Murder: A Social History of the Crime Story*, London: Pluto.

MANNING, P. (1998), 'Media Loops', in F. Bailey and D. Hale (eds), *Popular Culture, Crime and Justice*, Belmont, Cal.: Wadsworth.

MARSH, H. L. (1991), 'A Comparative Analysis of Crime Coverage in Newspapers in the United States and Other Countries From 1960–1989: A Review of the Literature', *Journal of Criminal Justice*, 19(1): 67–80.

MASON, P. (1996), 'Prime Time Punishment: The British Prison and Television', in D. Kidd-Hewitt and R. Osborne (eds), *Crime and the Media*, London: Pluto.

—— (2003a), 'The Screen Machine; Cinematic Representations of Prison', in P. Mason (ed.), *Criminal Visions*, 278–97, Cullompton, Devon: Willan.

—— (ed.) (2003b), *Criminal Visions*, Cullompton, Devon: Willan.

MATHEWS, T. D. (1994), *Censored*, London: Chatto and Windus.

MATHIESEN, T. (1997), 'The Viewer Society: Michel Foucault's "Panopticon" Revisited', *Theoretical Criminology*, 1(2): 215–34.

MAWBY, R. C. (1998), 'The Changing Image of Policing in Television Drama 1956–96', *Journal of the Police History Society*, 13: 39–44.

—— (1999), 'Visibility, Transparency, and Police-Media Relations', *Policing and Society*, 9(3): 263–86.

—— (2001), 'Promoting the Police? The Rise of Police Image Work', *Criminal Justice Matters*, 43: 44–5.

—— (2002), *Policing Images: Policing, Communication and Legitimacy*, Cullompton, Devon: Willan.

—— (2003), 'Completing the "Half-formed Picture"? Media Images of Policing', in P. Mason (ed.), *Criminal Visions*, Cullompton, Devon: Willan.

MAWBY, R. I. and BROWN, J. (1983), 'Newspaper Images of the Victim', *Victimology*, 9(1): 82–94.

McCAW, N. (2011), *Adapting Detective Fiction: Crime, Englishness and the TV Detectives*, London: Continuum.

MEDVED, M. (1992), *Hollywood vs. America*, London: Harper Collins.

MERTON, R. (1938/1957), 'Social Structure and Anomie', *American Sociological Review*, 3: 672–82. Reprinted in R. Merton, *Social Theory and Social Structure*, Glencoe, Ill.: Free Press, 1957; revised edn, 1963.

MESSNER, S. F. and ROSENFELD, R. (2000), *Crime and the American Dream*, 3rd edn, Belmont, Cal.: Wadsworth.

MEYERS, R. (1981), *TV Detectives*, San Diego, Cal.: Barnes.

—— (1989), *Murder on the Air*, New York: The Mysterious Press.

MILLER, F. (1994), *Censored Hollywood: Sex, Sin and Violence on Screen*, Atlanta, Ga.: Turner.

MURDOCK, G. (1982), 'Disorderly Images', in C. Sumner (ed.), *Crime, Justice and the Mass Media*, 104–23 (Cropwood Papers 14), Cambridge: Institute of Criminology.

NELLIS, M. and HALE, C. (1982), *The Prison Film*, London: Radical Alternatives to Prison.

NEWBURN, T. and HAYMAN, S. (2001), *Policing, CCTV and Social Control*, Cullompton, Devon: Willan.

NORRIS, C. and ARMSTRONG, G. (1999), *The Maximum Surveillance Society: The Rise of CCTV*, Sussex: Berg.

—— and McCAHILL, M. (2006), 'CCTV: Beyond Penal Modernism', *British Journal of Criminology*, 46(1): 97–118.

NYBERG, A. K. (1998), 'Comic Books and Juvenile Delinquence: A Historical Perspective', in F. Bailey and D. Hale (eds), *Popular Culture, Crime and Justice*, 61–70, Belmont, Cal.: Wadsworth.

OLIVER, M. B. and ARMSTRONG, G. B. (1998), 'The Color of Crime: Perceptions of Caucasians' and African-Americans' Involvement in Crime', in M. Fishman and G. Cavender (eds), *Entertaining Crime*, New York: Aldine De Gruyter.

OSBORNE, R. (1996), 'Crime and the Media: From Media Studies to Post-modernism', in D. Kidd-Hewitt and R. Osborne (eds), *Crime and the Media*, 25–48, London: Pluto.

OUSBY, I. (1976), *Bloodhounds of Heaven: The Detective in English Fiction From Godwin to Doyle*, Cambridge, Mass.: Harvard University Press.

—— (1997), *The Crime and Mystery Book*, London: Thames & Hudson.

PALMER, J. (1978), *Thrillers*, London: Edward Arnold.

PANDIANI, J. (1978), 'Crime Time TV: If All We Knew Is What We Saw . . .', *Contemporary Crises*, 2: 437–58.

PARK, W. (1978), 'The Police State', *Journal of Popular Film*, 6(3): 229–38.

PEARSON, G. (1983), *Hooligan: A History of Respectable Fears*, London: Macmillan.

PEAY, J. (1998), 'The Power of the Popular', in T. Newburn and J. Vagg (eds), *Emerging Themes in Criminology*, Loughborough: British Society of Criminology.

PEELO, M., FRANCIS, B., SOOTHILL, K., PEARSON, J., and ACKERLEY, E. (2004), 'Newspaper Reporting and the

Public Construction of Homicide', *British Journal of Criminology*, 44(2): 256–75.

PHILLIPS, M. (1996), *The Observer Review*, 8 December: 2.

PORTER, B. (1981), *The Pursuit of Crime*, New Haven, Conn.: Yale University Press.

POWERS, S. P., ROTHMAN, D. J., and ROTHMAN, S. (1996), *Hollywood's America: Social and Political Themes in Motion Pictures*, Boulder, Col.: Westview.

RAFTER, N. (2006), *Shots in the Mirror: Crime Films and Society*, New York: Oxford University Press.

—— and BROWN, M. (2011), *Criminology Goes to the Movies: Crime Theory and Popular Culture*, New York: NYU Press.

RAWLINGS, P. (1992), *Drunks, Whores, and Idle Apprentices: Criminal Biographies of the Eighteenth Contury*, London: Routledge.

—— (1998), 'Crime Writers: Non-Fiction Crime Books', in T. Newburn and J. Vagg (eds), *Emerging Themes in Criminology*, Loughborough: British Society of Criminology.

REINER, R. (1978), 'The New Blue Films', *New Society*, 43(808): 706–708.

—— (1981), 'Keystone to Kojak: The Hollywood Cop', in P. Davies and B. Neve (eds), *Politics, Society and Cinema in America*, Manchester: Manchester University Press.

—— (1994), 'The Dialectics of Dixon: The Changing Image of the TV Cop', in S. Becker and M. Stephens (eds), *Police Force, Police Service*, London: Macmillan.

—— (2000a), *The Politics of the Police*, 3rd edn, Oxford: Oxford University Press.

—— (2000b), 'Romantic Realism: Policing and the Media', in F. Leishman, B. Loveday, and S. Savage (eds), *Core Issues in Policing*, London: Longman.

—— (2000c), 'Crime and Control in Britain', *Sociology*, 34(1): 71–94.

—— (2001), 'The Rise of Virtual Vigilantism: Crime Reporting Since World War II', *Criminal Justice Matters*, 43: 4–5.

—— (2003), 'Policing and the Media', in T. Newburn (ed.), *Handbook of Policing*, Cullompton, Devon: Willan

——, LIVINGSTONE, S., and ALLEN, J. (2000), 'No More Happy Endings? The Media and Popular Concern About Crime Since the Second World War', in T. Hope and R. Sparks (eds), *Crime, Risk and Insecurity*, London: Routledge.

——, ——, and —— (2001), 'Casino Culture: Media and Crime in a Winner-Loser Society', in K. Stenson and R. Sullivan (eds), *Crime, Risk and Justice*, Cullompton, Devon: Willan.

——, ——, and —— (2003), 'From Law and Order to Lynch Mobs: Crime News Since the Second World War', in P. Mason (ed.), *Criminal Visions*, Cullompton: Willan.

ROBERTS, J. V. and STALANS, L. J. (2000), *Public Opinion, Crime and Criminal Justice*, Boulder, Col.: Westwood.

ROBERTS, M. (2001), 'Just Noise? Newspaper Crime Reporting and Fear of Crime', *Criminal Justice Matters*, 43: 10–11.

ROCK, P. (1973), 'News As Eternal Recurrence', in S. Cohen and J. Young (eds), *The Manufacture of News*, London: Constable.

ROSHIER, B. (1973), 'The Selection of Crime News By the Press', in S. Cohen and J. Young (eds), *The Manufacture of News*, London: Constable.

ROSOW, E. (1978), *Born to Lose*, New York: Oxford University Press.

ROSS, J. I. (1998), 'The Role of the Media in the Creation of Public Police Violence', in F. Bailey and D. Hale (eds), *Popular Culture, Crime and Justice*, Belmont, Cal.: Wadsworth.

RUBIN, M. (1999), *Thrillers*, Cambridge: Cambridge University Press.

SACCO, V. F. (1995), 'Media Constructions of Crime', *The Annals of the American Academy of Political and Social Science*, 539: 141–54.

SASSON, T. (1995), *Crime Talk: How Citizens Construct A Social Problem*, New York: Aldine De Gruyter.

SAYERS, D. (ed.) (1936), *Tales of Detection*, London: Dent.

SCHLESINGER, P. (1989), 'Rethinking the Sociology of Journalism: Source Strategies and the Limits of Media-Centrism', in M. Ferguson (ed.), *Public Communication: The New Imperatives*, London: Sage.

—— and TUMBER, H. (1992), 'Crime and Criminal Justice in the Media', in D. Downes (ed.), *Unravelling Criminal Justice*, London: Macmillan.

—— and —— (1993), 'Fighting the War Against Crime: Television, Police and Audience', *British Journal of Criminology*, 33(1): 19–32.

—— and —— (1994), *Reporting Crime*, Oxford: Oxford University Press.

——, MURDOCK, G. and ELLIOTT, P. (1983), *Televising "Terrorism" : Political Violence in Popular Culture*, London: Commedia.

——, DOBASH, R., and MURDOCK, G. (1991), 'The Media Politics of Crime and Criminal Justice', *British Journal of Sociology*, 42(3): 397–420.

——, ——, and WEAVER, C. (1992), *Women Viewing Violence*, London: British Film Institute.

SCHRAMM, W., LYLE, J., and PARKER, E. B. (1961), *Television in the Lives of Our Children*, Stanford, Cal.: Stanford University Press.

SEAL, L. (2009), 'Issues of Gender and Class in the Mirror Newspapers' Campaign for the Release of Edith Chubb', *Crime Media Culture: An International Journal*, 5, 1:57–78.

—— (2010), *Women, Murder and Femininity: Gender Representations of Women Who Kill*, Basingstoke: Palgrave Macmillan.

SHADOIAN, J. (1977), *Dreams and Dead Ends*, Cambridge, Mass.: MIT Press.

SHALE, S. (1996), 'Listening to the Law: Famous Trials on BBC Radio 1934–69', *Modern Law Review*, 59(6): 813–44.

SHERIZEN, S. (1978), 'Social Creation of Crime News: All the News Fitted to Print', in C. Winick (ed.),

*Deviance and Mass Media*, Beverly Hills, Cal.: Sage.

SIGNORIELLI, N. (1990), 'Television's Mean and Dangerous World: A Continuation of the Cultural Indicators Perspective', in N. Signorielli and M. Morgan (eds), *Cultivation Analysis: New Directions in Media Effects Research*, Newbury Park: Sage.

SKIDMORE, P. (1996), 'Telling Tales; Media Power, Ideology, and the Reporting of Child Sexual Abuse in Britain', in D. Kidd-Hewitt and R. Osborne (eds), *Crime and the Media*, London: Pluto.

SKLAR, R. (1975), *Movie-Made America*, New York: Vintage.

SMITH, S. (1984), 'Crime in the News', *British Journal of Criminology*, 24(3): 289–95.

SOLOMONS, S. (1976), *Beyond Formula: American Film Genres*, New York: Harcourt, Brace, Jovanovich.

SOOTHILL, K. and WALBY, S. (1991), *Sex Crime in the News*, London: Routledge.

SPARKS, R. (1992), *Television and the Drama of Crime*, Buckingham: Open University Press.

—— (1993), 'Inspector Morse', in G. Brandt (ed.), *British Television Drama in the 1980s*, Cambridge: Cambridge University Press.

—— (2000), ' "Bringin' It All Back Home": Populism, Media Coverage, and the Dynamics of Locality and Globality in the Politics of Crime Control', in K. Stenson and R. Sullivan (eds), *Crime, Risk and Justice*, Cullompton, Devon: Willan.

—— (2001), 'The Media, Populism, Public Opinion and Crime', *Criminal Justice Matters*, 43: 6–7.

STABILE, C. (2006), *White Victims, Black Villains: Gender, Race and Crime News in US Culture*, New York: Routledge.

STENSON, K. and SULLIVAN, R. (eds) (2000), *Crime, Risk and Justice: The Politics of Crime Control in Liberal Democracies*, Cullompton, Devon: Willan.

STEPHENSON-BURTON, A. (1995), 'Through the Looking-Glass: Public Images of White Collar Crime', in D. Kidd-Hewitt and R. Osborne (eds), *Crime and the Media*, London: Pluto.

SUMNER, C. (1982), ' "Political Hooliganism" and "Rampaging Mobs": The National Press Coverage of the Toxteth "Riots" ', in C. Sumner (ed.), *Crime, Justice and the Mass Media*, Cropwood Papers 14, Cambridge: Institute of Criminology.

SURETTE, R. (1998), *Media, Crime and Criminal Justice: Images and Realities*, 2nd edn, Belmont, Cal.: Wadsworth.

SWANSON, C. (1955), 'What They Read in 130 Daily Newspapers', *Journalism Quarterly*, 32(4): 411–21.

SYMONS, J. (1972), *Bloody Murder*, London: Penguin.

THOMPSON, J. (1993), *Fiction, Crime and Empire: Clues to Modernity and Postmodernism*, Urbana, Ill.: University of Illinois Press.

THOMPSON, J. B. (1995), *The Media and Modernity: A Social Theory of the Media*, Cambridge: Polity Press.

TOMBS, S. and WHYTE, D. (2001), 'Reporting Corporate Crime Out of Existence', *Criminal Justice Matters*, 43: 22–23.

TUMBER, H. (1982), *Television and the Riots*, London: British Film Institute.

TUSKA, J. (1978), *The Detective in Hollywood*, New York: Doubleday.

TYLER, T. (2006), 'Viewing *CSI* and the Threshold of Guilt: Managing Truth and Justice in Reality and Fiction', *Yale Law Journal*, 115(5): 1050–85.

VALVERDE, M. (2006), *Law and Order: Images, Meanings, Myths*, London: Routledge.

WAKSHLAG, J., VIAL, V., and TAMBORINI, R. (1983), 'Selecting Crime Drama and Apprehension About Crime', *Human Communication Research*, 10(2): 227–42.

WALL, D. (ed.) (2001), *Crime and the Internet*, London: Routledge.

WARTELLA, E. (1995), 'Media and Problem Behaviours in Young People', in M. Rutter and D. Smith (eds), *Psychological Disorders in Young People*, London: Wiley.

WATSON, C. (1971), *Snobbery With Violence: English Crime Stories and Their Audience*, London: Eyre Methuen.

WILLIAMS, P. and DICKINSON, J. (1993), 'Fear of Crime: Read All About It? The Relationship Between Newspaper Crime Reporting and Fear of Crime', *British Journal of Criminology*, 33(1): 33–56.

WILLIAMS, T. M. (ed.) (1986), *The Impact of Television: A Natural Experiment in Three Communities*, New York: Academic Press.

WILSON, C. P. (2000), *Cop Knowledge: Police Power and Cultural Narrative in Twentieth-Century America*, Chicago: University of Chicago Press.

WINSTON, R. (2004), 'Seeing is Believing', *Guardian G2*, 7 January.

—— and MELLERSI, N. (1992), *The Public Eye: Ideology and the Police Procedural*, London: Macmillan.

WOBER, M. (1978), 'Televised Violence and Paranoid Perception: The View From Great Britain', *Public Opinion Quarterly*, 42(3): 315–21.

WREN-LEWIS, J. (1981/2), 'TV Coverage of the Riots', *Screen Education*, 40: 15–33.

WYKES, M. (2001), *News, Crime and Culture*, London: Pluto.

YOUNG, A. (2007), 'Images in the Aftermath of Trauma: Responding to September 11th', *Crime, Media, Culture: An International Journal*, 3(1): 30–48.

YOUNG, J. (1971), *The Drug-Takers*, London: Paladin.

—— (1999), *The Exclusive Society*, London: Sage.

—— (2004), 'Constructing the Paradigm of Violence: Mass Media, Violence and Youth', in H.-J. Albrecht, T. Serassis, and H. Kania (eds), *Images of Crime II*, 187–98, Freiburg: Max Planck Institute.

ZILLMAN, D. and WAKSHLAG, J. (1987), 'Fear of Victimisation and the Appeal of Crime Drama', in D. Zillman and J. Bryant (eds), *Selective Exposure to Communication*, Hillsdale, NJ: Erlbaum.

# 10

# PUBLIC OPINION, CRIME, AND CRIMINAL JUSTICE

*Mike Hough and Julian V. Roberts*

Deciding how to accommodate public opinion in criminal justice policy provokes fundamental questions about the way in which democracies should function. For most of the last century, politicians have tended to assume that public opinion about crime and punishment was something to be *managed*. The death penalty in Britain provides the clearest example of this: for 50 years majorities of the public have wanted to bring back executions—and the majority of MPs have voted against reinstatement on several occasions. In the last two decades, however, we have witnessed signs of increasing political responsiveness to public opinion. Whether this trend should be seen as mere populism or as a long-overdue sensitivity to the public depends partly on one's reading of political motives and partly on whether public opinion can be regarded as sufficiently informed to justify consideration in penal policy-making. Whatever the case, no system of justice can ignore community views entirely.

Why should we care about the public's views of criminal justice? There are several reasons. First, as a matter of democratic principle the electorate should have some influence over public policies and services—including criminal justice. Second, the system depends on public cooperation to function. If people have a negative view of the police or the justice system, they may be disinclined to report crimes. Once a charge is laid, the justice system requires the assistance of the public who may be involved as witnesses, jurors, or as lay magistrates. In short, the effective administration of the justice system depends upon the support of the public. Finally, and crucially, the institutions of justice need to be seen by the public to exercise legitimate authority. If the police and the courts lose public trust, they also lose their perceived legitimacy and public commitment to the rule of law may be weakened. As we shall see, institutional legitimacy flows partly from public beliefs that the system treats people fairly, respectfully, and according to the rules.

In addition, there is also a strong normative element to compliance with the law; people need to see a reasonable alignment between their own norms and values and those implicit in the criminal law. Our system of justice exists in part to censure offenders for their wrongdoing (see Ashworth and Roberts, this volume). The expression of censure represents an appeal to the morality of the offender to desist; censure is only possible if the censuring agent is perceived to be legitimate. For all these reasons we need to know the extent to which criminal justice policy and practice (including sentencing policies) command public confidence and reflects community values (see discussion in Morgan 2005; Roberts 2011).

On the other hand, few would advocate a justice system which blindly followed the opinions of the public; crafting crime policies that were tightly aligned with majority opinion could result in a very poor system of justice. Enforcing the law is quintessentially about the resolution of conflict, and some other basis for doing this is needed beyond simply adopting majority views. Whatever stance is adopted towards public opinion, criminal justice officials need to be dispassionate when deciding about competing rights, and well-informed when choosing between competing policies.

A large body of research has by now accumulated on public attitudes to crime and criminal justice. Governments of all political orientations routinely canvass the views of the public to see where people stand with respect to possible criminal justice reforms. Much of this work consists of polls which pose short, usually simple, questions about criminal justice policies; but there is also a substantial scholarly literature drawing upon a range of methodologies, both quantitative and qualitative (see Roberts, Feilzer, and Hough 2011; Tendayi Viki and Bohner 2009). We therefore now have a rich research record on which to draw. Of all the topics included in this *Handbook*, public opinion is possibly of widest relevance to other jurisdictions and within the limits of a relatively brief chapter we illustrate the discussion with examples from around the world.

This chapter is structured in four parts. The first part summarizes research on public knowledge of crime and criminal justice. Interpreting public attitudes to criminal justice requires an assessment of the knowledge on which those attitudes are based. We demonstrate that most people are misinformed about trends in crime and justice; for example, the public assume that crime rates are constantly rising, and people underestimate the severity of the criminal justice system. The second part moves from public *knowledge* to public *attitudes*. Unsurprisingly, given public misperceptions, most people are critical of the justice system, and believe it is structured to benefit offenders at the expense of victims. The third part links these two domains by investigating the relationship between levels of knowledge and attitudes to criminal justice. The final part explores the issues of trust, confidence and perceived legitimacy.

## PUBLIC KNOWLEDGE OF CRIME AND CRIMINAL JUSTICE

### KNOWLEDGE OF CRIME TRENDS

Surveys of the public in many countries have asked people to answer factual questions about crime and justice. The results have revealed considerable misperception. For example, although crime rates in most Western nations have been declining steadily since the mid-1990s, the public appear unaware of this important trend. Thus between 1992 and 2008, the property crime rate declined in the US from 325 to 134 incidents per 1,000 households, a decline of 59 per cent (Sourcebook of Justice Statistics 2011). Reported incidents of violent crime fell from 51 per 1,000 population to only 19 over the same period, a drop of almost two-thirds (Sourcebook of Justice Statistics 2011). Yet when asked about crime trends most Americans continued to believe that there was more crime than the year previously. Over the period 1996–2009 the percentage of respondents believing that crime was rising averaged 62 per cent (Sourcebook of Criminal Justice Statistics 2011). Similar trends are observed elsewhere including Australia (Roberts and Indermaur 2009; Butler and McFarlane 2009) and Canada (Doob and Roberts 1988).[1]

In England and Wales crime has been falling or steady for the 15 years since 1995 according to the British Crime Survey (BCS), with an overall decline of 50 per cent (Flatley et al. 2010); but in any year over this period, between three-quarters and two-thirds of the population thought that crime nationally was rising (Flatley et al. 2010; see also Ashcroft 2011). There is, however, a growing divergence in beliefs about national and local crime trends. In 1996, 55 per cent of BCS respondents endorsed the opinion that crime was rising in their local area, a figure that had fallen to 31 per cent by 2009/10. In other words, by 2010 the majority of the population thought that crime was *not* rising in their own area, but *was* rising nationally.

Similar distortions exist with respect to trends involving specific offences, particularly serious crimes of violence. Consider the most serious crime, and the one which attracts the most media stories. murder. Convictions for murder peaked at 317 cases in 2004/5 and have since declined (Mitchell and Roberts 2010). However, when the public are asked about murder trends, only about 5 per cent were correct; most people believed the murder rate had been increasing. Other misperceptions have been documented. Thus most people over-estimate:

- the proportion of crime that involves violence. Over three-quarters of the public in a number of countries including Britain, the US, Canada, Australia, New Zealand, and Barbados over-estimated the proportion of crime involving violence (Doob and Roberts 1988; Roberts and Hough 2001; Amelin et al. 2000; Nuttall et al. 2003; Roberts and Indermaur 2009);

- the volume of offending committed by people on bail and people on parole or licence (Paulin et al. 2003; Doob and Roberts 1988); and

- the recidivism rates of offenders released from prison (Roberts 1988a; Redondo et al. 1996; Paulin et al. 2003; Mitchell and Roberts 2010).

This general pattern of findings should not be surprising. In the first place, the measurement of crime is far from straightforward (see Maguire, this volume), even if the evidence is clear that crime has fallen in many western countries. Second, the reality is that crime rose in most industrialized nations for most of the second half of the twentieth century, leading people to assume that crime always rises; and people's mindsets

---

[1] It is worth noting, however, that while public knowledge of crime trends is poor, people do seem to have a more realistic sense of crime in their own neighbourhood. When pollsters ask two questions—one about the national crime trends and a second about local crime rates—people tend to be more accurate about the latter. This suggests that media coverage of crime is responsible for misperceptions of crime trends on the larger level.

may change only slowly. Third, the fact that claims about crime trends are contestable inevitably means that politicians *do* contest them. For example, there was no political consensus about crime trends over the first decade of this century in Britain, even if academic criminologists and statisticians were in broad agreement that crime had fallen; and politicians took every opportunity to attack their opponents if and when they claimed that crime was falling. Finally, the news values of the mass media, and the priority placed on dramatic and worrying stories, ensure that reports of rising crime attract much more coverage in newspapers, television and radio than declining crime rates (see Reiner, this volume). In other words, there are many factors that lead people to think that crime 'out there' is still rising, even if they do not think that this is true for their own neighbourhoods, about which they can make more informed judgments.

## KNOWLEDGE OF THE CRIMINAL PROCESS

Misperceptions also abound with respect to the workings of the justice system. Researchers in several countries have asked people to estimate the imprisonment rate for various crimes. Here too, the public appear misinformed: most people under-estimate the severity of the courts. This has been repeatedly documented in Britain using the British Crime Survey. For example, in 2007/8, almost all (97 per cent) of convicted rapists were sentenced to custody. However, when BCS respondents were asked to estimate the imprisonment rate for this offence, a third estimated that less than half of all offenders convicted of rape were imprisoned; another third estimated between 50 and 80 per cent. Comparable misperceptions have been found for burglary[2] (see also Mattinson and Mirrlees-Black 2000) and murder (Mitchell and Roberts 2010). Similar trends have been found in Canada (Doob and Roberts 1988), Australia (Roberts and Indermaur 2009) and the United States (California Assembly Committee on Criminal Procedure 1975).

### Self-reported knowledge levels

Table 10.1 summarizes the responses of the British public when asked to describe how much they know about various components of the criminal justice system (MORI [now Ipsos MORI] 2003). As can be seen, people report knowing most about the police—presumably because they are the most visible criminal justice professionals and the ones people are most likely to encounter. Self-reported levels of knowledge are much lower for other parts of the justice system. Thus well over half the sample admitted knowing hardly anything about youth offending teams, and between a third and a half knowing hardly anything about the probation service, the Crown Prosecution Service, or youth courts. These branches of criminal justice are generally invisible to most people, unless and until they become involved in the system as a victim or witness. The most recent polling finds similar trends: fully 85 per cent of the public

---

[2] Analysis conducted by one of the authors (MH) for a speech by Lord Judge (2009);  details available from the authors on request.

**Table 10.1** Self-reported level of knowledge about criminal justice agencies in Britain

| | A great deal/ a fair amount | Not very much | Hardly anything/ nothing |
|---|---|---|---|
| Police | 74% | 19% | 7% |
| Courts | 51% | 32% | 17% |
| Prisons | 30% | 38% | 31% |
| Probation service | 23% | 40% | 37% |
| Crown Prosecution Service | 27% | 41% | 33% |
| Youth courts | 18% | 38% | 45% |
| Youth offending teams | 13% | 28% | 59% |

*Source:* MORI (2003); Q: 'How much do you know about each of the following…?'

admitted that they were not informed about sentencing in England and Wales (MORI 2009).

The factors that shape public knowledge—or lack of knowledge—about the criminal justice system are very probably linked to knowledge about crime itself. Those people—perhaps the majority—who think that crime trends are a function of the deterrent capacity of the justice system may assume that sentencing *must* be too soft given that they believe that crime is rising. In addition, media coverage of the courts tends to focus on dramatically unusual sentences—especially where judges appear to have been unreasonably lenient.

## PUBLIC ATTITUDES TO CRIMINAL JUSTICE

### PURPOSES OF THE CRIMINAL JUSTICE SYSTEM

The criminal justice system serves multiple purposes, seeking to prevent crime before it occurs as well as to punish convicted offenders. Criminal policies—and media coverage—generally pay more attention to punishment rather than prevention. Crime prevention programs such as Neighbourhood Watch are less newsworthy than sentencing laws such as the 'three strikes' mandatory penalties. It is often alleged that the public are more interested in punishment than prevention; indeed the public are often described as being more punitive than the courts—a description we will contest later in this chapter.

### THE POLITICS OF PUNISHMENT VS. PREVENTION

Politicians often believe that getting tough with offenders—or talking tough—carries political benefits. The consequence is punitive populism (e.g. Roberts *et al.* 2003; Pratt 2007). Politicians in a number of Western jurisdictions have promoted punitive criminal justice policies such as mandatory sentencing more with an eye to winning votes than to actually reducing crime.[3] There appears to be a widespread perception that the public sees crime prevention as representing a 'soft' approach to crime, and prefer tougher options. The former British Prime Minister Tony Blair was well-known for using the slogan, 'Tough on crime, tough on the causes of crime'. The first part was clearly aimed at balancing what was seen as the 'softer' philosophy behind the second phrase.

The emergence of penal populism raises a number of questions. The first is whether politicians are good at 'reading' the popular mood and are able to craft their policies to respond to this mood. The right answer, in all probability, is that they are, at least for most of the time—and that they are certainly more sensitive to public preferences than academic criminologists. Being seen to be soft on crime is a vote-loser—and being tough on crime can be electorally decisive (see Downes and Morgan 2007, for a discussion). Behind this question is a more complex one, about the political legitimacy of responding to public preferences that are poorly informed. We shall return to this question, but first, let us review the evidence about public support for 'tough on crime' penal policies.

First, when a national sample of the UK public was asked to identify the best response to crime—effectively to express a preference for one of the two elements in the Blair slogan—they were far more likely to support prevention. Thus, two-thirds of the polled public favoured addressing the causes of crime while less than one third favoured tougher punishment (Roberts and Hastings 2011). Second, US research shows that there could be clear electoral benefits to be gained by promoting crime prevention: a poll found that over four-fifths of respondents stated that they would be much *more* likely to vote for a political candidate who endorsed investing in crime prevention programs (Peter Hart Research Associates 2002; Cooper and Sechrest 2008). In comparison, a much lower proportion of respondents said they would be more likely to support a candidate who endorsed tougher sentencing.

The public are aware that crime is caused by more than individual decision-making, and that crime reduction is therefore not a task exclusively for the criminal justice system. As long ago as 1947, when Americans were asked to identify the causes of crime, 'lack of parental control and supervision' headed the list (47 per cent of the sample; see Erskine 1974). This finding is echoed in polls conducted in many other countries (see Roberts and Hastings 2011). On four occasions over the decade 2000–9, MORI asked the British public to identify the most effective ways to reduce crime. On every occasion better parenting and better discipline were chosen most often—usually by over half the respondents, and by over two-thirds in the most recent administration (2009). The 'get tough' option—'put more offenders in prison' was seen as being effective by the fewest proportion of respondents, usually around only one in ten (MORI 2010).

Public support for non-punitive responses to crime is not limited to the issue of crime reduction. When asked to identify the best way to prevent reoffending, there was much more support for rehabilitation than punishment (MORI 2010). Similarly, the US public have been repeatedly asked to identify the most effective way of preventing

---

[3] Few politicians are likely to admit to this publicly, of course, so the evidence about populist motives is almost always circumstantial.

crime. Given a choice between punishment and crime prevention through social development, the public have repeatedly chosen the former, as can be seen in Table 10.2. On the face of it, this message appears lost on politicians who perceive the public to be very supportive of punitive responses to crime.

## THE LOPSIDED SCALES OF JUSTICE?

Most people hold a general belief that leniency is pervasive in the criminal process and this emerges from their responses to factual questions. In reviewing polls conducted over the past 40 years, it is clear that people believe that the justice system goes to excessive lengths to protect the rights of defendants. One manifestation of this is a public perception that the scales of justice are skewed in favour of the suspect, accused, or offender, at the expense of the victim. According to the public, 'criminals' are treated better, and have more rights than crime victims. Thus 70 per cent of Americans polled on the issue agreed that the laws and the courts are more concerned with protecting the rights of criminals than they are with protecting the rights of victims (Cole 1991) and almost three-quarters of respondents to a MORI poll in Britain agreed that: 'the law works to the advantage of the criminal and not victims' (MORI 2000).

## COURTS

Sentencing represents the apex of the criminal process and the element of the justice system which attracts most media attention and public interest. This stage has also accounted for more research on public opinion than all the other components of the justice system. When people think about criminal justice, sentencing is most likely to come to mind. When a sample of the public was asked to identify the most important crime problem, lenient sentencing was cited by the highest proportion of respondents (MORI 2010).

Public views,—or rather views ascribed to the public—appear to have fuelled a more punitive response to offending on the part of sentencers. For example, penal

Table 10.2 Attitudes toward approaches to lower the crime rate (US)

|  | Address social problems | More law enforcement |
|---|---|---|
| 1989 | 61% | 32% |
| 1990 | 57% | 36% |
| 1992 | 67% | 25% |
| 1994 | 57% | 39% |
| 2000 | 68% | 27% |
| 2003 | 69% | 29% |
| 2006 | 65% | 31% |
| 2010 | 64% | 32% |
| Average | 64% | 31% |

Source: Adapted from Sourcebook of Criminal Justice Statistics (2011)

policies in England and Wales over the period 1992–2007 became tougher in part because successive administrations cited the need to respond to public views. Thus the Conservative Home Secretary introduced proposals for tougher sentencing by noting they were necessary to maintain public confidence (see Ashworth and Hough 1996). The subsequent Labour Government expressed a desire to align policies more closely with its perception that the public demanded more punitive responses to crime and anti-social behaviour (Allen and Hough 2008). Research in several jurisdictions, including England and New Zealand, has identified sentencers' responsiveness to public pressure as a cause of harsher sentencing (e.g. Millie *et al.* 2005; Pratt 2007). Many punitive and ineffective sentencing policies of recent years such as 'three strikes' sentencing laws have been linked to public opinion (Roberts *et al.* 2003). The historical record is therefore not especially encouraging for advocates of greater public consultation. Seen from this perspective the public represent a source of pressure towards more punitive sentencing.

A great deal of research going back 40 years has contrasted public sentencing preferences with the practice of the courts with a view to determining how closely the two correspond. We have learned important lessons from this body of literature. First, if general questions are asked such as, 'Are the courts too lenient, too harsh or about right?', the weight of opinion will always be that they are too lenient. The reasons for this take us back to the issue of public knowledge. When people think of the typical crime, the typical image of an offender that comes to mind is of a violent crime committed by a recidivist (Indermaur 1987). Similarly when people think about sentences they have read about, they are likely to recall some sentence that appeared so lenient that it attracted media coverage. In short, people's 'top of the head' reactions to sentencing are likely to draw upon an unrepresentative archetype of crimes and punishments.

This finding on attitudes to sentencing has been replicated over time, using different methodologies and across disparate jurisdictions. For example, 85 per cent of respondents in South Africa expressed the view that sentences were too lenient (Schonteich 1999) and 74 per cent in Scotland (Justice 1 Committee 2007). Comparable findings emerge from other countries, including Belgium (Parmentier *et al.* 2004), Germany (Kury *et al.* 2002) and Barbados (Nuttall *et al.* 2003). US polls also reveal little variation over time in the percentage perceiving sentences to be too lenient. This did not vary outside a narrow range from 79 per cent in 1975 to 67 per cent in 2002 (Sourcebook of Criminal Justice Statistics 2011). The same pattern emerges from Australian and Canadian polls over the same period (see Roberts and Indermaur 2009; Roberts *et al.* 2007).[4]

The sheer volume of such findings leads many politicians to take for granted that the public are much more punitive than the courts. However, a poll using a simple and very general question asking if sentences are tough enough is an inappropriate method of seeing whether opinion and sentencing practice are in step, if only because it takes no account of respondents' level of knowledge. Researchers have therefore

---

[4] The perception of leniency is only part of the story; courts are also criticized for being out of touch with 'what ordinary people think'. Thus 82 per cent held this view of judges in England and Wales (Hough and Roberts 1998).

given people summaries of actual cases and asked them to impose sentence. In this way participants are more informed, having been given the details of the crime and the offender. Public 'sentences' emerging from this method are then compared to the sentences that were actually imposed in these cases. The advantage of this approach is that it sidesteps problems of ignorance about actual practice. Assessed in this way, public sentencing preferences and judicial practice are usually much closer together—the 'punitiveness gap' diminishes.

One example of this in England and Wales comes from the British Crime Survey, which has since 1996 asked a sub-sample to 'sentence' a 23-year-old burglar with previous convictions who broke into an old man's home and stole electrical goods. The case on which the vignette was modelled had actually attracted a sentence of three years, reduced on appeal to two (Hough and Roberts 1998). However, when the public were asked to sentence this case, only 54 per cent of the sample favoured imprisonment, with an average sentence length of twelve months. Clearly, then, the attitudes of the public and the practice of the courts are much closer than polls would suggest. This general finding has been replicated on numerous occasions in Britain and elsewhere (see Hough and Roberts 2005 for a review).

The argument that public punitiveness is a myth should not be overstated, however. Crime raises strong emotions of anger and anxiety in people, not only when it involves serious harm against vulnerable victims but also in more mundane cases of burglary, for example, vehicle crime and vandalism. Being the victim of crime is at the very least a significant irritant, and at worst a life-deforming experience. It is not surprising that people expect politicians to find an effective response to it. Whether this response should be simply punitive turns partly on questions of effectiveness—but it also depends in part on what a *properly informed* public would support.

## RELATIONSHIP BETWEEN KNOWLEDGE AND OPINION

A considerable literature has arisen around attempts to change public attitudes—to improve the public image of criminal justice—by providing information about the system. The hypothesis being tested is that if knowledge levels improve, attitudes will become more accepting of current practice; one approach to changing attitudes or to increase confidence might simply be to dispel some of the most persistent and prevalent misperceptions. The general research strategy in this field has been to provide some members of the public with information about a particular issue such as the death penalty, community sentencing, or parole—and then to measure attitudes to the issue in question. These peoples' attitudes are then compared to those held by the general public or by other participants who have not been provided with information. Since many of these studies have used an experimental approach—involving random assignment to condition—we can confidently attribute differences in attitudes or changes in opinions to the role of information.

Two studies are illustrative. The first involved a 'deliberative poll' carried out in England in 1994 (Fishkin 1995), in which almost 300 people were recruited to spend a weekend together in a hotel, hearing lectures, receiving information on crime and punishment, and being given opportunities to 'deliberate' on the issues. The idea was to see to what extent public views differed from their 'top of the head' opinions, and to see if any change was durable over time. Re-analysis of 'before and after' surveys—including a follow-up survey 10 months after the event—showed significant and lasting change, at least on some issues (Hough and Park 2002). On balance, attitudes shifted in a liberal direction. The importance of this experiment lies in its demonstration that considered views *are* genuinely different from those charted by straightforward polls.

A second example is reported by Mitchell and Roberts (2011) who explored the role of knowledge in shaping public attitudes to sentencing for murder. Having established that most people hold the opinion that sentences imposed for murder are too lenient, these authors tested the hypothesis that providing information about sentencing for this most serious crime would change opinions. Most people believe that offenders sentenced to life imprisonment are free once they leave prison on licence; in fact, these offenders are subject to recall for the rest of their life. Half the respondents to a nation-wide survey were given a brief factual description of what actually happens to offenders convicted of murder; the other half of the sample received no such information. All respondents were then asked a series of questions about sentencing in cases of murder. The researchers found that participants who were given the additional information were less critical of sentencing, and less punitive in the sentences that they imposed in case histories.

Other demonstrations of the way that attitudes are dependent on information include the following:

- Sanders and Roberts (2000) found that Canadians who had been given information about community penalties were significantly less likely to support imposing a prison sentence when asked to sentence offenders. Part of the strong public support for imprisonment can therefore be explained by the lack of familiarity with alternative sanctions.

- Doble (2002) asked members of the American public to impose sentence in a number of crimes; having done so he then provided them with the complete range of alternatives to imprisonment and asked if they wished to change the sentences they had imposed. Once they were aware of the alternative sentences, support for imprisoning the offenders declined greatly. Hough and Roberts (1998) report similar findings for England and Wales.

- Jones and Weatherburn (2010) found that Australians who know more about criminal justice trends and sentencing practices have higher levels of confidence in the justice system.

These studies demonstrate that it is possible to change attitudes and improve public confidence through the provision of information. This is not to say that public cynicism about justice can be traced exclusively to misinformation about crime and punishment. As discussed above, it would be naïve to ignore the deep-seated anger with which some people respond to crime, and even more naïve to think that this could be effectively countered by public education initiatives (see Loader and Sparks 2011, for a discussion). Increasing public levels of knowledge is not easy, however, and attitude change does not always occur; the challenge is to attract peoples' attention and to counter news media misrepresentations of justice (see Feilzer 2007, for discussion). At the same time, the evidence is overwhelming that public misunderstanding is at least a contributory factor to the overheated nature of political debate about crime and punishment.

So how should politicians respond to public opinion about crime and punishment, given that people's opinions are often demonstrably misinformed? We can only offer political—or normatively laden—answers to this question. In the first place, politicians may often themselves have only a partial grasp of the empirical evidence relating to crime and punishment—and indeed may share many of the misperceptions of their electorate. One can only hope that political elites make every effort to ensure that they are as fully informed as possible on the issues. Where they are informed in this way, they may then face the difficult choice of offering the public policies that they *need* or policies that they *want*. It is obviously electorally more advantageous—at least in the short term—to do the latter. However, the former—which might involve explaining the reasons for particular policy choices—strikes us as a more mature and more preferable form of politics. Many politicians would agree with this, of course—but, unlike criminologists, have to take account of the impact of coverage of their decisions by the mass media—which are quick to portray nuance as muddle-headedness, and cautious attention to evidence as dithering.

## TRUST, CONFIDENCE, AND PERCEIVED LEGITIMACY

Public trust or confidence has become one of the most researched issues in the field of public opinion and justice. Recognizing the importance of maintaining public faith in justice, almost all Western nations have conducted surveys to measure levels of public confidence in criminal justice (see Hough and Roberts 2004 for a review). These polls have revealed low levels of public confidence in justice across many countries. As a result, a number of jurisdictions have also launched initiatives to promote public confidence in the administration of justice.

### EFFECT OF MANDATE OF THE JUSTICE SYSTEM ON PUBLIC CONFIDENCE

An important factor to take into account when interpreting findings on confidence in, or satisfaction with, the criminal justice system concerns the mandate of the system. Speaking of the lack of public confidence in the courts, Kritzer and Voelker (2002) wrote that: 'It is not surprising that courts generate dissatisfaction; they are associated with unpleasant things such as criminals, injuries, divorces and the like. Many, perhaps most people are probably as likely to choose voluntarily to go to court as they are to choose to have their wisdom teeth extracted' (p. 59). Comparison with the National

Health Service is instructive. The patient's well-being is the foremost concern of the NHS, and of the professionals who work in the system. However, when crime victims get caught up in the justice process, the justice system has many functions besides responding to the victims' needs. For many victims, the protracted nature of legal proceedings, the experience of being cross-examined in court, or their inability to influence sentencing may all create frustration. This helps to explain the negative views of the justice system expressed by many victims of crime.

### ROLE OF PUBLIC IDEOLOGIES RELATING TO CRIME CONTROL

There is also an ideological component to public evaluations of criminal justice professionals, and this is not the case with respect to other public services such as the armed forces or the medical profession. People often have a theory regarding the way that the system should respond to offenders, and when criminal justice practices contradict that theory—for example, when offenders appear to be treated with leniency—ratings of the justice system and its professions suffer. Evaluations of other public services are more pragmatic, less based on ideology. For example, public evaluations of the health service are not guided or influenced by any ideological perspective or theory of health-care delivery. People want expeditious and effective treatment, and ratings of health professionals simply reflect the extent to which they perceive these goals to have been achieved. We therefore need to be cautious in our interpretation of findings from surveys in this area. It is unreasonable to expect public confidence in the justice system, or public performance ratings to be as high as for other institutions such as the armed forces or the National Health Service.

### CONFIDENCE IN THE LOCAL AND NATIONAL RESPONSE TO CRIME

In 2003, respondents in Britain were asked the following question about their confidence in the justice system: *Overall, how confident are you about the way crime is dealt with*? The question was posed with respect to the respondent's area, and the country as a whole, with very different outcomes. When the question asked about confidence in the *local* response, significantly more people were confident than not—with almost two-thirds (63 per cent) reporting confidence, and 34 per cent lacking confidence. When the confidence question shifted to the *national* level, 47 per cent expressed confidence, 51 per cent lacked confidence.

These findings suggest that different factors affect public confidence in justice at the local and national levels. Conclusions about levels of confidence in criminal justice can therefore only be drawn having first made a distinction between the local and national levels. At the local level, a strong majority of the public has confidence in the criminal justice response to crime. At the national level, a slim majority *lacks* confidence. Which evaluation reflects the true state of public confidence in criminal justice? We are inclined to the view that public attitudes to the local response are more important. Knowledge about crime across the country, and the nature of the criminal justice response, comes from the news media, and is indirect in nature. Public confidence in local authorities' response to crime is far more likely to reflect direct experience.

## CONFIDENCE IN SPECIFIC FUNCTIONS OF JUSTICE

Considerable variability exists in public levels of confidence with respect to specific functions of the criminal justice system. A MORI poll in 2009 found that confidence levels are much higher for some functions than for others. Over three-quarters of the public have confidence that the system respects the rights of accused persons and treats them fairly, but less than one quarter of the polled public are confident that the system is effective in dealing with young people accused of a crime. A clear distinction emerged between perceptions of the effectiveness as opposed to the fairness of the criminal justice system: people were significantly more likely to have confidence in the fairness of the system than in its effectiveness. Thus 60 per cent of the public were confident that the system is fair while only 40 per cent were confident that it was effective in reducing crime (MORI 2009). Similar trends have recently been found in Australia (Jones and Weatherburn 2010).

A more detailed picture of the functions that attract the lowest levels of public confidence may be derived from a MORI survey. There is a clear discrepancy between public perceptions of the importance of different objectives of criminal justice, and the extent to which people are confident that these objectives are being achieved. Specifically, people were asked (a) to rate the importance of specific functions such as 'bringing people who commit crimes to justice' and (b) to express their level of confidence that these objectives were being realized. Respondents were asked about more than 20 criminal justice objectives.

As can be seen in Table 10.3, the objectives people rated as being most important tended to be ones that attracted the least amount of confidence. Thus 'creating a safe society' was ranked second in importance, but tenth in the level of confidence that this objective was being achieved. Similarly, 'reducing the level of crime' was one of the highest ranked in importance (sixth) but attracted a very low confidence ranking (17th). In general, people gave high confidence scores to functions such as protecting the rights of offenders, and lower scores to effectiveness in terms of preventing crime or protecting the public. The nature of the functions on the list is also revelatory. It suggests that much of the public's lack of confidence springs from concern about public safety. People appear to have the least amount of confidence that the system is dealing with crimes of high visibility: mugging, burglary, and drug dealing for example. It is also interesting that the lowest confidence rating occurs for the issue of preventing reoffending. This finding is consistent with a number of other polls that have found that people believe reoffending rates are high, and that the system is incapable of addressing the problem.

## COMPARISONS WITHIN THE CRIMINAL JUSTICE SYSTEM

Most countries have now conducted surveys in which people are asked to rate their level of confidence or trust in specific branches of the justice system. The British Crime Survey has repeatedly measured public ratings of the various elements of the criminal justice system. When asked to rate the performance of the police and other professions a clear hierarchy emerges. Table 10.4 summarizes public ratings of seven branches of criminal justice, averaged over six administrations of the BCS between 2002 and 2008.

**Table 10.3** Public rankings of importance and confidence in criminal justice system functions

|  | Importance ranking (based on % rating function as 'absolutely essential') | Confidence ranking (based on % responding 'very' or 'fairly confident') |
|---|---|---|
| Treating all people fairly, regardless of race | 1. 72% | 2. 61% |
| Creating a society where people feel safe | 2. 69% | 14. 41% |
| Bringing people who commit crimes to justice | 3. 68% | 10. 50% |
| Dealing effectively with sex offenders | 4. 68% | 11. 51% |
| Dealing effectively with violent crime | 5. 67% | 6. 53% |
| Reducing the level of crime | 6. 63% | 17. 40% |
| Stopping offenders from committing more crimes | 7. 60% | 20. 24% |

*Source*: MORI (2003); Questions: 1. 'How important, if at all, do you regard each of the following aspects of the criminal justice system? For each, please give me a number from 1–10, where 1 is not at all important and 10 is absolutely essential; 2. How confident are you that the system is performing this function?'.

**Table 10.4** Public performance ratings of criminal justice system components: 2002–8

|  | Percentage of respondents choosing 'good' or 'excellent' |
|---|---|
| 1. Police | 50% |
| 2. Magistrates | 29% |
| 3. Judges | 27% |
| 4. Crown Prosecution Service | 27% |
| 5. Prisons | 25% |
| 6. Probation | 24% |
| 7. Youth Courts | 16% |

*Source*: Smith (2010); Question: 'How good a job do you think each criminal justice group is doing?'.

As can be seen the police attract the most positive ratings, with exactly half rating them as good or excellent. Ratings of the other elements of the justice system are very similar—and all rated less positively. The public appear most critical of youth courts, with only 16% of the public over this period perceiving youth courts as good or excellent (Table 10.4).

The hierarchy of confidence—with the police at the top and the courts at the bottom—is found in all other countries in which people have been asked their reaction to specific branches of the system. For example, when Canadians were asked how much confidence they had in various agencies of the criminal justice system, 37 per cent were very confident in the police, but only 7 per cent expressed this level of confidence in the courts. The lowest confidence levels emerged with respect to the prison and parole systems; even fewer respondents (3 per cent) had this much confidence in these institutions (Roberts 2007). Similarly, three-quarters of the New Zealand public gave the police excellent or good ratings. Only 45 per cent of New Zealanders rated the courts in such a positive way (Paulin *et al.* 2003).

## Comparisons across jurisdiction in public confidence

How do absolute levels of confidence in Britain compare with findings from surveys in other countries? Inconsistencies in the wording of specific questions in different countries make it hard to make direct comparisons. Nevertheless, some conclusions may be drawn.

Lappi-Seppälä (2011) reports that (according to the 2005 World Values Survey) England and Wales has lower levels of social trust and trust in justice than Scandinavian countries, the Netherlands, Australia, and New Zealand. However, it emerges better than many other European countries, and considerably better than ex-communist countries.

## TRUST IN JUSTICE AND COMPLIANCE WITH THE LAW

As the above discussion shows, much research on public knowledge and opinion in this field has aimed to identify the penal policies that the public will or will not tolerate. It has been conducted in a somewhat a-theoretical way; insofar as any hypotheses were made explicit, these tested and challenged the prevailing political assumptions about public punitivity. To the extent that research measured confidence in justice, it did so largely because public confidence in any public service was reckoned to be of self-evident value, and thus worth monitoring. Alongside this research, however, a parallel body of work has emerged over the last two decades that places findings on public knowledge and attitudes more firmly within sociological theory. There is an important and growing body of work tracing the linkages between trust in justice, perceptions of legitimacy, and public compliance and cooperation with the law. These 'compliance theories' can be located within a broader set of theories of normative compliance, which can be traced back to Durkheimian and Weberian thinking about the roots of social order. On the one hand, there has been increasing (or perhaps, more accurately, rediscovered) interest over the last two decades in the relationship between 'political economy', which trace the connections between the social distribution of wealth and attachment to—or detachment from—social norms; such theories well fall outside of the scope of this chapter.

However, there are also compliance theories about the impact on societal norms of the institutions of formal social control. Thus Robinson and Darley (1997) argue that if the law's potential for building a moral consensus is to be exploited, sentences must be aligned at least to some degree with public sentiments. Tyler (e.g. 2006, 2010, 2011) emphasizes the need for justice institutions to pursue fair and respectful *processes*—in contrast to *outcomes*—as the surest strategies for building trust in justice, and thus institutional legitimacy and compliance with the law. This is the central hypothesis in procedural justice theory. Procedural justice theories offer the possibility of resolving the tension that is often thought to exist between effective crime control and the respecting of people's rights. They suggest that fair, respectful, and legal behaviour on the part of justice officials is not only ethically desirable, but is a prerequisite for effective justice.

Clearly, the relationships between public trust in justice, public perceptions of institutional legitimacy, and public compliance and cooperation with the law will vary from jurisdiction to jurisdiction. Sherman (2002) identifies three domains affecting public confidence in justice: (i) the practice of the justice system and of criminal justice professionals; (ii) changing values and expectations of the culture the system serves; (iii) the images of criminal justice projected by the media. He argues that changes in modern society have left the procedures and behaviour of criminal justice officials out of tune with popular values. To this list we would add public knowledge of crime and criminal justice statistics, and experience with the system as a witness, juror, or crime victim. It also seems likely that trust in justice co-varies with levels of social trust and political trust, which themselves will be associated with factors such as social mobility and income inequality.

There is a growing body of British (and comparative) survey research on trust in justice and its relationship to perceptions of legitimacy, and cooperation and compliance with the law (see, e.g. Hough *et al.* 2010; Hough and Sato 2011; Jackson *et al.* 2011). In general terms, the expected relationships are found between procedural fairness, trust, perceptions of legitimacy, cooperation with the law, and compliance with the law. In other words, there is evidence that the way in which the institutions of justice treat people can support or erode their consent to the rule of law. It should be stressed, however, that there are limits to the ability of survey research to capture such subtle processes accurately (see Hough 2012, in press). There are problems of measurement—for example in devising sensitive measures of trust and perceptions of legitimacy, and in measuring people's compliance with the law through self-report measures.

Difficulties also arise in establishing the direction of causal relationships, especially in cross-sectional (snapshot) surveys: does distrust in the police reduce obedience to the law, for example, or does law-breaking prompt distrust? There are also problems of 'reach' in survey research of this sort, in that the most important groups to research—marginalized young men, for example—are least likely to take part in survey interviews. Despite the limitations, research of this sort is important; deriving a better understanding of the relationships between people's moral norms, their consent to the rule of law, and their perceptions and experience of the justice system is a major enterprise—and one which in our view goes to the heart of the criminological enterprise.

### ■ SELECTED FURTHER READING

For reviews of the literature see: J. V. Roberts and M. Hough (2005), *Understanding Public Attitudes to Criminal Justice*, Maidenhead: Open University Press; F. Cullen, B. Fisher, and B. Applegate (2000), 'Public Opinion about Punishment and Corrections', in M. Tonry (ed.), *Crime and Justice. A Review of Research*, Chicago: University of Chicago Press. A good summary of MORI polling on criminal justice topics can be found in B. Duffy *et al.* (2008), *Closing the Gaps: Crime and Public Perceptions*, London: MORI. A review of public attitudes towards the justice system can be found in S. Van de Walle and J. Raine (2008), *Explaining attitudes towards the justice system in the UK and Europe*, London: Ministry of Justice. For a review of public opinion and sentencing around the world, see J. van Kesteren (2009), 'Public Attitudes and Sentencing Policies Across the World', *European Journal of Criminal Policy Research*, and a good discussion of the psychology of punitiveness can be found in S. Maruna and A. King (2009), 'Once a Criminal, Always a Criminal?: "Redeemability" and the Psychology of Punitive Public Attitudes', *European Journal of Criminal Policy Research*. These volumes contain readings on a range of issues: J. Wood and T. Gannon (eds) (2009), *Public Opinion and Criminal Justice*, Cullompton: Willan; J. V. Roberts and M. Hough (eds) (2002), *Changing Attitudes to Punishment*, Cullompton: Willan Publishing.

## ■ REFERENCES

ALLEN, R. and HOUGH, M. (2008) 'Does it matter? Reflections on the effectiveness of institutionalised public participation in the development of sentencing policy', in K. Gelb and A. Freiberg (eds), *Penal Populism: Sentencing Councils and Sentencing Policy*, Cullompton: Willan Publishing.

AMELIN, K., WILLIS, M., BLAIR, C., and DONNELLY, D. (2000), *Attitudes to Crime, Crime Reduction and Community Safety in Northern Ireland*, Review of the Criminal Justice System in Northern Ireland, Research Report No. 1, Belfast: Northern Ireland Office.

ASHCROFT, LORD (2011), *Crime, Punishment and the People*, London: House of Lords.

ASHWORTH, A. and HOUGH, M. (1996), 'Sentencing and the Climate of Opinion', *Criminal Law Review*, 776–87.

BUTLER, A. and MCFARLANE, K. (2009), 'Public Confidence in the NSW Criminal Justice System' Available at: www.lawlink.nsw.gov.au/sentencingcouncil.

CALIFORNIA ASSEMBLY COMMITTEE ON CRIMINAL PROCEDURE (1975), 'Public Knowledge of Criminal Penalties', in R. Henshel and R. Silverman (eds), *Perception in Criminology*, Toronto: Methuen.

COLE, G. (1991), *Thinking about Crime: the scope of the Problem and shifts in Public Policy, The Public Perspective*, 2: 3–6.

COOPER AND SECHREST ASSOCIATES (2008), *Third Way Crime Poll Highlights*, Washington: Cooper and Sechrest Associates.

DOBLE, J. (2002), 'Attitudes to punishment in the US: punitive and liberal opinions', in J. V. Roberts and M. Hough (eds), *Changing Attitudes to Punishment: Public opinion around the Globe,* Cullompton, Willan Publishing.

DOOB, A. N. and ROBERTS, J. V. (1988), *Public Punitiveness and Public Knowledge of the Facts: Some Canadian Surveys*, in N. Walker and M. Hough (eds), *Public Attitudes to Sentencing*, Aldershot: Gower.

DOWNES, D. and MORGAN, R. (2007), 'No turning back: The politics of law and order into the millennium', in M. Maguire, R. Morgan, and R. Reiner (eds), *The Oxford Handbook of Criminology*, 4th edn, Oxford: Oxford University Press.

ERSKINE, H. (1974), 'The Polls: Causes of Crime', *Public Opinion Quarterly*, 50: 288–98.

FEILZER, M. (2007), 'The Magic Bullet', *Prison Service Journal*, 170: 39–44.

FISHKIN, J. (1995), *The Voice of the People*, New York: Vail-Baillou Press.

FLATLEY, J., KERSHAW, C., SMITH, K., CHAPLIN, R., and MOON, D. (2010), *Crime in England and Wales 2009/10*, London: Home Office.

HOUGH, M. (2012, in press), 'Researching trust in the police and trust in justice. A UK perspective', *Policing & Society*

—— and PARK, A. (2002), 'How Malleable are Public Attitudes to Crime and Punishment?', in J. Roberts and M. Hough (eds), *Changing Attitudes to Punishment: Public opinion around the Globe*, Cullompton: Willan Publishing.

—— and ROBERTS, J. V. (1998), *Attitudes to punishment: findings from the British Crime Survey*, Home Office Research Study No. 179, London: Home Office.

—— and —— (2004), *Confidence in Justice: An International Review*, London: Home Office.

——, JACKSON, J., BRADFORD, B. *et al.* (2010), 'Procedural Justice, Trust and Institutional Legitimacy', *Policing: A Journal of Policy and Practice*, 04(3): 203–10.

—— and SATO, M. (2011), *Trust in justice: why it is important for criminal policy, and how it can be measured: Final report of the Euro-Justis project*, Helsinki: HEUNI.

INDERMAUR, D. (1987), 'Public Perception of Sentencing in Perth', *Australian and New Zealand Journal of Criminology*, 20: 163–83.

JACKSON, J., BRADFORD, B., HOUGH, M., KUHA, J., STARES, S. R., WIDDOP, S., FITZGERALD, R., YORDANOVA, M., and GALEV, T. (2011), 'Developing European Indicators of Trust in Justice', *European Journal of Criminology*, 8(4): 267–85.

JONES, C. and WEATHERBURN, D. (2010), 'Public Confidence in the NSW Criminal Justice System: A Survey of the NSW Public', *Australian and New Zealand Journal of Criminology*, 43: 506–25.

JUSTICE 1 COMMITTEE (2002), *Public attitudes towards sentencing and alternatives to imprisonment.*

KRITZER, H. and VOELKER, J. (1998), 'Familiarity Breeds Respect: How Wisconsin Citizens View Their Courts', *Judicature*, 82: 58–64.

KURY, H. (2002), 'Introduction to special issue: International Comparison of Crime and Victimization: The ICVS', *International Journal of Comparative Criminology*, 2: 1–9.

LAPPI-SEPPÄLÄ. T. (2011), 'Explaining Imprisonment in Europe', *European Journal of Criminology*, 8(4): 303–28.

LOADER, I. and SPARKS, R. (2011), *Public Criminology?*, London: Routledge.

MATTINSON, J., and MIRRLEES-BLACK, C. (2000), *Attitudes to Crime and Criminal Justice: Findings from the 1998 British Crime Survey*, Home Office Research Study No. 200, London: Home Office, Research, Development and Statistics Directorate.

MILLIE, A., JACOBSON, J., and HOUGH, M. (2005), 'Understanding the Growth in the Prison Population in England and Wales', in C. Emsley (ed.), *The Persistent Prison*, London: Francis Boutle Publishers.

MITCHELL, B. and ROBERTS, J. V. (2010), *Public Opinion and the Law of Murder*, London: Nuffield Foundation.

—— and —— (2011), 'Public Attitudes Towards the Mandatory Life Sentence for Murder: Putting Received Wisdom to the Empirical Test', *Criminal Law Review*, 6: 454–65.

MORGAN, R. (2005), 'Privileging public attitudes to sentencing?', in J. V. Roberts and M. Hough (2005), *Understanding Public Attitudes to Criminal Justice*, Maidenhead: Open University Press.

MORI (2000), *Crime and Punishment Poll*. MORI poll 16 July 2000. Available at: www.mori.com/polls/2000/ms000714.shtml.

—— (2003), *Public Confidence in Criminal Justice*, London: Ipsos MORI.

—— (2009), *Sentencing—Public Attitudes Survey*, London: Ipsos MORI.

—— (2010), *Where are the public on crime and punishment?* London: Ipsos MORI.

NUTTALL, C., EVERSLEY, D., RUDDER, I., and RAMSAY, J. (2003), *Views and Beliefs about Crime and Criminal Justice*, Bridgetown, Barbados: Barbados Statistical Department.

PARMENTIER, S., VERVAEKE, G., DOUTRELPONT, R., and KELLENS, G. (eds) (2004), *Popular Perceptions and their implications for policy-making in western countries*, Brussels: Politeia Press.

PAULIN, J., SEARLE, W., and KNAGGS, T. (2003), *Attitudes to Crime and Punishment: A New Zealand Study*, Wellington: Ministry of Justice.

PETER HART ASSOCIATES (2002), *Changing Public Attitudes toward the Criminal Justice System*, Washington: Open Society Institute.

PRATT, J. (2007), *Penal Populism*, London: Routledge.

REDONDO, S., LUQUE, E., and FUNES, J. (1996), 'Social Beliefs about Recidivism in Crime', in: G. Davies, S. Lloyd-Bostock, M. McMurran, and C. Wilson (eds), *Psychology, Law, and Criminal Justice*, New York: Walter de Gruyter.

ROBERTS, J. V. (1988), 'Early Release: What do the Canadian Public Really Think?', *Canadian Journal of Criminology*, 30: 231–39.

—— (2007), 'Public Confidence in Criminal Justice in Canada: A Comparative and Contextual Analysis', *Canadian Journal of Criminology and Criminal Justice*, 49: 153–85.

—— (2008), 'The Role of public opinion in the development of sentencing policy and practice', in A. Freiberg and K. Gelb (eds), *Penal Populism, Sentencing Councils and Sentencing Policy*, Cullompton: Willan Publishing.

—— (2011), 'Community Views of Sentencing: Intuitive and Principled Responses to Offending', in M. Tonry (ed.), *Punishment Futures*, Oxford: Oxford University Press.

——, CRUTCHER, N., and VERBRUGGE, P. (2007), 'Public Attitudes to Sentencing in Canada: Exploring Recent Findings', *Canadian Journal of Criminology and Criminal Justice*, 49: 75–107.

——, FEILZER, M., and HOUGH, M. (2011), 'Measuring Public Attitudes to Criminal Justice', in D. Gadd, S. Karstedt, and S. Messner (eds), *Handbook of Criminological Research Methods*, London: Sage Publications.

—— and HASTINGS, R. (2011), 'Public Opinion and Crime Prevention', in D. Farrington and B. Welsh (eds), *The Oxford Handbook of Crime Prevention*, New York: Oxford University Press.

—— and HOUGH, M. (2001), 'Public Opinion, Sentencing and Parole: International Trends', in R. Roesch, R. Corrado, and R. Dempster (eds), *Psychology in the courts*, Amsterdam: Harwood.

—— and —— (2005a), 'The State of the Prison: Exploring Public Knowledge and Opinion', *The Howard Journal of Criminal Justice*, 44: 286–307.

—— and —— (2005b), 'Sentencing Young Offenders: Public Opinion in England and Wales', *Criminal Justice*, 5: 211–32.

——, STALANS, L. S., INDERMAUR, D., and HOUGH, M. (2003), *Penal Populism and Public Opinion. Lessons from Five Countries*, Oxford: Oxford University Press.

—— and INDERMAUR, D. (2009), *What Australians think about crime and justice*. Canberra: Australian Institute of Criminology.

ROBINSON, R. and DARLEY J. (1997), 'The Utility of Desert', *Northwestern University Law Review*, 91: 453–99.

SANDERS, T. and ROBERTS, J. V. (2000), 'Public Attitudes toward Conditional Sentencing: Results of a National Survey', *Canadian Journal of Behavioural Science*, 32: 199–207.

SCHONTEICH, M. (1999), *Sentencing in South Africa. Public Perception and Judicial Practice*, Occasional Paper No. 43, Institute for Security Studies.

SHERMAN, L. (2002), 'Trust and Confidence in Criminal Justice', *National Institute of Justice Journal*, 248: 22–31.

SMITH, D. (2010), *Public Confidence in the Criminal Justice System: findings from the British Crime Survey 2002–2008*, London: Ministry of Justice.

Sourcebook of Criminal Justice Statistics (2011). Available at: http://www.albany.edu/sourcebook/.

Tendayi Viki, G. and Bohner, G. (2009), 'Achieving accurate assessment of attitudes toward the criminal justice system: methodological issues', in J. Wood and T. Gannon (eds), *Public Opinion and Criminal Justice*, Cullompton: Willan.

Tyler, T. R. (2006), *Why People Obey the Law*, 2nd edn, New Haven: Yale University Press.

Tyler, T. R. (2010), *Why People Cooperate? The Role of Social Motivations*, New Jersey: Princeton University Press.

—— (2011), 'Trust and legitimacy: policing in the US and Europe', *European Journal of Criminology*, 8(4): 254–66.

# PART III

# DIMENSIONS OF CRIME

# 11

# CASINO CAPITAL'S CRIMES: POLITICAL ECONOMY, CRIME, AND CRIMINAL JUSTICE

*Robert Reiner*

When the capital development of a country becomes a by-product of the activities of a casino, the job is likely to be ill done

(Keynes 1936: 159)

Modern bourgeois society...is like the sorcerer who is no longer able to control the powers of the nether world whom he has called up by his spells...In these crises...Society suddenly finds itself put back into a state of momentary barbarism

(Marx and Engels 1848: ch. 1)

## INTRODUCTION: POLITICAL ECONOMY AND CRIME: RETURN OF THE REPRESSED?

Contemporary criminology and criminal justice policy are characterized by a peculiar absence, the virtual disappearance until very recently of a perspective that criminology was rooted in, and had been a largely taken for granted truism of thinking about crime and its control: political economy. As will be shown, political economy was expelled from criminology after the mid-1970s by a set of pincer movements. It is only in the last decade that the consequences of this, in particular for criminal justice debate and policy, but also for the (mis)understanding of crime, have forced the repressed back into consciousness.

The notion that there exists some sort of connection between crime and economic circumstances, especially deprivation, is age-old, as the etymology of the terms 'villain' and 'rogue' indicate for example.[1] The exploration of such links has been a prominent

---

[1] The Oxford English Dictionary states that 'villain' derives from the medieval French for peasant, and 'rogue' from the Latin for beggar. By contrast 'propriety' and 'property' share a common root, indicating a connection between economic class and conceptions of 'good' behaviour (Neocleous 2000: 39).

activity within criminology. Much of this was conducted within an implicit (or sometimes explicit) economic determinist model, 'the proposition that economic life is fundamental and therefore the determining influence upon which all social and cultural arrangements are made' (Taylor 1997: 266).[2] The literature on the role of economic factors in crime and criminal justice will be reviewed in this chapter, but the title 'political economy' is intended to signify a broader approach than simply spotlighting the significance of the economic, let alone economic determinism. The economic must be seen as part of a complex set of interdependencies with individual, moral, cultural, and other social dimensions. It is this dialectical interplay of levels of analysis that the label 'political economy' is intended to convey.

## WHAT IS POLITICAL ECONOMY?

The term 'political economy' is used nowadays in contradictory ways. Although it most frequently signifies a perspective that is distinct from 'economics', it is also sometimes treated as synonymous with it. *The Journal of Political Economy*, for instance, is the title of the house journal of the Chicago School, most famously associated with Milton Friedman and other exponents of neo-classical economics. It was *The Journal of Political Economy* that initiated the application of neo-classical economics to crime with seminal articles by Gary Becker and Isaac Ehrlich in the late 1960s and early 1970s (Becker 1968; Ehrlich 1973). The journal's title is explicable because economics as a discipline emerged out of classical political economy in the late nineteenth century, but the neo-classical perspective that the Chicago School espouses is frequently seen as diametrically opposed to 'political economy'.

What is now practised and taught as 'economics' is very different from the 'political economy' that was its origin. The most famous work of eighteenth century political economy, Adam Smith's *The Wealth of Nations*, 'was part of a much broader inquiry into the foundations of society. It was inseparable from moral philosophy' (Haakonsen 2006). Over time it fed into what is now referred to as 'classical political economy', the leading exponents of which were Malthus, Ricardo, James Mill, and his son John Stuart Mill (ibid.: ch. 7). Marx saw himself as heir to this tradition, synthesizing it with the dialectical philosophy of Hegel and with French St Simonian socialism, and indeed 'political economy' is sometimes used as virtually a synonym for Marxism.

'Economics' grew out of political economy in the late nineteenth century as a distinct discipline focusing on the economic in abstraction from these wider dimensions.[3] There was a parallel emergence of other social science disciplines out of the broad discourses of political economy and philosophy: political science, sociology, psychology—and indeed criminology. This was interrelated with the growing separation between

---

[2] The late Ian Taylor wrote the chapter on 'The Political Economy of Crime' for the first two editions of *The Oxford Handbook of Criminology*. Sadly he died before completing a revised version for the third edition. He brought a breadth of knowledge, penetrating insight, and profound moral and political commitment to his analysis that are impossible to emulate.

[3] The label 'economics' now refers primarily to a supposedly apolitical, value-free, 'scientific' enterprise, analysing the 'economic' using primarily mathematical models based on particular axioms about human motivation, decision-making processes, and forms of social organization of a highly abstract and simplified kind.

what came to be seen as different social and institutional fields. Liberal capitalism was characterized by ideal and to some extent actual distinctions between the spheres of the 'private' and 'public'; 'civil society' and 'the state'; 'the economy' and 'the polity'; 'criminal' and 'civil' law, each constituted and studied by an autonomous discipline (Neocleous 2000: 13–14; Lea 2002: chs 1–3).

## POLITICAL ECONOMY AS 'FULLY SOCIAL THEORY'

The most explicit exposition in criminology of the formal elements of a perspective rooted in political economy is the sketch of 'a fully social theory of deviance' in *The New Criminology* (Taylor, Walton, and Young 1973: 268–80). This was explicitly intended as 'a political economy of criminal action, and of the reaction it excites', together with 'a politically informed social psychology of these ongoing social dynamics' (ibid.: 279). It was an attempt 'to move criminology out of its imprisonment in artificially segregated specifics... to bring the parts together again in order to form the whole' (ibid.). Specifically it postulated that a 'fully social theory' must include analysis of:

> 1) The wider origins of the deviant act... a *political economy of crime*... 2) Immediate origins of the deviant act... a *social psychology of crime*... 3) The actual act... 4) Immediate origins of social reaction... a *social psychology of social reaction*... 5) Wider origins of social reaction... a *political economy of social reaction*... 6) The outcome of the social reaction on deviant's further action... 7) The nature of the deviant process as a whole [ibid.: 270–8].

Probably the closest attempt to incorporate all these elements into the study of one specific phenomenon was the magisterial study of mugging and the reaction to it by Stuart Hall and his associates, *Policing the Crisis* (Hall *et al.* 1978, for recent discussions see the symposium 'Policing the Crisis 30 Years On', *Theoretical Criminology*, 4 January 2008; Coleman *et al.* 2009). Starting from a particular robbery in Birmingham, and the sentencing of its perpetrators the book analysed the mass media construction of a 'moral panic' about 'mugging', and police responses to this. It then proceeded to a wide-ranging account of British economic, political, social, and cultural history since the Second World War to explain the deeper concerns that 'mugging' condensed. The later chapters offered an account of the impact of transformations in the political economy on black young men in particular, and how this structured the formation of specific subcultures in which robbery was more likely to be perpetrated. Altogether, *Policing the Crisis* remains a uniquely ambitious attempt to synthesize macro-, middle-range, and micro-analysis of a particular offence and the reaction to it, embodying all the facets of political economy as 'fully social theory'.

Most research studies inevitably focus on a narrower range of phenomena or policy issues, using more limited methodological tools and explanatory variables. But the value of the checklist of elements for a 'fully social theory' is to be a constant reminder of the wider contexts in which particular aspects of deviance and control are embedded, and their mediations and interrelationships. Even so the framework can be criticized for not including enough. Despite its emphasis on the need for social psychology as well as political economy, one of its co-authors argued recently that it remains a fundamentally structuralist perspective, precluding adequate exploration of the psychodynamics of crime and control (Jefferson 2008). Despite recognizing the need to incorporate analysis of the dynamics of deviant acts themselves, it brackets off the existentialist appreciation of 'the seductions of crime' from the perspective of offenders (Katz 1988), and more generally downplays cultural, interpretive, and symbolic dimensions (which are foregrounded in cultural criminology cf. Hayward and Young, this volume). Furthermore, it does not suggest practicable crime control policies, the basis of the subsequent 'Left Realist' auto-critique (Taylor 1981; Lea and Young 1984).

These critiques, however, have now in turn produced an unjustifiable neglect of structural and macro-social dimensions of crime and control. The pincer pressures of the Realist and the interpretive turns (see Loader and Sparks; Rock, this volume) have squeezed out recognition of the significance of the political economy as a key to understanding crime and control (Currie 1997: 147–51, 2009; Reiner 2007, 2011; Hall *et al.* 2008; Hall and MacLean 2009; Hall 2011; Bell 2011). Re-emphasizing the importance of the economic, as this chapter does, is not intended to encourage a reverse one-sided accentuation. But it is intended to show that without the holistic sensibility that political economy connotes it is impossible to explain patterns and trends in crime and control.

The next part of the chapter will review the fluctuating influence of political economy on criminological theorizing. The third section examines the empirical, primarily econometric, literature on the role of economic factors in explaining crime and criminal justice. As argued earlier, whilst not neglecting these variables, political economy sees them within a wider political, social, and cultural context. How do different kinds of political economy in their routine as opposed to pathological functioning impact on crime and criminal justice? This will be considered in the fourth section of this chapter, which will show how different types of political economy are related to comparative and historical variations in crime and criminal justice across space and time. Finally, the conclusion will assess the significance of political economy for understanding crime and control.

# POLITICAL ECONOMY AND CRIMINOLOGICAL THEORY

This section will review the influence of political economy in the history of criminological theory. Whilst there have been key stages in which political economy played a major role in attempts to theorize crime and criminal justice, there have also been long periods when its role has been denied or marginalized.

## THE SCIENCE OF POLICE AND THE DAWN OF CRIMINOLOGY

The standard account of the history of criminology sees its origins in the 'classical' perspective associated with Beccaria's 1764 book *Dei Delitti e Delle Pene*, and its profound influence, via Blackstone, Bentham, and others, on the Enlightenment movements for reform of criminal law and punishment (Taylor, Walton, and Young 1973: ch. 1). David Garland has called the application of the label 'criminology' to these eighteenth century thinkers 'altogether misleading' (Garland 1985: 14–15, 2002: 7–25). Apart from anachronistic terminology—the word 'criminology' was only coined in the late nineteenth century—it is argued that the 'classical' perspective did not concern itself much with aetiological questions, presuming a voluntaristic, rational, economic actor model of offenders. Beirne has shown that this was not true of Beccaria, who was strongly influenced by the emerging 'science of man' in the discussions of the philosophers and political economists of the Scottish Enlightenment, notably Hume, Adam Ferguson, and Adam Smith (Beirne 1993: ch. 2). This was a deterministic discourse concerned with explaining the causes of human conduct and society. Nonetheless, the primary focus of the classical school was not on the causation of crime but on its control by criminal law and justice.

Textbook histories of criminology usually neglect the relationship between political economy and Enlightenment discussions of crime and criminal justice and political economy, reflected partly in the work of Beccaria.[4] Political economy was intertwined particularly with the 'science of police' that flourished in the eighteenth and early nineteenth centuries, but has been overlooked by criminologists until recently.[5] It is well-known that the term 'police' originally had a much broader meaning, essentially coterminous with the internal policies of governments. What is less acknowledged is the intimate intertwining of 'police' and political economy. In his 1763 *Lectures on Justice, Police, Revenue and Arms* Adam Smith defined 'police' as 'the second general division of jurisprudence. The name is French, and is originally derived from the Greek "politeia" which properly signified the policy of civil government, but now it only means the regulation of the inferior parts of government, viz: cleanliness, security and cheapness of plenty' (cited in Radzinowicz 1956: 421).

The eighteenth century 'science of police' was a vast body of work that flourished across Europe. Its remit was correspondingly capacious, as summed up in the title of a 1760 treatise by von Justi, *Foundations of the Power and Happiness of States, or an Exhaustive Presentation of the Science of Public Police* (cited in Pasquino 1978: 44). Gradually this all-encompassing 'science' of happiness or 'police' came to be separated out into an array of distinct fields and disciplines, as liberalism sought to delimit the appropriate role of the state (Neocleous 2000: chs 2 and 3).

In England the leading exponent of the 'science of police' was the magistrate Patrick Colquhoun. Colquhoun is most commonly remembered as a precursor of the modern British police in the narrow post-1829 sense. However, he wrote extensively on political economy, crime, and criminal justice, and his work can be seen as a precursor of a 'fully social' criminology. Unlike the radical 1970s version of this, however,

---

[4] Beccaria himself was appointed to a Chair of 'Political Economy and Science of Police' at Milan in 1768, where he delivered lectures on the 'Elements of Political Economy' (Pasquino 1978: 45).

[5] The main exception is Radzinowicz, who discussed it extensively in the third volume of his *History of the English Criminal Law* (Radzinowicz 1956). Originally rediscovered by Foucault and some of his followers in the late 1970s (Foucault 1977; Pasquino 1978), it has been increasingly influential in recent years, above all in Foucaultian discussions of 'governmentality' but more generally in attempts to reconnect criminology with broader issues of the state and political economy (Reiner 1988, 2011; Neocleous 2000; Garland 2001: 31–4; Dubber 2005; Zedner 2006a; Dubber and Valverde 2006).

Colquhoun was a staunch conservative, both in his practice as a magistrate and as a political economist.

'Colquhoun's starting point is the insecurity of property' (Neocleous 2000: 49). Wealth depended on labour, but the maintenance of incentives to labour required that the working class remained poor, creating a perennial problem of order (Colquhoun 1806: 7–8). The task of police 'is to prevent the poverty-stricken class from becoming a criminalized and pauperised rabble' (ibid.). To achieve this police (in the widest sense) had to be both tough (and smart) on crime, *and* on the (multi-layered) causes of crime.

To Colquhoun crime and criminal justice were not independent phenomena that could be considered in isolation from broader issues of social and economic structure. Colquhoun was engaged not in criminology or economics as autonomous disciplines, but political economy and the 'science of police', embracing the totality of social and cultural relations. His proposals for the prevention and control of crime were rooted in empirical investigation of crime patterns. Colquhoun's analysis located the ultimate causes of crime in the overall structure of economy and society, but he was concerned to trace down the social and cultural mediations generating criminality and conformity. Crime was 'the constant and never-failing attendant on the accumulation of wealth', providing the opportunities and temptations for misappropriation (Colquhoun 1800: 155–6). Crime (mainly theft) was attributable to the poor, but not all the poor. Colquhoun saw a crucial distinction between poverty and indigence (Neocleous 2000: 49–56). Poverty did not determine crime, and was inevitable and indeed beneficial (as the crucial incentive for labour). The 'evil' was indigence—the inability or unwillingness to labour in order to relieve poverty (Colquhoun 1806: 7–8).

The task of analysis and control or 'police' was to minimize indigence. Indigence arose for both structural and cultural reasons. Structural factors included variations in the opportunities for training available to different ethnic groups (such as Ashkenazi as distinct from Sephardi Jews, according to Colquhoun, cf. Radzinowicz 1956: 273–4), and downturns in the economic cycle. But cultural and informal moral controls (such as religion and the promotion of uplifting rather than 'bawdy' forms of popular pastimes) were also important to encourage 'manners' that were 'virtuous' rather than 'depraved'.

The reform of formal policing arrangements for which Colquhoun is best known was only a relatively minor aspect of the policies required to prevent crime. Effective deterrence by regular police patrol was important, and certainly more effective than harsh punishment. Even the operation of formal policing was primarily important in symbolic and cultural rather than instrumental, utilitarian terms. The beneficial effects of police patrol were more to encourage moral discipline than to deter or catch perpetrators. Its terrain was to be 'upon the broad scale of General Prevention—mild in its operations—effective in its results; having justice and humanity for its basis, and the general security of the State and Individuals for its ultimate object' (Colquhoun 1800: 38).

Overall the analysis of security, order, crime, and policing advanced by Colquhoun and the 'science of police' were more sensitive to the interplay of politics, law, and justice with criminality than the later nineteenth-century 'science of the criminal'.

As with the contemporaneous displacement of political economy by economics, the apparent gain in 'scientific' rigour was bought at a high price in terms of the obscuring of the political, economic, and ethical dimensions of crime and welfare.

## POLITICAL ECONOMY, AND POSITIVIST CRIMINOLOGY

The term 'positivism' in histories of criminological theory is used to refer to the project of seeking causal explanations of crime on the methodological and logical model attributed to the natural sciences. As a specific and self-conscious movement, positivism is associated with Lombroso and his influence in the last quarter of the nineteenth century, but the broad quest to analyse crime causally had already existed for some time in a diversity of forms. The Lombrosian school primarily emphasized individual constitutional factors, although social and economic aspects were also considered. But the most significant pioneers of the exploration of economic dimensions of crime were the 'moral statisticians' of the early nineteenth century (Rock, this volume; Beirne 1993: chs 3–4).

### The moral statisticians

The acknowledged pioneers of sociological criminology were Andre-Michel Guerry and Adolphe Quetelet, who took advantage of the development of national crime statistics in France in the 1820s to explore the contours of criminality. They anticipated many of the patterns and complexities subsequently found in the later econometric studies that will be reviewed in the next section. Guerry found, for example, that contrary to the common belief that poverty was associated with crime, there were higher rates of property crime (but not violence) in wealthier regions of France. He attributed this to an opportunity effect—there was more to steal in richer areas by the poor within them.

This was confirmed by Quetelet's later more detailed analysis of the new crime statistics. He showed that the young, male, poor, unemployed, and uneducated were more likely to commit offences—but in places where there were more wealthy people to steal from. In his analysis crime was a function both of social pressures stemming from inequality *and* of the distribution of targets and temptations.

The most fundamental discovery made by Quetelet was the relative constancy of the rates and patterns of crime (and many other social phenomena) over substantial periods of time, which stimulated the later development of an explicitly sociological perspective by Tarde (Beirne 1993: ch. 5). Quetelet has been widely attacked for his supposed ultra-rigid determinism. Certainly he made remarks that invited such criticism. Perhaps the best known was his claim to be 'able to enumerate in advance how many individuals will stain their hands with the blood of their fellow creatures, how many will be forgers, how many poisoners' (cited in Beirne 1993: 90–1). But he intended only to offer descriptions of social patterns that were probabilistically, not inevitably, related to individual actions. He regarded crime as fundamentally a function of morality, but social factors such as lack of education or poverty made immoral decisions more likely, because they increased temptations and impeded the development of a prudent character. Overall the explorations of the 'moral statisticians' paved the way for the much more elaborate analyses of subsequent sociological criminology, above all the theory of anomie.

## Anomie theory

Merton's anomie theory is the most influential and cogent formulation of a political economy of crime outside the Marxist tradition (for a fuller account of its sources and influence see, Rock, this volume). Merton adopted the concept of anomie from Durkheim's 1897 book *Suicide*. Durkheim suggested that healthy societies require effective cultural definition and regulation of people's aspirations (which are otherwise potentially insatiable). Rapid social change dislocated such controls, producing anomie, characterized by restlessness, dissatisfaction, agitation, and other maladies conducive to suicide and other deviance. Amongst the key sources of this, argued Durkheim, was the economic cycle. Both economic downturns *and* upturns can disrupt the regulation of aspirations and produce anomie.

Merton's theory picked up on this analysis in a brief but seminal article, originally published in 1938, offering a framework for explaining variations in deviance between and within societies (Merton 1938). Despite the ritual slaying of Merton's analysis (arguably misrepresented, cf. Reiner 1984) in countless textbooks and exam answers over the decades, Merton remains the paradigm for a structural social theory of crime (Lea and Young 1984: 218–25; Young 2003b; Messner and Rosenfeld 2006; Special Issue of *Theoretical Criminology*, 11 January 2007).

Most accounts of Merton's analysis of anomie represent it as 'strain' theory. They focus on one aspect of his paper: the argument that a society combining *cultural* encouragement of common material aspirations by a mythology of meritocracy, and a *structural* reality of unequal opportunities, generates anomic pressures, leading to a variety of deviant reactions. Contemporary American versions frequently reduce Merton's structural political economy to a social psychology of deviance, attributing it to a psychic gap between individual aspirations and achievement (Agnew 1992). Merton's analysis was only partly directed at explaining the individual or even subcultural pattern of deviance within a society, although his typology of possible reactions to societal anomic pressure is probably the most frequently reproduced section of his paper (Merton 1957: 140). This aspect was also most influential in policy terms, leading—via Cloward and Ohlin's development of the concept of opportunity structures—to some of the 'Great Society' programmes of the early 1960s (Cloward and Ohlin 1960).

Merton's analysis of anomie as an explanation of intra-societal variations in crime was only part of a broader account aimed at understanding differences between societies. Anomie arose not only from a strain between culturally prescribed goals and structurally limited legitimate means to fulfil them. Anomie was also a consequence of the nature of the goals encouraged by particular cultures. A highly materialistic culture—especially one that defines success almost exclusively in monetary terms[6] (like the USA)—is prone to anomie, and hence to crime at *all* levels, not just among the relatively deprived lower classes. This is especially so if the goals of material attainment are extolled at the expense of consideration of the legitimacy of the means used to attain them.

---

[6]  Money as a definer of success is 'indefinite and relative' (Merton 1957: 136), and hence *ipso facto* liable to generate anomie.

Merton is a paradigm for a political economy of crime, suggesting links between a materialistic culture and overall problems of moral regulation. He also sketches how different tendencies to deviance can arise within a society in relation to the distribution of legitimate opportunities. But it is not an economically determinist account. It is not inequality or deprivation *per se* that generate anomie and deviance. The cultural significance these material factors have in different social settings is crucial to how they are experienced. The brief typology of possible reactions also points to many other factors mediating between structural pressure and human reaction. The informal moral controls in particular cultures are significant, for example, as shown in Merton's account of 'ritualism'.

For all its strengths, however, Merton's theory has been rather out of fashion in recent decades. Its social democratic critique of unbridled capitalism made him too 'cautious' a rebel for the radical criminology of the 1960s/1970s (Taylor, Walton, and Young 1973: 101), too radical for post-1980s neo-liberal triumphalism, and too structuralist for postmodernists.

### Political economy and realism

Since the mid-1970s mainstream criminology, especially in the USA, has been increasingly dominated by pragmatic realism, concerned with 'what works?' in immediately practicable policies. This was initially predicated on an explicit rejection of 'root cause' theories such as Merton's that sought to explain crime by macro-social causes (Wilson 1975: xv). Causal explanation was not eschewed altogether, but it has been pursued at individual (Wilson and Herrnstein 1985), situational, or community levels. These are more amenable to policy interventions that do not raise questions of wider social justice or reform. Whilst realism has largely ousted political economy, paradoxically it has been associated with a resurgence of studies of the economics of crime. There has also been a broader revival of neo-classical perspectives based on an 'economic man' model of the offender, such as rational choice theory (Zedner 2006b; Rock, this volume offer cogent critiques).

## POLITICAL ECONOMY AND RADICAL CRIMINOLOGY

### Marx, crime, and law

Until the flowering of radical criminology in the 1960s and 1970s little systematic attention was given by Marxists or others on the Left to crime or criminal justice. Marx and Engels themselves wrote little specifically on crime (Taylor, Walton, and Young 1973: ch. 7). Critics have often dismissed Marx's analysis as simple economic determinism. This has been countered by arguments stressing Marx's humanism (mainly from his early work), and the attention he gave to ideology and to the autonomy of human action within structured limits. It is of course possible to construct several alternative readings of Marx's voluminous corpus of work, and, given its political significance, all interpretations are highly contested (Reiner 2002: 239–52).

It is widely stated that in his mature theoretical work Marx did not systematically address issues of law, crime, or criminal justice. Chapter 10 of *Capital*, however, is a lengthy historical analysis of the emergence of the Factory Acts in early nineteeth century England (Marx 1867/1976: ch. 10). It constitutes a pioneering case study of criminalization and of what would nowadays be called corporate crime[7] (see Nelken, Chapter 21 this volume). Marx's account is very far from the economic determinism attributed to him, and gives weight to both structure and action, in complex interaction (Reiner 2002: 240–6).

The emergence of the Factory Acts presented something of a puzzle to Marx (as did the welfare state more generally for later generations of Marxists). How could legislation that restricts the autonomy of manufacturers be passed by a state that was not only rhetorically 'a committee for managing the common affairs of the whole bourgeoisie', as the 1848 *Communist Manifesto* had claimed (Marx and Engels 1848/1998: 37), but also some decades away from even the beginning of working-class enfranchisement?

Marx starts his explanation with structuralist factors. Without external regulation competitive pressures constrained factory owners to increase the hours and intensity of work by their employees, to a point that threatened the long-term viability of the system of production. However benign or enlightened they might be individual capitalists could not introduce more humane conditions unilaterally, so legislation compelling them to do so on an equal footing was necessary. Legislation required effective human action however. Marx shows the role of progressive factory owners, workers themselves, and (once they were established) the Factory Inspectors in the formulation and enforcement of the new laws.

At first legislation was symbolic rather than effective. Marx says of the Acts preceding the 1833 Factory Act that 'Parliament...was shrewd enough not to vote a penny for their compulsory implementation' (Marx 1867/1976: 390). He documented the subsequent ebb and flow of struggle by the Factory Inspectors to enforce the new 'law in the books' and ensure it became the 'law in action'. There was a continuous struggle between the Inspectors and deviant owners over avoidance devices introduced by the latter, stretching and testing the limits of the law. Marx traced this conflict up to the 1860s, showing how the extent of law-breaking, and the fluctuations in the strictness of case law and new legislation, were shaped by a complex interplay of shifting balances of economic and political forces (for example the split between the agricultural and manufacturing capitalists) and the success of human strategies within these changing structural pressures and opportunities.

Human actors operated within constraints that were shaped by histories and wider circumstances beyond their control, but could and did act in ways that could not be simply read off from an analysis of their structural position. Marx gave due credit, for example, to the efforts of more philanthropic capitalists, and to the 'bourgeois' Factory Inspectors (on whose reports he heavily relied). Altogether, this long chapter is a significant but neglected early example of a political economy of crime and control.

## EARLY TWENTIETH CENTURY RADICAL CRIMINOLOGY

Willem Bonger, a Dutch professor, made the first attempt to develop a systematic Marxist analysis of crime (Bonger 1916/1969). Bonger was in many ways an ethically

---

[7] Its specific subject matter, the creation and violation of laws regulating safety and other conditions of work, has of course been developed by later criminological studies, notably Carson 1970, 1981; Slapper 1999; Tombs and Whyte 2007).

inspiring figure, who pioneered many themes of subsequent radical (and indeed liberal) criminology (Cohen 1998), but whose work has usually been treated harshly, not least by later radical criminologists (Taylor, Walton, and Young 1973: 222–36 for example), who fail to give Bonger his due as a pioneer of the political economy of crime and control.

In Bonger's analysis the structure of capitalism generates particular criminogenic pressures and conflicts. In common with Marxism in general he has been accused of economic determinism, but his attempt to spell out the mediating links between structural roots and criminal acts is complex, and allowed scope for individual autonomy and moral responsibility. To Bonger the main way in which capitalism was related to crime was through the stimulation of a culture of egoism, at all levels of society. This enhanced the material aspirations of workers and the poor, and weakened their internal controls against predation in times of hardship.

In terms that anticipated Merton's analysis of anomie, Bonger talked of the stimulation of material desires by modern marketing and retail methods, so that 'the cupidity of the crowd is highly excited' (Bonger 1916/1969: 108). This explained not only proletarian crime but also crimes of the powerful. The egoism engendered by capitalism was particularly virulent higher up the social scale, so that 'although cupidity is a strong motive with all classes of our present society, it is especially so among the bourgeoisie, as a consequence of their position in the economic life' (ibid · 138).

Bonger recognized a complex multiplicity of linkages between the structural conflicts of capitalism, with its general egoism, and particular forms of crime. He acknowledged for example the need to analyse internalized controls as a factor preventing offending in the face of motives for crime generated by the egoistic culture (Bonger 1916/1969: 401). He also saw the problem of understanding the immediate situation and process of criminal action, not just its antecedent precipitating factors (ibid.). The root causes of crime in the larger immorality and injustices of capitalism did not remove the moral accountability of offenders (Bonger 1935: 23). Individual psychology as well as contingent factors such as suddenly occurring temptations had also to be considered (Bonger 1916/1969: 36). For recognizing the complexity of causal webs and relations leading to crime Bonger has been accused of 'eclecticism' (Taylor, Walton, and Young 1973: 227–8). However, it is difficult to see how to draw a principled line between 'eclecticism' and the checklist of elements of a 'fully social' theory of deviance, most of which Bonger seems to have been aware of.

Bonger introduced many ideas that were explored in later critical criminology. He recognized that legal conceptions of crime reflected disproportionately the interests of the powerful, anticipating subsequent labelling theory (Bonger 1916/1969: 24). But whilst acknowledging that class and power influenced the content and operation of the legal system, he nonetheless saw that it contributed to the maintenance of order in general, which benefited all classes. Some aspects of law were controversial, and enforcement might sometimes be biased, but most criminal law had the moral approval of the population. Bonger's recognition and condemnation of the harms inflicted by much crime was castigated by later radical criminologists (Taylor, Walton, and Young 1973: 232, 235). They attribute to him (as to Marx and Engels) a 'correctionalist' bourgeois distaste for disorder, and a failure to 'appreciate' crime as diversity (ibid.: 232–3). In many ways, however, Bonger anticipated the arguments of the subsequent auto-critique by these writers when they espoused 'Left Realism' in the 1980s (Cohen 1998: 125–6). Not only did he acknowledge the harm done by much conventional crime, he also saw it as particularly inflicting pain on the least powerful.[8]

The other significant contribution to political economy by early twentieth century radical criminology was Rusche and Kirchheimer's historical study of punishment (Rusche and Kirchheimer 1939). Two of the Frankfurt School refugees from Nazism who came to the USA in the late 1930s, Rusche and Kirchheimer published *Punishment and Social Structure* in 1939. The book was largely neglected for some 30 years, but republished in 1968, in an era of efflorescence for critical criminology. Its long-term historical analysis of trends in punishment since the early medieval period attempted to demonstrate that the development of penal measures was shaped by changes in the mode of production, in particular fluctuations in the supply of and demand for labour power.

Subsequent scholars, whether working within this broad tradition or critical of it, have qualified Rusche and Kirchheimer's account in two main ways. Empirically their history has been subject to detailed critique and qualification. Theoretically it has been attacked for excessive economic determinism. Although Rusche and Kirchheimer recognized the role of cultural, political, and other factors, it was left to later studies to spell these out in much more elaborate detail, considerably qualifying the economism of their account.[9]

## Political economy and critical criminology

Political economy had a central but fluctuating place in the critical criminologies that began to flourish in the 1960s. The labelling theory that developed in the early 1960s owed much more to symbolic interactionism and other micro-sociologies than to political economy (Rock, this volume). But labelling theorists began exploring how the structurally patterned play of power and advantage shaped the emergence and enforcement of criminal law and other definitions of deviance (Becker 1963; Chapman 1968).

Political economy assumed a central position with the Marxist-influenced radical criminologies that became prominent in the early 1970s, above all the 1973 book *The New Criminology*, with its conception of a 'fully social' theory of crime as discussed above (Taylor, Walton, and Young, op. cit.). The 'Left Realist' auto-critique that some of these radical criminologists offered in the 1980s explicitly distanced itself from straightforward economic analyses of crime (Lea and Young 1984: ch. 3). These economic models were associated with a supposed 'aetiological crisis' of radical criminology, as the reductions in poverty and unemployment associated with the post-war Keynesian welfare state failed to stop crime from rising (Young 1986). The Left Realist emphasis was on the need for and possibility of immediate steps to control crime in

---

[8] For his recognition of the oppression of women see Bonger 1916/1969: 58–60. He was also sensitive to the prevalent persecution of gay people and ethnic minorities, cf. Bemmelen 1960.

[9] A comprehensive but judicious exposition and critique of Rusche and Kirchheimer can be found in Garland 1990: ch. 4. Examples of later research on the political economy of punishment that qualifies their economistic Marxism are Ignatieff 1978; Cohen and Scull 1983; de Giorgi 2006; Lacey 2008.

the shape of more effective policing and criminal justice, not the 'root causes' approach attributed to earlier 'left idealism'.

Nonetheless, in so far as Left Realists concerned themselves with crime causation, this was largely by incorporating into their analyses earlier political economy perspectives such as relative deprivation and anomie, even if the origin of these ideas was scarcely acknowledged (e.g. Lea and Young 1984: ch. 6; Webber 2007). In the 1990s the erstwhile 'Left Realists' moved back to more macro-analyses of the relationship between crime, criminal justice, and late modernity or market society (Young 1999, 2007; Taylor 1999), in combination with cultural analysis (Chapter 4, this volume). These and other attempts to develop a political economy of contemporary trends in crime and control will be considered in the fourth section of this chapter. First, however, the next section will review the empirical evidence about the role of economic factors in explaining crime.

# ECONOMIC FACTORS AND CRIME: WHAT IS THE EMPIRICAL EVIDENCE?

## CRIME AND ECONOMY: A COMPLEX CONNECTION

The idea of an association between economic conditions and crime is embedded deeply in our culture and in the history of criminology. At a straightforward empirical level it is amply indicated by official statistics and surveys on patterns of formally labelled offending and victimization (see Maguire; Hoyle, this volume). As Braithwaite's 1979 review of self-report studies concluded, 'lower-class adults commit those types of crime which are handled by the police at a higher rate than middle-class adults', and the same applies to juveniles[10] (Braithwaite 1979: 62). This is true *a fortiori* of those who are processed by the criminal justice system as offenders, as summed up sharply in the title of Jeffrey Reiman's critical text—*The Rich Get Richer and the Poor Get Prison* (Reiman and Leighton 2009) and one might add the poor also get victimized.

However, in recent decades it has become fashionable to play down the role of the political economy in explaining crime. The dominant trend, on the political left and the right, in criminological research, policy, and politics, has been 'Realism', what works? 'What is to be done?' is Realism's key question (an ironic echo of Lenin surviving in the political discourse of market societies). Left Realists emphasize the value (or at any rate, potential) of criminal justice and policing in delivering security *now*, whilst

---

[10] Braithwaite's caveat is of course vitally important. By definition this pattern of greater 'lower-class' crime or punishment is not true of corporate or state crime, but these 'crimes of the powerful' are notoriously unrecorded and unsanctioned by the criminal justice system (Nelken, Chapter 22; Green and Ward, this volume; Slapper and Tombs 1999; Green and Ward 2004; Gobert and Punch 2003; Hillyard *et al.* 2004; Chambliss *et al.* 2010). The differential treatment accorded to tax and social security fraud is a prime example, cf. Cook 2006.

not denying altogether the significance of the political economy. Realists of the Right sought to banish political economy from discussion of crime policy. Throughout the 1980s Margaret Thatcher's Government vehemently denied Labour allegations that their neo-liberal economic policies stoked the pressures generating crime, above all attacking the view that crime was due to unemployment. If there was no such thing as society, it certainly could not be an explanation of crime. The paradox is that this turn away from political economy coincided with the emergence of the strongest evidence of precisely such connections.

*A priori*, economic factors might be expected to impact on crime in a variety of ways. For a crime to occur there are several logically necessary preconditions, which can be identified as: labelling, motive, means, opportunity, and the absence of control (Reiner 2007: ch. 4). Economic factors are potentially relevant to all of these.

1. *Labelling.* As 'labelling theory' re-emphasized in the 1960s, acts and actors that might be regarded as harmful, immoral, or anti-social are not necessarily seen as deviant or criminal. To become part of the apparent problem of crime requires a process of 'labelling'. Labelling processes are contingent and fluctuating. Legal categories of crime change and evolve: acts are criminalized and de-criminalized. Only a small and unrepresentative sample of all acts or actors that could be treated as criminal end up being recorded as such in any type of criminal statistics or subject to criminal justice processing of any sort.

Economic factors shape these labelling processes at all levels. Studies of the emergence of criminal law have accorded significant weight to changes in the political economy (Lacey, Wells, and Quick 2010). Fluctuations in the propensity of victims to report crimes, and/or the police to record them, are also influenced by economic factors, such as the proliferation of high-value stealable consumer goods and insurance cover for them, or the impact of managerial performance management in policing (Reiner 2007: ch. 3). The application of criminal labels to individuals is patterned by police deployment strategies and enforcement decisions. In turn these are influenced by perceptions of particular (usually poorer) areas as high crime hotspots, or stereotypes of particular groups (usually low in power and advantage) as likely offenders— 'police property' (Newburn and Reiner, this volume; Chapman 1968). The official labelling of crimes and criminals which underpins the apparent problem of crime is thus shaped in part by political economy.

2. *Motive.* A crime will not occur unless there is someone motivated to commit it. Most criminological theories have been directed at uncovering the sources of motivations tempting, seducing, or driving people to commit crimes, whether within the individual offender or their social position. Economic factors have been emphasized by most sociological and social psychological analyses of criminal motivation. Anomie theory, discussed earlier, is probably the most influential sociological attempt to explain the sources of criminal motivation, and centres on the significance of economic aspirations and strains. Developmental theories also identify economic variables such as poverty, unemployment, and relative deprivation as risk factors precipitating individuals towards criminal motivations, in conjunction with other aspects of family context and socialization (McAra and McVie, this volume).

Although in the 1980s neo-liberals such as Mrs Thatcher denied a link between economic conditions and crime, it is a straightforward inference of neo-classical economic theory that economic fluctuations affect the perceived costs and benefits of legitimate as compared with illegitimate actions (Becker 1968; Fielding, Clarke, and Witt 2000: 1–14 and pt I). An unemployed person dependent on benefits, for example, will find the relative rewards of illegitimate activity higher than someone earning legitimate wages, and, especially when legitimate work opportunities are restricted by recession, will find the costs of acquiring a criminal record lower. From the point of view of conventional economic analysis, a utility-maximizing rational economic actor will commit crimes if the reward is higher than available legitimate wages, so crime should fluctuate with the buoyancy of labour markets (Grogger 2000: 268–73). Although in economic theory (as in classical 'criminology') offenders are not presumed to have different motivations from the law-abiding, it is their changing economic circumstances that determine whether people will be motivated to commit crimes or not.

3. *Means*. The capacity to commit crimes of various types will be affected by economic developments. The availability of illegal markets for stolen goods, and the shifting attractiveness of different goods on them, will structure changes in crime patterns (Sutton 1998; Sutton *et al.* 2001; Fitzgerald *et al.* 2003; Hallsworth 2005: 112). Changes in the labour market also affect the capacity to commit offences. Unemployment may affect crime in various ways, but one is the time and idle pair of hands it provides for the Devil, as conveyed by the old adage. Conversely, different types of employment offer varying means for the commission of crimes at work. Prosperity increases the means to purchase and consume socially the intoxicating drink and drugs that fuel fights (Field 1990)

4. *Opportunity*. The availability of targets for crime is affected by economic development. The proliferation of valuable and easily stolen consumer goods—cars, videos, mobile phones, etc.—since the mid-1950s has often been seen as a key factor in the growth of crime. Field for example has shown that 'thefts and burglaries are both linked to the stock of crime opportunities, represented by the sum of real consumer expenditure... For every 1 per cent increase in this stock, burglary and theft have increased by about 2%' (Field 1999: 7). Economic development also changes the 'routine activities' of different groups, shifting their vulnerability to victimization (Felson 2010). For example, 'when people have money, they tend to spend more time away from their homes earning and spending, increasing the vulnerability of persons and property to crime' (Field 1999: 3). In these and other ways it is true in part that 'opportunity makes the thief' (Felson and Clarke 1998).

5. *Absence of controls*. A motivated offender with the means and opportunity to commit a labelled crime may still desist or be deterred because of internalized or informal controls, or external prospects of sanctioning. The occurrence of a crime requires the absence of effective controls, whether the 'inner police' of conscience (Eysenck 1965: 261), or the threat of external policing and punishment.

Economic factors affect the functioning of both informal and formal controls. Employment is amongst other things a direct and indirect form of discipline. Directly it limits the opportunity and temptation to commit offences (although it may also provide workplace opportunities). Indirectly it facilitates the possibility of effective education and of marriage, which are also important control factors (Currie 1985, 1998a, 1998). The availability, resourcing, deployment, and management of the formal controls of policing and punishment are also heavily influenced by economic factors, such as changes in the politics of public expenditure.

## CRIME AND ECONOMY: THE EMPIRICAL LITERATURE

In 1987 the late Steven Box published a seminal analysis of the relationships between 'recession, crime and punishment' (Box 1987). This was 14 years after the slump triggered by the 1973 oil crisis, and eight years on from Margaret Thatcher's enthusiastic espousal of monetarism, which produced huge increases in unemployment, inequality, and poverty, reversing the gains of the post-war decades. Box's literature search found 50 econometric studies up to the mid-1980s testing for relationships between unemployment and crime levels. Simply taking all these studies at face value, there were 32 which found that higher unemployment was associated with more crime, while 18 found the opposite: the result that would be predicted by anomie theory, radical criminology, and neo-classical economics. But the scoreline was far from overwhelming! Those espousing theoretical perspectives making the opposite prediction, that recession reduces crime by decreasing the available targets of crime and increasing the number of unemployed 'guardians' staying at home (e.g. situational crime prevention and routine activities theories), could take some comfort from the fact that nearly half the studies went their way.

Box also highlighted the methodological weaknesses of many of the studies. In particular several use measures of crime such as arrest or conviction rates that are even more problematic than the officially recorded crime rates with all their well-known limitations. There were also important conceptual and methodological issues concerning which variables should be controlled for in order to try and isolate the relationship between unemployment and crime, and what measures of unemployment were used. Box further underlined the rather small relationship between unemployment and crime uncovered in most of the studies, in either direction, meaning that whilst on balance they provided some support for the hypothesis of a link, it was a weak one.

Box also reviewed econometric studies probing links between income inequality and crime levels. Theoretically it would be expected that these variables were closely associated, because inequality would be likely to produce a sense of relative deprivation, motivating property crime in particular. Of the 17 studies reviewed by Box, 12 reported a positive relationship between inequality and crime and five did not. The five exceptions were all studies of homicide, so there was unanimous support for the view that greater inequality was associated with more property crime.

There are crucial limitations of all econometric studies from a criminological perspective that must be borne in mind in assessing their results. One is that the variables measured by econometricians have at best a rough and ready correspondence to the concepts in the criminological theories being tested. Unemployment or inequality rates, for example, may be related to anomie, but they are not direct measures of it.

The social and psychological meaning of economic variables such as employment or income will vary according to different social, cultural, and individual circumstances and interpretations. At best econometrics can establish correlations between economic indicators and official crime measures (with all the pitfalls of these statistical indices), not causal relationships. Interpreting such associations as causal explanations requires assumptions about the direction of causality. More fundamentally, the relationships have to be 'adequate at the level of meaning' as Weber put it (Weber 1947/1964: 99–100). There have to be plausible narratives linking the variables as sequences of comprehensible human action.

It is important to note that the studies reviewed by Box were all carried out before the mid-1980s. The social character, meaning, and impact of such variables as unemployment and inequality changed fundamentally in the years immediately before Box's book, indeed that was what prompted him to write it (Box 1987: Preface). This means that the data for the studies he reviewed were gathered mainly in the post-Second World War decades of virtual full employment, during which unemployment would have been mainly transitional and voluntary. Theoretically there would be little reason to expect such unemployment to be associated with crime.

After 1973, however, the recession and the advent of monetarism resulted in long-term, sometimes permanent, exclusion from legitimate livelihoods of growing numbers of young men. The social impact and meaning of this, especially in an increasingly consumerist culture, is quite different from what unemployment represented in earlier decades. It signified a fatal combination of enhanced anomie and an erosion of the controls represented by legitimate work, and indeed marriage and family responsibilities (Campbell 1993; Currie 1998a, 1998b; Davies 1998). The changed meaning of unemployment after the mid-1970s would be expected to produce a closer association between unemployment and crime levels than in earlier decades.

This is confirmed by research carried out more recently than Box's 1987 book (Marris 2000; Witt et al. 1999; Field 1999: Pt II; Kleck and Chiricos 2002; Deadman and Macdonald 2002; Hale 2005; Arvanites and Defina 2006; Lin 2008; Hooghe et al. 2011). Although most studies conducted since the 1980s do find positive relationships between higher unemployment and higher crime rates (especially property crime), the strength of the association remains fairly modest. In part this may be because measures of total unemployment continue to include both voluntary and involuntary unemployment. Robin Marris has tried to estimate the significance of this, by assuming that unemployment rates below 4 per cent mainly involve transitional, voluntary unemployment and only levels above 4 per cent signify involuntary unemployment. He demonstrates that there were very strong associations during the 1980s and early 1990s between burglary and *involuntary* unemployment (estimated by including only levels over 4 per cent: Marris 2000: 73–4).

Furthermore, unemployment statistics have become an *increasingly* problematic measure of levels of prosperity or economic hardship. Partly this is because official statistics on unemployment were considerably revised during the 1980s, as a result of the increasingly controversial increases in unemployment due to the Thatcher Government's neo-liberal economic policies (Hale 2005: 332).

It has also been argued that unemployment fluctuations lag behind changes in economic conditions. In a recession, for example, earnings will begin to fall before employment statistics do, because of wage-cuts, reduced overtime, and greater resort to part-time work. These cuts in conditions will generate stronger incentives for property offending *before* unemployment begins to rise, dampening the apparent effect of subsequent rises in the unemployment statistics (Pyle and Deadman 1994).

Wider transformations in the structure of the labour market, associated with the change from Keynesian economic management to neo-liberalism, have also made unemployment statistics a less crucial measure of economic exclusion and relative deprivation. Chris Hale has demonstrated the criminogenic significance of the emergence of a 'dual labour market' since the 1970s (Hale 1999, 2005: 333–4; see also Krivo and Peterson 2004; Wadsworth 2006). There is an increasing contrast between a *primary* or core sector of skilled workers, enjoying relative security, and buoyant earnings, benefits, and employment rights, and a *secondary*, peripheral sector—mainly in service industries—lacking these advantages. Employment in the peripheral sector is low skilled, unstable, insecure, poorly paid, and without employment rights and benefits. These 'McJobs' are much less likely to reduce crime in the way that work in the primary sector traditionally did. De-industrialization in the wake of neo-liberalism during the 1980s enormously increased the peripheral relative to the primary sector. This was associated with increasing crime rates, especially in economic downturns when earnings in the secondary sector are squeezed even more (Grogger 2000). Machin and Meghir have shown that declining wages for unskilled workers were associated with increasing property crime (Machin and Meghir 2003). Conversely, the introduction of the minimum wage in 1999 was followed by greater decreases in crime in areas with disproportionately high numbers of workers previously earning less than the minimum, who thus gained most from the new policy (Hansen and Machin 2003). Whilst the changing structure of the labour market explains much of the growth and fluctuations in crime, it also means that the division between unemployment and marginal employment in the secondary sector becomes less clear-cut and significant.

Another factor complicating the crime-unemployment relationship is the contradiction between the motivational and opportunity effects of economic prosperity or hardship (Cantor and Land 1985; Kleck and Chiricos 2002). Simon Field's work for the Home Office has shown that both are important, but in different ways (Field 1990, 1999; Dhiri *et al.* 1999). Analysing data between the Second World War and the late 1990s, Field found that the short-term cyclical effects of economic change must be distinguished from the long-term consequences of economic growth. In the short run there is an inverse relationship between economic fluctuations[11] and property crime, and hence recorded crime overall. In the long term, however, crime has increased as affluence has grown. This discrepancy was accounted for by the contradictory

---

[11]  Field used the level of consumption expenditure as the main indicator of the business cycle. He found that unemployment was not associated with crime if consumption was taken into account (Field 1990: 7). This does not mean it was not associated with crime fluctuations, but that on his analysis it was only related to crime through its effects on consumption. Subsequent analyses of the time-series relationship between crime trends since the Second World War and economic variables, using different modelling techniques and assumptions, confirmed the link with consumption levels, but also found associations between crime and Gross Domestic Product and unemployment (Pyle and Deadman 1994; Hale 1998). Altogether this is a powerful body of evidence confirming the negative relationship between fluctuations in prosperity and property (and overall) crime levels.

short- and long-run effects of prosperity. In the short term economic upturns reduce *motivations* for property crime, but the long-run result of affluence is the expansion of criminal opportunities.

It was noted earlier that Box's 1987 study already showed overwhelmingly strong evidence that greater inequality was related to more property and violent crime, but not homicide (Box 1987: 87). Since then there has continued to be a sharp increase in economic inequality (Dorling 2011). More recent studies, in Britain and the USA, have continued to confirm the strong association between inequality and crime (Hale 2005: 334–6).

A significant change, however, is that homicide is no longer an apparent exception. Studies in several countries show strong associations between greater inequality and more homicide (these are summarized in: Wilkinson 2005: 47–51, ch. 5; Wilkinson and Pickett 2009: ch. 10. The Wilkinson and Pickett book has attracted some attempted refutations from conservative think tanks. For a discussion and reply cf. www.equalitytrust.org.uk). The difference from the earlier period studied by Box is probably due to increases in the proportion of homicides involving poor young men as victims and perpetrators (Dorling 2004).

The clear conclusion indicated by a review of the econometric evidence is that there is a plethora of material confirming that crime of all kinds is linked to inequality, relative deprivation, and unemployment (especially if it is an index of long-term social exclusion cf. Reiner 2007: ch. 4). The downplaying of economic 'strain' factors in criminal justice policy discourse since the 1970s was due to shifts in dominant political and intellectual perspectives, not evidence that there are no significant economic correlates—arguably 'root causes' (*pace* Wilson 1975)—of crime. Examination of the seminal work of Ehrlich, for example, shows this. In his 1970s papers that pioneered the revival of interest in the economics of crime, Ehrlich's data clearly showed strong associations between poverty, inequality, unemployment, and crime levels (Ehrlich 1973, 1975: 409–13). The emphasis on the significance of deterrence variables (probability and severity of sanctions) by Ehrlich himself and his primary audience of neoliberals was because policing and punishment were seen as desirable and available policy levers, whilst the economic factors either could not or should not be reversed by government action.

## POLITICAL ECONOMIES, CRIME, AND CRIMINAL JUSTICE: COMPARATIVE AND HISTORICAL PERSPECTIVES

The econometric evidence reviewed above focuses on the relationships between economic factors and crime within particular social orders. Ian Taylor pointed out in his chapter on 'Political Economy' in the first and second editions of *The Oxford Handbook of Criminology* that the econometric literature was primarily concerned with 'the causal relations between "economic crisis", "the business cycle", or other *departures from normal economic conditions or circumstances* and the outgrowth of crime. There is often very little curiosity, in this pragmatic "political economy" tradition, about the ways in which the routine functioning of economies organised around the capital-labour relation or around individual self-interest may in itself be a factor in crime' (Taylor 1997: 266). In this section comparative and historical evidence will be reviewed, showing that the overall character of different political economies is related to variations in their patterns of crime and violence, and the style of criminal justice they develop.

## CRIME AND JUSTICE: CONTEMPORARY COMPARISONS

In the last few years there has been a notable resurgence of interest in the political economy of penality. The seminal text has been David Garland's *The Culture of Control* (Garland 2001), a magisterial analysis of the epochal shift from the penal welfarism to more punitive and pervasive penal and preventive policies (for critical discussions see Zedner 2002; Matravers 2009; Nelken 2010: ch. 4. See also Young 1999, 2007; Reiner 2007; Simon 2007; Lacey 2008; Wacquant 2009; Bell 2011 for overviews of transformations in crime control).

This re-awakening of criminological interest in political economy has largely been focused on analysing punishment, above all understanding what is widely seen as a new populist punitiveness (Pratt *et al.* 2005, 2006; for a critique see Matthews 2005, 2009). The most wide-ranging book explicitly utilizing a political economy framework has been Michael Cavadino and James Dignan's influential *Penal Systems: A Comparative Approach* (Cavadino and Dignan 2006). This provides a cogent analysis of systematic differences in penal systems in the contemporary world. It reports on a comparative study of 12 industrial, liberal-democratic countries, seeking to relate variations in their penality to differences in their political economies. The material on particular countries was provided by expert criminologists in each one, responding to detailed questions from the volume's authors, with the final versions written by Cavadino and Dignan themselves.

The book is explicitly set within the context of globalization (op. cit.: 10–12), in the sense of massively heightened flows of information, global commodity and financial markets, with increasing economic and cultural domination by the USA and its neo-liberal economic strategy. In the criminal justice realm, Cavadino and Dignan note that US models such as 'zero tolerance' spread with unprecedented rapidity in the discourse and policies of practitioners and governments around the world, leading to talk of penal convergence (for a detailed analysis of the issue of policy transfer see Jones and Newburn 2006). But whilst there may be common international pressures and trends, and increasing American cultural domination, this does not entail homogenization (Nelken 2010, and Nelken, Chapter 5, this volume).

There have been many attempts in the last 15 years to characterize the 'varieties of capitalism' (Hall and Soskice 2003) that may still be distinguished in the contemporary world. Despite a shared trajectory of globalization under neo-liberal, 'Washington consensus' auspices, there remain significantly different models and 'real worlds' of welfare capitalism and corporatism (Glyn 1999; Olssen 2010). Developing these analyses (especially the seminal typology formulated by Esping-Anderson 1990), Cavadino and Dignan suggest a distinction between four ideal-type, contemporary political economies. These are:

1. *Neo-liberalism*—minimal welfare state, extreme income and wealth differences, formal status egalitarianism, individualism with limited social rights, increasing social exclusion, right wing political dominance (the USA is the closest exemplar).

2. *Conservative corporatism*—status-related welfare state, pronounced but not extreme income differentials, moderately hierarchical status rankings, moderate social rights, some social exclusion, centrist politics (e.g. Germany).

3. *Social democratic corporatism*—universalistic, generous welfare state, limited income differentials, egalitarian status system, relatively unconditional generous social rights, limited social exclusion, left political dominance (e.g. Scandinavian states).

4. *Oriental corporatism*—private sector based paternalistic welfare, limited income differentials, traditional status hierarchy, quasi-feudal corporatist duties, little social exclusion but alienation of 'outsiders', centre-right politics (e.g. Japan).

The nub of Cavadino and Dignan's analysis is the demonstration that this typology of political economies corresponds to clear differences in the punitiveness of both penal policy and culture. The chapters on individual countries, and on particular aspects of policy (privatization, youth justice), show the complexity and internal variations that any summary must ignore or over-simplify. Nonetheless the four types of political economy appear to differ qualitatively in penal practice and culture—although not in a linear way. In terms of punitiveness of *policy* as measured by the (admittedly crude and problematic) data on official imprisonment rates, four fundamentally different groups can be discerned (Cavadino and Dignan 2006: 29–32): neo-liberal countries are the most punitive (rates ranging from 701 per 100,000 population in the USA to 115 in Australia); conservative corporatist next (imprisonment rates varying from 93 to 100 per 100,000); social democracies considerably lower (70–73 per 100,000); with the oriental corporatism of Japan having the lowest imprisonment rate (53). There are also overlaps between the groupings, although South Africa, the USA, and England and Wales (all in the neo-liberal group) score the highest by a long way.

These differences correspond also to variations in styles of penal policy. Neo-liberal regimes are much more receptive than social democracies to prison privatization, for example. They also differ in their modes of punishment, with social democracies and Japan more inclined to inclusionary rather than exclusionary methods. The penal ideologies of these regimes differ fundamentally. Neo-liberalism is associated with a dominant politics of 'law and order', whilst conservative corporatism emphasizes rehabilitation, and social democracies[12] a rights-based approach.

---

[12] The significance of differences in political economy, but also their tenuousness in the face of the common globalizing forces all are subject to, albeit with differing degrees of resistance, is illustrated by detailed comparison of the UK and Scandinavian social democracies, notably Sweden. The stronger survival of a social democratic welfare state in Scandinavian countries seems to have mitigated the rise both in crime and in punitive penal policy, but threats to both are becoming apparent (Tham 1998; Bondeson 2005; Tham and

Cavadino and Dignan's important analysis demonstrates the variations in criminal justice policy between different types of political economy in the contemporary world,[13] even though all are subject to similar pressures and tendencies resulting from globalization. It is important to emphasize that the explanatory variable they are looking at is *political economy*, not economics. Their theoretical model explicitly rejects economic determinism. It is a pluralist framework that gives weight to the interaction between material and cultural dimensions, as well as to political conflicts and the practices of individual actors and groups (op. cit.: 12–14). Other studies have developed the analysis of the *political* in political economy, demonstrating the significance of variations in political institutions and culture (in addition to economic policy) for explaining variations in penality (Sutton 2004, 2010; Simon 2007; Lacey 2008). The broad shift towards more punitive penality has also been related to changing modalities of control of the labour force and the at best marginally employed underclass with the development of neo-liberalism (di Giorgi 2006; Wacquant 2009; Cheliotis and Xanakis 2010; Bell 2011).

There is no systematic comparative study of the relationship between crime and political economy, analogous to Cavadino and Dignan on penal policy. An obvious issue is that the problems of comparison between recorded crime rates in different jurisdictions are vastly greater than the acknowledged difficulties in comparing penal severity (see the discussion of the severe problems of comparative criminology in Nelken, Chapter 5, this volume). The well-known hazards of interpreting national crime statistics are amplified into another dimension altogether by the huge variations in legal definitions, police practices, and cultural conceptions of crime, order, and morality affecting public perceptions and reporting.

Since 1989 a group of criminologists in different countries have mounted several sweeps of the 'International Crime Victims Survey' (ICVS) seeking to overcome some of these issues (van Dijk *et al.* 2007 reports on the fourth sweep). They have attracted particular media attention in the UK because they show England and Wales as one of the highest of the countries surveyed in overall incidence of reported victimization, well above the USA, often assumed to be the developed world's crime capital (van Dijk *et al.* 2007: 43).

The survey is scrupulously rigorous in its methodology, and open about its possible limitations (such as the use of telephone interviewing). It is clearly an ambitious and interesting undertaking, representing a state-of-the-art attempt to provide data on comparative crime patterns and trends. For all that, the results obtained seem bizarre from the point of view of analysis in terms of political economy or indeed any other theoretical framework, and defy any attempt at interpretation or explanation

Hofer 2009). Similar arguments apply to the recent reversal of the Netherlands' relatively liberal penal policy (Downes and van Swaaningen 2007).

[13]  Beckett and Western found similar patterns in their analysis of variations between different states in the USA (Beckett and Western 2001; Western 2006). States with relatively higher spending on welfare tended to have lower rates of imprisonment, whether analysed over time or cross-sectionally. Downes and Hansen have shown that the same applies cross-nationally: countries with lower welfare expenditure are more punitive, and vice versa (Downes and Hansen 2006; Downes 2011).

(Young 2003a, 2004). The authors themselves do not offer any account of the pattern of differences, beyond noting its consistency across the sweeps.

The ordering of the countries by the ICVS bears no relationship to the types of political economy distinguished by Cavadino and Dignan, nor to the rankings of punitiveness. It is equally mysterious to liberals, political economists, or deterrence theorists, supporting Jock Young's acerbic dismissal of the surveys as 'maverick results' (Young 2003a: 36–7), owing more to cross-cultural vicissitudes in perceptions of order and indeed official interviewers than to crime patterns. As Young suggests, the league tables of different societies run so counter to expectation that it is plausible that higher-ranked societies may be ones paradoxically where the relative *absence* of serious violence makes respondents more sensitive to low-level incivility, and thus more likely to report incidents to interviewers, boosting the survey rate!

There are fewer problems of international comparison of homicide statistics (for obvious reasons not included in the victim surveys), because there is less diversity in legal definitions and recording practices (Barclay and Tavares 2003: 10). The international pattern of homicide rates *does* correspond systematically to variations in political economies—indeed it fits the typology developed by Cavadino and Dignan as closely as their analysis of penal systems (Reiner 2007: 106). The neo-liberal countries have the highest rates. South Africa is by far the highest at 55.86 per 100,000 population. The USA is next at 5.56 (for all the celebrations of the sharp decline in American murder rates since the early 1990s). New Zealand, England and Wales, and Australia are somewhat lower (with 2.5, 1.6, and 1.87 respectively). The 'conservative corporatist' countries, Italy, Germany, the Netherlands, and France, are next: rates respectively of 1.5, 1.15, 1.51, and 1.73--all lower than any of the 'neo-liberal' group. Social-democratic Sweden is lower still: 1.1. As the other two Nordic social democracies, Denmark and Norway, are comparably low (respectively, 1.02 and 0.95), it seems that Finland is for some reason an anomaly to the general pattern of much higher homicide rates in neo-liberal than social-democratic countries.[14] Japan is the lowest of the Cavadino and Dignan set of 12 countries at 1.05, although this is higher than social-democratic Denmark and Norway. The overall conclusion is clear: rates of lethal violence are highest in neo-liberal political economies, and lowest in social democracies.

Many recent studies have offered cogent analyses of why serious violent crime rates could be expected to be much higher in neo-liberal than social democratic political economies (Currie 1985, 1997, 1998a, and 1998b, 2009; James 1995; Hall 1997, 2011; Davies 1998; Dorling 2004; Hallsworth 2005; Hall *et al.* 2008; Hall and McLean 2009). The earlier review of econometric studies showed considerable evidence that inequality, relative deprivation, and involuntary, exclusionary unemployment are linked to more property crime and serious violence, and neo-liberalism is associated with much greater inequality, long-term unemployment, and social exclusion (Reiner 2007). In addition to economic inequality and deprivation, Currie has spelled out several other mediating links between political economy and greater pressures towards violent

[14] Examination of the table for the capital cities of these 39 countries adds a further complication. The homicide rate in Helsinki is lower than for Finland as a whole, unlike the general pattern for capitals to have higher rates than the rest of the country (Barclay and Tavares 2003: 11).

crime (Currie 1997: 154–66). These include 'the withdrawal of public services and supports, especially for women and children; the erosion of informal and communal networks of mutual support, supervision, and care; the spread of a materialistic, neglectful, and "hard" culture; the unregulated marketing of the technology of violence; and...the weakening of social and political alternatives' (op. cit.: 154). This link between neo-liberal political economies and higher propensities towards serious crime is further supported by historical evidence about long-term trends in crime and disorder in many societies.

## CRIME, JUSTICE, AND POLITICAL ECONOMY: HISTORICAL DIMENSIONS

The post-Enlightenment incorporation of the mass of the population in industrial capitalist, liberal democracies into a common status of citizenship was associated with a secular decline in violence and disorder. Manuel Eisner has recently synthesized and updated the results of numerous historical studies exploring long-term trends in homicide in Europe (Eisner 2001; cf. also Spierenberg 2008; Roth 2010 on the USA for similar evidence). Eisner builds on the seminal work of Ted Robert Gurr and colleagues, which had earlier estimated long-term trends in violence in a number of European countries, as well as the USA and Australia (Gurr 1981).

The long-term trajectory from the medieval period can be summarized roughly as a J-curve (Eisner 2001: 629). Homicide rates fall sharply up to the late eighteenth century. There is then a period of increase up to the middle of the nineteenth century, but much smaller than the earlier fall, taking the level back only to that of a century earlier. After the middle of the nineteenth century the decline resumes, until the last quarter of the twentieth century, when there is a return to the levels of the mid-Victorian period.

Focusing on the trend since the early nineteenth century in greater detail suggests a U-shape pattern in homicide and other serious crime over this period. Gurr shows this for the USA, Britain, Australia, and some European countries. Crime rates increased between the late eighteenth and mid-nineteenth century, declined in the later nineteenth century, and were fairly stable until the later twentieth century, when there was a return to rising crime (Gurr 1981: 325). Gatrell's detailed analysis of the trends in theft and violence in England during the nineteenth and early twentieth centuries supported this picture of decline in the later nineteenth century, followed by rough stability for the first quarter of the twentieth[15] (Gatrell 1980).

There have also been a number of historical studies showing a similar U-shaped pattern for the extent of violence in political and industrial disorders: secular decline from the mid-nineteenth to the last quarter of the twentieth century, with an increase

---

[15] The validity of the English statistics on which these analyses rely has been called into question by Howard Taylor, in a series of papers attempting to demonstrate that even the homicide figures are essentially driven by 'supply-side' factors, the shifting exigencies and strategies of the authorities responsible for producing the data, primarily the Home Office and police forces (Taylor 1998a and 1998b, 1999). Taylor's evidence and arguments certainly offer a sharp and salutary reminder of the need for caution in interpreting all criminal statistics (they have been challenged in turn by other historians, notably Morris 2001. For a review of the arguments see Emsley 2010: ch. 2).

thereafter. This has gone hand in hand with a similar trend in the militarism of polic-ing tactics (Geary 1985; Waddington and Wright 2008). Recent econometric evidence further underlines an association between economic fluctuations and political unrest and violence: in essence, 'austerity' is linked to 'anarchy' (Bohlken and Sergeant 2010; Ponticelli and Voth 2011).

Attempts to explain these long-term trends must involve a complex mix of interde-pendent considerations. Eisner and Gurr themselves primarily invoke Norbert Elias's analysis of a broader 'civilizing process' (Elias 1939/1994). This depicted a secular cul-tural, social, and psychic tendency of greater sensitization towards control and dis-play of bodily processes generally, including violence, during modernization (Garland 1990: ch. 10). Whilst the emphasis in Elias's analysis is on cultural and psychic sensi-bilities, these are seen as interlocked with developments in state formation, as well as disciplinary and stabilization processes associated with the emergence of markets and factories (Fletcher 1997: 36, 64). The state came to monopolize the means of violence, as part of a process of pacification of social and economic life,[16] with the police emerg-ing as the institutional locus for this (Silver 1967; Bittner 1970; Brodeur 2007).

The changes in cultural sensibilities analysed in Elias's account of the civilizing process were bound up with broad shifts in the political economy. A sharpening of social conflicts, crime, and disorder in the early stages of industrial capitalism dur-ing the late eighteenth and early nineteenth centuries was succeeded by a long-term process of inclusion of the majority of the population in legal, political, and (to a lesser extent) economic and social citizenship (Marshall 1950). This was the precondition for the mix of mass seduction and discipline represented by 'penal welfarism' during the first three-quarters of the twentieth century (Garland 1985, 2001: ch. 2), as well as the development of 'policing by consent' (Reiner 2010a: ch. 3; 2010b).

The sharp upturns in crime and violence experienced throughout the Western world in the last third of the twentieth century (with somewhat different periodicity in terms of onset) were largely associated with the displacement of Keynesian welfarist social management by the increasingly triumphant neo-liberalism of the 'Washington consensus' that has come to dominate the globalized political economy. Of course the profound changes in social order, crime, and control over the last three decades have complex, multiple, interacting sources, but the shift in political economy plays a pivotal role.

The only challenge to this view is the conservative account that places the primary if not sole explanatory weight on 'permissiveness', the undermining of social controls by liberalism. As Currie has argued most cogently, this either/or approach

begins to get in the way of understanding both the multiplicity and the interconnect-edness of the forces that operate to increase the risks of violent crime in specific, real world social circumstances. When we examine patterns of youth violence in, say, South Chicago or South London, we don't see evidence of 'strain' and *not* disorganisation, for example, and *not* a weakening of 'parental' controls. We are likely to see great structural inequalities *and* community fragmentation and weakened ability of parents to monitor

---

[16] This is obviously similar to Weber's analysis of the state, but Elias placed much less emphasis on the *legitimacy* of state monopolization of violence, seeing this as an ambiguous and problematic notion (Elias 1939/1994: 450; Fletcher 1997: ch. 3).

and supervise their children—and a great many other things, all going on at once, all entwined with each other, and all affecting the crime rate—with the combination having an impact that is much greater than the sum of its parts [Currie 1997: 150].

It is precisely this holistic analysis that is represented by political economy, as argued earlier.

The emergence of the globalized neo-liberal political economy has been associated with social and cultural changes that are likely to aggravate crime, and to displace all frameworks for crime control policy apart from 'law and order' (Reiner 2007). The spread of consumerist culture, especially when coupled with increasing social inequality and exclusion, involves a heightening of what Merton called anomie, to a degree that Jock Young has aptly characterized as social 'bulimia' (Young 1999; Messner and Rosenfeld 2006). It generates a broader culture of narcissistic aspiration for ever more consumer goods that are perpetually out of reach of the legitimate means of many, the seductive edge for crime (Hayward 2004, Hallsworth 2005; Hall *et al.* 2008). At the same time the egoistic culture of a 'market society', with its zero-sum, 'winner–loser', survival of the fittest ethos, erodes conceptions of ethical means of success being preferable, or of concern for others limiting ruthlessness, and ushers in a 'new barbarism' across the social spectrum. This is indicated by Karstedt and Farrall's study of 'The Moral Maze of the Middle Class', charting the growth of fraud and unethical business practices in the UK and Germany, and the techniques of neutralization facilitating it (Karstedt and Farrall 2004). The corruption of the highest levels of economic power is demonstrated by the growth of corporate malpractice, whether illegal, on the borderline, or tolerated by a criminal law that has increasingly defined down such egregious activities as tax avoidance by the use of offshore havens (Nelken, Chapter 21, this volume; Shaxson 2011). Informal social controls, the inculcation of a 'stake in conformity', through family, education, and work, become forlorn dreams (Currie 1985, 1998a, 1998b; Ruggiero 2000). The eclipse of social democratic hopes shuts off prospects of alleviating deprivation (absolute or relative) by legitimate collective industrial or political action, leaving the 'responsibilized' individual to sink or swim. Sometimes, as neo-classical economics would predict, offending is the 'rational choice' in adverse labour market conditions. The reversal of the 'solidarity project' (Garland 2001: 199), the long-term incorporation of the mass of the population into a common status of citizenship, which underpinned the 'civilizing process' of declining violence and crime, has formed the dark couple of rising crime and harsher control efforts (Reiner 2010b).

In the 1990s recorded crime figures and victimization survey rates began to fall, first in the USA, but then in most Western countries, including the UK (Blumstein and Wallman 2000; Tonry and Farrington 2005; Reiner 2007: ch. 3; van Dijk *et al.* 2007; Zimring 2007). The dramatic fall in New York City, formerly seen as a world crime capital, attracted particular media attention. This has caused a reverse 'aetiological crisis' to that associated with the 1950s crime rise (Young 2004: 24–5). No 'grand narrative' seems satisfactory. Neo-liberalism, the Left's prime suspect, retains its global economic hegemony. But conversely there has not been any reversal of 'permissiveness', the Right's dominating bête noire. The favourite criminal justice accounts all have some plausibility, but not as complete explanations.

The zero-tolerance policing explanation, celebrated by many promoters of the supposed New York miracle, has been demolished definitively by close analyses. The precise timing of the crime changes in New York does not fit the zero-tolerance account, and many US cities showed similar falls in crime without the same policing changes (Bowling 1999; Karmen 2000; Jones and Newburn 2006: ch. 6). In so far as policing changes contributed to the fall, it was the 'smart' rather than the 'tough' aspects of the NYPD reforms that were crucial—the managerial and intelligence-analysing reforms referred to as 'Compstat' (Punch 2007).

Nor has the enormous expansion of punitiveness, above all the staggering and gross levels of imprisonment, contributed more than marginally (Spelman 2000, 2005; Tonry and Farrington 2005). More mundane improvements in the effectiveness of crime prevention, referred to by Garland as the 'criminologies of everyday life' (Garland 2001: 127–31), have played an important part in the reduction of 'volume crimes' such as burglary and car theft (Farrell *et al.* 2011).

Within the array of explanations, economic factors are certainly significant, if peculiarly unheralded by governments wishing to appear 'tough on crime' (Downes and Morgan: ch .7 above; Downes 2010). But they cannot provide more than part of the explanation. Unemployment has certainly been at much lower levels than during the crime explosion of the 1980s. This has been achieved, however, largely by the expansion of secondary labour market jobs. In the USA there has been no reduction in poverty or inequality. In the UK, the minimum wage had a significant crime reduction effect in some areas. But overall there has not been any significant change in the extreme level of economic inequality and insecurity that New Labour inherited. The crime drop remains something of a mystery, defying any simple account. But economic factors are an important part of the explanation, and the Coalition's policy of cuts is likely to hugely exacerbate the drivers of crime and disorder (as the return of protest and riot in 2011 already indicates clearly).

## CONCLUSION: MARKETS, MEANINGS, MORALS

Political economy and other primarily structural perspectives have been sidelined in the last 30 years, by a number of 'turns' in intellectual, cultural, and political life (Hall 2011). They have been caught in a pincer movement from right and left, denying the reality of 'society', or at any rate structural causes and grand narratives. In criminology specifically, political economy perspectives were first attacked by the right wing 'Realist' critique advanced most noisily in the mid-1970s by James Q. Wilson's polemic against 'root cause' perspectives (Wilson 1975: xv). Subsequently 'Left Realism' pointed to a supposed 'aetiological crisis' of earlier Left criminology (Young 1986), and argued for the necessity and possibility of short-term crime control strategies. More recently, 'cultural criminologists' have claimed that political economy and structural perspectives are over-deterministic and simplistic, and fail to be true to the subjective meanings and seductions of deviance and crime (Hayward and Young, this volume). These critiques have been buttressed by a belief that the econometric evidence itself called into question any postulated relationships between crime and economic factors.

This chapter has sought to rehabilitate political economy approaches from these various critiques, and restate their importance for understanding patterns and trends in crime and criminal justice. As argued earlier, political economy stands for a holistic approach, but one that recognizes the dialectical complexity of mediations and interactions between macro-structures and individual actions. As Weber put it long ago, explanation has to be both 'causally adequate' and 'adequate at the level of meaning' (Weber 1947/1964: 99–100). *Verstehen* and structural pressures are each necessary elements of explanation, complementary not contradictory. Nor (again following Weber's venerable lead) are understanding or explanation incompatible with ethical judgements or policies (Reiner 2011: Introduction).

Contrary to the critiques of 'Realists' of the Left, Right, or centre, recognition of the existence of 'root causes' does not mean that it is unnecessary or undesirable to explore also all possible avenues of immediate crime reduction, victim support, or penal reform. What this chapter has tried to demonstrate is the theoretical viability of political economy perspectives, and that there is empirical evidence both of the importance of economic factors in crime, and of variations between types of political economy and patterns of crime and punishment.

Specifically it has shown that neo-liberal as distinct from social-democratic political economies tend to have a 'dark heart' (Davies 1998) of both serious crime and cruel punishment (Reiner 2007). Short-term pain and symptom relief are helpful and ethical, but only provided they do not become 'liddism' (Rogers 2002), a futile struggle to hold down the lid on what remain 'root causes'. The discourse and practices of law and order which have become increasingly dominant since the late 1970s have exacerbated criminality, 'the tendency of our society to produce criminals' (Currie 2000). During the 1980s and early 90s, when crime rates exploded, this was evident in official statistics. The decline in recorded crime since then was not because we have got tough on crime, let alone on its causes. It is primarily because enhanced security has held the lid down, and because the very mild and *sotto voce* social democratic policies implemented by New Labour (and now largely reversed by the Coalition) afforded some hope of justice and progress to the socially excluded.

The crime control discourse and policies associated with neo-liberalism embody an image of people as necessarily selfishly egoistic and asocial, requiring tough, exclusionary forms of discipline to maintain order and security. This is quite different from the social democratic conception of criminals as people who have acted wrongly, often because of socio-economic and cultural pressures that are themselves targets of reform, but remain capable of rehabilitation and reintegration. New Labour's espousal of law and order in the early 1990s was a Faustian pact to secure re-election, but which (together with its broader embrace of neo-liberalism) has precipitated its destruction.

The paradox is that social democratic policies—coupled with smarter crime prevention, policing, and penal policy as first-aid responses to crime—*can* deliver lower crime rates. Periods of Labour government have generally been associated with lower crime (Downes and Young 1987; Reiner 2007: chs 3, 4). Neo-liberalism has fanned the fames of social breakdown and crime, stimulating an ever more insatiable popular lust for harsher punishments. The media have of course been important cheerleaders for this (Greer and Reiner: ch. 9 above).

Social peace requires getting tough on the 'root causes' of crime that realism scorned. Whilst this perspective has for the time being lost the political battle, it does not follow it has lost the argument. There are still mysteries in explaining the sudden rise of neo-liberalism to dominance in the 1970s, sweeping away so rapidly the post-World War II social democratic consensus that had delivered so much in terms of widely shared growth in material prosperity and security, as well as relatively low crime and benign control strategies by historical standards. Many of the standard accounts assume the success of neo-liberalism is attributable to fatal rather than contingent flaws in the social democratic or Keynesian models it supplanted. Whilst in economics and political philosophy this conclusion is vigorously contested (e.g. Harvey 2005, 2006, 2010; Dumenil and Levy 2010; Cohen 2009, 2010; Judt 2010; Hacker and Pierson 2011; Eagleton 2011) as yet it has had little echo in criminology.

Even more important, and at least as mysterious: where are we going now? For a brief moment when credit crunched in late 2007 the neo-liberal model seemed discomfited if not totally discredited in all circles. Even Alan Greenspan, former Chair of the Fed and high priest of neo-liberalism in its heyday, admitted his free market faith had been refuted ('Greenspan: I Was Wrong About the Economy', *The Guardian*, 24 October 2008). But within a couple of years its savagely deflationary prescriptions for dealing with the sovereign debt crisis (resulting from governmental support for banking to cope with the 2007 banking debacle) are the new orthodoxy, espoused by the British Coalition, increasing swathes of erstwhile social democratic Europe, and the tax cutting, anti-government spending US Tea Party that seems to have burst the bubble of hope brought by Obama's election. How can this zombie neo-liberalism be explained? And what will it mean for criminal justice in Britain, in the hands of the new Conservative-led Coalition?

Many liberals were impressed and surprised by early signs of Coalition willingness to reverse some of the trends to harsher punitiveness and the erosion of civil liberties under New Labour (and the Michael Howard regime at the Home Office before that). For the first time in nearly 20 years, there was government questioning of Howard's mantra that prison works. It was sadly predictable that these liberal ambitions would be frustrated in practice by increasing crime and disorder flowing from the financial cuts and downturn. As before, the 'freeing' of the economy was likely to engender a strong state penal and policing response to the social dislocation it produces. The growth of demonstrations and protests against the Coalition's cuts and the unjust burden placed on the relatively poor by the legal tax avoidance of the rich, spearheaded by heroic groups like UK Uncut, and the harsh policing tactics they have been met with, have indicated this clearly. So too does the return of rioting to British cities in August 2011, uncannily replaying the outbursts that met the genesis of neo-liberalism under Margaret Thatcher in the early 1980s.

Neo-liberalism inevitably fans social injustice, and feeds the barbarisms of disorder *and* order (Hall *et al.* 2008; Hall 2011). An alternative narrative to neo-liberal instrumentalism and egoistic aspiration is needed, evoking the mutualism of Buber's ideal of 'I-thou' (as argued by Benjamin 2010 in relation to financial markets). This echoes the ethics of the Golden Rule that underpinned social democracy (Reiner

2011). Criminology must help chart a way forward to reviving the conditions for security and peace, which social democratic political economies had begun gradually to deliver. This will entail new economic, social, and criminal justice policies that may again advance the security and liberty of the majority of people. The signs are not propitious, but the alternative (as Rosa Luxemburg put it a century ago) is barbarism.

## ■ SELECTED FURTHER READING

For analyses of recent crime and criminal justice trends incorporating political economy see Currie, E. (1998b), *Crime and Punishment in America*, New York: Holt; Taylor, I. (1999), *Crime in Context*, Cambridge: Polity; Young, J. (1999), *The Exclusive Society*, London: Sage; Garland, D. (2001), *The Culture of Control*, Oxford: Oxford University Press; and Reiner, R. (2007), *Law and Order: An Honest Citizen's Guide to Crime and Control*. Cavadino, M. and Dignan, J. (2006), *Penal Systems: A Comparative Approach*, London: Sage and Lacey, N. (2008), *The Prisoners' Dilemma: Political Economy and Punishment in Contemporary Democracies* offer pioneering comparative analyses of the political economy of penal systems.

## ■ REFERENCES

AGNEW, R. (1992), 'Foundations for a General Strain Theory of Crime and Delinquency', *Criminology*, 30: 47–87.

ARVANITES, T. and DEFINA, R. (2006), 'Business Cycles and Street Crime', *Criminology*, 44(1): 139–64.

BARCLAY, G. and TAVARES, C. (2003), *International Comparisons of Criminal Justice Statistics 2001*, London: Home Office.

BECKER, G. (1968), 'Crime and Punishment: An Economic Approach', *Journal of Political Economy*, 76: 175–209.

BECKER, H. (1963), *Outsiders*, New York: Free Press.

—— (1967), 'Whose Side are We On?', *Social Problems*, 14: 32–40.

BECKETT, K. (1997), *Making Crime Pay*, New York: Oxford University Press.

—— and SASSON, T. (2000), *The Politics of Injustice*, Thousand Oaks, Cal.: Pine Forge.

—— and WESTERN, B. (2001), 'Governing Social Marginality: Welfare, Incarceration and the Transformation of State Policy', *Punishment and Society*, 3: 43–59.

BEIRNE, P. (1993), *Inventing Criminology*, Albany, NY: State University of New York Press.

BELL, E. (2011), *Criminal Justice and Neoliberalism*, London: Sage.

BEMMELEN, J. M. (1960), 'Willem Adrian Bonger', in H. Mannheim (ed.), *Pioneers in Criminology*, London: Stevens.

BENJAMIN, J. (2010), 'The Narratives of Financial Law', *Oxford Journal of Legal Studies*, 30(4): 787–814.

BITTNER, E. (1970), *The Functions of the Police in Modern Society*, Maryland: National Institute of Mental Health.

BLUMSTEIN, A. and WALLMAN, J. (eds) (2000), *The Crime Drop in America*, Cambridge: Cambridge University Press.

BOHLKEN, A. T. and SERGEANT, E. J. (2010), 'Economic growth and ethnic violence: An empirical investigation of Hindu-Muslim riots in India', *Journal of Peace Research*, 47(5): 589–600.

BONDESON, U. (2005), 'Levels of Punitiveness in Scandinavia: description and explanations', in J. Pratt, D. Brown, M. Brown, S. Hallsworth, and W. Morrison (eds), *The New Punitiveness*, Cullompton, Devon: Willan.

BONGER, W. (1916/1969), *Criminality and Economic Conditions*, Bloomington: Indiana University Press.

—— (1935), *An Introduction to Criminology*, London: Methuen.

BOWLING, B. (1999), 'The Rise and Fall of New York Murder', *British Journal of Criminology*, 39: 531–54.

BOX, S. (1987), *Recession, Crime and Punishment*, London: Macmillan.

BRAITHWAITE, J. (1979), *Inequality, Crime and Public Policy*, London: Routledge.

BRODEUR, J-P. (2007), 'An Encounter With Egon Bittner', *Crime, Law and Social Change* 48(3–5): 105–32.

CAMPBELL, B. (1993), *Goliath: Britain's Dangerous Places*, London: Methuen.

CANTOR, D. and LAND, K. C. (1985), 'Unemployment and Crime Rates in Post World War II United States: A Theoretical and Empirical Analysis', *American Sociological Review*, 50: 317–32.

CARSON, W. G. (1970), 'White-collar Crime and the Enforcement of Factory Legislation', *British Journal of Criminology*, 10: 383–98.

—— (1981), *The Other Price of Britain's Oil*, Oxford: Martin Robertson.

CAVADINO, M. and DIGNAN, J. (2006), *Penal Systems: A Comparative Approach*, London: Sage.

CHAMBLISS, W. (ed.) (1969), *Crime and the Legal Process*, New York: McGraw Hill.

——, MICHALOWSKI, R., and KRAMER, R. (eds) (2010), *State Crime in the Global Age*, Cullompton: Willan.

CHAPMAN, D. (1968), *Sociology and the Stereotype of the Criminal*, London: Tavistock.

CHELIOTIS, L. and XENAKIS, S. (2010), 'What's Neoliberalism Got to Do With It? Towards a Political Economy of Punishment in Greece', *Criminology and Criminal Justice*, 10/4: 353–73.

CHIRICOS, T. G. (1987), 'Rates of Crime and Unemployment', *Social Problems*, 34: 187–211.

CLOWARD, R. and OHLIN, L. (1960), *Delinquency and Opportunity*, New York: Free Press.

COHEN, G. (2009), *Why Not Socialism?*, Princeton: Princeton University Press.

—— (2010), *On the Currency of Egalitarian Justice*, Princeton: Princeton University Press.

COHEN, S. (1988), *Against Criminology*, New Jersey: Transaction Books.

—— (1998), 'Intellectual Scepticism and Political Commitment: The Case of Radical Criminology', in P. Walton and J. Young (eds), *The New Criminology Revisited*, London: Macmillan.

—— and SCULL, A. (eds) (1983), *Social Control and the State*, Oxford: Martin Robertson.

COLEMAN, R., SIM, J., TOMBS, S., and WHYTE, D. (eds) (2009), *State, Power, Crime*, London: Sage.

COLQUHOUN, P. (1796), *A Treatise on the Police of the Metropolis*, 2nd edn, London: H. Fry.

—— (1800), *Treatise on the Commerce and Police of the River Thames*, London: J. Mowman.

—— (1806), *Treatise on Indigence*, London: J. Hatchard.

COOK, D. (2006), *Criminal and Social Justice*, London: Sage.

CURRIE, E. (1985), *Confronting Crime*, New York: Pantheon.

—— (1997), 'Market, Crime and Community: Toward a Mid-range Theory of Post-industrial Violence', *Theoretical Criminology*, 1: 147–72.

—— (1998a), 'Crime and Market Society: Lessons From the United States', in P. Walton and J. Young (eds), *The New Criminology Revisited*, London: Macmillan.

—— (1998b), *Crime and Punishment in America*, New York: Holt.

—— (2000), 'Reflections on Crime and Criminology at the Millenium', *Western Criminology Review*, 21(1): 1–15.

—— (2009), *The Roots of Danger: Violent Crime in Global Perspective*, Harlow: Prentice-Hall.

DAVIES, N. (1998), *Dark Heart*, London: Verso.

DEADMAN, D. and MACDONALD, Z. (2002), 'Why Has Crime Fallen? An Economic Perspective', *Economic Affairs*, 22: 5–14.

DHIRI, S., BRAND, S., HARRIES, R., and PRICE, R. (1999), *Modelling and Predicting Property Crime Trends in England and Wales*, London: Home Office.

DIGIORGI, A. (2006), *Rethinking the Political Economy of Punishment*, Aldershot: Ashgate.

DORLING, D. (2004), 'Prime Suspect: Murder in Britain', in P. Hillyard, C. Pantazis, S. Tombs, and D. Gordon (eds), *Beyond Criminology*, London: Pluto.

—— (2011), *Injustice*, Bristol: Policy Press.

DOWNES, D. (2011), 'What Went Right? New Labour and Crime Control', *Howard Journal*, 49(4): 394–7.

—— and YOUNG (1987), 'A Criminal Failure: The Tories' Law and Order Record', *New Society*, 13 May.

—— and HANSEN, K. (2006), 'Welfare and Punishment in Comparative Perspective', in S. Armstrong and L. McAra (eds), *Perspectives on Punishment*, Oxford: Oxford University Press.

—— and VAN SWAANINGEN (2007), 'The Road to Dystopia? Changes in the Penal Climate of the Netherlands', in M. Tonry and C. Bijleveld (eds), *Crime and Justice in the Netherlands*, Chicago: Chicago University Press.

—— and ROCK, P. (2007), *Understanding Deviance*, 5th edn, Oxford: Oxford University Press.

DUBBER, M. (2005), *The Police Power*, New York: Columbia University Press.

—— and VALVERDE, M. (eds) (2006), *The New Police Science*, Stanford: Stanford University Press (forthcoming).

DUMENIL, G. and LEVY, D. (2010), *The Crisis of Neoliberalism*, Cambridge: Harvard University Press.

EAGLETON, T. (2011), *Why Marx Was Right*, New Haven: Yale University Press.

EHRLICH, I. (1973), 'Participation in Illegal Activities: A Theoretical and Empirical Investigation', *Journal of Political Economy*, 81: 521–63.

—— (1975), 'The Deterrent Effect of Capital Punishment', *American Economic Review*, 65: 397–447.

EISNER, M. (2001), 'Modernisation, Self-control and Lethal Violence: The Long-term Dynamics of European Homicide Rates in Theoretical Perspective', *British Journal of Criminology*, 41: 618–38.

ELIAS, N. (1939/1994), *The Civilising Process*, Oxford: Blackwell.

EMSLEY, C. (2010), *Crime and Society in England 1750–1900*, 4th edn, London: Longman.

ESPING-ANDERSON, G. (1990), *The Three Worlds of Welfare Capitalism*, Cambridge: Polity.

EYSENCK, H. (1965), *Fact and Fiction in Psychology*, London: Penguin.

FARRELL, G. TILLEY, N., TSELONI, A., and MAILLEY, J. (2010), 'Explaining and Sustaining the Crime Fall in Industrialised Countries', *Crime Prevention and Community Safety*, 12(1): 24–41.

FARRINGTON, D., GALLAGHER, B. MORLEY, L., St. LEDGER, R. J., and WEST, D. J. (1986), 'Unemployment, School Leaving and Crime', *British Journal of Criminology*, 26(4): 335–56.

FELSON, M. and BOBA, R. (2010), *Crime and Everyday Life*, 4th edn, Thousand Oaks, Cal.: Sage.

—— and CLARKE, R. (1998), *Opportunity Makes the Thief*, London: Home Office.

FIELD, S. (1990), *Trends in Crime and Their Interpretation: A Study of recorded Crime in Post-war England and Wales*, London: Home Office.

—— (1999), *Trends in Crime Revisited*, London: Home Office.

FIELDING, N., CLARKE, A., and WITT, R. (eds) (2000), *The Economic Dimensions of Crime*, London: Palgrave.

FITZGERALD, M., STOCKDALE, J., and HALE, C. (2003), *Young People and Street Crime*, London: Youth Justice Board.

FLETCHER, J. (1997), *Violence and Civilization*, Cambridge: Polity.

FOUCAULT, M. (1977), *Discipline and Punish*, London: Penguin.

GARLAND, D. (1985), *Punishment and Welfare*, Aldershot: Gower.

—— (1990), *Punishment and Modern Society*, Cambridge: Cambridge University Press.

—— (2001), *The Culture of Control*, Oxford: Oxford University Press.

—— (2002), 'Of Crime and Criminals', in M. Maguire, R. Morgan, and R. Reiner (eds), *The Oxford Handbook of Criminology*, 3rd edn, Oxford: Oxford University Press.

GATRELL, V. (1980), 'The Decline of Theft and Violence in Victorian and Edwardian England', in V. Gatrell, B. Lenman, and G. Parker (eds), *Crime and the Law*, London: Europa.

GEARY, R. (1985), *Policing Industrial Disputes*, Cambridge: Cambridge University Press.

GLYN, A. (ed.) (1999), *Social Democracy in Neo-Liberal Times*, Oxford: Oxford University Press.

GOBERT, J. and PUNCH, M. (2003), *Rethinking Corporate Crime*, London: Butterworths.

GOODIN, R., HEADEY, B., MUFFELS, R., and DIRVEN, H. J. (1999), *The Real Worlds of Welfare Capitalism*, Cambridge: Cambridge University Press.

GREEN, P. and WARD, T. (2004), *State Crime*, London: Pluto.

GROGGER, J. (2000), 'An Economic Model of Recent Trends in Violence', in A. Bloomstein and J. Wallman (eds), *The Crime Drop in America*, Cambridge: Cambridge University Press.

GURR, T. R. (1981), 'Historical Trends In Violent Crime', in M. Tonry and N. Morris (eds), *Crime and Justice*, 3, Chicago: Chicago University Press.

HAAKONSEN, K. (ed.) (2006), *The Cambridge Companion to Adam Smith*, Cambridge: Cambridge University Press.

HACKER, J. S. and PIERSON, P. (2011), *Winner Take-All Politics*, New York: Simon and Schuster.

HALE, C. (1998), 'Crime and the Business Cycle in Post-war Britain Revisited', *British Journal of Criminology*, 38: 681–98.

—— (1999), 'The Labour Market and Post-war Crime Trends in England and Wales', in P. Carlen and R. Morgan (eds), *Crime Unlimited*, London: Macmillan.

—— (2005), 'Economic Marginalization and Social Exclusion', in C. Hale, K. Hayward, A. Wahidin, and E. Wincup (eds), *Criminology*, Oxford: Oxford University Press.

HALL, P. and SOSKICE, D. (eds) (2003), *Varieties of Capitalism*, Oxford: Oxford University Press.

HALL, S. (2011), *Theorising Crime and Deviance*, London: Sage.

——, WINLOW, S., and ANCRUM, C. (2008), *Criminal Identities and Consumer Culture: Crime, Exclusion and the New Culture of Narcissism*, Cullompton: Willan.

—— and McLEAN, C. (2009), 'A tale of two capitalisms: Preliminary Spatial and Historical Comparisons of Homicide', *Theoretical Criminology* 13/3: 313–39.

——, CRITCHER, C., JEFFERSON, T., CLARKE, J., and ROBERTS, B. (1978), *Policing the Crisis*, London: Macmillan.

HALLSWORTH, S. (2005), *Street Crime*, Cullompton, Devon: Willan.

HANSEN, K. and MACHIN, S. (2003), 'Spatial Crime Patterns and the Introduction of the UK Minimum Wage', *Oxford Bulletin of Economics and Statistics*, 64: 677–97.

HARVEY, D. (2005), *A Brief History of Neoliberalism*, Oxford: Oxford University Press.

HAY, D., LINEBAUGH, P., THOMPSON, E. P., RULE, J. G., and WINSLOW, C. (1975), *Albion's Fatal Tree*, London: Penguin.

HAYWARD, K. (2004), *City Limits*, London: Glasshouse.

HILLYARD, P., PANTAZIS, C., TOMBS, S., and GORDON, D. (eds) (2004), *Beyond Criminology: Taking Harm Seriously*, London: Pluto.

HOOGHE, M., VANHOUTTE, B., HARDYNS, W., and BIRCAN, T. (2011), 'Unemployment, Inequality, Poverty and Crime: Spatial Distribution Patterns of Criminal Acts in Belgium 2001–6', *British Journal of Criminology*, 51/1: 1–20.

IGNATIEFF, M. (1978), *A Just Measure of Pain*, London: Macmillan.

JAMES, O. (1995), *Juvenile Violence in a Winner-Loser Society*, London: Free Association Books.

JEFFERSON, T. (2008), 'Policing the Crisis Revisited: The State, Masculinity, Fear of Crime and Racism', *Crime Media Culture*, 4/1: 113–21.

JONES, T. and NEWBURN, T. (2006), *Policy Transfer and Criminal Justice*, Maidenhead: Open University Press.

JUDT, T. (2010), *Ill Fares the Land*, London: Allen Lane.

KARMEN, A. (2000), *New York Murder Mystery*, New York: New York University Press.

KARSTEDT, S. and FARRALL, S. (2004), 'The Moral Maze of the Middle Class: The Predatory Society and its Emerging Regulatory Order', in H.-J. Albrecht, T. Serassis, and H. Kania (eds), *Images of Crime II*, Freiburg: Max Planck Institute.

KATZ, J. (1988), *Seductions of Crime*, New York: Basic Books.

KEYNES, J. M. (1936), *The General Theory of Employment, Interest and Money*, London: Macmillan.

KLECK, G. and CHIRICOS, T. (2002), 'Unemployment and Property Crime: A Target-Specific Assessment of Opportunity and Motivation as Mediating Factors', *Criminology*, 40: 649–79.

KRIVO, L. T. and PETERSON, R. D. (2004), 'Labour Market Conditions and Violent Crime Among Youth and Adults', *Sociological Perspectives*, 47(4): 485–505.

LACEY, N. (2008), *The Prisoners' Dilemma: Political Economy and Punishment in Contemporary Democracies*, Cambridge: Cambridge University Press.

——, WELLS, C. and QUICK, O. (2010), *Reconstructing Criminal Law*, 4th edn, Cambridge: Cambridge University Press.

LEA, J. (2002), *Crime and Modernity*, London: Sage.

—— and YOUNG, J. (1984), *What is to be Done about Law and Order?*, London: Penguin.

LIN, M-J. (2008), 'Does Unemployment Increase Crime? Evidence From US Data 1974–2000', *Journal of Human Resources*, 43/3: 413–36.

MACEWAN, A. (1999), *Neo liberalism or Democracy?*, London: Zed Books.

MCLAUGHLIN, E., MUNCIE, J., and HUGHES, G. (2001), 'The Permanent Revolution: New Labour, New Public Management and the Modernization of Criminal Justice', *Criminal Justice*, 1: 301–18.

MACHIN, S. and MEGHIR, C. (2004), 'Crime and Economic Incentives', *Journal of Human Resources*, 39: 958–79.

MARRIS, R. (2000), *Survey of the Research Literature on the Economic and Criminological Factors Influencing Crime Trends*, London: Volterra Consulting.

MARSHALL, T. H. (1950), *Citizenship and Social Class*, Cambridge: Cambridge University Press.

MATTHEWS, R. (2005), 'The Myth of Punitiveness', *Theoretical Criminology*, 9/2: 175–201.

—— (2009), 'Beyond "So What?" Criminology', *Theoretical Criminology*, 13/3: 341–62.

MARX, K. (1867/1976), *Capital Vol. 1*, London: Penguin.

—— and ENGELS, F. (1848/1998), *The Communist Manifesto*, London: Verso.

MATRAVERS, M. (ed.) (2009), *Managing Modernity*, London: Routledge.

MERTON, R. (1938), 'Social Structure and Anomie', *American Sociological Review*, 3: 672–82 (revised in R. Merton (1957), *Social Theory and Social Structure*, London: Free Press).

MESSNER, S. and ROSENFELD, R. (2006), *Crime and the American Dream*, 4th edn, Belmont, Cal.: Wadsworth.

MORRIS, R. (2001), '"Lies, Damned Lies and Criminal Statistics": Reinterpreting the Criminal Statistics in England and Wales', *Crime, History and Societies*, 5: 111–27.

NELKEN, D. (2010), *Comparative Criminal Justice*, London: Sage.

NEOCLEOUS, M. (2000), *The Fabrication of Social Order*, London: Pluto.

OLSSEN, M. (2010), *Liberalism, Neoliberalism, Social Democracy*, London: Routledge.

PASQUINO, P. (1978), 'Theatrum Politicum: The Genealogy of Capital—Police and the State of Prosperity', *Ideology and Consciousness*, 4: 41–54.

PONTICELLI, J. and VOTH, H-J. (2011), *Austerity and Anarchy: Budget Cuts and Social Unrest in Europe 1919–2009*, Discussion Paper 8513, London: Centre for Economic Policy Research.

PRATT, J. (2006), *Penal Populism*, London: Routledge.

PYLE, D. and DEADMAN, D. (1994), 'Crime and the Business Cycle in Post-war Britain', *British Journal of Criminology*, 34: 339–57.

RADZINOWICZ, L. (1956), *A History of the English Criminal Law Vol. 3*, London: Stevens.

REIMAN, J. and LEIGHTON, P. (2009), *The Rich Get Richer and the Poor Get Prison*, 8th edn, Boston: Allyn and Bacon.

REINER, R. (1984), 'Crime, Law and Deviance: The Durkheim Legacy', in S. Fenton, *Durkheim and Modern Sociology*, Cambridge: Cambridge University Press.

—— (1988), 'British Criminology and the State', *British Journal of Criminology*, 29(1): 138–58.

—— (2002), 'Classical Social Theory and Law', in J. Penner, D. Schiff, and R. Nobles (eds), *Jurisprudence*, London: Butterworths.

—— (2006), 'Beyond Risk: A Lament for Social Democratic Criminology', in T. Newburn and P. Rock (eds), *The Politics of Crime Control*, Oxford: Oxford University Press.

—— (2007), *Law and Order: An Honest Citizen's Guide to Crime and Control*, Cambridge: Polity.

—— (2010a), *The Politics of the Police*, 4th edn, Oxford: Oxford University Press.

—— (2010b), 'Citizenship, Crime. Criminalisation: Marshalling A Social Democratic Perspective', *New Criminal Law Review*, 13/2: 240–61.

—— (2011), *Policing, Popular Culture and Political Economy: Towards A Social Democratic Criminology*, Farnham: Ashgate.

ROGERS, P. (2002), *Losing Control: Global Security in the Twenty-first Century*, London: Pluto.

ROTH, R. (2010), *American Homicide*, Cambridge: Harvard University Press.

RUGGIERO, V. (2000), *Crime and Markets*, Oxford: Oxford University Press.

RUSCHE, G. and KIRCHHEIMER, O. (1939/2003), *Punishment and Social Structure*, New Jersey: Transaction.

SHAXSON, N. (2011), *Treasure Islands: Tax Havens and the Men Who Stole the World*, London: Bodley Head.

SILVER, A. (1967), 'The Demand For Order in Civil Society', in D. Bordua (ed.), *The Police*, New York: Wiley.

SIMON, J. (2007), *Governing Through Crime*, New York: Oxford University Press.

SLAPPER, G. (1999), *Blood in the Bank*, Aldershot: Ashgate.

—— and TOMBS, S. (1999), *Corporate Crime*, London: Longman.

SPELMAN, W. (2005), 'Jobs or Jails? The Crime Drop in Texas', *Journal of Policy Analysis and Management* 24/1: 133–65.

SPIERENBURG, P. (2008), *A History of Murder*, Cambridge: Polity Press.

SUTTON, J. R. (2004), 'The Political Economy of Imprisonment in Affluent Western Democracies, 1960–1990', *American Sociological Review*, 69(1): 170–89.

—— (2010), 'Imprisonment and Opportunity Structures', *European Sociological Review*, advance access 11 August: 1–16.

SUTTON, M. (1998), *Handling Stolen Goods and Theft: A Market Reduction Approach*, London: Home Office.

——, SCHNEIDER, J., and HETHERINGTON, S. (2001), *Tackling Theft With the Market Reduction Approach*, London: Home Office.

TAYLOR, H. (1998a), 'The Politics of the Rising Crime Statistics of England and Wales 1914–60', *Crime, History and Societies*, 2: 5–28.

—— (1998b), 'Rising Crime: The Political Economy of Criminal Statistics Since the 1850s', *Economic History Review*, 51: 569–90.

—— (1999), 'Forging the Job: A Crisis of "Modernisation" or Redundancy for the Police in England and Wales 1900–39', *British Journal of Criminology*, 39: 113–35.

TAYLOR, I. (1981), *Law and Order: Arguments for Socialism*, London: Macmillan.

—— (1997), 'The Political Economy of Crime', in M. Maguire, R. Morgan, and R. Reiner (eds), *The Oxford Handbook of Criminology*, 2nd edn, Oxford: Oxford University Press.

—— (1999), *Crime in Context*, Cambridge: Polity.

——, WALTON, P., and YOUNG, J. (1973), *The New Criminology*, London: Routledge.

THAM, H. (1998), 'Crime and the Welfare State: the Case of the United Kingdom and Sweden', in

V. Ruggiero, N. South, and I. Taylor (eds), *The New European Criminology*, London: Routledge.

—— and HOFER, H. V. (2009), 'Individual Prediction and Crime Trends', *European Journal of Criminology*, 6(4): 313–35.

TOMBS, S. and WHYTE, D. (2007), *Safety Crimes*, Cullompton, Devon: Willan.

TONRY, M. and FARRINGTON, D. (eds) (2005), *Crime and Punishment in Western Countries 1980–1999*, Chicago: Chicago University Press.

VAN DIJK, J., VAN KESTEREN, J., and SMIT, P. (2008), *Criminal Victimisation in International Perspective*, The Hague: Boom.

WACQUANT, L. (2009), *Punishing the Poor: The Neoliberal Government of Social Insecurity*, Durham, N.C.: Duke University Press.

WADDINGTON, P. A. J. and WRIGHT, M. (2008), 'Policing Public Order and Political Contention', in T. Newburn (ed.), *Handbook of Policing*, 2nd.edn, Cullompton, Devon: Willan.

WADSWORTH, T. (2006), 'The Meaning of Work: Conceptualising the Deterrent Effect of Employment on Crime Amongst Young Adults', *Sociological Perspectives*, 49(3): 343–68.

WEBER, M. (1947/1964), *The Theory of Social and Economic Organisation*, Glencoe, Ill.: Free Press.

WEBBER, C. (2007), 'Revaluating Relative Deprivation Theory', *Theoretical Criminology*, 11/1: 97–120.

WESTERN, B. (2006), *Punishment and Inequality in America*, New York: Russell Sage.

WILKINSON, R. (2005), *The Impact of Inequality*, New York: New Press.

—— and PICKETT, K. (2009), *The Spirit Level: Why More Equal Societies Almost Always Do Better*, London: Allen Lane.

WILSON, J. Q. (1975), *Thinking About Crime*, New York: Vintage.

—— and HERRNSTEIN, R. (1985), *Crime and Human Nature*, New York: Simon and Schuster.

WITT, R., CLARKE, A., and FIELDING, N. (1999), 'Crime and Economic Activity: A Panel Data Approach', *British Journal of Criminology*, 39: 391–400.

YOUNG, J. (1986), 'The Failure of Criminology: The Need for a Radical Realism', in R. Matthews and J. Young (eds), *Confronting Crime*, London: Sage.

—— (1988), 'Radical Criminology in Britain', *British Journal of Criminology*, 28: 159–83.

—— (1999), *The Exclusive Society*, London: Sage.

—— (2003a), 'Winning the Fight Against Crime? New Labour, Populism and Lost Opportunities', in R. Matthews and J. Young (eds), *The New Politics of Crime and Punishment*, Cullompton, Devon: Willan.

—— (2003b), 'Merton With Energy, Katz With Structure: The Sociology of Vindictiveness and the Criminology of Transgression', *Theoretical Criminology*, 7: 389–414.

—— (2004), 'Voodoo Criminology and the Numbers Game', in J. Ferrell, K. Hayward, W. Morrison, and M. Presdee (eds), *Cultural Criminology Unleashed*, London: Glasshouse.

—— (2007), *The Vertigo of Late Modernity,* London: Sage.

ZEDNER, L. (2002), 'The Dangers of Dystopias in Penal Theory', *Oxford Journal of Legal Studies*, 22: 341–66.

—— (2006a), 'Policing Before the Police', *British Journal of Criminology*, 46: 78–96.

—— (2006b), 'Opportunity Makes the Thief-Taker: the Influence of Economic Analysis on Crime Control', in T. Newburn and P. Rock (eds), *The Politics of Crime Control*, Oxford: Oxford University Press.

ZIMRING, F. (2007), *The Great American Crime Decline*, New York: Oxford University Press.

# 12

# GENDER AND CRIME

*Frances Heidensohn and Marisa Silvestri*

## INTRODUCTION

Men commit crime at higher rates than women, are involved in more serious and violent offending, and are more prone to recidivism. While this statement has been called 'one of the few undisputed "facts" of criminology' (Lauritsen *et al.* 2009: 362) it was an unconsidered one for much of the subject's history. That it is now a central and much debated matter is due largely to the advent of feminist criminology which took this 'gender gap' in recorded crime as one of its key themes.

Gender is now an established and central topic in criminology and studies of criminal justice (Heidensohn, forthcoming). This chapter reflects this status by outlining the development of the feminist critique, the present state of the art in key fields of research and debate: women, girls and crime, history, police, and men. Later sections cover significant areas in gender and justice, particularly major shifts in the treatment of women in the criminal justice system in the twenty-first century. As will be apparent, continuity and change are central themes of our survey: thus some of the questions raised by the pioneer scholars in the foundational years, such as the gender gap, are still being vigorously debated today (see below and Heidensohn 2010a and Miller 2010).

## THE EARLY FEMINIST CRITIQUE OF CRIMINOLOGY

One of the first tasks in second-wave feminism from the 1960s onwards was to develop a comprehensive critique of the discipline. The early critique has been well rehearsed elsewhere (see, e.g., Heidensohn 1996). It has frequently focused on the two main themes of amnesia or neglect and distortion. Women account for a very small proportion of all known offenders, and as a consequence relatively little attention has been given to them. The majority of studies of crime and delinquency prior to the 1980s were of men's crime and delinquency (Leonard 1982; Scraton 1990). A second theme in the critique is that, even when women were recognized, they were depicted in terms of stereotypes based on their supposed biological and psychological natures. Whilst critical criminology challenged the assumptions of positivism in explaining men's crime, it neglected to acknowledge how such assumptions remained most prevalent in academic and popular conceptions of women's crime. Similarly, while analyses of class structure, state control, and the political nature of deviance gained credibility, the study of women's crime remained rooted in notions of biological determinism and an uncritical attitude towards the dominant sexual stereotypes of women as passive, domestic, and maternal (Smart 1976). Tracing the continuance of sexist assumptions from Lombroso to Pollak and beyond, Smart (1976) examined how assumptions of the abnormality of female offenders came to dominate both theory and criminal justice policy—despite evidence of more critical thinking in relation to men and men's crime. Women were ignored, marginalized, or distorted, both in their deviancy and in their conformity. The exposure of criminology as the criminology of men marked the starting point of feminists' attempts to find alternative modes of conceptualizing the social worlds of deviance and conformity, punishment and control.

Dominant strands in the development of feminist perspectives in criminology have included empirical illuminations about discriminatory practices as we show later in the chapter. New ways of viewing matters—the different ways in which conformity is produced for instance—were also developed. Heidensohn (1985, 1996) concluded her review of women, crime, and criminal justice by arguing for a return to the sociology of gender and for the use of insights from other studies of women's oppression. Such a redirection helped expose the explicit and informal controls exercised over women—in the home and at work—and, above all, focused on the rather peculiar notion of 'normal behaviour'. A number of writers have made apparent the correspondences between the policing of everyday life and policing through more formal mechanisms of social control (see Heidensohn 2000). A large body of empirical work drew attention to the experiences of female victims of crime and to female victims' and offenders' experiences of criminal justice processes (see, e.g., Walklate 2004). Again, as we show later, some of the focus on women and criminal justice developed from important feminist work in this area.

Daly and Chesney-Lind (1988) raise two key questions in relation to criminological theory. First, they ask whether theories generated to describe men's or boys' offending can apply to women and girls (what they call the 'generalizability problem'). Secondly, they ask why women commit less crime than men (what they term the 'gender ratio problem'). In other words, they express concern about 'gender', the implication being that theories of crime must be able to take account of both men's and women's (criminal) behaviour, and that they must also be able to highlight factors which operate differently on men and women. Daly and Chesney-Lind also urge criminologists to read at first hand of women's experiences rather than relying on distorted, received wisdom about women, for these accounts of experience have not only enriched feminist thought, but become a central part of feminist analyses and epistemological reflections. There is also encouragement for criminologists to reflect on the ethnocentricity inherent in mainstream criminological thinking: the fact that the questions posed by criminologists are generally those of white, economically privileged men.

While the battle to make gender a central concern of contemporary criminology can be said to have been won (Heidensohn, forthcoming) struggles continue over particular areas. Thus both Zedner (2002) and Gelsthorpe (2004) provide lengthy reviews of Garland's *Culture of Control* (2001) in which, while they praise his work, they focus on its limitations due to his neglect of gender issues: 'greater attention to the influence of feminism and the treatment of female offenders and victims would have enriched his interpretation of the culture of control' (Gelsthorpe 2004: 76). She makes a very similar point in reviewing Wacquant on penality and welfare:

> important as it is, I want to suggest that Wacquant's analysis would have benefited from some of the work of feminist criminologists (Gelsthorpe 2010: 377).

Wacquant does argue, she stresses, that 'the public aid bureaucracy serves to promote employment and "inculcate" the duty of working for work's sake among poor women...other agencies serve to control men' (op. cit. 2010: 376). There has, in short, been a 'double regulation' of the poor in the USA in the late twentieth century which reflects a 'remasculinizing' of the state (Wacquant 2009: 15). More than 40 years on from the first feminist critiques of criminological and penological theory, there are still limitations in the way many authors engage with the topic of gender, although as we set out below, there have been major shifts in attitudes and understanding. See Heidensohn (forthcoming) for a review.

If we characterize the first two main developments in feminist criminology as *feminist empiricism* (as evidenced in the wide-ranging criminological research on women, crime, control, and justice to counterbalance the absence of women from conventional work), and *feminist standpointism* (drawing attention to the need to place women's experience at the centre of knowledge), the third is best described as *feminist deconstructionism* (Naffine 1997) since it draws on postmodern insights relating to the problematizing of language and concepts.

These are foundational feminist contributions to criminology and to methodological thinking. One key feature of feminist contributions to criminology is the push to recognize gender as a social construct and not simply as a statistical 'variable'. Whilst early feminist work focused on the need to incorporate women in all areas of criminological debate, later work introduced a more critical consideration of the concept of gender (Daly 1997; Walklate 2004). Feminist criminologists have encouraged theorizations of gender, gender differences, gender relations, gender order, and the meaning of gender as a subjective lived experience rather than merely an ascription, within a context of power relations and patriarchy.[1] There have been some criticisms of the focus on gender to the neglect of other dimensions of lived realities (in relation to race and ethnicity for example), but there have nevertheless been significant steps towards a sophisticated understanding of gender. As Chesney-Lind (2006) has put it:

> Contemporary approaches to gender and crime...tend to avoid the problems of reductionism and determinism that characterize early discussions of gender and gender relations, stressing instead the complexity, tentativeness, and variability with which individuals, particularly youth, negotiate (and resist) gender identity [2006: 8].

---

[1]  Literally meaning 'the power of the father', but more generally referring to systems of power, hierarchy, and dominance that oppress women.

# WOMEN, GIRLS, AND CRIME

The differences between male and female rates of crime, variously termed 'the gender gap' or the 'sex crime ratio', has become one of the key themes of modern feminist criminology and of the wider field of gender-related studies of crime. In recent years the idea of a convergence between male and female rates of crime has gained ascendancy within criminological, public, and policy discourses. In particular, such ideas have increasingly come to dominate discourses in relation to the behaviour of girls and young women. In this section we review the extent and nature of women's involvement in criminal activity, paying particular attention to the current disquiet and growing concern over the level of criminality amongst girls and young women.

### CONVERGENCE IN CRIMINAL ACTIVITY

Arguments about whether female crime was rising at a faster rate than male, and that thus the female share was going up, have been highly contended criminological issues since the 1970s. Indeed, this is one of the few topics to do with women and crime to excite widespread attention (Heidensohn 1989). The issue was first raised by Freda Adler (and in a more modified form by Rita Simon) who argued that female crime rates had been rising more rapidly in the late 1960s and early 1970s; that women offenders were changing their patterns of offending to more 'masculine' styles, becoming more aggressive and violent; and that this was due to the growth of the modern women's movement. 'Liberation', in short, 'causes crime' (Adler 1975). Well into the twenty-first century, the concept of liberation causing crime is still very much alive and is clearly evidenced in media representations of young women's participation in the public sphere, delinquency, and in crime (Jewkes 2004; Chesney-Lind 2006). The unprecedented media attention and reporting of the emergence of the 'ladette', the 'mean girl' (Ringrose 2006), and the 'shemale' gangster (Young 2009) provide much fuel for those seeking evidence of a convergence in the behaviour of girls and boys. Headlines such as 'Violent Women: Binge Drinking Culture Fuels Rise in Attacks by Women (Clout 2008, The Guardian), 'Binge-drinking Blamed for Rise in Girl Violence' (Alleyne 2008, Daily Telegraph), 'Why are Girls Fighting Like Boys (Geoghegan 2008, BBC News Magazine) and 'Ladettes on a Crime Spree' (MacAskill 2004, Daily Telegraph) all provide ample evidence of the unease surrounding the behaviour of girls and young women.

While this concern is not new, Sharpe and Gelsthorpe (2009) point to a notable shift in terms of its focus, moving from a concern over girls' sexuality towards a concern over the level of violence they are engaged in. This is not to say that girls' sexual behaviour does not remain under scrutiny, indeed, Sharpe's (2009) analysis of youth worker referral records shows that 7 out of 11 girls had been referred to a Youth Inclusion Support Panel because they were 'sexually promiscuous' or 'sexually active'—by comparison, none of the 44 boys had been referred for this reason.

Nonetheless, the concern over violence amongst girls and young women has been cited as a growing problem within youth justice systems internationally—the problem of girls' violence has been reported in Scotland (Burman and Batchelor 2009; Burman

2009), the United States (Chesney-Lind and Irwin 2008; Putallaz and Bierman 2004), the Netherlands (Beijerse and Swaaningen 2006), and Australia (Carrington 2006). The extent to which such concern is justified is difficult to establish, as Sharpe and Gelsthorpe (2009: 203) note: 'The ubiquity of such popular representations of 'ladettes', violent girls and girl gang members has not been matched by either empirical research or policy attention'. There are, however, a range of official data sources that provide statistical data on gender and crime. Given what we know of the limitations of such data (see Maguire, this volume), great caution is necessary in interpreting crime statistics. It is useful at this point to remind ourselves of the problematic nature of studying women's participation in crime given their small number. The low number of women engaged in criminal behaviour has very significant impacts on those seeking to study them—it is a well-established fact that small numerical increases or decreases can make a great deal of difference in terms of reported rises and reductions.

Conviction data for England and Wales indicates that 'theft and handling stolen goods' remains the most common indictable offence group for which both males and females are prosecuted. Figures for 2009 show that 44 per cent of females were prosecuted for this offence type compared to 28 per cent of males. The reported increase in women and girls' violence is located in police-recorded arrest data. Here the figures show that 'violence against the person' is the most common offence for both women and men. In 2008/9, 34 per cent of all adult females arrested and 31 per cent of all males arrested were suspected of committing violence against the person, which was consistent with trends since 2006/7. Arrest data indicates a significant rise in the number of women and girls arrested for violence, showing an increase from 37,100 in 1999/2000 to 88,100 in 2007/8 (Hand and Dodd 2009). It is important to stress here, however, that figures for 2008/9 also show that the number of juveniles, both female and male, arrested for 'violence against the person' were at their lowest for five years (Ministry of Justice 2010).

Given that the increase in girls' arrest rates for violence occurred during a period in which the British Crime Survey reports violent crime falling by 23 per cent, Hedderman (2010: 487) suggests that 'it is reasonable to think that some of the change in arrest statistics is explained by a change in police behaviour'. Indeed commentators have suggested a range of factors that can influence a rise and a reduction in crime statistics. Changes to sentencing patterns, law and policy have all been cited as central to understanding women's increased appearance in the criminal statistics. There is also a growing awareness of the impacts of such media-fuelled narratives about women's violence on criminal justice practitioners themselves. Some insight into these factors is essential if we are to make sense of women's changing position in the criminal statistics.

Two studies carried out by Steffensmeier and his colleagues (2005 and 2006) test out hypotheses about recent trends in girls' violence and increase in female violence more generally. For the former, they compare Uniform Crime Report (UCR) data from the FBI with victim surveys and self-report studies. They 'find that the rise in girls' violence as counted in police arrest data is not borne out in unofficial longitudinal sources' (Steffensmeier et al. 2005: 395). The rise in girls' violence, they suggest, is due to a variety of factors, some of which may include differential arrest policies and social constructionist penal policies:

Recent changes in law enforcement practices and the juvenile justice system have apparently escalated the arrest proneness of adolescent females. The rise in girls' arrest for violent crime and the narrowing gender gap have less to do with underlying behavior and more to do, first, with net-widening changes in law and policing toward prosecuting less serious forms of violence in …private settings…and second, with less biased or more efficient responses to girls'…aggression (Steffensmeier *et al.* 2005: 389–90).

In their second study, the same group compare all female and male violent crime rates in the USA over two decades, again using the UCR and the National Crime Victimization Survey (NCVS). Recorded increases in crime showed that between 1980 and 2003 the female percentage of all arrests increased from one-fifth to one-third for simple assault (Steffensmeier *et al.* 2006). This time they tested two simpler hypotheses of behaviour change and policy change (Steffensmeier *et al.* 2006). Again their key conclusion is that 'there has been no meaningful or systematic change in women's involvement in crimes of interpersonal violence and in the gender gap in the past couple of decades' (op. cit.: 93). Instead, they find a strong case for the policy change thesis: 'we have changed our laws, police practices, and policies in…ways toward enhanced identification and criminalization of violence in general and of women's violence in particular' (op. cit.: 94). In the same journal issue, Chesney Lind argues that one specific policy, that of mandatory arrests for domestic violence, has led to dramatic jumps in rates of female violence (2006: 15). However, Lauritsen and her colleagues challenged Steffensmeier *et al.*'s study, reanalysed the NCVS data, and achieved very different results (Lauritsen *et al.* 2009). 'Our NCVS findings stand in stark contrast to their findings and conclusions…we find that the gender ratios of assault, robbery…have increased over time, which indicates a narrowing of the gender gap' (op. cit. 2009: 386). They go on to argue that both the economic marginalization of poor women, plus the civilizing effects of more women being present in public life, where they act as 'capable guardians' and restrain male violence, may be more plausible hypotheses than the policy change thesis put forward by Steffensmeier *et al.* (2006). In the same issue of *Criminology* Schwartz *et al.*, including Steffensmeier, respond robustly and insist that their interpretation is still valid and that the gender gap, especially in more serious and predatory forms of violence, remains stable. They also conclude that triangulation of their data from other sources shows 'a lack of evidence for a narrowing gender gap in serious violence' (Schwartz *et al.* 2009: 418), both from surveys and a variety of qualitative studies. The response to this from Lauritsen *et al.* indicates that they disagree and that this debate will continue and, while much of it is highly technical, it is extremely important both because it reflects a key issue raised by feminist criminologists in the pioneer era and, as all these authors acknowledge, the media and public debate about female violence have often been misled by exaggerated and sensational treatment of this topic (Heimer *et al.* 2009). There is no questioning of Lauritsen *et al.*'s insistence that 'Our findings show that female rates of violent offending have declined over time; clearly, *a new violent female offender has not emerged*' (op. cit. 2009: 385) our italics.

Other studies have sought to explain women's increased participation in violence through a closer examination of their changing participation in other forms of crime. Hedderman (2010: 487) for example, suggests that the '*proportion* of arrests related to violence has increased partly because the number of arrests rose but also because the *number* of women arrested for theft and handling, fraud and forgery, burglary, drugs and sexual offences fell by over 27,000' between 1999–2008. Sharpe and Gelsthorpe (2009: 198) also argue that violent acts constitute a high proportion of girls' recorded offences 'principally because of their non-participation in other crimes—notably driving related matters and serious offences. Thus changes within the criminal justice system that result in a statistical inflation of violent crimes by drawing on low-level assaults and physical altercations—including playground fights and domestic disputes—into the criminal justice system, will affect girls disproportionately'.

In this way the reported increase in girls' violence is attributable more to changes in the labelling and criminalization of girls' bad behaviour than to changes in their behaviour. Such re-labelling of offences is also reported by Chesney-Lind (2006) who observes that girls previously ignored by the criminal justice system may now find themselves being redefined as violent offenders. Worrall follows this general view of girls and violence across the English-speaking world with a detailed dissection of recent British policies which, she argues, have resulted in the ' "welfarization" and "soft policing" of young women's behaviour by both formal and informal social control mechanisms having given way to straightforward "criminalization" of that same behaviour, with increasing numbers of young women being incarcerated not on spurious benevolent welfare grounds, but on spuriously equitable "justice" grounds' (Worrall 2004). In short, more bad behaviour by girls is being redefined as criminal, particularly fighting.

Burman and Batchelor (2009: 271) position the growing concern around violent and disorderly young female offenders in Scotland against a broader social and political context in which they identify an increasing politicization of youth crime since the mid-1990s and major changes in youth justice policy. In their analysis of the readiness and ease within which young women in Scotland have become problematized, they argue that 'young women depicted as drunk and disorderly, out of control and looking for fights have increasingly been identified as a new source of the "youth problem" '. A possible consequence of this they argue is that 'what we are witnessing is not an increase in violent offending *per se* , but the increased reporting, recording and prosecuting of young women accused of violent offences' (Burman and Batchelor 2009: 275). As a result 'statistics and their analysis can *influence* system responses, thus having direct material consequences for (certain) young women' (Sharpe and Gelsthorpe 2009: 196, emphasis in original). This is confirmed by Chesney-Lind (2006) and Steffensmeier and Schwartz (2009) who suggest a 'self-fulfilling' effect of increased reporting and policing of girls' disorderly behaviour following statistical rises.

The extent to which the media commentaries noted above affect and shape practitioners' perceptions of women and girls who offend is difficult to establish and the research in this area is underdeveloped. Steffensmeier *et al.*'s (2005) US study suggested that sentencers, as members of the public, are inevitably affected by such 'moral panics' about girls. Evidence from Sharpe's (2009) study on the extent to which media representations of 'ladettes' and girls' violence are evident in contemporary professional ideology in England concurs. Following interviews with a range of criminal justice practitioners, she notes that whilst the views expressed by professionals interviewed were both complex and contradictory, the idea that 'today's girls are rapidly getting "worse" has made inroads into professional youth justice discourse' (Sharpe

2009: 65). Furthermore, practitioner accounts revealed that they had 'been influenced by media and cultural stereotypes that gender role convergence, or "equal opportunities", *must be a factor* in the widely-publicized "rise" in girls' offending' (ibid.: 263).

Self-report studies have become important sources of data on gender-gap issues and offer some interesting perspectives on these topics. A study of alcohol, crime, and disorder among young people found that '[m]ales were more likely to binge drink (48 per cent) than females (31 per cent)' (Richardson and Budd 2003: vii). The same researchers found that 'almost half of the men reported taking an illegal drug compared with just over a third of women' (2003: 27). When disorderly activity was compared: 'young men were significantly more likely to admit offending than young women' (33 and 13 per cent). Self-report data from a recent longitudinal analysis, *Offending, Crime and Justice Survey 2003–06,* showed that female respondents aged 10–25 years were significantly less likely to have been offenders than males. Males were more likely than females to admit to an offence in each major offence category (Hales *et al.* 2009). Data from the US shows no upward trend in girls' self-reported criminality, in fact they show a decline (Chesney-Lind 2004; Chesney-Lind and Belknap 2004; Steffensmeier *et al.* 2005).

For those women and girls who are engaged in violent behaviour, there is much to be gained from those studies that have investigated the nature of their violence. For instance, among Alder and Worrall's (2004) findings are that, while there were instances of recorded increases in girls' violent offending in Australia, the UK, and Canada, their convictions were often for the most minor forms of offending not involving weapons, and many of their victims were care workers or police officers, suggesting that girls' normal resistance to discipline is more readily criminalized and punished today, where once it was treated as a welfare issue. Young's (2009) work examining the rise of the so-called 'shemale' gangster in the UK between 2000 and 2007 also notes that the data does not show that young women who are in gangs are more likely to be involved in serious violence. Rather, statistics show that co-offending by young females is largely confined to criminal damage and shoplifting offences and the violence they enact tends to be of a low-level nature. Interviews carried out by Young (2009: 234) with young women identified their use of violence as 'peer related and the result of perceived provocation, and not gang related'. Burman and Batchelor (2009: 275) also stress that the majority of young female offending is non-violent and that when compared to young men, violence remains an overwhelmingly male activity—figures taken from the Scottish Government 2008 show that for 2006/7 69 women had a charge for a non-sexual crime of violence proven against them compared with 719 crimes of violence committed by young men.

At the same time, there are some interesting studies which have emphasized the resourcefulness of some of the most marginal and oppressed subjects, deviant women and girls who are conventionally seen as passive and submissive. Lisa Maher, in a study of gender, race, and resistance in a Brooklyn drug market, describes 'the tactics women use to resist and contest the constraints that shape their occupational lives' (1997: 199). Lopez *et al.*'s (2009: 247) study on girls who use drugs also provides much evidence of their agency in 'breaking out of culturally proscribed constraints and crafting their own versions of femininity and survival'. Miller's (2001, 2002) accounts of women's participation in street robbery in the USA, also address the question of the agency of women who have few channels of expression yet find their own. There are also a number of studies in the US that have focused on young women's creation of street identities and enactments of violence (Cobbina *et al.* 2010; Brunson and Stewart 2006, Ness 2004; Miller and Mullins 2006). Such studies concur in suggesting that girls' use of street violence has much to do with their attempts to establish identity, maintain respect, and build status and reputation.

The notion of conformity has been central to understandings of women's lack of participation in crime. Heidensohn (1996) emphasized that one of the most striking things about women's behaviour was not their criminality but their conformity to social norms. Building on this notion, Toor's (2009) work provides a fresh insight into the important role played by honour (*izzat*) and shame (*sharam*) on the lives of British Asian girls. Whilst the extent of Asian girls' involvement in offending is unknown,[2] she argues that '[t]here are key dynamics embedded in Asian cultures that effectively preclude female activity in criminal and deviant spheres' (ibid.: 241).

The idea that 'women commit far less crime than do men' was the standard introduction to this topic for a long time and whilst closer examination has led to some qualifications above, a number of established observations about female crime remain valid and the differences between women and men remain remarkable and robust. The overall female share of recorded crime appears to be fairly stable and the ratios have changed very little in the second half of the twentieth century. Women commit fewer and less serious offences—figures for those cautioned or convicted of more serious (indictable) offences in England and Wales, by sex and type of offence in 2007, show that over 60 per cent of offences by women and girls were theft related, compared to only 36 per cent of those for which men and boys were responsible (Ministry of Justice 2010). Despite the fact that the number of women and girls arrested for violence has more than doubled since 1999/2000 from 37,100 to 88,100 in 2007/2008, Hedderman (2010: 487) reminds us that the 'number of men arrested for violence has risen over this period from 218,400 to 389,600; and remains four times the number of women and as such remains an overwhelmingly male activity. Women desist from crime more readily; girls reach their peak age of offending sooner than boys. Women's criminal careers are shorter and tend to peak in the mid- rather than late-teens (Home Office 2003; Gelsthorpe *et al.* 2006). Given these observations, commentators have increasingly expressed concern over the scale of increase in women and girls' incarceration in recent years; we return to these concerns later in the chapter.

## GENDER, CRIME, AND HISTORY

Modern historical work on crime has experienced a renaissance, and studies of women offenders have been one offshoot of this. They enrich, and also complicate, the patterns

---

[2] The Youth Justice Board's Annual Workload Data (previously Annual Statistics) does provide statistics by gender and ethnicity, but not on the two aggregated together.

of crime we are trying to unravel. We have already shown the importance of the gender gap to modern criminological analysis, and it has occupied historians of crime too. In her comprehensive study of seventeenth century Cheshire court records, Walker urges close analysis of discourses on violence. She found that there was 'little difference in actual methods of fighting by men and by women', (Walker 2003: 270), yet men claimed the privileges of manhood and honour to explain their actions, not an option open to women. Walker presents a fascinating comparison of two gendered sources of reprieve before the courts: benefit of clergy and benefit of belly (pregnancy) and shows that women were not morally equivalent, nor indeed successful; many women gained only temporary reprieve because of their pregnancy and were later executed (op. cit.: 197–201). Writing of Britain in the eighteenth century, McLynn states that '[o]nly 12 per cent of the accused in the home counties in 1782–7 were female' (1989: 128). Nonetheless, Feeley and Little (1991), taking a sample of Old Bailey cases tried between 1687 and 1912, found that 45 per cent of defendants were women.[3]

However, figures for these, and earlier, periods need to be treated with even more circumspection than those from today. In particular, Zedner notes that: 'Overall there was a considerable decline in those designated as the "criminal classes". Over the period 1860–90 they fell by more than half. The number of women fell at roughly the same rate as men, remaining at around a fifth of the total in this category over the period' (Zedner 1991: 20). She concludes that this relatively low rate was due to the exclusion of prostitutes, vagrants, and tramps. In terms of convictions, Zedner notes that 'overall, women's crimes made up a steady 17 per cent of all summary convictions' (ibid.: 34), with drunkenness, assault, and larceny the commonest types of offence. In contrast to the steady state in summary jurisdiction, 'over the second half of the nineteenth century, women formed a declining proportion of those proceeded against by indictment '(from 27 per cent of the total in 1867 to only 19 per cent by 1890) (ibid.: 36). Zedner's detailed work on nineteenth century data confirms on the whole the 'modest share' view of female crime as compared with male. She also notes some reporting of a decline in convictions of women for serious offences by the end of the century (ibid.: 23).

While gendered, historical accounts of crime and the criminal justice system are important in their own right, it is for the contribution to contemporary discourse that they have most salience for criminology. Wiener's (1998) view of the 'vanishing female' in Victorian crime figures is that this was partly due to the increasing prominence and visibility of the male criminal. In his analysis of male and female workplace appropriation (embezzlement) in mid-nineteenth century Yorkshire, Godfrey (1999) provides support for modern arguments which attribute female conformity to greater levels of social control and the harsh effects of punishment

> Women clearly faced many disincentives to appropriate workplace materials, ranging from the physical and the supervisory structures of the factory, to the deterrence of punishments which were particularly severe for women—the loss of children and future employment... foremen and employers preferred to use informal punishments (Godfrey 1999: 147).

---

[3] See Beattie 1975 on women's role in the food riots in the pre-modern period.

Godfrey (1999) also contributes to the debates on leniency, or chivalry, towards women in the criminal justice system. He found that, although the evidence is mixed, courts were perceived by manufacturers who were their employers to excuse women.

In a study of street violence in the late nineteenth century in Manchester and Salford, Davies describes how 'young working-class women on occasion fought each other, and assaulted men (including police officers) in the streets' (1999: 87). He also found evidence of gender discrimination in sentencing and of the use of informal controls. For instance, he found that 'girls who were occasionally rough were kept out of the clutches of the police' and notes, 'the cycle of repeat offending that seems to have affected young lads' (Godfrey 2004: 34). Girls were willing to fight and to take risks, but he argues that the risks they took had more to do with unprotected sex and illegal abortion than with violence. All these examples illustrate the ways in which gendered historical perspectives on crime both illuminate their subject matter and inform current debates.

## GENDER AND POLICING

The entry of women into policing in the USA, the UK, Australia, and parts of Europe, was a product of first wave feminism (Heidensohn 2000). It was a cause promoted in the late nineteenth and early twentieth centuries precisely to provide protection to female and juvenile offenders and victims which, it was felt, they did not receive from an all-male force (Carrier 1988; Feinman 1986). For more than 50 years, until integration in the 1970s, small numbers of female officers worked in this fashion in all these systems.

While there was an international, concerted, and ultimately successful early twentieth century effort to support the cause of the policewomen's movement, the results in this century vary considerably. Whereas in England and Wales in 2010 26 per cent of the total police strength were females, a figure close to that of previous years (Sigurdsson and Dhani 2010), their share in the USA was much lower and had actually declined at the turn of the Millennium (Heidensohn 2008). A major review of the data noted that, despite America being the first country where women were appointed as law enforcement officers 'during the 1990s and 2000s the percentage of sworn officers who were women increased only slightly in federal, state and local agencies' (Langton 2010: 1). By 2008, they comprised 20 per cent across several large federal agencies but this proportion was less in others (op. cit.).

A study of gender equity in Australian and New Zealand policing found an increase in the percentage of women from 22 per cent in 2003/4 to 24 per cent in 2007/8 in Australia, while in New Zealand it stood at only 17 per cent in that year (Prenzler *et al.* 2010: 592). European 'pioneer' states on the other hand, show notably larger proportions of women with their making up 44 per cent of the intake of the Swedish Police Academy in 2005. The comparable level for Britain is about 30 per cent. The Netherlands also has about 40 per cent of lower rank positions held by women (NB. these are both countries with dual level entry to policing).

Findings from studies with a gender perspective throw light on the role and position of women in law-enforcement, reconstruct the notion of police culture, and form part of the basis for 'modernization' in many agencies around the world. Martin (1980), Jones (1986), and Heidensohn (1992), for example, have respectively looked at the notion of 'defeminized' women who compete directly with their male colleagues and 'deprofessionalized' women who accept subordinate roles and routine tasks in the station house; 'traditional' and 'modern' types of woman officer; and work identities which revolve around a sense of mission regarding values of law and order and a perception of a duty to keep the peace. Paradoxically, this could lead some women to take, or be perceived as taking, a deviant stand by challenging custom and practice: this could be in cases of alleged police corruption, in bullying, or by exposing their organization to public scrutiny through legal challenges (Heidensohn 1994).

In a later project, Brown and Heidensohn (2000) compared the experiences of an international sample of policewomen and, as with others, found widespread evidence of a macho cop culture, manifested in sexual discrimination and sexual harassment of women officers by their male colleagues. The authors developed a comparative framework for this study, grouping police organizations around the world into four categories of cops, colonials, transitionals, and gendarmeries. They noted the relationship between these models, the impact of police culture on women officers, and the attitudes to the victimization of women. The theme of how 'deviant' and threatening women officers could still seem was apparent. More recent research reflects the growing levels of recruitment of women into policing and their promotion to the highest levels: the first female chief constable was appointed in Britain in 1995 and there have been several since. Westmarland (2001) argues that women may now have a better chance of achieving promotion than men since they specialize in areas such as child protection which are part of a new and vital agenda of policing. However, other evidence suggests a more cautious interpretation. Westmarland herself found an 'anti-women' atmosphere in police departments with very low numbers of females (ibid.: 85). In a study of senior women officers, Silvestri (2003) found that female officers could not afford to be seen as feminists and focused on 'representation and retention issues rather than changing the culture'.

Two more recent assessments of gender, culture, and police reflect the ways in which changes in the *external* modern demands of diversity policies have an impact on the interior world of the police and how officers themselves adapt and react to these. Loftus (2008) studied one English force and found that what she terms 'a recalcitrant perspective had emerged from white, heterosexual male officers towards the new realities. The revised emphasis on diversity was considered to be excessive and unwarranted' (Loftus 2008: 762). Many minority officers, she found, continued to feel excluded (op. cit.: 769) even if this came in 'more subtle forms of discrimination, while a quarter of the force were female and all the minorities had their own support groups'. This dominant and discriminatory discourse was, she observed, still expressed by the white, male majority who continued to espouse intolerant views but in what she terms 'white space' where they can comfortably do so (op. cit.: 770).

Chan and her colleagues use data from their longitudinal study of the New South Wales Police to examine how their subjects, mid-career officers, 'do and undo gender' in their everyday lives. In this research, females as well as males accepted and used the gendered division of labour and even gender stereotypes in order to 'negotiate their (multiple) identities' (Chan *et al.* 2010: 442). This project focuses much more than the first one on change over time, the different stages of a career in law enforcement, suggesting that rookies first 'do policing' with 'doing gender' only coming to the fore as a strategy later on, once they are secure in the accomplishment of the former.

Women's entry into law enforcement and their roles, careers, and contributions are the most widely researched of all the gender issues in relation to professionals in the criminal justice system. While these studies are of course significant in their own right, this is not least because 'studies of policing are somewhat distinctive in that the importance of gender had been accepted, albeit in a very different way, almost from the earliest studies of policing' (Heidensohn 2003: 556). Other professionals in the criminal justice system face similar problems (Martin and Jurik 1996; Thomas 2005). Commitment to diversity in all aspects of criminal justice is slowly changing this situation.

## THEORIZING MEN, MASCULINITIES, AND CRIME

That men and boys are responsible for the majority of offending behaviour remains an uncontested feature within criminology and debates on gender and crime. Official arrest data for 2008–9 shows that 83 per cent of adult men were arrested for committing violence against the person; 97 per cent for sexual offences; 91 per cent for robbery; 92 per cent for burglary; 78 per cent for theft and handling stolen goods; 75 per cent for fraud and forgery; 87 per cent for criminal damage, and 88 per cent for drug offences (Ministry of Justice 2010). A sociology of masculinity has emerged from feminist work on gender, and from men's involvement in feminism, as well as the growing field of gay and lesbian studies. A vital change came in asking what it is about men as men and 'not as working-class, not as migrants, not as underprivileged individuals but *as men*, that induces them to "commit crime"' (Grosz 1987). A broad base of criminological studies identify the participation of boys and men for most street crimes (Hallsworth 2005; Mullins 2006; Cobbina *et al.* 2010); crimes of violence (Collier 1998; Oliver 1994; Anderson and Umberson 2001; Gadd 2003); drugs (Simpson *et al.* 2007); alcohol (Dingwall 2005); crimes associated with the night-time economy (Winlow 2001; Hobbs *et al.* 2003); sexual offences (Thomas 2005); and corporate crime (Beirne and Messerschmidt 2007).

Connell (1995) looked at the key concepts of patriarchy, domination, oppression, and exploitation through which men are deemed the powerful (and women the 'other'); and suggested that masculinity is negotiated and practised in varying ways in different contexts. This at once draws together feminist perspectives on the social construction of gender and puts the contestation of power at the centre of an analysis of masculinities. Over time, the focus on masculinity has been transformed into an understanding of complex and multiple masculinities: 'hegemonic' masculinities (associated with heterosexuality, toughness, power, authority, and competition) or 'subordinated' masculinities (associated with gay men, for example). Silvestri and Crowther-Dowey

(2008) point to four major insights provided by Connell's work. Firstly, that Connell has consistently shown that it is not simply a case of looking at men on the one hand and women on the other hand. Rather, masculinity is not something linked exclusively to men and the male body, thus women may also adopt masculinity. Secondly, masculinity is not static and changes over time and place. Thirdly, there is no single masculinity but multiple masculinities and finally, despite there being no clear-cut and fixed identities, there are ideal types of masculinity sustaining hierarchical relation, especially patterns of male dominance.

Messerschmidt's (1993) analysis has been the most extensive attempt to apply Connell's framework to the study of crime. He developed the idea of gender as a 'situational accomplishment' and of crime as a means of 'doing gender'. Following Connell, Messerschmidt addresses race and class alongside gender in his theorization of these categories as 'structured action' (1997). In line with critical, radical and Left Realist criminologists he draws attention to those groups marginalized and excluded from labour markets, but rather than arguing that these factors push men into crime, he describes how men who cannot access economic and material resources commit crime as a method of 'doing masculinity' and the assertion of manliness.

The rise of a more psychosocial approach to understanding men and crime has perhaps provided the most significant challenge to the work of Connell and Messerschmidt. Jefferson (1997, 2002) argues that notions of hegemonic masculinity are problematic because they are based on an overly socialized view of masculinity. For Jefferson, the key issues are how in reality men deal with their own life histories and psychic formations with regard to masculinities. This is done intersubjectively because of the centrality of 'biographically mediated difference between men' (Gadd 2003: 333). The psychosocial approach draws attention towards men's subjectivities and the workings of unconscious processes. Such ideas have been elaborated upon by Gadd and Farrall's (2004) work on men's criminal careers and desistance.

With this in mind, Hall and Winlow (2005) have pointed to the disintegration of traditional forms of community and social order and the rise of 'competitive individualism and instrumentality' as key to understanding men's violence. They assert that one of the main factors in the recent rise of crime and violence among working-class men in the north east of England is the 'individual's need for a technique of satisfying these ambitions and desires and thus releasing over-stimulated psychic tension' (Hall and Winlow 2005: 46). A focus on men's individual biographies is also central to their latest work exploring persistently violent men (Winlow and Hall 2010). Drawing on a psychosocial framework they argue that 'violent men often address unfolding social interaction as a means of taking control of painful and humiliating memories, rewriting the past and rehabilitating the self from its previous failures' (ibid.: 288). Focusing on the emotional feelings of 'humiliation' and 'regret', they outline how violent incidents from earlier stages of men's life courses can be drawn upon 'both directly and indirectly, as motivational and justificatory instruments in potentially violent interactions in the here and now' (ibid.: 285).

Though such studies show a marked attempt to take psychosocial processes more seriously, Connell's framework remains salient to the study of men, masculinity, and crime. Connell and Messerschmidt (2005) have addressed some of the criticisms by amplifying how the concept of hegemonic masculinity does not equate to social reproduction, and by recognizing more the social struggles in which subordinated masculinities influence dominant forms. They suggest a reformulation of the concept by introducing a more complex model of gender hierarchy (acknowledging the agency of women more), by giving explicit recognition to the geography of masculinities (acknowledging the interplay between local, regional, and global levels), by giving specific greater attention to embodiment in contexts of privilege and power (acknowledging transgender practices along the way), and by giving stronger emphasis to the dynamics of hegemonic masculinity (through life histories, for example). Certainly this reformulation is more likely than previous formulations to recognize constructions of racialized and gendered identities and to recognize that psychological as well as sociological factors are essential to analysis. Jody Miller (2002) has advanced Messerschmidt's analysis by looking at the strengths and limitations of 'doing gender' for understanding street crime, and in particular by challenging gender dualism and focusing on the transformative aspects of social action to capture the dynamic nature of agency as it impacts on 'doing gender' and creating identity (see also Messerschmidt 2002). Cobbina *et al.*'s (2010: 596) analysis of African-American young men's narratives of violence further contributes to this strand of analysis. Their research highlights how street reputation and associated violence is central to some young black men's identities in contexts of concentrated disadvantage. Here, men's use of violence emerges in response to concerns that emphasize 'autonomy, respect and the defense of reputation, and is indicative of the import of hegemonic masculinities on the streets'.

Our aim here has been to highlight some of the theoretical reasoning regarding masculinity and masculinities studies promoted, at least in part, by feminist insights into conceptions and practices of gender. Criminological theory has certainly been enriched by this growing body of work but there is further work to be done in relation to crime and victimization, and in relation to the need to recognize the state (and the criminal justice system) as a gendered institution.

## GENDER AND JUSTICE

Much modern research on women and crime has been marked by its engagement with debates from the past. One enduring belief is that women offenders are protected from the full rigours of the law; but a series of concepts which modify the notion of chivalry have been advanced and discussed. These include the notions of double deviance and double jeopardy, of stigma, and of the importance of formal and informal controls in the lives of women. In this section we summarize earlier studies that have noted the importance of such issues. We review the sentencing of women offenders, paying particular attention to the number of studies that have pointed to the stark increase in the rate of women's incarceration as a significant departure from the past. We then draw out the literature on women's prisons and provide an insight into women's experiences of and responses to incarceration. Finally, we provide an overview of some of the more recent changes that have occurred in relation to the way in which the criminal justice system deals with women offenders—since the previous edition of this chapter, there has been a significant shift in Britain towards developing more gender-specific and responsive policy.

## CHIVALRY, DOUBLE DEVIANCE, AND DOUBLE JEOPARDY

Several authors have reviewed and/or researched the respective treatment of women and men by the courts although few offer straightforward support for chivalry or leniency towards women unrelated to offence seriousness (see Gelsthorpe 2001 for an overview of early studies). Allen's study (1987) is perhaps exceptional in suggesting that violent women offenders received more sympathetic and individualized justice for serious crimes than men. Most British researchers point to the complexities in sentencing. Eaton (1986), for instance, noted that men and women conforming to conventional roles were better treated than those such as homosexuals or single mothers, who did not. Carlen (1983) also found that Scottish sheriffs distinguished between 'good' and 'bad' mothers and were prepared to sentence them accordingly. Worrall (1990) discerned a still more complex situation in which various agents and agencies contrived to make female offenders in the system invisible. In the USA, Daly (1989a) found that it was children and the family, rather than women themselves, who were the focus of chivalry, or 'judicial paternalism', as the courts sought to support and conserve the fabric of society. Using a sample of matched pairs, in a study of a New Haven felony court, Daly concluded that men and women were not sentenced differently for like crimes (1994b).

To explore some of the above points further, women's low share of recorded criminality has significant consequences for those women who do offend: they are seen to have transgressed not only social norms but gender norms as well. As a result they may, especially when informal sanctions are taken into account, feel that they are doubly punished. Carlen (1983, 1985) notes the prevalence of informal punishment of women by their partners. Several observers have stressed that concern over the anomalous position of deviant women leads to excessive zeal in their treatment, in remands in custody for reports, and in more medicalized interventions (Heidensohn 1981; Edwards 1984). Steward's (2006) study of remand decisions in London magistrates' courts in the twenty-first century, however, found a more complex and individualized pattern in decision-making. Such approaches are particularly marked towards young girls, whose minor sexual misdemeanours seem consistently to be more harshly handled than those of boys (Webb 1984; Cain 1989; Gelsthorpe and Sharpe 2006). Such bias is not, as Gelsthorpe emphasizes (1989), the sole determining factor in the way young people are handled by agencies, however; other variables, such as organizational features, are important as well. Nevertheless, there is accumulated evidence to suggest that women and their families suffer especially from the stigma associated with deviance (Heidensohn 1996; Condry 2006). Whilst the small number of women in prison continues to be an enduring feature of the criminal justice system (figures for January 2011 indicate that there are 4,125 women and girls in prison compared to 80,330 men; Howard League for Penal Reform 2011), it is the alarming rate of increase in the number of women being imprisoned that has caused much concern among commentators.

## SENTENCING

The numbers of women sentenced to immediate imprisonment in England and Wales grew faster than comparable figures for males for much of the 1990s and into the twenty-first century. Between 1992 and 2002 the average female inmate population grew by over 173 per cent, the male by only 50 per cent (Home Office 2005). In a more recent appraisal, Hedderman (2010) notes an increase of 68 per cent between 1997 and 2008 (from 2,675 to 4,505 women)—this compares to a 35 per cent increase for men during this period. The massive growth of overall rates of imprisonment in both Britain and the USA, despite the decline in recorded crime, has led some analysts to point to a new penality as part of a wider culture of control (Garland 2001: 14) and to seeming punitiveness towards women. It is now common ground between most participants in policy-making and analysis for women offenders that 'the evidence suggests that courts are imposing more severe sentences on women for less serious offences' (Home Office 2004: 3). Hedderman's detailed study of why more women are being sentenced to custody in England and Wales concludes that the changes are not due to changes in offending rates: 'there is little to suggest that female offending....has become more prevalent or more serious' (2004: 86). What has changed, on the other hand, is the custody rate: '40% of the women sentenced in the Crown Court are now being given custodial sentences compared to under a quarter eight years ago...at the magistrates' court....the rate of increase has been higher....custody is now used five times more frequently than in 1992' (op. cit.: 89).

Other research suggests that sentencers are imposing longer prison sentences for serious crimes and are more likely to imprison those appearing before the courts today than 10 years ago (Hough *et al.* 2003). Convictions for drug offences in 1996–7 for example, explain a significant part of the growth in incarceration rates since they attract longer sentences (Woodbridge and Frosztega 1998). More recent examination by Hedderman (2010) identifies an increasing number of women being received into prison on very short sentences (less than six months); 63 per cent of women sentenced to custody received sentences of up to six months compared with less than half (46 per cent) of men.

In contrast, Carlen (1998) uses a series of interviews with prisoners and staff to illustrate her argument that the increases are due to more women falling into the category of social and economic deprivation—a category traditionally more vulnerable to imprisonment, and to an increased punitiveness by the courts to women. Gelsthorpe and Morris, however, are more cautious in their analysis of the reasons for increased penality towards women. They argue that:

> [t]here is some evidence of increased punitiveness because a greater proportion of women are being sentenced to imprisonment and more women are being received into prison for short periods,...although the 'type' of woman imprisoned remains much the same.... However,...there is little evidence of an increased punitiveness solely towards women [2002: 287].

Despite the varied, complex, and at times contradictory explanations presented above, the paradox remains that women's relatively minor offending, and distinctive 'troubled' rather than 'troublesome' status as offenders (Gelsthorpe and Loucks 1997), have led to what is widely seen as a dramatic and extraordinary increase.

## PRISONS FOR WOMEN AND WOMEN IN PRISON

Since the start of incarceration as punishment, women have been subject to broadly the same prison system as men, but with distinctive variations introduced from time to time. Welfare objectives have sometimes been to the fore, especially in the nineteenth century and in relation to women said to be in moral danger. Rafter has catalogued the history of one such institution in the USA and noted how the lofty intentions of its founders led it to becoming additionally repressive of its female inmates who were infantilized by middle-class maternalism (1985). Zedner (1991) describes two schemes in Britain primarily designed for women: diversion from the penal system, care and welfare of offenders, and moral protection. In the first programme from 1898 to 1914, a number of inebriate reformatories for habitual female drunkards were founded, the purpose being 'quite simply, to create of the enfeebled and degraded drunk a model of healthy, domesticated femininity' (ibid.: 237). This initiative was followed by another in which assumptions about female deviance had changed and centred on a switch to 'feeble-mindedness' as a prime cause of female crime and deviance, and, indeed, wider social evils (Simmons 1978). Barton has examined the history of what she terms a 'semi penal institution', one of many, neither formal nor informal, but which 'used ... regulatory methods and disciplinary techniques ... to contain, supervise and control and ... to normalise deviant women back to an acceptable standard of feminine behaviour' (Barton 2005: 3). While her focus is on a church-owned institution, once a refuge for destitute women, latterly a bail hostel for women, she finds continuity with present-day developments and its past history. She found 'a regime that whilst claiming to "empower", actually led to the infantilisation of its residents' (op. cit.: 155).

Such case histories are highly instructive. They show that when women are the subjects of special penal treatment, it frequently results in the development of benevolently repressive regimes which emphasize dependency and traditional femininity and fail to facilitate rehabilitation. Secondly, such programmes tend to be determined by the assumed characteristics and needs of women, rather than well-explored evidence. Such examples are not just historical. The rebuilding of Holloway Prison, London, in the 1970s was based on views about women offenders being physically or mentally sick, or both, and thus needing a therapeutic environment. The case was not proven, and the design of the prison proved unsatisfactory and controversial (RAP 1969; Rock 1996). Several studies of the attempts made in Canada to set up a more woman-centred programme of provision have described their failure (Hannah-Moffat 2001, 2002; Hayman 2006; Shaw 1991). In particular this work exposes the ways in which despite well-intentioned, radical proposals in the Task Force Report on Federally Sentenced Women (1990), women offenders with high treatment needs come to be reclassified as 'high-risk'. Moreover, through a treatment discourse heavily characterized by notions of 'empowerment', women offenders become increasingly 'responsibilized'. Thus it becomes '*their* responsibility to take programmes and to change, and *their* responsibility to take measures seen by *others* as likely to reduce their re-offending' (Shaw and Moffat 2000: 169).

Indeed, Carlen attributes her development of the term 'carceral clawback' (meaning the ideological mechanisms necessary to the existence of the maintenance of prisons) to the inspiration and understanding she gained from this work (Carlen and Worrall 2004: 91). She argued that we should resist the myth that, as a result of feminist-informed reforms, women's prisons were becoming benign places of treatment and rehabilitation. She and many others are particularly concerned about the application of programmes of cognitive skills training, based on male norms and male models, to female prisoners (ibid.; Carlen and Worrall 2004; Hannah-Moffat and Shaw 2000). Since female inmates may be required to complete such programmes despite their lack of fit, they will have poorer outcomes (Hedderman 2004: 241). By contrast, Mason's (2006) study on the development of the Dochas centre in Dublin reports no such problems. Her study shows that despite initial setbacks and ongoing challenges, the underlying aspirations of developing such a gender-specific penal initiative remained intact.

Early women's prison studies reflected dominant themes in relation to studies of men's prisons: the process of prisonization and the existence of inmate subcultures (see Liebling and Crewe, this volume). Certainly much research on prisons for women in the USA has used the now rather dated features of such studies to explore women's reactions—with some interesting findings which point to the salience of sexual and emotional relations in female correctional establishments and the idea that the penal life of women, largely because of their small numbers and restricted provision, was distinctive. Female felons in the USA were said to feel the pains of imprisonment (the loss of family and home) more acutely and therefore set up alternative sexual relationships with one another, or formed 'pseudo families' to replace their missing kin (Ward and Kassebaum 1965; Giallombardo 1966). Several studies found women's commitment to inmate codes to be less than men's (Tittle 1969; Kruttschnitt 1981).

In Scotland, Carlen (1983) found little evidence of inmate solidarity, or indeed the presence of subcultures. One of the paradoxical conclusions of a review of research on female subcultures is that they are weaker and more diffuse than male (Pollock-Byrne 1990) yet, certainly in Britain, women perceive the pains of imprisonment as sharper and react with greater vehemence against them (Heidensohn 1975, 1981; Casale 1989; Mandaraka-Sheppard 1986; Carlen 1985). A higher proportion of women are charged with disciplinary offences, tranquillizers are more frequently prescribed, and there is a significantly greater incidence of self-mutilation (Sim 1990). A new generation of women's prison studies provides both confirmation and challenge to the earlier accounts. Owen's ethnographic study of a Californian women's prison on the whole supports a gendered and importational view of female experiences of imprisonment. She observed three critical areas of life: '(1) negotiating the prison world (2) styles of doing time and [3] involvement in the "mix"' (Owen 1998: 167). The 'mix' comprises a number of problems inside the prison—drugs, homosexuality, fighting. Avoiding trouble meant keeping out of these. Kruttschnitt et al. compared two other women's prisons (CIW and VSP), also in California. While 'how women at CIW talked about their experiences... [had] important similarities, including diverse styles of adaptation, the importance placed on primary group relationships, and the absence of serious violence or racial conflict....women's adaptations at VSP—anomic, suspicious and detached' were quite different (2000: 712). They attributed these differences to the quite distinct institutional features of the two institutions. VSP represented the new, harsher penology, and CIW a historic, maternal, therapeutic culture. Their conclusion is that

> women's adaptations to prison may not be as fundamentally structured by gender in
> many of the ways traditionally assumed... The adaptations described in so many other

studies of women in prison are likely as much or more a product of the nature of women's corrections at a particular time and place as they are a product of the nature of women themselves [ibid.: 713].

Bosworth's (1999) study of power relations in three women's prisons in Britain also found distinctive responses. Her subjects resist the regime imposed on them and construct new identities (see also Barton 2005: 155).

While scholars may differ on how far experience of imprisonment is distinctly gendered, there is a growing policy consensus in Britain that women offenders should be differentially treated. Carlen argues that this is essential because of the nature and the context of female offending: they are already more severely sentenced and subject to a double form of regulation (Carlen 1998: 153). There is also now a convincing evidence base that demonstrates the distinctive and complex vulnerability and underlying needs of women offenders as they enter and progress through the criminal justice system. Research has increasingly pointed to the poor physical and mental health, the social effects of poverty, addictions, and physical and sexual abuse as characteristic of women offenders (Eaton 1993; Carlen and Worrall 2004; Worrall and Gough 2008). Other studies have emphasized women's disadvantage beyond their time in custody. Whilst women have many of the same resettlement needs as men, there are additional factors relating to their caring responsibilities, histories of abuse, and discrimination in the labour market that further compound their vulnerability. It has also been estimated that 18,000 children experience having their mothers sent to prison each year and a third of women in prison are lone parents (Corston 2007). A study by the New Economics Foundation (2008) suggests that when added up, the social, environmental, and economic costs of sending non-violent mothers to prison results in a total of £17 million over 10 years.

Given the awareness of women's complex underlying needs, a concern over the quality of care that women in custody receive has been the focus of various criminological, official, and campaigning studies (HMCIP 1997, HMCIP 2000; Prison Reform Trust 2000; Scottish Executive 2002; Scottish Parliament 2009; Fawcett Society 2004; Corston Report 2007). Prompted by such concern there does appear to be a clear change in direction in the criminal justice response to women offenders over the past decade. This chapter does not permit a full review of the various interventions that have taken place; we therefore encourage readers to consult previous editions of this chapter for a more comprehensive overview of the interventions that have occurred over time.

## WORKING WITH WOMEN OFFENDERS IN THE COMMUNITY

In terms of constructing alternative realities, there has certainly been no shortage of alternative proposals to deal with women offenders ranging from Heidensohn's (1986 and 2010b) identification of two models of justice: Portia (rational, judicial, and masculine) and Persephone (relational, informal, feminine) which broadly reflect

Gilligan's (1982) analysis of gendered morality,[4] to Carlen's (1990) notion of 'a wom-enwise penology' which aims to ensure that penal policy for women does not increase their oppression as women further and that penal policy for men does not brutalize them to the extent that they become more oppressive to women (see also Daly 1989b). These studies, combined, amount to a sophisticated critique of the administration of justice and the structures in which it operates.

The *Women's Offending Reduction Programme* (WORP 2004–7) provides a good starting point from which to make sense of some of the more recent policies aimed at developing more community-based approaches for women offenders. The pro-gramme's action plan outlined two key long-term objectives: reducing women's offending and reducing the number of women in custody. The programme focused on improving community-based services and interventions that were better tailored to the needs of women by encouraging collaboration between government departments and other agencies within the framework of the new National Offender Management Service and the new sentencing powers of the Criminal Justice Act 2003 (Gelsthorpe *at al*. 2007).

More recently, the Corston Report (2007) has brought about a renewed vigour and momentum to the study of women offenders. Critical of previous efforts to address the needs of women offenders, Corston (2007) reported little improvement in their treat-ment and called for a radical change to the way in which women are treated through-out the whole criminal justice system. At the heart of her investigation was a focus on women's distinctive vulnerabilities and their marginalization in a criminal justice system designed largely by men for men. She called for gender-specific understandings and a community-based support system for women. In doing so, she called for a more 'distinct, radically different, visibly-led, strategic, proportionate, holistic and woman-centred, integrated approach' to both women who offend and those at risk of offending (Corston 2007: 79). Instrumental in raising the visibility of the female offender, the Corston Report (2007) has played a key role in developing the greater use of 'normal' community facilities to address the needs of women offenders. Evans and Walklate (2011:6) draw out this significance when they state that:

> In listening to women's voices Corston developed an approach that contextualised women's offending in the wider social and economic circumstances linked to being born a female in late modernity. From this position, women who offend are seen as being subjected to wider social harms inflicted upon them both by social norms and expecta-tions and the structural position of women in society at large. Corston recognized that the effect of these harms, when combined in certain configurations (individual to the woman concerned but generally present for all women) can precipitate crises that propel particular women into behaviour destructive to themselves and those around them.

---

[4] See also Spader's (2002) later work on the morality of justice and the alternative morality of care which similarly draws on Gilligan's work; Spader set out the different conceptions of justice and poses questions about the superiority of the care model, whether it can operate as a separate and equal model or whether elements of the care model might be integrated into the justice model, although she does not come to any clear-cut conclusions. Riley *et al*. (2005) also outline a feminist vision of justice which asserts that interde-pendence, responsibility, respect for and relationship with the environment, and an ethics of care are the foundation for a more reasoned and reasonable practice of justice, although translating these ideas into practice may be another matter.

The Government accepted just over half (25) of Corston's 43 recommendations for change in their entirety and a further 14 in principle or in part (Ministry of Justice 2007). The influence of the Corston Report (2007) is apparent in the setting up of a cross-departmental Criminal Justice Women's Unit to manage and coordinate the work on Corston across all relevant departments, and the establishment of the *National Service Framework: Improving Services to Women Offenders* (2008) which provides a strategy for dealing with women offenders 'at all stages of their journey through the criminal justice system, with the aim of breaking cycles of reoffending and keeping socially excluded women and the risk of offending out of custody' (Ministry of Justice 2008a: 4). Furthermore, the *Offender Management Guide to Working with Women Offenders* (2008) highlights current good practice and provides additional information to offender managers working with women offenders.

## WOMEN-CENTRED APPROACHES

In the last edition of this chapter we noted that strong claims for examples of good practice in England and Wales were being made but that this was more talk of strategy than practice (Scottish Office 1998; Her Majesty's Chief Inspectorate of Prisons (HMCIP) 2000). There has been much movement in this field since then and there is now a growing body of work which supports interventions which are informed by a women-centred approach.

Evaluations of community-based approaches for women offenders indicate that there is much to be optimistic about (see Gelsthorpe *et al.* 2007 for a good overview of community-based provision). In particular, the positive work being carried out at The Asha Women's Centre and 218 Centre[5] was identified by the Home Office in 2005 as a basis for the development of the Together Women Programme (TWP). In March 2005 the Government made available £9.15 million for the development of a one-stop shop provision with linked key workers to facilitate women's access to services in the community. TWP began operating in 2006 and early 2007 at five 'women-only' centres in two areas in England: the North West, and Yorkshire and Humberside National Offender Management Services (NOMS). The main objective of TWP is to offer a one-stop-shop centre providing holistic and individual support packages for women to reduce reoffending, divert women offenders from prosecution and custody, and to divert 'women at risk' of offending from becoming offenders. Services on offer include training on issues such as parenting, managing mental health, life skills, thinking skills, and addressing offending behaviour. This approach is underpinned by the following nine key principles identified by Gelsthorpe *at al.* (2007). Provision for women offenders in the community should:

1. Be women-only to foster safety and a sense of community and to enable staff to develop expertise in work with women.

2. Integrate offenders with non-offenders so as to normalize women offenders' experiences and facilitate a supportive environment for learning.

---

[5] 218 Centre is a community based resource for women offenders in central Glasgow (sponsored by the Scottish Executive).

3. Foster women's empowerment so they gain sufficient self-esteem to directly engage in problem-solving themselves, and feel motivated to seek appropriate employment.

4. Utilize ways of working with women which draw on what is known about their effective learning styles.

5. Take a holistic and practical stance to helping women to address social problems which may be linked to their offending;

6. Facilitate links with mainstream agencies, especially health, debt advice, and counselling.

7. Have the capacity and flexibility to allow women to return to the centre or programme for 'top up' or continued support and development where required.

8. Ensure that women have a supportive milieu or mentor to whom they can turn when they have completed any offending-related programmes, since personal support is likely to be as important as any direct input addressing offending behaviour.

9. Provide women with practical help with transport and childcare so that they can maintain their involvement in the centre or programme.

The work carried out by TWP has received much positive feedback and the service has been commended for providing both practical and emotional support within an 'enabling and empowering' culture (Hedderman *et al.* 2008; Jackson 2009). However, an evaluation of the Together Women (TW) centres (Joliffe *et al.* 2011) did not find robust enough data to draw firm conclusions about 'the impact of TW on "re-offending or other desirable social exclusion outcomes"'. This does not mean that these projects were not successful 'but that [this] cannot be demonstrated by the TW centres'. Such findings are echoed in evaluations of the 218 Centre in Glasgow, where women offenders report a range of positive outcomes, including a reduction in the frequency and seriousness in their offending behaviour, a reduction in substance misuse, and improvements in relationships with family and children (Easton and Matthews 2010)—the authors also report significant cost benefits of such a service.

There have been a number of reinforcing policy developments since then, Ministry of Justice (MOJ) policy frameworks and good practice guides have followed (MoJ 2008a, 2008b). The MOJ has further committed £25 million to voluntary organizations to take the lead with statutory agencies to provide extra and enhanced community support for women at risk of offending. Building on the Conditional Caution, September 2008 saw the development of a new condition in England and Wales aimed at low-level, low-risk women offenders, known as the 'women specific condition' (WSC). The WSC is a conditional caution where there is a rehabilitative condition requiring the woman offender to attend a TWP centre for a 'needs assessment'. Whilst the evaluators of this programme outline a number of positive changes in women offenders' lives, they also express some concern over the capacity of the agencies involved (the police, CPS, and TWP) to work together effectively. They also note the potential punitive effects of such women-centred reform for some women (Easton *et al.* 2010).

## NET-WIDENING/UP-TARIFFING

One of the key concerns identified by those seeking to divert women away from custody is the extent to which diversionary strategies actually result in drawing more women into the criminal justice system. Indeed one of the perennial problems associated with diversion strategies is that they can lead to net-widening or up-tariffing. Evidence of up-tariffing has been cited in studies examining the introduction of conditional cautions and conditional bail (Blakeborough *et al.* 2007; Brown 1998; Hucklesby 2001). Easton *et al.*'s study (2010) suggests that WSCs had been issued to women offenders who might otherwise have only received a simple caution. A further concern of such initiatives is the suggestion that women could easily end up in prison if found breaching a community order/conditional caution (Hedderman 2010; Easton *et al.* 2010). Such outcomes were also reported in relation to girls by the Youth Justice Board (2009)—figures show the number of young girls being sentenced for breaching a statutory order increased by 38 per cent between 2004/5 and 2007/8.

Despite Scotland's commitment to reducing the number of women in prison, Burman and Batchelor (2009) point to a worsening situation in which the female prison population (all ages) increased by 87 per cent, whereas the male prison population increased by 20 per cent between 1998/99 and 2007/8. An alternative account of the situation in Scotland can be found in the work of Easton and Matthews (2010). They note that while the numbers of women over 21 sentenced to prison had significantly increased across Scotland as a whole, Glasgow City had seen a reduction of nearly 25 per cent of women sentenced to prison. There has also been a significant reduction in the rate at which women are sentenced to prison in Glasgow as a proportion of the total in Scotland—from 33 per cent in 1998/9 to 13 per cent in 2008/9. Easton and Matthews (2010:64) point out that:

> While it is not possible to attribute such changes in sentencing to the presence of the 218 Service alone, it is significant that the rate of imprisonment of women offenders in Glasgow has not increased at the same rate as that for Scotland as a whole and has in fact resisted a wider international trend over a sustained period.

Studies have also been critical of gender-specific initiatives for treating women offenders as a homogenous group. A recent HM Inspectorate Report (Scottish Government 2009) has re-emphasized the unfavourable facilities and opportunities available to young women when compared to their male counterparts. With Scottish youth criminal justice policy aimed primarily at boys and gender-specific programmes aimed at adult women, Burman and Batchelor (2009) conclude that girls and young women 'fall between two stools' and remain the 'forgotten few'. Not only are girls absent from the focus of gender-specific programmes but there is evidence to suggest that more girls than ever are now subject to greater intervention. Sharpe (2009) reasserts Chesney-Lind and Irwin's (2008) notion of a 'protective-punitive confluence' to characterize the increase of girls in the youth justice system when she states that '[i]n the third millennium, rather than one paradigm displacing the other, "welfare" and "justice" or responsibilization explanations and practices co-exist' (Sharpe 2009: 265–6). Furthermore, the growing body of literature that situates girls and women's pathways into crime in the context of their experience of victimization has not translated down into how offending girls are perceived. Sharpe (2009) notes that only 26 per cent of professionals interviewed suggested that girls' offending might be a consequence of their experience of abuse. Rather, whilst acknowledging that a large number of young offenders (both boys and girls) had been abused, professionals 'rejected the notion that this might be a gendered phenomenon' (ibid.: 258). In explaining these views, Sharpe suggests that '[s]uch views arise in part from a misplaced concern about "equal opportunities", whereby to highlight a characteristic or need as being distinct to, or more prevalent amongst, girls was believed to constitute discrimination against *boys*' (ibid.: 258).

## EMPOWERMENT

In addition to concerns about net-widening and up-tariffing, the notion of 'empower-ment' as a guiding principle of women-centred policy has also come under increas-ing scrutiny in recent years. The contradictions inherent in the idea of empowering women whilst they are in prison have been well rehearsed elsewhere (Hannah-Moffat 2001; Pollack and Kendall 2005). Pollack's more recent paper provides (2010) an inter-esting discussion of the relationship between empowerment and debates about 'risk'. In applying this premise to women offenders, she argues that the:

> [c]onnections between risk and empowerment take on a particular gendered form across the penal-welfare system. The interpretive frame of dependency and self-esteem is used to construct women involved with welfare and penal systems as in need of empowerment (generally in the form of therapy) (Pollack 2010: 1268).

Whilst it may seem counterintuitive to suggest that the provision of such women-centred services are not empowering for women offenders, the reality may not be as straightforward as it first appears. Easton *et al.* (2010) explain this paradox when they note that whilst it may be the case that the increased requirement to engage with sup-port services over a period of time may result in an overall positive benefit on women offenders' lives, the WSC was not intended to require women offenders to engage with support but rather to encourage their voluntary engagement. Despite the voluntary nature of engagement with the support services on offer at TWP, some women offend-ers in their study expressed the 'coercive' element of such support; indeed there was also some misunderstanding among practitioners regarding the conditions of support being offered. Such a situation is echoed in Pollack's (2010: 1275) study of women in prison in which she argues that women are 'often required to "perform empowerment" in order to gain access to parole, passes and programming'. In this way '[m]andated empowerment is a contradiction in terms' (ibid.: 1273). On a more practical note it is also worth remembering that those women offenders with the gravest need of support might not be best positioned to be empowered, as Easton *et al.* (2010: 29) argue:

> [i]t is important to recognise that women offenders often have "multiple presenting prob-lems" which may make it difficult for them to make empowered decisions (particularly while in police custody) or for them to attend support services.

It is difficult to offer a definitive commentary on the effects of such women-centred initia-tives listed above, not least because of the very real methodological difficulties encoun-tered by researchers. There appears a consensus among researchers that the small number of women offenders involved in such initiatives, coupled with the lack of a control group, inconsistent 'outcome' measures, and a variation in the data collection mechanisms across agencies, remain key obstacles to developing any robust conclusions (Loucks *et al.* 2006; Hedderman *et al.* 2008; Easton *et al.* 2010; Easton and Matthews 2010).

## CONCLUDING THOUGHTS

'The study of gender and crime has become one of the strongest and most enduring areas in criminology' (Heidensohn forthcoming). There is evidence of striking achievements in both research and public policy. Female offenders now attract serious, if not always welcome attention (Snider 2003). Notions of gender are no longer as simplistic nor as taken for granted as they once were; women's experiences of criminal justice have been extensively studied and some concerns addressed (ibid.).

Progress has not been entirely smooth, of course. Whilst gender perspectives and feminist issues have formed part of the cutting edge of criminology in recent years, it is striking that there is still sometimes a need to press the case for women's experiences not to be forgotten or marginalized, and for men's subjectivities to be recognized—we need to raise at least as many points about what happens to men, especially if they are young and poor, and come from minorities, as we do about women. There are awakenings in some quarters of criminology and this is reflected in theory, research, teaching, and policy developments. In other quarters, there is 'selective deafness'.

Earlier editions of this chapter have expressed both pessimism and optimism with regard to the impact of feminist perspectives and the attention to gender more generally. At the same time lively feminist debates and intellectual advances in criminology abound in the Women's Division of the American Society of Criminology (the ASC) and in the recent launch of the Women and Crime and Criminal Justice network as part of the British Society of Criminology (the BSC). The journal *Feminist Criminology* is continuing evidence of intellectual interest and scholarship.

There remain gaps and limitations: giving priority to gender over race and class in feminist approaches, is undoubtedly a valid one. Writers have, however, acknowledged this tendency in constructive ways (see Daly and Stephenson 1995). Moreover, we have indicated that some of the important theoretical developments regarding 'doing gender' include race and class issues (Jefferson 1997; Miller 2001). Contributors to Daly and Maher's (1998) review of the crossroads and intersections of criminology and feminist work on crime and justice highlight these themes too. Chesney-Lind (2006) and Burgess-Proctor (2006) enjoin others in recognizing that proper treatment of the race, gender, punishment nexus is critical to the development of feminist criminology. It is also fair to say that Rafter and Heidensohn (1995) present *International Feminist Perspectives* as a genuine attempt to contribute to our understanding of such issues.

There is also evidence of an impact of feminism on criminological research, policy, and practice (see, for instance, Lacey 2001; ESRC Violence Programme 1998; Prison Reform Trust 2000), at least in the kinds of questions asked, if not in the end result. It is notable that the same questions have to be rehearsed time and time again, but it is also heartening that there is currently a Home Office gender network involving academics as well as policy-makers and practitioners from statutory and voluntary agencies (Fawcett Society 2009).

The need for a 'gender conscious', 'feminist' visible, and strategic leadership has been identified as pivotal in driving forward successful reform agendas (Silvestri 2003). Referred to as 'femocrats' (Sawer 1995) such individuals are concerned with putting women's concerns centre stage on both policy and governmental agendas. Recent years have seen some important inroads being made here. The former government established a cross-departmental criminal justice women's unit to manage and coordinate the work on Corston across all relevant departments at an official level; and an Inter-Ministerial Subgroup was established to progress Corston's recommendations. With a key role in the Government Equalities Office during 2008–10, the then minister of state, Maria Eagle, appears to have shown a genuine interest in translating Corston's aspirations (Evans and Walklate 2011). A number of Criminal Justice 'Champions' have also been identified with a key role to promote and increase gender awareness in policy and practice. Such an approach is also evident in Scotland where a commitment has been made to create a *Women Offenders Forum* to provide strategic leadership, monitoring, and evaluation in relation to women offenders. Though powerful in presence, Evans and Walklate (2011) emphasize the self-limiting nature of such advocates when they argue that change can only be achieved within the context of existing government culture, ideology, and rhetoric.

The previous edition of this chapter was written under a New Labour Government, and whilst some have been critical of New Labour policy of 'doing too little, too late' for women offenders, there is little doubt that at the end of their term in office, much had been done to deal more effectively with the social exclusion needs of women offenders (Hedderman 2010; Evans and Walklate 2011). The capacity to develop such positive activism through a continued focus on gender however is increasingly questionable given the advent of the new Coalition (Conservative/Liberal Democrat) government in May 2010. We have already noted Carlen's concept of 'carceral clawback' in relation to women's imprisonment— the concept is also useful when thinking about recent moves to more community-based interventions. Carlen (2002) argued that non-custodial projects were also vulnerable to 'carceral clawback, to the extent that they were dependent on state funding and accreditation and therefore warned of the need to be vigilant that the woman-centred principles are not compromised by the demands of contemporary penal policy' (Worrall and Gelsthorpe 2009: 336). The extent to which the Coalition Government will be able to demonstrate a commitment (financial or otherwise) remains to be seen but a healthy dose of realism may be warranted here. The possibility of sustaining funding for such women-focused services looks increasingly bleak.

Despite such forecasts, some commentators have drawn out some optimism regarding the possible outcomes. Evans and Walklate (2011:11) for example note the potential opportunities presented under such a government when they state that:

> As the public spending review takes a grip, it is always possible, that the community alternatives proposed by Corston, could be the means to which both politicians and policy-makers (it will need the like mindedness of both groups) turn in order to manage female offending. This turn, of course, will not be generated from within the ethos of holism that featured so strongly in Corston, but will be driven instead by cost-effectiveness. This may be an unintended consequence of the present financial crisis, of that there is no doubt, but it is a consequence that may be possible, and which could result in some benefits for those female offenders for whom at present the penal response does very little.

It is remarkable to be able to record that a chapter on gender and crime which was, in the first edition of this *Handbook*, a comparative innovation, and included a number of cautious statements has survived in various forms into the fifth and, we would insist, is highly likely to continue to do so. The reasons are basically the same as they were in the foundational texts in this subject: the relatively modest female share of recorded crime is still an intellectually interesting and policy relevant topic to study. Doing so, as has been done with increasing success and impact over the intervening decades, has produced some of the most lively and important work in criminology. There remains much to explore and more and better concepts are needed to do so, but we have no doubt that this can be done.

## ■ SELECTED FURTHER READING

For further coverage on some of the topics in this chapter see S. Walklate (2004), *Gender, Crime and Criminal Justice* (Cullompton, Devon: Willan). For those new to the study of gender and crime, see M. Silvestri and C. Crowther-Dowey (2008), *Gender and Crime* (London: Sage) for an overview of both women and men's experiences of the criminal justice system—it also offers an insight into the potential of a human rights agenda for the study of gender and crime. See also K. Evans and J. Jamieson (2008) (eds), *Gender and Crime: A Reader* (Open University Press) for an overview of a range of classic and groundbreaking studies, key contributions, and debates. For some cross-cultural information see *The Encyclopedia of Women and Crime* (Phoenix, Ariz.: Onyx Press, 2000) edited by N. H. Rafter. For an overview of working with women offenders in the community see R. Sheehan, G. McIvor, and C. Trotter (eds) (2010), *Working with Women Offenders in the Community* (Routledge).

In relation to feminism and criminology, L. Gelsthorpe and A. Morris (eds) (1990), *Feminist Perspectives in Criminology* (Buckingham: Open University Press), and N. H. Rafter and F. M. Heidensohn (eds) (1995), *International Feminist Perspectives in Criminology* (Buckingham: Open University Press) cover the broad feminist critique of criminology and its theoretical parameters. F. Heidensohn (ed.) (2006), *Gender and Justice* (Cullompton, Devon: Willan) provides a collection of essays which reflect research and theory.

For gender theory relating to masculinities, see R. Connell (2002), *Gender* (Cambridge: Polity) and M. Mac an Ghaill and C. Haywood (2003), *Men and Masculinities* (Buckingham: Open University Press). In relation to masculinity and criminology, see I. Newburn and E. Stanko (eds) (1994), *Just Boys Doing Business* (London: Routledge), R. Collier (1998), *Masculinities, Crime and Criminology* (London: Sage), and S. Tomsen (ed) (2008), *Crime, Criminal Justice and Masculinities* (Ashgate).

Useful websites for information about women and criminal justice:

Fawcett Society: www.fawcettsociety.org.uk

Women in Prison: www.womeninprison.org.uk

Home Office/ Research Development, Statistics www.homeoffice.gov.uk/rds/

Ministry of Justice: www.justice.gov.uk/ (see for details of section 95 Statistics on Women and the Criminal Justice System and a range of reports on women offenders).

Scottish Centre for Crime and Justice Research: www.sccjr.ac.uk/

US Bureau of Justice http://bjs.ojp.usdoj.gov/

Key online journals:

*Women and Criminal Justice* website:

http://www.tandf.co.uk/journals/titles/08974454.asp

*Feminist Criminology* website:

http://fcx.sagepub.com/

# ■ REFERENCES

ADLER, F. (1975), *Sisters in Crime*, New York: McGraw Hill.

ALDER, C. and WORRALL, A. (eds) (2004), *Girls' Violence*, New York: State University of New York Press.

ALLEN, H. (1987), *Justice Unbalanced: Gender, Psychiatry and Judicial Decisions*, Milton Keynes: Open University Press.

ALLEYNE, R. (2008), 'Binge-drinking Blamed for Rise in Girl Violence', *Daily Telegraph*, 15 May.

ANDERSON, K. and UMBERSON, D. (2001), 'Gendering Violence: Masculinity and Power in Men's Accounts of Domestic Violence', *Gender & Society* 15(3): 358–80.

ARNOT, M. and USBORNE, C. (eds) (1999), *Gender and Crime in Modern Europe*, London: UCL Press.

BARTON A. (2005), *Fragile Moralities and Dangerous Sexualities*, Aldershot: Ashgate.

BEATTIE, J. (1975), 'The Criminality of Women in Eighteenth Century England', *Journal of Social History*, 8: 80–116.

BEIJERSE, J. and SWAANINGEN, R. (2006), 'The Netherlands: Penal-welfarism and Risk Management', in J. Muncie and B. Goldson (eds), *Comparative Youth Justice*, London: Sage.

BEIRNE, P. and MESSERSCHMIDT, J. (2007), *Criminology*, 4th edn, Oxford: Oxford University Press.

BOSWORTH, M. (1999), *Engendering Resistance: Agency and Power in Women's Prisons*, Aldershot: Ashgate.

BROWN, J. and HEIDENSOHN, F. (2000), *Gender and Policing*, Basingstoke: Macmillan/Palgrave.

BRUNSON, R. K. and STEWART, E. (2006), 'Young African American Women, the Street Code, and Violence: An Exploratory Analysis', *Journal of Crime & Justice* 29(1): 1–19.

BURGESS-PROCTOR, A. (2006), 'Intersections of Race, Class, Gender and Crime', *Feminist Criminology*, 1(1): 27–47.

BURMAN, M. (2004a), 'Turbulent Talk: Girls' Making Sense of Violence', in C. Alder and A. Worrall (eds), *Girls' Violence*, New York: SUNY Press.

—— (2004b), 'Breaking the Mould: Patterns of Female Offending', in G. McIvor (ed), *Women Who Offend*, London: Jessica Kingsley.

—— (2009), Breaking the Mould? Patterns of Female offending', in G. McIvor (ed.), *Women who Offend*. London: Jessica Kingsley.

——, BATCHELOR, S., and BROWN, J. (2001), 'Researching Girls and Violence: Tracing the Dilemmas of Fieldwork', *British Journal of Criminology*, 41(3): 443–59.

—— BATCHELOR, S. A. (2009), 'Between Two Stools: Responding to Young Women who Offend', *Youth Justice*, 9(3): 270–85.

BENNETT, T. and HOLLOWAY, K. (2004), 'Gang Membership, Drugs and Crime in the UK', *British Journal of Criminology*, 44(3): 305–23.

BLAKEBOROUGH, L., PIERPOINT, H., BENNETT, T., MAGUIRE, M., PINTO, C., WREFORD, L., and SMITH, D. (2007), *Conditional Cautions: An examination of the early implementation of the scheme*, Research Summary 7, London: Ministry of Justice.

BROWN, D. (1998), *Offending on bail and police use of conditional bail*, Home Office Research Findings 72, London: Home Office.

CAIN, M. (1989), *Growing Up Good. Policing the Behaviour of Girls in Europe*, London: Sage.

CARLEN, P. (1983), *Women's Imprisonment*, London: Routledge & Kegan Paul.

—— (1985), *Criminal Women*, Oxford: Polity Press.

—— (1990), *Alternatives to Women's Imprisonment*, Buckingham: Open University Press.

—— (1998), *Sledgehammer*, Basingstoke: Macmillan/Palgrave.

—— (ed.) (2002), *Women and Punishment: The Struggle for Justice*, Cullompton, Devon: Willan.

—— and WORRALL, A. (eds) (2004), *Analysing Women's Imprisonment*, Cullompton, Devon: Willan.

CARRIER, J. (1988), *The Campaign for the Employment of Women as Police Officers*, Aldershot: Gower.

CARRINGTON, K. (2006), 'Does Feminism Spoil Girls? Explanations for Official Rises in Female Delinquency', *The Australian and New Zealand Journal of Criminology*, 39(1): 34–53.

CASALE, S. (1989), *Women Inside. The Experience of Women Remand Prisoners in Holloway*, London: Civil Liberties Trust.

CHAN, J. (1996), 'Changing Police Culture', *British Journal of Criminology*, 36: 109–34.

—— (1997), *Changing Police Culture*, Cambridge: Cambridge University Press.

CHAN, J., DORAN, S., and MAREL, C. (2010), 'Doing and undoing gender in policing', *Theoretical Criminology*, 14(4), 425–46.

CHESNEY-LIND, M. (2006), 'Patriarchy, Crime, and Justice: Feminist Criminology in an Era of Backlash', *Feminist Criminology*, 1(1): 6–26.

CHESNEY-LIND, M. and BELKNAP, J. (2004), 'Trends in Delinquent Girls; Aggression and Violent Behavior', in M. Putallaz and K. L. Bierman (eds) (2004), *Aggression, Anti-Social Behaviour and Violence among Girls*, New York: Guilford.

—— and IRWIN, K. (2008), *Beyond Bad Girls: Gender, Violence and Hype*, New York: Routledge.

CLOUT, L. (2008), 'Violent Women: Binge Drinking Culture Fuels Rise in Attacks by Women', *The Telegraph*, 31 July 2008.

COBBINA, J. E., LIKE-HAISLIP, T., and MILLER, J. (2010), 'Gang Fights versus Cat Fights: Urban Young Men's Gendered Narratives of Violence', *Deviant Behavior*, 31(7): 596–624.

COLLIER, R. (1998), *Masculinities, Crime and Criminology*, London: Sage.

CONDRY, R. (2006), 'Stigmatised Women: Relatives of Serious Offenders and the Broader Impact of

Crime', in F. Heidensohn (ed.), *Gender and Justice: New Concepts and Approaches*, Cullompton, Devon: Willan.

CONNELL, R. (1995), *Masculinities*, Cambridge: Polity Press.

—— and MESSERSCHMIDT, J. (2005), 'Hegemonic Masculinity. Rethinking the concept', *Gender and Society*, 19(6): 829–59.

CORSTON, J. (2007), *The Corston Report: A Review of Women with Particular Vulnerabilities in the Criminal Justice System*, London: Home Office.

—— (2011), *Second Report on Women with Particular Vulnerabilities in the Criminal Justice System*, London: Home Office.

DALY, K. (1989a), 'Rethinking Judicial Paternalism: Gender, Work-Family Relations and Sentencing', *Gender and Society*, 3(1): 9–36.

—— (1989b), 'Criminal Justice Ideologies and Practices in Different Voices: Some Feminist Questions about Justice', *International Journal of the Sociology of Law*, 17: 1–18.

—— (1994a), 'Criminal Law and Justice System Practices as Racist, White and Racialised', *Washington and Lee Law Review*, 15(2): 431–64.

—— (1994b), *Gender, Crime and Punishment*, New Haven: Yale University Press.

—— (1997), 'Different Ways of Conceptualizing Sex/Gender in Feminist Theory and Their Implications for Criminology', *Theoretical Criminology*, 1(1): 25–51.

—— and CHESNEY-LIND, M. (1988), 'Feminism and Criminology', *Justice Quarterly*, 5(4): 498–538.

—— and MAHER, L. (1998), *Criminology at the Crossroads. Feminist Readings In Crime and Justice*, Oxford: Oxford University Press.

—— and STEPHENSON, D. (1995), 'The "Dark Figure" of Criminology: Toward a Black and Multi-Ethnic Feminist Agenda for Theory and Research', in N. Rafter and F. Heidensohn (eds), *International Feminist Perspectives in Criminology*, Buckingham: Open University Press.

DAVIES, A. (1999), '"These Viragoes are No Less Cruel Than the Lads": Young Women, Gangs and Violence in Late Victorian Manchester and Salford', *British Journal of Criminology*, 39(1): 72–89.

DINGWALL, G. (2005), *Alcohol and Crime*, Cullompton: Willan Publishing.

EASTON, H. and MATTHEWS, R. (2010), *Evaluation of the 218 Service: Examining Implementation and Outcomes*, Scottish Government Research Office.

EASTON, H., SILVESTRI, M., EVANS, K., MATTHEWS, R., and WALKLATE, S. (2010), 'Conditional cautions: Evaluation of the women specific condition pilot', *Ministry of Justice Research Series 14/10*.

EATON, M. (1986), *Justice for Women?*, Milton Keynes: Open University Press.

—— (1993), *Women After Prison*. Buckingham: Open University Press.

ECONOMIC and SOCIAL RESEARCH COUNCIL (ESRC) (1998), *Research Programme on Violence*, Swindon: ESRC.

EDWARDS, S. (1984), *Women on Trial*, Manchester: Manchester University Press.

EVANS, K. and JAMIESON, J. (2008), *Gender and Crime; A Reader*, Open University Press.

EVANS, K. and WALKLATE, S. (2011), 'The Corston Report: Reading even further between the lines', *Prison Service Journal*, March No. 194: 6–11.

FAWCETT SOCIETY (2004), *Commission on Women and the Criminal Justice System*, London: Fawcett Society.

—— (2006), *Gender and Justice Policy Network* (minutes of meetings), London: Fawcett Society.

—— (2009), Engendering Justice—from Policy to Practice, *Final report of the Commission on Women and the Criminal Justice System*, London: Fawcett Society.

FEELEY, M. and LITTLE, D. (1991), 'The Vanishing Female: The Decline of Women in the Criminal Process, 1687–1912', *Law and Society Review*, 25(4): 719–57.

FEINMAN, C. (1986), *Women in the Criminal Justice System*, New York: Praeger.

GADD, D. (2003), 'Reading between the Lines: Subjectivity & Men's Violence', *Men and Masculinities*, 5(3): 1–22.

—— and FARRALL, S. (2004), 'Criminal Careers, Desistance and Subjectivity: Interpreting Men's Narratives of Change', *Theoretical Criminology*, 8(2): 123–56.

GARLAND, D. (2001), *The Culture of Control*, Oxford: Oxford University Press.

GELSTHORPE, L. (1989), *Sexism and the Female Offender, An Organizational Analysis*, Aldershot: Gower

—— (1990), 'Feminist Methodologies in Criminology: A New Approach or Old Wine in New Bottles?', in L. Gelsthorpe and A. Morris (eds), *Feminist Perspectives in Criminology*, Buckingham: Open University Press.

—— (2001), 'Critical Decisions and Processes in the Criminal Courts', in E. McLaughlin and J. Muncie (eds), *Controlling Crime*, 2nd edn, London: Sage.

—— (2004), 'Female Offending: A Theoretical Overview', in G. McIvor (ed.), *Women Who Offend*, London: Jessica Kingsley.

—— (2010), 'Women, Crime & Control', *Criminology & Criminal Justice*, 10: 375–86.

—— and LOUCKS, N. (1997), 'Magistrates' Explanations of Sentencing Decisions', in C. Hedderman and L. Gelsthorpe (eds), *Understanding the Sentencing of Women*, Home Office Research Study 170, London: Home Office.

—— and MORRIS, A. (eds) (1990), *Feminist Perspectives in Criminology*, Buckingham: Open University Press.

—— and MORRIS, A. (2002), 'Women's Imprisonment in England and Wales in the 1990s: A Penal Paradox', *Criminal Justice*, 2(3): 277–301.

GELSTHORPE, L. and SHARPE, G. (2006), 'Gender, Youth Crime and Justice', in B. Goldson and J. Muncie (eds), *Youth Crime and Justice*, London: Sage.

GELSTHORPE, L., SHARPE, G., and ROBERTS, J. (2007), *Provision for Women Offenders in the Community*, London: Fawcett Society.

GEOGHEGAN, T. (2008), 'Why are Girls Fighting like Boys?', *BBC News Magazine*, 5 May 2008.

GIALLOMBARDO, R. (1966), *Society of Women: A Study of a Women's Prison*, New York: Wiley.

GILLIGAN, C. (1982), *In a Different Voice*, Cambridge, Mass.: Harvard University Press.

GODFREY, B. (1999), 'Workplace Appropriation and the Gendering of Factory "Law": West Yorkshire, 1840–80', in M. Arnot and C. Usborne (eds), *Gender and Crime in Modern Europe*, London: UCL Press.

—— (2004), 'Rough Girls, 1880–1930: The "Recent" History of Violent Young Women', in C. Alder and A. Worrall (eds), *Girls' Violence: Myths and Realities*, Albany: State University of New York Press.

GROSZ, E. (1987), 'Feminist Theory and the Challenge to Knowledge', *Women's Studies International Forum*, 10(5): 208–17.

HALES, J., NEVILL, C., PUDNEY, S., and TIPPING, S. (2009), *Longitudinal analysis of the Offending, Crime and Justice Survey 2003–06*, Home Office Research Report 19. http://rds.homeoffice.gov.uk/rds/pdfs09/horr19c.pdf.

HALL, S. and WINLOW, S. (2005), 'Anti-nirvana: Crime, culture and instrumentalism in the age of insecurity, *Crime, Media, Culture*, 1(1): 31–48.

HALLSWORTH, S. (2005), *Street Crime*, Cullompton: Willan.

HAND. T. and DODD, L. (2009), 'Arrests and Detentions', in D. Povey and K. Smith (eds), *Police Powers and Procedures England and Wales 2007/08*. Home Office Statistical Bulletin 07/09, London: Home Office.

HANNAH-MOFFAT, K. (2001), *Punishment in Disguise. Penal Governance and Federal Imprisonment of Women in Canada*, Toronto: University of Toronto Press.

—— (2002), 'Creating Choices? Reflecting on the Choices', in P. Carlen (ed.), *Women and the Struggle for Justice*, Cullompton, Devon: Willan.

—— and SHAW, M. (2000), 'Thinking about Cognitive Skills? Think Again!', *Criminal Justice Matters*, 39: 8–9.

HAYMAN, S. (2006), 'The Reforming Prison: A Canadian Tale', in F. Heidensohn (ed.), *Gender and Justice: New Perspectives*, Cullompton, Devon: Willan.

HEDDERMAN, C. (2004), 'Why are More Women Being Sentenced to Custody?', in G. McIvor (ed.), *Women Who Offend*, London: Jessica Kingsley.

—— (2010), 'Government policy on women offenders: Labour's legacy and the Coalition's challenge', *Punishment and Society*, 12(4) 485–500.

HEDDERMAN, C., PALMER, E., and HOLLIN, C. (2008), *Implementing Services for Women Offenders and Those 'At Risk' of Offending: Action Research with Together Women*, Ministry of Justice Research Series 12/08, London: Ministry of Justice.

HEIDENSOHN, F. (1975), 'The Imprisonment of Females', in S. McConville (ed.), *The Use of Imprisonment*, London: Routledge & Kegan Paul.

—— (1981), 'Women and the Penal System', in A. Morris and L. Gelsthorpe (eds), *Women and Crime*, Cambridge: Cropwood Conference Series 13.

—— (1985), *Women and Crime*, London: Macmillan.

—— (1986), 'Models of Justice: Portia or Persephone? Some Thoughts on Equality, Fairness and Gender in the Field of Criminal Justice', *International Journal of Sociology of Law*, 14: 287–98.

—— (1992), *Women in Control? The Role of Women in Law Enforcement*, Oxford: Oxford University Press.

—— (1994), 'From Being to Knowing: Some Reflections on the Study of Gender in Contemporary Society', *Women and Criminal Justice*, 6(1): 13–37.

—— (1996), *Women and Crime*, 2nd edn, Basingstoke: Macmillan.

—— (2000), *Sexual Politics and Social Control*, Buckingham: Open University Press.

—— (2002), 'Gender and Crime', in M. Maguire, R. Morgan, and R. Reiner (eds), Oxford Handbook of Criminology, 3rd edn, Oxford: Clarendon Press.

—— (2003), 'Gender and Policing', in T. Newburn (ed), *Handbook of Policing*, Cullompton, Devon: Willan.

—— (2006) (ed), *Gender and Justice: New Concepts and Approaches*, Cullompton, Devon: Willan.

—— (2010a), 'On writing "The Deviance of Women": observations and analysis', *British Journal of Sociology*, Vol. 61, Virtual Issue.

—— (2010b), 'Women Offenders in the Criminal Justice System: Cinderella, Portia or Persephone?', 2010 Frank Dawtry Memorial Lecture, University of Leeds, 8 December.

HER MAJESTY'S CHIEF INSPECTORATE OF PRISONS (HMCIP) (1997), *Women in Prison: A Thematic Review*, London: Home Office.

—— (2000), *An Unannounced Follow-up Inspection of HM Prison Holloway*, London: Home Office.

HEIMER, K., LAURITSEN, J. L, and LYNCH, J. P. (2009), 'The National Crime Victimisation and the Gender Gap in Offending: Redux', *Criminology*, 47(2): 427–37.

HOBBS, D., HADFIELD, P., LISTER, S., and WILLOW, S. (2003), *Bouncers*, Oxford: Oxford University Press.

HOME OFFICE (2003), *Statistics on Women and the Criminal Justice System, Section 95 Report*, London: Home Office.

—— (2004), *Statistics on Women and the Criminal Justice System, Section 95 Report*, London: Home Office.

—— (2005), *Statistics on Women and the Criminal Justice System, Section 95 Report*, London: Home Office.

HOUGH, M., JACOBSON, J., and MILLIE, A. (2003), *The Decision to Imprison: Sentencing and the Prison Population*, London: Prison Reform Trust.

HOWARD LEAGUE FOR PENAL REFORM (2011), Weekly Prison Watch http://www.howardleague.org/women.

HUCKLESBY, A. (2001), 'Police bail and the use of conditions', *Criminal Justice*, 1(4): 441–63.

JACKSON, M. (2009), *Together Women Project. Key lessons learned to date*, Report, London: Ministry of Justice.

JEFFERSON, T. (1997), 'Masculinities and Crimes', in M. Maguire, R. Morgan, and R. Reiner (eds), *Oxford Handbook of Criminology*, 2nd edn, Oxford: Clarendon Press.

—— (2002), 'Subordinating Hegemonic Masculinity', *Theoretical Criminology*, 6(1): 63–88.

JEWKES, Y. (2004), *Media and Crime*, London: Sage.

JOLLIFFE, D., HEDDERMAN, C., PALMER, E., and HOLLIN, C. (2011), *Re-offending Analysis of Women Offenders Referred to Together Women (TW)*, Ministry of Justice Research Series 11/11.

JONES, S. (1986), *Policewomen and Equality*, London: Macmillan.

KING, P. (1999), 'Gender, Crime and Justice in Late Eighteenth Century and Early Nineteenth Century England', in M. Arnot and C. Usborne (eds), *Gender and Crime in Modern Europe*, London: UCL Press.

KRUTTSCHNITT, C. (1981), 'Prison Codes, Inmate Solidarity and Women: A Re-examination', in M. Warren (ed.), *Comparing Female and Male Offenders*, Newbury Park, Cal.: Sage.

——, GARTNER, R , and MILLER, A. (2000), 'Doing Her Own Time? Women's Response to Prison in the Context of the Old and the New Penology', *Criminology*, 30(3): 681–717.

LACEY, N. (2001), 'Beset by Boundaries. The Home Office Review of Sex Offences', *Criminal Law Review*, January: 3–14.

LANGTON, L. (2010), 'Women in Law Enforcement, 1987–2008', *Bureau of Justice Statistics*, NCJ 230521, Washington DC.

LAURITSEN, J. L., HEIMER, K., and LYNCH J. P (2009), 'Trends in the Gender Gap In Violence: Re-evaluating NCVS and Other Evidence', *Criminology*, 47(2): 361–400.

LEONARD, E. (1982), *Women, Crime and Society: a Critique of Criminology Theory*, New York: Longman.

LOFTUS, B. (2008), 'Dominant Culture Interrupted', *British Journal of Criminology*, (48): 756–77.

LOPEZ, V., JURIK, N., and GILLIARD-MATTHEWS, S, (2009), 'Gender, Sexuality, Power and Drug Acquisition Strategies Among Adolescent Girls Who Use Meth', *Feminist Criminology*, 4(3): 226–51.

LOUCKS, N., MALLOCH, M., MCIVOR, G., and GELSTHORPE, L. (2006), *Evaluation of the 218 Centre*, Edinburgh: Scottish Executive Justice Department.

MACASKILL, M. (2004), ' "Ladettes" on Crime Spree', *The Times*, 2 May 2004.

MCLYNN, F. (1989), *Crime and Punishment in the Eighteenth Century*, Oxford: Oxford University Press.

MAGUIRE, M., MORGAN, R., and REINER, R. (eds) (1994; 1997; 2002), *Oxford Handbook of Criminology*, Oxford: Clarendon Press.

MAHER, L. (1997), *Sexed Work*, Oxford: Oxford University Press.

MANDARAKA-SHEPPARD, A. (1986), *The Dynamics of Aggression in Women's Prisons in England*, Aldershot: Gower.

MARTIN, S. and JURIK, N. (1996), *Doing Justice, Doing Gender*, Thousand Oaks, Cal.: Sage.

MARTIN, S. E. (1980), *Breaking and Entering*, Berkeley, Cal.: University of California Press.

MASON, B. (2006), 'A Gendered Irish Experiment—grounds for Optimism?', in F. Heidensohn (ed.), *Gender and Justice: New Concepts and Approaches*, Cullompton, Devon: Willan.

MESSERSCHMIDT, J. (1993), *Masculinities and Crime: Critique and Reconceptualisation of Theory*, Lanham, Md.: Rowman and Littlefield.

—— (1997), *Crime as Structured Action: Gender, Race, Class and Crime in the Making*, Thousand Oaks, Cal.: Sage.

—— (2002), 'On Girl Gangs, Gender and Structured Action Theory: A Reply to Miller', *Theoretical Criminology*, 6(4): 477–80.

MILLER, J. (2001), *One of the Guys. Girls, Gang, and Gender*, New York: Oxford University Press.

—— (2002), 'The Strengths and Limits for "Doing Gender" for Understanding Street Crime', *Theoretical Criminology*, 6(4): 433–60.

—— (2010), 'Commentary on Heidensohn's "The Deviance of Women": continuity and change over four decades of research on gender, crime and social control', *British Journal of Sociology*, Vol. 61, Virtual Issue.

—— and MULLINS, C. W. (2006), 'Stuck Up, Telling Lies, and Talking Too Much: The Gendered Context of Young Women's Violence', in K. Heimer and C. Kruttschnitt (eds), *Gender and Crime: Patterns of Victimization and Offending*, New York: New York University Press.

MINISTRY OF JUSTICE (2008a), *National Service Framework. Improving Services to Women Offenders*, London: Ministry of Justice, NOMS

—— (2008b), *Offender Management Guide to Working with Women*, London: Ministry of Justice, NOMS.

—— (2009), *Statistics on Women and the Criminal Justice System: A Ministry of Justice publication under Section 95 of the Criminal Justice Act 1991*, London: Ministry of Justice.

—— (2010), *Statistics on Women and the Criminal Justice System. A Ministry of Justice publication under Section 95 of the Criminal Justice Act 1991*, London: Ministry of Justice.

MULLINS, C. W. (2006), *Holding Your Square. Masculinities, Street life and Violence*, Cullompton: Willan Publishing.

NEW ECONOMICS FOUNDATION (2008), *Unlocking Value: How we all benefit from realistic alternatives to prison for women offenders*, London: New Economics Foundation.

NAFFINE, N. (1997), *Feminism and Criminology*, Cambridge: Polity.

NESS, C. D. (2004), 'Why Girls Fight: Female Youth Violence in the Inner City', *The Annals of the American Academy of Political and Social Sciences*, 595(1): 32–48.

NEWBURN, T. and STANKO, E. (eds), (1994), *Just Boys Doing Business? Men, Masculinities and Crime*, London: Routledge.

OAKLEY, A. (2000), *Experiments in Knowing. Gender and Method in the Social Sciences*, Cambridge: Polity.

OLIVER, W. (1994), *The Violent Social World of Black Men*, New York: Lexington Books.

OWEN, B. (1998), *'In the Mix': Struggle and Survival in a Women's Prison*, Albany: State University of New York Press.

POLLOCK-BYRNE, J. (1990), *Women, Prison and Crime*, Belmont, Cal.: Wadsworth.

POLLACK, S. (2010), 'Labelling Clients "Risky": Social Work and the Neo-Liberal Welfare State' *British Journal of Social Work*, (40): 1263–78.

—— and KENDALL, K. (2005), 'Taming the shrew: mental health policy with women in Canadian federal prisons', *Critical Criminology: An International Journal*, 13(1): 71–87.

PRENZLER, T., FLEMING, J., and KING, A. (2010), 'Gender equity in Australian and New Zealand policing: a five year review', *International Journal of Police Science & Management*, 12(4): 584–95.

PRISON REFORM TRUST (PRT) (2000), *Justice for Women: The Need for Reform*, Report of the Committee on Women's Imprisonment. Chaired by Professor Dorothy Wedderburn, London: Prison Reform Trust.

PUTALLAZ, M. and BIERMAN, K. L. (eds) (2004), *Aggression, Anti-Social Behaviour and Violence among Girls*, New York: Guilford.

RAFTER, N. (1985), 'Chastizing the Unchaste: Social Control Functions of a Women's Reformatory', in S. Cohen and A. Scull (eds), *Social Control and the State*, Oxford: Blackwell.

—— (ed.) (2000), *The Encyclopedia of Women and Crime*, Phoenix, Ariz.: Onyx Press.

—— and HEIDENSOHN, F. (eds) (1995), *International Feminist Perspectives in Criminology*, Buckingham: Open University Press.

RAMAZANOGLU, C. and HOLLAND, J. (2002), *Feminist Methodology. Challenges and Choices*, London: Sage.

RAP (1969), *Radical Alternatives to Prison*, London: Christian Action Publications.

RICHARDSON, A. and BUDD, T. (2003), *Alcohol, Crime and Disorder: A Study of Young Adults*, Home Office Research Study 263, London: Home Office.

RILEY, J., TORRENS, K., and KRUMHOLZ, S. (2005), 'Contemporary Feminist Writers: Envisioning a Just World, *Contemporary Justice Review*, 8(1): 91–106.

ROCK, P. (1996), *Reconstructing a Women's Prison*, Oxford: Clarendon Press.

SAWER, M. (1995), 'Femocrats in Glass Towers?: The office of the status of women in Australia', in D. M. Stetson and A. G. Mazur (eds), *Comparative State Feminism*, London: Sage.

SCHWARTZ, J., STEFFENSMEIER, D., ZHONG, H., and ACKERMAN, J. (2009), 'Trends in the Gender Gap in Violence: Re-evaluating NCVS and Other Evidence', *Criminology*, 47(2): 401–25.

SCOTTISH EXECUTIVE (2002), *A Better Way: The Report of the Ministerial Group on Women's Offending*, Edinburgh: Scottish Executive.

SCOTTISH OFFICE (1998), *Women Offenders—A Safer Way*, Edinburgh: Social Work Services and Prisons Inspectorate for Scotland.

SCOTTISH PARLIAMENT (2009), *Female Offenders in the Criminal Justice System*, 3rd Report of the Equal Opportunities Committee, Edinburgh: Scottish Parliament.

SCRATON, P. (1990), 'Scientific Knowledge or Masculine Discourses? Challenging Patriarchy in Criminology', in L. Gelsthorpe and A. Morris, (eds), *Feminist Perspectives in Criminology*, Buckingham: Open University Press.

SHARPE, C. (2009), 'The Trouble with Girls Today: Professional Perspectives on Young Women's Offending', *Youth Justice* 2009; 9(3): 254–69.

SHARPE, C. ALRIDGE, J., and MEDINA, J. (2006), *Delinquent Youth Groups and Offending Behaviour: Findings from the 2004 Offending, Crime and Justice Survey*. London: Home Office.

SHARPE, G. and GELSTHORPE, L. (2009), 'Engendering the Agenda: Girls, Young Women and Youth Justice', *Youth Justice*, 9(3): 195–208.

SHAW, M. (1991), *The Federal Female Offender*, Ottawa: Solicitor General of Canada.

—— and HANNAH-MOFFAT, K. (eds) (2000), *An Ideal Prison? Critical Essays on Women's Imprisonment in Canada*, Halifax: Fernwood Publishing.

SHEEHAN, R., McIVOR, G., and TROTTER, C. (2010), *Working with Women Offenders in the Community*, Routledge.

SIGURDSSON, J. and DHANI, A. (2010), *Police Service Strength England and Wales, 31 March 2010*, Home Office Statistical Bulletin 14/10, London.

SILVESTRI, M. (2003), *Women in Charge: Policing, Gender and Leadership*, Cullompton, Devon: Willan.

SILVESTRI, M. and CROWTHER-DOWEY, C. (2008), *Gender and Crime*, London: Sage.

SIM, J. (1990), *Medical Power in Prisons*, Milton Keynes: Open University Press.

SIMMONS, H. (1978), 'Explaining Social Policy: The English Mental Deficiency Act of 1913', *Journal of Social History*, 11(3).

SIMPSON, M., SHILDRICK, T., and MACDONALD, R. (eds) (2007), *Drugs in Britain: Supply, Consumption and Control*, Basingstoke: Palgrave Macmillan.

SIMON, R. (1975), *Women and Crime*, Toronto: Lexington.

SMART, C. (1976), *Women, Crime and Criminology*, London: Routledge & Kegan Paul.

SNIDER, L. (2003), 'Constituting the Punishable Woman: atavistic Man Incarcerates Postmodern Woman', *British Journal of Criminology*, 43(2): 354–78.

SPADER, D. (2002), 'The Morality of Justice and the Morality of Care: Are there Distinct Moral Orientations for Males and Females?', *Criminal Justice Review*, 27(1): 66–88.

STEFFENSMEIER, D. J., SCHWARTZ, J., ZHONG, H., and ACKERMAN, J. (2005), 'An Assessment of Recent Trends in Girls' Violence using Diverse Longitudinal Sources: Is the Gender Gap Closing?', *Criminology*, 43(2): 355–405.

——, and ZHONG, H., ACKERMAN, J., SCHWARTZ, J., and AGHA, S. (2006), 'Gender Gap Trends for Violent Crimes, 1980 to 2003: A UCR-NCVS Comparison', *Feminist Criminology*, 1(1): 72–98.

STEFFENSMEIER, D. and SCHWARTZ, J. (2009), 'Trends in Girls' Delinquency and the Gender Gap: Statistical Assessment of Diverse Sources', in M. Zahn (ed.), *The Delinquent Girl*, Philadelphia: Temple University Press.

STEWARD, K. (2006), 'Gender Considerations in Remand Decision-Making', in F. Heidensohn (ed.), *Gender and Justice: New Concepts and Approaches*, Cullompton, Devon: Willan.

TASK FORCE REPORT ON FEDERALLY SENTENCED PRISONERS (TFFSW) (1990), *Creating Choices—The Report of the Task Force on Federally Sentenced Women*, Ottawa: Solicitor General of Canada.

THOMAS, C. (2005), *Judicial Diversity in the United Kingdom and Other Jurisdictions*, London: Commission for Judicial Appointments.

TITTLE, C. (1969), 'Inmate Organization: Sex Differentiation and the Influence of Criminal Sub Cultures', *American Sociological Review*, 34: 492–505.

TOMSEN, S. (ed) (2008), *Crime, Criminal Justice and Masculinities*, Aldershot: Ashgate.

TOOR, S, (2009), 'British Asian Girls: Crime and Youth Justice', *Youth Justice*, 9(3): 239–253.

WACQUANT, L. (2009), *Punishing the Poor*, Durham: Duke University Press.

WALKER, G. (2003), *Crime, Gender and Social Order in early Modern England*, Cambridge: Cambridge University Press.

WALKLATE, S. (2004), *Gender, Crime and Criminal Justice*, Cullompton, Devon: Willan.

WARD, D. and KASSEBAUM, G. (1965), *Women's Prison*, London: Weidenfeld.

WEBB, D. (1984), 'More on Gender and Justice: Girl Offenders on Supervision', *Sociology*, 18.

WESTMARLAND, L. (2001), *Gender and Policing*, Cullompton, Devon: Willan.

WIENER, M. (1998), 'The Victorian Criminalization of Men', in P. Spierenburg (ed.), *Men and Violence: Gender, Honor and Rituals in Modern Europe and America*, Columbus, Ohio: Ohio State University Press.

WINLOW, S. (2001), *Badfellas,* Oxford: Berg.

WINLOW, S. and HALL, S. (2010), 'Retaliate first: Memory, humiliation and male violence', *Crime, Media, Culture*, 5(3): 285–304.

WOODBRIDGE, J. and FROSZTEGA, J. (1998), *Recent Changes in the Female Prison Population*, London: Home Office.

WORRALL, A. (1990), *Offending Women*, London: Routledge.

—— (2004), 'Twisted Sisters, Ladettes, and the New Penology. the Social Construction of "Violent Girls" ', in C. Alder and A. Worrall (eds), *Girls' Violence*, New York: State University of New York Press.

—— and GOUGH, M. (2008), *Giving them back their dignity: a review of the Adelaide House Outreach Project for Women Offenders*, London: Butler Trust.

—— and GELSTHORPE, L. (2009), 'What works with women offenders: The past 30 years, *Probation Journal*, 56(4): 329–45.

YOUNG, T. (2000), 'Girls and Gangs: "Shemale" Gangsters in the UK?', *Youth Justice*, 9(3): 224–38.

YOUTH JUSTICE BOARD (2009), *Girls and Offending—Patterns, Perception and Interventions*, London: Youth Justice Board.

ZEDNER, L. (1991), *Women, Crime and Custody in Victorian England*, Oxford: Oxford University Press.

—— (2002), 'Dangers of Dystopias in Penal Theory-Extended Review of David Garland "The Culture of Control" ', *Oxford Journal of Legal Studies*, 22: 341–66.

# 13

# ETHNICITIES, RACISM, CRIME, AND CRIMINAL JUSTICE

*Coretta Phillips and Ben Bowling*

Since the birth of the discipline, criminologists have been fascinated by the relationship between crime and markers of 'ethnic' or 'racial' difference. From Lombroso to the present day, scholars have wondered whether physical features such as skin colour and hair texture correlate with criminal behaviour. In many places over the years—starting in Italy and then across Europe and the Americas—studies have shown that convicts tend, on average, to be darker-skinned than the people who live in the countries or regions surrounding the prisons in which they are held. This observation has prompted some people to conclude that there is a direct link between 'race' and crime; certain racial groups, they argue, have a greater than average propensity to engage in criminal behaviour.

Many people writing in this field have rejected the very premise of this claim; pigmentation, they argue, is only skin deep and tells us nothing about human character, least of all about a social construct like crime. Moreover, the critics argue, the very act of labelling dark skin as a marker of criminality is to make a 'self-fulfilling prophecy' (Merton 1968: 477). From this perspective, the belief that black and brown people are crime-prone leads police, courts, prisons, and wider society to discriminate against them based on racist stereotypes. Racial discrimination increases the chance that minority ethnic groups will be suspected, arrested, convicted, and imprisoned. From this perspective, the criminological problem is not 'race' but racism and the task is to explain how racial prejudice and discrimination cause the over-representation of certain groups in prison.

This chapter explores the dimensions of this 'race and crime debate' through an analysis of the criminological research set in historical and social context. It examines criminal statistics, contemporary theoretical and empirical work on patterns of crime, and the functioning of the criminal justice system from policing to prisons. It also touches on other important issues that deserve examination, such as the experience of minority ethnic groups as victims of crime in such contexts as racist violence and street gangs. Ethnicity, racism, and diversity evidently also play a role *within* criminal justice institutions. This leads us to look at racialized social relations in prisons and the experiences of people from minority ethnic backgrounds working in criminal justice professions. Our goal is to explore some long-standing questions and to raise some new ones so as to broaden the agenda for future research in this field.

## HISTORICAL, CONCEPTUAL, AND CONTEMPORARY CONTEXT

Racial ideologies have helped to shape the ways in which ethnicity, crime, and criminal justice have been conceptualized. The pseudo-scientific idea that humanity can be divided into distinct and hierarchically arranged 'races' originated in the ideas of European Enlightenment. For philosophers and physical scientists such as Hume, Kant, de Gobineau, Linne, and Blumenbach, reason and civilization were synonymous with the 'white people' of northern Europe while those of 'other racial' origins were regarded as naturally inferior in moral, intellectual, and evolutionary potential. Images of the 'Negro race' differed sharply from the Mongolian or Malay but all were assumed to be fixed in a hierarchical position below the Caucasian (Bowling and Phillips 2002: 1–5, 57–9).

Lombroso (1876), the most influential of the new 'scientific criminologists', made a direct link between 'race' and crime. In *Criminal Man* he concluded that 'many of the characteristics found in savages, and in the coloured races, are also to be found in habitual delinquents'. These physical features included low cranial capacity, receding foreheads, darker skin, curly hair, and large, handle-shaped ears. These 'inferior' traits were also ascribed to racially 'other' whites including Irish and Jewish people. The themes of racist thinking—what Gilroy (2000) refers to as 'raciology' legitimized practices of slavery and indentured labour, becoming embedded in imperialism and colonial policies. Racial science was also integral to Nazi Germany and the ideological roots of the Holocaust.

Following World War II there was a sustained attempt within academia to disentangle racial ideologies from the physical and social sciences. The 1951 UNESCO *Statement by Experts on Race Problems* concluded that there was no scientific basis for defining some racial groups as naturally inferior to others. Rather than being a scientifically objective classification, 'race' was a fallacy based on a social and ideological construction; in short, it was *Man's Most Dangerous Myth* (Montagu 1943). However, the persistence of 'race' in the public (and criminological) imagination has meant that it has not yet been eclipsed by 'ethnicity', a term carrying less ideological baggage. Ethnicity eschews a biological focus, referring to self-defined collectivities among people who share either an internal or external sense of distinctiveness (Kleg 1993). Although the idea of an 'ethnic group' implies common geographical origin and culture, it allows for variation according to local socio-cultural systems unlike 'race' which fixes human difference as though it were an unchanging ahistorical biological essence (Barth 1969; Gilroy 1987b).

The issues explored in this chapter are relevant to other parts of the world, but to understand them in any particular country requires knowledge of the relevant demographic, social, and political context in which they unfold. Our substantive focus is Britain, and although people of African and Asian origin have lived in this country for centuries, arguably the most important context is migration from its former colonies as the Empire declined and fell. Britain was destined to become an ethnically diverse society by virtue of its imperial past, not least because colonial subjects were entitled to a British passport. Citizenship rights were gradually withdrawn from the newly independent nation states, but not before many people had taken up their entitlement to travel to Britain and settle here.

The political and popular reaction to migrants echoed earlier concerns about the perceived problems of 'racial' degeneration and the view that 'bad stock' would pollute the 'British race'. In Notting Hill and Nottingham in 1958, this hostility escalated into widespread racist violence (Bowling 1999). In his notorious 'rivers of blood' speech in Birmingham in 1968, Enoch Powell MP described 'coloured immigration' as a 'preventable evil' which was like 'a nation busily engaged in heaping up its own funeral pyre'. 'Race' war, he implied, was the inevitable result. Although he was sacked from the shadow cabinet for his outspoken views, Powell garnered much public support and the anti-immigrant views, to which he gave a voice, defined the politics of 'race' for many decades.

By the end of the 1960s the major political parties had all committed themselves to reducing and then stopping immigration by which time about one million people from the New Commonwealth had already settled in Britain. Primary migration was soon followed by the arrival of dependents and the birth of a new generation. By the time of the 2001 census, there were 4.6 million people of ethnic minority backgrounds—about 8 per cent of the general population—including migrants as well as their British-born children and grandchildren. The most recent population estimates are shown in Table 13.1. Despite the significant demographic change over the past 50 years, Britain remains a country in which most people—nearly nine out of ten—are 'white'. The nature of our topic means, therefore, that much of our discussion is of people from *minority* ethnic groups in the context of a majority 'white' society.

The administrative categories used in the UK census and for the purposes of 'ethnic monitoring' under section 95 of the 1991 Criminal Justice Act are problematic for various reasons. They are a curiously inconsistent mixture of 'race' or colour (e.g. 'white'), nationality (e.g. Indian), and geographic origin (e.g. African); they reify a discredited and essentialist notion of 'race'; and they obscure the internal heterogeneity of the groups they are supposed to describe (Bowling and Phillips 2002). Although it is tempting to conclude that the categories are entirely meaningless, the data to which they give rise offer the only opportunity to assess how experiences vary among different ethnic groups. Given the widespread hostility towards migration to Britain from the New Commonwealth that was manifest from the 1960s onwards, it is not surprising to find that this had an impact on life chances of migrants themselves in terms of housing, employment, and education.

Many people migrating from the former colonies settled in urban areas that had suffered significant war casualties or population losses as the indigenous population moved to the suburbs (Solomos and Back 1996). More generally, migrants settled where there were jobs that the indigenous community did not want. For these reasons, Britain's minority ethnic communities are not evenly spread across the country.

**Table 13.1** Population of England and Wales by ethnic group, mid-2009

|          | %  |
|----------|----|
| White    | 88 |
| Asian    | 5  |
| Black    | 3  |
| Mixed    | 1  |
| Chinese  | 1  |
| Other    | 1  |

*Source*: Population Estimates By Ethnic Group Mid 2009 (Experimental) http://www.ons.gov.uk/ons/taxonomy/index.html?nscl=Population+Estimates+by+Ethnic+Group

Mostly, they are concentrated in London and the cities and towns of the South East, the Midlands and North West of England. Some minority ethnic communities are *only* to be found in major conurbations and within some boroughs make up a large minority of the general population. In some places the 'white' population is itself comprised of 'ethnic minorities' originally from Southern and Eastern Europe.

Early surveys found that people from minority ethnic groups were consistently in jobs below the level to which they were qualified and were overtly excluded from adequate public and private sector housing by an informal 'colour bar' (Daniel 1968). The legacy of early discrimination has contemporary resonance as social inequalities among Britain's minority ethnic groups have been sustained over time, although with increasing differentiation. Collectively, minority ethnic communities remain geographically concentrated in urban neighbourhoods where unemployment and social deprivation are greatest. Housing conditions are poorest for those of Pakistani and Bangladeshi origin, followed by those of African and Caribbean origin. There are signs that people of Indian origin have made greater economic progress in suburban areas of London and the major conurbations (Phillips 2010).

Educational under-achievement among children and young people from minority ethnic backgrounds has been a major concern for many years. Contemporary secondary school attainment levels based on GCSE examination results present a complex picture with a high-attaining cluster of ethnic groups (Chinese, Indian, White and Asian, and Irish), a mid-range cluster (White British, White and black African, Bangladeshi, and black African) and two tiers of a lower attaining cluster of pupils (Caribbean and Pakistani, Irish Traveller and Gypsy/Romany origin) with extremely low rates of educational attainment. When account is taken of social economic status, black people appear to face the greatest disadvantage in education (Strand 2008) but those of white working class origins also have low achievement levels.

Studies of the labour market show that minority ethnic men and women are more likely than average to face unemployment. Whilst this is least marked for those of Indian and Chinese origin, the evidence points to 'ethnic penalties'—of which racial discrimination represents a large part—disadvantaging most minority ethnic groups, once qualifications have been taken into account (Heath and Cheung 2006). In all these areas of social policy, there is cumulative evidence of a complex interplay of socio-economic, demographic, institutional, structural, and cultural factors—alongside direct and indirect racial discrimination—which contributes to disadvantage among minority ethnic groups.

# THE SOCIAL CONSTRUCTION OF ETHNICITY AND CRIMINALITY

Crime has often been portrayed as something alien to the 'British way of life'. Media-fuelled 'crime panics' have often used words imported from other countries such as 'Hooligan' (Ireland), 'garrotting' (Spain), or 'mugging' (USA) to describe supposedly foreign types of criminality (Pearson 1983; Hall *et al.* 1978; Bowling and Phillips 2002: 77). Crime and deviance are well documented in British history, of course, but there has also been a 'racial' undertone in discussions with home-grown 'British criminality' seen as the result of the 'disease' of 'racial degeneration' (Pearson 1983: ix-xi, 69–73).

The 'race and crime' debate heated up with the arrival in Britain of minority ethnic groups migrating from the former colonies. Although people of the so-called 'darker races' were widely seen as inclined towards deviance in the colonies, until the mid-1970s, the official view was that crime was not a significant problem among the people from Africa, the Caribbean, and the Indian sub-continent settling in Britain. As a House of Commons Select Committee stated in 1972: '[t]he conclusions remain beyond doubt: coloured immigrants are no more involved in crime than others; nor are they generally more concerned in violence, prostitution and drugs. The West Indian crime rate is much the same as that of the indigenous population. The Asian crime rate is very much lower' (House of Commons 1972: 71).

Official views changed markedly soon afterwards with some minority ethnic communities increasingly being seen as a crime and disorder problem (House of Commons 1976). From the mid-1970s sensationalist media reports appeared with headlines such as 'black crime shock' based on the publication of selective police statistics on robbery in inner city areas (Hall *et al.* 1978). Public discussion of the urban disorders of the late 1970s and 1980s fuelled by media images of 'black criminality' served to lend credence to views about the pathological nature of minority ethnic communities, their family structure, values, and culture (Gilroy 1987a). As a result, images of black people as prone to violence, drug abuse, and disorderly behaviour became entrenched in the public consciousness (Gilroy 1982, 1987b).

Asian communities were for many years portrayed as conformist, passive, inward-looking, and self-regulating (Wardak 2000; Webster 1997). More recently, with media panics about 'Asian gangs', Pakistani and Bangladeshi communities have been portrayed as increasingly violent and disorderly (Alexander 2000). The riots of 2001 involving pitched battles between young Asian youth and the police in the northern towns of Bradford, Burnley, and Oldham also contributed to that image (Cantle 2001). Asian communities have also been portrayed as culturally separatist and resisting integration within British society, and as the source of home-grown Islamic terrorism. The media representation of the 7 July 2005 London bombings and the fact that the perpetrators were British-born Muslims also served to cement the image of minority ethnic groups as a security threat (McGhee 2008). Numerous critics have also pointed out that ethnicity and culture always come to the fore when black and Asian people commit crime (Gilroy 1987a) a point which is reinforced by the absurdity of describing football violence, child sex abuse, serial killing, or corporate manslaughter as 'white on white' crime (Heaven and Hudson 2005: 376).

Critics approaching this issue from a social constructionist perspective do not deny that people from minority ethnic groups commit crime (Hall *et al.* 1978). It would be surprising if people concentrated in urban areas, often in the worst parts of those areas, experiencing social and economic exclusion, poor housing, and schools were never involved in crime. The key issue is that the media, sometimes based on a selective use of police statistics, have created distorted or exaggerated images of crime within particular groups in society. In this light, any attempt to discover the 'real' rate of crime among different ethnic groups must clearly proceed with great caution, if at all.

# CRIMINOLOGICAL RESEARCH AND STATISTICS ON ETHNICITY AND CRIME

There are a number of ways in which criminologists have attempted to compare patterns of crime among different ethnic groups, all of which are flawed in one way or another. In the next sections, we consider what can be learned from official records, victims' descriptions and crime surveys.

## OFFICIAL STATISTICS

Many accounts of 'race and crime' rely on official statistics—based on records of arrest, criminal convictions, and prison populations—to make comparisons among different groups (Coleman and Moynihan 1996, Bowling and Phillips 2002: 83–7). The obvious advantage of these statistics is that they are relatively robust 'head counts' of people arrested by the police or sent to prison by the courts. They rest on the assumptions that there is sufficient evidence of wrongdoing to justify official action and that the ethnic origin of the subject has been accurately recorded. The major weakness of these data for this purpose is that they are accounts of decisions taken by criminal justice officials rather than evidence of offending *per se*. Any bias—intentional or otherwise—in the administration of criminal justice will obviously have the effect of creating a skewed picture.

Statistics on the ethnic origin of prisoners have consistently shown a much higher rate of imprisonment for black people since they were first published in the mid-1980s (Home Office 1986). This is true for male and female prisoners and people of both British and foreign nationality. In June 2008, incarceration rates for British nationals of Asian origin (fewer than 1.8 per 1,000) were slightly above those of 'white 'people (1.3 per 1,000) but were markedly lower than the very high incarceration rate for black people (6.8 per 1,000) and people of mixed backgrounds (3.7 per 1,000). People from 'Chinese and other' groups had the lowest rate of imprisonment at 0.5 per 1,000 (MOJ 2009). These figures mask significant differences within these broad categories and are significantly higher if foreign national prisoners are included (Bowling and Phillips 2002: 192–9).

A similar picture can be found at the entry point to the criminal justice system in statistics based on people arrested by the police. Table 13.1 shows that compared with the 'white British' population there are slightly elevated arrest rates for those of 'Other White', Pakistani, and Bangladeshi origin but the rates are more than twice that of the 'white' ethnic group for black people and those of mixed ethnic origins. The lowest per capita rates in 2008/9 were Indian, Chinese, and people identified as 'mixed–white/ Asian'.

Arrest statistics show that black people are over-represented in most offence categories, but most markedly for fraud and forgery, drug offences, and robbery. Asian suspects are over-represented in arrests for sexual offences and for fraud and forgery. Black and Asian people were under-represented in burglary and criminal damage offences, a pattern which has been reflected in prison populations since 1985 (MOJ 2010). With the exception of robbery and homicide (see below) there has been no empirical research on the possibility of 'ethnic specialization' in different types of offending.

## VICTIM AND WITNESS DESCRIPTIONS

Victims of crime can tell us about the 'ethnic appearance' of the people whom they suspect of committing crimes against them by describing them to the police or in victimization surveys. About 40 per cent of victims surveyed in the British Crime Survey were able to describe the person they knew or believed to be their assailant, typically in 'contact offences' such as assault, robbery, and theft (Clancy et al. 2001). Victims' descriptions should be treated with caution because the crimes in which they can describe the offender may not be representative of those where they cannot, and also because eye-witness identification is not always reliable (Coleman and Moynihan 1996).

Analysing the 2000 British Crime Survey, Clancy et al. (2001) found that, where victims could judge the ethnic origin of their assailant, 85 per cent described them as white, compared with 15 per cent who said they were from a visible minority group. Minority ethnic groups make up a small proportion of suspected offenders for most offences with some notable exceptions. For example, among 203 victims of 'mugging' identified in the survey, 63 (3 out of 10) described their assailant as black (ibid.). 'Mugging', a term without legal standing but essentially meaning street robbery, accounts for less than 2 per cent of recorded crime and has been the focus of media panics since the early 1970s (Hall et al. 1978).

The police have collected ethnically coded descriptions of offenders for selected offences—typically street robbery—since the mid-1970s (Hall et al. 1978; Bowling and Phillips 2002: 78–9). Several recent Home Office studies have examined victims' descriptions in police reports of particular crimes in selected locations. Harrington and Mayhew (2001: 41) found that in the London borough of Westminster, two-thirds of suspects of mobile phone theft were black and 3 out of 10 were white, whereas in Stockport three-quarters of suspects were white and only 10 per cent were black. In Birmingham, only 10 per cent of suspects were white compared with more than half who were black and one-third Asian. Smith (2003: 26) found that the majority of robbery suspects were black in six out of the nine police areas he studied. The exceptions were Stockport, Preston, and Blackpool where 99 per cent of the suspected offenders were white.

## HOMICIDE STATISTICS

The police recorded 2,228 victims of murder, manslaughter, or infanticide in England and Wales in a three-year period ending March 2008, just under 750 people per year. In this period, nearly three-quarters of victims (73 per cent) were white, 11 per cent were 'black', 8 per cent were Asian, and 3 per cent were from other minority ethnic groups. Twenty-one homicides were recorded as 'racially motivated' in this period. There is a marked over-representation of minority ethnic groups among homicide victims: black people are about five times as likely to be murdered by comparison with their white counterparts and people of Asian origin were nearly twice as likely (MOJ 2009).

The detection rate for homicide is relatively high in comparison with other offences but it is more common for those involving black victims to remain unsolved (41 per cent) in comparison with Asian (36 per cent) or 'white' victims (33 per cent) (MOJ 2009). This may be because of the method of killing (e.g. those involving strangers and guns are less likely to be solved), or because witnesses are less likely to come forward. There is a widely held perception within minority ethnic communities, that the police are less interested in these cases, make mistakes, or mishandle investigations (Clancy *et al.* 2001). Since homicide data were first published in 1997, the overwhelming majority of homicides were *intra*-ethnic. Where a suspect was identified, about 9 out of 10 'white' victims were killed by someone of the same ethnic group and this was the case in two-thirds of Asian victims and between two-thirds and three-quarters of black victims (Bowling and Phillips 2002: 95–8, MOJ 2009).

Recent years have seen increased public anxiety about gun and knife crime within black communities in the UK. While guns hardly featured in the crime scene until the late 1980s, murders involving guns became increasingly prevalent during the 1990s. Despite public concern and media attention, there still remains only a handful of journalistic accounts of gun crime within black communities and a very limited amount of research (Bullock and Tilley 2002; Hales 2006; Pitts 2008; Gunther 2010). It is important to keep these crimes in perspective. Gun homicide remains relatively rare: in the three year period to April 2008 an average of 22 black people were victims of gun murder each year compared with around 44 white people and 5 Asians (MOJ 2009). Black murder victims are much more likely to have been shot (26 per cent) than 'white' (4 per cent) or Asian (8.5 per cent) victims and account for four out of ten of those murdered with guns in England and Wales. Bullock and Tilley's (2002) study of shooting in Manchester found that of the 32 offenders identified in 46 shooting incidents they examined, 22 were black, eight were white, and two were Asian. There was a clear overlap between victims and offenders. Of the 32 offenders identified, eight had previously been shot and three were subsequently shot dead.

## Gangs

Traditionally regarded as the preserve of the US, increasingly, media and political attention has been paid to the problem of street gangs, and as Hallsworth and Young (2008: 185) have observed, 'the gang is always seen to wear a black or brown face' (see also Alexander 2000). For Hagedorn (2007) membership reflects those disadvantaged by economic restructuring, the neo-liberal retrenchment of welfare, and social exclusion, a view echoed by Pitts (2008) in his study of gangs in East London.

Hagedorn (2007) suggests that organized gang members assert their oppositional religious, ethnic, or cultural identities in urban areas, although Hales *et al.* (2006) show that gangs exist in predominantly white areas of England as well as more ethnically diverse neighbourhoods (see also Aldridge and Medina 2008). Gangs can be loosely structured, bound by territorial identification by 'postcode' or 'housing estate'. Some, but not all gangs are involved in drug-dealing and the illicit economy and where they are this often reflects segmentation along class and ethnic lines (Ruggiero 2000). Long-standing rivalries with other groups are the context for 'beef' which can lead to violent conflict as protagonists respond to masculine slights or 'disrespect'. Violence is used more instrumentally, and thus sparingly, in more organized gangs involving older white men who might be participants in middle-level drug markets (Hales *et al.* 2006). Estimating the extent and nature of gang membership is plagued by definitional and methodological issues and a lack of systematic research (Hallsworth and Young 2008; see also Goldson 2011).

## VICTIMIZATION AND FEAR OF CRIME

The 2008/9 British Crime Survey (BCS) estimates that the risk of being a victim of crime was highest for those describing themselves as 'mixed' (35 per cent) compared with black (24 per cent), white (23 per cent) or Asian (26 per cent) (MOJ 2010). This is broadly consistent with BCS data over the past decade, but earlier sweeps found that minority ethnic respondents were more likely to be victims of burglary and vehicle theft than 'white' respondents, while those of mixed race experienced substantially higher levels of household and personal crimes (Clancy *et al.* 2001). Multivariate analysis of the BCS found factors such as age, low income, unemployment, inner-city residence, and a lack of academic qualifications, were more important than ethnic origin in explaining minority ethnic groups' higher levels of victimization (Clancy *et al.* 2001; Salisbury and Upson 2004). Nevertheless, some of these factors, such as inner-city residence and unemployment, may themselves be partly explained by discrimination in housing and employment. Moreover, it is as yet unclear why risks are significantly higher for people of mixed heritage, as this could not be explained on the basis of their age, type of area, levels of economic activity, or housing tenure (Salisbury and Upson 2004). The BCS also found that minority ethnic groups were significantly more anxious about crime (Clancy *et al.* 2001; MOJ 2009).

## RACIST VICTIMIZATION

Minority ethnic groups' experience as crime victims has rarely been at the heart of the 'race and crime debate'. For reasons that we discuss below, the Stephen Lawrence Inquiry was the moment when *racist* victimization—where an individual is selected as a target because of their race, ethnicity, or religion—gained full public recognition (Bowling 1999). Racist violence was nothing new—local monitoring groups have been highlighting the problem since the 1970s (e.g. Bethnal Green and Stepney Trades Council 1978). Similarly, Islamophobia has been brought to the fore through the work of the European Monitoring Centre on Racism and Xenophobia and community-based organizations (Allen and Nielsen 2002).

Police-recorded racist incidents increased dramatically from 4,400 incidents in 1988 to a peak of 61,300 in 2006/7 declining to 55,900 in 2008/09 (MOJ 2010). BCS data show a drop in racist victimization since 1995, which gives indications of both increased reporting to and recording by the police, and may well represent a downward trend (Docking and Tuffin 2005). Whilst the perpetrators of racist violence are not exclusively white, elements of a defensive form of whiteness can assume significance in offending behaviour. Salisbury and Upson (2004) found 4 per cent of mixed race respondents, 3 per cent of Asians, and 2 per cent of black and Chinese/other origin respondents had been the victim of racially motivated crime in the previous year, compared with less than one per cent of white respondents.

The number of recorded racist incidents is, as one might expect, higher in areas with relatively large minority ethnic populations, but Maynard and Read (1997) found that *per capita rates* of racist victimization were highest in provincial police force areas. This is consistent with accounts of rural racism and the victimization of asylum seekers and refugees dispersed outside of Britain's centres of minority ethnic concentration (see Chakraborti and Garland 2004). Brincombe *et al.*'s (2001) analysis of racist victimization in East London supported the hypothesis that attacks cluster where minority ethnic individuals form a small but growing proportion of the population (see also Hesse *et al.* 1992; Sampson and Phillips 1992, 1996; Bowling 1999; Ray *et al.* 2004).

Although victimization surveys go further than official statistics in documenting the extent of racist violence, they do not capture the process and nature of victimization, with its complex and repeated interactions and its cumulative impact on the victim (Bowling 1993). Sampson and Phillips, (1992) showed that racist victimization tends to be of an ongoing nature, with both 'minor' abuse and incidents of physical violence interwoven in a pattern of harassment and intimidation—a fact often unacknowledged by statutory agencies who respond to single, discrete incidents (Bowling 1999; Phillips and Sampson 1998).

## SELF-REPORT SURVEYS

Self-report surveys provide a solution to the problem of using information collected by police, courts, and prisons. These data come straight from the offenders themselves and have none of the potential biases introduced by agents of the criminal justice system. On the other hand, they inevitably rely on the honesty of interviewees to disclose dishonest and violent behaviour (see Maguire, this volume). Nonetheless, large numbers of people do admit to their crimes, many providing great detail, and the method is generally agreed to be valid and reliable (Sharp and Budd 2005). In the first UK study of this kind, Graham and Bowling (1995) found that among a sample of 2,500 young people white and black respondents had very similar rates of offending (44 per cent and 43 per cent), while those of Indian, Pakistani, and Bangladeshi origin (30 per cent, 28 per cent, and 13 per cent) had very much lower rates (see also Flood-Page *et al.* 2000). The Offending, Crime and Justice Survey of 12,000 people found that white people and those of mixed ethnic origin were the most likely to say that they had committed a crime (around 40 per cent), compared with those of Asian, black, or other ethnic origin (21 per cent, 28 per cent, and 23 per cent) (Sharp and Budd

2005: 8). Surveys in secondary schools in deprived areas found the highest rates of offending among the mixed group (61 per cent) with white (55 per cent) and black (50 per cent) respondents having similar rates with those of Asian origin significantly lower (33 per cent) (Armstrong *et al.* 2005: 19).

Since the early 1990s, at least nine Home Office self-report surveys have compared drug use among different ethnic groups, producing remarkably similar findings (see Bowling and Phillips 2002: 101). Sharp and Budd (2005) found that amongst males, respondents of mixed ethnicity were most likely to have used drugs—mostly cannabis—in the last year (27 per cent) compared with 16 per cent of both their black and white counterparts, 13 per cent of other ethnic groups, and 5 per cent of Asians. Class A drug use in the last year was similar for males of white, mixed, and other ethnic origins (6 per cent) and much lower for Asian and black males (1 per cent and 2 per cent respectively). Among females, drug use (both cannabis and Class A) was higher among white respondents and those of mixed ethnic origin and lower among Asian and black people (ibid.).

## 'RACE AND CRIME': AN INTERIM CONCLUSION

Crime statistics paint a complex picture of patterns of crime when comparisons are made among communities defined in terms of ethnicity. On one hand, black people and those of other ethnic groups are over-represented in arrest and prison statistics. People of Asian origin are over-represented in some statistics and under-represented in others. Black people also appear substantially over-represented in victims' and witness descriptions of some forms of crime but not others and again, the picture for people of Asian origin is more mixed. On the other hand, self-report studies—based on *admitted* offending—are consistent with official data in indicating that offending rates among the Asian population are very much lower than their white counterparts, but contrast sharply with their indication that offending is no more common among the black population than among the white population. There are three possible explanations for this discrepancy:

- self-report studies may accurately reflect the extent of crime within minority ethnic communities while arrest and other official statistics create a distorted picture as a result of racial discrimination in policing and the criminal justice process;
- people from minority ethnic groups may be less willing to admit their offending to crime surveys. No research evidence exists to support this view in the UK (Budd and Sharp 2005), although studies in the US and the Netherlands have found that some ethnic groups are more likely to conceal their offending than others (Hindelang *et al.* 1981; Junger 1989, 1990, cf. Bowling 1990); or
- the two methods measure different things. Self-report surveys may be best suited to measuring the extent of criminal behaviour in the *general population* but less useful for shedding light on the small number of the most serious offenders who are often missed by household surveys.

This debate could be considered simply 'empiricist haggling' over crime statistics and we have sympathy with those who eschew the whole enterprise of classifying crimes according to offenders' skin colour (Gilroy 1982: 146). However, this debate will continue with or without the benefit of research evidence. Moreover, the question of patterns of crime within minority ethnic communities contributes to the framing of discussions about the fairness of policing and the criminal justice process and it is to these issues that we now turn our attention. We start with the police, the first and most frequent point of contact between citizen and state.

# THE POLICE AND POLICING MINORITY ETHNIC COMMUNITIES

Mistrust, resentment and suspicion between the police and minority ethnic communities can be traced back to the anti-immigrant attitudes and insensitive policing of the early years of post-colonial migration to the UK (Whitfield 2004). In the 1960s The West Indian Standing Conference reported that police officers were going 'nigger hunting...to bring in a coloured person at all costs' (Hunte 1966: 12). Allegations of oppressive policing against black and Asian communities—such as mass stop and search operations, the inappropriate use of paramilitary tactics, excessive surveillance, unjustified armed raids, police violence and deaths in custody, and a failure to respond effectively to racist violence— recur throughout the 1970s and 1980s (Institute of Race Relations 1987; Bowling and Phillips 2002: 128–9). The collective experience of minority ethnic communities—including marginalized white minorities such as the Irish community—in the UK is of being 'over-policed and under protected' (Reiner 2010; Macpherson 1999).

## STOP AND SEARCH, INVESTIGATION, AND TARGETING

With the exception of deaths in police custody, stop and search has been the most contentious aspects of the relationship between the police and minority ethnic communities (Bowling, Phillips, and Parmar 2007). Under the 1824 Vagrancy Act, the so-called 'sus' law, a person could be arrested and prosecuted by the police and convicted at court for 'loitering with intent' to commit a crime. This power was used extensively and often arbitrarily against black communities. In April 1981, the London Metropolitan Police conducted a mass stop and search called 'Operation Swamp', triggering the Brixton riots amid allegations of racist and abusive policing (Scarman 1981). After the abolition of 'sus', section 1 of the Police and Criminal Evidence Act 1984 authorized stop and search where police have 'reasonable suspicion' of wrongdoing (see also Sanders and Young, this volume). However, allegations that minority ethnic groups were being targeted persisted and the first 'ethnically coded' statistics painted a clear picture of disproportionality, a pattern that persists to this day.

In the year ending April 2009, the police carried out more than 1,140,000 searches. Of the people stopped, 15 per cent were black, 9 per cent Asian, 3 per cent were of mixed ethnicity, and 1 per cent were Chinese (MOJ 2010). Black people were, *per capita*, nearly seven times more likely to be searched than white people and Asians twice as likely. The number of searches increased by 30 per cent for white people since 2004, but the number of black people stopped and searched increased by 70 per cent and while the number of searches carried out by police forces has varied, the level of disproportionality has increased steadily since ethnic monitoring data were first published. The figures conceal very significant differences *within* these crude ethnic categories (Waddington *et al.* 2004). In particular, the experiences of white minorities such as the Irish, travellers and migrants from Eastern Europe—differ markedly from those of the white majority community, but are subsumed in the catch-all white (Mooney and Young 2000; James 2005).

BCS data are broadly consistent with police statistics, indicating that black and Asian people are more *frequently* stopped, more often *repeatedly* stopped (in vehicles and on foot) and subject to more *intrusive* searches (Skogan 1990; Newburn and Hayman 2001). Formal action is also more common in stops involving black people compared with other ethnic groups (Norris *et al.* 1992; Bucke and Brown 1997). When stopped, people from minority ethnic groups are much less likely to think that the police acted politely and fairly (Clancy *et al.* 2001).

The use of section 60 of the Criminal Justice and Public Order Act, 1994 which permits a police officer to stop and search a person *without suspicion* when serious violence is anticipated, has increased from 8,000 searches annually in the late 1990s to more than 150,000 in 2008/9 (MOJ 2010). At the same time, the use of this power against black people has risen by 600 per cent. For every 1,000 people searched under this Act, 42 are black whilst 1.6 are white—making black people nearly 27 times more frequently stopped and searched. Asians were more than six times as likely to be stopped in comparison to their white counterparts (ibid.).

'Suspicionless searches' authorized under section 44 of the Terrorism Act 2000 have also been used disproportionately against black and Asian people. After the 7/7 London bombings there has been a sharp increase in the use of these powers and they were used very extensively against minority ethnic communities, Muslims in particular (Parmar 2011). In March 2005, Home Office minister Hazel Blears commented that it was a 'reality' that anti-terrorist stops and searches would be targeted disproportionately at the Muslim community'. In 2010, the European Court of Human Rights ruled in the case of *Gillan and Quinton v United Kingdom* that section 44 was unlawful on the grounds that it was used arbitrarily and lacked sufficient safeguards. Innes *et al.*'s (2011) review of Prevent policing suggests a complex picture with police interventions receiving some support from Muslim communities in four diverse research sites with national BCS data reporting largely positive views about the police, although ratings of the police were slightly lower among young Muslim men compared with their non-Muslim counterparts.

But why are people from minority ethnic communities more frequently stopped and searched by the police? One view is that police officers deliberately target minority groups because of widespread racial prejudice, stereotyping, and overt discrimination. Certainly, numerous prominent black people including Dr John Sentamu (Archbishop of York), senior civil servants, police officers, and Members of Parliament, have been stopped without justification (Bowling and Phillips 2007). Qualitative research on police culture in the 1980s found that racist language—such as 'Paki', 'nigger', 'coon', and 'spade'— were accepted and expected' and reflected deep-seated racist beliefs about ethnicity and criminality (Smith and Gray 1985). Police officers unapologetically used 'colour as a criterion' for targeting stop and search on the basis that this reflects ethnic differences in patterns: 'police officers tend to make a crude equation between crime and black people, to assume that suspects are black and to justify stopping people in these terms' which, for Smith (1994: 1092), was a 'rational explanation' in line with victims' descriptions of offenders.

Police officers seem now to be more hesitant in admitting to overt targeting, also that explicit racist language is less common and that officers feel less able to carry out unjustified stop and search 'fishing trips' without proper grounds (Foster *et al.* 2005: 30). However, racist attitudes and behaviour may simply have gone 'underground' (ibid.) In October 2003 a BBC documentary *The Secret Policeman* covertly filmed extreme racist attitudes among a group of recruits, several of whom said quite explicitly that they were targeting people from minority ethnic communities, particularly Asians, for stop and search. Searches where officers have wide discretion to use their own intuition, stereotypes, and prejudices are most likely to be discriminatory (FitzGerald 1993). It is perhaps for this reason that disproportionality tends to be widest in drugs searches (Quinton *et al.* 2000) and those that require no element of reasonable suspicion (Bowling and Philips 2002).

People from minority ethnic communities are also stopped and searched more frequently due to social and demographic factors including age, employment, and leisure activities. As some researchers have argued, being more frequently 'available' at the times and in the places where stop and search occurs, particular ethnic groups 'place themselves at risk of being stopped by the police through their differential use of public space' (MVA and Miller 2000; Waddington *et al.* 2004). From this perspective, disproportionality is an unintended result of the fact that policing bears down more heavily upon people who more frequently use public space and these happen to be black and Asian people (Waddington *et al.* 2004). Whatever the explanation, the disproportionate use of stop and search is clearly a problem: it seems inherently unfair, contributes to the criminalization of minority ethnic communities, and undermines public support for the police (Bowling and Phillips 2007, Equality and Human Rights Commission 2010).

## THE STEPHEN LAWRENCE INQUIRY

The murder of Stephen Lawrence in south-east London in 1993 and the public inquiry which followed in 1999 into the failed Metropolitan Police murder investigation brought the issues of racist violence, stop and search, and policing racism to the top of the political agenda (Bowling 1999, Hall *et al.* 2009). The Inquiry concluded that the initial investigation into the murder was 'marred by a combination of professional incompetence, institutional racism and a failure of leadership by senior officers' (Macpherson 1999: 46.1). Institutional racism—the 'collective failure of an organization to provide an appropriate and professional service to people because of their colour, culture, or ethnic origin'—could be 'seen or detected in processes, attitudes and behaviour which amount to discrimination through unwitting prejudice, ignorance, thoughtlessness and racist stereotyping which disadvantage minority ethnic people' (Macpherson 1999: 34). The report criticized the police for denying the racist motive for the murder, stereotyping Stephen's friend, Duwayne Brooks at the scene (Hall *et al.* 1998), using inappropriate and offensive language, and insensitive and patronizing handling of the Lawrence family throughout the investigation. It confirmed research and community accounts revealing dissatisfaction with the police failure to investigate reported racist attacks and to bring offenders to justice. The Stephen Lawrence Inquiry had an 'explosive impact on the workings of the criminal justice system' (Rock 2004: 481). The government response was to establish a Ministerial Priority for the police service 'to increase trust and confidence in policing amongst minority ethnic communities', as well as a range of other measures (Home Office 1999a).

## THE CRIMINAL JUSTICE PROCESS

The claim that the criminal justice process is dominated by 'whiteness' and maleness has been explored by Hudson (2006; 1993). She notes that white criminal justice practitioners may see minority ethnic 'others' through stereotypical, imperialist mythologies and representations which lead to the over-penalizing and criminalization of racialized subjects. In relation to police detention and court processes, empirical research has found evidence of both direct and indirect racial discrimination.

### INDIRECT RACIAL DISCRIMINATION

Research conducted in the 1980s and 1990s showed how minority ethnic suspects and defendants could be cumulatively disadvantaged by practices reliant on their cooperation with police officers or prosecutors. At the police station, minority ethnic suspects were less likely to opt for legal advice, exercise their right of silence, or to admit offences during interview or before trial (Phillips and Brown 1998; Bucke and Brown 1997). Refusing to admit to offences means that defendants are ineligible for a caution or a sentencing discount. Whilst such decisions are, in *a formal sense*, racially neutral, mistrust of the police may operate to deny minority ethnic offenders the benefits of cooperation.

Minority ethnic groups are also more likely than average to fall into the socio-economic and demographic categories for whom a remand in custody is likely. Housing inequalities and a perceived lack of 'communities' for black defendants in particular, may be regarded as contributing to a risk of absconding. This can lead to higher rates of custodial remands and the added risk of a custodial sentence if convicted. Hudson (1993: 164) notes the irony that the 'characteristics of the penalized population are so often the very characteristics we are building in to various formalised decision-making criteria, adherence to which we take as evidence that we are dispensing impartial criminal justice'. Supposedly non-discriminatory practices are therefore enshrined in long-established rituals of the criminal justice system and may work to the advantage of some ethnic groups but the disadvantage of others. This amounts to indirect racial discrimination but is defended on the ground that such practices are necessary to run the criminal justice system efficiently. For Smith (1997: 753), deciding 'which decision-making criteria are justifiable or legitimate raises deep and difficult problems in the philosophy of law'.

## DIRECT RACIAL DISCRIMINATION

Evidence of direct racial discrimination comes from a small number of methodologically rigorous research studies which have typically employed multivariate statistical analysis to tease out the independent effects of ethnicity as a predictor of a disproportionately severe outcome for people from ethnic minority communities. Newburn *et al.* (2004), for example, found that, black people were twice as likely to be strip searched at a police station even once the reason for the arrest, outcome of detention, and the age and sex of the offender had been taken into account. Similarly, in Phillips and Brown's (1998) study of 1,175 defendants, being from an ethnic minority group predicted an increased chance of case termination by the CPS, after controlling for previous convictions and the type and seriousness of the offence. Mhlanga's (1999) study of young suspects indicated that police officers may have been charging some black and Asian suspects without sufficient evidence or where it was not in the public interest to prosecute.

The writing of pre-sentence reports by probation officers for magistrates to consider before passing sentence presents another opportunity for racial bias to creep in with negative and stereotypical attitudes represented in reports on minority ethnic defendants. Hudson and Bramhall's (2005) qualitative study in a North-West probation area found that probation officers highlighted assumed behavioural problems and used more 'distancing' language in reports for Asian offenders which cast them as less remorseful than white offenders. Subjective assertions based on demographic, familial, cultural, and socio-economic differences between ethnic groups underline how unwitting discrimination can permeate risk assessments.

An area which has received little research attention in the UK until recently is juries. Thomas's (2010) study of jury verdicts provided little indication of biased decision-making by all white or racially diverse juries. At a *prima facie* level, recent conviction rates suggest discrimination, as these were lower for both adults and juveniles from black, Asian, and other minority ethnic groups in the magistrates' courts, although ethnic variation was less apparent in Crown Court convictions (MOJ 2010). The Denman Inquiry (2001: 107) concluded that the CPS could be construed as 'discriminating against minority ethnic defendants by failing to correct the bias in police charging decisions and allowing a disproportionate number of weak cases against minority ethnic defendants to go to trial'. Similarly, sentences of immediate custody were more likely to be given to adult minority ethnic defendants (42 per cent–52 per cent) for indictable offences than white defendants, of whom 29 per cent were sentenced to prison. However, without further research it is impossible to know whether there were legally relevant factors (such as seriousness of the offence) which might explain such patterns.

### Direct discrimination in sentencing

Hood's (1992) pioneering study of *Race and Sentencing* in five Crown Courts in the West Midlands produced definitive evidence of discrimination in sentencing. It estimated that black people had a 5 per cent greater probability of being sentenced to custody compared with their white counterparts, once all conceivable legally relevant case characteristics had been controlled for. In guilty plea cases, Asian defendants were, on average, sentenced to nine months longer and black defendants three months longer than white defendants. These differences were most often observed in the middle range of offence seriousness where judicial discretion was high. The study also found that unequal treatment of black defendants was more common in the suburban Dudley Crown Court by comparison with the Crown Court in Birmingham, a more cosmopolitan city. Hood's (1992) study was invaluable in documenting direct discrimination in sentencing and its contribution to racial disproportionality in prison (Bowling and Phillips 2002: 183–7). This landmark study was carried our more than 20 years ago, however, and there has been little research since which has produced such conclusive evidence of indirect or direct racial discrimination in decisions regarding bail or sentencing.

## Youth justice

Feilzer and Hood's (2004) analysis of over 31,000 Youth Offending Team (YOT) records found that young black people were substantially over-represented and young Asian people under-represented in YOT caseloads, although this did vary by area. In contrast, May *et al.* (2010) found that whilst two-thirds of arrests resulted from reactive policing, minority ethnic young people were more often the subject of proactive arrests mostly for drug and traffic offences compared with their white counterparts. Both studies consistently reported higher case termination rates among black boys. Taken together the studies uncovered several stages at which black, Asian, and mixed race youths were disadvantaged in the criminal justice process including pre-court disposals, case termination, remands, acquittals, committals to Crown court, pre-sentence report sentence recommendations, and higher tariff sentencing, but these were not consistent across all minority ethnic groups in either study. Nonetheless, both Feilzer and Hood (2004) and May *et al.* (2010) conclude that these findings are consistent with racially discriminatory treatment in the youth justice process.

## THE OVER-REPRESENTATION OF MINORITY ETHNIC GROUPS IN PRISON

By the end point of the criminal justice process, the cumulative effects of social exclusion, direct, and indirect discrimination can be seen in the disproportionate rates of imprisonment for people from minority ethnic groups. On 30 June 2009 there were 22,292 people from minority ethnic groups in custody amounting to 35 per cent of the male prison population and 27 per cent of the female population. Of these, one-third of the male and over one-half (55 per cent) of the female minority ethnic population were foreign nationals (MOJ 2010). The massive increases in the prison population in recent years have been more marked for minority ethnic communities. Among British nationals, the white male prison population increased by 41 per cent between 1985 and 2009, while the black and Asian male prison population grew by 104 per cent and 261 per cent respectively (Home Office 1986; MOJ 2010). The picture for women is equally stark, especially for foreign national prisoners (Sudbury 2005).

## 'Race' and racism in prisons

'Race relations' policies were introduced into prisons in the early 1980s in response to allegations of racism among prison staff and anxiety about the growing minority ethnic prison population. Genders and Player's (1989) comprehensive study of *Race Relations in Prison* found evidence of direct racial discrimination. Black prisoners were stereotyped by prison officers as being arrogant, lazy, noisy, hostile to authority, with values incompatible with British society, and as having 'a chip on their shoulder'. These stereotypes informed allocations to the least favoured prison jobs and contributed to harsher discipline. Evidence of discriminatory treatment by prison officers has regularly resurfaced ever since alongside mutual support and resistance by prisoners (Wilson 2003; Bosworth 1999).

Claims of serious racist brutality and discrimination in Feltham, Parc, and Brixton prisons led to a formal investigation by the Commission for Racial Equality in 2003. Seventeen counts of unlawful racial discrimination by the Prison Service included failures to protect prisoners and staff from racist abuse, violence, and intimidation, failing to meet the religious and cultural needs of Muslim prisoners, denying some black prisoners access to jobs and earned privileges, and in disproportionate disciplinary action (Commission for Racial Equality (CRE) 2003). This failure of protection was brought graphically to light in 2000 by the murder of Asian prisoner Zahid Mubarek, beaten to death by Robert Stewart, a very disturbed young white man diagnosed with psychopathic personality disorder, who shared his cell. The independent public investigation concluded that Zahid's death had been preventable. Individual officers had failed to take account of Stewart's previously disturbed, violent, and overtly racist behaviour. Institutional failures included allowing a climate of overt and covert racism against staff and prisoners to exist (House of Commons 2006).

Cheliotis and Liebling's (2006) survey of the *Quality of Prison Life* in 49 prisons found that 42 per cent of black, 41 per cent of Asian, 30 per cent of Chinese/Other, and 9 per cent of white prisoners agreed that black and Asian prisoners are treated unfairly by comparison to white prisoners. Their statistical analyses found minority ethnicity predicted a more negative perception of race equality in prison, but this varied across prisons, and with prisoners' age and gender. Discretionary decisions about earned privileges, discipline, information, and requests were central to perceptions of fairness. Edgar and Martin (2004) refer to 'informal partiality' in prison where prison officers' use of discretion lacks managerial oversight and monitoring. The role of discretion in unequal outcomes was similarly underlined in the NOM (2008) *Race Review*, conducted five years after the CRE formal investigation. This found that black prisoners were still 30 per cent more likely than white prisoners to be on the 'basic' regime (without any privileges), 50 per cent more likely to be held in a segregation unit, and 60 per cent more likely to have force used against them.

Prison officers and prisoners seem to live in 'parallel worlds'. Officers tend to perceive 'race relations' with prisoners more positively and assume that the greatest problems are among prisoners themselves (HMIP 2005). Officers in the five prisons studied by Beckford *et al.* (2005) downplayed blatant racism by staff, with some suggesting that Muslim prisoners made false claims about discriminatory treatment which they called 'playing the race card'. For their part, prisoners were concerned about racist banter and discriminatory treatment in their requests for jobs and education courses. A recent Prisons Inspectorate thematic review found that Muslim prisoners' perceptions of their treatment were significantly worse than non-Muslims with prisoner-staff relations described as 'distant' (HM Inspectorate of Prisons 2010). Many prisoners worried about being stereotyped as 'Islamic terrorists' and a 'security risk' in prison, and there were concerns about the provision of halal food.

Recent research by Phillips (2008, forthcoming) suggests a complex picture of wary and ambivalent relations among white and minority ethnic prisoners in an adult male prison and a Young Offenders' Institution. Potent undercurrents of racist sentiment sometimes surfaced amidst a professed 'multicultural conviviality'. White prisoners often struggled to navigate their encounters with culturally assertive black prisoners which caused anxiety, envy, and resentment which sometimes erupted into confrontation. This work suggests that understanding the contemporary experience of prison life must consider the complex intersections between identities forged around masculinity, ethnicity, class, and neighbourhood (Phillips 2008; Earle and Phillips 2009; Phillips, forthcoming).

## PROBATION

The imperialist roots of probation lie in the practice of religious missionaries seeking to save the souls of the intemperate. The needs and experiences of minority ethnic groups came to be recognized in probation policies from the 1980s onwards, but policy development was uneven and inconsistent. In a thematic inspection on racial equality, concerns centred on the quality of supervision of black offenders, particularly in terms of reduced levels of contact during the later stages of probation orders (HM Inspectorate of Probation 2000, 2004). Calverley et al.'s (2004) study of 483 black and Asian probation clients found that 86 per cent felt they had been treated fairly by their supervisor, most of whom were white. There were mixed views on whether having a minority ethnic supervisor would have positive benefits (one-third thought it would), and most subject to attendance on a structured group-work programme felt mixed ethnic groups rather than separate provision was the best option.

A key issue has been the extent to which probation officers have considered the role of racism in contributing to offending behaviour. Calverley et al. (2004) found that while minority ethnic offenders had similar levels of socio-economic disadvantage to their 'white' counterparts, one-fifth said they had experienced racism at school, and many claimed that racial discrimination in the labour market had limited their opportunities to engage in legitimate activities. Black empowerment programmes have been implemented in a small number of probation areas, typically incorporating sessions on black history, the dynamics of racism, exclusion, and offending, with some mentoring, training, or community support for participants to counteract negative self-beliefs. There is some indication that such programmes may have higher completion rates and contribute to reduced reoffending among participants, although evaluative evidence is scarce (Williams 2006). The gendered experiences and needs of minority ethnic female offenders, however, remains rather neglected in both the policy and academic arena (Gelsthorpe 2005).

## PERCEPTIONS OF FAIRNESS AND EQUALITY

After the Lawrence Inquiry, increasing minority ethnic confidence in the agencies of the criminal justice system has been a key government objective. In general, the British Crime Survey has found that minority ethnic respondents generally hold *more favourable* attitudes than white respondents towards the criminal justice system (Smith 2010). The more negative assessments tend to relate to perceptions of unfair treatment as suspects and a lack of respect for the rights of the accused, especially by the police (Hood *et al.* 2003). This is particularly the case for young men of all ethnic groups and people of Caribbean origin. These demographic groups are, of course, those most likely to come into coercive contact with the police and other criminal justice agencies. This has significant implications, since it remains the case that, if policing and criminal justice practices are seen as inequitable and illegitimate, this can breed defiance for authority which, in turn, can have the effect of undermining voluntary compliance with the law (Tyler 1990). Perceptions of fairness also have a significant impact on the willingness of minority ethnic communities to join the police and other criminal justice professions.

## MINORITY ETHNIC EMPLOYMENT IN THE CRIMINAL JUSTICE SYSTEM

Ensuring that criminal justice organizations have a workforce that reflects the diversity of the communities they serve is substantively important in its own right. It is a marker of a fair society and supports integration into the labour market. It has also been argued that minority ethnic representation will increase confidence and trust in the criminal justice system and enhance its legitimacy. This argument assumes that black and minority ethnic police officers, lawyers, magistrates, judges, and prison officers will act in a more even-handed and sensitive way than white officers. With 'cultural competence', they will avoid stereotyping and foster understanding and respect while specific skills, such as being multilingual, will offer operational benefits for delivering criminal justice in a multicultural setting (Bowling *et al.* 2004). On the other hand, black and Asian officials may simply find themselves co-opted into an all-encompassing occupational culture in which racialized stereotyping is maintained regardless (Cashmore 1991, 2002). In the US, for example, the research evidence reveals similar arrest and use of force rates for minority and white police officers (Walker, Spohn, and DeLone 2004).

In the wake of the Lawrence Inquiry, the Home Office (1999b) published targets for the increased recruitment, retention, career progression, and senior level representation of police, prisons, and probation services and Home Office staff from minority ethnic groups. Table 13.2 illustrates the continued under-representation of minority ethnic groups in the police and prison services, in the magistracy, judiciary, and Parole Board. Efforts to recruit a more diverse police and prison service continue to be hampered by negative perceptions exacerbated by the high-profile employment tribunals and allegations of racial discrimination. Abbas's (2005) review of access to the senior judiciary points to the significance of fewer minority ethnic students studying law at the elite universities which recruit to the Bar, as well as the influence

Table 13.2 Proportion of minority ethnic officers in the
criminal justice professions in 2009

| Agency | % |
| --- | --- |
| Police | 4 |
| Prison officers | 5 |
| Judiciary (Recorders) | 5 |
| Parole Board | 5 |
| Magistracy | 8 |
| Solicitors | 11 |
| Barristers | 11 |
| Crown Prosecution Service | 12 |
| Probation officers | 13 |
| Youth Offending Team | 16 |

Source: *Statistics on Race and the Criminal Justice System* (MOJ 2010).

of secret soundings to informally assess candidates, which disadvantage candidates from minority ethnic communities.

The Morris Inquiry (2004) into the management of diversity in the Metropolitan Police Service documented 'management by retreat' as managers expressed fear and anxiety about managing the process such that poor performance by minority ethnic officers was less likely to be tackled via structured supervision, development, or training, so there was no opportunity for improvement before formal action was taken. This contributed to the disproportionate numbers of minority ethnic officers being subjected to internal investigations and suspensions. The findings of the Butt Inquiry (2010) six years later were almost identical.

Research since the Lawrence Inquiry has found that police officers believe that overt and blatant racism so prevalent in the occupational cultures of the 1970s and 1980s has disappeared. This is a welcome development but officers also express concern about more subtle forms of discrimination. Unequal treatment persists, limiting access to informal routes for career advancement. Isolation, marginalization, and the use of veiled comments to avoid disciplinary action, have all been complained about. Such experiences may be further compounded by sexism and sexual harassment for women (Holder *et al.* 2000). Moreover, people from minority ethnic groups remain underrepresented in senior positions in most agencies (typically less than 5 per cent), with the exception of the CPS (MOJ 2010).

Professional associations run by minority ethnic groups have been set up in all of the criminal justice professions to provide support networks and training. In many cases they also have a campaigning and lobbying function. Phillips' (2005b, 2007) interviews with Chairpersons of seven minority ethnic-led professional associations (such as the Association of Black Probation Officers) found that perceptions of subtle and direct discrimination were widespread. Being given impossible work tasks, inadequate supervision and training, more severe judgements on work performance leading to disciplinary charges, were common complaints. Holdaway (2009) has likened the collective action of black police associations to that of 'new social movements'. Working within constabularies, they have highlighted racial prejudice and discrimination and engaged at a senior level within the organization to seek remedies to these problems.

## CONCLUSION

The striking over-representation of black and brown people in prisons remains a disturbing conundrum for British criminologists as it does in other parts of the world. Michael Tonry's (1994) observation that racial disproportionality is higher in England (and Australia) than in the USA remains true today, but things have not remained static. Political discourse has hardened against offenders and governments' appetite for punishment has grown. The number of crimes on the statute book has increased and meanwhile, the police have been granted more powers which they are using more frequently. More people from minority ethnic communities have experience of stop and search, more are being arrested and facing criminal trials and experiencing prison. As fast as the prison population has grown, the imprisonment of people from minority ethnic communities has grown faster still. These trends are a clearly visible sign of malign neglect (Tonry 2005) and, as we argued a decade ago, the criminalization of Britain's black and other ethnic minority populations has not occurred unwittingly, but 'knowingly, as a matter of policy' (Bowling and Phillips 2002: 261).

The question of differences in offending among different ethnic groups remains a live issue (House of Commons 2007). Self-report surveys show that black and white people have, in general, an equal likelihood of being involved in crime and that people of Asian origin are much less likely to say they have been involved in crime. On the other hand, police arrest data, victimization surveys, and witness descriptions conclude that black people are disproportionately more likely to commit some specific criminal offences. The evidence points to social and economic inequality and the penalization of poverty as key to explaining these differences. From this perspective, the key to the puzzle is socio-economic exclusion not race or ethnicity.

Other commentators have argued that cultures of crime or of resistance have been 'imported' to an otherwise peaceful United Kingdom. This view can easily be criticized because it over-simplifies the cultural complexity of life in Britain and neglects the context of socio-economic inequality. At the same time, there is good evidence that racial discrimination operates in various forms at each stage of the criminal justice process. Police stereotyping plays a role in the targeting of black and Asian people for stop and search on the basis of unjustified assumptions rather than reasonable suspicion, and combined with 'racial profiling' and police deployment in areas where minority ethnic groups are more 'available', they are exposed to the criminal justice system more than their white counterparts. Direct discrimination and the application of supposedly neutral criteria when police, magistrates, and judges during arrest, charge, and sentencing decisions can also disadvantage minority ethnic suspects and defendants.

In his contribution to the early editions of the *Oxford Handbook of Criminology*, David Smith (1994, 1997) insisted that conceptualizing the divergent outcomes for people of black and Asian origin could not be explained by 'generalized racism'. Most persuasively, he pointed to the extensive economic and social exclusion of people of Pakistani and Bangladeshi origin who were, nonetheless, not over-represented among arrestees or prisoners. This perspective, however, overlooks the evidence that modern racism has, since its origins, constructed very different images of particular ethnic groups and these have inspired markedly different social responses. It also neglects the possibility of change. British officials were convinced in 1972 that black people were no more likely than their white neighbours to be involved in crime, but four years later this had turned 180 degrees. Similarly, in recent times the communities of the Indian subcontinent, hitherto portrayed as law-abiding and self-contained, have now become the focus of the police. In our view, conceiving of racism as a complex and socially situated phenomenon *can* explain the criminal justice experiences of different ethnic groups (Bowling and Phillips 2002). Thus, patterns of selective enforcement and harsher criminal justice outcomes are consistent with unjustified heightened suspicion of black people (and more recently Asians, especially Muslims) based on stereotypes. For this reason, we reject notions of a uniform, static, and monolithic form of racism in favour of one rooted in historical and spatial specificity.

Racism interacts with class disadvantage to produce patterns of social inequality experienced differently by minority ethnic groups; that is to say that racism has relative autonomy from class relations. Crime clusters in conditions of social and economic exclusion and these material conditions mean that offending among minority ethnic groups is more likely to occur in public places, is more visible and subject to surveillance and police attention. Compounded by racial discrimination within the criminal justice process, a disproportionate number of people within black and other minority ethnic communities acquire stop and search histories, intelligence files, entries on the police national computer, criminal convictions, and prison records. This is illustrated starkly by the Equality and Human Rights Commission (2009) estimate that within the black male population, one-third of men and three-quarters of youth (16–24 years) have records on the national DNA database holding samples of those arrested for a recordable offence.

More than a decade ago, the Lawrence Inquiry was hailed as a watershed in the pursuit of justice for minority ethnic groups in Britain, but despite the volumes of research, policy development, legislation, innovation, and training that followed in its wake, progress has been slow. Racialized exclusion and discrimination is not yet a thing of the past and in fact things have got worse rather than better for many people from minority ethnic communities. 'Tough' crime policies have resulted in funnelling increasing numbers of people through the criminal justice process and into prison, impacting particularly severely on minority ethnic communities. And yet these policies have not achieved their stated goal of making all communities safe and peaceful places to live. The challenge for students of criminology and criminal justice is to envision ways to create a safer society without sacrificing freedom, fairness, and justice.

# ■ SELECTED FURTHER READING

This chapter develops the ideas explored in the authors' *Racism, Crime and Justice* (Longman 2002); a more recent text is Colin Webster's *Understanding Race and Crime* (Open University Press, 2007), and Patel and Tyrer's *Race, Crime and Resistance* (Sage, 2011). On ethnicity and victimization, see Ben Bowling's *Violent Racism* (Clarendon Press, 1999) and *Hate Crime* by Nathan Hall (Willan, 2005). *Policing, Race and Racism* by Michael Rowe (Willan, 2005) provides an overview and a historical perspective is provided by James Whitefield in *Unhappy Dialogue: the Metropolitan Police and London's West Indian Community* (Willan, 2004). For the other key areas of criminal justice see Tiggey May and colleagues' (*Differential Treatment in the Youth Justice System* (EHRC 2010), *Race and Probation* by Lewis et al. (Willan, 2005). The starting point for a critical perspective on these issues is Stuart Hall and colleagues' (1978) *Policing the Crisis*. Mary Bosworth, Ben Bowling, and Maggy Lee (2008), attempt to open up new directions in research on *Globalisation, ethnicity and racism* in a special issue of *Theoretical Criminology* (Vol. 12(3): 263–73).

# ■ REFERENCES

ABBAS, T. (2005), *Diversity in the Senior Judiciary: A Literature Review of Research on Ethnic Inequalities*, London: The Commission for Judicial Appointments.

ALDRIDGE, J. and MEDINA, J. (2008),*Youth Gangs in an English City: Social Exclusion, Drugs and Violence*, End of Award Report (RES-000-23-0615), Swindon: Economic and Social Research Council.

ALEXANDER, C. (2000), *The Asian Gang: Ethnicity, Identity, Masculinity*, Oxford: Berg.

ALLEN, C. and NIELSEN, J. S. (2002), *Summary Report on Islamophobia in the EU after 11 September 2001*, Vienna: European Monitoring Centre on Racism and Xenophobia.

ARMSTRONG, D., HINE, J., HACKING, S., ARMAOS, R., JONES, R., KLESSINGER, N., and FRANCE, A. (2005), *Children, risk and crime: the On Track Youth Lifestyles Surveys*, Home Office Research Study 278, London: Home Office.

BARTH, F. (1969), *Ethnic Groups and Boundaries: The Social Organisation of Cultural Difference*, London: George Allen and Unwin.

BECKFORD, J. A., JOLY, D., and KHOSROKHAVAR, F. (2005), *Muslims in Prison—Challenge and Change in Britain and France*, Basingstoke: Palgrave.

BETHNAL GREEN AND STEPNEY TRADES COUNCIL (1978), *Blood on the Streets*, London: Bethnal Green and Stepney Trades Council.

BOSWORTH, M. (1999), *Engendering Resistance: Agency and Power in Women's Prisons*, Aldershot: Dartmouth Publishing Company.

BOWLING, B. (1990), 'Conceptual and Methodological Problems in Measuring "Race" Differences in Delinquency: A Reply to Marianne Junger', *British Journal of Criminology*, 30: 483–92.

—— (1993), 'Racial Harassment and the Process of Victimization: Conceptual and Methodological Implications for the Local Crime Survey', *British Journal of Criminology*, 33(2): 231–50.

—— (1999), *Violent Racism: Victimisation, Policing and Social Context* (revised edn), Oxford: Oxford University Press.

—— and PHILLIPS, C. (2002), *Racism, Crime and Justice*, London: Longman.

—— and —— (2007),'Disproportionate and Discriminatory: Reviewing the Evidence on Police Stop and Search', *Modern Law Review*, 70, 936–61.

——, PHILLIPS, C., CAMPBELL, A., and DOCKING, M. (2004), *Policing and human rights: eliminating discrimination, xenophobia, intolerance and the abuse of power from policework*, Geneva: United Nations Research Institute for Social Development.

——, PARMAR, A., and PHILLIPS, C. (2008), 'Policing minority ethnic communities', in Newburn, T. (ed.), *Handbook of policing*, 2nd edn, Cullompton: Willan Publishing.

BRINCOME, A., RALPHS, M., SAMPSON, A., and TSUF, H. (2001), 'An Analysis of the Role of Neighbourhood Ethnic Composition in the Geographical Distribution of Racially Motivated Incidents', *British Journal of Criminology*, 41(2): 293–308.

BUCKE, T. and BROWN, D. (1997), *In Police Custody: Police Powers and Suspects' Rights Under the Revised PACE Codes of Practice*, Home Office Research Study 174, London: Home Office.

BULLOCK, K. and TILLEY, N. (2002), *Shootings, Gangs and Violent Incidents in Manchester: Developing a Crime Reduction Strategy*, Crime Reduction Research Series Paper 13, London: Home Office.

BUTTS, C. (2010), *Race and Faith Inquiry Report*, London: MPA.

CALVERLEY, A., COLE, B., KAUR, G., LEWIS, S., RAYNOR, P., ASADEGHI, S., SMITH, D. A., VANSTONE, M., and WARDAK, A. (2004), *Black and Asian Offenders on Probation*, Home Office Research Study 277, London: Home Office.

CANTLE, T. (2001), *Community Cohesion: A Report of the Independent Review Team*, London: Home Office.

CASHMORE, E. (1991), 'Black Cops Inc.', in E. Cashmore and E. McLaughlin (eds), *Out of Order?: Policing Black People*, London: Routledge.

—— (2002), 'Behind the Window Dressing: Ethnic Minority Police Perspectives on Cultural Diversity', *Journal of Ethnic and Migration Studies*, 28(2): 327–41.

CHAKRABORTI, N. and GARLAND, J. (2004) (eds.), *Rural Racism*, Cullompton: Willan Publishing.

CHELIOTIS, L. K. and LIEBLING, A. (2006), 'Race Matters in British Prisons: Towards a Research Agenda' *British Journal of Criminology*, 46(2): 286–317.

CLANCY, A., HOUGH, M., AUST, R., and KERSHAW, C. (2001), *Crime, Policing and Justice: the Experience of Ethnic Minorities: Findings from the 2000 British Crime Survey*, Home Office Research Study 223, London: Home Office.

COLEMAN, C. and MOYNIHAN, J. (1996), *Understanding Crime Data: Haunted by the Dark Figure*, Milton Keynes: Open University Press.

COMMISSION FOR RACIAL EQUALITY (2003), *A Formal Investigation by the Commission for Racial Equality into HM Prison Service of England and Wales—Part 2: Racial Equality in Prisons*, London: Commission for Racial Equality.

DANIEL, W.W. (1968), *Racial Discrimination in England*, Harmondsworth: Penguin.

DENMAN, S. (2001), *The Denman Report—Race Discrimination in the Crown Prosecution Service*, London: Crown Prosecution Service.

DOCKING, M. and TUFFIN, R. (2005), *Racist Incidents: Progress since the Lawrence Inquiry*, Online Report 42/05, London: Home Office.

EARLE, R. and PHILLIPS, C. (2009,) '"Con-Viviality" and Beyond: Identity Dynamics in a Young Men's Prison', in M. Wetherell (ed.), *Identity in the 21st Century: New Trends in Changing Times*, Basingstoke: Palgrave.

EDGAR, K. AND MARTIN, C. (2004), *Perceptions of Race and Conflict: perspectives of minoitry ethnic prisoners and of prison officers*, London: Home Office Online Report 11/04.

EQUALITY AND HUMAN RIGHTS COMMISSION (2009), *The Equality and Human Rights Commission's Response to the Government's Consultation on: Keeping the Right People on the DNA Database*, London: EHRC.

—— (2010), *Stop and Think: a critical review of the use of stop and search powers in England and Wales*, London: EHRC.

FEILZER, M. and HOOD, R. (2004), *Difference or Discrimination?*, London: Youth Justice Board.

FITZGERALD, M. (1993), *Ethnic Minorities in the Criminal Justice System*, Home Office Research and Statistics Department, Research Study No. 20, London: HMSO.

FLOOD-PAGE, C., CAMPBELL, S., HARRINGTON, V., and MILLER, J. (2000), *Youth Crime: Findings from the 1998/99 Youth Lifestyle Survey*, Home Office Research Study No. 209, London: Home Office.

FOSTER, J., NEWBURN, T., and SOUHAMI, A. (2005), *Assessing the Impact of the Stephen Lawrence Inquiry*, Home Office Research Study 294, London: Home Office.

GELSTHORPE, L. (2005), 'The Experiences of Female Minority Ethnic Offenders: The Other "Other"', in S. Lewis, P. Raynor, D. Smith, and A. Wardak (eds), *Race and Probation*, Cullompton: Willan Publishing.

GENDERS, E. and PLAYER, E. (1989), *Race Relations in Prison*, Oxford: Clarendon Press.

GILROY, P. (1982), 'Police and Thieves', in Centre for Contemporary Cultural Studies, *The Empire Strikes Back*, London: Hutchinson.

—— (1987a), *There Ain't No Black in the Union Jack*, London: Hutchinson.

—— (1987b), 'The Myth of Black Criminality', in P. Scraton (ed.), *Law, Order and the Authoritarian State: Readings in Critical Criminology*, Milton Keynes: Open University Press.

—— (2000), *Between Camps: Race, Identity and Nationalism at the end of the Colour Line*, London: Allen.

GOLDSON, B. (ed) (2011), *Youth in Crisis?: 'Gangs', Territoriality and Violence*, London: Routledge.

GUNTER, A. (2010), *Growing up bad: black youth culture and badness in an East London neighbourhood*, London: Tufnell Press.

GRAHAM, J. and BOWLING, B. (1995), *Young People and Crime*, Home Office Research Study No. 145, London: Home Office.

HAGEDORN, J. (ed.) (2007), *Gangs in the Global City: Alternatives to Traditional Criminology*, Chicago: University of Illinois Press.

HALL, N., GRIEVE, J., and SAVAGE, S. (eds) (2009), *Policing and the Legacy of Lawrence*, Cullompton: Willan.

HALL, S., CRITCHER, C., JEFFERSON, T., CLARKE, J., and ROBERTS, B. (1978), *Policing the Crisis: Mugging, the State and Law and Order*, London: Macmillan.

HALES, G., LEWIS, C., and SILVERSTONE D., (2006), *Gun crime: the market in and use of illegal firearms*, Home Office Research Study 298, London, Home Office.

HALL, S., LEWIS, G., and MCLAUGHLIN, E. (1998), *The Report on Racial Stereotyping* (prepared for Deighton Guedalla, solicitors for Duwayne Brooks, June 1998), Milton Keynes: Open University.

HALLSWORTH, S and YOUNG, T (2008), 'Gang talk and gang talkers: a critique', *Crime Media and Culture*, 4(2):175–95.

HARRINGTON, V. and MAYHEW, P. (2001), *Mobile Phone Theft*, Home Office Research Study 235, London: Home Office.

HEATH, A. and CHEUNG, S. (2006), *Ethnic penalties in the labour market: Employers and discrimination*.

Research Report No. 341, London, Department for Work and Pensions.

HEAVEN, O. and HUDSON, B. (2005), 'Race, Ethnicity and Crime', in C. Hale, K. Hayward, A. Wahidin and E. Wincup, *Criminology*, Oxford: Oxford University Press.

HER MAJESTY'S INSPECTORATE OF PRISONS (2005), *Parallel Worlds: A Thematic Review of Race Relations in Prisons*, London: HMIP.

—— (2010) *Muslim Prisoners' Experiences: A Thematic Review*, London: HMIP.

HER MAJESTY'S INSPECTORATE OF PROBATION (2000), *Towards Race Equality. Thematic Inspection*, London: Home Office.

—— (2004), *Towards Race Equality: Follow-up Inspection Report*, London: Her Majesty's Inspectorate of Probation.

HESSE, B., RAI, D.K., BENNETT, C., and McGILCHRIST, P. (1992), *Beneath the Surface: Racial Harassment*, Aldershot: Avebury.

HINDELANG, M., HIRSCHI, T., and WEIS, J. (1981), *Measuring Delinquency*, Beverly Hills: Sage.

HOLDAWAY, S. (2009), *Black Police Assocations: An Analysis of Race and Ethnicity within Constabularies*, Oxford: Oxford University Press.

HOLDER, K. A., NEE, C., and ELLIS, T. (2000), 'Triple Jeopardy? Black and Asian Women Police Officers' Experiences of Discrimination', *International Journal of Police Science and Management*, 3(1): 68–87.

HOME OFFICE (1986), *The Ethnic Origins of Prisoners: The Prison Population on 30 June 1985 and Persons Received, July 1984–March 1985*, London: Home Office.

—— (1999a), *Action Plan, Response to the Stephen Lawrence Inquiry*, London: HMSO.

—— (1999b), *Race Equality—The Home Secretary's Employment Targets: Staff targets for the Home Office, the Prison, the Police, the Fire and the Probation Services, a Home Office Publication under section 95 of the Criminal Justice Act 1991*, London: Home Office.

—— (2000), *Prison Statistics England and Wales 1999*, London: Home Office.

—— (2005a), *Code A: Police and Criminal Evidence Act Code of Practice for the Exercise of Statutory Powers of Stop and Search. Effective from 1 January 2006*, London: Home Office.

—— (2005b), *Stop and Search Manual*, London: Home Office.

HOOD, R. (1992), *Race and Sentencing*, Oxford: Clarendon Press.

HOOD, R., SHUTE, S., and SEEMUNGAL, F. (2003), *Ethnic Minorities in the Criminal Courts: Perceptions of fairness and equality of treatment*. Research Series 2/03. London: Lord Chancellor's Department.

HOUSE OF COMMONS (1972), Select Committee on Race Relations and Immigration Session 1971–2, *Police-Immigrant Relations*, London: House of Commons.

—— (1976), Select Committee on Race Relations and Immigration Session 1975–6, *The West Indian Community*, London: House of Commons.

—— (2006), *Report of the Zahid Mubarek Inquiry*, London: The Stationery Office.

—— (2007), Home Affairs Select Committee, *Young Black People and the Criminal Justice System*, London: House of Commons.

HUDSON, B. (2006), 'Beyond white man's justice: Race, gender and justice in late modernity', *Theoretical Criminology*, 10(1): 29–47.

HUDSON, B. (1993), *Penal Policy and Social Justice*, Basingstoke: Macmillan.

—— and BRAMHALL, G. (2005), 'Assessing the Other: Constructions of "Asianness" in Risk Assessments by Probation Officers', *British Journal of Criminology*, 45(5): 721–40.

HUNTE, J. (1966), *Nigger Hunting in England?*, London: West Indian Standing Conference.

INNES, M., ROBERTS, C., INNES, H., LOWE, T., and LAKHANI, S. (2011), *Assessing the Effects of Prevent Policing: A Report to the Association of Chief Police Officers*, Cardiff Universities' Police Science Institute.

INSTITUTE OF RACE RELATIONS (1987), *Policing Against Black People*, London: IRR.

JAMES, Z. (2005), 'Policing Space: Managing New Travellers in England', *British Journal of Criminology*, 46(3): 470–85.

JUNGER, M. (1989), 'Discrepancies between police and self-report data for Dutch racial minorities', *British Journal of Criminology*, 29(3): 273–84.

—— (1990), 'Studying Ethnic Minorities in Relation to Crime and Police Discrimination: Answer to Bowling', *British Journal of Criminology*, 30(4). 493–502.

KLEG, M. (1993), *Hate Prejudice and Racism*, Albany, NY: Suny Press, ch.4, pp. 85–113.

LOMBROSO, C. (1876), *L'Uomo Delinquente*, Turin: Fratelli Bocca.

MACPHERSON, W. (1999), *The Stephen Lawrence Inquiry*, Report of an Inquiry by Sir William Macpherson of Cluny, advised by Tom Cook, The Right Reverend Dr John Sentamu and Dr Richard Stone, Cm 4262 1, London: The Stationery Office.

McGHEE, D. (2008), *The End of Multiculturalism: Terrorism, Integration and Human Rights*, Maidenhead, Open University Press.

MAYNARD, W. and READ, T. (1997), *Policing Racially Motivated Incidents*, Police Research Group, Crime Detection and Prevention Series No. 59, London: Home Office.

MERTON, R. K. (1968), *Social Theory and Social Structure*, New York: Free Press.

METROPOLITAN POLICE AUTHORITY (2004), *Report of the MPA Scrutiny on MPS Stop and Search Practice*, London: Metropolitan Police Authority.

MHLANGA, B. (1999), *Race and Crown Prosecution Service Decisions*, London: The Stationery Office.

MOJ (2009), *Statistics on Race and the Criminal Justice System 2007/8*, London: MOJ.

—— (2010), *Statistics on Race and the Criminal Justice System 2008/9*, London: MOJ.

MONTAGU, A. (1943), *Man's Most Dangerous Myth: The Fallacy of Race*, London: AltaMira Press.

MOONEY, J. and YOUNG, J. (2000), 'Policing Ethnic Minorities: stop and search in North London', in A. Marlow and B. Loveday, *After Macpherson: policing after the Stephen Lawrence Inquiry*, Lyme Regis: Russell House Publishing.

MORRIS, W. (2004), *The Report of the Morris Inquiry the Case for Change: People in the Metropolitan Police Service*, London: Metropolitan Police Authority.

MVA and MILLER, J. (2000), *Profiling Populations Available for Stops and Searches*, Police Research Series Paper No. 131, London: Home Office.

NEWBURN, T. and HAYMAN, S. (2001), *Policing, Surveillance and Social Control: CCTV and Police Monitoring of Suspects*, Cullompton: Willan Publishing.

NEWBURN, T., SHINER, M., and HAYMAN, S. (2004), 'Race, Crime and Injustice? Strip Search and the Treatment of Suspects in Custody', *British Journal of Criminology*, 44(5): 677–94.

NOMS (2008), *Race Review 2008: Implementing Race Equality in Prisons—Five Years On*, London, NOMS.

NORRIS, C., FIELDING, N., KEMP, C., and FIELDING, J. (1992), 'Black and Blue: an Analysis of the Influence of Race on Being Stopped by the Police', *British Journal of Sociology*, 43(2): 207–23.

PARMAR, A (2011), Counter-terrorist or counter-productive, *Policing and Society*, 21(44): 369–82.

PEARSON, G. (1983), *Hooligan: a History of Respectable Fears*, London: Macmillan.

PHILLIPS, C.(2005), 'Facing inwards and outwards?: Institutional racism, race equality and the role of Black and Asian professional associations', *Criminology & Criminal Justice*, 5(4): 357–77.

—— (2007), 'The re-emergence of the "black spectre": minority professional associations in the post-Macpherson era", *Ethnic and racial studies*, 30(3): 375–96.

—— (2008), 'Negotiating Identities: Ethnicity and Social Relations in a Young Offenders' Institution', *Theoretical Criminology*, 12(3): 313–31.

—— (2009), 'Ethnic Inequalities: Another Ten Years of the Same?', in J. Hills, T. Sefton, and K.Stewart (eds), *Towards a More Equal Society? New Labour, Poverty, Inequality and Exclusion*, Bristol: Policy Press.

—— (Forthcoming), *The Multicultural Prison: Ethnicity, Masculinity and Social Relations among Prisoners*, Oxford: Oxford University Press.

—— and EARLE, R. (2010), 'Reading difference differently?: identity, epistemology and prison ethnography', *British Journal of Criminology*, 50(2): 360–78.

——. and BOWLING, B. (2003), 'Racism, Ethnicity and Criminology: Developing Minority Perspectives', *British Journal of Criminology*, 43(2): 269–90.

—— and BROWN, D. (1998), *Entry into the Criminal Justice System: a Survey of Police Arrests and Their Outcomes*, Home Office Research Study No. 185, London: Home Office.

—— and SAMPSON, A. (1998), 'Preventing Repeated Victimisation: an Action Research Project', *British Journal of Criminology*, 38(1):124–44.

PITTS, J. (2008), *Reluctant Gangsters: the changing face of youth crime*, Cullompton: Willan.

QUINTON, P., BLAND, N., and MILLER, J. (2000), *Police Stops, Decision-Making and Practice*, Police Research Series Paper No. 130, London: Home Office.

RAY, L., SMITH, D., and WASTELL, L. (2004), 'Shame, Rage and Racist Violence', *British Journal of Criminology*, 44(3): 350–68.

REINER, R. (2010), *The Politics of the Police*, Oxford, 4th edn, Oxford University Press.

ROCK, P. (2004), *Constructing Victims' Rights: The Home Office, New Labour, and Victims*, Oxford: Oxford University Press.

RUGGIERO, V. (2000), *Crime and Markets: Essays in Anti-Criminology*, Oxford: Oxford University Press.

SALISBURY, H. and UPSON, A. (2004), *Ethnicity, Victimisation and Worry About Crime: Findings from the 2001/2002 and 2002/3 British Crime Surveys*, Findings 237, London: Home Office.

SAMPSON, A. and PHILLIPS, C. (1992), *Multiple Victimisation: Racial Attacks on an East London Estate*, Police Research Group Crime Prevention Unit Series Paper 36, London: Home Office.

—— (1996), *Reducing Repeat Victimisation on an East London Estate*, Police Research Group Crime Prevention Unit Crime Prevention and Detection Paper 67, London: Home Office.

SCARMAN, L. (1981), *The Scarman Report*, London: HMSO.

SHARP, C. and BUDD, T. (2005), *Minority Ethnic Groups and Crime: the Findings from the Offending, Crime and Justice Survey 2003*, Home Office Online Report 33/05.

SKOGAN, W.G. (1990), *The Police and the Public in England and Wales: A British Crime Survey Report*, Home Office Research Study No. 117, London: HMSO.

SMITH, D. (2010), *Public Confidence in the Criminal Justice System: Findings from the British Crime Survey 2002/03 to 2007/08*, MOJ Research Series 16/10, London: MOJ.

SMITH, D.J. (1994), 'Race, Crime and Criminal Justice', in M. Maguire, R. Morgan, and R. Reiner (eds), *The Oxford Handbook of Criminology*, 1st edn, Oxford: Clarendon Press.

—— (1997), 'Ethnic Origins, Crime and Criminal Justice', in M. Maguire, R. Morgan, and R. Reiner (eds), *The Oxford Handbook of Criminology*, 2nd edn, Oxford: Oxford University Press.

—— and GRAY, J. (1985), *Police and People in London*, London: Policy Studies Institute.

SMITH, J. (2003), *The Nature of Personal Robbery*, Home Office Research Study 254, London: Home Office.

SOLOMOS, J. and BACK, L. (1996), *Racism and Society*, London: Macmillan.

STRAND, S. (2008), *Minority Ethnic Pupils in the Longitudinal Study of Young People in England: Extension Report on Performance in Public Examinations at Age 16*, DCSF RB029, London: DCSF.

SUDBURY, J. (2005), ' "Mules", "Yardies" and Other Fold Devils: Mapping Cross-Border Imprisonment in Britain', *Global Lockdown: Race, Gender, and the Prison-Industrial Complex*, London: Routledge.

THOMAS, C. (2010), *Are Juries Fair? MOJ Research Series 1/10*, London: MOJ.

TONRY, M. (1994), 'Racial Disproportion in US Prisons', *British Journal of Criminology*, 34, Special Issue: 97–115.

—— (1995), *Malign Neglect: Race, Crime and Punishment in America*, New York: Oxford University Press.

TYLER, T. (1990), *Why People Obey the Law*, London: Yale University Press.

WADDINGTON, P. A. J., STENSON, K., and DON, D. (2004) 'In Proportion: Race and Police Stop and Search', *British Journal of Criminology*, 44: 889–914.

WALKER, S., SPOHN, C., and DELONE, M. (2004). *The Color Of Justice: Race, Ethnicity, And Crime In America*. 2nd edn, Belmont, CA: Wadsworth.

WARDAK, A. (2000), *Social Control and Deviance: A South Asian Community in Scotland*, Aldershot: Ashgate.

WEBSTER, C. (1997), 'The Construction of British "Asian Criminality"', *International Journal of the Sociology of Law*, 25: 65–86.

WEBSTER, C. (2007), *Understanding Race and Crime*, Buckingham: Open University Press.

WHITFIELD, J. (2004), *Unhappy Dialogue: The Metropolitan Police and Black Londoners in Post-War Britain*, Cullompton: Willan.

WILLIAMS, P. (2006), 'Designing and Delivering Programmes for Minority Ethnic Offenders', in S. Lewis, P. Raynor, D. Smith, and A. Wardak (eds), *Race and Probation*, Cullompton: Willan Publishing.

WILSON, D. (2003), ' "Keeping Quiet" or "Going Nuts": Some Emerging Strategies Used by Young Black People In Custody at a Time of Childhood Being Re-Constructed', *Howard Journal of Criminal Justice*, 42(5): 411–25.

# 14

# VICTIMS, THE CRIMINAL PROCESS, AND RESTORATIVE JUSTICE

*Carolyn Hoyle*[1]

## INTRODUCTION

In recent years, conventional conceptions of victimization have been challenged by new studies of previously hidden victims: of corporate and white-collar crime (Croall 2009); 'non-conventional' crimes such as consumer fraud, bribery, and computer-related offences (Van Dijk *et al.* 2010); trafficking (Hoyle *et al.* 2011), and genocide, armed conflict, torture, terrorism, and crimes of the state (Karstedt 2010). Studies of secondary victimization and the collateral effects of crime and punishment draw attention to the families of primary victims (Young 2000), prisoners (Travis and Waul 2004), those convicted of serious offences (Condry 2007), and those sentenced to capital punishment or executed in jurisdictions that retain the death penalty (Vandiver 2009). These studies, alongside academic research and the political impact of legislation, policy-making, and lobbying by interest groups, both expand and render problematic the concept of victim. The promotion of victims' interests on the national and international stage has driven radical policy development in respect of victims' service and procedural rights, including restorative justice; reforms that purport to enhance justice for victims.

[1] I would like to thank Marie Manikis for her research assistance and Rod Morgan, David Rose, Lucia Zedner, Polly Rossetti from Victim Support, Lizzie Nelson from the Restorative Justice Council, and Christine Magill from CPS headquarters for their helpful comments on a previous draft.

# THE NATURE AND DISTRIBUTION OF VICTIMIZATION

## SOURCES OF DATA

### Survey data

Since the 1960s victimization surveys have sought to quantify the unreported 'dark figure' of crime, and thereby generated criminological interest in victims. The National Crime Victimization Surveys (NCVSs) and the British Crime Survey (BCS) collected data on victimization incidence and prevalence as well as risk, impact, and fear of crime. National crime surveys are also carried out in Scotland (MacLeod 2009) and in Northern Ireland (Toner and Freel 2010), and over 70 countries are included in national or international comparative studies. Further data are generated by the International Crime Victimization Survey programme (ICVS), covering approximately 48 countries (Alvazzi del Frate and Van Kesteren 2004). Recently, the European Commission's Action Plan on the Hague Programme (2004–9), updated in the Stockholm Action Plan (2010–14), commits the European Commission to develop a comparative victimization survey.

These surveys seek a more accurate picture of victimization than police records supply and identify the social, economic, and demographic characteristics of victims as well as victims' responses to crime (although for discussion of methodological limitations see Maguire, this volume). Comparative surveys of levels of concern about crime, show that Britons are much more concerned than other Europeans, and even Americans, with 43 per cent of the UK population considering crime and violence to be one of the most worrying issues in their lives—more than double the level in Germany and significantly higher than in America (Duffy *et al.* 2007).

The World Health Organization (WHO) and various non-governmental organizations (NGOs), such as Amnesty International (AI) and Human Rights Watch, regularly publish reports on crimes; including, violence against women and children, violence against minorities, human rights abuses, torture, 'disappearances', 'death squads', trafficking, terrorism, as well as on the justice system; particularly, the death penalty, arbitrary detention, unlawful killings, unfair trials, and deaths in custody. The annual reports on human rights published by the United Kingdom Foreign and Commonwealth Office[2] and UN special rapporteurs' reports are further sources of information on victims of extra-judicial killings, torture, terrorism and the death penalty, as well as specific abuses against women and children.

### Academic research

Academic empirical studies, since Sparks, Genn, and Dodd's study (1977) of London, have attempted to overcome the limitations of recorded data by adopting qualitative methods and focusing on local smaller samples in order to document the uneven

---

[2] See www.fco.gov.uk/en/publications-and-documents/publications1/annual-reports/human-rights-report.

distribution of risk, by race, sex, age, class, and locale (see Maguire, this volume) and the differential fear of crime (Farrall and Lee 2008). For example, rural victim surveys challenged the presumption that crime is primarily an urban problem (Mawby 2007b).

Local surveys set crime in its broader social context by including questions about racial and sexual harassment and anti-social behaviour, as well as victim perceptions of police priorities, service delivery, and accountability. Several local or specialized surveys suggest levels of sexual crime against women far higher than those revealed by national victim surveys and police records (Walby and Allen 2004). The chief difficulty with these studies is that differences in approach, wording, and categorization of responses have generated widely differing estimates of victimization. These limitations led many academics, particularly those committed to empirical study of the experiences of vulnerable groups, to abandon the survey for in-depth qualitative work. Examples include studies on intimate partner violence (Hoyle and Sanders 2000), including within ethnic minority and marginal communities (Parmar *et al.* 2005), at the intersections of race and class (Sokoloff 2005), in same-sex relationships (Donovan and Hester 2010), and violence against both children and men in the home (Hester, Pearson, and Harwin 2007; Dobash and Dobash 2004). Such research has exposed the problems of male rape (Allen 2002), date rape (Fisher *et al.* 2005), and rape within marriage (Basile 2008).

Qualitative research by Hamill (2002) illustrates the less than ideal status of victims of paramilitary punishments in Northern Ireland, while Borer (2003) challenges the binary approach to victims and offenders through an analysis of the South African Truth and Reconciliation Commission. These studies make clear that there can be considerable overlap between populations of victims and offenders. This is not only because victims and offenders tend to share the same socio-demographic features, but that in some cases offending can—causally—lead to an increase in victimization and victimization can—to a lesser extent—lead to an increase in offending (Bottoms and Costello 2010).[3] Quantitative academic research also reveals the inadequacies of recorded crime data. Shepherd *et al.* found that only 23 per cent of people injured in assaults who attended Bristol Accident and Emergency department appeared in police records of woundings (Shepherd *et al.* 1989).

A relatively new area of 'radical-critical' victims research concerns victims of crimes of the state, armed conflict, and crimes against humanity. Despite intense media coverage of the atrocities in Srebrenica in 1995 and the 1994 genocide in Rwanda, as well as state crimes committed in Zimbabwe over the past decade and the current crimes against humanity being committed in Syria and the Ivory Coast, criminology has only recently begun to recognize and take interest in the scale and effects of such violence (Moon 2011). Recent empirical and theoretical studies of genocidal victimization suggest that this is a fruitful area of research (Hagan and Rymond-Richmond 2009), although it poses methodological challenges for criminology (Parmentier 2011).

---

[3] Victim Support's report, 'Hoodie or Goodie', shows a link between victimization and offending behaviour in young people (see: www.victimsupport.com/About%20us/Publications/~/media/Files/Publications/ResearchReports/hoodie-or-goodie-report).

Recently, the difficulties inherent in identifying a 'typical trafficking narrative', have persuaded many that small-scale, local studies are preferable to those that make more sweeping generalizations regarding routes in and out of trafficking (Tyldum 2010). However, gaining access to subjects can frustrate those focused on in-depth qualitative research (Bosworth *et al.* 2011).

With a few notable exceptions, there has been insufficient comparative research on victims or policies responding to victimization. While academics in the UK draw on research from the US, and occasionally from Australia, they rarely cite work from other European jurisdictions. However, in recent years, comparative research has appeared on victim compensation (Miers 2007), on European responses to racial and religious victimization (Goodey 2007), and on victims and policy-making (Hall 2010), but as with other criminological research, the comparative method remains underused.

## THE NATURE AND SCOPE OF VICTIMIZATION

### National data

The BCS consistently shows that while the chance of being a victim of a minor offence is relatively high, the risk of suffering a more serious offence is small, and recent surveys provide evidence of an overall falling crime rate. The 2009–10 BCS estimated that there were 2,087,000 violent incidents against adults in England and Wales, although around 50 per cent of these did not result in any lasting injury to the victim. Violent crime rates have fallen by 50 per cent since reaching a peak in 1995, with murder rates in 2009–10 at their lowest for more than a decade. Victimization falls unequally on particular individuals and groups. Risk of victimization generally is closely related to geographical area, and risk of personal victimization correlated with age, sex, and patterns of routine activity, such as going out in the evenings and consuming alcohol (Flatley *et al.* 2010: 63). Much crime is endogenous—victims, witnesses, and offenders are recruited from substantially the same groupings and are more likely to be (quite literally) in contact with one another. Age is a key determinant: young men between the ages of 16 and 24 are most at risk, with 13.3 per cent experiencing criminal violence in the past year (Flatley *et al.* 2010: 45). Domestic violence is the only category for which the risks for women (0.4 per cent) are higher than for men (0.2 per cent) (domestic violence is the largest cause of morbidity worldwide in women aged 19–44; Home Office 2005a: 2). Risks of violence by strangers and acquaintances are substantially greater for men than for women; 2.2 per cent of men were victims of stranger violence in 2009–10, compared with 0.6 per cent of women (Flatley *et al.* 2010).

Women are most likely to be raped by men they know: 54 per cent of rapes are committed by intimates, and 29 per cent by other known individuals, with 50 per cent of cases involving repeat offences by the same person (Walby and Allen 2004). Although 6 per cent more sexual offences were recorded by the police in 2009–10 than in the previous year (54,509 offences, including 13,991 rapes of women and 1,174 rapes of men), this increase should be interpreted with caution, as the Association of Chief Police Officers has made efforts to enhance the recording of serious sexual offences. Approximately 2 per cent of women aged 16 to 59 and less than 1 per cent of men of the same age had experienced a sexual assault (including attempts) in 2009–10 (Flatley *et al.* 2010: 57).

The risk of being a victim of either burglary or vehicle-related theft has halved since 1995 and is much reduced for other property crimes. Household theft halved between 1995 and 2009–10 and domestic burglaries fell by 6 per cent between 2008–09 and 2009–10 (Flatley *et al.* 2010: 21); results that may surprise those expecting a rise in property-related crime during the recession.

For many types of crime, in particular street robberies, both African-Caribbeans and Asians are more at risk than whites, possibly because they are over-represented in socio-economic and age groups particularly prone to crime. The risk of being the victim of a racially motivated offence is highest among those of mixed ethnicity. Assaults, threats, and vandalism are those offences most often thought to be committed for racial reasons (Salisbury and Upson 2004: 1–3).

In 2009, children aged 10–15 experienced between 248,000 and 1.7 million incidents of violence (depending on the approach used to analyse the data) (Millard and Flatley 2010: 8). Until very recently there was no national database to document crimes of sexual abuse against children. The National Society for the Prevention of Cruelty to Children (NSPCC) contacted every police force in the UK, and estimated that there were 21,000 child victims in 2009–10.[4] The Home Office made a commitment to centrally record this information from April 2011.

Those living with mental health problems in the community, like other 'vulnerable groups' such as older people and people with learning disabilities, experience high rates of crime and victimization. Seventy one per cent of respondents to a MIND study had experienced crime or harassment in the two years prior to the study and nearly 90 per cent of those living in local authority housing had been victimized (MIND 2007).

### International data

The 2005 ICVS revealed that in most countries for which trend data are available the level of victimization peaked in the middle of the 1990s and has since shown a slow but steady decline, particularly in burglary and other property crimes, with changes in violent crime being more variable (van Dijk *et al.* 2005, 16). The sixth ICVS survey took place in 2009 in six countries (Canada, Denmark, Germany, the Netherlands, Sweden, and the UK). While the report is not yet available, preliminary findings show reductions in fear of crime across all jurisdictions except Denmark, and reductions in rates of victimization across 10 'common crimes', except Denmark and Germany, where they had increased slightly.[5]

The US National Crime Victimization Survey (2008) shows that US rates of violence declined 6.9 per cent from 2007 to 2008, with violence and property crime rates in 2008 at or near their lowest levels in over three decades (Rand 2009). Nonetheless, in the US, 700,000 women report being raped or sexually assaulted each year (Krug *et al.* 2002: 151). Evidence from other continents, particularly from Africa, suggests that high rates of sexual violence are endemic. For example, the South African police statistics for 2008–9 recorded 30,000 sexual offences against women (Amnesty International 2010a), while in Haiti, during the first six months of 2009, more than half of the 136

---

[4] www.nspccannualreview.org.uk/#!/campaigns/.
[5] http://62.50.10.34/icvs/About_ICVS_2010/News_and_updates/Latest_news/Conference_report_ICVS_Final_Conference_Freiburg_October_13th_2010.

rape victims reporting to a Haitian women's organization were children (Amnesty International 2010b: 162).

Domestic violence is common and in some countries endemic: in Turkey it is estimated that between a third and a half of women are victims of physical violence in the home (Amnesty International 2005: 5). It accounts for a significant proportion of female murder victims (between 40 and 70 per cent in Australia, Canada, Israel, South Africa, and America; Krug *et al.* 2002: 93). Amnesty International has documented significant shortcomings in state responses to rape and sexual violence in countries that are often praised on gender equality, such as the Nordic countries (2010b).

There has been growing awareness over the past decade of particularly heinous forms of domestic abuse, such as acid attacks and murder as a consequence of dowry disputes, so-called 'honour killings', and forced marriage, within the UK as well as beyond (the UK Government's Forced Marriage Unit dealt with approximately 1,600 reported incidents of suspected forced marriage in 2008).

Notwithstanding an emerging problem in the West, UN data show that dowry murder occurs predominantly in South Asia. In many societies rape victims and women suspected of engaging in premarital sex or adultery are murdered by their male relatives in 'honour killings'. According to the Human Rights Commission of Pakistan, 647 women were killed in the name of 'honour' in 2009.[6] In December 2009, London Metropolitan Police reported that there had been a huge rise in such crimes between April and October, with 211 incidents reported in London.[7]

While research on victims of political violence suggests that the victim label can be contested—associated with either weakness or strength, depending on the audience (Ferguson *et al.* 2010)—it has become clear that victimization within armed conflicts and state-sponsored aggression demands criminological attention. Some 70 per cent of casualties in recent conflicts were non-combatants, mostly women and children. Women are frequent victims of abduction, rape, sexual abuse, forced pregnancy, and slavery. Deliberate HIV infection of women and mass gang rape is a common tool of ethnic warfare (Rehn and Johnson Sirleaf 2002). According to the UK Foreign and Commonwealth Office, over two million children have been killed in conflicts over the last decade and many more have been orphaned, maimed, abducted, and abused. Furthermore, trafficking thrives in conflict zones, with girls in particular being at a high risk of sexual violence (Hoyle *et al.* 2011).

Finally, government statistics and research data on Internet crimes such as the distribution of child pornography and 'grooming' of minors by predatory sex offenders suggest victims of such offences may be in their thousands, albeit for the most part hard to identify or reach (O'Donnell and Milner 2007).

## IMPACT OF VICTIMIZATION

The BCS shows that the vast majority of victims—almost nine in ten—are emotionally affected in some way by their experience of being victimized (Flatley *et al.* 2010).

---

[6] www.hrcp-web.org/pdf/Annual%20Report%202009.pdf.
[7] www.bbc.co.uk/ethics/honourcrimes/crimesofhonour_1.shtml.

Most are angry but a significant minority will experience more severe symptoms such as depression and panic attacks (Walker *et al.* 2009). Victim surveys tell little about the impact of victimization. This is better captured by qualitative research focusing on particular types of crime or of victim, for example, victims of: burglary (Mawby 2007a); domestic violence (Hague and Mullender 2005); sexual assault and stalking (Finney 2006); rape (Coy 2009); hate crime (Walters and Hoyle 2011); forced marriage (Chantler, Gangoli, and Hester 2009); victimization of prostituted teens (Williams 2010); child victims (Hartless *et al.* 1995)—including violence in teenage intimate relationships (Bates *el al.* 2009); and of the elderly (Heisler 2007). Together these studies highlight the acute stress and adverse physical, practical, and financial effects suffered by victims of more serious crimes.

Studies also show the differential experiences of those who are already vulnerable when victimized; for example, rape victims who are dependent on alcohol and drugs (Lovett and Horvath 2009), or are young or suffering from mental health problems (Stanko *et al.* 2007), or victims of domestic and sexual violence who have learning or physical disabilities (see various chapters in Itzin, Taket, and Barter-Godfrey 2010). While significant proportions of assault victims develop post-traumatic stress disorder (Kessler *et al.* 1995), factors that exacerbate mental health effects include repeat victimization, unemployment, and low levels of innate resilience (Shepherd and Bisson 2004), with child abuse victims being particularly vulnerable to impaired self-esteem, poor physical and psychological health, learning problems, withdrawal, and regressive behaviour (Wolfe 1999).

Studies of abuse by intimate partners reveal immediate and lasting mental and physical health effects (Harne and Radford 2008). Children who routinely witness abuse frequently exhibit similar behavioural and psychological disturbances as those who are abused (Krug *et al.* 2002: 103). The failure of criminal justice to provide an effective response for some victims has led to alternative responses, including specialized domestic violence courts (Eley 2005) and restorative justice (Strang and Braithwaite 2002).

Property crimes can also adversely affect victims. One study of 545 victims of burglary found that many felt angry (72 per cent), shocked (55 per cent), worried (43 per cent), and fearful or scared (39 per cent) after the burglary, with over a third suffering depression and anxiety as a direct result of their victimization (Victim Support 2005: 13). White-collar, corporate, environmental, or business crime can also cause its victims to suffer significant, enduring trauma (Croall 2009; Tombs and Williams 2008).

Repeat or series victimization compounds the impact suffered with each repeated occurrence. A very small percentage of victims experience a disproportionate amount of crime (Farrell and Pease 2007) and the burden of repeat victimization falls disproportionately on the most vulnerable victims. Racial harassment is an important example of ongoing victimization the mere counting of individual incidents cannot capture (Bowling 1998). And the wider impact of crime on secondary or indirect victims is increasingly recognized, with the most telling example being the immediate grief and long-term trauma of the families of murder victims (Rock 1998; Victim Support 2006).

## VICTIMS' MOVEMENTS AND VICTIMS' JUSTICE

In the United States, a strongly rights-based victim movement emerged in the 1960s and 1970s. Consisting of the unlikely bedfellows radical feminists and conservative 'law and order' groups (Barker 2007), it typically sought ever-harsher criminal laws and more punitive responses to offenders in the courts (Dubber 2001), and in some states was associated with demands for the retention or reintroduction of the death penalty (Hodgkinson 2004).

In Britain, the central organ of the victim movement, Victim Support, has a very different history. Established nearly four decades ago in Bristol, Victim Support grew to over 370 local federated schemes covering England and Wales, which in 2008 merged to create a single national charity. Victim Support resolved from the first that it would not comment on sentencing, but it has recently taken a position on the use of Victim Personal Statements (VPSs), expressing regret that they 'are used far too rarely and victims feel their views are not taken into account as intended even when they are used' (Victim Support 2010: 21). It also recommended that 'every victim should be helped and encouraged to make a VPS so that all victims have an equal opportunity to formally state the impact of crime upon them' (ibid.: 22). More recently the organization called for the widespread availability of VPS in order that 'magistrates and judges [can] determine the most effective and appropriate sentence, and appropriate levels of compensation' (Victim Support 2011).

Victim Support provides practical help and emotional support to victims of all crime types. Its staff and volunteers speak with more than 1,500 new victims of crime each day, to assess their needs and provide targeted support. They also assist victims with their applications for compensation, helping to secure more than £27m in 2010 for those affected by violent crime (Victim Support 2010). Victim Support now aims to contact victims by phone, text, or email, within 48 hours of getting their details from the police and carry out a structured needs assessment (Victim Support 2009). It is currently piloting ways of encouraging more victims to contact them, and targeting vulnerable and repeat victims. Over the past decade it has developed specialist services for victims of serious crime—including domestic abuse and homicide—but continues to provide a service to victims of burglary, robbery, and theft. This expansion of its remit has led—perhaps inevitably—to a (mutually consensual) separation from its former 'child' organization, Support after Murder and Manslaughter (SAMM).

Other established organizations include the NSPCC, a predominantly campaigning body, and Childline—which merged with the NSPCC in 2006—which provides a free 24-hour helpline for children in distress or danger. In 2009–10 Childline counsellors responded to 508,943 contacts from children asking directly for help, advice, and protection and referred nearly 10 per cent to the police.[8]

About 450 women's refuges currently support victims of domestic violence in the UK, and in 2007–08 17,406 women and 25,384 children stayed in refuge

---

[8] www.nspccannualreview.org.uk/#!/helpline/.

accommodation. However, refuges are struggling to provide sufficient places. In London, during 2006–7, 21 providers turned away over 2,300 requests for refuge because they were full (Commons Home Affairs Committee 2008) and the National Domestic Violence Helpline is currently able to respond to only 65 per cent of the 175,000 calls it receives.

Lobbying by some victim interest groups has contributed to a trend towards increasingly punitive policies, but also a greater role for victims in the state response to crime. Those promoting victims' rights to participate in justice have included Sara Payne MBE, mother of Sarah Payne who was murdered by a paedophile. After years of campaigning, in 2009 Payne was appointed Victims Champion, a role superseded by the Commissioner for Victims and Witnesses. Similarly, Helen Newlove, who became a champion of victims' rights and campaigned against drink-related violence following her husband's murder by a gang of teenagers in 2007, was made a peer of the House of Lords in 2010.[9]

The victim has been invoked as a potent rhetorical device: what Ashworth calls 'victims in the service of severity' (2000: 186) and Garland describes as 'the projected, politicized, image of "the victim"…as an all-purpose justification for measures of penal repression' (2001: 143). Similarly, the naming of criminal laws and penal measures after individual victims uses the plight of the victim to legitimate more extensive controls and new punitive measures (Wood 2005; 'Megan's Law' in America, recently superseded by 'Marsy's Law', following a Californian case in 2008, and 'Sarah's Law' in Britain, named after Sarah Payne. Sarah's Law allows parents to check if someone in contact with their child is a sex offender and, after a successful pilot, was extended to all 43 police forces in England and Wales in spring 2011[10]).

Under Labour in Britain, a more general political commitment to 'rebalance' justice in favour of victims and to promote 'victims' justice' was a central plank of government policy (Home Office 2002), one that seems to have continued under the current Coalition Government. One outcome was the Victims Advisory Panel, chaired by the Minister of State with responsibility for victims' issues. It comprised officials and representatives of victims' organizations and 10 lay members, who themselves had been victims of crime, and discussed the impact of crime and considered new government policies (Victims Advisory Panel 2003/04). In 2010 the first Commissioner for Victims and Witnesses—Louise Casey—was appointed, to report on the treatment of victims and witnesses and to review the operation of the Code of Practice for Victims of Crime. A year later she had resigned and as yet the Ministy of Justice has no plans to replace her. Also in 2010, a new National Victims Service was created by the Home Office to provide victims of crime and anti-social behaviour with their own caseworker, an assessment of their needs, and a tailored plan to address them.[11] However, this scheme was soon withdrawn, a victim of the current fiscal constraints.[12]

[9] www.bbc.co.uk/news/uk-england-merseyside-10644120.

[10] www.bbc.co.uk/news/uk-12952334.

[11] www.justice.gov.uk/news/speech270110a.htm.

[12] This has not been the only casualty of the current financial crisis in public funding. In spring 2011 the Government stopped funds to the Poppy Project, the pioneer of specialist services for victims of sex trafficking, and the biggest and most established organization of its kind. The £4m contract for services went instead to the Salvation Army (*The Observer,* 17 April 2011; www.guardian.co.uk/society/2011/apr/17/prostitution-human-trafficking).

## VICTIMS IN THE CRIMINAL JUSTICE PROCESS

From the late 1980s mounting criticism within the academy and victim support organizations of the marginalization of victims within the criminal process made victims the focus of intense policy interest on both the national and international stage. This started over a quarter of a century ago, with the UN Declaration of Basic Principles of Justice for Victims of Crime and Abuse of Power, but it took most countries a long time to implement the principles within the Declaration in national legislation and policies. There have been further UN measures concerning offences against children and against women in the home and, most recently, the Protocol to Prevent, Suppress and Punish Trafficking in Persons, Especially Women and Children (2000), binding those states that ratify them to incorporate their provisions into domestic laws, and the Basic Principles and Guidelines on the Rights to a Remedy and Reparation for Victims of Gross Violations of International Human Rights Law and Serious Violations of International Humanitarian Law (2005).

As Hall (2010: 69) points out, the main achievement of these UN measures lies in building up 'a framework of language in which victim issues can be discussed...and providing the context and political precedent to allow (and compel) individual governments to move ahead with such measures'. The Council of Europe, the European Union, and various other transnational organizations have added their own conventions and recommendations on matters relating to victims. Finally, the International Criminal Court has afforded victims of the most serious offences a role in the justice response to their victimization (Hoyle 2011). However, despite international consensus on the importance of victims' rights to information, as well as the number of instruments that codify this right, research suggests that many victims are inadequately informed as to the progress of their case due to state agencies' breaches (Brienen and Hoegen 2000).

### PUTTING RIGHTS INTO PRACTICE

To the extent it is possible to speak of 'rights' for victims, they can be categorized under two headings. 'Service rights' refer to services which do not affect procedure, such as information provided about case progress. 'Procedural rights', such as victims' rights of allocution, give victims a voice in the criminal process and may be detrimental to the defendant (Ashworth 2000). Although this distinction is analytically useful, and helps to structure the following discussion, it breaks down in respect of those service rights that have procedural implications; for example, the screening of vulnerable victims in court may have an adverse impact on defendants' rights to a fair trial.

### Service rights

In Britain, the Home Office has made progressive attempts to improve the ways in which victims are kept informed by police and prosecutors. Two *Victims' Charters* published in the 1990s (Home Office 1990; 1996) set out standards of service to ensure that victims received better information about case progress, that their views were obtained and considered, and that they received proper facilities and assistance in court (Hoyle *et al.* 1999: 41–2).

The Charters have been replaced by a Code of Practice introduced under the Domestic Violence, Crime and Victims' Act 2004 (section 32). In force since April 2006, the Code sets out minimum standards of service that victims and witnesses can expect from criminal justice agencies. For example, most victims (the Code does not extend to corporate victims) have the right to information about decisions relating to case progress, to be reported within specified time-scales, shortened in the case of vulnerable or intimidated witnesses.[13] These include bail and remand decisions, whose omission under the OSS scheme had been a source of dissatisfaction to victims (Hoyle *et al.* 1998). They also include notification about some cases reviewed as possible miscarriages of justice by the Criminal Cases Review Commission (CCRC). Under the Code (section 15), and under its own victim notification policy, the CCRC is committed to inform victims if 'their' case is referred for an appeal or, in a non-referral outcome, if the victim has already been made aware of the CCRC's review.[14] Under the Crown Prosecution Service (CPS) 'Direct Communication with Victims' (DCV) programme—launched in 2001, as a result of the recommendations in the Glidewell and Macpherson Reports—the CPS took over from the police the responsibility to communicate any decision to discontinue or substantially alter the charge directly to the victim (Spencer 2010), and the 'Prosecutors Pledge', published in 2005, sets out the level of service that victims can expect from prosecutors.[15]

Witness Care Officers, working within Witness Care Units, support the witnesses of crime in those cases going to court, providing a single point of contact, needs assessment, information, and support. Although the work of Witness Care Officers does not affect the responsibilities of the decision-making lawyer under the provisions of DCV, they are responsible for providing information to victims, about the progress and outcome of their case. Despite these developments, an audit conducted by the CPS Inspectorate in 2007 found that compliance had been patchy (Spencer 2010), although a follow-up inspection by the HMCPSI found it had improved since 2007.[16] Nonetheless, the then Victims' Champion, Sara Payne, interviewed hundreds of victims and concluded that the delivery of the right to information remains inadequate. Although there is considerable information about the criminal justice system available to victims, many wanted specific information about their case, which was too often lacking (Payne 2009).

The Witness Service, run by Victim Support, and covering all criminal courts across England and Wales, provides advice, information, and support to help witnesses through the stress of a court appearance, including pre-trial visits to court and helping witnesses make sense of the court process. From April 2004, the 'No Witness No Justice' initiative established joint CPS/Police Witness Care Units across England

---

[13] Vulnerable victims are defined as persons under the age of 17 and those with mental or physical disabilities. The definition of intimidated victims is very broad, deriving from socio-demographic and offence-related factors that provide evidence of likely intimidation or potential further victimization.

[14] www.ccrc.gov.uk/documents/VICTIMS_OF_CRIME-_CCRC_CONTACT.pdf.

[15] www.cps.gov.uk/publications/prosecution/prosecutor_pledge.html.

[16] www.hmcpsi.gov.uk/documents/services/reports/AUD/DCV_FU_Oct09_audit.pdf.

and Wales.[17] Witness Care Officers act as a single point of contact, providing information about case progress, and coordinating other support agencies. Pilot studies in 2003 found that the Units improved witness attendance at court by nearly 20 per cent, reduced the number of trials adjourned due to witness issues by 27 per cent, and led to a 17 per cent drop in cracked trials due to witness issues.[18] However, Victim Support reports (2010) that victims are often left without a full understanding of the sentence given to the perpetrator of their crime. While Witness Care Units have a duty to explain sentences to victims, they are not obliged to provide the kind of detailed explanation offered to offenders (Victim Support 2010). Prosecutors or, if prosecutors are unavailable, other representatives of the CPS, are supposed to introduce themselves at court and later explain the sentence, but only if the victim is referred to the CPS for an explanation by the joint police/CPS Witness Care Units.[19]

Recognition of the secondary victimization experienced by vulnerable witnesses such as rape victims, who can be subjected to intensive and embarrassing questioning, has led to many procedural innovations and changes in the rules of evidence (Stern Review 2010). While reports on these reforms suggest that practice has improved somewhat, they also note geographical variations and continued causes for concern. Many of the recommendations made in research and by previous enquiries and audits have not been implemented consistently (Brown *et al.* 2010).

There is now a good deal of policy and guidance on the needs of vulnerable and intimidated witnesses in the system, most notably the Youth Justice and Criminal Evidence Act 1999 (YJCEA), recently amended by the Coroners and Justice Act 2009. The YJCEA provides for a range of 'special measures' for prosecution and defence witnesses, including the provisions for screening the defendant, having the judge and counsel remove gowns and wigs, giving evidence by electronic live link, video-recorded evidence in chief, and the permission for intermediaries to assist witnesses giving evidence. It provides also for the protection of certain witnesses from cross-examination by the accused in person; and restricts the cross-examination of rape complainants about their sexual history. Under the Criminal Justice Act 2003 vulnerable and intimidated witnesses can give evidence via a live video link but occasionally so can witnesses in cases where this is required 'in the interests of the efficient or effective administration of justice', such as where the witness lives a very long way from the trial court. Of course, these are not rights, but special measures that defence and prosecution counsel can apply for and their permission is always at the discretion of the court.

Evaluation of provisions for vulnerable and intimidated witnesses suggests that the administrative and legislative measures in place are not fully implemented and leave significant unmet needs (Burton *et al.* 2006). Research shows that court familiarization visits and explanations about how the special measures benefit vulnerable witnesses, as well as the use of intermediaries, appear to reduce anxiety and improve the quality of the evidence given (Plotnikoff and Woolfson 2009). Early identification of vulnerable and intimidated witnesses by the police and CPS is vital if these measures are to

---

[17] www.cps.gov.uk/legal/d_to_g/direct_communication_with_victims_/introduction/.

[18] www.cps.gov.uk/publications/docs/NWNJ_pilot_evaluation_report_291004.pdf.

[19] Victims Code of Practice, para 7.12.

be used appropriately, but Burton *et al.* (2006) found that these organizations continue to experience difficulties identifying those in need. Recently, the Home Office created five pilot schemes of support services for young victims of crime which, among other objectives, run a campaign to inform them about special measures at court to encourage them to come forward as witnesses (Home Office 2008).[20]

### Compensation

In Britain, victims retain their theoretical but rarely exercised right to damages against the offender in a civil action, but have no right in criminal proceedings to compensation. They have either to rely upon the court to make a compensation order or to make claims against the state Criminal Injuries Compensation Scheme.

Unlike jurisdictions such as France or Germany where victims have the right to pursue civil claims for compensation within the criminal process, in Britain compensation is payable by the offender as an ancillary order to the main penalty in cases where 'injury, loss, or damage' has resulted (under the Criminal Justice Act 1972). Reparation was one of the main purposes of sentencing under the Criminal Justice Act 2003, Part 12, section 142(1) and the Ministry of Justice Business Plan for 2011–15 includes a specific commitment to 'ensure better reparation to victims', a commitment it reiterates in the current Green Paper which promises to increase the use of compensation orders (2010a). Compensation orders can be made in respect of personal injury; losses through theft of, or damage to, property; losses through fraud; loss of earnings; medical expenses; travelling expenses; and pain and suffering; and the Criminal Justice Act 2003 makes it possible to order compensation pre-trial under conditional cautions. The total amount of compensation awarded in 2009 was approximately £29.1 million, paid by 48,176 offenders. However, this is still only 14.7 per cent of all those sentenced, suggesting, as Victim Support (2011) recently pointed out, that there is considerable scope to radically increase the use of compensation orders, although the court must take account of the offender's circumstances and ability to pay.

While the courts have wide powers to enforce payment, including imprisonment, a significant proportion of compensation is either never paid, or is paid in very small amounts over a long period of time. Indeed, the amount of compensation paid within the same year it is ordered stands at just over 40 per cent, and the total outstanding amount is increasing by nearly 20 per cent a year (Magistrates' Association Judicial Policy and Practice Committee 2010). Victim Support (2011) found that a failure to properly enforce compensation orders causes significant discontent among victims, and proposes that the Government takes responsibility for paying compensation upfront and in full to victims, recouping the money directly from offenders.

Compensation is also made through the state-funded Criminal Injuries Compensation Authority (CICA) set up in 1964—just a year after the first known scheme was established in New Zealand. In an attempt to curb the spiralling cost of payments and improve administrative efficiency, a tariff scheme—grouping injuries of comparable severity into 25 bands—was introduced under the Criminal Injuries Compensation Act 1995 (Miers 2001b). The scheme was criticized for unduly limiting

---

[20]  http://webarchive.nationalarchives.gov.uk/20100413151441/press.homeoffice.gov.uk/press-releases/funding-young-victims.html.

maximum awards, excluding consideration of the complexities of individual cases, failing to take full account of loss of earnings, excluding victims of crimes other than violence, and removing parity between state compensation payments and civil awards (Duff 1998). A controversial aspect of the scheme was, and remains, the regard given to the victim's character and history. Where an applicant behaved provocatively or has convictions for serious offences, however unconnected with the offence in question, compensation is generally withheld.

An updated scheme was introduced in 2001, bringing about minor modifications; including, further eligibility exclusion for those who are deemed to have contributed to their victimization by the excessive consumption of alcohol or illicit drugs. Most of the tariffs remained the same, with the exception of compensation for child victims of sexual abuse, which was increased to reflect criticisms of the previous scheme (Rock 2004: 283). Further revisions to the scheme were made in 2008, allowing for compensation for mental injury. Typically this is only when it has occurred *in addition to* physical injury but it can be made in cases where a victim is put in reasonable fear of immediate physical harm or has witnessed significant injury to a person with whom they have a close loving relationship. The fixed tariff system remains, with, for example, the standard lump sum payment of £11,000 when the primary victim has died as a result of criminal injuries (with no discretion to alter this sum). The 2008 scheme introduced geographically based CICA teams, focused on improving relations with local criminal justice agencies, and a new case working model for claims. As with previous schemes, this one is criticised for trying to cut costs and utilizing compensation as a tool for facilitating victims' cooperation with the criminal justice system (Hall 2010: 180).

Given the prohibition against compensating those in an existing relationship with the offender, it should be of no surprise that victim recourse to the CICA is declining. Compared with nearly 80,000 claims in 2001/2, in 2009–2010 the Authority decided over 70,000 cases and paid out over £209 million in tariff compensation (Criminal Injuries Compensation Authority 2010). Moreover, approximately a third of all applications for compensation are refused because of the applicant's conduct or unspent convictions (Goodey 2005: 146).

### Procedural rights

While few object to service rights, procedural rights are contentious because they can threaten defendants' due process rights and undermine fairness (Ashworth 2010: 382). Arguments against allowing victims a greater say include: the intrusion of private views into public decision-making; limitations on prosecutorial discretion; the danger that the victim's subjective view undermines the court's objectivity; disparity in sentencing of similar cases depending on the resilience or punitiveness of the victim (Ashworth 1993); and, lastly, that to increase their involvement may further burden victims while raising their expectations unrealistically (Reeves and Dunn 2010). Nevertheless, partly as a result of lobbying by particular victim interest groups, there has been a significant expansion of victims' rights to influence decisions in respect of cautioning and charging decisions, plea negotiations, sentencing, parole, and release. For example, the probation service is now obliged to contact the victims of life-sentenced prisoners, and of other particular categories of prisoner, to ascertain if they have concerns about the conditions attached to the offender's release, which the Parole Board is required to take into account in determining licence conditions (Roberts 2009).

In Britain Victim Personal Statements (VPSs) were introduced under the Victims' Charter 1996, inviting victims to state the physical, financial, psychological, social, or emotional effects the offence had on them or their family (Hoyle *et al.* 1999). Since then they have been rolled out across the country but their limits remain unclear (Hoyle 2011). The current Green Paper, *Breaking the Cycle: Effective Punishment, Rehabilitation and Sentencing of Offenders* (paragraphs 75–7) invites further consideration on their use. The Judiciary of England and Wales' response to this invitation is broadly positive but warns that:

> …the expectations of the alleged victim must be managed. The court can of course take the VPS into account but must not be bound by it. The court needs to take a consistent approach to sentencing and cannot increase a sentence because one victim reacts differently to another. If victims do not understand this it will inevitably lead to disappointment if the court chooses not to act on the potentially emotive VPS.[21]

Advocates of victim input have argued that it promotes more informed, accurate and democratic sentencing decisions; recognizes the victim's status as the person harmed by the offence; helps victims to recover; increases their satisfaction and cooperation with the criminal justice system; helps victims recover from crimes committed against them; and can promote rehabilitation by confronting the offender with the impact of his crime (Tobolowsky 1999; Cassell 2009). Opponents argue that VPS impair the objectivity of the process; shift the focus away from legitimate sentencing factors and towards inappropriate considerations of victim retaliation and vengeance; risk disparate and disproportionate sentencing; erode the prosecutor's function; or further traumatize victims by creating unmet expectations or by obliging them to participate in the sentencing process against their wishes (Tobolowsky 1999; Bandes 2009).

Victim personal statements were introduced in Australia in the early 1990s (Cook *et al.* 1999), and have more recently been introduced into some European countries, for example the Netherlands and Poland (Wemmers 2005). Studies of their efficacy suggest that victims are generally pleased with their experiences of providing victim impact evidence (Roberts and Erez 2010), although there are differences of opinion in how to interpret the data. For example, Hoyle *et al.* (1998) found that victims' expectations were raised but their hopes for benefits from impact evidence not always satisfied, leaving some frustrated, while Leverick *et al.* (2007) found that the vast majority of those who submitted an impact statement concluded that it had been the right thing to do. A recent review of empirical research concludes that victims benefit from the experience (Roberts 2009) although misunderstandings about the purpose of statements and, in particular, an expectation that the statement will have a significant impact on the sentence, can lead to disappointment (Roberts and Erez 2010). Victim Support (2010) found that only 16 per cent of victims both recall being offered the

---

[21] www.judiciary.gov.uk/Resources/JCO/Documents/Consultations/judicial-response-green-paper-breaking-the-cycle.pdf

opportunity to give a victim personal statement and felt their views were taken into account when they took up this offer.

In England and Wales, Family Impact Statements were introduced experimentally in trials for murder and manslaughter in five Crown Court Centres in 2006 (the Victims Advocate Scheme, of which the impact statements were a central plank, also included enhanced pre-trial support and personal and social legal advice; Sweeting *et al.* 2008). In 2007—before the pilot project was complete and the report of the evaluation published—the Government rolled out nationally the Victim Focus Scheme for homicides, but also included corporate manslaughter, deaths in custody, and road traffic accidents.[22] The delivery was restricted to written statements passed to the judge or presented orally by counsel. Rock (2010) found that the statements had only a modest effect on the families' satisfaction and very little effect on sentencing.

In New Zealand, the Victims' Rights Act 2002 allows family statements to influence sentences, whereas in New South Wales they must not affect sentencing (Kirchengast 2008). The Criminal Code of Canada's definition of 'victim' is broad and can include statements from family members and recently an appellate court confirmed that victim impact evidence of ancillary harm by family members is an aggravating factor in sentencing (Roberts and Manikis 2010).

In the US, the federal government and the majority of states have constitutional or legislative provisions (or both) that require victim notification of important events and actions in the criminal process and allow, to varying degrees, victim presence and hearing at critical stages of the criminal process. While victims' right to be heard at sentencing has been widely adopted, the role of victim impact evidence in capital sentencing hearings remains controversial. Just over 20 years ago the US Supreme Court overruled previous judgments to pave the way for the admission of victim impact evidence in death penalty cases (*Payne v Tennessee*),[23] and recent empirical evidence shows that such statements make a death sentence more likely (Paternoster and Deise 2011).

Victim impact statements at parole are controversial. Parole Boards' role is to determine the offender's risk of re-offending, as well as to evaluate the likelihood that he will benefit from release into the community. The victim is unlikely to provide information relevant to either determination. Additionally, there is no expressive or communicative role for the victim at parole, except for certain limited security concerns the victim may have, such as ensuring that the prisoner does not live on the same street (Padfield and Roberts 2010). However, research suggests that positive and negative victim input at parole is *not* a significant predictor of parole release (Caplan 2010).

Over the past three decades the role of the victim in the criminal justice system has clearly expanded considerably. Victims now have certain 'rights' to allocution, 'rights' to provide information that could influence sentences, 'rights' to receive information about 'their case', and a much closer relationship with the prosecution. However, the extent to which these various reforms create *real* rights for victims is debatable. The Human Rights Act 1998 lacks any clear statement of victims' rights (Ashworth 2000: 188), although it has established that ECHR Articles relating to the protection of life, liberty, and security of a person may be invoked in relation to victims (Doak 2008).

[22] http://www.cps.gov.uk/legal/v_to_z/victim_focus_scheme/.
[23] 501 U.S. 808, 827 (1991).

Even though the Code of Practice sets out the 'obligations of service providers', failure to comply does not, of itself, result in liability to legal proceedings (Home Office 2005b). Although victims have the right to complain to their MP and eventually to the Parliamentary Ombudsman should they feel that service providers have failed to abide by its provisions, the continuing limits of enforceability and the political nature of this complaints process make it questionable whether the Code generates substantive rights for victims (Manikis 2010).

Moreover, criminal justice or penal theory has not changed sufficiently to accommodate these 'reforms' or 'rights' to the system. Sentencing philosophies are still offender focused: courts punish for the purposes of retribution, deterrence, incapacitation, or rehabilitation, not to make the victim feel better or, to adopt the American cliché, to provide 'closure'. Retributivists have locked horns with advocates of restorative justice, but neither has adequately provided a theoretical framework to describe these changes. Gruber examines the theoretical bases for victim-centred reforms that aim to balance the punishment of offenders with the repair (emotional and otherwise) of victims, taking into account the harms caused to the victim, or, more likely, articulated by them. She makes a convincing case for understanding changes to the role of victims in the criminal process as 'distributive': 'In popular politics as well as case doctrine, victims' interests now stand alongside and even trump concerns over retributive fault and social utility' (Gruber 2010: 57).

As Gruber explains, reforms challenge two central tenets of the criminal law: first, that crimes are offences against the state, not individual victims, second, that all people are equal before the law. Victim impact evidence clearly challenges both of these doctrines, not least because it can result in punishment of offenders being—at least in part—a consequence of their victim's status.

However, Gruber's distributive theory does not apply so well to restorative justice. Unlike victims' rights that seek to give victims their 'due' by increasing the pain apportioned to offenders, restorative justice theorists centralize the role of the victim but underscore the curative value of forgiveness, dialogue, and relationship building. In the ideal restorative justice world, offenders and victims profit from participating in proceedings that promote healing. Like social programs that seek to 'increase rather than divide "the pie", restorative justice seeks to increase pleasure for victims and offenders, not utilize the criminal law to distribute the scarce resources of pleasure between them' (Gruber 2010: 45). Restorative justice is presented as an exception to the 'zero-sum' logic that sees the granting of due process protections to offenders as a denial of justice for victims. In this sense, it cuts across the trend in recent decades of increasing the rights of victims in part to further punish offenders.

## RESTORATIVE JUSTICE—A MOVE AWAY FROM THE 'ZERO SUM' LOGIC?

From the late 1980s, victims' rights groups began to advocate that specific legal rules be introduced to give greater weight to victims' interests, and to provide them with restitution and compensation. In some jurisdictions, for some cases, this heralded the emergence of restorative justice.[24]

## WHAT IS RESTORATIVE JUSTICE?

While some have focused on developing a theory of restorative justice, others have attempted to define restorative justice by practices, describing as 'restorative' any new initiative that does not follow the typical trajectory of arrest, prosecution, conviction, and punishment. The development of a clear understanding of restorative justice is frustrated by this confusing application of the label to a variety of, often disparate, practices.

In the absence of a universally agreed definition of 'restorative justice', the concept has become deeply contested among its proponents and critics. Most restorative theoretical frameworks encompass values, aims, and processes that have in common attempts to repair the harm caused by criminal or other types of anti-social behaviour. Restoration addresses emotional as well as material loss, safety, damaged relationships, and the dignity and self-respect of victims and other stakeholders. Accordingly, restorative justice is concerned with ensuring appropriate reparation to victims and their communities. But it is also aimed at lessening fear of crime, strengthening the sense of community, and addressing the needs of all of those harmed, including the perpetrators (Hoyle and Young 2002).

The two most frequently discussed examples of restorative justice within the extant literature are victim–offender mediation and restorative or family group conferences. These practices typically involve a face-to-face meeting between the victim and offender (or those involved in conflict where disputants cannot be categorized as such) in a safe environment to discuss the incident, the harms it has caused, and how these harms should be repaired. Conferences, unlike victim–offender mediation, typically include supporters of the disputants and other concerned community members, and sometimes representatives of the state, such as police officers, social workers, or housing officers. The meetings should be empowering and inclusive, and enable all stakeholders to reveal fully how the incident has affected them, with no-one silenced by domination. Restorative justice can also be facilitated through indirect or 'shuttle' mediation; victims and offenders discuss their case individually with a restorative facilitator, who then feeds information back to the other party.

Restorative justice programs operating throughout the UK are, for the most part, administered by the police or Youth Offending Teams (YOTs) and available primarily for 'shallow-end crime' (Cunneen and Hoyle 2010). In 1998, police cautions for young offenders were replaced with 'reprimands' and 'warnings', influenced by restorative principles. In 2009, just over half (53 per cent) of juveniles received an out-of-court disposal, 69 per cent of which were reprimands and 31 per cent final warnings (Ministry of Justice 2010b). Scope for restorative practices and a consultative role for victims are also provided by the power given to the courts to impose reparation orders and action

---

[24] Various European countries also established institutions, legal frameworks, and policies aimed at providing redress, justice, and restitution to victims of crime, although—within these civil law systems—this did not require a paradigm shift in notions of justice.

plan orders on young offenders (Fionda 2005). In 2008–9 there were 25,865 referral orders given (14 per cent of all disposals) and 4,720 reparation orders (3 per cent of all disposals) (Ministry of Justice 2010b).

Since 1999 there has been a mandatory sentence of 'referral order' to a 'Youth Offender Panel' for most young offenders pleading guilty and appearing before a youth or magistrates' court for the first time (and just recently this has been extended to second offences). The procedures followed at a panel meeting, and any activities specified in the resulting contract, should be informed by principles of restorative justice: taking responsibility for the consequences of offending behaviour; making reparation to the victim; and achieving reintegration (or integration) into the community. However, victims attend panel meetings in less than 10 per cent of cases (Crawford and Newburn 2003). Adult cautions with reparative conditions attached—'conditional cautions'—were introduced in 2003, but few police services are regularly issuing restorative, conditional cautions and almost none involve victims (Hoyle 2008). Most recently the Ministry of Justice has outlined, in its Business Plan for 2011–15, its plans to pilot—in the summer of 2011—Neighbourhood Justice Panels to divert low-level offences from court to be heard by panels of community volunteers, overseen by criminal justice practitioners.[25]

Those restorative measures introduced over the past decade or two have too often found themselves upstaged by a sudden need for a shot of political adrenalin. High-profile cases, especially those involving child offenders, have been exploited to justify various control measures imposed on ever-younger 'feral youths' and their 'inadequate' parents. When governments demand a crackdown on high profile offences, restorative conferencing is likely to take a back seat, as was seen in the English Thames Valley Police service in the early years of the new millennium when pressure was put on the service to focus resources on reducing the number of street robberies (Hoyle 2009).

There are some examples of restorative experiments being carried out for more serious offences and offenders: in prisons (Elliott 2007); for serious offences (Shapland *et al.* 2006); for sexual (Daly 2006) and racial crimes (Hudson 1998); for hate crimes (Walters and Hoyle 2010); for domestic violence (Hudson 2002; Stubbs 2007); with families of homicide victims (Umbreit *et al.* 2003), including those cases where the offender is awaiting execution (Umbreit and Vos 2000); for disputes and bullying in schools and workplaces (Morrison 2006); with complaints against the police (Young *et al.* 2005); and with victims of human rights abuses and even genocide (Weitekamp *et al.* 2006). These diverse initiatives have the potential to restore victims and reintegrate offenders—other, of course, than those facing execution (Hoyle and Young 2003). However, those cases that are disposed of using restorative practices in the UK tend not to be serious. While mediation is the primary response to domestic abuse in Austria and frequently used in Belgium, in England and Wales only a handful of schemes use restorative processes for abuse in the family. Similarly, while restorative processes are used for sexual violence in some American states (e.g. RESTORE in Arizona) and in New Zealand, and while some regions in England and Wales make use of Circles of Support

---

[25] www.justice.gov.uk/news/business-plan-2011–15.htm.

and Accountability, only a few cases of sexual violence are dealt with by way of restorative meetings (the exception being the work done by AIM in Manchester).

In Northern Ireland there is considerably more restorative activity for youths. Since the Justice (Northern Ireland) Act 2002, youth conferences have been used for all types of offences, except those that would attract a life sentence if the offender was an adult, while offenders can receive a youth conference referral on more than one occasion. There the use of restorative processes alongside retributive punishments, including custody (under the Youth Conference Plans), give the courts and probation boards more scope for meeting the needs of society as well as young people in trouble. And Restorative Assistance Panels ensure adequate community involvement.

In New Zealand, since the Children, Young Persons and their Families Act 1989, about a quarter of cases—the most serious (except murder and manslaughter) and those involving repeat young offenders—have received restorative interventions, with the majority of cases reaching an agreement that avoids prosecution (Maxwell and Morris 2006).

With the recent publication of the Green Paper, *Breaking the Cycle*, and the new crime strategy, *A New Approach to Fighting Crime*, the government has made clear its commitment to greater use of restorative justice in the youth justice system (Ministry of Justice 2010a: 61–9), a commitment that has the support of victims' organizations, including Victim Support (2011). However, it is not committed to developing national, centrally-funded initiatives, rather, restorative justice is being promoted as part of its localism agenda—encouraging people to become involved in the response to crime in their local areas and to consider restorative processes as part of those responses. So what are the chances of increasing use of restorative justice in the near future?

The police use of restorative approaches for minor crimes is likely to increase, because they will benefit financially as well as seeing directly the benefits to victims and offenders (the Youth Restorative Disposal evaluation by the Youth Justice Board (unpublished) found that using restorative justice instead of issuing a reprimand saved seven hours of officer time, and about £400 a case). The changes to the 'counting rules' outlined in *A New Approach to Fighting Crime* will produce further financial benefits. The Government has shown its commitment to restorative justice and, in particular, the quality of restorative processes, by its endorsement of the Restorative Justice Council's (RJC) Best Practice Guidance 2011, and by the start-up funding provided to the RJC to develop practitioner registration. However, there is no central funding for restorative justice and—as yet—no further legislation to increase the use of restorative justice for serious offences at the later stage of the criminal process (the RJC response to *Breaking the Cycle* argues that these need to be in place). While the Government may like to see restorative justice used for more serious offences, the cost-incentives are largely absent here. For example, if restorative justice is delivered pre-sentence, by the Probation Service, any savings would be spread across the criminal justice system. Under current fiscal constraints, in the absence of legislation, adult, serious offenders are not likely to receive restorative interventions.

## RESTORATIVE JUSTICE: A VICTIM-CENTRIC APPROACH?

Restorative justice, more than any other initiative since the establishment of the modern criminal justice system, has the power to reinstate the victim centre stage (Travis

2006). Research suggests that many victims want a less formal process where their views count, more information about both the progress and outcome of their case, to participate in its resolution, and to receive material reparation and emotional restoration, including an apology (Strang 2002).

Despite concerns expressed by both critics and advocates about the role of victims in restorative justice, a consistent picture of high aggregate victim satisfaction with police-led processes emerges from the research. At their best, restorative encounters appear to alleviate victims' feelings of anger or fear towards their offender, or crime more generally, and bring about genuine remorse on the part of the offender, encouraging a greater sense of victim empathy. Victims can, and often do, receive explanations, apologies, and occasionally compensation (Sherman and Strang 2007).

While not all victims are equally satisfied, and a small minority of victims feels worse, the data on different schemes show that victims who meet with offenders in the presence of other affected parties are much more likely to feel that they had experienced a fair and inclusive process than victims who are involved in 'shuttle mediation', whereby a trained mediator passes information from one party to another (Cunneen and Hoyle 2010). While the recent initiative evaluated by Shapland *et al.* achieved victim participation in 91 per cent of conferences (2006: 49), low rates of victim participation are common in the UK. On current evidence it is far from clear that restorative justice is principally about victims. Furthermore, a review of restorative justice programmes in 12 European countries found that only one country (Denmark) claimed to be victim-oriented; a further five are offender-oriented; in two countries the orientation varies with the particular programme; and in the remaining four the orientation is mixed (Miers 2001a: 79).

The question then arises: how much is restorative justice promoted in the interests of victims and how much in the interest of offenders or crime reduction? While academics' support for restorative justice is typically motivated by the benefits to victims and to the wider communities from which victims and offenders come, for most policy-makers, and many practitioners, the litmus test remains its ability to impact on offending. Criminological research across the world has produced conflicting evidence on the impact of restorative justice on offending, although there are very few examples of it increasing recidivism and rather more of it reducing it (Sherman and Strang 2007).

Shapland and her team evaluated three restorative schemes in Thames Valley, London, and Northumbria and found that the offenders who participated committed significantly fewer offences in the subsequent two years than offenders in the control group, while there were almost no differences between the types of offenders or cases which lead to better reconviction rates (Shapland *et al.* 2008).

### INTEGRATING RESTORATIVE AND CRIMINAL JUSTICE

Early restorative treatises, that saw restorative justice as a 'new lens' through which to see crime (Zehr 1990), were aspirational, even evangelistic, but rather unsophisticated. In promoting the benefits of restorative justice they found it necessary to reject outright criminal justice and, in order to justify this rejection, to present it as little more than victim-insensitive, state-sponsored vengeance. Failing to acknowledge the various victim-centred and reparative measures that were already being introduced into the criminal justice system, they presented restorative and retributive justice in dichotomous terms, with the former representing all that was good about community responses to crime and the latter all that was harmful with the state monopoly over justice. But in reality restorative justice is—and should be—part of the criminal justice system (Cunneen and Hoyle 2010). This, of course, raises the most difficult questions, not yet answered to the satisfaction of either critics or advocates, concerning the place of restorative justice in the criminal process and, in particular, its relationship to the state, including who should facilitate meetings and whether outcomes should be guided by principles of proportionality (Young and Hoyle 2003; Hoyle 2008).

Restorative principles have historically been incorporated somewhat awkwardly into the existing punitive framework (Zedner 1994). Opinions differ as to the extent to which restorative justice should be bound by principles of due process. Some consider proportionality as paramount (Ashworth 2002) and some do not (Braithwaite 2002), with others arguing for reparative processes and outcomes within upper and lower limits of proportionality (Cavadino and Dignan 1997; Braithwaite 2002).

While there is by no means consensus on the compatibility of restorative and retributive justice, it is clear that restorative justice (on the whole) does not reject all punitive measures associated with retributive justice and that the court system is not devoid of all restorative elements. So, it is not inevitable that certain crimes should be dealt with restoratively and others by way of prosecution and the courts. Restorative justice can play a role in responses to most offences, from shop theft, through violence in the home, to crimes against humanity. Each of these, and other offences, will likely require different combinations, or a different balance, of restorative and retributive justice (Cunneen and Hoyle 2010). As long as it does not lead to net-widening, restorative justice could serve as a 'cooling device' to our current 'hot criminological climate', which seems determined to ratchet up sentencing and incarcerate greater numbers of offenders (Loader and Sparks 2011) with too few benefits to victims.

## CONCLUSION

Victims of conventional crimes now attract an unprecedented level of interest, both as a subject of criminological enquiry and as a focus of criminal justice policy. Victim research has profoundly altered our picture of crime by uncovering a vast array of hidden offences, many against the most vulnerable members of society. Academic scholarship has shifted, over the last few years, with less attention given to the impact of crime on victims and more focus on the contentious questions about the role of victims in the criminal process. Political pressure, too, has raised the victim's profile. It has greatly expanded the provision of services, and information, and has allowed victims' interests to inform key decisions in the criminal process. At a time when the impulse to punish dominates, the current commitment to restorative justice, especially for young offenders, is an important countertrend. How far restorative justice serves the interests of victims, however, remains a matter of live debate.

## ■ SELECTED FURTHER READING

Bottoms and Roberts' (2010) edited collection is a useful source of essays exploring the evolving relationship between the state and the victim and the role of the victim in the criminal process. Davis *et al.* (2007), now in its third edition, provide a synopsis of the contemporary literature and debates, including newer areas of criminological interest such as elder abuse, school-based violence, and victims of terrorist acts. For contemporary academic, policy, and political debates on the nature, extent, and impact of criminal victimization and policy responses to it, see Walklate (2007). On the development of the victims' movement, Rock (2004) still provides the authoritative account. Mathew Hall (2010) presents much needed comparative analysis of the development of victims' policies and practices in nine jurisdictions. Dignan's (2004) exploration of the origins of and the relationship between victims policy and restorative justice is still a useful starting point for students. On restorative justice see Braithwaite (1989; 1999), Hoyle and Cunneen (2010), Johnstone (2011), and Shapland, Robinson, and Sorsby (2011). Of the many edited collections on restorative justice, its potential and its limits, Von Hirsch *et al.* (2003) and Johnstone and Van Ness (2006) remain useful resources.

## ■ REFERENCES

ALLEN, S. (2002), 'Male Victims of Rape: Responses to a Perceived Threat to Masculinity', in C. Hoyle and R. Young (ed.), *New Visions of Crime Victims* 23–48, Oxford: Hart Publishing.

ALVAZZI EL FRATED. F. and VAN KESTEREN, J. N. (2004), *Criminal Victimisation in Urban Europe. Key Findings of the 2000 International Crime Victims Survey*, Turin: UNICRI.

AMNESTY INTERNATIONAL (2005), *Amnesty International Report 2005: the state of the world's human rights*, London: Amnesty International Publications.

—— (2010a), *The state of human rights in the world*, London: Amnesty International Publications.

—— (2010b), *Case Closed, Rape And Human Rights In The Nordic Countries Summary Report*, Amnesty International ACT 77/001/2010.

ASHWORTH, A. (1993), 'Victim Impact Statements and Sentencing', *Criminal Law Review*, 498–509.

—— (2000), 'Victims' Rights, Defendants' Rights and Criminal Procedure', in A. Crawford and J. Goodey (eds), *Integrating a Victim Perspective within Criminal Justice*, Aldershot: Ashgate.

—— (2002), 'Responsibilities, Rights and Restorative Justice', *British Journal of Criminology*, 42(3): 578–95.

—— (2010), *Sentencing and Criminal Justice*, Cambridge: Cambridge University Press.

BANDES, S. (2009), 'Victims, "Closure", and the Sociology of Emotion', *Law and Contemporary Problems*, 72: 1–26.

BARKER, V. (2007), 'The Politics of Pain: A Political Institutionalist Analysis of Crime Victims' Moral Protests', *Law and Society Review*, 41: 619–64.

BASILE, K. C. (2008), 'Histories of violent victimization among women who reported unwanted sex in marriages and intimate relationships: Findings from a qualitative study', *Violence Against Women*, 14(1): 29–52.

BATES, C., MCCARRY, M., BERRIDGE, D., and EVANS, K. (2009), *Partner exploitation and violence in teenage intimate relationships*, NSPCC.

BORER, T. A. (2003), 'A Taxonomy of Victims and Perpetrators: Human Rights and Reconciliation in South Africa', *Human Rights Quarterly*, 25(4): 1088–116.

BOSWORTH, M., HOYLE, C., and DEMPSEY, M. (2011), 'Researching Trafficked Women: On Institutional Resistance and the Limits to Feminist Reflexivity', *Qualitative Enquiry*, 17(9): 769–79.

BOTTOMS, A. and COSTELLO, A. (2010), 'The phenomenon of victim-offender overlap: a study of offences against households', in A. Bottoms and J. V. Roberts (eds), *Hearing the Victim: Adversarial justice, crime victims and the State*, Cullompton: Willan.

BOTTOMS, A. and ROBERTS, J. V. (2010), *Hearing the Victim: Adversarial justice, crime victims and the State*, Cullompton: Willan.

BOWLING, B. (1998), *Violent Racism: victimization, policing, and social context*, Oxford: Oxford University Press.

BRAITHWAITE, J. (1989), *Crime, shame and reintegration*, Cambridge: Cambridge University Press.

—— (1999), 'Restorative Justice: Assessing Optimistic and Pessimistic Accounts', in M. Tonry (ed.), *Crime and Justice, A Review of Research*, Vol. 25, Chicago: University of Chicago Press.

—— (2002), 'In search of restorative jurisprudence', in L. Walgrave (ed.), *Restorative Justice and the Law*, Cullompton: Willan.

BRIENEN, M. E. I. and HOEGEN, E. H. (2000), *Victims of Crime in 22 European Criminal Justice Systems: The Implementation of Recommendation (85) 11 of the Council of Europe on the Position of the Victim in the Framework of Criminal Law and Procedure*, Nijmegen: Wolf Legal Productions.

BROWN, J., HORVATH, M. A. H., KELLY, L., and WESTMARLAND, N. (2010), *Connections and disconnections: Assessing evidence, knowledge and practice in responses to rape*, London: Government Equalities Office.

BURTON, M., EVANS, R., and SANDERS, A. (2006), 'Implementing Special Measures for Vulnerable and Intimidated Witnesses: The Problem of Identification', *Criminal Law Review*, 229–40.

CAPLAN, J. (2010), 'Parole release decisions: Impact of victim input on a representative sample of inmates', *Journal of Criminal Justice*, 38: 291–300

CASSELL, P. (2009), 'In Defence of Victim Impact Statements', *Ohio State Journal of Criminal Law*, 6: 611–48.

CAVADINO, M. and DIGNAN, J. (1997), 'Reparation, Retribution and Rights', *International Review of Victimology*, 4(4): 233–54.

CHANTLER, K., GANGOLI, G., and HESTER, M. (2009), 'Forced Marriage in the UK: Religious, Cultural, Economic or State Violence?', *Critical Social Policy* 29(4): 587–612.

COMMONS HOME AFFAIRS COMMITTEE (2008), *Domestic Violence, Forced Marriage and "Honour"-Based Violence, Sixth Report of Session 2007 8*, London: The Stationery Office Limited.

COMMISSION FOR RACIAL EQUALITY (1988), *Learning in Terror: A Survey of Racial Harassment in Schools and Colleges*, London: Commission for Racial Equality.

CONDRY, R. (2007), *Families Shamed: The Consequences of Crime for Families of Serious Offenders*, Cullompton: Willan.

COOK, B., DAVID, F., and GRANT, A. (1999), *Victims' Needs, Victims' Rights: Policies and Programs for Victims of Crime in Australia, Research and Public Policy Series No. 19*, Canberra: Australian Institute of Criminology.

COY, M. (2009), 'Invaded spaces and feeling dirty: women's narratives of violation in prostitution and sexual violence', in M. A. H. Horvath and J. Brown (eds), *Rape: Challenging contemporary thinking*, Cullompton: Willan.

CRAWFORD, A. and GOODEY, J. (eds) (2000), *Integrating a Victim Perspective within Criminal Justice*, Aldershot: Ashgate Dartmouth.

CRAWFORD, A. and NEWBURN, T. (2003), *Youth Offending and Restorative Justice: implementing reform in youth justice*, Cullompton: Willan.

CRIMINAL INJURIES COMPENSATION AUTHORITY (2010), *Annual Report and accounts 2009–10*, London: HMSO.

CROALL, H. (2009), 'White Collar Crime, Consumers and Victimization', *Crime, Law and Social Change*, 51: 127–46.

CROWN PROSECUTION SERVICE (2009), *Violence against Women crime report* 2008–9. www.cps.gov.uk.

CUNNEEN C. and HOYLE, C. (2010), *Debating Restorative Justice*, Oxford: Hart.

DALY, K. (2006), 'Restorative Justice and Sexual Assault: An Archival Study of Court and Conference Cases', *British Journal of Criminology*, 46(2): 334–56.

DAVIS, R. C., LURIGIO, A. J., and HERMAN, S.A. (2007), *Victims of Crime*, Thousand Oaks: Sage.

DIGNAN, J. (2005), *Understanding Victims and Restorative Justice*, Maidenhead: Open University Press.

DOAK, J. (2008), *Victims' Rights, Human Rights and Criminal Justice: Reconceiving the Role of Third Parties*, Oxford: Hart.

DOBASH, R. P. and DOBASH, R. E. (2004), 'Women's Violence to Men in Intimate Relationships', *British Journal of Criminology*, 44(3): 324–49.

DOMESTIC VIOLENCE, CRIME AND VICTIMS ACT 2004, c. 28.

DONOVAN, C. and HESTER, M. (2010), 'I Hate the Word "Victim": An Exploration of Recognition of Domestic Violence in Same Sex Relationships', *Social Policy and Society*, 9(2): 279–89.

DUBBER, M. K. (2001), 'Policing Possession: The War on Crime and the End of Criminal Law', *Journal of Criminal Law and Criminology*, 91, 829–996.

DUFF, P. (1998), 'The Measure of Criminal Injuries Compensation: Political Pragmatism or Dog's Dinner?', *Oxford Journal of Legal Studies*, 18(1): 105–42.

DUFFY, B., WAKE, R., BURROWS, T., and BREMNER, P. (2007), 'Closing the gaps: crime and public perceptions', London: Ipsos MORI.

ELEY, S. (2005), 'Changing Practices: The Specialised Domestic Violence Court Process', *Howard Journal of Criminal Justice*, 44(2): 113–24.

ELLIOTT, E. (2007), 'Security, Without Care. Challenges for Restorative Values in Prison', *Contemporary Justice Review*, 10(2): 193–208.

EUROPEAN COMMISSION (2004–9), *Action Plan on the Hague Programme*.

EUROPEAN COMMISSION (2010–14), *Stockholm Action Plan*.

FARRALL, S. and LEE, M. (2008), *Fear of Crime: Critical Voices in an Age of Anxiety*, Abingdon: Routledge-Cavendish.

FARRELL, G. and PEASE, K. (2007), 'Victims and Victimization', in S. Shoham, O. Beck, and M. Kent (eds), *International Handbook of Penology and Criminal Justice*, Taylor and Francis Publishing.

FERGUSON, N., BURGESS, M., and HOLLYWOOD, I. (2010), 'Who are the Victims? Victimhood Experiences in Postagreement Northern Ireland', *Political Psychology*, 31(6): 857–86.

FINNEY, A. (2006), *Domestic Violence, Sexual Assault and Stalking: Findings from the 2004/2005 British Crime Survey* (on-line report 12/06), London: Home Office.

FIONDA, J. (2005), *Devils and Angels: Youth Policy and Crime*, Oxford: Hart Publishing.

FISHER, B. S., CULLEN, F. T., and DAIGLE, L. E. (2005), 'The Discovery of Acquaintance Rape', *Journal of Interpersonal Violence*, 20: 493–500.

FLATLEY, J., KERSHAW, C., SMITH, K., CHAPLIN, R., and MOON, D. (2010), *Crime in England and Wales 2009/2010: Findings from the British Crime Survey and police recorded crime,* London: Home Office.

GARLAND, D. (2001), *The Culture of Control: Crime and Social Order in Contemporary Society,* Oxford: Oxford University Press.

GLIDEWELL, I. (1998), *Review of the Crown Prosecution Service* (Cmnd 3960), London: Home Office.

GOODEY, J. (2005), *Victims and Victimology: Research, Policy and Practice,* Harlow: Pearson Education.

—— (2007), 'Racist Violence in Europe: Challenges for official data collection', *Ethnic and Racial Studies,* 30(4): 570–89.

GRUBER, A. (2010), 'A Distributive Theory of Criminal Law', *William and Mary Law Review,* 52(1): 1–73.

HAGAN, J. and RYMOND-RICHMOND, W. (2009), *Darfur and the Crime of Genocide,* Cambridge: Cambridge University Press.

HAGUE, G. and MULLENDER, A. (2005), 'Listening to women's voices', in T. Skinner, M. Hester, and E. Malos (eds), *Researching Gender Violence,* Cullompton: Willan.

HALL, M. (2010), *Victims and Policy Making,* Abingdon: Willan Publishing.

HAMILL, H. (2002), 'Victims of paramilitary punishment attacks in Belfast', in C. Hoyle and R. Young (eds), *New Visions of Crime Victims,* Oxford: Hart Publishing.

HARNE, L. and RADFORD, J. (2008), *Tackling Domestic Violence: Theories, Policies and Practices,* Maidenhead: Open University Press.

HARTLESS, J., DITTON, J., NAIR, G., and PHILLIPS, S. (1995), 'More Sinned Against than Sinning: A study of young teenagers' experience of crime', *British Journal of Criminology,* 35(1): 114–33.

HEISLER, C. J. (2007), 'Elder Abuse', in R. C. Davis, A. J. Lurigio, and S. Herman (eds), *Victims of Crime,* 3rd edn, Thousand Oaks: Sage.

HESTER, M., PEARSON, C., HARWIN, N., and ABRAHAMS, H. (2007), *Making an Impact—Children and Domestic Violence,* A Reader, 2nd edn, London: Jessica Kingsley.

HODGKINSON, P. (2004), 'Victims: meeting the needs of the families of the homicide victim and the condemned', in P. Hodgkinson and W. Schabas (eds), *Capital Punishment: Strategies for Abolition,* Cambridge: Cambridge University Press.

HOME OFFICE (1990), *Victim's Charter: A Statement of the Rights of Victims,* London: HMSO.

—— (1996), *Victim's Charter,* London: HMSO.

—— (2002), Justice for All, London: HMSO.

—— (2005a), *Rebuilding Lives: supporting victims of crime,* London: Home Office.

—— (2005b), Code of Practice for Victims of Crime, London: HMSO.

—— (2008) *Youth Crime Action Plan 2008* London: Home Office.

HOYLE, C. (2008), 'Restorative Justice, Victims and the Police', in T. Newburn (ed.), *Handbook of Policing,* 2nd edn, Cullompton: Willan.

—— (2009), 'Restorative Justice Policing in Thames Valley', *Journal of Police Studies,* 2(11): 189 (Special Issue on Restorative Policing edited by L. G. Moor, T. Peters, P. Ponsaers, and J. Shapland).

—— (2011), 'Can International Justice Be Restorative Justice? The Role of Reparations', in N. Palmer, D. Granville and P. Clark, (eds), *Critical Perspectives in Transitional Justice,* Intersentia Press.

——, BOSWORTH, M., and DEMPSEY, M. (2011), 'Victims of Sex Trafficking: Exploring the borderland between rhetoric and reality', *Social & Legal Studies,* 20(3): 313–30.

——, CAPE, E., MORGAN, R., and SANDERS, A. (eds) (1998), *Evaluation of the 'One-Stop Shop' and Victim Statement Pilot Projects,* London: Home Office.

——, MORGAN, R., and SANDERS, A. (1999), *The Victim's Charter: an evaluation of pilot projects,* London: Home Office.

—— and SANDERS, A. (2000), 'Police Response to Domestic Violence: From Victim Choice to Victim Empowerment?', *British Journal of Criminology,* 40(1): 14–36.

—— and YOUNG, R. (2002), 'Restorative Justice: assessing the prospects and pitfalls', in M. McConville and G. Wilson (eds), *The Handbook of the Criminal Justice Process,* 525–48, Oxford: Oxford University Press.

—— and YOUNG, R. (2003), 'Restorative Justice, Victims and the Police', in T. Newburn (ed.), *Handbook of Policing,* 680–706, Cullompton: Willan.

HUDSON, B. (1998), 'Restorative Justice: The Challenge of Sexual and Racial Violence', *Journal of Law and Society,* 25(2): 237.

—— (2002), 'Restorative Justice and Gendered Violence: Diversion or Effective Justice?', *British Journal of Criminology,* 42(3): 616–34.

HUMAN RIGHTS COMMISSION OF PAKISTAN (2010), *State of Human Rights in 2009,* Lahore: Maktaba Jadeed Press.

ITZIN, C., TAKET, A., and ARTER-GODFREY, S. (2010), *Domestic and Sexual Violence and Abuse: Tackling the Health and Mental Health Effects,* Abingdon: Routledge.

JOHNSTONE, G. (2011), *Restorative Justice: Ideas, Values, Debates,* 2nd edn, Abingdon: Routledge.

JOHNSTONE, G. and VAN NESS, D. (eds) (2006), *Handbook of Restorative Justice.* Cullompton: Willan.

KARSTEDT, S. (2010), 'From absence to presence, from silence to voice: victims in transitional justice since the Nuremberg trials', *International Review of Victimology,* 17: 1.

KESSLER, R. C., SONNEGA, A., BROMET, E., HUGHES, M., and NELSON, C. B. (1995), 'Post-traumatic stress disorder in the national comorbidity survey', *Archives of General Psychiatry,* 52: 1048–60.

KIRCHENGAST, T. (2008), 'Sentencing Law and the "Emotional Catharsis" of Victim's Rights in NSW Homicide Cases', *Sydney Law Review,* 30: 615–37.

KRUG, E. G., DAHLBERG, L. L., MERCY, J. A., ZWI, A. B., and LOZANO, R. (2002), *The World Report on Violence and Health,* Geneva: World Heath Organisation.

LEVERICK, F., CHALMERS, J., and DUFF, P. (2007), *An Evaluation of the Pilot Victim Statement Schemes in Scotland.* Available at www.scotland.gov.uk/ publications

LOADER, I. and SPARKS, R. (2011), 'Criminology's Public Roles: A Drama in Six Acts', in M. Bosworth and C. Hoyle (eds), *What is Criminology?,* Oxford, Oxford University Press, 17–34.

LOVETT, J. and HORVATH, M. A. H. (2009), 'Alcohol and drugs in rape and sexual assault', in M. A. H. Horvath and J. Brown (eds), *Rape: Challenging contemporary thinking,* Cullompton: Willan.

MACLEOD, P., PAGE, L., KINVER, A., and ILIASOV, A. (2009), *2008/09 Scottish Crime and Justice Survey: First Findings.* www.scotland.gov.uk/Resource/ Doc/296333/0092084.pdf.

THE MAGISTRATES' ASSOCIATION JUDICIAL POLICY AND PRACTICE COMMITTEE (2010), 'Compensation fund'. www.magistrates-association.org.uk/dox/ consultations/1274599675_compensation_fund_ policy_22_april_2010.pdf?PHPSESSID=qtlrgg2er asgl91tu51qjvst05.

MANIKIS, M. (2010), *Victims' information 'rights' and responses to their breaches: Exploring the efficacy of the Code of Practice for Victims of Crime,* MSt Thesis, Faculty of Law, University of Oxford.

MAWBY, R. I. (ed.) (2007a), *Burglary,* Farnham: Ashgate.

—— (2007b), 'Crime, place and explaining rural hotspots', *International Journal of Rural Crime,* 1(1): 21–43.

MAXWELL, G. and MORRIS A. (2006), 'Youth Justice In New Zealand: Restorative Justice in Practice?', *Journal of Social Issues,* 62(2): 239–58.

MACPHERSON, SIR WILLIAM (1999), *The Stephen Lawrence Inquiry: The Report of an Inquiry,* London: HMSO.

MIERS, D. (1997), *State Compensation for Criminal Injuries,* Oxford: Oxford University Press.

—— (2001a), *An international review of restorative justice,* London: Home Office.

—— (2001b), 'Criminal Injuries Compensation: The New Regime', *Journal of Personal Injuries,* 4. 371–95.

—— (2007), 'Looking Beyond Great Britain: the development of criminal injuries compensation', in S. Walklate (ed.), *Handbook of Victims and Victimology,* 337–62, Cullompton: Willan Publishing.

MILLARD, B. and FLATLEY, J. (2010) *Experimental statistics on victimisation of children aged 10 to 15: Findings from the British Crime Survey for the year ending December 2009,* London: Home Office.

MINISTRY OF JUSTICE (2010a), *Breaking the Cycle: Effective Punishment, Rehabilitation and Sentencing of Offenders,* London: Ministry of Justice.

—— (2010b), *Criminal Statistics: England and Wales 2009 Statistics Bulletin,* London: Ministry of Justice.

MOON, C. (2011), 'The crime of crimes and the crime of criminology: genocide, criminology and Darfur', *The British Journal of Sociology,* 62(1): 49–55.

MORRISON, B. (2006), 'Restorative Justice in Schools and Workplaces', in G. Johnstone and D. Van Ness (eds), *Handbook of Restorative Justice,* Cullompton: Willan.

NATIONAL AUDIT OFFICE, Ministry of Justice (2010), *Financial Management Report 2010,* London: HMSO.

NATIONAL SOCIETY FOR THE PREVENTION OF CRUELTY TO CHILDREN (2010), *Delivering more for children, NSPCC annual review, report and accounts 2009/2010,* http://www.nspccannualreview.org. uk/#!/helpline/).

O'DONNELL, I. and MILLNER, C. (2007), *Child pornography crime, computers and society,* Cullompton: Willan.

PADFIELD, N. and ROBERTS, J. V. (2010), 'Victim impact at parole: probative or prejudicial?', in A. Bottoms and J.V. Roberts (eds), *Hearing the Victims: Adversarial justice, crime victims and the State,* 255–84, Cullompton: Willan.

PARMAR, A., SAMPSON, A., and DIAMOND, A., (2005), *Tackling domestic violence: providing advocacy and support to survivors from Black and other minority ethnic communities,* London: Home Office.

PARMENTIER, S. (2011), 'The Missing Link: Criminological Perspectives on Dealing with the Past', in M. Bosworth and C. Hoyle (eds), *What is Criminology?,* Oxford: Oxford University Press.

PATERNOSTER, R and DEISE, J. (2011), 'A Heavy Thumb on the Scale: The Effect of Victim Impact Evidence on Capital Decision Making', *Criminology,* 4(1), 129–61.

PAYNE, S. (2009), *Redefining justice: Addressing the individual needs of victims and witnesses,* London: Victims' Champion Report.

PLOTNIKOFF, J. and WOOLFSON, R. (2009), *Measuring Up? Evaluating implementation of Government Commitments to young witnesses in criminal proceedings,* London: Nuffield Foundation & NSPCC.

RAND, M. (2009), *Criminal Victimization bulletin 2008. Bureau of Justice Statistics National Crime Victimization Survey,* Washington, DC: US Department of Justice.

REEVES, H. and DUNN, P. (2010), 'The status of crime victims and witnesses in the twenty-first century', in A. Bottoms and J. V. Roberts (eds), *Hearing the Victim: Adversarial justice, crime victims and the State,* Cullompton: Willan.

REHN, E. and JOHNSON SIRLEAF, E. (2002), *Women, War and Peace: The Independent Experts' Assessment on the Impact of Conflict on Women and Women's Role in Peace-building,* United Nations Development Fund for Women (UNIFEM).

ROBERTS, J.V. (2009), 'Listening to the Crime Victim: Evaluating Victim Input at Sentencing and Parole', in M. Tonry (ed.), *Crime and Justice,* Vol. 38, Chicago: University of Chicago Press.

—— and EREZ, E. (2010), 'Communication at sentencing: the expressive function of Victim Impact Statements', in A. Bottoms and J. V. Roberts (eds),

*Hearing the Victims: Adversarial justice, crime victims and the State*, Cullompton: Willan.

—— and MANIKIS, M. (2010), 'Victim Impact Statements at Sentencing: Exploring the Relevance of Ancillary Harm', *Canadian Criminal Law Review*, 15(1): 1–26.

ROCK, P. (1998), *After Homicide: Practical and Political Responses to Bereavement*, Oxford: Oxford University Press.

—— (2004), *Constructing Victims' Rights: the Home Office, New Labour, and Victims*, Oxford: Oxford University Press.

—— (2010), 'Hearing victims of crime: the delivery of impact statements as ritual behaviour in four London trials for murder and manslaughter', in A. Bottoms and J. V. Roberts (eds), *Hearing the Victims: Adversarial justice, crime victims and the State*, Cullompton: Willan.

SALISBURY, H. and UPSON, A. (2004), *Ethnicity, Victimisation and Worry about Crime: findings from the 2001/02 and 2002/03 British Crime Surveys Research Findings No. 237*, London: Home Office.

SHAPLAND, J., ATKINSON, A., ATKINSON, H., CHAPMAN, B., COLLEDGE, E., DIGNAN, J., HOWES, M., JOHNSTONE, J., ROBINSON, G., and SORSBY, A. (2006), *Restorative Justice in Practice: The second report from the evaluation of three schemes*, Sheffield: Centre for Criminological Research University of Sheffield.

——, ATKINSON, A., ATKINSON, H., CHAPMAN, .B, COLLEDGE, E., DIGNAN, J., HOWES, M., JOHNSTONE, J., ROBINSON, G., and SORSBY, A. (2008), *Does restorative justice affect reconviction? The fourth report from the evaluation of three schemes. Home Office Findings No. 10/08*, London: Home Office.

——, ROBINSON, G., and SORSBY, A. (2011), *Restorative Justice in Practice: Evaluating What Works for Victims and Offenders*, Cullompton: Willan.

SHEPHERD, J. P., SHAPLAND, M., and SCULLY, C. (1989), 'Recording of violent offences by the police: an accident and emergency perspective', *Medicine, Science and the Law*, 29: 251–57.

—— and BISSON, J. I. (2004), 'Towards integrated health care: a model for assault victims', *The British Journal of Psychiatry*, 184: 3–4.

SHERMAN, L. and STRANG, H. (2007), *Restorative Justice: The Evidence*, London: The Smith Institute.

SOKOLOFF, N. J. (2005), *Domestic Violence at the Margins: Readings in Race, Class, Gender, and Culture*, Piscataway, NJ: Rutgers University Press.

SPARKS, R., GENN, H., and DODD, D. J. (1977), *Surveying Victims*, London: Wiley.

SPENCER, J. (2010), 'The victim and the prosecutor', in A. Bottoms and J. V. Roberts (eds), *Hearing the Victim*, Cullompton: Willan.

STERN, V. (2010), *The Stern Review: A Report by Baroness Vivien Stern CBE of an Independent Review into How Rape Complaints are Handled by Public Authorities in England And Wales*, London: Home Office.

STANKO, B., NORMAN, J., and WUNSCH, D. (2007), *The Attrition of Rape Allegations in London: A Review*, London: Metropolitan Police Service.

STRANG, H. (2002), *Repair or Revenge: Victims and Restorative Justice*, Oxford: Clarendon Press.

—— and BRAITHWAITE, J. (eds) (2002), *Restorative Justice and Family Violence*, Cambridge: Cambridge University Press.

STUBBS, J. (2007), 'Beyond apology? Domestic Violence and Critical Questions for Restorative Justice', *Criminology and Criminal Justice*, 7(2): 169–87.

SWEETING, A., OWEN, R., TURLEY, C., ROCK, P., GARCIA-SANCHE, M., WILSON, L., KHAN, U. (2008), *Evaluation of the victims' advocate scheme pilots*, London: Ministry of Justice Research Series 17/08.

TOBOLOWSKY, P. M. (1999), 'Victim Participation in the Criminal Justice Process: Fifteen Years After the President's Task Force on Victims of Crime', *New England Journal on Criminal and Civil Confinement*, 25(1): 21–106.

TOMBS, S. and WILLIAMS, B. (2008), 'Corporate Crime and its Victims', in B. Stout, J. Yates, and B. Williams (eds), *Applied Criminology*, London: Sage.

TONER, S. and FREEL, R. (2010), *Experience of Crime: Findings from the 2009/10 Northern Ireland Crime Survey*, Research and Statistical Bulletin 4/2010, Northern Ireland: Department of Justice.

TRAVIS, A. (2006), 'Victims of Crime Reject Notion of Retribution', *The Guardian*, London.

TRAVIS, J. and WAUL, M. (eds) (2004), *Prisoners Once Removed: The Impact of Incarceration and Reentry on Children, Families, and Communities*, Washington, DC: Urban Institute Press.

TROWELL, J., UGARTE, B., KELVIN, I., BERELOWITZ, M., SADOWSKI, H., and LE COUTEUR, A. (1999), 'Behavioural psychopathology of child sexual abuse in schoolgirls referred to a tertiary centre: A North London study', *European Child and Adolescent Psychiatry*, 8(2): 107–116.

TYLDUM, G. (2010), 'Limitations in Research on Human Trafficking', *International Migration*, 48(5): 1–12.

UMBREIT, M. S., BRADSHAW, W., and COATES, R. (2003), 'Victims in Dialogue with the Offender: Key principles, practices, outcomes, and implications', in E. G. M. Weitekamp and H.-J. Kerner (eds), *Restorative Justice in Context: International practice and directions*, Cullompton: Willan..

UMBREIT, M. S. and VOS, B. (2000), 'Homicide Survivors Meet the Offender Prior To Execution: Restorative Justice Through Dialogue', *Homicide Studies*, 4(1): 63–87.

UN PROTOCOL TO PREVENT, SUPPRESS AND PUNISH TRAFFICKING IN PERSONS, ESPECIALLY WOMEN AND CHILDREN (2000)

UN BASIC PRINCIPLES AND GUIDELINES ON THE RIGHTS TO A REMEDY AND REPARATION FOR VICTIMS OF GROSS VIOLATIONS OF INTERNATIONAL HUMAN RIGHTS LAW AND SERIOUS VIOLATIONS OF INTERNATIONAL HUMANITARIAN LAW (2005).

VAN DIJK, J., MAYHEW, P., VAN KESTEREN, J., AEBI, M., and LINDE, A. (2010), *Final Report on the Study on Crime Victimisation*, Netherlands: INTERVICT.

VAN DIJK, J., VAN KESTEREN, J., SMIT, P. (2005), *Criminal Victimization in International Perspective: Key findings from the 2004–2005 ICVS and EU ICS*, The Hague: Ministry of Justice WODC.

VANDIVER, M. (2009), 'Capital Punishment and the Families of Victims and Defendants', in C. S. Lanier, W. J. Bowers, and J. R. Acker (eds), *The Future of America's Death Penalty*, Durham, North Carolina: Carolina Academic Press.

VICTIMS ADVISORY PANEL (2003/4), *Listening to Victims—the first year of the Victims' Advisory Panel*, London: HMSO.

VICTIM SUPPORT (2005), *Investigating the practical support needs of burglary victims*, London: Victim Support.

—— (2006), *In the Aftermath: the support needs of people bereaved by homicide*, London: Victim Support.

—— (2009), *2009–12 building our future*, London: Victim Support.

—— (2010), *Victims Justice? What victims and witnesses really want from sentencing*, London: Victim Support.

—— (2011), *Breaking the Cycle: Effective Punishment, Rehabilitation and Sentencing of Offenders: A response by Victim Support*, London: Victim Support.

VON HIRSCH, A., ROBERTS, J. V., BOTTOMS, A., ROACH, K., and SCHIFF, M. (eds) (2003), *Restorative justice and criminal justice: competing or reconcilable paradigms?*, Oxford: Hart Publishing.

WALBY, S. and ALLEN, J. (2004), *Domestic Violence, Sexual Assault and Stalking: Findings from the British Crime Survey*.

WALKLATE, S. (2007), *Handbook on Victims and Victimology*, Cullompton: Willan.

WALTERS, M. and HOYLE, C. (2011), 'Exploring the Everyday World of Hate Victimisation through Community Mediation', *International Review of Victimology*.

—— and —— (2010), 'Healing Harms and Engendering Tolerance: the promise of restorative justice for hate crime', in N. Chakraborti (ed.), *Hate Crime: Concepts, policy and future directions*, Cullompton, Willan.

WEITEKAMP, E. G. M., PARMENTIER, S., VANSPAUWEN, K., VALINAS, M., and GERITS, R. (2006), 'How to Deal with Mass Victimization and Gross Human Rights Violations. A Restorative Justice Approach', in U. Ewald and K. Turkovic (eds), *Large-Scale Victimisation as a Potential Source of Terrorist Activities*, 217–41, Amsterdam: IOS Press.

WEMMERS, J. A. (2005), 'Victim Policy Transfer: Learning From Each Other', *European Journal on Criminal Policy and Research*, 11/1: 121–33.

WILLIAMS, L. M. (2010), 'Harm and Resilience among Prostituted Teens: Broadening our Understanding of Victimisation and Survival', *Social Policy & Society*, 9(2): 243–54.

WOLFE, D. A. (1999), *Child Abuse: implications for child development and psychopathology*, 2nd edn, Thousand Oaks, CA: Sage.

WOOD, J. K. (2005), 'In Whose Name? Crime Victim Policy and the Punishing Power of Protection', *National Women Studies Association Journal*, 17(3): 1–17.

YOUNG, R. (2000), 'Integrating a Multi-Victim Perspective into Criminal Justice through Restorative Justice Conferences', in A. Crawford and J. Goodey (eds), *Integrating a Victim Perspective within Criminal Justice*, 227–51, Aldershot: Ashgate Dartmouth.

—— and HOYLE, C. (2003), 'Restorative Justice and Punishment', in S. McConville (ed.), *The Use of Punishment*, 199–234, Cullompton: Willan.

——, HOYLE, C., COOPER, K., and HILL, R. (2005), 'Informal Resolution of Complaints Against the Police: A quasi-experimental test of restorative justice', *Criminal Justice*, 5(3): 279–317.

ZEDNER, L. (1994), 'Reparation and Retribution: Are They Reconcilable?', *Modern Law Review*, 57(2): 228–50.

ZEHR, H. (1990), *Changing Lenses: A New Focus for Crime and Justice*, Scottdale, PA: Herald Press.

# 15

# MENTALLY DISORDERED OFFENDERS, MENTAL HEALTH, AND CRIME

*Jill Peay*

Mentally disordered offenders are, as Webb and Harris (1999: 2) observe, categorically awkward; being neither exclusively ill nor uncomplicatedly bad, such offenders 'totter between two not always compatible discourses of state intervention'. Are they offenders who have mental disorders, or people with mental disorders who have offended? Or both? When and where should we be treating illness or punishing infractions? Should such offenders be in penal institutions, in hospital, or in the community? This is a challenge faced by health and criminal justice personnel, and by criminologists. Can they agree about into whose remit mentally disordered offenders should fall? And what prospect is there of supportive and coherent legal reform, particularly at a time of economic restraint?

While it is clear that mentally disordered offenders do not represent some single, easily identifiable group, not much else is straightforward. This chapter charts a path through already muddied waters. It is perhaps unsurprising that it embodies much of the incoherence and many of the mixed philosophies evident in the responses of the law and of practitioners, policy-makers, and the caring professions to 'mentally disordered offenders'. However, one theme recurs. If mentally disordered offenders are not a distinct group, to treat them as such for reasons of beneficence exposes them, in an era when the shift to risk-based sentencing dominates policy, to being dealt with more harshly. An alternative approach, the plurality model (Peay 1993) might provide some guide to a less discriminatory approach, since it takes as its starting point the notion that 'mentally disordered offenders' ought to be treated alike with 'ordered' offenders. Proportionality in sentencing, access to therapeutic regimes and crime reduction interventions, and questions of reparation ought to apply equally. This would not be to suggest that a standard criminal justice model should simply embrace offenders with mental health problems, but rather that that model requires reform to be informed by issues pertinent to the capacity of the offender both to be held criminally responsible and to be a proper subject of treatment. And all the time our mental condition defences remain inadequate for properly distinguishing those who should be held responsible for their offending and those who should not

(Mackay 1995; Law Commission 2010) then we cannot begin to deal fairly even with the first issue.

The chapter is divided into six sections with a primary focus on England and Wales. The first section reviews developments in policy and sets the context of conflicting themes. Questions of individual justice and the effectiveness of interventions, questions which rightly apply for all offenders, are writ large where the neutrality of an 'intervention' becomes imbued with the apparent beneficence of 'treatment'. The second section examines the concept of mentally disordered offenders: do such offenders constitute an isolated category meriting special provision, or do the issues raised by this 'group' have wider implications for the study of criminology? The third addresses the problem of definition and incidence. What is meant by a 'mentally disordered offender', are such offenders a minority group, what is their impact on the criminal justice system, and what are the mechanisms for diverting offenders outwith the penal system? The fourth section examines the fundamental justification for separate provision, namely treatment. It takes a critical look at evidence of the relationship between mental disorder and crime, and then focuses on a key problematic group—offenders suffering from personality disorder—who straddle the ordered–disordered offending continuum. There is also a brief examination of the new pilot services for 'dangerous people with severe personality disorder' ('DSPD'). The fifth section tackles some hidden agendas—bifurcation, detention for protective purposes, due process in discharge and release mechanisms— and the final section formulates some conclusions.

## POLICY DEVELOPMENT IN ENGLAND AND WALES: A CONTEXT OF CONFLICTING THEMES

Encapsulating policy in mental health and crime in a single theme is problematic. At face value the dominant policy is humane and therapeutic: Home Office Circular 66/90, which encourages the placement of mentally disordered offenders, wherever possible, into the care of health and personal social services, has arguably received considerable recent support from both the recommendations of the Bradley Review (2009) and the Ministry of Justice (2010d). However, these 'rehabilitative revolutions' are invariably accompanied by riders which stress the need properly to protect the public; such a nuanced approach is captured by Ken Clarke's Ministerial Foreword to *Breaking the Cycle*:

> We will work with the Department of Health to divert more of the less serious offenders with mental illness and drug dependency into treatment rather than prison, as long as the safety of the public is not compromised. (Ministry of Justice 2010d: 2)

And it is these perceptions and attributions of risk which have had a greater influence on policy development (see, for example, Loader and Sparks, this volume, and for a somewhat contrary view Seddon 2008). Offenders with mental disorders are peculiarly 'at risk' of being perceived as posing an unquantifiable danger, and thus, peculiarly apt for the ubiquitous focus on risk management. As risk is transposed into danger, dangerous individuals are singled out for special attention, and the responsibility for preventing and managing risk is transferred to those professionals dealing with or caring for them (Douglas 1992).

What evidence is there of this duality in policy? A treatment-based approach treats offenders who are mentally disordered primarily in terms of their mental disorder, relegating questions of risk and reoffending to secondary status. Thus, the report of the Government's Expert Committee on the necessary scope of mental health legislation (Richardson 1999) would, with its emphasis on patient autonomy, non-discrimination, and issues of capacity, have aligned mental health law much more with medical than penal law (Fennell 2001).

However, the then Government's contrary emphasis on risk management, the reduction of reoffending and early intervention, rejected this approach. Its White Paper (Department of Health/Home Office 2000) took issues relating to the safety of the public as being of key importance, and built on proposals for new DSPD orders; in essence, a form of indefinite detention for some people with personality disorder (Home Office 1999); policy developments which were arguably accomplished by the 2007 amendments to the Mental Health Act 1983 (see Peay 2010). But it is also notable that the introduction of indeterminate sentencing under the Criminal Justice Act 2003 (Ashworth 2010) and the Multi-Agency Public Protection Arrangements (MAPPA) introduced in April 2001 (see generally Home Office/National Probation Service 2004) pre-dated these mental health amendments and effectively achieved many of the then Government's protective ambitions. Indeed, Rutherford's (2010) review of the convergence of mental health and criminal justice systems documents the 'blurring' of former boundaries between these fields.

The annual reports for MAPPA (see Ministry of Justice 2010a) detail the scheme, but in essence MAPPA are designed to ensure the identification of serious sexual and violent offenders in the community, the sharing of information among those agencies involved in the assessment of the risk, and the management of that risk as offenders move from conditions of security into the community. The scheme embodies many of the conflicting themes pursued here for MAPPA embrace both registered sex offenders, violent and other sex offenders, either sentenced or disposed of as mentally disordered offenders, and some other offenders whom it is thought may cause serious harm to the public. On 31 March 2010 there were 48,338 MAPPA eligible offenders; 9,636 offenders were actively managed during 2009/10 by the multi-agency arrangements as they fell into the two highest risk categories. Psychiatrists are involved in these arrangements and since the passage of the Criminal Justice Act 2003, the various agencies have a duty placed on them to cooperate with the responsible authority in each of the 42 MAPPA areas. Yet a psychiatrist's primary responsibility is to the health of their patients; and psychiatrists, like other health professionals, have a duty of confidentiality towards those patients, a duty that does not sit easily with the concepts of information sharing embraced by MAPPA. The tensions are evident, and not only in respect of information sharing (Royal College of Psychiatrists 2004), but also in respect of the very relevance of psychiatric knowledge to the broad ambit of general offending:

> the contribution of psychiatry to risk assessment and management is confined to those with a mental disorder, and that the ability of psychiatrists accurately to assess risk is

limited. There is otherwise a danger of perceived risk being seen as a reason for psychiatric involvement. Any such tendency would result in the unjustified 'pathologising' of ex-prisoners, which would be both unethical and impractical in its service implications. (ibid.: 12)

The shift towards indeterminacy, of controlling offenders in the community, and of the role of risk in underpinning these developments, had all been presaged by a number of warning signs evident in earlier editions of this *Handbook* (see Peay 2007: 499). Indeed such developments were only one manifestation of a wider trend towards greater repression (see Ashworth and Roberts; Loader and Sparks, this volume). But for mentally disordered offenders this trend would have been magnified by concerns about reoffending by former psychiatric patients fuelled by the introduction in 1994 of *mandatory* inquiries into homicides committed by those who had had contact with the specialist mental health services (Peay 1996). The spate of negative publicity the inquiries brought to psychiatric patients, services, and personnel (see Rumgay and Munroe 2001) did much to kindle an underlying public misconception of a relationship between mental disorder and violence.

Yet it had been repeatedly demonstrated that reoffending rates are no higher for disordered than ordered offenders. The most recent reconviction statistics (Ministry of Justice 2010b: 6) not only support this but suggest, and accepting all the difficulties of drawing such comparisons, that the reconviction rates for restricted patients discharged from psychiatric hospitals remain comparatively low (see Ministry of Justice 2010: 72–4). Indeed, homicides by mentally ill people have declined (Taylor and Gunn 1999) and when psychiatric patients kill, they are much more likely to kill themselves than others (Appleby *et al* 2006). Mythology and reality are not always easy to dissect but the announcement in 2001, that inquiries after homicide were no longer to be mandatory, may reflect a recognition both that there were limits to what could be learned from such inquiries and that mentally disordered offenders were not exceptional offenders.

The policy context clearly embodies both positive and negative messages. On the one hand, calls for diverting mentally disordered offenders from the damaging effects of the criminal justice system remain persistent (Bradley 2009). Notions of early intervention are also consistent with a philosophy that 'treatment works'; people can be changed, diverted, distracted, or protected from inappropriate or damaging experiences. Yet on the negative side, there appears to be a persistent distrust of therapeutic disposals for some mentally disordered offenders.

Much of the confusion arises because of the tensions inherent across the continuum both of ordered–disordered behaviour and that of law-abiding–law breaking behaviour. Notions of care and treatment are seen as appropriate for the seriously disordered, provided this does not arise in conjunction with offending of a worrying nature. Similarly, notions of protection and custodial punishment have been traditionally reserved for serious offenders, again assuming an absence of obvious disorder. Yet these tensions are confounded where it is argued that disorder and offending exist side by side in one individual, or, more confusingly still, interact. The resulting amplification of discriminatory practices for mentally disordered offenders has led to calls for capacity-based legislation to apply to both mentally ordered and mentally disordered offenders (see Szmukler *et al.* 2010).

The key statutory provision dealing with mentally disordered offenders, the Mental Health Act 1983, continues uneasily to embrace both legalism and welfarism. The 1983 Act's emphasis on treating people for who they are has also sat uncomfortably alongside a criminal justice approach which has traditionally emphasized what people have done as the basis for a proportionate intervention. It is therefore notable that the Criminal Justice Act 2003 has the reform and rehabilitation of offenders as one of its five purposes of sentencing (section 142(1)), albeit that mentally disordered offenders dealt with under the 1983 Act are explicitly exempted from this (see section 142(2)(d)). Arguably, therefore, there has been something of a fusion between mental health and criminal justice objectives, with both sets of professionals now being expected to engage in the potentially competing tasks of reformation and risk management, with the latter taking precedence where the former is in peril.

Finally, there is the impact of the Human Rights Act 1998. The European Convention on Human Rights (ECHR) has had a powerful influence on the relationship between the executive and the continuing detention of those with psychiatric disorders; an influence which has generally permeated discretionary decision-making. Yet, the ECHR is not a document that naturally lends itself to the protection of those with mental disorders. Indeed, it permits the detention and treatment of those of 'unsound mind'. Nonetheless, the first declaration of incompatibility under the Human Rights Act occurred in a case concerning an offender-patient detained in a psychiatric hospital.[1] Perhaps this is mere coincidence. But perhaps it reflects the presence of conflicting tensions permeating the practices of all who work in this field, whether they are based in the police station or at the Court of Appeal (Eastman and Peay 1999).

## MENTAL DISORDER AND OFFENDERS: A CASE FOR SPECIAL PROVISION?

Should mentally disordered offenders be treated as a separate topic, in the same way that gender, race, youth, and victims are isolated from the mainstream? Arguably not, since mental disorder is not a fixed characteristic of an offender. Yet what these topics do have in common is their 'inconvenience' for a criminology imbued with male, adult, mentally healthy, formerly non-victimized values. It is the premise of this chapter that the lessons to be learned from how we deal conceptually, practically, and in principle with those deemed 'mentally disordered offenders' have as much to say about topics regarded as central to, or ranging across, the scope of criminology as they have to say about 'marginal' groups. Thus, mentally disordered offenders should not be seen as a Cinderella area.

Indeed, to argue for the existence of a discrete group of mentally disordered offenders would presuppose a category of mentally ordered offenders. This falsely comforting notion echoes Gilman's (1988) observation that setting the sick apart sustains the

---

[1]  *R (on the application of H) v Mental Health Review Tribunal* [2001] 3 WLR 512.

fantasy that we are whole. The criminal law broadly adopts such an approach, presuming rationality in the absence of proof of its complete loss (see Smith and Hogan 1988: 200). But such a clear-cut division is problematic. Even the reasonable man on the Clapham omnibus can experience a seeming moment of madness if he alights at the Common. In turn, scientific advances in our understanding of the structure, functioning, and chemistry of the brain have generated a more medical approach to some forms of offending and the neurological syndromes which may underlie them (Eastman and Campbell 2006). In the area of so-called normal offending, defences are frequently advanced or mitigation constructed which draw on elements of 'diminished responsibility', 'unthinking' behaviour, or uncontrolled responses to extreme social stress. Concepts of limited rationality will be familiar to criminologists. Yet few of these offenders would wish for the special treatment that may follow a finding of 'defect of reason' integral to a finding of 'not guilty by reason of insanity'. Why not? Is it a recognition of the punishing aspects of such treatment? Or a desire not to be stigmatized along with those deemed mad? As Porter (2004) observed, it might be preferable to be criminalized and maintain one's free will than to be psychiatrized and lose it.

Or is it that we recognize that some level of disordered thinking ought to alleviate punishment, if not excuse it altogether? Mentally disordered offenders find themselves confined in hospitals, prisons, therapeutic regimes within prisons, and, most notably, within the remand population. Mentally disordered offenders exist in one shape or form across the entire criminal justice system, and 'disorder' may be found to a greater or lesser extent—partly dependent on the incentives for its construction—throughout offending populations.

Accordingly, one dominant theme here is a plea that the component parts of the concept be disaggregated: mentally disordered offenders are first and foremost people; whether they may have offended or whether they may be disordered will be matters for individual resolution. Prioritization of one aspect (the mentally disordered element) of an individual's make-up readily leads to neglect of other, perhaps more pertinent, aspects. Mentally disordered people may have other needs deriving from other 'defining' features such as gender, race, or age; particular offender groups such as sex offenders or substance misusers may need prioritization; similarly, people with personality disorders, or sensory disabilities, or brain damage, or learning disabilities may also require special provision. This range of offenders will manifest themselves amongst the homeless, amongst victims, and as witnesses to crime. Indeed, as James et al. (2002: 88–9) have noted from their study of court diversion, the majority of 'mentally disordered offenders' may be more aptly described as the 'offending mentally disordered' since they are known psychiatric patients who are, in essence, accessing care through the criminal justice system and who have more similarities with those being admitted directly from the community than with 'those committing serious offences, who are subsequently found to be mentally ill'. And this distinction is important because it has implications for where expanding services should be focused (that is, in general not forensic psychiatry) and for the likely success of different forms of intervention (providing services to meet basic needs like poverty and housing can reduce the likelihood of the repetition of particular offences, e.g. stealing to eat). Thus, the very concept of the 'mentally disordered offender' may undermine the need for flexibility within the mental health and criminal justice agencies; a flexibility vital to bridge the gap between expectations and provision.

## THE PROBLEM OF DEFINITION AND INCIDENCE

Hale (2010: 145) notes that 'The fact that a person who is alleged to have committed a criminal offence may be mentally disordered can affect the normal processes of the criminal justice system at several points' and admirably details those interactions. An individual's mental state may affect detention, interrogation, diversion, prosecution, conviction, disposal, treatment, and release (see also Criminal Justice Joint Inspection 2009). But what is 'mental disorder'? In short, it is a term of acute terminological inexactitude. Section 1 of the amended Mental Health Act 1983 defines mental disorder as 'any disorder or disability of the mind', a definition so broad as seemingly to include the world at large. Yet, the concept 'mental disorder' acts like a concertina, expanding and contracting depending on the context in which it is applied in order to accommodate different client groups with little or no coherence. This mismatch frequently results in uncertainties and anomalies (see Peay 2002: 753–5). And as was pointed out to the Joint Scrutiny Committee on the 2004 Draft Mental Health Bill, this definition was broad enough to include those who engaged in the smoking of cigarettes and would encompass all individuals with personality disorder.[2] Whether the implications of this had been fully thought through in respect of all of the points at which it would apply to those involved in the criminal justice process is a moot point; but it was clearly intended to include personality-disordered offenders, and hence those with DSPD (see below), within the ambit of compulsory treatment.

In this context mentally disordered offenders are unlikely to constitute a minority group. They will contribute to the totality of offending, interact with all stages of the criminal justice system, and make up a significant proportion of custodial populations.

Dealing with the last issue first: are the mentally disordered over-represented in custodial populations? Parallels here may be made with the arguments about race and offending. Mental disorder may correlate with certain kinds of offending, but is rarely causative; yet there is a progressive concentration in the criminal justice system of those suffering from mental disorder (compare Singleton *et al.* 1998 with Meltzer *et al.* 1995). Quite why this should be is not clear. However, passage through both processes, of mental health and criminal justice, entails a significant exercise of discretion. Most law-breakers are neither convicted nor sentenced. Most of those with mental disorder are treated without the use of compulsion. Thus, the scope for selective inclusion of more visible offenders is obvious; combining notions of inept offending with the range of views held by the relevant 'gatekeepers' as to the needs of this problematic group will undoubtedly contribute to a highly skewed criminal justice 'output'. Earlier in

---

[2] See www.publications.parliament.uk/pa/jt200405/jtselect/jtment/79/7906.htm#a20.

the process it is difficult to disentangle the impact of various policies and diversion schemes; on the one hand they serve to filter offenders away from the formal process, while on the other hand net-widening remains an issue. It is, however, important to note that surveys of the incidence of mental disorder at the earliest stages will be an under-representation as the police, the Crown Prosecution Service (CPS), and the courts are likely to identify only those with the most obvious symptomatology, while surveys of custodial populations are likely to be an over-representation since they will include those whose disorders have been exacerbated, or brought about, by the process of prosecution and punishment, and those who would not be sufficiently disordered to bring them within the ambit of the 1983 Act's requirements for compulsory admission. Similarly, any tendency to remand into custody to obtain psychiatric reports will contribute to this concentration effect. Again, the tension between a desire to obtain treatment for the 'deserving' mentally disordered offender, and protective concerns where that desire may be frustrated, plays itself out amongst a shifting population.

The contribution that the mentally disordered make to the totality of offending is too complex a question to be answered here (see Peay 2010); but, like juvenile offenders, their offences are frequently highly visible, petty, and repeated. The majority of mentally disordered offenders are to be found not on psychiatric wards but in local facilities supported by health, housing, and social services. It has already been argued that properly resourcing these facilities could have a major preventive impact. It is paradoxical, therefore, as Burney and Pearson (1995: 309) observe, that 'a court appearance may be the only way that their needs will become apparent'; yet that very involvement with the criminal justice system may constitute the reason why community services are more problematic to access for these individuals. And with respect to violence, the best epidemiological evidence comes from the United States: it indicates that major mental disorder accounts for at most 3 per cent of the violence in American society (Monahan et al. 2001) and that drugs and alcohol are more likely precursors.

The interaction of mentally disordered offenders with the criminal justice system is more muddied. The effectiveness of the policy (Home Office Circular No. 66/90) is questioned by the numbers of disordered offenders consistently to be found within the criminal justice system who could benefit under alternative regimes.

The relationship between a progressive trend to care for mentally disordered people in the community and its impact on their subsequent contact with the criminal justice system is also complex. Factors that underpin poor quality of care in the community (homelessness, the co-morbidity of alcohol, drug, and mental health problems, and the associated stress) also increase the likelihood of criminal infractions. Burney and Pearson's (1995) report on a diversion scheme based at one magistrates' court details the range of competing needs; whilst only a small number of offenders require psychiatric hospitalization, there is a larger number of repeat petty offenders, and a third amorphous group of people leading marginal lives where it is not clear whether or what type of intervention might be appropriate. Diversion accordingly becomes something of a logistical nightmare. Ideally, the problem requires the relevant personnel to be alive to the problem groups, having access to specialized services and permeability between service providers; this is a model which has been broadly mirrored in the mental health court pilots (Pakes et al. 2010). Yet, however effective diversion schemes become there will always be offenders with mental disorders in the penal system, either because of late onset of the disorder, or where the nature of the offending and/or disorder makes a penal disposal inevitable. Such offenders are supposedly not to be denied access to treatment. Accordingly, provision exists either for treatment within prison (on a voluntary basis), or for transfer within or outwith the prison system. So, crudely put, the issues become those of identification, diversion, integration with custodial populations, and transfer to therapeutic regimes. At the start of the process, one is looking for a needle in a haystack; at the end, at remand populations being 'swamped' by those with unmet mental health needs.

## IDENTIFICATION

Despite the existence of diversion schemes at the police station and the introduction of the 'appropriate adult' scheme under the 1984 Police and Criminal Evidence Act (PACE)—whereby independent visitors attend police interviews to advise and protect vulnerable arrested persons—research shows that the police both overuse the police station as a place of safety (Docking *et al.* 2007) whilst failing to identify some of those in need of special services (Robertson *et al.* 1995; Littlechild 2001). As to disposal, Robertson *et al.* (1995) noted a degree of bifurcation; those identified with mental illness were four times as likely to be released without further action as other detainees, but slightly more likely to be charged where persistence or violence was involved. Moreover, Vaughan *et al.*'s (2001) study notes that even police stations with diversion schemes fail to pick up, on average, 7 per cent of individuals who would be suitable for diversion, while inappropriately continuing to refer for diversion those who are not mentally disordered.

Under PACE 1984, if a police officer has any suspicion that a person may be mentally disordered or otherwise mentally vulnerable all of the protections and additional rights should be triggered to which the mentally vulnerable are entitled, including the right to have an appropriate adult present during questioning (Home Office 2008: Code C, para. 1.4). Since personality disorder falls within the new definition of mental disorder under the Mental Health Act 1983 it would be interesting to know how frequently the police's definition of, for example, a 'psychopath' impels them to adhere to these special protections. This may be another area where the mismatch between different agencies' expectations for, and definitions of, 'the mentally disordered' impedes the full protection to which that 'group' is entitled in law.[3]

## COURT ASSESSMENT AND DIVERSION SCHEMES

Court diversion schemes, which bring together a psychiatrist, the CPS, the mentally disordered alleged offender, and the sentencer, can prevent offenders being remanded in custody for reports merely because they do not enjoy stable community ties or because of the absence of bail hostels. Moreover, they can also facilitate successful outcomes where offenders are admitted to hospital (James *et al.* 2002); successful both in terms of addressing a patient's clinical needs and in respect of subsequent reconviction rates.

---

[3] Notably, in February 2011 the Code of Practice issued in 2008 still seemed to be making reference to the old definitions of mental disorder under the unamended 1983 Act.

Indeed, James's study reported two-year reconviction rates as being half that for those given non-medical disposals at court (2002: 88). However, NACRO's (2005) survey of court diversion and criminal justice mental health liaison schemes indicates not only that has there been a drop-off in the total number of schemes operating (from a peak of 150 in 1999) but also that, of those schemes remaining active, 25 per cent reported a decrease in their staffing levels and a third were operating with only one member of staff. These statistics support the reported sense that mentally disordered offenders were a low priority for agencies in almost a quarter of those schemes responding to the survey. It is evident that the recommendations of the Bradley Review (2009) for more effective diversion have much to redress.

In addition to the various diversion schemes, there are also formal powers under the 1983 Act to divert offenders into the hospital system. Sections 35 and 36 permit remand to hospital for reports and treatment respectively; section 38 provides for interim hospital orders, to avoid a 'once and for all' disposal to hospital under a section 37 hospital order. Although a punitive order should not follow where an offender responds to treatment and is returned to court for sentence, a punitive approach may be adopted where it becomes apparent that no 'cure' is possible. However, none of these orders is used frequently, albeit there has been some recent increase in their popularity (The NHS Information Centre 2010); carrying out psychiatric reports in prison remains the default position.

Should the mentally disordered be exempt from prosecution altogether? Views vary. Although the Code for Crown Prosecutors classifies mental disorder as a public interest factor tending against prosecution, prosecutors are required to balance the offender's needs, the victims' views, and the likelihood of a repetition of serious offending (CPS 2010: para. 4.17 g and j). Home Office Circular 66/90 also distinguishes those forms of mental disorder made worse by the institution of proceedings and those which come about by reason of instituting proceedings. Yet, the presence of disorder may make prosecution more likely where a guilty plea is anticipated and intervention is regarded as beneficial. Hence, in the decision to prosecute, the presence of mental disorder may act as a mitigating factor and pre-empt action, or it may act as an incentive to proceedings being taken.

Problems of due process also dog the diversion arena. Does the earlier involvement of psychiatrists inevitably favour welfarism over legalism? How is a balance to be achieved between the rights of the defendant and those of the victim? And, as Fennell notes (1991: 336–7), assuming an offender is prepared to be diverted, 'hospital authorities and local authorities have considerable discretion as to whether to accept responsibility for that person. If he is a persistent petty offender, or is potentially disruptive, he is unlikely to be afforded priority status in the queue for scarce resources.' Indeed, the James et al. (2002) study would suggest that those admitted to hospital via the courts are less needy than those admitted direct from the community, and it is only the trigger of criminal justice involvement that enables them to cross the threshold for admission. With the drop at district level in in-patient beds for the adult mentally ill, from around 150,000 in the 1950s to approximately 63,000 in the early 1990s, and a reluctance by some to see offender-patients integrated with 'non-offenders', diversion and community care may have real limits to their ability to absorb all those whom the courts might wish so to allocate. It is also notable that with the new community treatment orders under the 1983 Act substantial numbers (4,103 from 2009/10 alone, made up of those on civil and criminal orders) of patients are now being supervised in the community, and some are supervised for 'long periods of time' (The NHS Information Centre 2010: 13).[4] Shaw *et al.* (2001) had previously observed the problems of maintaining contact with 'diverted' patients, with one in three losing contact. Is this potentially a case of needles returning to the haystack?

## PRISON POPULATIONS

In discussing remands to hospital while awaiting trial, Hale (2010: 156) provocatively asks whether it is worse to languish in hospital without trial, or in prison without treatment. This question has real force, given the extent of mental disorder within the prison population. Examination of this (i) details the range of disorders recognized by psychiatrists amongst an offending population; (ii) underlines the 'irrelevance' to many of these offenders of their mental disorder (since it has not resulted in their being subject to special provisions); and (iii) re-emphasizes the central point that offenders with mental disorder are not some minority group of only marginal concern.

Studies of the prevalence of mental disorder in prison populations have consistently found substantial levels of disorder. The 1997 national survey of psychiatric morbidity (Singleton *et al.* 1998), found 7 per cent of sentenced men and 10 per cent of men on remand probably to have functional psychotic disorders. Of the five disorders surveyed in the research (personality disorder, psychosis, neurosis, alcohol abuse, and drug dependence), fewer than one in ten prisoners showed no evidence of any of these disorders.

Are these figures shocking in absolute terms? Yes. First, because the problem is in no sense new. Over 20 years earlier, Gunn *et al.* (1978) reported an incidence of 31 per cent with psychiatric disorders in the south-east prison population, of whom 2 per cent were psychotic. This high level of disorder (in its broad sense) but 'low' level of psychosis (the latter then comparable with that in the community) is a common finding. Whether the increase over the 20 years reflects more disorder or differential diagnostic practices is less clear; that it remains there at all to be diagnosed at these levels is the principal concern.

Secondly, the figures are shocking because of the related incidence of suicide and self-harm in prison. Whilst the suicide rate has declined over the last 10 years attributable to suicide prevention policies and first night centres—in 2009 there were 60 suicides in prisons in England and Wales—it remains a persistent problem. Taking their most rigorous measure—suicide attempts in the week prior to interview—Singleton *et al.* (1998) note that 2 per cent of the male remand population reported attempting suicide.

Thirdly, the prison population on 11 February 2011 stood at 84,785. By extrapolation this would mean up to 5,934 prisoners with functional psychosis, prisoners certainly

---

[4] A marked contrast with the infrequent use of community orders with a mental health requirement (Seymour *et al.* 2008).

in need of treatment and probably in need of transfer to hospital. And even if services for people with personality, sexual, and substance misuse disorders were developed in prisons, and even with the new mental health 'in-reach' services provided by the NHS (Department of Health *et al.* 2001) transfer to hospital for the seriously mentally ill is the only current viable option. Only in hospital can drugs be given compulsorily, victimization by other prisoners avoided, and violent or self-harming behaviour be better controlled. Yet hospital bed occupancy has been consistently over 90 per cent and the available secure bed total falls manifestly short of the latent demand in the prison population. There simply are not enough secure beds.

However, considering the number and variety of hurdles that mentally disordered offenders have to jump in order not to be diverted from the prison population, the presence of nearly 6,000 seriously mentally ill people would suggest a number of additional hypotheses. First, these filters may fail effectively either to divert or even identify offenders since abnormal behaviour on reception can be misinterpreted as a discipline problem. Secondly, the mismatch between the criteria for disposal under the 1983 Act at the point of sentence and the subsequent broad clinical diagnosis of disorder will substantially account for the finding of fewer than one in ten with no diagnosable disorder. Many disordered offenders have historically not met the 1983 Act criteria for hospital disposal or transfer, or if they have met them, a bed has not been available. Moreover, the tautological relationship between personality disorder/drug/alcohol and sexual problems, and offending behaviour will also skew the figures. Many of these offenders could benefit from transfer to a therapeutic community like Grendon. However, even with the new Grendon-type prison at Marchington, provision falls short of demand (Genders and Player 2010).

Lastly, disagreements among doctors about treatability and the lack of suitable facilities for those suffering from personality disorder and sexual deviation will result in imprisonment by default. Treatment in hospital for some types of offender is simply not a probable outcome; difficult or violent behaviour may discount a therapeutic disposal. While the courts may perceive a need for a psychiatric referral, this is not always matched by service provision.

Thus, although the sentencing of mentally disordered offenders is predicated on notions of diversion and treatment, the possibility of a penal disposal exists where there are elements of culpability (or predicted dangerousness) that require punishment (or control). Indeed, even where doctors are willing and able to treat an offender, the courts may still insist upon a penal sentence.[5]

## TRANSFER TO HOSPITAL

The development of mental disorder *after* imprisonment, together with a persistent failure to identify all those needing treatment at an earlier stage, makes necessary some transfer mechanism. Transfer from prison to hospital has a history plagued with

---

[5] *R v Birch* (1989) 90 Cr App R 78.

problems. Again the basic premise is difficult to contest, namely that detention in prison is inappropriate for those whose mental disorder is sufficiently serious to justify transfer to hospital; yet transfer was historically consistently under-used (Grounds 1991). Bed-blocking in the special hospitals, attributable to problems with moving patients either to less secure hospitals, or back to prison, reduced bed availability for those coming from prison.

Notably, nearly three times as many restricted patients enter hospital as transfers from prison, as come directly from the courts (for 2008, 926 compared with 343 Ministry of Justice 2010c); transferring prisoners at the end of their sentences causes particular problems with respect to their subsequent motivation for treatment. But, do these numbers suggest greater flexibility in the use of transfer provisions *per se*, or a growing reluctance by the courts to use therapeutic disposals in the first instance? The answer is difficult to unpick, but what is clear is that there has been an absolute increase over the last ten years in offenders transferred *after* sentence. Of course, some transfers may be motivated primarily by a desire to protect the public (Grounds 1991), and this would be particularly pertinent in the case of the transfer of DSPD patients almost at the end of determinate prison sentences. Moreover, hospital and limitation directions (a sentence of imprisonment with a direction that the offender be admitted to hospital; Eastman and Peay 1998) now apply to all those suffering from mental disorder. Although the numbers of such orders remain tiny (Ministry of Justice 2010c) they may yet prove attractive to those judges who are prepared to risk a therapeutic disposal only with the backdrop of a protective prison sentence.

As Fennell (1991: 333) concluded, 'it is likely that, despite current policies of diversion, significant numbers of mentally disordered offenders will remain in prisons, and therefore there is an urgent need to consider how a humane and therapeutic psychiatric service might be provided within the prison system'. And here is the nub of the problem; mentally disordered offenders cannot be neatly packaged and swept into the caring system, for, on a broad definition of the term, they make up some 90 per cent of the prison population. Thus, some means of offering effective 'treatment' (if not compulsory treatment) within prison has to be considered.

Hence the resurgence of a treatment movement within criminology. Although its genesis may lie equally in disillusionment with just deserts and humane containment for what is evidently a 'damaged' population, the presence and extent of mentally disordered offenders in the prison population constitutes a compelling force. While the view was ominously expressed in 1991 by the Home Office that 'offenders are not given sentences of imprisonment by the courts for the purposes of ensuring their rehabilitation' (para. 1.28), attempts to reduce subsequent offending by specific groups have grown in scale, especially through the cognitive behavioural programmes developed under the 'What Works' agenda (see Raynor, this volume). With rehabilitation back in vogue, albeit in a more instrumental guise (Ministry of Justice 2010d; Ashworth and Roberts, this volume), the perceived contribution that sentencing can make to crime reduction through working with offenders under sentence—both during and after a period of imprisonment— will only serve to reinforce this trend.

## MENTAL DISORDER, OFFENDING BEHAVIOUR, AND TREATMENT

Treatment is the fundamental justification for separate provision for mentally disordered people who have committed offences. But it is not readily clear what is meant by treatment, or what treatment is attempting to alter—the 'underlying disorder', the offending behaviour, or the link, if any, between the two? Or are our efforts really devoted largely to alleviating the distress and emotional problems offenders suffer, those either pre-existing or post-dating the offending? If it is the likelihood of criminal behaviour *per se*, the justification for treatment will not be confined to a 'mentally disordered' subgroup of offenders. Accordingly, an examination of the relationship between disorder and offending is critical. This leads into the final section of this chapter, on protection. Here, the argument is turned on its head: where mental disorder provides a basis, not for a therapeutic disposal, but for a lengthier custodial disposal than would be proportionate to the seriousness of the offence. Should there then be a compensatory right to treatment for that disorder (Hale 2004)?

### WHAT IS THE RELATIONSHIP BETWEEN MENTAL DISORDER AND OFFENDING BEHAVIOUR?

As Prins (1990, 2005) has amply demonstrated, the relationship between mental disorder and criminality is an uncertain one, concluding (1990: 256), '[m]ost psychiatric disorders are only very occasionally associated with criminality'. Establishing either a causal relationship or the direction of any such relationship is fraught (Peay 2010).

The primary focus has been on mental disorder and *violence* yet the overwhelming correlates of violence are male gender, youth, lower socio-economic class, and the use/abuse of alcohol or drugs, and not the diagnosis of major mental disorder. However, the belief that mental disorder predisposes people to behave violently is widely held and enduring. As Rubin (1972: 398) notes,

> certain mental disorders [are] characterized by some kind of confused, bizarre, agitated, threatening, frightened, panicked, paranoid or impulsive behaviour. That and the view that impulse (i.e. ideation) and action are interchangeable support the belief that all mental disorder must of necessity lead to inappropriate, anti-social or dangerous actions.

The relationship has been highly problematic to research. Results from the major MacArthur study of mental disorder and violence (Monahan *et al.* 2001) are revealing. With respect to criminological factors the authors observe first, that men are no more likely to be violent than women over the course of a one-year follow-up, although the nature of their violence differs (this is consistent with other studies of mental disorder, but not with the criminological literature generally); secondly, that prior violence and criminality are strongly associated with post-discharge violence; thirdly, physical abuse as a child, but not sexual abuse, was associated with post-discharge violence; and neighbourhood disadvantage—in short, poverty—was significantly associated with violence. This finding helps us to understand why using individual-level predictors of violence—for example, race—can be so misleading. For although African-American racial status was associated with violence (odds ratio 5 2.7), this was halved when neighbourhood disadvantage was taken into account, and in absolute terms the effect of 'poverty' was more significant (ibid.: 58–9). With respect to clinical factors, the presence of a *co-occurring diagnosis of substance abuse or dependence* was critical. More surprising was that a diagnosis of schizophrenia was associated with lower rates of violence, making schizophrenia a protective factor compared with depression or *personality disorder*. Notably, although psychopathy was a strong predictor of violence, the predictive power of the screening version of the Hare Psychopathy Checklist (Hart *et al.* 1995) derived from its 'anti-social behaviour' factor and not its 'emotional detachment' factor. Neither delusions nor command hallucinations were associated with higher rates of violence (making prescient Monahan and Steadman's (1983) question as to why those with paranoid delusions should be any more or less likely to attack their tormentors than those who are in fact being tormented). Failure to support the previous findings that lack of control and associated violent behaviour may be a prerogative of the *currently actively psychotic* conflicts with some dearly held psychiatric notions (see for an extensive discussion Peay 2010).

Whilst considering mental disorder and violence it is important to stress two matters. First, the complexity of the causes of violence amongst those with mental disorder (and, in all probability, amongst those without mental disorder) means that there will be no single solution to violence. Accordingly, any single treatment approach is likely to be of limited efficacy, and predictions of future violence will remain extremely hazardous. Secondly, mental disorders account for only a tiny proportion of violence despite the considerable literature devoted to such medicalized explanations. Moreover, medicalized explanations are attended by considerable problems: are not all offences equally open to medicalization? Even seemingly comprehensible property offences may, especially where trivial items are involved, require some less readily accessible explanation than mere acquisitiveness. Secondly, a medicalized explanation precedes a medicalized solution. But if treatment is adopted and then fails, what follows?

## TREATMENT IN PRISON

In 1990 the Home Office observed, '[f]or most offenders, imprisonment has to be justified in terms of public protection, denunciation and retribution. Otherwise it can be an expensive way of making bad people worse' (para. 2.7). Since then, evidence-based treatment programmes, both in prison and in the community, have gained considerable momentum, under the general heading of the 'What Works' initiative (Home Office 2001). The latter has had a significant impact on the philosophy of imprisonment, with the focus being largely on treating offending, rather than mental disorder *per se*. Cognitive behavioural programmes for sex offenders, offence-focused problem-solving (the McGuire 'Think First' programme), substance-abuse treatment programmes, controlling and managing anger (CALM), and cognitive self-change programmes for violent offenders capture the flavour of these initiatives (see also Raynor; Hollin, this volume).

However, the extent to which treatment endeavours can be both sustained and effective remains questionable. Achieving effectiveness will be jeopardized by two enduring factors: prison overcrowding and the use of short sentences, both of which can disrupt programme completion. Moreover, if sentencers come to believe that imprisonment will secure access to beneficial treatment programmes for persistent offenders, 'ordered' offenders may find themselves at as great a risk as disordered offenders of therapeutic sentencing, further accelerating the problem of overwhelming demand.

Emphasis is also shifting on to the importance of resettlement and providing through-care from prisons into the community. Yet, as Grant (1999) observed, this 'through-care' has had a worryingly narrow focus on crime reduction where multi-agency working has had as its objective pragmatic restraint rather than treatment *per se*. He argues that it is no easy task to support the health needs of less serious offenders while managing the risk they pose and the fear they engender. The shift from broadly based rehabilitation to offence-specific crime reduction initiatives has also had an impact on Grendon (psychiatric) Prison. Genders and Player (1995) admirably detail the way in which therapeutic endeavours and security considerations are difficult to reconcile. Yet Grendon's record of success in *controlling* problematic prisoners is notable. Similarly, Taylor (2003) has found statistically significant reductions in violent incidents amongst 55 prisoners held in the DSPD pilot assessment unit at HMP Whitemoor. Perhaps, as Genders and Player (1995) pointed out, the knowledge by all concerned that the rest of the prison system provides a very different form of containment may have a positive effect on prisoner behaviour.

Lastly, prison remains an inappropriate location for patients with psychotic disorders. Most notably, the UK has been found in violation of Article 2 of the ECHR—the right to life—following the killing of one mentally disordered man by another; both had been on remand and held in the same cell in Chelmsford Prison.[6]

This minefield may be crudely summarized:

1. 'Treatment' may mean many different things—ranging from the administration of anti-psychotic medication to the acquisition of social survival skills. There may be a mismatch between health and criminal justice personnel in respect of the objectives of treatment.

2. If the relationship between the disorder and the offending behaviour is not primarily causal, there is less justification for excusing from punishment, and offenders should remain entitled to protection of their rights as offenders while not being denied access to treatment.

3. Even if there is some causal element, punishment for the partially responsible (and hence, 'partially guilty') can be combined with voluntary treatment.

4. Successful treatment for a disorder may have no bearing on future criminality; mentally disordered offenders should be accorded proportionality in the length of confinement; release should not be determined on the basis of unreliable predictions of future offending.

5. As Campbell and Heginbotham (1991: 135) argue, where an offender is treatable and there is some causal connection between the disorder and his or her offending behaviour, there may be less (or no) justification for continued detention after treatment.

---

[6] *Paul and Audrey Edwards v The UK* (2002) Application No. 46477/99.

6. In the existing context, the balance between jurisprudential logic, which may sanction punishment for the 'culpable' mentally disordered offender, and decades of a humanitarian response endorsing a commonsense preference for treatment rather than punishment, ought to be reversed in favour of the former only where treatment can be demonstrated to be inappropriate.

## PERSONALITY DISORDER

Personality disorder (a clinical concept), psychopathy (a trait measurable by the Hare Psychopathy Checklist: Hare 1991) and DSPD (dangerous severe personality disorder—a political/policy concept) are all terms used when exploring the association between disorders of personality and criminality. It is inevitable that there will be some association between personality and criminality since the concepts are by definition, in varying formats, linked.

In addition to its interpersonal and affective elements, Hare's characterization of psychopathy includes the behavioural predisposition that 'psychopaths' are 'impulsive and sensation seeking, and they readily violate social norms' (Hare 1991: 3). Where psychiatrists employ clinical concepts of personality disorder, it is inevitable that therapeutic, conceptual, and legal difficulties will result (Grounds 1987; Peay 2011).

But what is psychopathy? Roth's definition (1990: 449) is noteworthy:

It comprises forms of egotism, immaturity, aggressiveness, low frustration tolerance and inability to learn from experience that places the individual at high risk of clashing with any community that depends upon cooperation and individual responsibility of its members for its continued existence. It has a characteristic sex distribution, age of onset, family history of similar symptoms and disorders and family constellations and influences that show a large measure of consistency in their course and outcome.

Yet people suffering from 'psychopathic disorder' rarely find themselves subject to civil commitment. So, are the traits associated with psychopathic disorder primarily troubling for the individual, or, more contentiously, advantageous?

From a criminological perspective, it is worth reiterating the findings of Monahan *et al.* (2001), above. 'Psychopathy' appears to have two dimensions: one relating to interpersonal and affective features (selfishness/callousness, etc.); and one to socially deviant behaviours (irresponsibility, anti-social behaviour, etc.). The relationship between psychopathy and violence appears, according to the Monahan *et al.* analysis (2001: 70), to be derived from the second dimension and to tap personality traits associated with a consistent record of impulsive, irresponsible, anti-social acts. The underlying emotional pathology appears less important. If so, this would have obvious implications for the likely success of any treatment regime.

Psychiatrists find themselves in a dilemma, being understandably wary of having to 'treat' psychopathic offenders. Some of the resultant slack has been taken up by psychologists, but even their enthusiasm may wane if the treatment is primarily containment and control. Paradoxically, psychiatrists have found themselves criticized both for a failure to offer treatment to those they regard as untreatable, and for releasing those they deem successfully treated.

## DANGEROUS PEOPLE WITH SEVERE PERSONALITY DISORDER

All of the difficulties outlined above are crystallized in the Government's DSPD initiative. This development (Home Office 1999; Department of Health/Home Office 2000) is the latest in a long line of legislative attempts to address the difficulties posed either by those with 'psychopathic disorder', or, in this case, by a subset of them. While this group has been portrayed as having

> high rates of depression, anxiety, illiteracy, poor relationships and loss of family ties, homelessness and unemployment. They have high rates of suicide and high rates of death by violent means. They have high rates of substance misuse. Their behaviour is often violent. Their behaviour is of immense distress to themselves and they are frequently in the position where they are asking for help and yet finding it very difficult to access suitable help [Home Office 1999: 34].

It is hard to resist the sense that the initiative stemmed not from concerns about treatment, justice, or due process, but explicitly from anxiety about reoffending by those 'prematurely' released from the hospital or prison system.

The DSPD proposals have become, since the earlier editions of this *Handbook*, a prime focus for service development and legislative provision (see Fennell 2001 and www.dspdprogramme.gov.uk/useful_information.html). DSPD individuals were thought to number some 2,400 men; but currently under 300 places are funded in high security services with the majority of offenders within prison rather than psychiatric units. To what extent this reveals an emphasis on containment rather than treatment, or the tacit recognition that treatment may not be successful, is unclear. *Breaking the Cycle* (Ministry of Justice 2010d: 37) envisages an expansion of the programme, but primarily in penal and community settings.

Generally, the DSPD initiative did not bode well. Although a research programme was initiated, legislation proceeded without any positive findings. This was not an evidence-based programme. And how, anyway, could it be? If there is no diagnosis and offenders are admitted to the programme who fall outside the specific criteria, no agreed treatment, no means of confidently assessing when the predicted risk may have been reduced, and no obvious link between the alleged underlying condition and the behaviour, how could outcome measures be agreed upon and then evaluated? Finally, the pilot programme, the results of which were themselves controversial (Tyrer *et al.* 2010), initially recruited volunteers; yet, the legislation enacted provided the basis for compulsory transfer and treatment.

# PROTECTIVE SENTENCING: PROCEDURAL SAFEGUARDS VERSUS TREATMENT

Reform in the area of the trial of offenders with mental disorder has been devoted primarily to increasing the court's sentencing options and not to addressing issues of prior culpability (Peay 2002: 765–72). This results in a 'double disadvantage' to those who remain to be sentenced on a 'conventional' basis (Eastman and Peay 1999: 12).

The bulk of offenders are sentenced with their mental disorder having little, if any, mitigating effect. Encouragingly, the Sentencing Guidelines Council did identify 'mental illness or disability' as one of the four factors that may 'significantly lower culpability' when the seriousness of an offence is assessed (Sentencing Guidelines Council 2004: para. 1.25). Statutory reform however has, to date, done little to address the issue, and the presence of mental disorder can still lead to disproportionately long sentences where paternalistic assumptions about the 'mental disorder' element, and protective-predictive ones about the offending element, leave prisoner-patients with more than their 'just' deserts. Unfitness to plead is under consideration (Law Commission 2010) but reform of the law *per se* still looks distant.

It is first worth reiterating that, like all offenders, those with mental disorder are overwhelmingly not dangerous. However, some are. Arguments favouring limited special measures have their attractions, if only to deal with that small but worrying group; but their *quid pro quo* is that the preventive rationale should be tempered by procedural safeguards. Similarly, the arguments for bifurcation are inherently appealing, where diversion into humanitarian care protects offenders from damaging penal sentences. Yet the implications of these two propositions under our existing arrangements are that the route into confinement will affect both the route out, and whether and what treatment will be given.

Concepts of dangerousness and its alleged association with mental disorder pepper the academic literature and the rhetoric of sentencing. Academics and policy-makers have been fiercely divided both on predictive grounds—will it work?—and on questions of rights. The argument embodies the distinction between statistical and legal-clinical decision-making; crudely put, the difference between risk factors associated with groups of people who have common characteristics (much of the risk-prediction literature is of this nature), and the determination of whether any one individual within that group will be amongst those where risk is realized. These kinds of difficult decisions are faced regularly by courts, Mental Health Tribunals (MHTs), discretionary lifer panels, the Parole Board, clinicians and the executive (see, e.g., Peay 1989; Padfield and Liebling 2000; Hood and Shute 2000; Boyd-Caine 2010). The findings of research concerning such decision-making bodies are consistent: despite actuarial evidence that would support the release of patients and prisoners, attributions of risk are central, overvalued, and very difficult to refute.

Should offenders be entitled to a proportional measure of punishment? Walker (1996: 7) argues that there may be no such 'right' where offenders have forfeited the presumption of being harmless because they have *previously* attempted or caused harm to others. But how is precautionary sentencing to be limited? And are mentally disordered offenders at greater risk of imposition of such a sentence? Dworkin (1977) described the restraint and treatment of the 'dangerously insane' as an insult to their rights to dignity and liberty—an infringement that could be justified not where crime reduction might result, but only where the danger posed was 'vivid'. Bottoms and Brownsword (1983: 21) unpacked this concept into its elements of seriousness, temporality (that is frequency and immediacy), and certainty. Certainty was pivotal to precautionary sentencing, but even a high probability of future offending should become relevant only if the behaviour anticipated involved causing or attempting 'very serious violence'. Thus, the right to a proportional measure of punishment would yield a *'prima facie* right to release for the prisoner at the end of his normal term', and this would apply—in the absence of 'vivid danger'—equally to the alleged 'dangerous offender'. But at this point theory and practice diverge.

The passage of the Criminal Justice Act 2003 (see Ashworth and Roberts, this volume) with its emphasis on crime reduction, risk management, reparation, and deterrence, alongside rehabilitation and deserved punishment, places mentally disordered offenders in triple, if not quadruple, jeopardy. Treatment for their underlying disorders, attempts to reduce independently their potential for crime through measures to change offenders' thinking strategies, and a deterrence philosophy which may impact even less successfully on offenders with mental disorders, are all likely to contribute to a greater than proportionate use of incapacitation with 'mentally disordered offenders'.

Under the Criminal Justice Act 2003 community sentences with a mental health treatment requirement have been little used (Seymour *et al.* 2008), in part attributable to the problem of finding a willing practitioner and a consenting patient. At the other end of the spectrum, the introduction of indefinite sentences under section 225 (life sentences or imprisonment for public protection for serious offences), where the court is of the opinion that there is 'significant risk to members of the public of serious harm', has drawn more mentally disordered offenders into the net of indeterminacy (Sainsbury Centre for Mental Health 2008). Notably, section 225 does not prevent the courts from making a hospital order with restrictions, where an offender satisfies the necessary conditions under the 1983 Act; indeed, only the mandatory life sentence following a conviction for murder has the capacity to trump a therapeutic disposal. However, in general protective confinement is self-justifying and difficult to resist.

Spelling out the involvement of predictions of dangerousness is a first step in ensuring that such predictions are made with due regard to the rights of an offender not to be unjustifiably detained. A second step is to ensure procedural fairness: the position of discretionary lifers has been somewhat improved by placing them on the same footing as restricted patients applying to MHTs; however, all the problems which bedevil tribunals are replicated in discretionary lifer panels. And even given a reversed burden of proof, mentally disordered offenders seeking their release on the ground of non-dangerousness will have an uphill struggle when doing so from conditions of security.[7]

## CONCLUSIONS

If the basic premise of this chapter is accepted—namely, that mentally disordered offenders are not, and should not be, treated as an isolated category—the conclusions that follow are of broader significance.

---

[7] The case of *H* above.

First, effort should be devoted to developing a pluralistic model of the criminal justice system. Piecemeal tinkering may provide solutions for the problems posed by specific offenders; it is insufficient as a basis for addressing problems across the ordered–disordered offending continuum. Equally, the temptation to solve problems by addressing only the back end of the process (namely, sentencing and disposal issues) distracts attention from the urgent need for the prior issues of culpability to be resolved on a fairer basis than is currently achieved.

Secondly, if the mentally disordered cannot effectively be identified and marginalized, diversion and transfer can never be the solution. Resource allocation needs to be across the board, not only in respect of a limited number of beds for potentially difficult offender-patients.

Thirdly, it is unrealistic to confine treatment to hospital settings. Treatment in prison, and in community settings, needs full consideration. The problem, of course, is the use of overt compulsion. What is clear is the need to think more carefully about the circumstances in which treatment will be offered, to whom, and what the consequences will be where it is deemed unwelcome, unsuccessful, or inappropriate. A pluralistic model would require the same limitations on intervention for all offenders, assuming they have the capacity to consent to treatment or undergo punishment. While adoption of a proportionality-based approach would constitute a sounder foundation for greater fairness between offenders, the risk-based/treatment approach looks set to dominate the field; in this context more thought needs to be given to the problematic aspects of multi-agency working where confidential 'health' information will seep into criminal justice agencies.

Fourthly, the justifications are many for singling out subsections of 'disordered offenders' for special treatment. But special treatment can readily become special control; to be seduced by the notion that risk can be managed through the containment of identifiable individuals is to allow discriminatory treatment for that group, while failing to tackle the roots of the problem.

Lastly, the failure to agree on a definition of what constitutes a mentally disordered offender, or to apply it consistently even if criteria could be agreed, is likely to result in there being a mismatch of expectations amongst the various personnel and agencies dealing with such offenders. As Watson and Grounds (1993) observed, greater liaison combined with overcoming the boundaries between different parts of the criminal justice and health agencies will be insufficient while the discrepancy in expectations remains.

## ■ SELECTED FURTHER READING

Whilst not mentioned explicitly in the text, Philip Bean's 'Madness and Crime' (2008) is recommended.

## ■ REFERENCES

APPLEBY, L., SHAW, J., KAPUR, N., WINDFUHR, K., ASHTON, A., SWINSON, N., AND WHILE, D. (2006), *Avoidable deaths: Five-Year Report of the National* *Confidential Inquiry into Suicide and Homicide by People with Mental Illness*, Manchester: University of Manchester.

ASHWORTH, A. (2010), *Sentencing and Criminal Justice*, 5th edn, Cambridge: Cambridge University Press.

BEAN, P. (2008), *Madness and Crime*, Cullompton, Devon: Willan Publishing.

BOTTOMS, A. and BROWNSWORD, R. (1983), 'Dangerousness and Rights', in J. W. Hinton (ed.), *Dangerousness: Problems of Assessment and Prediction*, London: Allen and Unwin.

BOYD-CAINE, T. (2010), *Protecting the Public? Executive Discretion in the Release of Mentally Disordered Offenders*, Cullompton, Devon: Willan Publishing.

BRADLEY, LORD KEITH (2009), *Lord Bradley's review of people with mental health problems or learning disabilities in the criminal justice system*, London: Department of Health, COI 2009.

BURNEY, E. and PEARSON, G. (1995), 'Mentally Disordered Offenders: Finding a Focus for Diversion', *The Howard Journal*, 34: 291–313.

CAMPBELL, T. and HEGINBOTHAM, C. (1991), *Mental Illness: Prejudice, Discrimination and the Law*, Aldershot: Dartmouth.

CRIMINAL JUSTICE JOINT INSPECTION (2009), *A joint inspection on work prior to sentence with offenders with mental disorders*, HMI Probation, HMI Court Administration, HMI Constabulary, and HM Crown Prosecution Service Inspectorate, http://webarchive.nationalarchives.gov.uk/+/http://www.justice.gov.uk/inspectorates/hmi-probation/docs/MDO_Joint_Report-rps.pdf.

CROWN PROSECUTION SERVICE (2010), *Code for Crown Prosecutors*, London: CPS.

DEPARTMENT OF HEALTH, HM PRISON SERVICE, and NATIONAL ASSEMBLY FOR WALES (2001), *Changing the Outlook: A Strategy for Developing and Modernising Mental Health Services in Prisons*, London: Department of Health.

—— and HOME OFFICE (2000), *Reforming the Mental Health Act: Part II High Risk Patients*, Cm 5016-ii, London: The Stationery Office.

DOCKING, M., GRACE, K., and BUCKE, T. (2007), 'Police Custody as a "Place of Safety": examining the use of section 136 of the Mental Health Act 1983', *Independent Police Complaints Commission*, Research and Statistics Series: Paper 11.

DOUGLAS, M. (1992), *Risk and Blame: Essays in Cultural Theory*, London: Routledge.

DWORKIN, R. (1977), *Taking Rights Seriously*, London: Duckworth.

EASTMAN, N. and PEAY, J. (1998), 'Sentencing Psychopaths: Is the "Hospital and Limitation Direction" an Ill-Considered Hybrid?', *Criminal Law Review*: 93–108.

—— and —— (eds) (1999), *Law Without Enforcement: Integrating Mental Health and Justice*, Oxford: Hart.

FENNELL, P. (1991), 'Diversion of Mentally Disordered Offenders from Custody', *Criminal Law Review*: 333–48.

—— (2001), 'Reforming the Mental Health Act 1983: "Joined Up Compulsion"', *Journal of Mental Health Law*: 5–20.

EASTMAN, N. and CAMPBELL, C. (2006), 'Neuroscience and legal determination of criminal responsibility', *Nature Reviews Neuroscience*, 7: 311–18.

GENDERS, E. and PLAYER, E. (1995), *Grendon: A Study of a Therapeutic Prison*, Oxford: Clarendon Press.

—— and —— (2010), 'Grendon: Ten Years On', *Howard Journal*, 49(5): 431–50.

GILMAN, S. (1988), *Disease and Representation. From Madness to AIDS*, Ithaca, NY: Cornell University Press.

GRANT, D. (1999), 'Multi-agency risk management of mentally disordered sex offenders: a probation case study', in D. Webb and R. Harris (eds), *Managing People Nobody Owns*, London: Routledge.

GROUNDS, A. (1987), 'Detention of "Psychopathic Disorder Patients" in Special Hospitals: Critical Issues', *British Journal of Psychiatry*, 151: 474–8.

—— (1991), 'The Transfer of Sentenced Prisoners to Hospital 1960–1983', *British Journal of Criminology*, 31(1): 54–71.

GUNN, J., DELL, S., and WAY, C. (1978), *Psychiatric Aspects of Imprisonment*, London: Academic Press.

HALE, LADY JUSTICE (2004), *What can the Human Rights Act do for my mental health?*, Paul Sieghart Memorial Lecture. Available from the British Institute of Human Rights website: www.bihr.org.uk/documents/paul-sieghart-lectures/what-can-the-human-rights-act-do-for-my-mental-health.

HALE, B. (2010), *Mental Health Law*, 5th edn, London: Sweet & Maxwell.

HARE, R. (1991), *The Hare Psychopathy Checklist—Revised*, Toronto: Multi-Health Systems.

HART, S., COX, D., and HARE, R. (1995), *The Hare Psychopathy Checklist: Screening Version*, Toronto: Multi-Health Systems.

HOME OFFICE (1990), *Crime, Justice and Protecting the Public*, Cm 965, London: HMSO.

—— (1991), *Custody, Care and Justice*, London: HMSO.

—— (1999), *Managing Dangerous People with Severe Personality Disorder. Proposals for Policy Development*, London: Home Office.

—— (2001), *What Works: Second Report of the Joint Prison/Probation Service Accreditation Panel*, London: Home Office.

—— (2008), *The Police and Criminal Evidence Act 1984 Code of Practice C*, rev. edn, London: The Stationery Office.

—— and NATIONAL PROBATION SERVICE (2004), *The MAPPA Guidance*. Probation Circular reference No. 54/2004, 14 October.

HOOD, R. and SHUTE, S. (2000), *Parole decision-making: weighing the risk to the public*, Home Office Research Findings 144, London: Home Office, Research Development and Statistics Directorate.

JAMES, D., FARNHAM, F., MOOREY, H., LLOYD, H., BLIZARD, R., and BARNES, T. (2002), *Outcome of psychiatric admission through the courts*, London: Home Office, RDS Occasional Paper No. 79.

LAW COMMISSION (2010), *Unfitness to Plead*, Consultation Paper No. 197.

LITTLECHILD, B. (ed.), (2001), *Appropriate Adults and Appropriate Adult Schemes: Service User, Provider and Police Perspectives*, Birmingham: Venture Press.

MACKAY, R. D. (1995), *Mental Condition Defences in the Criminal Law*, Oxford: Clarendon Press.

MELTZER, H., GILL, B., PETTICREW, M., and HINDS, K. (1995), *OPCS Surveys of Psychiatric Morbidity in Great Britain, Report 1: The prevalence of psychiatric morbidity among adults living in private households*, London: The Stationery Office.

MINISTRY OF JUSTICE (2010a), 'Multi-Agency Public Protection Annual Reports 2009/10', Ministry of Justice, Statistics Bulletin.

—— (2010b), 'Compendium of reoffending statistics and analysis', Ministry of Justice, Statistics Bulletin.

—— (2010c), 'Statistics of Mentally Disordered Offenders 2008 England and Wales', Ministry of Justice, Statistics Bulletin. www.justice.gov.uk/publications/mentally-disordered-offenders.htm.

—— (2010d), *Breaking the Cycle: Effective Punishment, Rehabilitation and Sentencing of Offenders* Cm 7972, London: The Stationery Office Ltd.

MONAHAN, J. and STEADMAN, H. (1983), 'Crime and Mental Disorder An Epidemiological Approach', in M. Tonry and N. Morris (eds), *Crime and Justice: An Annual Review of Research*, Vol. 4, 145–89, Chicago: University of Chicago Press.

——, STEADMAN, H., SILVER, E., APPELBAUM, P., ROBBINS, P., MULVEY, E., ROTH, L., GRISSO, T., and BANKS, S. (2001), *Rethinking risk assessment: The MacArthur study of mental disorder and violence*, New York: Oxford University Press.

NACRO (2005), *Findings of the 2004 Survey of Court Diversion/Criminal Justice Mental Health Liaison Schemes for mentally disordered offenders in England and Wales*, London: NACRO Publications.

PADFIELD, N. and LIEBLING, A. (2000), *An exploration of decision-making at discretionary lifer panels*, Home Office Research Study No. 213, London: Home Office, Research and Statistics Directorate.

PAKES, F., WINSTONE, J., HASKINS, J., and GUEST, J. (2010), 'Mental Health Court pilot: feasibility of an impact evaluation', Ministry of Justice, Research Summary 7/10.

PEAY, J. (1989), *Tribunals on Trial: A Study of Decision-Making Under the Mental Health Act 1983*, Oxford: Clarendon Press.

—— (1993), 'A Criminological Perspective', in W. Watson and A. Grounds (eds), *Mentally Disordered Offenders in an Era of Community Care*, Cambridge: Cambridge University Press.

—— (ed.) (1996), *Inquiries after Homicide*, London: Duckworth.

—— (2002, 2007), 'Mentally disordered offenders, mental health and crime', in M. Maguire, R. Morgan, and R. Reiner (eds), *The Oxford Handbook of Criminology*, 3rd/4th edn, Oxford: Oxford University Press.

—— (2010), *Mental Health and Crime*, Routledge: Abingdon, Oxon.

—— (2011), 'Personality Disorder and the Law: Some Awkward Questions', *Philosophy, Psychiatry and Psychology*, 18(3): 231–44.

PORTER, R. (2004), 'Is mental illness inevitably stigmatizing?', in A. Crisp (ed.), *Every Family in the Land. Understanding prejudice and discrimination against people with mental illness*, London: Royal Society of Medicine.

PRINS, H. (1990), 'Mental Abnormality and Criminality—an Uncertain Relationship', *Medicine, Science and Law*, 30(3): 247–58.

—— (2005), *Offenders, Deviants or Patients?*, 3rd edn, London: Taylor & Francis.

RICHARDSON, G. (1999), *Review of the Mental Health Act 1983*, Report of the Expert Committee, London: Department of Health.

ROBERTSON, G. , PEARSON, R., and GIBB, R. (1995), *The Mentally Disordered and the Police*, Research Findings No. 21, London: Home Office, Research and Statistics Department.

ROTH, M. (1990), 'Psychopathic (Sociopathic), Personality', in R. Bluglass and P. Bowden (eds), *Principles and Practice of Forensic Psychiatry*, Edinburgh: Churchill Livingstone.

ROYAL COLLEGE OF PSYCHIATRISTS (2004), *Psychiatrists and Multi-Agency Public Protection Panels: Guidelines on representation, participation, confidentiality and information exchange*, London: RCP.

RUBIN, D. (1972), 'Predictions of Dangerousness in Mentally Ill Criminals', *Archives of General Psychiatry*, 27: 397–407.

RUMGAY, J. and MUNROE, E. (2001), 'The Lion's Den: Professional Defences in the Treatment of Dangerous Patients', *Journal of Forensic Psychiatry*: 357–78.

RUTHERFORD, M. (2010), *Blurring the Boundaries: The convergence of mental health and criminal justice policy, legislation, systems and practice*, London: Sainsbury Centre for Mental Health.

SAINSBURY CENTRE FOR MENTAL HEALTH (2008), *In the dark: The mental health implications of imprisonment for public protection*, London: Sainsbury Centre.

SEDDON, T. (2008), 'Dangerous Liaisons: Personality disorder and the politics of risk', *Punishment and Society*, 10: 301–17.

SENTENCING GUIDELINES COUNCIL (2004), *Overarching Principles: Seriousness*, Final Guideline, London: SGC.

Seymour L., Rutherford M., Khanom H., and Samele C. (2008), 'The Community Order and the Mental Health Treatment Requirement', *Journal of Mental Health Law*, 53–65.

SHAW, J., TOMENSON, B., CREED, F., and PERRY, A. (2001), 'Loss of contact with psychiatric services in people diverted from the criminal justice system', *Journal of Forensic Psychiatry*, 12: 203–10.

SINGLETON, N., MELTZER, H., and GATWARD, R. (1998), *Psychiatric morbidity among prisoners in England*

*and Wales*, Office for National Statistics, London: The Stationery Office.

SMITH, J. C. and HOGAN, B. (1988), *Criminal Law*, 6th edn, London: Butterworths.

SZMUKLER, G., DAW, R., and DAWSON, J. (2010), 'A model law fusing incapacity and mental health legislation', *Journal of Mental Health Law*, 11–22.

TAYLOR, P. and GUNN, J. (1999), 'Homicides by people with mental illness: myth and reality', *British Journal of Psychiatry*, 174: 9–14.

TAYLOR, R. (2003), 'An assessment of violent incident rates in the Dangerous Severe Personality Disorder Unit at HMP Whitemoor', Home Office Research Findings, No. 210, London: Home Office.

THE NHS INFORMATION CENTRE (2010), *In-patients formally detained in hospitals under the Mental Health Act 1983 and patients subject to supervised community treatment Annual Figures, England 2009/10*

The NHS Information Centre, Community and Mental Health. www.ic.nhs.uk.

TYRER, P., DUGGAN, C., COOPER, S., CRAWFORD, M., SIEVEWRIGHT, H., RUTTER, D., MADEN, A., BYFORD, S., and BARRETT, B. (2010), 'The successes and failures of the DSPD experiment: the assessment and management of severe personality disorder', *Medicine, Science and the Law*, 50: 95–99.

VAUGHAN, P., KELLY, M., and PULLEN, N. (2001), 'The working practices of the police in relation to mentally disordered offenders and diversion services', *Medicine, Science and the Law*, 41: 13–20.

WALKER, N. (ed.) (1996), *Dangerous People*, London: Blackstone Press.

WATSON, W. and GROUNDS, A. (eds) (1993), *Mentally Disordered Offenders in an Era of Community Care*, Cambridge: Cambridge University Press.

WEBB, D. and HARRIS, R. (eds) (1999), *Managing People Nobody Owns*, London: Routledge.

# 16

# DEVELOPING SOCIO-SPATIAL CRIMINOLOGY

*Anthony Bottoms*

A chapter on the spatial distribution of crimes and offenders has appeared in each of the four previous editions of the *Oxford Handbook of Criminology*, with the present writer as an author or co-author on each occasion. Each of those chapters has attempted a general survey of the field at the time of publication. With the agreement of the editors, the chapter for this edition is somewhat different, and I shall begin by explaining why this approach has been adopted.

In the fourth edition, I identified three different 'groups of scholars working in the field of socio-spatial criminology' (Bottoms 2007: 570; this source is hereafter identified by the symbol '4thEd'). These three groups were: (i) researchers focusing on the study of criminal events, mainly adopting a 'routine activities' and/or a 'rational choice' theoretical perspective; (ii) those studying the social structures and social dynamics of neighbourhoods, with a special interest in the effects of neighbourhood life on the development of criminality, particularly among adolescents; and (iii) those following a more ethnographic and/or 'cultural criminology' approach—an approach which, although not incompatible with either of the first two traditions, has for most of the last 20 or 30 years been largely neglected by both. A central argument of the chapter was that these three groups were conducting their work too much in isolation from one another, and therefore that 'there remain significant and necessary steps to be taken to achieve better empirical and theoretical integration within socio-spatial criminology itself' (4thEd: 567).

Since the publication of the fourth edition in 2007, the broad field of socio-spatial criminology has been enriched by a number of publications of very high quality. In some of this recent scholarship, one can identify welcome moves towards better integration, yet it remains the case that much work in the field continues to be conducted in what contemporary management-speak calls 'separate silos'. Given this, but given also that each of the three traditions has (at least in my judgement) contributed importantly to criminological knowledge, the principal purpose of this chapter is to take some further steps towards an improved synthesis of the field.

Pursuing this goal necessarily entails that some aspects of socio-spatial criminology—particularly more technical aspects—will receive little attention here. For example, the chapter in the fourth edition contained a detailed discussion of one type of crime (thefts of and from vehicles) as an illustration of some of the difficulties involved in conceptualizing and measuring the geographical distribution of offences (4thEd: 537–40); but there is no space to pursue such topics here.

One further introductory remark is necessary, and this concerns the term 'socio-spatial criminology' itself. Readers should be aware that this term is not in common use. However, it seems to me to constitute a definite improvement on the two main alternatives, namely 'environmental criminology' and 'the geography of crime'. Both of these terms well describe the 'spatial' dimension of this field of study, but neither fully captures what I will argue is its necessarily intertwined 'social' dimension. Additionally, the term 'environmental criminology', although indeed used in early editions of this *Handbook*, now has the dual disadvantages (i) that it is sometimes used to refer to the important emerging field of 'green' criminology, and (ii) that it seems increasingly to be claimed as a self-defining label by just one of the three traditions of scholarship described above (see, e.g., Wortley and Mazerolle 2008).

## THREE SCHOLARLY TRADITIONS

As an essential foundation to the main argument of the chapter, this first section will briefly outline some principal features of the three main traditions of scholarship. In this inevitably truncated account, I shall focus on the *historical origins* and *main substantive focus* of each tradition, as well as the *principal theoretical frameworks* that each utilizes.

### THE NEO-CHICAGOANS: NEIGHBOURHOOD EFFECTS AND COLLECTIVE EFFICACY

Historically, the scholarly study of the spatial dimensions of criminality began in earnest in the University of Chicago in the period between the two World Wars, as part of the work of the celebrated 'Chicago School of Sociology' (see 4thEd for more details). The main criminological work of the Chicago School started by mapping the location of offender residences (especially those of juvenile delinquents), initially in Chicago itself and later in other cities. Researchers then attempted to explain these observed distributions by reference to wider understandings of the city, as derived from the field of urban sociology. Accordingly, this work emphasized the *social-structural and cultural conditions of the neighbourhoods* within which juvenile delinquents resided. In particular, the Chicago researchers noted that, over time, the rates of offender residence remained highest in the same inner city neighbourhoods, despite the fact that such neighbourhoods were—in early twentieth century America—successively occupied by waves of immigrants from different countries. Hence, Chicago School researchers made the claim that the social conditions of these neighbourhoods helped to generate delinquency among the adolescents living there, in a process that has more recently come to be described as the *production of a neighbourhood effect*.

For various reasons, scholarly interest in the concept of neighbourhood effects declined in the decades after the Second World War. However, it was powerfully rekindled by William Julius Wilson's seminal book, *The Truly Disadvantaged* (1987), which generated a fresh wave of research and writing in neighbourhood studies (see the citation data in Sampson, Morenoff, and Gannon-Rowley 2002). But in an increasingly individualistic, neo-liberal political culture, not everyone was convinced. Within criminology, for example, James Q. Wilson and Richard Herrnstein (1985) expressed scepticism about the very existence of neighbourhood effects (as opposed to individual or family effects) on individuals' crime careers, although their stance was effectively refuted some years later by Wikström and Loeber's (2000) important analysis of data from the longitudinal Pittsburgh Youth Study. In their research, Wikström and Loeber showed that, after one had controlled for various individual 'risk factors' for offending (such as impulsivity, poor parental supervision, and low school motivation), neighbourhood factors remained causally important in generating adolescent criminality, at least in the poorest neighbourhoods (for a fuller summary, see 4thEd: 558–60).

Some scholars have, however, continued to insist that even tightly-controlled analyses such as that of Wikström and Loeber are not conclusive, because they are not 'experimental' (i.e., they do not contain any randomized controls), and therefore the postulated 'neighbourhood effects' could in principle have arisen through a selection effect.[1] Doubts of a similar kind in the broader sociological field of neighbourhood effects led to the funding of a large-scale US experimental study known as the *Moving to Opportunity* project, which will be considered in a later section.

A leading recent writer within the 'neo-Chicagoan' criminological tradition (i.e., principally studying neighbourhoods and neighbourhood effects) has been Robert Sampson of Harvard University, notably through his work on the major Project on Human Development in Chicago Neighborhoods (PHDCN). Sampson's principal theoretical contribution has been creatively to adapt a concept developed by the original Chicago School, that of *social disorganization*. Chicago researchers had used this term when attempting to explain the geographical distribution of offender residences (see Kornhauser 1978: 61–82; 4thEd: 531–2), and they appeared to have in mind as its obverse an implicit model of a 'well-functioning community', or 'urban village' (see Sampson 2006). They therefore tended to regard close social relations among neighbours as a necessary feature of 'socially organized' communities. Sampson took seriously the evidence that in contemporary Western societies many middle-class, low offender rate neighbourhoods do not display this characteristic. Instead, families in such areas often 'keep themselves to themselves', although they do so within an

---

[1] The experimental stance is well described by Ludwig *et al.* (2008: 149) as an anxiety about 'classic omitted variable bias'; that is, 'people choose or in other ways end up in neighborhoods for reasons that ... may ... correlate with their outcomes'. In the case of a well-controlled non-experimental research study like that of Wikström and Loeber, this position requires one to argue that adolescents living in different kinds of neighbourhoods have systematic individual differences over and above those controlled for in the six individual risk factors. This is theoretically possible, but Robert Sampson's (2008: 216n) comment seems applicable: 'at some point, the burden is on the "unobserved heterogeneity" theorists to posit a coherent, plausible and nonmysterious explanation' that adds up to a 'substantial confounding' of the alleged findings of nonrandomized but well-controlled studies.

underlying framework of what has been called 'thin trust' (Smith, Phillips, and King 2010) that enables them to act collectively and cohesively in pursuit of specific goals where necessary (for example, if there were to be a clear threat to neighbourhood interests, such as a proposal to build a road through a park used by neighbourhood children). Sampson accordingly developed a theory known as *collective efficacy* (adapting Bandura's (1997) concept of the same name in his book on self-efficacy), defined as *the institutional ability to achieve what a group or community collectively wishes to achieve*. Methodologically, collective efficacy has been operationalized within neighbourhood studies through survey items measuring two linked concepts: first, the willingness of residents to intervene for the common good in certain defined situations (such as children spray-painting graffiti on a building); and secondly, the existence or otherwise of 'conditions of cohesion and mutual trust among neighbors' (since 'one is unlikely to take action in a neighborhood context where the rules are unclear and people mistrust each other': Sampson and Raudenbush 1999: 612). Thus, the concept of neighbourhood collective efficacy incorporates both a static 'underlying relations of [thin] trust' dimension and a more action-oriented 'willingness to intervene' dimension. Empirically, it has proved to be of considerable value in a number of research studies (see, e.g., the meta-analysis by Pratt and Cullen 2005).

However, consistent with the approach of the original Chicago School, Sampson does not regard collective efficacy as a stand-alone concept. He is very clear that it needs to be connected to macro-level understandings of social structure and power, and for this reason he decisively rejects criticism that the theory is 'merely an attempt to push the burden of social control or support onto residents, "blaming the victim" as some have claimed' (Sampson 2006: 155). Figure 16.1 presents an 'oversimplified sketch' in which Sampson attempts to portray these connections. Collective efficacy predicts an absence of violence and disorder; but is itself predicted by the density of social ties in an area, by good 'organizational infrastructure', and by an absence of concentrated poverty and residential instability. ('Organizational infrastructure' here refers to the ability to 'sustain capacity for social action in a way that transcends traditional personal ties'.) Additionally, 'spatial proximity' is seen as sometimes important—a point to which we will return (Sampson 2006: 155–6).

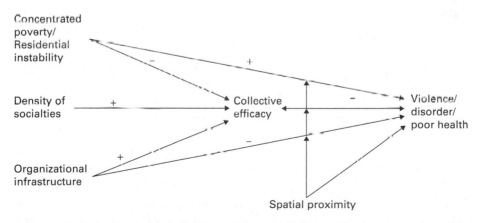

**Figure 16.1**  Main lines of emphasis in collective efficacy theory
*Source*: Sampson (2006: 156)
'Collective efficacy theory: lessons learned' by R.J. Sampson from TAKINGSTOCK: The Status of Criminological Theory by Francis Cullen (Figure 5.1)

A further conceptual matter relevant to the understanding of collective efficacy is that, as Sampson (2006: 157) has pointed out, criminogenic 'neighbourhood effects' on an individual can in principle be of two different types. Type One is a *dispositional (or developmental) neighbourhood effect*; that is, conditions in the neighbourhood could influence the individual's (usually, a young person's) moral values, or ability to exercise self-control (see Wikström 2006) so that he/she is less/more likely to commit offences, wherever he/she happens to be (in the neighbourhood or out of it). Type Two is a *situational neighbourhood effect;* that is, neighbourhood social conditions could make it less/more likely that anyone currently in that neighbourhood (resident or visitor) would commit offences, but this effect would not be operative once the person had left the neighbourhood. (Of course, these two conceptualizations overlap, but it remains analytically valuable to make the distinction.) Wikström and Loeber's (2000) Pittsburgh analysis provides strong evidence for the first type of effect. As regards collective efficacy, however, while the empirical evidence for this is generally strong (see above), that research also suggests that it achieves its effects in a situational rather than a dispositional way (Sampson 2006: 165; Sampson 2008: 195n).

## THE ECCA/HSP GROUP: FOCUSING ON CRIMINAL EVENTS

Researchers in the Chicago School, when they researched the geography of crime, focused on data plotting *the areas where offenders lived*. But offenders do not always commit crimes close to home (for example, they might shoplift in the city centre), so an alternative focus for socio-spatial criminology is to undertake a detailed study of the *location of offences*. Surprisingly, this type of study did not emerge strongly within criminology until the 1970s; but it has remained powerful ever since, and is now arguably the dominant voice in the field. One factor assisting its growing influence has been the advent of computerized 'crime mapping', which allows for the easy display and analysis of topographical information, replacing the laborious 'pin maps' of not so long ago. Crime mapping is now routinely utilized in all police departments, with a principal focus on the mapping of offence locations (see Chainey and Ratcliffe 2005). Indeed, the British Government has recently followed the lead of most jurisdictions in the United States in requiring local police forces in England and Wales to make crime maps available on the Internet to the general public, and these maps offer a rich source of data to contemporary students.

The two leading theoretical frameworks deployed to analyse crime events have been *routine activities theory* and the *rational choice perspective*. Routine activities theory (RAT) was originally developed by Cohen and Felson (1979) in a paper where they sought to explain crime rate trends by reference not to offenders' dispositions, but rather to social changes leading to increased opportunities for crime—specifically, the increasing proportion of adult women in the workforce, leading to more houses being unguarded during the day. Thus, it has been well stated that RAT embodies two key ideas: first, 'that the structure of routine activities in a society influences what kinds of situations emerge', and secondly, that 'people commit acts of crime in response to situational conditions' (Wikström *et al.* 2010: 59).

Cohen and Felson (1979: 590) articulated what has since become the classic formulation of RAT, which has three elements (italicized):

> The probability that a violation will occur at any specific time and place might be taken as a function of the convergence of *likely offenders* and *suitable targets* in the absence of *capable guardians*.

It is important to note—though this point is rarely made in the literature—that the 'capable guardians' dimension of this formulation allows links to be made between RAT and collective efficacy theory. This is because, on average, the residents in a neighbourhood with high collective efficacy are by definition more capable guardians than are residents of other areas. However, unlike collective efficacy theory, RAT has not developed any systematic theorization linking routine activities to macro-social issues.

The key *motivational* (as opposed to situational) concept in the outline formulation of RAT is that of the 'likely offender'. However, the criminologist who jointly developed and subsequently principally promoted RAT, Marcus Felson, has for most of the last 30 years focused much more attention on 'suitable targets' and 'capable guardians' than on offenders and their routine activities. (Not long ago, he said that RAT 'today has much more to say about offenders than its original rendition' (Felson 2008: 74), but his own view is still that 'criminology as a field works best when it focuses on crime, not criminals' (Felson 2011: 171)). Fortunately, however, within the broad grouping of those who focus their research on criminal events, Paul and Patricia Brantingham (2008) have made good this lacuna with their 'crime pattern theory', to be described in a later section (see p. 460).

The second principal theoretical approach in the study of crime events has been the *rational choice perspective*, developed particularly by Ronald Clarke and Derek Cornish (see Cornish and Clarke 1986). While employed as a senior researcher at the then Home Office Research and Planning Unit, Clarke began to develop a programme of research and action under the generic title *situational crime prevention* (StCP). This was based on the insight, derived from psychological research, that often human behaviour is situation-specific; it follows therefore that people might act in a different way if the immediate context is altered. A striking example of this truth was presented in an article by Clarke and Pat Mayhew (1988). They showed that the suicide rate had dropped suddenly in Britain in the 1970s when the source of domestic gas supplies was switched from coal gas (toxic) to natural gas from the North Sea (non-toxic), and they argued that there was no plausible explanation of this decline other than the change in the nature of the gas supply. In other words, even people desperate enough to try to end their own lives often did not turn to alternative methods when the immediate context was altered. Given this and other evidence of the apparent strength of influence of immediate situations, Clarke and his colleagues therefore studied the specific circumstances in which different offences are committed, with a view to modifying those situations to produce a reduction in crime. (Typically, this might involve strategies such as making goods harder to steal by strengthening security at potential targets; reducing the availability of means to commit certain crimes (e.g. guns, knives); or environmental management (e.g. separating the fans of opposing teams at football matches)). Such strategies have often led to beneficial results, and there are now many examples of successful StCP initiatives (see Clarke 1997).

Theoretically, StCP adopted a particular view of offending behaviour: 'offending was regarded as goal-oriented and offenders as rational actors seeking to obtain a variety of satisfactions from their crimes, at least risk and effort to themselves' (Cornish and Clarke 2003: 57). The preventive task was therefore seen as being to anticipate offenders' likely intentions, and then to thwart or deflect those intentions by the manipulation of situations. The theoretical assumption that offenders are to be viewed as *agents exercising rational choice* has subsequently remained central to the StCP perspective, although the rational choice perspective is described in modest terms by Cornish and Clarke (2008: 44, 38) as 'more a set of sensitising concepts than a conventional criminological theory', and as a 'good-enough theory' which was 'conceived primarily to assist the development of situational prevention'.[2]

Although they are not identical, there are some important similarities between the routine activities and the situational crime prevention/rational choice approaches (see generally Clarke and Felson 1993); and both also have links to the Brantinghams' 'crime pattern theory'. Specifically, all these approaches have a common focus on the crime event, and an explicit interest in crime reduction as a main goal for scholarship. Accordingly, these scholars jointly formed an organization known as 'ECCA' (Environmental Crime and Crime Analysis), which is devoted to the furtherance of research and policy in this tradition (for an edited volume setting out key features of this approach, see Wortley and Mazerolle 2008). More recently, a further subgroup with a broadly similar orientation has emerged, focusing its attention especially on so-called 'Crime Hotspots' (locations where many crimes occur), and on the development of police strategies to prevent crime at such locations ('hotspots policing' or HSP). This subgroup is not organizationally part of ECCA, but it shares both their micro-locational and their crime-preventive foci, and for this reason I shall hereafter use the shorthand term 'ECCA/HSP' to embrace all the subgroups. The leading scholar in the HSP tradition is David Weisburd, and in a recent monograph he and colleagues summarized their position in these words: 'we..argue that the police can be more effective if they shift the primary concerns of policing from people to places' (Weisburd, Telep, and Braga 2010: 7). Given such a claim, it is clear that the work of the HSP subgroup must feature strongly in a chapter on socio-spatial criminology. However, unlike the ECCA subgroups the HSP subgroup has no distinctive theoretical standpoint; indeed, it explicitly draws upon routine activities and rational choice perspectives as principal theoretical resources (see Braga and Weisburd 2010: ch. 3). But it has also recently become interested in the concept of legitimacy, which has the potential to link it more closely to broader sociological approaches (see further below).

---

[2] Elsewhere in the social sciences, much more robust claims are made for rational choice approaches. See for example the statement by James Bohman (1992: 207): 'Many philosophers, sociologists and political scientists defend the claim that rational choice theory can provide the basis for a unified and comprehensive theory of social behavior'. (For a good collection of papers in support of and against this view, see the edited volume in which Bohman's essay appears.)

## CULTURE, SEMIOTICS, AND THE SIGNAL CRIMES PERSPECTIVE

This third type of work in socio-spatial criminology has a less clear-cut history and identity than the first two groups, but it is of current importance in the field, and requires separate treatment because its main preoccupations are different. Its key distinguishing feature is its emphasis on *culture,* understood as in the following classic definition by A.L. Kroeber and C. Kluckhorn (Gould and Kolb 1964: 165):

> Culture consists of patterns, explicit and implicit, of and for behaviour acquired and transmitted by symbols....; the essential core of culture consists of traditional (i.e. historically derived and selected) ideas and especially their attached values; culture systems may, on the one hand, be considered as products of action, on the other hand as conditioning elements of further action.

Within this definition, the key terms are '*symbols*' and '*values*'; so we are here in the realm of metaphor and norms—topics that scarcely feature in some kinds of criminology, yet are of unquestionable importance for people's daily lives in cities.

Symbols are the special focus of a field of study known as *semiotics* ('the science of signs and symbols'), which focuses especially with the operation of such symbols in communication (both language and visual media). There is no doubt that semiotics is relevant to socio-spatial criminology, since the signs emitted at particular locations can send messages that significantly affect behaviour; for example, the architecture and the ambience of a particular hotel or shop might be fashioned to carry the message 'don't enter unless you have money'.

The cultural dimension within socio-spatial criminology stretches back to the work of the Chicago School, since that school had a strong ethnographic tradition (see Matza 1969). More recently, some 'cultural criminologists', notably Keith Hayward (2004), have shown a strong interest in linking cultural issues—including the cultural symbols of a consumerist society—to the study of 'crime in the city', but this work has not been strongly enough connected to mainstream debates in socio-spatial criminology to make a real impact on most scholars in the field.

A much more influential recent development has been Martin Innes's (2004) 'signal crimes perspective' (SgCP), which in a few short years has made a very distinctive contribution to socio-spatial criminology. As Innes and Roberts (2007: 245) have pointed out, SgCP draws explicitly both on Umberto Eco's (1976) pragmatist social semiotics, and on Erving Goffman's (1971) work on 'relations in public' (which itself is, at least loosely, part of the symbolic interactionist tradition in sociology). The distinctive voice of the signal crimes perspective will be fully discussed in a later section.

## THE ORGANIZATION OF THIS CHAPTER

The remainder of this chapter has three main sections. It is organized initially by *spatial scale,* because, as will become clear, this is now an important topic within socio-spatial criminology. Accordingly, in the first section I shall consider *neighbourhoods,* with special attention to the issue of neighbourhood effects. The second section then narrows the spatial gaze to focus on *micro-locations* within neighbourhoods, particularly *crime hotspots*. In the third section the recently burgeoning field of research into *incivilities in public spaces* is discussed. The best-known theoretical approach in this field is Wilson and Kelling's (1982) 'broken windows theory' (BWT), which is a significant point of reference throughout the section. Since BWT considers both micro-events (the broken window) and their alleged consequences for the escalation of criminality in the neighbourhood, this section necessarily embraces both micro- and meso-spatial levels. The opportunity is also taken, however, to examine studies relating to the semiotic dimensions of incivilities, and this is ultimately found to be a more promising line of research than BWT.

## NEIGHBOURHOODS AND NEIGHBOURHOOD EFFECTS

Consider first some basic data about a reasonably representative English city: Sheffield (population 535,000).[3]

The map drawn at Figure 16.2(a) shows 339 small areas of the city ('lower-level super output areas') according to their status on the official governmental Index of Multiple Deprivation (IMD). Some 124 (37 per cent) of these areas, situated predominantly in the east of the city, were among the one-quarter most deprived areas in England; hence, in aggregate Sheffield is not an affluent city. Yet it is definitely a city of contrasts, because alongside the real deprivation in many of these areas, some 53 small areas (16 per cent: mostly in the south-west) were counted among the one-quarter most affluent areas in England. So there are definitely 'two Sheffields', and indeed residents' average life expectancy declines by about 10 years as one moves from west to east.

Consider now the social and geographical distribution of offenders' residences in Sheffield at a similar time period (Figure 16.2(b)).

As will be seen, eastern Sheffield had many more offenders living in it than western Sheffield; indeed a rank order correlation between the IMD and the offender rate in lower-level super output areas showed a very close association between the two variables (Spearman's rho = -.935; P<.001). But where did these offenders commit offences *when they offended against other households* (as opposed to business premises, etc.)? Police-recorded data for residential burglaries are shown in Figure 16.2(c).[4] *A priori*, one might reasonably have hypothesized that burglars would, in large numbers, travel the short distance from east to west Sheffield in order to take advantage of the more

---

[3] I am most grateful to my Sheffield colleague Dr Andrew Costello for preparing the maps shown in Figure 16.2. The offender and crime data shown in Figure 16.2(b) and Figure 16.2(c) are derived from his long-standing research collaboration with the South Yorkshire Police.

[4] Residential burglary has been selected because research has shown that offenders on average travel further from their residential base to commit this offence than they do for other offences against households, e.g. criminal damage against residential properties.

*(a) Map showing Area Ratings on Index of Multiple Deprivation (IMD), 2007*

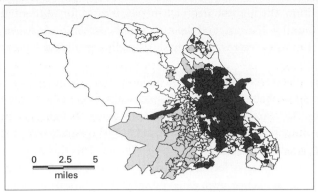

Key: Grey = amongst 25% most affluent areas in England;   White = middle 50%;
Black = amongst 25% most deprived areas in England. Data for IMD 2007 are from 2005–6.

*(b) Map of offender residences for the period September 2004–August 2006*
(in quintiles, highest rate darkest)

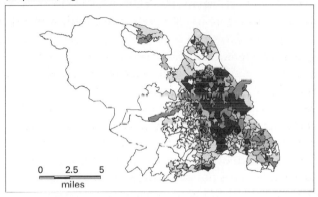

*(c) Map of victimizations for offences of residential burglary, September 2004–August 2006* (in quintiles, highest rate darkest)

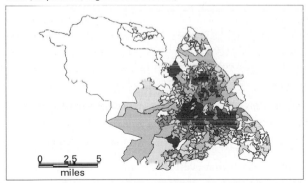

**Figure 16.2** City of Sheffield: geographical distribution of (a) social deprivation, (b) offender residences and (c) victimizations for residential burglary. (All maps are based on lower level super output areas)

lucrative theft opportunities to be found there. However, although there is clearly some movement in this direction, the highest area victimization rates for residential burglary were again to be found in the east, and the rank order correlation between IMD and the small-area victimization rate was highly statistically significant (Spearman's rho = -.294, P<.001).

Why is this so? From the general literature of socio-spatial criminology one can readily identify two main probable reasons (and specifically for Sheffield, see Wiles and Costello 2000). First, 30 years ago the Canadian criminologists Patricia and Paul Brantingham (1981; see more recently Brantingham and Brantingham 2008) proposed a theory that has since become known as *crime pattern theory*. This theory postulates that most offenders, like most people, feel much more comfortable in areas that they know reasonably well; in consequence, even when potential burglars are engaging in a search pattern for a suitable target, it is hypothesized that they will usually not wish to venture into residential areas that are completely unknown to them (as much of western Sheffield is to many offenders resident in the east). In other words, the suggestion is that offenders will usually commit crimes in areas already known to them through their routine activities. While this theory has not been tested to the extent that one would ideally wish, the research evidence that is available supports it (for details, see 4thEd: 543–7; also now Wikström *et al.* 2010: 76).

A second potential reason why residential burglaries tend to be clustered close to offenders' residences can be discerned from a feature of the rational choice perspective. Clearly, in eschewing searches for affluent targets in the west of the city, Sheffield's burglars are not acting with full rationality. But, as rational choice theorists have repeatedly emphasized, we need to consider not only full rationality, but also what has been termed 'bounded rationality'; that is, the more truncated (but still rational) choices that most people make on an everyday basis (for example, as regards choices like buying clothes or booking a holiday). The main features of a bounded rationality process have been described as follows (Gigerenzer and Selten 2001: 8, slightly adapted):

(1) The person engages in a simple search for relevant information.

(2) The search is usually terminated by simple 'stopping rules' (for example, 'I can only afford to spend one afternoon on buying a new outfit'; 'I will rent the first flat that meets my basic requirements'). Such rules frequently 'do not involve optimization calculations'.

(3) The decision-making process is simple: one makes a decision on the basis of the information within the framework of the 'stopping rule'.

It is not hard to see that the thought processes of many burglars might fit this pattern. We know from ethnographic research that even active and recidivistic burglars tend to commit crimes especially when they are confronted with what they perceive as a 'pressing need'—for example, a financial crisis connected to the need to pay the rent or to get the next drugs fix (Wright and Decker 1994). It therefore makes sense that they should then search for the first target that will meet their basic aspiration level (i.e., to 'tide them over' for the time being). If such a process is engaged in, it will tend to result in many offences being committed quite close to their residential base.

The preceding paragraphs have some important implications. The original Chicago School criminologists focused only on the study of high *offender rate* areas, and this has tended also to be the main interest of many of their Neo-Chicagoan successors; by contrast, the overwhelming focus of the ECCA/HSP group is on *criminal events* and the circumstances (including the locations) in which they occur. But it turns out that in the real world, these two topics (location of offender residences and location of criminal events) are by no means unconnected. Indeed, an empirical proposition that is well supported in the research literature is: *other factors being equal, a neighbourhood close to a high offender area will have more crimes committed in it than a similar neighbourhood more distant from a high offender area* (see, e.g., Wikström 1991: 227). Perhaps in this finding lies a first clue as to how we might begin to work towards a more integrated field of socio-spatial criminology.

The most important recent research project on neighbourhood effects and crime is the 'Moving to Opportunity' (MTO) experiment (see above), in which subsidized opportunities were provided for selected residents to move away from very poor areas in the US. To pave the way for the discussion of MTO, the next subsection therefore considers evidence relating to socially deprived neighbourhoods, focusing on *why they have high offender rates*, and also on the *extent of victimization* of residents in such areas.

## AREAS OF HIGH SOCIAL DEPRIVATION

Empirical findings of the kind shown in Figure 16.2(b) are not confined to Sheffield. For example, Roger Houchin (2005) collected data on the pre-prison residential addresses of men in Scottish prisons on a given night in 2003, and found a steeply rising imprisonment rate as the poverty level increased: from less than 10 per 10,000 males in the most affluent areas to nearly 100 in the most deprived.

These are stark findings, which should engage the attention of anyone interested in the spatial dimensions of crime and criminality. How are they to be explained? This is a very complex question, but in summary the following matters are relevant:

First, it is of course possible that there is systematic social bias in at least some aspects of the criminal justice system. However, such potential bias is the province of other chapters in this *Handbook,* so I shall leave it aside here.

Secondly, the finding certainly reflects in part the housing market constraints that many offenders experience. Known offenders frequently find it difficult to obtain any employment, let alone well-paid employment. In consequence, they tend to be forced into the poorer sectors of the housing market; and of course, cheap accommodation is most readily available in poorer areas. Thus, the offender rate/IMD correlation is in part a direct consequence of the operation of the housing market.

Thirdly, although the relevant research literature is complex, there is empirical evidence suggesting that the social conditions within poorer areas might themselves generate a higher level of criminality among young people growing up in such areas (see in particular Wikström and Loeber 2000; for a summary of other research, see 4thEd: 561–3). It has been suggested, for example, that such a consequence can arise because of the stresses of parenting in economically deprived circumstances (see especially Weatherburn and Lind 2001); and/or a 'school effect' arising from poor educational facilities available to children in such areas; and/or a 'peer effect' for 'youths of low educational status and with a preference for unsupervised routine activities' (typically in the streets) (Oberwittler 2007a; see also Oberwittler 2007b). The evidence for such effects is, however, stronger in the United States than in European research (Oberwittler 2007a), possibly because of the more extreme poverty levels that are found in the most deprived housing areas in the US.

Fourthly, however, it is important not to overstate the deprivation/offender rate connection, because it is not universal. Thus, 20 years ago researchers from Sheffield University reported a case study of two adjacent public housing areas, with virtually identical demographic and economic profiles, in which one area had offender rates *three times* that of the other (Bottoms, Mawby, and Xanthos 1989). This was part of more general research work in Sheffield showing the importance of housing markets in relation to the offender rates of areas (see Baldwin and Bottoms 1976; Bottoms and Wiles 1986), a finding that has since been confirmed by other studies (e.g. Wikström 1991; Hope and Foster 1993: see further, 4thEd: 563–5). Such studies therefore lead one to caution against any over-simple interpretations of data such as those shown in Figure 16.2.

Turning now to victimization, it is necessary to recognize that living in a deprived area can have direct human costs in terms of both crime victimization and unavoidable daily confrontations with what are usually termed 'incivilities' (such as graffiti, or the detritus associated with drug use and drug markets). Table 16.1 presents relevant summary data from the British Crime Survey (BCS) on these issues. In this table, responses are grouped according to the ACORN neighbourhood classification system, with the most affluent areas in the left-hand column and the most deprived in the right-hand column.[5] An unusual category that requires some explanation is the relatively affluent 'urban prosperity' group (second from left), which mainly consists of dwellings in gentrified or 'student accommodation' areas, often located not far from deprived neighbourhoods.

Looking first at Part A of the table, on household victimizations, we observe a general tendency for the victimization rate to rise as one moves from left to right of the table, with the exception of the 'urban prosperity' group. However, the contrast between the richest and poorest areas is certainly not as stark as when offender rates were considered. In summary, two main reasons lie behind this important difference. First, many offences are committed not against households but against businesses in the city centre or elsewhere; such offences do not of course appear in tables such as Table 16.1, but those who commit them necessarily live somewhere, and are therefore included in maps such as Figure 16.2(b). Secondly, offenders do to an extent venture outside their own areas to other areas, especially if reasonably lucrative targets are to be found nearby—which is indeed the main reason for the high victimization rates in 'urban prosperity' areas.

Part B of Table 16.1 introduces data on frequent incivilities. Here, the main point of interest is that the rates of repeated experience are very high—44 per cent of those in 'hard-pressed' areas report experiencing a 'social incivility' (see foot of table for a

[5] ACORN means 'A Classification of Residential Neighbourhoods'. It classifies small areas in different parts of the country according to their demographic, employment, and housing characteristics, and then groups them together into categories. There are five principal area types (as shown in Table 16.1), each of which contains a number of more specific 'basic area types' (of which there are 56 in all).

**Table 16.1** Respondents' reported experience of property crime victimization and frequent local incivilities by ACORN residential area types, British Crime Survey 2004–5

|  | Wealthy achievers | Urban prosperity | Comfortably off | Moderate means | Hard-pressed |
|---|---|---|---|---|---|
| *A. Crime: % of households victimized once or more* | | | | | |
| Criminal damage | 5.1 | 8.0 | 6.7 | 9.7 | 7.8 |
| Vehicle-related theft* | 5.1 | 11.9 | 7.8 | 11.4 | 10.1 |
| Burglary | 1.6 | 4.6 | 2.0 | 2.9 | 3.8 |
| *B. Disorder: % of survey respondents reporting experience of frequent local incivilities (at least once a week)* | | | | | |
| Physical incivilities† | 3 | 8 | 6 | 9 | 11 |
| Social incivilities†† | 23 | 38 | 32 | 42 | 44 |

* Data given are % victimization of households with vehicle
† Physical incivilities = Litter or Graffiti
†† Social incivilities = Young people hanging around; drug use or drug dealing; drunk or rowdy behaviour; or noisy neighbours
*Sources*: Part A: Nicholas *et al.* (2005) : Table 4.08, p. 69
Part B: Davenport (2010): Table 5.9

definition) in their neighbourhood *at least once a week*, a rate much higher than any other in the table.

In summary, therefore, people living in deprived areas are at risk of suffering relatively high rates of victimization for household crimes, and very high rates of repeated incivilities. Given these data, it requires little imagination to recognize that living in the most socially deprived areas can be tough, and that bringing up children in these conditions might have deleterious consequences for them, including an enhanced probability of their acquiring a criminal record. These are important background observations as we move on to consider the Moving to Opportunity (MTO) project in the United States.

## THE MOVING TO OPPORTUNITY EXPERIMENT

The MTO Project has been described as 'one of the most ambitious social experiments ever attempted' (Briggs, Popkin, and Goering 2010: 51). It arose, in large part, out of the scepticism previously described as to whether one could ever demonstrate a 'neighbourhood effect' (for any outcome variable) unless an element of experimental randomization were built into the design of a major research study.

In MTO, families living in public housing in selected very poor census tracts in five major US cities (Baltimore, Boston, Chicago, Los Angeles, and New York) were invited to apply for a 'housing voucher' to move to a 'low poverty' area.[6] Not all those living in the specified census tracts were eligible; in particular, households were only registered for MTO if the family unit included one or more children under 18 and if 'the household did not contain anyone with a criminal record' (Ludwig *et al.* 2008: 154). Those accepted as eligible (a total of 4,248 families) were then randomly assigned to one of three experimental conditions: (i) a control group, who received no special assistance; (ii) an experimental group, who received a subsidized voucher enabling them to rent a property in a low-poverty area, together with some limited advice about how best to use this voucher; and (iii) an intermediate group who received vouchers enabling them to move to any area, but with no additional advice. For simplicity, I will confine the discussion to comparisons between the experimental and control groups.

In practice, only just under half (47 per cent) of those receiving an experimental voucher actually moved under the experiment, and—not surprisingly—these families were found to differ significantly in a number of ways from those who received a voucher but did not use it. Following the language of randomized clinical trials in medicine, those within the MTO experimental group who moved are described as 'experimental compliers' (= 'took the medicine correctly').

The principal scientific reason for conducting a randomized trial is to eliminate selection bias in the samples subjected to the experimental and control treatments; in other words, to be able to say with certainty that there are no significant differences in the background characteristics of the experimental and control groups. This remains a valid approach where, as in MTO, there is a sizeable 'non-complier' subgroup within the experimental group, *but only if one treats the experimental group as a whole* (i.e. compliers plus non-compliers) when making experimental-control comparisons. (This procedure is known as an ITT (or 'intention to treat') analysis, because the experimental group consists of all those intended to receive the experimental treatment, whether or not they did receive it.) Where, as in MTO, the 'non-complier' subgroup is large, it becomes harder to demonstrate statistically significant effects as between experimentals and controls, given that one is trying to discern whether or not a 'neighbourhood effect' exists, using—in this instance—an experimental group half of whom did not actually move neighbourhoods within the terms of the experiment.

### The MTO evaluation

Families who moved within the framework of the MTO experiment did so sequentially in the years 1994 to 1997 inclusive. In 2002 (four to seven years after random assignment), a large-scale 'interim evaluation' of MTO was conducted, including surveys of adults and youth in all five cities and in all three experimental conditions (see Orr *et al.* 2003; Kling, Liebman, and Katz 2007). A 'final evaluation', on the same comprehensive basis, has recently been undertaken, but results are not yet available. Between the interim and final evaluations, two research studies of a more qualitative nature were undertaken, with smaller samples and extensive use of long descriptive interviews. One of these qualitative studies, the 'Three Cities' study (conducted in

---

[6] The baseline census tracts all had a 'poverty rate' of at least 40%, i.e., 40% of families living in the area were officially classified as 'poor'. The experimental group were required to move to a 'low poverty area', i.e., with a poverty rate of less than 10%.

Boston, Los Angeles, and New York) has been published in full (Briggs, Popkin, and Goering 2010); the other, the 'Two Cities' study (conducted in Baltimore and Chicago), has not, but its researchers have recently produced a very interesting article on criminality (Clampet-Lundquist *et al.* 2011).

The main experimental outcomes of MTO at the time of the interim evaluation (using an ITT approach) have been usefully tabulated by Kling, Liebman, and Katz (2007: 90), and Table 16.2 presents a simplified version of their summary. In brief, adults in the experimental group experienced an improvement in mental health, but not in economic self-sufficiency or physical health; experimental girls experienced extensive benefits; but for experimental boys, the findings were much less encouraging, with no outcome showing a positive sign. Criminologists will of course be particularly interested in the headline contrast between the results on 'risky behaviour' for adolescent girls (encouraging) and adolescent boys (not encouraging); it will be necessary to consider this result in more detail shortly.

## Social conditions for experimentals and controls

Before one can interpret the MTO results adequately, it is necessary to know something about the social conditions actually experienced by the experimental and control groups. A first point to note is that the MTO families were, at the beginning of the experiment, among the most deprived in American society. For example, Sampson (2008: 196) calculated that only about 5 per cent of his PHDCN sample in Chicago would have qualified for MTO under its eligibility criteria, which, he comments, 'shows how far into the extreme tail of the [American] poverty and race distributions the MTO study reaches'. In the five MTO cities taken together, over 90 per cent of family heads in the study were black or Hispanic, and most households were female-headed.

Given that all families eligible for MTO had children, it is not surprising that just under half of adults surveyed said that they applied to join the experiment in the hope of securing better schooling for their children. But, less predictably, this was not the most frequently stated reason for applying: *as many as three-quarters* of adults (in each

Table 16.2 Summary of main outcomes from MTO research

|  | Adult | Adolescent males | Adolescent females |
|---|---|---|---|
| Economic self-sufficiency | NS | * | * |
| Absence of mental health problems | + | NS | + |
| Absence of physical health problems | NS | – | NS |
| Education | * | NS | + |
| Absence of risky behaviour | * | – | + |
| Aggregate assessment | NS | – | + |

\* = not applicable
+ = experimental group better than control group (P<.05)
– = experimental group worse than control group (P<.05)
NS = no significant difference between experimentals and controls
*Source*: derived from Kling, Liebman and Katz (2007: 90)

of the experimental conditions) said they had applied in the hope of securing a move to an area with fewer crime and drug problems (Ludwig and Kling 2007: 496; see also Briggs, Popkin, and Goering 2010). Thus, issues of perceived neighbourhood safety actually lie at the heart of the MTO experiment, though this point is not always prominent in the project literature.

Given the design of the MTO experiment, the social conditions in which the experimental compliers were living at the time of the interim evaluation were of course not as poor as those of the control sample. However, the difference between the samples was less marked than expected, for two reasons: some control group families moved to less poor areas during the experiment, while some experimental families moved on from their first destination, usually back towards a poorer district. These subsequent moves among experimentals frequently occurred because of housing market constraints (for example, within a generally buoyant economic context, the new landlords might increase the rent, or decide not to accept vouchers any longer); but such moves also occurred for more personal reasons, such as wishing to be closer to relatives left behind in the baseline neighbourhood. Additionally, continuing family links to the baseline neighbourhood sometimes led to regular visits back to that area by experimental compliers, even where there was no second move (see generally Briggs, Popkin, and Goering 2010).

A further point in the MTO experience has importance for an emerging 'units of analysis debate' in socio-spatial criminology; readers are therefore asked to bear with the detail, even though it might not seem immediately relevant. In brief, although in general MTO experimental compliers moved to *less poor* areas, they largely remained housed in *racially segregated* areas (Clampet-Lundquist and Massey 2008; Sampson 2008). Sampson's analysis of this issue is of special interest. He begins by noting previous research showing that 'African-Americans face a unique risk of ecological proximity to disadvantage that goes well beyond local neighborhoods', and he emphasizes that this difficulty is faced even by middle-class black families. He accordingly re-coded the MTO empirical data for Chicago not—as MTO does—by small census tracts, but according to a widely-used classification of broader 'community areas'. This analysis showed 'a striking social reproduction of disadvantage among MTO participants, experimental and control group members alike ... *the patterns of neighborhood attainment flows in the two groups are indistinguishable, suggesting a profound structural restraint*' (p. 211, emphasis added). In other words, at least in the Chicago MTO site, poor people did not move to any fairytale 'opportunity' (as the policy rhetoric of 'choice' that underpins housing voucher schemes might suggest); instead, the argument is that, because of the broader social-structural conditions within which the experiment was necessarily conducted, they moved 'to inequality, with opportunities embedded in a rigid and likely reinforcing ... social structure' (p. 213). If Sampson is right (and he has certainly developed a strong case), then it is not difficult to see why the adults in the MTO experiment did not improve their economic self-sufficiency.

But it is important to remember that, for the MTO participants themselves, signing up for the scheme was not primarily about improving their economic opportunities; instead, the primary motivation was improved safety for their family. Given such an aim, relocation to a nearby safer neighbourhood (regardless of its socio-structural difficulties) could be sufficient to meet participants' 'bounded rationality' goals;

moreover, *there is firm evidence that such aims for improved safety were often achieved.* Thus, in the interim evaluation, the ITT analysis showed that experimental households were significantly less likely than control group households to report feeling unsafe at night, seeing drugs in the area recently, being a victim of a crime, seeing public drinking locally, or believing that the police in the area 'do not respond when called'; and, in two 'collective efficacy' questions, they were also significantly more likely to say that neighbours would intervene to do something about kids skipping school and kids spraying graffiti on a local building (Ludwig *et al.* 2008: 160–1). These are not inconsiderable differences, even though they occurred within the 'profound structural restraints' described by Sampson.

What therefore emerges from this discussion is the significance for social analysis—including criminological analysis—of *both* large-neighbourhood social-structural constraints on socio-economic opportunities (Sampson's point), *and* small-area differences in safety within such larger structurally-constrained neighbourhoods (the MTO participants' point). This dual focus, I believe, has an importance well beyond MTO, and will assist us in the quest for a better-integrated socio-spatial criminology (see below).

## The youth crime gender difference

Finally, I turn to the surprising MTO results about 'risky behaviour' for adolescents, as outlined in the summary by Kling, Liebman, and Katz (2005) (see Table 16.2). In their summary, the authors used a rather limited definition of 'risky behaviour';[7] but when other measures are used, the results are similar. In particular, the arrest data for MTO youth up to the end of 2001 (at which time their average age was 19) show that girls in the experimental group accrued significantly *fewer* arrests for both violent and property arrests than did the controls; but experimental boys had a significantly *higher* number of arrests for property crime (though not for violent crime) than their controls (Kling, Ludwig, and Katz 2005: 100). This result for boys was of course unexpected, given that experimental compliers moved, on average, to less poor areas with lower crime rates (see above). Nevertheless, the subsequent qualitative analyses of both the Three-Cities Study (Briggs, Popkin, and Goering 2010) and the Two Cities Study (Clampet-Lundquist *et al.* 2011) indicate that the results are probably not spurious (though there are questions to be asked about the validity of the arrest data—see below). Additionally, in the interim evaluation, a self-reported 'behavioral problem index' (relating to minor behavioural matters such as lying, temper outbursts, and disobedience at home) also showed experimental boys reporting significantly higher problems than controls (Kling, Ludwig, and Katz 2005: 100).[8]

How are these results to be explained? This is a very difficult question to answer, because while randomized experiments provide a rigorous methodology to ascertain

---

[7] 'Marijuana in past 30 days; smoking in past 30 days; alcohol in past 30 days; ever pregnant or gotten someone pregnant': Kling, Liebman, and Katz (2007: 90).

[8] A self-reported delinquency index showed no significant difference between experimentals and controls for either boys or girls; however, the researchers considered that the levels of self-reported behaviour were 'unrealistically low', an observation that they thought was supported by the fact that young people also self-reported many fewer arrests than appeared on their official records (Kling, Ludwig, and Katz 2005: 100, 102, 103n).

*whether* an effect exists, the experimental method in itself does nothing to explain *why* a demonstrated effect exists. Sometimes (as in clinical trials of new drugs in medicine), the cause of the effect can be easily discerned, since the difference in the treatment (experimental drug versus placebo) is the only plausible explanation of a significant effect. However, the complicated circumstances of MTO allow no straight-forward inferences of this kind; and in such a situation, the cause of any effect has to be inferred by the researchers through an interpretation of all relevant data, including non-experimental data.

This explains the strange fact that, in the MTO literature, there are three principal papers on the male-female differences in youth criminality, each of which offers a different explanatory account of the observed effects (Kling, Ludwig, and Katz 2005; Briggs, Popkin, and Goering 2010, ch. 5; Clampet-Lundquist *et al.* 2011). Given space limitations, I shall not discuss these differences here;[9] instead, I shall distil some com-mon features of the two most recent research accounts. It appears from these studies that adolescent boys (but not girls) in the experimental complier group continued, in their new environments, to practise the dominant leisure activity they had learned in the baseline neighbourhoods, namely 'hanging out' with one another in public places. But they found themselves less accepted by existing residents in the new areas than did their sisters. (This was possibly because such residents had no fear of girls from stigmatized public housing projects, but adolescent boys from such areas were viewed more warily.) Moreover, the new areas had higher collective efficacy than the baseline neighbourhoods (and therefore more adult interventions with teens); hence, according to the Two Cities study, 'a negative side of collective efficacy' seemed to be apparent, i.e. adult interventions were made, but they led to resentment from the boys (Clampet-Lundquist *et al.* 2011: 1171). Moreover, according to the same researchers, experi-mental boys were 'more likely than any other group ... to describe being questioned or hassled by the police' (1169)—which might perhaps have led to artefactually high arrest data. Given the above, it is not surprising that whereas girls in the experimental group expressed significantly greater satisfaction with their current neighbourhood than did their controls, among boys there was no such difference. Similarly, while experimental girls were significantly less likely than controls to have continuing links with their baseline neighbourhoods, this was not the case for boys (Kling, Ludwig, and Katz 2005: 109). Boys, it appears, were simply not adjusting as well as girls to their new neighbourhoods, and this was leading to at least some enhanced behaviour problems. Overall, there seems little doubt that what is being described is a series of gender-related differences in reactions to a change of neighbourhood, leading to differences in behaviour: in other words, a *gendered neighbourhood effect.*

---

[9] The two main suggested explanations not discussed in the text are: (1) Kling, Ludwig, and Katz (2005: 114) consider the best explanation to be that male 'experimental youth have a comparative advantage [over the controls] in exploiting the set of theft opportunities in their new neighborhoods'; (2) on the basis of their qualitative data, researchers in the Three Cities Study postulate that low-poverty neighbourhoods 'are pro-tective for girls in a way that they are not for boys', in that girls were enabled to experience a 'dramatically reduced' fear of 'sexual harassment, coercion and rape' than they experienced in the baseline neighbour-hoods (Briggs, Popkin, and Goering 2010: 94ff). However, Clampet-Lundquist *et al.* (2011: 1183) report that in the Two Cities Study, while researchers did not systematically ask about sexual harassment, 'few girls in either program group [experimentals or controls] volunteered such experiences'.

## DISCUSSION

In the light of the preceding discussion, what conclusions can reasonably be drawn about the study of neighbourhoods and neighbourhood effects in relation to crime and criminality? I would suggest that five conclusions are of special importance.

*First,* and most obviously, some neighbourhoods can, by reason of the crime and disorder within them, be experienced as very unpleasant places to live. It speaks volumes that in the MTO experiment, despite the very high levels of poverty in the baseline neighbourhoods, the wish to move to a safer area was the most important reason for families to apply to participate. Fortunately, the residents of deprived areas in Britain do not usually encounter such adverse social conditions, yet the problems experienced by their residents remain substantial (Table 16.1).

*Secondly,* it is now clear beyond doubt (taking MTO results together with previous research such as that of Wikström and Loeber) that neighbourhood effects on the criminality (or compliance) of individual residents do sometimes exist. We are, however, still a long way from being able to specify the precise nature of these effects.

*Thirdly,* it is also clear that in trying to understand such matters, it is sometimes necessary to take account of macro-level social-structural arrangements—such as the historic patterns of segregation and lack of opportunity in Chicago neighbourhoods, as described by Sampson. In other words, factors beyond the immediate locality are sometimes of great importance in shaping the daily experience of residents.

*Fourthly,* as the 'risky behaviour' results of MTO so well show, the shaping of social life and social effects can be very complex, and they can differ for different population groups in the same neighbourhood. Complex results of this kind emerge from subtle interactions of structure, culture, and agency within areas, which social scientists (including criminologists) need to understand more fully. Also, where (as in MTO) the participants in an experiment, and people with whom they interact, are aware of the special circumstances of the experiment, that knowledge itself becomes part of the subtle set of interactive dynamics.

*Fifthly,* and in more methodological vein, the MTO experiment seems to have a wider significance than simply its contribution to debates on 'neighbourhood effects'. In a period when it is sometimes rather loosely claimed that the randomized experiment is a methodological 'Gold Standard' within criminology, the complex debates around MTO are a salutary reminder that randomized experiments, while they are certainly in principle the best design for eliminating selection bias, can also sometimes pose many interpretive problems.[10] (On these issues in relation to MTO, see the balanced and insightful assessment by Sampson 2008.)

---

[10] The particular difficulty with the 'Gold Standard' metaphor is that it encourages unthinking acceptance of *any* randomized design as providing a close-to-perfect methodological solution. More thoughtful advocates of randomization, such as the authors of the widely-cited 'Maryland Scientific Methods Scale' (Farrington *et al.* 2002), make clear that this is not so. Thus, these authors specifically state that the principal advantage of randomized designs relates to *internal validity* only (pp.16–17); that even in this sphere there can be a threat to validity if 'professionals or [experimental] subjects know about the experimental design' (p.14); and that sometimes experiments have implementation problems that reduce their methodological rigour (pp. 17–18).

I will conclude with a concrete illustration of the fourth of the above points. In a widely-cited recent paper, David Kirk (2009) analysed re-offending data for Louisiana ex-prisoners in the wake of the Hurricane Katrina tragedy of 2005, following which many residential areas were devastated. Careful statistical analysis showed that parolees forced by these circumstances to move to a different geographic area had substantially lower rates of reincarceration. The mechanisms by which this reduction occurred could not be ascertained from the available data; nevertheless, Kirk claims that some 'significant policy implications' can already be identified. He argues that 'a logical next step' for policy-makers is 'to consider how to disperse the population of ex-prisoners on a large scale', though he concedes that 'forcing ex-prisoners to move away from their old neighborhoods is neither realistic nor ethical' (Kirk 2009: 501). Yet there are some obvious problems with this proposed policy inference. First, the special circumstances of the Louisiana disaster meant that the baseline neighbourhoods were physically devastated; this would not be the case if a general 'dispersal' policy for all ex-prisoners were to be implemented, so the Louisiana research results might not be generalizable to these different circumstances. Secondly, Kirk's 'dispersal' suggestion is reminiscent of some extrapolations that were made from the early results of MTO—for example, in September 2000 a Yale law professor argued, based on MTO, that one should try to move all poor inner-city families to the suburbs (cited in Sobel 2006: 226). But, as Sobel goes on to point out, moving *all* inner-city families would almost certainly have very different aggregate social effects than moving out a relatively small number of families in a special experiment.

This final comment in turn reminds us that, because of what might be termed the 'individualistic turn' in much contemporary social science, the scholarly community might be in danger of focusing its discussions of 'neighbourhood effects' too much on *individual effects*, with insufficient focus on the possibilities for *changing communities* (see also Kirk and Laub 2010). This important possibility is, however, taken up in various ways in the remaining sections of this chapter.

## SPECIFIC PLACES AND THEIR CRIME PROBLEMS

In this section, there is a change of spatial focus. We are no longer considering neighbourhoods; instead, the focus switches to much smaller geographical units—specific places, especially those at which much crime is committed. The discussion will be in two subsections, the first of which focuses on the 'hotspots policing' literature, and the second on two recent research studies that—in different ways—have considered micro-locations from the perspective of prospective offenders.

### HOTSPOTS AND HOTSPOTS POLICING

The 'hotspots' literature in criminology effectively began with a seminal paper by Sherman, Gartin, and Buerger (1989) using police call data for Minneapolis. These authors uncovered a very skewed distribution of the extent to which micro-locations in the city attracted crime-related calls: 50 per cent of the calls related to just 3.3 per cent of the locations. The study further showed that if one measures crime rates at a *neighbourhood* level, a misleading picture of crime locations can easily be generated, because what looks like a 'high crime area' using a large unit of measurement will usually consist of many different micro-locations, some of which are indeed serious 'hotspots' of crime, but others of which are relatively crime-free.

In the years since the Minneapolis study, these initial findings have been developed through two different kinds of research—one relating to crime analysis, and the other to crime prevention.

As regards *crime analysis*, a recent specialist volume draws specific attention to 'the problem of units of analysis in geographic criminology' (Weisburd, Bernasco, and Bruinsma 2009: 24). It documents a trend towards the use of 'increasingly smaller units of analysis'; it also applauds that trend, and urges researchers to turn away from neighbourhood-level studies because of the issue of within-neighbourhood heterogeneity. It is important to note, however, that the primary focus of attention throughout the volume is the accurate identification of *offence locations*. I shall shortly argue that the authors' argument is correct within that frame of reference, but that other considerations are also relevant to a fully-developed socio-spatial criminology.

Turning then to *crime prevention*, it was of course obvious from early hotspots analyses that the heavy concentration of criminal events in specific locations offered an apparent potential for successful crime prevention. However, there were several further issues that required exploration before researchers could confidently recommend to policymakers a preventive strategy based on hotspots. These were:

(1) Perhaps the identified hotspots were ephemeral, so that a different set of hotspots would appear if one were to conduct the analysis for a later year, or a series of years?

(2) Perhaps crime prevention initiatives targeted on specific places would not actually reduce crime at the hotspot?

(3) Even if the crime prevention effort was successful at the hotspot, perhaps those committing crimes in that location would simply move their activities elsewhere (a phenomenon known as 'crime displacement')?

These were reasonable questions, but subsequent research has convincingly dispelled doubts. Detailed summaries of the evidence relating to these matters will be found in two important recent overviews of the 'hotspots policing' (HSP) literature (Weisburd, Telep, and Braga 2010; Braga and Weisburd 2010), and little purpose would be served by repeating the details here. Briefly, however, longitudinal analyses have now shown that hotspots in given cities are usually enduring, not ephemeral; rigorous evaluative studies have now shown that HSP strategies can be effective; and displacement is rarely a problem. On the second and most important of these points, the evaluative evidence has been summarized and assessed in two authoritative sources: first, a Committee to Review Research on Police Policy and Practices, set up by the US National Research Council (Skogan and Frydl 2004); and secondly, a Campbell Collaboration Systematic Review of Hotspots Policing Programmes (Braga 2005).

This above constitutes, without question, an impressive contribution to scholarship by HSP researchers. Nor is that all, because more recently they have begun to explore a further topic, which is of great interest to the quest for synthesis being pursued in this chapter; namely, the *legitimacy* of crime prevention initiatives at hotspots. (On legitimacy and criminal justice see Tyler 2003; Bottoms and Tankebe 2012.)

In their chapter on this topic, Braga and Weisburd (2010: ch. 6) present a diagram (see Figure 16.3) that sets out in schematic form three different models by which police could in principle seek to control crime at hotspots: namely, the 'traditional' model, which is incident-driven and reactive; a proactive 'enforcement' model; and a proactive 'situational' model. The authors' preferred model is the 'situational' model, which incidentally illustrates the way in which HSP policies often build on previously-developed ECCA approaches. Interestingly, however (and definitely not derived from ECCA), a principal reason given by Braga and Weisburd for preferring the 'situational' to the 'enforcement' approach is the potential for legitimacy deficits if the police were to adopt an unvarnished enforcement strategy (such as the widely-discussed 'zero tolerance' approach to policing). Such 'overly aggressive and indiscriminate arrest-based strategies', say the authors, 'are more likely to generate community concern and poor relations' (Braga and Weisburd 2010: 229).

It is worth adding one further comment on this (surely correct) argument, which is that in rightly taking account of the possible 'community concern', the authors in effect situate the crime hotspot within a wider social context. In so doing, while maintaining the focus of analysis and crime prevention on the hotspot itself, they widen the spatial scale of the issues that must be considered when responding to the hotspot.

## BRINGING OFFENDERS INTO THE UNDERSTANDING OF HOTSPOTS

In interesting contrast to many writers in the ECCA/HSP tradition, two recent research studies of offence locations have fruitfully focused—in very different ways—on offenders' use of space, and/or their understandings of specific locations. Both these studies confirm important aspects of ECCA's rational choice/routine activities approach; but

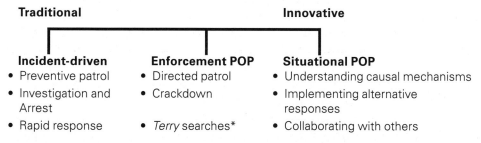

**Figure 16.3** Types of police strategies to control crime hot spots

\* This refers to the 1968 U.S. Supreme Court case of *Terry v Ohio*, allowing a safety frisk where police officers 'have reason to believe that such persons may be armed and dangerous to the police or others'.
*Source*: Braga and Weisburd (2010: 159).

both have also drawn explicitly on collective efficacy theory, thus moving towards a welcome synthesis of the neo-Chicagoan and the hotspots traditions.

### Hotspots in a high-poverty Chicago neighbourhood

Peter St. Jean (2007) conducted his research in a randomly-selected police beat (population 3,400) within the most economically disadvantaged police district in Chicago—an area very similar to the 'baseline' neighbourhoods in the MTO project. Even within this small high-crime neighbourhood there was a marked geographical skew in the distribution of police-recorded offences: for example, in the year 2000 five of the 59 'address blocks' within the studied police beat 'contributed 60 per cent of the narcotics violations, 53 per cent of the robberies and 44 per cent of the batteries' (St. Jean 2007: 28). These data therefore provide strong additional support for the recommendation that, when studying crime data, a micro-locational rather than a neighbourhood focus is essential (Weisburd, Bernasco, and Bruinsma 2009).

The primary purpose of St. Jean's research was to explain why offences were committed at particular hotspots, *from the perspective of offenders*. He focused on only three offences, of varying types: drug dealing ('entrepreneurial'), robbery ('predatory'), and battery ('grievance'); I shall discuss only the first two here. The assumption was made (without specific research) that the social deprivations of the area, plus the high levels of drug dependency, created a strong motivation to offend among a significant segment of the local population; research attention was therefore focused on where and how this motivation became manifest in action (St. Jean 2007: 22).

Part of the research tested collective efficacy theory, with mixed results. In brief, most 'high collective efficacy [address] blocks' had low crime, but 'low collective efficacy blocks were observed to be almost equally crime hotspots and coldspots' (St. Jean 2007: 197). The crime hotspots were clustered in two particular sub-areas within the police beat; these contained the busiest intersections and a majority of the business premises (such as grocery stores, liquor stores and 'check cashing outlets'). The author's interviews with drug dealers and robbers suggested that 'such blocks are attractive [to offenders] mainly because the businesses within them bring different people together—people who can be clandestine clients of drug dealers, or easy targets for robbers' (p. 197). In more residential areas, however, collective efficacy was sometimes clearly relevant: for example, 'there were several instances when collective action by residents resulted in a decline in narcotics sales on a particular street block' (p. 206), and 'watchful neighbors...sometimes serve as effective constraints against neighbourhood robberies' (p. 208). Thus, offenders' rational perceptions of criminal opportunities in the 'busy intersection/business outlet' micro-locations explained a large part of the local offence distribution, but in the more purely residential areas collective efficacy (or its absence) was more relevant.

### Situational action theory

In recent years, Per-Olof Wikström has developed a fresh theoretical approach within criminology, known as 'Situational Action Theory' or SAT (Wikström 2006). The theory postulates that to understand how criminality arises, one needs to consider two matters: first, an individual's *propensity* to commit crime (defined as consisting of both the person's morality and his/her ability to exercise self-control); and secondly, his/her *exposure to situations of varying criminogenic potential* (where 'criminogenic exposure' is defined as 'the moral rules of the [social and environmental] settings in which a person takes part, and their enforcement': Wikström *et al.* 2010: 61). The theory therefore envisages a possible *interaction* as between criminal propensity and environmental conditions.

Wikström and his colleagues are conducting a longitudinal study of adolescent development in Peterborough, a medium-sized town in eastern England. While longitudinal studies now have a fairly lengthy pedigree in criminology (see McVie and McAra, this volume), the Peterborough study is the first such study to have examined in detail how an unselected sample of adolescents spend their time, using for this purpose a detailed diary of a four-day period ('space-time budget'). Some key findings from the Peterborough space-time analysis are shown in Table 16.3: this is based on an aggregate of the data, for each individual, from five administrations of the space-time budget (at yearly intervals at ages 13–17: that is, 20 days in total). The columns of this table show whether an individual's 'crime propensity was assessed as low, medium, or strong, while the data shown are the 'rates of (self-reported) crime per 1000 hours' spent in various conditions during the days studied in the space-time budgets. The mean rate of self-reported crime was 0.7 per 1000 hours, or the equivalent of four crimes per respondent per year (Wikström *et al.* 2010: 79).

As the authors comment, this analysis appears to be a criminological 'first', because never before has anyone studied empirically 'the convergence *in time and space* of people's crime propensity, criminogenic exposure and acts of crime' (Wikström *et al.* 2010: 79, emphasis in original).

**Table 16.3**  Crimes per 1,000 hours exposure in different settings, Peterborough adolescent study

|  | Crime Propensity of Subject | | | |
|---|---|---|---|---|
|  | Low | Medium | Strong | Total |
| **A. Exposure Condition A**[†] |  |  |  |  |
| When in exposure condition | 0.0 | 2.3 | 11.3 | 4.4 |
| When not in exposure condition | 0.0 | 0.4 | 2.2 | 0.6 |
| Significance | NS | P<.003 | P<.001 |  |
| **B. Exposure Condition B**[††] |  |  |  |  |
| When in exposure condition | 0.0 | 1.3 | 9.0 | 3.4 |
| When not in exposure condition | 0.0 | 0.4 | 1.9 | 0.6 |
| Significance | NS | NS | P<.001 |  |

[†] Exposure Condition A = 'Unsupervised with peers in area with high public entertainment'
[††] Exposure Condition B = 'Unsupervised with peers in area with poor collective efficacy'
*Source*: Wikström *et al.* (2010: 80)
Springer Journal of Quantitative Criminology, 26, 2010, 55–87, 'Activity fields and the dynamics of crime: advancing knowledge about the role of the environment in crime causation', Wikström, P-O.H., Ceccato, V., Hardie, B., and Treiber, Table 8; with kind permission from Springer Science+Business Media B.V.

Two main types of 'criminogenic exposure' were considered: being unsupervised with peers in an area with high public entertainment (Exposure Condition A), and being unsupervised with peers in an area with poor collective efficacy (Exposure Condition B). Not surprisingly, taking the population as a whole (final column of the table), substantially more crimes were committed when the young people were in conditions of hypothesized criminogenic exposure than when they were not (for example, 4.4 crimes per 1000 hours when in Exposure Condition A as against 0.6 when they were not). For those with a 'strong' criminal propensity, the difference in the rate of crime commission when 'in' or 'not in' a criminogenic environment was particularly marked (for both exposure conditions). On the other hand, those with a low crime propensity committed no crimes whether or not they were in criminogenic exposure conditions; for them, their strong anti-crime dispositions were able to override any temptations offered in criminogenic exposure conditions. Thus, the results show a genuine interaction effect as between propensity and environment.

Comparing the results for the two exposure conditions, it is interesting that 'time spent unsupervised with peers in areas with high public entertainment' appears to exert a slightly stronger criminogenic effect than 'time spent unsupervised with peers in areas with poor collective efficacy'. (This result has some similarities—in a completely different context—with St. Jean's findings in Chicago.) Moreover, 'time spent unsupervised with peers in areas with poor collective efficacy' had a slightly stronger criminogenic effect than a more general measure of 'total time spent unsupervised with peers'. Thus, the results are consistent with collective efficacy theory, although with the proviso that collective efficacy is irrelevant for those with low criminal propensity. The results also, of course, show the great importance of the routine activities of adolescents in contributing to the spatial distribution of crime.

## DISCUSSION

The findings presented in this section show beyond question that, when one is analysing specific crime events, it is vital to adopt a micro-locational focus. Additionally, scholars specializing in hotspots policing, building on the foundational insights of the ECCA group, have done criminology a service in bringing the importance of hotspots to attention. But one has to add that they have spent little time in analysing hotspots from the offender's point of view, nor have they devoted much attention to the key explanatory question—namely, exactly *why* do these particular micro-locations have high crime, while others do not? That explanatory question has been fruitfully addressed in different ways in both the Chicago and the Peterborough studies. Interestingly, these research studies each suggest that, for a full explanation, one needs to consider *both* the ECCA group's emphases on opportunities and routine activities, *and* the neo-Chicagoans' key concept of collective efficacy. These findings in turn suggest that to understand fully the events (including the crime) in a given hotspot, one needs to consider both meso-spatial (neighbourhood) and macro-spatial matters. Thus, the need for effective synthesis of the neighbourhood and the micro-locational traditions is evident.

## INCIVILITIES: BREACHES OF SOCIAL NORMS AND THEIR CONSEQUENCES

A few years ago, Robert Sampson and Steven Raudenbush (2004: 319) claimed that 'the concept of neighborhood disorder once again has assumed priority in the social sciences'. In making this comment, they had particularly in mind the famous 'broken windows theory' (BWT) of Wilson and Kelling (1982; see also Kelling and Coles 1996) according to which:

> ...minor forms of public disorder lead to serious crime and a downward spiral of urban decay...The presumed reason is that visual clues such as graffiti, public intoxication, garbage and abandoned cars are thought to attract criminal offenders, who assume from these cues that residents are indifferent to what goes on in the neighborhood (Sampson and Raudenbush 2004: 319).

The specific hypotheses of the sequential stages of BWT are set out in Figure 16.4, which reproduces a helpful graphic prepared by Ralph Taylor (2001). It should be said at once that BWT has a paradoxical status in criminology. On the one hand, perhaps because of its straightforward causal message and its evocative title, 'few ideas [have been]...more influential in the urban policy world' (Sampson 2009: 8). On the other hand, the supporting empirical evidence for the theory, when tested on a longitudinal basis, is decidedly meagre (see especially Sampson and Raudenbush 1999; Taylor 2001; Harcourt and Ludwig 2006; also 4thEd: 554–6). These studies strongly suggest that disorder is a less strong predictor of serious crime than is the neighbourhood structural context.

Recent research projects may between them help to throw further light on this complex situation. Consider first some important experimental work by Dutch psychologists Keizer, Lindenberg, and Steg (2008) on 'the spreading of disorder'. A central theoretical feature of this work lies in its emphasis on the *norm-violating character* of incivilities, a point that has also been stressed in a recent Australian survey on

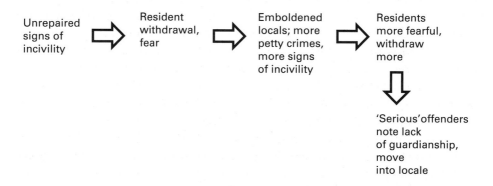

**Figure 16.4** The Incivilities Thesis of Wilson and Kelling (1982)
*Source*: Taylor (2001: 98)
Copyright © 2000, Ralph Taylor. Reprinted by permission of Westview Press, a member of the Perseus Books Group.

encounters with 'rude strangers' (Smith, Phillips, and King 2010).[11] Following Cialdini *et al.* (1991), Keizer and his colleagues distinguish two connotations of the term 'social norm': *first,* the existence in a given community or neighbourhood of 'common (dis) approval of a particular kind of behavior (*injunctive norm*)'; and secondly, the presence of 'particular behavior common in a setting (*descriptive norm*)' (p. 1681, emphasis added). They go on to suggest that the kind of incivilities envisaged in BWT are social settings in which an injunctive norm (e.g. 'streets should be kept tidy and pleasant for public use') is in conflict with a descriptive norm (e.g. 'it seems that everyone is dumping rubbish in this street'). The authors' primary research question asked whether injunctive norms are seen as more persuasive when, in a particular setting, they are accompanied by a congruent message from descriptive norms.

A series of ingenious experiments delivered a strongly affirmative answer to this question. For example, at the entrance to an indoor car park that was located next to a supermarket, a prominent notice stated: 'Please return your shopping carts' (injunctive norm). On two different days, the researchers placed advertising flyers under the driver's side windscreen wipers of all cars in the car park. On one of these days, the researchers ensured that there were no unreturned shopping carts in the car park; on the other day, four shopping carts were 'standing around in disarray'. In the second condition (scattered carts), drivers returning to their cars were, by comparison with the first condition, twice as likely to throw the advertising flyer to the ground rather than to take it with them (58%/30%, P< 002). A similar result, though with a lower level of significance because absolute injunctive norm-violation rates were lower, was reported from two experiments involving the more serious act of stealing a 5-euro note visibly stuffed (in an envelope) into the opening of a mailbox.

These results are supportive of a main contention of BWT, namely that people observing the violation of a norm will be more likely to breach that same norm (by littering public space) or another norm (by stealing). However, although the results are congruent with BWT, they do not fully confirm it, given that the theory postulates a number of sequenced and interlinked hypotheses (Figure 16.4). Two other pieces of recent research evidence are relevant to other aspects of the theory.

First, later experiments by Keizer (2010) showed that compliance as well as disorder can be influenced by nearby behaviour. More precisely, when members of the public observe people complying with a norm, this can enhance their own compliance with that norm, or a related norm. Thus for example, in one experiment in a public street, a confederate of the researchers was wheeling a bicycle along a street and 'accidentally' dropped some oranges while s/he was trying to put them into a bag (all the time continuing to hold the bicycle). Would passers-by help the confederate pick up the oranges? Answer: in the 'baseline' condition (as described above), 40 per cent of passers-by helped the cyclist/confederate; but in a second condition, when a further

---

[11] In this survey, the dominant emotional response to the rude encounter was anger (reported by 60%). The authors interpret this result (Smith, Phillips, and King 2010: 68–70) by reference to Durkheimian sociology, with its emphasis on the moral bonds that hold societies together (*conscience collective*) and the anger generated by breaches of the normative standards underpinning such bonds.

confederate could be seen and heard sweeping up rubbish nearby, the helping rate for the cyclist doubled (83%; P<.001) (Keizer 2010: ch.3). As the author concludes, these results therefore 'support the expectation that subtle clues of [respect or disrespect] for a norm' can, at least momentarily, influence 'behavior on the streets' (51). This is important because it goes beyond the propositions of BWT: that theory suggests that to avoid the causal sequence shown in Figure 16.4 one needs to 'repair the broken window', but Keizer's research suggests that pro-social normative behaviour unrelated to the broken window could have a similar effect.

For the second piece of relevant research we return to Peter St. Jean's (2007) work in Chicago. As previously noted, that research focuses on the perspectives of serious offenders—a perspective which, within BWT, is of great importance within the final hypothesized stage (Figure 16.4). Unfortunately for the advocates of BWT, St. Jean's research produced little evidence to support this hypothesis. As regards so-called physical disorders (such as graffiti and rubbish, but also of course 'broken windows'), it was found that such conditions were of no interest to serious offenders (drug dealers and robbers)—for them, very different factors affected whether a location seemed to offer lucrative opportunities (see earlier discussion). As regards social disorder, the results were quite similar to those found for collective efficacy—that is, there was a statistical association between social disorder and drug dealing/robberies, but this association 'was mostly due to the observation that those crimes do not flourish in the absence of social disorder'; by contrast, 'high social disorder was insufficient to produce high crime rates' (St Jean 2007: 202).

In summary, in this subsection I have outlined some complex results. Most prior research on BWT, based on studies of neighbourhoods over time, has shown very limited support for its hypotheses, yet the recent work of Keizer *et al.* (2008) supports the proposition (central to BWT) that 'disorder spreads'. On the other hand, the final-stage hypothesis of BWT ('serious offenders, sensing opportunities, move in to the area') receives very little support from St Jean's research; while Keizer's recent research suggests that disorder can be reduced in many subtle ways other than simply 'nipping the first disorder in the bud'. Between them, these last findings seem to offer some compelling reasons why there is limited overall empirical support for BWT. The research of Keizer and his colleagues also opens up for exploration a rich realm of normative behaviour, and normative influences on behaviour in public, reminiscent—in a different context—of the work of Erving Goffman (1971). A strong implication of this Dutch research is that syntheses of work in socio-spatial criminology need to take serious account of these normative issues. I shall return to this point shortly, but first it is necessary to examine a relatively neglected but important issue about incivilities in public places—repetition.

## REPEATED INCIVILITIES

Frank Field, Member of Parliament for Birkenhead, vividly describes meeting a group of his constituents who were very distressed about incivilities in their neighbourhood: 'young lads who ran across [my constituents'] bungalow roofs, peed through their letterboxes, jumped out of the shadows as they returned home at night, and, when they were watching television, tried to break their sitting room windows' (Field 2003: 10).

Field shrewdly noted, however, that these incivilities usually differed from crimes in one important respect:

> [T]he distinguishing mark of anti-social behaviour is that [unlike a crime such as bur-glary] each single instance does not by itself warrant a counter legal challenge. It is in its regularity that anti-social behaviour wields its destructive force (Field 2003: 45).

This last observation has recently been confirmed empirically in research commissioned by H.M. Inspectorate of Constabulary (HMIC). Ipsos MORI (2010) conducted for HMIC a survey of people who had reported an incivility to the police in England and Wales in September 2009. In linked research, Innes and Weston (2010: 22–3) used this dataset to assess individual differences in the extent to which victims perceived incivilities as having an adverse impact on their quality of life ('vulnerability'). They found that *repeat [incivilities]victimization is the key factor shaping levels of vulnerability* (emphasis added). They further found that this vulnerability becomes particularly acute where people experiencing repeated incivilities 'also report a long-term illness, or self-define as disabled' (23). Precisely this combination of adverse circumstances was involved in the tragic high-profile case of Fiona Pilkington, who in 2007 killed herself and her disabled daughter after repeated intimidation from local youths that had not been adequately handled by the local police (Independent Police Complaints Commission 2011).

How common are repeated incivilities? This topic has been illuminated by a recent analysis of British Crime Survey (BCS) data. When information is published about national levels of incivilities in England and Wales, the data cited is almost always derived from a series of seven BCS questions known as 'perceived anti-social behaviour' (or 'PASB') questions. (For a literature review on PASB, from BCS and elsewhere, see Mackenzie *et al.* 2010.) In these questions, the respondent is asked whether s/he perceives a specified type of behaviour (for example, 'rubbish or litter lying around') to be 'a very big problem', 'a fairly big problem' (etc.) in his/her neighbourhood. However, in recent years BCS interview schedules have also contained another set of 'incivilities' questions; these ask the respondent whether in the last 12 months s/he *has personally witnessed*, in the local neighbourhood, any of five specific types of behaviour (listed in Table 16.4). Results from these 'experienced incivility' questions are not normally published by the Home Office, the main exception being a section in a report by Upson (2006). However, BCS 'experience' data for 2004/5 have recently been analysed by Ryan Davenport (2010) of the University of Sheffield, and he has very kindly allowed me to publish some of his findings.[12]

From the BCS 'experience' questions, data relating to 'repeated incivilities' can be compiled. Table 16.4, taken from Ryan Davenport's work, shows that among those experiencing incivilities repeat experiences greatly outnumbered single experiences (Part A of the table); whereas, in the same year, those experiencing victimization for crimes were much more likely to be single victims than repeat victims (Part B of the table). In other words, empirically speaking, *repeated exposure is much more commonly experienced by victims of incivilities than of crimes*. Moreover, a minority of

---

[12] These analyses form part of Ryan Davenport's Ph. D. dissertation. He is currently preparing papers which will report the results more fully.

**Table 16.4** Frequency of repeated experience of incivilities and crimes, British Crime Survey 2004/5 (% of whole sample)

| | No experience | Single experience | Less frequent repeats | Frequent repeats† | Total |
|---|---|---|---|---|---|
| **A. Disorders** | | | | | |
| [Fresh] vandalism or graffiti | 62 | 5 | 27 | 7 | 100 |
| Drug use or drug dealing | 86 | 2 | 7 | 5 | 100 |
| Drunk or rowdy behaviour | 58 | 1 | 22 | 18 | 100 |
| Noisy neighbours | 87 | 1 | 6 | 6 | 100 |
| Young people hanging around | 39 | 1 | 14 | 46 | 100 |
| All incivilities combined | 28 | 5 | 38 | 30 | 100 |
| **B. Crimes** [Any repeat] | | | | | |
| Property crime | 79 | 17 | 4 | | 100 |
| Personal crime | 93 | 5 | 2 | | 100 |
| All crime combined | 75 | 20 | 6 | | 100 |

† = Frequent repeats are at least once a week
*Source*: Davenport (2010: 129 and 126)

respondents had the misfortune to experience 'frequent repetitions' (at least once a week) of noisy neighbours, drug use, drunken behaviour, or fresh graffiti or rubbish in their area. The repetitions were not necessarily by the same person or group; nevertheless, the extent of repetition for incivilities is an important finding, particularly bearing in mind the anger that can be generated by even a one-off breach of a deeply-held norm (see note 11). That is especially the case when the evidence of Table 16.1 is recalled, showing that repeat incivilities are most common in the most deprived (and therefore already very disadvantaged) areas (see also Ipsos MORI 2010: 33).

## THE SIGNAL CRIMES PERSPECTIVE

The 'Signal Crimes Perspective' (SgCP) originated in discussions around the turn of the millennium between senior police officers and researchers from the University of Surrey. The police were concerned that they seemed to be dealing with a new problem. According to both police and BCS data, crime rates were falling, yet public anxiety about crime remained high. Why was this happening, and what should the police response be?

A key conceptual move made by the researchers in response to this puzzle was to argue that, as Martin Innes (2004: 336) later put it, the criminological literature lacked 'a coherent explanation of the public understanding of crime and disorder, and how such understandings are imbricated in the wider symbolic construction of social space'. To fill this gap, the researchers' 'central proposition' was that *some crime and disorder incidents matter more than others to people in terms of shaping their risk perceptions*' (Innes 2004: 336, emphasis added). Thus, for example, three spouse murders in a medium-sized town in a year would be unusual, but would not necessarily create widespread fear, or a sense of threat, in the community at large, because they would be seen as 'private matters'. By contrast, the abduction and murder of a local schoolgirl on her way to school would almost certainly generate much more fear, and a sense of threat, in the area, because of the *normative signal* it would transmit about potential risks in the community. In the light of this signal, ordinary people might freshly consider as 'risky' certain places, people, or situations that they might easily encounter in their everyday lives; hence signals are 'social semiotic processes by which different crimes and disorders might have a disproportionate effect' in terms of fear and perceived threat, often in relation to specific locations (Innes and Fielding 2002: Abstract).

These core ideas were subsequently developed by Innes in work with the police as part of the National Reassurance Policing Programme (NRPP: for an excellent evaluation of this programme see Tuffin, Morris, and Poole 2006). Innes and colleagues conducted detailed qualitative interviews in 16 NRPP areas, asking representative respondents in each area what they would identify as the key *potential threats to neighbourhood safety* in their area. Not surprisingly—and congruently with the HSP emphasis on the importance of micro-locations—there was a good deal of local variation in the perceived threats identified in different localities. Nevertheless, a key result was that various kinds of disorders (such as youths hanging around, drugs, litter/graffiti, and public drinking) featured strongly as perceived threats in the public responses *in all areas*. Indeed, such items were usually perceived as a greater threat than residential burglary (see, for example, the diagram at 4th Ed: 552). These results appeared, in part, to be explained by the fact that the disorders seen as threatening were *events occurring in public space*, often with a strongly repetitive dimension; such events therefore seemed to send a powerful message to residents that 'my area is out of control'. As one respondent put it to Innes (2004: 348):

> Yes, it is daft, it is almost daft, but graffiti is the thing that sort of bothers me more, because it is in my face every day. I mean obviously rape and murder are more horrendous crimes, but it is graffiti that I see.

This respondent's sentiments were subsequently endorsed by the Ipsos MORI (2010) sample. Respondents took the clear view that the police should, when allocating their resources, prioritize crimes such as residential burglaries and street robberies; but in addition, 'the large majority of respondents continue to cite the importance of focusing efforts to tackle anti-social behaviour' (Ipsos MORI 2010: 31).

In short, the evidence suggests that even quite minor incivilities in an area can, especially if persistent ('in my face every day')—be perceived as significant threats to peaceable daily living. Such results have been interpreted by Innes and Roberts (2007: 241) as being linked to the more general social insecurities of late modern societies (Loader and Sparks, this volume).

As noted, the generic name for Innes's theoretical approach is the 'Signal Crimes Perspective' (also embracing 'signal disorders'). There is, however, a further dimension within the perspective, known as 'control signals', and this is highly congruent with Keizer's (2010) psychological research on pro-social influences (as in the case of the 'sweeping confederate'). The core idea behind control signals is that certain acts by authoritative persons or institutions, or by other residents, can 'send signals' to residents and businesses in an area, in a way that may promote confidence and a sense of social order (or, of course, the converse if the acts are not taken). Space precludes full discussion of control signals, but interested readers are referred to my discussion of this issue, with examples, in Bottoms (2009).

Because both SgCP and BWT place emphasis on incivilities, people often ask how the two approaches differ. Responding to this question, Innes and Roberts (2007: 245) say, first, that, in contrast to BWT, SgCP 'does not seek to arrange disorderly and criminal conduct in a causal sequence, whereby the former begets the latter' (see Figure 16.4 for this sequence). They add, secondly, that while BWT treats disorder 'as a broadly undifferentiated mass', for SgCP it is important to focus on the specific features of individual disorders, as they 'occur within and have resonances to particular community contexts'. In addition to these points, I would suggest that further differences can be identified. For example, in its proposed sequencing BWT largely assumes that people will act instrumentally (Tyler 2011: 256), but SgCP focuses to a greater extent on normative and cultural mechanisms. In a related fashion, BWT recommends dealing quickly and effectively with the initial disorders ('mending the broken window'), but SgCP has a wider understanding of 'control signals', and the broader normative messages they can send.

Another important comparison concerns similarities and differences between SgCP and HSP. These approaches have several characteristics in common; in particular, both have a strong commitment to a careful understanding of, followed by an intelligent response to, specific local circumstances in micro-locations. There remain, however, some important differences of emphasis between the two approaches. In particular, HSP scholars would presumably be critical of SgCP, as they are of BWT, on the grounds that it 'encourages the police to be concerned with problems of disorder, and moves crime itself to a secondary, or at least second-stage goal of the police'. Additionally, it is argued that by including disorders this kind of approach 'expands...the police function' (Braga and Weisburd 2010: 49; on the last point see also Loader 2006). As we have seen, this automatic prioritization of crimes is not shared by SgCP, which sees a focus on disorder as, in some circumstances, vitally necessary to allay perceived threats to the peaceable use of important areas of public space (see for example the response to Loader by Innes and Roberts 2008: 259–60).

As a final comment on SgCP, it is necessary to note that the disorder described as 'youths hanging around' has often been prominent when SgCP-style analyses of neighbourhood safety have been conducted (see the Figures at 4thEd: 552 and Innes and Weston 2010: 20).[13] This is a qualitatively different finding from that shown in Table 16.4, since that table refers only to 'youths hanging around' being *experienced* in the neighbourhood, while Innes's analyses refer to their being *seen as a threat to neighbourhood safety*. The reasons for findings of this kind—which are not unique

---

[13] Innes and Weston's (2010) analysis, derived from BCS data, focuses on what are described as 'the relative harms' of different incivilities, using a graph showing the 'intensity of effect on individuals' as the x-axis, and the number of people affected as the y-axis. (For example, it is shown that litter affects many people but has only a low effect on people's lives; abuse and intimidation is suffered by few people, but greatly affects their lives.) The incivility 'teens hanging around in public space' is shown to affect many people (as many as does litter), and its intensity of effect on individuals is assessed as medium.

to Innes—remain insufficiently explored, and require further research. One point is, however, clear from the research of a Keele University research team, which pre-dated Innes's work. This team reported that, in the small town they studied (Macclesfield, Cheshire) 'the unsupervised gathering of groups of male and female teenagers in public places' was 'perhaps the principal source of adult concern about youth' (Girling, Loader and Sparks 2000: 81). However, their ethnographic research also established that:

> residents interpret the presence and behaviour of these teenagers in contrasting ways and invest it with varying degrees of significance, and these interpretations *cannot* simply be read off from actual levels of disorderly or criminal activity (2000: 82, emphasis in original).

This raises the very important issue of the relationship between 'objective' and 'subjective' perceptions of disorder, which the final subsection will discuss.

## PERCEIVED DISORDER AND ITS CONSEQUENCES

In 2008, Robert Sampson was chosen to deliver the prestigious British Journal of Sociology (BJS) Annual Lecture at the London School of Economics. In the lecture, visible disorder was taken as the starting point for a wider sociological discussion of themes such as social stratification and immigration (Sampson 2009b). Two topics raised in the lecture are of special interest in the present context: they are the relationship between 'perceived' and 'objectively-measured' disorder, and the long-term consequences of perceived disorder.

Sampson and Raudenbush (2004) developed an innovative method for 'objectively' measuring disorder, known as 'Systematic Social Observation' (SSO). In this method, a sports utility vehicle (SUV) is equipped with cameras and staffed by trained observers; it then drives systematically and slowly around selected streets of a city, recording everything that is seen. When tested in particular areas, it was found that this 'objective' data partly but not wholly explained perceptions of disorder.[14] As well as objective disorder, the other principal factor predicting perceptions of disorder was the racial composition of the area; *both black and white respondents* perceived disorder as a greater problem in predominantly black areas than in other areas. This finding is explained by saying that individuals necessarily 'draw on their prior beliefs' (Sampson 2009b: 12) in forming their subjective assessments of disorder, and that the narrative of race in American culture constitutes an important element of these beliefs. In the BJS lecture, Sampson (2009b: 20) develops this line of argument with an empirical investigation as to whether 'shared perceptions of disorder in one's environment predict an *individual's* perception of disorder many years later, adjusting for current levels of observed disorder, poverty and an individual's social perception?' (emphasis in original). The answer was affirmative, which Sampson considered to be

---

[14] There have been some methodological criticisms of SSO, but it is not appropriate to pursue such issues here. Another way of comparing 'objective disorder' with 'perceived disorder' is by cross-tabulating the answers to survey questions on 'experience of disorder' and on 'perception of disorder as a problem'. Such a comparison was carried out by Davenport (2010) using BCS data; comparably to Sampson's results, he found that on similar items the two measures were highly correlated, but by no means identical.

'rather remarkable', and testimony to 'the sensitivity of humans to the evaluations of others' (ibid.). As one of the commentators on the BJS lecture added, this analysis is highly innovative, since it attempts to incorporate studies of 'cognitive processes' into analyses of 'structural patterns of racial composition, segregation of poverty and the... social production of space in the city' (Davis 2009: 41); that is, it seriously tries to integrate social psychology with structural sociology.

Interestingly, however, the Sampson/Raudenbush findings have not been fully replicated in Britain. A sophisticated statistical analysis of BCS data by Joanna Taylor, Liz Twigg, and John Mohan (2009) suggested that, at a neighbourhood level, the differential ethnic composition of an area did *not* affect perceived incivilities—rather, 'deprivation and poverty, rather than [ethnic] diversity, are most strongly associated with perceived high levels of antisocial behaviour'. This is clearly a very important cross-cultural difference that requires further research.

The second main disorder-related point made in Sampson's (2009) BJS lecture concerned the apparent long-term effects of perceived incivilities. As he summarized the matter at the end of his lecture:

> Setting details aside and focusing on the big picture, I found that systematically *observed* disorder had *no independent association with later poverty*... [but] shared *perceptions [of disorder]* were as strong if not stronger in predicting later poverty than population composition by race and even prior poverty itself (Sampson 2009: 22, emphasis added).

In one sense, this reinforces Sampson and Raudenbush's (1999) earlier conclusion that disorder is inextricably linked to structural disadvantage; and it certainly reinforces these authors' scepticism about BWT. (For BWT, disorder causes serious crime; for Sampson, disorder is primarily linked to long-term poverty.) But a further, and crucial point is added, namely that '*social perceptions* reinforce later disorder and potentially poverty, absent an exogenous intervention' (p. 18, emphasis added). At first blush, this seems to be a remarkable result; but on more careful reflection the finding makes a great deal of sense. It is after all, a matter of everyday knowledge that perceptions of local disorder contribute to the broad-brush and impressionistic assessments of local areas by people such as 'prospective homebuyers, real estate agents, insurance agents, investors, the police and politicians'; and of course they also shape 'the perceptions of residents who might be considering moving out' (Sampson 2009: 9). Thus, perceived disorder influences individual and corporate decisions; and individual and corporate decisions shape the long-term social trajectories of neighbourhoods (Taub, Taylor, and Dunham 1984). In this sense, the results are a salutary reminder of the sociological truism that perceptions, even if inaccurate, can have very real social consequences. More specifically in relation to socio-spatial criminology, the analysis has brought us back full circle to the importance of housing markets in relation to crime and criminality, discussed in an earlier section. As Sampson (2009a: 90) has rightly commented, 'because housing markets act as a mechanism of allocation... they... need to be better integrated into sociological and criminological theory'.

Yet one must finally note an important qualifying clause in the quotation at the beginning of the previous paragraph, where Robert Sampson reports that perceptions of disorder predict long-term social effects '*absent an exogenous intervention*'. In the BJS lecture, Sampson did not expand this qualifier, but in my commentary on the lecture (one of several published in the BJS), I drew attention to it, and linked it to Innes's concept of control signals (Bottoms 2009). In other words, it would seem that what look like potential long-term neighbourhood trajectories can, under the right conditions, be turned around by appropriately-deployed control signals (see further, Sampson 2009a: 89). Thus, there remains hope even in apparently very unpromising contexts.

## DISCUSSION

Two principal conclusions emerge from the analysis in this section: one substantive, the other methodological. First, despite its high public profile, broken windows theory now seems to have little to offer either to criminology or to public policy; hence, criminologists and policy-makers would do better to concentrate instead on the incivility-related research of Sampson and Innes. These two scholars offer distinctive insights, both of which are of great importance. One (Sampson) focuses on the long-term reproduction of structural disadvantage, and the role of perceived disorder within it; the other (Innes) concentrates on the symbolic importance of disorders in the perceptions of citizens as they use public space on a day-to-day basis. Given that disorder is the breach of a significant social norm, both analyses also draw attention to the sometimes neglected importance of norms in daily social life.

Secondly, the analysis in this section has devoted significantly greater attention than previous sections to the linked issues of *perceptions, culture,* and *norms*. Hopefully, it has been demonstrated that this is a vital dimension of social life that needs to be fully integrated into future analyses of both neighbourhoods and micro-locations. Sampson's BJS lecture is a strong example of just such integration; so this is, perhaps, an appropriately optimistic note on which to conclude the quest for better synthesis that has been pursued in this chapter.[15]

## CONCLUSION

I shall not prolong this chapter with a lengthy conclusion. I have reviewed an extensive amount of recent research in the fields of neighbourhood effects, crime prevention efforts in micro-locations, and incivilities. This has required a wide-ranging analysis embracing, for example, (i) experimental and quasi-experimental studies, very practically-focused crime prevention projects, and analyses of social and cultural perceptions; (ii) offender-focused research, crime-focused research, and disorder-focused research; and (iii) both neighbourhood research and research in micro-locations. I have tried to show that all of these kinds of research have contributed fruitfully to socio-spatial criminology; and that, despite the separate 'silos' into which some researchers might try to retreat, the subject will be best advanced by pulling these strands together. As I have shown, some have already begun this synthesizing task in promising ways, but they are still in a minority.

---

[15] After this chapter was completed, news broke that a Dutch professor of psychology, Diederik Stapel, had admitted to fabricating data in a number of experimental studies. One of the relevant papers was co-authored by Siegwart Lindenberg, although he was not involved in the data collection for that paper. Lindenberg is also a co-author of the Keizer *et al.* (2008) study discussed in this section. For the avoidance of doubt, it should be said that there is no reason to question the validity of the data in the Keizer *et al.* research.

I will conclude with some wise words by Ralph Taylor (2001: 20). These words were written within the specific context of incivilities, but the spirit of his message has a wider applicability to the field:

> Theorizing on incivilities needs to reconnect more firmly with works in the areas of urban sociology, urban political economy, collective community crime prevention and organizational participation. Changes in neighborhood fabric, neighborhood crime rates and residents' safety concerns are each tangled topics with a range of causes. To gain a clearer picture of these processes, it is necessary to break away from [incivilities] per se, and broaden the lines of inquiry.

In other words, socio-spatial criminology, although it properly and fruitfully often focuses on crimes and disorders in micro-locations, needs to do this with a wide vision encompassing different academic specialisms and a broad awareness of different aspects of urban life. It is, therefore, a reasonable claim that socio-spatial criminology, when well conducted, is an important sub-field within the study of social order in the contemporary world.

## ■ SELECTED FURTHER READING

An excellent overview of the work of the ECCA group is provided in the collection of essays edited by Richard Wortley and Lorraine Mazerolle (2008), *Environmental Criminology and Crime Analysis* (Willan). A similarly helpful overview of the 'hotspot policing' literature will be found in Anthony A. Braga and David L. Weisburd's (2008), *Policing Problem Places* (Oxford University Press).

The best introduction to collective efficacy theory is Robert Sampson's essay in Francis Cullen, John Wright, and Kristie Blevin's (2006) edited collection, *Taking Stock: The Status of Criminological Theory* (Transaction). Robert Sampson's work on incivilities is best approached through his very stimulating *British Journal of Sociology* lecture; this paper also has the advantage of carrying commentaries by seven authors of varying interests and theoretical persuasions (*British Journal of Sociology*, Vol. 60, No. 1, 2009).

Martin Innes's various contributions to the signal crimes perspective have not yet been collected together in a convenient single source. The best starting-point is his *British Journal of Sociology* paper on 'Signal crimes and signal disorders' (Vol. 55, 2004).

Two major authors in this field had books in press at the time this chapter was completed. Neither volume has been consulted in the preparation of the chapter, but both texts will undoubtedly contribute substantially to the field. They are Robert Sampson's (2012), *Great American City: Chicago and the Enduring Neighborhood Effect* (University of Chicago Press) and Per-Olof Wikström, Dietrich Oberwittler, Kyle Treiber, and Beth Hardie's (2012), *Breaking Rules: The Social and Situational Dynamics of Young People's Urban Crime* (Oxford University Press).

## ■ REFERENCES

BALDWIN, J. and BOTTOMS, A. E. (1976), *The Urban Criminal*, London: Tavistock.

BANDURA, A. (1997), *Self-Efficacy: The Exercise of Control*, New York: W.H. Freeman.

BOHMAN, J. (1992), 'The limits of rational choice explanation', in J. S. Coleman and T. J. Fararo (eds), *Rational Choice Theory: Advocacy and Critique*, London: Sage.

BOTTOMS, A. E. (2007), 'Place, space, crime and disorder', in M. Maguire, R. Morgan, and R. Reiner (eds), *The Oxford Handbook of Criminology*, 4th edn, Oxford: Oxford University Press.

—— (2009), 'Disorder, order and control signals', *British Journal of Sociology*, 60: 49–54.

—— and TANKEBE, J. (2012), 'Beyond procedural justice: a dialogic approach to legitimacy in criminal justice', *Journal of Criminal Law and Criminology*, (forthcoming).

—— and WILES, P. (1986), 'Housing tenure and residential community crime careers in Britain', in A. J. Reiss and M. Tonry (eds), *Communities and Crime*, Chicago: University of Chicago Press.

——, MAWBY, R.I., and XANTHOS, P. (1989), 'A tale of two estates', in D. Downes (ed.), *Crime and the City*, London: Macmillan.

BRAGA, A. A. (2005), 'Hot spots policing and crime prevention: a systematic review of randomized controlled trials', *Journal of Experimental Criminology*, 1: 317–42.

—— and WEISBURD, D. L. (2010), *Policing Problem Places*, Oxford: Oxford University Press.

BRANTINGHAM, P. L. and BRANTINGHAM, P. J. (1981), 'Notes on the geometry of crime', in P. J. Brantingham and P. L. Brantingham (eds), *Environmental Criminology*, Beverly Hills, Cal.: Sage Publications.

—— and —— (2008), 'Crime pattern theory', in R. Wortley and L. Mazerolle (eds), *Environmental Criminology and Crime Analysis*, Cullompton, Devon: Willan.

BRIGGS, X. DE S., POPKIN, S. J., and GOERING, J. (2010), *Moving to Opportunity: The Story of an American Experiment to Fight Ghetto Poverty*, Oxford: Oxford University Press.

CHAINEY, S. and RATCLIFFE, J. (2005), *GIS and Crime Mapping*, Chichester: John Wiley.

CIALDINI, R. B., KALLGREN, C. A., and RENO, R. R. (1991), 'A focus theory of normative conduct: a theoretical refinement and re-evaluation of the role of norms in human behavior', in M. P. Zanna (ed.), *Advances in Experimental Social Psychology*, Vol. 24, San Diego, CA: Academic Press.

CLAMPET-LUNDQUIST, S. and MASSEY, D.S. (2008), 'Neighborhood effects on economic self-sufficiency: a reconsideration of the Moving to Opportunity experiment', *American Journal of Sociology*, 114: 107–43.

——, EDIN, K., KLING, J. R., and DUNCAN, G. J. (2011), 'Moving teenagers out of high-risk neighborhoods: how girls fare better than boys', *American Journal of Sociology*, 116: 1154–99.

CLARKE, R. V. (ed.) (1997), *Situational Crime Prevention: Successful Case Studies*, 2nd edn, Guilderland, NY: Harrow and Heston.

—— and FELSON, M. (1993), *Routine Activity and Rational Choice*, New Brunswick, NJ: Transaction.

—— and MAYHEW, P. (1988), 'The British gas suicide story and its criminological implications', in M. Tonry and N. Morris (eds), *Crime and Justice: A Review of Research*, Vol. 10, Chicago: University of Chicago Press.

COHEN, L. E. and FELSON, M. (1979), 'Social change and crime rate trends: a routine activities approach', *American Sociological Review*, 44: 588–608.

CORNISH, D. B. and CLARKE, R. V. (eds), (1986), *The Reasoning Criminal: Rational Choice Perspectives on Offending*, New York: Springer.

—— and —— (2003), 'Opportunities, precipitations and criminal decisions: a reply to Wortley's critique of situational crime prevention', in M. J. Smith and D. B. Cornish (eds), *Theory for Practice in Situational Crime Prevention*, Monsey, NY: Criminal Justice Press.

—— and —— (2008), 'The rational choice perspective', in R. Wortley and L. Mazerolle (eds), *Environmental Criminology and Crime Analysis*, Cullompton, Devon: Willan.

DAVENPORT, R. A. (2010), 'Incivilities, Crime and Social Order: the Role of Repeat Experience', Unpublished Ph.D. thesis, University of Sheffield.

DAVIS, D. E. (2009), 'Taking place and space seriously: reflections on "Disparity and Diversity in the Contemporary City"', *British Journal of Sociology*, 60: 39–47.

ECO, U. (1976), *A Theory of Semiotics*, Bloomington: Indiana University Press.

FARRINGTON, D. P., GOTTFREDSON, D. C., SHERMAN, L. W., and WELSH, B. C. (2002), 'The Maryland Scientific Methods Scale', in L. W. Sherman, D. P. Farrington, B. C. Welsh, and D. L. MacKenzie (eds), *Evidence-Based Crime Prevention*, London: Routledge.

FELSON, M. (2008), 'Routine activity approach', in R. Wortley and L. Mazerolle (eds), *Environmental Criminology and Crime Analysis*, Cullompton, Devon: Willan.

—— (2011), 'Sort crimes, not criminals', in M. Bosworth and C. Hoyle (eds), *What is Criminology?*, Oxford: Oxford University Press.

FIELD, F. (2003), *Neighbours from Hell: The Politics of Behaviour*, London: Politico's.

GIGERENZER, G. and SELTEN, R. (eds) (2001), *Bounded Rationality: the Adaptive Toolbox*, Cambridge, Mass: MIT Press.

GIRLING, E., LOADER, I., and SPARKS, R. (2000), *Crime and Social Change in Middle England: Questions of Order in an English Town*, London: Routledge.

GOFFMAN, E. (1972), *Relations in Public: Microstudies of the Public Order*, London: Allen Lane the Penguin Press.

GOULD, J. and KOLB, W. L. (eds) (1964), *A Dictionary of the Social Sciences*, London: Tavistock.

HARCOURT, B. E. and LUDWIG, J. (2006), 'Broken windows: new evidence from New York City and a five city social experiment', *University of Chicago Law Review*, 73: 271–320.

HAYWARD, K. J. (2004), *City Limits: Crime, Consumer Culture and the Urban Experience*, London: Glass House.

HOPE, T. and FOSTER, J. (1993), *Housing, Community and Crime: The Impact of the Priority Estates Project*, Home Office Research Study 131, London: HMSO.

HOUCHIN, R. (2005), *Social Exclusion and Imprisonment in Scotland*, Glasgow: Glasgow Caledonian University.

INDEPENDENT POLICE COMPLAINTS COMMISSION (2011), *IPCC Report into the Contact between Fiona Pilkington and Leicestershire Constabulary, 2004–2007*, London: IPPC.

INNES, M. (2004), 'Signal crimes and signal disorders: notes on deviance as communicative action', *British Journal of Sociology*, 55: 335–55.

—— and FIELDING, N. (2002), 'From community to communicative policing: "signal crimes" and the problem of public reassurance', *Sociological Research Online*, 7(2).

—— and ROBERTS, C. (2008), 'Reassurance policing, community intelligence and the co-production of social order', in T. Williamson (ed.), *The Handbook of Knowledge-Based Policing: Current Conceptions and Future Directions*, Chichester: John Wiley and Sons.

—— and WESTON, N. (2010), *Rethinking the Policing of Anti-Social Behaviour*, London: H. M. Inspectorate of Constabulary.

IPSOS MORI (2010), *Policing Anti-Social Behaviour: The Public Perspective*, London: H. M. Inspectorate of Constabulary.

KEIZER, K., (2010), 'The Spreading of Disorder', Unpublished Proefschrift, University of Gröningen.

——, LINDENBERG, S., and STEG, L. (2008), 'The spreading of disorder', *Science*, 322: 1681–5.

KELLING, G. and COLES, C. M. (1996), *Fixing Broken Windows*, New York: Free Press.

KIRK, D. S. (2009), 'A natural experiment on residential change and recidivism: lessons from Hurricane Katrina', *American Sociological Review*, 74: 484–505.

—— and LAUB, J. H. (2010), 'Neighborhood change and crime in the modern metropolis', in M. Tonry (ed.), *Crime and Justice: A Review of Research*, Vol. 39, Chicago: University of Chicago Press.

KLING, J. R., LIEBMAN, J. B., and KATZ, L. F. (2007), 'Experimental analysis of neighborhood effects', *Econometrica*, 75: 83–119.

——, LUDWIG, J., and KATZ, L .F. (2005), 'Neighborhood effects on crime for female and male youth: evidence from a randomized housing voucher experiment', *Quarterly Journal of Economics*, 120: 87–130.

KORNHAUSER, R. R. (1978), *Social Sources of Delinquency*, Chicago: University of Chicago Press.

LOADER, I. (2006), 'Policing, recognition and belonging', *Annals of the American Academy of Political and Social Science*, 605: 201–21.

LUDWIG, J. and KLING, J. R. (2007), 'Is crime contagious?', *Journal of Law and Economics*, 50: 491–518.

——, LIEBMAN, J. B., KLING, J. R., DUNCAN, G. J., KATZ, L. F., KESSLER, R. C., and SANBONMATSU, L. (2008), 'What can we learn about neighborhood effects from the Moving to Opportunity experiment?', *American Journal of Sociology*, 114: 144–88.

MACKENZIE, S., BANNISTER, J., FLINT, J., PARR, S., MILLIE, A., and FLEETWOOD, J. (2010), *The Drivers of Perceptions of Anti-Social Behaviour*, Research Report No. 34, London: Home Office.

MATZA, D. (1969), *Becoming Deviant*, Englewood Cliffs, NJ: Prentice Hall.

NICHOLAS, S., POVEY, D., WALKER, A., and KERSHAW, C. (2005), *Crime in England and Wales 2004–5*, Home Office Statistical Bulletin 11/05, London: Home Office.

OBERWITTLER, D. (2007a), 'Social Exclusion and Youth Crime in Europe—The Spatial Dimension', in K. Aromaa (ed.), *Penal Policy, Justice Reform, and Social Exclusion*, Plenary presentations held at the Fifth Annual Conference of the European Society of Criminology, 31 August–3 September 2005, Krakow, Poland. Helsinki: European Institute for Crime Prevention and Control (HEUNI).

—— (2007b), 'The Effects of Neighbourhood Poverty on Adolescent Problem Behaviours: A Multi-level Analysis Differentiated by Gender and Ethnicity', *Housing Studies*, 22: 781– 803.

ORR, L., FEINS, J. D., JACOB, R., BEECROFT, E., SANBONMATSU, L., KATZ, L. F., LIEBMAN, J. B., and KLING, J. R. (2003), *Moving to Opportunity: Interim Impacts Evaluation*, Washington, DC: US Department of Housing and Urban Development.

PRATT, T. and CULLEN, F. (2005), 'Assessing the relative effects of macro-level predictors of crime: a meta-analysis', in M. Tonry (ed.), *Crime and Justice: A Review of Research*, Vol. 32, Chicago: University of Chicago Press.

ST JEAN, P. K .B. (2007), *Pockets of Crime: Broken Windows, Collective Efficacy and the Criminal Point of View*, Chicago: University of Chicago Press.

SAMPSON, R. J. (2006), 'Collective efficacy theory: lessons learned', in F. T. Cullen, J. P. Wright, and K. R. Blevins (eds), *Taking Stock: The Status of Criminological Theory*, New Brunswick: Transaction Publishers.

—— (2008), 'Moving to inequality: neighborhood effects and experiments meet social structure', *American Journal of Sociology*, 114: 189–231.

—— (2009a), 'Analytic approaches to disorder', *British Journal of Sociology*, 60: 83–90.

—— (2009b), 'Disparity and diversity in the contemporary city: social (dis)order revisited', *British Journal of Sociology*, 60: 1–31.

—— and RAUDENBUSH, S. W. (1999), 'Systematic social observation of public spaces: a new look at disorder and crime', *American Journal of Sociology*, 105: 603–51.

—— and —— (2004), 'Seeing disorder: neighborhood stigma and the social construction of "broken windows"', *Social Psychology Quarterly*, 67: 319–42.

——, MORENOFF, J. D., and GANNON-ROWLEY, T. (2002), 'Assessing "neighborhood effects": social processes and new directions in research', *Annual Review of Sociology*, 28: 443–78.

SHERMAN, L. W., GARTIN, P. R., and BUERGER, M. E. (1989), 'Hot spots of predatory crime: routine activities and the criminology of place', *Criminology*, 27: 27–55.

SKOGAN, W. G. and FRYDL, K. (eds) (2004), *Fairness and Effectiveness in Policing: The Evidence* (Committee to Review Research on Police Policy and Practice), Washington, D.C.: The National Academies Press.

SMITH, P., PHILLIPS, T. L., and KING, R. D. (2010), *Incivility: The Rude Stranger in Everyday Life*, Cambridge: Cambridge University Press.

SOBEL, M. E. (2006), 'Spatial concentration and social stratification: does the clustering of disadvantage "beget" bad outcomes?', in S. Bowles, S. N. Durlauf, and K. Hoff (eds), *Poverty Traps*, New York: Russell Sage Foundation.

TAUB, R., TAYLOR, D. G., and DUNHAM, J. D. (1984), *Paths of Neighborhood Change*, Chicago: University of Chicago Press.

TAYLOR, J., TWIGG, L., and MOHAN, J. (2010), 'Investigating perceptions of antisocial behaviour and neighbourhood ethnic heterogeneity in the British Crime Survey', *Transactions of the Institute of British Geographers (NS)*, 35: 59–75.

TAYLOR, R. B. (2001), *Breaking Away from Broken Windows: Baltimore Neighborhoods and the Nationwide Fight against Crime, Grime, Fear and Decline*, Boulder, Col: Westview.

TUFFIN, R., MORRIS, J., and POOLE, A. (2006), *An Evaluation of the Impact of the National Reassurance Policing Programme*, Home Office Research Study 296, London: Home Office.

TYLER, T. R. (2003), 'Procedural justice, legitimacy and the effective rule of law', in M. Tonry (ed.), *Crime and Justice: A Review of Research*, Vol. 30, Chicago: University of Chicago Press.

—— (2011), 'Trust and legitimacy in the USA and Europe', *European Journal of Criminology*, 8: 254–66.

UPSON, A. (2006), *Perceptions and Experience of Antisocial Behaviour. Findings from the 2004/2005 British Crime Survey*, Home Office Online Report 21/06, London: Home Office.

WEATHERBURN, D. and LIND, B. (2001), *Delinquent-Prone Communities*, Cambridge: Cambridge University Press.

WEISBURD, D., BERNASCO, W., and BRUINSMA, G. J. N. (eds) (2009), *Putting Crime in its Place: Units of Analysis in Geographic Criminology*, New York: Springer.

——, TELEP, C. W., and BRAGA, A. A. (2010), *The Importance of Place in Policing: Empirical Evidence and Policy Recommendations*, Stockholm: Swedish National Council for Crime Prevention (Brå).

WIKSTRÖM, P-O. H. (1991), *Urban Crime, Criminals and Victims: The Swedish Experience in an Anglo-American Comparative Perspective*, New York: Springer-Verlag.

—— (2006), 'Individuals, settings, and acts of crime: situational mechanisms and the explanation of crime', in P-O. H. Wikström, and R. J. Sampson (eds), *The Explanation of Crime: Context, Mechanisms, and Development*, Cambridge: Cambridge University Press.

—— and LOEBER, R. (2000), 'Do disadvantaged neighborhoods cause well-adjusted children to become adolescent delinquents?: a study of male serious juvenile offending, individual risk and protective factors, and neighborhood context', *Criminology*, 38: 1109–42.

——, CECCATO, V., HARDIE, B., and TREIBER, K. (2010), 'Activity fields and the dynamics of crime: advancing knowledge about the role of the environment in crime causation', *Journal of Quantitative Criminology*, 26: 55–87.

WILES, P. and COSTELLO, A. (2000), *The 'Road to Nowhere'. The Evidence for Travelling Criminals*, Home Office Research Study 207, London: Home Office.

WILSON, J. Q. and HERRNSTEIN, R. J. (1985), *Crime and Human Nature*, New York: Simon and Schuster.

—— and KELLING, G. (1982), 'Broken windows', *The Atlantic Monthly*, (March): 29–38.

WILSON, W. J. (1987), *The Truly Disadvantaged: The Inner City, the Underclass and Public Policy*, Chicago: University of Chicago Press.

WORTLEY, R. and MAZEROLLE, L. (eds) (2008), *Environmental Criminology and Crime Analysis*, Cullompton, Devon: Willan.

WRIGHT, R. T. and DECKER, S. H. (1994), *Burglars on the Job: Street Life and Residential Break-ins*, Boston: Northeastern University Press.

# 17

# YOUTH CRIME AND JUSTICE: REDISCOVERING DEVOLUTION, DISCRETION, AND DIVERSION?

*Rod Morgan and Tim Newburn*

## INTRODUCTION

Histories of social policy are often periodized in order to highlight shifts in ways of thinking and method. It is clearly dangerous to suggest the occurrence of a policy sea change on the basis of short-term evidence. But the economic crisis of 2008–11 and the formation of the Coalition Government following the General Election 2010 has undoubtedly prompted some fundamental re-thinking in the field of criminal justice generally. This is having an impact on youth justice in particular. The autumn 2010 Spending Review White Paper announced the deepest public expenditure cuts in a generation (HM Treasury 2010), alongside a criminal justice Green Paper suggesting a significant change of policy direction from that of the preceding administration (Ministry of Justice 2010a). The Green Paper contained only a brief chapter on youth justice in which few radical changes were indicated, a pattern confirmed in the Government's response to the consultation on the Green Paper (Ministry of Justice 2011). Nevertheless, read alongside the rest of the document, together with other elements of the Coalition's proposed legislative programme, it seems likely that youth justice during the second decade of the millennium will be following imperatives different from those pursued under New Labour during the period 1997–2010. We characterize this new mood as one of *austerity and parsimony*, austerity because it seems clear that there is to be less spending on youth justice by the state, and parsimony because the dominant message is that criminal justice interventions should be scaled back.

This policy shift is striking for at least two reasons. First, because all the evidence is that the public remains as concerned about the threat of anti-social behaviour and crime by young people as was ever the case (Jones 2010). Secondly, because recent years have seen the apparent emergence of a particularly grave form of youth crime.

Namely, gang-related youth-on-youth murders in which knives or guns have been used. Though the latest official statistics indicate that homicides of this nature are rare, and the incidence of serious violence is today lower than in past years, these events, some of them shocking in their apparently casual brutality, have attracted huge amounts of publicity which in previous years have precipitated loud political alarums and short-term repressive measures.

Yet in the face of such pressures the mood in the corridors of Westminster and Whitehall appears, for a variety of reasons, to be one of determined calm. There will be no new slew of criminal justice legislation other than that initially required to 'simplify' the welter of existing statutes and restore to the judiciary the discretion judges need to determine 'the just sentence in each case' (ibid.: paras 165–7). Meanwhile the Youth Justice Board (YJB), which since 1998 has overseen the youth justice system reformed by New Labour, may be abolished and powers given back to the localities and the professionals to decide how services should best be provided and what form of intervention, before or after a court hearing, should be taken to reduce re-offending (ibid.: ch. 5). It is a singular change of emphasis following a General Election during which, for the first time in many a year, 'law and order' did not figure prominently (see Downes and Morgan, this volume).

In previous editions of this *Handbook* there have been separate chapters on youth culture and crime and youth justice. In this edition we have brought the topics together. We have done so in order better to integrate the evidence on youth crime and the manner in which we respond to it. And also because, having charted much of the history and current administration of youth crime and justice in previous editions, we propose briefly summarizing that history and administration here and concentrating in greater detail on contemporary developments. We recommend that readers refer to earlier editions of this *Handbook* for the more detailed historical accounts and administrative detail.

## YOUTH CULTURE AND OFFENDING

### YOUTH AND CRIME IN HISTORICAL CONTEXT

Concerns about youthful (mis)behaviour are far from new (Pearson 1983). Although youth cultures in Britain are generally thought of as a post-war phenomenon, they have been observable for far longer. In this section of the chapter we explore aspects of continuity and change in youth cultures, beginning by considering the emergence of the idea of 'adolescence' as a distinct period in individual development, before moving on to examine youth culture in post-war Britain and current patterns of youth crime.

In England and Wales no child may be guilty of a criminal offence below the age of 10. Moreover, between the ages of 10 and 18 young offenders are dealt with in the youth justice system largely separately from adult offenders. Such a separation is relatively new and reflects, in part, increasing concerns about the particular vulnerability of young people. Indeed, from the seventeenth century onward, childhood was progressively extended and increasingly separated from adulthood. In Aries' (1973) view, it is only since that time that we have become preoccupied with the physical, moral, and sexual development of young people. As childhood as a separate category evolved, so there developed with it the idea that children were a responsibility—that they required protection—and, moreover, that children were creatures with the potential for good and evil, discipline being required to ensure that the former predominated over the latter.

As these two phases in the life-cycle were progressively separated and the transition between them extended through restrictions on work and the formalization of education, so the opportunity for the development of a further, intermediary phase increased. This is the phase that has come to be referred to as 'adolescence'. The distinctively modern adolescent started to appear in the nineteenth century. The Factory Acts limited working hours, compulsory education began to develop from the 1870s—albeit slowly—and urban working-class young people were developing what can perhaps be regarded as the first modern youth subcultures (Davis 1990; Savage 2007), such as the 'scuttlers' and 'peaky blinders' (Humphries 1981). Institutions were developed for delinquents and for those *at risk* of delinquency—the 'perishing classes'—and it was out of these that the modern juvenile justice system grew. By the turn of the century, young people in the new cities and manufacturing towns were experiencing considerable economic independence and leisure time was expanding. It was at this time that heightened concerns about delinquency and hooliganism emerged (Rook 1899; Booth 1902).

Most official indicators of the level of juvenile crime suggested that it rose fairly steadily during the 1930s, and rose sharply, though with some ups and downs, during the Second World War. War-time conditions—the black-out, high wages for youth labour, family disruption, the closure of schools and youth clubs—were blamed for much delinquency (Bailey 1987). In the late 1940s and 1950s, with the advent of the welfare state, there was some expectation that crime would return to its pre-war levels. This proved not to be the case, and by the late 1950s recorded crime statistics were rising sharply.

## YOUTH IN POST-WAR BRITAIN

The number of known juvenile offenders began to rise substantially from about 1955, as did public concern about youth in general. Young people were beginning to enjoy a degree of autonomy that was significantly greater than that of previous generations and at the heart of this was their generally increasing affluence (Abrams 1959). This led to the growth of increasingly distinctive youth styles based around the conspicuous consumption of 'leisure and pleasure' (Frith 1983), linked with the emergence of what became known as 'mass culture' and the development of its most spectacular offshoot, youth culture.

Although the subcultural styles that developed were, seemingly, distinctly class-based, there were aspects of 'youth' in post-war Britain that appeared to transcend class and the widespread concern over youth as a whole. The development of phrases such as the 'generation gap' gave expression to the prevalent feeling that it was the differences between age groups as opposed to classes that were the more problematic, a view that received some support in sociological quarters. 'Youth' were crucially perceived to be one of the most striking indications of social change. For the moral entrepreneurs of the period, 'youth' was a problem and 'a cornerstone in the construction of understandings, interpretations and quasi-explanations *about* the period' (Clarke *et al.* 1976: 9).

The first of the major post-war subcultures was the 'Teds'. The appearance of rock 'n' roll in Britain lit the touch paper of respectable moral outrage (Gillett 1983). Moral concern was focused in the main on the sporadic violence at rock 'n' roll movies, on the occasional confrontations between rival groups of 'Teds', and on the so-called 'race riots' of the late 1950s. However, concerns about the general behaviour of young people in post-war British society focused both on sexual and criminal behaviour, and images of juvenile delinquency, and more generalized forms of rebellion or resistance, were closely intertwined. It was not just violence associated with the 'Teds', therefore, but the blatant sexuality of what Melly (1972: 36) called 'screw and smash' music—'a contemporary incitement to arbitrary fucking and mindless vandalism'—which terrified older generations. Though post-war thinking—influenced by Fabianism and positivism—looked for solutions in increasing prosperity, it seemed clear that 'consensus, affluence and consumerism had produced, not the pacification of worry and anxiety—their dissolution in the flux of money, goods and fashion—but their reverse: a profound, disquieting sense of moral unease' (Hall *et al.* 1978: 233). The more liberal atmosphere of the 1960s, illustrated in the reform of the laws on obscenity, abortion, theatre censorship, capital punishment, homosexuality, divorce, and licensing, was counterbalanced, at least in part, by moral campaigns to check the 'permissive revolution' (Newburn 1991).

A succession of white working-class subcultures followed in the wake of the 'Teds', and with what appeared to be increasing speed. These included 'Mods' (Hebdige 1976) and, from lower down the social scale (Barker and Little 1964) and in opposition, sometimes literally, always stylistically, the Rockers (Willis 1978). Perhaps the most starkly aggressive of all subcultural styles were the skinheads, who appeared in the late 1960s, espoused traditional, even reactionary, values and, through their association with football violence and attacks on ethnic minorities and gays, quickly obtained folk devil status. Their racism, defence of territory, opposition to hippy values, their social origins (unskilled working class) and particular construction of style or 'bricolage' (Clarke 1976b) were seen by subcultural theorists as representing 'an attempt to recreate through the "mob" the traditional working class community' (Clarke 1976a: 99).

It was not until the late 1960s that a distinctly British school of subcultural theory emerged. Its distinctiveness lay in taking the American subcultural tradition and locating it within cultural and historical time and place. This was in part a response to the perceived shortcomings of *anomie* theory, but also because North American theory was felt inapplicable to the British context in a number of ways (Downes and Rock 1982; and Rock, this volume). Nevertheless, despite any differences, the two waves shared a great deal: 'Both work with the same "problematic"... growing up in a class society; both identify the same vulnerable group: the urban male working-class late adolescent; both see delinquency as a collective solution to a structurally imposed problem' (Cohen 1980: iv). Early British work, such as John Barron Mays' *Growing Up in the City* and Terry Morris' *The Criminal Area,* formed the basis of a distinctly

British form of sociological criminology which really took off from the late 1960s after the publication of Downes' *The Delinquent Solution* (Downes 1966). From this view delinquency is not at heart rebellious, but conformist. The conformity is to working class values. Consequently, he effectively rejected the idea—so far as the area he was studying was concerned—of delinquent subcultures and, rather, saw delinquency as a 'solution' to some of the structural problems faced by young men. Aligning himself with American sociologists such as Matza and Sykes, Downes argued that many of the young people he studied dissociated themselves from school and work and emphasized leisure:

> There is some reason to suppose, however, that the working-class 'corner boy' both lays greater stress on its leisure goals, and has far less legitimate access to them, than male adolescents differently placed in the social structure. This discrepancy is thought to be enough to provide immediate impetus to a great deal of group delinquency, limited in ferocity but diversified in content. (ibid.: 250)

As British subcultural theory developed, so its focus moved gradually away from delinquency and increasingly towards leisure and style (the main exceptions being Patrick 1973; Parker 1974; and Gill 1977). Parker's is a study of criminal subculture in which theft from cars provided a profitable adolescent interlude before the onset of a more respectable adult life or a more serious and long-term criminal career. Both his and Patrick's study—in which the focus was on the machismo of the 'hard man'—brought insights from labelling theory to bear on the study of subcultures. Parker's 'boys' used theft as a means of dealing with some of the problems they faced, dissociating themselves in part from the values of the dominant social order and, like the delinquents in Downes' pathbreaking study, responding within the physical and material conditions which constrained their range of choice and freedom.

For later writers in particular, subcultures emerged not just as a response to the problems of material conditions—their class circumstances, schooling, and so on—they were also taken to represent a symbolic critique of the dominant culture in which 'style' was read as a form of resistance. Subcultures, at least from the viewpoint of the more radical commentators of the 1970s, were essentially oppositional rather than subordinate, and gave rise to the kinds of societal reaction that Stan Cohen described as 'moral panics' (1980: 9). For their members, subcultures allowed the possibility of providing solutions to material and socio-cultural problems, albeit through solutions that were symbolic. Thus, as Phil Cohen (1972: 23) put it, the latent function of subculture was to 'express and resolve, albeit "magically", the contradictions which appear in the parent culture'.

Such solutions were largely expressed through style rather than crime. It was at this point that the vocabulary of cultural studies met various strands of the sociology of deviance. Discerning 'the hidden messages inscribed in code on the glossy surfaces of style, to trace them out as maps of meaning' (Hebdige 1979: 18), became the key task. The dominant focus of British subcultural theory in the 1970s was on white, working-class, male culture (Dorn and South 1982). There were, at least in the earliest years of such writing, few attempts to understand either female delinquency or the styles associated with female subcultures, though the work of Angela McRobbie was both an early and a consistent exception to this (McRobbie 1980, 1991). Because much 'girl culture' was a culture of the bedroom rather than the street, together with young women's lesser involvement in crime, McRobbie (1980: 40) argued, most subcultural theorists:

> in documenting the temporary flights of the Teds, Mods or Rockers,...fail[ed] to show that it is monstrously more difficult for women to escape (even temporarily) and that these symbolic flights have often been at the expense of women (especially mothers) and girls. The lads'...peer-group consciousness and pleasure frequently seem to hinge on a collective disregard for women and sexual exploitation of girls.

By comparison with the 1960s, the early 1970s were a relatively quiet time on the youth subcultural front, though they did see the blossoming of African-Caribbean cultural resistance, in part associated with, and reinforced by, the mugging panic of the mid-1970s (Hall *et al.* 1978). Up to this point there appears to have been no explicit association between black youth and crime. Subsequently, however, as Gilroy (1987: 109) puts it, the 'view of the blacks as innately criminal, or at least more criminal than the white neighbours whose deprivation they share, [...] became "common sense" during the early 1970s, [and was] crucial to the development of new definitions of the black problem and new types of racial language and reasoning' (Gilroy 1987: 109). From 'rude boys' and ska to reggae and Rastafarianism, Hebdige sought to explain elements of black youth culture as expressions of resistance, and as products of an increasingly problematic relationship with elements of British society—not least the police.

Through the late 1970s and into the 1980s, social and economic conditions for many young people became dramatically tougher. The key defining features were unemployment and racism, and it was against this background that African-Caribbean cultural resistance burgeoned and 'punk' appeared (Savage 1991). From the late 1970s onwards, youth unemployment became a permanent feature of the social landscape, access to benefits was restricted, and a raft of new training schemes emerged. The major consequence of these structural changes was to extend and complicate the transition from dependent childhood to independent adulthood (Furlong and Cartmel 1997), with the consequence that a small proportion of young people fell through the net, ending up outside education (often having been excluded), training, or work. This was the group around which many concerns about criminal activity tended to coalesce (Williamson 2004).

As the world of work has retreated as a realistic prospect for many, so, it is argued, lifestyles dominated by consumption have come closer to the foreground: youth culture 'became more of an advertising medium than ever before' (Redhead 1990: 105). The late 1980s and 1990s saw the emergence of dance-based, drug-associated youth cultural styles, to which the acid house subculture and subsequent rave 'movement' or 'scene' were central. Such partying—or 'hedonism in hard times' (Redhead 1993: 4)—was somewhat in contrast with the drabber youth culture of the late 1970s and early 1980s. Where 'punk had rejected such obvious pleasure a decade before...youth hedonism was now back, with a vengeance. A fortnight's holiday in the sun became packed into a single weekend— then the next weekend and the next' (McKay 1996: 105). Despite the declining frequency in recent times with which new subcultural styles have emerged and been played out as a form of 'symbolic guerrilla warfare' (Thompson

1998: 48) moral panics around youth, and especially youthful deviance and criminality, continue to be a regular feature of the political and cultural landscape.

Most recently, such concerns have tended to coalesce around the issue of 'gangs'. Long associated with youthful deviance in the United States (Thrasher 1963; Miller 1982), the emergence of gangs is held to be a much more recent phenomenon in Britain (Pitts 2008; though see Davies 1998), though the existence of a 'gang culture' remains contested (Hallsworth and Silverstone 2009). Media reporting surrounding a spate of gun-related homicides and concerns about possibly increasing levels of knife-crime have, in recent years, been elided with talk of gangs to underpin arguments suggesting that the problem of serious youth violence is undergoing significant change. In fact, the picture is extremely complex, with data on gun-related crime being rather limited and difficult to interpret (Squires *et al.* 2008). Notwithstanding the definitional problems of what constitutes a 'gang' (Pitts 2008), there is some evidence indicating that young people claiming to be involved in such groupings are much more likely to admit having carried a gun (Marshall *et al.* 2005; Bennett and Holloway 2004). Ethnographic research in the north of England, however, found that gang members did not specialize in violence, though violence played an important role in member's lives, particularly symbolically and rhetorically (Aldridge *et al.* 2008). The study found that gang members earned money from a *combination* of legal and illegal opportunities but, perhaps contrary to expectations, drug dealing was neither central to such earning, nor was control over drugs markets the primary cause of gang-related violence.

## YOUNG PEOPLE, CRIME, AND VICTIMIZATION

A significant proportion of crime is committed by young people. Indeed, Hirschi and Gottfredson (1983: 552) argue that the age-crime distribution 'represents one of the brute facts of criminology'. This, in tandem with adult fears about youthful deviance, leads to young offenders occupying the 'dubiously privileged position', in changing guises, as society's number one folk devil (Muncie *et al.* 1995). Though official statistics can only ever provide a crude estimate of juvenile offending, they nevertheless suggest that almost one-fifth of all those cautioned or convicted in any one year for indictable offences are aged 10–17 and one-third are under 21 (*Criminal Statistics* 2009).

Self-report studies confirm that offending in the teenage years is relatively common; Home Office research in the mid-1990s found that over half of males and almost one-third of females aged between 14 and 25 admitted to committing one or more criminal offences at some point in their lives (Home Office 1995a). More recent self-report studies have found that 10- to 17-year-olds were responsible for 35 per cent of the incidents measured even though they comprised 14 per cent of the sample (Budd *et al.* 2005) and that approximately one-quarter of young males and just under one-fifth of young females aged 10–25 reported having committed at least one offence in the past year (see Figure 17.1; figures are largely consistent with those reported in Youth Justice Board 2010).

What of overall levels of youth crime? Neither official statistics nor victimization surveys offer a straightforward means of assessing trends, though *Criminal Statistics* data indicate that the proportion of convictions and cautions accounted for by those aged under 21 has dropped significantly since the late 1980s (Smith 2010). Within

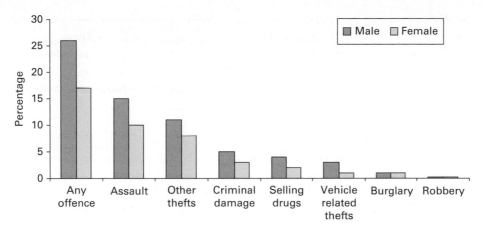

**Figure 17.1** 10-25 year olds committing an offence in last 12 months, by sex (%)
*Source*: Roe and Ashe 2008

this general trend, there is some evidence of an increase in the number of young people being convicted for violent crimes in the last decade (though the changes in the counting rules make the data extremely hard to interpret; see Maguire, this volume). Self-report studies appeared to show something of an increase in the prevalence of offending among 14–17-year olds, and a decrease among young adults during the 1990s (Flood-Page *et al.* 2000), but subsequent studies found little or no significant change up to 2008 (Roe and Ashe 2008; YJB 2000). Though all such data need to be treated with considerable caution, there is little indication from across these sources of any substantial increase in youth crime in the last decade and a half.

Considerable criminological research has focused on the 'shape' of criminal careers', exploring their beginning (onset), end (desistance), and length in between (duration), together with the risk and protective factors associated with each (Piquero *et al.* 2007). Estimates of the peak age of offending vary but generally place it somewhere between 15 (MORI 2004) and 18 (*Criminal Statistics* 2009). The estimated peak age of offending is higher for males than it is for females. Home Office self-report survey data, though now somewhat old, identify the 16–17-year age group as that with the highest prevalence of offending for males, with that for females being slightly younger at approximately 14–15 (see Figure 17.2). Official statistics also suggest that the peak age of known male offending has increased; it was 14 years in 1971, 15 in 1980, and increased to 18 by 1990, where it remains. The location of the peak age of offending in the mid to late adolescent years has traditionally been taken as indicating that a significant proportion of young people will simply 'grow out of crime' (Rutherford 1992).

The first Youth Lifestyles Survey (YLS) provided new evidence about the prevalence of offending for different age groups (Graham and Bowling 1995). The data showed that the peak age of offending for males to be 14 for 'expressive property offences', 16 for violent offences, 17 for serious offences, and 20 for drug offences. Among females, the peak age of offending was 15 for property, expressive, and serious offences, 16 for violent offences, and 17 for drug offences. Looking, however, at the proportions of males at different ages who admitted to having committed various offences within a one-year period, Graham and Bowling found that expressive and violent offences

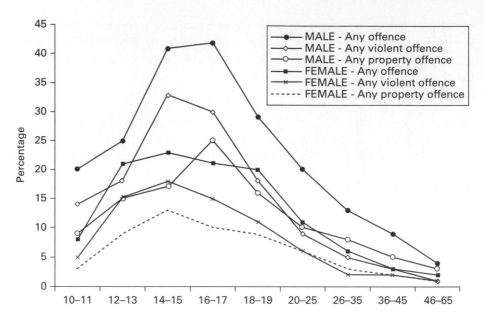

**Figure 17.2** Last year prevalence of offending, by age (%)
*Source*: Budd *et al.* 2005

were most prevalent among 14–17-year-olds, property offences (excluding fraud and theft from work) among 18–21-year-olds, and theft of motor vehicles among 22–25-year-olds. When fraud and theft from work were included within the property crime category, 22–25-year-olds had the highest rate of offending. They concluded that, among males, while the rate of participation in offending does not change significantly between the ages of 14 and 25, it does change markedly in character. Most particularly, they suggested that young men did not appear to be desisting from property offences in their early 20s, thus casting some doubt on the idea that young people tend to 'grow out of crime'. The second YLS, which had an extended age range (12 to 30) and a larger sample size, again found that rates of property offending differed from rates of criminal damage and violence, remaining fairly stable between the ages of 18 and 25, and also found that the proportion declined thereafter, possibly suggesting a somewhat delayed pattern of 'desistance' (Flood-Page *et al.* 2000).

Frequency of offending varies markedly and there is now a considerable criminological literature looking at persistent and serious offending by juveniles. Early research by Wolfgang and colleagues (1972) identified what they described as 'chronic offenders'. This small group—representing just over six per cent of the cohort studied—accounted for more than half of all the arrests experienced by the whole group. There has been considerable policy interest in such offenders for a decade or more and a large body of longitudinal and cross-sectional research has examined the backgrounds and offending histories of such 'frequent', 'high rate', or 'life course persistent' offenders (West and Farrington 1977; Farrington and West 1993; Huizinga *et al.* 1995). Similarly, the 2006 OCJS uses self-report data to distinguish between what it refers to as 'frequent offenders' (those who committed six or more offences in the last 12 months); 'serious offenders' (those who committed one or more of the following: theft of a vehicle; burglary; robbery; theft from the person; assault resulting in injury; and selling Class A drugs), and 'frequent serious offenders (being those that had committed a serious offence at least six times in the last 12 months). The results can be found in Table 17.1 below.

Table 17.1 Serious and frequent offending in the last 12 months by age and sex

|          | Offender | Serious offender | Frequent offender | Frequent serious offender |
| -------- | -------- | ---------------- | ----------------- | ------------------------- |
| **Males**   | **26** | **12** | **8**  | **1** |
| 10 to 11 | 22 | 9  | 3  | 0 |
| 12 to 13 | 26 | 12 | 7  | 2 |
| 14 to 15 | 37 | 18 | 15 | 3 |
| 16 to 17 | 33 | 16 | 11 | 2 |
| 18 to 25 | 21 | 11 | 7  | 1 |
| **Females** | **17** | **8** | **3** | **1** |
| 10 to 11 | 12 | 4  | 4  | 2 |
| 12 to 13 | 24 | 12 | 3  | 1 |
| 14 to 15 | 26 | 14 | 8  | 3 |
| 16 to 17 | 23 | 10 | 4  | 1 |
| 18 to 25 | 13 | 5  | 2  | 1 |

*Source*: Roe and Ashe (2008)

## ETHNIC MINORITY YOUTH AND CRIME

It was not until the 1970s that there was any explicit association made between black youth and crime (Hall *et al.* 1978; see Phillips and Bowling, this volume). The increased concern arose partly out of the 'mugging panic' early in the decade and other signs of poor or deteriorating relationships between the police and black youth. This was reinforced by the release of statistics by the Metropolitan Police suggesting that crime rates were particularly high among African-Caribbean youth in the capital. Other sources of data showed black youth to be over-represented at all stages of the criminal justice process, a pattern confirmed by later research on prosecution rates (Landau and Nathan 1983), charging patterns (Audit Commission 1996), and remands and sentencing to custody (Feilzer and Hood 2005).

Given the now strong popular association between black youth and crime, it is perhaps surprising how little rigorous, empirical research has been conducted in the area. There are a number of useful exceptions to this, including the first YLS which included a booster sample of young people from ethnic minorities (Graham and Bowling 1995) as well as the 2005 Offending Crime and Justice Survey (OCJS) (Sharp and Budd 2005). The data from the YLS were striking. They suggested that, in general, white and African-Caribbean youth have similar rates of participation in offending, though these are significantly higher than self-reported participation by South Asian youth. Data from the more recent self-report OCJS show slightly higher levels of self-reported offending among black or black British respondents compared with white respondents (see Figure 17.3).

Both groups report higher levels of lifetime offending than either Asian or Asian British respondents or those of mixed ethnic origin. However, a slightly higher proportion of white respondents (23 per cent) reported having ever committed a 'serious' offence compared with mixed (20 per cent), black or black British (20 per cent), or Asian or Asian British respondents (15 per cent). The 2005 OCJS also included a series of questions about anti-social and other 'problem' behaviours. The results showed slightly higher overall levels of anti-social behaviour among white young people aged 10 to 15, but the differences were not significant. The more sizeable differences appeared to be in relation to treatment within the criminal justice system which, in some instances at least, were 'consistent with discriminatory treatment' (Feilzer and Hood 2005).

## YOUNG PEOPLE, DRUGS, ALCOHOL, AND CRIME

Close associations between youth subcultures and illicit drug use have been noted since at least the hippy counter culture of the 1960s (Young 1971). However, far from being perceived as problematic, 'during the 1960s and 1970s it was fashionable in social science and liberal circles to question whether the prevailing concern about drug use might not be an example of…"moral panic"' (Dorn and South 1987: 2). This all changed in the late 1970s, and the years 1979–81 were the watershed during which 'the heroin habit' really began to take off and when, for the first time, its use became associated with the young unemployed (Pearson 1987). The number of known addicts trebled between 1979 and 1983, and research in the late 1980s confirmed the impression of a significant spread of heroin use (Parker *et al.* 1988). Public concern about increasing heroin use was followed by fears of a possible 'crack' epidemic, though, in the main, the worst of these fears have not been realized. Research in the 1990s suggested that 'the picture now is one of continuing widespread availability of a great variety of drugs, use being shaped by familiar factors such as local supply, contexts of

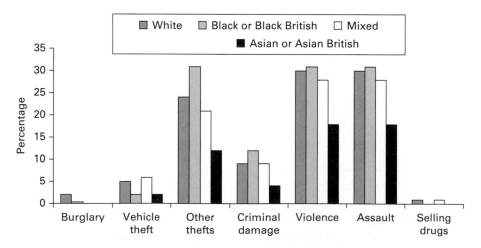

**Figure 17.3** Percentage of 10–15-year-olds who have 'ever offended' by ethnic group
*Source*: Sharp and Budd (2005)

use, preferred styles of consumption and purpose or intent' (see Measham and South, this volume).

Data on the incidence and prevalence of drug use among young people are now available as a result of a number of important surveys (latterly, Goulden and Sondhi 2001; Budd *et al.* 2004; Hoare and Moon 2010). Prevalence for 15–20-year-olds varies between approximately 10–35 per cent in the national samples and 5–50 per cent in local samples, with cannabis the most popular drug. Drug use and age are clearly linked. Use of illicit drugs is rare in early teenage years, increases sharply in the mid to late teens, and is generally shown to peak in the late teens or early twenties (ISDD 1994; Hoare and Moon 2010). See Figure 17.4.

Both national and local surveys appeared to indicate that drug use by young people was on the increase during the 1990s; Mott and Mirrlees-Black (1993), for instance, noting that the percentage of 16–19-year-olds reporting cannabis use more than doubled between 1983 and 1991. The most recent national surveys of youthful drug use (Hoare and Moon 2010) suggest that prevalence rates have generally been in decline for much of the past decade—the major exception being cocaine use which has shown significant increases since the mid-1990s (see Figure 17.5). To what extent this is a 'cohort effect' (i.e. a product of the aging of a particular generation rather than a more generalized change in behaviour) is not as yet clear (Aldridge 2008).

Research in the 1990s, in particular from local surveys, indicated something of a decline in gender differences in drug use among adolescents and young adults—in particular in lifetime measures of drug use. There is continuing evidence that the

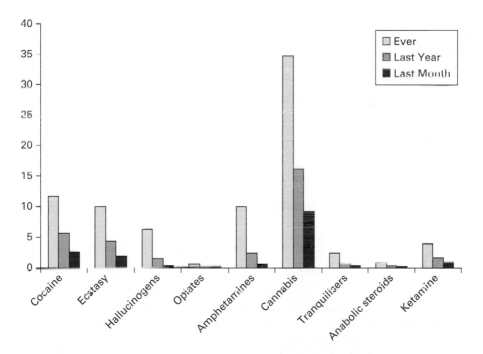

**Figure 17.4** Proportion of 16–24-year-olds reporting use of drugs 'ever', 'in the last year', and 'in the last month' (%)
*Source*: Hoare and Moon (2010) (Tables 2.6–2.8)

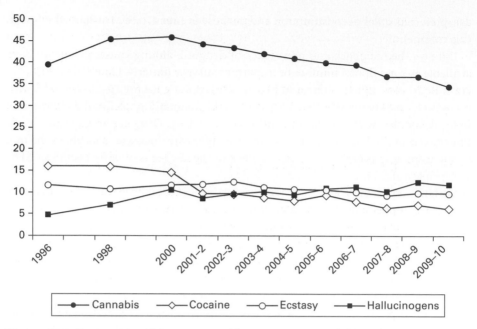

**Figure 17.5** Proportion of 16–24-year-olds reporting use of drugs *ever* in their life-time, 1996–2009/10 (BCS)

*Source*: Hoare and Moon (2010)

gender gap in the youngest age groups researched (11–15-year-olds) remains small (op. cit.).

In recent times, alcohol consumption has become an increasingly prominent feature of adult concern about youth lifestyles and, indeed, school-age young people are more likely to report having drunk alcohol at least once (54 per cent) than to have ever used illicit drugs (around 25 per cent) or to have smoked cigarettes (33 per cent) (Fuller 2008). Although the prevalence of teenage drinking has declined since the 1980s, the amount drunk by those that do so has nearly doubled in the last decade or so (Fuller 2008). More particularly, it is what has become known as 'binge drinking'—essentially, intermittent, high consumption drinking patterns—that has become the key concern. Studies have shown that a majority of those arrested late at night in city centre areas are intoxicated with alcohol (Deehan *et al.* 2002), and Home Office research indicates that 15 per cent of all 12–17-year-olds had been involved in some form of anti-social behaviour during or after drinking and that 'frequent drinkers' were more likely to have behaved anti-socially (Richardson and Budd 2003).

A growing body of research has highlighted the particularly 'vulnerable' position of young offenders (Becker and Roe 2005). An analysis of the first YLS found that a higher proportion of offenders aged 12–17 were frequent drinkers (36 per cent) than non-offenders (20 per cent), and that this was consistent across the age range (Harrington 2000). The second YLS found that three-quarters (74 per cent) of 'persistent offenders' reported lifetime use of drugs, and almost three-fifths (57 per cent) reported having used drugs in the past year (Goulden and Sondhi 2001). In addition to raised general prevalence rates, the survey also suggested that the rates of use of drugs such as crack and heroin are significantly higher among young serious and/ or persistent offenders than they are in the general population, a finding reinforced by studies of adult offending populations (Bennett 2000). Work on young offenders largely confirms this general picture (Hammersley *et al.* 2003). The 2004 OCJS, for example, shows higher rates of offending among drug users when compared with non-users, and higher levels still among Class A drug users and frequent users (see Figure 17.6).

## YOUNG PEOPLE, VICTIMIZATION, AND THE POLICE

When the words 'youth' and 'crime' are linked, the picture in most minds is frequently of the young person as an offender. Young people, however, are frequently victims of crime. Outside those studies which have focused specifically on child abuse and domestic violence, most criminological studies of victimization have paid scant attention to young people's experiences as victims of crime (though for some exceptions see Morgan and Zedner 1992; Aye Maung 1995; Hartless *et al.* 1995; see also Hoyle, this volume).

Initial sweeps of the BCS focused on the experiences of those aged 16 or older, though the fourth included questions for 12–15-year-olds. The results were illuminating. They showed that 12–15-year-old boys and girls are at least as much at risk of victimization as adults, and for some types of crime, more at risk than adults and older teenagers (Aye Maung 1995). So important are such developments in our understanding considered to be that the decision was taken that from January 2009 the BCS would be extended to cover children aged 10 to 15. Initial exploratory work as part of this development sought to test a number of different ways of classifying incidents involving children: *all in law*—include all incidents reported by children that are in law a crime; *all in law*

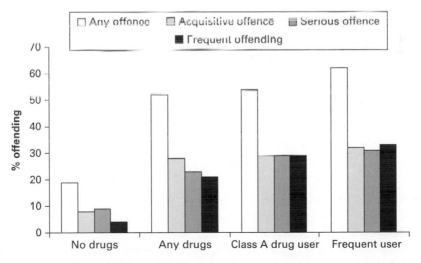

**Figure 17.6** Proportion of 10–25-year-olds committing different types of offences, by drug status
*Source*: Budd *et al.* (2005b) (Table A7.3)

*outside school*—as above, but excluding incidents within school; *victim perceived*—all incidents that are in law a crime and are thought by victims themselves to be crimes; a *norms-based* measure which applies an explicit set of normative rules to exclude relatively minor incidents (see Figure 17.7).

Making a direct comparison with victimization risks from the BCS is problematic, but the authors of this most recent work point out that the proportion of adults who were victims of any personal crime was 6 per cent in the same period. Thus, even the most conservative measure above shows children's risks as being at least as great as that of adults, and by three of the measures significantly higher. Looking at individual characteristics, the BCS data showed boys had a higher risk of being victims than girls, particularly in relation to violence and theft from the person, and boys aged 13–15 had the highest risk of being a victim of theft from the person (see Table 17.2).

Further analysis of this new data source suggests that a little under a quarter of children have had contact with the police in the past year (23 per cent) and that this contact was most commonly initiated by the police (Hoare *et al.* 2011). Slightly over one-fifth of children (22 per cent) reported having been bullied in the past year in a way which either frightened or upset them, of whom about one quarter reported 'cyber-bullying' (i.e. having been sent unwanted and nasty emails, texts, or messages or having something nasty posted about them on a website) (2011: 49). The analysis of the BCS also considered young people's experiences of public safety, finding that the vast majority (81 per cent) reported that they hung around with friends in public spaces, and that one-fifth of respondents had experience of having been moved on by the police in the previous 12 months. Intriguingly, over one-third of children (35 per cent) reported finding young people hanging around in their local area a problem,

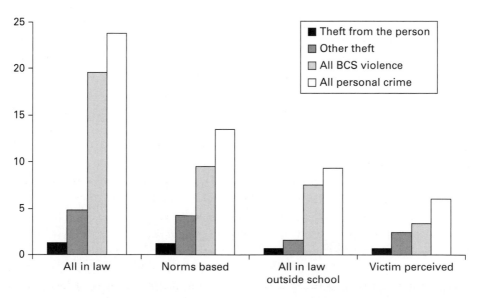

**Figure 17.7**  Risk of being a victim of personal crime for children aged 10–15 (%)
*Source*: Millard and Flatley (2010)

**Table 17.2** Proportion of children aged 10–15 who were victims of personal crimes by age and sex

|  | All in law | Norms based | All in law outside school | Victim perceived |
|---|---|---|---|---|
| **All** | 17.2 | 13.5 | 9.3 | 6.0 |
| **Boys** | 21.9 | 17.8 | 11.9 | 7.6 |
| 10–12 | 23.1 | 18.1 | 10.8 | 6.6 |
| 13–15 | 20.8 | 17.5 | 12.9 | 8.6 |
| **Girls** | 12.4 | 9.1 | 6.5 | 4.3 |
| 10–12 | 12.3 | 8.4 | 5.0 | 3.0 |
| 13–15 | 12.4 | 9.7 | 8.0 | 5.6 |

*Source:* Millard and Flatley (2010)

with those living in the most deprived areas being significantly more likely to do so than those living in the least deprived areas.

## YOUTH JUSTICE

### HISTORICAL DEVELOPMENT AND PARADIGMS

There has been a formally separate system of youth justice in England and Wales for just over a century. We described the key developmental features of this system in an earlier version of this chapter (Morgan and Newburn 2007). It will suffice to say here that: in 1908 juvenile courts (renamed youth courts in 1991) were established; thereafter separate sentences were introduced for child and young offenders; and from the late nineteenth century onwards separate institutions were created within which young offenders were to be held apart from adults. This separation, which was strengthened in a series of steps during the inter-war and immediate post-war years, was designed to protect children, in recognition of their lack of maturity and experience, from danger and exploitation. However, the separation was never watertight and remains porous to this day. The juvenile court was little differentiated from the adult court. Some juvenile offenders continued to be held in predominantly adult prisons. And young offenders found guilty of serious crimes continued to be liable to custodial sentences of the same duration as those provided for adults. This remains the case.

If criminal justice systems involve a tension between the objectives of punishment and welfare (Garland 1985) then juvenile justice systems illustrate it acutely. Despite occasional assertions to the contrary (see Home Office 1997, para. 2.1–2) there are inherent contradictions between what we may term the *punishment*, or just deserts, and the *welfare* paradigms. The former treats the child as a responsible person exercising choice, the bearer of rights which must be respected through legal due process, but ultimately deserving of punishment proportionate to culpability. The latter views the child as having limited responsibility because his or her capacity has yet to be realized, is deserving of protection, and has needs which should be met as a duty owed the child by society. All juvenile justice systems embody a compromise between these two paradigms. Indeed McAra (2010) argues that contemporary juvenile justice systems tend to accommodate elements of two additional paradigms, the *restorative* and the *actuarial*. The former recognizes both the child's responsibilities *and* entitlements, aims to make good the harm caused by the offence, and, by bringing the offender and victim together, build a more inclusive society. The latter sees the child in terms of a capacity for wrongdoing with interventions justified on preventive grounds proportionate to the risk of future harms posed.

The balance between competing paradigms changes over time and it is possible, with a fair level of agreement between analysts, to periodize the historical development of juvenile justice policy and make comparisons between jurisdictions. In England and Wales the twentieth century, up to the late 1960s, marked the gradual ascendancy of a welfarist approach to juvenile justice, support for which gathered pace in the postwar period. Local authority children's departments were established in 1948. In 1963 the age of criminal responsibility was raised from eight to ten. Finally, the Children and Young Persons Act 1969, 'the most developed application of welfare principles to criminal justice ever seen in an English statute' (Bottoms and Stevenson 1992: 36), laid the basis for a fundamental departure from the classical, just deserts response to youth crime. The Act provided for the abolition of prosecution of any child under 14 for all criminal offences except homicide. It also restricted civil care measures for young children, favouring, wherever possible, that they be dealt with outside court. Prosecution of 14–16-year-olds was to remain an option but non-criminal care proceedings, the preferred alternative in most cases, were also to be available. For those young offenders prosecuted, there were to be two main disposals available—the care order and the supervision order—both to be supervised by social workers given considerable discretion. Penal custody for offenders aged 14 to 16 was to be phased out and the juvenile court was to become a welfare-providing agency 'of last resort' (Rutter and Giller 1983).

In the event the 1969 Act was only partly implemented and its radically welfarist vision never realized. The Labour Government that introduced the legislation lost the 1970 General Election and when the Party was returned to power in 1974 it abandoned its commitment to reform. Criminal proceedings were retained for 10–14-year-olds, the juvenile courts continued to function largely as before, and the powers relating to 14–16-year-olds were not restricted. Though care proceedings on the commission of an offence were now possible, they were used sparingly and the number of custodial sentences more than doubled during the decade. Though much of the 1969 Act was not implemented and practice became more punitive and 'justice' oriented, the fact that it was on the statute book led, ironically, to the vision it embodied being scapegoated for all the youth crime and justice ills of the 1970s. There was a significant backlash against welfarism, the criticisms coming from all points on the political spectrum. Commentators on the right were critical of what they took to be the insufficiently tough approach characteristic of contemporary juvenile justice. Those on the left felt that behind all the talk of 'treatment', restrictive and potentially punitive forms of intervention were on the increase which required a renewed emphasis on due process rights.

Following the Thatcher-led Conservative electoral victory in 1979, 'short sharp shock' detention centre regimes were experimentally introduced, and despite being found wanting in terms of re-offending rates, were extended to all detention centres. Yet though youth justice policy appeared now to be a far cry from that envisaged by the 1969 Act, the Thatcher 'law and order' years witnessed the emergence of countervailing tendencies. The Criminal Justice Act 1982 limited the use of custody for young offenders, shortened the detention centre sentence, and, via the new Youth Custody Order, signalled the end of borstals and indeterminate sentences. Against this background a significant and sustained decline in the numbers of young people being processed by the courts took place in the latter half of the 1980s. The use of police cautions greatly increased and there was a significant fall in the number of children and young people in custody.

What explains these apparently surprising trends in the 1980s? Several factors contributed. There were the restrictions placed on the use of custody. There was the introduction of a range of non-custodial penalties to which requirements could be added, used increasingly as a high tariff option. Most important was diversion from court, resulting in a significant decline in the number of juveniles prosecuted in the latter half of the decade. So successful was this policy believed to be that in 1988 the Government signalled its intention to transfer the lessons learnt in juvenile justice to policies for offenders generally;

> Most young offenders grow out of crime as they become more mature and responsible. They need encouragement and help to become law abiding. Even a short period of custody is quite likely to confirm them as criminals, particularly as they acquire new criminal skills from the more sophisticated offenders. They see themselves labelled as criminals and behave accordingly (Home Office 1988: paras 2.17–2.19).

Yet though diversion from custody and court proceedings was emphasized the Children Act 1989 removed civil care proceedings from the juvenile court and the Criminal Justice Act 1991 extended the court's remit to include 17-year-olds. From now on criminal and care proceedings were radically separated, the renamed youth court having no power to remit cases to the family court. 'Justice' rather than welfare was now pre-eminent in youth court proceedings, though Pratt (1989) discerned the emergence of a form of 'corporatism'. Centralized authority and bureaucratic control over decision-making was driving a system increasingly characterized by multi-agency working, in which the aims of 'economy' and 'efficiency' were of growing importance in the management of those caught up in the system. Pratt presciently anticipated the preoccupation with risk management, what McAra terms the actuarial paradigm, which increasingly characterized youth justice under New Labour after 1997.

The major changes in English youth justice in the 1990s were triggered by several events. There were the well-publicized urban disturbances of 1991 and the moral panic about so-called 'persistent young offenders'. This led in 1993 to the introduction of the secure training order (STO), aimed at those 'persistent juvenile offenders whose repeated offending makes them a menace to the community' (Hansard, 2 March 1993, col. 139). The measure was applied to 12–14-year-olds convicted of three imprisonable offences who had proved 'unwilling or unable to comply with the requirements of supervision in the community while on remand or under sentence'.

In 1993 there occurred the highly publicized abduction and murder of two-year-old James Bulger by two 10-year-old boys, Jon Thomson and Robert Venables. This case 'inspired a kind of national collective agony' (Young 1996: 113), the importance of which can scarcely be exaggerated and the shadow of which, as we shall see, hangs over the English youth justice debate to this day. Tony Blair, then an Opposition Home Affairs spokesman, pontificated on the case and Michael Howard, then Home Secretary, responded by embracing 'populist punitive' (Bottoms 1995) rhetoric and introducing a package of measures, at the heart of which was the reassertion of the centrality of custody. The Criminal Justice and Public Order Act 1994 doubled the maximum sentence in a Young Offenders Institution (YOI) for 15–17 year-olds to two years.

These punitive measures met with little criticism from the Labour Party which was gearing up to outflank the Conservatives over 'law and order' (Downes and Morgan 2002) and did so in the General Election three years later. The predictable consequence was a rise in the use of youth custody. The number of 15–17-year-olds given custodial sentences rose by almost four-fifths between 1992 and 1998.

The Audit Commission, established in 1982 to promote economy, efficiency, and effectiveness in public services, became increasingly influential in criminal justice during the 1990s. The Commission's report on youth crime and justice, *Misspent Youth* (Audit Commission 1996) was hugely influential, and strikingly similar to that in a discussion document simultaneously produced by the Labour Party (1996), still the Opposition but shortly to assume government. The call in both documents was for an emphasis on 'criminality prevention'.

The Audit Commission was highly critical of existing youth justice arrangements, considering them uneconomic, inefficient, and ineffective. The Commission was particularly critical of repeat police cautioning, the lack of programmes directed at offending behaviour, and what it judged to be the absence of coordinated working. Its most damning indictment was that 'overall, less is done now than a decade ago to address offending by young people. Fewer young people are now convicted by the courts, even allowing for the fall in the number of people aged 10–17 years, and an increasing proportion of those who are found guilty are discharged' (ibid.: para. 69). The system, the Commission argued, needed to be streamlined, speeded up, and greater attention given to early preventive work focusing on 'risk factors' which longitudinal research associated with offending by juveniles.

After New Labour's 1997 election victory the Commission's analysis and proposals were taken up in the Crime and Disorder Act 1998. The Act was heavily managerialist in approach, emphasizing inter-agency cooperation, the necessity of an overall strategic plan, the creation of key performance indicators, and active monitoring of aggregate information about the system and its functioning. To a youth justice system that had been the site of competing philosophies, approaches, and ideologies—notably welfarism, punitive just deserts, and systems management—New Labour added actuarial managerialism and its own potent blend of populist communitarianism. Some commentators saw it as the emergence of a 'new youth justice' (Goldson 2000). The framework laid down in 1998 remains largely in place today and it is to that framework to which we turn next. But before we leave this brief reprise it should be explained that Scotland and Northern Ireland pursued different approaches to juvenile justice than England and Wales.

Until the 1970s the Scottish system was characterized by a tension between welfare and punishment not dissimilar to that south of the border. In 1971, however, there was introduced what became known as the 'hearings' system, implementing the radically welfarist recommendations of the 1964 Kilbrandon Report. 'The welfare of that child throughout his childhood' became the 'paramount consideration', a principle enshrined initially in the Social Work (Scotland) Act 1968 and reaffirmed in the Children (Scotland) Act 1995. The age of criminal responsibility remained eight years but prosecution was avoided wherever possible. The vast majority of offences committed by 8–15-year-olds are referred to and investigated by a 'reporter' whose task is to consider whether statutory grounds for referral have been met and whether compulsory measures of care are necessary. If so, the case proceeds to a hearing. The child and parents must accept the grounds for the referral (i.e. there must be an admission of guilt in cases where offending is alleged): without which the case proceeds to the sheriff court. Serious cases, a small minority, go directly to the sheriff court, which also deals with most offences committed by 16- and 17-year-olds as with adults (though 16- and 17-year-olds can be referred for hearings and a minority are).

Children's hearings are private and usually involve three members of a lay panel, the child and the child's parents, a lawyer or advisor, the reporter, a social worker, and, where appropriate, other professionals such as a teacher or psychologist. Apart from discharging the case there are two primary intervention options: residential and non-residential supervision. The former involves placing the child in a residential establishment; the latter means that the child continues to live at home, most likely under the supervision of a social worker.

In 1999 the government of Scotland was substantially devolved from Westminster to Edinburgh. Though Scotland has always had a legal and education system separate from England and Wales the Scottish Parliament now gained separate legal competence including that for all aspects of youth justice. The Scottish Government immediately instituted a review of youth justice by appointing an Advisory Group on Youth Crime, the focus being on the interventions available to children's hearings and the courts when dealing with persistent young offenders. The Advisory Group recommended a multi-agency approach which was not fully realized. The outcome was the introduction of several 'get tough' measures and a risk-based, managerialist approach based on standard assessment tools similar to those in use in England and Wales. Regional Community Justice Authorities were set up and specialist sheriff youth courts instituted (Burman *et al.* 2010).

Though the Scottish system retains a welfarist character and still differs markedly from that in England and Wales, it has been beset by tensions often associated with welfarist approaches. When Westminster youth justice politics drifted towards popular punitivism in the 1980s and '90s the Scottish system was enviously regarded by many practitioners and commentators in England. North of the border it was 'inextricably linked to a sense of Scottishness' (McAra 2006). Scottish devolution, paradoxically, seems to have undermined that distinctive identity. According to McAra, civil culture in Scotland went into a 'period of drift' with the Labour/Liberal coalition governments in Scotland finding ideological common ground with the New Labour Government at Westminster. The result was some convergence in Scottish and English youth justice thinking, or 'detartanization' (McAra and McVie 2010).

Juvenile justice arrangements in Northern Ireland roughly tracked those in England and Wales after 1900, but the radically welfarist statutes enacted in the rest of the United Kingdom in the late 1960s found no parallel in the province. The 1979 Black Report made recommendations which anticipated the radical separation of care and criminal proceedings set out in the Children Act 1989 in England and Wales, but this step was not taken in Northern Ireland until 1996. Youth courts thereafter dealt, as in England and Wales, with child offenders aged 10–17 inclusive. Not until 2003 did Northern Ireland introduce its distinctive contribution to UK youth justice thinking. The Justice (Northern Ireland) Act 2002 initiated a system of restorative conferences the inspiration for which no doubt grew out of the desperate 'troubles' in Northern Ireland and the need for warring factions to come together, negotiate, and achieve amicable compromise.

Restorative conferences normally comprise a meeting, chaired by an independent, trained, youth conference facilitator, attended by the youth, parents or guardians, victims, if they agree to attend, and a police officer. Conferences are not intended for use in minor matters, which are normally dealt with by way of warnings or police cautions, and are either diversionary or court ordered. In either case the young offender must have either admitted the offence or pleaded guilty in court. The courts must refer all young offenders for youth conferences except those pleading guilty to offences liable to a mandatory life sentence. This means, in effect, that restorative conferencing is in Northern Ireland the first youth justice measure for all young offenders except those who have committed a small number of very serious offences.

By 2010 there were within the United Kingdom three distinctively different youth justice systems exhibiting, to different degrees, all of the youth justice paradigms which McAra (2010) has distinguished. Northern Ireland was giving primacy to a restorative approach set against a traditional just deserts court arrangement. Scotland retained a welfarist emphasis, though that approach was showing some signs of convergence with the more managerialist/actuarial and just deserts framework south of the border. And in England and Wales there were awakening signs of interest in the Scottish and Northern Irish arrangements. It is to the immediate background to that awakening of interest to which we now turn.

## NEW LABOUR'S 'NEW YOUTH JUSTICE'

The key elements of the new system after the 1998 Act comprised: the establishment of the Youth Justice Board (YJB), the creation of local authority youth offending teams (YOTs), and the restructuring of the non-custodial penalties available to the youth court. The principal aim of the system was 'to prevent offending by children and young persons' (section 37) by:

- having a clear preventive strategy;
- making offenders, and their parents, face up to their offending behaviour and take responsibility for it;

- earlier, more effective intervention when young people first offend;
- faster, more efficient procedures from arrest to sentence;
- and a partnership between all youth justice agencies to deliver more effective interventions.

New Labour sought, as in so many aspects of its social policy, to impose order from the centre. Labour's former chief advisor on youth justice and the principal author of the 1996 Audit Commission report were installed as Chairman and Chief Executive respectively of the YJB, whose principal functions were to establish appropriate performance measures, monitor the operation of the youth justice system in the light of national standards, conduct research, promulgate good practice, and advise ministers. These functions were subsequently expanded in 2000 to include the commissioning of all custodial provision for under 18-year-olds.

The YOTs were not to be directed by the YJB. They were and still are appointed by their local authorities and accountable to them. But the YJB oversaw their performance and though the bulk of YOT funding (currently 81 per cent: Ministry of Justice 2010c: Table A2) came from contributing local services, the 'advice' over standards and performance issued by the YJB was given and received in a directive manner fully justifying the appellation 'systematic managerialism' (Bottoms 1995; for a study of the cultural changes that YOT formation involved see Souhami 2007).

The YOTs were the most significant innovation in the new system. Whereas youth justice teams prior to 1998 comprised mainly social workers, YOTs had to include representatives of both criminal justice and welfare agencies—social services, the police, probation, education, and health. Whether local authorities cooperated to form a joint YOT, or provided their own, was a matter for them with the result that arrangements have varied from one area to another and to some extent shifted over time. There are currently 156 YOTs in England and Wales with great variation between them in size, composition, funding (there is no funding formulae), and line management arrangements (see Audit Commission 2004).

The original constitution of YOTs mirrored the Multi-Agency Diversion Panels of the 1980s (particularly the Northampton Diversion Scheme, which was given a good press by the Audit Commission). However, their composition and functions differed. First, whereas the majority of YOT staff were originally seconded by the contributing agencies, over time most became permanent YOT workers. As a result YOTs have arguably become silos in their own right rather than the multi-agency teams originally intended, something which the Audit Commission (2004) recommended should be reversed. Secondly, unlike the Diversion Panels, YOTs were charged with targeting and intervening rather than diverting.

The result is that local authority youth justice plans are heavily influenced by the performance framework developed by the YJB. This, in turn, has reflected the performance framework developed initially by the Home Office and, following its creation in 2007, the Ministry of Justice, which provides the bulk of the YJB's budget. From 1997–2010 the ostensibly devolved youth justice system was locked into New Labour's increasingly rigorous performance and reporting framework at the apex of which was the cross-ministry National Criminal Justice Board meeting monthly to review performance against an elaborate set of targets.

New Labour promised increased, and earlier, interventions in the lives of young offenders and those 'at risk' of becoming young offenders. The Crime and Disorder Act scrapped the caution (informal and formal) and replaced it with a reprimand (for less serious offences) and a final warning which, excepting a substantial lapse of time, could be used only once. There was introduced, therefore, a high degree of automaticity: it was to be 'two strikes' and, no matter how minor the subsequent offence, 'you're out' or, rather, into court. Further, all young offenders receiving a final warning were to be referred to the YOT with a view to assessment and participation in a rehabilitation programme (in which reparation was expected generally to be present). This provision opened up the possibility of restorative justice, repairing the harm done to victims and in some cases bringing offenders and victims together. Other measures were designed to prevent up-tariff responses both upstream and downstream of reprimands and final warnings. Responding to research evidence highlighting the link between early and frequent offending and later, extended criminal careers, the YJB developed several early prevention schemes.

- Youth Inclusion and Support Panels (YISPs) to work with 8–13-year-olds identified as at risk of offending, the aim being to support the young people and their families in accessing mainstream services.

- Youth Inclusion Programmes (YIPs) which aim to engage through positive activities and improved access to mainstream services the 50 young people in an area who the key agencies identify as most at risk of offending.

- Parenting programmes, mostly voluntary, often as an adjunct to YISPs and YIPs, but in a minority of cases through Parenting Contracts or Parenting Orders (section 8 of the 1998 Act).

- Safer Schools Partnerships (SSPs) in which police officers are more or less intensively attached to schools with a view to reducing crime and victimization, making the school and its environment safer and reducing truancy and exclusions.

These initiatives, none of which were without controversy on the grounds that they represented an expansion of the criminal justice orbit and risked stigmatizing environments, children, and their families with potentially net-widening consequences, grew rapidly in number. By 2010 most YOTs had a number of early prevention schemes, some of them contracted out to voluntary sector providers.

Alongside these early preventive, risk-based initiatives New Labour firmly emphasized the responsibility of young children for their offending behaviour and developed a controversial menu of anti-social behaviour (ASB) initiatives which, initially in many parts of the country at least, sat outside the multi-agency YOT structures.

Prior to 1988 English law made a distinction between children aged 10–13 and those aged 14–17. The former were subject to the *doli incapax* rule, the rebuttable common law presumption that young children do not know the difference between right and wrong and therefore cannot be convicted. This provision was removed on the grounds, as Home Secretary Jack Straw argued at the time, that: 'The presumption that children aged 10 to 13 do not know the difference between serious wrongdoing and simple naughtiness flies in the face of common-sense and is long overdue for reform'. Thus 20 years after the Children and Young Persons Act had provided for the minimum age of criminal responsibility to be raised to 14, New Labour moved the system in the opposite direction.

In Opposition New Labour had been much influenced by the 'Broken Windows' thesis (Wilson and Kelling 1982; see Bottoms and Newburn and Reiner, this volume) and now introduced a range of measures where there was no necessity for there to be the commission of a criminal offence but enabling local agencies to tackle 'low-level disorder'. Most controversial was the anti-social behaviour order (ASBO) designed to combat behaviour 'likely to cause harassment, alarm or distress to one or more persons not of the same household'.

ASBOs are civil orders lasting a minimum of two years, breach of which is a criminal offence carrying a maximum sentence, in the Crown Court, of five years. The order can be applied for by persons other than the police (and the Anti-Social Behaviour Act 2003 extended that list of persons), most local authorities early established ASB units, and there was no statutory obligation on applicants for ASBOs with respect to juveniles to consult with or inform the YOT. As such ASBOs potentially lay outside the newly coordinated, multi-agency youth justice system and in many local authorities lay outside it in practice. This was not a huge problem initially because there was widespread reluctance to use the controversial new powers. But in 2003 the ASBO policy was given high-profile political impetus by, *inter alia*, setting up a unit within the Home Office (ASBU, later re-titled the 'Respect' Unit) which encouraged use of the new powers, including those enabling courts to impose ASBOs post-conviction for a criminal offence (known colloquially as CRASBOs) The number of ASBOs imposed, including those on children, increased dramatically despite pointed international and domestic criticism (European Commissioner for Human Rights 2005: paras 109–11; see also Simester and Von Hirsch 2006; Millie *et al.* 2005).

Serious concerns were by now being expressed regarding the impact of ASBOs on children and young people. The minimum order was so long and the number of prohibitions imposed so often excessive, that breach was made likely. Despite guidance being issued emphasizing the desirability of full consultation with the relevant YOT prior to an order being sought (YJB/ACPO/Home Office 2005), there was evidence that in some parts of the country the YOTs, and thus the partnership spirit of the 1998 reforms, were effectively being circumvented, not least because ASBO applications were normally heard in adult courts not covered by YOT representatives. This was arguably disproportionate because in some areas ASBOs were being sought and granted without the recommended lower tier measures (home visits, warnings letters, and acceptable behaviour contracts (ABCs)) first being tried. Finally ASBOs, following breach, were dragging into custody some young people who would not previously have got there or, possibly more commonly, were providing an evidential short cut for the police to fast track persistent young offenders into custody (Home Affairs Committee 2005). These criticisms led to the introduction, at the end of 2005 and early 2006, of ASBO reviews after 12 months and a practice direction that ASBO applications relating to juveniles be heard, whenever possible, by youth court magistrates.

New Labour also advanced the Conservatives' custodial plans. The secure training centre (STC) building programme continued and a new, generic custodial sentence, the Detention and Training Order (DTO), was introduced. DTOs are from 6 to 24 months, half the sentence being served in custody and half in the community.

They replace the Secure Training Order (for 12–14-year-olds) and detention in a YOI (for 15–17-year-olds). DTOs, available to the youth court, sit alongside existing provisions whereby grave offences, in the case of murder, mandatorily, are committed to the Crown Court and liable to 'long-term detention' (to distinguish the sentence from a DTO), the sentence maxima being the same for adults. After the Criminal Justice Act 2003 young offenders also became liable for indeterminate sentences for public protection (IPPs) and by the end of 2007 51 boys under 18 were serving such sentences (HMI Prisons/HMI Probation 2008: para. 6.3).

The DTO represented an increase in the powers of the youth court to impose custodial sentences. The maximum period of detention in a YOI for 15–17-year-olds had been six months for a single offence: the DTO has a maximum of two years. Further, though the STO for 12–14-year-olds already provided for a two year maximum, New Labour replaced the strict criteria for offenders under 15 relating to 'persistence' with the provision that the sentence be available where the court 'is of the *opinion* that he is a persistent offender'. The courts, including the Court of Appeal, interpreted this power rather broadly.

Though New Labour relaxed the criteria for use of custody it also increased the scope for reparation and restorative justice. The most important of the new provisions embodying this vision was the referral order, the mandatory sentence in the youth court for 10–17-year-olds convicted for the first time for an imprisonable offence, unless the offence is serious enough to warrant custody or so minor that an absolute discharge will suffice. Referral orders may be for three to twelve months. They involve referring the young offender to a youth offender panel (YOP) the design of which draws on the Scottish hearings system, family group conferencing, and victim offender mediation. Panels comprise one YOT member and at least two community panel members, one of whom leads the panel. Parents are expected to attend all panel meetings and it is not intended that legal representatives participate. To encourage the restorative aspect victims may be encouraged voluntarily to attend, the aim being to devise a 'contract' making good whatever harm has been done.

## 'NEW YOUTH JUSTICE' 2007–10: THE RECORD

Assessing the effectiveness of New Labour's 'new youth justice' policy is complex. In what follows we consider the youth justice record from different angles, beginning with two recent, important overview statements, the first from the incoming Coalition Government and the second from an independent commission.

The Coalition announced their general plans for criminal justice in a Green Paper late in 2010. One brief chapter concerned youth justice. It was conceded that:

> some progress had been made in recent years. Both the number of young people entering the system and the number of young people in custody have reduced. Yet this progress sits alongside an unacceptably high level of re-offending. 75% of young people released from custody and 68% of young people on community sentences reoffend within a year (Ministry of Justice 2010a: 67).

This judgement echoed that from an independent commission reporting in summer 2010. Though there had been a reduction in the number of children prosecuted and sent to custody, it was pointed out that this had been in the preceding 18 months only and the returns from the youth justice system generally:

> in terms of crime prevention, reduced reoffending and helping children to deal with the issues that lead them into criminal behaviour remain unimpressive (Independent Commission 2010: 25).

Already, in these two summary judgements, a number of different tests are referred to. Let us take each of them in turn.

### The number of children and young people criminally sanctioned

Table 17.3 shows the number of children and young people sanctioned as a result of pre-court decisions or following a finding of guilt in court. There is no evidence that the trend it describes reflects shifts in the overall incidence of youth crime which, as we have seen, all the evidence suggests has changed very little in recent years. On the contrary the pattern since the Crime and Disorder Act provisions came into force suggest strongly that the number of young people dealt with by the system has had more to do with political and managerial initiatives affecting how the system reacts to children and young people.

Apart from the marked decline in 2008–9 the number of children brought before the courts changed very little over the 10-year period. The spike in overall numbers sanctioned from 2004–7 was attributable almost entirely to the introduction in 2003 of penalty notices for disorder (in effect, on-the-spot fines  see Padfield, Morgan, and Maguire, this volume) for 16–17-year-olds combined with increased use of the traditional out-of-court sanction, the caution, now named either a reprimand or a final warning. In 2008–9 there was a marked drop-off in the use of all types of formal sanctions. To what was this very considerable expansion and then contraction attributable? The answer is simple. It was almost wholly the result of the Government setting national targets for offences brought to justice (OBTJs) to which both PNDs and police

Table 17.3 Children and young people sanctioned pre-court or found guilty in court 1999–2009

|  | PNDs | Reprimands & Final Warnings | Findings of Guilt | Total |
| --- | --- | --- | --- | --- |
| 1999 | - | 104,000 | 90,000 | 194,000 |
| 2000 | - | 97,600 | 91,000 | 188,600 |
| 2001 | - | 98,100 | 96,000 | 194,100 |
| 2002 | - | 86,500 | 95,000 | 181,500 |
| 2003 | 600* | 91,900 | 93,000 | 185,500 |
| 2004 | 3000* | 105,000 | 97,000 | 205,000 |
| 2005 | 12,500 | 118,900 | 97,000 | 228,400 |
| 2006 | 19,600 | 129,100 | 92,000 | 240,700 |
| 2007 | 19,200 | 127,300 | 97,400 | 243,900 |
| 2008 | 14,500 | 98,100 | 86,000 | 198,600 |
| 2009 | 11,700 | 78,700 | 81,500 | 171,900 |

Source: Ministry of Justice (2010d: Chapters 3, 4, and 6, including supplementary tables (* = estimated))

cautions contribute: these out-of-court sanctions were heavily used by the police to meet their OBTJ targets, a fact acknowledged by Sir Ronnie Flanagan in his major review of policing. The target had:

> the unintended effect of officers spending time investigating crimes with a view to obtaining a detection, even when that is clearly not in the public interest. An example of such would be a low level playground common assault (Flanagan Report 2008: 10).

This perverse consequence was most marked in relation to minor offences committed by children and young persons, the so-called 'low hanging fruit'. Use of PNDs, reprimands, and final warnings rose most steeply for juveniles, particularly children under 14 years, and when in 2007 the OBTJ target was modified so as to focus now on 'serious, violent, sexual and acquisitive offences', and was finally abandoned altogether in 2010 by the incoming Coalition Government, the fall was steepest for juveniles (see Farrington-Douglas and Durante 2009: 12–14): the police no longer got brownie points for recording minor youth offences and criminalizing youth. Given that the best research evidence suggests that, *ceteris paribus,* criminalizing children is criminogenic—that is, the likelihood of re-offending is increased rather than diminished (see McAra and McVie 2007)—it seems probable that New Labour's managerialist, target-driven, policing policies in the first decade of the twenty-first century exacerbated the problem of youth crime and has left a legacy of adult, career criminality which could have been avoided.

### First-time entrants

The second test of youth justice effectiveness adopted in recent years is reduction in the number of first time entrants to the system (FTEs). This test was the *quid pro quo* demanded by the Treasury in 2004–5 for agreement to allocate additional funds to the YJB for investment through YOTs in early prevention schemes. The rationale was simple. If interventions of various kinds with young children at risk are effective, this should result in fewer children above the minimum age of criminal responsibility committing offences and being drawn into the youth justice system: the youth offender supply tap should partly be closed. The view that early interventions of proven effectiveness represent the most cost-beneficial use of government expenditure in the field of youth justice is now a mantra lent credibility by evidential meta-analyses of a large range of interventions (see Aos *et al.* 2004).

The YJB began collecting FTE data in 2005 and the computed figure of FTEs for 2005–6 became the baseline for the YJB target of a 5 per cent reduction by March 2008 (YJB 2006: 10). Controversy clouded early assessments of outcome, however. The database employed was seriously incomplete. In 2008 the YJB reported that the FTE target had, with a 10 per cent reduction, been greatly exceeded. The burgeoning use of PNDs was excluded, however, on the grounds that PNDs lay outside the formal youth justice system, a nonsensical omission given that the principal rationale for the introduction of PNDs was the *displacement* of low-level offences and offenders from the formal system (Morgan 2009; see Padfield, Morgan, and Maguire, this volume). When PNDs were eventually included and a systematic assessment undertaken based on police national computer (PNC) data going back to 2000/1 the evidence suggested that there had been a literally *breathtaking* reduction in the number of FTEs: down 45 per cent

**Table 17.4** 10–17-year-olds first-time entrants to youth justice system living in England and Wales 2000/1–2009/10

| Number of children receiving.... | 2000/1 | 2001/2 | 2002/3 | 2003/4 | 2004/5 | 2005/6 | 2006/7 | 2007/8 | 2008/9 | 2009/10 |
|---|---|---|---|---|---|---|---|---|---|---|
| reprimand, warning, or conviction | 89,857 | 88,902 | 83,266 | 88,213 | 95,670 | 107,187 | 110,188 | 100,105 | 79,851 | 61,422 |
| PND, reprimand, warning, or conviction | 89,857 | 88,902 | 83,266 | 88,213 | 97,720 | 112,730 | 118,164 | 107,269 | 85,354 | 64,761 |

*Source*: Ministry of Justice (2010e): Table 1. PNDs became available for 16- and 17-year olds in 2004–5.

in 2009–10 from the high point for the criminalization of children in 2006–7, and a 28 per cent reduction since the early days of the youth justice reforms in 2000–1. See Table 17.4.

It is doubtful that these data represent the last word on the FTE test because, as the statistical note attached to the Ministry of Justice statistical bulletin conceded, PNC data are subject to recording delays and inaccuracies. Further, it is far from clear to what extent the reduction in the number of FTEs over the decade is attributable to youth justice early intervention programmes with children above and below the age of 10. The bulk of the decline since 2006/7 is manifestly attributable to the amendment and then removal of the OBTJ target (see above). Aspects of this are illustrated in the FTE data. The biggest increase and fall in the number of children sanctioned during the period 2004/5 to 2008/9 was for 14- and 15-year-old boys, reprimanded, for summary offences (ibid.: Charts 6 to 8). This is clear evidence of 'low hanging fruit': it was almost certainly not in the public interest that many of these children were drawn into the criminal justice system, no matter how apparently innocuous the stain on their record.

The YJB, understandably, attributed the greater than-expected reduction in FTEs to their funding of early intervention initiatives. Then and since the YJB has cited the impact of YIPs, YISPS, parenting programmes, and SSPs. These schemes were said collectively to have prevented 20,448 young people entering the criminal justice system in 2008–9 (see, for e.g., YJB Press Statement of 26 November 2009). This is more than the evidence will bear, a point to which we return below. There is no evidence that the recent reductions in the number of children and young people criminalized reflects change in the criminal behaviour of young people generally and it is unclear to what degree it is a consequence of targeted early interventions with children at risk delivered through YOTs (though see Mackie *et al.* 2008)

### Reduced re-offending

Apart from what can be gleaned from self-report studies (see Maguire, this volume) we only know about re-offending committed by known offenders resulting in convictions. It follows that the target 'reduced re-offending' is a misnomer: the measure, correctly termed, is 'reduced reconvictions.'

Reduced reconvictions, like reduced convictions, may be desirable or undesirable. Desirable if it reflects less offending, signifying that rehabilitation has taken place or deterrence achieved, or, if the re-offending is so minor, that it would be counterproductive to reconvict. Undesirable perhaps if, as New Labour repeatedly claimed, '5% of young people are responsible for over half of all youth crime' (HM Government 2008: 4). The Government was from the outset committed to 'closing the justice gap' (Home Office 2001: para. 28) by 'bringing more offenders to justice', thereby reducing impunity: that was the basis of the OBTJ target. In which case, it might be judged regressive to divert from prosecution any known re-offending behaviour (Morgan 2008: 21).

The historical record of reduced reconvictions under New Labour is complex. High claims have been made which, for various methodological and data deficiency reasons, have subsequently had to be retracted (see Solomon and Garside 2008: 49–52). The estimates of re-offending now being made are, despite the continuing reconviction–reoffending misnomer, more sophisticated than those of a decade ago. Estimates are now made of the *frequency, seriousness, actual*, and *predicted* rates of proven re-offending based on PNC data. The predicted rates allow for changes in offender characteristics over time. The latest evidence (Ministry of Justice 2010f) is encouraging. When offender characteristics are taken into account the proportion of proven offenders re-offending between 2000 and 2008 fell by 7.6 per cent (from 40.2 to 37.3 per cent), though the fact that the drop off was greatest in the last two years, when proactive actions against children fell substantially, suggests that it remains unclear whether *actual re-offending* has reduced significantly. The same doubt, for the same reason, attaches to the 25 per cent reduction in the frequency rate from 151.4 to 113.9 offences per 100 offenders since 2000. On the other hand the fact that serious offences are unlikely to have been greatly affected by reduced police keenness to arrest young people, the 7.3 per cent fall in the number of severe offences per 100 offences is more convincing and thus promising.

What can be said about re-offending rates for offenders sanctioned in different ways?

The relative effectiveness of different sanctions cannot be assessed because, as the Ministry of Justice statisticians put the matter, 'there is no control for known differences in offender characteristics or other factors that may affect both reoffending and the type of sentence given' (ibid.: 18). Not surprisingly the least intrusive sanctions, the out-of-court penalties and referral orders, have by far the lowest re-offending rates and the most intrusive sanctions, the intensive community penalties and custodial sentences, by far the highest. The re-offending rate associated with custody has remained largely the same during the decade (75.7 and 74.3 per cent in 2000 and 2008 respectively) and the rates for the most intensive community orders have got marginally worse, though the frequency of re-offending for both custody and community supervision has decreased (ibid.: Table A5).

## Sanctioning trends

If the evidence suggests that, *ceteris paribus*, criminalization, social exclusion and, in particular, incarceration in penal institutions, is criminogenic, then there is merit in scaling back the use of criminal sanctions, particularly those that are most exclusionary and stigmatizing. What was sanctioning practice under New Labour's new youth justice?

If the data in Tables 1 and 3 are brought together and considered alongside the longer-term trend (see Morgan and Newburn 2007: Fig 30.2), the first point to note is the current low in the total number of sanctions imposed, but the proportionately high use of criminal court proceedings. If all PNDs, reprimands, warnings, and court sentences of 10–17-years-olds are aggregated then in 2009 146,251 children were criminally sanctioned—the lowest *total* since 1997—of whom 56 per cent were sentenced in court—the highest *proportion* since 1997. The trend is clear. The number of children criminally sanctioned rose steadily until 2006, since when it has fallen dramatically (down 31 per cent). But the fall off has been most marked in use of out-of-court sanctions: in 2006 court sentences comprised only 44 per cent of all sanctions, and in the early 1990s the figure was one-third or less. Most children were then dealt with by means of police cautions.

It follows that if parsimony is to be the new youth justice watchword, there has been a welcome retreat from the criminalizing bonanza of New Labour's middle period but, if historic practice is any guide, the retreat could go considerably further. Given that there is now in place more systematic assessment and engagement with child offenders pre-court, there are arguably many children still appearing before the youth court who could have been dealt with out-of-court.

This viewpoint is lent support by analysis of what happens to children brought before the courts. The big change since 1997 has, as Table 17.5 shows, been the significant decline in the use of discharges and fines and their displacement by the referral order, potentially the jewel in the crown in New Labour's youth justice reform panoply. However, the referral order has to date not fulfilled its restorative justice potential. As early assessments and later YJB monitoring data attest, a very small proportion of referral orders result in the active participation of victims and there are big variations in the proportion who do from one YOT to another (Crawford and Newburn 2003; Morgan and Newburn 2007). There is now a case for many offenders being dealt with not post prosecution and conviction by YOTs, but by out-of-court panels, along the lines of Scottish hearings or restorative justice conferences similar to those in use in Northern Ireland. On the grounds that there is overwhelming evidence that restorative justice conferences in which victims participate results in greater victim satisfaction

Table 17.5 Court sentences for all children sentenced in all courts 1998–2009 (%s and totals)

| Sentence | 1998 | 1999 | 2000 | 2001 | 2002 | 2003 | 2004 | 2005 | 2006 | 2007 | 2008 | 2009 |
|---|---|---|---|---|---|---|---|---|---|---|---|---|
| Discharge | 31 | 30 | 25 | 18 | 15 | 15 | 13 | 13 | 13 | 13 | 12 | 12 |
| Fine | 24 | 23 | 23 | 23 | 16 | 15 | 16 | 15 | 12 | 11 | 10 | 10 |
| Referral Order | - | - | 1 | 2 | 20 | 27 | 27 | 31 | 32 | 33 | 33 | 35 |
| Community Sentence | 34 | 34 | 39 | 43 | 37 | 32 | 32 | 32 | 33 | 35 | 35 | 34 |
| Custody | 8 | 8 | 8 | 8 | 8 | 7 | 7 | 6 | 7 | 6 | 6 | 6 |
| Other | 3 | 4 | 4 | 6 | 4 | 4 | 5 | 3 | 3 | 3 | 3 | 3 |
| Total Sentenced | 86294 | 90160 | 91480 | 95485 | 94458 | 92531 | 96188 | 96203 | 93806 | 97387 | 88375 | 81490 |

*Source*: Ministry of Justice (2010g): supplementary tables

and frequency of re-offending reduced (Shapland *et al.* 2008) this is the argument and recommendation of the Independent Commission (2010: ch. 4), which would also like to see court-ordered restorative conferencing take place.

Though, at 34 per cent, the proportion of young offenders dealt with by means of community orders has remained almost constant since 1987, significant changes have taken place within this category. First, in 2009 the Community Punishment Order was replaced, following the Criminal Justice and Immigration Act 2008, by the Youth Rehabilitation Order (YRO). This provides the court with no fewer than 18 requirements which can be attached to an order, ranging from activity or curfew requirements to intensive fostering or intensive supervision and surveillance (ISSP). The latter requirement is the legacy of ISSPs introduced by the YJB in 2001 as an alternative to custody. ISSP has independently been evaluated (Moore *et al.* 2004; Gray *et al.* 2005) the principal findings being that:

- ISSP was being targeted at relatively serious and persistent offenders (burglary and robbery being the most common index offences, with on average 12 offences in the preceding two years);
- a high proportion of the offenders would likely have received a custodial sentence had ISSP not been an option (though it was conceded that there has been some net-widening effect);
- though the headline two-year reconviction rate of 91 per cent was very high, the rate for offenders with as many pre-convictions released from custodial sentences was at 95 per cent higher still;
- the frequency of re-offending was down by 40 per cent and the seriousness of those further offences down 13 per cent;
- there was substantial engagement in education and other positive activities with offenders' multiple practical problems being addressed;
- however, a comparison group of offenders eligible for ISSP but not receiving it (refused bail, placed on a community order, or sentenced to a DTO) did just as well in terms of re-offending.

The latter finding led some critics (Green 2004) to suggest that investment in ISSPs was not worthwhile. It seems more likely, however, that the intensity of ISSP surveillance means that the further offences of the young people involved are more likely to be detected. Further, though the introduction of ISSP did not lead to reduction in the use of custody in the areas where it was available, the fact that ISSP has been targeted at offenders at high risk of custody, and that sentencers reportedly have confidence in the programme, makes it likely that the proportionate use of custody would have been greater had it not been for the existence of ISSP. The availability of ISSP is probably contributing to the reduced use of custody.

The introduction of the YRO was accompanied by the rolling out of what the YJB termed 'the scaled approach' (YJB 2009). This mirrors Probation Service practice and involves use of the YJB's long-standing assessment tool, ASSET, to combine four static and 12 dynamic risk factors scaled so as to produce an aggregate score, for which the maximum number of points is 64, for each offender, scores which are then banded so as to produce an indicative supervision level and type. The managerial principle being honoured is one of risk-supervision proportionality.

The 'scaled approach' is the YJB's response to the Audit Commission's critique that most young offenders were in 2003 getting no more face-to-face supervision, an average of roughly an hour a week, than was the case when the Commission reviewed the youth justice system in 1996 (Audit Commission 2004: 4). The risk with a scaled approach is that it is overly bureaucratic and mechanistic (Case and Haines 2009), that it will serve to ratchet up overall levels of intervention and bear most heavily on vulnerable young offenders least able to comply with multiple requirements (Morgan 2009b), and, because it focuses on future risk rather than past deeds, it conflicts with the general principle of proportionality in sentencing (Graham 2010).

## Children in custody

The most controversial sanction available for children, however, is custody, use of which had by the end of New Labour's third administration fallen both proportionately and absolutely, but which nevertheless still stood substantially higher in 2010 than had been the case 20 years previously and remained the highest in Western Europe. In 2007 one of us, Rod Morgan, then Chairman of the YJB, resigned over the punitive trend and though, shortly thereafter, the Board abandoned its previous target to reduce the custodial population, numbers have since come down considerably from over 3,000 in 2007/8 to less than 2,000 in early summer 2011. This despite the continuing rise in the adult prison population and the fact that the tri-ministerial *Youth Crime Action Plan* (HM Government 2008) continued to emphasize the language of 'punishment' and 'enforcement' rather than 'welfare' (Graham 2010). The unsustainably high costs of custody—the Independent Commission (2010: 24) calculated that in 2008/9 more was being spent on keeping 3,000 young offenders in custody than the total budget for YOTs dealing with 127,197 offenders—and the depressingly high re-offending outcome, which despite the generally acknowledged improvement in custodial conditions showed no real sign of improving, led successful, behind-the-scenes reductive initiatives to be taken. The penal and children's pressure groups published highly critical reports regarding the high use of custody: for very young children who have not committed grave crimes (Glover and Hibbert 2009); for children on remand (Gibbs and Hickson 2009); who have learning difficulties (Talbot 2010); or have multiple disadvantages (Jacobson et al. 2010). These followed reports on the high reliance on physical restraint within custodial institutions (Carlile Report 2006) and the repeated deaths of children in custody (Coles and Goldson 2005).

This welter of criticism and the suggestion that part or all of the costs of child custody might be transferred from central government, in the shape of the YJB, to the local authorities (HM Government 2008: para 5.7; New Economics Foundation 2010) galvanized several high custody local authority areas and their YOTs to take up the offer of a Prison Reform Trust consultancy to analyse decision-making locally. The result, in combination with overall shrinkage in the number of children being drawn into the youth justice system generally (see Allen 2011), has been a dramatic fall in custody rates in some localities, contributing to the significant fall nationally.

## Social equality, human rights, and public confidence

No youth justice system should be judged solely in terms of managerial targets. How well did New Labour's reformed youth justice system perform in terms of other criteria?

Somewhat surprisingly, given the importance attached by the Government to confidence in the police, public confidence in youth justice was never the specified objective of the Home Office, Ministry of Justice, or the YJB. Nor is there good recent survey evidence on the issue. However, it is unlikely that matters have improved much since Hough and Roberts' (2004) data. Most people over-estimate the proportion of crime committed by youth and know less about the youth justice system than any other branch of criminal justice. Furthermore, the overwhelming majority think youth justice is doing a poor job and most people, despite their ignorance, think the system too soft. In fact, as is generally the case, when people are presented with scenario offence and offender cases and asked what intervention or sentence would be appropriate, they are much more supportive of existing practice and less punitive practices than these initial reactions suggest (see Hough and Roberts, this volume). But regrettably New Labour tended generally to stress the 'tough on crime' rather than the 'tough on the causes of crime' aspect of their policy slogan. Little political leadership was provided or educational effort invested in a more welfare-oriented approach. The result, as we have seen, is that more young and multiply-disadvantaged children were drawn into the system. The evidence of this has repeatedly been summarized and it would be redundant do so again here. Suffice it to say that criminalized, and particularly incarcerated, children are typically drawn from the most deprived families and communities in the country and have normally several educational and health deficits (see Morgan and Newburn 2007; Morgan 2009c: 68–70).

The increase in the number of girls, including young girls, being drawn into the system has been greater than for boys despite there being no evidence of the self-reported rates of girls' offending increasing (Phillips and Chamberlain 2006). In 1990, the number of girls in custody was so small that the Government seriously considered abolition of secure custody for all girls other than those convicted of grave crimes. In 2009, 381 girls were given sentences of immediate custody, the first year since 1987 that the number fell below 400: in two of those preceding years the figure rose above 500.

The evidence suggests that ethnic minority young offenders have always been over-represented in the new youth justice system, as are adults in the criminal justice system generally (see Phillips and Bowling, this volume). This aspect of youth justice was commented on critically by the Audit Commission (2004: para 73) and in 2005, following an in-depth study (Feilzer and Hood 2004), the YJB responded by requiring all YOTs to audit their practice and develop action plans to improve equal treatment (YJB 2005: 8). According to the most recent statistics, 14 per cent of all the children and young people drawn into the system and whose ethnicity was recorded were from the minority ethnic or mixed race groups, of whom just under half were black (Ministry of Justice 2010c: Table 1.3). Both the House of Commons Home Affairs Committee (2007) and government (HM Government 2008) have expressed concerns about this over-representation which the evidence suggests is the product of discrimination in policing and each subsequent stage in the criminal justice process, but the phenomenon has not so far diminished.

As far as respect for human rights is concerned the English youth justice system has attracted severe criticism from international human rights bodies. In addition to the adverse results from the UNICEF (2007) survey of child well-being in Britain, the ages of criminal responsibility in the UK are among the lowest in the world and are regarded as unacceptably low by the corpus of United Nations bodies whose rules and guidance relating to children suggest 12 years is the absolute minimum (Cipriani 2009). The European Court of Human Rights was critical of the fact that the young killers of James Bulger were tried in the Crown rather than the youth court thereby making it difficult for the defendants to participate in the proceedings. Though this matter was subsequently considered by the Auld review of the criminal courts, which recommended that in future all juvenile cases be dealt with in the youth court (Auld 2001: paras 207–11; a recommendation recently endorsed by the Independent Commission (2010)), the recommendation was not acted on. The high use of arrest and custody under New Labour scarcely accords with our international obligation to ensure that both powers are 'used only as a measure of last resort and for the shortest appropriate period of time' (UN Convention on the Rights of the Child 1989, Article 37(b)). The British member of the Council of Europe Working Party which devised the European Rules for Juvenile Offenders Subject to Sanctions or Measures 2008 has opined that our compliance is 'sorely lacking' (Graham 2010: 133). Finally the use of ASBOs for children was excoriated by the European Commissioner for Human Rights in 2005 (paras 109–11). Our youth justice system is not regarded internationally as a beacon of civilization: quite the contrary.

## CONCLUSION: FUTURE PROSPECTS

Youth culture and crime is volatile terrain, as is the youth justice system which responds to it. Following New Labour's 1998 youth justice reforms there was no legislative stability but constant amendment of police powers, court sentencing options, and youth justice practice. No fewer than 27 criminal justice statutes were passed during the 1990s (Ministry of Justice 2010a: para 165) many of them affecting youth justice. This constant change suggests that there is never a good time to review and explain the system and summer 2011 seems a particularly unpropitious time at which to consider the future. The incoming Coalition Government has announced dramatic public spending cuts (HM Treasury 2010) which threaten central and local government spending on the full range of child-related services, including the YOTs and the voluntary sector services with whom they work in partnership. There is huge uncertainty among practitioners. According to the Coalition's criminal justice Green Paper, the YJB is to be abolished and its functions taken over by a Youth Justice Division within the Ministry of Justice led by the former YJB chief executive (Ministry of Justice 2011: paras 34–5), though at the time of writing there remains uncertainty as to whether this change will be implemented. The pause for thought has been prompted by the major disorders of 5–10 August 2011 in which, the evidence suggests, young people, and even some children, took a prominent part (see Downes and Morgan, this volume).

Given that 'localization' of policy is allegedly to be the watchword, meaning an end to 'high level performance monitoring' so beloved by New Labour, and YOTs being given even greater freedom to innovate (ibid.: para 35), the question is being asked as to whether a youth justice sense of direction from the centre will best be delivered by largely anonymous civil servants from within the Ministry of Justice as opposed to the arms-length, specialized YJB.

A series of 'payment by results' pathfinders have been announced, the outcome sought being further reductions in the number of young people in custody (Ministry of Justice 2010a: 72). The context for youth is in similar turmoil. The Coalition Government has announced major structural changes in the organization and funding of the police, the health service, education, and local government all of which will have a bearing on the nature and extent of children's and child-related services. The best that one can do is distil indicators of the likely direction of policy travel all of which suggest both threats and positive opportunities.

There is as yet no real suggestion of a swing of the pendulum towards *welfarism*, away from *punishment* and *just deserts*. The youth court, it would seem, is to remain, as is the age, at 10, of criminal responsibility and custody of the majority of young people in the hands of the Prison Service. Moreover, everything the Coalition Government has so far said about the desirable nature of unpaid work (or 'community payback' as they are keen to brand it) and custodial regimes connotes punitiveness, the 'tough discipline of regular working hours', 'tougher curfews', 'hard work', offenders paying back 'the debt they owe to society' (ibid.: 14–16). Such phrases are of course capable of being operationalized in very different ways, particularly within the context of a genuine 'rehabilitation revolution'. 'Hard work' may suggest sewing mailbags or publicly digging ditches dressed in orange fatigues, but could turn out to be much better resourced education and employment training programmes for young people notably ill-prepared for the labour market. Furthermore, though the Government is keen to ensure that were 'a Bulger case' to reoccur, that grave offenders as young as Thompson and Venables would continue to be prosecuted (Downes and Morgan 2012), they may nonetheless take up the recommendation that children under 12 not be prosecuted except for the gravest of offences (Barnardos 2010) or that all prosecutions be heard in the youth court, in serious cases by senior judges (Independent Commission 2010).

What is clearer is that the Coalition Government wishes to see more parsimonious use made of criminalization for young offenders generally and custody in particular, the manifest imperative being that public expenditure must be reduced, but the proffered justification being that the public would be as well or better protected from youth re-offending were it so and other control measures or lesser criminal justice sanctions used instead. To this end the *restorative* paradigm is preyed in aid as is a move away from the rigidities of *actuarilism*. It is not suggested that the 'scaled approach' be abandoned, but targets mostly have been and greater discretion in decision-making is to be granted to local authorities, the police, youth justice workers, and sentencers (Ministry of Justice 2010a, 2011). These propositions chime well with measures for which most critics have been calling. Less reliance on criminalization, exclusion and punishment, more reliance on prevention (parenting programmes, mentoring, education support, intensive foster care, and so on), more emphasis on restorative justice, and better integration of children in trouble (Independent Commission 2010; Smith 2010b).

The problem is that the same public expenditure cuts which will likely prompt less reliance on unsustainably expensive criminalization and incarceration simultaneously threaten community-based, child-support services, be they provided by the state or the voluntary sector. Though the Government is promoting 'payment by results'— the providers of services being rewarded with bonuses if re-offending or incarceration is reduced (Ministry of Justice 2010a)—it is far from clear whether that approach can be made to work and since there is to be no new money on the table, it is apparent that only a small proportion of any savings made will be transferred from custodial to community services or from the criminal justice to the civil budget. Finally, this difficult transition will be taking place at a time of rising youth unemployment, that is, when the welfare needs of young people in trouble will almost certainly be intensifying. 2011 heralds the beginning of a decade in which there is a real possibility of the Government substantially reversing New Labour's expansionist youth justice programme. Whether that contraction will be sustained in the face of possible social strains and occasional dreadful events—of which the urban riots of early August 2011 were possibly a grim foretaste—remains to be seen. Firm commitment, a clear political nerve, and conspicuous leadership will be required for that to happen.

## ■ SELECTED FURTHER READING

David Garland's *Punishment and Welfare* (1985) is the best history of the emergence of a separate youth justice system in Britain. The 1998 youth justice reforms cannot be fully appreciated without a reading of the two key documents, the Audit Commission's *Misspent Youth* (1996) and New Labour's subsequent White Paper, *No More Excuses* (Home Office 1997), which informed the Crime and Disorder Act 1998. John Muncie's (2009) *Youth and Crime*, 3rd edn (2009) and Roger Smith's (2007) *Youth Justice: Ideas, policy and practice*, 2nd edn are the best general introductions to the recent history of the system. Michael Tonry and Anthony Doob's (2004) edited collection of essays *Youth Crime and Youth Justice*, contains authoritative accounts of juvenile justice provision in Great Britain, Canada, New Zealand, the Netherlands, Denmark, Sweden, and Germany, and provides a useful comparative overview. Finally, the Youth Justice Board website (or the Ministry of Justice, if the YJB is abolished) provides access all the key policy statements regarding youth justice as well as national youth justice statistics.

## ■ REFERENCES

ABRAMS, M. (1959), *The Teenage Consumer*, London: Routledge & Kegan Paul.

ALDRIDGE, J. (2008), 'Decline but no fall? New millennium trends in young people's use of illegal and illicit drugs in Britain', *Health Education*, 108(3): 189–206.

——and MEDINA, J. (2008), 'Youth Gangs in an English City: Social Exclusion, Drugs and Violence', *Final report to the ESRC*, RES-000–23-0615.

ALLEN, R. (2011), *Last resort? Exploring the reduction in child imprisonment 2008–11*, London: Prison Reform Trust.

ANDERSON, S., KINSEY, R., LOADER, I., and SMITH, C. (1994), *Cautionary Tales*, Aldershot: Avebury.

AOS, S., LIEB, R., MAYFIELD, J., MILLER, M., and PENNUCCI, A. (2004), *Benefits and Costs of Prevention and Early Intervention Programs for Youth*, Olympia, WA: Washington State Institute for Public Policy.

ARIES, P. (1973), *Centuries of Childhood*, Harmondsworth: Penguin.

AUDIT COMMISSION (1996), *Misspent Youth: Young people and crime*, London: Audit Commission.

AUDIT COMMISSION (2004) *Youth Justice 2004: A review of the reformed youth justice system*, London: Audit Commission.

AULD REPORT (Lord Justice Auld) (2001), *Review of the Criminal Courts of England and Wales: Report*, London: The Stationery Office.

AYE MAUNG, N. (1995), *Young people, victimisation and the police: British Crime Survey findings on the experiences and attitudes of 12–15 year olds*, Home Office Research Study No. 140, London: HMSO.

BAILEY, V. (1987), *Delinquency and Citizenship: Reclaiming the young offender 1914–1948*, Oxford: Clarendon Press.

BARKER, P. and LITTLE, A. (1964), 'The Margate offenders—a survey', *New Society*, 4(96): 6–10.

BARNARDOS (2010), *From Playground to Prison: the case for reviewing the age of criminal responsibility*, London: Barnardos.

BECKER, J. and ROE, S. (2005), *Drug use among vulnerable groups of young people: Findings from the 2003 Crime and Justice Survey*, London: Home Office.

BENNETT, T. (2000), *Drugs and Crime: The results of the second developmental stage of the NEW-ADAM programme*, Home Office Research Study No. 205, London: Home Office.

BENNETT, T. and HOLLOWAY, K. (2004), 'Gang membership, drugs and crime in the UK', *British Journal of Criminology*, 44.

BOOTH, C. (1902), *Life and Labour of the People of London*, London: Macmillan.

BOTTOMS, A. E. (1995), 'The philosophy and politics of punishment and sentencing', in Clarkson, C. M. V. and Morgan, R. (eds), *The Politics of Sentencing Reform*, Oxford: Oxford University Press.

—— and STEVENSON, S. (1992), 'What went wrong? Criminal justice policy in England and Wales 1945–1970', in D. Downes (ed.), *Unravelling Criminal Justice*, Basingstoke: Macmillan.

BUDD, T., SHARP, C., WEIR, G., WILSON, D., and OWEN, N. (2005b), *Young People and Crime: Findings from the 2004 Offending, Crime and Justice Survey*, Home Office Statistical Bulletin 20/05, London: Home Office.

BURMAN, M., JOHNSTONE, J., FRASER, A., and MCNEILL, F. (2010), 'Scotland', in F. Dunkel *et al.* (eds), *Juvenile Justice Systems in Europe: Current Situation and Reform Developments*, Mönchengladbach, Germany: Forum Verlag Godesberg.

CARLILE REPORT (Lord Carlile of Berriew) (2006), *The Carlile Inquiry: An Independent Inquiry into the Use of Physical Restraint, Solitary Confinement and Forcible Strip Searching of Children in prisons, Secure Training Centres and Local Authority Secure Children's Homes*, London: Howard League.

CASE, S. and HAINES, K. (2009), *Understanding Youth Offending: Risk factor research, policy and practice*, Cullompton: Willan.

CASHMORE, E. (1983), *Rastaman,* London: Allen and Unwin.

CIPRIANI, D. (2009), *Children's Rights and the Minimum Age of Criminal Responsibility: A Global Perspective*, Farnham: Ashgate.

CLARKE, J. (1976a), 'The skinheads and the magical recovery of community', in S. Hall and T. Jefferson (eds), *Resistance Through Rituals*, London: Hutchison.

—— (1976b), 'Style', in S. Hall and T. Jefferson (eds), *Resistance Through Rituals*, London: Hutchison.

COHEN, P. (1972), 'Subcultural conflict and working class community', in S. Hall *et al.* (eds), *Culture, Media, Language*, London: Hutchison.

COHEN, S. (1980), *Folk Devils and Moral Panics*, London: Martin Robertson.

COLEMAN, J. and HENDRY, L. (1990), *The Nature of Adolescence,* London: Routledge.

COLES, D. and GOLDSON D. (2005), *In the Care of the State? Child Deaths in Penal Custody*, London: Inquest.

CRAWFORD, A. and NEWBURN, T. (2003), *Youth Offending and Restorative Justice: Implementing reform in youth justice,* Cullompton: Willan.

DAVIES, A. (1998), 'Youth gangs, masculinity and violence in late Victorian Manchester and Salford', *Journal of Social History*, 32(2):349–369.

DAVIS, J. (1990), *Youth and the Condition of Britain*, London: Athlone Press.

DEEHAN, A., MARSHALL, E., and SAVILLE, E. (2002), *Drunks and disorder: a description of alcohol-related crime and disorder in two late night city centres*, London: Home Office.

DORN, N. and SOUTH, N. (1982), 'Of males and markets: A critical review of youth culture theory', *Research Paper 1, Centre for Occupational and Community Research*, London: Middlesex Polytechnic.

—— and —— (eds) (1987), *A Land Fit for Heroin? Drug policies, prevention and practice*, Basingstoke: Macmillan.

DOWNES, D. (1966), *The Delinquent Solution*, London: Routledge & Kegan Paul.

—— and MORGAN, R. (2002), 'The skeletons in the cupboard: the politics of law and order at the turn of the millennium', in M. Maguire, R. Morgan, and R. Reiner (eds), *The Oxford Handbook of Criminology*, Oxford: Oxford University Press.

and MORGAN R. (2012), 'Waiting for Ingleby? The minimum age of criminal responsibility: a red line issue?,' in T. Newburn and J. Peay (eds), *Policing: Politics, Culture and Control. Essays in Honour of Robert Reiner*, Oxford: Hart.

—— and ROCK, P. (1982), *Understanding Deviance*, Oxford: Oxford University Press.

EUROPEAN COMMISSIONER FOR HUMAN RIGHTS (2005), *Report by Mr Alvaro Gil-Robles, Commissioner for Human Rights, on his Visit to the United Kingdom 4–12 November 2004*, Strasbourg: Council of Europe.

FARRINGTON, D. and WEST, D. J. (1993), 'Criminal, penal and life histories of chronic offenders: Risk and protective factors and early identification', *Criminal Behaviour and Mental Health*, 3, 492–523.

FARRINGTON-DOUGLAS, J. and DURANTE, L. (2009), *Towards a Popular Preventative Youth Justice System*, London: IPPR.

FEILZER, M. and HOOD, R. (2005), *Differences or Discrimination: Minority Ethnic Young People in the Youth Justice System*, London: Youth Justice Board.

FLANAGAN REPORT (2008), *The Review of Policing by Sir Ronnie Flanagan: Final Report*, London: HMIC.

FLOOD-PAGE, C., CAMPBELL, S., HARRINGTON, V., and MILLER, J. (2000), *Youth Crime: Findings from the 1998/99 Youth Lifestyles Survey*, Home Office Research Study No. 209, London: Home Office.

FULLER, E. (ed.) (2008), *Drug use, smoking and drinking among young people in England in 2007*, National Centre for Social Research, National Foundation for Educational Research

FURLONG, A. and CARTMEL, F. (1997), *Young People and Social Change*, Buckingham: Open University Press.

GARLAND, D. (1985), *Punishment and Welfare*, Aldershot: Gower.

GIBBS, P. And HICKSON, S. (2009), *Children: Innocent until proven guilty. A report on the overuse of remand for children in England and Wales and how it can be addressed*, London: Prison Reform Trust.

GILL, O. (1977), *Luke Street: Housing policy, conflict and the creation of the delinquent area*, London: Macmillan.

GILROY, P. (1987), *There Ain't No Black in the Union Jack*, London: Hutchinson.

—— and LAWRENCE, P. (1988), 'Two tone Britain: white and black youth and the politics of anti-racism', in P. Cohen and H. S. Bains (eds), *Multi-Racist Britain*, London: Macmillan.

GLOVER, J. and HIBBERT, P. (2009), *Locking up or giving up? Why custody thresholds for teenagers aged 12, 13 and 14 need to be raised. An analysis of the cases of 214 children sentenced to custody in England in 2007–8*, London: Barnardos.

GOLDSON, B. (ed.) (2000), *The New Youth Justice*, Lyme Regis: Russell House.

GOULDEN, C. and SONDHI, A. (2001), *At the margins: drug use by vulnerable young people in the 1998/99 Youth Lifestyles Survey*, Home Office Research Study No. 228, London: Home Office.

GRAHAM, J. (2010), 'Responding to youth crime', in D. J. Smith (ed.), *A New Response to Youth Crime*, Cullompton: Willan.

—— and BOWLING, B. (1995), *Young People and Crime*, London: Home Office.

GRAY, E., TAYLOR, E., ROBERTS, C., MERRINGTON, S., FERNANDEZ, R., and MOORE R. (2005), *ISSP: The Final Report*, London: YJB.

GREEN, D. (2004), *The Intensive Supervision and Surveillance Programme*, London: Civitas.

HALL, S., CRITCHER, C., JEFFERSON, T., CLARKE, J., and ROBERTS, B. (1978), *Policing the Crisis. Mugging, the State and Law and Order*, London: Macmillan.

HALLSWORTH, S. and SILVERSTONE, D. (2009), ' "That's life innit": A British perspective on guns, crime and social order', *Criminology and Criminal Justice*, 9(3): 359–377.

HAMMERSLEY, R., MARSLAND, L., and REID, M. (2003), *Substance use by young offenders: the impact of the normalization of drug use in the early years of the 21st century*, London: Home Office.

HARRINGTON, V. (2000), *Underage drinking: Findings from the 1998–99 Youth Lifestyles Survey*, London: Home Office.

HARTLESS, J., DITTON, J., NAIR, G., and PHILLIPS, S. (1995), 'More sinned against than sinning: A study of young teenagers' experiences of crime', *British Journal of Criminology*, 35(1): 114–33.

HEBDIGE, D. (1976), 'The Meaning of Mod', in S. Hall and T. Jefferson (eds), *Resistance Through Rituals*, London: Hutchison.

—— (1979), *Subculture: The meaning of style*, London: Methuen.

—— (1987), *Cut 'n' Mix. Culture, Identity and Caribbean Music*, London: Routledge.

HIRSCHI, T. and GOTTREDSON, M. (1983), 'Age and the explanation of crime', *American Journal of Sociology*, 89: 552–84.

HM GOVERNMENT (2008), *Youth Crime Action Plan 2008*, London: HM Government

HMI PRISONS/HMI PROBATION (2008), *The Indeterminate Sentence for Public Protection: a thematic review*: London. HMI Prisons/HMI Probation.

HOARE, J. and MOON, D. (eds) (2010), *Drug Use Declared: Findings from the 2009/10 British Crime Survey*, London: Home Office.

——, PARFREMENT-HOPKINS, J., BRITTON, A., HALL, P., SCRIBBINS, M., and FLATLEY, J. (2011), *Children's experience and attitudes towards the police, personal safety and public spaces: Findings from the 2009/10 British Crime Survey interviews with children aged 10–15*, Statistical Bulletin 8/11, London: Home Office.

HOME AFFAIRS COMMITTEE (2005), *Anti-Social Behaviour*, Fifth Report, London: Stationery Office.

HOME OFFICE (1988), *Punishment, Custody and the Community*, Cm 424, London: HMSO.

—— (1997a), *No More Excuses—A New Approach to Tackling Youth Crime in England and Wales*, Cm 3809, London: Home Office.

—— (1997b), *Tackling Youth Crime*, London: Home Office.

—— (2001), *Criminal Justice: The Way Ahead*, Cm. 5074, London: HMSO.

HOUGH, M. and ROBERTS, J. (2004), *Youth Crime and Youth Justice. Public Opinion in England and Wales*, Bristol: Policy Press.

HOUSE OF COMMONS HOME AFFAIRS COMMITTEE (2007), *Young Black People and the Criminal Justice System*, Second Report of Session 2006–7, London: The Stationery Office.

HUIZINGA, D., LOEBER, R., and THORNBERRY, T. (1995), *Recent Findings from the Program on the Causes and Correlates of Delinquency*, Report to the Office of Juvenile Justice and Delinquency Prevention, Washington DC.

HUMPHRIES, S. (1981), *Hooligans or Rebels? An oral history of working class childhood and youth, 1889–1939*, Oxford: Basil Blackwell.

INDEPENDENT COMMISSION (2010), *Time for a fresh start: The report of the Independent Commission on Youth Crime and Antisocial Behaviour*, London: Police Foundation/Nuffield Foundation.

JACOBSON, J., BHARDWA, B., GYATENG, T., HUNTER, G., and HOUGH, M. (2010), *Punishing Disadvantage: a profile of children in custody*, London: Prison Reform Trust.

LANDAU, S. and NATHAN, G. (1983), 'Selecting delinquents for cautioning in the London metropolitan area', *British Journal of Criminology*, 23(2): 128–49.

MACKIE, A., HUBBARD, R., and BURROWS, J. (2008), *Evaluation of the Youth Inclusion Programme*, London: Morgan Harris Burrows/YJB.

MARSHALL, B., WEBB, B., and TILLEY, N. (2005), *Rationalisation of Current Research on Guns, Gangs and Other Weapons: Phase 1*, Jill Dando Institute of Crime Science, University College, London.

MCARA, L. (2006), 'Welfare in Crisis? Key developments in Scottish Youth Justice', in J. Muncie and B. Goldson (eds), *Comparative Youth Justice*, London: Sage

—— (2010), 'Models of Youth Justice', in D. J. Smith (ed.), *A New Response to Youth Crime*, Cullompton: Willan.

—— and MCVIE, S. (2007), 'Youth Justice? The Impact of System Contact on Patterns of Desistance from Offending', *European Journal of Criminology*, 4(3): 315–45.

—— and —— (2010), 'Youth Crime and Justice in Scotland', in H Croall, G. Mooney, and M. Munroe (eds), *Criminal Justice in Scotland*, Abingdon: Willan.

MCGALLAGLY, J., POWER, K., LITTLEWOOD, P., and MEIKLE, J. (1998), *Evaluation of the Hamilton Child Safety Initiative*, Crime and Criminal Justice Research Findings No. 24, Edinburgh: Scottish Office.

MCKAY, G. (1996), *Senseless Acts of Beauty: Cultures of resistance since the sixties*, London: Verso.

MCROBBIE, A. (1980), 'Settling accounts with subcultures: A feminist critique', *Screen Education*, 39.

—— (1994), 'A cultural sociology of youth', in A. McRobbie (ed.), *Postmodernism and Popular Culture*, London: Routledge.

MELLY, G. (1972), *Revolt into Style*, Harmondsworth: Penguin.

MILLARD, B. and FLATLEY, J. (eds) (2010), *Experimental Statistics on the Victimization of Children Aged 10–15: Findings from the British Crime Survey for the year ending 2009*, London: Home Office.

MILLER, W. B. (1982), *Crime by Youth Gangs and Groups in the United States*, Washington DC: US Department of Justice.

MILLIE, A., JACOBSON, J., McDONALD, E., and HOUGH, M. (2005), *Anti-social behaviour strategies: finding a balance*, Bristol: Policy Press and Joseph Rowntree Foundation.

MINISTRY OF JUSTICE (2010a), *Breaking the Cycle: Effective Punishment, Rehabilitation and Sentencing of Offenders*, London: TSO.

—— (2010b), *Green Paper Evidence Report: Breaking the Cycle: Effective Punishment, Rehabilitation and Sentencing of Offenders*, London: Ministry of Justice.

—— (2010c), *Youth Justice Annual Workload data 2008/09: England and Wales*, London: Ministry of Justice.

—— (2010d), *Criminal Statistics England and Wales*: Statistics Bulletin, London: Ministry of Justice/National Statistics.

—— (2010e), *Youth Crime: Young people aged 10–17 receiving their first reprimand, warning or conviction 200–1 to 2009–10*, London: Ministry of Justice.

—— (2010f), *Re-offending of Juveniles: Results from the 2008 Cohort*, London: Ministry of Justice.

—— (2010g), *Sentencing Statistics: England and Wales 2009*, London: Ministry of Justice.

—— (2011), *Breaking the Cycle: Government Response*, London: Ministry of Justice.

MOORE, R., GRAY, E., ROBERTS, C., MERRINGTON, S., WATERS, I., FERNANDEZ, R., HAYWARD, G., and ROGERS, R. (2004), *ISSP: The Initial Report*, London: YJB.

MORGAN, J. and ZEDNER, L. (1992), *Child Victims: Crime, impact and criminal justice*, Oxford: Oxford University Press.

MORGAN, R. (2008), *Summary Justice: Fast but Fair?* London: Centre for Crime and Justice Studies, Kings College, London.

—— (2009a), 'Out-of-court summary justice: more smoke and mirrors', *CJM*, June, 10–12.

—— (2009b), 'The Risk of Risk-Preoccupation: Criminal Justice Policy in England,' in C. Hood and P. Miller (eds), *Risk and Public Services*, London: ESRC, LSE, and University of Oxford.

—— (2009c), 'Children and Young People: Criminalisation and Punishment', in M. Barry and F. McNeill (eds), *Youth Offending and Youth Justice*, London: Jessica Kingsley.

—— and NEWBURN, T. (2007), 'Youth Justice', in M. Maguire, R. Morgan, and R. Reiner (eds), *The Oxford Handbook of Criminology*, Oxford: Oxford University Press.

MORI (2004), *MORI Youth Survey 2004*, London: Youth Justice Board.

MOTT, J. and MIRRLEES-BLACK, C. (1993), *Self-reported Drug Misuse in England and Wales: Main finding from the 1992 British Crime Survey*, London: Home Office.

MUNCIE, J., COVENTRY, G., and WALTERS, R. (1995), 'The politics of youth crime prevention: developments in Australia and England and Wales', in L. Noaks, M. Levi, and M. Maguire (eds), *Issues in Contemporary Criminology*, Cardiff: University of Wales Press.

NATIONAL AUDIT OFFICE (2010), *The Youth Justice System in England and Wales: Reduced Offending by Young People*, London: NAO.

NEW ECONOMICS FOUNDATION (2010), *Punishing costs: How locking up children is making Britain less safe*, London: NEF.

NEWBURN, T. (1991), *Permission and Regulation: Law and morals in post-war Britain*, London: Routledge.

PARKER, H. (1974), *View From The Boys*, London: David and Charles.

PATRICK, J. (1973), *A Glasgow Gang Observed*, London: Methuen.

PEARSON, G. (1983), *Hooligan: A history of respectable fears*, Basingstoke: Macmillan.

PHILLIPS, C. and CHAMBERLAIN, V. (2006), *MORI Five Year Report: an analysis of youth justice data*, London: YJB.

PIQUERO, A., FARRINGTON, D., and BLUMSTEIN, A (2007), *Key Issues in Criminal Career Research*, Cambridge: Cambridge University Press.

PITTS, J. (2008), *Reluctant Gangsters: The changing face of youth crime*, Cullompton: Willan.

PLANT, M., PECK, D., and SAMUEL, E. (1985), *Alcohol, Drugs and School Leavers*, London: Tavistock.

PRATT, J. (1989), 'Corporatism: The third model of juvenile justice', *British Journal of Criminology*, 20(3): 236–54.

RAMSAY, M. and PERCY, A. (1996), *Drug Misuse Declared: Results of the 1994 British Crime Survey*, Home Office Research Study 151, London: Home Office.

REDHEAD, S. (1990), *The End of the Century Party: Youth and pop towards 2000*, Manchester: Manchester University Press.

—— (1993), 'The end of the end-of-the-century party', in S. Redhead (ed.), *Rave Off*, Avebury: Aldershot.

RICHARDSON, A. and BUDD, T. (2003), *Alcohol, Crime and Disorder: A study of young adults*, London: Home Office.

ROE, S. and ASHE, J. (2008), *Young People and Crime: findings from the 2006 Offending, Crime and Justice Survey*, London: Home Office.

ROOK, C. (1899), *The Hooligan Nights*, London: Grant Richards

RUTHERFORD, A. (1992), *Growing Out of Crime: The New Era*, Winchester: Waterside Press.

RUTTER, M. and GILLER, H. (1983), *Juvenile Delinquency: Trends and perspectives*, Harmondsworth: Penguin.

SAVAGE, J. (2007), *Teenage: The creation of youth 1875–1945*, London: Chatto and Windus.

SHAPLAND, J., ATKINSON, A., ATKINSON, H., DIGNAN, J., EDWARDS, L., HIBBERT, J., HOWES, M., JOHNSTONE, J., ROBINSON, G., and SORSBY, A. (2008), *Does restorative justice affect reconviction? The fourth report from the evaluation of three schemes*, London: Ministry of Justice.

SHARP, C. and BUDD, T. (2005), *Minority Ethnic Groups and Crime: Findings from the Offending, Crime and Justice Survey 2003*, London: Home Office.

SIMESTER, A. P. and VON HIRSCH, A. (2006), 'Regulating Offensive Conduct through Two-Step Prohibitions', in A. Von Hirsch and A. P. Simester (eds), *Incivilities: Regulating Offensive Behaviour*, Oxford: Hart Publishing.

SMITH, D. J. (2010a), 'Time trends in youth crime and in justice system responses', in D. J. Smith (ed), *A New Response to Youth Crime*, Cullompton: Willan.

—— (ed.) (2010b), *A New Response to Youth Crime*, Cullompton: Willan.

SOLOMON, E. and GARSIDE, R. (2008), *Ten years of Labour's youth justice reforms: an independent audit*, Centre for Crime and Justice Studies, Kings College, London.

SOUHAMI, A. (2007), *Transforming Youth Justice: Occupational identity and cultural change*, Cullompton: Willan.

SQUIRES, P., GRIMSHAW, R., and SOLOMON, E. (2008), *'Gun Crime': A review of evidence and policy*, London: Centre for Crime and Justice Studies.

STREET REPORT (Dame Sue Street) (2009), *Safeguarding the Future: A Review of the Youth Justice Board's Governance and Operating Arrangements*, London: YJB.

TALBOT, J. (2010), *Seen and Heard: supporting vulnerable children within the youth justice system*, London: Prison Reform Trust/Association of YOT Managers.

THOMPSON, K. (1998), *Moral Panics*, London: Routledge.

THRASHER, F. (1963), *The Gang*, Chicago, University of Chicago Press.

UNICEF (2007), *Child Poverty in Perspective: An overview of child well-being in rich countries. A comprehensive assessment of the lives and well-being of children and adolescents in the economically advanced nations*, Florence, Italy: UNICEF.

WEST, D.J. and FARRINGTON, D. (1977), *The Delinquent Way of Life*, London: Heinemann Educational.

WILKINSON, R. G. and PICKETT, K.E. (2009), *The Spirit Level: Why More Equal Societies Almost Always Do Better*, London: Allen Lane.

WILLIAMSON, H. (2004), *The Milltown Boys Revisited*, London: Berg.

WILLIS, P. (1978), *Profane Culture*, London: Routledge & Kegan Paul.

WILSON, J. Q. and KELLING, G. (1982), 'Broken Windows', *Atlantic Monthly*.

WOLFGANG, M., FIGLIO, R. M., and SELLIN, T. (1972), *Delinquency in a Birth Cohort*, Chicago: University of Chicago Press.

WOOD, M. (2005), *The victimisation of young people: findings from the Crime and Justice Survey 2003*, Home Office Findings 246, London: Home Office.

YOUNG, A. (1996), *Imagining Crime: Textual outlaws and criminal conversations*, London: Sage.

YOUNG, J. (1971), *The Drugtakers*, London: Paladin.

YOUTH JUSTICE BOARD (2005), *Offender Management Caseload Statistics 2004*, London: YJB.

—— (2006), *Annual Report and Accounts 2005/06*, London: YJB.

—— (2008), *Youth Justice Annual Workload Data 2006/7*, London: YJB.

—— (2009), *The Scaled Approach*, London: YJB.

—— (2010), *Youth Survey 2009*, London: YJB.

YJB/ACPO/Home Office (2005), *Anti-Social Behaviour: A guide to the role of Youth Offending Teams in dealing with anti-social behaviour*, London: Youth Justice Board.

# 18

# CRITICAL DEBATES IN DEVELOPMENTAL AND LIFE-COURSE CRIMINOLOGY

*Lesley McAra and Susan McVie*

## INTRODUCTION

Any overview of the theoretical and methodological debates within criminology (as they have evolved over the past 200 years) will highlight deep and continuous divisions in respect of: the primary object of analysis (mind vs. body, culture vs. structure, individual vs. social); the methods through which it should be studied (scientific-empirical vs. hermeneutic vs. deconstruction); and the normative and political purpose of such interrogation (there are, as yet, no settled answers to the following questions—what is criminology for, who or what interests does/should criminology serve, whose side should the criminologist be on). Never has debate been so visceral than in responses (mostly from critical criminologists) to the contribution of positivism (the scientific-empirical) to criminology. Positivism—as manifested in developmental criminology—is chided variously for being too focused on the individual 'delinquent', for embracing an outmoded and crude form of scientism as method, and for being inherently conservative in orientation. As John Muncie, a key critic of this perspective, has written (2010: 303–4):

> [this] research typically transforms and dehumanises the dynamic, interactive process of offending into a list of measurable developmental anomalies. Its simplified analyses and policy proposal[s] take us further from any informed and reasoned assessment of the nature and meaning of offending. ... Any notion that future behaviour can be predicted in a scientific way and pre-empted by government agencies flagrantly side steps any commitment to democracy and social justice.

The brief given to the authors of this chapter was to provide a critical conspectus of developmental and life-course criminology with a particular focus on the key theoretical, methodological, and policy debates. In fulfilling this brief, our aim has not been to mount a full-scale operation to rescue developmental criminology from its detractors, nor has it been to side wholeheartedly with a critical criminological position.

As researchers and criminological scholars, we have found ourselves bestriding such epistemological and methodological divides. In our corpus of published work we have sustained a strong belief in the radical possibilities of the scientific-empirical approach to study, utilizing findings from the Edinburgh Study of Youth Transitions and Crime (a prospective longitudinal study) to challenge contemporary approaches to juvenile justice across the UK (and beyond), to develop new theoretical ideas, and to proclaim the need for greater social justice.

If our role as criminologists is (as we believe) to engage in public and policy debate on matters of crime control and penal practice and to be transformative in matters of social and criminal justice, then it behoves us to be critically aware of the links between knowledge and context, and to be open to the theoretical and methodological possibilities offered by variant paradigms in our search for greater understanding of behaviours, cultural constructions, and institutional functioning. In developing this position, our chapter is divided into five interrelated sections. The first part comprises a critical review of the context in which developmental and life-course criminology emerged and the (later) dominance of risk-focused prevention strategies within policy circles (utilizing the USA and the UK as case studies). In the second, third, and fourth parts we set out respectively some of the core terminology and the theoretical and methodological debates within the paradigm. The chapter concludes in the fifth part with a critical review of the nature and efficacy of programmes which have been promulgated by developmental and life-course scholars for preventing and reducing crime.

# THE HISTORICAL AND CONCEPTUAL EMERGENCE OF DEVELOPMENTAL CRIMINOLOGY

The term 'developmental and life-course criminology' is widely used to describe the field of study which explores age-based changes in individual offending behaviour. It is distinct from other related fields of enquiry by its conceptual focus on crime and anti-social behaviour *across the life-span* of the *individual* (i.e. *within* individual change) and is characterized by a methodological approach which involves longitudinal exploration of key developmental stages and transitions over the life-course.

## CONTEXTUALIZING THEORY

In order to illustrate where developmental criminology fits both conceptually and historically within the wider discipline, we have set out a potted history of criminological theory in Table 18.1. This is not intended to present an exhaustive picture of theoretical developments; however, it serves to highlight some of the key paradigms of relevance here and to illustrate the epistemological and methodological divisions between them.

As shown in Table 18.1, developmental criminology emerged in the early to mid-twentieth century (drawing inspiration from the statistical movement led, *inter alia*,

Table 18.1 Paradigmatic developments in criminology: a potted history

| Paradigm | Classicism | Biological and physical positivism | Early sociological and ecological criminology | Developmental criminology | Radical criminology | Postmodern and cultural criminologies |
|---|---|---|---|---|---|---|
| Date of emergence | 18th century | 19th century | Late 19th to early 20th century | Early to mid-20th century | Late 20th century (following labelling theory from late 1950s/1960s) | Late 20th to early 21st century |
| Primary unit of analysis | Mind | Body | Social structure | Bio-psycho-social | Socio-economic structure | Cultural narrative |
| Method of interrogation | Deontic | Scientific-empirical | Scientific-empirical | Scientific-empirical | Dialectical materialism | Deconstruction |
| Concept of Personhood: | Individuals constitutionally self-interested | Individuals a product of bodily constraint | Individuals a product of social constraint | Individuals a product of experience | Individuals born free but structurally constrained | Individuals negotiate identity in the context of variant discursive framings |
| Individual Offender | Offender as rational and responsible | Offender as non-rational, irresponsible | Offender as constrained, limited responsibility | Offender as constrained, limited responsibility | Offender constrained by class position (brutalizing consequences of social marginalization) but also agentic (proto-revolutionary) | Offender as rational—choice within constraints |
| Social relations | Contractual, state vs. individual citizen | Primacy of individual | Structure functionalist | Primacy of individual within immediate family and peer context—functionalist | Functionalist, state determined by economic structure, serves interests of dominant classes | State as cultural product, serves interests of moral entrepreneurs |

by Quetelet in the mid-nineteenth century, and the expert knowledge-base of social work and psychiatry which had evolved from the late nineteenth century onwards). The methodological roots of developmental criminology lie firmly in a scientific-empirical approach to the study of crime. It is predicated on the notion that knowledge is progressive, perfectible, and universalizable. Core assumptions of the developmental paradigm are that human behaviour is measurable and quantifiable, and that there are law-like regularities in social encounters and individual responses which enable predictions to be made. It is in these ways that developmental criminology is, at heart, a 'modernist creation' (Garland 1994).

The *scientific* ambition of the embryonic developmental perspective had much in common with early sociological theories and variants of biological and physiological positivism. However, a key difference was its primary unit of analysis. Rather than focusing solely on the body (as per biological and physiological positivism) or social 'facts' (as per early sociological criminology), the developmental approach initially adopted what may be termed a 'bio-psycho-social' approach to the study of the individual.

Sheldon and Eleanor Glueck were amongst the earliest protagonists of the developmental approach. During the 1930s they instigated a longitudinal research project following a cohort of 1,000 boys in Boston. Their core object of study was the body, the mind, as well as the social milieu of the individual youngster. They concluded that early onset of delinquency was a strong predictor of adult criminality. Family relationships were key, with weak discipline, sundered emotional ties, and social deprivation all featuring in the lives of the youngsters at greatest risk of long term criminal careers. Other contributing factors were low IQ, mental disturbance, and body shape, with mesomorphic tendencies being linked to delinquent propensity (Glueck and Glueck 1950).

The developmental perspective mushroomed over the course of the twentieth century, gaining particular purchase within US criminology from the 1970s onwards. Of key salience was a study by Wolfgang *et al.* (1972), *Delinquency in a Birth Cohort,* which highlighted the fact that a small group of young offenders was responsible for a disproportionately high number of offences. This was a major source of inspiration for the subsequent focus on 'criminal careers' research in the US, taken forward by the Panel on Research on Criminal Careers led by a group of leading scholars and funded by the National Institute of Justice in 1983. One of the outcomes of this was a proliferation of longitudinal studies, including a collective group known as the *Causes and Correlates* studies which comprised the Pittsburgh Youth Survey launched in 1987 (see Loeber *et al.* 2003), the Rochester Youth Development Study (see Thornberry *et al.* 2003), and the Denver Youth Survey (see Huizinga *et al.* 2003). As we will demonstrate in the third part of this chapter, this was an especially productive time for developmentalists, and some of the most innovatory contributions to theory and method stem from this period. However, it was also a time when it faced particularly harsh criticism from the emergent radical and later postmodern and cultural criminological perspectives.

These perspectives eschewed the precepts of scientific criminological inquiry, with radical criminologists shifting the emphasis of theory and method onto definitional rather than motivational questions, (with a specific focus on the functioning of the state's power to criminalize and punish) and later postmodern and cultural criminologists focusing on the deconstruction of cultural narratives and the shifting nature of identities. Adherents to such critical perspectives generally dismissed developmental approaches as oversimplifying individual experiences and failing to take sufficient account of structural contexts and cultural difference (see Case and Haines 2009).

## DURABILITY OF THE PARADIGM

Given that developmental criminology is modernist in orientation, it is particularly intriguing that it has continued to survive and, indeed, flourish within advanced liberal (late modern) societies and in the light of the theoretical challenges posed by the radical and other critical perspectives summarized in Table 18.1 (see Young 1988). Why has the developmental perspective remained so *resilient* in the face of such 'assaults'?

Part of its durability can be attributed to a disciplinary migration (particularly from the 1970s onwards in the USA) by those interested in criminological study from other fields (with greater expertise in quantitative research), including psychology, psychiatry, education, medicine, and public health; coupled with a vast increase in computational power and rapid advances in statistical modelling (see the fourth part of this chapter). Arguably, however, key sources of its longevity, have also been: (i) the manner in which protagonists within the paradigm have functioned as 'policy entrepreneurs', harnessing governmental research monies and seeking to shape (with varying degrees of success) the criminal justice agenda in both the US and the UK; and (ii) that the solutions proffered by developmentalists continue to 'make sense' to policy-makers and practitioners, as one element of a complex and contradictory set of frameworks which have come to characterize youth justice policy in the twenty-first century (especially in the context of the UK, see McAra 2010).

### Policy entrepreneurs

The advent of radical criminology in the late 1960s and early 1970s laid the ground work for a range of up-and-coming scholars to disengage from the policy process. It culminated in the early to mid-1980s with the sociological turn in the study of punishment, which disconnected the study of punishment from the study of criminal behaviour and encouraged a breed of criminological scholars with rather more theoretical than applied policy ambition (see Garland and Young 1983). The policy field was then left open for any entrepreneurial criminologist to colonize.

Developmentalists on both sides of the Atlantic have been highly active in engaging with policy-makers and practitioners (with varying degrees of success). In North America, for example, such scholars have made efforts to extend their policy influence by developing intervention programmes as part of their research and testing their efficacy (as for example the multi–modal intervention programme developed by Tremblay *et al.* 1995 and the Seattle Social Development Project developed by Hawkins *et al.* 1991, see the fifth part of this chapter for further details). Within the UK, David Farrington has been heavily involved in government-sponsored Working Groups, as well as a range of international and UK-based campaigning and expert research groups such as the Campbell Collaboration (a network which is aimed at improving the evidence base for government decision-making through systematic research review, see www.campbellcollaboration.org/about_us/index.php). As co-directors of the Edinburgh Study of Youth Transitions and Crime, the authors of this chapter have also actively sought direct engagement with government, and our findings have now shaped the ethos of the 'whole-system' approach to youth justice currently being developed in Scotland (see www.scotland.gov.uk/Topics/Justice/crimes/youth-justice/reoffending).

### Key narratives 'make sense'

The second key factor contributing to the longevity of the developmental approach has been the ways in which some (but not all) of the solutions stemming from longitudinal research have played a key role in legitimizing and sustaining an increasingly complex and contradictory policy portfolio, over the course of the late 1990s and the first decade of the twenty-first century.

Over this period, youth justice policy, particularly in a UK context, has increasingly become framed by a set of conflicted imperatives—policy is variously punitive, restorative, and actuarial in orientation, whilst also retaining some vestiges of older-style penal welfarism (see McAra 2010, Morgan and Newburn, this volume). It combines a range of complex sensibilities from the retributive and exclusionary impulses of the more punitive elements of the framework, to the more scientific rationalist approach to knowledge production embodied within the concept of evidence-led policy. The developmental paradigm has had a key role to play in this mix, manifested in the shift towards preventative strategies in youth crime and the gradual elision which has occurred between the youth justice, community safety, and social inclusion agendas (McAra 2010, 2011).

A number of commentators have argued that core dimensions of contemporary policy narratives (particularly populist punitivism and actuarialism) are tied into the conditions of late modernity. Just as the emergence of theory is closely linked to its temporal and spatial context, so too do such policy responses reflect the uncertainties and anxieties produced by the risk society, the loss of nation state sovereignty, and the growth of what Sparks terms 'structurally redundant populations' in the context of macro socio-economic transformations (Sparks 2006; Armstrong and McAra 2006). Arguably, however, these broader changes have also opened up a conceptual 'space' in which narratives of certainty (predictability) are found to be politically comforting as is a lexicon which talks of (individual) resilience rather than fundamental transformation of extant structures. The developmental perspective has offered policy-makers a concrete set of 'solutions' which are measurable (to an extent) and above all make it appear as if the government is having an impact. We will return to the nature and efficacy of these solutions later in the fifth part of the chapter.

Having set out the context within which developmental and life-course criminology emerged and reasons for its subsequent longevity, we now turn to a more detailed exposition and critique of its contemporary conceptual, methodological, and theoretical framings.

## KEY CONCEPTS IN DEVELOPMENTAL AND LIFE-COURSE CRIMINOLOGY

Here we introduce some of the key terms which are core to developmental and life-course criminology (DLC): the age-crime curve; criminal careers; and risk factors. These terms underpin much of the theoretical development within the paradigm, have influenced research methodologies, and played a major role in shaping policy solutions to the problem of crime.

### AGE, CRIME, AND CRIMINAL CAREERS

At the heart of DLC is the universally accepted fact that crime has a strong relationship with age, which is typified by a characteristic pattern in the data. The ubiquitous 'age-crime curve' is a peak found in aggregate crime data when it is plotted against age. Typically, it shows a sharp rise in offending during the teenage years, peaking in the late teens or early twenties and then declining, steeply at first and then steadily, into adulthood (Farrington 1986).

The first recorded illustration of an age-crime curve was published by Adolphe Quetelet in 1831. In a subsequent essay Quetelet stated that:

> of all the causes which influence the development of the propensity to crime, or which diminish that propensity, age is unquestionably the most energetic. Indeed, it is through age that the physical powers and passions of man are developed, and their energy afterwards decreases with age (Quetelet 1842, republished 1996: 23).

Figure 18.1 uses Quetelet's original statistical data recorded in France between 1826 and 1829 to illustrate the shape and form of the age-crime curve for three forms of violent offending, which shows that the peak age of offending was between 25 and 30 years.

Research on the relationship between age and crime flourished during the 1970s and 1980s and the characteristic shape of Quetelet's age crime curve was replicated a sufficient number of times to substantiate its existence (see Farrington 1986, Tittle and Grasmick 1997). The precise shape of the curve and the age at which the peak emerges varies depending on a range of factors, including the type of data used (convictions data tend to show a later peak than self-report survey data), gender (peaks are shallower for females than males), era (the peak age of offending has tended to get younger over time), and jurisdiction (peculiarities in justice systems and recording practices can impact on the shape of the age-crime curve). Nevertheless, the omnipresent nature of its existence within crime data has led to it being described as one of the 'brute facts of criminology' (Hirschi and Gottfredson 1983: 552).

While the existence of this unimodal pattern in the data may be uncontested, its meaning for the study of crime and deviance remains contentious. As indicated in the above quotation, Quetelet proposed that the age-crime curve was based on a change in individual propensity to offend underpinned by three main elements: physical strength, passion, and reason (or judgement). He proposed that man's (*sic*) propensity

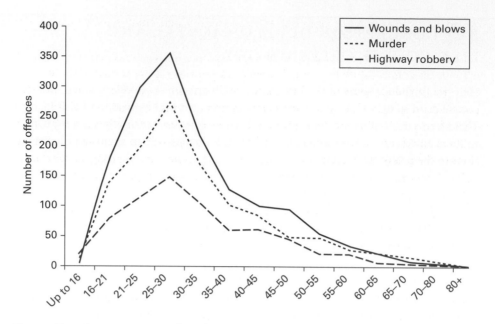

**Figure 18.1** Age-crime curve based on crime data from France, 1826-1829

*Source*: Abridged version of M. A. Quetelet (1842) *A Treatise on Man and the Development of his Faculties*, Edinburgh: Chambers, republished in J. Muncie, E. McLaughlin, and M. Langan (1996), *Criminological Perspectives*: A Reader, London: Sage. The data were taken from Table 2.7 on p. 25.

to offend reached its maximal effect (or peaked) at the age when his strength and passion had attained their maximum levels, but his ability to reason had not acquired sufficient power to govern their combined influence. More than a hundred years later, similar notions of criminal propensity and maturational development became central to several modern theoretical perspectives about crime. For example, Gottfredson and Hirschi's (1990) 'general theory of crime' hypothesized that the development of self-control in childhood (established through good child rearing processes) was essential in minimizing an individual's propensity to commit crime. This propensity manifested itself particularly during the teenage years, when maturational developments associated with the process of ageing led to an increase in anti-social behaviour, hence the distinctive pattern of the age-crime curve. Hirschi and Gottfredson (1983) were dismissive of the need to study any further underlying dimensions of the aggregate age-crime curve. In their view, age itself was a causal factor.

The relationship between age and crime was also a major preoccupation for the criminal careers paradigm. In simple terms, a criminal career is 'the characterization of the longitudinal sequence of crimes committed by an individual offender' (Blumstein *et al.* 1986a: 12). In other words, it is the study of how engagement in offending (on a range of dimensions) changes with age. Criminal careers can span from single, isolated acts to a sustained level of involvement in crime (Petersilia 1980); although the focus tends to be on the study of offending histories which extend over a considerable period of time and involve many different offences, rather than those which involve one-off or occasional acts. The paradigm is concerned with heterogeneity (or differences) in offending between individuals as well as both 'stability' and 'change' in criminal activity over time within the individual (see Smith 2007).

Rather than attempting to explain the aggregate age-crime curve, criminal careers scholars partitioned the curve into different components on the basis that these could affect the shape of the curve in different ways (Blumstein *et al.* 1986a). The two main components of relevance here were 'participation' (who is engaged in offending and who is not) and 'frequency' (the rate of offending amongst active offenders). Analysis of data using these two components revealed that the age-crime curve was explained to a greater extent by changes in participation. Frequency of offending was far more stable over time, although it did increase with age for some types of offence and subgroups of offender (Blumstein *et al.* 1986a).

Notably, Gottfredson and Hirschi (1986, 1987) launched a vigorous critique against Blumstein and colleagues. Gottfredson and Hirschi's theoretical perspective indicated that the most important focus of the research on age and crime was to distinguish between offenders and non-offenders (i.e. participation in offending, rather than frequency of offending). In response, Farrington (1986) demonstrated that the shape and structure of the age-crime curve was subject to considerable variance over time, place, and different groups. Further, he showed that the age-crime curves for individuals did not resemble the aggregate curve, there was no uniformity in the age at which offending behaviour peaked within individuals, nor was there consistency between individuals in their frequency of offending over the life-course. He concluded that the pattern of the age-crime curve was most likely to be explained by changes in participation in offending driven by 'decreasing parental controls, a peaking of peer influence in the teenage years, and then increasing family and community controls with age' (1986: 236). Blumstein, Cohen, and Farrington (1988) further argued that criminal offending could not simply be driven by one underlying theoretical construct of criminal propensity, otherwise all aspects of an individual's criminal career (such as when they started, when they stopped, and how frequently and seriously they offended) would be interconnected and explained by the same correlates and predictors.

Although an important empirical question, the relationship between participation and frequency in offending and age has received relatively little attention and the research evidence has been mixed (see Piquero *et al.* 2007); however, recent studies have indicated that decline in the age-crime curve reflects a combination of both decreasing individual offending participation and frequency after the peak (see Petras *et al.* 2010).

As well as contributing to the age-crime debate, the criminal careers paradigm has significantly advanced knowledge about some of the key dimensions of individual criminal behaviour. For example: when it starts (onset), when it slows down or stops (desistance), how long it lasts (duration), why people continue to offend (persistence), why offending increases and decreases at specific times (escalation and de-escalation), what type of crimes are committed (seriousness), the nature of the crime mix (specialization), and whether involvement in offending is a collective activity (co-offending). However, this approach paid little attention to the factors or events that influenced the dimensions of criminal careers (see Piquero *et al.* 2003). Other emergent developmental approaches have been more specifically aimed at identifying factors that increase the risk of offending behaviour and identifying methods of intervention to prevent offending behaviour.

## RISK AND PREVENTION

The 'risk factor prevention paradigm' emerged during the 1990s, building on the work of the criminal careers scholars. Risk factors are typically adverse characteristics, circumstances, or behaviours that are identified and measured at a point prior to the onset of a particular outcome. The outcome may be onset of offending or it may be some other aspect of the individual's criminal career, such as increased frequency, seriousness, or persistence. In order to establish whether a risk factor has a causal relationship with the outcome, good quality longitudinal data are needed to establish the ordering of events and allow for the testing of a variety of confounding variables. One of the principal advocates of the risk factor approach, David Farrington, has stated that:

> a key advantage of the risk factor prevention paradigm is that it links explanation and prevention, fundamental and applied research, and scholars and practitioners. Importantly, the paradigm is easy to understand and to communicate, and it is readily accepted by policy makers, practitioners, and the general public. Both risk factors and interventions are based on empirical research rather than theories (Farrington 2007: 7).

For many researchers and policy-makers, the risk factor paradigm represents a significant breakthrough in understanding and explaining offending behaviour, especially in terms of serious and violent offending (see Loeber and Farrington 1998). A review of the developmental literature over the last 20 years reveals that a growing number of criminologists have embraced the concept of risk factors and there is no shortage of studies identifying correlates of crime and anti-social behaviour. As a result, a vast array of risk factors for the early onset of offending have been identified. According to Farrington (2003: 224), they include: individual factors (low intelligence, low school achievement, hyperactivity/impulsiveness and risk-taking, and anti-social behaviour in childhood such as aggression and bullying), family factors (poor parental supervision, harsh discipline and physical abuse, inconsistent discipline, cold parental attitude and child neglect, poor parent-child involvement, parental conflict, broken family, criminal parents and delinquent/criminal siblings); socio-economic factors (low family income, large family size); peer factors (delinquent peers, peer rejection, and low popularity), school factors (high delinquency rate school) and neighbourhood factors (high crime neighbourhood).

It should be noted that the bulk of risk factor research has been targeted at early childhood and adolescence, and there have been far fewer studies on risk factors in adulthood. However, Laub and Sampson's (2003) study of men in their 70s found that desistance from offending in late adolescence and adulthood was predicted by several more dynamic life events, including being married, having a stable and satisfying job, moving to a better area, and joining the military. Generally speaking, there is a lack of distinction in the literature between 'risk factors' and 'life events' and they tend to be incorporated under the general heading of risk factors.

Other gaps in knowledge are the mechanisms and processes by which risk factors have causal effects on offending and the extent to which this differs within individuals, since much of the research has been focused on between-individual differences. There are also gaps in knowledge about risk factors which may be causes of offending or indicators of the same underlying construct, or both (for example, heavy drinking may cause crime, or it may be caused by the same underlying construct such as anti-social personality, or both). While knowledge of family and individual risk factors, specifically those that occur in childhood, is comprehensive (see Farrington 2007) there is less known about biological, peer, school, or neighbourhood risk factors and less about the risk factors that cause late onset of offending. There is also limited research evidence about protective factors, and whether these are just the opposite of risk factors, and how other factors mediate or counteract their effects.

A key claim of the paradigm is that successful identification of risk factors in early childhood may enable us to predict future offending and, therefore, enable early prevention. Such an idea is inherently attractive to politicians and, as noted earlier, has been at the core of the early intervention policies promulgated across the UK in recent years (a point to which we return in the fifth part of the chapter). Many studies have demonstrated that persistent offending in adolescence and adulthood is associated with early onset of a wide range of temperamental, personality, social, and environmental risk factors during childhood (West and Farrington 1977; Lahey *et al.* 2003). For example, using data from the Dunedin Multidisciplinary Health and Development Study, Caspi (2000) found strong continuities in personality development amongst individuals from age 3 to age 21 and concluded that early temperament had a profound influence on life-course development and impacted on criminal offending in early adulthood. However, while these studies are often compelling, they fail to address a fundamental paradox: that while offending in adulthood is strongly predicted by anti-social behaviour in childhood, most anti-social children do not go on to become offenders in adulthood (Sampson and Laub 1993). In other words, it is not inevitable that an anti-social child will become an anti-social adult because there is such a large degree of heterogeneity between individual offenders. In fact, most life-course research has been only moderately successful in attempting to prospectively predict future offending amongst young people. The greatest degree of homogeneity tends to be found amongst a very small group of individuals who are at the most extreme end of the offending spectrum (Rutter *et al.* 1998), and yet even they are difficult to identify prospectively.

A key point of controversy is whether predictions made using such risk factors have a high degree of accuracy. Also using data from the Dunedin Study, White *et al.* (1990) found that the predictive power of early childhood measures diminished over time. They looked at a wide variety of characteristics of children at ages 3 and 5 in an effort to predict later conduct disorder at ages 11 and 15. Using discriminant function analysis to identify the five most important predictor variables from childhood, they correctly predicted the anti-social outcomes for 81 per cent of the children; however, at age 15 they correctly predicted only 65 per cent of adolescents as delinquent or not. Moreover, their results showed a high false positive rate for the prediction of anti-social outcomes at age 11, since 85 per cent of those predicted to be anti-social at this age only 15 per cent of them developed stable and pervasive anti-social behaviours. They concluded that the predictive power of early childhood measures extends only modestly into adolescence, and that other factors need to be identified to explain behaviour at that age. Looking at a longer cohort of data from age 7 to 70, Sampson and Laub (2004) found that even using a multitude of childhood and adolescent risk factors to predict long-term patterns of offending, the majority of offenders desisted from offending by their middle adult years and prospective analysis of troubled children did not allow them to identify distinct offender groups.

While the criminal careers perspective contributed significantly in a descriptive way to the study of individual offending, some commentators argued that it made little progress in terms of theory (see Tittle 1988). Marvell and Moody (1991: 239), for example, pointed to an abundance of speculative reasons for offending, including:

> the physical ability to accomplish strenuous criminal acts, chemical factors such as testosterone levels that might predispose persons to crime, innate recklessness of juveniles, level of moral development, inability to balance immediate gains against long-term effects of crime, participation in peer groups consisting of frequent offenders, opportunities for gainful legitimate employment, extent of family ties, and greater legal penalties given adults and repeat offenders.

However, they criticized the lack of empirical support for these ideas and the absence of theory to explain the existence of such a relationship. Over the last two decades, a number of theoretical perspectives have emerged which have attempted to explain the distinctive pattern of the age crime curve and the nature of individual change in offending over the life-course. It is to these that we now turn.

## THEORETICAL DEBATES

We do not have the space to provide a comprehensive review of theory here, so we have overviewed five perspectives which demonstrate a range of approaches and underlying concepts, and which illustrate the breadth and versatility of developmental hypotheses.

### DUAL TAXONOMY THEORY

One of the most influential theories within developmental and life-course criminology has been that put forward by Moffitt (1993, 2003). Using data from the Dunedin Multidisciplinary Health and Development Study, Moffitt utilized a taxonomic approach to identify two distinct categories of anti-social behaviour which she labelled 'life-course persistent' (LCP) and 'adolescence limited' (AL). Moffitt hypothesized that LCP offending began during early childhood and manifested itself in a range of problematic behaviours (such as temper tantrums and periods of hyperactivity). It continued to exhibit itself throughout the life-course, although the specific forms of anti-social behaviour changed to reflect the age and stage of the individual. She proposed that anti-social behaviour was a highly stable trait amongst LCP, not because early offending locked them into a cycle of later offending, but because the causal factors that underpinned their anti-social behaviour tended to be present throughout their lives. By contrast, AL offending was described as temporary, starting in early adolescence (around the age of puberty), rapidly escalating, and then de-escalating after the peak age of offending.

The causal explanations proposed for these two types of offending were very different. LCP was said to be underpinned by a neuropsychological deficit (i.e. a deficiency in the executive function of the brain), which was exacerbated by family-adversity risk factors in the child's early social environment, whereas, AL offending was a reaction to various exogenous (external) risk factors during the teenage years, combined with maturational reform and associated rebellion against controls which mimicked the actions of the LCP offenders (Caspi and Moffitt 1995). Importantly, Moffitt's work demonstrated that the aggregate age-crime curve was a combination of two underlying curves representing different sub-populations with different underlying aetiologies and social experiences. The characteristic shape of the curve reflects the surge in offending amongst the much larger group of AL offenders between early to late adolescence, but conceals the fact that the much smaller group of LCP offenders maintain a constant underlying presence in the data. In other words, the age-crime curve conceals important trajectories of offending.

## AGE-GRADED THEORY OF INFORMAL SOCIAL CONTROL

Sampson and Laub's (1993) Age-graded Theory is essentially a social control theory extended into adulthood. Using data collected by the Gluecks in their Boston Study and following the cohort of men into their 70s, Sampson and Laub theorized that social bonds were key to explaining involvement in offending, and that strength of bonding was dependent on attachments to parents, schools, peers, and siblings and socialization processes such as discipline and supervision. People who bond well with conventional others build social capital: a store of positive relationships emanating from social networks built on norms of reciprocity and trust, upon which the individual can draw for support. Offending during the peak teenage years is linked to the importance of attachment to delinquent peers at that time. However, adulthood involves a series of transitions (including marriage and entry into employment) which may change a person's life trajectory in pro-social directions, which Sampson and Laub call turning points. Structural background and individual factors have indirect effects on offending, as they impact on informal social control but, importantly, age-graded theory strongly emphasizes human agency.

## INTERACTIONAL THEORY

Like the age-graded theory of informal social control, Thornberry's (1987, 2005) Interactional Theory explains involvement in delinquency as stemming from weakened bonds to society. Based on analysis of data from the Rochester Youth Development Study, Thornberry hypothesized that weakened bonds did not occur in a vacuum but were linked to structural variables, including social class position and residential area. Causal influences vary over the life-course, as well as stage in criminal career, and these are not always uni-directional. Delinquency can be both the outcome of weak bonds but, in turn, it can also cause the weakening of the bonds themselves.

Thornberry hypothesized that there was interaction between causal factors and their outcomes. In other words, delinquency itself is part of a larger causal network, affected by social factors but also affecting the development of those social factors over time.

## INTEGRATED COGNITIVE ANTI-SOCIAL POTENTIAL (ICAP) THEORY

Farrington's ICAP Theory (2003, 2008), which is based on analysis of data from the Cambridge Study in Delinquent Development, also looks at the interaction and sequencing of variables. However, he draws on a wider range of traditional criminological theories, including strain, control, learning, labelling, and rational choice. It is ambitious in that it is designed to explain within-individual and between-individual variations in male offending throughout life, and to explain the different dimensions of the criminal career. The key concepts in ICAP Theory are anti-social potential (AP), which is a person's potential to engage in crime, and 'cognition', which is the thinking or decision-making process that turns potential into actual behaviour. Farrington distinguishes between individuals with long-term, persisting, between-individual differences in AP, and those with short-term, within-individual variations in AP. Long-term AP is dependent on impulsiveness, strain, modelling, socialization processes, and life events, while short-term AP is dependent on motivational and situational factors.

According to Farrington, absolute levels of AP vary with age, but peak in the teenage years because of within-individual change in risk factors that influence long-term AP (i.e. the declining influence of parents and the increasing influence of peers). In line with strain theory, the motives that lead to long-term AP include long-term energizing factors (e.g. desire for material gain, high status, excitement, and sexual satisfaction), but only where these motives cannot be satisfied by legitimate means. It also relies on attachment and socialization processes (e.g. poor parenting), exposure to anti-social models (e.g. delinquent peers or family members), significant life events, and individual impulsivity. Short-term AP is dependent on short-term energizing factors (e.g. boredom, anger, alcohol, frustration, or male peers) and the availability of criminal opportunities and suitable victims. The consequences of offending have implications for long-term AP, through social learning, especially if the consequences are reinforcing or punishing. Desistance occurs for both social and individual reasons and occurs at different rates according to a person's level of AP.

## NEGOTIATED ORDER THEORY

Finally, findings from the Edinburgh Study of Youth Transitions and Crime have provided the groundwork for a theory of offending and desistance based on the concept of Negotiated Order (McAra 2005, McAra and McVie, forthcoming 2012). Drawing on labelling theory, we focus on the role which formal and informal regulatory practices play in the development of offender and non-offender identities. Formal regulatory orders comprise schools, the police, social work, the courts, etc. Informal orders include parenting, peer interactions, and street culture. The practices of these orders ascribe a range of (sometimes) competing identities to young people. In order to retain a sense of self-integrity (ego continuity) youngsters are required to negotiate a pathway through the regulatory framework and actively engage with ascribed identities, absorbing them or fighting back.

Contemporary modes of formal regulation are, in practice, profoundly exclusionary for certain categories of young people. The working cultures of the police and juvenile justice agencies serve to repeatedly target the same groups of young people (particularly young boys from disadvantaged backgrounds), who are recycled again and again within the system (McAra and McVie 2005, 2007). Importantly, exclusion by formal orders appears to limit the capacity to negotiate actively, leading to a downward spiral of increased marginalization. A symbiotic relationship exists between exclusion by formal agencies and inclusion in informal (deviant) groupings and this inhibits capacity to change. One of the principal ironies of such processes is that systems of juvenile justice reproduce the conditions of their own existence, a point to which we return in the fifth part of this chapter.

There are a number of other developmental theories which are not summarized here, such as the Social Development Model (Catalano and Hawkins 1996), Integrative Multilayered Control Theory (LeBlanc 1997), Developmental Pathways Theory (Loeber 1996), Situational Action Theory (Wikström 2010), and many others. This weight of evidence demonstrates that developmental criminology has generated a large number of theoretical frameworks for explaining offending. Nevertheless, there is general agreement amongst scholars that the number of theories needs to be reduced and (ironically, given its scientific-empirical focus) there is a high degree of controversy over how this should be achieved. This in turn raises a number of questions with regard to the method of theory building and it is to such methodological debates that we now turn.

## METHODOLOGICAL DEBATES

The growth in availability of individual level longitudinal data has fostered a large number of empirical studies aimed at addressing key criminological issues, such as patterns of criminal offending across the full or partial life-course (Laub and Sampson 2003), the existence of offender trajectories (Nagin and Land 1993, D'Unger et al. 1998), possible correlates or explanations of different offender trajectories (Blockland et al. 2005), and the ability to predict future offending using trajectories and covariates (Sampson and Laub 2004). In general, methodological issues around survey design and statistical analyses tend not to inspire active debate amongst criminologists within the wider discipline which, in part, reflects the deliberate disengagement from positivist approaches discussed in the first part of this chapter. It is worth noting here, however, that the lack of engagement in such debate (amongst UK scholars) may stem from a much wider, deep-rooted lack of quantitative methods training for social scientists within higher education. The authors of a recent review found that 'the qualitative/quantitative divide is particularly stark in British criminology, and this is seen as unsatisfactory and the topic of much debate' (Lynch et al. 2007). The same is not true in the US where quantitative methods training is integral to higher education.

Amongst developmental criminologists, there have been interesting debates raised by the methodological and analytical opportunities available, such as whether and how analyses should be undertaken, how the research design might impact on data, and which forms of statistical analyses provide the most robust and valid solutions. The question of how method relates to theory is also an important topic of discussion. It is not possible to provide a full exposition of the debates here, so we shall concentrate on three key issues that have been identified as important to the development of the DLC approach: the advantages and disadvantages of official or administrative data versus self-report survey data; whether longitudinal data are superior to cross-sectional data; and a comparison of different approaches to statistical modelling.

## OFFICIAL STATISTICS VERSUS SELF-REPORT DATA

Developmental studies have tended to use data from two main sources: official statistics (usually data on convictions, arrests, or other forms of criminal justice contact) and self-reported offending surveys (information collected directly from individuals about their engagement in offending). While valuable for many purposes, the limitations of official data as an accurate measure of individual offending are well documented (Weis 1986; see also Maguire, this volume). For example, they provide very limited data on offences and offenders, they cover only a small proportion of all crimes committed (since most crime does not come to the attention of the police) and they tend to present a distorted picture of offending (for example, more serious crimes seem more prevalent because they are more likely to be reported). Since around the 1960s, self-report studies have been more commonly used to collect information on prevalence and frequency of offending. They are more suited to the purpose for a number of reasons, for example: they collect information about offences that are never reported to the police; they can contain detailed questions on the nature of offending behaviour; and they enable researchers to collect a wider set of data about the characteristics, background, and behaviours of the offender in order to test aetiological theories of crime.

The use of self-report offending studies increased dramatically both in the US and across Europe, in part due to the fact that they demonstrated the level of bias in official statistics, since a great many people who had offended had no criminal record (Junger-Tas and Marshall 1999). One of the main concerns about self-report studies has centred around the issue of validity. Critics feared that data may be inaccurate due to a failure on the part of respondents to report accurately their offending behaviour (either deliberately or through some other kind of response error); however, such concerns are generally accepted to be unfounded (Elliott 1994). The evidence substantiating the validity between self-report and official data, reviewed by Smith (2007), indicates that the self-report method is the most appropriate for the life-course approach to criminology; however, high standards of quality in survey methodology are crucial. Research design and administration problems, such as systematic sample bias, measurement error, poor instrument validity, and lack of integrity or data quality seriously impair the value of self-report studies (McVie 2009). Despite the limitations of official data, most of the largest and most influential studies have collected both official and self-report records for reasons of testing validity (Piquero *et al.* 2003), although it is disappointing that few of these studies have taken the opportunity to explore the potential impact of criminal justice intervention on offending behaviour (exceptions include Huizinga *et al.* 2003 and McAra and McVie 2010).

## LONGITUDINAL VERSUS CROSS-SECTIONAL

Another area of methodology that has inspired critique and debate, especially in the early years, is whether longitudinal data are required to study the age-crime relationship or whether cross-sectional data are sufficient. Developmental criminologists strongly advocate the need for longitudinal data (repeated measures taken at intervals from the same group of individuals) as opposed to cross-sectional data (one-off or repeated measures taken from different groups of individuals each time) in order to be able to draw causal inferences about the impact of early events on later ones (Petersilia 1980). As noted earlier, Hirschi and Gottfredson (1983) hypothesized that the effect of age on crime was stable over time. This meant that cross-sectional studies were sufficient to explore the age-crime relationship. They were critical of time-consuming and expensive longitudinal studies which they felt were unjustified. However, Greenberg (1991) points out that the causal effect of age on crime cannot be adequately tested or explained using cross-sectional data because they typically understate the importance of variables where their effect is time-lagged. So if, as the criminal careers approach proposes, crime is the result of dynamic processes, longitudinal data are required to estimate the causal effects of potential explanatory variables or risk factors. According to Piquero *et al.* (2003) cross-sectional designs are suitable only for taking a snap-shot of an individual's offending behaviour at one point in time, but do not allow for the study of within-individual variation over time.

The use of longitudinal data does not, however, resolve the problem of potentially confounding age, cohort, and period effects (Rutter 1995). Age effects are variations in risk that depend entirely on the age of the individual; cohort effects are variations in risk that apply to all individuals within a specified group or who share a common experience (e.g. are born in a year that is characterized by a particular event); and period (or secular) effects are variations in risk over time that tend to apply to an entire generation. Using cross-sectional survey data the effect of age on crime may be confounded by the characteristics of the cohort under study (i.e. factors that affect a particular cohort of individuals may make them different to other cohorts, which may obscure a real age effect). On the other hand, with a longitudinal survey, the effect of age may be confounded by period effects (i.e. secular change or environmental influences may affect the aging cohort). Farrington (1986: 214) stresses the advantages of the longitudinal design over cross-sectional studies (particularly in terms of studying continuity and discontinuity between different ages, the sequencing of events, and establishing causation) but concedes that 'the best solution is to combine methods, if possible, by following up multiple cohorts and by deriving information both from official records and from self-reports'.

## APPROACHES TO STATISTICAL MODELLING

As indicated earlier, developmental studies have shown that the age-crime curve is an amalgam of underlying micro-curves that varied widely in shape, and may represent quite different combinations of change in terms of both frequency and prevalence of offending (Brame and Piquero 2003; McVie 2005). Advances in computational power and statistical modelling allowed developmental criminologists to explore the dynamics of these curves.

Statistical approaches to exploring criminal careers typically fall into two categories: semi-parametric group-based (or trajectory) modelling (Nagin 2005; Piquero *et al.* 2007) and other random effects growth-curve models (Raudenbush and Bryk 2002; Skrondal and Rabe-Hesketh 2004). Such analyses are appropriate only for longitudinal data, although they can be applied equally well to official data and self-report offending data, or even a combination of the two. These advanced statistical techniques take into account both homogeneity and heterogeneity in the population of study; in other words some pathways may be similarly aligned while others will vary between individuals, and that any such variations may be caused by a range of different influences, from birth to old age.

Early efforts to explore population differences in offending involved relatively crude or arbitrary methods of grouping individuals (see, e.g., Wolfgang *et al.* 1972; Blumstein *et al.* 1985). Semi-parametric group-based models, however, enabled radically different types of individual to be distinguished using statistical algorithms (see Nagin and Land 1993). This method is well-suited to longitudinal data as it identifies an optimal number of developmental trajectories within a population based on measures of offending recorded at different ages. Discrete groups of offenders are estimated which are internally homogenous (individuals are similar to each other within the group) but externally heterogeneous (the groups as a whole differ from each other). A key advantage of the method is that it can accommodate missing data in estimation which allows individuals with incomplete data to be included in analysis (an important consideration for longitudinal studies where attrition and non-response can be problematic issues).

Using data from the Cambridge Study in Delinquent Development, Nagin and Land (1993) applied group-based modelling techniques to study trajectories of criminal propensity. They identified four latent classes grouped on the basis of their patterns of conviction (including one class of individuals who were never convicted). In line with Moffitt, these included a long-term, high-rate trajectory that matched the life-course persistent offender group and a late-onset, short-term trajectory that matched the adolescence limited group. In addition, however, they identified a low-rate chronic class of offenders that did not conform to Moffitt's Dual Taxonomy Theory. This class was distinguishable from all the others in terms of their disproportionately low IQ, although it was quite distinctively different from the high-rate chronic class on a host of dimensions. Nagin and Land (1993: 355) conclude that the 'low-rate chronics appear to be comparatively docile individuals who, because of their low intelligence, either blunder into or are easily led into crime'.

The question of how many groups of offenders exist in the data remains an unanswered, and controversial, one (D'Unger *et al.* 1998). A range of other studies have found various numbers of latent classes with strikingly different offending trajectories. For example, an Australian study by Livingston *et al.* (2008) found three groups of offenders; Chung *et al.* (2002) identified five offending trajectories using data from the Seattle Social Development Project; and using data on a sample of young men convicted and committed to the California Youth Authority, Ezell and Cohen (2005) found six distinct classes of offender. D'Unger *et al.* (1998) found that different samples of data produced different numbers of latent classes (although four or five tended to be sufficient) and concluded that the shapes of offending trajectories by age were heavily dependent on the nature of the data used to measure offending (such as self-report, arrest, or convictions data), the nature of the cohort under study, and the context of the community from which the sample was drawn.

Each of the developmental studies mentioned here used group-based modelling techniques (Nagin 2005); however, studies have also used *a priori* or deductive approaches (similar to Moffitt's) to identify more than two groups. Using a dynamic classification procedure developed by Loeber *et al.* (1991) which places individuals into categories based on changes in levels of delinquent behaviour over time, Ayers *et al.* (1999) examined eight mutually exclusive categories of offenders to see whether they could be distinguished from each other. They found that there were distinctions between the groups, although the extent of the distinction varied considerably depending on the comparison groups and according to gender.

Osgood (2005) notes that the motivation behind the typological approach may have been driven by theory, but the method itself is atheoretical and exploratory, similar to factor or cluster analysis. Even Nagin, a key proponent of semi-parametric group-based modelling, has made clear that it is a heuristic device and that the groups identified cannot be interpreted as reflecting real underlying discrete groups in the population (Nagin and Land 1993, Nagin 2005).

In response to the criticism that absolute groups of offenders may not exist in reality, an alternative approach adopted by some scholars is the random effects growth-curve model. This method is equivalent in many respects to the latent class approach, in the sense that it seeks to identify patterns in the data over time. Rather than placing individuals into groups, however, the approach estimates *individual* growth-curves (or trajectories). A regression model is then used to estimate the relationships between individual characteristics and differences between growth-curves. Restrictions placed on the data ensure that the growth curves are 'smoothed', which means that the curves are artificially adjusted to look smoother than they may actually be. Sharp changes or chaotic patterns can sometimes be obscured. As a result, such models are efficient for plotting long-term, gradual change, but less good for reflecting short-term or erratic change in behaviour. When growth-curves are interpreted, it is generally assumed that all the within-individual change is being measured; however, Osgood (2005) estimates that growth-curves typically account for less than half of all within-individual variance (in other words, some aspects of change are not being reflected). He argues that this is not necessarily a shortcoming of the method, but it is important for analysts to interpret the results of such models carefully and accurately: 'growth-curves are useful summaries of the more consistent aspects of patterns of change, but they are only a partial picture, not some deeper reality' (Osgood 2005: 205).

Using data from the Cambridge Study in Delinquent Development, Kreuter and Muthen (2006) carried out a comparison of these two types of model, and also included two further types which are not discussed here (growth mixture models and non-parametric growth mixture models). They found that the random effects growth model did not fit the data as well as the latent class model and the mixture model alternatives. However, Osgood (2005) argues that growth-curve models are preferable over the grouping approach for three reasons. Firstly, comparisons of trajectory typologies show that the number and distribution of the typologies varies depending on the underlying measures used. Second, there is a danger that despite the warnings of scholars such as Nagin, researchers will treat and interpret them as 'real' groups. And third, policy-makers presented with offender groups may be more punitive towards those in the 'high chronic' groups without justification.

Eggleston *et al.* (2004) have also been critical of the group-based approach and argue that there has been a lack of sensitivity analysis to determine how the results of this method vary according to various methodological problems in criminological data. They took three common problems faced by longitudinal self-report studies (differential length of follow up, missing data, and the 'extrapolation' problem caused by lack of offending data either due to incarceration or death). While they found a certain degree of model robustness, they also found that aspects of the models (such as the number of groups identified, the shape of the trajectories, and the groups to which individuals were assigned) varied depending on the data being used. Nagin (2004) agreed that such data issues could alter trajectory models in important ways; however, he also argued that this was a problem that was generic to all forms of longitudinal analysis, including growth-curve models.

Importantly, the use of such statistical methods has been criticized for its atheoretical approach to life-course criminology. While developmental criminologists who utilize such techniques have been responsible for presenting a number of important and influential theories (see the third part of this chapter), Sampson *et al.* (2004) have argued that there is still a greater need for the analytical methods used in criminological research to be more tightly linked to theory development. In particular, they argue that developmental criminologists must take a longer-term view to exploring how trajectories may be socially produced.

## CONTRIBUTIONS TO POLICY AND PRACTICE

In this final section of the chapter we overview the programmes and policy solutions which have been offered by the developmental and life-course perspective to the problem of crime. As with the theoretical and methodological controversies just outlined, there is keen debate within the field over the application of findings to policy. Such debate has focused around: the groups and/or population on whom intervention should be targeted; the particular stages in the life-course and/or criminal career when intervention may be most effective; and the nature and scope of the interventions themselves.

## WHO OR WHAT TO TARGET AND WHEN?

There are some differences within the broader developmental literature in terms of who or what to target, and the appropriate level of service provision (see also Crawford and Evans, this volume). Hawkins *et al.* (2010) for example differentiate between three core levels: universal targeting—developing services and support for a whole population without differentiating between those who may be more or less risky; selective targeting—focusing services on those groups who may not yet be involved in offending/anti-social behaviour, but whose background and family context suggest that they are at risk; and indicative targeting—providing support for those who are beginning to demonstrate problematic behaviours. Within the UK-based research report '*Support from the Start*' (Sutton *et al.* 2004), variant levels of intervention are described as primary (universal support targeting whole communities), secondary (providing support and services for families and schools where individual children have been identified as being at risk of offending), and tertiary levels of prevention (interventions aimed at preventing re-offending provided by youth justice specialists). Aside from consideration of the particular groups to be targeted, the timing of intervention is also of key importance. This has been a particular concern of criminal-career-based scholars. Their accounts indicate the need for policy-makers to match appropriate forms of intervention to different *stages* in the criminal career: onset, persistence, and desistance.

Research by Aos and colleagues has shown that secondary prevention programmes which selectively target at-risk families can have cost-benefits (Lee *et al.* 2008). While universal services are often regarded as expensive and there are concerns about uptake amongst the most needy groups, they may also be cost-effective in the longer term. Farrington *et al.* (2006) found that many self-reported offenders do not have criminal convictions (around half of all self-reported offenders in the Cambridge Study who were followed-up at age 50 had not been convicted) and thus may be unknown to service providers. Similarly, the Edinburgh Study has shown that of those involved in violent offending at age 17, just over three-quarters (76 per cent) had no convictions and were unknown to agencies (McAra and McVie 2010). As a consequence there is an urgent need to develop open-door, voluntary sector, outreach projects to support some of the most vulnerable and challenging populations. Primary prevention programmes targeting whole communities may therefore have a longer-term pay-off in connecting with such 'hidden' groups and reducing the risk that they undoubtedly pose.

## WHAT INTERVENTIONS WORK AND HOW DO WE KNOW?

Turning to more specific applications of theory into practice, space precludes a detailed overview of this burgeoning and extensive field. Instead, we overview some of the most prominent programmes developing from the risk factor paradigm. Table 18.2 sets out key risk factors identified in the literature, a range of strategies which have been recommended as logical modes of tackling such factors, and some examples of programmes which extant evaluations suggest can have positive outcomes.

Family-focused approaches include a raft of programmes aimed at supporting and educating parents (in particular new mothers) and parent management training (Smith

**Table 18.2** Risk-focused prevention—examples of effective strategies

| Risk factors | Strategies | Examples of programmes |
|---|---|---|
| Early involvement in problem behaviour (hyperactivity and impulsivity, conduct disorders) Poor parental supervision and discipline Family conflict and history of problem behaviour Parental involvement in/attitudes condoning problem behaviour Low family income Poor housing | **Family** Pre-natal services Family support using home visitors Parenting information and support | Oregon Study (child-rearing—Patterson 1982) Universal Parent Management (Mason et al. 2003) 'Triple P' Programme (positive parenting, Sanders et al. 2000) Functional Family Therapy (Sexton and Alexander 2003) The Incredible Years Programme (Webster-Stratton 1984) Elmira Study (intensive home-visiting—Olds et al. 1986) Montreal Study—Multi-modal intervention (Tremblay et al. 1995) Multi-dimensional Treatment Foster Care (Chamberlin 2003) |
| Low achievement beginning in primary school Aggressive behaviour including bullying Lack of commitment to school including truancy School disorganization | **School and pre-school** Pre-school education Family literacy and reading schemes Reasoning and social skills education School organizational changes (whole school ethos, teacher training and support) Preventing/tackling truancy and exclusion Further education for disaffected young people | High/Scope Perry Pre-School Project (Schweinhart and Weikart 1980) Child-Parent Centre (CPC) Programme (Reynolds et al. 2001) Seattle Social Development Project—multiple component programme (Hawkins et al. 1991) Promoting Alternative Thinking Strategies (Greenberg et al. 1995) |
| Friends involved in problem behaviour Alienation and lack of social commitment | **Youth** After-school clubs Mentoring Youth employment with education Youth work programmes | Multi-systemic Therapy (multiple component programme—Henggeler et al. 1992) Children at Risk (Harrell et al. 1999) Participate and Learn Skills (constructive leisure pursuits—Jones and Offord 1989) Job Corps (enhancing employability—Schochet et al. 2008) |
| Disadvantaged neighbourhoods Community disorganization and neglect High turnover/low neighbourhood attachment | **Community** Community mobilization Peer-led community programmes | Communities that Care (Harachi et al. 2003) |

*Source: Adapted from Anderson et al.* (2008), Hawkins *et al.* (2010).

2004). The Elmira Study is one of the best known home visit programmes for new parents in the US. Developed by David Olds and colleagues in New York, it involved intensive home visits by nurses, both pre and post-natal, and aimed to improve pregnancy outcomes, ensure that mothers gave better care to their children, and support the personal development of mothers (see Hawkins *et al.* 2010). Four hundred women were recruited to the study and randomly assigned to intervention and control groups. The research found significantly lower levels of child abuse and neglect in the intervention group during the first two years of life in comparison with a control group. A 15-year follow-up repeated these findings and also indicated that youngsters from the intervention group had significantly fewer arrests (20 per cent as contrasted with 45 per cent of the controls—see Olds *et al.* 1998).

A raft of parent management training programmes have been developed aimed at promoting effective child rearing techniques, including modes of discipline. Research by Patterson (1982) has shown that careful monitoring of child behaviour, clear and consistent rules, negotiation in the context of conflict (to inhibit escalation), and non-punitive forms of disciplining can be effective in minimizing offending and anti-social behaviour. Indeed a meta-analysis of 10 evaluations conducted by Farrington and Welsh (2003) found that such programmes reduced anti-social behaviour and delinquency by 20 per cent. Examples of parenting management programmes implemented within the UK include the Triple P programme (initially developed in Australia) and the Incredible Years programme.

Turning to school and pre-school strategies, programmes here are generally aimed at enhancing educational attainment and fostering greater attachment to school amongst young people as well as improving school organization and ethos. One of the most famous programmes is the Perry High/Scope Pre-School project (implemented in Ypsilanti, Michigan USA). Groups of disadvantaged ethnic minority youngsters were assigned to intervention and control groups. Those in the intervention group were made subject to a daily pre-school programme, plus home visits on a weekly basis over two years. The overall aim of the programme was to provide intellectual enrichment, improve reasoning skills, and thus have a longer-term impact on school attainment. Follow-ups from the programme at age 19 and again at age 40 indicated important benefits including better educational outcomes, greater employability, and lower levels of arrests (for a range of crimes) amongst the intervention group in comparison with the controls (Schweinhart *et al.* 1993, 2005).

A further important school-based programme is the Seattle Social Development Project. This is an example of a multi-component programme (tackling a range of different aspects of risks and at different levels). It combined parent management techniques, teacher training, and skills training for the youngsters involved. Five hundred first-grade children (aged around 6 years) were randomly assigned to experimental and control groups. Follow-ups at age 12 and again at age 18 demonstrated the efficacy of this approach. At age 12, boys in the experimental group from low-income families were significantly less likely to be involved in delinquency in comparison with controls, and girls were less likely to be involved in drug use (O'Donnell *et al.* 1995). Similarly, at age 18 the intervention group were less likely to be involved in violence and alcohol abuse (Hawkins *et al.* 1999).

Multi-systemic Therapy is also a programme which (as its name suggests) involves a range of different components—with a focus on the individual, family, school, and community. This programme was initially developed within the USA but has been implemented on a pilot basis within the UK. The programme targets serious young offenders and mixes and matches the variant dimensions of programme content to the particular needs of the young person. A core premise of the programme is the interconnectedness between the problems facing young offenders. It is run by trained therapists and intensive work can be done to improve home-school links, and to enhance cognitive skills amongst the young people. The first experimental test of the programme involved 84 young people and had promising results. At a two-year follow-up the intervention group had fewer arrests, reported lower levels of delinquency, and experienced better improvements in family functioning than the control group (Henggeler 1993). Five large-scale experiments conducted at a later stage reported positive benefits, although some evaluations have had more equivocal outcomes (including an evaluation in Canada by Leschied and Cunningham 2002, and a meta-analysis of MST undertaken by Littell 2005).

Finally, as shown in the table, a key exemplar of a community-based strategy is the Communities that Care (CTC) programme (initially developed in the US). The programme aims to involve the whole community in prevention of crime risks amongst young people. A coalition of key groups is constructed from all sectors of the community including schools, youth services, law enforcement agencies, health, business groups, religious groups, residents etc. It is intended that this coalition will work together to identify local prevention needs and then draw on a range of prevention activities from a specified list of tried and tested interventions. The coalition has responsibility for the implementation of the programme and for monitoring and tracking offenders involved with it. Early evaluations indicated very positive outcomes, with the CTC communities experiencing significant reductions in delinquency and alcohol use in comparison with controls (Feinberg *et al.* 2007). CTC was introduced into the UK by the Joesph Rowntree foundation on a pilot basis in 1998 (France and Crow 2001), and has now been implemented in over 35 locations.

## THEORY INTO PRACTICE; KEY CHALLENGES

While the list of programmes set out in Table 18.2 is certainly not exhaustive, it is evident that most energy is being expended by researchers in developing individual-, family-, and/or school-based programmes. Rather fewer programmes can be found tackling risk factors in whole communities and/or the nature and functioning of the community dynamics which underpin these. It should also be noted that the overwhelming majority of these programmes have been evaluated in a US/Canadian context. Indeed there is a questionable assumption within the broader literature that such programmes can be readily transported from jurisdiction to jurisdiction without the need to consider differences in the cultural and social context within which such measures are to be implemented (Muncie 2002, Muncie and Goldson 2006).

While developmentalists are keen to be involved in applied policy debate, it is interesting to note that some of the more radical implications of their research are not wholly followed through. The research consistently shows that the young people most at risk of offending are those who are the most socially disadvantaged and from the most impoverished backgrounds. Policy suggestions from developmentalists tend to be strongly focused on the individual child or immediate social environment, rather than tackling the broader *structural supports* for some of the adversities which they face. Rather than teaching resilience in a context of risk, justice demands that efforts be made to transform such macro-level processes.

Importantly, the findings from the Edinburgh Study challenge the assumption that targeted interventions are always and everywhere the most effective solution to the problem of crime. As we have shown in previous analysis (McAra and McVie 2005, 2007, 2010), a key difficulty with early targeted intervention is its capacity to stigmatize and criminalize. The risk factor paradigm in itself risks creating a self-fulfilling prophecy—targeted intervention may turn out to be iatrogenic in its own right.

In our 2007 article, we looked at three crucial decision-making stages of the juvenile justice process: the decision of police officers to 'charge' the young person with committing a crime; the decision of police officers to refer the young person to the juvenile justice system on offending grounds; and the decision of the officials within the system to bring the young person to a formal hearing. We found that selection effects were operating at each of these three stages in a way that ensured that certain categories of young people—'the usual suspects'—were propelled into a repeat cycle of referral into the system, whereas others involved in equally serious offending escaped the attention of formal agencies altogether.

Quasi-experimental analysis was conducted which allowed individuals who experienced these three progressively more intensive forms of intervention to be paired up with a group of similar young people, statistically matched on a range of characteristics (including serious offending), who had not had formal system intervention. The results of our analysis showed that the deeper young people who were identified as the usual suspects penetrated the youth justice system, the more likely it was that their pattern of desistance from involvement in serious offending was *inhibited*. These findings are significant because they highlight that even a system as inherently child-centred as the Scottish juvenile justice system (which should be better placed than most other Western juvenile justice systems to reduce offending) can contribute to a process of repeated targeting and labelling. The paper concludes that the key to tackling serious and persistent offending lies in a maximum diversion approach.

## CONCLUSIONS

In this chapter we have overviewed the emergence of developmental and life-course criminology within the wider framework of criminological history. We have critically considered the contribution of this field of criminology to conceptual, theoretical, and methodological debates within contemporary criminology and reviewed its continued policy salience.

This journey has reinforced to us the importance of remaining open to the variant epistemological and ontological framings of our discipline and for all scholars to have purchase on normative and political debates. The findings from the developmental and life-course perspective remind us that young people who offend most seriously, and those who come into conflict with the law, are amongst the most vulnerable and victimized groups in our society. If we abandon attempts to model the social world according to scientific-empirical precepts, then we run the danger of overlooking those who are the most needy and abandoning action for ivory towers.

We know from extant research that institutions create the conditions of their own existence, that in spite of a raft of 'effective' programmes, the same young people are recycled into the criminal justice system again and again. In challenging the operational practices of these institutions, and in facilitating an understanding of the complex negotiations which frame day-to-day interactions, then we are better placed to effect justice for all. In our view a critical positivism is possible and we urge our comrades to engage.

## ■ SELECTED FURTHER READING

Seminal texts in the field of developmental criminology are the two volumes of essays edited by A. Blumstein, J. Cohen, J. A. Rosh, and C. Visher (1986a and 1986b), which laid the groundwork for this paradigm.

For a critical evaluation of the study of the age-crime relationship and the developmental perspective, M. Gottfredson and T. Hirschi's (1990), *A General Theory of Crime* is an excellent starting point.

For key theoretical and methodological debates, the books by J. H. Laub and R. J. Sampson (2003), R. J. Sampson and J. H. Laub (1993), and by A. R. Piquero, D. P. Farrington, and A. Blumstein (2007) offer a broad review of the issues and consideration of analytical techniques.

The policy perspective is well captured in the collection of essays edited by D. J. Smith (2010), *A New Response to Youth Crime*.

## ■ REFERENCES

ANDERSON, B., BEINART, S., FARRINGTON, D. F., LANGMAN, J., STURGUS, P., and UTTING, D. (2008), *Summary of Risk and Protective Factors Associated with Youth Crime and Effective Interventions to Prevent it*. London: Youth Justice Board for England and Wales. www.yjb.gov.uk/publications/scripts/prodview.asp?idproduct=246&eP=.

ARMSTRONG, S. and McARA, L., (2006), 'Audience, Borders, Architecture: The Contours of Control', in S. Armstrong and L. McAra (eds), *Perspectives on Punishment: The Contours of Control*, Oxford: Oxford University Press.

AYERS, C. D., WILLIAMS, J. H. HAWKINS, J. D., PETERSON, P. L., CATALANO, R. F., and ABBOTT, R. D. (1999), 'Assessing correlates of onset, escalation, de-escalation and desistance of delinquent behaviour', *Journal of Quantitative Criminology*, 15: 277–306.

BLOCKLAND, A., NAGIN, D. S., and NIEUWBEERTA, P. (2005), 'Life Span Offending Trajectories of a Dutch Conviction Cohort', *Criminology*, 43: 919–53.

BLUMSTEIN, A., FARRINGTON, D. P., and MOITRA, S. (1985), 'Delinquency careers: innocents, desisters and persisters', in M. Tonry and N. Morris (eds), *Crime and Justice: A Review of Research*, Vol. 6, Chicago: Chicago University Press.

BLUMSTEIN, A., COHEN, J., ROTH, J. A., and VISHER, C.A. (eds) (1986a), *Criminal Careers and 'Career Criminals'*, Vol. I, Washington DC: National Academy Press.

——, ——, ——, and —— (eds) (1986b), *Criminal Careers and 'Career Criminals'*, Vol. II, Washington DC: National Academy Press.

BLUMSTEIN, A., COHEN, J., and FARRINGTON, D. P. (1988), 'Criminal career research: Its value for criminology', *Criminology*, 26(1): 1–35.

BRAME, R. and PIQUERO, A. (2003), 'The role of sample attrition in studying the longitudinal relationship between age and crime', *Journal of Quantitative Criminology*, 19: 107—27.

CASE, S. and HAINES, K. (2009), *Understanding Youth Offending: Risk Factor Research, Policy and Practice*, Cullompton: Willan Publishing.

CASPI, A. (2000), 'The child is father of the man: Personality continuities from childhood to adulthood', *Journal of Personality and Social Psychology*, 78: 158–72.

—— and MOFFITT, T. E. (1995), 'The continuity of maladaptive behaviour: from description to understanding in the study of antisocial behaviour', in D. Cicchetti and D. Cohen (eds), *Developmental Psychopathology*, Vol. 2, New York: Wiley.

CATALANO, R. F. and HAWKINS, J. D. (1996), 'The social development model. A theory of antisocial behaviour', in J. D. Hawkins (ed.), *Delinquency and Crime: Current theories*, Cambridge: Cambridge University Press.

CHAMBERLIN, P. (2003), *Treating chronic juvenile offenders: Advances made through the Oregon Multi-dimensional treatment Foster Care Model*, Washington DC: American Psychological Association.

CHUNG, I-J., HILL, K. G., HAWKINS, J. D., GILCHRIST, I. D., and NAGIN, D. S. (2002) 'Childhood Predictors of offense trajectories', *Journal of Research in Crime and Delinquency*, 39(1): 60–90.

D'UNGER, A. V., LAND, K. C., MCCALL, P.L., and NAGIN, D. S. (1998), 'How many latent classes of delinquent/criminal careers? Results from mixed Poisson regression analyses', *American Journal of Sociology*, 103(6): 1593–630.

EGGLESTON, E. P., LAUB, J. H., and SAMPSON, R. J. (2004), 'Methodological sensitivities to latent class analysis of long-term criminal trajectories', *Journal of Quantitative Criminology*, 20(1): 1–26.

ELLIOT, D. S. (1994), 'Longitudinal Research in Criminology: Promise and Practice', in E. G. M. Weitekamp and H.-J. Kerner (eds), *Cross-National Longitudinal Research on Human Development*, Dordrecht: Kluwer.

EZELL, M. E. and COHEN, L. E. (2005), *Desisting from crime: Continuity and change in long-term crime patterns of serious chronic offenders*, Oxford: Oxford University Press.

FARRINGTON, D. P (1986), 'Age and crime', in M. Tonry and N. Morris (eds), *Crime and justice: An annual review of research*, Vol. 7: 189–250.

—— (2003), 'Developmental and life-course criminology. Key theoretical and empirical issues—the 2002 Sutherland Award address', *Criminology*, 41(2): 221–55.

—— (2007), 'Childhood risk factors and risk-focused prevention', in M. Maguire, R. Morgan, and R. Reiner (eds), *The Oxford Handbook of Criminology*, 4th edn, Oxford: Oxford University Press.

FARRINGTON, D. P. (2008), 'The Integrated Cognitive Antisocial Potential (ICAP) Theory', in D. P. Farrington (ed.), *Integrated developmental and life-course theories of offending: Advances in criminological theory*, Vol. 14, New Brunswick: Transaction Publishers.

—— and WELSH, B. C. (2003), 'Family-based Prevention of Offending. A Meta-analysis', *Australian and New Zealand Journal of Criminology*, 36: 127–51.

——, COID, J., HARNETT, L., JOLLIFFE, D., SOTERIOU, N., TURNER, R., and WEST, D. J. (2006), *Criminal careers up to age 50 and life success up to age 48: new findings from the Cambridge Study in Delinquent Development*, 2nd edn, Home Office Research Study, 299.

FEINBERG, M. E., GREENBERG, M. T., OSGOOD, D., SARTORIUS, J., and BONTEMPO, D. (2007), 'Effects of the Communities that Care Model in Pennsylvania on Youth Risk and Problem Behaviours', *Prevention Science*, 8(4): 261–70.

FRANCE, A. and CROW, I. (2001), *The Story So Far: An Interim Evaluation of Communities that Care*, York: Joseph Rowntree Foundation.

GARLAND, D. (1994), 'Of crimes and criminals: the development of criminology in Britain', in M. Maguire, R. Morgan, and R. Reiner (eds), *Oxford Handbook of Criminology*, 1st edn, Oxford: Oxford University Press.

—— and YOUNG, P. (eds) (1983), *The Power to Punish: Contemporary Penality and Social Analysis*, Aldershot: Ashgate.

GLUECK, S. and GLUECK, E. (1950), *Unravelling Juvenile Delinquency* New York: The Commonwealth Fund.

GOTTFREDSON, M. and HIRSCHI, T. (1986), 'The true value of lambda would appear to be zero: An essay on career criminals, criminal careers, selective incapacitation, cohort studies and related topics', *Criminology*, 24: 213–33.

—— and —— (1987), 'The methodological adequacy of longitudinal research on crime', *Criminology*, 25: 581–614.

—— and —— (1990), *A general theory of crime*, Stanford, California: Stanford University Press.

GREENBERG, D. F. (1991), 'Age, crime and social explanation', *American Journal of Sociology*, 91(1): 1–21.

GREENBERG, M. T., KUSCHE, C. A., COOK, E. T., and QUAMMA, J. P., (1995), 'Promoting emotional competence in school-aged children: the effects of the PATHS curriculum', *Development and Psychopathology*, 7(1): 117-36.

HARACHI, T. W., HAWKINS, J. D., CATALANO, R. F., LAFAZIA, A. M., SMITH, B. H., and ARTHUR, M. W. (2003), 'Evidence-based Community Decision-making for Prevention: Two Case Studies of Communities that Care', *Japanese Journal of Sociological Criminology*, 28: 26–37.

HARRELL, A., CAVANAUGH, S., and SRIDHARAN, S. (1999), *Evaluation of the Children at Risk Programme: Results One Year After the End of the Programme. Research in Brief*, Washington DC: National Institute of Justice.

HAWKINS, D., WELSH, B., and UTTING, D. (2010), 'Preventing Youth Crime: Evidence and Opportunities', in D. Smith. (ed), *A New Response to Youth Crime*, Cullompton, Devon: Willan.

HAWKINS, J. D., CATALANO, R. F., KOSTERMAN, R., ABBOTT, R., and HILL, K. G. (1999), 'Preventing Adolescent Health-Risk Behaviours by Strengthening Protection During Childhood,', *Archives of Paediatrics and Adolescent Medicine*, 153: 226–34.

HAWKINS, J. D., VON CLEVE, E., and CATALANO, R. F. (1991), 'Reducing Early Childhood Aggression: Results of a Primary Prevention Programme', *Journal of the American Academy of Child and Adolescent Psychiatry*, 30(2): 208–17.

HENGELLER, S. W., MELTON, G. B., and SMITH, L. A. (1992), 'Family Preservation Using Multi-systemic Therapy: An Effective Alternative to Incarcerating Serious Juvenile Offenders', *Journal of Consulting and Clinical Psychology*, 60(6): 953–61.

—— (1993), 'Multisystemic Treatment of Serious Juvenile Offenders: Implications for Treatment of Substance-Abusing Youths', *National Institute on Drug Abuse Research Monograph* 137, DHHS Pub. No. (ADM) 88–1523, Washington, DC: US Government Printing Office: 181–99.

HIRSCHI, T. and GOTTFREDSON, M. (1983), 'Age and the Explanation of crime', *American Journal of Sociology*, 89: 552–84.

HUIZINGA, D., SCHUMANN, K., EHRET, B., and ELLIOT, A. (2003), *The effects of juvenile justice processing on subsequent delinquent and criminal behaviour: a cross-national study*, Washington: final report to the National Institute of Justice.

JONES, M. B. and OFFORD, D. R. (1989), 'Reduction of Anti-social Behavior in Poor Children by Non-school Skill-development', *Journal of Child Psychology and Psychiatry*, 30: 737–50.

JUNGER-TAS, J. and MARSHALL, I. H. (1999), 'The self-report methodology in crime research', *Crime and Justice*, 25: 291–367.

KREUTER, F. and MUTHEN, B. (2006), 'Analyzing criminal trajectory profiles: Bridging multilevel and group-based approaches using growth mixture modelling', *Journal of Quantitative Criminology*, 24(1): 1–31.

LAHEY, B. B., MOFFITT, T. E., and CASPI, A. (2003), *Causes of conduct disorder and juvenile delinquency*, New York: The Guilford Press.

LAUB, J. H. and SAMPSON, R. J. (2003), *Shared beginnings, divergent lives. Delinquent boys to age 70*, Cambridge, MA: Harvard University Press.

LEBLANC, M. (1997), 'A generic control theory of the criminal phenomenon: The structural and dynamic statements of an integrative multilayered control theory', in T. P. Thornberry (ed.), *Developmental theories of crime and delinquency (Advances in criminological theory, Vol 7)*, New Brunswick, N.J.: Transaction.

LEE, S., AOS, S., and MILLER, M. (2008), *Evidence-based programmes to prevent children from entering and remaining in the child welfare system. Benefits and costs for Washington*, Olympia: Washington State Institute for Public Policy, Document No. 08–07-3901.

LESCHIED, A. W. and CUNNINGHAM, A. (2002), *Seeking Effective Interventions for Serious Young Offenders: Interim Results of a Four-Year Randomized Study of Multisystemic Therapy in Ontario, Canada*. http://www.lfcc.on.ca/seeking.html.

LITTELL, J. H. (2005), 'Lessons Learned from a Systematic Review of Multi-systemic Therapy', *Children and Youth Services Review*, 25: 445–63.

LIVINGSTON, M., STEWART, A., and ALLARD, T. (2008), 'Juvenile Offending Trajectories: Implications for Crime Prevention', *Australian and New Zealand Journal of Criminology*, 41(3): 345–63.

LOEBER. R. (1996), 'Developmental continuity, change and pathways in male juvenile problem behaviours and delinquency', in J. D. Hawkins (ed.), *Delinquency and crime: current theories*, Cambridge: Cambridge University Press.

—— and FARRINGTON, D. P. (1998), *Serious and violent juvenile offenders: Risk factors and successful interventions*, Thousand Oaks, Cal.: Sage.

——, STOUTHAMER-LOEBER, M. S., VON KAMMEN, W., AND FARRINGTON, D. P. (1991), 'Initiation, escalation and desistance in juvenile offending and their correlates', *Journal of Criminal Law and Criminology*, 82:36-82.

——, ——, STOUTHAMER-LOEBER, M. S., MOFFITT, T. E., CASPI, A., WHITE, H. R., WEI, E. H., and BEYERS, J. M. (2003), 'The development of male offending: Key findings from fourteen years of the Pittsburgh Youth Study', in T. P. Thornberry and M. D. Krohn (eds) *Taking stock of delinquency: An overview of findings from contemporary longitudinal studies*, New York: Kluwer/Plenum.

LYNCH, R., MAIO, G., MOORE, G., MOORE, L., ORFORD, S., ROBINSON, A., TAYLOR, C., WHITFIELD, K. (2007), ESRC/HEFCW Scoping Study into Quantitative Methods Capacity Building in Wales. www.esrc.ac.uk/_images/Scoping_Study_into_Quantitative_Capacity_Building_in_Wales_tcm8–2724.pdf.

MARVELL, T. B. and MOODY, C. E. (1991), 'Age structure and crime rates: The conflicting evidence', *Journal of Quantitative Criminology*, 7(3): 237–73.

MASON, W. A., KOSTERMAN, R., HAWKINS, J. D., HAGGERTY, K. P., and SPOTH, R. L. (2003), 'Reducing Adolescents' growth in Substance Use and Delinquency: Randomized Trial Effects of a Preventative Parent-Training Intervention', *Prevention Science*, 4( 3): 203–12.

McARA, L. (2005), 'Negotiated Order: Gender, Youth Transitions and Crime', *British Society of Criminology* e-Journal, Vol. 6.

—— (2010), 'Models of Youth Justice', in D. Smith (ed.), *A New Response to Youth Crime*, Cullompton, Devon: Willan.

—— (2011), 'The Impact of Multi-Level Governance on Crime Control and Punishment', in A. Crawford. (ed.), *International and Comparative Criminal Justice and Urban Governance: Convergence and Divergence in Global, National and Local Settings*, Cambridge: Cambridge University Press.

—— and McVIE, S. (2005), 'The Usual Suspects? Street-life, Young Offenders and the Police', *Criminal Justice*, 5(1): 5–36.

—— and —— (2007), 'Youth Justice? The Impact of Agency Contact on Desistance from Offending', *European Journal of Criminology*, 4(3): 315–45.

—— and —— (2010), 'Youth Crime and Justice: Key Messages from the Edinburgh Study of Youth Transitions and Crime', *Criminology and Criminal Justice*, 10: 211–30.

—— and —— (2012 forthcoming), 'Negotiated Order: Deviance, Identity and Desistance', Special Edition on Negotiated Order, *Criminology and Criminal Justice*.

McVIE, S. (2005), 'Patterns of deviance underlying the age-crime curve: the long term evidence', *British Society of Criminology* e-Journal, Vol. 7.

—— (2009), 'Self-report delinquency surveys in European Countries: Britain and Ireland', in R. Zauhermann (ed.), *Self-Reported Crime and Deviance Studies in Europe, Current State of Knowledge and Review of Use*, Brussels: VUB Press.

MOFFITT, T. E. (1993), '"Life-course persistent" and "adolescent-limited" anti-social behaviour: A developmental taxonomy', *Psychological Review*, No. 100: 674–701.

—— (2003),' Life-course-persistent and adolescence-limited antisocial behaviour: A 10-year research review and a research agenda, in B. B. Lahey, T. E. Moffitt, and A. Caspi (eds), *Causes of conduct disorder and juvenile delinquency*, New York: The Guilford Press.

MUNCIE, J. (2002), 'Policy transfers and what works: Some reflections on comparative youth justice', *Youth Justice*, 1(3):27–35.

—— (2010), 'Book Review: S Case and K Haines, Understanding Youth Offending: Risk Factor Research, Policy and Practice, Willan Publishing, Cullompton, 2009', *Youth Justice: An International Journal*, 10: 302–4.

—— and GOLDSON, B. (2006), *Comparative youth justice*, London: Sage

NAGIN, D. S. (2004), 'Response to methodological sensitivities to latent class analysis of long-term criminal trajectories', *Journal of Quantitative Criminology*, 20(1). 27–35.

—— (2005), *Group-based modelling of development*, Cambridge, MA: Harvard University Press.

—— and LAND, K. C. (1993), 'Age, criminal careers and population heterogeneity: specification and estimation of a non-parametric, mixed poisson model', *Criminology*, 31(3): 327–62.

O'DONNELL, J., HAWKINS, J. D., CATALANO, R. F., ABBOTT, R. D., and DAY, L. E. (1995), 'Preventing School Failure, Drug Use and Delinquency Among Low-Income Children: Long-Term Intervention in Elementary Schools', *American Journal of Orthopsychiatry*, 65(1): 87–100.

——, HENDERSON, C. R. Jr., CHAMBERLIN, R., and TATELABUM, R. (1986), 'Preventing Child Abuse and Neglect: A Randomized Trial of Nurse Home Visitation', *Paediatrics*, 78(1): 65–78.

OLDS, D. L., HENDERSON, C. R. Jnr., CHAMBERLIN, R., AND TATELBAUM, R. (1986), 'Preventing child abuse and neglect: a randomised trial of nurse home visitation', *Paediatrics*, 78(1): 65–78.

——, ——, COLE, R., ECKENRODE, J., KITZMAN, H. R., and LUCKEY, D. (1998), 'Long-term Effects of a Nurse Home Visitation on Children's Criminal and Anti-social Behaviour: 15-year Follow-up of a Randomized Control Trial', *Journal of the American Medical Association*, 280(14): 1238–44.

OSGOOD, D. W. (2005), 'Making sense of crime and the life-course', *The Annals of the American Academy of Political and Social Science*, 602: 196–211.

PATTERSON, G. R. (1982), *A Social Learning Approach. Vol. 3: Coercive Family Process*, Eugene, Oregon: Castalia Publishing.

PETERSILIA, J. (1980), 'Criminal career research: A review of recent literature', in N. Morris and M. Tonry (eds), *Crime and Justice*, Vol. 2, Chicago: University of Chicago Press.

PETRAS, H., NIEUWBEERTA, P., and PIQUERO, A. R. (2010), 'Participation and frequency during criminal careers across the life span', *Criminology*, 48(2): 607–37.

PIQUERO, A. R., FARRINGTON, D. P., and BLUMSTEIN, A. (2003), 'The criminal career paradigm', *Crime and Justice*, 30: 359–506.

——, FARRINGTON, D. P., and BLUMSTEIN, A. (2007), *Key issues in criminal career research: New analyses of the Cambridge Study in Delinquent Development*, Cambridge: Cambridge University Press.

QUETELET, A. (1842), 'Of the development of the propensity to crime', in J. Muncie, E. McLaughlin, and M. Langan (eds) (1996), *Criminological Perspectives: A Reader*, London: Sage Publications.

RAUDENBUSH, S. W. and BRYK, A. S. (2002), *Hierarchical Linear Models: Applications and data analysis methods*, 2nd edn, Thousand Oaks, CA: Sage.

REYNOLDS, A. J., TEMPLE, J. A., ROBERTSON, D. L., and MANN, E. A. (2001), 'Long-term Effects of an Early Childhood Intervention on Educational Achievement and Juvenile Arrest; A 15-Year Follow up of Low-Income Children in Public Schools', *Journal of the American Medical Association*, 285(18): 2339–46.

RUTTER, M. (1995), 'Causal concepts and their testing', in M. Rutter and D. Smith (eds), *Psychosocial disorders in young people: Time trends and their causes*, Chichester: Wiley and Sons.

——, GILLER, H., and HAGELL, A. (1998), *Antisocial behaviour by young people*, Cambridge: Cambridge University Press.

SAMPSON, R. J. and LAUB, J. H. (1993), *Crime in the making: pathways and turning points through life*, Cambridge, MA: Harvard University Press.

—— and —— (2004), 'Life-course desisters? Trajectories of crime among delinquent boys followed to age 70', *Criminology*, 41(3): 301–39.

——, ——, and EGGLESTON, E. P. (2004), 'On the robustness and validity of groups', *Journal of Quantitative Criminology*, 20(1): 37–42.

SANDERS, M. R., MARKIE-DADDS, C., TULLY, L. A., and BOR, W. (2000), 'Triple P-Positive Parenting

Program: a comparison of enhanced, standard, and self-directed behavioural family intervention for parents of children with early onset conduct problems', *Journal of Consulting and Clinical Psychology*, 68(4): 624–40.

SCHOCHET, P. Z., BURGHARDT, J., and McCONNELL, S. (2008), 'Does Job Corps Work? Impact Findings from the National Job Corps Study', *American Economic Review*, 98: 1864–86.

SCHWEINHART, L. J. and WEIKART, D. P. (1980), *Young Children Grow-Up: The Effects of the Perry Preschool Programme on Youths Through Age 15*, Ypsilanti, MI: High/Scope Press.

——, BARNES, H. V., and WEIKART, D. P. (1993), *Significant Benefits. The High/Scope Perry Preschool Study Through Age 27*, Ypsilanti, Michigan: High/Scope Educational Research Foundation.

——, MONTIE, J., ZONGPING, X., BARNETT, W. S., BELFIELD, C. R., and NORES, M. (2005), *Lifetime Effects: The High/Scope Perry Preschool Study Through Age 40*, Ypsilanti, Michigan: High/Scope Educational Research Foundation.

SEXTON, T. L. and ALEXANDER, J. F. (2003), 'Functional Family Therapy: A Mature Clinical Model for Working with At-risk Adolescents and their Families', in T. L. Sexton, G. R. Weeks, and M. S. Robbins (eds), *The Handbook of Family Therapy*, New York: Taylor and Francis.

SKRONDAL, A. and RABE-HESKETH, S. (2004), *Generalized latent variable modelling. Multilevel, longitudinal and structural equation models*, Boca Raton, FL: Chapman and Hall/CRC.

SMITH, D. J. (2004), *Parenting and Delinquency at ages 12 to 15*, Edinburgh: Edinburgh Study of Youth Transitions and Crime Research Digest Series No. 3. www.law.ed.ac.uk/cls/esytc/findings/digest3.pdf.

—— (2007), 'Crime and the life-course', in M. Maguire, R. Morgan, and R. Reiner (eds), *The Oxford Handbook of Criminology*, 4th edn, Oxford: Oxford University Press.

—— D. J. (ed.) (2010), *A New Response to Youth Crime*, London: Willan.

SPARKS, R. (2006), 'Ordinary Anxieties and States of Emergency: Statecraft and Spectatorship in the New politics of Insecurity', in S. Armstrong, and L. McAra (eds), *Perspectives on Punishment: The Contours of Control*, Oxford: Oxford University Press.

SUTTON, C., UTTING, D., and FARRINGTON, D. P. (2004), *Support from the Start: Working with Young Children and their Families to Reduce the Risks of Crime*

*and Antisocial Behaviour*, London: Department for Education and Skills (Research Brief 524).

THORNBERRY, T. P. (1987), 'Toward an interactional theory of delinquency', *Criminology*, 25(4): 863–91.

—— (2005), 'Explaining multiple patterns of offending across the life course and across generations', *Annals of the American Academy of Political and Social Science*, 602: 296–302.

——, LIZOTTE, A. J., KROHN, M. D., SMITH, C. A., and PORTER, P.K. (2003), 'Causes and consequences of delinquency: Findings from the Rochester Youth Development Study', in T. P. Thornberry and M. D. Krohn (eds), *Taking Stock of Delinquency: An Overview of Findings from Contemporary Longitudinal Studies*, New York: Kluwer/Plenum.

TITTLE, C. R. (1988), 'Two empirical regularities (maybe) in search of an explanation: Commentary on the age/crime debate', *Criminology*, 26: 75–86.

—— and GRASMICK, H. G. (1997), 'Criminal Behavior and Age: A Test of Three Provocative Hypotheses', *Journal of Criminal Law and Criminology*, 88: 309–42.

TREMBLAY, R. E., PAGANI-KURTZ, L., MÂSSE, L. C., VITARO, F., and PIHL, R. O. (1995), 'A bimodal preventive intervention for disruptive kindergarten boys: Its impact through mid-adolescence', *Journal of Consulting and Clinical Psychology*, 63(4): 560–8.

WEBSTER-STRATTON, C. (1984), 'Randomized Trial of Two-Parent-Training Programs for Families With Conduct-Disordered Children', *Journal of Consulting and Clinical Psychology*, 52(4): 666–78.

WEIS, J. J. (1986), 'Issues in the measurement of criminal careers', in A. Blumstein, J. Cohen, J. A. Roth, and C. A. Visher (eds), *Criminal careers and 'career criminals'*, Vol. II, Washington DC: National Academy Press.

WEST, D. J. and FARRINGTON, D. P. (1977), *The delinquent way of life*, London: Heinemann.

WHITE, J., MOFFIT, T., EARLE, F., ROBINS, L., and SILVA, P. (1990), 'How Early Can we Tell? Predictors of Childhood Conduct Disorder and Adolescent Delinquency', *Criminology*, 28(4): 507–33.

WIKSTRÖM, P-O. (2010), 'Situational action theory', in F. Cullen and P. Wilcox (eds), *Encyclopaedia of criminological theory*, Beverley Hills: Sage Publications.

WOLFGANG, M. E., FIGLIO, R. M., and SELLIN, T. (1972), *Delinquency in a birth cohort*, Chicago: University of Chicago Press.

YOUNG, J. (1988), 'Radical Criminology in Britain: the emergence of a competing paradigm', *The British Journal of Criminology*, 28: 159–83.

# PART IV

# FORMS OF CRIME

# 19

# VIOLENT CRIME

## Fiona Brookman and Amanda Robinson

## INTRODUCTION

Violence is a controversial and highly emotive topic, arousing both fear and fascination, condemnation and condonement. We can be attracted to acts of violence or violent individuals in one context, repelled in another. Our perceptions of the individuals involved—their brutality, their vulnerability, their culpability—also inform our judgements of their behaviour. On the one hand, unprovoked attacks of violence can unleash a wave of public anger and abhorrence. On the other, we may sympathize with an individual who retaliates against long-term abuse with an act of premeditated violence. Public attitudes are also affected by factors such as media coverage (itself influenced by government, police, and corporate agendas) and people's own (and their friends' and neighbours') personal experiences of crime.

This chapter will focus on violent behaviour in early twenty-first century Britain. However, 'violence' is clearly a dynamic concept that varies greatly across time and place. In a different century the violent actions routinely condemned in modern Britain might not have been illegal—indeed, might even have been encouraged— domestic abuse being a case in point. Wood (2004: 23) noted that in eighteenth century England, '[v]iolence was not merely a reluctantly acknowledged "fact of life": rather, the early modern state, community and home were all arenas in which violence was an accepted—indeed, an expected—means of expressing legitimate social power'.

Similar considerations apply to contemporary cross-national differences. In some parts of the world, it is still not the case that wife-beating constitutes a criminal act. In others, extreme violence on behalf of ruling parties or warring factions is commonplace and 'routine'. Our knowledge of violence is mainly derived from research conducted within a fairly recent segment of human history, and often from a sociological or psychological perspective. In contrast, we tend to take little notice of the contributions that could be made to our understanding of violence by drawing from archaeological studies of early human societies, or from evolutionary psychology. For these reasons, a broad understanding of violent crime requires careful 'unpicking' of existing terminology, and clarity in defining the kinds of violent behaviour to which we are referring. In this chapter, while we touch upon others, we concentrate mostly on those types of (mainly interpersonal) violent behaviour that are the primary focus of crime control and preventive activities in the UK. The chapter therefore offers only a small and partial snapshot of the phenomenon and cannot be regarded as an exhaustive exploration.

The chapter first explores briefly what is known about the extent and seriousness of *interpersonal violence* in comparison with other significant classifications of violence, most notably *state and political violence* and *corporate violence*. We next look at the likelihood of becoming a victim of interpersonal violence; firstly in relation to the four basic social categories of gender, age, social class, and race and, secondly, in terms of 'dynamic' risk factors such as type and place of work, alcohol/drug use, and mental health. This is followed by an examination of the different ways in which scholars from a variety of disciplines have tried to account for the nature and extent of various forms of violent behaviour. Finally, recent trends and developments in attempts to control or reduce violence are briefly reviewed, focusing firstly on the more traditional approaches adopted by the criminal justice system, before examining the growing role of multi-agency partnerships whose remit is to address violence and the harm that it causes to individuals and communities.

## TYPES OF VIOLENCE: RELATIVE SCALE AND SERIOUSNESS

Violence is a highly contested and context-dependent concept. The elasticity of its borders, whilst partially liberating (in allowing one to cast the net wide when exploring violence) also makes the task of capturing the extent and nature of the phenomenon, let alone its causes or scope for prevention—extremely challenging, if not impossible.

First of all, there is no generally agreed definition to guide its measurement. Most social scientists would agree that such a definition should include psychological as well as physical harm and should not be restricted to legally prescribed violent offence categories; however, this remains debatable. For example, Henry (2000: 13) defined violence as 'the use of power to harm another, whatever form it takes' noting that it may encompass many aspects beyond the physical (e.g. psychological, emotional, economic, identity, ethical, etc.). Some critics point out, however, that definitions can become 'so broad that almost any situation that a person finds disagreeable would qualify as a form of violence' (Waddington *et al.* 2004: 158; Platt 1992).

Secondly, certain types of violence tend to be afforded significantly more attention than others by governments, the media, and criminologists alike, and hence the amount of reliable information available varies widely between them. Notably, corporate or state violence has generally failed to ignite the sustained level of concern or coverage which is aroused by various forms of street violence or, more recently, both domestic violence and terrorism. Moreover, even within crime categories that attract attention, certain types of victims or aspects of the violence tend to be neglected. For example, it is only recently that attention has been paid to domestic violence within same-sex relationships (Ristock 2009) or against men by women (Dobash and Dobash 2004) and there continues to be a neglect of violence perpetrated against individuals within institutions such as children's homes, hospitals, prisons, and homes for the elderly (Cooper *et al.* 2008; Evans 2010). There is also a general neglect of crime committed by and against the elderly compared to a perennial preoccupation with the 'problem' of youth crime (Estrada 2001). Finally, the language routinely used to describe certain acts of violence—such as child, sexual, or elder 'abuse'—fails to represent the essentially violent reality of the acts involved and their impact on the victims. The language often adopted to describe war-time violence is similarly dilutive (e.g. terms such as conflict, skirmish, and casualties).

As noted above, our focus in this chapter will be largely upon *interpersonal violence*. Other major forms of violence are discussed in other chapters (including state violence by Green and Ward, terrorism by Innes and Levi, and corporate violence by Nelken). However, in order to contextualize our analysis a little more, we begin by contrasting the scale of interpersonal violence in relation to *state and political violence* and *corporate violence*.

The World Health Organization (somewhat exceptionally) acknowledges the importance of producing a broad picture of this kind. Their threefold classification of violence-related deaths moves us beyond the conventional focus upon interpersonal violence and, when combined with data from the International Labour Organization (ILO), we gain a picture of violence that is quite at odds with most official publications (such as those that emanate from the Home Office). Hence, as illustrated in Figure 19.1, deaths due to corporate negligence or neglect make up the greatest proportion of global violence-related deaths (57 per cent), followed by suicide (21 per cent), homicide (14 per cent), and war-related deaths (8 per cent). Of course, this is just one way to divide up violence but hopefully illustrates how the lens through which we view violence may be tilted in different directions and, in some cases, the shutter fails to open leaving the extent, nature, or impact of some forms of violence unexplored.

## STATE AND POLITICAL VIOLENCE

State and political violence refers to those acts of lethal and non-lethal violence perpetrated by formal governments and quasi-governmental entities. Whilst attempts to

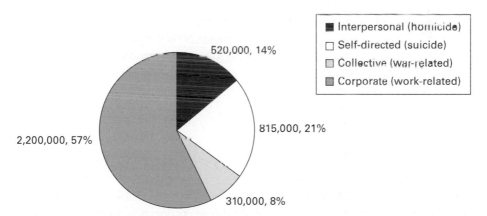

**Figure 19.1** Global violence-related deaths

*Source*: Adapted from WHO (2002), *World Report on Violence and Health*\* and ILO (2005), *World Day for Safety and Health at Work*.

\* *The WHO received data from over 100 countries in order to compile the World Report on Violence and Health (2002), including mortality data, police and judiciary records, crime laboratory, government, and legislative records as well as surveys and special studies (see Chapter 1 for full methodological details).*

quantify violence perpetrated by the state are fraught with difficulty (due to genuine difficulties in recording such deaths coupled with a desire by state officials to conceal its extent) it is apparent that violence resulting from action or inaction by governments is a significant problem. As indicated in Figure 19.1, the WHO estimated that about 310,000 people died from war-related injuries in 2000. This approximation falls at the conservative end of the spectrum however, with other commentators providing estimates some eight times greater. For example, Rummell (1994) estimated that 262 million people died at the hands of governments between 1900 and 1999 through acts such as genocide and mass murder. Over a quarter of a million people are estimated to have been killed in the 10 years since 2001 in Iraq, Afghanistan, and Pakistan[1] (Eisenhower Study Group 2011: 1).

Many other forms of violence, both lethal and non-lethal, accompany war. For example, it has been estimated that up to 60,000 women were raped in Bosnia and Herzegovina during the conflict between 1992 and 1995 (Randall and Haskell 1995) with inevitable long-lasting physical and psychological impacts. Mass rape as an element of warfare has also been unearthed in Congo, Darfur, Rwanda, and Liberia and in same cases has persisted after wars have ended (Kristof 2009).

Torture continues to be practised in a significant proportion of UN member states, including some of the richest and the most democratic (Morgan 2010). For example, its 2011 report concluded that 98 out of the 157 countries it examined had tortured or ill-treated people, despite most of them being party to the UN Convention against torture and other ill-treatment (Amnesty International 2011). The actual extent of torture is difficult to decipher given the secrecy surrounding security-led 'interrogations'.

Finally, the indirect effects of state-sanctioned violence are similarly immense. For example, untold suffering is experienced by individuals who may have to flee their homelands as refugees, infant mortality generally increases during times of conflict, and communicable diseases can increase to epidemic proportions. Famine alone related to conflict or genocide in the twentieth century killed around 40 million people (WHO 2002).

While we have focused upon some of the more extreme examples of state violence, it is important to recognize that state crime is pervasive and is not confined to a few 'rogue' states or countries with authoritarian regimes (Williams 2010). In fact, Green and Ward (this volume) suggested that modern states perpetrate or instigate most of the world's serious illegitimate violence whilst simultaneously claiming a monopoly over the legitimate use of violence. Perhaps more so than any other category of violence, state violence remains under-researched by social scientists and the focus of little attention by policy-makers.

## CORPORATE VIOLENCE

It is notoriously difficult to find reliable data on the extent of corporate violence. Nevertheless, as Figure 19.1 indicates, deaths due to corporate negligence and neglect (much of it is wilful) dwarf all other kinds of homicides that are routinely counted.

---

[1] This figure includes allied military, allied security, insurgents, civilians, journalists, and humanitarian workers (Eisenhower Study Group 2011: 4).

From the mass casualties produced by industrial disasters (e.g. Bhopal, approximately 20,000 deaths) through to the more routine deaths and injuries of workers, it is evident that harm from corporate violence is immense.

Broadly speaking, crimes of corporate violence fall into three categories: (i) those committed against consumers (e.g. the sale of unfit goods or provision of unsafe services); (ii) those that arise out of the employment relationship (e.g. health and safety at work); and (iii) crimes against the environment (e.g. air pollution) (Tombs 2008). If we just take one example from each category the scale of corporate violence quickly becomes apparent.

Unfit goods and services is a broad category that includes unsafe transport systems, unfit foods, contaminated water, unsafe medicines, and so forth. We will just consider transport safety briefly. Air crashes alone kill an average of 1,178 people each year globally and have killed over 11,000 people in the last decade.[2] Whilst many are ultimately deemed to have occurred because of pilot error, it is also apparent that the industry itself creates the conditions under which safety is compromised including those occasions when managers have insisted that planes fly to schedule despite deficiencies in safety (Tombs 2008).

Turning now to deaths and injuries in the workplace, the ILO estimated that, at a bare minimum, 2.2 million workers die across the globe each year through work-related 'accidents' and diseases (ILO 2005: 1). This translates to more than 5,000 work-related deaths every day. The Health and Safety Executive recorded over 26,000 major injuries to workers in 2009/10 and 152 fatalities to British workers. However, Tombs (2010: 889) is critical of these statistics, arguing that a multiplier of between 5 and 6 is required, bringing the total deaths of workers in 2009/10 to around 900. If we add to these figures the thousands of people who die from occupational cancers (HSE 2010) it becomes clear that work kills at least four times more people in the UK in an average year than those 'real' homicides (i.e., murder, manslaughter, and infanticide) recorded by the Home Office.

Finally, the WHO estimated that air pollution causes the annual premature death of two million people worldwide (WHO 2008) whilst in the UK an estimated 24,000 die prematurely every year because of air pollution (Thornton and Beckwith 2004: 291).

Despite the enormous death tolls and broader harms caused by corporate entities, many argue that their injurious activities are invariably not perceived as 'real crime' or punished as such (Box 1989; Snell and Tombs 2011[3]). In the UK, the first successful conviction for corporate homicide was brought in February 2011, some three years after the Corporate Homicide and Manslaughter Act 2007 came into force.[4] Nevertheless, the emergence of this new legislation does mark an important departure from the former position where corporations fell well below the radar of prosecution.

---

[2] Aircraft Crashes Records Office (ACRO) Geneva, Switzerland: www.baaa-acro.com/.

[3] See also Families Against Corporate Killers at: www.hazardscampaign.org.uk/fack/.

[4] Alex Wright, a 27-year-old geologist, died in September 2008 when working for Cotswold Geotechnical Holdings Limited in a 3.5 metre deep trench when it collapsed. Cotswold were fined £385,000 when the jury found that their system of work in digging trial pits was wholly and unnecessarily dangerous and well recognized health and safety guidance was ignored (CPS 2011—news release www.cps.gov.uk/news/press_releases/107_11/).

## INTERPERSONAL VIOLENCE

Despite the scale and importance of state, political and corporate violence, the form of violence most frequently measured, by governments and other organizations, is interpersonal violence. Society's preoccupation with certain kinds of violence is reflected in the two sets of data that are now published together annually in *Crime in England and Wales* (Flatley *et al.* 2010), police-recorded crime statistics, and the results of the British Crime Survey (BCS). Both are products of particular perceptions and definitions of violence, and are unreliable for a host of reasons (Maguire, this volume). They are also often mistrusted by the public (Bailey *et al.* 2010). Despite their limitations, they do give us a picture of the numbers of people who are willing to report having been victimized each year, and the levels of injuries they sustained. These figures can also be translated into 'risks' of being assaulted, in comparison to, for example, being burgled (see next section).

The recorded crime statistics on violence cover a disparate collection of offences that have reached the statute books over the years, ranging from murder to harassment, and including 'new' forms of violence (e.g. corporate manslaughter) and some historical anomalies (e.g. endangering life at sea). They currently divide violent crime broadly into three main categories: *violence against the person, sexual offences*, and *robbery*. The first group is subdivided into those offences that result in injury and those that do not. The BCS makes a similar distinction between injurious and non-injurious violence. The offences covered by the BCS estimates do not map directly on to those in the police figures. Looking at the two together, however, provides a broad indication of the extent to which interpersonal violent crime remains hidden from official notice. In the 2009/10 BCS interviews, in 55 per cent of the violent incidents recalled by victims, the police did *not* come to know about the matter (Hall and Innes 2010: 47).[5]

As shown in Table 19.1, police in England and Wales recorded approximately one million 'violent crimes' in 2009/10. As illustrated by Table 19.2, BCS estimates of violence tend to be significantly larger, in the order of about twice as many violent incidents against adults per year, compared to the number recorded by police (Flatley *et al.* 2010: 28). The BCS estimated almost five times as many robberies, and eight times as many sexual offences, as those recorded by police[6] (Flatley *et al.* 2010; see also Hall 2011: 84). It is important to point out that incidents resulting in serious injury were relatively small in number compared with those that resulted in minor injuries.[7] Indeed, around half of both BCS and police-recorded incidents of violence against the person involved no physical injury (Table 19.2).

[5] Whilst it is tempting to presume that at least twice as much violent crime occurs as is recorded by the police this would not be accurate given the large differences in reporting rates across offence categories; for example, sexual violence is more susceptible to under-reporting than acquisitive crimes such as burglary. Moreover, the victims of certain crimes are not likely to come into contact with researchers or, if they did, be prepared to speak to them (e.g. victims of human trafficking).

[6] BCS estimates of sexual assaults include attempts, making comparisons with police figures particularly difficult.

[7] Specifically, in the police figures for 2009/10, only about 6% of the 'with injury' category consisted of 'inflicting grievous bodily harm (GBH) with intent' whereas 89% consisted of the less serious 'actual bodily harm (ABH) and other injury' category. Furthermore, the 619 homicides recorded amounted to 0.06% of all violent offences and 0.01% of all recorded crime (Coleman *et al.* 2011).

**Table 19.1** Violent offences recorded by the police, England and Wales, 2009/10

| Offence group | Number 2009/10 |
|---|---|
| Violence against the person | 871,419 |
| (with injury) | 401,629 |
| (without injury) | 469,790 |
| Robbery | 75,105 |
| (business property) | 8,182 |
| (personal property) | 66,923 |
| Sexual offences | 54,355 |
| (Most serious) | 43,439 |
| (Other) | 10,916 |
| Total violent offences | 1,000,879 |

*Source*: Adapted from Flatley *et al.* (2010), *Crime in England and Wales 2009/10.*

**Table 19.2** Recorded violent crimes and BCS violence, comparable subset, 2009/10

| | Offence totals (to nearest 1,000) | | |
|---|---|---|---|
| | Police recorded | BCS estimate | Ratio Police: BCS |
| *Comparable offences* | | | |
| Assault with injury and wounding | 402,000 | 927,000 | 1:2.3 |
| Assault without injury | 470,000 | 821,000 | 1:1.7 |
| Robbery[8] | 67,000 | 334,000 | 1:5.0 |
| **Totals** | **939,000** | **2,082,000** | **1:2.2** |

*Source*: Adapted from Flatley *et al.* (2010), *Crime in England and Wales 2009/10.*

### Recent trends

According to BCS data, violence has decreased 50 per cent from its peak in 1995 (Osborne 2010). Police-recorded violence has also declined in recent years. This is consistent with research from the US, Canada, and Europe which has found overall declines in crime since the mid-1990s (Van Dijk *et al.* 2008; Tseloni *et al.* 2010). That said, there is evidence of a rise in violent crime since 2002 in certain parts of Western Europe—particularly Nordic countries. Nevertheless, these rises are outweighed by a decline in the number of violent crimes in the eastern part of the European Union, notably in Lithuania, Slovakia, Poland, Bulgaria, and the Czech Republic (Tavares and Thomas 2010).[9]

### The importance of context

In ending this section, it is important to emphasize that, aside from the limitations already mentioned, the official statistics on interpersonal violence do not adequately

---

[8] When making these comparisons robbery does not include incidents against business property.

[9] For discussion of international homicide trends see Brookman (2010).

capture the social and situational context of violence or other nuanced aspects of it (e.g. the relationship between offenders and victims, whether their roles merged or overlapped during the violent encounter, the role of bystanders, whether violence was planned or spontaneous or whether it occurred amongst individuals or groups). Moreover, the crude bifurcation of violence along the dimension of injury or absence of injury implies that physical injury is the key issue for the victim—when in reality this may not always be the case.[10] For this kind of detail one needs to look at research on specific forms of violence in different contexts, an issue we revisit later. We now turn our attention to the victims of violence, and in particular the risks of assault faced by different groups in the population.

## RISKS OF VICTIMIZATION

Based on the results of the 2009/10 BCS, the overall risk of being a victim of violent crime in that year was 3.0 per cent. Translated into crude 'risk' figures, the BCS results suggest at first sight that about one in 33 adults are likely to fall victim to violent offences (and 1 in 71 to violence by a *stranger*) each year. However, as we shall see, such figures have little relevance at the individual level, as some people will fall victim several times, and the distribution of risk among different social groups is highly skewed. In this section we explore a selection of static and dynamic factors that increase one's risk for violent victimization (risks for offending are covered by McAra and McVie, this volume). Although these may be established *correlates* of violence, and thus indicate where risk increases, we are not claiming they have a *causal* influence on violence.

### STATIC RISKS: GENDER, AGE, SOCIAL CLASS, AND RACE

We begin by briefly examining risk of victimization in terms of gender, age, social class, and race.

### Gender

It is impossible to understand the risk of victimization without considering gender (see also Heidensohn and Silvestri in this volume). In the 2009/10 BCS men were more than twice as likely as women to have experienced one or more violent crimes in the year prior to interview (4.2 per cent compared to 1.8 per cent) (Hall and Innes 2010). Men also had higher levels across all legally defined categories of crime (wounding, assault, etc). On the other hand, women were at greater risk of domestic violence (4.6 per cent compared to 2.6 per cent).[11] Furthermore, the data show that women suffer

---

[10] For example, domestic violence studies have shown that emotional pain has more lasting negative impacts when compared to physical pain (Chen *et al.* 2008).

[11] Is well-known that domestic violence is likely to be under-reported in face-to-face BCS interviews so data from a self-completion module on all types of intimate violence are used to supplement the figures derived from face-to-face interviews.

both *more serious* and *more frequent* domestic assaults than men; for example, 1 in 9 women reported having experienced 'severe force' from a partner since the age of 16, compared to 1 in 20 men. Risk of serious sexual assault was also found to be far greater for women (1 in 20 women compared to 1 in 331 men; op. cit. Table 3.14). A similar gendered pattern is apparent in homicide, in that, although men have a higher risk overall, women are at a much higher risk of domestic homicide: for example in 2009/10, 54 per cent of female victims aged 16 or over had been killed by their part-ner, ex-partner, or lover compared to 5 per cent of male victims (Coleman *et al.* 2011: Table 1.07).[12]

## Age

Age profoundly affects one's risk of victimization. Young people are more at risk than older people of becoming victims of violence, and risk steadily decreases as age increases for all types of violence. According to BCS figures, 13 per cent of 16–24-year-old males were assaulted in 2009/10, compared with 6 per cent of those aged 25–34, 3 per cent of those aged 35–44 and dwindling down to 0.2 per cent for those aged 75 or older (Hall and Innes 2010: Table 3.03). The equivalent figures for females were 4 per cent for the youngest group (16–24) and 0.1 per cent for the oldest (75+ years). Young people aged 16–29 were also the second most at-risk age group for homicide, at a rate of 17 per million population.[13] Such patterns are often explained in terms of differences in 'lifestyle' (discussed later); for example, young people tend to go out drinking at night more often than older people (Mattinson 2001). Indeed, characteristics of 'the young' such as being a full-time student, visiting bars and nightclubs, and living in privately rented flats are all associated with a higher likelihood of violence.[14]

### Social class

Research from the UK and elsewhere has demonstrated a robust negative correlation between social class and many types of violence both within and outside the home (Hall 2011; Lauritsen and Heimer 2010; Lauritsen and Schaum 2004; Ray 2010; Renzetti 2009). A range of factors can be drawn upon as indicators of social class including income, type of housing, and employment status. The 2009/10 BCS showed in multi-variate analysis that employment status and occupation were important predictors of violent victimization (Hall and Innes 2010: Table 3.07); equally, those living in areas such as 'blue-collar communities' and 'constrained by circumstances' were more likely to fall victim to violence than those in 'prospering suburbs'.[15] Similar patterns hold for homicide, where victimization is highly correlated—for both victims and offenders—with income inequality and social class (Brookman 2005; Daly, Wilson, and Vasdev 2001; Polk 1994; Rennison 2000). Thus, it seems evident that it is the poor who are

---

[12] By contrast, the overall homicide rate for men was 16 per million population and 7 for women.

[13] The most at-risk age group is children aged less than one year (Coleman *et al.* 2011; Table 1.07).

[14] The 2006 Offending, Crime and Justice Survey (OCJS) also found a higher risk for violence amongst those aged 10–15 compared to those aged 16–25, and this was observed for both males and females (Roe and Ashe, 2008: Table 4.1). Most assaults took place at school.

[15] These are categories defined by the ACORN classification, which groups postcodes according to demographic, employment, and housing characteristics.

most likely to be injured and killed, whether by violence as conventionally defined or by injury at work or at the hands of the state.[16]

### Race and ethnicity

In a reversal of earlier trends, the 2009/10 BCS indicated that white respondents were at higher risk of violence compared to black and minority ethnic (BME) respondents (3.1 per cent compared to 2.4 per cent). Furthermore, white respondents remained at higher risk of violence even after controlling for other socio-demographic and 'lifestyle' factors such as age, gender, marital status, and visits to nightclubs (Hall and Innes 2010: Table 3.07). This unexpected finding will undoubtedly be thoroughly dissected in future publications produced by the Home Office.[17] Nevertheless, it should be noted that violence against BME groups often includes racial motives, which can greatly magnify the impact on victims even of apparently 'minor' offences such as common assault and harassment. Furthermore, some of the 'new' forms of crime drawing attention in the UK fall disproportionately on BME groups, so-called 'honour-based' violence being a prime example (for further discussion, see Phillips and Bowling, this volume).

In the case of homicide, people from BME groups are more at risk than white people. Although these differences are less striking than in the USA, minority groups in Britain are consistently represented in homicide figures at levels that exceed their representation in the general population. Adding gender into the equation illustrates further the variation in risk across groups, as black males had the highest homicide rate (90 per million population), followed by males of other races (43 per million), Asian males (24 per million), and finally white males (15 per million). Although females generally have a lower homicide rate than males, examining the 'intersection' between race and gender shows black females at a higher risk than all other female groups, and even higher than white males (19 versus 15 per million) (Coleman *et al.* 2011: Table 1d).

### DYNAMIC RISK FACTORS

The distribution of risk of victimization is also affected by a number of factors that are 'dynamic', or amenable to change. Here we consider only a few examples: occupation/workplaces, 'lifestyle' factors such as alcohol/drug use, and mental health. Clearly these increase risk of violent victimization but they are also amenable to change, either by individual decision-making (e.g. how often to visit nightclubs) or broader policy interventions (e.g. to reduce assaults against workers, or to provide assistance to mentally ill homeless persons).

### Place and type of work

Most of our time is spent either at home or work, so it should come as no surprise that research finds a relationship between workplace characteristics and violence.

---

[16] For example, the WHO (2002: 11) estimated that less than 10% of global violence-related deaths occur in high income countries.

[17] The most recent version of 'Statistics on Race and the Criminal Justice System' was not available at the time of writing.

Attention to workplace violence from researchers and policy-makers has not gener-ally included the sorts of 'corporate violence' discussed earlier. Rather, it has focused mainly on attacks on staff by members of the public and is therefore criticized as being constructed primarily as a problem for public sector workers when, in reality, injury and harm to workers is much more widespread, as illustrated earlier.

A special analysis of responses to the 2002/3 British Crime Survey produced an estimate that over the year, just under 1 per cent of working adults had been victims of actual assaults and a further 1 per cent had been threatened in the workplace (Upson 2004: 5). A more recent study showed that physical violence at work (including threats, violence, and injury) was experienced by 4.9 per cent of 3,979 employed respondents (Jones *et al.* 2011). Workplace violence varies substantially by occupation, with work-ers in protective service occupations, such as police officers, being most at risk, and workers in health and social welfare, such as nurses, also reporting relatively high risks (Upson 2004). More recent work also highlights certain aspects of the workplace that significantly increase the risk of violence: public and third sector (compared to private sector), particular industries (health/social work and public administration/defence, which includes police officers), and occupations (e.g. personal service occupa-tions) (Jones *et al.* 2011).

### 'Lifestyle' factors

The frequency with which people consume alcohol or drugs, or visit pubs, bars, and nightclubs, has unambiguous implications for their risk of violence. According to the 2009/10 BCS, respondents who had visited pubs or bars in the evening more than once a week were more than twice as likely to fall victim to violence than those who had not (Hall and Innes 2010: 63). An even stronger effect was observed for visits to nightclubs, which increased the risk of violence by nearly six times. The most recent OCJS data also showed that assaults of 16–25-year olds most often took place in a pub, bar, or nightclub (Roe and Ashe 2008). Additional insight into the risk associated with these behaviours is provided by victim reports indicating that offenders were under the influence of alcohol in one-half, and the influence of drugs in one-fifth, of all vio-lent incidents (Hall and Innes 2010: 60). These 'lifestyle' factors significantly increase one's risk of experiencing multiple types of violence, and it is notable that they do so even after taking into account other key determinants of risk such as gender and age.

### Mental health

In comparison to the risk factors discussed thus far, the relationship between mental health and vulnerability to violence has received far less research attention, as most research in this area focuses on mental health and offending and how to manage the potential dangerousness of mentally ill persons (see Peay, this volume). There is ample evidence that persons with mental illness are at much higher risk of criminal victimi-zation, and violence in particular, compared to the general population (see Snowden and Lurigio 2007 for a review). For example, an American study found twice the levels of violent victimization in a patient sample compared to a comparison sample drawn from the same neighbourhoods (15 per cent compared to 7 per cent) (Silver 2002). This is consistent with results from the only British study which found twice the rate of vio-lence in a sample of community-dwelling patients compared to the BCS rates at that time (16 per cent compared to 7 per cent) (Walsh *et al.* 2003). The heightened risk of violent victimization amongst mentally ill persons has been explained by their symptomatology (e.g. delusions, symptom severity, functioning), and their greater risk of homelessness, drug or alcohol abuse, and involvement in conflicted social relationships (Hiday *et al.* 2001; Silver 2002; Teasdale 2009). Mentally ill women, especially those that are also homeless, can experience very high rates of physical and sexual violence (Khalifeh and Dean 2010; Goodman 1995).

Finally—and perhaps and most importantly—a vast body of research identifies a close association between offending and victimization, to the extent that it can 'be considered one of the most consistent of all criminological facts' (Reiss and Roth 1993) and one that is amplified within the context of violence (Piquero *et al.* 2005). As offenders and victims are frequently drawn from the same group of individuals, it makes sense to keep the risks for violent victimization in mind when reading the next section on theoretical explanations of offending. Specifically, it is important to consider how victims and offenders appear to share similar characteristics, and also how they can be empirically distinguished from each other.

## EXPLAINING VIOLENCE

Setting out to 'explain violence' immediately raises some important questions. Given the enormous heterogeneity of forms of violence discussed earlier, is it plausible that any one theory or theoretical paradigm can account for all these manifestations, or even serve as a common thread in all of them? Should we therefore be seeking only explanations of particular types of violence? And should we restrict ourselves to criminal violence, or include violence that is widely regarded as legitimate (such as violence perpetrated during wartime, violent sports, or executions of criminals)? Equally important, what sort of explanation are we looking for? An explanation of why this person committed that act in a particular place and time? Or why particular kinds of individual tend to acquire criminal histories of violent offending? Are we interested in the immediate triggers (proximate factors) or background influences (distal factors)? Alternatively, are we searching for an explanation of different *rates* of violence in different locations, geographical areas, or countries, and/or over time? Or of different rates of offending or victimization, by occupation, age, ethnicity, and gender? Or of patterns in relationships between offenders and victims? Different sorts of answers are required for different aims and levels of explanation. When judging the explanations given, it is also necessary to assess whether it can make sense of *non*-violence as well as of violence. The accounts that come closest to helping us understand why this person committed that crime on that particular occasion are retrospective reviews; however, the motivating factors they reveal are much more common than violent behaviour, even if one takes into account opportunity variables.

Within the space available we shall attempt to give a flavour of the multiplicity of perspectives by focusing upon individual, structural, cultural, and situational theories of violence. We will end by discussing the value of integrating these levels in order to more fully understand the complexity of violence (see also Rock, this volume, for additional theoretical discussion).

## THE 'CRIMINAL BEING': BIOLOGICAL, CLINICAL, AND EVOLUTIONARY APPROACHES

Biologically-based explanations of violence are, in a sense, where modern criminology began, with the work of Lombroso (1835–1909) and his focus upon the physical attributes and indicators of criminality (Brookman 2005). They are also perhaps the most often critiqued theories. While there is little doubt that some acts of violence are committed by individuals with some form of pathology (e.g. a neurological or personality disorder[18]), and some evidence that certain people simply enjoy hurting and killing other people (Schinkel 2004), most criminologists would agree that these represent exceptions rather than the rule (Brookman 2010). For example, psychopathology might be more likely amongst domestic violence offenders, but only a minority of all abusive men are psychopaths (Harris *et al.* 2001). Hence, the most convincing work in this area acknowledges the link between the individual and environmental stimuli (Niehoff 1999; Roth 2011). As Walby and Carrier (2010: 276) acknowledge 'in today's biocriminology, fewer claims are posited about direct causality'. Nevertheless, they have not gone away completely (DeLisi *et al.* 2008) and scientific advances have made it increasingly attractive to pursue and isolate criminal genes[19] and to probe ever closer into brain structural and functional impairments (see Fabian 2010 for a review of the latter). However, even amongst biologists, there is an increasing recognition that the way in which genes are expressed 'depends on social factors' (Rafter 2008: 246). In short, biological approaches are extremely limited in their explanatory capacity due to a failure to acknowledge the interactional nature of much violence and the power of the situation. So whilst the focus of biocriminology has moved from the 'outer observable body to its infinitesimal insides' ('jug ears to genes', see Walby and Carrier 2010: 275) the essential weaknesses remain.

Evolutionary psychology, on the other hand, offers a rather more sophisticated appraisal of the possible roots of violence and has paved the way for a 'biosocial' criminology that acknowledges the complex interplay of the biological being within the social environment. Most recently there has been a revival of interest in such approaches, not least due to historians making their presence felt in the search for links between our violent past and present (e.g. May 2011 special issue of the *British Journal of Criminology*). In seeking to understand how, why, and when violence was adaptive (i.e., increased human chances of survival) some historians, evolutionary psychologists, and archaeologists suggest that violence may be 'hard-wired' and emerge when, for example, environmental conditions necessitate competition for limited resources (Buss 2005; Roth 2011). Daly and Wilson, well-known proponents of

---

[18] There are important debates regarding the validity of diagnostic tools in relation to mental illness generally and, specifically, ongoing debates regarding the links between certain mental disorders, such as psychopathy, and involvement in violent crime (Skeem and Cooke 2010).

[19] See Beaver *et al.*'s (2010) study of a specific MAOA gene, dubbed the 'thug' or 'warrior gene', and the apparent links to gang violence.

evolutionary psychology in relation to homicide, proposed that homicide should vary inversely with the degree of genetic relatedness between the offender and victim (e.g. most family homicides occur amongst spouses as opposed to blood-relatives). Indeed Daly and Wilson (1996) found that victim and killer were genetic relatives in just 6 per cent of the total number of solved cases that they analysed from Detroit police records.[20] Furthermore, there is research evidence that stepchildren incur an elevated risk of lethal and non-lethal abuse as compared to those living with their biological parents (known as the 'Cinderella effect') offering further support for the evolutionary perspective (Daly and Wilson 2008; Burgess and Drais 1999).[21]

Other theories emphasizing 'individual pathology' focus on the effects of various substances upon the body and mind, notably work on the psychopharmacological effects of drugs and alcohol (Kuhns and Clodfelter 2009) but also research on the effects on the brain (and ultimately behaviour) of, for example, exposure to lead (Stretesky 2001) or of lower-than-normal sugar or cholesterol levels or elevated testosterone levels (see Brookman 2005 for a review). Research on the former illustrates that mediating and moderating factors (such as the social and environmental elements of the situation in which drug use or crime takes place) are crucial elements that cannot be isolated from any psychopharmacological effects (Bennett and Holloway 2005). It is, for example, very rare for people to be violent *every* time that they consume alcohol, so it cannot be said that the drink is a sufficient or even a necessary explanation of their violence. That said, the opportunities for certain types of interaction offered by heavy alcohol use, combined with an aggressive male 'drinking culture' (Tomsen 1997) strongly implicate alcohol in the process of becoming violent and hence offer a useful starting point from which to build theoretical explanations of at least some forms of violence[22] (see Bennett and Holloway 2009 and 2010 for a comprehensive discussion of the relationship between substance misuse and crime).

## STRUCTURAL EXPLANATIONS OF VIOLENCE

A contrasting account is provided by structural theorists, who are primarily concerned with explaining certain striking patterns in the social characteristics of victims and offenders. They try to unravel, for example, how and why certain conditions such as poverty, deprivation, social disorganization or inequality (in relation to dimensions such as race or gender) may explain patterns of violence. As such they focus broadly upon the organization (or rather *dis*organization) of society and how it can foster the conditions for violence.

There are many published studies documenting the apparent links between structural disadvantage and violent offending. Moreover, there is evidence that both offenders and victims of interpersonal violence often come from the same communities.

---

[20]  Brookman's 2005 similar analysis produced a figure of 14% for Britain.

[21]  However, if one considers the killing of babies aged less than one year it is apparent that the great majority are killed by a biological parent (rather than step-parents, other carers, or strangers)—an observation not easily compatible with evolutionary theory (see Coleman *et al.* 2011; Brookman 2005).

[22]  Of course, there are many types of violence for which it offers *no* explanation: for example, most political, corporate, and state-sponsored violence. Furthermore, violence is found even where the use of alcohol or illegal drugs is condemned or rare (e.g. Muslim countries).

As Papachristos (2009: 75) noted, 'individuals of minority groups, especially males between the ages of 17 and 28, who live in poor, isolated neighbourhoods bereft of social and human capital are the most likely perpetrators and victims of murder'. Other scholars have focused more specifically upon the links between marginalization and the development of violent forms of masculinity (e.g. Polk 1994; Brookman 2005; Treadwell and Garland 2011). This research provides a powerful reminder of how hegemonic masculinity is more likely to manifest within certain communities.

Structural approaches are also particularly useful in understanding the continued and widespread prevalence of violence against women and girls across the globe. The historical toleration, and in some cases encouragement, of abuse against females by male partners and family members continues to the present day. For example, control over women is maintained in different societies through established cultural concepts such as romantic love, duty, or notions of 'honour' and shame (Dobash and Dobash 1979; Gill 2008). Indeed, gendered crimes are impossible to understand fully *without* considering the unequal position of women in society. However, women are a heterogeneous group; those with fewer resources or additional vulnerabilities such as mental health problems tend to experience more domestic and sexual violence. For example, national surveys in the US and UK found that the risk for victimization was highest amongst young, single women with children, particularly those with lower incomes living within disadvantaged areas (Hall 2011; Lauritsen and Schaum 2004). As noted earlier, homeless women with mental health problems are especially vulnerable to domestic and sexual violence (Khalifeh and Dean 2010), further illustrating the pernicious impact of interlocking forms of structural disadvantage.

Similarly, there is a good deal of evidence from international research that street gangs emerge and flourish where inequality and marginality prevail. Vigil (2006: 22) for example, argued that the street gang is an outcome of 'the relegation of certain persons or groups to the fringes of society where social and economic conditions result in powerlessness'. Closer to home, Pitts's (2008: 56) research into youth gangs points to 'seismic economic and political changes' in the UK in the past two decades which have led to the appearance of US-style armed youth gangs. These changes include: (a) the widening gap between rich and poor; (b) the concentration of the poorest sections of the population in social housing; and (c) structural youth unemployment (due to the decline of Britain's industrial base). At the time of writing rioting has taken place for the fifth consecutive night across a number of cities in England. The violence (including arson attacks, looting, robbery, assault, and murder) predominantly perpetrated by youths, many of whom are believed to be gang-affiliated, was initially sparked by the shooting of a young man by the Metropolitan Police in North London. It has been suggested that economic recession, poverty, a culture of despair and consumerism explains, in part, the unprecedented scale and level of violence (Ponticelli and Voth 2011; Rogers 2011; BBC News Magazine 2011).

The question that immediately follows of course is how the scene, once set, actually plays out? Which actors come centre stage and play a violent role? When, instead, do they fade backstage or stand down? It is essentially on this basis that the structural approach has been subject to sustained criticism. As Levi (1997: 860) noted, macro-level accounts 'seldom generate anything close to a causal account which makes sense of nonviolence as well as of violence'. Put another way, the vast majority of individuals who live in conditions of poverty or disadvantage do not resort to violence at any time. Hence, in order to understand the patterns of violence that actually occur, it is imperative to study the *social experiences* of those who engage in it (Athens 1992). As will be shown, a variety of psychological, situational, and cultural perspectives can help us to take account of such social experiences and more clearly understand how violence unfolds in particular social settings.

## COGNITIVE AND BEHAVIOURAL PSYCHOLOGY

Over the last 30 years, a major contribution to the study of violence has been made by cognitive and behaviourist psychologists, especially social learning theorists, who adopt an integrated cognitive-behavioural approach (Bandura 1977), which provides important insights into how violent individuals interpret environmental cues and how they may have *learned* to behave violently. For example, the behaviourist theory of differential reinforcement indicates that crime occurs in an environment in which, in the past, the actor was positively reinforced for behaving in this manner and whereby any adverse consequences were such that they did not prevent the response (Jeffery 1965). Goldstein (1999) argued that low-level aggression can escalate to violence across incidents as the perpetrator's use of aggression is rewarded and reinforced over time, and inhibitions to aggressive behaviour diminish. Importantly, patterns of reinforcement and punishment are unlikely to be identical or constant between individuals or for the same person over time. Hence, the person's involvement in violence depends upon their unique interaction with the social environment—with some individuals having gained rewards for violence and others suffering adverse consequences.[23] Risks include the chance of arrest and imprisonment or the social and personal costs to one's reputation of 'backing down' from a challenge. Rewards could include the kudos accrued from a successful violent episode, the buzz associated with committing a daring violent offence, or the financial benefits associated with some violent offences such as robbery.

Cognitive-behaviourists focus more closely upon the specific cognitive processes that individuals use and how people deal with verbal and non-verbal information during interactions (i.e., how we encode information, make mental representations of the situation, and construct and decide upon a response). Biases or cognitive distortions can occur at any of these stages, leading to violent responses (Palmer 2006). In essence, cognitive explanations hypothesize that violent offenders interpret and appraise social information in a way that favours selection of an aggressive behavioural response (Crick and Dodge 1994; Seager 2005). Cognitive distortions can arise for various reasons and are linked to broader attitudes and beliefs about oneself, others and the role of violence (Collie *et al.* 2007) as well as a failure to mature normally and develop empathy and 'moral reasoning'. For example, Bandura (1990) proposed a theory of moral disengagement whereby offenders develop a number of cognitive techniques which allow them to avoid feeling guilty for their offences—such as displacement or

---

[23] 'Rational choice theory' (which provides the theoretical underpinning for 'situational crime prevention'—see Crawford, this volume) also focuses upon the relative risks and rewards of committing criminal acts including violence.

diffusion of responsibility, distorting the consequences of an action, or dehumanizing the victim. Such individuals may also be likely to lack social and interpersonal skills which assist people to resolve potential conflicts.

A number of attempts have been made to synthesize ideas from a variety of psychological theories of aggression. One that has recently been attracting attention from the designers of offending behaviour programmes is the General Aggression Model (GAM) (Anderson and Bushman 2002). GAM works on the premise that each individual brings a unique set of characteristics to a situation, such as genetic predispositions, personality traits, attitudes and learning experiences, which shape their arousal and cognitive responses to a given situation. Specifically, an inherent predisposition towards aggression combines with a series of experiences that prepare the individual to behave aggressively in different situations. This then leads to the acquisition of 'well-rehearsed and eventually automated aggressive knowledge structures that are retrieved habitually' (Gilbert and Dafern 2010: 171).

As discussed by both Hollin and Raynor in this volume, cognitive-behavioural theories have been influential in the development of 'offending behaviour programmes', which are currently attended by large numbers of offenders in prisons and probation areas across England and Wales. These include programmes aimed specifically at high-risk violent and sexual offenders, in which participants are taught to recognize and overcome their own cognitive distortions and practise more appropriate ways of handling situations through exercises and role-plays. An interesting aspect of such theories, with important implications for programmes, is their continued tendency to focus on *impulsive* behaviour, and on violence characterized by anger and a loss of self-control. This can draw attention away from a rather different kind of violence in which anger may be largely absent: broadly speaking, what Megargee (1983) called 'instrumental' (as opposed to 'expressive' or 'reactive') violence.[24] Such violence may be committed in order to obtain an economic benefit; for example, to keep other drug dealers off one's territory or away from one's crime proceeds (Stelfox 1998) or to obtain money or valuables through robbery. A reputation for violence can also be economically functional in, say, protection rackets or other activities involving 'gangsters' or organized criminal groups (Gambetta 1994). In practical terms, this issue raises questions about the suitability of interventions directed predominantly at 'impulsiveness' and 'anger management' (as are most programmes for offenders), for people who already use violence in a very controlled manner when, for example, committing robberies or rape: there may be a risk that this simply teaches some of them to do so more effectively.

## SITUATIONAL AND INTERACTIONIST APPROACHES

There still remain questions about why particular acts of violence occur at particular moments in time: why here? why now? why this victim? Situational and interactionist

---

[24] Ultimately, such a dichotomy of motives is far too crude. For example, many robbers also obtain a 'high' from the instrumental violence or threats they employ (Katz 1988) while apparently 'expressive' violence can also be used (instrumentally) as a means of controlling people (e.g. to obtain domestic or sexual services).

approaches address such questions by focusing upon the micro-environment of crime, and acknowledging that violence is a dynamic and evolving event where the 'actors' (i.e., victims, offenders, and bystanders) mould each other's behaviour within a particular physical and social context.

Research into the micro-environment of violence is vast (see Brookman 2005 for an overview). One of the most illuminating early analyses of violent interactions was Luckenbill's (1977) paper on homicide. Extant research had showed how victims precipitated or contributed to the escalation of violence, resulting in their death, but missing was a detailed understanding of how 'transactions of murder are organised and how they develop' (Luckenbill 1977: 176). His research, based on the analysis of 70 homicides, described in detail the dynamic interchange of moves and counter-moves between offenders, victims, and, often, bystanders of homicide. He saw these interactions as proceeding through six stages where the key players develop lines of action shaped in part by the actions of each other and predominantly focused towards saving or maintaining 'face' and reputation and demonstrating 'character'.

Group or collective violence is perhaps especially amenable to micro-situational analysis. Smeulers and Hoex (2010), in their exploration of the microdynamics of the Rwandan genocide, aptly demonstrated how many 'normal' individuals (i.e., otherwise non-violent, law abiding citizens) became involved in genocide due to complex interactional dynamics between the planners and instigators and those that chose to join in the violent situation. The involvement of these otherwise non-violent individuals in extreme and brutal violence could not be explained by the sudden onset of some biologically-based pathology, as individuals joined killer groups for reasons including ethnic hatred, greed, to feel part of a group, or for personal safety. Once embedded in such groups, many became caught up in the violence and have since claimed to have enjoyed killing and committing acts of cruelty (such as raping women, mutilating men, and throwing children against walls)[25] whilst others reported that the more Tutsis they killed the greater respect they gained within the group. Overall, the authors concluded that 'when killings are sanctioned by authorities and committed in groups in which compliance and consensus mechanisms are operational, many ordinary and otherwise law-abiding people join in simply because they think...that it is the right thing to do' (Smeulers and Hoex 2010: 452).

Finally, mention should be made of a scholar who has made an important and original contribution to interactionist studies of violence. Athens (1997) analysed the accounts of violent offenders, focusing upon their interpretations of situations in which they committed violence compared to situations in which they *almost* committed violence, their self-images, and their violent criminal careers. Athens discovered that individuals who had committed violent criminal acts (including homicide) formed one of four possible interpretations of the situation: (a) physically defensive; (b) frustrative; (c) malefic; or (d) frustrative-malefic. Particularly illuminating was his account of occasions when individuals *almost* resorted to violence, but did not (it is rare for criminologists to focus on such 'near misses'). A 'restraining judgement' was shown to be important, allowing them to escape the tunnel vision that often

---

[25] See Katz (1988) on the emotional state of killers at the moment in which they become involved in violent altercations.

characterized the violent events, instead redefining the situation as *not* requiring violence. There were various reasons for the change of interpretation such as: perceiving that the attack would fail, fear of jeopardizing an important relationship, fear of legal sanctions, or a change in the course of action of the other person (e.g. the potential victim conceded in some way or apologized). Athens's work moves us much closer to the moment of the interaction and reminds us that people form restraining judgements far more often than not: fortunately, more violent acts are begun than are ever completed (Athens 1997: 52–3). Collins similarly noted that 'most acts of violence are aborted' (2009:10), arguing that the dominant emotion in violent confrontations is tension, sometimes elevated to paralysing fear, almost always making the performance of violent acts inaccurate and incompetent.

## CULTURAL AND COMMUNITY EXPLANATIONS: THE IMPORTANCE OF PLACE

A broad account of cultural criminology is provided in this volume by Hayward and Young and we shall make only brief comment on aspects of it here. Cultural explanations locate violence within its social setting (e.g. at a community or neighbourhood level) whilst often acknowledging the broader structural factors that contribute to establishing the living conditions within such settings.

There is no shortage of work that places the aetiology of violence firmly within particular communities;[26] for example, the now widely cited subculture of violence thesis (Wolfgang and Ferracuti 1967). In line with other subcultural theories of the time, the authors argued that violent behaviour is learned from other members of peer groups who espouse certain sets of values that differ from those of the dominant culture of conventional society. Their main focus was on subcultures made up of young black people in inner cities, which appeared to produce higher rates of homicide and serious violence than those found elsewhere in the US. Such subcultures, they argued, promoted value systems in which violence comes to be regarded as *normal and expected* in certain social situations—indeed, to such an extent that those who avoid it are 'punished' by becoming ostracized or disrespected. The theory has been heavily criticized on both empirical and theoretical grounds: for example, that the supposed 'subculture' is not as homogeneous as implied by the authors, that poverty and social inequality are better predictors of violence,[27] and that it fails to explain satisfactorily the emergence of such a culture. Nevertheless, it was considerably influential on later work.

Research in this area has burgeoned recently with various criminologists exploring emergent forms of violent street culture, or 'codes of the street' and how these demand violent responses to interpersonal confrontation, and vengeance or retaliation for infractions (Anderson 1999; Brookman *et al.* 2011; Hochstetler and Copes 2003; Jacobs and Wright 1999). Two recent examples which together have grimly topical connotations, are Sandberg's (2008) study of ethnic minority youths and violence

---

[26] This line of work can be traced back to the Chicago School of sociology in the 1930s (see Rock, this volume for a detailed discussion of sociological theories).

[27] The extent to which structure or culture best explains violence continues to be debated most notably amongst American academics (see Pridemore and Freilich 2006).

on the streets of Oslo, and Treadwell and Garland's (2011) paper on racially-motivated violence based on three case studies of members of the English Defence League. Sandberg uses the concept of 'street capital' to show how marginalized young men find a sense of power in the context of structural oppression:

> for young ethnic minority men without labour and income, street culture is one of the very few arenas where their habitus can be transformed into social status and economic gains (Sandberg 2008: 165).

Specifically, these young men turned their ethnic status to their advantage and enacted 'the stereotype of the "dangerous foreigner"' in order to demand respect. In this way they accumulated symbolic capital or power and can be seen to have made a conscious choice (i.e., used their 'agency') to turn a negative situation into a positive. Treadwell and Garland (2011: 621) made similar observations about white racist violence. In a paper which resonates powerfully given the horrific shootings that recently took place near Oslo, they described the psychological processes by which perceptions of marginalization and disadvantage (socio-structurally generated) can evolve into scapegoating the Islamic 'other' and hence into justifications of violence.

More generally, some scholars have recently re-focused attention upon the criminogenic nature of the 'culture' of particular neighbourhoods. For example, taking forward Anderson's work on street codes, Steward and Simons (2010: 591) recently tried to unpick the relative influences of neighbourhood street culture (i.e., is violence embedded in the social context of the neighbourhood?) and individual-level street code values (i.e., to what extent do individuals within the culture partially or fully subscribe to the norms of the street culture?). They discovered that neighbourhood street culture has a direct influence on violence *above* the effect of individual-level street code values,[28] and in so doing reignite the Chicago School tradition of the criminogenic nature of particular areas as opposed to the inhabitants *per se*. As scholars attempt to disentangle the *relative* importance of cultural and individual-level processes, they remind us of how both structure *and* agency must be analysed in the aetiology of violent offending.

## INTEGRATED APPROACHES

Though we have presented explanations of violence under distinct headings above, it is increasingly the case that scholars seek to integrate elements from different disciplines or to focus upon multiple aspects of violence (e.g. the event, the individuals involved, and the broader social or structural context). For example, in his exploration of the dramatic surge in New York murder in the 1980s, Bowling (1999) linked the macro-structural forces of economic recession and poverty to the emergence of despair and relative deprivation at the community and individual level, while also acknowledging the importance of the development of lucrative crack and heroin markets and the widespread availability of guns. Hobbs *et al.* (2005) documented the emergence of

---

[28] Their research, like much of the research of street culture that emanates from the US, was restricted to African American adolescents. Presumably there are white subcultures of violence yet these are rarely researched.

'bouncers' in post-industrial Britain, showing how they developed a powerful sub-culture rooted in routine violence and intimidation. They demonstrated how post-industrial restructuring and the expansion of an essentially unregulated night-time economy paved the way for the development of this particular manifestation of violent coercion.

Other researchers have focused more upon the relation between negative neighbourhood conditions and psychological processes, noting that stress strips those affected of their coping skills and this can impact negatively upon their assessment of risk: minor insults are seen as major threats (Bernard 1990; Niehoff 1999; Vigil 2006) and a 'soldier mentality' characterized by heightened sensitivity to threats and a constant preparedness for action prevails (Sampson and Lauritsen 1994). In addition are those who make links between the biological and social-situational, as discussed earlier. The benefits of such integrated theories are seemingly obvious—they allow for a degree of latitude in terms of acknowledging the multiple influences that can converge and lead to violence.

In conclusion, explanations of violence are extremely diverse. The questions asked are highly variable as are the initial suppositions held by researchers. For example, debates continue as to whether violence is essentially functional and rewarding or pathological (Eisner 2009; Felson 2009, Collins 2009). Questions have also been raised recently about whether or not a general theory of violence is possible (see Karstedt and Eisner 2009) and whether a number of existing criminological theories can explain the overlaps between offending and victimization (Schreck *et al.* 2008). What is evident is that as new disciplines contribute to the endeavour (such as historians and archaeologists as of late) our knowledge becomes a little richer and new avenues of enquiry emerge.

## RESPONSES TO VIOLENCE

Violence always occupies a key position in discussions of how society should respond to crime problems. Over the past few decades, it has been the main focus of numerous 'law and order' initiatives designed to make governments appear tough (for a classic study on this see Hall *et al.* 1978; see also Garland 2001; Jones and Newburn 2007; Downes and Morgan, this volume). It is therefore unsurprising that we continue to locate primary responsibility for social responses to violence with the police and criminal justice agencies, rather than, say, education, health, or social care. Nevertheless, it has increasingly been recognized that a range of other systems and institutions have a major role to play, and these have gradually been brought into both formal and informal partnership initiatives with justice agencies in attempts to provide more effective and holistic responses to violence. Partnership responses are now common across the UK, arguably making multi-agency working the new criminal justice paradigm in contemporary Britain (Crawford and Evans, this volume).

We shall return to partnership shortly. First, however, we briefly outline trends in more traditional responses to violence involving the police, courts, prisons, and probation. This section should be read alongside other chapters in the *Handbook* which cover criminal justice responses to crime in general (especially Newburn and Reiner (policing); Sanders and Young (prosecution); and Ashworth and Roberts (sentencing)).

## CRIMINAL JUSTICE RESPONSES TO VIOLENCE

### Policing violence

Responding to violent crime always has been viewed as 'real police work'—both by the police and by the public—especially when it involves what are seen as core policing tasks and methods, such as covert surveillance on gang members, tackling knife crime, investigating homicide, and so on. Although the policing of violence is always a priority for the police, the nature of their response and the types of violence they prioritize, have changed over time. Apart from the growing prominence of partnership approaches, to be discussed later, recent efforts to improve the police response to violence have included the creation of more specific policies and procedures to guide professional judgement: for example, more guidance and structured information-gathering tools to use when responding to violent crime (e.g. DASH 2009 for domestic incidents, the MIM and MIRSAP for homicide investigation).[29] They have also included government pressure on the police to adopt more 'get tough' responses to violent crime. For example, 'offenders brought to justice' targets introduced during the 1990s contributed to an increase in the proportion of offences of violence against the person that led to convictions, cautions, or other out-of-court penalties (Morgan and Maguire, this volume), from 20 per cent to 29 per cent (Ministry of Justice 2009a). In addition, there have been specific initiatives such as recent guidelines on knife crime which promote charging all those who not only use, but carry, knives (and this applies to adults as well as 16–17 year olds), again with the stated objective of bringing more offenders before the courts (ACPO 2009).

### Sentencing and subsequent control of violent offenders

The basic trend in the sentencing of violent offenders has been towards more and longer custodial sentences. In 2009, roughly 43,200 people were sentenced for offences of violence against the person, an increase of 20 per cent since 1999 (Ministry of Justice 2009b).[30] The numbers sent to immediate custody rose from 14,000 in 1994 to a high of more than 22,000 in 2009, the latter figure representing a third of all those sentenced in that year. There was also a rapid increase in the use of Suspended Sentence Orders (SSOs) from 2006, the first full year they were introduced; in contrast, the use of fines has decreased markedly.

---

[29] DASH (Domestic Abuse, Stalking and Harassment and Honour-Based Violence), a new risk assessment tool, was made available to all forces in 2009 (Robinson 2010a). The Murder Investigation Manual (MIM) was first published in 2000 and is now in its second edition. It guides Senior Investigating Officers through all phases of the investigation and is supplemented by the Major Incident Room Standard Administration Procedures (MIRSAP) (ACPO Centrex 2006).

[30] The 2009 figure includes 39,000 sentences for 'malicious wounding etc', an increase of 1,600 on 2008. 1,200 of these were for possession of a knife in a public place, reflecting the more robust approach to policing knife crime described above.

Not only are more offenders being prosecuted and imprisoned for violent crimes, they are also receiving longer sentences. Between 1999 and 2009 the average length of custodial sentence for offences of violence against the person increased from 16 to 18 months, and for sexual offences from 38 to 49 months (Ministry of Justice 2009b). Among all the main offence groups, sexual offences and robbery (along with drugs offences) attract by far the longest average sentences: by comparison, the average sentence in 2009 for theft and handling offences was four months.

Sentencing trends for violent and sexual offenders have direct consequences for the size and structure of the prison population. Since 2005, the population has been swelled by high numbers receiving indeterminate sentences of Imprisonment for Public Protection (IPPs, see Padfield, Morgan and Maguire, this volume), to the extent that the number of prisoners serving open-ended sentences—all of them for sexual or violent offences—is currently about three times what it was in 2000 (Ministry of Justice 2011a, 2011b). By 2010, moreover, 54 per cent of the entire sentenced prison population, and over three-fifths of the long-term prison population were there for violence, including sexual violence (Ministry of Justice 2010a; Liebling and Crewe, this volume). Such figures are particularly striking when one remembers that violent and sexual offences make up only about 23 per cent of officially recorded crime (Maguire, this volume).

In addition, as Padfield, Maguire and Morgan show in this volume, mechanisms for early release from prison, have been greatly restricted for sexual and violent offenders. As a result, the proportion of time actually served for determinate sentences rose from 57 per cent in 2000 to 61 per cent in 2007. The average length of tariff (or minimum term which the offender must serve in prison) set by the courts for indeterminate sentences has also increased and most indeterminate sentence prisoners are kept in prison well beyond their tariff date (Ministry of Justice 2011a, 2011b).

Moreover, once released, violent and sexual offenders are now subject to strict controls, often going well beyond the full duration of the sentence. Offenders released from IPP sentences remain on license for at least 10 years. Sexual offenders are placed on the sex offender register and obliged to notify the police of their whereabouts for a minimum of five years. They can also be placed under a Sexual Offences Prevention Order (SOPO), which can be made by a court at the time of sentencing, or may be applied by the court following an application by the police. The courts imposed 1,828 SOPOs in 2009/10 compared with 1,512 in 2008/9 (Ministry of Justice 2010b). SOPOs apply for a minimum of five years and in some cases the remainder of the offender's life. If failing to comply with the requirements of the order, he or she can be taken back to court and may be liable for up to five years' imprisonment.

Multi-agency public protection arrangements (MAPPA) are yet another way in which post-release control over serious offenders has increased. These entail a statutory requirement for the prison service, the police, and probation to work together to 'manage the risks posed by dangerous offenders in the community' and can involve police surveillance, regular home visits, and other control measures (Maguire *et al.* 2001; Kemshall 2001, 2008). Recent increases have been observed in the number of MAPPA-eligible offenders, the number of restrictive orders imposed by the courts, and the number of offenders cautioned or convicted for breach of their requirements (Ministry of Justice 2010b).

What all of this means is that, while some vestiges of rehabilitative thinking still play some part in criminal justice and penal responses to violent—and especially sexual—offending, they have been largely swamped by draconian 'risk management' approaches built around incapacitation, surveillance, and control. Even so, as we shall now see, there are continuing efforts to expand the policy landscape and involve other agencies, with different philosophies and priorities, in social responses to violent behaviour.

## A CHANGING LANDSCAPE? THE ROLE OF PARTNERSHIP

In recent years UK government policy on violent crime has focused particularly on domestic violence, sex offending, knife crime, and gang violence. Although punishment and incapacitation have been highly visible components of policies in these areas, all have also contained other key features: in particular, efforts to support and expand multi-agency partnership work, and to give victims greater care, support, and opportunities to engage with criminal justice 'on their terms'. It is noticeable that these developments have survived a change in government and have been maintained through an economic crisis, giving the feeling that they are 'here to stay' rather than short-term political whims.

Both the Labour and Coalition governments have argued that partnership approaches are essential for reducing violent crime and that criminal justice agencies must work with other systems and organizations if they hope to achieve positive results in this area. This message was present in the description of how government aimed to progress all seven key objectives in the *Action Plan for Tackling Violence 2008–11* (HM Government 2008) and has reappeared in the recently published *A New Approach to Fighting Crime* (Home Office 2011) which gives support to multi-agency approaches such as Community Safety Partnerships, MAPPAs, and 'local incentives schemes'. While insisting on a strong focus on risk assessment and improved targeting, detection, and control of offenders, they also emphasize the value of broader and longer-term approaches to violence prevention, even though some would say this represents a fundamental clash of philosophies (Hughes 2007).

### Partnership in practice: knife crime, domestic violence, and sexual violence

We now briefly give some examples of how the concept of multi-agency partnership has been turned into practice in relation to specific types of violent crime. First, in a recent initiative against knife crime in 16 police force areas, a 'robust' enforcement approach was combined with education and prevention initiatives (Ward *et al.* 2011). The programme involved partnership between, among others, the police, Home Office, Department for Education, Ministry of Justice, and the Department of Health. Funding was fairly evenly distributed among the three objectives of enforcement, education and engagement, and prevention and communication activities.

Secondly, responses to domestic and sexual violence epitomize the convergence of the two policy trends described previously, as contemporary approaches—without exception—aim to provide specialist care and support of victims within a multi-agency framework. Considerable fast-paced change has occurred in recent years, as government has acknowledged the effectiveness of this approach and supported its expansion. Partnership work is the cornerstone of the premier multi-agency tool for domestic violence known as Multi-Agency Risk Assessment Conferences, or MARACs.[31] As noted in the original research on the first MARAC, these meetings embody a 'cooperative multi-agency spirit' in a way not seen previously, as '[r]epresentatives from voluntary support agencies, statutory agencies, and criminal justice agencies are working together in the same room, at the same time, and on a regular basis to devise strategies to protect victims' (Robinson 2006: 784). Currently there are estimated to be 250 MARACs operating across England and Wales, which discuss around 45,000 high-risk cases of domestic violence annually (Robinson 2010a, 2010b; Steel *et al.* 2011). They could not function effectively without the participation of police, who usually chair the meetings and deliver many of the actions required to address the safety needs of the victims and their children at highest risk of violence. The other key players in MARACs are the specialist support providers that represent the 'voice of the victim' at the meetings, known as Independent Domestic Violence Advisors or IDVAs.[32] These specialist workers navigate multiple systems to coordinate a range of services that meet the needs of individual victims (Robinson 2009a). Their pivotal role has been repeatedly evidenced, and government has invested substantially in these posts.[33]

Partnership work on sexual violence is less established, but recent developments indicate that multi-agency responses will continue to become more central. Sexual Assault Referral Centres (SARCs) are 'one-stop-shops' providing a range of services for victims under one roof, often with police or health at the helm (Robinson *et al.* 2008). SARCs, along with specialist projects located in the voluntary sector such as Rape Crisis Centres, provide different, yet complementary models of service provision for victims of sexual violence but it is noteworthy that both rely on a partnership approach (Robinson and Hudson 2011). ISVAs, like their IDVA counterparts, are crucial workers in both of these models as they help bring together a range of services on behalf of victims while also supporting victims to access justice on 'their own terms' (Robinson 2009b; Robinson *et al.* 2011). Finally, the applicability of using MARACs for high-risk cases of sexual violence is currently being considered by government.

The increased number of successful prosecutions for violent offences, described earlier, provides a potential indication of how criminal justice outcomes can be improved via the use of partnership approaches, particularly when these include providing better support and care to victims. Specialist domestic violence court systems illustrate this well, as these multi-agency initiatives include police, prosecutors, magistrates, court staff, the Probation Service, and specialist support services for victims (such as IDVAs) and have been linked with higher rates of successful case outcomes in recent

---

[31] MARACs are aimed at very high-risk victims of domestic violence and their children (see Robinson 2010a, 2010b for further information). CAADA, the charity that provides the MARAC quality assurance programme on behalf of the Home Office, has published many useful resources on MARACs (see www.caada.org.uk).

[32] IDVAs are usually based in specialist domestic violence projects located in the voluntary sector, and often provide the ongoing support and contact for the victim (Robinson 2009a; CAADA 2010a; Howarth *et al.* 2009).

[33] Even so, only a fraction of the IDVAs actually needed for full coverage of England and Wales is actually in post (see CAADA 2010b).

years (CPS 2008, 2010; Robinson 2010b). Partnership approaches allow justice agencies to share the 'burden' of responding to violence with others in the community while at the same time enabling these same partners to monitor and help improve their performance (a process known as 'institutional advocacy', of particular importance in improving the state response to domestic and sexual violence).

### Changing MAPPA and 'Integrated Offender Management'

Finally, it is worth making brief mention of some changes that appear to be occurring in relation to Multi-Agency Public Protection Arrangements (MAPPA), as well as the development of Integrated Offender Management (IOM) systems. As pointed out earlier, MAPPA have been primarily managed and operated by criminal justice agencies, despite the presence of other agencies at meetings, and their approach has often been dominated by the aims of surveillance and control. However, it has increasingly been recognized that this alone may not be the most effective way of reducing re-offending by these kinds of offenders, and that other agencies—including voluntary organizations—can contribute greatly, for instance by relating to offenders in a less impersonal manner and reducing their social isolation (for example, through the setting up of 'circles of support'—see Hoyle, this volume), engaging the public in sensible forms of risk management, or providing support and information to parents, children, and communities (Maguire and Brookman 2005; Harrison 2011; Kemshall and Wood 2007; Kemshall 2008; Wilson *et al.* 2008).

IOMs, which have some parallels with these newer approaches to MAPPA, are currently being piloted in a number of areas (Ministry of Justice 2010c). They involve a range of partners including police, probation, prisons, local authorities, and voluntary agencies working together to monitor and control a wider range of offenders who are identified as causing substantial harm in their communities, while at the same time providing services to support their rehabilitation. These include violent as well as property offenders. In contrast to MAPPA, the IOM approach is based on a joint analysis of the most problematic crime and offending issues confronting a community, whether or not the offenders are subject to statutory supervision. They are also in many cases operated on a voluntary rather than compulsory basis, whereby the offender is offered services to address social or criminogenic needs in return for cooperation with the scheme.

## CONCLUSION

It has been emphasized throughout this chapter that violence is a diverse and elusive concept subject to varied perceptions, explanations, and responses. Certain forms of violence are virtually absent from the criminological gaze (e.g. self-directed violence or eco-violence), while others gradually make their way onto the horizon (e.g. corporate violence). Although the risks of falling victim to violence are not equally distributed among us, inevitably violence will affect us all in some way or another. The human, social, and economic costs of violence, regardless of the type examined, are very real for both the individuals directly affected and society as a whole. Estimating the true 'costs' of violence to society is probably impossible, but even conservative figures provide startling indications of their magnitude. Walby (2004), for example, approximated the human and emotional cost of domestic violence at £17 billion *annually* in the UK.

Explaining violence remains fraught with difficulties. Whilst we have learned a great deal, particularly over the last 40 years, about possible factors that contribute to violence (from the individual to the structural) we are still not able to explain the non-violence of most people, all or most of the time, in many situations that seem conducive to violence. Furthermore, how we explain and respond to violence depends, to a large extent, upon the particular form of violence in question. Can we really begin to understand acts as diverse as street robbery, rape, corporate violence, terrorism, child cruelty, or rioting within the same theoretical framework? Clearly some acts of violence will be better understood in terms of individual pathology whilst others make little sense at all divorced from their social contexts.

Responses to violent crime are becoming more varied and often more sophisticated. Traditional criminal justice approaches are being combined with other preventative, rehabilitative, and multi-agency work, and extended to arenas not even considered 'criminal' even a few decades ago (for example, domestic violence or hate crime). It is notable that, even in a time of austerity, substantial government funding has been committed to specialist services for victims of domestic and sexual violence. Despite demonstrable growth in victim and offender services, however, efforts to tackle some of the more complex contributory factors of violence (such as poverty, inequality, and marginalization) are woefully lacking. Much of the energy and investment in relation to violent offending revolves around trying to provide improved responses to it and is, therefore, designed to work 'after the event'.

Finally, official data and large-scale surveys are playing an ever-increasing role in shaping public opinion and policy in relation to violence. Young (2011: viii) recently challenged the use of quantitative research methods and those devoid of theory and called for a return to methods involving time, patience and human contact, stating; 'Science abhors the blurred, the constantly contested and the subjective'—those indelible characteristics of all violent interactions. Yet criminologists must continue to strive to make a rigorous and indeed scientific contribution to public discourses about crime and criminality. The continuing challenge, therefore, is to take stock of what we know, what we think we know, and what we need to know about violence and to tailor a research and policy agenda to meet these needs.

### ■ SELECTED FURTHER READING

The recently published *Handbook of Crime* (Willan, 2010) contains over 17 chapters dealing with violent crimes as diverse as homicide, arson, armed robbery, elder abuse, hate crime, terrorism, torture and corporate, domestic and youth gang violence. This resource is valuable for both its breadth and depth of coverage, as each chapter details the nature of specific types of violence, providing theoretical analysis and discussion of contemporary responses. The *Routledge Handbook of Deviant Behaviour* (2011) is another extensive collection that includes many chapters on specific types of violence. For a multidisciplinary analysis of the concept and phenomenon of violence, the edited collection by Bufacchi (2010) entitled *Rethinking Violence* (Routledge) is worth consulting. Ray also provides a readable overview of key concerns in *Violence and Society* (Sage, 2011). Other recent works focus on particular forms of violence and are valuable for their originality, such as Kinnell's (2008) *Violence and Sex Work in Britain* (Willan), Brown and Walklate's (2011) *Handbook of Sexual Violence* (Sage), Romito's (2008) *A Deafening Silence: Hidden Violence against Women and Children* (Policy Press, translated from the Italian), Pitts's (2008) *Reluctant Gangsters: The Changing Face of Youth Crime* (Willan), and Winlow and Hall's (2006) *Violent Night* (Berg).

The complexity of identifying suitable responses for violent and sexual offending are provided by Harrison's (2011) *Dangerousness, Risk and the Governance of Serious Sexual and Violent Offenders* (Routledge), while a gendered analysis is offered by Wykes and Welsh (2009) in *Violence, Gender and Justice* (Sage). The challenge of responding effectively to violence against women in a global context is the focus of a special issue in the *International Journal of Comparative and Applied Criminal Justice* (2008), while the fourth edition of *Responding to Domestic Violence* (Buzawa, Buzawa, and Stark 2012) provides a comprehensive overview of the American experience.

Finally, a number of recent special issues in academic journals are recommended. *The International Journal of Conflict and Violence* published a series of papers devoted to violence in 2009, raising interesting questions about the possibility of a general theory of violence and in 2011 an issue was dedicated to violence and violence research in the Global South. A recent special issue of the *British Journal of Criminology* (May 2011) on 'Violence in Evolutionary and Historical Perspective' usefully reminds us of the importance of taking a longer view when studying violence.

## ■ REFERENCES

ASSOCIATION OF CHIEF POLICE OFFICERS (ACPO) (2009), *Guidance on the investigation, cautioning and charging of knife crime offences 2009*.

ACPO CENTREX (2006), *Murder Investigation Manual* 3rd edn, Bedfordshire: Centrex.

AMNESTY INTERNATIONAL (2011), *Annual International Report 2011: The State of the World's Human Rights*, London: Amnesty.

ANDERSON, C. A. and BUSHMANB, B. J. (2002), 'Human aggression', *Annual Review of Psychology*, 53: 27–51.

ANDERSON, E. (1999), *Code of the Street: Decency, Violence and the Moral Life of the Inner City*, New York: W. W. Norton.

ATHENS, L. H. (1980), *Violent Criminal Acts and Actors: A Symbolic Interactionist Study*. London: Routledge & Kegan Paul.

—— (1992), *The Creation of Dangerous Violent Criminals*, Chicago: University of Illinois Press.

—— (1997), *Violent Criminal Acts and Actors Revisited*, Chicago: University of Illinois Press.

BAILEY, R., ROFIQUE, J., and HUMPHREY, A. (2010), *Public Confidence in Official Statistics 2009*, London: National Centre for Social Research.

BANDURA, A. (1977), *Social Learning Theory*, Englewood Cliffs, NJ: Prentice Hall.

—— (1990), 'Mechanisms of moral disengagement', in W. Reich (ed.), *Origins of terrorism: Psychologies, ideologies, theologies, states of mind*, ). Cambridge: Cambridge University Press.

BBC NEWS MAGAZINE (2011), *The competing arguments used to explain the riots, 11th August 2011*. www.bbc.co.uk/news/magazine-14483149.

BEAVER, K. M., DELISI, M., VAUGHN, M. G., and BARNES, J.C. (2010), 'Monoamine Oxydase: A Genotype Is Associated with Gang Membership and Weapon Use', *Comprehensive Psychiatry*, 51(2): 130–4.

BENNETT, T. H. and HOLLOWAY, K. (2005), *Understanding Drugs, Alcohol and Crime*, Berkshire: Open University Press.

—— and —— (2009), 'The causal connection between drug use and crime, *British Journal of Criminology*, 49: 513–31.

—— and —— (2010), 'Drug- and alcohol-related Crime', in F. Brookman, M. Maguire, H. Pierpoint, and T. Bennett (eds), *Handbook on Crime*, Cullompton: Willan.

BERNARD, T. J. (1990), 'Angry aggression among the truly disadvantaged', *Criminology*, 28(1): 73–96.

BOWLING, B. (1999), 'The Rise and fall of New York Murder', *British Journal of Criminology*, 39(4): 531–54.

Box, S. (1989), *Power, Crime and Mystification*, London: Tavistock.

Brookman, F. (2005), *Understanding Homicide*, London: Sage.

—— (2010), 'Homicide', in F. Brookman, M. Maguire, H. Pierpoint, and T. Bennett (eds), *Handbook on Crime*, Devon: Willan.

——, Bennett, T., Hochstetler, A., and Copes, H. (2011), 'The "Code of the Street" and the Generation of Street Violence in the UK', *European Journal of Criminology*, 8(1): 17–31.

Burgess, R. L. and Drais, A.A. (1999), 'Beyond the Cinderella Effect: Life History Theory and Child Maltreatment', *Human Nature*, 10(4): 373–95.

Buss, D.M. (2005), *The Murderer Next Door: Why the Mind is Designed to Kill*, New York: Penguin.

CAADA (2010a), *The MARAC guide 2010—From principles to practice*, Bristol: CAADA.

CAADA (2010b), *Saving lives, saving money: MARACs and high risk domestic abuse*, Bristol: CAADA.

Chen, Z., Williams, K. D., Fitness, J., and Newton, N. C. (2008), 'When Hurt Will Not Heal: Exploring the Capacity to Relive Social and Physical Pain', *Psychological Science*, 19(8):, 789–95.

Coleman, K., Eder, S., and Smith, K. (2011), 'Homicide' in K. Smith *et al.* (eds), *Homicides, Firearm Offences and Intimate Violence 2009/10.* HOSB 01/11, London: Home Office.

Collie, R. M., Vess, J., and Murdoch, S. (2007), 'Violence-related cognition: Current research', in T. A. Gannon, T. Ward, A. R. Beech, and D. Fisher (eds), *Aggressive offenders' cognition: Theory, research and practice*, Chichester, England: Wiley.

Collins, R (2009), 'Micro and Macro Theories of Violence', *International Journal of Conflict and Violence*, 3(1): 9–22.

Cooper, C., Selwood, A., and Livingson, G. (2008), 'The Prevalence of Elder Abuse and Neglect: A Systematic Review', *Age and Ageing*, 37: 151–60.

CPS (2008), *Justice with safety: Specialist Domestic Violence Courts Review 2007–2008*.

CPS (2010), *Violence against women crime report 2009 2010*. Crown Prosecution Service. Management Information Branch.

Crick, N. R. and Dodge, K. A. (1994), 'A review and reformulation of social information processing mechanisms in children's social adjustment', *Psychological Bulletin*, 115: 74–101.

Daly, M. and Wilson, M. (1996), 'The Evolutionary Psychology of Homicide', *Demos*, 8 December: 39–45.

—— and —— (2008), 'Is the "Cinderella Effect" controversial?', in C. Crawford and D. Krebs (eds), *Foundations of Evolutionary Psychology*, New York, NY; Abingdon, Oxon: Taylor and Francis.

——, ——, and Vasdev, S. (2001), 'Income inequality and homicide rates in Canada,' *Canadian Journal of Criminology*, 43: 219–36.

Delisi, M., Beaver, K., Wright, J., and Vaughn, M. (2008), 'The Etiology of Criminal Onset: The Enduring Salience of Nature and Nurture', *Journal of Criminal Justice*, 36(3): 217–23.

Dobash, R. E. and Dobash, R. P. (1979), *Violence Against Wives*, New York: The Free Press.

—— and —— (2004), 'Women's Violence to Men in Intimate Relationships', *British Journal of Criminology*, 44(3): 324–49.

Eisenhower Study Group (2011), *The Costs of War Since 2001: Iraq, Afghanistan, and Pakistan*, Watson Institute for International Studies, Brown University: Eisenhower Research Project.

Eisner, M. (2009), 'The Uses of Violence: An Examination of Some Cross-Cutting Issues', *International Journal of Conflict and Violence*, 3(1): 40–59.

Estrada, S. (2001), 'Juvenile Violence as a Social Problem: Trends, Media Attention and Societal Response', *British Journal of Criminology*, 41: 639–55.

Evans, J. (2010), 'Institutional Abuse and Children's Homes', in F. Brookman, M. Maguire, H. Pierpoint, and T. Bennett (eds), *The Handbook on Crime*, Devon: Willan.

Fabian, J.M. (2010), 'Neuropsychological and neurological correlates in violent and homicidal offenders: a legal and neuroscience perspective', *Aggression and Violent Behavior*, 15(3): 209–23.

Felson, R. B. (2009), 'Violence, Crime, and Violent Crime', *International Journal of Conflict and Violence*, (1): 23–39.

Flatley, J., Kershaw, C., Smith, K., Chaplin, R., and Moon, D. (eds) (2010), *Crime in England and Wales 2009/10, Findings from the British Crime Survey and police recorded crime*, HOSB 12/10, London: Home Office.

Gambetta, D. (1994), *The Sicilian Mafia*. Cambridge, Mass.: Harvard University Press.

Garland, D. (2001), *The Culture of Control*, Oxford University Press

Gilbert, F. and Daffern, N. (2010), 'Integrating contemporary aggression theory with violent offender treatment: How thoroughly do interventions target violent behavior?', *Aggression and Violent Behavior*, (15): 167–180.

Gill, A. (2008),'"Crimes of Honour" and Violence Against Women in the UK', *International Journal of Comparative and Applied Criminal Justice*, 32(2): 243–63.

Goldstein, A.P. (1999), *Low level aggression: First steps on the ladder to Violence*, Illinois: Research Press.

Goldstein, P.J. (1985), 'The Drugs/Violence Nexus: A Tripartite Conceptual Framework', *Journal of Drug Issues* 15: 493–506.

Goodman, L.A. (1995), 'Episodically homeless women with serious mental illness: prevalence of physical and sexual abuse', *American Journal of Orthopsychiatry*, 65: 468–73.

HM Government (2008), *Saving Lives, Reducing Harm, Protecting the Public: Action Plan for Tackling Violence, 2008–11*, London: Home Office.

Hall, P. (2011), 'Intimate Violence: 2009/10 BCS', in K. Smith *et al.* (eds), *Homicides, Firearm Offences and*

*Intimate Violence 2009/10*, HOSB 01/11, London: Home Office.

—— and INNES, J. (2010), 'Violent and Sexual Crime', in J. Flatley *et al.* (eds), *Crime in England and Wales 2009/10, Findings from the British Crime Survey and police recorded crime*. HOSB 12/10, London: Home Office.

HALL, S., CRITCHER, C., JEFFERSON, T., CLARKE, J., and ROBERTS, B. (1978), *Policing the crisis*, London: Macmillan.

HARRIS, G. T., SKILLING, T. A., and RICE, M. E. (2001), 'The construct of psychopathy', in M. Tonry (ed.), *Crime and Justice: An Annual Review of Research*, Chicago: University of Chicago Press.

HARRISON, K. (2011), *Dangerousness, Risk and the Governance of Serious Sexual and Violent Offenders*, London: Routledge.

HEALTH AND SAFETY EXECUTIVE (2010), *The Health and Safety Executive Statistics 2009/10*, London: National Statistics. Available at: http://www.hse.gov.uk/statistics/overall/hssh0910.pdf.

HENRY, S (2000), 'What's the Scope of Violence in School Violence', *The Critical Criminologist,* 10(2):13–16.

HIDAY, V. A., SWANSON, J. W., SWARTZ, M. S., BORUM, R., and WAGNER, H. R. (2001), 'Victimization: a link between mental illness and violence?', *International Journal of Law and Psychiatry*, 24: 559–72.

HOBBS, D., HADFIELD, P., LISTER, S., and WINLOW, S. (2005), *Bouncers: Violence and Governance in the Night-Time Economy*, Oxford: Oxford University Press.

HOCHSTETLER, A. and COPES, H. (2003), 'Situational construction of masculinity among male street thieves', *Journal of Contemporary Ethnography*, 32: 279–304.

HOWARTH, E., STIMPSON, L., BARRAN, D., and ROBINSON, A. L. (2009), *Safety in Numbers: A multisite evaluation of Independent Domestic Violence Advisor Services*. www.caada.org/Research/Safety-in-Numbers-Full-report.pdf.

HUGHES, G. (2007), *The politics of crime and community*, Basingstoke: Palgrave Macmillan.

INTERNATIONAL LABOUR ORGANIZATION (2005), *World Day for Safety and Health at Work 2005: A Background Paper*, Geneva: International Labour Office.

JACOBS, B. and WRIGHT, R. (1999), Stick-up, street culture, and offender motivation', *Criminology*, 37: 149–74.

JEFFERY, C.R. (1965), 'Criminal Behaviour and Learning Theory', *Journal of Criminal Law, Criminology and Police Science*, 56(3): 294–300.

JONES, T. and NEWBURN, T. (2007), *Policy Transfer and Criminal Justice: Exploring US influence over British crime control*, McGraw Hill: Open University Press.

——, ROBINSON, A., FEVRE, R., and LEWIS, D. (2010), 'Workplace Assaults in Britain: Understanding the Influence of Individual and Workplace Characteristics', *British Journal of Criminology*, 51: 159–178.

KEMSHALL, H. (2001), *Risk assessment and management of known sexual and violent offenders: A review of current issues*, Police Research Series Paper 140, London: Home Office.

—— (2008), *Understanding the Management of High Risk Offenders*, Buckingham: Open University Press.

—— and WOOD, J. (2007), 'Beyond public protection: An examination of community protection and public health approaches to high-risk offenders', *Criminology and Criminal Justice*, 7(3): 203–22.

KHALIFEH, K., and DEAN, K. (2010), Gender and violence against people with severe mental illness, *International Review of Psychiatry, 22(5):* 535–46.

KRISTOF, N. D. (2009), *After Wars, Mass Rapes Persist*, New York Times.

KUHNS, J.B. CLODFELTER, T.A. (2009), 'Illicit drug-related psychopharmacological violence: The current understanding within a causal context', *Aggression and Violent Behavior*, 14: 69–78.

LAURITSEN, J. L. and HEIMER, K. (2010), 'Violent victimization among males and economic conditions: The vulnerability of race and ethnic minorities', *Criminology and Public Policy,* 9(4): 665–92.

—— and SCHAUM, R. J. (2004), 'The social ecology of violence against women', *Criminology*, 42(2): 323–57.

LEVI, M. (1997), 'Violent crime', in M. Maguire, R. Morgan, and R. Reiner (eds), *The Oxford Handbook of Criminology*, 2nd edn, Oxford: Oxford University Press.

LUCKENBILL, D. F. (1977), 'Criminal homicide as a situated transaction', *Social Forces*, 25: 176–86.

MAGUIRE, M. and BROOKMAN, F. (2005), 'Violent and sexual crime', in N. Tilley (ed.), *Handbook of Crime Prevention and Community Safety*, Devon: Willan.

——, KEMSHALL, H., NOAK, L., WINCUP, E., and SHARPE, K. (2001), *Risk management of sexual and violent offenders: The work of public protection panels*, Police Research Series Paper 139, London: Home Office.

MATTINSON, J. (2001), *Stranger and acquaintance violence: Practice messages from the British Crime Survey*, Briefing Note 7/01, London: Home Office.

MEGARGEE, E. (1983), 'Undercontrolled and overcontrolled personality types in extreme antisocial aggression', *Psychological Monographs*, 80 (3, whole No. 611).

MINISTRY OF JUSTICE (2009a), *Criminal statistics: England and Wales.*

—— (2009b), *Sentencing statistics: England and Wales.*

—— (2010a), *Offender management caseload statistics: England and Wales.*

—— (2010b), *Multi-Agency Public Protection Arrangements Annual Report 2009/10.*

—— (2010c), *Breaking the Cycle: Effective punishment, rehabilitation and sentencing of offenders* (Green Paper Evidence Report).

—— (2011a), *Offender Management Statistics Quarterly Bulletin, October to December 2010, England and Wales.*

—— (2011b), *Provisional figures relating to offenders serving indeterminate sentence of imprisonment for public protection (IPPs).*

MORGAN, R. (2010), 'Torture', in F. Brookman, M. Maguire, H. Pierpoint, and T. Bennett (eds), *Handbook on Crime*, Devon: Willan.

MORRS, P. and GRAYCAR, A. (2011), 'Homicide Through a Different Lens', *British Journal of Criminology*, 51(5): 823–38.

NIEHOFF, D. (1999), *The Biology of Violence*, New York: Free Press.

OSBORNE, S. (2010), 'Extent and Trends', in J. Flatley et al. (eds), *Crime in England and Wales 2009/10, Findings from the British Crime Survey and police recorded crime*, HOSB 12/10, London: Home Office.

PALMER, E.J. (2006), 'Cognitive-Behaviourism', in E. McLaughlin and J. Muncie (eds), *The Sage Dictionary of Criminology*, London: Sage.

PAPACHRISTOS, A. V. (2009), 'Murder by Structure: Dominance Relations and the Social Structure of Gang Homicide', *American Journal of Sociology*, 115(1): 74–128.

PIQUERO, A. R., MACDONALD, J., DOBRIN, A., DAIGLE, L., and CULLEN, F. T. (2005), 'The relationship between violent offending and death by homicide: A test of the general theory of crime', *Journal of Quantitative Criminology*, 21: 55–71.

PITTS, J. (2008), *Reluctant Gangsters: The Changing Face of Youth Crime*, Cullompton: Willan.

PLATT, T. (1992), 'The Concept of Violence as Descriptive and Polemic', *International Social Science Journal*. 44(2): 185–191.

POLK, K. (1994), *When Men Kill: Scenarios of Masculine Violence*, Cambridge: Cambridge University Press.

PONTICELLI, J. and VOTH, H. (2011), *Fact: There is a link between cuts and riots*, The Guardian Newspaper online (www.guardian.co.uk), 10 August 2011.

PRIDEMORE, W.A. and FREILICH, J.D. (2006), 'A test of recent subcultural explanations of white violence in the United States', *Journal of Criminal Justice*, 34: 1–16.

RAFTER, N. (2008), *The Criminal Brain: Understanding Biological Theories of Crime*, New York: New York University Press.

RANDALL, M. and HASKELL, H. (1995), 'Sexual violence in women's lives: findings from the women's safety project, a community-based survey', *Violence Against Women*, 1:6–31.

RAY, L. (2010), *Violence and society*, London: Sage.

RENNISON, C. M. (2000), *Criminal victimization 1999 Changes 1998–99 with trends 1993–99*, NCJ-182734, Washington, DC: Department of Justice, Office of Justice Programs.

REISS, A. J., Jr. and ROTH, J. (eds) (1993), *Understanding and preventing violence*, Washington, DC: National Academy Press.

RENZETTI, C. (2009), 'Intimate partner violence and economic disadvantage', in E. Stark and E. S. Buzawa (eds), *Violence against women in families and relationships: Vol.1: Victimization and the community response*, Santa Barbara, CA: Praeger.

RESSLER, R.K., BIRGESS. A.W., and DOUGLAS, J.E. (2006), 'Serial Killers: Antecedent Behaviors and the Act of Murder', in P. Cromwell (ed.), *In Their Own Words: Criminals on Crime An Anthology*, 4th edn, Los Angeles: Roxbury Publishing Company.

RISTOCK, J. L. (2009), 'Understanding violence in lesbian relationships', in E. Stark and E. S. Buzawa (eds), *Violence against women in families and relationships: Vol.1: Victimization and the community response*, Santa Barbara, CA: Praeger.

ROBINSON, A. L. (2006), 'Reducing Repeat Victimisation among High-Risk Victims of Domestic Violence: The Benefits of a Coordinated Community Response in Cardiff, Wales', *Violence Against Women*, 12(8): 761–88.

—— (2009a), *Independent Domestic Violence Advisors: A process evaluation*, School of Social Sciences: Cardiff University.

—— (2009b), *Independent Sexual Violence Advisors: A process evaluation*, Home Office Research Report 20, London: Home Office.

—— (2010a), 'Risk and intimate partner violence', in H. Kemshall and B. Wilkinson (eds), *Good practice in risk assessment and risk management*, 3rd edn, London: Jessica Kingsley Publishers.

—— (2010b), 'Domestic violence', in F. Brookman, M. Maguire, H. Pierpoint, and T. Bennett (eds), *Handbook of Crime*, Devon: Willan.

——, HUDSON, K., and BROOKMAN, F. (2008), 'Multi-agency work on sexual violence: Challenges and prospects identified from the implementation of a Sexual Assault Referral Centre (SARC)', *Howard Journal of Criminal Justice*, 47(4): 411–28.

—— and HUDSON, K. (2011), 'Different yet complementary; two approaches to supporting victims of sexual violence in the UK', *Criminology and Criminal Justice*, 11(5): 515–33.

——, —— and MORGAN, A. (2011), 'Specialist support services for victims of sexual violence in the UK: context, mechanisms, outcomes' [under review].

ROE, S. and ASHE, J. (2008), *Young people and crime: findings from the 2006 Offending, Crime and Justice Survey*, Home Office Statistical Bulletin 09/08, London: Home Office.

ROGERS, S. (2011), *England riots: was poverty a factor?* The Guardian Newspaper on-line (www.guardian.co.uk), 16 August 2011.

ROTH, R. (2011), 'Biology and the Deep History of Homicide', *British Journal of Criminology*, 51(3): 535–55.

RUMMELR. J. (1994), *Death by government: genocide and mass murder since 1900*, New Brunswick, NJ, and London: Transaction Publications.

SAMPSON, R. and LAURITSEN, J. (1994), 'Violent victimization and offending: individual-, situational-, and community-level risk factors', in A. J. Reiss and J. A. Roth (eds), *Understanding and Preventing Violence: Vol. 3, Social Influences*. Washington, DC: National Academy Press.

SANDBERG, S. (2008), 'Street capital: ethnicity and violence on the streets of Oslo', *Theoretical Criminology*, 12(2): 153–71.

SCHINKEL, W. (2004), 'The will to violence', *Theoretical Criminology*, 8(1): 5–31.

SCHRECK, C., STEWART, E., and OSGOOD, D. (2008), 'A Reappraisal of the Overlap of Violent Offenders and Victims', *Criminology*, 46(4): 871–906.

SEAGER, J. A. (2005), 'Violent men: The importance of impulsivity and cognitive schema', *Criminal Justice and Behavior*, 32: 26–49.

SKEEM, J. and COOKE, D. (2010), 'Is Criminal Behavior a Central Component of Psychopathy? Conceptual Directions for Resolving the Debate', *Psychological Assessment*, 22(2): 433–45.

SILVER, E. (2002), 'Mental disorder and violent victimization: The mediating effect of involvement in conflicted social relationships', *Criminology*, 40(1): 191–212.

SMEULERS, A. and HOEX, L. (2010), 'Studying the Microdynamics of the Rwandan Genocide', *British Journal of Criminology*, 50(3): 435–54.

SNELL, K. and TOMBS, S. (2011), '"How do you get your voice heard when no-one will let you?" Victimization at Work', *Criminology and Criminal Justice*, 11(3):207–23.

SNOWDEN, J. and LURIGIO, A. J. (2007), 'The mentally ill as victims of crime', in R. C. Davis, A. J. Lurigio and S. Herman, (eds),*Victims of crime*, 3rd edn, Los Angeles, CA: Sage Publications.

STEEL, N., BLAKEBOROUGH, L., and NICHOLAS, S. (2011), *Supporting high-risk victims of domestic violence: a review of Multi-Agency Risk Assessment Conferences (MARACs)*, London: Home Office Research Report, 55.

STEWART, E. and SIMONS, R. (2010), 'Race, code of the street, and violent delinquency: A multilevel investigation of neighborhood street culture and individual norms of violence', *Criminology*, 48: 569–605.

STRETESKY, P.B. (2001), 'The Relationship Between Lead Exposure and Homicide', *Archives of Pediatric Adolescent Medicine*, 155: 579–82.

TAVARES, C. and THOMAS, G. (2010), Crime *and Criminal Justice, Statistics in focus*, Eurostat 58/2010, Luxembourg: Office for Official Publications of the European Communities.

TEASDALE, B. (2009), 'Mental disorder and violent victimization', *Criminal Justice and Behavior*, 36: 513–35.

THORNTON, J. and BECKWITH, S. (2004), *Environmental Law*, 2nd edn, London: Sweet and Maxwell.

TOMBS, S. (2008), 'Corporations and Health and Safety', in J. Minkes and L. Minkes (eds), *Corporate and White Collar Crime*, London: Sage.

—— (2010), 'Corporate Violence and Harm', in F. Brookman, M. Maguire, H. Pierpoint, and T. Bennett (eds), *Handbook on Crime*, Cullompton, Devon: Willan.

TOMSEN, S. (1997), 'A Top Night. Social Protest, Masculinity and the Culture of Drinking Violence', *The British Journal of Criminology*, 37(1): 90–102.

TRAVIS, A. (2011), *'Prison population hits record high in England and Wales'*, www.guardian.co.uk, Friday 19 August 2011.

TREADWELL, J. and GARLAND, J. (2011), 'Masculinity, Marginalization and Violence: A Case Study of the English Defence League', *British Journal of Criminology*, 51(4): 621–34.

TSELONI, A., MAILLEY, J., FARRELL, G., and TILLEY, N. (2010), 'Exploring the International Decline in Crime Rates', *European Journal of Criminology*, 7(5): 375–94.

UPSON, A. (2004), *Violence at Work: Findings from the 2002/3 British Crime Survey*, London:Home Office.

VAN DIJK, J.J.M., VAN KESTEREN, J.N., and SMIT, P. (2008), *Criminal Victimisation in International Perspective, Key findings from the 2004–2005 ICVS and EU ICS*, The Hague: Boom Legal Publishers. http://rechten. uvt.nl/icvs/pdffiles/ICVS2004_05.pdf.

VIGIL, J. D. (2006), 'A multiple marginality framework of gangs', in A. Egley, C. Maxson, J. Miller, and M. Klein (eds), *The Modern Gang Reader*, 3rd edn, Oxford: Oxford University Press.

WADDINGTON, P.A.J., BADGER, D., and BULL, R (2004), 'Appraising the Inclusive Definition of Workplace "Violence"', *British Journal of Criminology*, 45(2): 141–64.

WALBY, S. (2004), *The Cost of Domestic Violence*, London: Women and Equality Unit.

—— and CARRIER, N. (2010), 'The rise of biocriminology: Capturing observable bodily economies of "criminal man"', *Criminology and Criminal Justice*, 10(3): 261–85.

WALSH, E., MORAN, P., SCOTT, C., MCKENZIE, K., BURNS, T., CREED, F., TRYER, P., MURRAY, R. M., and FAHY, T. (2003), 'Prevalence of violent victimisation in severe mental illness', *The British Journal of Psychiatry*, 183: 233–8.

WARD, L., NICHOLAS, S., and WILLOUGHBY, M. (2011), *An assessment of the Tackling Knives and Serious Youth Violence Action Programme (TKAP)—Phase II*, London: Home Office Research Report 53.

WILLIAMS, K. S. (2010), 'State Crime', in F. Brookman, M. Maguire, H. Pierpoint, and T. Bennett (eds), *The Handbook on Crime*, Devon: Willan.

WILSON, R., MCWHINNIE, A., and WILSON, C. (2008), 'Circles of support and accountability: An international partnership in reducing sexual offender recidivism', *Prison Service Journal, 178*: 26–36.

WOLFGANG, M. E. and FERRACUTI, F. (1967), *The Subculture of Violence: Towards an Integrated Theory in Criminology*, London: Tavistock.

WOOD, J. C. (2004), 'A Useful Savagery: The Invention of Violence in Nineteenth-Century England', *Victorian Culture*, 9(1): 22–42.

WORLD HEALTH ORGANIZATION (2002), *Word Report on Violence and Health* (edited by E. G. Krug., L. L. Dahlberg., J. A. Mercy., A. B. Zwi, and R. Lozano), Geneva: WHO.

—— (2008), World Health Organisation Air Quality and Health, Fact Sheet No. 313. www.who.int/mediacentre/factsheets/fs313/en/index.html.

YOUNG, J. (2011), *The Criminological Imagination*, Oxford: Wiley.

# 20

# THE ORGANIZATION OF SERIOUS CRIMES FOR GAIN

*Michael Levi*

## INTRODUCTION

In this chapter, we will briefly critique legal and operational definitions of organized crime, and suggest more meaningful ways of thinking about them; discuss what we know about the criminal careers of 'organized criminals', about how criminals organize themselves, and how criminal markets work; and finish with a brief appreciation of the importance of understanding the interrelationship between crime control mechanisms—criminal justice and prevention, including private sector controls— and the ways in which criminals get together to commit serious crimes for profit. For space reasons, its focus will be on the way that global issues affect the organization of crimes in the UK and to a lesser extent, the rest of Europe, but it examines models that have more universal application.

'Organized crime' has been a significant part of the popular discourse of American politicians and movies since the 1920s. Italy excepted, its place in the Western European cultural lexicon has been less prominent. From the early 1970s, the European components of this international 'connection' have been popularized by films such as *The Godfather* and *The French Connection*, although far less 'Hollywoody' national versions (e.g. British films such as *The Krays*, *Get Carter*, *The Long Good Friday*, and *Lock, Stock and Two Smoking Barrels*) portrayed a more banal and parochial British reality more similar to the racecourse gangs depicted in *Brighton Rock* (1947 and 2010) than to their real or fictional American or even French or Italian counterparts.[1] The rise of illicit drugs and labour markets since the 1960s reflects that often sloppily analysed term 'globalization', manifested locally. But the causes, form, and policy responses cannot sensibly be handled by the term 'organized crime', which provides little more than a 'floating signifier' of social danger, allowing interpreters to read what they like into it (Levi-Strauss 1987). *The Godfather*'s alien import conspiracy model has been a

---

[1] This may have reflected differences in the nature of criminal organization (influenced by Prohibitionist policies) in the US and the UK.

core part of the US mindset (Woodiwiss and Hobbs 2009); threat imagery within and beyond Europe is provided by Italy and by the ex-communist and 'Balkan' countries of Eastern Europe, and by China (for people trafficking and cybercrime).

The nature and extent of organized crime threats remain deeply contested terrain (Edwards and Levi 2008; van Duyne and Van der Beken 2009; Zoutendijk 2010). There is controversy over (i) the scaling of the relative harmfulness of illicit activities, including but not restricted to drugs (Nutt *et al.* 2010) and sex work, and (ii) the extent to which user health and criminogenic damage from some drugs is aggravated rather than reduced by law enforcement and by health policies. It is increasingly questioned whether beyond excluding legitimate firms from offering competition, repression by law enforcement and paramilitary methods do and can have much of an impact on the supply, availability, and price of unlawful goods and services. Data—well-founded or speculative—play a role in the harm advocacy process (Andreas and Greenhill 2010). In the cultural struggle over harm prioritization, the terminology can become blurred. If the women know at the point of transportation that they are going to become sex workers, the proper term is 'smuggling'; if they do not know this, it is 'trafficking' or even (when sold by their relatives) 'slavery'. In practice, adults seeking a better economic future are often told lies about the nature of their future employment, but it is hard to verify *ex post facto* what they were told. Some feminist and religious fundamentalist groups consider that women cannot validly consent to become sex workers and therefore that all such transportation is 'trafficking'; others that (though not an ideal occupation) selling sex voluntarily is a right. Much migrant sex and other work involves exploitation, but it is unlikely that any transporting network would survive long if most of those whose families paid to emigrate failed to reach their destinations alive or to send funds back to repay and help their families. Davies (2009) has critiqued the exaggerations in advocacy groups' estimates of sex workers trafficked to the UK. Estimates of global money laundering in the trillions of dollars (Unger 2009; Walker and Unger 2009) have a very poor analytical and evidential basis but become 'facts by repetition' (van Duyne and Levi 2005; Levi and Reuter 2006).[2] Worldwide, criminal markets are very large and generate proceeds (if not profits) in the billions. The mistake is to move from the defensible proposition that harmful impacts are considerable, to the indefensible propositions that these impacts can be specified with certainty (or even with reasonable plausibility) and that they arise from a common coherent delivery mechanism called 'organized crime'.

Post '9/11', terrorism replaced organized crime as a core governmental concern. But since 2010 (much earlier in the UK and Australia), organized crime has re-emerged somewhat as an American priority (ACC 2011; Cabinet Office 2011; Home Office 2004, 2009; White House 2011). Irrespective of controversies over how much organized crime there is and how much money 'it' makes, however, we start this chapter from

---

[2] Money laundering in legal terms means any act of concealment of proceeds of crime, including thieves placing funds in their own bank accounts in their own names. However, given the lifestyles of most offenders, they typically save very little so to calculate laundering we would need to know something about the distribution of profits from crime (subtracting operational costs including corruption), how much offenders save, and in what media they do so. From a country's point of view, one might need to know how much of other countries' proceeds of crime they handle and how much of their gross domestic criminal product gets exported.

the 'realist' premises that (i) there are a lot of profitable crimes about, and, (ii) these crimes need 'organizing' (throughout, we prefer the connotations of the verb 'organizing crime' to that of the noun 'organized crime'). Some components of these crimes—from financing through obtaining the tools of crime to concealing the proceeds from law enforcement and from other criminals—*usually* involve moving money, people, and chemicals/weaponry across national borders. Not that any of this is so surprising, since most licit economic activities have similar requirements, down to those that enable us to buy at the corner shop the high-energy bar required to get readers through this chapter.

## POLICY RESPONSES AND MODELS OF ORGANIZED CRIME

In the period 1988–2005, no fewer than four United Nations Conventions were devoted to serious economic and organized crime issues.[3] At a European level, there has been a proliferation of measures attending to the threat of money laundering and organized crime. These commenced with the 1990 Council of Europe Convention and the first EC Money Laundering Directive of 1991, and accelerated in the late 1990s and early part of this century, to (in 2005) the EC Third Directive and the Council of Europe Warsaw Convention No. 198,[4] which also cover the financing of terrorism. Following the Hague and Stockholm programmes, the EU Internal Security Strategy set out the challenges, principles, and guidelines for dealing with security issues within the EU. To implement this strategy, the European Commission (2010) adopted the communication 'EU Internal Security Strategy in Action', which proposed 41 actions, including a shared agenda to disrupt criminal and terrorist networks, protect citizens, businesses, and societies against cybercrime, increase EU security by smarter border management, and strengthen the EU's readiness and response to 'security crises' (which might include large flows of illegal immigrants).

Policy makers' enthusiasm for combating organized crime has generated expansive *legal* definitions that set the boundaries of punishment both within nation states and, increasingly, outside them. As defined by the EU and UN, 'organized crime' can mean anything from major Italian syndicates in sharp suits or Sicilian peasant garb to three very menacing-looking burglars with a window cleaning business who differentiate their roles by having one act as look-out, another as burglar, and a third as money launderer. If any component of what they do involves a foreign country, they

---

[3] The UN Conventions are the Vienna Drugs Convention 1988; the Convention for the Suppression of the Financing of Terrorism 2000; the Transnational Organized Crime Convention 2000; and the Convention against Corruption 2003, all of which are now in force.

[4] These are the EC Third Directive on the prevention of the use of the financial system for the purposes of money laundering or terrorist financing, and the Council of Europe Conventions of 1991 and 2005 on the laundering, freezing and confiscation of the proceeds from crime and on the financing of terrorism. (See Fijnaut and Paoli 2004 and Gilmore 2011, for some rich description of these policy trends.)

become 'transnational organized criminals'! Almost all drugs and fraud money laundering—including placing funds even in a local bank account in one's own name—qualifies as organized crime, making its scale very large.

These legislative framework changes have been accompanied by the unprecedented growth of (often informal, 'soft law') international bodies such as the Financial Action Task Force whose task is to monitor compliance with a multitude of rules—a quite recent phenomenon of transnational governance, whose limits remain unclear (Levi and Gilmore 2002). Internationalization of law enforcement and intelligence by the US has proceeded apace from an already substantial anti-drugs and anti-insurgency presence in the 1970s (Andreas and Nadelmann 2007; White House 2011). The Serious Organised Crime Agency, established in the UK in 2006 specifically as a harm-reduction rather than law enforcement body (to emphasize its broader strategic intervention role),[5] is second only to the US in the number of intelligence/liaison staff working overseas. SOCA will be merged in 2013 into a broader National Crime Agency, and will have a formal UK/US investigative cooperation arm (Home Office 2011).

However, this is not a chapter reviewing those fascinating and socially important developments in international law-making, policing, and criminal justice: there is no space to do that. Rather it represents an attempt to look at the nature of the criminal phenomena that are the justification for changes in law creation and crime control—and that, to the extent that the controls have had an impact, have also been moulded by them. It will be seen that there is a spectrum of academic opinion, ranging from:

1. those who see crimes as very well *organized* (whatever that means), to

2. those who see crimes typically as intermittently or more regularly *networked* but not in any stable hierarchy (Edwards and Levi 2008; Levi 2008b; Morselli 2009).

Even the latter group agree that there are pockets of hierarchical, tightly organized crime in some countries, which only occasionally transplant successfully elsewhere (Varese 2011). It is implausible that there is a natural progression to vertically organized crime groups operating laterally across multiple crime types and throughout large geographical regions. We might more profitably ask what, given the existing conditions of crime networks, corruption, and public and private sector control efforts, represents an 'adequate' minimum way of organizing particular forms of crime.

Many forms of organized crime involve the supply of desired but illegal products, whether they are:

1. wholly illegal (like criminalized drugs);

2. counterfeit (on a spectrum from poor quality pharmaceuticals—such as antibiotics or 'stamina pills' that do not work as advertised—super-carcinogenic cigarettes, and movies badly filmed in cinemas to high quality digital DVDs and expertly copied generic pharmaceuticals that work as well as the originals); or

3. tax-evaded but otherwise legal (smuggled genuine booze, fuel oil, or tobacco).

---

[5] The complexities of harm assessment are too great to be discussed here, nor is there space in this chapter for more than a cursory review of the control of organized crime.

Though most individuals involved in drug dealing, extortion, credit card fraud, armed robberies, sex work, etc. may not do any international business as part of their daily routines, some aspects of these businesses—including 'gun crime' (Hallsworth and Silverstone 2009)—are transnational. There is no 'criminal organization gene' whose DNA it is our scientific task to unravel. An over-simplified focus on organizational *structures* of offending is part of the emotional baggage of hierarchy associated with 'The Mafia'. (See Innes and Levi, this volume, for analogies with the over-hierarchical image of 'Al-Qaeda', which subsequently morphed into much more loosely networked, even solo 'Al-Qaeda-*inspired*' terrorism.) Our image of who the offenders are is shaped by the disproportionate publicity given to the most overtly threatening and apparently cohesive groups who conform to 'news values' (Levi 2008a). Media, police, and politicians unwittingly or cynically exaggerate some transnational threats and the prospective effect of their proposed remedies.[6] In the context of analysing business conspiracies to fix contracts in the Dutch building industry, van Duyne (2005) and van de Bunt (2010) ask why we do not label corporate cartels as organized crime in the same way that we do the Colombian cartels. It seems easier to generate negative labels for people who (we believe) do only bad things; when people are engaged in some socially positive activities, they get less condemnation or even get support. Thus, as Pablo Escobar in Colombia and Christopher Coke in Jamaica showed, drugs traffickers may be popular if they are generous in their neighbourhoods and spend liberally in local car dealerships, liquor stores, and restaurants, especially if other significant education and opportunities are unavailable. However, business cartels operating in the legal sector are seldom noted for generosity to 'their' communities.

The amounts and the organization of crimes in any given society are affected by how competently/vigorously controls are implemented and/or perceived by motivated offenders. This simple insight is captured in routine activities and situational crime prevention models (see the valuable contributions to Bullock *et al.* 2010; Levi and Maguire 2004). 'Controls' here include not just legal norms and their enforcement but the broader sets of activities that shape crime opportunities, most of them in developed economies occurring in the private sector. Examples include technological factors such as the effective introduction in Europe (and elsewhere, except the US) of Chip and PIN to neutralize the skimming of data from the magnetic stripes on our credit and debit cards; or measures like one-time only passwords to frustrate phishing, 'key logging', and other Trojan-like viruses as a way of capturing our passwords for on-line banking. (Such controls over elites and organized criminals in the commercial sector are largely ignored by the literature on nodal governance: see Jones, this volume.) What is more difficult to address is the ways in which *criminal justice* practices (as well as history, motivations, and skills) shape the extent and *organization* of offending: except for the impact of corruption within criminal justice systems on increasing the impunity of offenders, the research evidence to date is poor.

Table 20.1 represents the three main 'non-traditional' approaches to the prevention of organized crime that can be found at present. Like situational prevention techniques,

---

[6] While underplaying other data not on the 'organized crime' radar such as civilian deaths in Iraq and other 'State crimes'—see Brookman and Robinson, this volume.

**Table 20.1**  Non-traditional approaches to organized crime prevention

| | |
|---|---|
| **Community approaches** | 1. Community crime prevention<br>2. Passive citizen participation: giving information about harms and risks, hotlines<br>3. Active citizen participation: civic action groups |
| **Regulatory, disruption, and non-justice system approaches** | 4. Regulatory policies, programmes, and agencies (domestic and foreign, including non-governmental organizations such as Global Witness and Transparency International, and inter-governmental organizations such as the IMF, OECD/FATF, UNODC, and World Bank)<br>5. Routine and suspicious activity reporting by financial institutions and other bodies<br>6. Tax policy and programmes<br>7. Civil injunctions and other sanctions<br>8. Military interventions<br>9. Security and Secret Intelligence Services<br>10. Foreign policy and aid programmes (e.g. annual US Presidential Determination on Major Illicit Drug Transit or Major Illicit Drug Producing Countries; counter-narcotics assistance/anti-corruption programmes) |
| **Private sector involvement** | 11. Individual companies' risk management/security<br>12. Professional and industry associations<br>13. Anti-fraud, cyber-attack  and money laundering software<br>14. Private policing<br>15. Private sponsorship of public policing |

*Source*: Modified from Levi and Maguire (2004)

this is a kind of 'natural history' classification of broad intervention methods, each of which may work by several mechanisms.

# ANALYTICAL ISSUES IN DEFINING THE NATURE OF 'ORGANIZED CRIME'

The term 'organized crime' denotes not just a set of criminal *actors* but also a set of criminal *activities* (Cohen 1977). Nowadays, these for-profit activities would be taken to include drugs trafficking; smuggling/trafficking in people; extortion; kidnapping for profit; illegal toxic waste dumping (environmental crime); identity frauds (including sophisticated credit and debit card fraud and social security/tax credit frauds); fraud against the European Union; smuggling to evade excise tax on alcohol and tobacco; intellectual property theft (video and audio piracy and product counterfeiting); Value-Added Tax (VAT) frauds; corruption of public officials to facilitate these offences and/or evade sanctions, etc.[7] (Council of Europe 2005; Europol 2011; SOCA 2010). Problematically, the term is usually used to describe those activities *only when carried out by underworld-type figures*, though all of the above 'threat assessment' reports broaden out this conventional imagery to include activities and people that facilitate and underpin—'enable'—serious crime. Indeed, the Europol mandate was changed from 'organized' to 'serious' crime in order to reduce the need to indulge in intellectual sophistry. Thus the collective noun 'organized crime' is constituted by both 'full-time' and 'part-time' criminals, many of whom may have multiple criminal and legitimate partners. The number of people available, motivated, *and technically competent* to commit serious crimes for financial gain and the ways they interact with existing crime networks are important to how crimes are organized and their frequency. The UK Serious Organised Crime Agency does not fall victim to conventional mythology, noting (soca.gov.uk/threats/organised-crime-groups) that there is much variation in levels of organization of crime in the UK:

> Organised crime is defined as 'those involved, normally working with others, in continuing serious criminal activities for substantial profit, whether based in the UK or elsewhere'. Organised criminals that work together for the duration of a particular criminal activity or activities are what we call an organised crime group.

Nevertheless, there is a conceptual problem of judging when a 'network' begins and ends. Moreover, counting organized crime groups is a matter of judgement (Gregory 2003). This remains so despite the UK's relatively disciplined Organised Crime Group mapping exercise which concluded that in the UK, there are around 38,000 organized criminals and around 6,000 organized crime groups (Home Office 2011).[8]

How do we know how 'organized crime' is constituted? Cressey (1969), using the surveillance tapes and interviews with Joseph 'the Canary that Sang' Valachi, set out the official version of Italian-American Mafia as a line management, vertically integrated, and horizontally coordinated organization (though it was left unstated how widely crime groups' 'licence to operate' charges extended to predatory crimes such as burglaries, robberies, frauds, etc.). (Note organizational imagery parallels with 'Islamic terrorism'.) Few academics have been convinced by the Valachi Boss-Underboss-Soldier model. Although Jacobs *et al.* (1994) and Jacobs and Gouldin (1999) put up a spirited evidence-backed defence that LCN (La Cosa Nostra) organized crime families do exist in cities like New York, there is little confirmed evidence of such gang *domination* of a broad range of criminal activity, even in the North-Eastern US.

The radical view that business and criminals are symbiotic (Chambliss and Block 1981; Woodiwiss 2005) ignores the often unwanted parasitical and predatory crimes

---

[7] Politicians find it difficult to resist adding to the list of competencies of agencies charged with organized crime control. Following feminist, human rights, and media campaigns, trafficking of women rose to a high priority in the West and UN, despite real concerns about whether some of this was just economic migration.

[8] From the references to the UK in the Home Office report, it appears that this would include the 4,066 individuals representing 367 serious organized crime groups in Scotland (Scottish Government 2009). For a sophisticated Australian discussion, see ACC (2011).

committed *against* business by crime groups. While hierarchical large-scale criminal organizations do exist in Italy, Mafia is more a method of extortion and patron/client relationships (including public sector contract procurement) than it is a specific body 'in charge' of all serious criminality. Hobbs (1997, 2001) argues that 'the Firm' was first rooted in and then uprooted from its English class and local environment. Later British work stresses the linkages between serious crimes for gain (especially drugs, extortion, and sex work) and the night-time economy, which flourishes in the relatively unsurveilled, age-segregated geographic sector of our towns and cities.

We should also pay close attention to the use of the term 'transnational': it is helpful to think of the tasks that need to be performed to commit serious crimes over a long period, most of these tasks being as easily accomplished at a local level as transnationally. These are:

1. obtain finance for crime;

2. find people willing and technically/socially competent to commit crimes (though this may not always be necessary);

3. obtain equipment and transportation necessary to commit the crimes;

4. convert, where necessary, products of crime into money or other usable assets;

5. find people and places willing to store proceeds (and perhaps transmit and conceal their origin);

6. neutralize law enforcement by technical skill, by corruption, and/or by legal arbitrage, using legal obstacles to enforcement operations and prosecutions which vary between states.

These procedural elements can be broken down further into much more concrete steps or 'scripts', when analysing the dynamics of particular crimes and/or criminal careers.[9] Some 'rogue' or 'collapsed' states (such as Afghanistan at times, following intervention by many international actors) are too weak and/or corrupted to deal with crime entrepreneurs and/or political rebels in their midst.[10] In practice, provided they are deemed to assist in restraining communism or 'Islamic fundamentalism'/terrorism, anti-crime measures may be subordinated to wider foreign and economic policy interests (Naylor 2005; Thoumi 2007). Specialized information sources may be tainted and the perspectives drawn from them partial. Some law enforcement officials may have *idées fixes* about 'organized crime', may lack adequate analytical skills or resources to carry out network analysis[11]—or they may simply pragmatically find the term to be a convenient myth to get more resources from politicians. Data matching and more sophisticated data mining techniques may reveal connections in, for example, insurance, social security, or tax fraud claims that were not otherwise apparent: but this does not mean that all crimes or other types of fraud are 'organized' by three or more people. Our judgements of how 'organized' crimes are can be disciplined by evidence drawn from a variety of methods including ethnographic and interview

[9] See Cornish (1994), Tremblay *et al.* (1994, 2001), Morselli (2005), Kleemans etc., Chiu *et al.* (2010).

[10] (Tilly 1985; Williams 2001).

[11] For glimpses of what is required, see Klerks (2003) or Coles (2001), the latter critiqued by Chattoe and Hamill (2005).

studies, especially of drug and people smuggling markets;[12] reviews of completed but not always prosecuted case files, which are easier to access in continental Europe than in the UK; and creative use of economic pricing analysis to infer patterns of monopoly and competition in criminal markets.[13]

## THE NATURE OF ORGANIZED CRIME AND 'ITS' MARKETS

There is no *a priori* reason why the organization of crime should be constant over time or between societies at any given moment, or should embody a trend towards syndicated crime. All ethnographic accounts focus on a complex set of patron/client relationships in which ethnic networks can sometimes supply a trust level that is important for smoothly functioning crime as it is for commerce. This research includes studies of networks of Colombians at home and abroad (e.g. Kenney 2007; Zaitch 2002), Canadian Hells Angels (Morselli 2009), Japanese (Hill 2003; Kaplan and Dubro 2003) and Turks (Bovenkerk and Yesilgöz 2007; Fijnaut *et al.* 1998), as well as Hobbs' (1997, 2001, 2004) and Levi's (2008a, 2008b) work in the UK. It collectively demonstrates the subtle linkages between the organization of crime and the organization of ordinary social relations and work. This is also true of other, more subject-specific studies such as crime in the diamond trade (Siegel 2009) and in the music and transport sectors (Vander Beken 2005). Social network analysis based on police intercept data has sometimes offered a fascinating and in some respects more 'objective' insight into the organization of crime (Morselli 2009), especially when supplemented by observation and interviews.

In brief, the accident of geography (where particular drugs can be easily produced, people want/need to emigrate, and direct supply routes), combined with the skill and contact set and (variable) trust values that offenders bring to the table, has led many to become involved in 'organized crime'. A variety of ethnicities supply and facilitate criminal goods and services to and within the US (Chin 1996, 2009; Finckenauer and Waring 1999; Finckenauer and Albanese 2005; Finckenauer and Chin 2010; Shelley 2010; Zhang and Chin 2008). Such groups nowadays make less use of Italian American Mafia dispute resolution services (including its former near-monopoly of local and state-level corrupt law enforcement and political contacts). Nor is there much vertical integration of organized crime groups in the US or Europe, even in drugs markets:[14] street-level criminals are normally independent of major crime syndicates, even where the latter do exist (Matrix 2007; McSweeney *et al.* 2008).

---

[12] (Dorn *et al.* 2005; Hobbs 2000, 2001; Matrix 2007; Pearson and Hobbs 2001; Rawlinson 2007; Ruggiero and Khan 2006; Webb and Burrows 2009; Wright 2006).

[13] (Caulkins and Reuter 2009, 2010; Fiorentini and Peltzman 1995; Levitt and Dubner 2005; Levitt and Venkatesh 2000; Naylor 2005, 2011; Reuter 1983; Reuter and Kleiman 1986).

[14] (Dorn *et al.* 1992, 1998, 2005; Gruter and van de Mheen 2005; Pearson and Hobbs 2001; Ruggiero and South 1995; Paoli 2001; Paoli *et al.* 2009; Zaitch 2002; Zaitch *et al.* 2003).

We should not expect criminal organization to take the same forms everywhere. In Mexico a small élite historically dominated the economy and political system and shared prosperous deals out among themselves. The scale of recent murders (approaching 40,000 in the four years since President Calderon launched his US-favoured 'War against the Mexican drug cartels') reveals the lethal blend of mass unemployment, *machismo* culture, group dynamics, and illicit money, not to mention the physiological effects of the drugs themselves (Reuter 2009; Vulliamy 2010). Ironically, the privatization of the economy in former communist countries in the name of freedom enabled oligarchs—whether connected or not to organized crime groups—to buy former state assets for far below their true value and to buy up cheaply the shares given to the workers and public (Baloun and Scheinost 2003). Privatization also provides easy avenues for money laundering where the authorities and banks cannot afford to be too inquisitive about the source of the funds. (Though sensible criminals may not wish to leave their funds too long in countries with no depositor or investor protection schemes, or where a liquidator of a bank that goes bust might demand to know the beneficial ownership and origin of the funds before paying compensation.) The era of ultra-violent entrepreneurship may have ended and consolidation occurred in Russia but there remains a substantial amount of economic crime emanating from Russian criminals. Some—like Nigerians—operate from diasporas outside the country, but internally, most are involved either in e-crime (hacking and identity fraud) at a less élite level, or in corporate raiding and blackmail (Firestone 2008, 2010; Galeotti 2004; Rawlinson 2009; Volkov 2002).

Among advanced industrial nations, the closest similarities to this 'political coalition' organizational model have been reported for Australia, where extensive narcotics, cargo theft, and labour racketeering rings with ties to state-level politicians and police were discovered during the 1970s and 1980s, with periodic and more limited discoveries since (Chan and Dixon 2007); and for Japan, where Yakuza and other racketeers specialize in vice and extortion (Kaplan and Dubro 2003; Hill 2003). In Britain, by contrast, though lobbying for profit is commonplace, links between politicians and organized crime groups have not been revealed to date. The disconnect is principally because the supply and consumption of alcohol, gambling, and (in many respects) prostitution remain legal and partly regulated (as was the case, for a while, for opiates). This reduces the profitability of supplying these goods and services criminally, although large profits can still be made by traffickers in women, who make them work in near-slavery conditions in massage parlours, saunas, and the like, in suburbia as well as in traditional red light districts; and worldwide (including intra-EU), differences on tax levels on alcohol make widespread evasion profitable. A host of groups are important in the supply of illegal drugs to and via Britain. But except for drug importers and wholesalers, cargo thieves who work at airports, and local vice, protection, and pornography syndicates, the historic evidence suggests that British 'organized criminals' tend to be relatively short-term groups drawn together on a local or regional basis for specific projects, such as fraud and armed robbery, from a pool of long-term professional criminals.

Europe has a large diversity of economies, extensive economic regulations, many loosely controlled borders to cross, and relatively small jurisdictions. This means that the largest illegal profits for European crime-entrepreneurs are to be gained in the drug market and in organized business crimes. If the normal (licit) business nucleus in Southern Italy, Turkey, or Pakistan is the extended family (Ianni and Reuss-Ianni 1972; Fijnaut *et al.* 1998; Bovenkerk and Yesilgoz 2007), in Northern Europe such socio-economic family units are much rarer and social bonds are more restricted, for example to people bound by loyalties of place: though the very fracturing of the social fabric that has led to so much concern about social exclusion also paradoxically may inhibit *criminal* solidarity. The exceptions are the crime-enterprises of minorities in Europe whose businesses are family matters, not impersonal 'syndicates' (Bovenkerk 2007).

In order to make profits, those who offer illegal goods and services must advertise, if only to selected 'affinity groups' derived from other sources and activities. Thus in the long run, the police will come to know about the criminality too. Unless they can rely on police tolerance or on other indicators of trustworthiness such as (paradoxically) long prison sentences (Gambetta 2009), to ensure freedom from the law, the criminals must therefore subvert any component of the criminal justice process: a major reason for concern about the impact of organized crime. (Though in reality, it is a side-effect of the prohibition of goods and services in popular demand, which exclude most legitimate firms from the market, and without which organized criminals would be operating in this area only as extorters from business.) Parts of the Italian state have at times collaborated with organized crime groups, but this is separate from the cosy or sometimes parasitic corrupt deals between politicians and businesspeople investigated mainly by the Milan magistrates. (To date, this produced much aggravation for Prime Minister Berlusconi but negligible final criminal justice outcomes.) Patron-client relationships permeate Italian society—for instance, the exchange network that generated corrupt refereeing and led to sanctions against several top Italian soccer clubs such as Juventus in 2006. The Neapolitan ambience of this was memorably encapsulated in the book (and film) *Gomorrah* (Saviano 2007). Glenny (2009) provides an excellent history of the way in which the hollowing out of Soviet-era governance, corruptly underpriced privatizations, combined with dismissed Secret Service personnel possessing both skills and trust, 'produced' East European gangsterism, even if his weaving of this into a global 'McMafia' is ill-supported by the evidence.

Alternatively, those crime entrepreneurs who are not confident about their abilities to subvert or sidestep the law might rationally choose to operate on a fairly small scale, while the supply of criminal labour generates the total volume of product demanded by the marketplace. The result is a that people and groups involved in supplying illegal goods and services are far more flexibly intertwined than the Organised Crime imagery would lead us to expect. This applies even to the so-called Cali and Medellin drug 'cartels', where collaborative authority structures made it most unlikely that long-term price fixing could ever be accomplished (Kenney 2007; Naylor 2004, 2011; Thoumi 2003). Finally, the consensus[15] suggests that the success of organized crime in Italy and Russia (and, one might further argue, in many parts of Latin America) depends also on the more general lack of trust in society and between citizens and government. This imposes some limits on expansion by Mafia-type groups, since

---

[15] Good contributions to the trust and organized crime issue include Gambetta (1994, 2010), von Lampe and Johansen (2004), Nelken (1997), and Varese (2001, 2011).

when they come up against societies in which trust is high, they are unsuccessful in the long term, despite the substantial funds at their disposal (Gambetta 2009; Varese 2011). Mafiosi often find themselves abroad due to the pressure of events, rather than through a strategic plan to colonize new territories. Varese (2011) spells out the conditions that lead to their long-term success, namely sudden market expansion that is neither exploited by local rivals nor blocked by authorities. Ultimately the inability of the state to govern economic transformations gives mafias their opportunity. Attempts to combat organized crime in low-trust countries require more than a merely institutional focus on governance if they want to succeed, i.e. more than whether there countries have something called an Independent Commission against Corruption and a panoply of intrusive surveillance and anti-laundering/asset forfeiture laws (Levi 2007, forthcoming; Sharman 2011).

## SKILLS AND PREREQUISITIES FOR CRIME

In predatory acts such as robbery, violence or its threat is a key element, and professional robbers—whether of commercial premises (Gill 2001; Shover 1996) or of passengers in the street—become highly skilled in its dramaturgy. In the drugs trade, violence occurs mostly in disputes over territory or over proceeds of crime stored in cash. In most Western societies, such violence happens when citizens cannot resort to law to settle disputes; though elsewhere, extortion or 'protection' ('roof' in Eastern Europe) can take place where a weak state is incapable of protecting all its people from such threats *and* where criminals (who can include police or even senior politicians and officials) have the motivation and aptitude to make convincing threats. In all of these cases, violence is instrumental, but it can simultaneously also express a need/wish to be shown 'respect' (Brookman and Robinson, this volume).

Despite the general social movement against corruption[16] in profit-driven crime, corrupt payments are not central, because predatory crimes do not require them, while drugs and other market offences give value to normally voluntary purchasers (addicts excepted). However, corruption may be a one-off or regular payment to neutralize law enforcement (Sherman 1974; Punch 2000) from where, once established, 'good governance' campaigns will not generate ready change without an internal seismic shift in patron-client relationships as has happened—at least temporarily—in Indonesia and the Philippines (see further, De Sousa *et al.* 2009; Quah 2011).

Once the offences have occurred, an integral part of the crime process involves fencing (resale) of goods—where goods or traceable money have been obtained—and laundering those proceeds that have not been spent and need to be stored. Sutton (1998) has shown how stolen goods tend to be recycled through pubs and informal neighbourhood networks: this can neutralize the official rhetoric about the threat of 'organ-

---

[16]  (See De Sousa *et al.* 2009; Transparency International 2006; Pieth 1999; Anechiarico and Jacobs 1998; World Bank 2006).

ized crime'. This focus on the embeddedness of crime with the local economy[17]may understate somewhat the use of supermarkets and local shops to sell unaccounted for produce from large hauls. In the 1970s, I interviewed someone who had stolen without knowing its content a truckload of yoghurt, which he could not have sold without its going off: selling alcohol and tobacco smuggled in from the Continent is relatively easy, not just because of there is a bigger market but also because there are fewer storage problems and easy rationalizations for both sellers and purchasers that 'the amount of duty the government charges is diabolical'.

Alongside these local markets, eBay offers opportunities for more remote sales of stolen property, though the need for developing a reputation as a 'good' seller can create vulnerability to enforcement surveillance and intervention. Internet user groups offer a graduated access to 'dark markets' in which personal details and card numbers can be exchanged for e-money, and given servers located in uncooperative jurisdictions, these can be hard to close down.

In his study of the global market for looted antiquities, Mackenzie (2005a, 2005b) notes the importance of 'techniques of neutralization' that are given some protection in law and by the inactivism of law enforcement and victims: unless a provenance (history of ownership and/or documented circumstances of excavation) adds to the value of an object, it usually is not mentioned. However, shifts in enforcement practices (e.g. in Greece during 2006) may have an effect on the market, whether on key nodal intermediaries or on private and public institutions for whom respectability is important.

## CRIMINAL CAREERS

The Dutch Ministry of Justice funded 'Organized Crime Monitor' gives us the best public knowledge about criminal careers of 'organized criminals' (Kleemans 2007; Kleemans and de Poot 2008, van Koppen et al. 2010).[18] Van Koppen et al. (2010), for example, show that in the Netherlands, 40 per cent of people in organized crime clusters were adult-onset offenders; 19 per cent had no previous criminal records, but 11 per cent were early starters and 30 per cent were persistent offenders. This is far more varied than the popular and law enforcement image of 'organized crime' as full-time career criminals might lead us to expect. These careers are affected by the networks in which motivated offenders find themselves and/or help to create by their social skills, abilities to generate fear, or other characteristics (including chance). For reasons of space, we will take as an example drugs trafficking (see also Measham and South, this volume).

---

[17] (See also Hobbs 2001; von Lampe 2006; Ruggiero 2000; and Shapland and Ponsaers 2009)

[18] Varese (2006, 2011) argues that features of the local economy—the presence of significant sectors of the economy unprotected by the state and a local rather than export orientation—generate a demand for criminal protection, and leads to successful transplantation. Contrary to established theories of social capital and trust, a high level of interpersonal trust among local law-abiding residents is not sufficient to stop the mafia from establishing itself elsewhere. Whether this is true outside Italy or other places where images of Mafia remain credible remains to be tested.

## DRUG TRAFFICKING NETWORKS AND OFFENDER CHARACTERISTICS

Much of the rising concern about organized criminality around the world has been because of its association with illegal drugs. There has been a gradual improvement in our understanding of drugs networks, where the greatest profits are thought to be in the 'middle market' in the supply chain. However, the term 'network' is often loosely used, and the literature review of upper level drug trafficking by Dorn *et al.* (2005) helpfully concludes (p. 9) that it is best understood as a way of describing the structure and/or everyday workings of *the market as a whole*, in the sense that the market can be regarded as a complex social network (*singular noun*), within which different participants have to network (*verb*) (to carefully seek out and interact with traffickers who may be like or unlike themselves.

Overall little research has taken place in the UK on the characteristics of drug traffickers although there are some studies of incarcerated sellers (Dorn *et al.* 2005; Matrix 2007; Decker and Chapman 2008) that suggest that drug dealing—even at a high level—requires few specialized skills, being essentially just brokerage activity between source and customers. However, some specific skills and knowledge do seem to be advantageous, and these are acquired mainly by working with an existing dealer, who 'produces' new dealers when selling is profitable, just as existing users introduce new ones. When the current number of sellers at these higher market levels is very small, the inflow of new dealers is also small; but in larger drug markets, the arrest of even hundreds of drug sellers would be unlikely to take out more than 10 per cent of sellers (Caulkins and Reuter 2009, 2010).

Figure 20.1 below shows the attrition involved at higher levels of drug trafficking (though actual numbers are highly approximate). Upper-level trafficking is taken to include: wholesale distribution within the source countries; export, international transit, and entry into Europe; and connections downwards to the city level. Middle- and low-level trafficking typically include small-scale cultivation of plants (such as opium poppy and coca bush); and, at the other end of the chain, retail sale and transactions (Dorn *et al.* 2005).

An interview-based study of British South Asian drug dealers by Ruggiero and Khan (2006: 478) found that there was more drugs-specialization at higher levels of

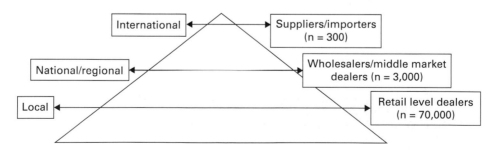

**Figure 20.1** A pyramidal market system
*Source*: May and Hough 2004: 555; Matrix Knowledge Group 2007: 2

the market than at middle levels, where fraud and guns were common adjuncts to drugs.

Dorn *et al.* (2005: 38) developed the following typology for upper level drug traffickers operating and networking in this market:

1. *'Politico-military' traffickers (unlikely to be found within the UK):* are insurgent or paramilitary groups in source countries who may impose 'taxes' on traffickers or may involve themselves in trafficking in order to support political or military activities from the revenues raised. They may also be concerned with achieving or maintaining a dominant position within existing political structures.

2. *'Business criminals':* are driven by a profit motive and tend to comprise of small, socially-integrated, and skilled business groups. Considered a highly risk-averse group keen to protect the safety of key players and other core assets, they are deemed highly resistant to law enforcement efforts.

3. *'Adventurers':* these are marginal groups and individuals who are active in a variety of dispensable and interchangeable roles. Generally risk-tolerant, they will adopt amateurish and sometimes dangerous short-cuts.

Within and between these trafficking 'types', there is an increasing tendency towards reciprocal learning and cooperation, with business criminals and professionals playing a prominent role in facilitating these links. However, there is no published evidence of how many professionals (or what percentage) are engaged in such facilitation. The same study found that at the higher levels of the market, traditional ties along ethnic, national, and related lines were eroding. However, SOCA threat assessments and this author's interviews state that strategic geographic placement in different supply chain countries by national groups (such as Colombians in Spain) does continue (see also Paoli *et al.* 2009 on the world heroin market).

Shared experience facilitates new bonds, trust, and, on release from prison, closer cooperation between 'different' groups, and the easier formation of multi-cultural/multi-national teams. As a result, the old barriers are breaking down fast. Whilst in the past it may have made sense for Law Enforcement Agency (LEA) reports to categorize some varieties of criminality along ethnic, national, or related lines, to do so today is open increasingly to question: networking has spilt over traditional channels. This does not mean that there are no risks in dealing with other cultural groups and with strangers, and for all the constant reiteration that criminals know no boundaries—only the police do—insufficient is known about the barriers to successful integration of criminals across national and international borders, which still exist, or there might be more territorial crime wars than there are.

## PROFITS FROM ORGANIZED CRIME AND MONEY LAUNDERING

Money laundering has been the subject of much mystification. Laundering in legal terms is simply the concealment of proceeds of crime (in a bank, in a wall safe, etc.), but more analytically ought to be viewed as the cleansing of funds so that they can be used in a way indistinguishable from legitimate money. What most people appear to mean by money laundering is the hiding of funds in accounts somewhere outside of the *current* surveillance capabilities of enforcement agencies and/or of 'responsibilized' professional intermediaries such as accountants, bankers, and lawyers. The latter have a legal duty to sensitize themselves to laundering typologies and to report suspicions or 'unusual' transactions to the authorities, on pain of lengthy imprisonment and large fines. If and when those official surveillance capabilities increase—as they did steadily during the 1990s, accelerating especially after the '9/11' attacks—funds that were just hidden become vulnerable to enforcement intervention and perhaps confiscation. Those 'organized criminals'—the great majority by volume, it appears (Shover 1996)—who spend their money on 'lifestyle' have no such problems of working out how to hide and store their money—they have very little savings.

There are currently no reliable estimates of the scale of money laundering in the UK or anywhere else in the world. Even the more disciplined of the speculative guesstimates often take the central figure within a wide error range as the 'real figure'; however, the actual amount could reasonably be a lot less or indeed more. In addition, estimates tend to take the gross sales of illicit commodities as the basis for calculating laundering, assuming that all income would be available to the criminals. However, proceeds of crime are much larger than profits from crime. What is spent on business costs (including corruption) or 'lifestyle' (travel and entertainment) is not saved and therefore not truly laundered by the offenders, though some large corruption payments may be saved. Although we know little about how much middle and upper market drugs or human traffickers save, we do know that most low-level offenders do not save significant sums (Dorn *et al.* 2005; Levi and Reuter 2006; Matrix 2007; Webb and Burrows 2009).

There have been some attempts to estimate the scale of proceeds of crime/money laundering within the UK that have been linked to target-setting by the Home Office. Dubourg and Prichard (2009: 72) state that 'the flow of criminal assets theoretically available for seizure is about £2bn per year in the UK, with a further £3.3bn of revenue sent overseas'. The Attorney General's Department (unpublished) estimated that UK criminals' assets thought to be abroad totalled £562.5 million in 2008 (Home Office 2009). If organized crime proceeds totalled £15–25 billion p.a. (Dubourg and Prichard 2009: ii), and confiscation plus criminal taxes unit efforts totalled £153.7m in 2008/9 (rising slightly the following year), then the Annual Laundering Gap would be at minimum just under £15 billion, and the total volume of laundered proceeds over a 10-year period might be £150 billion, depending on how successful crime reduction measures and asset recovery are. This broader 'recovery deficit' representing what offenders have got away with dwarfs the attrition issue between value of confiscation orders sought and value of orders imposed, which was 38 per cent for drug supply cases (£71.5 million vs. £44 million), and 34 per cent for all non-drugs offences (£120 million vs. £79.1 million) (Bullock *et al.* 2009: 13). Whichever way one looks at that data, much remains to be achieved, though lower levels of proceeds intervention could have an impact on offenders' intensity of involvement in crime.

Webb and Burrows (2009) conducted interviews with 45 prisoners convicted of human smuggling/trafficking offences to examine the costs and profits associated with these crimes. They found that the prices charged for a single smuggled person ranged from £1,500 in Romania to £50,000 in China. Koser's (2008) study of human smuggling from Pakistan to the UK also showed a wide variation in the prices charged, in this case, for different modes of travel: for example, the costs of indirect transport were much lower ($4,000) than direct flights ($13–14,000). The costs did, however, depend partly on the numbers of trafficked people, in other words, costs were lower if more people were smuggled together.

The actual income derived from smuggling or trafficking operations is dependent upon the volume of business and the charges made, set against the overheads incurred. Box 20.1, below, provides an illustration of the income generated from a 'typical' business.

Income from human trafficking can be generated in a variety of ways. Traffickers may for example sell the victim on to a third party for a one-off sum. Alternatively they may retain the trafficked individual as a form of income for themselves; in other words, the trafficked victim will be forced to work and their wages, or a proportion of them, may then be taken by the trafficker. Another source of income can be derived from providing accommodation for the trafficked individuals. Webb and Burrows (2009) interviewed one individual who indicated that these activities could bring in about £35 per week per tenant; which in the example described, involved 70 tenants in ten houses. Within the trafficking market, different people and groups will assume different responsibilities and so any profit will need to be split across these groups. For example, girls could be collected from UK entry points and purchased for £3,000 to £4,000 (although very occasionally figures of around £700 were quoted). This money would be paid in cash and taken back to the originating country where it would be split between the initial recruiters, the central supplier, and, if applicable, the escort who ensures that the girl is delivered to the purchaser. For those interviewed, the profits that could be achieved outweighed any perceived risks. Indeed, the risks were considered low: business dealings would be done in cash, much of which would then be exported to other countries. Despite recent initiatives to combat money laundering, transferring money abroad was not considered difficult by those interviewed. The proceeds from facilitation were often returned to the home country where land and property were then bought. Facilitators based in the UK kept the bulk of the money here

---

**Box 20.1 A 'TYPICAL' INCOME GENERATED BY A HUMAN TRAFFICKING ORGANIZATION**

A partly legitimate business that specialized in supplying false documentation for entry via commercial airlines spent about a third of its income from each immigrant (about £1,500–£2,000 per immigrant) on overheads (including offices, regular staff, and specialist services). The business reportedly supplied false documentation for about 600–700 immigrants over a 12-month period, accounting for a net profit of between £300,000 and £500,000. They also operated a supplementary service of providing entry by car with false documents (using a team of drivers), and this was reported to provide a form of regular trade, albeit not yielding the same levels of profit as that received for air travel.

for disposable income and for investment in property and businesses such as shops, hotels, restaurants, and sweatshops.

An interview-based study of UK-imprisoned drug dealers provides some insights in to how they launder their money: 37 per cent bought property or other assets; 21 per cent laundered money through legitimate business; and 16 per cent sent money overseas (Matrix 2007: 39). The findings point to relatively unsophisticated money laundering techniques and a tendency to use friends and family (by investing in their businesses or storing in their bank accounts for example). This echoes research elsewhere in Europe (van Duyne and Levi 2005; Levi and Reuter 2006), though studies based on convicted samples are likely to under-estimate the sophisticated techniques and networks available to the most serious offenders, especially fraudsters and very large scale traffickers, where money laundering charges are seldom laid.

## THE EVOLUTION OF CRIME ORGANIZATION

The explanation of how and why crime groups develop in the way that they do is important, but a focus on definitions of 'organized crime' and on which groups might or might not qualify as such imposes a false (fantasy) grid of coherence on what is really a very diverse set of people and activities. As UK policing enters the Age of Austerity, despite increased confiscations and the political heralding of such work (Home Office 2011), even the shift from fraud to financial investigation for asset recovery (Gannon and Doig 2009) may be imperilled as Constabularies move away from work other than 'front-line policing' and 'signal crimes' such as homicides and phone hacking largely associated with News International.

The organization of crimes results from the interaction of crime opportunities, offender and prospective offender motivations, skills and networks, and control efforts (whether through the criminal law, administrative law, or disruption). It is thus a *dynamic* process that evolves as offenders adapt (or fail to adapt) to their changing environment, including facilities offered by the legal commercial environment, such as air travel, container lorries and ships, car repair firms (Tremblay *et al.* 2001), drug laboratories (Chiu *et al.* 2011), payment card issuers and merchants (Levi 1998; Glenny 2011), telemarketing of 'investment opportunities' (Shover *et al.* 2003; International Mass-Marketing Fraud Working Group 2010), and relationships with financial institutions and professionals (contributors to the Special Issue introduced by Levi *et al.* 2005; Levi and Reuter 2006). In some cases, for example 'missing trader' or 'carousel' VAT frauds, the opportunities result from structural weaknesses in EU regulations on how VAT is administered in intra-EU trades, resulting in billions of pounds of losses annually in the UK and some other EU countries, only some of them known to be attributable to 'organized crime' figures in the conventional sense[19] though they

---

[19] (Author interviews with Revenue and Customs officials). Missing trader fraud is a complex VAT scam, involving cross-border sales, typically of high-value products such as mobile phones or computer chips. The fraud is perpetrated by an importer who supposedly collects VAT on behalf of the government when

do meet the EU criteria for organized crime and featured as a major issue in the UK's Organised Crime Threat Assessment (SOCA 2010 and earlier). HM Revenue and Customs in 2006 won permission from the EU to change the way it applies VAT to trades of mobile phones and computer chips, the favourites among fraudsters because they are of high value but are small in bulk. From early 2007, VAT has been chargeable when the phones arrive at a retailer and are not refundable when the goods cross an EU border. The Internet has transformed the crime opportunities for global e-theft and sale of both material and e-commodities via eBay and digital fora such as the Dark Market (Glenny 2011; Wall 2007). There are many cases where crime networks adapt to police preventative tactics even in the course of one series of frauds or (in e-crime) within days or even hours; and the losses of drugs or excise-evaded shipments constitute mainly opportunity costs, from which higher members of crime groups either develop counter-intelligence strategies or just accept risks and losses of (often poor third world female) 'mules'.

Aggregate changes in routine activities, fashion, decriminalization and prevention technology—as well as in criminal networks—may produce changes or apparent changes in modes of 'organized criminality'. Yet though all the ethnographic, policing, and survey datapoint to the dramatic rise in the size of illegal drug markets, it is not easy to pinpoint changes in their *organization*.

If the world of crime were to parallel Elias's analysis of the civilizing process, one might expect a drift away from *macho* criminality to the softer arts of the fraudster, where less police interest and lower sentences can be found. However, though there has been a significant rise in frauds available to traditional criminals, such as insurance and payment card fraud, there appear to be cultural, skill, and formal qualification barriers to entry into many areas of fraud which have inhibited this transformation for most predatory and market criminals (Levi 2008b; Diih, forthcoming). Several armed robbers turned to long-firm (bankruptcy) frauds as early as the late 1960s, and later to credit card fraud, social security fraud, and even to carousel, VAT, and other frauds against the European Union—either alongside or subsequent to drug dealing—but this move into the moderately upmarket areas of fraud has hardly dented those other types of crime, so arguably it is expansion rather than displacement. In focusing on these shifts by criminals with 'previous' (convictions), we may risk neglecting systematic frauds and other crimes by people who are not previously known to the authorities. The link between identity thieves (or rather, duplicators), fraudsters and 'ordinary' organized crime groups is not well understood, though some linkages occur, and whether voluntarily or by extortion,

---

the goods are sold in this country. Instead, the importer becomes a 'missing trader' who pockets the tax and disappears. The goods can then be exported, at which point the government is expected to pay a VAT refund. When the fraud is repeated many times, it is known as 'carousel fraud'. Goods are imported repeatedly and re-exported in a series of contrived transactions, with VAT stolen by the importer and a refund claimed by the exporter every time the goods are moved to another state. Sometimes, the goods are non-existent and are simply created on paper. Trade figures have shown a rapid escalation in fraudulent cross-border trade, suggesting that the Exchequer's losses from the fraud will run into several billion pounds in 2006. In August 2006, official data showed that exports linked to missing trader fraud rose by almost 50% in the second quarter to a record £9.7bn. About £1 in every £10 of Britain's exports in 2006 were linked to the fraud. Since the changes were made, volumes of this fraud have dropped markedly.

they may be expected to develop economies of scale. Some Russian crime syndicates (including wealthy businesspeople based in the US) have shown the capacity to engage in vast international frauds, but so too have long-term Caribbean and Swiss residents operating businesses globally for decades without being defined as part of the 'organized crime problem' (Block and Weaver 2004; van Duyne and Block 1994; Williams 2001). This applies also to corrupt kleptocrats in developing countries and tax evaders in the developed and developing worlds (Sharman 2011; Shaxson 2011).

An interview-based study of bankruptcy fraudsters found substantial variations in the organization of that form of crime during the 1960s and 1970s, but since the sixteenth century, fraudsters in particular have found cross-border crime attractive because it creates problems of legal jurisdiction, investigative cost, and practical interest by police, prosecutors, and even creditors themselves (Levi 2008c).

Fluidity and brokerage roles—often temporary social arrangements—in putting people and skills are central to serious crime group activity in the UK and elsewhere (Hobbs 1997; Coles 2001; Kleemans and de Poot 2008; Morselli 2009). Indeed, it is these connectors or 'nodes' rather than the most central or highest-ranking figures who may be the most crucial lubricants of serious crime (Jackson *et al.* 1996).The rapid career development of some major criminals demonstrates that the rewards (and risks) of playing such a key entrepreneurial role can be very high (Barnes *et al.* 2000; Kleemans 2007; van Koppen *et al.* 2010). Thus, while acknowledging the importance of missing data about the waxing and waning of relationships over time and place (Sparrow 1991; McAndrew 1999), Coles (2001: 586) argues:

> It is possible to contemplate the situation where unsophisticated groups fail to use brokers and have no links to other groups; more sophisticated groups, particularly large and stable groups might employ a number of relatively static individuals as brokers; and, the most sophisticated, aggressively entrepreneurial groups would utilise a range of capable brokers operating themselves in chains of brokers. The identification of any varying usage of brokers in this way might provide an indication of the sophistication or degree of 'organization' of a criminal network.

The role of fences, criminal professionals (accountants, lawyers), money launderers, and transportation firms may be important in facilitating networks, though they themselves may have to be 'brokered', an aspect somewhat neglected in Gambetta's (2009) account. Such an enforcement intelligence methodology may bring increased risks for those elite or marginal upperworld members whose connections with the underworld may not previously have been noticed: but if neither the person nor the activity is part of the police and intelligence surveillance set, they may still remain safe from intervention. High volumes of suspicious activity reports (SARs) from regulated bodies like banks and lawyers may mean that those who are not already suspects may not be investigated in the UK. In 2009–10, the UK Financial Intelligence Unit—SOCA—received 240,582 SARs, though approximately half of them were submitted by four banks, and 20 reporters submitted 75 per cent of all SARs. Some other European jurisdictions (e.g. in 2009, Germany—9,046; Switzerland—896, rising to 1,159 in 2010) have much lower volumes of reports, and processing them consumes fewer resources. In Switzerland, 86.5 per cent of reports have a sufficient basis to be passed onto prosecutors; in the UK, such utilization data are not available, but the *proportion* acted upon would be much smaller.

There is a relatively risk-free zone of experimentation in economic crime attempts, whether by e-crime or more conventional forms, so long as experiments do not involve hacking into defence establishments or other critical national infrastructure, which arouse the concern of the authorities transnationally.

The proposition that criminal organization/networking has changed over the years—with a shift from solid hierarchy or collegiality to the chameleon-like flexible networks—may reflect dominant academic and law enforcement opinion (though the latter, like governments, appears publicly glued to the language of 'organized crime'). However, this proposition is by no means proven. To test it, we would need the following: (i) a distinct and replicable method for exploring and demonstrating criminals' management of their affairs, in relation to organization/networking; (ii) sufficient confidence in that method to be able to say that it could track changes over time in forms of organization/networking; (iii) to be clearer than perhaps we are at present whether the proposition would refer to 'all' forms of serious crime (corporate, public corruption, terrorism, state crime) or only to particular aspects (drugs and people trafficking, major VAT/excise tax frauds); and (iv) to delineate which periods of time and corresponding crime control/policing/private sector regulatory policies we are referring. For example, we might wish to contrast 1990s developments (including regulation and policing, national and EU third pillar and international cooperation), with the current period, post '9/11', with its mix of (a) often US-driven polices connecting 'failed states', anti-terrorism, the terrorism-OC linkage, and business clean-up agendas, and (b) (Euro financial crises notwithstanding), continuing tendencies to European harmonization if not integration post-Lisbon Treaty. This is far beyond current data capability in academia or police intelligence circles, and even the Dutch Organized Crime Monitor is stretched to illuminate the shift fully.

As things stand, in spite of the abundant scholarship reviewed here (and the even more abundant global material omitted for reasons of space), we have barely set out the methods for such testing, let alone applied them to specific periods, policies, and crime sectors: hence no generalization is safe. The field is open for research students as well as established scholars to make a real contribution here, both in fine-tuning methodology and in terms of careful focused efforts to fill the knowledge gaps. It could be useful to focus our professional communication capabilities  websites, journal special issues, etc.—on first attaining some degree of common language on this recurrent question, moving on to collate sectoral and then possibly general answers. The fruits should be of interest in a practical policy sense as well as moving forward the discipline of explaining patterns of serious criminality.

## SUMMARY AND CONCLUSIONS

All areas of criminological explanation are difficult, but accounting for changes in how and why people get together to commit a large range of serious crimes for profit is indeed challenging. This chapter has involved us thinking, first, about concepts and the utility of many terms in common use; second, the epistemology of how we would recognize 'organized crime' if we saw it; and finally, what we would need to get a better appreciation of the influences (including criminal justice and prevention influences) on the patterning of serious crime. The fact that many of these questions are not conceptually or empirically settled may distress readers looking for the sort of confident clarity conveyed in some textbooks and media accounts: but as eyewitness testimony research shows, there is no correlation between confidence and accuracy, and if understanding is to increase, it is better to start with an awareness of what we do not reliably know. What we know is that there has been a boom in illicit trade over recent decades, and that the digitization of products and the development of electronic communications have had a significant impact, though not as great as Castells (2000) predicted. Technology opens up new methods of surveillance as well as new methods of communication and crime commission, and we need to comprehend its effects in enabling (a) the networking of strangers, and (b) the industrialization of false and 'borrowed' identities for fraud and other criminal purposes. The organization of serious crimes for gain is influenced by levels of market demand, skills barriers, the willingness of professionals to enable crimes, communication technologies, and corruption. Although we need to take account of transnational aspects of many crime trades, demand and supply are experienced often at the local level also, and a focus on crime entrepreneurship and on criminal 'upcomers' and 'downcomers' is important to understand the shaping of criminal organization.

### ■ SELECTED FURTHER READING

There are several sorts of approach to the study of organized crime and its control, spanning political science, international criminal law and international relations, social network analysis, socio-legal studies, etc.

Clear analysis of the organization of crime is to be found in Naylor, R. T. (2003), 'Towards a general theory of profit-driven crimes', *British Journal of Criminology*, 43:81–101. A good collection of essays may be found in Edwards, A. and Gill, P. (eds) (2003), *Transnational Organized Crime: Perspectives on Global Security*, London: Routledge; the special issue of *Criminology and Criminal Justice* (December 2008) edited by Levi, M. and Edwards, A.; Paoli, L. (ed.) (2012), *The Oxford Handbook of Organized Crime,* New York: Oxford University Press; and the annual European collections edited by Van Duyne and colleagues, published by Wolf Legal Publishers, www.wolfpublishers.nl/.

In addition to national governmental websites, useful websites and bibliographic sources include the United Nations (www.unodc.org/unodc/index.html); Net L-3 (2010), *The Global Literature on Organized Crime: An Interpretive Report on the Development and Meta-Analysis of an Annotated Bibliographic Database for Canadian Policy Makers,* http://publications.gc.ca/collections/collection_2011/sp-ps/PS4–97-2010-eng.pdf; and the on-line journal *Trends in Organized Crime.* A short historical overview that has never been bettered is McIntosh, M. (1975), *The Organization of Crime,* London: Macmillan.

For good drugs-focused work on organization of crime, see Dorn, N., Oette, L., and White, S. (1998), 'Drugs Importation and the Bifurcation of Risk: Capitalization, Cut Outs and Organized Crime', *British Journal of Criminology*, 38; 537– 60; Dorn, N., Levi, M., and King,

L. (2005), *Literature review on upper level drug trafficking*, Home Office RDS OLR 22/05, www.homeoffice.gov.uk/rds/pdfs05/rdsolr2205.pdf. See also the Royal Society of Arts, www.thersa.org/__data/assets/pdf_file/0006/2868/rsa-illegal-drugs-report-2007.pdf; and the drugs reports of the Beckley Foundation, www.beckleyfoundation.org/policy/reports.html and of the UK Drug Policy Commission, www.beckleyfoundation.org/2011/04/03/the-global-initiative-for-drug-policy-reform/.

The policing of organized crime has been examined mostly in the context of drugs, but useful reviews include contributions to Beare, M. (ed.) (2003), *Critical Reflections on Transnational Organized Crime, Money Laundering and Corruption*, Toronto: Toronto University Press; Harfield, C., 'SOCA: A paradigm shift in British policing', *British Journal of Criminology*, 2006, 46(4): 743–61; Levi, M., 'Organised and Financial Crime', in T. Newburn, (ed.) (2008), *Handbook of Policing*, Cullompton: Willan, 2008, and Sheptycki, J., *Issues in Transnational Policing* (2000), London: Routledge. For a good review of policing in England and Wales, see also HMIC (2009), *Getting organised: A thematic report on the police service's response to serious and organised crime*, www.hmic.gov.uk/media/getting-organised-20080330.pdf. For discussions of organized crime prevention, see the contributions to Bullock, K., Clarke, R., and Tilley, N. (eds) (2010), *The Situational Prevention of Organised Crime*, Cullompton: Willan. See also, reviewing the Dutch experience, Bunt, H. van de and Schoot, C. van der (2003), *Prevention of Organised Crime: a Situational Approach*, Cullompton: Willan, and Schoot, C. van der, *Organised Crime Prevention in the Netherlands*, http://repub.eur.nl/res/pub/7385/manuscript_proefschrift_cathelijne_4_december_2005_bladwijze.pdf; and, more generally, Levi, M. and Maguire, M. (2004), 'Reducing and preventing organised crime: An evidence-based critique', *Crime, Law and Social Change*, 41(5): 397–469.

## ▪ REFERENCES

ACC (2011), *Organised Crime in Australia 2011*, Canberra: Australian Crime Commission.

ANDREAS, P. (2000), *Border Games: Policing the US-Mexico Divide*, New York: Cornell University Press.

—— and NADELMANN, E. (2007), *Policing the Globe: Criminalization and Crime Control in International Relations*, New York: Oxford University Press.

—— and GREENHILL, K. (eds) (2010), *Sex, Drugs, and Body Counts: The Politics of Numbers in Global Crime and Conflict*, Ithaca: Cornell University Press.

ANECHIARICO, F. and JACOBS, J. (1998), *The Pursuit of Absolute Integrity*, Chicago: University of Chicago Press.

ARLACCHI, P. (1986), *Mafia Business: the Mafia Ethic and the Spirit of Capitalism*, London: Verso.

—— (1998), 'Some observations on illegal markets', in V. Ruggiero, N. South, and I. Taylor (eds), *The New European Criminology*, London: Routledge.

BALOUN, V. and SCHEINOST, M. (2003), 'Financial crime in the Czech Republic: its features and international extension', in P. van Duyne, K. von Lampe, J. Newell, *Criminal Finances and Organising Crime in Europe*, Nijmegen: Wolf Legal Publishers.

BARNES, T., ELIAS, R., and WALSH, P. (2000), *Cocky: the Rise and Fall of Curtis Warren Britain's Biggest Drug Baron*, London: Milo.

BEARE, M. (ed.) (2003), *Critical Reflections on Transnational Organized Crime, Money Laundering and Corruption*, Toronto: Toronto University Press.

VAN DER BEKEN,, T. (2005), *Organised Crime and Vulnerability of Economic Sectors: The European Transport and Music Sector*, Antwerp: Maklu Uitgevers.

BLOCK, A. and CHAMBLISS, W. (1981), *Organizing Crime*, New York, Elsevier.

BOVENKERK, F. (2007), 'Half-baked Legalization Won't Work', in F. Bovenkerk and M. Levi (eds), *The Organized Crime Community*, Dordrecht: Springer.

—— and YESILGÖZ, Y. (2007), *Turkish Mafia*, London: Milo.

BULLOCK, K., MANN, D., STREET, R., and COXON, C (2009), *Examining attrition in confiscating the proceeds of crime*, Home Office Research, Development and Statistics Directorate Research Report 17.

——, CLARKE, R., and TILLEY, N. (eds) (2010), *The Situational Prevention of Organised Crime*, Cullompton: Willan.

BUNT, H. VAN DE (2010), 'Walls of secrecy and silence: The Madoff case and cartels in the construction industry', *Criminology and Public Policy*, 9(3): 435–53.

—— and SCHOOT, C. VAN DER (2003), *Prevention of Organised Crime: a Situational Approach*, Cullompton: Willan.

CABINET OFFICE (2011), *The National Security Strategy of the United Kingdom: Security in an interdependent world*, London: Cabinet Office.

CASTELLS, M. (1998), *End Of Millennium*, Oxford: Blackwell Publishers.

CAULKINS, J. and REUTER, P. (2009), 'Toward a Harm Reduction Approach to Enforcement', *Safer Communities*, 8(1): 9–23.

—— and —— (2010), 'How Drug Enforcement Affects Drug Prices', in M. Tonry (ed.), *Crime and Justice: an Annual Review of Research*, Chicago: University of Chicago Press.

CHAN, J. and DIXON, D. (2007), 'The politics and police reform: ten years after the RoyalCommission into the New South Wales Police Service', *Criminology and Criminal Justice*, 7(4): 443–68.

CHATTOE, E. and HAMILL, H. (2005), 'It's Not *Who* You Know—It's What You Know About People You *Don't* Know That Counts: Extending the Analysis of Crime Groups as Social Networks', *British Journal of Criminology*, 45: 860–76.

CHIN, KO-LIN. (1996), *Chinatown Gangs: Extortion, Enterprise, and Ethnicity*, New York, NY: Oxford University Press.

—— (2009), *The Golden Triangle: Inside Southeast Asia's Drug Trade*, Ithaca: Cornell University Press.

CHIU, Y-N., LECLERC, B., and TOWNSLEY, M. (2011), 'Crime Script Analysis of Drug Manufacturing in Clandestine Laboratories', *British Journal of Criminology*, 51: 355–74.

COHEN, A.K. (1977), 'The concept of criminal organisation', *British Journal of Criminology*, 17: 97–111.

COLES, N. (2001), 'It's not *what* you know—it's *who* you know that counts: analysing serious crime groups as social networks', *British Journal of Criminology*, 41: 580–94.

COUNCIL OF EUROPE (2005), *Organised Crime Situation Report 2005, Strasbourg, Council of Europe*. http://www.coe.int/t/dghl/cooperation/economiccrime/organisedcrime/Report2005E.pdf.

CORNISH, D. (1994), 'The procedural analysis of offending and its relevance for situational prevention', in R. Clarke (ed.), *Crime Prevention Studies*, Monsey: Criminal Justice Press.

CRESSEY, D. (1969), *Theft of the nation; the structure and operations of organised crime in America*, New York: Harper & Row.

CUELLAR, M. (2003), 'The Tenuous Relationship Between the Fight Against Money Laundering and the Disruption of Criminal Finance', *Journal of Criminal Law and Criminology*, Winter/Spring, 93(2–3): 311–466.

DAVIES, N. (2009), 'Prostitution and trafficking—the anatomy of a moral panic', *The Guardian*, 20 October 2009.

DE SOUSA, L., LAMOUR, P., and HINDESS, B. (2009), *Governments, NGOs and Anti-Corruption*, London: Routledge.

DECKER, S. and CHAPMAN, M. (2008), *Drug Smugglers on Drug Smuggling: Lessons from the Inside*, Philadelphia: Temple University Press.

DIIH, S. (forthcoming), *Infiltration of New York's Financial Market by Organized Crime*, New York: Columbia University Press.

DORN, N. (2003), 'Proteiform criminalities: the formation of organised crime as organisers' responses to developments in four fields of control', in A. Edwards and P. Gill, (eds), *Transnational Organised Crime*, London: Routledge.

——, MURJI, K., and SOUTH, N. (1992), *Traffickers*, London: Routledge.

——, OETTER, L., and WHITE, S. (1998), 'Drugs Importation and the Bifurcation of Risk: Capitalization, Cut Outs and Organized Crime', *British Journal of Criminology*, 38: 537–60.

——, LEVI, M., and KING, L. (2005), *Literature review on upper level drug trafficking*, London: Home Office, RDS OLR 22/05.

DUBOURG, R. and PRITCHARD, S. (eds) (2009), *Organised Crime: Revenues, Economic and Social Costs, and Criminal Assets Available for Seizure*, London: Home Office.

EDWARDS, A. and LEVI, M. (2008), 'Researching the Organisation of Serious Crimes', *Criminology and Criminal Justice*, 8(4): 363–88.

EUROPEAN COMMISSION (2010), *The EU Internal Security Strategy in Action: Five steps towards a more secure Europe*, Brussels: EC COM(2010) 673 final.

EUROPEAN COURT OF JUSTICE (2005), Judgment Of The Court (Grand Chamber), Action for annulment–Articles 29 EU, 31(e) EU, 34 EU, and 47 EU–Framework Decision 2003/80/JHA, 13 September, Luxemburg: European Court of Justice, http://curia.europa.eu.

EUROPOL (2011), *Organised Crime Threat Assessment 2011*, The Hague: Europol.

FIJNAUT, C., BOVENKERK, F., BRUINSMA, G., and VAN DER BUNT, H. (1998), *Organised Crime in the Netherlands*, The Hague : Kluwer.

—— and PAOLI, L. (eds) (2004), *Organised Crime in Europe*, Dordrecht: Springer.

FINCKENAUER, J. (2006), 'Review of Wages of Crime', *Crime, Law and Social Change*, 45(3): 27–30.

—— and WARING, E. (1999), *Russian Mafia in America*, Boston: Northeastern University Press.

—— and ALBANESE, J. (2005), 'Organized crime in North America', in P. Reichel (ed.) (2005), *Handbook of Transnational Crime & Justice*, Thousand Oaks: Sage.

—— and CHIN, K. (2010), *Researching and Rethinking Sex Trafficking: The Movement of Chinese Women to Asia and the United States for Commercial Sex*, Final report submitted to National Institute of Justice for Grant #2006-IJ-CX-0008, Washington DC: NIJ.

FIORENTINI, G. and PELTZMANN, S. (eds) (1995), *The Economics of Organised Crime*, Cambridge: Cambridge University Press.

FIRESTONE T. (2008), 'Criminal Corporate Raiding in Russia', *The International Lawyer*, 1207–29.

—— (2010), 'Armed injustice: abuse of the law and complex crime in post-soviet Russia', *Denver Journal of International Law & Policy*, 38(4): 555–79.

FRIMAN, R. and ANDREAS, P. (eds) (1999), *The Illicit Global Economy and State Power*, Lanham, Md: Rowman and Littlefield.

GALEOTTI, M. (2004), 'The Russian "Mafiya": Consolidation and Globalisation', *Global Crime*, 6(1): 54–69.

GAMBETTA, D. (1994), *The Sicilian Mafia*, Cambridge, Mass: Harvard University Press.

—— (2009), *Codes of the Underworld*, Princeton University Press.

GEOPOLITICAL DRUG DISPATCH (2001), Special issue of *Crime, Law and Social Change*.

GILL, M. (2001), 'The Craft of Robbers of Cash-in-transit Vans: Crime Facilitators and the Entrepreneurial Approach', *International Journal of the Sociology of Law*, 29: 277–91.

GILL, P. (2000), *Rounding Up the Usual Suspects?*, Aldershot: Ashgate.

GILMORE, W. (2012), *Dirty Money: The Evolution of Money Laundering Counter-Measures*, 4th edn, Strasbourg: Council of Europe Publishing.

GLENNY, M. (2009), *McMafia: Seriously Organised Crime*, London: Vintage.

—— (2011), *DarkMarket: Cyber Thieves, Cyber Cops and You*, London: Bodley Head.

GOMEZ-CESPEDES, A. (1999), 'Organised crime in Mexico,' in F. Brookman, L. Noaks *et al*, (eds), *Qualitative Research in Criminology*, Brookfield, VT: Ashgate.

GREGORY, F. (2003), 'Classify, Report and Measure: the UK Organised Crime Notification Scheme,' in A. Edwards and P. Gill (eds), *Transnational Organised Crime*, London: Routledge.

GRUTER, P. and VAN DE MHEEN, D. (2005), 'Dutch cocaine trade: the perspective of Rotterdam cocaine retail dealers', *Crime, Law and Social Change*, 44(1): 19–33.

HALLSWORTH, S. and SILVERSTONE, D. (2009), '"That's life innit": A British perspective on guns, crime and social order', *Criminology and Criminal Justice*, 9(3): 359–77.

HARFIELD, C. (2006), 'SOCA: A paradigm shift in British policing', *British Journal of Criminology*, 46(4): 743–61.

HILL, P. (2003), *The Japanese Mafia: Yakuza, Law and the State*, Oxford: Oxford University Press.

HOBBS, D. (1997), 'Professional crime: change, continuity, and the enduring myth of the Underworld', *Sociology*, 31(1): 57–2.

—— (1998), 'Going Down the Glocal: the local context of organised crime', *The Howard Journal*, 37(4): 407–22.

—— (2001), 'The Firm: organizational logic and criminal culture on a shifting terrain', *British Journal of Criminology*, 41: 549–60.

—— (2004), 'Organised crime in the UK', in C. Fijnaut and L. Paoli (eds) (2004), *Organised Crime in Europe*, Dordrecht: Springer.

HOME OFFICE (2004), *One Step Ahead: A 21st Century Strategy to Defeat Organised Crime*, London: Home Office.

—— (2009), *Extending Our Reach*, London: Home Office.

—— (2011), *The National Crime Agency: A plan for the creation of a national crime-fighting capability*, London: Home Office.

IANNI, F.A. and REUSS-IANNI, E. (1972), *A Family Business; Kinship and social control in organised crime*, London, Routledge & Kegan Paul.

IANNI, F.A. (1974) 'Authority, power and respect: the interplay of control systems in an organised crime "family"', in S. Rottenberg (ed.) (1974), *The economics of crime and punishment*, Washington D.C.: American Enterprise Institute for Public Policy Research.

INDEPENDENT MONITORING COMMISSION (2006), *10th Report*, Belfast and Dublin.www.official-documents.gov.uk/document/hc0506/hc10/1066/1066.pdf.

INTERNATIONAL MASS MARKETING FRAUD WORKING GROUP (2010), *Mass-Marketing Fraud: A Threat Assessment*, London: SOCA.

JACKSON, J., HERBRINCK, J., and JANSEN, R. (1996), 'Examining criminal organisations: possible methodologies', *Transnational Organized Crime*, 2/4: 83–105.

JACOBS, J., WORTHINGTON, J., and PANARELLA, C. (1994), *Busting the Mob*, New York: New York University Press.

—— and GOULDIN, L. (1999), 'Cosa Nostra's Last Stand?', in M. Tonry (ed.), *Crime & Justice: An Annual Review of Research*, Vol. 24, Chicago: Chicago University Press.

KAPLAN, D. and DUBRO, A. (2003), *Yakuza: Japan's Criminal Underworld*, expanded edn, Berkeley: University of California Press.

KELLY, L. (2005), '"You Can Find Anything You Want": A Critical Reflection on Research on Trafficking in Persons within and into Europe', *International Migration* 4(1–2): 235–65.

—— and REGAN, L. (2000), *Stopping Traffic: Exploring the Extent of, and Responses to, Trafficking in Women for Sexual Exploitation in the UK*, Police Research Series Paper 125, London: Home Office.

KENNEY, M. (2007), 'The Architecture of Drug Trafficking: Network Forms of Organization in the Colombian Cocaine Trade', *Global Crime* 8: 233–59.

KLEEMANS, E. R. (2007), 'Organized crime, transit crime, and racketeering', in M. Tonry and C. Bijleveld (eds), *Crime and justice in the Netherlands. Crime and justice. A review of research* 35: 163–215, Chicago: University of Chicago Press.

—— and DE POOT, C. (2008), 'Criminal Careers in Organized Crime and Social Opportunity Structure', *European Journal of Criminology*, 5(1): 69–98.

KLERKS, P. (2003), 'The network paradigm applied to criminal organizations: theoretical nitpicking or a relevant doctrine for investigators? Recent developments in the Netherlands', in A. Edwards and P. Gill (eds), *Transnational Organised Crime: Perspectives on global security*, London: Routledge.

VAN KOPPEN, M., DE POOT, C., KLEEMANS, E., and NIEUWBEERTA, P. (2010), 'Criminal Trajectories in organised crime', *British Journal of Criminology*: 50, 102–123.

KOSER, K. (2008), 'Why Migrant Smuggling Pays', *International Migration*, 46(2): 3–26.

LACZKO, F. (2005), 'Data and Research on Human Trafficking', *International Migration*, 43(1–2): 5–16.

VON LAMPE, K. (2006), 'The cigarette black market in Germany and in the United Kingdom', *Journal of Financial Crime*, 13/2: 235–54.

—— and JOHANSEEN, P. (2004), 'Organised Crime and Trust: On the conceptualization and empirical relevance of trust in the context of criminal networks', *Global Crime*, 6(2): 159–84.

LASCOUMES, P. and GODEFROY, T. (with contributions by J. Cartier-Bressonand M. Levi (2002), *Emergence du Problème des 'Places Off Shore' et Mobilisation Internationale*, Paris: CEVIPOP-CNRS.

LEVI, M. (2003), 'Organising and controlling payment card fraud: fraudsters and their operational environment', *Security Journal*, 16(2): 21–30.

—— (2002), 'Money Laundering and its Regulation', *The Annals of the American Academy of Social and Political Science*, July.

—— (2006), 'The media construction of financial white-collar crimes', *British Journal of Criminology*, 46: 1037–57.

—— (2008a), 'White-collar, organised and cyber crimes in the media: some contrasts and similarities', *Crime, Law and Social Change*, 49: 365–77.

—— (2008b), "Organised Fraud": Unpacking Research on Networks and Organisation', *Criminology and Criminal Justice*, 8(4): 389–420.

—— (2008c), *The Phantom Capitalists*, 2nd edn, Aldershot: Ashgate.

—— (forthcoming), 'Money laundering and organized crime', in L. Paoli (ed.), *The Oxford Handbook of Organized Crime*, New York: Oxford University Press.

—— and GILMORE, B. (2002), 'Terrorist finance, money laundering and the rise and rise of mutual evaluation: a new paradigm for crime control?', *European Journal of Law Reform*, 4(2): 337–64.

—— and MAGUIRE, M. (2004), 'Reducing and preventing organised crime: An evidence-based critique', *Crime, Law and Social Change*, 41(5): 397–469.

—— and NAYLOR, T. (2000), *Organised crime, the Organisation of Crime, and the Organisation of Business*, Essay for the Crime Foresight Panel, London: Department of Trade and Industry.

—— NELEN, H. and LANKHORST, F. (2005), 'Lawyers as crime facilitators in Europe: An introduction and overview', *Crime, Law and Social Change*, 42 (2–3): 117–121.

—— and REUTER, P. (2006), 'Money Laundering: A Review of Current Controls and their Consequences', in M. Tonry (ed.), *Crime and Justice: an Annual Review of Research*, Vol. 34, Chicago: Chicago University Press.

LEVI-STRAUSS, C. (1987), *Introduction to Marcel Mauss*, London: Routledge,.

LEVITT, S. and DUBNER, S. (2005), *Freakonomics: A Rogue Economist Explores the Hidden Side of Everything*, London: Allen Lane.

—— and VENKATESH, S. (2000), 'An Economic Analysis of a Drug-selling Gang's Finances', *The Quarterly Journal of Economics*, 115: 755–89.

MCANDREW, D. (1999), 'The structural analysis of criminal networks', in D. Canter and L.Alison (eds), *The Social Psychology of Crime: Groups, Teams and Networks*, Aldershot: Ashgate.

MCINTOSH, M. (1975), *The Organisation of Crime*, London: Macmillan.

MCSWEENEY, T., TURNBULL, P., and HOUGH, M. (2008), *Tackling Drug Markets and Distribution Networks in the UK*, London: The UK Drug Policy Commission.

MACK, J. and KERNER, H. (1975), The Crime Industry, Lexington: Saxon House.

MACKENZIE, S. (2005a), *Going, Going, Gone: Regulating the Market in Illicit Antiquities*, Leicester: Institute of Art and Law.

—— (2005b), 'Dig a Bit Deeper: Law, Regulation and the Illicit Antiquities Market', *British Journal of Criminology*, 45(3): 249–68.

MATRIX KNOWLEDGE GROUP (2007), *The illicit drug trade in the United Kingdom*, Home Office Online Report 20/07, London: Home Office.

MAY, T. and HOUGH, M. (2004), 'Drug markets and distribution systems', *Addiction Research & Theory*, 12(6): 549–63.

MITSILEGAS, V. (2003), *Money Laundering Counter-Measures in the European Union: A New Paradigm of Security Governance versus Fundamental Legal Principles*, Amsterdam: Kluwer Law International.

MONZINI, P. (2005), *Sex Traffic: Prostitution, Crime and Exploitation*, London: Zed.

MORSELLI, C. (2005), *Contacts, Opportunities and Criminal Enterprise*, Toronto: University of Toronto Press.

—— (2009), *Inside Criminal Networks*, New York: Springer.

NAYLOR, R. (2003), 'Towards a general theory of profit-driven crimes', *The British Journal of Criminology*, 43: 81–101

—— (2005), *Wages of Crime: Black Markets, Illegal Finance, and the Underworld Economy*, 2nd edn, Ithaca: Cornell University Press.

—— (2011), *Crass Struggle: Glitz, Greed, and Gluttony in a Wanna-Have World*, Montreal: McGill/Queens University Press.

NCIS (2001), *UK Threat Assessment, 2001*, London: NCIS.

NELKEN, D. (1996), 'The judges and political corruption in Italy', in M. Leviand, D. Nelken (eds), *The Corruption of Politics and the Politics of Corruption Special Issue, Journal of Law and Society*, 23: 95–112.

—— (1997), 'The Globalization of crime and criminal justice: prospects and problems', in M. Freeman (ed.), *Law and Opinion at the end of the 20th Century*, Oxford: Oxford University Press.

NUTT, D., KING, L., and PHILLIPS, L. (2010), 'Drug harms in the UK: a multicriteria decision analysis', *The Lancet*, 376: 1558–65.

PAOLI, L. (2001), *Illegal Drug Markets in Russia*, Freibourg: Max Planck Institut.

—— (2002), 'The paradoxes of organized crime', *Crime, Law and Social Change*, 37: 51–97.

—— (2003), *Mafia Brotherhoods*, New York: Oxford University Press.

——, GREENFIELD, V., and REUTER, P. (2009), *The World Heroin Market: Can Supply Be Cut?*, New York: Oxford University Press.

PEARSON, G. and HOBBS, D. (2001), *Middle Market Drug Distribution*, HORS 227, London: Home Office.

PIETH, M. (1999) 'The Harmonisation of Law against Economic Crime', *The European Journal of Law Reform*, 1,4: 7–45.

PUNCH, M. (2000), 'Police Corruption and its Prevention', *European Journal on Criminal Policy and Research*, 8(3): 301–24.

QUAH, J. (2011), *Curbing Corruption in Asian Countries An Impossible Dream?*, London: Emerald Books.

RAWLINSON, P. (2007), 'Mission impossible? Researching organized crime', in R. King and E. Wincup (eds), *Doing Research on Crime and Justice*, Oxford: Oxford University Press.

RAWLINSON, P. (2009), *From Fear to Fraternity*, London: Pluto.

REICHEL, P. (ed.) (2005), *Handbook of Transnational Crime & Justice*, Thousand Oaks: Sage.

REUTER, P. (1983), *Disorganized crime: Illegal markets and the Mafia*, Cambridge, Massachusetts: MIT Press.

—— (2009), 'Systemic violence in drug markets', *Crime, Law and Social Change*, 52(3): 275–89.

—— and RUBINSTEIN, J. (1978), 'Fact, Fancy, and Organized Crime', *The Public Interest*, 53: 45–68.

—— and KLEINMAN, M. (1986), 'Risks and Prices: An Economic Analysis of Drug Enforcement', in M. Tonry and N. Morris (eds), *Crime and Justice: A Review of Research*, Vol. 7, Chicago: Chicago University Press.

RUGGIERO, V. (2000), *Crime and Markets: Essays in Anti-Criminology*, Oxford: Clarendon Press.

—— and SOUTH, N. (1995), *Eurodrugs*, London: Routledge.

—— and KHAN, K. (2006), 'British South Asian communities and drug supply networks in the UK. A qualitative study', *International Journal of Drug Policy*, 17: 473–83.

SAVIANO, R. (2007), *Gomorrah: Italy's Other Mafia*, London: Pan.

SHAPLAND, J. and PONSAERS, P. (eds) (2009), *The informal economy and connections with organised crime: the impact of national social and economic policies*, The Hague: Boom Juridische Uitgevers, Reeks Het groene gras.

SHARMAN, J. (2011), *The Money Laundry: Regulating Criminal Finance in the Global Economy*, Ithaca: Cornell University Press.

SHELLEY, L. (2010), *Human Trafficking: A Global Perspective*, Cambridge: Cambridge University Press.

SHEPTYCKI, J. (2000), *Issues in Transnational Policing*, London: Routledge.

—— and WARDAK, A. (eds) (2005), *Transnational and Comparative Criminology*, Glasshouse Press.

SIEGEL, D. (2009), *The Mazzel Ritual: Culture, Customs and Crime in the Diamond Trade*, New York: Springer.

SHATFORD, J. and DOYLE, W. (2005), *Dome Raiders: How Scotland Yard Foiled the Greatest Robbery of All Time*, London: Virgin.

SHAXSON, N. (2011), *Treasure Islands: Tax havens and the men who stole the world*, London: Bodley Head.

SHERMAN, L. (1974), *Police Corruption: A Sociological Perspective*, Garden City, NJ: Doubleday.

SHOVER, N. (1996), *Great Pretenders: Pursuits and Careers of Persistent Thieves*, Boulder: Westview Press.

——, COFFEY, G., and HOBBS, D. (2003), 'Crime on the line: Telemarketing and the changing nature of professional crime', *British Journal of Criminology*, 43 (July): 489–505.

SOCA (2010), *The United Kingdom Threat Assessment of Organised Crime 2009/10*, London: Serious and Organised Crime Agency.

SPARROW, M. (1991), 'The application of network analysis to criminal intelligence: an assessment of the prospects', *Social Networks*, 13: 251–74.

STELFOX, P. (2003), 'Transnational Organised Crime: a police perspective', in A. Edwards and P. Gill, *Transnational Organized Crime: Perspectives on Global Security*, London: Routledge.

STILLE, A. (1996), *Excellent Cadavers*, London: Vintage.

SUTTON, M. (1998), *Handling stolen goods and theft: A market reduction approach*, Home Office Research Study 178, London: Home Office.

THOUMI, F. (2003), *Illegal Drugs, Economy and Society in the Andes*, Baltimore: Johns Hopkins University Press.

—— (2007), 'The Rise of Two Drug Tigers: the development of the illegal drugs industry and drug policy failure in Afghanistan and Colombia', in F. Bovenkerk and M. Levi (eds), *The Organized Crime Community*, Dordrecht: Springer.

TILLY, C. (1985), 'War making and State making as Organized Crime', in P. Evans, D. Reuschemeyer, and T. Skocpol (eds), *Bringing the State Back In*, Cambridge: Cambridge University Press.

TRANSPARENCY INTERNATIONAL (2006), *Global Corruption Report*, Berlin: Transparency International.

TREMBLAY, P., CLERMONT, Y., and CUSSON, M. (1994), 'Jockeys and joyriders: changing car theft opportunity structures', *British Journal of Criminology*, 34(3): 307–21.

——, TALON, B., and HURLEY, D. (2001), 'Body Switching and related adaptations in the resale of stolen vehicles', *British Journal of Criminology*, 41: 561–79.

UNGER, B. (2009), 'Money Laundering—A Newly Emerging Topic on the International Agenda', *Review of Law & Economics*, 5(2): Article 1.

VAN DUYNE , P. (1993), 'Organised Crime and Business-Crime Enterprises in the Netherlands', *Crime, Law and Social Change*, 19: 103–42.

—— (1996), 'The Phantom and Threat of Organised Crime', *Crime, Law and Social Change*, 24: 341–77.

—— (1998), 'Money-Laundering: Pavlov's Dog and Beyond', *The Howard Journal*, 37(4): 359–74.

—— (2005), 'Criminal subcontracting in the Netherlands: the Dutch "koppelbaas" as crime-entrepreneur', in P.C. van Duyne and K. von Lampe (eds), *The organised crime economy*, Nijmegen: Wolf Legal Publishers.

—— and BLOCK, A. (1994), 'Organized Cross Atlantic Crime', *Crime, Law and Social Change*, 22(2): 127–47.

—— (2004), 'The creation of a threat image: media, policy making and organised crime', in P. van Duyne, M. Jager, K. von Lampe, and J. Newell (eds), *Threats and phantoms of organised crime, corruption and terrorism*, Nijmegen: Wolf Legal Publishers.

——, GROENHUIJSEN, M.S., and SCHUDELARO, A.A.P. (2005),'Balancing financial threats and legal interests in money-laundering policy', *Crime, Law and Social Change*, 43(2): 117–47.

—— and LEVI, M. (2005), *Drugs and Money: Managing the Drug Trade and Crime-Money in Europe*, London: Routledge.

—— and VAN DIJCK, M. (2007), 'Assessing organised crime: the sad state of an impossible art', in F. Bovenkerk and M. Levi (eds), *The Organized Crime Community*, Dordrecht: Springer.

—— and VAN DER BEKEN, T. (2009), 'The incantations of the EU organised crime policy making', *Crime, Law and Social Change*, 51: 261–81.

VARESE, F. (2001), *The Russian Mafia*, Oxford: Oxford University Press.

—— (2006), 'How Mafias Migrate: The Case of the 'Ndrangheta in Northern Italy", *Law & Society Review*, 40: 411–44.

—— (2011), *Mafias on the move: how organized crime conquers new territories*, Princeton, NJ: Princeton University Press.

VOCKS, J. and NIJBOER, J. (2000), 'The promised land: a study of trafficking in women from central and eastern Europe to the Netherlands', *European Journal on Criminal Policy and Research*, 8(3): 379–88.

VOLKOV, V. (2002), *Violent Entrepreneurs*, Ithaca: Cornell University Press.

VULLIAMY, E. (2010), *Amexica: War Along the Borderline*, London: Bodley Head.

WALKER, J. and UNGER, B. (2009), 'Measuring Global Money Laundering: "The Walker Gravity Model"', *Review of Law & Economics*, 5(2).

WALL, D. (2007), *Cybercrime: The transformation of crime in the information age*, Cambridge: Polity.

WEBB, S. and BURROWS J. (2009), *Organised immigration crime: a post conviction study*, Home Office Research Report 15, London: Home Office.

WILLIAMS, P. (2001), 'Transnational criminal networks', in J. Arquillaand and D. Ronfeldt (eds), *Networks and Netwars: the Future of Terror, Crime and Militancy*, Santa Monica: RAND.

WOODIWISS, M. (2001), *Organized Crime and American Power: a History*, Toronto: University of Toronto Press.

—— (2005) *Gangster Capitalism: The United States and the Global Rise of Organized Crime*, London: Constable and Robinson.

—— and HOBBS, R. (2009), 'Organized Evil and the Atlantic Alliance: Moral Panics and the Rhetoric of Organized Crime Policing in America and Britain', *Br J Criminol* 49(1): 106–28.

WORLD BANK (2006), *The Many Faces of Corruption: Tracking Vulnerabilities at the Sector Level*, Washington DC: World Bank.

WHITE HOUSE (2011), *Strategy to Combat Transnational Organized Crime*, Washington DC: The White House.

WRIGHT, A. (2006), *Organized Crime*, Cullompton: Willan.

ZATICH, D. (2002), *Trafficking Cocaine. Colombian Drug Entrepreneurs in the Netherlands*, The Hague: Kluwer Law International.

——, BOVENKERK, F., and SIEGEL, D. (2003), 'Organized crime and ethnic reputation manipulation', *Crime, Law & Social Change*, 2003(1): 23–38.

ZARTMAN, W (1995), *Collapsed States*, Boulder: Lynne Rienner.

ZHANG, S. and CHIN, K. (2008), 'Snakeheads, mules, and protective umbrellas: A review of current research on Chinese organized crime', *Crime, Law and Social Change*, 50(3): 177–95.

# 21

# WHITE-COLLAR AND CORPORATE CRIME

*David Nelken*

## INTRODUCTION

The media regularly report cases of business or professional people caught out in serious offences, sometimes for behaviour that they did not expect to be treated as criminal, and for which it is often difficult to secure a criminal conviction. Recent cases from the USA, and elsewhere, include numerous reports of insider dealing, million dollar settlements by a pharmaceutical company to settle a claim that it fraudulently tried to stop competition with one of its anti- depressant drugs, multi -millionaire settlements by banks after admitting criminal wrongdoing in helping rich people shelter from taxes (one of which included an agreement not to bring a prosecution as long as the bank concerned accepted to be monitored to see that it did not continue with the offending), deaths by poisoning caused a the dumping of toxic waste, and the loss of 11 lives along with the largest and most devastating oil spill yet documented, caused by errors in drilling by BP off the gulf of Mexico.

Such Jekyll and Hyde contradictions between respectability and crime raises questions that are unlike those posed by many other types of criminal behaviour. Why do they do it when they have so much to lose? How representative are these cases of the practices of other businessmen, or of professional and business life in general? Is there one law for the rich and another for the poor? These questions, as will be seen in the last section of this chapter, have taken on added significance in the light of the major global economic implosion of 2008 linked to risky and fraudulent behaviour by some leading bankers and others in the USA and Europe.

One of the biggest difficulties in approaching this subject is to find a way of putting dramatic and newsworthy cases of business misbehaviour into some sort of context and proportion. Study of the distribution and frequency of white-collar crimes is made problematic by the fact (not in itself unimportant) that, especially in the common law countries where the concept was first formulated, most white-collar crimes are not included in the official statistics which serve as the basis for debates about 'the crime problem'. The usual difficulties of interpreting the statistics of crime are greatly magnified here (Levi 1985). The information recorded by specialized enforcement agencies (often not even made public) serves mainly as a source for describing methods of control rather than the misbehaviour being controlled. Neither can it be assumed that there is any uniformity in the meaning of data obtained in this way. A few agencies are reactive, and depend on complaints; others are proactive, but the level of enforcement is restricted by limited resources (in Britain factories are inspected for safety offences on average once every four years). Much regulation is geared to using prosecution as a last resort—thus the number of prosecuted offenders says little about the theoretical level of crime; conversely, the number of visits or warnings cannot be used as an index of the incidence of deliberate law-breaking. There is a danger of double-counting where the same behaviour is dealt with by different agencies, or where one firm has more subunits than another. This also creates problems about defining recidivism—which were ignored by Sutherland in his pioneering study (Sutherland 1949). There are problems of classifying the date and location of some of these offences (a factor which often helps secure their immunity). Shifts in legislative mandates, and in the number, expertise, politics, and motivation of enforcers, make a treacherous basis for studies of changes in offending patterns over time. Lastly, supplementing official statistics with victim reports is difficult because the victims are often unaware of their victimization; and even where this is not the case, as in organizations subject to fraud, there is often unwillingness to admit to vulnerability.

These difficulties mean that many discussions of the subject in textbooks are forced to rely unduly on newspaper reports or on the activities of crusading journalists (see, e.g., Coleman 1985). Obtaining information in this way complicates the task of assessing the accuracy, frequency, or representativeness of the cases reported. 'Scandals' by definition are unrepresentative of normal life, but they may also expose typical practices and mechanisms of 'institutionalized deviance'. Were the billions lost through the gambles of Nick Leeson of (the now— thanks to him—defunct) Barings bank—or Jérome Kerviel of Société Générale—the result of actions of 'rogue traders'? Or were they no more than extreme examples of normal and acceptable risk-taking by dealers who were highly valued when they were bringing in good profits? What is clear is that newspapers, or those who feed them their stories, initiate crime control campaigns for reasons which may have little to do with the long-term trend in the misbehaviour at issue. It is therefore often hard to tell, here as elsewhere, whether business or financial crimes are increasing or are just more newsworthy, or to decide if apparent change is the result of an increase in a given kind of misbehaviour or more the consequence of a trend towards the use of formal and legal, rather than informal, means to deal with it.

Despite these problems there have been some useful studies drawing on agency records to survey the rate of corporate offending (Clinard and Yeager 1980), or even on court records to establish the type of offenders normally apprehended for what the authors call 'middle-class crimes' (Weisburd et al. 1991). What we know about white-collar crime also comes from interviews with enforcers as well as observation of their work (e.g. Carson 1970; Hawkins 1984; Hutter 1988, 1997; and cf. Nelken 1991); interviews with businessmen (e.g. Lane 1953; Braithwaite 1984); biographies of and retrospective accounts by offenders (e.g. Geis 1968); participant observation in offending organizations (e.g. Nelken 1983: ch. 2); experimental techniques such as those used by consumer organizations (Green 1990: ch. 2), as well as other sources (and for useful methodological hints on researching these type of offences, see Levi 1985).

Although most of the literature on white-collar crime is American, major contributions have been made by other English-language scholars, such as Braithwaite, Carson, and Levi. The equivalent term for 'white-collar crime' is also widely found in other languages, and even used in foreign court proceedings. There are also interesting contributions, sometimes in foreign languages, which could serve as a useful starting point for comparative research (e.g. Tiedemann 1974; Cosson 1978; Magnusson 1985; Clarke 1990b; Delmas-Marty 1990; Ziegler 1990; Van Duyne 1993; Passas and Nelken 1993; Savelsberg 1994). But the common use of the term can be misleading. Despite the similarities of modern industrialized economies, there are important differences in general and legal culture that affect the meaning of and response to white-collar crime (and its contrasting category of ordinary crime). These contrasts have not yet been sufficiently explored (see Nelken 1994a; Levi and Nelken 1996; Nelken 2000). In civil law countries such as Italy there are few of the special enforcement agencies used to deal with occupational offences found, for example, in America, Britain, and Australia. Instead, normal police forces, often spearheaded by specialized financial police, conduct investigations of economic crime, and businessmen or politicians with white collars regularly see the inside of prisons (though few seem to stay there for long). American outrage over business misbehaviour may be connected to what Wright-Mills (1943/1963) saw as the small-town values of American social reformers, as well as to a peculiar, American love–hate relationship with big businesses (are they the ultimate proof of capitalist success, or a threat to the market and to the individual?). In countries with a strong Catholic heritage the respectability attached to capitalist profit-making may be less secure than in Protestant countries (Ruggiero 1996).

Much of the literature on white-collar crime continues to be concerned to demonstrate the seriousness and diffuseness of such offending, and to show that its costs and damages dwarf those of conventional, or ordinary, crime (for a recent summary of attempts to measure the impact of white-collar crime, see Slapper and Tombs 1999: 37–41, 54–84). It is difficult to count the numbers of victims caused by the unsustainable risks taken by leading financial institutions in the early 2000s (Barak 2012 speaks of 30 to 40million people being affected). More than any other type of crime, as the behaviour of bankers recently again demonstrates, white-collar offences undermine the basis of trust that holds society together by discrediting those in authority or positions of privilege who are supposed to be models of respectability.

Colossal fines and settlements are imposed in cases of some financial crimes, for example, Michael Milken, the junk bond king, paid over $650 million in court-ordered restitution even before sentence. The collapse of the savings and loan institutions (similar to what in Britain are described as building societies) in the United States in the late 1980s may end up costing a trillion dollars. This is many times the cost of the Marshall Plan or the Korean War; but the real impact is blunted because the costs are to be covered by a US Government 50-year loan (Pontell and Calavita 1993; Calavita et al. 1997; Zimring and Hawkins 1993). Contrary to what is supposed by some definitions (e.g. Edelhertz 1970), there is also no reason to exclude violence and death from the province of white-collar crime. There are a number of case studies which document this, even without going into more controversial but important calculations of the overall number of fatal accidents or diseases occurring at work which could have been prevented and prosecuted (Box 1983: 28ff.; Hills 1988; Slapper 1991).

Carson's study of the loss of life in the exploration for oil in the North Sea (confirmed by later events such as the blowing up of the Piper Alpha oil rig in 1988 with the loss of 168 lives), for instance, showed that many lives could have been saved with rudimentary attention to safety considerations (Carson 1982). The devastating consequences of the nuclear disaster at Chernobyl, the chemical explosion at Bhopal, the suffering caused by the sale of the drug thalidomide, or the contraceptive known as the Dalkon shield, are other well-known examples. But even victims of economic and business offences involving fraud and deception suffer a large number of physical as well as economic consequences (Croall 2009). Between 20 and 30 per cent of investors who lost money as a result of the collapse of Enron also reported extreme or major harm to their marital relations, friendships, and physical health, typically consequences similar to or greater than those caused by violent crime (Boyd 2006).

Despite such evidence, white-collar crimes are still subjected to very different interpretations. Durkheim argued that societies consider dangerous those behaviours they respond to as criminal, rather than the other way round. But many authors insist that it is levels of social harm that should matter (Hillyard, Pantazis, Tombs, and Gordon 2004). Showing that white-collar crime causes more harmful consequences than street crime is seen as a way of influencing the social definition of such conduct—and debates over the causes and control of white-collar crime often connect to different political evaluations of the misdeeds of business or capitalism. Political conservatives tend to favour structural explanations of business malpractice rather than personal guilt— thus changing places with liberals in comparison with their positions on ordinary crime (as noted by Zimring and Hawkins 1993). On the other hand, even some authors critical of capitalism argue that corporate crime requires 'a shift from a humanist to a structuralist problematic'—though they continue nonetheless to apply the criminal label to the behaviour which results from such a structural problematic (Slapper and Tombs 1999: 17). Whilst many authors will emphasize the harm caused to workers, investors, savers, and pensioners through the failure of leading corporations or banks others will be more worried by the social costs of their continuing economic 'success' (Prashad 2002).

An important relevant recent line of study is the effort to show that the response to crimes of the upper-world intersects with that towards more conventional crimes and that both depend on larger political economic changes. Hagan, for example, writing about the USA, tells us that over-extending sub-prime mortgages—an important cause of the 2008 financial crash—actually helped reduce crime in the inner cities by increasing home stability for minority groups even as it also facilitated mortgage fraud and played a part in what became toxic packages of securities (Hagan 2010). He also stresses the way different crime threats are ' framed'. Over the period running from Roosevelt to that of Reagan 'crimes of the streets' were increasingly vilified as compared to 'crimes in the suites'. Whilst risk-taking was advocated for those in the business world, self-control was the mantra for underdogs (Hagan 2010). Where, on the one hand there was increasing deregulation for suite crime, on the other hand we witness a strong state approach to policing and large-scale imprisoning of the poor engaged in street crime (see also Waquant 2009). Those who challenge this view would no doubt argue that the two kinds of risk-taking are not analogous in their cause or their consequences. But this depends exactly on how the harms caused by business are framed.

# SEVEN TYPES OF AMBIGUITY

Why is there still so much disagreement over white-collar crime? As with the equivocal designs produced by Gestalt psychologists, do we find it difficult to see 'the criminal' and 'the respectable person' in one and the same figure? Following Aubert (1952) I shall argue that ambiguity about the nature of white-collar crime, and the best way of responding to it, forms an essential key to the topic and can be used to provide insights into this type of crime as well as the 'ordinary' crime to which it is contrasted. As the subject has become more established scholars have either tended to abandon Aubert's insight, or to concentrate on only one or two of the sources of ambiguity that will be considered here. They also tend to divide into those, on the one hand, who point to the ambiguous features of white-collar crime so as to explain and/or justify special treatment for this misbehaviour, and those, on the other hand, who claim that ambiguity is a socially constructed smoke-screen that ought to be dispelled. Why for example, is mortgage fraud the so-called 'worst crime no one has ever heard of'?

In this chapter I do not purport to settle the question of how far the features that supposedly make white-collar crime more ambiguous than ordinary crime are (merely) socially constructed. I shall, however, try to do something to clarify the uncertainties produced by the literature itself by offering a critical review both of those arguments which assert that ambiguity is intrinsic to the misbehaviour itself and of those which attempt to prove that white-collar crime is 'essentially' the same as ordinary crime but is transformed by the social reaction to it. I shall seek to illustrate seven different sources of ambiguity that surround this topic (using the term 'ambiguity' loosely to embrace the various forms of equivocalness, uncertainty, and ambivalence referred to in and produced by discussions of the characteristics of white-collar crime).

The first ambiguities that I shall consider arise in trying to define what is meant by 'white-collar crime'. The ambiguous way the concept is used in the criminological literature means that it is not clear what range of crimes is being referred to. From the outset, Sutherland's concept has also been criticized for seeking to apply the crime label to behaviours whose definition as crime is legally or sociologically controversial. The second set of ambiguities belongs more to discussions of the causes of white-collar crime. While many scholars try to apply the usual criminological frameworks of explanation to this kind of offending, others have used the topic precisely so as to place these schemes in doubt. Ambiguity also surrounds discussions of the commission of these offences. Thus some writers stress the point that this type of offending behaviour takes place in a more respectable context than most other crimes, and that it is the product of more ambiguous intentions than is the case for ordinary crime. The third set of ambiguities derives from the regulation and handling of white-collar crime. White-collar crimes are often controlled in a different, and more ambivalent, way than ordinary crime, and it is controversial how far this reflects, reinforces, or even creates its ambiguity. The uncertain status of these crimes may also be seen to reflect a process of transition and social change in which the public is not yet ready for more outright criminalization of these behaviours. It is also argued that control of these offences is hampered by problems of competing values and social costs that do not arise in repressing ordinary crime.

I shall be taking these various ambiguities one by one, partly for purposes of exposition and partly because there are important differences amongst the sources and types of ambiguity. Taken as a whole, however, many of these ambiguities are mutually reinforcing and thus help to shape the perceived character of white-collar crime as a social phenomenon. If, for example, different and predominantly administrative methods of enforcement are used in dealing with white-collar as opposed to ordinary crimes, this will shape public opinion concerning their relative seriousness. Benson and Simpson (2009: 141) emphasize that white-collar criminals do not see themselves as criminal—and nor does the general public. At the same time, such (alleged) differences in public attitudes also serve as justifications offered by legislators and regulators for their different treatment of white-collar crimes. On the other hand, any given source of ambiguity may have implications under a number of different headings. For example, the fact that white-collar crimes generally take place in private settings represents a special feature of their causation that may facilitate their commission. This also serves as an impediment to normal policing methods, which helps to explain the use of other forces and forms of enforcement. Finally, the importance of respecting 'privacy' as a value also figures as an argument in policy debates over the appropriateness or otherwise of strengthening controls.

## WHITE-COLLAR CRIME AS A CONTESTED CONCEPT

If Sutherland merited a Nobel prize, as Mannheim thought, for pioneering this field of study, he certainly did not deserve it for the clarity or serviceableness of his definition. What, if anything, is there in common between the marketing of unsafe pharmaceuticals, the practice of insider trading, 'long-firm' fraud, computer crime, bank embezzlement, and fiddling at work? The paedophilia allegations levelled against many Catholic priests in the early 2000s refer to offences that fit Sutherland's definition perfectly, but few have thought to investigate them through this lens. A recent text argues that we should look more to the nature of the offence(s) than to that of the offender. Focusing on offences such as deception, abuse of trust, and conspiracy it emphasizes the importance of the many (objective and subjectively perceived) *opportunities* to commit fraud in health-care, consumer services, banking and securities (Benson and Simpson 2009). On the other hand, it also draws attention to the under-representation of women and some minorities in these crimes. And it would be a mistake to lose sight of who were the offenders if we think of the role of some of the leading figures on Wall Street who first helped create the financial crash of 2008 and were then entrusted with managing the consequences.

Though Sutherland claimed to be interested in reforming criminological theory, rather than changing society, the appeal of this topic, particularly through the 1970s and 1980s, was unquestionably linked to its progressive connotations and its implicit accusations of bias in the making and enforcing of criminal law (Yeager 1991). The apparent success of the label in finding public acceptance, while lacking a clear or agreed referent, may testify less to its coherence than to its capacity to name a supposed threat. Not all examples of white-collar crime are ambiguous (e.g. embezzlement), just as not all ambiguous deviance is white-collar crime. But considerable disagreement over the range of misbehaviour referred to, as well as doubts about the coherence of those behaviours it does include, makes the category as a whole rather ambiguous (Passas and Goodwin 2004). And, peculiarly enough, those white-collar offences whose criminal character seems most unambiguous—such as bank embezzlement or (on some definitions) credit card fraud—are the ones least likely to illustrate the theoretical or policy-relevant features of white-collar crime in which Sutherland and his successors have been most interested.

We will not deal here with the intrinsic difficulties built into Sutherland's definition of white-collar crime as a crime committed by 'a person of high status in the course of his occupation' (1949: 9), a matter that was discussed in the first edition of this *Handbook*. Nor will we illustrate the point that the problem of definition cannot just be put aside in order to get on with more interesting matters, because the solution found for this problem ultimately determines the findings of any investigation (see earlier editions of this work). If at one extreme there can be problems in distinguishing ordinary business behaviour from business crime, at the other, there continues to be uncertainty about where to draw the line between white-collar crime and organized crime. As predicted in the first edition of this *Handbook* (Nelken 1994b), the overlap between these types of enterprise crime has become an important new focus of research (though one already anticipated in the theory of illegal enterprises put forward by Smith and others in the 1980s). Ruggiero, for example, claims that Sutherland created an unsatisfactory distinction between these two types of criminal behaviour (leaving only gangsters in the category of organized crime) that has wrongly been taken over by later criminologists. He argues that white-collar/organized crime should be seen as a normal rather than pathological aspect of business life, and its causes should be sought in wealth and power rather than greed as such. Organized crime, he insists, once we get away from ethnic stereotypes, involves the same flexible consumer-oriented behaviour that characterizes all successful business behaviour. Offering a wealth of examples of business-type crimes, Ruggiero argues that both white-collar and organized criminals use similar techniques, share the same illegal know-how, and share the same values—even if perpetrators come from different backgrounds. Their crimes are performed in or by organized structures, thrive on collusion, and normally enjoy the connivance of administrators and legislators (Ruggiero 1996).

In part we may be witnessing real changes in the phenomena pointed to by these different criminological labels. In the first place, business crime may be taking on some of the characteristics of organized crime. As Reichman observes, 'insider trading as practiced in the 1980s is a form of crime that combines elements of the traditional categories of occupational and organizational crime' (Reichman 1992: 56). Likewise, traditional organized crime groups, such as the Mafia or the Camorra in Italy, or the Chinese or Taiwanese Triads, have become increasingly capitalistic in orientation and ethos (see, e.g., Arlachi 1985 on the Mafia and the Protestant ethic, or Gambetta's (1994) thesis of the Mafia as an industry of private protection). In post-communist countries which are without a recent history of capitalist markets, it may indeed be artificial to draw a line between business and organized crime. More broadly, globalization may be leading to similar forms of structural integration of legitimate and illegitim-ate business activities, making regular collaboration between business and organized criminals both more possible and more necessary (Nelken 1997a). An important topic for research is global tax avoidance and evasion, and the role of professionals such as lawyers and accountants on both sides of the fence as facilitators and enforcers (see, e.g., Levi *et al.* 2005).

On the other hand, this thesis should not be pushed too far. Claims concerning a symbiotic relationship between ordinary business, white-collar crime, and organized crime presuppose important differences rather than total overlap. Organized crime groups are able to gain legitimacy, respectability, protection, access, expertise, suppli-ers, customers, investment opportunities, or various other advantages from such rela-tionships, and these benefits would be attenuated if the differences were to disappear. Both white-collar crime and organized crime cover such a continuum of activities that there will clearly be some that fall outside any attempt to categorize them together (think, on the one hand, of a small food shop breaking hygiene regulations, and, on the other, of a classical protection racket based on territorial domination). What is certainly true is that the distinction between these types of crime will vary according to the type of crime and the structure of the industry under consideration.

By common agreement, Sutherland's definition is not considered a helpful starting point for doing research into white-collar crime. Apart from its internal contradictions (for example, are we dealing with crimes committed for, by, or against organizations?), changes in class structure, forms of business activity, organizational forms, and cul-tural valuations all threaten to undermine its empirical coherence. But what other definitions can be found which do not simply rely on selecting the most appropriate-seeming crimes from the official criminal statistics? One common inductive strategy is to start from the data produced by the non-police administrative agencies generally entrusted with dealing with business offences (especially in common law countries). This was the source of data used in the comprehensive Clinard and Yeager study which focused on various federal regulatory bodies (Clinard and Yeager 1980). Non-police agencies in Britain included the Post Office, British Transport Police, Customs, water authorities, local government, Ministry of Agriculture, etc. (see Royal Commission 1980). But though these agencies may have some enforcement practices in common it would be quite wrong to describe all the types of offenders they prosecute (many from poor backgrounds) as white-collar criminals.

Another strategy is to seek to develop typologies of different kinds of crime which fit under the general heading of 'white-collar crime'. Many writers work with subcat-egories such as crimes against the environment, crimes in the workplace, and eco-nomic crimes. The difficulty here is that the categories thus created are still likely to end up as containers for somewhat disparate behaviours. Green (1990) distinguishes organizational occupational crime, state authority occupational crime, professional occupational crime, etc. But these headings cannot pretend to be either theoretically defined, or even coherent classifications of types of crime. The offences considered as state crime range from bribe-taking to genocide; whilst the chapter on individ-ual occupational crime—which is admitted to be a 'catch-all' category—includes behaviours as different as employee theft and securities crimes. The drawbacks to inductivism are evident in the artificial distinctions that lead Green to discuss the crimes committed by bribe-givers in a different chapter from those of bribe-takers. Nonetheless, the range of crimes brought under the rubric of the white-collar crime concept continues to grow and new typologies are regularly proposed (see, e.g., Simpson 2008, Friedrichs 2010).

There are also various attempts to re-think Sutherland's concept in a more deductive fashion, such as Clarke's extended definition of business crime in terms of its distinguishing features (Clarke 1990a). Of greater value are the more ambitious efforts aimed at finding a key theoretical variable which could produce a coherent focus for further research. There continue to be efforts to understand white-collar crimes as elite crimes or crimes of the powerful, most recently treating them as examples of grievous human rights breaches. A more focused approach is Shapiro's prescient warning of the increasing need to trust agents and the consequent exposure to various forms of abuse of such trust in which agents subordinate the interests of their principals to their own gain (Shapiro 1989). Coleman and others stress the importance of the growth of organizational actors in what has been called the 'asymmetric society' (Gross 1980; Coleman 1992). These approaches may include more or less than the offences that Sutherland covered: Shapiro's proposal, for example, seems to be derived from her previous empirical research interests in securities frauds and would not be applicable, say, to pollution crimes; its focus on agents also lets principals off the hook. But such approaches promise to be theoretically more productive than Sutherland's concept.

## IS WHITE-COLLAR CRIME REALLY CRIME?

If there are basic uncertainties about what is being referred to when talking of white-collar crime, there are also long-standing doubts whether or not all the mis behaviours discussed under this rubric can be considered to count as crime. Most of the continuing controversy, as well as the stimulus, generated by this topic is due to the fact that it appears to straddle the crucial boundary between criminal and non-criminal behaviour. Since this is a well-aired problem, and the debates can be found in all the readers on this subject (e.g. Geis 1968), I will confine myself to drawing out their relevance to the issue of ambiguity. Many scholars have argued that the misbe-haviours discussed by Sutherland or his followers do not always satisfy the legal criteria for crime; some even go so far as to insist on the necessity for a penal conviction at court (e.g. Tappan 1947). It is, admittedly, ironic that Sutherland himself was unable to publish the names of the companies whose administrative violations he described in his book, because of his publisher's fears that he would then be exposed to claims of libel for describing them as criminal (this was remedied only in the uncut version published much later: Sutherland 1983). Restricting attention to those crimes found in the ordinary criminal statistics, however, too easily robs the term of all its sense. The results of following such a definition make it possible to argue that white-collar crime is an otiose category and that white-collar criminals, like most ordinary criminals, are young, feckless, and unsuccessful (see Hirschi and Gottfredson 1987, 1989; and the criticism by Steffensmeier 1989). Others have made the opposite point, complaining that many white-collar crimes are merely technically criminal and are not socially considered on a par with ordinary crimes; hence they do not satisfy the requirements of a sociological definition of crime (see, e.g., Burgess 1950, criticizing Hartung 1950). While this is a more acute criticism, it tends to assume the unchanging circularity of social definitions and under-estimates the potential for change (a process in which criminology can play a part).

The fact that such opposite criticisms can be raised is confirmation of the ambiguity of this concept—which is also reflected in the use of descriptions such as 'regulatory crimes' or 'mala prohibita'. Sutherland, and many later scholars, chose to include in their definition of white-collar crime not only misbehaviours with criminal penalties, but also those that carried only civil or administrative sanctions. This was done precisely so as not to invoke the question whether the choice of these different and generally lighter sanctions was justified (or only a sign of the political and economic power of the offenders involved). But it is only a small (if significant) step from this to argue for the inclusion in the category of white-collar crime of other types of harmful business behaviour that have succeeded (through much the same political and economic pressures) in avoiding being subject to any sanctions at all.

Must we use law to draw the line? One of the contributions made by the topic of white-collar crime to criminology lies in this very difficulty of assimilating all that Sutherland was getting at without breaking the boundaries of the discipline. Should the definition of crime adopted for sociological purposes be the same as that of the law? What are the dangers of tying criminology to a starting point defined by another—politically conditioned—discipline? If we allow the political process to define what counts as crime, is this a politically conservative choice? Or is it just good tactics—a way to avoid alienating the 'liberals' (as Box 1983 argues)? Leading writers insist that we must refer to the law because otherwise it would be impossible to decide who is to define what should count as business deviance (Coleman 1987). But this was exactly the decision that the labelling perspective tried to force criminologists to face. The topic of white-collar crime thus illustrates the possibility of divergence between legal, social, and political definitions of criminality—but in so doing it reminds us of the artificiality of all definitions of crime.

## EXPLAINING THE CAUSES OF WHITE-COLLAR CRIME

Can white-collar crime be explained using the normal frameworks of criminological explanation? In previous editions I argued that the motives usually attributed to white-collar criminals (greed and power) were too often left unexplored and that more effort needed to be made to 'appreciate' the perspective of those engaged in white-collar crime, however politically distasteful this might be for some scholars (Nelken 1994b, 1997b). But much progress is being made. The insider stories which emerge from former participants, especially in the world of high finance, describe a subculture where the excitement for young men of living life in the fast lane is as important as the money benefits themselves (Portnoy 1997). There are also a large number of insider accounts of what went on in the major US investment banks before and during the financial crash of 2008. In his valuable contributions Punch argues that business studies students can get as indignant as the next person about the social and human costs of business misbehaviour. But once they are asked to role-play as managers having to make hard choices in risky situations, the same students regularly opt for 'macho', high-risk strategies. In the 'real world' of the organization the pressure 'to deliver the goods' or protect market share or just one's own career are potent motivations. Behind the 'surface solidity of the business organisation' he describes a' fluctuating and even turbulent reality of managerial "backstage" behaviour'. In this 'world of power struggles, ideological debate, intense political rivalry, manipulation of information, and short term problem solving, managers emerge as something of amoral chameleons, buffeted by moral ambiguity and organizational uncertainty; they survive this "messy not to say dirty" environment by engaging in Machiavellian micro-politics'. Managers have to negotiate such ambiguity (including the ambiguity of white-collar crime itself), to learn how to bend rules and speak to different audiences. Success makes everything forgiven (Punch 1996, 2008).

More generally, however, the problem of what exactly needs to be explained continues to confuse the search for causes. Is white-collar crime conventional or unconventional behaviour for those who commit it? If it is conventional, why is so much effort put into keeping criminal activities secret even from other members of the same organization (Hirschi and Gottfredson 1987)? Where the explanatory approach adopted is to look for the individual motivations of what is taken to be clearly criminal behaviour, white-collar crime becomes just another test of standard theories of crime causation. Its novelty, if any, is tied to the emergence of new opportunities, for new groups, to commit old offences—for example, through the use of computers to carry out frauds. Where, instead, the issue becomes the criminogenic properties of business, of capitalism, or organizational behaviour in general, then the normative fabric of everyday business life seems placed in doubt and the actual evidence of white-collar crime seems to fall short of what would be possible.

These difficulties have not discouraged a series of attempts to explain the causes of white-collar crime, and there are even a number of good reviews of such work (see, e.g., Braithwaite 1985, who concludes, however, that 'only banal generalisations are possible', or Coleman 1987, who furnishes a (banal?) synthesis of existing work in terms of opportunity and motivation theory). I shall comment on explanations concerned with the whole area of white-collar crime. But, as already noted, the search for causes may—and perhaps should—be limited to typologies of crime, such as crimes by professional people, or even to specific offences. And obviously, where the topic is theoretically reformulated this will affect what needs to be explained. For Shapiro, for example, the study of white-collar crime belongs to the wider study of the maintenance and abuse of trust (see also Nelken 1994a; Friedrichs 2003). Attention should focus on the rising need to rely on agents and the consequent increased exposure to the risks of their malpractices. Trust is required in so far as it is difficult to tell when agents are putting their self-interests above those of their principals, especially as they tend to be the 'repeat players', and to act at a distance; but efforts to limit their discretion are self-defeating. To understand causation there therefore needs to be 'the marriage of a systematic understanding of the distribution of structural opportunities for trust abuse with an understanding of the conditions under which individual or organisational fiduciaries seize or ignore these illicit opportunities' (Shapiro 1989: 353).

The concept of white-collar crime was certainly not invented in order to provide comfort for standard approaches to causation in criminology. Sutherland hoped to use these misbehaviours as ammunition against the reigning tendency to explain crime in terms of individual or social pathology. By ridiculing the idea that businesses or businessmen could be said to misbehave because of their difficult childhoods, he intended to reform criminological theory and show that only his theory of 'differential association' could account for all forms of criminal behaviour. There is ample evidence of the diffusion of definitions favourable to white-collar forms of law-breaking in business circles, whether these are based on loyalty to the firm, the alleged requirements of business life, or dislike of government regulation. But Sutherland's theory is nevertheless now regarded as flawed and superficial, and the search for a universal theory of crime has lost its attractions. Ironically, those who are most committed to the subject of white-collar crime are now under attack by criminologists who argue that there is no need for this special category of criminal behaviour precisely because it gets in the way of general explanations of the crime phenomenon (Hirschi and Gottfredson 1987; Gottfredson and Hirschi 1990: ch. 9).

Proponents of both 'strain' and of 'control' theories have tried to make sense of white-collar crime. Whatever his original focus may have been, most strain theories of corporate crime find their inspiration in Merton's concept of anomie. White-collar crimes can be seen, for example, as an 'innovative' response on the part of businesses (or particular roles such as middle management) to the strain of conforming to cultural prescriptions to maintain profits even in difficult circumstances (Passas 1990; Vaughan 1996; Slapper and Tombs 1999). The strain may be located in the business environment as such, in particular industries, or in particular firms. A classical study of the conditions under which the major car manufacturers in the USA constrain their car dealers to operate showed the pressure put on dealers to cut corners if they wanted to survive economically (Leonard and Weber 1970); other situations may 'facilitate' rather than directly 'coerce' criminal solutions (Needleman and Needleman 1979; Nelken 1994c). In explaining the financial excesses of recent years, resort is made to Durkheim's original idea of anomie as a lack of stable normative regulation (Hagan 2010).

Control theories, on the other hand, are premised on the initial question: why don't we all commit crimes when the temptations are so strong? The reply given is that most of us, the generally law-abiding, have too much invested in relationships and in legitimate society. The best way to rob a bank may indeed be to own one—or work in one—but, we assume, most of those in this position do not take advantage of it. This approach is a weak candidate for explaining white-collar crime because it finds it difficult to account for how middle-class criminals (and even most of those who find themselves in a position to embezzle) ever achieved their social positions in the first place. It also needs to show why they would be willing to risk their investment (Wheeler 1992). One neglected argument that is suggested here is based on the idea of 'over-investment'. The findings of Weisburd and his colleagues in their sample of middle-class criminals were that 'many of our offenders have the material goods associated with successful people but may barely be holding their financial selves together' (Weisburd *et al.* 1991: 65).

This could be interpreted as meaning that such offenders are, if anything, so strongly tied to social expectations and obligations that they are even willing to offend to maintain their position (and so anomie and control theories meet up)! In any case, whatever its general bearing, more specific ingredients of control theory, such as the importance of 'neutralization' of social controls through the use of justifications (learned within or outside the company), are regularly adopted in explaining white-collar crime. Typical theoretical syntheses in textbooks dealing with white-collar crime in fact draw both on the 'strain' elements of capitalist competition and striving for business or individual success, and on the large possible variety of such 'techniques of neutralization' (see, e.g., Box 1983; Coleman 1987; Green 1990) including denying responsibility or damage to victims. Common excuses include relying on experts, higher orders, and loyalty to the organization.

The labelling approach has, strangely, been relatively neglected in the study of white-collar crime. One reason for this could be that criminologists here line up with those doing the labelling (see Katz 1980; Yeager 1991). There is of course the apparent paradox that it is the 'insiders' rather than the 'outsiders' who are being labelled—but the paradox normally disappears once the details of who is really affected become clearer. In any case, few would now want to deny the importance of legislative or other battles over the labelling of business misbehaviour. The perspective would seem peculiarly relevant given the relative recency of many laws regulating business, the sharp swings between political projects of regulation and deregulation, and the divergent views of different groups as to the appropriateness of criminalization. Some attention has been given to the success of techniques of 'non-labelling' or 'de-labelling' used by lawyers and accountants in diluting or avoiding the imposition of the criminal label, for example in shaping the (mis)behaviour involved in some tax-avoidance schemes (McBarnet 1991; McBarnet and Whelan 1999). In my study of the social construction of landlord crime (Nelken 1983) I examined the process of criminal labelling and de-labelling in this area of business misbehaviour. I showed that those actually apprehended for landlord crime were small, immigrant landlords involved in disputes with their tenants (for similar findings for other white-collar crimes, see Hutter 1988; Croall 1989). With some effort it was possible to portray their self-help methods as criminal, but the malpractices characteristic of large business landlords stayed immune to criminalization because of their similarity to ordinary business behaviour—a 'limit' of the legal process which was, paradoxically, concealed by actually exaggerating the capacity of law to control such behaviour (Nelken 1983). White-collar crimes and the reaction to them seem, perhaps more than other crimes, to be subject to interrelated cycles of expansion and reform. The apparent growth of political corruption in the 1980s, followed by widespread crackdown in the 1990s, is a good example (Nelken and Levi 1996).

The attempt to explain white-collar crime within the 'normal science' approaches used in criminology shows itself not only in theories of causation, but also in the effort to follow the 'careers' of such criminals (Weisburd and Waring 2001). Many writers adopt a positivist search for the peculiar characteristics that distinguish offenders from non-offenders. Sutherland (1949, 1983) was keen to show the widespread nature of white-collar offences but also to identify the major culprits. He examined infringements of rules governing fair labour practices by General Motors and others, violations of rules against the restraint of trade, especially common in the major companies in the film industry, infringements of patents, and misrepresentation in advertising involving household names such as Bayer aspirin, Quaker Oats, Carnation milk, Phillips milk of magnesia, Hoover vacuum cleaners, and Encyclopedia Britannica. He particularly stressed the duration of some offences and the 'recidivism' of some of the companies concerned.

Clinard and Yeager (1980), in the most wide-ranging documentary study of corporate crime to date, examined all the federal administrative, civil, and criminal actions initiated in 1975 and 1976 by 25 federal agencies against 582 of America's largest corporations. The violations they examined were divided into non-compliance with agency regulations; environmental pollution; financial crimes, such as illegal payments or tax offences; labour discrimination, including unsafe working practices; manufacturing offences, such as the distribution of unsafe products; and unfair trading practices, including price-fixing arrangements. Going beyond Sutherland, they tried to control comparisons for the time available to commit offences and the different size of the companies they investigated. They found that three-fifths of their sample had charges brought against them in those years. While 13 per cent of the companies accounted for just over half the violations, large, medium, and small companies were all well represented amongst the violators. Where Sutherland had found the film, mercantile, and railroad industries particularly engaged in violations, Clinard and Yeager found their black sheep in the oil, pharmaceutical, and motor vehicle industries, which all had more than their proportional share of violations. The oil industry, for example, was involved in three-fifths of all serious violations, with 22 of 28 oil-refining firms guilty of at least one violation in the period under consideration; car manufacturers were responsible in all for one-sixth of all the violations discovered and for a third of the manufacturing violations overall; pharmaceutical manufacturers accounted for one-tenth of all violations, and all 17 companies were found to have committed at least one violation.

Some of Clinard and Yeager's findings were artifacts which resulted from using data which depended on the vagaries of regulatory regimes: the higher offending rates of diversified firms, for example, may simply mean that they were more exposed to different regulatory agencies (though the firms concerned may also have faced problems in maintaining oversight of their different operations). Their investigation produced some statistical support for the proposition that violations increased as financial performance became poorer; this was particularly marked for environmental and labour offences. On the other hand, firms with higher than average growth rates were more likely to have engaged in manufacturing violations. The authors admitted that the causal variables on which they concentrated—size, growth rate, diversification, and market power and resources—had only limited predictive power. Even the more confident of their claims concerning crime rates and economic performance have been questioned in the later literature (Braithwaite 1985). Their study was unable to allow for the complicating factor of why and when agencies choose to uncover violations, and has been criticized for taking agency records as the measure of corporate crime and for failing to see such behaviour as endemic to capitalism (Young 1981). A valuable study by Haines (1997) examines the way companies react after they have been involved in safety violations on the hypothesis that the same causes which explain violation would also account for what was done or not done afterwards to put things right. Her findings were that managers in larger companies were less likely to take a 'blinkered' view of what should be done to avoid recurrence and could afford to take a broader and longer-term approach to the problem of reconciling profit and safety.

A central debate amongst scholars of white-collar crime in fact concerns the extent to which corporate and business crime should be seen as an inevitable consequence of capitalism. Box (1983), in a Marxist-influenced application of Merton, argues that corporations are criminogenic because, if legal means are blocked, they will resort to illegal means so as to maintain or increase profitability. As and when necessary, they will use techniques aimed at competitors (e.g. industrial espionage or price fixing), at consumers (e.g. fraud or misleading advertising), or at the public at large (e.g. environmental pollution). Those recruited to work in corporations learn to justify such behaviour on the grounds that 'business is business' (cf. Pearce 1976; Punch 1996). This is particularly true for those who rise to the top and who then have a disproportionate influence over the ethos of their firms (although they generally take care not to be directly involved or informed of the illegal activities made necessary by their drive for profit). For those who subscribe to this theory businessmen comply with the law in so far as they see it enforced strictly (thereby denying competitive advantage to those who would break it). Where there are few effective controls, as in the third world, capitalism shows its true face, selling unsafe products, paying low wages, and exploiting the complaisance of poor and corrupt governments and regulators (see Slapper and Tombs 1999: ch. 7).

On the other hand, it is well to bear in mind some reservations about the idea that capitalism as such is criminogenic. If Merton's anomie theory is to be pressed this far it is at least necessary to go on to discuss the alternative, non-criminal modes of responding to 'strain', and (what Merton did not do) offer an explanation of when and why each mode is chosen. The argument appears to predict too much crime and makes it difficult to explain the relative stability of economic trade within and between nations, given the large number of economic transactions, the many opportunities for committing business crimes, the large gains to be made, and the relative unlikelihood of punishment. This theory also has difficulty in accounting for improvements in safety and increases in the quality of goods under capitalism. If it is somewhat oversimplified to argue that only a small proportion of businessmen are 'bad apples', it is not much more convincing to assume that all businesses act as 'amoral calculators' and would choose to offend but for the availability of serious sanctions (Pearce and Tombs 1990, 1991). The desires to continue in business, and to maintain self-respect and the goodwill of fellow businessmen, go a long way to explaining reluctance to seize opportunities for a once-only windfall. Trading competitors (as well as organized consumer groups, unions, and others) can serve as a control on illicit behaviour for their own reasons. Law-abidingness can often be definitely in the competitive interests of companies. Braithwaite (1985) illustrates how American pharmaceutical companies able to obtain Federal Drug Administration authorization for their products are in this way guaranteed lucrative markets in countries that cannot afford their own expensive drug-testing facilities. It could be said that the clear evidence of exploitation and the sale of dangerous goods in third world countries reflects an anomalous situation which is at least partly the result of the excessive freedom of manoeuvre of powerful multinational companies which are not exposed to sufficient competition. On the other hand, we should not underestimate the role of state regulation in all this. Current pressures of globalization that may be leading to a 'de-coupling' of politics and economics, both at home and abroad, could have dire consequences.

Marxist theory has no need to assume that all business crime will be tolerated. Many forms of business misbehaviour made into crimes may reflect changing forms of capitalism or inter-class conflict. At any given period, some corporate crimes, such as antitrust offences, will not be in the interest of capitalism as a whole, so it is important to distinguish what is in the interests of capitalism from what suits particular capitalists. Even if the latter may succeed in blocking legislation or effective enforcement, at least in the short term, this does not prove that it is capitalism as such which requires the continuation of specific forms of misbehaviour. Moreover, capitalism is a set of practices and not just an important set of social actors. Practices may remain free from effective control even if the group concerned is not particularly economically powerful. Thus the relative immunity from control of abuses of the Rent Acts committed by private business landlords in Britain has been attributed less to their importance within the social structure and more to objective difficulties in controlling their behaviour without affecting normal commercial transactions (Nelken 1983). When professional criminals succeed in getting away with serious forms of business-related crime such as 'long-firm' fraud, it is implausible to say that this is in the interest of any capitalist group (Levi 1985). The same can be said of many of the large frauds carried out by previously respected insiders against companies.

We should not under-estimate the fruitfulness of hypotheses based on the capacity of capitalism to generate business crime. But care needs to be taken in connecting macro and micro levels of explanation. All organizations, and not only the corporate form of trading, can be criminogenic in so far as they tend to reward achievement even at the expense of the outer environment (Kramer 1992). This would help to explain why public organizations such as the army, the police, or government bureaucracies also generate crime and corruption (these behaviours are increasingly being included in textbooks on white-collar crime). Likewise, the far from positive record of the former communist regimes in matters of worker safety, environmental pollution, or corruption cannot be blamed on the pressures of competition. Even in capitalist societies it is often the absence of market pressures that explains some types of business misbehaviour, such as the ease with which government subsidy programmes are diverted to improper uses (Passas and Nelken 1993; Nelken 2002).

## WHITE-COLLAR CRIME IN ITS EVERYDAY SETTINGS

We have seen so far that there are, on the one hand, doubts about how far the same explanations will work for white-collar crime as for ordinary crime, and, on the other hand, risks of over-explanation in accounts which relate it too closely to ordinary business behaviour. For some commentators, however, the central issue concerns the extent to which white-collar crimes come about in similar ways to other criminal behaviour. Clarke's book on business crime, for example, argues strongly that these misbehaviours are typically 'less criminal' in their inception and motivation than much ordinary crime (Clarke 1990a). Whereas many textbook presentations of white-collar crime simply list a variety of dangerous behaviours in a way that emphasizes their harmful consequences and implies that these are incurred deliberately, or at least recklessly, Clarke attempts to recover their sense by putting them back into their everyday business context.

For Clarke there is a series of factors that distinguish the commission of business crimes. Their location in the midst of ordinary business and occupational activity both facilitates their achievement and helps to prevent their detection by colleagues and superiors as well as outside authorities. As compared to ordinary crimes such as burglary, the perpetrator has every justification to be present at the scene of the crime. Indeed, Clarke claims that unlike ordinary crimes, where a crucial clue is presence at the scene, with white-collar crimes the problem is to discover whether there has been an offence rather than to identify the culprit. Police or regulatory agencies are reluctant to enter private settings without invitation, and are often not called upon even where an offence has been committed. White-collar crimes are frequently what we could call 'complainantless crimes', and those who suffer the consequences of them cannot be relied upon to act as a reliable source of criminal intelligence. Clients of professionals are often unable to assess their performance– this is why they need to turn to them in the first place. Workers may simply be unaware of the risks to which they have been exposed; consumers will often not appreciate what they have lost; competitors will be unaware of collusive practices. The behaviour that constitutes white collar crime is often indistinguishable on its surface from normal legal behaviour. For example, for fraud to be accomplished, it must obviously succeed in mimicking the appearance of legitimate transactions, and it is not unusual for those guilty of this crime to remain undetected for years or even a lifetime. Unlike all except 'victimless crimes' the involvement of the victim is apparently voluntary (though sometimes the result of the lure of easy money).

A further claim concerning the supposed distinctiveness of white-collar crime is more or less true by definition. The criminal aspects of the business or occupational activities under consideration are often secondary or collateral features, both in priority and in the succession of events, of an undertaking pursued for other, legitimate purposes. Criminal consequences, such as damage to the health of workers or to the environment, often come about either as a result of omissions, or because of financial pressures or unanticipated opportunities for gain; they are not inherent to the economic activity as such. Such criminality is difficult to recognize (in time) because of the narrow and constantly changing line between acceptable and unacceptable business behaviour. Even such essential features of outright crooked schemes as the deliberate withholding of payment to creditors may exist as practices in the legitimate world of business—for example, as a desperate manoeuvre by small businesses trying to survive on tight margins, or as a more cynical use of market strength by large enterprises exploiting the dependence on their patronage of small contractors. This makes it difficult for all concerned—creditors, regulators, and others—to tell whether, or at what point, the intention permanently to avoid payment was formed.

Ambiguity surrounds not only the goals of the activity in the midst of which white-collar crime is encountered, but also, it is argued, the degree of intentionality involved. There are certainly notorious cases of cold-blooded calculation, such as the way Ford went ahead with its dangerous design for the Ford Pinto rear engine because it estimated that the potential payment of damages would be less than the cost of recalling the cars (Dowie 1988), or the manner in which the P&O shipping company disregarded repeated requests for the installation of bow warning-lights to improve safety on their 'on-off' ferries (see Punch 1996; Slapper and Tombs 1999). But, it is claimed, these are the exceptions (and even these cases did not end in criminal convictions). But they are not exceptions in the sense that similar disasters can be easily predicted for the future. The 2010 BP Deepwater Horizon rig explosion, according to a Presidential Report, was the result not of 'aberrational but systematic decisions', that 'whether purposeful or not, clearly saved time and money', (conduct overlooked by understaffed regulators clearly not up to the job). On the other hand, it is often difficult to distinguish malevolence from incompetence; and, as Clarke insists, in business and professional life, we are often more concerned about the harmful effects of the latter. Professionals are specifically valued for their competence rather than for their honesty as such (which is perhaps taken for granted); in large organizations and bureaucracies there is considerable scope for laziness or disinterest that may have tragic consequences. These points, it is said, are less true of more conventional crimes.

On the other hand, many scholars insist that these aspects of the setting and commission of white-collar crimes mainly point to problems of detection and do not negate the essential similarities between these and ordinary crimes. Businesses involved in offending behaviour often do their best to organize so as to minimize the costs of their infractions (concealing compromising knowledge from directors, 'appointing vice presidents responsible for going to jail', etc.). Conversely, as explained in previous editions of this *Handbook*, there are also occasions where enforcement against ordinary crime has to overcome similar difficulties of categorization. Like so much concerning the social definition of white-collar crime, the question of intention therefore easily lends itself to social construction. Much ambiguity, or, conversely, the provision of a cover of ostensible legality, is a contingent product of social processing. Thus accountants and barristers may use their professional skills to help businesses construct tax-avoidance schemes which must then appear as anything but deliberate attempts to evade tax (McBarnet 1991; McBarnet and Whelan 1999). Even if a case reaches trial, defence lawyers work hard to redefine the misconduct as not having been deliberate (Mann 1985). White-collar criminals may even find that they have allies in the redefinition of their behaviour in those trying their misbehaviour. In the course of research into deviance by professionals I made a study of the (confidential) proceedings of English family practitioner tribunals, which deal with cases where dentists (and other professionals) are alleged not to have complied with their National Health Service contracts. Here everything is done to avoid the impression that potentially criminal behaviour is at issue even though, in cases where misconduct is proved, fixed withholdings from payment serve the function of fines. In one case, for example, a dentist admitted to 'fraud' in deliberately claiming for more work than he had done, only to find the tribunal members pleading with him to retract his admission (and claim inadvertence) so that they could retain jurisdiction.

While it is debatable how far the ambiguous aspects alleged to characterize the commission of white-collar crime are intrinsic features restricted to this type of misbehaviour, there are certainly some important cases where criminals deliberately exploit the appearance of legitimate business. In fact the overlap between white-collar crime and more clear-cut kinds of crime, such as organized crime, has so far been relatively neglected in comparison to the attention given to the boundary between white-collar crime and ordinary business behaviour. Professional or organized criminals may create ambiguity by fostering the impression of genuine business enterprises, if necessary by trading normally for an initial period. At other times they may penetrate legitimate companies, especially when these have fallen on hard times, and use them to launch purely criminal activities such as 'long-firm' frauds (Levi 1981). Organized criminal businesses may seek to monopolize the market for legitimate goods and services, such as public construction projects or waste processing, beating their competitors with their lower marginal costs and using violence or corruption against competitors or those with the power to award lucrative contracts, as with Camorra enterprises in the Campania area of Italy and the activities of many of the *cosche* of the New Mafia (Arlachi 1985).

The division of labour between legitimate and illegitimate business can represent an attempt to disguise the criminal presuppositions of legal enterprises. Legitimate businesses may call upon the service of criminals for particular operations such as loan repayment, money laundering, or tax evasion (Block 1991: chs 5 and 6). They may also take indirect advantage of the operation of international criminals. For example, major electrical companies apparently find it financially profitable to buy and resell (at the expense of other wholesalers) examples of their own products illegally smuggled on to the market (Van Duyne 1993). Legal enterprise may rely on organized criminals to supply a disciplined workforce, as in the New York construction industry (New York State Organized Crime Task Force 1988), or to get rid of industrial waste products in illegal ways so as to reduce their external costs of production (Szasz 1986). Conversely, organized criminals may call upon legitimate businesses, such as printers or supermarkets, in developing major frauds like those against the EU agricultural subsidy programmes (Passas and Nelken 1993); such symbiosis is also essential for the purpose of recycling money earned in illegal activities. The steady growth in international and transnational trading—and the changing face of national and economic borders in Europe—is also leading to an increase in different types of criminals seeking to profit from the opportunities these changes offer them (Passas and Nelken 1993; Van Duyne 1993; Nelken 2002). Current research on white collar crime is increasingly concerned with exploring the relationship between legal, semi-legal, and illegal economic activities—and such enquiry is likely to be intensified as regional groupings increasingly use harmonized crime control as a badge of identity. This requires giving attention to the comparative dimension, because the relationships between businessmen, professionals, and organized criminals vary in different countries and because many of these crimes have an international dimension which exploits differences between national legal systems (Ruggiero 1996; Nelken 1997a). Appreciation of the political and economic structures conducive to such operations requires the criminologist to be open to concepts pioneered in disciplines other than sociology, including ideas about clientilism in political science, legal and illegal monopolies in economics, and risk analysis in accounting and management science.

## THE AMBIVALENT RESPONSE TO WHITE-COLLAR CRIME

The above discussion will have already illustrated various ways in which the control of white-collar crime can also play a part in its causation. Government and business may share similar imperatives that coincide to favour offending. Carson's description of the importance of 'speed' in the calculations of both the Treasury and the oil companies in the exploitation of North Sea oil, and the consequent sacrifice of ordinary safety standards, is an extreme example of such objective coincidence of interests (Carson 1981). The Bank of England may be caught between its duties as regulator of the banking system and its desire not to compromise the credibility of one of the major clearing banks (*The Economist* 1992). But, even where government and offenders are clearly opposed, weak regulatory regimes or moves towards deregulation can still provide an incentive to offending. One common strategy that leads to increased crime is the combination of removing legal or informal constraints on a business sector with the simultaneous use of (new) criminal penalties to be available as a last resort. Complex and changing regulatory regimes, especially those involving government payment schemes, may in themselves provide the opportunity for crime (Calavita *et al.* 1997; Nelken 2002; Passas and Nelken 1993; Vaughan 1983). In using rational choice, opportunity, or situational approaches to explaining the causes of white-collar crime we should remember that the key opportunity here is that of writing or rewriting the rules.

The methods adopted in responding to white-collar crime play a particularly important part in shaping this type of behaviour, inasmuch as the difficulty of relying on complainants means that the accent must be put on prevention and proactive enforcement. In this way our information about these types of misbehaviour often tells us more about the theories and priorities of the controllers than anything else (for example, the belief that small firms are more likely than large ones to bend the rules will inevitably find confirmation in the statistics of violations discovered). New forms of enforcement contribute to the construction of '"postmodern" policing' (Spalek 2001). When dealing with the type of offence which is seen to overlap with organized crime (such as international fraud or money laundering) the (often misleading) accounts of who is responsible for such activity which are put forward by enforcers have a large role in creating the type of policing then put in place (see Nelken 1997a).

But the main issue that needs to be discussed under this heading is the charge that the different enforcement methods used to respond to white-collar as compared to ordinary crimes reinforce their ambiguous status and indirectly contribute to their causation. Is the difference in handling the cause or consequence of the distinctiveness of white-collar crime? Many scholars stress the fact that white-collar crimes are difficult to detect and control. It is difficult to prove intention when dealing with decisions taken within an organization (and legal thinking has not yet caught up with the importance of organizations); trials are long and expensive; juries have problems in understanding the evidence in complex fraud cases; professional advisers acting for businessmen can delay or defeat prosecution. In current cases brought against the collapsed US bank Bear Stearns for example the difficulty is showing that the defendants knew the funds they were trading were in trouble. A premium is therefore placed on achieving compliance without the need for prosecution (although this is used as a threat, the need actually to resort to it is seen as failure). It is considered still better to rely on self-regulation by an industry or by the business itself. But reliance on self-policing can easily lead to conflicts of interest, as when banks find themselves both as potential participators in money laundering and as required to detect and deter it (Levi 1991a, 1991b).

Some scholars (such as Clarke 1990a, but here his views are more widely shared) argue that the way white-collar crimes are handled reflects the special circumstances of these offences. It makes sense to use compliance in the regulation of occupations because the offender can easily be found at his or her place of occupation and it is feasible to put repeated pressure on him. Violations of safety or pollution standards are difficult and costly to conceal. Even the apparently self-defeating practice of giving advance warning of inspection visits does not therefore lead to concealment of offending. The difficulty in other business offences, Clarke argues, is to identify the commission of an offence rather than find the offender. But even here offenders in organizations do tend to leave a 'paper trail' of their actions.

Different interpretations of the nature of white-collar crime lead to corresponding views concerning the best way to handle them. Clarke argues that an approach based on criminal prosecution is inappropriate for all but a few cases of business crime because complainants are mainly interested in recompense and go to the police only if all else fails; the criminal process polarizes the parties, involves delay, carries risks of failure, and, above all, does nothing to secure future improvement in the relevant working practices. Existing enforcement practices make more sense; suggestions for improvement should be based mainly on trying to internalize better methods of control within businesses themselves rather than to increase prosecution (Stone 1975 is a classic discussion of this theme). But the opposite point of view is also well supported. Green summarizes an extensive American literature that offers various proposals for improving the effectiveness of prosecution against white-collar crimes (Green 1990: ch. 8; see also Groves and Newman 1986). The assumption behind much of this work is that business behaviour is in fact particularly well suited to the application of deterrent criminal sanctions. Offences, it is alleged, are strictly instrumental and offenders have much to lose from prosecution; prison, if only it were to be used regularly, would be more potent than for ordinary criminals. The main problem in current practice is that of producing a level of fines sufficient actually to deter business. Solutions such as stock dilution, equity fining, or ceding shares to the state may all work, but in cases where there has been physical injury they may give the wrong message that everything can ultimately be paid for. Informal and formally initiated negative publicity is unlikely to put a firm out of business, but it can and does have collateral effects and may help to produce beneficial procedural changes within firms (Fisse and Braithwaite 1985).

For many observers the difficulties of controlling white-collar crime, and the need to rely on compliance techniques, should rather be attributed to a lack of political will to provide the resources necessary for a full-blown prosecution approach. In Britain proportionally few policemen are assigned to the Fraud Squad; the prestige of such assignments is low and term of service short (Levi 1987). For the United States, Calavita and Pontell argue that the savings and loans crash was partly due to the lack of trained thrift examiners and the overloaded FBI agents directed to clear up the scandal (Calavita and Pontell 1992; Calavita *et al.* 1997). Even the famous and feared American Securities and Exchange Commission (SEC), according to Shapiro, is forced to choose between detection or enforcement and uses the criminal sanction only in around 11 per cent of its cases (Shapiro 1984).

The actual combination of objective difficulties and political priorities in decisions over prosecution is often concealed by ideologically loaded communication. Much white-collar crime is subject to regulation under the heading of strict liability by which, in theory, even unintentional offending can be held criminally culpable. Criminal law textbooks and philosophic writers discuss whether or not this is justified by the difficulty of proving intention in complex, modern, industrial processes. However, investigations of the 'logic in use' of the inspectorates responsible (at least in common law countries) for some of the most important areas of social regulation, such as those concerning worker safety or environmental pollution, tell a different story. In practice, apart from cases in which accidents have taken place, breaches of rules will normally be subject to sanctions only if *mens rea*—and even recidivism—has been shown by a refusal to correct matters pointed out by the inspector in warning visits and letters (Carson 1970; Hawkins 1984; Hawkins and Thomas 1984; Hutter 1988, 1997). The inspectors involved in such enforcement activity refuse to see themselves as 'industrial policemen', seeing their role rather as one geared to advising and cajoling the majority of fundamentally law-abiding businessmen.

One consequence (perhaps even an intended one, see Carson 1974, 1980) of this difference between theory and practice is that the imposition of strict liability reduces the stigma associated with these offences so as to reinforce the impression that they represent behaviour that is merely 'mala prohibita' rather than 'mala in se'. Enforcement techniques that concentrate on consequences rather than intentions, by collapsing the distinction between incompetence and deliberateness, thus often end up diluting rather than extending criminal stigma. Recent efforts to convict corporations for crime, especially in the area of safety, have had some success. But despite a series of disasters, moves towards more effective regulation have been slow (Wells 1993; Slapper 1999). How far criminal law can help is a moot point: in Italy, employers found guilty of serious safety offences at work are regularly subject to sanctions in the ordinary courts. But Italy has one of the highest rates in Europe of what they refer to as 'white death' (a point missed by Gobert and Punch (2003) when they praise the relevant Italian legislation).

Difficulties of enforcement may often be exaggerated to conceal other decisions (or non-decisions) about responding to crimes committed by economically influential groups. In an important study, Carson argued convincingly that the causes of accidents on North Sea oil-rigs were little different from those which lead to accidents in factories or construction (Carson 1981). The claim that the high level of injuries was due to the difficulty of regulating activities operating 'at the frontiers of technology' at hitherto untried depths of oil exploration at sea was not supported by his careful examination of the relevant case records. The crucial issue was the fact that the responsibility for ensuring compliance with the normal standards of safety had not been assigned to the factory inspectors of the Health and Safety Inspectorate (here being seen in more heroic light than in Carson's earlier work) but to the Department of Energy. But since this was also the body responsible for encouraging oil exploration to proceed as fast as possible in the interests of the British balance of payments, there was an inevitable conflict of interests in which those of the weakest groups were sacrificed.

Since Sutherland, the subject of white-collar crime has also been the focus of attempts to prove that the rich and powerful are treated more favourably by the criminal justice system. Some caveats should be entered here. The main basis for the relative immunity of businessmen in the criminal process (at least in Anglo-American jurisdictions) derives from political choices regarding which behaviour to make criminal in the first place, and only to a lesser extent from the way their offences are categorized. Those effectively criminalized for business-related offences tend to be small businessmen, quite often from immigrant backgrounds (Nelken 1983; Croall 1989). It is thus a mistake to confuse the macro (legislative) and micro (enforcement) logics which keep criminality and respectability apart. Many of those working in the criminal justice system would actually be interested in (and have an interest in) successful prosecutions of 'the powerful'. Thus apparently ineffective legislative outcomes are often best studied as a product of 'coherence without conspiracy' (Nelken 1983). This does not mean, of course, that there cannot also be more explicit cases of prejudice, and there have rightly been many attacks on alleged bias and injustice in the handling of white-collar crimes, from enforcement to trial and beyond. As with most accusations of bias, however, the difficulty is in ensuring that like is being compared with like.

A well-known debate over the alleged leniency involved in using 'compliance' methods for dealing with white-collar regulatory offences is that between Pearce and Tombs, on the one hand, and Hawkins on the other (Pearce and Tombs 1990, 1991; Hawkins 1990, 1991). Pearce and Tombs began by criticizing Hawkins's and other descriptions of the compliance approach, for giving the appearance of being persuaded by the 'logic in use' of those whose enforcement strategy they described. In this way, it was alleged, they (indirectly) confirmed an unfair status quo instead of supporting the adoption of stricter methods that could reduce the level of harm caused by such offences. Hawkins fiercely challenged this as a misreading of the role of interpretive sociology (which was not directed towards policy evaluation), but then went on to endorse the compliance strategy in general terms without necessarily agreeing with all its tactics or the level of severity of the sanctions applied. For their part, Pearce and Tombs recommended that prosecution should begin at an earlier stage; they favoured the imposition of (low) fines rather than simply warning notices and wanted there to be more use of other sanctions such as the withdrawal of licences. In his reply, Hawkins pointed out that very few of the violations noted in routine proactive enforcement do eventually turn out to be the cause of serious harm and that it is not possible to predict which will do so. In his view, unless Pearce and Tombs really want to cut back sharply on enforcement discretion, their proposals are unlikely to produce much change in current practice.

And to insist on legal action each time a violation is revealed, as was tried for a time by the American OSHA mines authority, tends to be counterproductive in terms of alienating the goodwill of those being regulated. It also risks producing a political backlash leading to deregulation, as happened in the case of this agency.

As this summary suggests, this and similar debates fail to make progress mainly because the policy arguments of Hawkins and others like him assume as givens exactly those political realities which their critics would like to see changed (see now Slapper and Tombs 1999). A useful study which points to this moral is Cook's comparison of the harsh response to those suspected of social security fraud with that met by those engaged in tax frauds of very similar kinds (Cook 1989). The very different treatment received by each group relates less to the practical possibilities of enforcement (more or less the same), or to fears of counterproductive effects from tougher penalties, but rather follows from a set of associated beliefs about the relative worth and importance of maintaining the goodwill of each set of offenders.

Some of the most fruitful proposals for strengthening the control of white-collar crime, which acknowledge the force of both sides of this debate, are those developed by Braithwaite on the basis of his research into the successes and failures of regulation in very different industries and businesses, such as drug-manufacturing, coalmining, and nursing homes. He suggests that businesses (beyond a certain size) should be obliged by government to write a set of rules tailored to the unique contingencies of their firm. These rules should be submitted for comment and amendment to interest groups, including citizen groups. Firms should have their own internal compliance unit with statutory responsibility on the director to report cases of violation, and the function of government inspectors would be to audit and (if necessary) sanction the performance of this unit (see Braithwaite 1995; Hutter 1997; Haines 1997).

It might be thought that the study of bias in the prosecution and trial of white-collar crimes should be more straightforward than an evaluation of the justifiability of its special style of enforcement; but even here there is no consensus. Analysis of the penalties meted out for serious frauds in Britain, as compared to other types of crime, certainly suggests that these are the crimes which are the most rewarding (Levi 1991c). Shapiro, in her study of securities offenders in the USA, detected a tendency for higher-status offenders to be less likely to receive criminal penalties instead of being dealt with by administrative and civil measures (Shapiro 1984, 1989). But in their more comprehensive American study, Weisburd *et al.* (even after double-checking) found that higher-status offenders were more likely to get prison sentences (Weisburd *et al.* 1991: 7). In their earlier study Wheeler *et al.*, using a sample of pre-1980 American social enquiry reports and case files, showed that penalties for white-collar crimes depended on the normal criteria for other crimes: prior record, seriousness of crime, degree of involvement of offender, the nature of harm to the victim, etc. There was, however, some limited evidence of judges identifying with the offender more than in cases of ordinary crimes, especially if the latter involve personal violence (Wheeler *et al.* 1988). The authors left it open whether the judges were merely reproducing (unconsciously or deliberately) the biases of the wider population.

Instead of demanding that white-collar criminals be treated like ordinary criminals, could we argue the reverse and seek to apply the methods used for dealing with businessmen and professionals to ordinary criminals? Much of what purports to be regulation or self-regulation of white-collar crime is bogus or ineffectual, and deserves to be attacked as such but there is also much to be learned from the variety of forms of regulation and self-regulation designed to reduce violations without criminalizing the offender. Even if it would probably be impossible to model the handling of ordinary crime too closely on that used for businessmen, the differences are not always as great as made out. Corporations often avoid penalties, for example in dumping of toxic waste cases, even where deaths result, because they offer or are asked to provide compensation. But all non-police agencies—even when not dealing with powerful offenders—put the emphasis on recovering money rather than securing convictions (Royal Commission on Criminal Procedure 1980). Ordinary criminals are not linked to their place of work as white-collar criminals are. But the problem of maintaining pressure on them is not as great as it seems: the police do know just where to lay their hands on juvenile delinquents—and quite a few other criminal suspects—and white-collar criminals have even more resources than ordinary criminals for covering their tracks when it becomes necessary.

In a sense compliance does already get used with ordinary criminals; Pearce and Tombs (1991) mention police control of prostitution and gambling as an example of compliance methods. But they use this to show the danger of collusion and corruption in the use of such methods. The role of social work and diversion (before trial) and probation or other techniques of rehabilitation (after conviction) is a better example. The choice between cooperation or compulsion is repeatedly offered to ordinary criminals from the stage of pleading guilty to obtaining parole. A crucial difference, however, is that it is usually necessary for an offender accused of ordinary crime to suffer the stigma of a conviction before consideration is given to compliance, whereas the opposite is true for business offenders handled in this way. We may be tempted to believe that, beyond a certain point, enforcement against ordinary crime is geared precisely to maximizing stigma even at the expense of effectiveness.

Pearce and Tombs do seem correct in tracing the difference in approach to the (untested) assumption that businessmen are basically disposed to respond well to a compliance approach whereas ordinary criminals are presumed to require punishment. But they prefer the equally untested assumption that businessmen should be dealt with as 'amoral calculators'. The evidence from interviews, however, is that managers say that they do not, for the most part, think in deterrence terms because only unethical managers are seen to respond to deterrence. Interviewees do concede that this process can get out of control and that it is difficult to be ethical when not running at a profit (Simpson 1992; Yeager 1995). But they insist that 'reputable' managers 'cut corners' only to try to save the company; they may bend the rules but do not violate them and they do not act for personal gain. It is reasonable to conclude that practical considerations regarding effective enforcement provide insufficient justification for the extent of the present contrast between methods used for ordinary and business crimes. A considerable merit of Braithwaite's long-standing search for an effective as well as just approach to the control of all types of crime—what he calls 're-integrative shaming' (Braithwaite 1989, 1995)—is that it builds in a series of attempts at compliance as a prelude to prosecution.

## WHITE-COLLAR CRIME AS AN INDEX OF SOCIAL CHANGE

Whatever the reasons or justifications for the methods used to control white-collar crime, the ambivalence of the social response to this sort of behaviour is also related to wider social factors which have both objective and subjective dimensions. For Aubert (as well as for writers such as E. A. Ross, who anticipated Sutherland's ideas on this topic) the ambiguity of white-collar crimes reflected the objective fact that they were the index of important transitions in social structure. A good example of this phenomenon is the practice of 'insider trading' on the stock exchange and in other financial institutions, which has only relatively recently come to be penalized in Britain. Even now practitioners can have difficulty in drawing the line between legal and illegal conduct (a problem exploited by defence lawyers) and can justify as good business the competitive testing of the limits of legality (Reichman 1992). As Clarke brilliantly puts it:

> It would have perplexed leading members of these institutions up to the end of the 1950s to be told that they were doing anything reprehensible in acting on such information. It was precisely because of the access to such information that one was part of the City, and one was part of the City in the clear expectation of making a considerable amount of money' (Clarke 1990a: 162).

The crime of insider trading therefore nicely symbolizes the change from a time when there were only 'insiders' (see also Stanley 1992). The attacks on political corruption in the 1990s are a further example of white-collar crime as an index of changing social structure.

Ambiguity and ambivalence are inevitable results of situations in which previously legal behaviour has only recently been redefined, and this is exacerbated when the boundaries are changed in ways that are to some extent outside the control of the community being regulated. We could also extend Aubert's analysis by saying that social and legal definitions of crime may be out of joint either because public attitudes have not yet caught up with the legal recognition of important economic and social changes, or because the law has not yet recognized the seriousness of behaviour which causes public concern (in both cases these processes will be fanned, resisted, or mediated by interest and pressure groups). As a further complication we should note that economic and legal definitions will not always coincide (insider trading is still seen as economically useful by some economists). Conversely, at any given time there will be some practices which are quite legal but of dubious economic value, a current example being corporate raiding so as to bid up the price of a business and sell on at a profit. It is therefore not always easy to tell when the time has arrived at which certain business practices have lost all economic justification.

In their stimulating work on the savings and loans frauds, Calavita and Pontell discuss the economic justifications of the type of practices which were the subject of prosecutions during and after the period of Reaganite relaxation of economic controls in the 1980s (Calavita and Pontell 1992; Calavita *et al.* 1997). This period saw the breaking down of barriers between banks and other financial institutions, and a great increase in the scale and internationalization of financial transactions. Drawing on the idea of the French economist Allais, they argue that much of what is produced in what he calls the 'casino economy' is of illusory economic benefit. If, for example, it takes only $12 billion of commercial trade to generate $400 billion of foreign exchange transactions, the opportunities for manipulating money are far in excess of the goods to which they correspond. The system is kept going only by trust in the backing of these transactions, but an excess of confidence can equally bring about disaster if it allows the production of 'junk bonds' or helps sustain unsound financial institutions. They point to various characteristic abuses of this period, such as corporate takeovers, currency trading and futures trading, 'land flips', 'daisy chains' and other forms of property speculation, and the switching of loans to confuse auditors regarding actual assets. Emblematic for them was the accumulation of enormous uncollectable loans relying on federal deposit insurance that were at the heart of the massive 'savings and loans' losses.

An interesting question is how far the practices that Calavita and others describe (which they associate with finance capital as opposed to industrial capital) can be controlled severely without putting at risk jobs and economically sound activities. Much of what they criticize, shorn of obvious abuses, may point to changes in what makes economic sense in a world where the costs of production increasingly favour countries other than the USA and Western Europe. It should also be noted that the savings and loans fiasco was as much the result of too generous government guarantees to bank investors, as it was of speculation and financial mismanagement. They themselves may be relying on an outdated model of industrial capitalism as the only proper conception of a functioning economy. This said, much white-collar and financial crime grows out of the opportunities to exploit objective changes in organizational forms of business trading (particularly marked in a period of increasing global competition) in ways which the law, especially national laws, are slow to deal with or incapable of catching in time. (See, e.g., Pearce and Snider 1995; Tombs 1995.) Other crimes are connected to the cycles of boom and bust that seem inherent in global capitalist expansion.

A more subjective source of ambivalence in the social response to white-collar crime is the assumption that there is less public concern about these behaviours—and therefore less support for severe sanctions, than is the case with more familiar street crimes—especially those involving violence (though this may be the result of existing methods of control). A series of studies has therefore sought to demonstrate that the public in fact ranks examples of these crimes quite severely as compared to ordinary crimes (see, e.g., Cullen *et al.* 1983; Green 1990: 47–57). Harsh attitudes towards such conduct, going well beyond the penalties actually imposed, can be documented in cases of culpable disasters caused by white-collar offenders (Calavita *et al.* 1991). On the other hand, some other attempts to measure public attitudes to white-collar crime do reveal greater leniency in public attitudes (see, e.g., Goff and Nason-Clarke 1989). Much depends on the way questions about different crimes are phrased and the extent to which an effort is made to refer to the possible side-effects of the use of certain sanctions (see, most recently, Almond and Colover 2010). But even if it were to be shown that there was greater public ambivalence towards white-collar crimes than towards ordinary crimes, writers such as Box would only regard this as a further challenge 'to sensitize people to not seeing processes in which they are victimised as disasters or accidents' (Box 1983: 233).

## THE COLLATERAL COSTS OF CONTROL

Many of the ambiguities discussed so far point to value conflicts and awkward policy dilemmas that are often cited as explaining, and even justifying, caution in seeking to curb white-collar crime. If risk-taking is really the motor of the capitalist economy then someone has to pay the price of the inevitable failures. The pursuit of greater health and safety (or even of greater bank transparency) has costs in terms of national and international competitiveness and jobs; it is not always easy to juggle competing pressures, and the interests of business and/or employment can be used to try to justify the acceptance of no more than a 'reasonable' level of safety or pollution. In many areas of business crime enforcers are obliged to choose between going for punishment (and stigmatization), or else achieving compliance or maximizing the amount of revenue recovered. Other dilemmas are more particular. If we are worried about money laundering, does this mean that we want to see banks become a crucial part of the justice system? What about the rights to privacy and confidentiality (Levi 1991a, 1991b)?

But we should not be too quick to assume that such post hoc philosophical dilemmas or justifications are the actual movers of political action. To explain the social weight given to these conflicting values we also need to provide a sociology of public policy choices. Starting from a Marxist perspective, Snider, for example, examines the dialectic between the state, business interests, pressure groups, public opinion (etc.) in an attempt to explain the contrasting fate of different types of regulation (Snider 1991; but see also the more hopeful analysis by Braithwaite 1995). She argues that the resistance to effective implementation of legislation concerning health and safety at work is explicable in terms of the fact that these laws are not in the interest of business itself (except where they can be used by large businesses to beat off the competition of smaller firms). Industry tends—with the collusion of the state—to balance the safety of workers against the increased costs of production. The victims of these crimes are diffuse, though not as diffuse as the victims of crimes against the environment. Antitrust legislation has more success because the state is interested in bringing down its costs as a major purchaser from the private sector, and at least parts of the business world are in favour of such laws. On the other hand, the monopolies and cartels that already control many major markets provide firm resistance, and, of less importance, unions may be ambivalent because of the threat to jobs which could follow the break-up of large conglomerations. Insider trading and stock market fraud, Snider claims, should encounter least resistance (as the success of the American Securities and Exchange Commission supposedly illustrates) because here the interests of the state and business coincide. Business needs to be able to raise money on the stock market, and government does not want to have to bail out defrauded investors. We will be reminded of the political dimension of these policy dilemmas if we accept that the control of ordinary crime may also have a number of negative side-effects—on the offender, his family, and the community—which tend to be ignored when the crucial criterion of policy choice is reduced to the need to continue business as usual.

## CORPORATE CRIME AND THE 2008 FINANCIAL CRASH: THEFT AS PROPERTY?

This chapter in the last handbook ended by asking whether the crimes connected to the so-called 'Enron stage of capitalism' (Prashad 2002) meant that white-collar crime was no longer shrouded in ambiguity (see also McBarnet 2006). In this edition we consider (instead) why there is still such an ambivalent institutional response to the misbehaviour of banks and other leading financial institutions that recently risked bringing about the collapse of large parts of the world's financial system. The courts have been able to impose convictions in some of the more clear-cut cases. But there have been few prosecutions of the leading players whose actions led to the crisis. Nor has there been much support for (re)introducing tough regulation (such as reinstating the US Glass Seagal Act, requiring the separation of investment and high street banks—though even this would not have avoided the collapse of the Lehman Brothers investment bank). Much more attention has been given to trying get back to business as usual at the cost of taxpayer-funded bailouts, sometime enriching those who were responsible for the crisis in the first place. A line continues to be drawn between behaviour which is treated as unquestionably criminal (and parasitic on normal business behaviour) and on the other hand, that where (as was said of the behaviour of those leading the Irish building societies that accumulated enormous debts)' greed, arrogance, incompetence and hubris may be the only charges that can be laid at their doors'.

We are back to the same question. Why is there not more open acknowledgement that capitalism is itself criminogenic? Why is it still apparently easier to generate 'moral panic' over less harmful conventional crimes? Even critical accounts of what happened admit that it is 'often difficult to distinguish white-collar crime from ordinary business transactions' (Hagan 2010). Barak (2012) proposes to discuss *analogous forms of social injury* not specifically prohibited' (italics in original) 'where consequences are *similar* to illegal acts' (my italics). The book titles of insider accounts of these events speak of excess, reckless greed, hubris, and mismanagement, rather than of crime.

It is difficult to provide a neat summary of the financial horse-trading whose very success depended on its complexity and lack of transparency (for useful non-technical accounts see Tett 2009 and Lanchester 2010). The essential background was an increasingly neo-liberal political and economic context characterized by privatization and the increasing 'disembedding' of market from state regulation. By contrast, city values, under the influence of what Lanchester (2009) calls 'Cityphilia', the culture of valuing short-term performance, shareholder value, and league tables colonized public life. Globalization and the migration of manufacturing meant that Western economies (especially the USA and the UK) increasingly specialized in financial services. The search for profitable investment opportunities led to the invention of ever more risky securities, including futures options and credit default swops, that magnified possible gains—but also losses. These were traded in ever greater amounts, often using borrowed money, and the risks of default were hedged (betting on failure) and insured against with giant insurers such as AIG.

At the final—and fatal—stage of this process, bonds based on packages including sub-prime mortgages (involving people with poor credit histories) were passed around and sold from bank to bank in a non-transparent way. By the end one in five mortgages were of this kind, and with the collapse of the housing market and consequent repossessions the bubble burst. Even Goldman Sachs, the most successful of the US investment banks, paid 60 million dollars to end investigation of its sub-prime practices (it sold 33 billion dollars' worth but stopped in time to save itself). Even banks did not know the full risk they were running and were reluctant to lend to each other, hence the credit crunch.

Angelo Mozillo the convicted CEO of Countrywide Trading, the largest US mortgage lender, supposedly realized that many so-called 'ninja' loans would not be repaid and acknowledged in private correspondence that he was selling the 'most dangerous products in existence'. But the difficulty of determining the intentions and knowledge of many of the other key players complicates any effort to answer the question whether the behaviour that led to the financial crash could have been treated as criminal. Some of the worst consequences did not follow from efforts to steal but from unwise business practices. Many building societies and banks came unstuck using short-term borrowing to finance long-term loans—and did not have a business model that allowed for a credit crunch. But, of course, much of this—with sufficient political will— could be redefined as crime. Many investors, let alone savers or pension holders, did not know or understand, let alone acquiesce, in the way their funds were gambled away.

There are obviously many overlaps between this crisis and other recent examples of white-collar and corporate crime. As with the Enron scandal, lobbying for deregulation was a crucial factor here—as in allowing over the counter selling of securities and resisting regulatory oversight over derivatives. Likewise, the 'financial engineering' that was central to new ways of making money, including methods of keeping debts 'off the books', went hand-in-hand with the use of 'legal engineering' so as to undermine regulations through 'creative compliance' (McBarnet 1991). Already in Enron there was an attempt to make money out of and not only defend against risk. Likewise, fraudulent over-extension of mortgages was as central to the massive 'Savings and Loans' debt crisis as to this one (Shover and Grabosky 2010). But there are also important differences. Here banks (and the whole banking system) were central to what happened, rather than just being indirect if significant players. The size and importance of these institutions meant that they were 'too big to fail'. In addition, unlike Enron, there were implications for the increasingly interconnected global financial system not witnessed since the 1929 Wall Street Crash.

Enron and related frauds raised the question of the consequences for society when corporations put the pursuit of profit for their shareholders above all wider interests (Bakan 2004). But the puzzle now is how capitalism can keep going in the face of patterns of risky and fraudulent behaviour that do not even presuppose the survival of the central institutions in which such conduct takes place. Admittedly, those banks who best survived, such as Morgan Stanley (Tett 2009), and also Goldman Sachs, were those most able to command loyalty from their staff. Did those working elsewhere fail to see the danger to their jobs or the organization? Did they hope that they would not need to work again—or just assume that there would be a bail out by the state? Participants' accounts—of which there are many—should not be treated as the last word (few assume that low-status criminals offer fully satisfactory criminological explanation of why they do what they do). Some authors talk of collective delusion or euphoria. Others speculate, on the contrary, that the explanation is masochism and a desire for self- destruction. What is beyond question, as the anthropologist, turned financial journalist, Gillian Tett, discovered, is that participants spoke a tribal language in which it was valid to discuss money in abstract, mathematical, ultra-complex terms, without any reference to tangible human beings (Tett 2010).

As with the Enron scandal there is also the question of how far hedge funds, derivatives, swaps and the other instruments that led to a major financial collapse can (also) be seen as examples of innovation. (It should be noted, of course, that innovation, as both Durkheim and Merton explained, is itself related to deviance.) Options and futures were originally introduced to help farmers who feared what might happen to their crops before harvest. Robert Merton Junior won a Nobel prize for making the risks of hedging with derivatives calculable, and argued later that any negative consequences were a result of the rest of the financial environment not being ready for it. On the other hand, Moody's former managing director described the behaviour of the hedge funds before the crisis as 'wolves, hunting in packs, eating what they killed', whereas rating agencies (such as his own) he saw as mere scapegoats whose primary function was 'to absorb the blame for the sins of the community'. Probably the world's most noted investor, Warren Buffet, called collateralized debt obligations (CDOs) 'financial arms of mass destruction' and George Soros compared them to 'taking out an insurance policy on someone with the right to kill them'. Some of the banks that survived the crash—such as Morgan Stanley—did so by exercising prudence over what they did with their innovations.

The recent crisis seems to have taken us even further than previous ones into the realm of a 'virtual' economy. The value of financial exchanges based on derivatives and other instruments far exceeds the economic activity it refers to; money seems to have been detached from economic growth. In one sense property is always an artificial creation of the law (for example, in the 1970s progressive thinkers were eager for welfare entitlements to be considered to be genuine property rights). And changes in patterns of economic life necessarily reshape what is considered theft, and this takes time (Hall 1958). But, if financial activities are paid for by debts, who does such 'wealth' belong to (Rossi and Prodi 2010)? If it could once be argued that 'property is theft' we now seem close to accepting the opposite. Options on securities are, at best, two removes from 'material value'; derivatives are considered contracts and not securities (and therefore not subject to securities regulation).

As this suggests, the role of 'knowledge' (including that put out by rating agencies) and technological artifacts was also crucial in a new way (Mackenzie 2008, 2010), and not only in multiplying the consequences of economic miscalculations and recklessness. Merton Junior's own investment vehicle, LTCM, imploded because of Russia defaulting on its debt obligations. The later derivatives-based trading that led to the credit crunch also failed to build in 'unthinkable' social and political events and under-estimated the 'linkage' between different factors in economic downturns. In addition, as the sociologist Donald Mackenzie' put it, in a series of notes from the front published in the *London Review of Books*, 'the crisis isn't just about the bursting of the US housing bubble and dodgy sub-prime lending. Nor is it merely a reflection of the perennial cycle in which greed trumps fear to create a euphoric disregard of risk, only for fear to reassert itself as the risk becomes too great. What is revealed by the end-of-the-world trade is that the current crisis concerns 'the collapse of public fact'. For him, even crucial indicators, such as the LIBOR index that defines interest lending rates, are created by those who may have 'interests' in the outcome. He sees no easy practical alternative to this.

In trying to tease out why ambivalence persists a useful contrast can be drawn between the fate of Bernie Madoff, treated as an arch-criminal who was sent to prison for 150 years for conducting a long-standing Ponzi scheme which lost billions of dollars, and the lack of criminalization of bankers who lost even larger amounts through speculation and miscalculation. The line between them, however, is in reality less clear (Barak 2012). Madoff managed to keep his fraud going for over 20 years whereas the derivatives-funded schemes organized by the leading investment banks collapsed in a few years. Many of Madoff's investors (possibly over half) made net gains—and many of the largest of these are themselves being sued. It is not known what proportion of those caught up in the banking crises were winners and losers but it is unlikely to be half. In both the Madoff fraud and the global financial crisis professionals acted without understanding the underlying logic of the transactions they made, and those who knew better ignored the signs of impending disaster; and in both cases, the failure of regulatory agencies was a large part of the problem.

Madoff's offending was certainly more crass and easier to prove. Even more than the normally closed world of investment bankers his fraudulent enterprise was run as a 'secret society' consisting of a handful of well-paid individuals that allegedly escaped the purview of his closest family members. But the assumption that prices would always rise is, in a broad sense, itself a sort of Ponzi scheme. And there was at least implicit collusion between Madoff and the so called 'feeder' organizations, including leading banks, who channelled him his funds (and collected large fees). Whilst some of these have been or will be exposed to law suits, few will face criminal trials. Hence an important part of the explanation for the difference in how other behaviour was treated must be the kind of concern about the collateral effects of pursuing the kinds of conduct by business that have been highlighted throughout this chapter.

Further evidence of the obstacles (or, supposed obstacles?) in curbing this sort of behaviour as compared to many other sorts of crimes may be seen in the caution shown in imposing solutions to avoid a repeat of the crisis. Without doubt, deregulation as well as the speed of changes of regulation are structural factors intrinsic to these offences. Poorly enforced regulation also played its part: the SEC not only failed to catch Madoff out on six inspections, he actually used this as a badge of propriety. Changes in fee structures for selling CDOs and restrictions on bonuses are some specific reforms that can be introduced but attempts to reign in the bankers face the threat (or bluff?) that they could move outside the UK, US, or even beyond Europe to more lightly regulated countries. Despite the admission by Alan Greenspan, long-serving chairman of the US Federal Reserve Bank, that he had over-estimated the market's self-regulatory capacities, many serious commentators continue to argue that market discipline (and social norms) are more effective in their sanctions than state regulation (even if this is needed as a supplement).

Remedies based on past malpractices can easily be side-stepped by new techniques, and may even be counterproductive (as with the so-called 'mark to market rule' for measuring assets introduced after the Enron scandal). Whilst, understandably, many call for a tightening of the rules to avoid risky behaviour by banks, others worry that this could be counterproductive by reducing needed flexibility. Some even claim that the blame for what happened should be laid at the door of a 'cowardly capitalism' that is not willing to shoulder risks. Insofar as capitalism is seen as inherently risky there is also some tendency to 'blame the victim' as in the refrain that investors 'need educating'.

As before, many critical criminologists insist that the crime label should be applied as much as possible to these latest examples of harmful business misbehaviour. But they do not always distinguish the supposed role of criminal law in prevention as compared to repression. They also say little about the fact that, comparatively, the USA is one of the places that is most proactive in seeking harsh sentences for white-collar crimes. A focus on criminality 'hardly captures all at stake in the financial market crisis' (Dorn 2010). But, as one of a spectrum of disciplines concerned with regulation, criminology does have something to offer in describing and explaining what went on (Barak 2012; Hagan 2010; Shover and Grabosky 2010), and showing how this was facilitated by the 'limits of regulatory common sense' (Dorn 2010; Snider 2009). There will always be a need for denouncing 'elite crime' and the many illegal, semi-legal, and legal ways businesses and professionals cause harm. Recent events should underline the costs of the severe underfunding of this sort of criminology. But practical experience, as well as theoretical considerations, suggest that there are severe difficulties in relying on criminal law alone as the means to control the groups most powerful within a given society.

## ■ SELECTED FURTHER READING

An essential starting point remains Edwin H. Sutherland (1983), *White-collar Crime: The Uncut Version* (New Haven: Yale University Press). Useful overviews of the field include David Nelken (ed.) (1994), *White-collar Crime* (Aldershot: Dartmouth); Gary Slapper and Steve Tombs (1999), *Corporate Crime* (Harlow: Longman); Hazel Croall (2001), *Understanding White-collar Crime* (Milton Keynes: Open University Press); James Gobert and Maurice Punch (2003), *Rethinking Corporate Crime* (London: Butterworths); David O. Friedrichs (2009), *Trusted Criminals: White-collar Criminals in Contemporary Society.* (Belmont: Wadsworth, 4th edn); and Michael Benson and Sally Simpson (2009), *White-Collar Crime: An Opportunity Perspective* (London: Routledge). More detailed case studies can be sampled in Kip Schlegel and David Weisburd (eds) (1992), *White-Collar Crime Reconsidered* (Boston: Northeastern University Press), Michael Tonry and Albert Reiss Jnr (eds) (1993), *Beyond the Law: Crime in Complex Organizations* (Chicago: Chicago University Press), and Maurice Punch (1996), *Dirty Business: Exploring Corporate Misconduct* (London: Sage). On the response to the sort of serious white-collar crime which gets dealt with by the ordinary courts in Britain the best work continues to be that by Mike Levi, see, e.g., *Regulating Fraud* (London: Tavistock, 1987).

A number of websites carry information about corporate crime (especially in the USA). See e.g. www.corporatepredators.org; or www.corpwatch.org; or www.paulsjusticepage.com/elite-deviance.htm. But a more effective use of the net would be to set the 'Google alert' facility so as to receive regular updates on a given type of offending (or style of response).

## ■ REFERENCES

ALMOND, P. and COLOVER, S. (2010), 'Mediating Punitiveness: Understanding Public Attitudes towards Work Related Fatality Cases', *European Journal of Criminology*, 7(5): 323–38.

ARLACHI, P. (1985), *Mafia Business*, Oxford: Oxford University Press.

AUBERT, V. (1952), 'White-collar Crime and Social Structure', *American Journal of Sociology*, 58: 263–71.

BAKAN, J. (2004), *The Corporation: The Pathological Pursuit of Profit and Power*, New York: Free Press.

BARAK, G. (2012), *Theft of a Nation: Wall street Looting and the Political Economy of Crime*, Lanham, MD: Rowman & Littlefield.

BENSON, M.L. and SIMPSON, S. (2009), *White-Collar Crime: An Opportunity Perspective*, London: Routledge.

BLOCK, A. (1991), *Perspectives on Organising Crime*, Boston/London: Kluwer.

BOX, S. (1983), *Power, Crime and Mystification*, London: Tavistock.

BOYD, N. (2006), 'Investment Fraud: The Victims of Enron Mortgage', *Paper presented at the annual meeting of the American Society of Criminology, Los Angeles, CA*, 1 November 2006.

BRAITHWAITE, J. (1984), *Corporate Crime in the Pharmaceutical Industry*, London: Routledge & Kegan Paul.

—— (1985), 'White-collar crime', *Annual Review of Sociology*, 11: 1–25.

—— (1989), *Crime, Shame and Integration*, Cambridge: Cambridge University Press.

—— (1995), 'Corporate Crime and Republican Criminological Praxis', in F. Pearce and L. Snider (eds), *Corporate Crime*, Toronto: University of Toronto Press.

BURGESS, E. (1950), 'Comment to Hartung', *American Journal of Sociology*, 56: 25–34.

CALAVITA, K. *et al.* (1991), 'Dam Disasters and Durkheim', *International Journal of the Sociology of Law*, 19: 407–27.

—— and PONTELL, H. (1992), 'The Savings and Loans Crisis', in M. Erdmann and R. Lundman (eds), *Corporate and Governmental Deviance*, Oxford: Oxford University Press.

——, ——, and TILLMAN, R. (1997), *Big Money Crime*, Berkeley, Cal.: University of California Press.

CARSON, W. G. (1970), 'White-collar Crime and the Enforcement of Factory Legislation', *British Journal of Criminology*, 10: 383–98.

—— (1974), 'Symbolic and instrumental dimensions of early factory legislation', in R. Hood (ed.), *Crime, Criminology and Public Policy*, London: Heinemann.

—— (1980), 'The Institutionalisation of Ambiguity: The Early British Factory Acts', in G. Geis and E. Stotland (eds), *White-collar Crime: Theory and Research*, London and New York: Sage.

—— (1981), *The Other Price of Britain's Oil*, Oxford: Martin Robertson.

CLARKE, M. (1990a), *Business Crime: Its Nature and Control*, Oxford: Polity Press.

—— (1990b), 'The Control of Insurance Fraud: A Comparative View', *British Journal of Criminology*, 30: 1–23.

CLINARD, M. and YEAGER, P. (1980), *Corporate Crime*, New York: Free Press.

COFFEE, JNR, J. C. (2002), 'Understanding Enron: It's About the Gatekeepers, Stupid', *Columbia Law & Economics Working Paper* No. 207 (30 July).

COLEMAN, J. W. (1985), *The Criminal Elite: The Sociology of White-Collar Crime*, New York: St Martin's Press.

—— (1987), 'Toward an Integrated Theory of White-collar Crime', *American Journal of Sociology*, 93(2): 406–39.

—— (1992), 'The Asymmetric Society', in M. Erdmann and R. Lundman (eds), *Corporate and Governmental Deviance*, Oxford: Oxford University Press.

COOK, D. (1989), *Rich Law, Poor Law*, Milton Keynes: Open University Press.

COSSON, J. (1978), *Les Industriels de la Fraude Fiscale*, Paris: Editions du Seuil.

CROALL, H. (1989), 'Who is the white-collar criminal?', *British Journal of Criminology*, 29: 157–74.

—— (2009), 'Community safety and economic crime', *Criminology and Criminal Justice*, 9(2): 165–185.

CULLEN, F. *et al.* (1983), 'Public Support for Punishing White-Collar Criminals', *Journal of Criminal Justice*, 11: 481–93.

DELMAS-Marty, M. (1990), *Droit Pénal des Affaires*, Paris: Presses Universitaires de France.

Dorn, N. (2010), 'The Governance of Securities: Ponzi Finance, Regulatory Convergence, Credit Crunch', *British Journal of Criminology*, 50: 23–45.

Dowie, M. (1988), 'Pinto Madness', in S.L. Hills (ed.), *Corporate Violence: Injury and Death for Profit*, Totowa, N. J.: Rowman and Littlefield.

Economist, The (1992), 'The Blue Arrow Affair', 7 March: 23.

Edelhertz, H. (1970), *The Nature, Impact and Prosecution of White-Collar Crime*, Washington DC: US Government Printing Press.

Fisse, B. and Braithwaite, J. (1985), *The Impact of Publicity on Corporate Offenders*, Albany, N.Y.: State University of New York Press.

Friedrichs, D. (2003), *Trusted Criminals: White-collar Criminals in Contemporary Society*, 2nd edn, Belmont: Wadsworth.

Gambetta, D. (1994), *The Sicilian Mafia: An Industry of Private Protection*, Oxford: Oxford University Press.

Geis, G. (1968), 'The Heavy Electrical Equipment Anti-Trust Cases of 1961', in G. Geis (ed.), *White-Collar Crime*, New York: Atherton Press.

Gobert, J. and Punch, P. (2003) *Rethinking Corporate Crime*, London: Butterworths.

Gorr, C. and Nason Clarke, N. (1989), 'The Seriousness of Crime in Fredericton, New Brunswick: Perceptions toward White-collar Crime', *Canadian Journal of Criminology*, 31: 19–34.

Gottfredson, M. and Hirschi, T. (1990), *A General Theory of Crime*, Stanford, Cal.: Stanford University Press.

Green, G. S. (1990), *Occupational Crime*, Chicago: Nelson Hall.

Gross, E. (1980), 'Organisational Structure and Organisational Crime', in G. Geis and E. Stotland (eds), *White Collar Crime: Theory and Research*, New York: Sage.

Groves, W. B. and Newman, G. (eds) (1986), *Punishment and Privilege*, Albany, N.Y.: Harrow and Heston.

Hagan, J. (2010), *Who are the Criminals?*, Princeton, Princeton University Press.

Haines, F. (1997), *Corporate Regulation: Beyond Punish or Persuade*, Oxford: Clarendon Press.

Hall, J. (1952), *Theft, Law and Society*, 2nd edn, Charlottesville: Indiana University Press.

Hall, S., Winlaw, S., and Ancru, C. (2008), *Criminal Identities and Consumer Culture*, Cullompton: Willan.

Hartung, F. (1950), 'White-collar Offences in the Wholesale Meat Industry in Detroit', *American Journal of Sociology*, 56: 25–34.

Hawkins, K. (1984), *Environment and Enforcement: Regulation and the Social Definition of Pollution*, Oxford: Clarendon Press.

—— (1990), 'Compliance Strategy, Prosecution Policy and Aunt Sally: A Comment on Pearce and Tombs', *British Journal of Criminology*, 30: 444–66.

—— (1991), 'Enforcing Regulation: More of the same from Pearce and Tombs', *British Journal of Criminology*, 31: 427–30.

—— and Thomas, J. M. (eds) (1984), *Enforcing Regulation*, Boston/London: Kluwer.

Hills, S. L. (ed.) (1988), *Corporate Violence: Injury and Death for Profit*, Totowa, N J: Rowman and Littlefield.

Hillyard, P., Panzatis, C. , Tombs, S., and Gordon, D. (2004), *Beyond Criminology: Taking Harm Seriously*, London: Pluto Press.

Hirschi, T. and Gottfredson, M. (1987), 'Causes of White-Collar Crime', *Criminology*, 25: 949–74.

—— and —— (1989), 'The Significance of White-Collar Crime for a General Theory of Crime', *Criminology*, 27: 359–72.

Hutter, B. (1988), *The Reasonable Arm of the Law?*, Oxford: Clarendon Press.

—— (1997), *Compliance: Regulation and the Environment*, Oxford: Clarendon Press.

Katz, J. (1980), 'The Social Movement Against White-collar Crime', *Criminology Review Yearbook*: 161–84.

Kramer, R. C. (1992), 'The Space Shuttle Challenger Explosion: A Case Study of State–Corporate Crime', in K. Schlegel and D. Weisburd, *White-Collar Crime Reconsidered*, Boston, Mass.: Northeastern University Press.

Lanchester, J. (2010), *Whoops!: Why everyone owes everyone and no one can pay*, London: Allen Lane.

Lane, R. (1953), 'Why Businessmen Violate the Law', *Journal of Criminal Law, Criminology and Police Science*, 44: 151–65.

Leonard, W. N. and Weber, M. G. (1970), 'Automakers and Dealers: A Study of Criminogenic Market Forces', *Law and Society Review*, 4: 407–24.

Levi, M. (1981), *The Phantom Capitalists*, London: Gower Press.

—— (1985), 'A Criminological and Sociological Approach to Theories of and Research into Economic Crime', in D. Magnuson (ed.), *Economic Crime – Programs for Future Research*, Report No. 18: 32–72, Stockholm: National Council for Crime Prevention, Sweden.

—— (1987), *Regulating Fraud*, London: Tavistock.

—— (1991a), 'Pecunia Non Olet: Cleansing the Money Launderers from the Temple', *Crime, Law and Social Change*, 16: 217–302.

—— (1991b), 'Regulating Money Laundering', *British Journal of Criminology*, 31: 109–25.

—— (1991c), 'Fraudulent Justice? Sentencing the Business Criminal', in P. Carlen and D. Cook (eds), *Paying for Crime*, Milton Keynes: Open University Press.

—— and Nelken, D. (eds) (1996), 'The Corruption of Politics and the Politics of Corruption', special issue of the *Journal of Law and Society*, 23: 1.

——, Nelen, H., and Lankhorst, F. (2005), 'Lawyers as crime facilitators in Europe: An introduction and overview,' *Crime, Law and Social Change*, 42(2–3): 117–121(5).

MACKENZIE, D. (2006), *An Engine, not a Camera: how Financial Models Shape Markets*, Boston: MIT Press.

—— (2007), 'The Material Production of Virtuality: Innovation, Cultural Geography, and Facticity in Derivatives Markets', *Economy and Society*, 36: 355–376.

—— (2008), ' End of the World Trade', *London Review of Books*, 30 :8 May 2008.

—— (2010), 'The Credit Crisis as a Problem in the Sociology of Knowledge', working paper, www. sps.ed.ac.uk.

MCBARNET, D.J. (1991), 'Whiter than White-collar Crime: Tax, Fraud Insurance and the Management of Stigma', *British Journal of Sociology*, 42: 323–44.

—— (2006), 'After Enron: Will whiter than white collar crime still wash', *British Journal of Criminology*, 46(6): 1091–109.

—— and Whelan, C. (1999), *The One Eyed Javelin-Thrower*, London: Wiley.

MAGNUSSON, D. (ed.) (1985), *Economic Crime— Programs for Future Research*, Report No. 18, Stockholm: National Council for Crime Prevention, Sweden.

MANN, M. (1985), *Defending White-collar Crime*, New Haven, Conn.: Yale University Press.

MINKES, J. and MINKES, L.(2008), *Corporate and White Collar Crime*, London: Sage.

MOOHR, G.S. ( 2003), 'An Enron lesson: the modest role of criminal law in preventing corporate crime', *Florida Law Review*, 55: 940.

NEEDLEMAN, M. L. and NEEDLEMAN, C. (1979), 'Organizational Crime: Two models of Crimogenisis', *Sociological Quarterly*, 20: 517–28.

NELKEN, D. (1983), *The Limits of the Legal Process: A Study of Landlords, Law and Crime*, London: Academic Press.

—— (1991), 'Why Punish?', *Modern Law Review*, 53: 829–34.

—— (1994a), 'Whom can you Trust? The Future of Comparative Criminology', in D. Nelken (ed.), *The Futures of Criminology*, 220–44, London: Sage.

—— (1994b), 'White-Collar Crime', in M. MAGUIRE, R. MORGAN, and R. Reiner (eds), *Oxford Handbook of Criminology*, 1st edn, 355–93, Oxford: Oxford University Press.

—— (ed.) (1994c), *White-collar Crime*, Aldershot: Dartmouth.

—— (1997a), 'The Globalisation of Criminal Justice', in M. Freeman (ed.), *Law and Opinion at the End of the Century*, Oxford: Oxford University Press.

—— (1997b), 'White-Collar Crime', in M. Maguire, R. Morgan, and R. Reiner (eds), *Oxford Handbook of Criminology*, 2nd edn, Oxford: Oxford University Press.

—— (2000), 'Telling Difference', in D. Nelken (ed.), *Contrasting Criminal Justice*, Aldershot: Dartmouth.

—— (2002), 'Corruption in the European Union', in M. Bull and J. Newell (eds), *Corruption and Scandal in Contemporary Politics*, London: Macmillan.

—— and LEVI, M. (1996), 'Introduction' to 'The Corruption of Politics and the Politics of Corruption', special issue of the *Journal of Law and Society*, 23(1): 1–17.

NEW YORK STATE ORGANIZED CRIME TASK FORCE (1988), *Corruption and Racketeering in the New York City Construction Industry*, New York: Cornell University Press.

PASSAS, N. (1990), 'Anomie and Corporate Deviance', *Contemporary Crises*, 14: 157–78.

—— (2000), 'Global Anomie, Dysnomie and Economic crime', *Social Justice*, 27: 16–44.

—— and NELKEN, D. (1993), 'The thin line between legitimate and criminal enterprises: subsidy frauds in the European Community', *Crime, Law and Social Change*, 19: 223–43.

——and GOODWIN, N. (eds) (2004), *It's Legal, but it ain't Right*, Ann Arbor:University of Michigan Press.

PEARCE, F. (1976), *Crimes of the Powerful: Marxism, Crime and Deviance*, London: Pluto.

—— and SNIDER, L. (1995), 'Regulating Capitalism', in F. Pearce and L. Snider (eds), *Corporate Crime*, Toronto: University of Toronto Press.

—— and TOMBS, S. (1990), 'Ideology, Hegemony and Empiricism: Compliance Theories of Regulation', *British Journal of Criminology*, 30: 423–43.

—— and —— (1991), 'Policing Corporate "Skid Rows" ', *British Journal of Criminology*, 31: 415–26.

PONTELL, H. N. and CALAVITA, K. (1993), 'The Savings and Loan Industry', in M. Tonry and A. Reiss Jnr (eds), *Beyond the Law: Crime in Complex Organizations*, Chicago: University of Chicago Press.

PORTNOY, F. (1997), *F.I.A.S.C.O: Blood in the Water on Wall Street*, London: Profile Books.

PRASHAD, V. (2002), *Fat Cats and Running Dogs: the Enron Stage of Capitalism*, London: Zed Books.

PUNCH, M. (1996), *Dirty Business: Exploring Corporate Misconduct*, London: Sage.

—— (2008),'The organization did it: Individuals, corporations and crime', in Minkes and Minkes (eds), *Corporate and White Collar Crime*, London; Sage.

REICHMAN, N. (1992), 'Moving Backstage: Uncovering the Role of Compliance Practices in Shaping Regulatory Practices', in K. Schlegel and D. Weisburd, *White-Collar Crime Reconsidered*, Boston, Mass.: Northeastern University Press.

ROSOFF, S. M., PONTELL, H. N., and TILLMAN, R. (1998), *Profit Without Honour: White Collar Crime and the Looting of America*, Upper Saddle River, N. J.: Prentice Hall.

ROSSI, G. and PRODI, P. (2010), *Non Rubare*, Bologna: Il Mulino.

ROYAL COMMISSION ON CRIMINAL PROCEDURE (1980), *Prosecutions by Private Individuals and Non-Police Agencies*, Research Study No. 10, London: HMSO.

RUGGIERO, V. (1996), *Organised Crime and Corporate Crime in Europe*, Aldershot: Dartmouth.

SAVELSBERG, J. (1994), *Constructing White-Collar Crime: Rationalities, Communication, Power*, Philadelphia, Pa: University of Pennsylvania Press.

SHAPIRO, S. (1984), *Wayward Capitalists*, New Haven, Conn.: Yale University Press.

—— (1989), 'Collaring the Crime, not the Criminal: Reconsidering "White-Collar Crime"', *American Sociological Review*, 55: 346–65.

SHOVER, N. and GRABOSKY, P. ( eds) (2010), 'The Global Economy, Economic Crisis and White Collar Crime', *Criminology and Public policy*, Special Issue, 9:3.

SIMPSON, S. S. (1992), 'Corporate Crime Deterrence and Corporate Control Policies, Views from the Inside', in K. Schlegel and D. Weisburd, *White-Collar Crime Reconsidered*, Boston, Mass.: Northeastern University Press.

SLAPPER, G. (1991), *Blood in the Bank*, Aldershot: Dartmouth.

—— and TOMBS, S. (1999), *Corporate Crime*, Harlow: Longman.

SMITH, D. J. Jnr (1980), 'Paragons, Pariahs and Pirates: A Spectrum-Based Theory of Enterprise', *Crime and Delinquency*, 26: 358–86.

SNIDER, L. (1991), 'The Regulatory Dance: Understanding Reform Processes in Corporate Crime', *International Journal of the Sociology of Law*, 19: 209–36.

—— (2000), 'Accommodating Power: The "Common Sense" of Regulators', *Social and Legal Studies*, 18: 179–97.

SPALEK, P. (2001), 'Policing the UK Financial System: The Creation of the New Financial Services Authority and its Approach to Regulation', *International Journal of the Sociology of Law*, 20(1): 75–88.

STANLEY, C. (1992), 'Serious Money: Legitimation of Deviancy in the Financial Markets', *International Journal of the Sociology of Law*, 20: 43–60.

STEFFENSMEIER, D. (1989), 'On the Causes of White collar Crime. An Assessment of Hirschi and Gottfredson's Claims', *Criminology*, 27: 345–58.

STONE, C. (1975), *Where the Law Ends: The Social Control of Corporate Behaviour*, New York: Harper and Row.

SUTHERLAND, E. H. (1949), *White-collar Crime*, New York: Holt, Rinehart and Winston.

—— (1983), *White-collar Crime: the Uncut Version*, New Haven, Conn.: Yale University Press.

SZASZ, D. (1986), 'Corporations, Organised Crime and the Disposal of Hazardous Waste: An Examination of the Making of a Criminogenic Regulatory Structure', *Criminology*, 24: 1–27.

TAPPAN, P. (1947), 'Who is the Criminal?', *American Sociological Review*, 12: 96–102.

TETT, G. ( 2009), *Fool's Gold*, New York: Free Press.

TIEDEMANN, K. (1974), 'Kriminologische und Kriminalistiche Aspekte der Subventionse—schteichung', in H. Schafer (ed.), *Grundlagen der Kriminalistik*, 13(1), Wirtschaftskriminalitat, Weissen-Kragen Kriminalitat, Hamburg: Steinton.

TOMBS, S. (1995), 'Corporate Crime and New Organizational Forms', in F. Pearce and L. Snider (eds), *Corporate Crime*, 132–47, Toronto: University of Toronto Press.

VAN DUYNE, P. (1993), 'Organised Crime and Business Crime Enterprises in the Netherlands', *Crime, Law and Social Change*, 19: 103–43.

VAUGHAN, D. E. (1983), *Controlling Unlawful Organizational Behaviour*, Chicago: University of Chicago Press.

—— (1996), *The Challenger Launch Decision*, Chicago: University of Chicago Press.

WACQUANT, L. (2009), *Punishing the Poor*, Durham, NC: Duke University Press.

WEISBURD, D. and WARING, E. J. (2001), *White Collar Crime and Criminal Careers*, Cambridge: Cambridge University Press.

WELLS, C. (1993), *Corporations and Criminal Responsibility*, Oxford: Clarendon Press.

WHEELER, S. (1992), 'The Problem of White-Collar Crime Motivation', in K. Schlegel and D. Weisburd, *White-Collar Crime Reconsidered*, Boston, Mass.: Northeastern University Press.

——, MANN, K., and SARAT, A. (1988), *Sitting in Judgement: The Sentencing of White-Collar Crimes*, New Haven, Conn.: Yale University Press.

—— WARING, E., and BODE, N. (1991), *Crimes of the Middle Classes: White-collar Offenders in the Federal Courts*, New Haven, Conn.: Yale University Press

WRIGHT-MILLS, C. (1943/1963), 'The Professional Ideology of Social Pathologists', in C. Wright-Mills, *Power, Politics and People*, 525–52, New York: Oxford University Press.

YEAGER, P. C. (1991), *The Limits of Law: The Public Regulation of Private Pollution*, Cambridge: Cambridge University Press.

—— (1995), 'Management, Morality and Law, Organizational Forms and Ethical Deliberations', in F. Pearce and L. Snider (eds), *Corporate Crime*, 147–68, Toronto: University of Toronto Press.

YOUNG, T. R. (1981), 'Corporate Crime: A Critique of the Clinard Report', *Contemporary Crises*, 5: 323–36.

ZIEGLER, J. (1990), *La Suisse Lave Plus Blanc*, Amsterdam: Uitgeverij Balans.

ZIMRING, F. and HAWKINS, G. (1993), 'Crime, Justice and the Savings and Loans Crisis', in M. Tonry and A. Reiss Jnr (eds), *Beyond the Law: Crime in Complex Organizations*, Chicago: University of Chicago Press.

# 22

# TERRORISM AND COUNTER-TERRORISM

*Martin Innes and Michael Levi*

## INTRODUCTION

Sutherland and Cressey (1955) famously defined criminology as a discipline gravitating around the study of the processes of 'making laws, breaking laws and reacting to the breaking of laws'. Albeit there have been some departures from these principal interests over the years, for the most part, the criminological enterprise has demonstrated a sustained interest in such themes. In this chapter we seek to develop and deploy a lens derived from this criminological perspective to the social problem of terrorism.

Until comparatively recently, criminologists have contributed little of note to either the theoretical or empirical study of terrorism. This is despite significant levels of engagement in trying to understand the social processes involved in many other kinds of violence, the work of criminal justice systems, and social reactions to deviant behaviour. Instead, the keynote contributions have come from other social science disciplines, most obviously international relations, social psychology, and political science. More recently though, in the midst of a more general expansion of interest and activity that itself reflects broader social trends (and significant tranches of funding to deal with the 'new Islamist threats'), a number of scholars with stronger and weaker affiliations to mainstream criminology have sought to contribute to knowledge about terrorism and counter-terrorism. Herein our aim is to review the nature of these contributions and to provide them with added impetus by thinking in a concerted fashion about how concepts and theories distilled from studies of other forms of violent and criminal conduct might broaden and deepen social understandings of terrorism.

In adopting this approach, it is not our intention to provide a systematic review of the scholarly activity directed towards terrorism and responses to it. Rather our aim is to explore more selectively how the kinds of perspectives and framings that are typically mobilized by criminologists can be profitably applied to the study of terrorism. Accordingly, the chapter is organized around five key sections. It commences by developing a framework for assessing the different ways in which terrorism is defined and the contests attached to the application of this label. This is followed by an overview of what is known about the 'moral careers' of terrorists and how people become involved in terrorist groups and actions. The third section attends to the social control of terrorism and the work of counter-terrorism agencies. This frames a subsequent discussion of the particularly important area of social reactions to terrorism and counter interventions, and the ways that public attitudes and perceptions shape the interactions that occur between terrorist and counter-terrorist interventions. By way of conclusion we seek to draw upon the preceding discussion to start to trace out the contours of the key elements of a criminological approach to the study of terrorism.

## THE IDEA OF TERRORISM

...deviance is not a quality of the act the person commits, but rather a consequence of the application by others of rules and sanctions to an 'offender'. The deviant is one to whom the label has successfully been applied; deviant behaviour is behaviour that people so label. (Howard Becker 1963, *Outsiders*: 9)

With its questioning stance towards the received institutionalized categories that we use to make sense of and attend to varieties of troublesome and problematic behaviour, Labelling Theory, as exemplified by Howard Becker's study of 'outsiders', has been profoundly influential upon several generations of criminological study. For this approach illuminates the frequently arbitrary relationship between the ontology of acts and behaviours, and the ways in which they come to be defined and treated in practice by criminal justice and extra-judicial systems. From this vantage point, the institutions of law and the processes of criminal justice are of interest not just because of their instrumental qualities, but because of the work they do in creating and sustaining particular orders of reality that conceptualize certain acts and actors as requiring interventions, whilst other ostensibly similar events are placed outside of their purview. Thus, the capacity and capability to successfully construct a social problem as a crime and particular social actors as 'criminals' is understood as an accomplishment irreducibly inflected by the distribution of economic and political power, and by ideologies and categories that refract that power.

Such considerations are directly relevant to the study of terrorism, which is pervaded by the problem of social constructionism. Scholars have long wrestled with the difficulties associated with establishing a coherent definition of terrorism. Almost every meaningful book-length study commences by rehearsing this definitional issue and grappling with the problem that, as the popular notion has it 'one man's terrorist is another man's freedom fighter'. Such definitional difficulties are similarly detectable in the policy environment. For instance, despite its major role in organizing and legitimating sanctions, the United Nations has failed to secure an agreed definition of terrorism at the international level, partly because of the views of post-colonial member states, many of whose leaders were themselves once defined as terrorists. Cognizant of these conceptual difficulties and debates, in this chapter we focus explicitly upon terrorism in democratic political contexts. In so doing, we are self-consciously accepting an implicit proposition that context matters and terrorism should be regarded differently in democratic settings when compared with non-democratic or occupied countries.

At a more local level, similar concerns frequently surface about how to construct a coherent definition of the situation in terms of distinguishing between some forms of crime and terrorism. This was exemplified by the case of Anders Breivik, the Norwegian man who, in 2011, shot 69 individuals on the island of Utoeya and killed another eight via a bomb he left in Oslo. Breivik was motivated by a far-right political discourse, and he displayed considerable intent and capability in conducting his acts. But ultimately what he did is probably better defined as a 'spree killing', than an act of terrorism. The same considerations can be applied to the Oklahoma City bombing in 1995.

Writing nearly a quarter of a century ago, Schmid and Jongman (1988) were able to list over 100 different definitions of terrorism, and more recent studies have suggested that there are now many more in circulation (Smelser 2007). As a consequence, several more recent surveys of the field have started to organize these definitions by introducing some 'meso-level' theoretical framings to identify where proposed conceptualizations gravitate around similar constructs. For example, Richard English (2008) draws a sharp distinction between 'analytic' approaches and the considerations that routinely inform more avowedly practical approaches. In contrast, Crelinsten (2009) suggests that the competing definitions can be grouped together under four broad headings: (1) 'tactical' definitions that are common in international legal conventions and accent the 'how' of terrorism; (2) 'perpetrator'-based approaches that pivot around 'who' the individuals and groups involved are'; (3) 'motive'-oriented accounts that focus upon 'why' they do what they do; or (4) a 'behavioural' approach that is most concerned with 'what' is done.

Adopting a different starting point Weston and Innes (2010) have suggested that disciplinary genealogies serve to subtly configure how different authors frame the problem that they are engaging with. So studies emanating from economics tend to accent and attend to different qualities than those from sociology or psychology.

Despite this and the variations present, it does seem possible to distil from the literature some common themes that appear in most (if not all) attempts to trace the conceptual contours of terrorism:

- political violence—there is widespread agreement that a necessary condition for defining an act as terrorist and thus distinguishing it from some other forms of violence is that it is conducted in pursuit of some political objective;

- communicative violence—accompanying the preceding point, almost all definitions acknowledge that terrorist acts are marked by a desire to communicate an intimidatory message beyond the immediate victims; and

- asymmetry of power—more contentiously perhaps, many contributions identify that terrorist violence tends to arise when a relatively powerless group identifies a need to mobilize a response to a more powerful adversary. For example, as part of his wider geometry of social relations, Black (2004) proposes that terrorism is frequently an attempt at social control and self-help by relatively weak minority positions.

All of these key elements are, for instance, present in Paul Wilkinson's (2005: 12–13) influential definition:

Terrorism is the systematic use of coercive intimidation, usually to service political ends. It is used to create and exploit a climate of fear among a wider target group than the immediate victims of the violence and to publicise a cause, as well as to coerce a target to acceding to the terrorists' aims.

As can be seen, Wilkinson is more equivocal about the role of the asymmetry of power element as necessarily being a defining quality of terrorism. In subsequent discussion he develops his basic position to recognize that terrorism is usually committed by relatively weak minorities against stronger opponents, but can be a method engaged by states. Following the established convention in the political science literature he elects to differentiate 'state terror' from the 'terrorism' of factional groups. He further seeks to sub-divide these types according to whether they are 'internal' or 'international' in orientation, albeit he reflexively questions the utility of such a distinction on the grounds that many forms of contemporary terrorism blend aspects of the local and global.

Whilst a number of other contributions to the debate on definitions of terrorism have more clearly differentiated state terror from terrorism, the adoption of such a position has been strongly contested. Cohen (2001) notes that there are nation states that invoke communicative violence against their own citizens in pursuit of their own political objectives, causing destruction, fear and panic (see also Green and Ward, this volume). Why should such acts be understood as either conceptually or morally separate from other forms of terrorism? Equally, the literature on insurgency and counter-insurgency identifies how similar tactics and motivations often feature in the conduct of 'low-intensity' wars and 'guerrilla' conflicts (Hoffman 2006; Kilcullan 2009).

These latter contributions on state crime and guerrilla combat are important to this discussion because they clarify how and why definitions matter so much. Coherent with the axioms of criminological labelling theory, definitions and labels are consequential in that they shape patterns of reaction and response (and are often framed with that in mind). English (2009) identifies that terrorist type activities can be, and indeed are, frequently embedded within the conduct of wars and ongoing serious criminality such as trafficking of minerals and diamonds, and of illegal commodities. As will be discussed in more detail in subsequent sections of this chapter, how such acts are categorized can play an important role in determining whether they are deemed to require a 'military' or 'criminal justice' response. To put it another way, should terrorism be understood as a form of crime, or as a form of war?

Those groups to whom the label of terrorist is trying to be applied will often contest it. In a particularly interesting example of the importation of criminological theories into the study of terrorism, Cromer (2001) usefully applied Sykes and Matza's (1957) 'techniques of neutralization' to examine how groups attempt to resist being defined as terrorists. Cromer showed how, depending upon their aims and orientations, different terrorist groups and organizations, seek to: deny responsibility; deny injury; deny the victim; condemn the condemners; and appeal to higher loyalties.

Originally developed to account for how individuals are able to break laws and rules that they otherwise support and believe in, Sykes and Matza argued that the invocation of these neutralizing techniques 'loosened' moral and social bonds sufficiently to facilitate deviant conduct whilst avoiding too much cognitive or affective stress. That similar invocations can be detected in the discourses and rhetorics of those labelled as terrorists points to a pivotal issue for those engaged in studying this configuration of violence—how and why do ordinary people come to engage in extra-ordinary acts?

In the annals of criminology it is now well documented that contrary to many mass media representations, the vast majority of criminals are not 'folk devils' made flesh but fairly ordinary individuals. Whilst the allure of the depiction of terrorists as pathological and psychotic individuals is seductive to the media and politicians, the best available research contests such views. For example, Horgan (2005) emphasizes the normality of most people who engage in terrorist activity and rejects the notion that it is associated with a unique psychopathology or personality type. Likewise, the data from in-depth interviews with participants in 'terrorist' groups presented by Atran (2010) clearly conveys their ordinariness.

If we stop to consider such matters for a moment, it makes eminent sense. Executing a successful terrorist attack often requires meticulous planning. It also requires an ability to operate covertly and discreetly in order not to arouse the suspicions of others, and avoid detection by the authorities. Moreover, terrorists often work in small cells requiring some form of social interactional competency. These are all elements of the 'tradecraft' of terrorism (Hoffman 2006) that are not suited to the participation of a wild and errant individual. Indeed, there are claims that many terrorist organizations such as Al-Qaeda are quite careful to avoid recruiting such dysfunctional individuals, albeit tempered by the fact that their selection processes may not be perfect and the pool of available motivated persons circumscribed. Although much of the research on these issues has been developed in and shaped by a post-'9/11' environment, it is clear that other conflicts yield different patterns, depending on the embeddedness of 'freedom struggles' within different social formations (see, e.g., Laqueur 2003).

## TERRORISM AS A 'CAREER'

By being willing, the subject may begin a process that neither holds him within its grip nor unfolds without him...To enter the process the invitational edge of the deviant phenomenon must somehow be hurdled...exthe next issue for the subject...is whether the phenomenon and those affiliated with it succdisexeed or fail in 'turning him on' or converting him. (Matza 1969: 117)

In his book *Becoming Deviant*, David Matza delineated the social processes negotiated by individuals and groups when engaging in illegal and deviant conduct. In so doing, he sought to contest the notion that some people are impelled to act in certain ways by dint of their exposure to particular social, political, or economic forces. He also identified distinct phases of involvement requiring explanation. Across the social sciences the concept of 'career' has been repeatedly developed and deployed to engage with such issues, being used to articulate a sense of trajectory in how individuals and groups come to enact a series of different tasks and roles. For example, the notion of the criminal career is widely discussed in attempts to explain patterns in the onset, escalation, and desistance of criminal offending. Likewise, sociologists routinely reference the notion of a 'moral career' in order to help them take apart the distinct phases involved in occupying particular roles and performing certain actions, and in particular the consequences for self and social identities (Goffman 1959). Here, informed by these other studies and research conducted on terrorist groups, we seek to develop the notion of 'the terrorist career'. The approach derived is based around three key phases:

1. Becoming a terrorist—is focused upon processes of radicalization and the acquisition of certain beliefs and attitudes; the formation and/or joining with a group of like-minded individuals; and the more pragmatic issues involved in developing the practical skills required to engage in terrorist acts.

2. Being and doing terrorism—shifts the focus to what is required to actually perform terrorist actions, and maintain a cell or organization (large or small) in order to pursue a campaign.

3. Desistance from terrorism—is the phase where either individually or collectively, a decision is made to move away from using tactics or strategy deemed by others as terrorist.

## BECOMING A TERRORIST

Reflecting increasing disenchantment with theories focused on individual psycho-pathologies, a number of recent accounts have started to weave together more subtle and sophisticated explanations of how individuals come to be motivated to engage in terrorism. Richardson (2006: 14) for example, argues that the causes of terrorism are grounded in subjective perceptions melding with:

> …a lethal cocktail containing a disaffected individual, an enabling community and a legitimizing ideology. I believe that terrorist behaviour can be understood in terms of both long-term political motivations, which differ across different types of groups, and more immediate short-term motives, which very different types of terrorists share.

Looking across manifestations of terrorism in varying contexts, she identifies that a necessary condition is the presence of 'a conducive surround'. Terrorist campaigns that acquire traction and a degree of longevity are typically situated in a social environment that is somewhat amenable to mounting a sustained campaign, frequently because it affords a degree of either tacit or explicit community support. If this explains the inception of a terrorist campaign, then it is a desire for 'revenge, renown, and reaction' that influences individual actors to participate in the campaign.

Richardson and other authors (e.g. Silke 2008) are starting to derive nuanced theories of how individuals and groups acquire the motivations to engage in particular forms of communicative violence in pursuit of their political beliefs. This aspect of the research effort could be typified as the search for 'incubators of terrorism'. Wiktorowicz's (2005) study of the membership of Al-Muhajiroun identifies that certain types of personal crises (e.g. losing a job; experiences of racism; bereavement; crime victimization) can create a 'cognitive opening' whereby people become more receptive to new perspectives and ideas. The creation of such an opening and rendering people receptive is a distinct issue from how they are 'programmed' with extremist ideas. Examining earlier studies of how people become indoctrinated into religious cults is potentially instructive in this regard. For example, John Lofland's (1966) ethnographic study of proselytization and indoctrination describes what he terms the 'involvement sequences' by which cult members came to join. That he writes of 'sequences' rather than 'a sequence' is significant, for his analysis captures that different members joined for different reasons and in different ways. So whilst there are common elements to the individual involvement sequences (such as: people who are in some way already predisposed to be receptive to alternative religious schemas; questioning the group's ideas and receiving answers to these queries that they deem satisfactory; bonding to the individual members of the group and disassociating from previous social contacts) these were arranged in different orders for different members.

In keeping with this developing perspective on the multiple career sequences involved in the initial participation in, and subsequent conversion to, terrorist campaigns, it is relevant that different groups tend to exploit different motivations. Groups engaging in 'terrorist' acts in pursuit of broadly nationalist aims, typically evidence greater levels of social support and participation, than do groups whose agenda pivots primarily around a political ideology, such as Germany's Red Army Faction (Baader-Meinhof Gang).

In his account of the motivations underpinning 9/11, Holmes (2005: 165) identifies the potency of an 'intense craving for retaliation' on the part of the plotters. In contrast to some other accounts, Holmes found that bin Laden almost never justified terrorism as a means of subjugating Western countries to the true Islamic faith. Rather his vocabulary of motives gravitated around the expression of a legitimate form of self defence. Several published accounts (Malik 2007; Maher 2007; and Husain 2007), record how large-scale conflicts (such as in Bosnia/Afghanistan/Iraq) and the symbolic violence of events such as reactions to 9/11, functioned to generate a generalized sense of anger within and across many Muslim communities. Anger that was reheated and re-worked by the dissemination of videos of abuses against Muslims and their faith symbols. Keppel (2004) develops aspects of this approach when he notes that the spectacular violence of 9/11 was designed as a provocation of such magnitude that in its over-reaction the US Government would unintentionally help to coagulate a hitherto factionalized Islamist consciousness. And as far as Keppel was concerned, it was partially successful, pushing together otherwise disparate groups under the ideological umbrella of Al-Qaeda, later refined to 'Al-Qaeda-inspired' or regional offshoots such as 'al Qaeda in Iraq'. This concurs with the findings from research on other forms of violent crime that point to the significance of anger as a motive for engaging in such acts (cf. Katz 1988).

There is though a second approach that suggests that becoming a terrorist and the social processes of 'incubation' depend not just upon the acquisition of a suitable motivation, but also upon social ties and relationships. Utilizing a form of social network analysis applied to 'open source' data, Marc Sageman (2004) has analysed the make-up of key members of Al-Qaeda (AQ). He argues that recruitment into AQ and its affiliates worked through established social relationships. This he dubbed the 'bunch of guys' theory. He maintains that one of the strongest predictors of becoming involved in AQ-inspired terrorism is knowing another individual already involved. A not dissimilar account is found in Atran's (2010) more qualitative approach, which serves to enrich our understanding of how social bonds can be harnessed to recruit and radicalize.

These social network analysis based approaches certainly appear to afford some compelling insights into the workings of AQ and its franchise organizations. They also tend to support the views proffered by analyses derived from other methods such as Burke (2004), who differentiate between an original tightly bonded core membership of AQ and subsequent more loosely affiliated activists. However, there must be some question about their overall generalizability. Situational context matters in terms of shaping how processes of recruitment and radicalization are enacted. Groups such as the Tamil Tigers, Hamas, or Hezbollah may operationalize very different approaches.

## 'BEING' A TERRORIST, 'DOING' TERRORISM

The metaphoric 'explosion' of interest in terrorism that has followed the real explosions that took place in America in 2001 has, to a significant degree, gravitated around the activities of Al-Qaeda and the perceived inception of what is referred to as 'internationalized' (Hoffman 2006) or 'transnational' (Enders and Sandler 2004) terrorism. However, the selection and depiction of these kinds of master-narrative, if presented too simplistically, have the potential to neglect the fact that in most places, most of the time, the primary causes for engaging in terrorism are localized (Laqueur 2003). Indeed, even though it has subsequently evolved as a 'network of networks' with global reach and franchises (Burke 2004), the historical orientations of AQ's core membership were towards 'the near enemy' (Wright 2007).

Evidence for this local orientation behind much terrorist activity is provided by LaFree *et al.* (2010). Based upon a database containing records of 73,961 terrorist attacks from 206 countries over a 36-year period up to and including 2006 they find a clear geographic concentration of attacks in particular countries and that these concentrations are fairly stable over time. Since 1970, 32 countries account for over three-quarters of all attacks in the database. As the authors note, such patterns of geographic and temporal clustering are remarkably reminiscent of the patterns that have been observed in relation to other kinds of serious and volume crime.

Randall Collins (2008) in his enquiry into violence across different social spaces and settings identifies an important axiom—that contrary to popular expectations, 'competent' violence is difficult to accomplish. Most of the violence that takes place in society is chaotic and messy, rather than calculating and clinical. This is particularly so at the interpersonal level and at close-quarters, where a basic 'confrontational tension' functions to render violence difficult. He contends that it is for this reason many terrorist groups adopt 'confrontation minimizing' tactics. The use of remote controlled bombs and IEDs is one example of this, but more contentiously he maintains that so is suicide bombing. According to Collins the tactic of suicide bombing enables the bomber to outwardly maintain the aura of normal appearances until the moment of detonation, thereby avoiding the need for direct interpersonal confrontation and remonstrations with potential victims. In effect, it keeps them 'de-personalized', cognitively easing the ability to envision their obliteration (though we would add that this concealment also makes it harder to stop them).

The process of converting human beings into 'human bombs' to combine dying with killing is one that appears to exert a 'gravitational pull' of fascination for a number of scholars. Unlike those who commit suicide, 90 per cent of whom are depressed or have diagnosable mental conditions, suicide attackers do not typically display such traits. Most bombers are young unmarried men, although not all are—globally around 15%

are female (Pape 2006). Suicide bombers tend to be comparatively well educated and from a higher social background when related to the communities to which they belong (Gambetta 2005; Pape 2006). In this sense their actions align fairly well with Durkheim's (1952/1897) construct of 'the altruistic suicide'.

Whilst suicide bombing is oftentimes an effective tactic, judged in terms of its capacity to secure public and political attention, and to elicit fear and fascination, it remains a relatively rare method even today. There are a panoply of other terrorist methods including kidnap, extortion, assassination, and hi-jacking that in aggregate have been more commonly deployed than suicide bombing. In respect of these methods, a frequently overlooked issue is how terrorist groups learn from each other in terms of 'what works', 'what doesn't', and 'what's promising'. There is quite literally an international trade in 'terrorist tradecraft'. For example, there is compelling evidence of contacts between the Basque separatist group ETA and Provisional IRA, and that the latter were also involved in training FARC groups in Columbia in the use of firearms and explosives.

Terrorist groups select particular methods owing to their capacity and capability to generate an asymmetric impact upon the social order. It takes only a relatively small number of motivated and skilled terrorists to induce significant social effects. For example, taking the contemporary concerns with Islamist violent extremism as an illustration, the former head of the Security Service, Dame Eliza Manningham-Buller, stated in November 2006 that the UK Security Service was monitoring some 200 networks, comprising at least 1,600 individuals, and was aware of close to 30 mass fatality plots being planned.[1] Subsequently, the Prime Minister revised these figures upwards in July 2007 to state that 2,000 individuals were being tracked.[2] The perceived need to monitor and control the activities of this comparatively small number of people was responsible for the development of an entire cross-departmental CONTEST strategy that has consumed hundreds of millions of pounds (discussed in more detail below).

## DESISTANCE FROM TERRORISM

Whilst the majority of literature on the conduct of terrorism has focused upon the prior two phases of the terrorist career, several notable recent contributions have addressed how and why people decide to cease terrorist actions. Broadly speaking, these accounts can be distinguished between those that focus upon individual decisions and those concerned with groups and collective desistance. In the former case, the key analytic issue is the processes by which individual actors elect to leave a terrorist group even though the campaign is being sustained. The latter instance concerns the processes involved in the cessation of whole campaigns and a joint decision by groups to forego future violence.

Bjorgo (2009) examined young people's disengagement from violent right wing groups based upon interviews with 50 people. He finds, in a similar manner to the

---

[1] Subsequently published as Manningham-Buller (2007). Only those with classified access can confirm or refute these data.

[2] See P. Wintour and A. Travis, 'Brown sets out sweeping but risky terror and security reforms', *The Guardian*, 26 July 2007.

factors facilitating engagement and participation, there are a range of 'pushes' and 'pulls' involved in individual patterns of desistance. Amongst the former set of factors identified are: negative social sanctions; a loss of faith in the ideology; a feeling that 'things have gone too far'; disillusionment with the inner workings of the group; a loss of status within the group; and a sense of exhaustion from the pressures of participating on an ongoing basis. In addition Bjorgo notes that disconnecting also occurs because of the attraction or 'pull' of: longing for the freedoms of a normal life; increasing physical and emotional maturity; the jeopardy created for personal future or career; new responsibilities with a spouse or children. It might be reasonably hypothesized that, over an extended period of time, the intensity of these push and pull factors is heightened by concerns about the viability of the strategy or tactics where progress in achieving aims is not evident.

Bjorgo's analysis attends to and accents a number of 'organic' social processes as causes for individual disengagement decisions. There are, of course, a number of more purposive programs whose design is to deliberately engineer the onset of desistance. One of the most high-profile examples of such approaches is the 'Saudi Counselling Program' intended to rehabilitate and reintegrate militant Islamist jihadists back into Saudi Arabian society. In a commentary upon the processes embedded within the programme, Boucek (2009) notes its base coherence with a number of other Saudi post-prison resettlement regimes, founded upon principles of benevolence and not vengeance or retribution. Acknowledging that there are only limited available data via which to measure the programme, Boucek reports that the Saudi authorities claim that as of November 2007 only 35 individuals (equating to 1–2 per cent) who have passed through the program have been re-arrested for security offences. There may of course be others whose continued offending has gone undetected, or who have subsequently acted to provide support to others.

As outlined above though, perhaps more significant than individually based unilateral decisions to leave terrorism behind is the issue of when a broader collective or social movement takes place. Cronin (2009: 203) describes the key issues succinctly in that terrorist campaigns have an uphill battle in trying to maintain momentum. Most terrorist groups disintegrate, falling under the weight of their own unpopular tactics. There is a consistent ongoing pressure upon individuals and their relationships with each other and a continual risk of implosion amongst groups emanating from mistakes, burnout, and collapse. Sometimes these stresses are nudged along by intelligent, carefully targeted pressure from the police or military.

Based upon a global, historical review of how different terrorist campaigns have ended she derives six principal conclusions:

1. Decapitation   is where the leadership of the group is either killed or captured. The consequences of such an event tend to depend upon the make-up of the group, although Cronin's analysis suggests that generally arrest induces more effect than assassination.

2. Negotiated endgame— rare examples such as the Northern Ireland Peace Process suggest that in some (limited) conditions and under some circumstances, it does appear possible to reduce violence through political processes and negotiation.

3. Achieving the objective—on occasion, terrorists cease their operations because they perceive that they have accomplished their principal objectives. The key example Cronin cites is the African National Congress in South Africa.

4. Implosion or marginalization—the decline of terrorist groups is frequently precipitated by the inability to sustain intra-group cohesion or to retain wider social support. Such tensions often present when mistakes are made in operational matters and a popular backlash is generated.

5. Repression—cases from Russia (Narodnaya Volya), Peru (Sendero Luminoso), and Turkey (Kurdistan Workers Party) amongst others provide evidence that terrorism can be concluded if overwhelming force can be leveraged in such a way as to avoid generating an increase in public support for the terrorists/freedom fighters.

6. Reorientation—participation in terrorist actions can decline should a group decide to 'transition' to an alternative *modus operandi*. For example, rather than terrorism there can be an escalation of the conflict to an insurgency or full war footing.

In outlining these ways in which terrorist campaigns decay and decline, Cronin is careful to convey that the process of moving away from terrorist violence is frequently difficult and challenging. It is not uncommon for 'splintering' to occur within the groups, and for some to try and escalate the violence to provoke a reaction and feed the conditions for sustenance of conflict, whilst at the same time their former collaborators denounce such moves. As such, even when a process of collective desistance is being progressed there is a real risk of 'spoilers'. These are acts deliberately timed and targeted to make the reduction of violence by either side more difficult. Actions by the 'Real IRA' or 'Continuity IRA' post-Peace Agreement are an example.

As Cronin's analysis intimates, appropriate interventions conducted by criminal justice agencies and/or the military, especially when they cohere with other trends, do have a role in promoting desistance from terrorism, though this is hard to separate out and quantify. Attempting to clarify this issue, Gary LaFree and his colleagues (2010) undertook to try and test precisely what impacts flow from criminal justice interventions. Informed by data on six key counter-terrorist interventions conducted in Northern Ireland between 1969 and 1992, they constructed two alternative hypotheses. The first was a 'deterrence model' founded on the belief that assertive policing would deter individuals and groups from future violence. The alternative proposition advanced was that such interventions would actually induce a 'backlash' and more violence. The analysis found that only one of the military surges appeared to have deterred violence, whereas three out of the six interventions appeared to have promoted 'backlash effects'. It is relevant in appraising these results though that the interventions tested were all assertive, intrusive, and coercive. As Wilkinson (2005: 102) contends, since 1969 the conflict in Northern Ireland exemplified a modality of counter-terrorism grounded in 'the use of military in aid of the civil power'. In this approach the military are operationalized in support of the police and civil authorities. Whilst distinct from the full militarization of counter-terrorism that has been seen elsewhere, nonetheless it represents something of a departure from the criminal justice based approach that Wilkinson maintains should always be the default option for liberal democratic polities. Thus the interventions being tested by LaFree and colleagues perhaps lacked some of the more 'soft power' dimensions that much research identifies as an important component of effective counter-terrorism.

## COUNTER-TERRORISM

The problem of crime control in late modernity has vividly demonstrated the limits of the sovereign state...In the complex, differentiated world of late modernity, effective, legitimate government must devolve power and share the work of social control with local organizations and communities. (David Garland 2001, *The Culture of Control*: 205)

In his 'culture of control' thesis, Garland (2001) crafts an argument that social order has been intentionally and unintentionally transformed by the desire to establish control over a range of criminal and disorderly behaviours. Central to Garland's argument is a process of 'responsibilisation' whereby national governments have increasingly sought to 'push' responsibility for responding to such issues 'down and out' from the centre of the state into communities and the lower echelons of their key institutions. To a significant degree, this resonates with what can be observed in relation to counter-terrorism. Taking the UK as an example, comparing the situations pre and post 2001, it is noticeable that in recent years the response to terrorism has increasingly been predicated upon enlisting communities, local policing, and other public agencies into a purportedly more holistic and rounded effort (see also Walker and Rehman, forthcoming).

The tenor of this response is exemplified in the UK Government's cross-departmental CONTEST strategy. This was first introduced in 2004 in recognition of the limitations exposed by the events of 11 September 2001 and has subsequently undergone a process of 'policy transfer' to provide the basis of the European Union's policy framework.[3] CONTEST is constructed around four key strands of activity: Prepare; Prevent; Protect; and Pursue. Of these strands the latter two most closely focus upon the kinds of activity traditionally associated with counter-terrorism. They tend to be less publicly visible, and are typically conducted by the assets of the state's security apparatus. In contrast, the former two are more innovative and public facing. They can be differentiated and defined as follows:

- Prepare—focuses upon ensuring that processes and systems are in place in anticipation of a range of different types of potential attack. This addresses both cross-governmental responses but also community resilience.

- Prevent—is concerned with activities designed to inhibit and interdict processes of violent radicalization, and those who seek to propagate extremist ideas. This will be discussed in more detail below.

[3] Strasbourg: 14469/05, 2005: 2. The Strategy is divided into the four pillars—Prevent, Protect, Pursue, and Respond—a taxonomy very redolent of the UK version.

- Protect—involves a range of activities, often derived from the principles of situational crime prevention, seeking to reduce risks and threats to elements of the critical national infrastructure. The idea being to minimize the opportunities for an attack and limit consequences should one occur.

- Pursue—is more in the traditions of police and security service involvement in counter-terrorism work. It focuses upon the identification and securing of motivated offenders.

## 'PREPARE' AND 'PROTECT'

The moves to better 'prepare' and 'protect' the social order in relation to a range of terrorist risks and threats have been credited with inducing significant shifts in the patterns of surveillance and social sorting (Lyon 2006; Gandy 2006). In an intriguing and innovative contribution, Neyland (2008) identifies how this has involved the monitoring of both people and things, with the latter altering the ontologies of a number of everyday objects. He posits that, in the post 9/11 environment, a number of hitherto mundane and ordinary things have been re-cast as potential terrorist weapons. The most obvious illustration of this would be the list of articles that it is now prohibited to take in hand luggage on board aeroplanes. Liquids, gels, and creams can only be carried in small quantities lest they carry the chemical components of a bomb. Whilst this contribution highlights how counter-terrorism considerations have come to be embedded in the routines of everyday life, it arguably neglects the significance of situation and setting in terms of how, when, and why object ontologies are adapted and altered. Most of the time knives, water, and fertilizer are just knives, water, and fertilizer. It is only through their introduction into particular social situations that the kinds of processes that Neyland identifies are triggered and gain traction.

These insights into the transformative impacts of the new, more holistic, counter-terrorism efforts on everyday situations can be developed by examining attempts to reduce what is increasingly termed 'threat finance' (Levi 2010), through the introduction of new controls and regulations within the banking system. Anti-money laundering regulations were first operationalized in 1986 as part of the 'War on Drugs'. Though some measures were developed by the Terrorist Finance Unit in Northern Ireland in the 1980s, they have been progressively 're-tooled' to respond to 'Islamist terrorism' (sic!) and 'rogue States' (Eckert and Biersteker 2010). Some money is moved via charities and via Money Service Businesses (like Western Union and MoneyGram) and by informal value transfers (Passas 2003, 2006). The latter are sometimes termed 'hawala banking' (a system that preceded formal banking and is cheaper and more efficient than banks in getting money to most developing countries).

Perhaps unsurprisingly, there are doubts about the efficacy of such approaches and debates over what the category of terrorist finance includes. Operationally, little money is required to mount a successful terrorist operation: '9/11' cost less than $500,000 to organize; and the London and Madrid bombings less than £10,000—the equivalent of fewer than 10 credit card frauds or even the savings of a few industrious workers. However, if by 'terrorist finance' one includes the costs of recruitment and preparation, and even broader ideological indoctrination, the sums involved are much larger. Whichever definition is used, it appears that cutting off the financial lifeblood of terrorism is harder to achieve in practice, than it is to urge as a solution 'in theory'.

This reflects how those interested in promoting violent extremism can obtain funds via a number of channels:

- wholly licit sources (including 'rogue states' as well as wealthy sympathizers);
- contraband (like smuggled alcohol, fuel, and tobacco);
- wholly illicit 'market offences' (e.g. drugs); and
- property crimes (fraud, robbery, and theft).

The latter three categories are covered by proceeds of crime controls, and as such, it is perhaps understandable why terrorists prefer to source their income from licit sources, bringing less risk of victim/law enforcement action against them before they have achieved their objectives. But if controls cut these sources off, displacement may occur to the easiest frauds (such as payment card frauds), or other crimes that lie within terrorist skill/contact sets.

In keeping with the more general 'direction of travel' identified previously, in order to effect these controls the banks have been 'responsibilized' (i.e. required to try to spot funds destined to aid terrorism). The expectation of the authorities is that the prospect of being identified: (a) puts potential donors on notice that they may lose their liberty and their assets for assisting terrorism or the purchase of components for proliferation, and (b) deters them from participation, or (c) leads to their apprehension and prosecution *pour décourager les autres*.

This responsibilization strategy can be traced back to the controls established in Italy in the late 1970s and in Ireland from the late 1980s to try to cut off the flow of funds to terrorists and paramilitaries. However, post-2001, such efforts accelerated markedly. The UN Security Council unanimously adopted Resolution 1373 (2001) and the EU followed, to put the funds beyond terrorist use by 'freezing' them. By the end of 2010, there were 578 Specially Designated Global Terrorists (OFAC 2011).

However, coherent with Neyland's analysis, such policy manoeuvres intrinsically raise questions about the grounds upon which particular activities or objects should generate suspicion? If bankers and other regulated bodies are to act against terrorist finance, they have to know names and/or behavioural characteristics to look for, preferably electronically, since there are billions of cross-border transactions daily and manual scrutiny is impossible. There is an inherent difficulty regarding the publication of advice on *modi operandi* of terrorism finance (and on the laundering of other forms of crime), since this inevitably gives rise to leakage to some sympathizers and to modifications (which may happen anyway).

The UK, but few other countries, has established small 'vetted groups' of Money Laundering Reporting Officers—MLROs—with formal security clearance, but general publication of suspects beyond the different sanctions lists has remained impracticable. After 9/11, substantial effort was expended within the private sector to try to develop profiles for terrorist finance. This was notwithstanding early findings from analysis of the financial background to the 9/11 plotters and operations, which showed that they were unpredictable and largely 'normal' (Roth *et al.* 2004), a view which applies to much (though not all) other terrorism financing. A substantial profitable industry has sprung up to supply automated checks on names on the various sanctions lists, which can be an expensive problem where names are capable of multiple English spellings (especially where the origins are in Arabic) and are (reasonably) presumed to be willing to engage 'fronts' to act for them. Third party firms operate only on government and court-decision-generated datasets, but will electronically check against lists of designated terrorists and Politically Exposed Persons (public officials and their immediate families) as a paid-for service. However, there are many false positives for common names, whether Arabic or not.

In practice then, controlling 'threat finance' is a modest element in the risk policing of terrorism, rather than being its core. Financial institutions have every incentive to identify terrorist financiers, but the task of building profiles without many false positives (which can serve to alienate customers) or false negatives (which alienate police and government officials) is simply too difficult. Further to which, in the case of terrorist groups financing their activities through crime, most of the offences in the West—payment card fraud, selling counterfeit goods, etc.—are not normally considered a priority by either reactive or intelligence-led policing, and are not plausibly preventable.

It is perhaps unsurprising therefore, that terrorist finance cases are not clogging up the courts or prisons. The number prosecuted in England and Wales 2001–9 was seven (in two cases in 2007 and 2008) (House of Lords 2009). As of January 2009, about £632,000 of suspected terrorist funds has been frozen under the Al-Qaida and Taliban Terrorism Order. Following cash seizures, 13 people were referred to the Metropolitan Police for suspected terrorist financing (House of Lords 2009), but what that means in practice is unclear. However, these are not the only yields. *After the event*, the pursuit of financial records enables linkages to be made; and controls may have a chilling effect on donations by the wealthy, who may fear incrimination even for *zakat* to some Islamic charities, some of whose funds may go to support terrorist group activities. But what such a situation does point to is the constraints that apply to the capacities and capabilities of government, police, and civil society actions to impact upon terrorist activities. As such, it is important to differentiate between the status of the 'law in books' and 'in action'. What governments intend through the introduction of new legislative instruments, and the tenor of public rhetoric and debate, should not be equated with what happens in practice.

### 'PREVENT'

> After all, a symptom is only a symptom, even if it does mark the place where you start digging. If, through whatever excising, you manage to lop off one symptom, and do nothing about the dynamics, another symptom is likely to pop up; it can have a quite different face and yet wear the same leer. (Goffman 1967: 138)

Erving Goffman here articulates one of the fundamental policy dilemmas in designing responses to all kinds of social pathologies—where to strike the balance between individual treatment and more collective pre-emptive intervention? In the environs of crime and terrorism, such considerations tend to be especially politically freighted because of the inevitable risks of false positives, and because preventative interventions often necessitate curtailing individual and collective liberty. For decision-makers though, such curtailments have to be weighed within a risk calculus of not doing something that could ultimately prevent mass destruction and death. It is for this reason that, in the post 9/11 environment, a precautionary posture has become increasingly evident. Many countries have, albeit to varying degrees, invested in developing preventative dimensions to their counter-terrorism programmes.

Of the four strands of the UK Contest strategy it is 'Prevent' that has proven to be the most politically contentious and publicly debated. There have been repeated allegations that it amounts to little more than a governmental programme to 'spy' upon communities (Kundani 2009) and has been profoundly alienating in terms of Muslim communities' relationships with the police and wider governmental apparatus. Given such claims, it is of note that Prevent has been subject to two systematic revisions, first in 2008 and then in 2011. The former was triggered by a sense that whilst the CONTEST strategy had been introduced in 2004, insufficient attention had been paid to developing genuinely preventative modes of working and as a consequence it was overly reliant upon more established 'Pursue' practices. The revisions in 2011 were more explicitly ideologically motivated by a change in government the year before. The new Coalition were of the view that whereas the previous iterations of Prevent focused upon integrating three key domains of: counter-radicalization; de-radicalization; and community cohesion building, they now wanted to establish a much clearer distinction between counter-terrorism work and activities addressing integration and cohesion.

That such revisions to Prevent have been deemed necessary is perhaps indicative of both how challenging it is to deliver counter-terrorism differently from established models and the issues that any such attempts necessarily turn up. In a recent study commissioned by the UK Government, Innes et al. (2011) sought to examine the effects of the police role in Prevent. Importantly, contra the oft levied charge that the instigation of Prevent has functioned to alienate Muslim communities, a number of indicators contained in the British Crime Survey revealed only limited evidence to support this claim. Overall, they found that people from Muslim faith backgrounds exhibit higher levels of trust and confidence in the police when compared with the general population. Young Muslim men had marginally more negative perceptions and attitudes than did their general population compatriots, but even then, nearly 4 out of 10 surveyed expressed positive views of policing.

An important component of this same study was in determining the strategies and tactics being engaged to deliver Prevent. The fieldwork evidence collated across four sites suggests several key areas of innovation. First, there is a shift to an overt counter-terrorism policing role. Whereas the classic mode of counter-terrorism policing has been in plain clothes and clandestine, Prevent officers were in uniform and explicitly presented themselves as 'counter-terrorism officers' when interacting with the public. The logic underpinning this approach being that, in being transparent with the public in this way, they are conveying that this area of police work is a legitimate area of concern. Several other studies have also identified the development of this overt counter-terrorism policing, but have also diagnosed a certain amount of public confusion stemming from the presence of overt and covert officers working in the same neighbourhoods (Thiel 2008; Pickering, McCulloch, and Wright-Neville 2008).

A second set of innovations identified centre upon the use of 'disruptions'. These are modes of intervention intended to impact upon illegal or troublesome activities without recourse to criminal law. For individuals who were 'of concern', rather than deemed as posing a clear threat, uniformed officers from the Prevent teams would pay them a visit and have a 'chat' with them. As one Inspector described it,

> Another Mosque in (xxxx) rang up one of my sergeants and said we've got three guys coming here, and they were doing the proper radicalization thing. They were trying to draw kids in, they were trying to have little meetings, they were being quite radical. We'd appreciate your support if you could come and help us, and speak to these three individuals because we don't want them here but we're a little bit concerned. So [Name]'s gone down, confronted the three individuals. The Mosque don't want you here, what are you about? Do you want to talk to me about it? They didn't. They went. We know where they went. (Innes *et al.* 2011: 28)

On the basis of the research conducted, Innes *et al.* identify that the delivery of Prevent has been evolving and developing over time. They suggest that four key intervention modes now underpin how it is being practised, conceptualized upon the basis of who defines the presence of a problem and who assumes responsibility for delivering the response. These four modes are set out in Table 22.1 below.

Table 22.1  The Four Prevent Policing Intervention Modes

|  | Police defined | Community defined |
|---|---|---|
| **Police delivered** | Protective | Type 1 Co-production |
| **Community delivered** | Type 2 Co-production | Mobilization |

- Protective—is where the police clearly 'own' the intervention. The tactics they engage can vary from disruption to law enforcement, but the crucial aspect is that the nature of the problem is determined and responded to by the police.

- Mobilization—is the converse to the above. In effect, the problem is identified by the community and they harness their informal social control resources to construct a self-help response. This response can range from violence through to awareness raising. Critically though, police and their local authority partners are reduced to bystanders, or indeed they may be wholly unaware of the activity.

- Type 1 Co-production—in some situations the police act to deal collaboratively with issues brought to their attention by the community. This type of collaborative working has been previously documented in other situations in the research literature. Within Prevent, this mode is engaged for two main reasons. First, because a problem is sufficiently troubling that it is beyond the scope of purely community-led interventions to impact upon it. Second, on some occasions police can fashion a response in order to build community trust and confidence.

- Type 2 Co-production—the final ideal-type is where police identify a problematic issue, but enable or encourage community-based actors to deal with it. This can either be through material/practical support, or more tacit forms of backing. Engaging this style of collaboration in Prevent work reflects that some of the problems encountered are complex and cannot be effectively treated through application of the criminal law. To the best of our knowledge, this style of working has not been previously identified by researchers.

In the US, the federal structure of law enforcement has meant that the impetus for reform of the counter-terrorism apparatus has manifested itself rather differently. Nevertheless, as in the UK there has been significant institutional reform introduced, most obviously with the inception of the Department for Homeland Security intended to improve coordination across America's complex counter-terrorism landscape. Moreover, although not tied into a systematic programme in the way that has happened in the UK, similar processes of co-opting local law enforcement into CT efforts have occurred.

In his study in Dearborne, Michigan, Thacher (2005) describes the emergence of joint-terrorism task forces (JTTFs). According to his analysis, JTTFs emerged as an improvised solution to the problem of getting local law enforcement agencies to engage more concretely in counter-terrorism policing. This was necessitated because police agencies were largely resistant to central government direction to implement proactive and intrusive counter-terrorism methods. Their preference instead was to implement 'community protection' strategies grounded in target-hardening and emergency response. The reason for this was that they felt that the kinds of surveillance required imperilled their crime control mission, in that it would cause minority communities to question the agencies overall legitimacy. The instigation of JTTFs was a way of trying to circumvent such resistance and to join-up the infamously complex policing and intelligence landscape of North America.

### Dilemmas, contradictions, and unintended consequences

What Thacher's (2005) account foregrounds are the complexities and unintended consequences that flow from attempts to convert policy into practice. This is a theme further developed in Fosher's (2009) ethnographic narrative of 'homeland security' work in and around the city of Boston. She focuses upon the interstices between national policy and local delivery, and in particular how the former is translated into the latter. Rather than a smooth and seamlessly operating machine, there is a confused and complex arena based largely upon improvised practices. Over time some of these improvisations sediment into routines, conventions and standard operating procedures, whilst others have to be periodically adapted and reconfigured. The picture she paints is of a constant effort to decode and interpret policy utterances and render them into forms that are meaningful and practically do-able. This activity of translation is conjoined with finding ways to coordinate the work of different agencies. Particularly in respect of counter-terrorism issues, these attempts to establish coordination across agencies are subverted by the 'need to know' secrecy principle that is frequently attached to information about terrorists and terrorism.

Secrecy as both a normative and operational imperative is a defining quality of counter-terrorism work (Innes and Thiel 2008). In an incisive contribution, Brodeur (2010) suggests that secrecy is applied in two main ways in 'high policing' forms of counter-terrorism. The first use he labels 'radical secrecy' which he connects to the 'absorbent' qualities of security and intelligence agencies. In relation to more mundane forms of intelligence used to fight crime in 'low policing' activities, he posits that the value of intelligence is defined by its operational usefulness. But this is not so in relation to terrorist threats against the state where agencies are driven by a more existential 'need to know'. Here there is a tendency for more and more data to be 'absorbed' by the institutional structures without any imperative for it to be translated into visible outputs. Brodeur refines his account by suggesting that from time to time, security and intelligence agencies may choose to partially 'lift the veil' over their activities and in so doing strategically operationalize a 'chilling effect' over selected adversaries.

Alongside the transformations of local institutional structures then, there have been similar manoeuvres at the international level. It has been argued that given the mobility of contemporary terrorist groups and actors there is a need to develop far more effective intelligence sharing mechanisms between states if they are to be able to respond effectively to the full range of risks and threats that they will encounter (Jacobsen 2006). For this reason it has been suggested that there is a pressing need to establish some form of multilateral intelligence clearing house in order that such data can be quickly moved between states that know about a threat to those that might need to know without comprising the source or its methods (Ganor 2005; Steven and Gunaratna 2004).

Attending to such developments is important in that they are illuminating how the institutional apparatus for counter-terrorism is being rendered more complex and sophisticated. For example, conceptual discussions of counter-terrorism in the academic literature typically distinguish 'military' and 'criminal justice' oriented modes (Steven and Gunaratna 2004), and between the adoption of 'offensive' and 'defensive' postures (Crelinstein 2009). The empirical examples noted above, suggest that such framings are potentially reductionist and liable to fail to capture some more subtle movements in how counter-terrorist responses are being arranged. In particular, there is a sense in which the offensive and defensive are being blended into each other so that key counter-terrorist agencies simultaneously enact more proactive and reactive measures. Likewise, whilst there is a case for suggesting that military and criminal justice responses are being 'joined up', an even more profound movement may be in the routinized connectivity being established between 'high' and 'low' policing. For example, the delivery of Prevent policing in the UK is predicated upon the absorption of a number of principles, processes, and practices originating in Neighbourhood Policing (Innes et al. 2011; Thiel 2008). Potentially even more consequential though, are the attempts to circumvent the criminal justice system to deal with potential terrorism risks through the use of disruptions. The involvement of citizens and the harnessing of informal social control in dealing directly with terrorism problems seems to be an area neglected in many extant conceptualizations.

Some commentators have questioned whether these contemporary configurations are sustainable. For example, Deflem (2010) is not convinced that it is possible to reconcile and harmonize the tensions that underlie the various components of the contemporary counter-terrorism apparatus. Pressures for unilateral action to defend against specific threats whilst simultaneously encouraging multilateral coordinated actions to degrade terrorist campaigns, whilst also sequencing military and criminal justice initiatives, may simply be too complex. Given the difficulties that inhere in reconciling such tensions, some commentators maintain that local domestic policing should be insulated from and eschew participation in counter-terrorism work (Manning 2010), such activities being the proper preserve of specialized central agencies.

In the previous section we saw that terrorism is communicative action deliberately designed to communicate a message. Herein, we have charted how the message of a series of terrorist acts has induced a profound institutional reconfiguration of the counter-terrorism apparatus in Western Europe and America. This perhaps elucidates how terrorist acts can function as signal crimes (Innes 2006). A signal crime is an illegal act that serves to signal the presence of wider risk and threat. Its significance is that it causes changes to how people think, feel, and behave (Innes 2004). Herein, we have observed how at an institutional level the ways in which states think, feel, and behave has undergone significant changes. This leads us on to the processes by which we perceptually apprehend acts of terrorism and their proponents.

## SOCIAL REACTIONS TO TERRORISM

There is never the fear of too much control, but of too much chaos. If we are losing control, we must try to take control. (Stan Cohen 1985, *Visions of Social Control*: 235)

In *Visions of Social Control,* Cohen plots the transformative 'master narratives' that explain how our collective responses to troublesome and problematic behaviours have been crafted around an expansion of 'hard' and 'soft' mechanisms of control that reach across and more deeply into the routines of social life. To a significant degree, the dominant trajectory in the evolution of the counter-terrorism apparatus, as described in the previous section, is coherent with these broader and deeper patterns. But what we have not yet addressed is the question of '*why* so many Western nation states have felt it necessary to develop such wide-ranging counter-terrorism programmes?' for, as several commentators have noted, applying an 'objective' risk calculus to terrorism, as a public problem, terrorism causes less harm to the majority of people than many other issues (Furedi 2007). It is in trying to answer this question of why terrorism is able to demand such attention, that the quotation from Cohen starts to hint at a potential explanation.

As acts of communicative violence designed to challenge normally taken for granted values and routines, terrorist incidents dramatically encode the limitations of the state's responsibility to protect its citizenry, and the potential vulnerability of key values and assumptions. It is for this reason that Smelser (2007: 85) contends that terrorism and counter-terrorism are effectively engaged in a 'rhetorical battle of symbols'. In Cohen's (1985) terms such assaults connote the capacity for chaos, if control cannot or will not be exerted.

One of the particular challenges associated with configuring a response that functions symbolically as well as practically is avoiding the potential for over-reaction. Numerous analyses now identify that one of the ways terrorism seeks to work is as a 'provocative intervention', whereby the state in fashioning its response, effectively over-reacts thereby unintentionally persuading more members of the public to sympathize with the terrorist cause. Generally then, terrorist attacks are designed to communicate two messages simultaneously to different audiences. For the general public, the act should instil terror. But at the same time, for those thought to be affiliated in some way with the cause (or at least with the potential to affiliate) the violence should work as a 'wedge issue' fracturing them away from any sense of belonging to the mainstream community. This is sometimes accomplished by virtue of the act itself, but more often by the counter-reaction on the part of the 'wounded' authorities.

The dynamics of these social processes of action and reaction, counter-action and counter-reaction are best articulated in Slucka's (1989) compelling and subtle ethnography of social support for the IRA and INLA in the Divis Flats housing estate in Belfast at the height of 'the troubles'. He shows how attempts to secure social support underpinned the actions of both terrorists and counter-terrorists.

Whereas most accounts bifurcate audiences into supporters and non-supporters of terrorism, Sluka suggests that in Catholic Belfast, whilst a minority of the local populace exhibited 'hard-line' support for the Provisional IRA (PIRA) and Irish National Liberation Army (INLA), the majority remained more ambivalent. For this latter group, their motivations and beliefs shifted and adapted in response to the actions undertaken by the active terrorists and their auxiliaries, and those interventions performed by the state-led Royal Ulster Constabulary and British military. Acknowledging the delicate and contingent position they thus occupied, the terrorist groups sought to provide a range of 'social services' to try and sustain active or, at least, passive, social support within the Catholic communities. The PIRA, for example, focused upon the provision of social control services in the absence of an effective order-maintenance presence by the police. As Sluka documents, engaging in such a role was fraught with problems and risks, and the fact that the IRA continued to perform it is indicative of how important the need to maintain social support was perceived to be. However, as he concludes, these efforts were far less significant as a determinant of social support than the influence of the coercive tactics and strategies applied by the British and Irish authorities.

In the context of moral claims and counterclaims to win over social audiences, one of the ways in which terrorists pursue their aims is by provoking states into a form of de-legitimizing over-reaction. During the 'troubles' in Northern Ireland it became clear that decisions to instigate a system of detention without trial and the so-called 'Diplock Courts' (the suspension of jury trials) were strategic mistakes resulting in significant increases in popular support for the IRA. The counterproductive effects of this policy was subsequently recognized and the Diplock system withdrawn. Yet, this retraction was of little consequence in offsetting the damage done to the legitimacy of the British authorities in the eyes of Irish Catholics. The cumulative impacts of the Government's legislative innovations, in conjunction with a series of specific coercive operations, led to the perception by Irish Catholics that they were being collectively viewed as a 'suspect community' (Hillyard 1993).

The need to secure and sustain legitimacy has motivated Bobbitt (2008), reflecting on the contemporary scene, to elevate this to a primary imperative and to urge states to avoid the tendency to over-react when challenged by terrorist provocations. Cognizant of how hard this can often be, he concedes that in order to facilitate effective responses the legislative frameworks deployed may require some reconfiguration.

Such considerations pose an obvious question about just how widespread support for terrorist actions tends to be. In relation to concerns about Islamist terrorism a number of estimates have been produced. For example, the former head of the Security Service stated on the basis of polling evidence, that some 100,000 UK citizens thought the attacks in 2005 were in some way justified (Manningham-Buller 2007). Whilst such categoric claims based upon polling data need to be treated with caution, that some younger Muslims are evincing increased support for more radical perspectives, is supported by other surveys. For instance, one survey of British Muslims in October 2006 found that 82 per cent of respondents believed British Muslims have become more politically radicalized and 81 per cent believe the 'war on terror' is really a 'war on Islam' (The 1990 Trust 2006). This is set against a backdrop of an increasing sense of separation (NOP 2006) where some young Muslims are turning to a politicized version of their religion in a search for identity and meaning (Kepel 2004; Policy Exchange 2007).

Looking beyond the UK, results of the Pew Global Attitudes Survey (2005) reported that 24 per cent of Muslim respondents thought there were times when suicide bombing is justifiable and 22 per cent felt the 7/7 London bombings were in some way justified. Not dissimilar patterns were evident in a YouGov survey in July 2005, where 24 per cent of respondents had some sympathy for the feelings/motivations of the 7/7 bombers and 56 per cent said they could understand why the 7/7 bombers behaved in that way (YouGov/Daily Telegraph Survey; 27 July 2005 http://cdn.yougov.com/today_uk_import/YG-Archives-pol-dTel-Muslims-050725.pdf). In the same survey, 14 per cent said they were aware of groups of young British Muslims who are preaching hatred of the West and 41 per cent said they believed Muslims would be reluctant to report suspicious behaviour to police for fear of getting other Muslims into trouble. In January 2007 the UK think tank Policy Exchange reported that 13 per cent of the Muslims aged between 16–24 surveyed said they 'admire organisations like Al-Qaeda that are prepared to fight the West'.

We know less about the dynamics of social support in relation to the many other far more localized terrorist campaigns that have taken place in countries around the world. This is perhaps inevitable given that both states and their terrorist adversaries are directly engaged in attempts to mould and mobilize public opinion towards their definition of the situation. Moreover, it is by no means clear how much support is required to prosecute an effective terrorist campaign. Indeed, the whole point of resorting to terrorism as a strategy is that it allows for a relatively small number of individuals, with relatively few social and economic resources, to contest and challenge a far more powerful opponent.

The counterpoint to the concern outlined above with understanding and gauging levels of social support for terrorism, is the consequences of terrorist acts for the perceptions and attitudes of the assailed population. Obviously terrorist attacks can sharpen and heighten public concerns about such attacks, but the extent to which and under what conditions, such assaults corrode mainstream public opinion is more ambiguous. Ganor (2005: 263) marshals a range of claims that, by the mid-1990s, the long-running situation in Israel had eroded almost any sense of personal security for Israeli citizens. It seems doubtful however, we can assume that such negative impacts can be detected elsewhere. It may well be that such impacts are relatively confined to long-running terrorist campaigns, and that in the shorter term greater community resilience might be more normal.

## CONCLUSION: FROM TERRORISM TO TERRORISMS

This chapter has sought to trace out some of the ways in which ideas originating in the study of crime and social reactions to crime might usefully be applied to understanding terrorism as a social problem in democratic societies. The argument propounded has not been that terrorism should be defined purely as 'crime', nor that it is directly analogous with criminal behaviour. Rather, the suggestion has been that some of the ways in which crime has been attended to, focusing especially upon how it is socially constructed, the 'career' paths of motivations and actions, and the social control responses to them, might illuminate new insights in respect of terrorism.

Conceptually this might promote a shift from talking about 'terrorism' to 'terrorisms'. As students of crime and its control have long recognized, definitions and labels matter. An adaptation in terminology might better acknowledge how the performance of terrorist acts encompasses a plurality of different combinations of motivations, technical skills, and social networks. Reference to a singular noun tends to obscure and obfuscate these differences. Following this line of thought, the research agenda should focus less upon trying to establish a comprehensive and all-encompassing definition, than constructing a theoretically and empirically coherent typology of the main species of terrorism. Just as we talk about and understand that there are different crimes, so we need to develop and agree a similar frame of reference for this kind of political violence.

An additional benefit that might be accrued from such an approach is in understanding more precisely what the connections between 'crimes' and 'terrorisms' actually are. A number of commentators have posited that terrorism should be treated as ontologically similar to particular types of crime—particularly organized crime. Based upon our reading of the extant literature though, such an approach seems to be both conceptually and empirically lacking. Some species of terrorism are quite closely aligned with the social organization of organized crime, but others are not. On occasion, terrorism has transitioned into organized crime, and vice versa. There are forms of terrorism effectively conducted by individual actors, devoid of any material support from others, whereas other types of terrorism are nurtured and supported by a vast array of illicit activities. There are still other modes where the illegal violence is undergirded by entirely legal and licit behaviours. Thus a preliminary framework for conceptualizing the different types of terrorisms should account for a range of factors, including: (i) the degree of social organization involved; (ii) motivations and aspirations of participants; (iii) whether the precursor activities are themselves criminal or legal acts; (iv) the particular techniques and technical skills involved in performing the violent act; (v) the extent of tacit and active social support present in the social environment; and (vi) the relationship of the act to its political surround.

Extending this line of thinking, in terms of comprehending how and why terrorism arises and diminishes, it is vital to attend to the influence of counter-terrorism measures. Fundamentally, there is an interactive relationship between terrorism and counter-terrorism as those arrayed on both sides seek to tactically and strategically out-manoeuvre their opponents. It is perhaps best conceptualized as a process of mutual adaptation whereby shifts or innovations by one side trigger or are liable to induce reactive alterations on the other.

In focusing upon the role of counter-terrorism there remains a profound question about why terrorism is able to command such attention? All democratic states have implemented elaborate security and intelligence apparatuses as part of their core operations, charged with managing the response to the range of terrorisms being confronted. This raises considerations, for example, of why policing agencies are thought to be insufficient for tackling this kind of violence? Obviously, police are enmeshed and engaged within the arrangements for preventing and responding to terrorism across all liberal democracies, but in almost all cases, they tend to be subservient to other more specialized military and intelligence arms of the state. Given that policing is a generalized repository for the states' capacity to respond to a range of socially harmful and individually injurious acts, what is it about terrorism that differentiates it so?

Might it be that some forms of terrorism acquire such salience on the grounds that they pose an existential threat to liberal democratic institutions? Again this returns us to the need to establish a satisfactory framework for conceptualizing the different terrorisms. In the case of situations such as those in Northern Ireland and Israel, the long-running campaigns of political violence have fundamentally altered the social order. But as reviewed in the previous sections, such cases tend to be outliers. Most terrorist groups 'organically' implode or are brought down by the countermeasures set for them. Moreover, when viewed in aggregate, the 'harm' caused by terrorism, in most cases, is probably less than the aggregate harm resulting from many other kinds of risks and threats.

Such equivocations notwithstanding, if one attempts to 'see like a state' (Scott 1999), it does appear that there is something different about terrorist attacks. This quality seems to derive from the 'signal value' of such assaults, rather than the actual material violence engaged. As forms of communicative violence, such acts matter because of how they are deliberately designed as assaults upon fundamental, core, shared values. Moreover, a successful terrorist attack dramatically illuminates the limits of these values, and the capacity of states founded upon them to afford protection. Thus it is in terms of what such acts intend to signal that such configurations of violence can be differentiated from other forms of violence that are more readily constructed as crimes.

## ■ SELECTED FURTHER READING

As noted in the chapter, the literature on terrorism and counter-terrorism, including both academic and informed comment, has been proliferating at a considerable rate in recent years. There are now a number of texts giving a general overview of the field. The best of these are Richardson (2006), Wilkinson (2001), and Hoffman (2006). A more explicitly sociological perspective is provided by Smelser (2007). This starts well but progressively loses its sense of incision and purpose. For those coming to the subject of terrorism from a criminological background the collection of articles in the *British Journal of Criminology*, July 2010 will be interesting. Grabosky and Stohle's (2010) short book also provides a clearly written overview of the key issues. It is worthwhile looking at some of the policy and practice documents issued by governments.

## ■ REFERENCES

ALTHEIDE, D. (2006), *Terrorism and the Politics of Fear*, Lanham, MD: Rowman & Littlefield.

ATRAN, S. (2010), *Talking to the Eneny: Violent Extremism, Sacred Values and What it Means to be Human*, London: Allen Lane.

BECKER, H. (1963), *Outsiders: Studies in the Sociology of Deviance*, Illinois: Free Press.

BJORGO, T. (2009), 'Processes of disengagement from violent groups of the extreme right', in T. Bjorgo and J. Horgan (eds), *Leaving Terrorism Behind*, London: Routledge.

BLACK, D. (2004), 'The geometry of terrorism', *Sociological Theory*, 22(1): 14–25.

BOBBITT, P. (2008), *Terror and Consent: The Wars for the Twenty First Century*, New York: Alfred Knopf.

BOUCEK, C. (2009), 'Extremist re-education and rehabilitation in Saudi Arabia', in T. Bjorgo and J. Horgan (eds), *Leaving Terrorism Behind*, London: Routledge.

BRATTON, W. and KELLING, G. (2006), *Policing Terrorism*, Civic Bulletin No. 43, Manhattan Lust for Policy Research. www.manhattan-institute.org/ html/cb_43.htm.

BRODEUR, J-P. (2010), *The Policing Web*, New York: Oxford University Press.

BURKE, J. (2004), *Al-Qaeda: The True Story of Radical Islam*, London: Penguin.

COHEN, S. (2001), *States of Denial: Knowing About Atrocities and Suffering*, Cambridge: Polity.

COLLINS, R. (2008), *Violence: A Micro-Sociological Perspective*, Princeton: Princeton University Press.

CRELINSTEN, R. (2009), *Counter-Terrorism*, Cambridge: Polity Press.

CROMER, G. (2001), 'Terrorist tales', in G. Cromer (ed.), *Narratives of Violence*, Aldershot: Ashgate.

DEFLEM, M. (2010), *The Policing of Terrorism: Organizational and Global Perspectives*, New York: Routledge.

DURKHEIM, E. (1952/1897), *Suicide: A Study in Sociology*, London: Routledge & Kegan Paul.

ENDER, W. and SANDLER, T. (2004), 'What do we know about the substitution effect in transnational terrorism', in A. Silke (ed.), *Research on Terrorism: Trends, Achievements and Failures*, London: Frank Cass.

ENGLISH, R. (2008), *Terrorism: How to Respond*, Oxford: Oxford University Press.

FOSHER, K. (2008), *Under Construction: Making Homeland Security at the Local Level*, Chicago: University of Chicago Press.

FUREDI, F. (2007), *Invitation to Terror: The Expanding Empire of the Unknown*, London: Continuum.

GAMBETTA, D. (2005), 'Can we make sense of suicide missions?', in D. Gambetta (ed.), *Making Sense of Suicide Missions*, Oxford: Oxford University Press.

GANDY, O. (2006), 'Data mining, surveillance and discrimination in the post 9–11 environment', in K. Haggerty and R. Ericson (eds), *The New Politics of Surveillance and Visibility*, Toronto. University of Toronto Press.

GANOR, B. (2005), *The Counter-Terrorism Puzzle: A Guide for Decision-Makers*, Edison, NJ.: Transaction.

GARLAND, D. (2001), *The Culture of Control*, Oxford: Oxford University Press.

GEARTY, C. (2007), 'Dilemmas of terror', *Prospect*, (October) 34–38.

GOFFMAN, E. (1959), 'The moral career of the mental patient', *Psychiatry*, 22(2): 123–42.

—— (1967), *Interaction Ritual: Essays on Face-to-Face Behaviour*, New York: Pantheon Books.

HILLYARD, P. (1993), *Suspect Community: Peoples' Experience of the prevention of terrorism Acts in Britain*, London: Pluto Press.

HOFFMAN, B. (2006), *Inside Terrorism*, 2nd edn, New York: Columbia University Press.

HOLMES, S. (2005), 'Al-Qaeda, September 11, 2001', in D. Gambetta, *Making Sense of Suicide Missions*, Oxford: Oxford University Press.

HORGAN, J. (2005), *The Psychology of Terrorism*, London: Routledge.

HOUSE OF LORDS (2009), *Money laundering and the financing of terrorism: Volume 2 Evidence*, European Union Committee, 19th Report of Session 2008–09, HL Paper 132–II.

INNES, M. (2004), 'Signal crimes and signal disorders: notes on deviance as communicative action', *British Journal of Sociology*, 55(3): 335–55.

—— (2006), 'Policing uncertainty: countering terror through community intelligence and democratic policing', *Annals of the American Academy of Political and Social Science*, 605: 222–41.

—— and THIEL, D. (2008), 'Policing Terror', in T. Newburn (ed.), *Handbook of Policing*, 2nd edn, Cullompton: Willan.

——, ABBOTT, L., LOWE, T., and ROBERTS, C. (2007), *Hearts and Minds and Eyes and Ears: Reducing Radicalisation Risks Through Reassurance-Oriented Policing*, London: ACPO.

JACOBSON, M. (2006), *The West at War: US and European Counterterrorism Efforts, Post-September 11*, Washington: Institute for Near-East Policy.

KEAN, T. and HAMILTON, L. (2004), *The 9/11 Commission Report*. New York: W.W. Norton.

KEPPEL, G. (2004), *The War for Muslim Minds: Islam and the West*, Cambridge, Ma.: The Belknap Press of Harvard University Press.

KILCULLAN, D. (2009), *The Accidental Guerrilla: Fighting Small Wars in the Midst of a Big One*, New York: Oxford University Press.

KUNDANI, A. (2009), *Spooked! How Not to Prevent Violent Extremism*, London: Institute of Race Relations.

LAFREE, G., MORRIS, N., and DUGAN, L. (2010), 'Cross-national patterns of terrorism: Comparing trajectories for total, attributed and fatal attacks 1970–2006', *British Journal of Criminology*, 50(4): 622–49.

LAPAN, H. and SANDLER, T. (1988), 'To bargain or not to bargain: That is the question', *American Economic Review*, 78(2):16–21.

LAQUEUR, W. (2001), *A History of Terrorism*, New York: Transaction.

—— (2004), *No End To War: Terrorism in the Twenty-First Century*, New York: Continuum.

LEVI, M. (2010), 'Combating the financing of terrorism: A history and assessment of the control of "threat finance"', *British Journal of Criminology Special Issue Terrorism: Criminological Perspectives*, 50(4): 650–69.

LYON, D. (2006), '9/11, synopticon, and scopophilia: watching and being watched', in K. Haggerty and R Ericson (eds), *The New Politics of Surveillance and Visibility*, Toronto: University of Toronto Press.

MANNING, P. (2010), *Democratic Policing in a Changing World*, Boulder: Paradigm.

MANNINGHAM-BULLER, E. (2007), 'The international terrorist threat to the United Kingdom', in P. Hennessy (ed.), *The New Protective State: Government, Intelligence and Terrorism*, London: Continuum.

OFAC (2011), *Terrorist Assets Report 2010*, Washington, DC: US Treasury Department, www.treasury.gov/resource-center/sanctions/Documents/tar2010.pdf.

PAPE, R. (2005), *Dying To Win: The Strategic Logic of Suicide Terrorism*, Random House. New York.

PASSAS, N. (2003), *Informal Value Transfer Systems, Money Laundering and Terrorism*, Washington D.C.: Report to the National Institute of Justice (NIJ) and Financial Crimes Enforcement Network (FINCEN). https://www.ncjrs.gov/pdffiles1/nij/grants/208301.pdf.

—— (2006), 'Fighting terror with error: the counter-productive regulation of informal value transfers', *Crime, Law and Social Change*, 45(4–5): 315–36.

PEW GLOBAL ATTITUDES PROJECT, *Islamic Extremism: Common Concern for Muslim and Western Publics*, July 2005. www.pewglobal.org/reports/display.php?ReportID=248

PICKERING, S., MCCULLOCH, J., and WRIGHT-NEVILLE, D. P. (2008), *Counter-terrorism Policing: Community, Cohesion and Security*, Springer: New York.

POPULUS/POLICY EXCHANGE LIVING SURVEY, *Living Apart Together: British Muslims and the Paradox of Multiculturalism*, January 2007.

www.policyexchange.org.uk/images/publications/pdfs/Living_Apart_Together_-_Jan__07.pdf.

POST, J., RUBY, K., AND SHAW, E. (2002), 'The radical group in context 1: An integrated framework for the analysis for group risk for terrorism', *Studies in Conflict and Terrorism*, 25(2): 73–100.

RICHARDSON, L. (2006), *What Terrorists Want: Understanding the Terrorist Threat*, London: John Murray.

RAPOPORT, D. (1988), 'Messianic sanctions for terror', *Comparative Politics*, 20: 195–213.

ROTH, J., GREENBURG, D., and WILLE, S. (2004), *Monograph on Terrorist Financing*, Staff Report to the Commission, Washington, DC: National Commission on Terrorist Attacks Upon the United States, www.9-11commission.gov/staff_statements/911_TerrFin_Monograph.pdf.

SAGEMAN, M. (2004), *Understanding Terror Networks*, Philadelphia: University of Pennsylvania Press.

SCHMID, A. and JONGMAN, A. (1988), *Political Terrorism: A Research Guide to Concepts, Theories, Data Bases and Literature*, Amsterdam: North Holland.

SCOTT, J. (1999), *Seeing Like a State*, New Haven: Yale University Press.

SILKE, A. (2004), 'The road less travelled: recent trends in terrorism research', in A. Silke (ed.), *Research on Terrorism: Trends, Achievements and Failures*, London: Frank Cass.

—— (2008), 'Holy Warriors. Exploring the Psychological Processes of Jihadi Radicalization', *European Journal of Criminology*, 5: 99–123.

SLUCKA, J. (1989), *Hearts and Minds, Water and Fish: Support for the IRA and INLA in a Northern Ireland Ghetto*, Connecticut: JAI Press.

SMELSER, N. (2007), *The Faces of Terrorism: Social and Psychological Dimensions*, Princeton: Princeton University Press.

STEVEN, G. and GUNARATNA, R. (2004), *Counter-terrorism: A Reference Handbook*, Santa Barbara: ABC Clio.

SUTHERLAND, D. and CRESSEY, D. (1955), *Principles of Criminology*, 5th edn, Philadelphia: Lippincott.

SYKES, G. and MATZA, D. (1957), 'Techniques of neutralization. A theory of delinquency', *American Sociological Review*, 22(6): 664–70.

THACHER, D. (2005), 'The local role in Homeland Security', *Law and Society Review*, 39(5): 635–76.

THIEL, D. (2008), *Policing Terrorism. A Review of the Evidence*, London: Police Foundation.

TURK, A. T. (2004), 'Sociology of Terrorism', *Annual Review of Sociology*, 30: 271–86.

WALKER, C. and REHMAN, J. (2012), 'Prevent Responses to Jihadi Extremism', in V. Ramraj, M. Hor, K. Roach, and G. Williams (eds), *Global Anti-Terrorism Law and Policy*, 2nd edn, Cambridge: Cambridge University Press.

WARDLAW, G. (1982), *Political Terrorism: Theory Tactics and Counter-Measures*, Cambridge: Cambridge University Press.

WILKINSON, P. (2001), *Terrorism Versus Democracy: The Liberal State Response*, Abingdon: Frank Cass.

WRIGHT, L. (2007), *The looming Tower: Al-Qaeda's Road to 9/11*, London: Penguin.

# 23

# DRUGS, ALCOHOL, AND CRIME

*Fiona Measham and Nigel South*

## INTRODUCTION

Illegal and legal drugs, including the most popular drug in the UK, alcohol, remain subjects of intense political, policy, and—for many people—personal interest. At the same time they are subjects surrounded by myths and confusions. The illegal status of some drugs but not others (e.g. medicines) reflects judgements and classifications in domestic laws and international agreements (Bennett and Holloway 2005: 2–5; McAllister 2000; Ruggiero 1999). In Britain the classification of illegal drugs is a tiered system reflecting official perceptions of their relative harmfulness at a particular moment in history. Thus Class A includes heroin and other strong opiates, cocaine, LSD, and ecstasy (MDMA); Class B includes amphetamines, cannabis, and barbiturates while Class C includes tranquillizers and some mild stimulants.

In terms of general effects, alcohol and drugs such as tranquillizers and heroin have a depressant effect on the nervous system; caffeine, amphetamines, cocaine, and tobacco are stimulants; LSD and magic mushrooms distort perceptions; whilst some drugs straddle these categories: for example, cannabis, a depressant drug, and ecstasy, a stimulant drug, both have mild hallucinogenic properties. However, in relation to all drug use, actual behaviour and subjective experience will be strongly shaped by other influences, such as culture, context, and expectations (Dalgarno and Shewan 2005; Zinberg 1984), as well as strength (e.g. alcohol content), routes of ingestion, and relative purity versus adulteration. Hence the socio-economic, political, and personal context to drug use, as well as pharmacology, can provide significant challenges when attempting to assess the harmfulness of individual drugs.

This chapter reviews trends in drug and alcohol use; situates drug control in the British and global contexts; and discusses data and debates concerning drugs and alcohol, crime and criminal justice.

## A REVIEW OF TRENDS IN DRUG AND ALCOHOL USE: 1950S TO 2011

Although most public and political attention tends to focus on illegal drugs as a source of social problems, this should not overshadow the significance of problems associated with legal drugs. For example, mass marketing and wide availability of prescribed and 'over the counter' pharmaceutical drugs, as well as solvents, may lead to misuse or dependency. More recently, novel psychoactive substances or so-called 'legal highs' have emerged as a challenge for public health and criminal justice agencies, as well as for the legislature (Birdwell *et al.* 2011). There has also been some debate about the extent to which drug use is not simply confined to personal leisure time but has intruded into the workplace leading some employers to introduce workplace drug testing on grounds of concerns about health and safety and lost productivity (Warren and Wray-Bliss 2009).

Undoubtedly, however, alcohol remains the most widely used and misused of psychoactive drugs in the UK. Alcohol consumption today is far higher than in the postwar years of the mid-twentieth century, although not yet at levels recorded in the nineteenth and early twentieth centuries before the two world wars. Increased consumption from the 1950s onward is related to increases in disposable income, changes in leisure patterns, the rise in social acceptability of female drinking, and the proliferation of outlets for sales and consumption. There are concerns about increased alcohol consumption and health problems posed such as the rise in liver disease among young people as well as evidence that middle and older age groups are also taking advantage of discounted prices for alcohol, increasing their risk of premature death due to heavy consumption (Alcohol Concern 2009), leading to a call by the Royal College of Psychiatrists for the recommended daily alcohol limit for older drinkers to be reduced. The contribution of alcohol to offending has been a recurrent issue with overall alcohol-related harm costing the UK an estimated £20 billion per year. Within this, the single largest area of expenditure is alcohol-related crime and anti-social behaviour, which has been estimated to cost the UK £7.3 billion per annum (Cabinet Office 2003). Lost productivity in the workplace costs another £6.4 billion. An updated estimate of the costs of alcohol harm to the NHS was more recently calculated at £2.7 billion (Department of Health 2008).

Mortality associated with tobacco and alcohol is considerably higher than deaths resulting from causes related to illegal drug misuse and complications. Deaths from the latter (mostly accidents) are difficult to determine, with various ways in which data may be recorded, misrecorded, or missed entirely. Recognizing these caveats, there has been a rise in drug-related deaths for England and Wales from about 860 in 1993 to around 2,182 in 2009 (Ghodse *et al.* 2010). Regarding alcohol, 'overall trends show that the rates of alcohol-related deaths, where alcohol has been identified as an underlying cause of death, have risen in England and Wales since World War II (1945). The number of deaths more than doubled from 2,506 in 1979 to 5,543 in 2000' (Alcohol Concern 2003: 2). Alcohol-related deaths peaked at 6,768 in 2008 and have fallen slightly since then (Health and Social Care Information Centre 2011: 76).

However, comparisons of drug-related deaths should not be interpreted as clear support for the view that illegal drugs should be legalized because 'they cause less harm than legal drugs'. The point is that legal drugs (even if restricted) are widely available, illegal drugs are not; the health-related consequences of widespread legal availability of presently illegal drugs are not known, nor are the effects of the new 'legal highs' being aggressively marketed online (EMCDDA 2010a: 21; Schmidt *et al.* 2011). Taylor (1999: 85) remarks that 'a selective decriminalisation of certain drugs could be one dimension in a serious campaign of harm-reduction, not least in disrupting the process of production of "outsider cultures"' formed by those suffering disadvantage and social exclusion related to forms of substance misuse. However, Taylor also notes Currie's (1993: 68) conclusion, based on the US inner-city experience, that '[p]roponents of full-scale deregulation of hard drugs ... tend to gloss over the very real primary costs of hard drug use ... and to exaggerate the degree to which the multiple pathologies surrounding drug use in America are an intended consequence of a "prohibitionist" regulatory policy'.

The legality of some drugs does not mean that they do not contribute to 'legal harms'. Drink and driving offences (including manslaughter deaths) (Corbett 2003) and alcohol-related violence and social disturbance result in high costs to the community and to health and emergency services (Shepherd and Lisles 1998; Pirmohamed *et al.* 2000). Despite their legal status, both alcohol and tobacco are attractive commodities for criminals engaged in theft or hijacking, and for smuggling if taxation to deter excessive consumption is raised too high.

## A SHORT HISTORY OF DRUG USE TRENDS—1900S–1940S

Historically, illegal drug use has frequently crossed class boundaries. During the early years of the twentieth century and into the 1920s, drug users included: medical-professionals who had abused their access to opiates and other drugs; 'therapeutic addicts' of different class backgrounds who had become dependent during the course of pain-killing treatment with opiate-type drugs; and working-class users of opiate-based patent medicines. In London, there were small numbers of recreational and addicted users on the bohemian fringes of high society, including socialites and entertainers, and within circles of young, white, male criminals and female prostitutes, whether using cocaine in the West End or as customers of East End 'opium dens' (Parssinen 1983: 216–17; Kohn 1992). However, while there was some considerable concern over drugs in this period (Kohn op. cit.), evidence suggests that the extent of use was limited and, by the end of the 1920s, in decline.

In the inter-war years illegal drug use attracted little attention in the UK. However, subsequently, the paramount concern of nations at war was to secure drugs for medical and military purposes, and the entry of the USA into the Second World War brought unusual developments. The USA became a repository, producer, and supplier of pain-killing opiate-type drugs for the allied war effort and on the international scene played a coordinating role in the strategy of purchasing opium for allied stocks and denying such supply to the Axis powers (McAllister 2000: 147–9). Furthermore, amphetamines were widely distributed to UK, US, German, and Japanese armed forces during the Second World War, to increase endurance (Rasmussen 2008).

## THE 1950S

During the early 1950s in Britain, both drug availability and official activity were minimal: 'The number of addicts known to the Home Office, most in medically related professions, remained low at between 300 and 400 ... But prosecutions for the use of cannabis began to rise' (Berridge 1999: 281). By the late 1950s a drug subculture was emerging in the West End of London linked to bohemian and jazz cultures (Tyler

1995: 169–70, 315–16). The availability of cannabis and heroin in these circles moved the Ministry of Health to establish the 1958 Inter-Departmental Committee on Drug Addiction under Sir Russell Brain, reporting in 1961. In the USA, popular anxieties and legislative responses were rather more pronounced. Accounts of the new youth fashions of the 1950s and purported links between rock and roll, the mixing of black and white youth, communism, and drugs (Shapiro 1999) were seen as alarms about America's vulnerability not only to external threats but also to subversion from within (Blackman 2004: 11–19).

## THE 1960S

Examining trends for the late 1950s, the 1961 Brain Committee reported that drug supply was 'almost negligible' and Britain had no drug problem of significance. However, the 1960 Home Office addict statistics had not been available for the Committee and rising numbers of addicts (from 454 in 1960 to 753 in 1964) (Mott 1991: 78–9) suggested that a new trend was emerging.

The period of the 1960s is now culturally represented as one of post-war release, artistic innovation, anti-establishment sentiments, and alternative cultures (Shapiro 1999). In this context alarm about drugs was partly related to the emergence of new, young, working class users of heroin, and the association between amphetamines, 'mods', and all-night dancing to soul music. Middle-class youth also used heroin but were particularly associated with images of a counter-culture—the 'hippy' lifestyle and drugs such as cannabis and LSD (Young 1971)—but it should also be remembered that for most youth, and adults, the intoxicant most widely used was (and remains) alcohol.

Official, medical, and other observers identified the irresponsible prescribing of opiate drugs by a small minority of either gullible or profit-motivated private practitioners as the cause of a rise in addicts centred on London's West End (Ruggiero and South 1995: 19–23; Mott 1991). The Brain Committee was re-convened in 1964 to report on changes and in 1965 made recommendations of considerable importance for the future of the British response to drug misuse (Pearson 1991: 176–8).

## FROM THE 1970S TO THE 1990S

With regard to opiate use, much of the 1970s presented a picture of relative stability and localized concentration, predominantly in the London area. By the tail of the decade, however, there were signs of further change and the 1980s saw a quite dramatic rise in use compared to the modest increases of the 1960s. Contrary to initial official perceptions, an increase in the availability of heroin was not a consequence of over-prescribing feeding the illegal market but of far less parochial developments. It was now the geopolitics of the international drug trade that demanded analysis and intervention. Cheap, high purity heroin was becoming readily available from the Golden Crescent region of South West Asia (Iran, Pakistan, and Afghanistan) and with a tighter prescribing policy adopted by the new Drug Dependency Units (DDUs; see below), the new sources of availability stimulated the market. Of crucial importance was that the new heroin imports could be *smoked*, the prepared drug being heated and the smoke inhaled ('chasing the dragon'), snorted, or sniffed (Auld *et al.* 1986). These methods overcame the deep psychological barrier associated with injecting and seemed familiar and 'ordinary' (Mott 1991: 85–6). Studies in various areas of England, Scotland, and Wales confirmed the rapid spread of heroin use, now cheaper in real terms than five years previously. At the same time, official and popular concern gathered around the 'threat' of 'crack' as a new smokeable form of cocaine. Initially a threat with little substance, a decade later the crack situation had changed. In the meantime, amongst a very different demographic group, from 1988, acid house and rave music had spiralled into a series of national and then international dance drug and clubbing cultures, chemically fuelled by ecstasy (MDMA), amphetamines, and LSD, which generated a new mix of hedonism and consumerism, and fed into the development of the British night-time economy of the 1990s (Hadfield and Measham 2009a; Hobbs *et al.* 2005; Measham *et al.* 2001; South 2004).

## THE 1990S AND INTO THE TWENTY-FIRST CENTURY

By the early 1990s, Britain had developed what remains a pattern of predominantly 'polydrug' use. Of course, mixing drugs, selection for different effects, and/or use of alternatives to the preferred 'drug of choice' in times of scarcity, were not new phenomena. What was new was the integration into young people's drug cultures of a pick 'n' mix approach (Parker and Measham 1994) to a growing repertoire of increasingly available legal and illegal drugs at reduced price across the 1990s (Davis and Ditton 1990; Parker *et al.* 1998; South 1999b). The ecstasy-fuelled dance culture proved distinctive, not least in involving relatively 'ordinary' people whose 'deviance' lay in being weekend enthusiasts of dance music and dance drugs but without pre-existing offending careers or drug dependency (Shapiro 1999; Sanders 2005; Hunt *et al.* 2010). Meanwhile, cocaine, crack, and heroin also saw increasing availability and use, generating serious crime and health problems, particularly in inner-city areas.

## PREVALENCE AND AVAILABILITY

There is a huge literature on 'why people take drugs' (Sumnall *et al.* 2006: 6–7) with the World Health Organization employing the following categories of use:

> experimental use that might or might not continue; functional use that serves some purpose, such as recreation, but does not cause problems for the user; dysfunctional use that leads to impaired psychological or social functioning; harmful use that causes damage to the user's physical or mental health; dependent use that could involve tolerance and/or withdrawal symptoms if use is ceased, and continued use [ibid.: 6].

A major preoccupation has been with drug users' careers and the question of 'when did (legal and illegal) drug use start'? Evidence suggests that teen (and early teen) years are significant; that for most young people, experimentation (and little more) with illegal drugs involves cannabis (Class B), and from the early 1990s onward, occasional to regular use of Class A drugs such as cocaine or ecstasy, and Class B stimulants such as amphetamines or more recently, 'legal highs' like mephedrone, controlled in the UK amidst much controversy in 2010. In the career of most drug users, 'escalation' to 'harder' drugs, long-term continuation of use and the development of dependency is confined to a minority.

While there are no current data on the drugs used by children aged 10 and under, in 2009 22 per cent of 11–15 year olds reported having tried illicit drugs at least once, falling from 29 per cent in 2001 (NHS Information Centre 2009). UK school pupils aged 15–16 years have consistently reported amongst the highest levels of lifetime use of any illegal drug compared with other European youth in the four-yearly ESPAD schools surveys (29 per cent for UK youth compared with an average of 21 per cent across Europe), although the UK youth prevalence rate has fallen considerably since the first ESPAD schools survey, from 42 per cent in 1995 to 29 per cent in 2007, with evidence of increasing convergence between countries with higher and lower levels of teenage drug use (Hibell *et al.* 2009: 372).

British Crime Survey (BCS) data also indicates that young people, aged 16–24 are more likely than older people to have tried drugs ever, in the last year and in the last month, although prevalence of drug use has been falling slightly in recent years across all age groups. However, this decline has been mostly due to a fall in cannabis use, with Class A drug use increasing in the general population from 1996–2009 (Hoare and Moon 2010).

A major change from the 1990s onward has been the increase in use of cocaine generally and by young people aged 16–24 in particular. Falling price (Corkery 2000; ISDD 1999) related to increased supply and hence easier availability, fashion, and social acceptability (Boys *et al.* 2001) may all be part of the explanation for this increase in the late 1990s. From the early 1990s to 2000, most crack or cocaine users in Britain seemed to be polydrug users, not using excessively and not developing heavy dependence (Druglink 1992: 6), but perhaps sometimes ill-informed about differences between cocaine and crack, and about risks, such as taking cocaine and alcohol together (Boys *et al.* 2001).

Importantly, Raistrick *et al.* (1999: 47) observe that:

> as drug use has become prevalent among adolescents, it has ceased to be a simple matter clearly to separate out the role of alcohol from the role of other substances. Drug misusers tend to have misused alcohol under age, younger than their peers and prior to use of most or all illegal drugs.

Parker *et al.* (1998) have suggested that a process of 'normalization' of 'recreational' drug use was under way from the early 1990s within the lifestyles and attitudes of the adolescents that they surveyed. 'Normalization' does not mean that all young people are now drug users, nonetheless acquaintance with 'recreational' drugs and/or users is no longer unusual and drug users are as likely to come from a range of 'normal' backgrounds across the social spectrum as be linked to social exclusion, which was a key risk factor for pre-1990s drug users. Others have been critical of this suggestion and its implications, arguing that prohibitions, peer-group resistance, parental attachment, and preference for alternative activities remain central and act as deterrents to drug use (Shiner and Newburn 1999). Both viewpoints have validity and this is reflected in ongoing arguments suggesting that we are seeing, if not a widespread normalization of use, at least a process of 'cultural normalisation' (Pearson 2001). The debate is significant (South 1999b, 2004), with the concept of normalization being refined across the last two decades (Aldridge *et al.* 2011; Measham and Shiner 2009) and now applied to drug use across the developed world from Denmark (Jarvinen and Demant 2011) and Finland (Hakkarainen *et al.* 2007), to Australia (Duff 2005; Pennay and Moore 2010; Wilson *et al.* 2010) and New Zealand (Hutton 2010).

In the late 1980s and at the start of the 1990s, heroin availability was still high. Signs and predictions that its use was in decline were short-lived and since the mid-1990s heroin use has seen a significant resurgence. Injecting is the main route of ingestion and in this respect, as well as many others, it is essential to note the health concerns associated with drug use which may include, for example, mental health problems or homelessness (Carrabine *et al.* 2004, 206–27; Green *et al.* 2005). Injecting is a dangerous practice *per se*, and in the 1980s its association with the spread of HIV/ AIDS was a key policy and practice issue. However, Hepatitis C is now well established as a virus transmitted via shared injecting equipment and yet receives far less media attention or health service provision (Advisory Council on Misuse of Drugs (ACMD) 2010). A further concern in recent years is that the falling purity of heroin, along with other Class A drugs, due to enforcement successes, has led to a drought on the streets, heavily adulterated street heroin, and displacement to benzodiazepines (Hallam 2011).

## SOCIAL DIVISIONS AND SOCIAL EXCLUSION

### Gender, drugs, and alcohol

Studies of women's use of drugs (legal or illegal) remain relatively rare compared to the volume of work focused on men and until recently, reproduced a narrow research agenda covering, for example, the role of men in introducing women to drug use and in assisting them in injecting; female users' roles as mothers and partners; and their involvement in prostitution. Informal care and support for problem drug and alcohol users is generally provided by women, and as Henderson (1999: 38) notes: 'A concern with women's drug use as it affects others still appears to dominate the gender and drug use literature'. Nonetheless, excellent studies do now exist (Taylor 1993; Maher 1997; May *et al.* 1999; Rosenbaum 1981) which increasingly focus on women's agency and pleasure in drug use (Henderson 1997; Hutton 2006; Measham *et al.* 2011a). It is no longer true that drug *use* is predominantly male to the extent that it has been in the past (Parker *et al.* 1998; Sharp *et al.* 2001) and the usually cited ratio of 2:1 male to female users is probably an under-estimate of the numbers of female users. As Best and Abdulrahim (2005: 3) note, this ratio may reflect uptake of services but under-estimate actual prevalence:

> The underlying debate around representation offers two broadly opposing possibilities: more men use drugs problematically than women, so the numbers seeking treatment and in treatment are broadly proportional, or drug-using women are 'hidden' and are under-represented in treatment, because of barriers that apply only to them, possibly relating to stigma and the structuring of treatment provision.

Possible barriers to women seeking treatment have now been examined quite systematically and are now better understood, including factors such as:

> stigmatisation and child protection issues; poor social support networks; weakness in maternity services; negative attitudes of health professionals; and ineffective interagency

working. Those women who do access drugs services often find that there are significant shortcomings in the provision they receive. From the literature review, we noted a lack of: childcare and transport facilities; women-only services; provision for black and ethnic minority women, and services within the Criminal Justice System (Becker and Duffy 2002: 11).

Drug *supply* remains a predominantly although not exclusively masculine territory, and there are familiar and predictable characteristics of criminal enterprise as well as sociocultural prejudices operating against women in the drugs economy that explain this. In addition, it has been argued that female drug users and suppliers may be particularly harshly treated when they come to official and media attention (Boyd 2004). US research (Fagan 1994: 186; Maher 1997) indicates openings in cocaine and crack markets for female suppliers, albeit with varying degrees of autonomy while Denton and O'Malley (1999) report on Australian research on female suppliers within the drug economy. In terms of alcohol, women's consumption has increased although this does not mean that gender-specific differences have disappeared; rather they continue to reflect prevailing norms and stereotypes (Ettorre and Riska 1995; Hunt *et al.* 2000; McDonald 1994; Plant *et al.* 2005).

## Ethnicity

Drug use within ethnic minorities remains a story largely hidden from the record (Akhtar and South 2000; Pearson and Patel 1998; Daly 2005; Whittington 1999). When the topic has received attention it has frequently been discussed in terms of 'the depiction of dangerous places defined by the linking of drugs, crime, race and violence' (Murji 1999: 49), a process that can sensationalize stories about drugs and minorities, 'racialize' certain forms of drug use and drug culture, and pathologize the places where the 'mugger' and the drug 'dealer' are said to reside (ibid.: 50–61).

Survey data on this subject face problems regarding reliability and coverage and although methods are increasingly sophisticated it remains worth noting that, as Murji (ibid.: 52) observes, while '[s]ome surveys report that some ethnic or racial minority groups declare higher drug use ... [others] have found the opposite'.

According to Edmonds *et al.* (2005: 16) 'community drug misuse needs assessments suggest distinct patterns of drug use exist between ethnic groups (Bashford *et al.* 2003)' and such patterns can be summarized: 'Drug use by South Asians was more characterised by the use of heroin than crack, and also the use of a wide range of drugs including ecstasy and LSD'; Black African reported use 'was characterised by the use of both heroin and crack, while Black Caribbean use was more characterised by crack, amphetamine and ecstasy'; 'Middle Eastern respondents reported no use of ecstasy, crack or heroin'. Across all ethnic groups, cannabis tends to be the most widely reported in terms of use.

In the national BCS, white and 'mixed' background respondents report higher levels of drug use than all British minority ethnic groups (Hoare and Moon 2010: 46). Amongst adults aged 16–59, 15 per cent of 'mixed' background respondents reported having taken any illicit drug in the past year, this being a higher result than for other categories (white, 11 per cent; black, 8 per cent; Chinese/other, 4 per cent; or Asian, 3 per cent). Amongst 16–24-year-olds, 25 per cent of white respondents reported past year use of any drug compared with 8 per cent of non-white respondents (Hoare and

Moone 2010: 48). Despite these lower levels of drug use amongst British minority ethnic groups, black and Asian drug users feature disproportionately in official statistics on drug offenders in part due to bias in the targeting of 'stop and search' street policing towards the black population (Ministry of Justice 2010).

### Drugs, deprivation, and social exclusion

Overall there seems to be some correlation between drug use and high rates of deprivation. The 1998 ACMD report on *Drug Misuse and the Environment* acknowledged that 'research points strongly to a statistical association between deprivation and problematic drug use' (ibid.: 3), and Foster (2000) revisited the site of a study undertaken 10 years previously and found deterioration on most measures of deprivation and a parallel increase in crime and drug use. In the case of Scotland, McCarron (2006: 29) reports that '[b]etween 1999 and 2001, in the 10 per cent most deprived areas there was a yearly average of 460 admissions to hospital for drug conditions per 100,000 population compared with 20 per 100,000 in the 10 per cent least deprived areas'. However, there may also be inverse relationships. Localities with high indices of deprivation may have low rates of use, while there are socially advantaged, middle-class areas with high rates of use, depending on drug type. Data from the 2000 BCS illustrated this mixed picture well, showing 'consistently higher levels of drug use among 16–29s living in affluent urban areas. Similar patterns are found for cocaine and Class A drugs. Heroin on the other hand, is more common in less affluent areas' (Sharp *et al.* 2001: 3). This picture has continued throughout the 2000s, with heroin and cannabis use associated with the lowest income households, and cocaine and stimulant drugs more generally associated with higher income households and urban areas. Both drug use generally and Class A drug use are highest in residential areas designated as 'urban prosperity' (Hoare and Moon 2010: 44).

From the late 1990s a series of policy initiatives aimed to reduce drug use and supply by addressing social exclusion, improving the living environment in run-down areas, and focusing on localities with concentrations of long-term and high youth unemployment to support the transition of young people (16–25) to adulthood (MacGregor 1998: 190; Social Exclusion Unit 2004).

## THE CONTROL OF DRUGS: BRITAIN AND THE GLOBAL CONTEXT

During the nineteenth century, opiate preparations were commonly marketed and widely used throughout Europe and North America (Berridge 1999), for example as medicines and tonics, analgesics, sedatives, remedies for cholera, and as children's 'quieteners'. Apart from such therapeutic uses, reports between the 1830s and 1860s describe the recreational use of opiates in factory districts, seaports, and the Fenlands (Parssinen 1983: 212), and the literature of the period indicates experimentation and familiarity with opium in literary and bohemian circles (Berridge 1999). However, the question of *control* was emerging.

The Industrial Revolution and other socio-economic developments promoted interest in the subject of public health, particularly in relation to the fitness of the urban working class. The common use of opiate preparations gave rise to some concern (although use for pleasure and pain relief among the middle class apparently received less disapproval and attention at this point) (Berridge 1999). A different provocation of public discussion about opiates was their common use as a means of sedating children—a practice resulting in many cases of children dying of opium poisoning (Parssinen 1983: 207; Pearson 1991: 170). Additionally, from around the 1870s onward, sensational accounts of Chinese 'Opium Dens' in London's East End provided sinister stereotypes of Oriental conspiracies and clandestine organizations (Kohn 1992: 18–20). There was, of course, considerable hypocrisy in the promotion of such images.

The original traffickers in the opium trade were the great colonial powers such as Britain and the Netherlands (McAllister 2000: 9–39) and Britain had invested heavily and engaged in two conflicts known as the Opium Wars (1839–42 and 1856–58) to secure the conditions of 'free trade' that enabled export of opium from India (then part of the British Empire) to China. China had sought to ban importation and when forced to accept this suffered a major trade deficit which it only managed to turn around by allowing domestic production of opium from 1880 (Chawla and Pietschmann 2005: 161). This investment in the opium trade makes the limited extent of domestic control over opiate use in Britain less surprising. Nonetheless, in the latter half of the century, moral opposition to Britain's opium trade was growing. Further, there was a shift in perception of opium use, from seeing it as an indulgence or habit to viewing it as a 'problem', classifiable in various ways by the discourses of the emergent medical profession (Berridge 1979, 1999). Prompted by an 'infant doping' scandal where 235 infants under one year old, 56 children aged one to four years, and 340 children aged five or over, died of opium poisoning in 1863–7, the 1868 Pharmacy Act, removed morphine and opium derivatives from the shelves of general stores and gave pharmacists the monopoly of dispensing.

As well as 'medical entrepreneurs', 'moral crusaders' were also active in seeking the introduction of new control measures. In 1874, the Society for the Suppression of the Opium Trade was formed, largely supported by Quaker campaigners, and subsequently securing parliamentary support from the radical wing of the Liberal party (Berridge 1999). The later Report of the Royal Commission on Opium published in 1895 was something of a 'whitewash' (ibid.: 186–7) but the important *economic* development was that, even as moral and political debates waxed and waned, by the early 1880s the 'signs of decline in the importance of opium as an Indian revenue item were already visible' and 'by 1885, China was probably producing just as much opium as she imported... In the 1890s, exports of Indian opium began to decline absolutely as well as relatively' (ibid.: 178). Furthermore, whilst Indian opium was important for international trade, opium imported into the UK in the nineteenth century came predominantly from Turkey and then Persia (Berridge 1978a). By 1906, it was neither an act of great moral conviction nor one incurring significant financial loss for a new Liberal Government to commit Britain to phasing out opium exports from India to China.

By the early years of the twentieth century a polarity had emerged between the medical view of drug use as addictive or a 'disease' and a moral view of it as a vice to be controlled and punished by law (Berridge 1979; Smart 1984). However, the concerns about vice that finally introduced the first significant penal response to drug use in Britain arose not as a result of peacetime lobbying but in the context of wartime emergency. During the early years of the First World War, press and public were aroused by accounts of prostitution and cocaine posing a threat to the discipline of allied troops (Kohn 1992: 23–66). Similarly, concern about the productivity of war workers in the factories prompted calls for restriction of alcohol availability. In 1916, Regulation 40B of the Defence of the Realm Act (DORA) made possession of cocaine or opium a criminal offence except for professionals such as doctors, or where supplied on prescription (Kohn 1992: 44). DORA regulations also introduced licensing laws restricting opening times of public houses and regulating alcohol sales. With hindsight, it was the control of alcohol that had the greatest long-term consequences but with regard to the cocaine 'threat', legal control of cocaine and opium was exercised and unauthorized possession was criminalized for the first time. A significant step had been taken and the role of the Home Office was brought to centre stage in the control of drugs, both domestically (Tyler 1995: 312–13; Pearson 1991: 172; Berridge 1978b: 293) and internationally (McAllister 2000).

Subsequently, various influences, such as the ambitions of the USA regarding prohibitionism and the agenda for drug control, as well as the final ratification of the 1912 Hague Convention on Opium via the post-war Versailles Treaty (Article 295) (Bruun et al. 1975: 12; McAllister 2000), all encouraged the extension of government legislation from troops to civilians in the form of the Dangerous Drugs Acts of 1920 and 1923. These confirmed possession of opiates and cocaine as illegal except where prescribed by a doctor. The Home Secretary gained powers to regulate the manufacture, distribution, and legitimate sale of these drugs, and policing practice and public perception reflected the new status of illegal drugs as a criminal matter (Parssinen 1983: 217; Pearson 1991: 172; Lee and South 2003).

Problems relating to excessive drinking or dependence have also been a source of moral, medical, and penal concern since the nineteenth century. Fines, imprisonment, or treatment programmes have been employed (Johnstone 1996: 33–100; Cabinet Office Strategy Unit 2004). However, while control regarding opium and cocaine was now set on a path of increasing prohibition in the twentieth century, control in relation to alcohol has largely been a story of increasing liberalization. DORA regulations were at first ignored and then lifted. The Licensing Act 1964 laid out the system for discretionary granting of licences to sell alcohol, originally by licensing magistrates but since the Licensing Act 2003 by licensing committees of local authorities. The Licensing Act 2003 brought together several licensing arrangements (for providing alcohol, entertainment, and late-night food and drink) under one arrangement and placed a duty on all licensing authorities to carry out four principal functions: the prevention of crime and disorder; public safety; the prevention of public nuisance; and the protection of children from harm. Public health was notably absent.

Liberalization of the alcohol laws began in the 1980s and in the following three decades successive governments have relaxed controls on availability. A variety of laws have defined and specified responses to drunken behaviour, from the Metropolitan Police Act 1839 and the Licensing Act 1872 to the Licensing Act 1964 and subsequent amendments. Certain Acts have focused on public order and providing powers to police and others, while provisions of local by-laws can also be used to enforce prohibition of drinking in designated places. In November 2005 the implementation of the Licensing Act 2003 allowed licensed premises to apply for permission to extend their licenses and increase their trading hours, in principle up to 24 hours a day, although this has been rarely utilized in practice. Proponents argued that extended trading hours would lead to a more relaxed, Mediterranean model of leisurely café bar alcohol consumption without the congestion and flashpoints for disorder that occurred with unified closing times, whilst critics predicted increases in 'binge drinking' and alcohol-related crime and disorder. An international review of changes in Australia, New Zealand, North America, and the UK concluded that in general the evidence points towards extended trading hours resulting in increased alcohol consumption and increased alcohol-related harms (Stockwell and Chikritzhs 2009). In the UK, research suggests that the Licensing Act 2003 reduced the peak of alcohol-related disorder around midnight and consequent pressure on emergency services, but extended the 'night out', with drinkers pre-loading on alcohol before entering the night-time economy, leaving home later, and stretching the resources of emergency services into the early hours of the morning (Hadfield and Measham 2009b; Hough and Hunter 2008; Humphreys and Eisner 2010).

## THE 'BRITISH SYSTEM' OF DRUG CONTROL

Following DORA and the 1920 Act, the Home Office made 'consistent attempts to impose a policy completely penal in direction' (Berridge 1984: 23). The response from the medical lobby was to result in a report to the Ministry of Health that laid the foundation for the 'British system' of response to drugs and indeed for a 'harm-reduction' approach. Chaired by Sir Humphrey Rolleston, President of the Royal College of Physicians, the 1926 Report of the Departmental Committee on Morphine and Heroin Addiction (known as the Rolleston Report) aimed to define the circumstances in which prescription was appropriate and the precautions to be taken to avoid the possibility of abuse (Ministry of Health 1926: 2; Tyler 1995: 313–14; Pearson 1991: 173). Hence, the Committee recommended prescription of heroin and morphine to enable gradual withdrawal, or to 'maintain' a regulated supply to those judged unable to break their dependence or those whose lives would otherwise suffer serious disruption.

Given the influential view that this development represents a profoundly different path to that taken by the USA, it is important to make two points. First, the view that Rolleston held of addicts was resolutely that they were 'middle class, middle aged, often from the medical profession and invariably an abuser of morphine. About five hundred such individuals existed nation-wide and rather than representing a threat they were to be pitied' (Tyler 1995: 313); only as 'an afterthought' was passing consideration given to the existence of working-class use of opiate-based patent medicines (ibid.). Secondly, looking at when drug-related criminality actually emerged in the USA can challenge the idea that it was the nature of the British response that avoided duplication of the US experience. As Parssinen (1983: 219) suggests:

> Although the Harrison Act [of 1914] probably strengthened the connections between narcotics addiction and the urban underworld, these connections were firmly in place

long before 1914. The increasingly hard-line American enforcement and treatment policy during the 1920s was less cause than effect of the emerging criminal-addict.

In other words, in terms of numbers of drug users, and the drugs-crime relationship, the British and US experiences were divergent already, ahead of the passing and subsequent interpretation of legislation. In Britain the drugs issue was receding in significance even as the Rolleston Committee deliberated: medical and recreational addiction was in decline. Press and public fascination persisted and sensational stories still made news (Kohn 1992) but, generally, such subcultures of use as had existed were fragile. Scarcity, related expense, and law enforcement efforts deterred both users and suppliers of cocaine and opiates. As Parssinen (1983: 220) argues, 'in Britain as in America, drug policy was less a cause than it was the effect of the addict population. Put simply, narcotic drug maintenance was accepted in Britain in the 1920s because the addict population was small, elderly and dying off'.

Various commentators (Smart 1984; Pearson 1991; Kohn 1992) agree that apparently dominant medical discourses of this time were in fact influenced by, and framed within, strong moral and penal positions. Nonetheless, one reason for a general acceptance of the success of 'Rolleston' is that through the 1930s to the late 1950s, Britain did indeed experience no serious problems with illegal drugs. Policy was seen as a continuing success despite being, in the words of Downes's (1977: 89) famous assessment, 'little more than masterly inactivity in the face of … an almost non-existent … problem'. Thus, as Berridge and Edwards (1987: 254) observed, the contrast between the American and British experience had rather less to do with the triumph of the Rolleston philosophy than with the 'enormously different social conditions in the cities of the two countries—different patterns of poverty, urban decay, ethnic under-privilege and entrenched criminal organization'. Despite this, for various reasons the 'British system' was (and continues to be) idealized by some, particularly a line of influential American commentators, thereby distorting debate in the USA and promoting 'an atmosphere of self-congratulation and complacency within the British medical elite' (Blackman 2004: 26).

Even so, between 1920 and 1964, Britain was a signatory to a long string of control measures, largely carried along by the momentum of international initiatives (McAllister 2000; Ruggiero and South 1995: 99–101). In 1961, the UN Single Convention on Narcotic Drugs drew together provisions of nine previous treaties signed between 1912 (Hague Convention) and 1953, and extended control to cover the plants poppy, coca, and cannabis. The 1960s also saw developments on the domestic scene. Nationally as well as internationally, drugs became a challenging social problem, associated with cultural and political change.

In Britain, in the wake of a 'mod' subculture fuelled by diversion of prescription amphetamines for recreational purposes (Osgerby 1998), the 1964 Drugs (Prevention of Misuse) Act was introduced to control possession, production, and supply of amphetamine (later adding control of LSD). In 1965, the Dangerous Drugs Act ratified the Single Convention and the reconvened Brain Committee published a new report. This was to lead to major legislation in the form of the Dangerous Drugs Act 1967. Prescribing was to continue but general medical practitioners were to be more tightly controlled by regulations and were to 'notify' the Home Office of new addicts not previously in treatment. The aim was to intervene to prevent seepage of prescribed opiates (and similar drugs) into the illicit market. Specialist Drug Dependency Units or 'clinics' were opened from 1968, initially in and around London, as the centres of expertise in treatment of addiction and with psychiatrists playing a leading role. Prescription of heroin and cocaine was now limited although general practitioners could still prescribe other drugs for treatment and there has been a long debate about the extent to which they are, can be, or should be involved in such specialist clinical work. In practice, the new clinics sought to break client dependence on street drugs by prescribing methadone as a 'substitute' drug, thought less attractive than heroin and suitable for detoxification or 'maintenance'. Thus medical *management* of addiction was endorsed, placing doctors in a role with responsibility for regulating supply and controlling the spread of dependence (Pearson 1991: 178–81; MacGregor 1999).

Debates aired around the dichotomies of 'soft' and 'hard' drugs, and 'users' and 'dealers', during the 1960s, were reflected in the core distinction made in the Misuse of Drugs Act 1971 between the offences of possession and supply. Drug users could be characterized as sad and vulnerable types corrupted by drug 'dealers' who were very bad types; the former needed counselling or treatment, the latter deserved harsh punishment. Hence, despite the liberalization of much other legislation in these 'permissive' years, drugs received quite conservative treatment; even a call by the respectable Advisory Council on Drug Dependence (the Wootton Committee 1968) for relaxation of the law on cannabis, was dismissively rejected (Young 1971: 198–201). As Berridge has argued (1984), if the much-lauded humanitarian model of heroin prescribing in the UK in the 1920s–60s was possible only because there was such a limited number of mostly middle class heroin addicts in that period, then once a much larger and more diverse drug user base developed from the late 1960s onwards, and heroin and cocaine prescribing shifted away from ordinary GPs, drug policy increasingly moved from medical to Home Office control.

The status of drug control as a 'war' can be traced to President Nixon's mobilization of American public and official sentiment in the 1970s when crime was ranked as pre-eminent among the problems facing US cities, with drugs close behind. In the 1980s President Reagan launched a renewed 'War on Drugs', and the coincidence of the conservative politics of the President and the new British Prime Minister, Mrs Thatcher, set the tone for the rhetoric—if not the practice—of drug control in that decade. Drugs in Britain in the 1980s became a political and politicized issue attracting a consensus that largely persists.

The Conservative Government produced two strategy documents: *Tackling Drug Misuse* (1985) and *Tackling Drugs Together* (1995), which proposed action around enforcement, education, prevention, and treatment. These elements continued in the Labour Government's *Tackling Drugs to Build a Better Britain* (HM Government 1998; updated 2002). However, it is noteworthy that strategy, and hence policy priorities and resources, focused on illegal drugs rather than alcohol and it was not until 2004 that an 'Alcohol Harm Reduction Strategy for England' was published (Cabinet Office Strategy Unit 2004).

Following Labour's re-election in 2001, commitment to cross-departmental, 'joined-up' thinking was patchy, with some return to traditional departmental divisions, a central role for the Home Office, and the creation of the National Treatment

Agency. Yet an emphasis on criminal justice remains paramount. The Drugs Act 2005 drew together several elements of past strategy and action, allowing testing of offenders when arrested for certain crimes, providing for intervention orders to be attached to Anti-Social Behaviour Orders (created under the Anti-Social Behaviour Act 2003), and requiring quasi-compulsory drug counselling. In Scotland, drugs strategy has been less dominated by a criminal justice approach (McCarron 2006: 32) though there have been innovations in this area including adaptations of the American Drug Court for the Scottish context (Glasgow and Fife) and creation of the Scottish Drug Enforcement Agency to coordinate both police and customs activities.

With the incoming Coalition Government, the focus in treatment services has shifted away from maintenance therapies—a key pillar of drug treatment from 1998–2010—towards a 'recovery' agenda and abstinence-based treatment programmes (HM Government 2010). One of the first pieces of drug legislation from the new Coalition Government was the flagship policy response to the emergence of novel psychoactive substances or so-called 'legal highs'—the Temporary Class Drug Orders introduced as part of the Police and Criminal Responsibility Act of 2011.

## LEGAL HIGHS

One of the biggest challenges for contemporary drug policy is how to respond to 'legal highs', a problem which emerged in the UK in 2009. 'Legal highs' developed from a catch-all term before 2009 referring to any uncontrolled drugs, to refer specifically to synthetic stimulants manufactured predominantly in China and the East and imported in increasingly large quantities to the UK from 2009 onwards. Although some seizures and public health concerns had been noted in Israel, Sweden, and elsewhere a few years earlier, it was during the summer festival season of 2009 that the consumption of substituted cathinones, notably mephedrone, came to public and police attention in the UK. The reason for the emergence and rapid increase in popularity of unregulated synthetic stimulants appeared to be in part related to availability (they could be purchased from high street 'head shops' or ordered from internet retailers and delivered within hours) and price (at £10/g substantially cheaper than established street drugs), combined with disillusionment by more experienced drug users such as weekend party-goers and clubbers at the reduced purity/availability of street drugs such as cocaine and ecstasy at that time (McElrath and O'Neill 2011; Measham et al. 2010).

A media furore unfolded, with politicians of all hues predictably eager for the assessment and control of apparently dangerous new drugs. This contrasted with liberal commentators criticizing the rapidity of control and the unnecessary widening of the net of prohibition (Measham et al. 2011b). Meanwhile, in the absence of an established body of scientific research on these substances—details of prevalence of use, drug-related harms, and drug-related deaths remained hotly disputed. Surveys of clubbers (Winstock and Power 2011) suggest that mephedrone rapidly became very popular amongst this group of generally more prolific drug users and the first national figures on mephedrone use in the BCS 2010/11 (Smith and Flatley 2011: 22) found that 4.4 per cent of 16–24-year-olds had mephedrone in the past year, the same as cocaine and less than only cannabis. The impact of the ban on drug use is currently being monitored, with surveys to date suggesting that legislative control has had some limited effect. For example, mephedrone had become the most popular club drug in London gay-friendly clubs by the summer of 2010, 10 weeks after it was banned, with evidence of an illegal street trade in the drug having developed both inside and outside the clubs (Measham *et al.* 2011c). Past year mephedrone use amongst this sample of predominantly gay clubbers was second only to cocaine. The annual Mixmag survey noted that by the autumn of 2010, there was evidence that respondents had switched from legal internet sites to illegal dealers and that the price had risen and suspected purity fallen (Winstock and Power 2011). Whilst demand for mephedrone has continued after its control, what is less apparent is evidence of displacement to other, currently unregulated 'legal highs' (Measham *et al.* 2011b, 2011c).

In fact, as Parliament has noted (House of Commons Public Accounts Committee 2010; Rolles and Measham 2011), there is little evaluation of legislation to provide evidence that prohibition acts as a deterrent to drug users or that the overall benefits of current drug policy outweigh the harms that it can produce (e.g. variable purity and adulteration of street drugs). The appeal of 'legal highs' both to underage adolescents who can easily acquire them in a non-regulatory environment without age or other sales restrictions, and to prolific and pharmacologically inquisitive young adult weekend polydrug users (Measham and Moore 2009), suggests that legislative restrictions alone will not stem importation. What has been advocated instead are firstly, an independent assessment of drug-related harm which is entirely 'decoupled' from determining punishments, as was recommended by the UK Parliamentary Science and Technology Select Committee (2006), secondly, a new Harmful Substances Control Act (Birdwell *et al.* 2011), and thirdly, a more robust framework for the regulation of trading standards and internet sales.

# LAW ENFORCEMENT AND DRUGS PREVENTION: CRIMINAL JUSTICE AND MULTI-AGENCY INITIATIVES

Various police forces and strategy commentators have supported the idea of 'low-level policing' aimed at disrupting street markets (Lee and South 2003: 433–6), diverting users from criminalization to counselling and treatment (Edmunds *et al.* 1999; Green *et al.* 2005), and more recently, the targeting of the 'middle market' (Pearson and Hobbs 2001; May and Hough 2004). Intelligence-led policing, use of informants, and collation of data have long been recognized as key features of effective drug law enforcement (Dorn *et al* 1992; Lee and South 2003). This has been reflected in the creation of a series of bodies from the 1973 Central Drugs and Illegal Immigration Unit to the 2006 Serious Organised Crime Agency (SOCA) with further re-organization announced in 2011 and a new National Crime Agency being established to absorb SOCA and also cover economic, border, and cybercrime. Transnational law-enforcement cooperation has grown extensively as well as in terms of sophistication since the 1980s. Drugs, money laundering, and latterly terrorism have been key targets (Lee and South 2003: 429–31; Matassa and Newburn 2003).

Given the volume of drugs now produced for the international market, improvements in enforcement effectiveness were thought to make only a modest impact on availability (Best *et al.* 2001), with little relationship between the size of seizures and either general availability or price. Even 'successful' enforcement—whether domestic or cross-border— might be ineffective in conditions where time and resource constraints mean that sections of a trafficking network are removed but quickly and easily replaced as the structure rebuilds itself. However, views have been changing regarding the success that can be attributed to supply-side interventions against trafficking outside, and importation into, the UK, or targeting of retail-level dealing. By the end of the 2000s, not only were SOCA and Europol noting significant enforcement successes along the whole supply chain, suppliers were reporting difficulties with importation resulting from significantly increased security at airports and ports of entry into the UK as a by-product of anti-terrorist and anti-trafficking measures. Cocaine, ecstasy, and heroin have plummeted in purity. As noted in Measham *et al.* (2010), 'cocaine seizures have risen sharply' (Hand and Rishiraj 2009: 6) and purity of cocaine seized by the police fell from over 60 per cent in 1999 to 22 per cent in the first quarter of 2009 (Hand and Rishiraj 2009). Similarly, about half of pills seized in 2009 contained no ecstasy and were as likely to be BZP party pills. For the first time in the history of drug control, it could be that enforcement *is* affecting the market (Hallam 2011). This has been at least one explanation for the timing of the rapid emergence and rise in use of 'legal highs' in the UK (Measham *et al.* 2010).

## ENFORCEMENT STATISTICS

A reappraisal of evidence of success has far-reaching implications. Politicians and the media like to see targets and impact measures, for example detection as reflected in annual seizure statistics. Of course this has always been recognized as a partial measure: years of high seizure have been greeted as either a sign of increased success of enforcement efforts, and/or a reflection of an increasing incoming volume of drugs requiring further enforcement resources. It is now widely acknowledged that seizure statistics must be treated with caution—a few seizures of very large amounts can inflate the figures unrepresentatively while low seizures do not mean low levels of importation or distribution. Evidently numerous consignments avoid detection and the Customs and police services of most countries are unlikely to feel able to claim much more than a 10 per cent interception rate. Drawing on global data for 2002, Chawla and Pietschmann (2005) note that 'nearly 1.1 million seizure cases were reported in the world' and that this represented a 'considerable increase from the 300,000 cases reported in 1992'. Furthermore, the United Nations (2011) annual report notes a significant decrease in production and trafficking in heroin and cocaine. Law enforcement statistics are subject to severe limitations, however, and it is unclear whether the recent reductions in availability/purity of Class A drugs in the UK will continue.

## DRUG OFFENCES SENTENCING

As Bennett and Holloway (2005: 4) remark, 'In practice, most official data on the drugs-crime connection come from government statistics on drug offences. Much less is known about drug-related crime other than drug offences.' Home Office data on 'Offenders dealt with' show a consistent rise in the number of persons found guilty, cautioned, or 'dealt with by compounding' for drugs offences under the Misuse of Drugs Act. In 1998/99, the total number of drug offences was 136,000 rising to 232,000 in 2010/11 (Chaplin *et al.* 2011: 45). 199,000 of these offences in 2010/11 (86 per cent) related to possession offences and of these, 160,000 (81 per cent) were specifically cannabis-related possession offences.

Unsurprisingly, the proportion of offenders known to the criminal justice system who have some form of alcohol or illicit drug problem is significantly high. According to the Office of National Statistics (Singleton *et al.* 1999), 58 per cent of remand and 63 per cent of sentenced prisoners reported hazardous levels of drinking in the year prior to entering prison while drug-testing of arrested people in eight sites across England and Wales found that 65 per cent tested positive for at least one illegal drug, 29 per cent for opiates and/or cocaine/crack (Bennett *et al.* 2001).

Assessment of the threat from organized serious crime is now undertaken on a frequent and sophisticated basis and it is recognized that criminal entrepreneurs will not necessarily be engaged in drugs-related activity alone. A range of techniques and targets are required and one that has become central, albeit with only partial success, is asset confiscation. The 1986 Drug Trafficking Offences Act meant that sentences could include asset confiscation and this was followed by the 2002 Proceeds of Crime Act and amendments such as the 2007 Serious Crime Act, all of which have been underpinned by government targets to increase recovery of criminal profits. This has proved a less effective tool than hoped despite allowing the presumption that assets are the proceeds of trafficking or other crime unless the defendant can prove otherwise.

Conclusions about the impact of sentencing are difficult to draw but imprisonment probably has little positive effect on drug or drug-related crime behaviour. Drugs are widely available in prisons and the sharing of injecting equipment makes risk of transmission of blood-borne viruses such as HIV and Hepatitis C a serious problem. Mandatory drug testing has encouraged use of drugs that are harder to detect, including a shift from cannabis to opiates.

## TREATMENT, REHABILITATION, AND DIVERSION

The issue of *treatment* of drug and alcohol users raises several key criminological questions, such as: what kinds of treatment are most efficacious in (a) reducing reliance on the illegal market for drug supply, and (b) reducing related criminal activity engaged in to generate funds for purchasing drugs? Some studies indicate that maintenance prescribing has little clear impact on criminal activity though there is some evidence that methadone treatment can help to reduce acquisitive crime rates in areas of heroin-based drug markets and that 'tailored' or 'flexible' therapeutic programmes can be effective. A key review of efficacy has been the National Treatment Outcomes Research Study (NTORS) and Gossop (2005: 5) notes that:

> Even without the numerous other tangible and intangible benefits in addition to the reductions in costs of crime to society, the financial costs of treating drug dependent patients provide a return that more than justified the cost of treatment. Initial calculations based upon savings associated with victim costs of crime and reduced demands

upon the criminal justice system, estimated that for every extra £1 spent on drug misuse treatment, there was a minimum return of more than £3 in terms of savings to the economy.

Even so, given the major reductions in public health funding, and problem drug and alcohol users not being a popular group with the public, funding for drug treatment is increasingly under threat, increasingly tied to payment by 'results' and increasingly rationed.

Drug Testing and Treatment Orders (DTTOs), lately superseded by Drug Rehabilitation Requirements (DRRs), were introduced as a new community sentence under the Crime and Disorder Act 1998 and while their use has increased there have been concerns about failure rates as well as geographical variations in terms of operational resources and practice. There is always some difficulty in determining whether success linked to such interventions can be attributed to the treatment *per se* or to personal history and situation (for example, users feeling that they are 'growing out of drugs' or are weary of the lifestyle). In practice, the argument for flexibility is precisely about being able to draw users into treatment at the point where they feel willing or need to change. It is also important to emphasize a further finding from NTORS, 'that crime and drug misuse do not inevitably go together. Half of the clients were not involved with acquisitive crime and more than two-thirds were not involved with drug selling crimes during the period before admission. Of those who were involved in crime, the majority were relatively infrequent offenders' (Gossop 2005: 3).

Treatment, abstinence, and tailored programmes can improve social conditions and personal relationships but have had a poor record in improving labour market skills or housing, financial, and personal circumstances. Increasingly treatment, rehabilitation, and diversion schemes are incorporating opportunities for gaining vocational skills-training and qualifications (South *et al.* 2001) and McCarron (2006: 31) notes the particular progress made in Scotland with this approach where the 'high rate of unemployment, low level of qualifications and relatively low working age of drug users entering treatment' led to development of 'research and guidance integrating access to education, training and employment with care pathways'. In relation to problem drinkers, Alcohol Concern (2000: 15) suggests that opportunities for treatment and prevention of re-offending are largely missed because of the absence of effective sentencing options. Many other problems here parallel those relevant to drugs, for example the need for specialist services within prisons and improved support arrangements on release from prison.

## DRUGS, ALCOHOL, AND CRIME

### DECRIMINALIZATION VERSUS PROHIBITION

Possession, supply, or preparation and manufacture of certain drugs are illegal. However some illegal drugs are argued to be relatively harmless compared to the Class A 'dangerous drugs' such as crack and heroin, and some legal drugs, such as tobacco, could be considered more harmful than some illegal ones. It should be noted that attempting to compare the relative harm of different drugs is both scientifically challenging and politically sensitive. A recent attempt to create a conceptual model to rank individual drug harms highlighted the inconsistencies between the scientific assessment of harms and the legal classification of individual drugs in the ABC classification system, as well as the complexities faced by any alternative modelling system (Nutt *et al.* 2010). Concerns have been expressed, however, at the subjectivity of such rankings, the integrating of drug harms with drug policy harms, as well as the flaws in such models of individual drugs which do not allow for the realities of polydrug use, varied routes of ingestion, the social context of use, and environmental influences on risk (Rolles and Measham 2011).

These points give rise to questions about whether the law is sensible, or whether legalization or other options are desirable (Police Foundation 2000). Proponents argue that the costly, counterproductive, and unsuccessful efforts of law enforcement as a response to drug use suggest that legalization is a wiser alternative. It is suggested that availability would not mean unacceptable rises in use, and that taxation of legal supply would provide funds for educational, health, and counselling responses. Regulation would ensure purity levels and hence reduce health hazards caused by adulterants; and legal availability would remove the profit motive that drives the criminal market (*The Economist* 2001; Nadelman 1989; Rolles 2010; see also Husak and de Marneffe 2005, where Husak argues in favour and de Marneffe against; and the analysis in MacCoun and Reuter 2001). Opponents (Inciardi and McBride 1989; Wilson 1990) argue that legalization *would* increase use, thereby increasing serious costs to society. The decriminalisation of cannabis use in the Netherlands has often been misunderstood, particularly by US prohibitionists. This is actually a case of a policy aimed at preserving 'market separation', keeping cannabis supply distinct from supply of drugs with an 'unacceptable risk', decriminalizing possession, and simply reflecting the flexibility that the 1961 UN Single Convention allows (Dorn 2004). However, whilst the Netherlands is now moving towards a stricter regime and closing half of its cannabis coffee shops under pressure from its European neighbours, Portugal decriminalized personal possession of all drugs in 2001. Evaluations of the first 10 years of Portuguese decriminalization suggest that it has not significantly adversely affected prevalence rates, with Portugal following a general trend across Europe of falling rates of drug use (EMCDDA 2011b) and with increased numbers of drug users in treatment, accompanied by falling HIV infection rates, overall it has had a positive effect on drug problems (Hughes and Stevens 2010).

In the UK, by contrast, the 2000s can be characterized as a period of extension of prohibition, with GHB, GBL, ketamine, substituted cathinones (e.g. mephedrone), and substituted pyrovalerones (e.g. naphyrone) all becoming controlled drugs in recent years, leading Measham and Moore (2008) to argue that we are seeing the 'criminalisation of intoxication' *per se* through 'proactive prohibition'. With reduced funding for harm reduction initiatives (Hunt and Stevens 2004), the focus of resources for recreational users has been on enforcement rather than education or treatment.

## DRUGS AND CRIME

The European Monitoring Centre for Drugs and Drug Addiction (2003: 33) has suggested that the term 'drug-related crime' might include 'criminal offences in breach of drug legislation, crimes committed under the influence of illicit drugs, crimes committed by users to support their drug habit (mainly acquisitive crime and drug dealing) and systemic crimes committed as part of the functioning of illicit markets (fight for territories, bribing of officials, etc.)' (see, e.g., McElrath 2004). Debates about the drugs/crime relationship generally follow one or other of the following propositions: 'criminal lifestyles may facilitate involvement with drugs'; or 'dependence on drugs then leads to criminal activity to pay for further drug use' (South 1995; Bennett and Holloway 2005: 11–12). There is no dispute that there is an association between drugs and crime but the relationship is not straightforward (Roberts 2003). It is straightforward that the very illegality of drugs will make their possession and supply an offence. Thereafter things are more complicated—does drug use lead to crime or does involvement in a criminal lifestyle lead to use of drugs? Daily and dependent heroin and crack users may be committing a considerable amount of acquisitive crime to fund their use (Bennett *et al.* 2001) but at the same time, as Seddon (2002) argues:

> a link between drugs and crime is in fact only found among a minority of drug users—the 3 per cent or so of illicit drug users who are termed 'problem' users. Within this group, the association is primarily between use of heroin and/or crack cocaine and commission of certain economic/property offences (especially drug selling, shoplifting, burglary and other theft).

It should also be noted that some heroin users remain occasional and non-problem users (Warburton *et al.* 2005). For others, the route to drug use may be through involvement in an array of delinquent and criminal lifestyles (Auld *et al.* 1986; Pudney 2002), and drugs are just one commodity bought and sold in the pleasure markets of the late modern illicit economy (Ruggiero and South 1997; Hobbs *et al.* 2005). Some work (Collison 1996; Parker 1996, South 2004) has noted a greater hedonistic attachment to a consumption-oriented lifestyle among young offenders using illegal drugs and/or alcohol, and that petty crime was routinely engaged in for support. Typically, drug-related crime is non-violent and acquisitive, involving theft, shoplifting, forgery, burglary, or prostitution. More serious drug-related crimes of violence and murder have been increasing in Britain, although still on a small scale by comparison with the USA.

### 'Involvement in criminal activity leads to drug use'

Some studies provide evidence that heroin or other serious drug users would already have been involved in delinquent or criminal activities before they started using these drugs. The argument on this side is that: (a) involvement in deviant/criminal-oriented subcultures or groups would be likely to lead a person to encounter the availability of drugs sold within that culture; (b) they would have a deviant lifestyle which would accommodate deviant drug use with relative ease; and (c) while money from criminal activity might then pay for the drugs, it was not drug addiction or use *per se* which led to the perpetration of crime.

### 'Involvement in drug use causes crime'

Of course, other studies argue that there *is* a *causal* link, and that drug use (particularly of heroin) causes crime. Some crimes seem to have a clear relationship with drug use, for example where drugs are stolen or where shoplifting or burglary generates funds that are used immediately to purchase drugs. There is a huge body of work supporting this proposition, albeit principally from the USA. The evidence is convincing but so too is the evidence from studies supporting the opposing proposition; furthermore and quite predictably, studies may uncover patterns in which 'participation in acquisitive crime (which mainly involves petty shoplifting) tends to precede the first use of drugs such as heroin and crack cocaine' but that 'participation in more serious crimes, such as street crime' may tend to occur after regular use has been established (Allen 2005: 356). The simple resolution of this debate is to agree with Nurco *et al.* (1985: 101), who over 20 years ago sensibly suggested that 'the long and continuing controversy over whether narcotic addicts commit crimes primarily to support their habits or whether addiction is merely one more manifestation of a deviant and criminal life-style seems pointless in view of the fact that addicts cannot be regarded as a homogeneous group'.

## ALCOHOL AND CRIME

Concerns about the relationship between alcohol and crime are not new. According to Lombroso (1911/1968: 95–6):

> Alcohol ... is a cause of crime, first because many commit crime in order to obtain drinks, further, because men sometimes seek in drink the courage necessary to commit crime, or an excuse for their misdeeds; again, because it is by the aid of drink that young men are drawn into crime; and because the drink shop is the place for meeting of accomplices, where they not only plan their crimes but squander their gains ... it appears that alcoholism occurred oftenest in the case of those charged with assaults, sexual offences, and insurrections. Next came assassinations and homicide; and in the last rank those imprisoned for arson and theft, that is to say, crime against property.

Contemporary studies and debates concerning the extent to which alcohol consumption is responsible for certain forms of criminal behaviour are extensive but inconclusive (Raistrick *et al.* 1999; All Party Group on Alcohol Misuse 1995, see Graham and Wells for review 2001), and have some similarities and some dissimilarities with those concerning drugs and crime, such as the debate between causation and correlation. Nonetheless, the National Alcohol Harm Reduction Strategy (Cabinet Office Strategy Unit 2004: 44) argued that:

> Alcohol misuse is a major contributor to crime, disorder and anti-social behaviour, with alcohol-related crime costing society up to £7.3bn per annum. The most visible areas of concern for most people include: alcohol-related disorder and anti-social behaviour in towns and cities at night; and under-age drinking. Less visible but equally significant concerns are: crime, disorder and anti-social behaviour—often caused by repeat offenders; domestic violence; and drink-driving.

It is alcohol rather more than illegal drugs that tends to be associated with aggression and violent crime, and hence, potentially, to crime with longer-term effects for victims and society (Alcohol Concern 2001; *Lancet* 1999). Estimates from the British Medical Association suggest that the offender or victim had been drinking in 65 per cent of murders, 75 per cent of stabbings, 70 per cent of beatings, and 50 per cent of fights or domestic assaults (ibid.). Raistrick *et al.* (1999: 54) similarly note that many perpetrators and victims of crimes of disorder or violence, including murder, as well as perpetrators of acquisitive crimes, such as burglary and theft, have alcohol in their blood at the time of the offence and one-fifth of violent crime occurs in or near licensed premises. Furthermore, as with other drugs, heavier users of alcohol are more likely to have criminal records and to admit to criminal acts than are lighter users or abstainers.

However, the existence of a causal relationship between alcohol and violent crime remains difficult to substantiate (Alcohol Concern 2001). Perhaps the key conclusion is that 'alcohol may be neither a necessary nor sufficient *cause* of crime, but may nonetheless *affect* crime' (Raistrick *et al.* 1999: 55). Research findings suggest that a variety of co-factors may play a significant role in alcohol-related aggression. As with illegal drug consumption, *belief* about how alcohol is 'supposed' to affect behaviour, *coupled* with the influences of immediate social context and wider culture, are as important for the behavioural outcome as the amount of alcohol consumed. A Home Office review of research concludes that situational and cultural variables may play a role in the relationship between alcohol and aggression, and that no direct pharmacological link between alcohol and violent behaviour is supported. More probably, alcohol influences the social and cognitive processes that may lead to aggression (Deehan 1999). Hence, socialization and cultural expectations, stereotypes and labelling, circumstances and significant others, all play their part in shaping people's identities as 'aggressive' and as 'drinkers' (Borrill and Stevens 1993). Such definitions change across time and cultures, and are also strongly influenced by positive and negative images of alcohol use in entertainment media and alcohol advertising. These findings all point to the importance of situational harm reduction and crime prevention through environmental design such as the development of 'safer bars' (Graham *et al.* 2004) and corporate responsibility in the retail alcohol trade.

The relationship between masculinity, alcohol, and violence is complex and deserves more attention (Tomsen 1997; Taylor 1999: 85–6). Hunt and Joe-Laidler (2001), for example, show how alcohol plays a significant role in gang life, contributing to cohesion, solidarity, and ways of maintaining group boundaries, but also being associated with internal violence including fights caused by rivalries or disputes over honour and respect. Alcohol may have a relationship with crime in other ways, for example:

> intoxication may shift some people over the threshold from contemplating crime to committing it; ... public disorder is commonly linked to open-air drinking by young people; ... alcohol use can serve as a financial motive for crime; alcohol problems can produce a home environment conducive to anti-social behaviours; ... drunk people may be amnesic regarding the negative consequences of their criminal actions, thus failing to learn from them; and alcohol intoxication can reduce inhibitions and judgement [Raistrick *et al.* 1999: 55].

Some of these factors may contribute to crimes in which there is a potential but unknown association with alcohol; in other words, there has been considerable research on alcohol and violence, sexual assault, and acquisitive crimes, but little on crimes such as 'fraud, tax evasion, smuggling, ... and other white-collar crimes' and the influence of alcohol (Raistrick *et al.* 1999: 56).

As Raistrick *et al.* (1999: 47) note, 'it is not known why some substance misusers become dependent on one substance, such as alcohol, and others on another, such as heroin, while most avoid dependence and grow out of substance misuse, or grow into a relatively stable and controlled pattern of alcohol or other drug use as adults'. Long-term, follow-up studies examining criminal careers and drinking careers suggest that 'criminality and alcohol abuse tend to run in parallel, as both have their peak incidence in young adults and tend to diminish with age' (d'Orban 1991: 298). Persistence of heavy drinking and petty crime into mid-life characterizes 'habitual drunkenness offenders' (ibid.), and some studies show a disproportionately higher level of alcohol problems among those arrested and prisoners than found in the general population (Raistrick *et al.* 1999). Cautions about inferring causality will still apply however: regardless of whether alcohol consumption precedes or succeeds offences (property or violent) and whatever the alcohol consumption levels involved (be it higher or lower than average) the drinking must still be considered in relation to specific criminal events.

### The binge drinking debate

From the mid-1990s significant changes occurred in young people's alcohol consumption which resulted in a significant increase in the quantity of alcohol consumed by both school pupils under 16 (Balding 2004) and young adults (ONS 2004), resulting in increased sessional consumption and a focus on drinking for maximum intoxication (Measham 1996). Increased consumption by young women proved to be a particular cause for concern, with associated concerns about the vulnerability and 'unfeminine' behaviour in emulation of male drunkenness by those who became known as 'ladettes' (Jackson and Tinkler 2007). Reasons for increased sessional consumption or 'binge drinking' and a notable desire for 'determined drunkenness' (Measham 2004), were associated with changes in the alcohol industry such as the development of café bars and fun pubs, flavoured alcoholic beverages ('alcopops'), and other high-strength bot-tled drinks (Measham and Brain 2005), alongside a broader expansion of the night-time economy (Hobbs *et al.* 2005), and excessive, sometimes titillating press coverage (Hayward and Hobbs 2007). As the 2000s drew to a close, a fall in alcohol consumption in the UK, particularly amongst young people, was linked to the economic reces-sion and associated job insecurities, whilst amongst older age groups and professional occupations increased home drinking, wine drinking, and weekday drinking are all increasing (Jayne *et al.* 2008; Valentine *et al.* 2007; Measham and Østergaard 2009). Thus whilst the acute criminal justice demands resulting from public drunkenness and associated problems on the streets may be waning, the chronic and public health concerns of the nation's 'favourite drug' implicate the targeting of a different socio-demographic group for alcohol education.

## CONCLUSIONS

In a 2011 report a new 'Global Commission on Drug Policy', with a membership that included former UN Secretary-General Kofi Annan, former leaders of Colombia, Mexico, and Brazil as well as writers, financiers, entrepreneurs, and politicians, argued that 'repressive strategies will not solve the drug problem' and called for an end to the criminalization of drug use and exploration of alternative legal approaches that could weaken criminal organizations and promote health and treatment responses. In California the case for legalization of marijuana use was put to the vote as 'Proposition 19' in November 2010 but despite the optimism of pro-reform lobbyists was rejected by voters. The debates about decriminalization and legalization are as lively as ever and one key reason for the protracted and unresolved nature of these debates is that there are strong arguments on both sides. The repressive approach is costly, is not evidently successful, and can present challenges to human rights in the formulation of laws and the operations of law enforcement and other agencies. Yet, a liberalized market, whether controlled or uncontrolled, could lead to an increase in consumption and problems of the kind that are associated with heavy use of any psychoactive substances—mental health illnesses, impairment while driving or working, absenteeism from work or study, as well as the cost of buying drugs.

One increasingly important issue to factor into the equation is the impact of both drug production and drug control on the environment. According to one estimate, in current conditions of clandestine production, for every gram of cocaine used, 4m square of rainforest have been destroyed in the process of cultivation (Laville 2008: 13) while laboratory processing results in chemical residues contaminating the land. Perversely, law enforcement efforts to eradicate drug crops also do this through their use of herbicides (de Olmo 1998: 272–7). At the same time, both traffickers and international police interception operations have become 'a serious but largely neglected impediment to conservation efforts' (Aldhous 2006: 6).

The dominant discourse around drug control remains Western-led and neglects comparative work that can throw light upon portraits of drug use in other cultures, and ways of managing matters in other contexts (Coomber and South 2004). On the domestic front, policy-makers and expert committees have reconsidered drugs law and treatment but despite acknowledging health issues, twenty-first century drug policy in the UK has so far shown no sign of a shift away from the legality/illegality anchor and the criminal justice preoccupations that accompany this. This distinction and state of affairs is rooted in legislation that is now over 40 years old (the Misuse of Drugs Act 1971) and shows signs of decrepitude in its creaky review process for individual drugs at a time when the Internet has marketed over 40 new compounds in the last year alone (Sumnall *et al.* 2011). There are now growing calls for a major review of UK legislation and an impact assessment of the MDA (Birdwell *et al.* 2011; Police Foundation 2000; Royal Society of Arts 2007; Transform 2009).

As the twenty-first century unfolds, the 'problems' that drugs (legal and illegal) pose will not disappear but it cannot be assumed that policy and legislation based on models from the 1960s and 1970s will provide the right way to address these.

### ■ SELECTED FURTHER READING

Useful websites with links to further sites are provided by Drugscope: www.drugscope.co.uk; by Alcohol Concern: www.alcoholconcern.org.uk; and by the Royal Society of Arts Drugs Commission: www.rsadrugscommission.org/. The Drugscope website provides access to *Drugsearch*, an online drugs encyclopaedia. P. Bean (2004), *Drugs and Crime* (Willan) and

R. Hammersley (2008), *Drugs and Crime* (Polity) focus on law enforcement and criminal justice debates; T. Bennett and K. Holloway (2005), *Understanding drugs, alcohol and crime* (Open University Press) and M. Simpson *et al.* (eds) (2007), *Drugs in Britain* (Palgrave) provide good general overviews. N. South (ed.) (1995), *Drugs, Crime and Criminal Justice*, Vols 1 and 2 (Dartmouth) reprint various classic and recent articles.

# ■ REFERENCES

ADVISORY COUNCIL ON MISUSE OF DRUGS (1998), *Drug Misuse and the Environment: A Report by the Advisory Council on the Misuse of Drugs*, London: Stationery Office.

—— (2009), *The primary prevention of hepatitis C among injecting drug users*, London: Home Office.

AKHTAR, S. and SOUTH, N. (2000), 'Hidden from heroin's history: heroin use and dealing within an English Asian community', in M. Hough and M. Natarajan (eds), *International Drug Markets: From Research to Policy*, Crime Prevention Studies, Vol. 11, New York: Criminal Justice Press.

ALCOHOL CONCERN (2001), www.alcoholconcern. org.uk/.

—— (2003), 'Alcohol and Mortality', *Acquire*: Alcohol Concern's Quarterly Information and Research Bulletin, Summer, London: Alcohol Concern. Available at www.alcoholconcern.org.uk/files/20030807_172030_mortality.pdf.

—— (2009), *Future Proof: Can we afford the cost of drinking too much?'*, London: Alcohol Concern, www.alcoholconcern. org.uk/.

ALDHOUS, P. (2006), 'Drugs, crime and a conservation crisis', *New Scientist*, 2nd September: 6.

ALL PARTY GROUP ON ALCOHOL MISUSE (1995), *Alcohol and Crime: Breaking the Link*, London: Alcohol Concern.

ALLEN, C. (2005), 'The links between heroin, crack cocaine and crime', *British Journal of Criminology*, 45(3): 355–72.

AULD, J., DORN, N., and SOUTH, N. (1986), 'Irregular Work, Irregular Pleasures: Heroin in the 1980s', in R. Matthews and J. Young (eds), *Confronting Crime*, London: Sage.

BACHUS, L., STRANG, J., and WATSON, P. (2000), 'Pathways to Abstinence: Two-Year Follow-up Data on 60 Abstinent Former Opiate Addicts', *European Addiction Research*, 6: 141–7.

BALDING, J. (2004), *Trends—Young People and Alcohol: Attitudes to drinking 1993–2001*, Exeter: Schools Health Education Unit.

RASHFORD, J., BUFFIN, J., and PATEL, K. (2003), *The Department of Health's Black and Minority Ethnic Drug Misuse Needs Assessment Project, Report 2: The Findings*, Preston: Centre for Ethnicity and Health.

BEAN, P. (2004), *Drugs and Crime*, Cullompton, Devon: Willan.

BECKER, J. and DUFFY, C. (2002), *Women Drug Users and Drugs Service Provision*, DPAS paper 17, London: Home Office.

BENNETT, T. and HOLLOWAY, K. (2005), *Understanding drugs, alcohol and crime*, Maidenhead: Open University Press.

——, ——, and WILLIAMS, T. (2001), 'Drug Use and Offending', *Findings*, 148, London: Home Office.

BERRIDGE, V. (1978a), 'Victorian Opium Eating: Responses to Opiate Use in Nineteenth-Century England', *Victorian Studies*, 21(4): 437–61.

BERRIDGE, V. (1978b), 'War Conditions and Narcotics Control: The Passing of the Defence of the Realm Act Regulation 40B', *Journal of Social Policy*, 7(3): 285–304.

—— (1979), 'Morality and Medical Science: Concepts of Narcotic Addiction in Britain, 1820–1926', *Annals of Science*, 36: 67–85.

—— (1984), 'Drugs and social policy: the establishment of drug control in Britain, 1900–1930', *British Journal of Addiction*, 79: 1.

—— (1999), *Opium and the People*, rev. edn, London: Free Association.

—— and EDWARDS, G. (1987), *Opium and the People*, 2nd edn, New Haven, Conn.: Yale University Press.

BEST, D. and ABDULRAHIM, D. (2005), *Women in Drug Treatment Services*, Research Briefing 6, London: National Treatment Agency.

—— et al. (2001), 'Assessment of a concentrated, high-profile police operation: No discernible impact on drug availability, price or purity', *British Journal of Criminology*, 41: 738–745.

BIRDWELL, J., CHAPMAN, J., AND SINGLETON, N. (2011), *Taking drugs seriously: A Demos and UK Drug Policy Commission report on legal highs*, London: Demos.

BLACKMAN, S. (2004), *Chilling Out*, Maidenhead: Open University Press.

BORRILL, J. and STEVENS, D. (1993), 'Understanding human violence: the implications of social structure, gender, social perception and alcohol', *Criminal Behaviour and Mental Health*, 3: 129–41.

BOYD, S. (2004), *From Witches to Crack Moms: Women, Drug Law and Policy*, Durham, N.C.: Academic Press.

BOYS, A., DOBSON, J., MARSDEN, J., and STRANG, J. (2001), *Cocaine Trends: A Qualitative Study of Young People and Cocaine Use*, London: National Addiction Centre.

BRANDT, S., SUMNALL, H., MEASHAM, F., and COLE, J. (2010), 'Second generation mephedrone: The confusing case of NRG-1', *British Medical Journal*, 6 July, 341: c3564.

BRUUN, K., PAN, L., and REXED, I. (1975), *The Gentlemen's Club: International Control of Drugs and Alcohol*, Chicago, Ill.: University of Chicago Press.

CABINET OFFICE (2003), *Alcohol Misuse: How much does it cost?*, London: Cabinet Office.

CABINET OFFICE STRATEGY UNIT (2004), *Alcohol Harm Reduction Strategy for England*, London: Cabinet Office.

CARRABINE, E., IGANSKI, P., LEE, M., PLUMMER, K., and SOUTH, N. (2004), *Criminology: A Sociological Introduction*, London and New York: Routledge.

CHAPLIN, R., FLATLEY, J., and SMITH, K. (eds) (2011), *Crime in England and Wales 2010/11: Findings from the British Crime Survey and police recorded crime*, 1st edn, Home Office Statistical Bulletin 10/11, London: Home Office.

CHAWLA, S. and PIETSCHMANN, T. (2005), 'Drug trafficking as a transnational crime', in P. Reichel (ed.), *Handbook of Transnational Crime and Justice*, Thousand Oaks, Cal.: Sage.

CHIVITE-MATTHEWS, N., RICHARDSON, A., O'SHEA, J., BECKER, J., OWEN, J., ROE, S., and CONDON, J. (2005), *Drug misuse declared: Findings from the 2003–04 British Crime Survey*, London: Home Office Statistical Bulletin 04/05.

COLLISON, M. (1996), 'In search of the high life: drugs, crime, masculinity and consumption', *British Journal of Criminology*, 36(3): 428–44.

CONDON, J. and SMITH, N. (2003), *Prevalence of Drug Use: Key Findings from the 2002/2003 British Crime Survey*, London: Home Office.

COOMBER, R. and SAITH, N. (eds) (2004), *Drug Use in Cultural Contexts 'Beyond the West': Tradition. Change and Post-Colonialism*, London: Free Association Books.

CORBETT, C. (2003), *Car Crime*, Cullompton, Devon: Willan.

CORKERY, J. (2000), *Drug Seizure and Offender Statistics, UK, 1998*, Statistical Bulletin 3/00, London: Home Office.

COWAN, R. (2006), 'Police raid Vietnamese cannabis factory', *Guardian Unlimited*, 16 March.

CURRIE, E. (1993), 'Towards a policy on drugs', *Dissent* (Winter): 65–71.

DALGARNO, P. and SHEWAN, D. (2005), 'Reducing the risks of drug use: the case for set and setting', *Addiction Research and Theory*, 13(3): 259–65.

DALY, M. (2005), 'Alien nation', *Druglink*, 20(4): 6–8.

DAVIS, J. and DITTON, J. (1990), 'The 1990s: Decade of the Stimulants?', *British Journal of Addiction*, 85: 811–13.

DEEHAN, A. (1999), *Alcohol and Crime: Taking Stock*, Policing and Crime Reduction Unit, London: Home Office.

DEL OLMO, R. (1998), 'The ecological impact of illicit drug cultivation and crop eradication programs in Latin America', *Theoretical Criminology*, 2(2): 269–78.

DENTON, B. and O'MALLEY, P. (1999), 'Gender, trust, and business. Women drug dealers in the illicit economy', *British Journal of Criminology*, 39: 513–30.

DEPARTMENT OF HEALTH (2008), *The cost of alcohol harm to the NHS in England*, London: Department of Health.

D'ORBAN, P. (1991), 'The Crimes Connection: Alcohol', in I. Glass (ed.), *The International Handbook of Addiction Behaviour*, London: Routledge.

DORN, N. (2004), 'UK policing of drug traffickers and users: policy implementation in the contexts of national law, European traditions, international drug conventions and security after 2001', *Journal of Drug Issues*.

——, MURJI, K., and SOUTH, N. (1992), *Traffickers: Drug Markets and Law Enforcement*, London: Routledge.

DOWNES, D. (1977), 'The Drug Addict as a Folk Devil', in P. Rock (ed.), *Drugs and Politics*, New Brunswick, N.J.: Transaction.

DRUGLINK (1992), 'Low Dependence and Use Typical of British Cocaine/Crack Users', *Druglink*, 7(3): 6.

—— (2005), 'Bengalis face heroin problem', *Druglink*, 20(4): 4.

DRUGSCOPE (2005), 'How many people die from using drugs?', Drugscope FAQs, www.drugscope.org.uk.

—— (2006), *Druglink Guide to Drugs (updated)*, London: Drugscope.

DUFF, C. (2005), 'Party drugs and party people: Examining the "normalisation" of recreational drug use in Melbourne, Australia', *International Journal of Drug Policy*, 16:161–70.

ECONOMIST, THE (2001), 'The case for legalisation: Time for a puff of sanity', *The Economist*; 26 July 2001.

EDMONDS, K., SUMNALL, H., MCVEIGH, J., and BELLIS, M. (2005), *Drug Prevention Among Vulnerable Young People*, Liverpool: National Collaborating Centre for Drug Prevention.

EDMUNDS, M., HOUGH, M., TURNBULL, P., and MAY, T. (1999), *Doing Justice to Treatment: Referring Offenders to Drug Services*, DPAS paper 2, London: Home Office.

ETTORRE, E. and RISKA, E. (1995), *Gendered Moods: Psychotropics and Society*, London: Routledge.

EUROPEAN MONITORING CENTRE FOR DRUGS AND DRUG ADDICTION (EMCDDA) (2010A), *Europol–EMCDDA Joint Report on a new psychoactive substance: 4-methylmethcathinone (mephedrone)*. Lisbon: EMCDDA.

—— (2011B), *Annual Report: the State of the Drugs Problem in Europe*, Lisbon: EMCDDA.

—— (2003), *The State of the Drugs Problem in the European Union and Norway*, Luxembourg: EMCDDA.

FAGAN, J. (1994), 'Women and drugs revisited: female participation in the cocaine economy', *Journal of Drug Issues*, 24(2): 179–225.

FORESIGHT PROJECT (2006), 'Ethical aspects of developments in neuroscience and drug addiction—Summary', *Drugs Futures 2025*, London: Office of Science and Technology.

FOSTER, J. (2000), 'Social Exclusion, Crime and Drugs', *Drugs: Education, Prevention and Policy*, 7(4): 317–30.

GHODSE, H., CORKERY, J., AHMED, K., NAIDOO, V., OVEFESO, A., and SCHIFANO, F. (2010), *Drug-related deaths in the UK Annual Report 2010*, National Programme on Substance Abuse Deaths (np-SAD), International Centre for Drug Policy, London: St George's, University of London.

——(2005), *Drug Misuse Treatment and Reductions in Crime*, Research Briefing 8, London: National Treatment Agency for Substance Misuse.

GRAHAM, K. AND WELLS, K. (2001), 'Alcohol and Crime: Examining the link', in N. Heather, T. Peters, and T. Stockwell (eds), *International Handbook on Alcohol Dependence and Problems*, Chichester: John Wiley and Sons.

GRAHAM, K., OSGOOD, W., ZIBROWSKI, E., PURCELL, J., GLIKSMAN, L., LEONARD, K., PERNANEN, K., SALTZ R., AND TOOMEY, T. (2004), 'The effect of the Safer Bars program on physical aggression in bars: Results of a randomised control', *Trial, Drug and Alcohol Review*, 23(1): 31–41.

GREEN, G., SMITH, R., and SOUTH, N. (2005), 'Court based psychiatric assessment: a case for an integrated and diversionary public health role', *Journal of Forensic Psychiatry and Psychology*, 16(3): 577–91.

GRINSPOON, L. (1999), 'Medical Marijuana in a Time of Prohibition', *International Journal of Drug Policy*, 10(3): 145–56.

HADFIELD, P. and MEASHAM, F. (2009a), 'A Review of Nightlife and Crime in England and Wales', in Hadfield, P. (ed.), *Nightlife and Crime*, Oxford: Oxford University Press.

—— and —— (2009b), 'Shaping the Night: How licensing, social divisions and informal social controls mould the form and content of nightlife', *Crime Prevention and Community Safety: An International Journal*, 11(3): 219–34.

HAKKARAINEN, P., TIGERSTEDT, C., and TAMMI, T. (2007), 'Dual-track drug policy: Normalization of the drug problem in Finland', *Drugs: Education, Prevention and Policy*, 14(6): 543–58.

HALLAM, C. (2011), *The Heroin Shortage in the UK and Europe*, International Drug Policy Consortium Briefing Paper, London: IDPC.

HAND, T. AND RISHIRAJ, A. (2009), *Seizures of Drugs in England and Wales, 2008/9*, Home Office Statistical Bulletin 16/09, London: Home Office.

HAYES, P. (2001), 'Driving up treatment standards: interview', *Access*, 4 (Drugs Prevention Advisory Service newsletter).

HAYWARD, K. and HOBBS, D. (2007), 'Beyond the Binge in "Booze Britain": Market-Led liminalization and the spectacle of binge drinking', *British Journal of Sociology*, 58(3): 437–56.

HENDERSON, S. (1997), *Ecstasy: Case Unsolved*, London: Pandora.

—— (1999), 'Drugs and Culture: the Question of Gender', in N. South (ed.), *Drugs: Cultures, Controls and Everyday Life*, London: Sage.

HM GOVERNMENT (1998), *Tackling Drugs to Build a Better Britain*, London: Stationery Office.

HIBELL, B., GUTTORMSSON, U., AHLSTRÖM, S., BALAKIREVA, O., BJARNASON, T., KOKKEVI, A., and KRAUS, L. (2009), *The 2007 ESPAD Report: Substance Use Among Students in 35 European Countries*, Stockholm: The Swedish Council for Information on Alcohol and Other Drugs.

HOBBS, R., HADFIELD, P., LISTER, S., and WINLOW, S. (2005), *Bouncers: violence and governance in the night time economy*, Oxford: Oxford University Press.

HOUGH, M. and HUNTER, G. (2008), 'The Licensing Act's impact on crime and disorder: an evaluation', *Criminology and Criminal Justice*, 8(3): 239–260.

HUGHES, C. and STEVENS, A. (2010), 'What can we learn from the Portuguese decriminalization of illicit drugs?', *British Journal of Criminology*, 50: 999–1022.

HUMPHREYS, D. and EISNER, M. (2010), 'Evaluating a natural experiment in alcohol policy: The Licensing Act (2003) and the requirement for attention to implementation' *Criminology and Public Policy*, 9(1): 41–67.

HUNT, G. and JOE-LAIDLER, K. (2001), 'Alcohol and violence in the lives of gang members', *Alcohol Research and Health*, 25(1): 66–71.

——, ——, and MACKENZIE, K. (2000), ' "Chillin", Being Dogged and Getting Buzzed": Alcohol in the lives of female gang members', *Drugs: Education, Prevention and Policy*, 7(4): 331–53.

HUSAK, D. and DEMARNEFFE, P. (2005), *The Legalization of Drugs*, Cambridge: Cambridge University Press.

HUTTON, F. (2006), *Risky Pleasures? Club Cultures and Feminine Identities*, Aldershot: Ashgate.

—— (2010), 'Kiwis, Clubs and Drugs: Club Cultures in Wellington, New Zealand', *Australian and New Zealand Journal of Criminology*, 43. 91–111.

INCIARDI, J. and MCBRIDE, D. (1989), 'Legalisation. A High Risk Alternative in the War on Drugs', *American Behavioural Scientist*, 32(3): 259–89.

INSTITUTE FOR THE STUDY OF DRUG DEPENDENCE (1999), 'Coke in the UK', *Druglink*, 14(6): 4.

JACKSON, C. and TINKLER, P. (2007), '"Ladettes" and "Modern Girls": "troublesome" young femininities', *The Sociological Review*, 55(2): 251–72.

JARVINEN, M. and DEMANT, J. (2011), 'The normalisation of cannabis use among young people: Symbolic boundary work in focus groups', *Health, Risk and Society*, 1(2): 165–82.

JAYNE, M., VALENTINE, G., and HOLLOWAY, S. (2008), 'Fluid Boundaries—British Binge Drinking and European Civility: Alcohol and the Production and Consumption of Public Space', *Space and Polity* 12(1): 81–100.

JOHNSTONE, G. (1996), *Medical Concepts and Penal Policy*, London: Cavendish.

KOHN, M. (1992), *Dope Girls: The Birth of the British Drug Underground*, London: Lawrence and Wishart.

*Lancet, The* (1999), 'Alcohol and Violence', *The Lancet*, 336: 1223–24, 17 November.

LAVILLE, S. (2008), 'Cocaine users are destroying the rainforest—at 4m2 a gram', *The Guardian*, 19 November: 13.

LEE, M. and SOUTH, N. (2003), 'Policing and drugs', in T. Newburn (ed.), *The Handbook of Policing*, Cullompton, Devon: Willan.

LOMBROSO, C. (1968), *Crime: Its Causes and Remedies*, Montclair, N. J.: Patterson Smith, originally published 1911.

MCALLISTER, W. (2000), *Drug Diplomacy in the Twentieth Century*, London: Routledge.

MCCARRON, M. (2006), 'Drugs: which policies work?', *RSA Journal*, February, 29–33.

MACCOUN, R. and REUTER, P. (2001), *Drug War Heresies: Learning from Other Vices, Times, and Places*, Cambridge: Cambridge University Press.

MCDONALD, M. (ed.) (1994), *Gender, Drink and Drugs*, Oxford: Berg.

MCELRATH, K. (2004), 'Drug Use and Drug Markets in the Context of Political Conflict: The Case of Northern Ireland', *Addiction Research and Theory*, 12(6): 577–90.

—— and O'NEILL, C. (2011), 'Experiences with mephedrone pre and post-legislative controls: Perceptions of safety and sources of supply', *International Journal of Drug Policy*, 22(2): 120–27.

MACGREGOR, S. (1998), 'Reluctant Partners: Trends in Approaches to Urban Drug-taking in Contemporary Britain', *Journal of Drug Issues*, 28(1): 185–98.

—— (1999), 'Medicine, Custom or Moral Fibre: Policy Responses to Drug Misuse', in N. South (ed.), *Drugs: Cultures, Controls and Everyday Life*, London: Sage.

MAHER, L. (1997), *Sexed Work: Gender, Race and Resistance in a Brooklyn Drug Market*, Oxford: Clarendon Press.

MATASSA, M. and NEWBURN, T. (2003), 'Policing and terrorism', in T. Newburn (ed.), *The Handbook of Policing*, Cullompton, Devon: Willan.

MAY, T. and HOUGH, M. (2004), 'Drug markets and distribution systems', *Addiction Research and Theory*, 12(6): 549–63.

——, EDMUNDS, M., and HOUGH, M. (1999), *Street Business: Links Between Sex and Drug Markets*, Crime Prevention Series Paper, London: Home Office Police Research Group.

MEASHAM, F. and BRAIN, K. (2005), 'Binge' drinking, British alcohol policy and the new culture of intoxication, *Crime, Media, Culture: An international journal*, 1(3): 263–84.

——and MOORE, K. (2008), 'The Criminalisation of Intoxication', in P. Squires (ed.), *ASBO Nation: The criminalisation of nuisance*, Bristol: Policy.

—— and ØSTERGAARD, J. (2009), 'The Public Face of Binge Drinking: British and Danish young women, recent trends in alcohol consumption and the European binge drinking debate', *Probation Journal*, Special Issue, 56(4): 415–434.

—— and SHINER, M. (2009), 'The Legacy of Normalisation: The role of classical and contemporary criminological theory in understanding young people's drug use', *International Journal of Drug Policy*, Special edition: Drug Policy Analysis, 20(6): 502–8.

——, ALDRIDGE, J, and PARKER, H. (2001), *Dancing on Drugs: Risk, Health and Hedonism in the British Club Scene*, London: FAB.

—— MOORE, K., and ØSTERGAARD, J. (2011b), 'Mephedrone, "Bubble" and Unidentified White Powders: The contested identities of synthetic "legal highs" ', *Drugs and Alcohol Today*, 11(3): 137–147.

——, WILLIAMS, L., AND ALDRIDGE, J. (2011a), 'Marriage, mortgage, motherhood: What longitudinal surveys can tell us about gender, "drug careers" and the normalisation of adult drug use', *International Journal of Drug Policy*, Special issues: Sociological and antropological approaches to drug policy, 22(6): 420–427.

——, MOORE, K., NEWCOMBE, R., and WELCH, Z. (2010), 'Tweaking, Bombing, Dabbing and Stockpiling: The emergence of mephedrone and the perversity of prohibition', *Drugs and Alcohol Today*, 10(1): 14–21.

——, WOOD, D., DARGAN, P., and MOORE, K. (2011c), 'The Rise in Legal Highs: Prevalence and patterns in the use of illegal drugs and first and second generation "legal highs" in south London gay dance clubs', *Journal of Substance Use*, 16(4): 263–272.

MINISTRY OF HEALTH (1926), *Report of the Departmental Committee on Morphine and Heroin Addiction*, London: HMSO.

MINISTRY OF JUSTICE (2010), *Statistics on Race and the Criminal Justice System—2008/09*, London: Ministry of Justice.

MOTT, J. (1991), 'Crime and Heroin Use', in D. Whynes and P. Bean (eds), *Policing and Prescribing: The British System of Drug Control*, London: Macmillan.

MURJI, K. (1999), 'White Lines: Culture, "Race" and Drugs', in N. South (ed.), *Drugs: Cultures, Controls and Everyday Life*, London: Sage.

MWENDA, L. (2005), *Drug Offenders in England and Wales*, Statistical Bulletin, 23/05, London: Home Office.

NADELMAN, E. (1989), 'Drug Prohibition in the United States: Costs, Consequences and Alternatives', *Science*, 245: 939–47.

NCSR/NFER (National Centre for Social Research/National Foundation for Education Research) (2005), *Smoking, Drinking and Drug Use among Young People in England in 2004*, London: Department of Health.

NHS INFORMATION CENTRE (2009), *Smoking Drinking and Drug use among Young People in England in 2009*, Leeds: The information centre. Available at: www.ic.nhs.uk/pubs/sdd09fullreport.

—— (2011), *Statistics on Alcohol: England, 2011*, Leeds: The Health and Social Care Information Centre.

NURCO, D., BALL, J., SHAFFER, J., and HANLON, T. (1985), 'The Criminality of Narcotic Addicts', *The Journal of Nervous and Mental Disease*, 173(2): 94–102.

NUTT, D., KING, L., and PHILLIPS, L. (2010), 'Drug harms in the UK: a multicriteria decision analysis', *The Lancet*, 376 (9752): 1558–65.

OFFICE FOR NATIONAL STATISTICS, (2004a), *Statistics on alcohol: England, 2004*, Statistical Bulletin 2004/15, London: The Stationery Office.

OSGERBY, B. (1998), *Youth in Britain since 1945*, Oxford: Blackwell.

PARKER, H. (1996), 'Alcohol, persistent young offenders and criminological cul-de-sacs', *British Journal of Criminology*, 36(2): 282–99.

—— and MEASHAM, F. (1994), 'Pick 'n Mix: changing patterns of illicit drug use amongst 1990s adolescents', *Drugs: Education, Prevention and Policy*, 1(1): 5–14.

——, ALDRIDGE, J., and MEASHAM, F. (1998), *Illegal Leisure: The Normalization of Adolescent Recreational Drug Use*, London: Routledge.

PARSSINEN, T. (1983), *Secret Passions, Secret Remedies: Narcotic Drugs in British Society, 1820–1930*, Manchester: Manchester University Press.

PATEL, K. (1999), 'Watching brief', *Druglink*, 14(5): 18–19.

PEARSON, G. (1987a), *The New Heroin Users*, Oxford: Basil Blackwell.

—— (1987b), 'Social Deprivation, Unemployment and Patterns of Heroin Use', in N. Dorn and N. South (eds), *A Land Fit for Heroin?: Drug Policies, Prevention and Practice*, London: Macmillan.

—— (1991), 'Drug Control Policies in Britain', in M. Tonry and J. Q. Wilson (eds), *Drugs and the Criminal Justice System, Crime and Justice*, 14: 167–227.

—— (2001), 'Normal drug use', *Substance Use and Misuse*, 36 (1 & 2): 167–200.

—— and HOBBS, D. (2001), *Middle Market Drug Distribution*. Research Study 27. London: Home Office.

—— and PATEL, K. (1998), 'Drugs, Deprivation and Ethnicity: Outreach among Asian Drug Users in a Northern English City', *Journal of Drug Issues*, 28(1): 199–224.

PENNAY, A. AND MOORE, D. (2010), 'Exploring the micro-politics of normalisation: Narratives of pleasure, self-control and desire in a sample of young Australian "party drug" users', *Addiction Research and Theory*, 18(5): 557–71.

PIRMOHAMED, M., BROWN, C., OWENS, L., LUKE, C., GILMORE, I., BRECKENRIDGE, A., and PARK, B. (2000), 'The burden of alcohol misuse on an inner-city general hospital', *QJM: International Journal of Medicine*, 93(5): 291–5.

PLANT, M., MILLER, P., and PLANT, M. (2005), 'The relationship between alcohol consumption and problem behaviours: gender differences among British adults', *Journal of Substance Use*, 10(1): 22–30.

POLICE FOUNDATION (2000), *Drugs and the Law: Report of the Independent Inquiry*, London: Police Foundation.

PRISON REFORM TRUST (2005), *Prison Factfile, May 2005*, London: PRT. www.prisonreformtrust.org.uk.

PUDNEY, S. (2002), *The Road to Ruin? Sequences of Initiation into Drug Use and Offending by Young People in Britain*, Home Office Research Studies 252, London: Home Office.

RAISTRICK, D., HODGSON, R., and RITSON, B. (eds) (1999), *Tackling Alcohol Together: The Evidence Base for a UK Alcohol Policy*, London: Free Association Books.

RASMUSSEN, N. (2008), *On Speed: The Many Lives of Amphetamine*, New York: New York University Press.

RESEARCH DEVELOPMENT AND STATISTICS DIRECTORATE (2003), *Ethnicity and drug use: key findings from the 2001/2002 British Crime Survey*, London: Home Office.

ROBERTS, M. (2003), *Drugs and Crime: From Warfare to Welfare*, London: NACRO.

ROLLES, S. (2010), 'Alternatives to the war on drugs', *British Medical Journal*, 341: c3360.

—— and MEASHAM, F. (2011), 'Questioning the method and utility of ranking drug harms in drug policy', *International Journal of Drug Policy*, 22: 243–46.

ROSENBAUM, M. (1981), *Women on Heroin*, New Brunswick, N.J.: Rutgers University Press.

ROYAL COLLEGE OF PHYSICIANS AND BRITISH PAEDIATRIC ASSOCIATION (1995), *Alcohol and the Young*, London: Royal College of Physicians.

ROYAL COLLEGE OF PSYCHIATRISTS (2011), *Our Invisible Addicts*, College Report CR165, London: Royal College of Psychiatrists.

ROYAL SOCIETY OF ARTS (RSA) Drugs Commission as (2006), 'News page' at www.rsadrugscommission.org/.

ROYAL SOCIETY OF ARTS Drugs Commission. (2007), *Drugs-Facing Facts: The Report of the RSA Commission on Illegal Drugs, Communities and Public Policy*, London: RSA.

RUGGIERO, V. (1999), 'Drugs as a password and the law as a drug: Discussing the legalisation of illicit substances', in N. South, *Drugs: Cultures, Controls and Everyday Life*,

—— and SOUTH, N. (1995), *Eurodrugs: Drug Use, Markets and Trafficking in Europe*, London: UCL.

—— and —— (1997), 'The Late-Modern City as a Bazaar: Drug Markets, Illegal Enterprise and "the Barricades"', *British Journal of Sociology*, 48(1): 55–71.

SANDERS, B. (2005), 'In the club: ecstasy use and supply in a London nightclub', *Sociology*, 39(2): 241–58.

SCHMIDT, M., SHARMA, A., SCHIFANO, F., and FEINMANN, C. (2011), '"Legal highs" on the net— Evaluation of UK-based websites, products and product information', *Forensic Science International*, 206(1): 92–97.

SEDDON, T. (2002), 'Five Myths about Drugs and Crime', *Safer Society*, 14, Autumn.

SHAPIRO, H. (1999), 'Dances with Drugs', in N. South (ed.), *Drugs: Cultures, Controls and Everyday Life*, London: Sage.

SHARP, C., BAKER, P., GAILDEN, C., RAMSAY, M., and SANDHI, A. (2001), *Drug Misuse Declared in 2000: Results from the British Crime Survey*, Findings 149, London: Home Office.

SHEPHERD, J. and LISLES, C. (1998), 'Towards Multi-Agency Violence Prevention and Victim Support', *British Journal of Criminology*, 38(3): 351–70.

SHINER, M. and NEWBURN, T. (1999), 'Taking Tea with Noel: The Place and Meaning of Drug Use in Everyday Life', in N. South (ed.), *Drugs: Cultures, Controls and Everyday Life*, London: Sage.

SINGLETON, N., FARREL, M., and MELTZER, H. (1999), *Substance Misuse among Prisoners in England and Wales*, London: Office of National Statistics.

SMART, C. (1984), 'Social Policy and Drug Addiction: A Critical Study of Policy Development', *British Journal of Addiction*, 79: 31–9.

SMITH, K. AND FLATLEY, J. (2011), *Drug Misuse Declared: Findings from the 2010/11 British Crime Survey, England and Wales*, Home Office Statistical Bulletin 12/11, London: Home Office.

SOCIAL EXCLUSION UNIT (2004), *A New Direction for the Social Exclusion Unit 2004–5: Improving Service Delivery to the Most Disadvantaged*, London: Office of the Deputy Prime Minister.

SOUTH, N. (ed.) (1995), *Drugs, Crime and Criminal Justice, Vol. 1*, Aldershot: Dartmouth.

—— (ed.) (1999a), *Drugs: Cultures, Controls and Everyday Life*, London: Sage.

—— (1999b), 'Debating Drugs and Everyday Life', in N. South (ed.), *Drugs: Cultures, Controls and Everyday Life*, London: Sage.

—— (2004), 'Managing work, hedonism and the borderline between the legal and illegal markets', *Addiction Research and Theory*, 122(6): 525–38.

——, AKHTAR, S., NIGHTINGALE, R., and STEWART, M. (2001), 'Idle Hands: The Role of Employment in Addiction Treatment', *Drug and Alcohol Findings*, 1(6): 24–30.

STOCKWELL, T. and CHIKRITZHS, T. (2009), 'Do relaxed trading hours for bars and clubs mean more relaxed drinking? A review of international research on the impacts of changes to permitted hours of drinking', *Crime Prevention and Community Safety*, 11(3): 153–70.

STRATEGY UNIT (2003), *Drugs Report, Parts 1 and 2*, London: Cabinet Office.

SUMNALL, H., McGRATH, Y., McVEIGH, J., BURRELL, K., WILKINSON, L., and BELLIS, M. (2006), *Drug Use Prevention Among Young People*, London: National Institute for Health and Clinical Excellence.

TAYLOR, A. (1993), *Women Drug Users*, Oxford: Clarendon Press.

TAYLOR, I. (1999), *Crime in Context: A Critical Criminology of Market Societies*, Cambridge: Polity.

TOMSEN, S. (1997), 'A Top Night: Social Protest, Masculinity and the Culture of Drinking Violence', *British Journal of Criminology*, 37(1): 90–102.

TRANSFORM DRUG POLICY FOUNDATION, (2009), *After the War on Drugs: Blueprint for Regulation*, Bristol: Transform.

TYLER, A. (1995), *Street Drugs*, London: Hodder & Stoughton.

UNITED NATIONS OFFICE ON DRUGS AND CRIME, (2011), World Drug Report 2011, Vienna: UNODC.

VALENTINE, G., HOLLOWAY, S.L., JAYNE, M., and KNELL C. (2007) *Drinking Places: Where People Drink and Why*, Leeds: Joseph Rowntree Foundation.

WARBURTON, H., TURNBULL, P., and HOUGH, M. (2005), *User perceptions of occasional and controlled heroin use*, York: Joseph Rowntree Foundation.

WARREN, S and WRAY-BLISS, E. (2009), 'Workforce drug testing: a critique and reframing', *New Technology, Work and Employment*, 24(2): 163–79.

WHITTINGTON, D. (1999), 'Nang Tien Nan: Princess Opium in Deptford', *Druglink*, 14(5): 13–14.

WILSON, J. (1990), 'Drugs and Crime', in M. Tonry and J. Q. Wilson (eds), *Drugs and Crime*, Chicago, Ill.: University of Chicago Press.

WILSON, H., BRYANT, J., HOLT, M., and TRELOAR, C. (2010), 'Normalisation of recreational drug use among young people: Evidence about accessibility, use and contact with other drug users', *Health Sociology Review*, 19(2): 164–75.

WINSTOCK, A. and POWER, M. (2011), Mixmag Drugs Survey. *Mixmag*, 49–59.

WOOTTON COMMITTEE (1968), *Cannabis: Report by the Advisory Committee on Drug Dependence*, London: HMSO.

YOUNG, J. (1971), *The Drugtakers: The Social Meaning of Drug Use*, London: Paladin.

ZINBERG, N. (1984), *Drug, Set, and Setting: The basis for controlled intoxicant use*, Connecticut: Yale University Press.

# 24

# STATE CRIME:
# A DIALECTICAL VIEW

*Penny Green and Tony Ward*

The core examples of state crime are generally easy to recognize: genocide, war crimes, torture, police violence, and 'grand corruption'—the organized plunder of national resources by a ruling elite. Exactly how state crime should be defined is nevertheless a controversial question. The structure of this chapter reflects our own preferred definition which captures the sometimes veiled and not always legally proscribed deviance of the state: state organizational deviance involving the violation of human rights. After an assessment of the extent of plainly criminal state activity in today's world, we analyse the two overlapping phenomena identified by that definition: organizational deviance by state agencies, and the violation of human rights. We then propose a dialectical approach to explain state crime and explore some of the innovative methods now used in state crime research.

## STATE CRIME IN THE WORLD

It takes little imagination to conjure up the evils committed by states: the ongoing genocide in Sudan's Darfur region; Mugabe's reign of terror in Zimbabwe; the Israeli bombing of Gaza at the end of 2009; the US torture of Iraqi prisoners in Abu Ghraib; the brutality of Ben Ali's Tunisian police state; the terror of Gadaffi's dictatorship and the corrupt enrichment of the Egyptian ruling elite. The scale of state killing and systematic theft by ruling elites is staggering and the organized and planned criminality of governments has resulted in immeasurable pain and suffering. Yet the shroud of secrecy, official resistance, and an ideological/juridical culture which confines hegemonic understandings of criminality to the actions of the powerless results in an absence of state crime statistics, a misplaced sense of public fear, and a resistance within criminology to invoke the state as perpetrator. Even for those crimes acknowledged in international law—torture, genocide, crimes against humanity, and war crimes—governments have shown at best only a selective interest in monitoring and measuring. There is no doubt that impunity, secrecy, and a lack of political will impose enormous challenges to the accurate recording of state criminality.

The few attempts there have been to quantify the scale of state crime are inevitably challenged by these complexities. R.J. Rummel, nonetheless, has calculated that 262 million people died between 1900 and 1999 through the 'murder of any person or people by a government including, genocide, politicide and mass murder' (Rummel n.d.). Amnesty International reported that in 2009, torture and ill-—treatment were perpetrated in at least 111 countries and those who perpetrated these and other human rights violations enjoyed impunity in 61 countries (Amnesty International 2010).

A further attempt to quantify state, militia, and insurgent killing has been undertaken by the NGO, Iraq Body Count (2011), with its estimate of between 99,704 and 108,856 violent deaths of civilians in Iraq between the 2003 invasion and January 2011. When the Wikileaks Iraq War Logs data on 15,114 new civilian deaths is added, the total figure of estimated civilian deaths rises to 123,960 (www.iraqbodycount.org/analysis/numbers/warlogs/). It is clear from these few attempts and from the countless reports and writings of journalists and academics in a range of disciplines, that state violence and corruption can no longer be left at the margins of criminology.

Modern states claim a monopoly over the legitimate use of violence (Weber 1970) but at the same time they also perpetrate or instigate most of the world's serious illegitimate violence, that is, the infliction of pain, injury, or death in contravention of legal or moral norms (Green and Ward 2004).

The combination of impunity and secrecy associated with state violence and political corruption creates a criminal opportunity structure which officials may also use to pursue private interests. Under the Argentinean and Brazilian military regimes, for example, police not only tortured detainees, and murdered them to cover up their torture, but became involved in a range of crimes such as smuggling, drug-dealing, and extortion, creating acute tensions and sometimes violent conflict within the apparatus of repression (Andersen 1993; Marchak 1999, Huggins *et al.* 2002). War too provides a very particular shield of secrecy and impunity, and increasingly we have seen crime shape the character of war. Mary Kaldor identifies human rights violations and war crimes as 'a central methodology' of modern armed conflict (Kaldor 2006:121–2). Rather than the isolated actions of criminal soldiers or criminal regiments, crimes of war now extend to the core of modern armed conflict and are fuelled by looting, illegal trading in diamonds, minerals and timber, corruption, and transnational criminal networks (Green and Ward 2004). The wars which characterized the second half of the twentieth century and into the twenty-first century have become both more frequent and considerably more deadly than their predecessors, particularly for civilian populations, with an estimated six times as many deaths occurring per war in the twentieth century as in the nineteenth (Sivard 1996). In the 1960s civilians accounted for 63 per cent of recorded war deaths, by the 1980s they accounted for 74 per cent and, according to the authors of the *World Military and Social Expenditures* report, that percentage grew higher again in the 1990s (Sivard 1996).

The World Health Organization (WHO) calculates that in 2000 some 310,000 people were killed as a result of war-related violence (2002: 10); this represents 20 per cent of all global violent deaths. The WHO acknowledges that this figure, which excludes domestic deaths at the hands of police and security forces, is the tip of an iceberg given the secrecy and denial which envelops so much state violence.

One measure of the coercive capacity of states is military expenditure. Evidence from the Stockholm International Peace Research Institute (2006) suggests that while the world saw an overall reduction in military expenditure following the end of the Cold War that decline has been sharply reversing since the late 1990s, driven largely by the United States.

As we write, details of the stolen wealth of Egypt's toppled regime are emerging: brutal dictator Hosni Mubarak is allegedly worth around $70 billion with much of that wealth secreted in Swiss and UK banks and in London property (Inman 2011) and several of his inner circle are multi-billionaires, three of whom were detained on corruption charges by the new government in the week following the revolution.

## STATES AS CRIMINAL ACTORS

State crime is a form of organizational deviance (Ermann and Lundman 1978). The modern state, however, is not a single organization, but rather a complex ensemble of different agencies (see Michalowski 2010). There are certain very general features of state agencies that carry with them a potential for criminal or deviant activity.

What connects these agencies into a single overarching organization, the state, is some common set of plans and rules. State agencies are expected to coordinate their policies in accordance with directives from a more or less centralized leadership, and to abide by legal and constitutional rules. At the same time, state agencies have a degree of autonomy and can adopt plans of their own which are not necessarily in accordance with those of the state as a whole. Thus the potential exists for organizational deviance by state agencies from the state's own laws and policies.

At the core of the state are agencies specializing in coercion—armed forces, police, and prisons (Engels 1968). These agencies claim to exercise *legitimate* force force which conforms to rules and goals acceptable to the population at large as well as to international audiences. The pressure to achieve organizational goals through coercion can, however, lead to violence that contravenes legal norms and accepted standards of legitimacy. What constitutes legitimate force is often fiercely contested, as in the case of the policing of the 1984 UK miners' strike (Green 1990).

States exercise a measure of control over resources in their territory and are sustained by the revenue they can obtain from those resources. For stable capitalist states, the most efficient way to extract resources is through maintaining a degree of legitimacy (so that taxes will be paid without direct coercion) and to align their policies with the economic interests of those who control the means of production (Gramsci 1971; Levi 1989; Tilly 1990). Liberal capitalist states tend to achieve a high degree of hegemony wherein the contradictions of class divided society are masked by a shared sense of common interest (Gramsci 1971). Some states, however, follow different models. One is state capitalism (often miscalled socialism) where the state directly controls the means of production, often in an extremely exploitative manner (Cliff 1988). Another is the predatory state where the elite rules in its own short-term economic interest rather than that of any other economic class. While much state crime scholarship has focused on the capitalist state (e.g. Barak 1991), these other types of political economy are even more criminogenic.

If 'to deviate is to stray, as from a path or standard' (Matza 1969: 10), then there are two kinds of path from which a state agency or individual official may stray: the path laid down by a higher-level organization or official and the path over which the organization claims a legitimate right of way. These paths do not necessarily coincide. Deviance from the first entails insubordination, from the second illegitimacy. The most obvious form of illegitimacy is illegality, but legal norms often contain vague or ambiguous terms such as 'reasonable force' or 'all necessary measures', and it can be argued that the modern law of war, for example, is a set of discursive resources for claiming or challenging legitimacy, rather than a rigid set of constraints that must be conformed to if legitimacy is to be maintained (Kennedy 2006). A state's interpretation of its own laws should not suffice to remove its conduct from the purview of criminology.

Insubordinate or illegitimate behaviour may be a purely individual matter, as when the proverbial 'bad apple' takes a bribe or beats up a suspect, without any encouragement or connivance by others in the organization. Friedrichs (1995) uses the term 'political collar crime' to distinguish this kind of activity from the crimes of state agencies as organizations. State crime is crime that arises out of some plan, whether official or unofficial, by which state officials coordinate their conduct.

Since deviance by state agencies can take the form of either illegitimacy or insubordination, an organization can find itself in a position where anything it does will be deviant from one perspective or another. Such appeared to be the predicament of the Egyptian army when it announced, to the presumed displeasure of its political masters, that it would not fire on what it recognized as legitimate protests. It would be strange to say that whatever the army did in this situation would amount to a state crime. Elsewhere we have suggested an answer to this definitional quandary (Green and Ward 2000): state crimes are not only deviant; they also involve violations of human rights.

## STATE CRIME AND HUMAN RIGHTS

One advantage of using human rights standards is that virtually all states at least pay lip service to international human rights law. Should criminologists base their definitions of crime on what they take to be sound legal arguments, or on what is in fact regarded as illegal or illegitimate by significant social audiences? Since different audiences, like different lawyers, may take different views, either approach requires the criminologist to take sides on contested questions of legitimacy: the question is whether to do this on explicitly moral and political grounds or on legal grounds (for an interesting discussion see Michalowski 2010). The Schwendingers' (1975) preferred approach of basing the definition of crime on the underlying purpose of human rights—to secure a range of basic human needs—has been developed by the present authors (Green and Ward 1999) and a number of other scholars (Barak 1990; Grewcock 2010; Pickering 2005; Faust and Carlson 2011).

Human rights are not timeless natural laws but rather arise, as Marx (1844) argued, in the transition from a feudal society where entitlements depend on status to one peopled by formally equal 'self-sufficient monad[s]'. Some contemporary liberal conceptions of human rights, however, are more expansive than the eighteenth-century 'rights of man' castigated by Marx. While this is not the place for elaborate arguments of political philosophy, any defensible conception of human rights must recognize rights to 'security and subsistence' (Shue 1996), or 'freedom and well-being' (Gewirth 1978)—in other words, to at least basic social and economic rights as well as civil and political rights. To put the point very simply, civil liberties are not much use to people who are too malnourished to exercise them. The criminological import of this point is that, without denouncing every less-than-ideal political system as 'criminal', it is important to include state-induced famine (de Waal 1997), the denial of basic welfare services as a result of corruption (Ruggiero 1994), and other denials of basic welfare rights, in the catalogue of state crimes.

The importance of human rights to criminology is not merely a matter of definition: they are also sociologically important as global social norms that have significant effects in international society. International relations scholarship offers two perspectives on human rights that translate easily into criminological terms. One is the 'spiral model' formulated by Risse *et al.* (1999) to provide a 'constructivist' account of the institutionalization of human rights norms. They argue that because political elites tend to care about the international image of their states, they are susceptible to a form of 'shaming'. Links between national and international NGOs (non-governmental organizations) facilitate a process (the 'boomerang effect') by which domestic criticisms of state abuses enter into the global media and political discourses. The resulting pressure may be sufficient to bring about tactical concessions, which lead to further pressure to make the notional acceptance of human rights norms a reality until the norms are institutionalized and contribute to genuine reform. The 'spiral model' suggests that, as in other areas of criminology, we need to attend to more subtle and informal processes of social control than legal punishment: which is not to deny that the internationalization of criminal punishment thorough *ad hoc* tribunals (Hagan 2003) and the International Criminal Court (Mullins 2011) may have significant symbolic effects.

Such effects will contribute to what a second important perspective in international relations would term the global hegemony of human rights discourse (Cox 1993). The idea of hegemony is used here in a Gramscian sense, to denote ideas diffused by civil society (here the 'global civil society' of NGOs and the media) and accepted as 'common sense' but which serve the interests of a politically and economically dominant bloc—here the USA and its allies (Chomsky 2004), or perhaps an 'Empire' (Hardt and Negri 2000) of international institutions. We argue elsewhere (Green and Ward 2004) that human rights can serve this purpose all the better because they furnish a discourse that can articulate genuinely universal human needs, but can also be selectively interpreted to serve a neo-liberal agenda.

## STATE CRIME IN ACADEMIA

In writing the first edition of *State Crime: Governments, Violence and Corruption* we were struck by how little criminology had to offer our understanding and knowledge of crime committed by states. Much of the work which addressed our direct concerns, and in particular offered insight into the perpetrators of state crime, was to be found in the literatures of anthropology, international relations, development studies, and psychology. The most prominent scholar of state crime was (and still is) Noam Chomsky, the MIT Professor of Linguistics who has devoted the latter part of his career to challenging US foreign policy.

The study of state crime owes much to three intellectual, political, and campaigning traditions each of which precedes the development of critical criminology—Marxism, the human rights movement, and those early scholars and journalists who openly scrutinized and exposed state deviance.

Long before criminologists became interested in studying state criminality we find a few examples of political and social commentators attempting to explore the socio-economic roots of state violence and corruption. Marx and Engels in their majestic studies of capital, class, and the state provided the intellectual framework for thinking about the relation of political conflict to the productive forces of the economy and have remained a central inspiration for critical criminology.

In the mid-nineteenth century the French Appeals Court judge and writer Louis Proal wrote his little known treatise *Political Crime*, published in English in 1898, in which he declared:

> There are no greater malefactors than the political malefactors who foment divisions and hatreds by their ambition, cupidity, and rivalries. Ordinary evil-doers who are judged by the courts are only guilty of killing or robbing some few individuals, the number of their victims is restricted. Political malefactors, on the contrary count their victims by the thousand. They corrupt and ruin entire nations (1898: vi).

Proal's legacy is significant because he went beyond documenting the crimes of individual powerful political actors to discuss 'crimes committed by *political systems*, based on craft and violence' (our emphasis 1898: viii), giving him a claim to the title of the first state crime scholar.

At the turn of the twentieth century we find another early pioneer of the field. In 1904, E.D. Morel, the journalist, writer, and socialist politician not only denounced King Leopold II's regime of slavery and brutality in the Congo Free State as criminal, but provided one of the first examples of a rigorous analysis of state crime (Morel 1904). While not a criminologist in the formal sense, he not only denounced Leopold's regime as criminal but systematically analysed its socio-economic roots (Ward 2005).

State crime was not entirely neglected by the 'founding fathers' of criminology. Sheldon Glueck (1946) devoted a monograph to the criminality of Nazi aggression. The book is a legal defence of the Nuremberg trials, with almost no criminological content, but it illustrates a major obstacle to the development of state crime research. If one focuses on the criminality of entire wars, as Glueck did and most opponents of the Vietnam war were later to do (e.g. Quinney 1979), it is not easy to subject them to anything like a conventional criminological analysis—*Unravelling Aggressive War* would have had to be a very different book from *Unravelling Juvenile Delinquency*.

More significantly, Robert Merton produced in 1948 a pioneering analysis of 'machine politics' and political corruption (Merton 1957: 72–82). While this work has certainly influenced—arguably not for the better—political scientists' understanding of corruption (e.g. Leff 1964), it has not become part of the criminological canon in anything like the way that 'Social Structure and Anomie' has done. Merton may have over-estimated both the prevalence of machine politics in the USA and its supposed beneficial effects (Williams 1981) but his understanding of clientelism, state-corporate collusion, and the way in which corruption and patron-client relations can create a parallel structure of power to the legally-constituted state foreshadowed major themes of state crime research.

State crime did not, however, emerge as a significant concern of mainstream criminology: Bryant's (1979) study of crime in and by the military is a notable, but isolated, exception. On the other hand, several classic studies of policing (e.g. Westley 1970, Muir 1977, Holdaway 1982) largely focused on police violence and deviance, even if they did not label it as 'crime'.

*The New Criminology* (Taylor *et al.* 1973) had little to say about state crime: the aim was to challenge the state's power to criminalize, not to criminalize the state. It was followed, however, by an edited volume (Taylor *et al.* 1975) which contained two important contributions to state crime research: Schwendinger and Schwendinger's (1975) manifesto for a criminology of human rights violations, and Chambliss's (1975) comparative study of urban political corruption in Ibadan and Seattle: a notable exception to the tendency of early state crime research to concentrate almost exclusively on the crimes of the advanced democracies. Chambliss went on to give a seminal presidential address to the American Society of Criminology (Chambliss 1989) which was a major stimulus to the growth of the field in the USA (see, e.g., Barak 1991; Ross 2000).

The most important British critical text of its period, Hall *et al.* (1978), while again saying little directly about state crime, coupled deviancy theory with a sophisticated analysis of the state founded on the Marxism of Gramsci and Poulantzas. In the 1980s, this strand of theoretical work coalesced with a growing resistance to police violence and racism within British and Northern Irish civil society (Sim *et al.* 1987) to produce a series of critical analyses of British state practices (e.g. Scraton 1985; Hillyard and Percy-Smith 1988; Green 1990). It was comparatively rare, however, for these practices to be explicitly framed as state or police *crime* and causally explained as such (Box 1983, is a notable exception). More recently, some of the key writers in this tradition have adopted the concept of 'social harm' in preference to that of crime (Hillyard and Tombs 2007). Social harm is clearly a much wider concept than crime or deviance (Ward 2004). For example Sim (2009) is concerned with the social harm caused by current forms of punishment even when they are clearly within the law and would be regarded by the state and most of its citizens as entirely legitimate.

An interesting question raised by this body of work is how different are the social and psychological processes involved in the production of 'legitimate' and 'deviant' harms. Pemberton (2004) proposes that 'moral indifference' is a central factor in the production of social harm. Such indifference, towards the suffering of prisoners, for example, might be an aspect of conventional morality as well as deviant attitudes to violence. Bauman (1989) sees the normal structures of the modern bureaucratic state as potentially conducive to genocide. From a different perspective, Waddington (1999) argues that the use of coercion in modern societies is a form of 'dirty work', engaging in which requires 'techniques of neutralization' even when no deviance is involved. We leave this question open, but the remainder of the chapter proceeds on the assumption that organizational deviance in the use of violence and the control of resources has a distinctive dynamic that is worth investigating from a criminological perspective.

## EXPLAINING STATE CRIME

Perhaps the two best known general approaches to the explanation of state crime are the 'integrated theory' and the 'crimes of obedience' model.

The 'integrated theory' was developed in the US by Ron Kramer and his collaborators (Kramer and Michalowski 1990; Kauzlarich and Kramer 1998; Matthews and Kauzlarich 2000). The theory is built on the simple insight that crimes of whatever kind are rarely if ever committed without a motive, an opportunity, and the failure of some form of control to prevent them (if no control mechanism at all is at work, it hardly makes sense to speak of a crime). State crimes, however, are not mere individual acts but are committed by people working for organizational units that in turn are part of an overarching organization, the state. Thus, a criminological explanation needs to study motives, opportunities, and failures of control on at least these three levels.

That, in a nutshell, is the integrated theory, and it might seem blindingly obvious were it not for the tendency of criminological theories to focus on motivation, opportunity structure *or* control rather than paying equal attention to all three, and to ignore organizational crime. Lasslett (2010) has persuasively challenged the integrated theory and other 'orthodox' approaches to crimes of the powerful for remaining on the surface of social phenomena, pointing out readily observable criminogenic factors and classifying them in ways that are highly abstract and consequently unenlightening. The theory remains, however, a useful heuristic and it has the attraction—especially for teachers introducing state crime to criminology students—of underlining the similarities between state crime and other behaviours studied in criminology. At its best, the theory provides insightful accounts of the organizational processes leading to criminal acts, as in Kramer's (1992) account of the 1986 Space Shuttle Challenger disaster and Kramer and Michalowski's (2005) analogy between the neo-conservative clique in US foreign policy and a delinquent subculture. The danger, however, is that merely rearranging goals, opportunities, and weaknesses of control to fit a ready-made template can be mistaken for theoretical analysis (Lasslett 2010).

The integrated theory rightly takes account of both macro-level (political economy) and micro-level (individual or psychological) factors. To date, however, scholarship in this vein has mainly focused on meso-level or organizational factors, making particularly valuable contributions to the study of state-corporate crime, i.e. 'illegal or socially injurious actions that result from a mutually reinforcing interaction' between the organizational goals and practices of state agents and private corporations (Kramer 1992: 215–16).

While the integrated theory emphasizes the similarities between state crime and 'street' crime, the 'crimes of obedience' approach (Kelman and Hamilton 1989) emphasizes the difference. As Smeulers puts it:

> a crime qualifies as a crime of obedience when it is supported by the authority structure.... This very fact turns the whole analytical framework which underlies criminological theory upside down because mainstream criminology studies people who break the law, people who *do not* live by the rules and people who are *deviant*. But within such a malignant governmental system, military organization or police unit, it is those people who...*abide* by the rules who become the perpetrators....[W]e have to focus on

the question why they are *obedient,* why they followed the group, why they *do* live by the (deviant and immoral) rules (Smeulers 2008: 236–7).

By referring to 'deviant rules', however, Smeulers' analysis raises the question as to whether this is really such a complete inversion of mainstream criminology. Employees of dishonest corporations and members of mafia-like organizations might also be said to live by deviant rules. They are under pressure to conform to the rules of their corporation or criminal fraternity, but are at the same time subject to other control mechanisms that define conformity to those rules as criminal behaviour.

The classic study of obedience to immoral orders is Milgram's (1974) notorious series of experiments (replicated *inter alia* by Burger 2009) in which a majority of subjects were prepared to inflict what they took to be high-voltage electric shocks on another participant (in reality an actor). In these experiments the subjects were confronted with unexpected demands in an unfamiliar, time-bound setting under the direct supervision of an authority figure (a white-coated 'scientist'). This is not a realistic model for the position of state-appointed torturers and murderers who must carry out extreme violence repeatedly over long periods, and not always under direct supervision. To understand the latter requires moving beyond the isolated order to an analysis of long-term political, social, and psychological processes.

The 'crimes of obedience' approach and the integrated theory each emphasize one side of a pervasive feature of state crime first noted by Chambliss (1989): the pressure of 'contradictory ideologies and demands'. State crime occurs when conformity to a state agency's demands requires or motivates conduct that runs counter to some rule or value that the agent would otherwise be disposed to uphold, or is under some pressure to uphold, and which is conducive to respect for human rights. To conform to one rule or demand is to deviate from another.

Scott Straus's (2006) analysis of the Rwandan genocide provides a striking example of the partial truth of both the integrated theory and the 'crimes of obedience' perspective. The mass killing was largely instigated and led by a mixture of economically impoverished violent young men, specialists in violence and hard-line political elites, who might well be characterized as deviants exploiting an opportunity structure created by political crisis and war, in the absence of effective controls from domestic law or the 'international community'. However, once a certain 'tipping point' had been reached in any district, participation in genocide became the norm to which the state demanded conformity by a much broader section of the population. The typical perpetrator of this 'crime of obedience' was ultimately indistinguishable from the average Hutu male.

The seemingly antithetical perspectives of 'crimes of obedience' and the integrated theory need to be synthesized in a manner that can aptly be termed *dialectical.* By a dialectical perspective we mean one that is not only attentive to contradictory beliefs and demands, but which understands the emergence and translation into action of those beliefs and demands as a process, rather than a sequence of discrete events, and understands the reaction of human agents to the contradictions they encounter in a manner summed up in Marx's famous dictum that people 'make their own history but they do not make it just as they please' (Marx 1968: 96). Such an approach requires a deeper analysis both of the structural determinants of state crime, and of individual responses to those 'determining contexts' (Scraton and Chadwick 1991) than is to be found in much of the existing literature on organizational deviance.

At an individual level, the contradiction often takes the form of 'cognitive dissonance' (Festinger 1962) between the norms an individual has internalized and the acts he or she performs. Outside Milgram's laboratory, normative conflicts are not simply situational; they evolve in a process with deep roots in political economy. Individual perpetrators do not merely make isolated choices to engage in violent or corrupt actions, but often undergo profound changes of moral sensibility through processes that may include training, exposure to propaganda, and informal socialization.

One of the most important attempts to connect the analysis of state formation with that of individual moral sensibilities is made in Norbert Elias's classic, *The Civilizing Process* (1939, 2000). For Elias, the monopolization of violence by the state has brought about profound changes in individual sensibilities, most importantly (for our purposes) an increased capacity for long-term planning, for disciplined compliance with the plans of authorities, and an abhorrence for most forms of interpersonal violence in everyday life. Pacification of this kind is a very long-term, and not necessarily linear, process, and it is doubtful whether Elias's analysis, which is explicitly confined to European history, can be generalized to states, such as Gadaffi's Libya, which displayed a persistent reliance on naked terror.

While terror can secure compliance in the short term, any regime needs to provide incentives to a sufficient number of followers for them to remain committed to sustaining the regime in power. The Weberian concept of 'sultanism' is useful in understanding states such as Libya and Belarus (Eke and Kuzio 2000). Sultanistic regimes are headed by a dictator who rules not primarily though charismatic authority or personal loyalty but through a combination of fear and rewards. Such regimes tend to be both violent and corrupt, and because they allow no mechanism for peaceful change their overthrow is likely to be violent (as witnessed in Libya in 2011). Family and tribal loyalties are also a crucial, but fragile, basis for commitment to the regime, as for example in Libya (Joffe 2011), Egypt (Inman 2011), and Iraq (Cockburn and Cockburn 2002). In Weberian terms such personal ties are characteristic of patrimonialism, of which sultanism is a variant. Events in Egypt and Libya in 2011 starkly underline the importance of understanding the internal dynamics of the military, and its role (particularly that of middle and lower-ranking officers) in sustaining or toppling regimes.

Somewhere between states of naked terror and stable democracies are those that have enjoyed a degree of stability and/or democratic legitimacy but have descended into extreme repression or violent conflict. It is in these societies that the contradiction between 'civilized' sensibilities (in Elias's sense) and the demands of the violent state are manifested most acutely. These conflicts have been the subject of several exemplary studies, including Schirmer's (1998) of the Guatemalan military in the 1980s, Huggins' work on Brazilian torturers and murders (Huggins *et al.* 2002), Haritos-Fatouros' (1988, 2003) and Gibson's (1990) work on torture under the Greek junta, and the work of Feitlowitz (1998), Marchak (1999), and others on Argentina. There is also, of course, a rich historical literature on Nazi Germany and other mid-twentieth century tyrannies from which state crime scholars can draw. In all these cases we see a highly planned use of systematic violence in a context where significant normative constraints have to be overcome; people have to be induced to engage in levels of violence that would previously have been unthinkable.

Whilst there are many nuances and regional particularities, we can identify a number of general explanatory themes in this body of scholarship. The first is a tendency for states which engage in systematic state violence to promote a monolithic sense of cultural identity (e.g. the project of the architects of the Turkish Republic). The 'imagined community' of monolithic indivisibility defines itself through exclusion of minorities whose claims to recognition and respect threaten the integrity of the monolith. When those claims take the form of active resistance against the state then clear ideological enemies are defined and the state may engage in a dehumanization process which excludes those enemies from the 'universe of obligation' (Fein 1990) within which ordinary moral rules apply. Monolithic cultures are frequently authoritarian in character and those agents of the state most likely to rise to its defence are found to be attracted to far right wing and fascist ideologies (Staub 1989).

A second theme that emerges clearly from the psychological research is that despite their capacity to engage in cruel and barbarous acts, torturers and purveyors of state terror are psychologically normal (Haritos-Fatouros 1988; Gibson 1990); they are generally not sadists or psychopaths. In order to become extremists in violence they require training, often of a very brutal and brutalizing nature, to counter long held socialized norms against the use of cruelty. Specialized elite units, such as those to which virtually all torturers of the Greek and Brazilian regimes belonged (Gibson and Haritos-Faturos 1986; Huggins *et al.* 2002) also appear to be essential; although as the case of Rwanda shows, specialists in violence can sometimes use their coercive power to recruit large numbers of killers who need no specialist training (Straus 2006). Violent states also commonly create 'enclaves of barbarism' (de Swaan 2001), segregated spaces in which the practice of state violence is both facilitated and rewarded while allowing the violent worker to return to an everyday life where ordinary social norms pertain.

The literature reveals, thirdly, that even when states portray torture and terror as essential to combat perceived threats to social order, there is a recognition on the part of state agents that this violence stands outside the bounds of political legitimacy (Cohen 1981; Green and Ward 2004). The versatile concept of 'techniques of neutralization' (Sykes and Matza 1957) helps to explain how state agents are able to define their actions in ways that make radical departures from conventional moral norms appear justifiable or excusable (Cohen 2001b; Alvarez 2010). A paranoid world-view, by exaggerating the threat posed by 'enemies of the state', also helps to neutralize inhibitions against violence (see, e.g., O'Kane 1991; Graziano 1992). Such paranoia can set states on a course of irrational self-destruction—the Khmer Rouge regime in Cambodia is one spectacular example—but can also make it easier to repress the real opponents of the state, such as the labour movement in 1970s Argentina (Píon-Berlin 1989).

There are many continuities between this research and that on the crimes committed by Western liberal democracies in the name of the 'war on terror' (Huggins *et al.* 2002; Jackson 2005; Blakeley 2009) and previous counter-insurgency campaigns. The School of the Americas (now the Western Hemisphere Institute for Security Co-operation) trained Central and South American dictatorships in the arts of counter-insurgency that included state terror and torture. The French lent the Argentine Junta their own expertise drawn from the campaign of terror they conducted in Algeria (MacMaster 2004). The administration of George W. Bush engaged in various attempts to re-define torture (Greenberg and Dratel 2005; Hersh 2005; Levinson 2004) and cultivated the now notorious black sites or 'enclaves of barbarism' in Eastern Europe and Asia where CIA instigated torture was orchestrated with impunity.

Of course Western liberal democracies like the United Kingdom and America are neither monolithic nor authoritarian, and their flourishing civil societies are well equipped to expose state criminality and to counter attempts to dehumanize its victims. As Vetlesen (2005: 164) argues, however, such market-driven and individualistic societies are prone to a 'dialectic of individualism and collectivism', whereby atomized individuals feel the lure of exclusivist ideologies which pit the imagined community against a scapegoated out-group. Dehumanization processes have been all too successfully applied to asylum seekers who, in countries including Australia, the UK, and America, have been subjected to mandatory detention (in desert camps in Australia), deaths in custody, border violence, voucher systems, and racist media campaigns (Poynting et al., 2004, Poynting and Mason 2007, Michalowski 2008, Pickering 2005, Grewcock 2010). One lesson to be learnt from the literature on genocide and ethnic cleansing is that scholars must be alert to the early stages of processes of exclusion.

In policing their own citizens, Western democracies do not always remain strictly within the boundaries of legitimate force. Some of the best-known works on the police, such as Westley (1971), Holdaway (1982), Chan (1997), and Choongh (1997) are very largely studies of manifestly criminal conduct, as are several studies of para-military policing (Jefferson 1990; Critcher and Waddington 1996; McCulloch 2001). Police crime has been addressed explicitly by Punch (1985, 2010), Skolnick and Fyfe (1993), and Geller and Toch (1996), among others, and there is a growing literature on police violence in middle-income countries (Chevigny 1995; Harriot 2000; Belur 2010; Hinton 2006; Hinton and Newburn 2008). For the purposes of state crime research it is important, but not always easy, to distinguish between individual deviance and deviance in pursuit of organizational goals (Sherman 1978). The formal organizational goal of upholding the law is readily transmuted into an informal goal of upholding police authority on the streets (Waddington 1999: 153–8).

As we noted above, criminologists have generally paid scant attention to war crimes. This is a remarkable omission as warfare is an activity in which issues of law and law-breaking loom large, and modern militaries increasingly engage in 'lawfare', the manipulation of legal rules to serve strategic goals (Kennedy 2006; Wheatley 2006). An influential body of scholarship about military affairs argues that the boundary between war and criminality has become increasingly blurred in the civil conflicts of the late twentieth and twenty-first centuries (van Creveld 1991; Kaldor 2006; Mueller 2004). In more high-tech conflicts, the ability of the US, Israeli, and other militaries to put forward legal defences of even their most outrageous acts of violence (e.g. Operation Cast Lead; and the murders of nine unarmed Palestinian supporters on board the Turkish Ship *Mavi Marmara*) reminds us of the dangerous ambiguities of legalistic definitions of crime (Goldstone 2009; Chomsky and Pappé 2010). The Iraq war has attracted some criminological attention, with Kramer and Michalowski (2005) providing a rare analysis of the crime of aggression, while Whyte (2007, 2010) focuses on the economic crimes of the occupation and Green and Ward (2009a, 2009b) on violence in the aftermath of invasion. Other notable contributions to a criminological understanding of armed conflict include Jamieson (1998), Ruggiero (2004, 2007), and Lilly (2007).

## CORRUPTION AND COLLUSION

Apart from illegitimate state violence, the other major form of state crime is that which involves the illegitimate use of state agencies' powers over the allocation and misuse of resources. Like violence, corruption involves a contradiction between two sets of norms or practices: on the one hand the 'official' rules and organizational goals by which state agencies publicly justify their activities and on the other the goals and plans that in reality shape organizational activity.

Since state agencies both control considerable resources of their own and exercise legal powers over the use that others may make of their resources (e.g. through planning permission and export licensing), they have ample scope for what economists call 'rent seeking', that is, obtaining a reward for the use of the resources they control. Corruption by isolated individuals or small groups cannot be regarded as state crime. It becomes a state crime when the 'dominant coalition' in an agency (Sherman 1978)— the people with the power to shape the organization's goals—adopt corrupt practices as a means to an organizational goal, or as a goal that in fact determines the organization's decisions, or where they tolerate corruption for organizational reasons.

One of the most important insights to emerge from the economic study of corruption is the tendency of states to gravitate towards either a high or low equilibrium, i.e. a stable level of corruption (Andvig and Feldstad 2000). Levels of corruption appear to be driven by either virtuous or vicious circles. In the virtuous circle, because corruption is rare, offering a bribe is risky and accepting one carries heavy 'moral costs' (guilt and the risk of detection). In the vicious circle, because corruption is common, offering a bribe stands a good chance of success with low risk of adverse consequences, and the costs of accepting a bribe are likely to be low. As in the case of violence, behaviour that is deviant according to one set of standards may amount to conformity to the expectations of those who can apply the most effective pressure to the individual actor. In a metaphor used by Hong Kong police officers, you can get on the bus (participate in corruption) or run alongside the bus (abstain from corruption but not interfere with it), but if you stand in front of the bus you are liable to be run over (Kutnjak Ivkovic 2005).

Corruption is important both as a major form of crime in its own right and as a factor in understanding some forms of state violence. For example, the vulnerability of certain populations to natural disasters (the 1999 Marmara earthquake, Hurricane Katrina in 2005, the Haitian earthquake, and the Pakistan floods of 2010) is directly attributable to corrupt decision-making processes and the resulting deaths can be considered a form of indirect state violence. Many states collude with criminal organizations to carry out violence as well as illicit business and numerous violent regimes rely on corrupt networks to sustain their power (see e.g. Heyman 1999; Green and Ward 2004).

Corruption is one way for corporations to exercise illicit influence over states, but criminal collusion between states and corporations occurs frequently even without corruption. One of the most studied examples is the reckless decision to launch the space shuttle Challenger in 1986 (Vaughan 1997; Kramer 1992). In these cases it is the 'mutually reinforcing interaction' between corporate and state organizational goals that results in 'illegal or socially injurious behavior' (Aulette and Michalowski 1993: 175).

At its most extreme, this contradiction between the formal rules of government and the real exercise of power manifests itself in a 'shadow state' (Reno 1995), where the legally constituted system is little more than a façade erected to secure international respectability and aid. In Weberian terms such states can be classed as 'neo-patrimonial' (Médard 2001)—patrimonialism (personal and economic ties between rulers and subordinates) is the real basis of the rulers' power, and of such domestic legitimacy as they may possess, but the formal structure of authority presents itself as a rational-legal one. Bayart *et al.* (1999) have discussed some extreme examples of the 'criminalization of the state in Africa', where relatively small states such as the Comoros Islands and Equatorial Guinea were largely financed by smuggling. Another extreme form of corruption is 'kleptocracy' where the theft of public resources by a ruling elite appears to be the ruling principle of the state. Examples include Liberia under (and before) Charles Taylor and Zaire under Mobutu (Schatzberg 1988).

Closely related to patrimonialism is clientelism, where a patron exercises power or influence in favour of a client who in turn responds with electoral support, political donations, or personal gifts. Clientelistic relationships can exist within predominantly rational-legal systems of government, in contrast to neo-patrimonialism which *is* a system of government, operating behind a rational-legal façade. While clientelistic relationships may be both legally and culturally acceptable, a climate in which exchanges of favours are the norm makes it easier for corruption to take root. Clientelism is a recognized and pervasive feature of many liberal democracies, including Italy, Ireland, Greece, and Turkey. In the United Kingdom, however, while not usually classified as such, informal exchanges of the kind described above characterize many interactions between the political and corporate elites. The link between party funding and peerages represents one of best known examples of political patronage.

## RESEARCHING STATE CRIME

Theory informs method and, given the strong Marxist antecedents informing the study of state violence and corruption, it is not surprising that research in the field has been impelled by three main drivers: (a) the political and economic context in which these crimes take place; (b) the primacy of victims' perceptions; and (c) an intimate examination of perpetrator agency. Combined with an implicit distrust of state-produced and packaged knowledge researchers are thus led to rely far more on the direct testimony of victims and perpetrators and detailed examinations of political economy.

Criminology has a narrowly drawn but important tradition of ethnographic research dating back to the Chicago School of the 1920s and Robert Park's injunction to young scholars to 'go out and get your hands dirty in real research' (Park 1966: 71).

Ernest Burgess, Lloyd Ohlin, Howard Becker, Clifford R. Shaw, Henry D. Mackay and those who followed explored the lives and normative codes of street corner gangs, drug users, gamblers, prostitutes, and juvenile delinquents in order to understand criminology's primary question—why people engage in behaviours which violate legal rules and social norms despite, typically, a degree of commitment to those same rules and norms. A revival of criminological ethnography in the late 1990s saw the method again confined to the marginalized and familiar constituents of criminology's oeuvre (see in particular Ferrell and Hamm 1998).

Where ethnography first begins to address state crime issues, however, is unsurprisingly within the domain, not of criminology, but of anthropology, the original home of ethnography (see Nordstrom and Robben 2004; and Jefferson and Jensen 2009). Lalli Metsola, for example, in studying the incorporation of former ex-rebel combatants into Namibia's police special field force and the human rights violations they have been widely accused of observes that 'structures of violence do not reproduce themselves without mediation . . . the structures and practices of violence are significant for the constitution of the force members' subjectivity . . .' (Metsola 2009: 116). The increasing cross-disciplinarity of the field has encouraged a new generation of criminologists to adopt ethnography in their attempts to shine a light on the wrongdoings of the powerful (Cameron 2010; Lasslett 2009, 2012 forthcoming; Franssen and MacManus 2012 forthcoming; Tombs and Whyte 2003).

When Tombs and Whyte published their important collection *Unmasking the Crimes of the Powerful* in 2003 they exposed the dearth of research within criminology on state and corporate crimes. Crimes committed by states were, by a significant margin, the least explored. Criminology has long suffered from 'an extremely intimate, indeed subservient relationship to the state' (Tombs and Whyte 2003: 26). The hegemonic influence of a criminology 'in the service of the state' has resulted in a field dominated by pragmatic empiricism. Stan Cohen noted the move within criminology to an increasingly criminal justice-centred character in the early 1980s (Cohen 1981). Increasingly the state-defined categories of criminality have defined the research agenda and this agenda has very explicitly excluded crimes of the powerful. A search in February 2011 for 'torture' results in the Home Office Research Development Statistics website, for example, produced 13 pages of results, all of which related to the UK Border Agency and pragmatic information relating to asylum applications and appeals. Ninety-eight per cent of the 122 reports listed were simply 'Country of Origin Information key documents', reporting secondary data on the developing world, three were immigration and asylum statistics; two 'fact finding missions' and a contracted research study by Oxford's Centre for Refugee Studies on asylum policy and integration. There were no research studies into torture at all.

Tombs and Whyte noted that access to state functionaries, to boardrooms and other inner sanctums of the powerful presented major methodological problems for researchers intent of investigating crimes of the powerful. States and corporations tend to be highly secretive organizations, skilled and equipped with extensive legal and administrative powers to conceal their wrongdoings from public scrutiny (Tombs and Whyte 2003; Matthews and Kauzlarich 2000; Power 2003: 151). A telling example to illustrate this point comes from research conducted by Kristian Lasslett into state-corporate criminality on the island of Bougainville in Papua New Guinea. Following a formal request to the Australian Government under the Freedom of Information Act 1982 and a number of communications with officials from the Department of Foreign Affairs and Trade (Freedom of Information Section) Lasslett received the following:

> Over 4,700 relevant pages were identified by the department in Canberra and at our overseas posts as falling within the scope of your request. Of these, approximately 4,670 pages are likely to be exempted from release. The estimated cost for processing your request is $17,814.92, requiring a 25 per cent deposit of $4,453.73 to proceed with the request. I am satisfied that the time required to assess the documents captured by your request by a qualified senior executive officer will be an unreasonable diversion of the Department's resources. It is estimated that over 900 hours of that officer's time will be required to process the application, examining each page line by line to determine if the information contained may be disclosed or whether it is covered by exemptions contained in the Act…affecting national security, defence and international relations, and communications in confidence from foreign governments…(Lasslett 2012 forthcoming).

This rebuff and a tenaciously inquiring spirit sent Lasslett in other surprisingly productive directions. Denied access to restricted documents by the Australian Government, the PNG Government, and University of Melbourne Archives, Lasslett sought informal avenues and struck gold with an American law firm, which was suing the mining company Rio Tinto plc on behalf of a number of Bougainvillean claimants over the company's role in facilitating the PNG Defence Force attacks on civilians and environmental damage caused by the mine. From this source Lasslett was afforded access to some 300 pages of memoranda and minutes and several hundred pages of sworn affidavits from company and government officials as well as internal company reports.

The difficulties in penetrating the 'armour of state and corporate secrecy' are manifest. However, in the decade since Tombs and Whyte made their observations research into state criminality has grown apace and, as we have seen, the difficulties they identified have encouraged a flourishing of methodological creativity.

Much state crime research is conducted in countries where language can be an issue. Both Cameron (2012, forthcoming) and MacManus (2012 forthcoming) found themselves manipulated and monitored by translators they had occasional need to employ. Cameron reported:

> The translator insisted on being present during all my meetings whether the services of a translator were required or not and in spite of my protestations. This clearly allowed the content of all conversations to be reported back to the government including the identities and responses of participants with whom contact had been arranged other than through the translator or key government officials. (Cameron 2010:24)

## INNOVATIONS

Researching perpetrators of state violence and corruption is not for the faint-hearted and the dangers involved foster particular forms of creative resourcefulness.

One of the most innovative methods of securing research access was conceived by the HHI and their local partners in the DRC, the Centre d'Assistance Medico-Psychosociale (CAMPS). In order to interview Mai Mai militia combatants active in the southern Kivu province and heavily involved in the perpetration of sexual and other violence, lead researcher Michael van Rooyen negotiated with a commanding colonel living in the forest outside the town of southern Kivu town of Kamituga. As Kamituga was under the control of the Congolese National Military, researchers negotiated a 48-hour amnesty for the combatants who were then required to disarm at the entrance to the town before entering for interviews (HHI 2009:13).

Innovative scholarship is increasingly informing the character of state crime research. Those working on state crime are, perhaps, predisposed to seek non-traditional and alternative data sources given the guarded nature of the subject. Accepting that the state does not provide neatly packaged statistical documentation on state deviance, and given the critical framework within which these scholars work, data is necessarily sought elsewhere. While fieldwork remains the central core of data gathering there are rich sources to be plumbed beyond the academy: eyewitness accounts from reputable journalists and quality print and broadcasting media (see especially the reports and films from Robert Fisk and John Pilger); civil society organizations, former state agents, legal firms, and NGOs can provide a wealth of valuable and reliable data.

During the Libyan uprising of February 2011 Google set up an account so that anyone in the country with a phone could call one of a range of numbers and leave a voice message about what was happening on the streets. The message was then automatically translated into a tweet in order to evade the communication blackout that Gaddafi's regime had imposed (Al Jazeera 2011). While not an immediately obvious research tool Google nonetheless provided a mechanism which allowed real time data to flow into the international public domain.

As we saw in the section on 'mapping', reliable quantitative data on state violence are hard to come by, and scholars often have to resort to 'meta-guesstimates' arrived at by averaging out the widely varying estimates available. Some more sophisticated demographic techniques for estimating death rates are discussed by Bijleveld (2008). Hagan and Rymond-Richmond used data from the Darfur Atrocities Documentation Project, the US State Department's survey into genocidal processes in Sudan[1] to advance their claim that genocide had taken place in Darfur; that a criminology of genocide was required; and that such a criminology could be used to advocate against genocide (Hagan and Rymond-Richmond 2008).

## LEAKS

In 2009 Wikileaks burst into public consciousness with the release of the Afghan and Iraq War Logs followed, beginning in June 2010 by the release of 251,287 leaked US Embassy Diplomatic Cables, which according to the website offers 'the largest set of confidential documents ever to be released into the public domain' (Wikileaks http://213.251.145.96/10.02.2011). The cables are an invaluable contribution to data sources at the disposal of those interested in the nuanced deliberations of states and their

---

[1] 1,136 eyewitnesses in refugee camps in Chad were interviewed by the research team, 'a sample large enough to be a statistically significant representation of the estimated 200,000 Darfuri refugees in Chad' Genocide Watch. www.genocidewatch.org/provinggenocidedarfur.html.

representatives. In the formerly secret Embassy cables, scholars have been provided with data which lays bare the organizational goals and decision-making processes which underpin the sometimes criminal and often deviant practices of the United States' foreign policy as well as their insights into the workings of criminal regimes such as Libya's (Peachey 2011).

In a similar vein was Al Jazeera's release in January 2011 of the 'Palestine Papers', containing some 1,700 files, including thousands of pages of diplomatic correspondence detailing the inner workings of the Israeli-Palestinian peace process. These documents, 'memos, e-mails, maps, minutes from private meetings, accounts of high level exchanges, strategy papers and even power point presentations' date from 1999 to 2010 (Al Jazeera 2011). For scholars researching the well-documented international crimes of Israel the leaked documents present an unparalleled opportunity to understand the organizational goals of Israeli, Palestinian, and US leaders, their commitment to international norms and laws, their consciousness of criminal conduct, and the concessions which they secretly negotiated.

While few scholars have yet to harness its full potential the advent of the 'leaked' data source offers state crime scholars a powerful and rich new resource. Julian Assange, the enigmatic founder of Wikileaks, is clear about the value of the leaked material for intellectual enquiry and registered surprise in an interview with John Pilger at the general lack of academic and journalistic interest in the leaked data. For Assange, '[t]he goal is justice, the method is transparency' (www.johnpilger.com/videos/julian-assange-in-conversation-with-john-pilger).

State crime scholars are only now beginning the task of analysing the data that the cables provide (see Green 2012 forthcoming; Lasslett 2012 forthcoming).

A newer methodology which has a particular value for the state crime scholar exploring state terror, ethnic cleansing, war crimes, and genocide is that of satellite earth observation imagery, already pioneered in archaeology for the protection and management of cultural heritage. Researchers may hire satellite capacity in order to monitor troop or militia movements; village destruction; population displacement; and the destruction of farm and pastureland. The costs remain high but the Satellite Sentinel Project which was launched by human rights organization Not on Our Watch to monitor troop movements in Southern Sudan in 2011 has demonstrated the potential of satellite data for researching criminal state practices. If the Sentinel project is successful it will reduce the waiting time for satellite images from 14 days to 36 hours. Images from the satellite will then be analysed by scholars at the Harvard Humanitarian Initiative and analysts at the UN (http://satsentinel.org/; McGreal 2010).

## COVERT PRACTICES

Investigating crimes of powerful state agents can be difficult, harrowing, and sometimes dangerous (Schirmer 1998; Nordstrom 2004; Green 2003). One of the reasons why so few researchers venture into empirically investigating crimes committed by generals, politicians, and state officials is the assumption that access to the powerful and their criminogenic processes will be denied. Access to powerful perpetrators may, however (with persistence and tenacity), be less difficult to secure than imagined, as the work of many of the authors cited above demonstrates. State crime researchers tend, however, to side with those for whom change brings freedom from state abuses. In so doing state crime researchers are adopting Scheper-Hughes' notion of 'ethical orientation' in which the personal accountability of the researcher is answerable to the 'other' (Scheper-Hughes 1992: 24). This ethical orientation speaks to a commitment to justice and moral alignment with the victims of state violence and corruption, in the pursuit of truth and change. When overt routes to knowledge are denied and secrecy characterizes the practices to be studied, clandestine methods may offer the only route to enlightenment.

Whyte's research on the criminal restructuring of the Iraqi economy following the 2003 invasion, by necessity, involved concealed methods. Iraq reconstruction meetings provided a uniquely valuable resource for those interested in researching post-invasion Iraq as they provided a rare opportunity to observe and participate in the corporate dealings of the occupation. The role of those meetings was to accelerate the reconstruction process by providing a mechanism for businesses to meet and discuss collaborations with government officials and the large prime contractors (including Halliburton, Bechtel, and Flour). Reconstruction meetings typically brought together politicians and state officials from both the Iraqi Government and the occupying powers. When Whyte's legitimate attempts to enter the internal corporate world of Iraqi reconstruction, via a press pass, were denied he employed deception:

> My credentials badge was coloured blue, indicating that I was not allowed entry into the main conference. Security was of course, very light. Yet no credentials were needed to get into the hotel for white men in suits.... I decided to just walk past security with my credentials obscured. This gave me entry to all of the high level government and corporate keynote addresses, the lively and often antagonistic responses to those speeches, the sumptuous lunches and the fringe meetings in rooms across the hotel. Once I was in, I covertly recorded the proceedings of the conferences,... using a digital sound device in the inside pocket of my suit.[2]

## CONCLUSION

State crime scholarship is moving into an exciting and expanding new phase of innovative research and the momentum which carries it is fuelled by an interdisciplinary commitment to exposing and understanding the violence and corruption of governments and their agents. Criminology can act as both a rendezvous discipline (see for example the International State Crime Initiative, www.statecrime.org) as well as making its own distinct contribution to understanding the processes involved in state criminality. The very fact that the *Oxford Handbook of Criminology* now includes a chapter devoted to state crime is progress.

It is over 150 years since Proal (1843: 2) began his pioneering study by quoting Seneca's observation that '[t]he desire to rule and the exercise of authority

---

[2] Personal Communication February 6th 2011.

teach fraud and violence'. If crime can be defined, as Gottfredson and Hirschi argued, as 'acts of force or fraud undertaken in pursuit of self-interest' (1990: 15) then criminology's recognition of Seneca's ancient insight is long overdue. In our first article on state crime (Green and Ward 2000) we alluded to the fact that the *Handbook* devoted only one sentence to the subject. Perhaps by the fifteenth edition there will be one chapter devoted to street crime in the developed world and 15 or so devoted to the crimes of government.

## ■ SELECTED FURTHER READING

CHAMBLISS, W., MICHALOWSKI, R., and KRAMER, R. (eds) (2010), *State Crime in the Global Age*, Cullompton: Willan Publishing.

COHEN, S. (2001b), *States of Denial: Knowing About Atrocities and Suffering*, Cambridge: Blackwell.

GREEN, P. and WARD, A. (2004), *State Crime: Governments, Violence and Corruption*, London: Pluto Press.

HUGGINS, M.K., HARITOS-FATOUROS, M., and ZIMBARDO, P.G. (2002), *Violence Workers: Police Torturers and Murderers Reconstruct Brazilian Atrocities*, Berkeley: University of California Press.

## ■ REFERENCES

AL JAZEERA (2011), 'How Did Egypt become so Corrupt?', *Inside Story* aired 7 February 2011. www.aljazeera.com/programmes/insidestory/2011/02/201128111236245847.htmlhttp://english.aljazeera.net/ palestinepapers/ 2011/01/201112214310263628.html.

ALVAREZ, A. (2010), *Genocidal Crimes*, London: Routledge.

AMNESTY INTERNATIONAL (2010), *Amnesty International report 2010: the state of the world's human rights*. http://thereport.amnesty.org/facts-and-figures.

ANDERSEN, M. E. (1993), *Dossier Secreto: Argentina's Desaparecidos and the Myth of the 'Dirty War'*, Boulder: Westview.

ANDVIG, J.C. and FELDSTAD, O-H. (2000), *Research on Corruption: A Policy Oriented Survey*, Oslo: Chr. Michelsen Institute and Norwegian Institute for International Affairs.

AULETTE, J. R. and MICHALOWSKI, R. (1993), 'Fire in Hamlet: A Case Study of State-Corporate Crime, ' in K. D. Tunnell. (ed.), *Political Crime in Contemporary America: A Critical Approach*, New York: Garland.

BARAK, G. (1990), 'Crime, Criminology and Human Rights: Toward an Understanding of State Criminality', *Journal of Human Justice*, 2(1): 11–28.

—— (1991), *Crimes by the Capitalist State: an Introduction to State Criminality*, New York: S.U.N.Y. Press.

BAUMAN, Z. (1989), *Modernity and the Holocaust*, Cambridge: Polity.

BAYART, J-F., ELLIS, S., and HIBOU, B. (1999), *The Criminalization of the State in Africa*, Oxford: James Currey.

BELUR, J. (2010), 'Why Do the Police Use Deadly Force? Explaining Police Encounters in Mumbai', *British Journal of Criminology*, 50(2): 320–41.

BIJLEVELD, C. (2008), 'Missing Pieces. Some Thoughts on the Methodology of the Empirical Study of International Crimes and other Gross Human Rights Violations', in A. Smeulers and R. Haveman (eds), *Supranational Criminology: Towards a Criminology of International Crimes*, Antwerp: Intersentia.

BLAKELEY, R. (2009), *State Terrorism and Neoliberalism: The North in the South*, Oxford: Blackwell.

BOX, S. (1983), *Power, Crime and Mystification*, Basingstoke: Macmillan.

BRYANT, C. D. (1979), *Khaki-collar Crime. Deviant Behaviour in the Military Context*, New York: Free Press.

BURGER, J.M. (2009), 'Replicating Milgram: Would People Still Obey Today?', *American Psychologist* 64(1): 1–11.

CARLSTROM, G. (2011), 'Introducing the Palestine Papers' http://english.aljazeera.net/%20palestinepapers/%202011/01/%20201112214310263628.html.

CAMERON, H. (2010), *Illuminating External bystander complicity in Genocide: Case Study Rwanda*, unpublished PhD thesis, University of Liverpool.

CHAMBLISS, W. J. (1989), 'State Organized Crime', *Criminology* 27: 183–208.

CHAN, J. (1997), *Changing Police Culture*, Cambridge: Cambridge University Press.

CHEVIGNY, P. (1995), *Edge of the Knife: Police Violence in the Americas*, New York: New Press.

CHOMSKY, N. (2004), *Hegemony or Survival: America's Quest for Global Dominance*, London: Penguin.

—— and PAPPÉ, I. (2010), *Gaza in Crisis*. London: Hamish Hamilton.

CHOONGH, S. (1997), *Policing as Social Discipline*, Oxford: Clarendon Press.

CLIFF, T. (1988), *State Capitalism in Russia*, London: Bookmarx.

COCKBURN, A. and COCKBURN, P. (2002), *Saddam Hussein: An American Obsession*, London: Verso.

COHEN, S. (1981), 'Footprints on the Sand: A Further Report on Criminology and the Sociology of Deviance in Britain', in M. Fitzgerald, G. McLennan, and J. Pawson (eds), *Crime and Society: Readings in History and Theory*, London: Routledge & Kegan Paul.

—— (2001b), *States of Denial: Knowing About Atrocities and Suffering*, Cambridge: Blackwell.

—— (2001c), 'Memory Wars and Peace Commissions', *Index on Censorship*, 30(1): 38–48.

COX, R. W. (1993), 'Gramsci, Hegemony and International Relations', in S. Gill (ed.), *Gramsci, Historical Materialism and International Relations*, Cambridge: Cambridge University Press.

CRITCHER, C. and WADDINGTON, D. (eds) (1996), *Policing Public Order: Key Issues and Controversies*, Aldershot: Avebury.

DE SWAAN, A. (2001), 'Dyscivilization, Mass Extermination and the State', *Theory, Culture & Society*, 18(2–3): 265–76.

DE WAAL, A. (1997), *Famine Crimes. Politics and the Disaster Relief Industry in Africa*, Oxford: James Currey.

EKE, S. M. and KUZIO, T. (2000), 'Sultanism in Eastern Europe: The Socio-Political Roots of Authoritarian Populism in Belarus', *Europe-Asia Studies*, 52(3): 523–47.

ELIAS, N. (2000), *The Civilizing Process*, Oxford: Blackwell.

ENGELS, F. (1968), 'Origins of the Family, Private Property and the State, ' in K. Marx and F. Engels (eds), *Selected Works*, London: Lawrence and Wishart.

ERMANN, M. D. and LUNDMAN, R. J. (1978), 'Deviant Acts by Complex Organizations: Deviance and Social Control at the Organizational Level of Analysis', *Sociological Quarterly*, 19: 55–67.

FAUST, K. L. and CARLSON, S. M. (2011), 'Devastation in the Aftermath of Hurricane Katrina as a State Crime: Social Audience Reactions', *Crime Law Soc. Change*, 55: 33–51.

FEIN, H. (1990), 'Genocide: A Sociological Perspective', *Current Sociology*, 38: 1–111.

FEITLOWITZ, M. (1998), *A Lexicon of Terror: Argentina and the Legacies of Terror*, Oxford: Oxford University Press.

FERRELL, J. and HAMM, M. (1998), *Ethnography at the Edge: Crime, Deviance and Field Research*, Boston: Northeastern University Press.

FRANSSEN, R. and MACMANUS, T. (2012 forthcoming), 'NGOs and Justice: researching state crime in West Africa', *State Crime* Vol.1(1) No. 2.

FESTINGER, L. (1962), *A Theory of Cognitive Dissonance*, Stanford: Stanford University Press.

FRIEDRICHS, D. O. (1995), 'State Crime or Governmental Crime: Making Sense of the Conceptual Confusion', in J.I.Ross (ed.), *Controlling State Crime: An Introduction*, New York: Garland.

GELLNER, W.A. and TOCH, H. (eds) (1996), *Police Violence*, New Haven, CT. Yale University Press.

GEWIRTH, A. (1978), *Reason and Morality*, Chicago: University of Chicago Press.

GIBSON, J.T. (1990), 'Factors contributing to the Creation of a Torturer', in P. Suedfeld (ed.), *Psychology and Torture*, New York: Hemisphere.

—— and HARTOS-FATOUROS, M. (1986), 'The Education of a Torturer', Copenhagen: Denmark Torture Rehabilitation Centre, RCT, 16 November: 50–8.

GLUECK, S. H. (1946), *The Nuremberg Trial and Aggressive War*, New York: Knopf.

GOLDSTONE, R. (2009), *Human Rights in Palestine and Other Occupied Arab Territories: Report of the UN Fact Finding Mission on the Gaza Conflict*. www2.ohchr.org/english/bodies/hrcouncil/specialsession/9/docs/UNFFMGC_Report.PDF.

GOTTFREDSON, M. R. and HIRSCHI T. (1990), *A General Theory of Crime*. Stanford, CA: Stanford University Press.

GRAMSCI, A. (1971), *Selections from the Prison Notebooks*, London: Lawrence & Wishart.

GRAZIANO, F. (1992), *Divine Violence. Spectacle, Psychosexuality and Radical Christianity in the Argentine 'Dirty War'*, Boulder: Westview.

GREEN, P. (1990), *The Enemy Without: Policing and Class Consciousness in the Miners' Strike*, Milton Keynes: Open University Press.

—— (2012 forthcoming), 'Wikileaks for state crime scholars: the Ankara cables', *State Crime*, Vol. 1(2).

—— and WARD, T. (2000), 'State Crime, Human Rights and the Limits of Criminology', *Social Justice* 27, 101–15.

—— and —— (2004), *State Crime: Governments, Violence and Corruption*, London: Pluto Press.

—— and —— (2009a), 'The Transformation of Violence in Iraq', *British Journal of Criminology*, 49(5): 609–27.

—— and —— (2009b), 'State-Building and the Logic of Violence in Iraq', *Journal of Scandinavian Studies in Criminology and Crime Prevention*, 10: 48–58.

GREENBERG, K.J. and DRATEL, J.L. (eds) (2005), *The Torture Papers: The Road to Abu Ghraib*, Cambridge: Cambridge University Press.

GREWCOCK (2010), *Border Crimes: Australia's "War" On Illicit Migrants*, Annandale: Federation Press.

HAGAN, J. (2003), *Justice in the Balkans: Prosecuting War Crimes in the Hague Tribunal*, Chicago: University of Chicago Press.

—— and RYMOND-RICHMOND, W. (2008), *Darfur and the Crime of Genocide*, Cambridge Studies in Law and Society, New York: Cambridge University Press.

HARDT, M. and NEGRI, A. (2000), *Empire*, Cambridge, MA: Harvard University Press.

HARITOS-FATOUROS, M. (1988), 'The Official Torturer: a learning model for obedience to an authority of violence', *Torture (RCT)* 26: 69–97.

—— (2003), *The Psychological Origins of Institutionalized Torture*, London: Routledge.

HARRIOTT, A. (2000), *Police and Crime Control in Jamaica: Problems of Reforming Ex-Colonial Constabularies*, Kingston: University of the West Indies Press.

HARVARD HUMANITARIAN INITIATIVE (HHI) (2009), *Characterizing Sexual Violence in the Democratic Republic of the Congo: Profiles of Violence, Community Responses, and Implications for the Protection of Women*, August 2009, Final Report for the Open Society Institute (Cambridge, MA: Harvard Humanitarian Initiative and Open Society Institute, 2009). Available at www.hhi.harvard.edu/images/resources/reports/final report for the open society institute—1.pdf.

HERSH, S. N. (2005), *Chain of Command*, London: Penguin.

HEYMAN, J. M. (ed.) (1999), *States and Illegal Practices*, Oxford: Berg.

HILLYARD, P. (1993), *Suspect Community*, London: Pluto.

——. and PERCY-SMITH, J. (1988), *The Coercive State*, London: Pinter.

—— and TOMBS, S. (2007), 'From "Crime" to Social Harm?', *Crime, Law & Social Change*, 48: 9–25.

HINTON, M. S. (2006), *The State in the Streets: Police and Politics in Argentina and Brazil*, Boulder: Lynne Rienner.

——M. S. and NEWBURN, T. (2008), *Policing Developing Democracies*, Abingdon: Routledge.

HOLDAWAY, S. (1982), *Inside the British Police*, Oxford: Blackwell.

Home Office research and development Statistics 2011 http://rds.homeoffice.gov.uk/rds/pubsintro1.html.

HUGGINS, M.K., HARITOS-FATOUROS, M., and ZIMBARDO, P.G. (2002), *Violence Workers: Police Torturers and Murderers Reconstruct Brazilian Atrocities*, Berkeley: University of California Press.

INMAN, P. (2011), 'Mubarak family fortune could reach $70 bn, say experts', *Guardian*, 4 February 2011

INTERNATIONAL STATE CRIME INITIATIVE (ISCI) www.statecrime.org.

IRAQ BODY COUNT (2011), www.iraqbodycount.org/database/.

JACKSON, R. (2005), *Writng the War on Terrorism: Language, Politics and Counter-Terrorism*, Manchester: Manchester University Press.

JAMIESON, R. (1998), 'Towards a Criminology of War in Europe', in V. Ruggerio, N. South, and I. Taylor (eds), *The New European Criminology*, London: Routledge.

JEFFERSON, T. (1990), *The Case Against Paramilitary Policing*, Milton Keynes: Open University Press.

JENSEN, S. and JEFFERSON, A. (2009), *State Violence and Human Rights: State Officials in the South*, London: Routledge.

JOFFE, G. (2011), 'Libya Past and Present?', *English Aljazeera*, http://english.aljazeera.net/indepth/opinion/2011/02/201122412934486492.html.

KALDOR, M. (2006), *New and Old Wars*, 2nd edn, Cambridge: Polity.

KAUZLARICH, D. and KRAMER, R.C. (1998), *Crimes of the American Nuclear State: At Home and Abroad*, Boston: Northeastern University Press.

KELMAN, H. C. and Hamilton, V. L. (1989), *Crimes of Obedience*, New Haven: Yale University Press.

KENNEDY, D. (2006), *Of War and Law*, Princeton: Princeton University Press.

KRAMER, R. C. (1992), 'The Space Shuttle Challenger Explosion', in J. Schlegel and D. Weisburd (eds), *White-Collar Crime Reconsidered*, Boston: Northeastern University Press.

—— and MICHALOWSKI, R. J. (2005), 'War, Aggression and State Crime: A Criminological Analysis of the Invasion and Occupation of Iraq', *British Journal of Criminology*, 45(4): 446–69.

—— and —— (1990), 'State-Corporate Crime', unpublished paper quoted in J. A. Aulette and R. Michalowski (1993), 'Fire in Hamlet: a case-study in State-Corporate Crime', in K. D. Tunnell (ed.), *Political crime in Contemporary America: A Critical Approach*, New York: Garland.

——, ——, and KAUZLARICH, D. (2002), 'The Origins and Development of the Concept and Theory of State-Corporate Crime', *Crime and Delinquency* 48(2): 263–82.

KUTNJAK IVKOVIC, S. (2005), *Fallen Blue Knights: Controlling Police Corruption*, New York: Oxford University Press.

LASSLETT, K. (2009), 'Winning hearts and mines: the Bougainville crisis, 1988–90', in R.Jackson, E. Murphy, and S. Poynting (eds), *Contemporary State Terrorism: Theory and Practice*, Routledge

—— (2010), 'Scientific Method and the Crimes of the Powerful', *Critical Criminology* 18: 211–28.

—— (2012 forthcoming), 'Stealing Fire from the Gods: Researching the criminal practices of the ruling class', in *State Crime*, 1(1).

—— (forthcoming), *Winning Hearts and Mines: The Bougainville Conflict 1987—1990*, London: Pluto Press.

LEFF, N.H. (1964), 'Economic Development through Bureaucratic Corruption', *American Behavioral Scientist*, 8: 8–14.

LEVI, M. (1989), *Of Rule and Revenue*, Berkeley: University of California Press.

LEVINSON, S. (ed.) (2004), *Torture. A Collection.* Oxford: Oxford University Press.

LILLEY, J. R. (2007), 'Counterblast: Soldiers and Rape: The Other Band of Brothers', *Howard Journal of Criminal Justice*, 46: 72–5.

MacMASTER, N. (2004), 'Torture: from Algiers to Abu Ghraib', *Race and Class*, 45: 1–21.

McCULLOCH, J. (2001), *Blue Army: Paramilitary Policing in Australia*, Melbourne: Melbourne University Press.

McGREAL, C. (2010), 'George Clooney and Google launch satellite plan to avert Sudan violence', *Guardian*, 29 December.

MARCHAK, P. (1999), *God's Assassins: State Terrorism in Argentina in the 1970s*, Montreal: McGill-Queen's University Press.

MARX, K. (1844), 'On *The Jewish Question*' http://www.marxists.org/archive/marx/works/1844/jewish-question/index.htm.

—— (1968), 'The Eighteenth Brumaire of Louis Napoleon', in K. Marx and F. Engels, *Selected Works*, London: Lawrence & Wishart.

MATTHEWS, R.A. and KAUZLARICH, D. (2000), 'The Crash of ValuJet Flight 592: A Case-study in State-corporate Crime', *Sociological Focus*, 3: 281–98.

MATZA, D. (1969), *Becoming Deviant*, New York: Free Press.

MÉDARD, J-F. (2001), 'Corruption in the Neo-patrimonial States of Sub-Saharan Africa', in M. Johnston and A. J. Heidenheimer (eds), *Political Corruption: Contexts and Consequences*, New Brunswick: Transaction.

MERTON, H. K. (1957), *Social Theory and Social Structure*, 2nd edn, New York: Free Press.

—— (1968), *Social Theory and Social Structure*, 3rd edn, New York: Free Press.

METSOLA, L. (2009), 'The Special Field Force and Namibian ex-combatant reintegration', in A. Jefferson and S. Jensen, *State Violence and Human Rights: State Officials in the South*, Abingdon, Oxon: Routledge-Cavendish.

MICHALOWSKI, R. J. (2010), 'In Search of "State" and "Crime" in State Crime Studies', in W. J. Chambliss, R. Michalowski, and R. C. Kramer (eds), *State Crime in the Global Age*, Cullompton: Willan.

—— and KRAMER, R. (2006), *State-Corporate Crime* New Brunswick, NJ: Rutgers University Press.

MILGRAM, S. (1974), *Obedience to Authority*, New York: Harper & Row.

MOREL, E. D. (1904), *King Leopold's Rule in Africa*, London: William Heineman.

MUELLER,. J. (2007), *The Remnants of War*, Ithaca: Cornell University Press.

MUIR, W. K. (1977), *Police: Streetcorner Politicians*, Chicago: University of Chicago Press.

MULLINS, C. W. (2011), 'The Current Status and Role of the International Criminal Court', in D. L. Rothe and C. W. Mullins (eds), *State Crime: Current Perspectives*, New Brunswick: Rutgers University Press.

NORDSTROM, C. (2004), *Shadows of War: Violence, Power, and International Profiteering in the Twenty-First-Century*, Berkeley, Los Angeles, London: University of California Press.

—— and ROBBEN, A. C. G. M. (2004), *Fieldwork under fire: contemporary studies of violence and survival*, Berkeley: University of California.

O'KANE, R. T. (1996), *Terror, Force and States*, Cheltenham: Edward Elgar.

PARK, R. E. (1966), 'Unpublished Statement made by Robert E. Park and Recorded by Howard Becker while a Graduate Student at Chicago in the Twenties', in J. C. McKinney (ed.), *Constructive Typology and Social Theory*, New York: Appleton-Century-Crofts.

PEACHEY, P. (2011), 'Leaked cables reveal Gaddafi's iron grip on corrupt regime', *The Independent*, 24 February.

PEMBERTON, S. (2004), 'A Theory of Moral Indifference', in P. Hillyard, C. Pantazis, S. Tombs, and D. Gordon (eds), *Beyond Criminology: Taking Harm Seriously*, London: Pluto.

PICKERING, S. (2005), *Refugees and State Crime*, Annandale: Federation Press.

PION-BERLIN, D. (1989), *The Ideology of State Terror. Economic Doctrine and Political Repression in Argentina and Peru*, London: Rienner.

POYNTING, S. and MASON, V. (2007), 'The Resistible Rise of Islamophobia: Anti-Muslim Racism in the UK and Australia before 9/11', *Journal of Sociology*, 43(1): 61–86.

POYNTING, S., NOBLE, G., TABAR, P., and COLLINS, J. (2004), *Bin Laden in the Suburbs: Criminalising the Arab Other*, Sydney: Sydney Institute of Criminology & Federation Press.

PROAL, L. (1898), *Political Crime*, London: T. Fisher Unwin.

PUNCH, M. (1985), *Conduct Unbecoming: the Social Construction of Police Deviance and Control*, London: Taylor and Francis.

—— (2010), *Shoot to Kill: Police Accountability, Firearms and Fatal Force*, Bristol: Policy Press.

QUINNEY, R. (1979), *Criminology*, 2nd edn, Boston: Little, Brown.

RENO, W. (1995), *Corruption and State Politics in Sierra Leone*, Cambridge: Cambridge University Press.

RISSE, T., ROPP, S. C., and SIKKINK, K. (1999), *The Power of Human Rights: International Norms and Domestic Change*, 1st edn, Cambridge: Cambridge University Press.

ROSS, J. I. (2000), *Controlling State Crime*, 2nd edn, New Brunswick: Transaction.

RUGGIERO, V. (2007), 'War, Crime, Empire and Cosmopolitanism', *Critical Criminology*, 15: 211–21.

—— (2004), 'Criminalizing War: Criminology as Ceasefire', *Social Legal Studies*, 14(2): 239–57.

—— (1994), 'Corruption in Italy: an Attempt to Identify the Victims', *Howard Journal*, 33: 319–37.

RUMMEL, R. J. (n.d.), '20th Century Democide', www.hawaii.edu/powerkills/20TH.HTM and www.hawaii.edu/powerkills/DBG.CHAP2.HTM.

SCHATZBERG, M. G. (1988), *The Dialectics of Oppression in Zaire*, Bloomington: Indiana University Press.

Scheper-Hughes, N. (1992), *Death without Weeping*, Berkeley: University of California Press.

Schirmer, J. (1998), *The Guatemalan Military Project*, Philadelphia: University of Pennsylvania Press.

Schwendinger, H. and Schwendinger, J. (1975), 'Defenders of Order or Guardians of Human Rights?', in I. Taylor, P. Walton, and J. Young (eds), *Critical Criminology*, London: Routledge & Kegan Paul.

Scraton, P. (1985), *The State of the Police*. London: Pluto.

—— and Chadwick, K. (1991), 'The Theoretical and Political Priorities of Critical Criminology', in K. Stenson and D. Cowell (eds), *The Politics of Crime Control*, London: Sage.

Sherman, L. W. (1978), *Scandal and Reform: Controlling Police Corruption*, Berkeley: University of California Press.

Shue, H. (1996), *Basic Rights*, Princeton: Princeton University Press.

Sim, J. (2009), *Punishment and Prisons: Power and the Carceral State*, London: Sage.

——, Scraton, P., and Gordon, P. (1987), 'Introduction: Crime, the State and Critical Analysis' in P. Scraton (ed.), *Law, Order and the Authoritarian State*, Milton Keynes: Open University Press.

Sivard, R. L. (1996), *World Military and Social Expenditures*, 16th edn, Washington, DC: Global Priorities.

Skolnick, J and Fyfe, J. (1993), *Above the Law*, New York: Free Press.

Smeulers, A. (2008), 'Perpetrators of International Crimes: Towards a Typology', in A. Smeulers and R. Haveman (eds), *Supranational Criminology: Towards a Criminology of International Crimes*, Antwerp: Intersentia.

Staub, E. (1989), *The Roots of Evil: The Origins of Genocide and Other Group Violence*, Cambridge: Cambridge University Press.

Stockholm International Peace Research Institute (2006), *SIPRI Yearbook*. Stockholm: SIPRI.

Straus, S. (2006), *The Order of Genocide: Race, Power and War in Rwanda*, Ithaca: Cornell University Press.

Sykes, G. and Matza, D. (1957), 'Techniques of Neutralization: a Theory of Delinquency', *American Sociological Review*, 22: 664–70.

Tatalović, M. (2011), First results from satellite watch over Sudan. www.scidev.net/en/new-technologies/digital-divide/news/first-results-from-satellite-watch-over-sudan.html.

Taylor, I., Walton, P., and Young, J. (1973), *The New Criminology*, London: Routledge & Kegan Paul.

—— Walton, P., and Young, J. (eds) (1975), *Critical Criminology*, London: Routledge & Kegan Paul.

Tilly, C. (1990), *Coercion, Capital and European States 990–1990*, Oxford: Blackwell.

Tombs, S. and Whyte, D. (eds) (2003), *Unmasking the Crimes of the Powerful: Scrutinizing States and Corporations*, New York: Peter Lang.

Van Creveld, M. (1991), *The Transformation of War*, New York: Free Press.

Vaughan, D. (1997), *The Challenger Launch Decision: Risky Technology, Culture, and Deviance at NASA*, Chicago: University of Chicago Press.

Vetlesen, A. J. (2005), *Evil and Human Agency*, Cambridge: Cambridge University Press.

Waddington, P. A. J. (1999), *Policing Citizens*, London: UCL Press.

Ward, T. (2004), 'State Harms', in P. Hillyard, C. Pantazis, S. Tombs, and D. Gordon (eds), *Beyond Criminology: Taking Harm Seriously*, London: Pluto.

—— (2005), 'State Crime in the Heart of Darkness', *British Journal of Criminology*, 45: 434–45.

Weber, M. (1970), 'Politics as a Vocation', in H. Girth and C. Wright Mills (eds), *From Max Weber: Essays in Sociology*, London: Routledge & Kegan Paul.

Westley, W. A. (1970), *Violence and the Police*, Cambridge, MA: MIT Press.

Wheatley, Col. K. D. (2006), 'Strategic Lawyering: Realizing the Potential of Military Lawyers at the Strategic Level', *Army Lawyer*, 1–16.

World Health Organization (2002), *World Report on Violence and Health*. www.who.int/violence_injury_prevention/violence/world_report/en/.

Whyte, D. (2007), 'The Crimes of Neo-Liberal Rule in Occupied Iraq', *British Journal of Criminology*, 47(2): 177–195.

—— (2010), 'The neo-liberal state of exception in occupied Iraq', in W. Chambliss and R. Michalowski (eds), *State Crime in the Global Age*, Collumpton: Willan.

—— (2012), 'Researching the Worlds of State-Corporate Elites', *State Crime*, 1(1).

Wikileaks (2011), Cablegate: 250, 000 US Embassy Diplomatic Cables http://213.251.145.96/index.html.

Williams, R. J. (1981), 'Political Corruption in the United States', *Political Studies*, 29: 126–9.

# PART V

# REACTIONS
# TO CRIME

# 25

# GOVERNING SECURITY: PLURALIZATION, PRIVATIZATION, AND POLARIZATION IN CRIME CONTROL AND POLICING

*Trevor Jones*

The increasing salience of 'security' in criminological writing over recent years is one of the latest manifestations of criminology's noted characteristic as a 'rendezvous subject' (Downes, in Rock and Holdaway 1998: 4). From being confined to subject areas such as international relations, war studies, and political science, the ideas and terminology of security have, in a relatively short period of time, come to occupy a central place in studies of crime control and policing. Yet security remains a slippery concept with a range of different meanings and usages. Security can have positive connotations suggesting the possibilities for a safer, more just, and inclusive society (Wood and Shearing 2007). On the other hand, the term can raise the spectre of oppressive interventions by the 'security state' in the lives of citizens, the persecution of minorities, and the suspension of due process protections (Hallsworth and Lea 2011). This chapter reviews the key themes of recent debates about security and the changing ways in which it is conceptualized and provided. It considers how security is being reconfigured, its current modes of governance, and how it might be better governed in the future. One of the challenges in reading the now quite extensive literature about security is that it is sometimes difficult to distinguish between conceptual, empirical, and normative themes. In Adam Crawford's words, empirical claims regarding developments in the security world—'a new set of things to look at'—can become conflated with conceptual arguments about 'a new way of looking at things' (Crawford 2008: 148). The picture is further complicated when normative evaluations and prescriptive suggestions about the way the world should and could be are added to the mix (Crawford 2006b). Thus for analytical clarity, whilst accepting that some degree of overlap is inevitable, this chapter makes conceptual, empirical, and normative issues the primary focus of separate respective sections. The first section explores conceptual issues regarding the meanings of 'security' and 'governance', and the ways in which they signify changed ways of thinking about the world of policing and crime control. The second section considers empirical claims about the contemporary security landscape and in particular, to what extent there are new things to think about. The third section considers normative aspects of what *should and could* be done about the governance of security, with a particular focus on the role of the state in security provision.

## CONCEPTUAL ISSUES: SECURITY AND GOVERNANCE

### SECURITY

The term security is a multi-dimensional concept which is deployed in a range of different ways. For example, it can be used to describe an objective state of being protected from threats or danger, a subjective feeling of safety, or the means of pursuit of either of these (Zedner 2003). As Johnston and Shearing (2003) note, this state of 'safety' can refer to protection from physical threats to life and limb, but also to those against emotional, psychological, and financial well-being. Some authors have cautioned against seeing security as an attainable state of affairs or a 'thing' at all, arguing that it is simply an 'umbrella term' denoting a range of different dynamic 'governing processes' (Valverde 2011).

Zedner (2009: 26–48) highlights various historical uses of the term, which 'are not so much sequential as cumulative' (2009: 26). 'Classical' notions of security were central in the writings of seventeenth century social contract theorists who saw protection from internal and external threat as the primary duty of the state. Following in this tradition, liberal theorists had a minimalist view of the state role, limited to ensuring 'negative liberty'—the protection of life and property—thus providing baseline conditions for the development of free markets. The emergence of the welfare state in the twentieth century brought with it ideas of 'positive liberty' or 'freedom to'. Security remained an important part of this conception of liberty, but conceptualized more broadly as 'social security' in the sense of collective insurance against threats of poverty, ill-health, poor education, bad housing, and unemployment (Timmins 2001). During the second half of the twentieth century the Cold War saw a heightened focus on issues of 'national security' focusing on the threats to sovereign nation states posed by external military forces or internal espionage (Barrass 2009; Williams 2008). The 1990s saw growing interest in the idea of 'human security', one that took the 'security of peoples' rather than the security of nation states as its primary focus (United Nations Development Programme 1994). The notion of human security presented a broad range of threats to be managed, including economic, environmental, housing, and health problems. Shaped by a range of disciplinary influences, including development economics and human rights law, the breadth of this notion—a product of 'cultivated ambiguity' (Paris 2001)—has been beneficial for coalition building and campaigning. However, critics have suggested that the amorphous nature of human security restricts its utility as a tool of research or policy analysis (Paris 2001). The importance of conceiving security broadly has been an important part of recent conceptualizations of security governance, as will be discussed further below. However, a more recent body of writing has warned of the negative consequences arising from the tendency of contemporary societies to reconfigure a range of social and economic problems as issues of security governance. 'Securitization' theorists have argued that this process results in other areas of social life becoming 'governed through security', with a range of resulting problems such as threats to civil liberties and the general distortion of public policies, practices, and resource allocation. These ideas, applied initially to the areas of asylum and migration (Huysmans 2006), have become influential in analyses of policing (Bigo 2000; Loader 2004; King and Sharp 2006; Virta 2008; Tregidga 2011) and have strong parallels to arguments about governing 'through crime' (Simon 2007) and the 'criminalization of social policy' (Rodger 2008).

It is possible to distinguish some broad conceptual commonalities shared between different ideas of security. The first concerns its future orientation. Whilst having contrasting versions of the nature of the primary 'threats', all conceptions of security provision involve 'intentional actions whose purpose is to provide guarantees of safety to subjects, both in the present and in the future' (Johnston and Shearing 2003: 15). This preventive, anticipatory logic contrasts sharply with the retrospective gaze of punishment which seeks to exact retribution for past wrongs. Future orientation chimes with broader 'risk' theories suggesting that contemporary social life is organized increasingly around attempts to predict and prevent (or at least ameliorate) future harms (Beck 1992). These social theories of risk have been very influential within criminological thinking. Feeley and Simon (1994) chart the emergence of an actuarial, managerial 'New Penology' in which risk-based discourses, objectives, and techniques challenge and overthrow those of traditional criminal justice approaches. Both Garland (2001) and Zedner (2006) demonstrate how risk-based orientations are underpinned by 'economic' theories of crime that view offenders as utility-maximizing individuals responding rationally to opportunities for offending. The second common feature of security discourse is the sense of urgency that the term conveys. The language of security is often invoked expressively to suggest that exceptional interventions are required that may override other valued social goods such as privacy or justice. The third feature concerns the expansionary tendencies of the concept. We see increasing links between security relating to internal and external threats to the nation state, between global events and national security, between national security and 'ordinary' crime at the local level (for example in the arena of counter-terrorism), between narrow and broader definitions of security, and between public and private security sectors (Zedner 2009).

## GOVERNANCE

'Governance' has now become a central theme within writing about crime control, security, and order (Edwards 2005; Loader and Sparks, this volume). Literally, the term denotes the activity (or activities) of 'governing'—self-conscious attempts to promote various collective outcomes. The term has come to be associated with a supposed shift in mentalities and practices of governing and a transformed role of the state within this (although public administration scholars have used it in a variety of ways, see Frederickson 2004). The use of the term governance in criminological debates relating to security draws upon several distinct bodies of work, all of which challenge state-centred conceptions of the way that governing power is exercised in contemporary polities.

Work within the 'governmentality' tradition has argued that in contemporary societies, governmental power aims to construct individuals who are capable of choice and action, but at the same time seeks to align their choices with the objectives of governing authorities (Foucault 1991). Individuals and non-state organizations are configured as active participants in their own government, and increasingly governance involves the reshaping of institutions in ways that encourage individuals to regulate themselves (Braithwaite 2000). Governmentality theorists highlighted the ways in which various neo-liberal reform programmes have separated the 'steering' and 'rowing' elements of governing (Osborne and Gaebler 1993) and pointed to a whole realm of government 'beyond the state' (Rose and Miller 1992). The social is reconfigured as a realm of government and the governmental process is dispersed throughout the social field, permeating a network of agencies rather than being concentrated in the institutions of the state. A second body of work that has influenced thinking about security emerged in the fields of political science and public administration. It proposed new ways of thinking about the ways in which societies are governed. In the UK, this has been most widely associated with Rhodes's critique of what he termed the 'Westminster model'. Rhodes (1997) contended that there has been a shift from 'government' to 'governance', because governing power now operates via attempts to steer 'self-organizing inter-organizational networks' rather than 'command and control' by state institutions. These changes are linked to developments associated with neo-liberal reforms such as privatization, contracting-out, and the creation of semi-autonomous service delivery agencies. The picture has been further complicated by the growing influence of supranational institutions such as the European Union. Such developments have, it is argued, reduced the central state's control over the implementation of policy and further encouraged the development of inter-organizational networks. A third branch of governance theory that has been applied to thinking about security is Castells's (1996) notion of the 'network society'. This work explores the impacts upon governing processes of the huge advances in information and digital technology, whereby information flows become the dominant feature of contemporary society. Castells sees the emergence of complex societies whose governance is undertaken via networks of communication flows defined by hubs where these flows cross. Both the ideas and terminology of the 'network society' are extensively used in the theories of 'nodal governance' discussed below. In their different ways, these three bodies of work highlight the importance of non-state actors in governing processes, and suggest a more limited role for state institutions, in contrast with traditional constitutional analyses of the process of government (Marshall 1984).

It is important not to overstate the historical novelty of the changes posited by new governance theorists. Only in the simplest of societies could a central governing power rule by direct command, and even at an early stage of development of sovereign nation states, central and local state institutions always needed to interact and bargain with other policy actors in order to develop and implement policy. There is a long tradition of pluralist analysis within political science, the starting point of which was that a focus on state governmental institutions obscured the reality of how political power is exercised in modern polities. Instead, pluralists focused upon the interplay of a range of groups, competing to organize and represent the interests of different segments of society (Atkinson and Coleman 1992; Dahl 1961; Polsby 1963). 'Governance' should be viewed both as a particular approach to *thinking about* the way that government operates, as well as pointing to some *new things* to think about. These new things arise from the fact that the fragmentation of the policy process has clearly become more marked in recent years, both in terms of the numbers of actors and networks involved in policy-making, and the complexity of the interrelationships between them. Whilst recognizing the importance of these developments, many scholars of governance accept the continued primacy of state institutions in the shaping of policy-making, at least in the context of Western democracies. Relationships between the various parties within networks are characterized by 'power dependence' (Stoker 1998). Since policy actors have access to different types and levels of resources—financial, political, legal, symbolic, or administrative—the policy process involves negotiation and bargaining between a myriad of bodies, both state and non-state. In many cases the central state maintains a key position because of greater financial, legal, and symbolic resources when compared with other actors. Despite the growing complexity of the policy process, in many spheres the state has significant capacity to define various interests as legitimate, give shape to political organization, and incorporate some societal actors (and not others) into the policy-making process. The relationship between state organizations and other parts of policy networks is characterized by 'asymmetric interdependence'. The governmental authorities rule by attempting to steer networks in the required direction, via a process of negotiation and bargaining, rather than central command.

Whilst political scientists have rarely applied theories of governance to the policy domain of crime control (though see Ryan *et al.* 2001 for an exception), scholars working within the field of criminology and related areas have used them to describe and explain changes in the nature of policing and security (Johnston and Shearing 2003). Indeed, it is suggested that developments in the security landscape—considered in the next section—are of such magnitude as to require an entirely new theoretical paradigm to make sense of them. It is argued that the ways that societies are governed are now best understood and explained within a framework of 'nodal governance' (Wood and Shearing 2007). Under conditions of nodal governance, collective outcomes are pursued within a network of 'nodes' some of which are state institutions, but the majority of which are made up of commercial or community actors. Wood and Shearing define nodes as 'sites of knowledge, capacity and resources that function as governance auspices or providers' (2007: 27). Whilst initial formulations of these ideas drew upon the imagery of 'networks', more recent versions have emphasized that different nodes are not necessarily linked together in operational relationships, and that the conceptual and empirical focus should be upon the nodes rather than the networks themselves (Shearing and Johnston 2010). Whether one focuses on 'networks', 'nodes', or both, the suggestion of these writers with regard to traditional police scholarship is clear. The 'polycentric' (McGinnis 1999) concepts and language of 'security governance' should replace considerations of 'police' and 'policing' which remain too wedded to anachronistic state-centric conceptions of governance (Shearing 2006). These conceptual claims have been contested robustly by some scholars in the field (see Reiner 2010: ch. 1). It remains open to debate whether or not the term 'policing' has outlived its conceptual usefulness, or more broadly that the idea of 'security governance' reflects a dramatically changed set of developments in the ways that societies are governed as we move into the twenty-first century. Nevertheless, scholarship about 'security governance' has been at the forefront of recent conceptual and empirical research on policing. Even those who contest the idea of a fundamental 'transformation' acknowledge the significance of some of the empirical developments that the concept of security governance attempts to capture (Jones and Newburn 2002; Crawford 2006b). It is to these developments that we now turn.

## EMPIRICAL CLAIMS: THE CHANGING FACE OF SECURITY GOVERNANCE

### DIVERSIFICATION

Whilst the security landscape has always been diverse, there is little doubt that it has become increasingly complex in recent decades. A variety of terms have been deployed to capture this phenomenon, including 'privatization' (Johnston 1992), 'multi-lateralization' (Bayley and Shearing 2001), and 'pluralization' (Loader 2000; Crawford et al. 2006; Jones and Newburn 2006). The growing complexity of security authorization and provision can be seen on a number of distinct levels (Loader 2000). In empirical terms, the most significant developments have been 'beyond' government in the corporate and commercial sector. The evidence for substantial change on other dimensions—within and below state government—is less clear. However, these areas too have seen some new developments and form an important element in new ways of thinking about security.

### Beyond state government

The growth of commercial security provision was the initial stimulus to debates about the diversification of security, and remains the most compelling element of empirical claims that the security world has changed fundamentally. There has undoubtedly been a major expansion in the market for commercial staffed security services, security equipment, and investigatory services in the UK and globally (Jones and Newburn 2006). Commercial provision has not just been restricted to the sphere of low policing, but a growing transnational security industry is engaged in the provision of military hardware and personnel, corrections, and policing operating across national boundaries (Johnston 2000; O'Reilly 2010). Indeed, commercial security is now centrally involved in military conflict with the involvement of private security firms in conflicts in Iraq and Afghanistan, and other parts of the world (Singer 2003). The major expansion of commercial security provision, numerically, functionally, spatially, and geographically has been widely evidenced. Various factors lie behind this expansion, including the increasing demands for policing and security services outstripping the resources of public providers, a degree of direct privatization and hiving off of policing functions, the changing nature of urban space, and a range of broader structural changes in contemporary industrial societies that have contributed to growing concerns about risk and insecurity (Jones and Newburn 2006).

As well as a proliferation of security providers, there has also been an expansion of the corporate auspices under which security is authorized and organized (Bayley and Shearing 2001). This reflects a deeper change in the nature of governance. Corporate entities not only contract in security provision themselves (sometimes from state providers) but also determine the nature of the order to be protected, the kinds of rules necessary to do this, and the manner in which compliance is achieved (Shearing 2006). Shearing has noted that much existing policing research—including work on the commercial security industry—overlooks the growing importance of private governments (McCauley 1986). These are defined as 'non-state entities that operate not simply as providers of governance on behalf of state agencies but as auspices of government in their own right' (Shearing 2006: 11). Increasingly, social life takes place within these non-state zones of governance, bringing into question the meaning of citizenship and the notion of a public sphere. Some such developments are related to the deliberate policies of privatization and responsibilization adopted by state governments (Garland 2001). But many have emerged independently of the state realm. The growing influence of private governance renders the notion of citizenship   tied to the idea of sovereign nation states—increasingly problematic. Indeed, it is argued that people should increasingly be thought of as 'denizens' of a range of distinct governmental domains, rather than citizens of a single, territorially-defined, sovereign state (Shearing and Wood 2003; Wood and Shearing 2007). Much of the initial discussion about the rise of commercial policing related its expansion to the growth of 'mass private property' (Shearing and Stenning 1981) in many countries. This is defined as large, geographically-connected holdings of commercially-owned property to which access is open to large numbers of people, such as shopping centres, holiday complexes, retail parks, educational campuses, leisure parks, and private residential complexes (or 'gated communities') (Jones and Newburn 1998). Shearing and Stenning (1981, 1987) have characterized the growth of mass private property as a form of new corporate feudalism, whereby private governments exist alongside state government and where responsibility for guaranteeing and defining the peace shifts progressively from the state to corporate entities (Shearing 1992: 425). Thus, many citizens increasingly live, work, shop, and spend their leisure time in these commercially-owned and governed spaces, rather than the traditional public sphere. It is clear that the changing spatial configuration of contemporary urban environments has important implications for the governance of security.

These spaces of 'non-state governance' are not, in themselves, 'new things' to think about. As Roberts (2005: 16) points out, privately-governed spaces 'are always there in centralized polities... this configuration is certainly not a unique feature of late capitalism, even if it takes on distinctive forms' (Roberts 2005: 16). But it does seem that there has been a growing degree of spatial complexity in contemporary urban environments, with a continuum of spatial types varying in terms of legal ownership and openness (Wakefield 2002; Kempa *et al.* 2004). The importance of private government has been illustrated by a number of legal cases relating to 'quasi-public space' in the UK, which have served to confirm the permissive rights of the owners of mass private property to exclude people from their land (Wakefield 2003). In 1995, in a ruling of 'feudal resonance' (Gray and Gray 1999: 46), the Court of Appeal upheld the right of the owners of a shopping centre in Wellingbrough in the English Midlands to ban permanently a group of youths from their property.[1] More recent examples have confirmed this position. In 1998 a group of residents from Washington in the North East of England attempted to organize a petition in the local shopping complex that had effectively become the local town centre, following sale of the land to a private property developer in the 1970s. Security guards requested the residents to leave because the corporation that owned the property banned the promotion of political or religious causes on their land. The civil liberties group Liberty later litigated this case in the European Court of Human Rights, arguing that in such 'quasi-public space' the residents should have the human right to peaceful protest.[2] In 2003, however, the ECHR ruled against Liberty, arguing that the existence of alternative places for public protest meant that the human rights of the residents had not been breached. In 2010, campaigners for better working conditions in Bangladeshi factories were prevented by private security, supported by the police, from petitioning passers-by on the pavement next to an out-of-town Asda supermarket (Astill 2010). Liberty continues to campaign for a change in the law that would render the owners of some forms of quasi-public space 'public authorities' under the Human Rights Act, which would provide the right to protest (Liberty 2008).

These developments confirm Crawford's (2006a) conclusion that the courts in England and Wales have provided private property owners with an almost unqualified right to exclude, which underlines the substantial powers of private governments. The use of banning orders in this way excludes some citizens from a major part of public life, given the increasing location of a range of employment, retail, and leisure facilities on such property (von Hirsch and Shearing 2000). Such policies circumvent due process safeguards that limit the application of the criminal law, and also allow for disproportionate 'punishment' in relation to the initial 'offence'. Thus, sovereignty itself—the authority to govern—is increasingly exercised by corporate private governments. These developments call into question the involvement of the state not only in security provision, but in governing social life more generally. There is certainly some evidence of significant growth in 'quasi-public' spaces in many countries, particularly those with substantial amounts of available land and relatively less stringent state planning regulations (MacLeod 2003; Glasze *et al.* 2006). In other national contexts, not least the UK and other European countries, the limited data available suggest that these trends are less marked, but are certainly still significant, particularly in the retail sector (Minton 2006; Jones and Newburn 1999).

As discussed in the next section, the expansion of some commercial types of private government has been accompanied by a substantial decline of other forms of governance 'below the state' over the past century. What is novel, then, is not non-state

---

[1] *CIN properties Ltd v Rawlins and others* [1995] 39 EG 148.
[2] *Appleby and others v United Kingdom* [2003] All ER (D) 39 (May).

government *per se*, but the distinctive nature and form that it takes in late modern societies. The most significant development is perhaps the corporatization of private governance. Many of the new communal spaces that are discussed in the literature are established and governed by commercial profit-making organizations (as compared with the greater influence of non-market forms of private government for earlier generations). This is reflected in the changed nature of activities that occur under the gaze of private governments, with more leisure, travel, and shopping activities from the late twentieth century, as compared with cultural, working, and religious activities in previous eras. It may well be the case, given these other shifts, that there has been a change in the nature of the populations subject to private forms of security governance. Much contemporary private governance is concerned with promoting a safe and amenable environment for the consumption activities of the better off. Disadvantaged communities are therefore less likely to be members of privately-governed organizations, and more likely to be subject to active exclusion from the spaces they cover. Finally, a key difference from former eras concerns the transnationalization of private government. Many of these zones of governance operate not only within nation states, but across and outwith national boundaries (Shearing 2006; Jones 2010).

### Within state government

The literature on security governance suggests that even within the realm of state government the arrangements for organizing and providing security are becoming much more diverse. Governmental complexity in the field of regulation has certainly grown due to the developments referred to earlier. In particular, it has been noted that the deregulation and privatization policies of the 1980s onwards have led, in practice, not to a shrinking of state regulation, but rather the emergence of a plethora of new forms of regulation and monitoring (Braithwaite 2000; Crawford 2006b). In terms of security provision more specifically, there have been some important new additions to the UK 'public' policing landscape in recent decades. These include the emergence of 'in-house' uniformed patrol services established by a number of local authorities during the 1980s and 1990s, and the spread of publicly-funded 'neighbourhood warden' schemes from 2000 onwards (Jones and Newburn 2006). The police service itself has 'diversified' its provision, following the introduction of 'Police Community Support Officers' (PCSOs) by the Police Reform Act 2002. There are currently about 6,000 such officers in England and Wales (Dhani and Kaiza 2011) and for almost a decade now they have performed an important role in local policing. However, the ambitious plan of the previous New Labour Government to expand the number of PCSOs to 28,000 was never realized, and there is now speculation about substantial reductions following the announcement of significant cuts in government expenditure on the police. Some of the PCSO functions may be taken over by 'Special Constables' who by 2011 numbered over 18,000 in England and Wales. These police auxiliaries have a long history, and despite some slight expansion in recent years, are still very substantially fewer than in the middle years of the twentieth century (Jones and Newburn 2002). Nevertheless, with the current government's plans to cut police budgets, and the wider 'Big Society' emphasis on the importance of volunteering, the role of Special Constables may receive more emphasis in the next few years. Another important aspect of the diversification of public policing concerns the increasingly complex contractual arrangements that now operate in the policing sphere. Since the 1980s, there has been a marked increase in budgetary devolution, contracting out, and the provision of sponsorship and commercial funding (Crawford 2008). In some areas, a quite complex local market for patrol of public spaces has emerged, including the 'private' funding of public policing (via sponsorship and charging of fees for specific policing services) alongside the public funding of private security (via public authorities contracting with security firms to undertake specific tasks) (Crawford and Lister 2006). As well as these new developments, the policing activities of state organizations outside of traditional police constabularies have increasingly been acknowledged as an important element in the patchwork of security. This broadened perception of what counts as 'policing' has illuminated a range of bodies that previously had been little discussed by policing scholars (Johnston 1992). Since the early years of the twentieth century (and in some cases earlier) a range of law enforcement and regulation tasks have been carried out by specialist bodies in national and local government other than public constabularies. These include special police forces (such as the British Transport Police (BTP)), and investigatory/regulatory bodies attached to national and local government (such as the Health and Safety Executive, Post Office Investigation and Security Services, environmental health officers, trading standards officers, benefit fraud investigators, etc.) (Jones and Newburn 2006; Newburn and Reiner, this volume). Whilst it would be misleading to present these long-established bodies as part of a radical transformation of security governance, they demonstrate further the diverse nature of security provision, even within the state itself.

### Below state government

Recent years have seen a considerable degree of criminological attention given to 'governing from below' in the form of order-definition and maintenance, rule-making, and regulation exercised by non-commercial community and voluntary organizations (Stenson and Edwards 2004; Lea and Stenson 2007). Part of this has arisen from new developments in the 'responsibilization' of non-state organizations to take control of their own security, and the spreading language of partnership and 'multi-agency' community safety (Garland 1996; Hughes 2007). Whilst much of this activity has involved commercial organizations, the part played by community and voluntary organizations is also important. The 'Big Society' ideas championed by the current Coalition Government in the UK support an enhanced role for voluntary, community, and faith groups in public service delivery (Cabinet Office 2010). A number of claims have been made about the nature and extent of the changes in community governance which are difficult to verify empirically due to a lack of reliable longitudinal data. It has been suggested that 'citizen-led' policing—in the form of neighbourhood watches, crime prevention associations, protective escort services, and monitors around schools, malls, and public parks—has expanded in a number of countries (Bayley and Shearing 1996: 587). Although there are no reliable data to enable measurement of trends in the levels or frequency of 'vigilantism', it has also been implied that such phenomena are increasing (Johnston 1992, 1996). The riots and looting that occurred in a number of English cities in August 2011 gave rise to a number of reports of community groups mobilizing in defence of their local areas (see, e.g., Beaumont *et al.* 2011; Williams *et al.* 2011). It remains to be seen whether such community patrols are best interpreted as contingent reactions to extraordinary events, or as signifying a new willingness on the part of citizens to engage in the governance of security 'from below'.

Indeed, *contra* recent reports, it might be speculated that 'community self-governance' in Britain was likely to have been a far more prevalent feature of relatively stable communities in the early and middle parts of the twentieth century—although perhaps not focused self-consciously and explicitly on the task of delivering physical security. The growing individualization of social life and the erosion of social solidarity in the last decades of the twentieth century has been a central feature of recent criminological and sociological analysis (Garland 2001). Increasing demands on the police and criminal justice system over recent decades probably reflect a *decreased* capacity and/ or willingness for individuals and organizations to 'sort things out themselves'. As Reiner argues, the period of relatively low crime rates in the UK in the middle part of the twentieth century reflected a form of highly effective 'governance from below' that has since declined substantially: 'Security, crime control and order maintenance depended on a complex network of informal social, economic and cultural controls of which the police were only one part' (Reiner 2010: 21). The literature on social capital has indicated long-term decline in civic engagement in Western societies (Putnam 2000) although the application of this to the UK has been disputed (Crowson *et al.* 2009). Nevertheless, whilst some new forms of civic participation may have grown, there does appear to have been a significant decline overall (in terms of mass industrial employment, membership of political parties and trade unions, participation in religious organizations, and involvement in a range of community and voluntary groups). For a large section of the British population a range of forms of non-state governance and community institutions, many of which were connected directly or indirectly to the existence of secure lifetime employment, literally collapsed during the latter part of the twentieth century (Mount 2005).

Whilst the declining influence of non-state governance—defined in this broader way relating to a range of economic, social, and cultural controls—is clearly true for much of the majority population, for some social groups, these forms of governance—many built around business and religious networks in particular communities—remain important. From the 1960s onwards, some immigrant communities responded to widespread disadvantage and discrimination in the housing and labour markets by developing high levels of home-ownership and self-employment (Jones 1996; Modood *et al.* 1997). As a range of working class institutions and forms of community organization have disintegrated amongst the white population in the de-industrialized regions of the UK, the influence of religious and community organizations as forms of non-state governance remains a central feature of the lives of some more recently arrived ethnic groups (Edwards 2002).

## RISK-BASED AND EMBEDDED FORMS OF SECURITY GOVERNANCE

The diversification of security organization and provision both reflects and contributes to a deeper change in the essence of contemporary security governance itself. This relates to a marked shift in the mentalities, technologies, and practices of security governance towards proactive and risk-oriented approaches (Loader and Sparks, this volume). As noted earlier, the very idea of security entails future-orientation and a preventive logic. The commodification of security has encouraged a forward-looking loss reduction mentality that rubs against the grain of traditional criminal justice approaches based on the retrospective punishment of past wrongs (Zedner 2007). Activities in the corporate sector are central to all these trends. Shaped by the instrumental objective of loss reduction, Johnston and Shearing (2003) show how risk oriented forms of thinking have a close fit with market sensibilities, but do not sit comfortably with more traditional punitive approaches. This has resulted in a proliferation of different kinds of security provision, which are more hidden and consensual than traditional forms. For example, they place more emphasis on surveillance (often using new technologies such as CCTV), and deploy a range of other interventions to modify behaviour. Security is increasingly embedded, both occupationally and functionally, throughout organizations. It is designed in to the physical structure of premises, so that the architecture and layout of the built environment reduces the possibility of non-compliance (Newman 1972; Coleman 1985). There is strong empirical evidence that these risk-based practices have become more widespread and influential in policing, criminal justice, and crime control, with a large and growing list of diverse examples such as 'early intervention' programmes, crime screening, intelligence-led policing, offender risk assessment instruments, special provision for the sentencing of 'dangerous' offenders, control orders for terrorist suspects, and so on (Kemshall 2003; Zedner 2007). Notwithstanding these very significant developments, however, the direction of change should not be interpreted as universal and unidirectional.

Risk-based mentalities and practices have not completely swept away what came before, but in some cases operate alongside more traditional punishment-oriented approaches. Kemshall and Maguire's (2001) analysis of the risk management of sex offenders in the community demonstrates the contested nature of such developments at the level of policy implementation. Although the language of risk looms large in policy documents and the discourse of managers, in practice this has been subject to a significant degree of resistance and reworking within and between particular criminal justice agencies. Similarly, Johnston (2000) shows how, within contemporary public policing, risk-based forms of thinking compete and co-exist in complex ways with more traditional punishment-oriented approaches. Other key contemporary developments in public policing and criminal justice more generally display this complex mingling of disciplinary and risk-oriented mentalities, technologies, and practices (Loader 1999; Wood and Shearing 2007). Furthermore, it is also possible to identify some countervailing trends whereby previously less visible and more informal kinds of social control have been replaced by an increasingly formalized and visible security presence. For example, there has been a very significant contraction of occupations that offered a degree of 'secondary social control' in public and quasi-public space. The last few decades have seen substantial falls in occupations such as bus and tram conductors, receptionists, ticket collectors and guards, rail and bus station staff, door-to-door delivery operatives, and park-keepers (Jones and Newburn 2002). In part, this has been a consequence of the development and spread of new labour-saving technologies such as self-purchasing ticket machines, automatic barriers, CCTV, and automated access control. Research on public and private policing in a London borough during the 1990s found that commercial security was undertaking activities that had previously been undertaken not by public police officers, but by a range of functionaries (such as caretakers, receptionists, teachers, school prefects, and park-keepers) for whom 'security' was, at most, a secondary part of their role (Jones and Newburn 1998). In these ways, security provision has become less—and not more—embedded, fragmented, and dispersed, and social control has arguably been weakened as a result.

## SOCIAL POLARIZATION AND EXCLUSION

One of the key concerns about the contemporary governance of security concerns its exclusionary and polarizing tendencies. This is one of the key paradoxes of security: that although security is often promoted as a universal good for the benefit of all, in practice its pursuit assumes and exacerbates social exclusion (Zedner 2003, 2009). It involves identification, targeting, and exclusion of those groups deemed to pose a threat. The growth of actuarial mentalities and practices, as outlined above, widens the gaze of those concerned with promoting security. They are now no longer simply concerned with investigating past wrongs and finding evidence about perpetrators but must consider the wider audience of all those who might *potentially* cause harms in the future. In combination with the economic forms of reasoning that configure all individuals as potential offenders, and the tendency to take pre-emptive action 'before the fact' in the name of security, the potential 'suspect' population expands. At the same time, suspicion continues to fall upon the usual populations: the poor, unemployed, homeless people, and ethnic/religious minorities. They are regarded as prime candidates against whom security-oriented measures are deployed, partly because of the threat they are seen to pose to the established order and the safety of the better off, but also because traditional forms of punishment are seen as being inevitably less effective with them. Such groups often operate on the margins of consumer society, have little purchasing power, and are less likely to be involved in regular legal employment. Thus, the cost/benefit rationality is likely to be less deeply embedded in their psyche. Excluded and marginalized populations literally have much less to lose (Zedner 2003). Some commentators have suggested that policy-makers are increasingly operating on the pragmatic assumption that the best that can be done is to contain the 'dangerous classes' as efficiently and economically as possible. The penal system thus performs a kind of social 'waste management' function for the better off majority in society (Lynch 1998).

As noted above, whilst risk-based approaches have become more widespread, they have not completely displaced traditional punitive forms of intervention. On the contrary, as will be discussed in more detail in the next section, a key characteristic of contemporary security governance is the simultaneous and linked expansion of state-based forms of intervention alongside corporate types of security provision. This combination has major implications for social polarization. Punitive forms of intervention have always had a greater impact upon less advantaged groups in society, whilst the better off are more likely to experience the embedded and consensual forms of security governance. Whilst the rich are increasingly protected within commercial-ly-governed spaces, the have-nots are excluded from these secure 'bubbles', and left to fend for themselves in more crime and disorder-ridden public spaces, policed by an increasingly militarized public police force (Davis 1990). Effective crime prevention in middle class districts and the spread of commercial forms of private governance work to exclude the poor at the same time as further displacing crime and disorder to disadvantaged areas. In addition, even in those public spaces that remain, security governance is increasingly following the exclusionary and risk-based policies of private government (Doherty *et al.* 2008; Crawford 2006a). The spread of crime prevention by environmental design, exclusionary use of 'anti-social behaviour orders' (ASBOs), and other such interventions (such as youth curfews), is working to privatize public space (Crawford 2006b). Although the spread of 'gated communities' in Britain is significantly less than has been the case in the USA, there is some evidence of increasing residential segregation of this type (Atkinson and Flint 2004; Webster 2002). This has major implications for the development of social trust and civic life (Blakeley and Snyder 1997). These developments also have the effect of exacerbating security concerns in the long run, a paradox to which we turn in the following section.

## EXPANSION

Contemporary forms of security governance bring with them a strong expansionist dynamic. As noted earlier, security concerns have a habit of feeding on themselves and a noted tendency to seep into other areas of social life and public policy. Although the idea of security suggests general reassurance, in practice its pursuit often fans the flames of public anxieties (Zedner 2003; Loader 1997). Furthermore and paradoxically, the diversification of security provision may contribute to further expansion of the state penal apparatus. Whereas in many other policy fields, the growth of privatization and contracting out has been accompanied by a decline in state provision, in the field of criminal justice these activities have been accompanied by a huge expansion of state expenditure and involvement (Braithwaite 2000). In many countries, public police forces now employ more staff than ever before. Public expenditure on the police, courts, and penal system continues to spiral; record numbers of people are incarcerated, and the penal sphere penetrates ever further into the family and civil society. Cohen's (1985) analysis of the dispersal and expansion of disciplinary control speaks to current developments more than two decades following its original publication. Privatization has been an addition to, not a replacement for public policing and punishment. It has allowed an expansion of surveillance, and is partly responsible for an increase in the formal reporting of matters to the police. There are more CCTV cameras, private security guards, wardens, and active citizens to direct police attention to incidents that at one time would have escaped official attention. Evaluations of some neighbourhood warden schemes have shown that their introduction was associated with an increase in recorded crime, because the existence of wardens actually meant that previously unreported incidents were now being dealt with by the police (NACRO 2003). In addition, the emergence of pragmatic and managerial approaches to crime control may have inadvertently added to the thirst for more punishment. The growing dominance of highly technical, apparently value-neutral, approaches to crime and punishment (and managerialist approaches such as reclassification of cannabis, and crime screening) may actually exacerbate punitive sentiments in the general public (Garland 2001).

Official responses to crime, such as crime prevention campaigns and a host of situational and target hardening measures, can have the unintended effect of heightening subjective feelings of insecurity. The increased visibility of security hardware and personnel sharpens the social perception of threat, and feeds the desire for yet more security. Tonry (2004) has argued that the emphasis of New Labour's anti-crime policies on disorder and anti-social behaviour may have made members of the public more sensitive to (and less tolerant of) minor infractions and incivilities. There are also other ways in which the ways in which current approaches to security are inherently expansionist. Loader (1997) argues that commercial security companies are active in constructing their own demand, by contributing through advertising to public insecurity. Similar claims can be made about senior public police officers, who whilst wanting to claim credit for reductions in crime, also may perceive some benefit from increased levels of crime and disorder in terms of support for resource claims. All these developments, along with a range of other structural and cultural changes, have contributed to 'insatiable demands' for more security (Morgan and Newburn 1997). Christie (2000) has demonstrated how the commodification of crime control in capitalist societies and the growing commercial corrections market has a self-generating dynamic. Christie argues that penal policy in many countries is increasingly influenced by the prison-industrial complex, an international alliance of commercial penal and industrial interests that profits from expansionist penal policies. These developments are the 'natural outgrowth of our type of society, not an exception to it' (2000. 170). There is strong evidence, at least in the USA, that commercial corrections corporations have been active in promoting greater demand for prison places, via helping to fund campaigns for tougher sentencing laws (Jones and Newburn 2005).

The growing spatial polarization discussed in the previous section also contributes to heightened fear of crime and increases in crime itself. By displacing crime and disorder away from richer areas, it exacerbates economic disadvantage and social disorganization in disadvantaged neighbourhoods, and increases the likelihood of further expansion of offending and incivilities. These trends also increase social polarization, and the tendency to perceive people from other social and economic groups as a threat (Zedner 2003). At a broader level still, a number of writers have observed a range of social developments that gathered pace in the latter part of the twentieth century that have contributed to a more generalized sense of 'ontological insecurity'. Such developments include: labour market restructuring and the virtual disappearance of secure lifetime employment; growing social and spatial mobility that has weakened the individual's ties with local places; the decline of participation in intermediate level institutions such as trade unions, local shops, churches, community groups, and clubs; and growing economic inequality and social polarization that leads to a heightened sense of (and fear of) the 'other' (Garland 2001). Whereas people used to see themselves primarily as members of one or more groups, increasingly people are defining their life goals in terms of individual personal development. The increased privatism and individualization of social life may reflect a degree of expanded opportunity for many people. But these developments have also eroded traditional bases of trust and stability, and individuals have increasingly become 'disembedded' and insecure (Giddens 1991). These processes are likely to have contributed significantly to the expansion of security concerns.

## NORMATIVE DEBATES AND POLICY PROPOSALS: NODAL GOVERNANCE OR RESTATING SECURITY?

This section considers debates about ways to govern security in democratic, just, and effective ways in the face of the challenges outlined above. Increasing levels of social diversity are accompanied by growing fragmentation and inequity, both in terms of authorizers and providers of security. The expanding influence of risk-based thinking leads to a further proliferation of policing and security providers (Johnston and Shearing 2003). This may lead to a patchwork that amounts to the 'worst of all possible worlds' that combines ineffectiveness with inequity. The challenge is to establish a system of security governance that is neither quantitatively excessive nor qualitatively invasive, and meets the requirements of public accountability, justice, and effectiveness (Johnston 2000). Most would agree that this is a desirable goal, but strong differences emerge on how best to address it. Many of these differences coalesce around views about the appropriate role of the state in security organization and provision. The section addresses the following three questions in turn. How far ought we to see 'security' as a desirable goal in itself and how might we begin to develop principles for assessing whether particular security interventions are morally justified? Should we accept that the state has had its day in dominating governance processes, and that the interests of citizens would be best served by recognizing and encouraging non-state forms of security provision? Alternatively, how far is it still realistic to see security as a public good, and in what ways is it possible and desirable for state-organized arrangements to assert more direction and control over its governance?

### THE DESIRABILITY OF SECURITY

Whilst it is understandable that governments and citizens would wish to do the utmost to reduce the risk of future harms, it is also the case that we can have 'too much security' (Zedner 2003). Total security, in the sense of a cast-iron guarantee of full protection from all possible harm, is an impossible goal. Even if it was attainable, it would certainly require social interventions with negative consequences for all citizens. Indeed, risk is by no means universally viewed as a negative aspect of contemporary life. Not only are certain forms of 'risky' behaviour widely viewed as exciting and attractive (Boutellier 2004), 'taking risks' is an essential part of innovation in capitalist economies (Dorn 2010). In short, security cannot be assumed necessarily to be a universal and unqualified good (Zedner 2003). Unchecked attempts to quench the thirst for more security can have serious negative impacts on other valued social goods such as liberty, justice, and privacy, and the economic virtues of innovation and profitability (Johnston 2000; Johnston and Shearing 2003). As the securitization theorists have demonstrated, security concerns have a tendency to migrate and contaminate other areas of social and economic policy. The promotion of security entails costs, and therefore requires explicit moral justification and we return to this below.

Whilst we must remain mindful of its actual and potential costs, security also clearly does have major social benefits. Loader and Walker (2006, 2007) highlight three beneficial public dimensions of security. First, the instrumental dimension reflects the fact that a degree of security is a necessary condition (or 'foundational presence') for the effective liberty of citizens and the attainment of other important social goods. Second, security has an important social dimension, in so far as the security of any particular individual depends in some essential way upon the security of others. A person's sense of their own security cannot be viewed independently of others: the very notion of 'private security' is a contradiction in terms (Loader 1997). The reconfiguration of security as a private commodity—something that can be and should be purchased by individual consumers in the market place—raises a number of tensions. Third, security has an important constitutive dimension, in that the promotion of security is fundamental to the establishment and sustenance of a sense of the social or the collective. The desire for protection from threats, and the ways in which collectivities realize such desires, plays a central role in establishing and maintaining trust, social identity, and a sense of community. In this sense, the pursuit of security 'helps to construct and sustain our "we feeling"—our very felt sense of "common publicness"' (Loader and Walker 2006: 191).

There are, then, important reasons why security should be viewed as a positive social good in itself. However, the costs of security, and in particular the ways in which its pursuit can impinge negatively on other social goals, remind us of the need for a principled framework to shape and optimize our security arrangements. This is quite a challenge. The development of principled frameworks for assessing proposed interventions with regard to crimes that have been proven—in the legal sense—to have happened in the past is difficult enough. To develop frameworks that could inform decisions about pre-emptive interventions with regard to events that *might* happen in the future is even more fraught with ethical and practical complexity. Zedner (2009: 167–74) begins this important task by drawing upon work on punishment philosophies to set out a series of 'due process' type principles which could inform decisions about what type of security and how much. These principles include necessity, minimalism, social defence, parsimony, transparency/accountability, proportionality, presumption against threat, compelling evidence (as to the nature and magnitude of the threat), fairness and equal impact, attention to human rights, and finally, adequate provision for redress. There is not the space to discuss these specific principles in detail here, but a key challenge for the future is to develop practical institutional forms that can realize and apply a framework of this kind.

## NODAL GOVERNANCE

A number of authors have suggested that not only have state-centric forms of security governance diminished in significance in conceptual and empirical terms, normatively this should be welcomed as providing a way forward for more democratic and effective security arrangements in the future. On this view, the concept of 'nodal governance' not only captures empirically the changed ways in which governing is currently undertaken in contemporary societies, but also provides the possibilities for a better future that should form the basis of policy directions. Despite general acknowledgement of the developments in the security landscape described in the previous section, Shearing

(2006) argues that much writing on policing continues to display 'state fetishism' and there is a need to escape this 'tenacious paradigm' in order to render new forms of security provision and governance both thinkable and doable. The failure to acknowledge private governments allows the relatively unfettered expansion of these forms of governance for the benefit of wealthy and privileged groups, who increasingly live their lives in the privately governed spaces of gated communities, shopping malls, holiday complexes, and leisure parks. To date, 'weak actors' have done less well out of these shifts in security governance than 'strong' ones (Wood and Shearing 2007: 98). A key objective for policy-makers should be to facilitate the participation of less advantaged groups within security markets, and to develop their own locally designed forms of private governance (Wood 2006; Wood and Shearing 2007).

This approach encourages the recognition and facilitation of other forms of government in which social orders are defined, rules are made, and compliance achieved by non-state bodies. The central state is ill-equipped for the organization and delivery of security. State organized provision has at best exhibited the inefficiencies of large, centralized public bureaucracies. At its worst, state policing has actively oppressed disadvantaged groups. Therefore, security provision based on locally designed and organized interventions, with minimal central state input, is more suited to current political conditions and more likely to achieve just and effective outcomes (Wood 2006). This suggests that contemporary trends in governance provide important opportunities to improve the governance of security for the less powerful. In particular, it rejects the position of those on the Left who simply attack neo-liberal policy programmes on principle and call for a return to the good old days of state provision. Furthermore, the leading proponents of this view go much further than intellectual theorizing and general exhortation. Some of the key writers in the 'nodal governance' school have been actively involved in the design and promotion of new arrangements for security governance in local communities in various parts of the world, most notably to date in South Africa and South America. Their approach is based on the implicit assumption that reversal of the dominant neo-liberal reform direction of recent decades is not politically feasible in the medium term. However, they share the concerns of many on the Left about the inequities and social polarization that seem to arise from these developments. At the same time, the nodal governance writers accept much of the Hayekian critique of the problems of state provision (Hayek 1955). Rather than a centralized, bureaucratic, and inefficient approach, they emphasize the need to empower local communities to build their own security arrangements that draw upon local capacities and knowledge. They argue that policy-makers should turn their attentions to frameworks that allow the poor and the weak to develop the power to compete and bargain effectively in a marketized world (Wood and Shearing 2007). What is required, therefore, is a radical devolution of governance, and the establishment and development of nodes governed by and for less advantaged communities.

These 'local capacity governance' approaches have been applied in a number of practical developments, most notably in developing or transitional countries. A key example was developed in the community of Zwelethemba in South Africa. This involved the establishment of 'peace committees'—made up of members of the local community—to engage in conflict resolution (peace-making) and preventive intervention to avoid similar conflicts arising again (peace building). The key aim is to draw upon local knowledge and capacity to develop imaginative, forward-looking solutions to community problems, rather than rely on the punitive and backward-looking mechanisms of traditional state policing. This has parallels to the way that security is managed in corporate settings, in that the main aim is to manage risks in order to better govern the future (rather than simply seek to punish past wrongs). When there is a conflict or problem in a local community, members of the local community can convene a Peace Gathering. These, chaired by a member of the Peace Committee, involve the range of relevant interested parties and seek to develop restorative solutions to these problems without recourse to formal criminal justice institutions (Shearing and Wood 2003; Johnston and Shearing 2003). Similar projects have been developed in Brazil and Argentina (Wood 2006; Wood and Cardia 2006). It should be noted that the kinds of community problem upon which these interventions focus include, but are not restricted to, a narrow 'security' focus. They articulate a broader notion of security, in parallel with the ideas of 'human security' outlined earlier, with the implication that solutions to narrow 'physical' security concerns are intimately connected with tackling broader issues of social and financial well-being (Wood and Shearing 2007).

The nodal governance approach has also been an important feature of policing reform proposals within one of the countries of the United Kingdom. Clifford Shearing was a member of the Independent Commission on Policing (ICP) in Northern Ireland which promoted the practical development there of a nodal conception of policing governance. The need for a broader vision of 'diverse' policing was a key element in the subsequent body of recommendations (Topping 2008). This recognized the existence of a wide range of community groups—not just paramilitary organizations—that had historically played a key role in conflict mediation and dispute resolution in both Republican and Loyalist communities. The Commission report reflected this in a number of ways, including the recommendation for the establishment of District Policing Partnership Boards—a committee of the local authority that would have the power to buy in extra local policing resources from providers other than the public police (Shearing 2000). The Commission also recommended that at force level, a Policing Board (not a Police Board) should be established that would have substantially more powers than the existing police authority (Walker 2000). It was suggested that this body might be given responsibility for regulating all policing providers including commercial firms, and coordinating provision across policing networks. In the event, the development of a less 'state-centric' and more nodal conception of policing in Northern Ireland has been limited. Topping (2008) argues that the Police Service of Northern Ireland (PSNI) has continued to treat 'non-state' actors in security provision with suspicion. The District Policing Partnerships (DPPs) have in practice exhibited the usual problems of police-community consultation panels, with low attendance, little engagement with grass roots community groups, and negligible influence over the daily routines of local police officers. In a similar vein, Ellison and O'Rawe (2010) posit that over a decade after the ICP report there is little evidence of a decline in state steering or rowing of security in Northern Ireland. They argue that this is primarily because of a deliberate strategy of 'colonization' of security by state organizations, involving a range of tactics aimed at perpetuating state dominance of security arrangements.

## RESTATING SECURITY GOVERNANCE: BRINGING THE STATE BACK IN

The work on nodal governance provides important challenges to the ways in which we conceptualize policing and security, but also a practical vision for a more just and effective governance of security in the future. However, concerns have been raised about the approach and its wider implications. Reiner (2010: 16–32) provides a detailed critique of the conceptual, empirical, and normative claims of what he terms the 'new policing theorists'. In his view, at least in the context of relatively stable liberal welfare states such as the UK, the case for a new conceptual paradigm, social reality, and normative value of 'nodal governance' is far from proven. There are a number of specific areas where it is difficult to imagine how effective and equitable outcomes might be advanced under the nodal governance model predicated upon an extremely limited (or absent) state. For example, where would responsibility lie for the monitoring and implementation of obligations under international law? What forms of intervention could deal with major environmental harms? How would serious and organized crimes that cross local community borders be effectively countered? How would the human rights of unpopular minorities be established and protected? With regard to this last point, Marks and Goldsmith (2006) suggest the nodal governance model is based on rather rosy assumptions about local community cohesiveness and the existence of a shared moral code that can act as the basis for locally organized security provision.

Contrary to the arguments of the nodal governance protagonists, it might be suggested that the central problem with contemporary security governance in crime-ridden impoverished areas is a lack of effective and equitable state provision. On this view, the last thing needed by populations who have long been abandoned by the market is to be abandoned by the state as well (Edwards and Hughes, forthcoming). In short, it is not state dominance that has undermined social justice but rather the *absence* of effective state institutions that have the necessary resources and legitimacy to coordinate and control security provision (Loader and Walker 2006). Put another way, the central problem to be addressed is the growing *impotence* of state institutions, rather than their unjust or ineffective deployment. Marks and Goldsmith (2006) argue that, rather than further devolve sovereignty, the state should reassert itself as 'the anchor of collective security provision'. Similarly, Loader and Walker (2007) underline the 'necessary virtues' of state provision, and suggest that state organizations must play a key role in a system of 'anchored pluralism' in security governance. Even if we accept the broader arguments of the nodal governance approach— that many aspects of local security provision can be better organized and provided by devolving responsibility and resources to local communities—it does appear that state institutions (or something akin to them) must continue to play a central role. As Crawford (2006b) notes, there are distinctive features of state action within contemporary security governance which set it apart from other 'nodes', at least in relatively stable Western democratic societies. These include its symbolic power and central authority, its claims to legitimacy for the vast majority of the population, the tactical resources and the sources of information at its disposal, and its position as the 'back-up' of last resort when forms of non-state governance fail.

Even in the particular nodal governance initiatives discussed above, there appears to be an implicit acceptance of the practical necessity of state bodies. First, there is at least a degree of (indirect) state funding via international aid. Although better local governance arrangements may in future facilitate growing local prosperity and an expanded local tax base, in the immediate future the kinds of disadvantaged communities where improvements in governance are most needed are likely to continue to be dependent upon resources raised through central taxation. For this to work it is vital that local communities—although they have their own particular concerns and interests—must be seen as part of a wider political community that is united by some general values. In addition, there must be institutional arrangements that allow for the collection of taxes and redistribution of resources to poorer communities, and there must be at least a degree of support for (or at least acquiescence to) such arrangements on the part of the wider political community. It is difficult to see how such an arrangement could work in the absence of some form of wider collective political institutional framework, or a more general sense of a public interest (Loader and Walker 2005, 2007). The nodal governance model works within a framework that requires local processes and outcomes to conform to human rights principles. This is necessary, for example, to guard against the development of localized forms of justice and security provision that might discriminate unfairly against minority groups. Such a framework of universal standards must ultimately be enforced if necessary by a body that transcends local community boundaries. Finally, individual members of local communities within the current nodal governance models always have the option of recourse to the formal state institutions of policing and criminal justice if they are dissatisfied with the local community forms of intervention. Thus, even within the nodal governance model, state-organized arrangements remain essential, albeit in the background.

There are thus strong arguments to suggest that we *should* retain and develop a generalized sense of security as a public good, and facilitate the development of collective political institutions to promote it (Loader and Walker 2006, 2007). Arguably, the nodal governance approach dismisses too readily the idea of the public interest in security and, in the extreme, it risks exacerbating the current polarization and expansion in security provision. As outlined above, Loader and Walker have argued, security—within limits—should be conceived of as a social good, one that is essential for the development of other public goods and the effective operation of citizens' liberties. There have clearly been huge problems with the ways in which states have historically attempted to deliver this public good, particularly in countries such as Argentina and South Africa, where many communities have good reason to remain suspicious of state-centred arrangements. However, it remains the case that in most polities the state both is, and should be, more than one node amongst many (Crawford 2006a).

Clearly, current state-centred arrangements remain problematic in a range of ways. One possible way forward, and one that pays due respect to the changed conditions of contemporary security governance but that also seeks to reassert the notion of security as a public good, has been suggested by Ian Loader (2000). He suggests the establishment of significant new accountability institutions—Policing Commissions—to take responsibility for coordinating and monitoring the range of bodies involved in policing and security provision at the local, regional, and national levels. Part of the membership of such Commissions would be directly elected, and part appointed to ensure adequate representation from a range of social groups. This leaves open the thorny question of how, in practice, to balance the claims of various constituencies in security governance. In short, how far should popular electoral pressures, the 'contributory expertise' of social scientists and researchers, and the professional knowledge and views of security professionals determine the content and implementation of security policies, and how are differences between these groups to be resolved?[3] Nevertheless, such proposals do offer an imaginative way forward in promoting state institutions that could bring about the fuller involvement of local community knowledge and capacities in security governance. They offer the possibility of public, democratic institutions that can provide more effective coordination of various security providers/authorizers, whilst promoting more equitable provision that tempers demands for 'more security' with reference to the possible impacts on other social goods.

## CONCLUSION

There have been important developments in the nature of security governance in recent decades. We have seen a significant diversification in security providers and authorizers, particularly in relation to the growth of the commercial sector. Furthermore, contemporary security governance is increasingly characterized by risk-oriented approaches and displays an expansionary tendency that exacerbates social inequality and polarization. The security field is becoming ever more complex and contradictory. Whilst 'nodal' scholars point to a reduced role for the state in security governance, others document with alarm increasing state incursions into social life justified by invocations of security. Some writers see the growth of non-state governance as an opportunity for fairer and more effective security provision, and others posit the empirical necessity and normative value of state anchoring of security. This high level of conceptual, empirical, and normative contestation is perhaps inevitable given that much of the work in the field is grappling with the formidable challenge of describing, understanding, and evaluating developments at quite a broad level of generalization. Criminological analyses have been crucial in shaping these debates, and continue to have much to offer to the field of security (Zedner 2009). At the same time, ideas and approaches from other disciplinary traditions can continue to help criminology make sense of contemporary developments. In particular, the sphere of political science, having provided the broader conceptual framework of 'governance' for the study of security, could also be fertile ground in providing middle-range concepts and methodological strategies to guide future criminological enquiry (see Edwards and Hughes, forthcoming). Political science has established traditions of empirical and conceptual analysis of policy formation that can shed light on the nature of *content* as well as the *processes* of governing security. Applying such approaches to the field

---

[3] See Edwards and Sheptycki (2009) for a helpful analysis of this issue in relation to crime control policy.

of security policy-making offers the potential for developing a better understanding of how security policies come to be the way they are, an essential precondition for bringing about progressive change.

## ■ SELECTED FURTHER READING

The key starting point for those interested in the conceptual and practical applications of the ideas of networked governance to the field of crime control and security is Johnston and Shearing's (2003), *Governing Security* (London: Routledge). A more recent exposition of the 'nodal governance' approach to security is Wood and Shearing's (2007) book, *Imagining Security* (Cullompton: Willan). Detailed critiques of the nodal governance approach are provided in Loader and Walker's (2007) book, *Civilizing Security* (Cambridge: Cambridge University Press), in the opening chapter of the fourth edition of Reiner's (2010), *The Politics of the Police* (Oxford: Oxford University Press), and in Zedner's (2009) book, *Security* (London: Routledge). This latter text also provides an excellent general discussion of the different dimensions of the concept of security and its growing importance within criminology. Chapters by leading supporters and critics of the nodal governance approach can be found in the edited collection by Wood and Dupont (2005), *Democracy, Society and the Governance of Security* (Cambridge: Cambridge University Press).

## ■ REFERENCES

ASTILL, K. (2010), 'The right to protest in a quasi-public space', *The Guardian*, 28 October. www.guardian.co.uk/commentisfree/libertycentral/2010/oct/28/protest-quasi public-space.

ATKINSON, M. and COLEMAN, W. (1992), 'Policy Networks, Policy Communities and the Problems of Governance', *Governance*, 5(2): 15–180.

ATKINSON, R. and FLINT, J. (2004), 'Fortress UK? Gated Communities, the Spatial Revolt of the Elites and Time-Space Trajectories of Segregation', *Housing Studies*, 19: 875–92.

BAYLEY, D. and SHEARING, C. (1996), 'The Future of Policing', *Law and Society Review*, 30(3): 585–606.

—— and —— (2001), *The New Structure of Policing*, Washington, DC: The National Institute of Justice.

BEAUMONT, P., COLEMAN, J., and LAVILLE, S. (2011), 'London Riots: People are fighting back. It's their neighbourhoods at stake', *The Guardian*, 10 August. www.guardian.co.uk/uk/2011/aug/09/london-riots-fighting-neighbourhoods.

BARRASS, G. (2009), *The Great Cold War: A Journey Through the Hall of Mirrors*, Stanford Ca.: Stanford University Press

BECK, U. (1992), *Risk Society: Towards a New Modernity*, London: Sage.

BIGO, D. (2000), 'Liaison Officers in Europe: New Officers in the European Security Field', in J. Sheptycki (ed.), *Issues in Transnational Policing*, London: Routledge.

BLAKELEY, E. and SNYDER, M. (1997), *Fortress America: Gated Communities in the United States*, Washington DC: Brookings Institution Press.

BOUTELLIER, H. (2004), *The Safety Utopia: Contemporary Discontent and Desire as to Crime and Punishment*, Berlin: Springer.

BRAITHWAITE, J. (2000), 'The New Regulatory State and the Transformation of Criminology', in D. Garland and R. Sparks (eds), *Criminology and Social Theory*, Oxford: Oxford University Press.

CABINET OFFICE (2010), *Building the Big Society*, London: Cabinet Office.

CASTELLS, M. (1996), *The Rise of the Network Society*, New York: Blackwell.

CHRISTIE, N. (2000), *Crime Control as Industry*, 3rd edn, London: Routledge.

CLARKE, R. (1997), *Situational Crime Prevention: Successful Case Studies*, 2nd edn, Albany, NY: Harrow and Heston.

COHEN, S. (1985), *Visions of Social Control: Crime, Punishment and Classification*, Cambridge: Polity Press.

COLEMAN, A. (1985), *Utopia on Trial: Vision and Reality in Planned Housing* London: Hilary Shipman.

CRAWFORD, A. (2008), 'The Pattern of Policing in the UK: Policing Beyond the Police', in T. Newburn (ed.), *The Handbook of Policing*, 2nd edn, Cullompton: Willan.

—— (2006a), 'Policing and Security as "Club Goods": The New Enclosures?', in J. Wood and B. Dupont (eds), *Democracy, Society and the Governance of Security*, Cambridge: Cambridge University Press.

—— (2006b), 'Networked Governance and the Post-Regulatory State? Steering, Rowing and Anchoring in the Provision of Policing and Security', *Theoretical Criminology*, 10(4): 449–79.

—— and LISTER, S. (2006), 'Additional Security Patrols in Residential Areas: Notes from the Marketplace', *Policing and Society*, 16(2): 164–88.

——, LISTER, S., BLACKBURN, S., and BURNE, J. (2005), *Plural Policing: The Mixed Economy of Visible Patrols in England and Wales*, Bristol: The Policy Press.

CROWSON, N., HILTON, M., and MCKAY, J. (2009), (eds), *NGOs in Contemporary Britain: Non-State Actors in Society and Politics Since 1945*, London: Palgrave.

DAHL, R. (1961), *Who Governs? Democracy and Power in an American City*, New Haven: Yale University Press.

DAVIS, M. (1990), *City of Quartz: Imagining the Future in Los Angeles*, London: Verso.

DHANI, A. and KAIZA, P. (2011), *Police Service Strength, England and Wales March 2011*, London: Home Office.

DOHERTY, J., BUSCH-GEERSEMA, V., KARPUSKIENE, V., KORHONEN, J., O'SULLIVAN, E., SAHLIN, I., TOSI, A., PETRILLO, A., and WYGNANSKA, J. (2008), 'Homelessness and Exclusion: Regulating Public Space in European Cities', *Surveillance and Society*, 5(3): 290–314.

DORN, N. (2010), 'The Governance of Securities: Ponzi Finance, Regulatory Convergence, Credit Crunch', *British Journal of Criminology*, 50(1): 23–45.

EDWARDS, A. (2002), 'Learning from Diversity: The Strategic Dilemmas of Community Based Crime Control', in G. Hughes and A. Edwards (eds)', *Crime Control and Community: The New Politics of Public Safety*, Cullompton: Willan.

EDWARDS, A. (2005), 'Governance', in E. McLaughlin and J. Muncie (eds), *The Sage Dictionary of Criminology*, 2nd edn, London: Sage.

—— and SHEPTYCKI, J. (2009), 'Third Wave Criminology: Guns, Crime and Social Order', *Criminology and Criminal Justice*, 9(3): 379–97.

—— and HUGHES, G. (forthcoming), 'Public Safety Regimes: Negotiated orders and political analysis in criminology', *Criminology and Criminal Justice*.

ELLISON, G. and O'RAWE, M. (2010), 'Security Governance in Transition: The Compartmentalizing, Crowding Out and Corralling of Policing and Security in Northern Ireland', *Theoretical Criminology*, 14(1): 31–57.

FEELEY, M. and SIMON, J. (1994), 'Actuarial Justice: The Emerging New Criminal Law', in D. Nelken (ed.), *The Futures of Criminology*, London: Sage.

FOUCAULT, M. (1991), 'Governmentality', in G. Burchill, C. Gordon, and P. Miller (eds), *The Foucault Effect: Studies in Governmentality*, Hemel Hempstead: Harvester Wheatsheaf.

FREDRICKSON, H. G. (2004), *Whatever Happened to Public Administration? Governance, Governance Everywhere*, Working Paper QU/GOV/3/2004, Belfast: Institute of Governance, Public Policy and Social Research, Queen's University Belfast.

GARLAND, D. (1996), 'The Limits of the Sovereign State', *British Journal of Criminology*, 36(4): 445–71.

—— (2001), *The Culture of Control: Crime and Social Order in Contemporary Society*, Oxford: Oxford University Press.

GLASZE, G., WEBSTER, C., and FRANTZ, K. (eds) (2006), *Private Cities: Global and Local Perspectives*, London: Routledge.

GIDDENS, Anthony (1991), *Modernity and Self-Identity: Self and Society in the Late Modern Age*, Cambridge: Polity.

GRAY, S. and GRAY, K. (1999), 'Civil Rights, Civil Wrongs and Quasi-Public Space', *European Human Rights Law Review*, 1: 46–102.

HALLSWORTH, S. and LEA, J. (2011), 'Reconstructing Leviathan: The Emerging Contours of the Security State', *Theoretical Criminology*, 15(2): 141–57.

HAYEK, F. (1953), *The Road to Serfdom*, London: Institute for Economic Affairs.

HUGHES, G. (2007), *The Politics of Crime and Community*, Basingstoke: Palgrave Macmillan.

HUYSMANS, J. (2000), 'The European Union and the Securitization of Migration', *Journal of Common Market Studies*, 38(5): 751–77.

JOHNSTON, L. (2000), *Policing Britain: Risk, Security and Governance*, London: Longman.

—— and SHEARING, C. (2003), *Governing Security: Explorations in Policing and Justice*, London: Routledge.

JONES, T. (1996), *Britain's Ethnic Minorities: An Analysis of the Labour Force Survey*, 2nd edn, London: Policy Studies Institute.

—— (2008), 'The Accountability of Policing', in T. Newburn (ed.), *The Handbook of Policing*, 2nd edn, Cullompton: Willan.

—— (2010), 'Governing Security in Tourist Spaces', in D. Botterill and T. Jones (eds), *Tourism and Crime: Key Themes*, Oxford: Goodfellow Publishing.

—— and NEWBURN, T. (1998), *Private Security and Public Policing*, Oxford: Clarendon Press.

—— and —— (1999), 'Urban Change and Policing: Mass Private Property Reconsidered', *European Journal on Criminal Policy and Research*, 7(2): 225–44.

—— and —— (2002), 'The Transformation of Policing? Understanding Current Trends in Policing Systems', *British Journal of Criminology*, 42(1): 129–146.

—— and —— (2005), 'Comparative criminal justice policy-making in the US and UK: the case of private prisons', *British Journal of Criminology*, 45(1): 58–80.

—— and —— (2006) (eds), *Plural Policing: A Comparative Perspective*, London: Routledge.

KEMPA, M., STENNING, P., and WOOD, J. (2004), 'Policing Communal Spaces: A Reconfiguration of the Mass Private Property Hypothesis', *British Journal of Criminology*, 44(4): 562–81.

KEMSHALL, K. (2003), *Understanding Risk in Criminal Justice*, Maidenhead: Open University Press.

—— and MAGUIRE, M. (2001), 'Public protection, partnership and risk penalty: The multi-agency risk management of sexual and violent offenders', *Punishment and Society*, 3(2): 237–64.

KING, M. and SHARP, D. (2006), 'Global Security and Policing Change: The Impact of "Securitization" on

Policing in England and Wales', *Police Practice and Research*, 7(5): 379–90.

LEA, J. and STENSON, K. (2007), 'Security, Sovereignty, and Non-State Governance "From Below"', *Canadian Journal of Law and Society*, 22(2): 9–27.

LIBERTY (2008), *Liberty's Supplementary Evidence to the Joint Committee and Human Rights: 'Policing and Protest'— Private Property*, London: Liberty.

LOADER, I. (1997), 'Private Security and the Demand for Protection in Contemporary Britain', *Policing and Society*, 7: 143–62.

—— (1999), 'Consumer Culture and the Commodification of Policing and Security', *Sociology*, 33(2): 373–92.

—— (2000), 'Plural Policing and Democratic Governance', *Social and Legal Studies*, 9(3): 323–45.

—— (2004), 'Policing, Securitisation and Democratisation in Europe', in T. Newburn and R. Sparks (eds), *Criminal Justice and Political Cultures: National and International Dimensions of Crime Control*, Cullompton: Willan Publishing.

—— and WALKER, N. (2001), 'Policing as a Public Good: Reconstituting the Connections between Policing and State', *Theoretical Criminology*, 5(1): 9–35.

—— . and —— (2005), 'States of Denial? Rethinking the Governance of Security', *Punishment and Society*, 6(2): 221–8.

—— and —— (2006), 'Necessary Virtues: The Legitimate Place of the State in the Production of Security', in J. Wood and B. Dupont (eds), *Democracy, Society and the Governance of Security*, Cambridge: Cambridge University Press.

—— and —— (2007), *Civilizing Security*, Cambridge: Cambridge University Press.

LYNCH, M. (1998), 'Waste Managers? The New Penology, Crime-Fighting and Parole Agent Identity', *Law and Society Review*, 32(4): 839–69.

MACLEOD, G. (2003), *Privatizing the City? The Tentative Push Towards Edge Urban Developments and Gated Communities in the United Kingdom*, Report for the Office of the Deputy Prime Minister, Durham: University of Durham.

MCAULEY, J. (1986), 'Private Government', in L. Lipson and S. Wheeler (eds), *Law and the Social Sciences*, New York: Russell Sage Foundation.

MCGINNIS, M. (ed.) (1999), *Polycentric Governance and Development: Readings from the Workshop in Political Theory and Policy Analysis*, Ann Arbor, MI: University of Michigan Press.

MARKS, M. and GOLDSMITH, A. (2006), 'The State, the People and Democratic Policing: The Case of South Africa', in J. Wood and B. Dupont (eds), *Democracy, Society and the Governance of Security*, Cambridge: Cambridge University Press.

MARSHALL, G. (1984), *Constitutional Conventions: The Rules and Forms of Political Accountability*, Oxford: Clarendon Press.

MINTON, A. (2002), *Building Balanced Communities: The US and UK Compared*, London: Royal Institute of Chartered Surveyors.

MODOOD, T. *et al*. (1997), *Ethnic Minorities in Britain: The Fourth National Survey*, London: Policy Studies Institute.

MORGAN, R. and NEWBURN, T. (1997), *The Future of Policing*, Oxford: Oxford University Press.

MOUNT, F. (2005), *Mind the Gap: The New Class Divide in Britain*, London: Short Books.

NACRO (2003), *Eyes and Ears: The Role of Neighbourhood Wardens*, Community Safety Practice Briefing, London: NACRO.

NEWMAN, O. (1972), *Defensible Space: Crime Prevention Through Urban Design*, New York: Macmillan.

O'REILLY, C. (2010), 'The Transnational Security Consultancy Industry: A Case of State-Corporate Symbiosis', *Theoretical Criminology*, 14(2): 183–210.

OSBORNE, D. and GAEBLER, T. (1993), *Reinventing Government: How the Entrepreneurial Spirit is Transforming the Public Sector*, New York: Penguin.

PARIS, R. (2001), 'Human Security: Paradigm Shift or Hot Air?', *International Security*, 26(2): 87–102.

POLSBY, N. (1963), *Community Power and Political Theory*, New Haven: Yale University Press.

PUTNAM, R. (2000), *Bowling Alone: The Collapse and Revival of American Community*, New York: Simon and Schuster.

REINER, R. (2010), *The Politics of the Police*, 4th edn, Oxford: Oxford University Press.

RHODES, R. (1997), *Understanding Governance: Policy Networks, Governance, Reflexivity and Accountability*, Buckingham: Open University Press.

ROBERTS, S. (2005), 'After Government? On Representing Law Without the State', *The Modern Law Review*, 68(1): 1–24.

ROCK, P. and HOLDAWAY, S. (1998), 'Thinking About Criminology. "Facts are bits of biography"', in P. Rock and S. Holdaway (eds), *Thinking About Criminology*, London: UCL Press.

RODGER, J. (2008), *Criminalizing Social Policy: Anti Social Behaviour in a De-Civilized City*, Cullompton: Willan Publishing.

ROSE, N. and MILLER, P. (1992), 'Political Power Beyond the State: Problematics of Government', *British Journal of Sociology*, 43(2): 173–205.

RYAN, M., SAVAGE, P., and WALL, D. (eds) (2001), *Policy Networks in Criminal Justice*, Basingstoke: Palgrave.

SHEARING, C. (1992), 'The Relation Between Public and Private Policing', in M. Tonry and N. Morris (eds), *Modern Policing*, Chicago: University of Chicago Press.

—— (2000), ' "A New Beginning" for Policing', *Journal of Law and Society*, 27(3): 386–393.

—— (2006), 'Reflections on the Refusal to Acknowledge Private Governments', in J. Wood and B. Dupont (eds), *Democracy, Society and the Governance of Security*, Cambridge: Cambridge University Press.

—— and BERG, J. (2006), 'South Africa', in T. Jones and T. Newburn (eds), *Plural Policing: A Comparative Perspective*, London: Routledge.

—— and JOHNSTON, L. (2010), 'Nodal Wars and Network Fallacies: A Genealogical Analysis of Global Insecurities', *Theoretical Criminology*, 14(4): 495–514.

—— and STENNING, P. (1981), 'Modern Private Security: Its Growth and Implications', in M. Tonry and N. Morris (eds), *Crime and Justice: An Annual Review of Research, Vol.3*. Chicago, IL: University of Chicago Press.

—— and —— (eds), (1987), *Private Policing*, Newbury Park, CA: Sage.

—— and WOOD, J. (2003), 'Nodal Governance, Democracy and the New "Denizen" ', *Journal of Law and Society*, 30(3): 400–19.

SIMON, J. (2007), *Governing Through Crime: How the War on Crime Transformed American Democracy and Created a Culture of Fear*, Oxford: Oxford University Press.

SINGER, P. (2003), *Corporate Warriors: The Rise of the Privatized Military Industry*, Cornell: Cornell University Press.

STENSON, K. and EDWARDS, A. (2004), 'Policy Transfer in Local Crime Control: Beyond Naive Emulation', in T. Newburn and R. Sparks (eds), *Criminal Justice and Political Cultures, national and international dimensions of crime control*, Cullompton: Willan.

STOKER, G. (1998) (ed), *The New Politics of British Local Governance*, Basingstoke: Macmillan.

TIMMINS, N. (2001), *The Five Giants: A Biography of the Welfare State*, London: Harper Collins.

TREGIDGA, J. (2011), *The Securitization of Routine Policing? A Case Study of the Impact of Counter Terrorism Policy on Local Policing*, Unpublished PhD. Thesis, Cardiff University.

TONRY, M. (2004), *Punishment and Politics: Evidence and Emulation in the Making of English Crime Control Policy*, Cullompton: Willan.

VALVERDE, M. (2011), 'Questions of Security: A Framework for Research', *Theoretical Criminology*, 15(1): 3–22.

VIRTA, S. (2008), *Policing Meets New Challenges: Preventing Radicalization and Recruitment*, Tampere: Tampere University Press.

VON HIRSCH, A. and SHEARING, C. (2000), 'Exclusion from Public Space', in A. Von Hirsch, D. Garland, and A. Wakefield (eds), *Ethical and Social Perspectives on Situational Crime Prevention*, Oxford: Hart.

WAKEFIELD, A. (2003), *Selling Security: The Private Policing of Public Space*, Cullompton: Willan.

WALKER, N. (2000), *Policing in a Changing Constitutional Order*, London: Sweet and Maxwell.

WEBSTER, C. (2002), 'Property Rights and the Public Realm: Gates, Green Belts, and Gemeinschaft', *Environment and Planning B: Planning and Design*, 29: 397–412.

WILLIAMS, D., KISIEL, R., and CAMBER, R. (2011), 'Right-wing extremists hijacking the vigilante patrols protecting against looters, warn police', *Mail Online*, 11 August. www.dailymail.co.uk/news/article-2024707/UK-riots-2011-Met-Polices-Tim-Godwin-warns-EDL-hijack-vigilante-patrols.html#ixzz1WPhJFfXM.

WILLIAMS, P. (2008) (ed.), *Security Studies: An Introduction*, London: Taylor and Francis.

WOOD, J. (2006), 'Research and Innovation in the Field of Security: A Nodal Governance View', in J. Wood and B. Dupont (eds), *Democracy, Society and the Governance of Security*, Cambridge: Cambridge University Press.

—— and CARDIA, N. (2006), 'Brazil', in T. Jones and T. Newburn (eds), *Plural Policing: A Comparative Perspective*, London: Routledge.

—— and DUPONT, B. (2006) (eds), *Democracy, Society and the Governance of Security*, Cambridge: Cambridge University Press.

WOOD, J. and SHEARING, C. (2007), *Imagining Security*, Cullompton: Willan.

ZEDNER, L. (2003), 'Too much security?' *International Journal of the Sociology of Law*, 31(3): 155–84.

—— (2006), 'Opportunity Makes the Thief-Taker: The Influence of Economic Analysis on Crime Control', in T. Newburn and P. Rock (eds), *The Politics of Crime Control*, Oxford: Oxford University Press.

—— (2007), 'Pre-Crime and Post-Criminology?', *Theoretical Criminology*, 11(2): 261–81.

—— (2009), *Security*, London: Routledge.

# 26

# CRIME PREVENTION AND COMMUNITY SAFETY

*Adam Crawford and Karen Evans*

The study of crime prevention has often been quite narrowly focused, limited to a discussion of the prevention and management of those crimes which are perceived to affect 'ordinary people' going about their daily business, concerned with finding solutions, largely technical, to particular crime problems. Its theoretical base has remained equally limited and its practice seen as largely divorced from political contexts and ideological frameworks. Drawn more broadly, however, crime prevention includes all pre-emptive interventions into the social and physical world with the intention, at least in part, of altering behaviour or the flow of events in a way that reduces the likelihood of crime or its harmful consequences. In more recent years there has been a recognition that the construction of the 'crime problem' and solutions proffered have become intensely ideological and used to further particular political ends (see, e.g., King 1989; O'Malley 1992). This chapter offers an overview of the ways in which the problem of crime has been constructed, the methods by which safety and security of communities and populations has been sought, and how certain theories of crime prevention have been allowed to predominate while others have been adapted and manipulated to meet the short-term goals of neo-liberal governance.

This chapter will present an overview of the contemporary rise of crime prevention and its institutionalization, specifically in England and Wales. Whilst similar developments are to be found in other advanced capitalist countries (Crawford 1998, 2009a; Hughes *et al.* 2002), often reflecting the global 'transfer' of crime prevention ideas and practices, the manner in which these have been implemented in different jurisdictions (and within jurisdictions) has been significantly shaped by divergent local political and cultural traditions and socio-legal contexts. The chapter begins by locating the contemporary rise of a preventive mentality in an historic context. It then explores the conceptions of crime, order, and security that inform key developments in crime prevention and community safety. It considers and critically analyses the claims and implications of different approaches to prevention. It will be argued that this shift to prevention together with the discourses, practices, and technologies that accompany it, is not premised upon a wholly coherent theoretical framework but a number of (sometimes competing) assumptions. In this light, the chapter then considers the infrastructure that has been assembled to deliver crime prevention over the last quarter of a century and the policy initiatives and political debates that have surrounded its implementation.

## THE FALL AND RISE OF PREVENTION

Our contemporary understanding of crime prevention is intrinsically coupled with the history of modern policing and the ambitions of the modern state which were built on claiming and accumulating the legitimate monopoly of physical force. Classical liberal thought in the eighteenth century promoted the governance of future life choices on the basis of rational calculations of the relative balance between pleasure and pain; reward and risk. The liberal subject at the heart of Bentham's writings was a prudent forward-planning rational actor—a *homo prudens*. Colquhoun and others publishing on the subject of policing around this time, advocated forms of crime prevention aimed at reducing opportunities and temptations which resonate with contemporary trends. Inspired by this thinking, Sir Robert Peel conceived of the 'new police' as an early form of preventative governance—their primary task, as made explicit in the Metropolitan Police's first instruction book published in 1829, was to be the 'prevention of crime'. Prior to this to 'police' was seen as a broad aspect of political economy and good governance (Zedner 2006). From the sixteenth until the early nineteenth century in Europe 'policing' referred to a general schema of regulation that included diverse institutions engaged in the promotion of public tranquillity and ensuring efficient trade and commerce. Crime was marginal to this body of police regulation. It was only with the combination of the institutional birth of the modern professional police and liberalism's intellectual claim to define policing in terms of the question of crime and the rule of law, that a narrower conception of policing, and concomitantly prevention, over time, firmly became located within the state and its paid agents.

As the police claimed ownership of crime prevention they subsequently shaped how it came to be understood. The period from the late nineteenth century saw the slow growth of an elaborate and complex division of labour in relation to the tasks of crime control. The resultant criminal justice infrastructure was built around responding to, processing, and seeking to know and correct, its object— the apprehended offender. Proactive crime prevention had little place, except as an element of the lingering general or individual deterrence engendered by the limited prospects of apprehension and punishment for those who transgressed criminal laws. So despite the explicit emphasis on prevention within Peel's vision of policing, the subsequent organizational history of the British police saw the increasing marginalization of crime prevention as an object of police activity and as a focus of governmental attention. Within the police, crime prevention was reduced to a small number of dedicated officers and the residual 'scarecrow' function of visible uniformed patrols. By the mid-1980s, Weatheritt observed:

> Whatever the expressed commitment of senior police officers and successive governments to the view that prevention is the primary objective of policing, the crime

prevention job remains an activity performed on the sidelines while the main action takes place elsewhere (1986: 49).

## GOVERNANCE RE-EMERGENCE OF PREVENTIVE GOVERNANCE

The last 30 years, however, have seen a re-emergence and explosion in crime reduction initiatives focused upon prevention. This contemporary emphasis prioritizes future governance (i.e. security) over re-ordering the past (i.e. justice) (Johnston and Shearing 2003), representing a 'major shift in paradigm' in criminal justice and crime control (Tuck 1988) fundamentally altering the way in which we manage crime and structure social relations. Consequently, 'preventive partnerships' have become a defining face of contemporary crime control. As Garland notes:

> Over the past two decades...a whole new infrastructure has been assembled at the local level that addresses crime and disorder in a quite different manner... The new infrastructure is strongly oriented towards a set of objectives and priorities—prevention, security, harm-reduction, loss-reduction, fear-reduction—that are quite different from the traditional goals of prosecution, punishment and 'criminal justice'. (2001: 16–17)

While conceptions of *preventive governance* are by no means new the re-emergence of these ideas has been associated with a loss of faith in the 'rehabilitative ideal' and in the effectiveness of institutions of criminal justice based on this ideal and most starkly evoked in Martinson's (1974) infamous phrase 'nothing works'.

In explaining the revival of crime prevention in the late twentieth century the following points are noteworthy:

- Recorded crime rates increased dramatically from the 1960s onwards, placing growing strain upon the reactive criminal justice system.
- Victimization surveys prompted the growing realization that most crimes do not come to the attention of formal institutions, and raised fundamental questions about the uncertain deterrent effects of state administered punishments. In addition, there has been a growth in social movements that championed previously ignored victims of crime.
- The importance of institutions and processes of informal control in sustaining order and conformity were increasingly acknowledged. This coincided with social and cultural trends in the post-war period that appeared to be loosening and undermining traditional bonds of family, kinship, and community.
- With the economic crisis of the mid-1970s, governments began to look to fiscal savings and cost efficiencies. Established modes of crime control came to be seen as representing a significant financial burden upon the public purse, prompting consideration of alternatives.

This shift reflected a broader crisis of public confidence, raising questions about the wider legitimacy of the crime control enterprise and prompting growing politicization of crime and criminal justice. Previously, crime control had been shielded from the gaze of political criticism by a broad consensus that it was best served by 'expert' judgement rather than public opinion. This insulation was increasingly breached as law and order became the subject of political debate from the 1970s. With declining clear-up rates, congested courts, and overcrowded prisons, the realization grew that welfarist promises ran ahead of government performance and that government was limited in its capacity to effect significant social change, particularly in the realm of behavioural modification. By the 1979 General Election, issues of law and order had reached the top of the political agenda where they have largely remained.

Influential in the revival of preventive governance was the publication of James Q. Wilson's (1975) *Thinking About Crime* which replaced ideas about reforming offenders through welfare-based programmes with classicist notions of deterrence combined with an emphasis on informal mechanisms of control and a new pragmatic realism. Wilson contended that criminology should be tied more closely to achievable public policy goals. To his mind, criminology had been preoccupied with questions of broad social and structural causation and social theories of crime which remained either unproven or impracticable. Instead, he argued, policy should focus upon what can be changed or manipulated. The new 'realist' logic was to seek interventions that could reduce the supply of criminal opportunities and increase the likelihood of apprehension. Motivational questions, whether they be social, structural, or psychological, in Ekblom's (2000) terms 'distal factors', were pushed into the background. In the 'new criminologies of everyday life' (Garland 1996) at the vanguard of a preventive mentality, 'proximal' (more individually motivated and immediate) factors were to be accorded greater salience. This precipitated a criminological shift away from the offender as the object of knowledge towards the offence— its situational and spatial characteristics—as well as the place and role of the victim.

## CONCEPTUALIZING PREVENTION

The development of a preventive mentality saw a number of conceptual shifts and innovations that began to chart the terrain, focus and technologies of governing through prevention. Brantingham and Faust's (1976) typology serves as a forceful reminder of the narrowness of the prevailing thinking about prevention. Drawing on an analogy with public health-care, they identified three typologies:

- *Primary prevention* entails work directed at general populations and places to address potentially criminogenic factors before the onset of the problem.

- *Secondary prevention* involves work with people or places identified as 'at risk' because of some predispositional factor.

- *Tertiary prevention* is directed towards preventing the recurrence of criminal events, by targeting known offenders, victims, or places that are already part of the crime pattern.

Rather like a health service that only focuses upon treating ill-people rather than ensuring that people live healthily, the modern state put all its crime preventive eggs in the tertiary basket. The criminal justice enterprise with its collection of specialists, professionals, and experts, appeared to be concentrating nearly all its resources in this narrow field and in the mid-1970s, very little explicit work could be said to be focused around secondary prevention and even less concerned with primary prevention. By the late 1990s, however, the task of crime prevention was drawn much more broadly. In the space of approximately two decades crime prevention had become embedded in government policies. The inflated cultural, social, and political salience accorded to crime and insecurity resulted in policies and strategies previously defined in terms of other outcomes increasingly redefined in terms of their possible crime preventive effects. Through this lens, the quality of education, nutrition, health, environment, housing, and social provisions more generally, frequently came to be viewed in terms of their criminogenic consequences or crime-potential, rather than merely as important public goods in their own right. Consequently, this preventive mentality has fostered a 'criminalization of social policy', whereby life is increasingly 'governed through crime and insecurity' or at least social policies are justified in terms of their crime reductive potential (Crawford 1997a: 228). The shift to prevention accords to crime an elevated place in the construction of social order such that fundamental public issues may become marginalized, except in so far as they are defined in terms of their crime preventive qualities. From this perspective, crime comes to constitute an organizing concept central to the exercise of contemporary authority such that 'we can expect people to deploy the category of crime to legitimate interventions that have other motivations' (Simon 2007: 4). Over the course of this chapter the theoretical and policy frameworks through which crime prevention has been traditionally practiced will be further explored.

## SITUATIONAL CRIME PREVENTION

Situational crime prevention involves the management, design, or manipulation of the immediate physical environment to reduce the opportunities for specific crimes. Its genesis is closely associated with the work of Ron Clarke and colleagues in the Home Office Research and Planning Unit during the early 1980s. Whilst their work was undoubtedly instrumental in conceptualizing and rationalizing disjointed developments, as well as fostering research and policy interest, situational prevention is probably better understood as an assortment of practices in search of a theory. It emerged through a plethora of locally-based and small-scale initiatives, innovations, and technological advances often arising from attempts to solve very specific problems many of which had their origins in the commercial sector. Simultaneously, a new band of researchers became interested in conceptualizing the crime preventive potential of practical initiatives. The pragmatic connection between emerging theory and practice made this interactive process particularly successful, driving innovation forward and Clarke later claimed situational prevention to be a 'framework for some practical and commonsense thinking about how to deal with crime' (1995: 93).

Moreover, situational, unlike social, factors, it was believed, would prove more easily manipulated and that it was easier to reduce opportunities and temptations than to change human dispositions. In place of a 'nothing works' pessimism emerged a renewed optimism that some things, however small, do impact upon the commission of crimes in specific locations, at particular times.

Opportunity reduction can take three interrelated forms:

- *increasing the perceived effort* involved in crime by making the targets of crime harder to get at or otherwise hindering the commission of crime;

- *increasing the perceived risks* of detection and apprehension;

- *reducing the anticipated rewards* of crime; in some cases this may involve removing the targets of crime altogether (Clarke 1995).

Pease (2002: 952) noted that the early emphasis on achieving opportunity reduction through 'bars, bolts and barriers' promoted misconceptions that primary prevention can be equated with target hardening and physical intervention. Partly in response to these perceptions, Cornish and Clarke (2003) added two further dimensions to include *reducing provocation* and *removing excuses*. Reducing the provocative elements in situations seeks to understand and limit the immediate triggers for criminal events. Removing excuses, by contrast, seeks to eliminate the possibility of someone responding that they did not know they were committing an offence or that they had no alternative but to commit a crime. Examples include signage reminding people of rules and alerting them to the consequences of breaking such rules. This approach constitutes a form of 'regulated self-regulation' that dovetails with the wider use of behavioural contracts (common in schools, housing, and youth justice) in governing future conduct (Crawford 2003). As Brantingham *et al.* note 'many of the specific techniques in this category of situational crime prevention represent activities typical of municipal government' (2005: 280). Here, we have a concept of prevention that is both extensive in its reach and accords closely with pre-nineteenth century concepts of policing. Consequently, prevention of crime is restored to an integral aspect of everyday good governance.

In this, situational prevention seeks to change people's behaviour through such routine and mundane modifications to the physical world that they become almost imperceptible. Control is embedded in the design and arrangement of things in a way that it is taken-for-granted, but nonetheless demands small adjustments to behaviour. The sleeping policeman (or hump) in the road does not require the motorist to engage in a finely grained calibration of the costs and benefits that attain from travelling at different speeds. It triggers a slight alteration of behaviour, in this instance with regard to speed. The promotion of behavioural changes through the use of different 'nudges' (Thaler and Sunstein 2008) has gained greater political popularity over the last few years and further entrenches the situational approach in wider policy agendas seeking to influence individual choices in regards to health, economic decisions, housing, schooling, and so on.

Collectively, situational prevention techniques represent the confluence of a number of different theoretical strands.

## ROUTINE ACTIVITY THEORY

Routine activity theory is a macro-level attempt to identify the supply of criminal opportunities and to understand crime patterns (Cohen and Felson 1979). It focuses on criminal events, their distribution and clustering over time and space, rather than criminal inclinations. The latter are not denied but rather the theory takes the supply of offenders as given. Routine activity theory identifies three minimal elements for a crime to occur:

- A *'likely offender'*—anyone who for any reason might commit a crime.
- A *'suitable target'*—an object or person likely to be taken or attacked by the offender.
- *The absence of 'capable guardians'*—someone who might intervene to stop or bear witness to an offence.

In this light, the rise in crime since the 1960s is explained by reference to the increasing proportion of empty homes in the day, in part due to the greater number of single person households and expanded participation of women in the workplace, and the increased availability of valuable, lightweight portable electronic goods. Social changes have produced more targets and fewer capable guardians. Conversely, it is proposed that the removal of any of the three constituent elements will disrupt criminal events. By implication, the supply of 'capable guardians' is crucial to prevention efforts. The most likely guardians against crime are not necessarily the police but rather neighbours, friends, and bystanders.

Routine activity theory has fostered meso-level crime pattern analysis, significantly facilitated by technological developments in geospatial mapping. This has allowed preventive energies to be targeted at high crime 'hot spots'. However, as routine activity theory dwells solely on the supply of opportunities provided by specific time-place conjunctions, it is unable to disentangle the conundrum as to whether places vary in their capacity to cause crime or merely serve to attract crime that would have occurred regardless. Sherman *et al.* phrase the question as follows: 'Are the routine activities of some hot spots criminogenic **generators** of crime, or merely more attractive **receptors** of crime?' (1989: 46). The answer is far from being resolved either theoretically or empirically but goes to the heart of situational prevention. Nonetheless, there has been considerable practical application of routine activity theory, in part due to its apparent simplicity and the pragmatic optimism it affords.

## RATIONAL CHOICE THEORY

At a micro-level, rational choice theory attempts to explain human decision-making. It revives neo-classical ideas about human motivations. At their base, people are pleasure maximizers. They seek-out avenues and opportunities that increase their individual pleasure and avoid those that may cause pain. This assumes that offenders choose to commit specific offences for the benefits they bring. Prevention is aimed at altering decision-making processes so as to increase the risks or effort involved in the commission of a crime and decrease any rewards associated with it. This challenges the established criminological wisdom that devoted attention to dispositional theories of crime. Notably, situational approaches presuppose crime to be a normal aspect of modern life and criminals to be essentially 'like us': no different from other rational actors. 'The reality', Felson opines, 'is that ordinary people can do ordinary crime—young and old. Everybody could do at least some crime some of the time' (1998: 11). He suggests that dominant criminological understandings and policy discourses tend to conform to a 'not me' fallacy: the idea that people who commit crime are somehow different from ordinary people 'like me'. By seeking to differentiate between criminals and law-abiding citizens, the focus has been on differences rather than similarities.

## ENVIRONMENTAL DESIGN

In the US, Jacobs (1961) presented a powerful critique of post-war urban planning, emphasizing its destructive impact on the natural processes of ordering within neighbourhoods. Drawing on these insights, Newman sought to identify architectural designs that would discourage criminality and foster preventive social controls. He elaborated a theory of 'defensible space' as 'a model for residential environments which inhibits crime by creating the physical expression of a social fabric that defends itself' (1972: 3). He argued that architectural design can release the latent sense of territoriality and community among inhabitants, so that these become accepted parts of residents' assumption of responsibility for preserving a safe and well-maintained living environment. Newman identified four key constituents of good design to encourage social control networks: territoriality, surveillance, image, and environment. Crucially, territoriality demands physical spaces that demarcate areas of control, whilst surveillance requires the design of buildings so as to allow and enable easy observation of territorial areas. The mass housing projects of the post-war period, he contended, squeezed out important processes of social control. In their place 'indefensible spaces' proliferated, including: anonymous walkways, underpasses, lifts, stair-wells, and long dark corridors, all with easy access to the public. These constitute 'confused' areas which belong to no-one, are cared for by no-one and which are observed by no-one. Smaller units which householders could supervise and be seen to be responsible for should engender a sense of ownership and community spirit, reviving important processes of control.

Newman's ideas had close affinity with a looser array of design practices which clustered under the heading of 'crime prevention through environmental design' (CPTED). Most prominent in the work of Jeffery (1971), CPTED sought to apply notions of environmental change and design to foster territoriality in situations beyond residential areas. These ideas attracted significant federal US funding to implement and evaluate. However, the results proved very disappointing. Subsequently, the interest in CPTED waned, in the US at least. More generally, the works of both Newman and Jeffery were accused of architectural determinism in their failure to consider the role of social variables and behaviour both directly and in mediating the effects of architectural designs.

In the UK, these ideas were resurrected by Coleman (1985), who identified a number of 'design disadvantages', the presence of which correlates with high levels of anti-social behaviour. She claimed empirical support for her thesis from the study of numerous public sector housing estates and sought to explain the social processes through which design affects crime. For her, situational and dispositional aspects of crime are identified, not as mutually independent but as 'two sides of the same coin'. Poor design encourages an environment in which crime is a 'learned response'. She argued that: 'Architectural situations that are highly vulnerable to crime can teach children to adopt criminal decisions, and this learned disposition can then cause them to see all situational weaknesses as rational opportunities for crime' (1989: 109–10). In sum, Coleman offers a vision of crime prevention in which situational modifications *cause* social and cultural change.

Coleman's analysis largely ignored the impact of wider social and cultural factors that influence the make-up of the people housed in poorly designed mass housing estates, such as the social stigma attached to certain estates, local authority allocation policies, and the character of housing estate management (Bottoms and Wiles 1986). Nevertheless, her work, along with that of Newman and Jeffery, has had an enduring legacy (Ekblom 1995) and been widely applied in planning designs by central and local governments.[1] In this light, police forces regularly employ architectural liaison officers to promote crime prevention thinking in planning designs. Furthermore, new houses are kite-marked as 'Secured by Design' if they conform to certain architectural standards.[2] However, Hillier and Shu contend that the debate on urban layout and crime over the past two decades has been 'long on ideology…but short on evidence' (2000: 224). They claim their research findings 'challenge many aspects of the current defensible space orthodoxy' and show that the built-in security advantages that defensible space proponents argue belong to cul-de-sacs 'in fact belong to the street, with its greater potential for movement, its greater mutual visibility for higher numbers of neighbours, and greater protection from the rear' (ibid.). Problematically, defensible space theory does not inform us of how places are actually used by people. Spaces may be defensible but not defended if the social apparatus and personnel for effective defence is lacking.

Possibly the most valuable insight provided by situational perspectives is that 'context matters'. Situational theory demands not merely that interventions are targeted at appropriate places rooted in an understanding of their specific crime problems but also that these should be regularly reviewed and renewed or adapted. As situational interventions are intended to effect behaviour, they need to be continuously checked, for their ongoing effectiveness will be dependent upon how crime patterns adapt and change over time. This acknowledges that crime patterns—like social, cultural, and technological worlds—are not static. From within a situational frame of reference, new criminal opportunities are being created all the time, notably through scientific innovations. Crime opportunities are highly specific, are concentrated in time and space, depend on everyday movements of activity, and are interconnected such that one crime may produce opportunities for another (Felson and Clarke 1998). As some opportunities may be closed or restricted consequent to situational endeavours others may be opened. Crucially, however, continual adaptation and evolution 'makes knowledge of what works in crime prevention a wasting asset' (Ekblom 2005: 230).

---

[1] For example, Department of the Environment circular 5/94 on *Planning Out Crime* and Government guidance on *Safer Places: The Planning System and Crime Prevention* produced in 2004 by the Home Office and Office of the Deputy Prime Minister.

[2] www.securedbydesign.com.

In essence, situational prevention privileges a particular kind of knowledge that is practical, empirical, and reflexive. This context specificity and temporal impermanence questions the generalizing claims about situational interventions made by many proponents of 'crime science' (Laycock 2005) and 'international crime prevention' (Farrington 2000), who advocate the application of 'science' to the control of crime and the transferability and replication of 'successful' prevention mechanisms and technologies across different settings. Situational prevention is essentially a 'bottom-up' approach that needs to be grounded in local knowledge and a reflexive engagement with the ongoing interactions between situations and people. This is very different from the scientific, evidence-based quest for 'what works' which dominates much crime prevention policy today. Situational prevention fits uneasily with efforts to generalize and provide evidence for rules distilled into universal 'tool-kits', yet, as Shapland (2000) notes, many of its proponents view situational prevention from a top-down governmental perspective which belies its knowledge-based assumptions. The inferences of contextual specificity are frequently lost in the application and implementation of situational prevention. Techniques developed in one context are often transferred to others with little regard to the context in which they are applied. One reason for this disjunction between theory and practice may lie in the fact that situational prevention embodies a universal image of human decision-making— that of the 'amoral' rational choice actor—which is easily and eminently generalizable. It evokes a 'de-differentiating' logic that cannot be housed in different, specialist, professional state institutions and that 'implies the generalization of crime control to meet the generality of crime' (Garland 2000: 13).

Situational crime prevention has proved attractive at a number of levels. As well as its pragmatism and its appeal to commonsense, piecemeal change with tangible results, situational prevention (re-)emerged at a favourable political moment. Its language of economic reasoning, personal choice, responsibility, and rationality fitted very well with the growing neo-liberal consensus within government, first articulated by the Thatcher governments of the 1980s, but subsequently reinforced and extended by later governments. Its appeal to the responsibilities of people and organizations throughout civil society meshed well with the growing political will to downsize and roll-back the state, in order to free-up entrepreneurial initiative. The neo-liberal mantra demanded a retreat from the 'illusion' that governments can provide social goods. In this context, situational prevention offered the promise of short-term and cost-effective, albeit small-scale, impacts. A situational mentality speaks the language of the market, of supply and demand, risk and reward, opportunities and costs, whilst appealing to regulation beyond the state through private and quasi-private auspices. It focuses as much on victims as on offenders. Furthermore, it contrasted with apparently discredited social welfare models of policy provision replacing 'socialized risk management with privatised prudentialism' (O'Malley 1992: 263).

Whilst originally promoted by a Conservative Government, Clarke (2000: 107–9) is correct to note that the ideas that inform situational approaches are by no means 'conservative'. Far from it, they eschew a moral agenda at the heart of conservative political philosophy, in preference for an instrumental understanding of both behaviour and the role of government. Neo-conservative ideas are to be found more clearly associated with community-based crime prevention (explored later), which sees the role of government as not merely implicated in freeing autonomy but crucially, also, in shaping it by inculcating a moralized vision of civic virtue.

## DISPLACEMENT—THE ACHILLES HEEL?

A central objection to situational prevention is that it merely deflects crime to other times or situations. Displacement can take a number of different forms including: *spatial, temporal, tactical, target,* and *type* of crime (Hakim and Rengert 1981). To complicate matters further, these forms of displacement may occur simultaneously or in combination. Clearly, displacement constitutes a major challenge for situational approaches and presents considerable difficulties for evaluating their effectiveness. However, it would be wrong to assume that displacement is either inevitable or complete. To do so would be to see crime prevention as analogous to squeezing a balloon which subsequently changes shape and distribution but does not change in volume. This 'hydraulic' interpretation assumes complete displacement which is unlikely in relation to many forms of crime, notably burglary, where the demands of time and effort are considerable. Displacement makes certain assumptions about crime. It presumes that incentives to commit a crime are sufficiently strong to survive the initial thwarting of intention—that 'bad will out'. Cornish and Clarke (1987) suggest that displacement is contingent upon the belief that different crimes can serve a functional equivalence for offenders. Instead, they claim that the willingness of an individual to substitute one offence for another depends upon the extent to which the alternative corresponds with the offender's goals and abilities. They point to the different 'choice structuring properties' of crimes, defined as the type and amount of pay-off, perceived risk, and skills needed that are 'perceived by the offender as being especially salient to his or her goals, motives, experience, abilities, expertise, and preferences' (ibid.: 935). The legitimate assumption is that displacement will not be random but is likely to be structured, or clustered, by certain factors (Guerette and Bowers 2009).

A significant difficulty arises where displaced crime shifts to a more serious offence or results in more harmful consequences. This 'malign' displacement might occur where offenders choose to use greater force or more harmful techniques in adapting to preventive interventions or where more vulnerable people are affected as a result of crime prevention. There was some evidence that the introduction of steering column locks in the UK—initially introduced on new cars only—whilst reducing theft of new cars made older cars almost twice as vulnerable (Webb 2005: 467). By implication, this shifted the risk of car theft onto those more likely to be less affluent. Likewise, we also need to acknowledge the possibility of 'benign' displacement, where a less serious offence or non-criminal act is committed or an act of similar seriousness is committed upon a victim for whom, or in a place where, it has less serious consequences.

Proponents of situational approaches point to a possible reverse effect by which crime reductive impacts may extend beyond the intended target in a 'diffusion of benefits' (Clarke and Weisburd 1994: 169). This 'halo' or 'free rider' effect highlights the processes that spread the crime reduction benefits beyond its primary targets. Poyner's (1992) evaluation of CCTV introduced in car parks at Surrey University found that neighbouring car parks outside the camera's field of vision also benefited from reductions in crime. Matthews (1992) study of the introduction of street closures to stop kerb crawling near Finsbury Park, north London, found that not only did prostitution decline but so did other offences indirectly associated with prostitution including bur- glary and car theft. This case study was also held to be an example of benign displace- ment. Where prostitutes were displaced, they often moved off the streets and into areas where the nuisance element was reduced and the prostitutes were likely to be safer.

Despite criticisms, the phenomenon of displacement points to the power of policy interventions not their weakness. Crime displacement might be seen as a potential tool of crime control policy rather than as an unwanted constraint upon crime preven- tion programmes (Barr and Pease 1990: 279). The displacement of crime, produced by forms of deliberate prevention, might be used to redistribute the burden of vic- timization in a more equitable manner. However, the attraction of explicit policies of crime redistribution is unlikely to be politically acceptable. Few people would wel- come redistributed crime into their neighbourhood. Nevertheless, this illuminates the political choices that constitute present patterns of crime.

## CRITIQUES OF SITUTATIONAL CRIME PREVENTION

Situational crime prevention has evoked considerable critique from within established criminology in part owing to its radical reframing of policy concern, research enquiry, and practical effort. It does not seek to explain, nor is it interested in, questions of aeti- ology—criminology's traditional focus. Offenders are constructed as 'abiographical individuals', abstracted from their social or structural contexts and personal histories (O'Malley 1992). Clarke and Cornish (1985) acknowledge the reality of 'limited rationality' in decision-making, in that choice is constrained by limits of time, ability, and the availability of relevant information. Nonetheless, this largely fails to address non-opportunistic crimes or the proposition that not all actors are economically self- interested. Situational prevention has little to say about non-instrumental factors, expressive crime, and the role of emotions. The attractions of risk-laden criminal acts that may express moral or cultural preferences are not easily comprehended within a framework of rational choice. In some contexts, the risk may itself be the attraction. Hence, situational approaches have less to say about crimes, such as joy-riding, drug- taking, hate crime, violence associated with binge-drinking and gang membership that may evoke some expressive dimension.

A further critique focuses on the lack of an ethical dimension to situational crime prevention theory. It appears to have no explicit concerns for equity built into it and affords no boundaries to its use or implications. Many proponents of situational approaches prefer to strip crime and prevention of any association with moral or normative debates (Felson 1998). Nevertheless, the way that situational prevention is used in an unequal society may well increase inequalities. Situational prevention has become associated, by some, with the rise of a 'fortress society' in which the logic of 'target hardening' is taken to its extreme in the form of 'gated communities' where people live secured behind walls, gates, and other security paraphernalia. Whilst the extent of gating in the UK has often been over-exaggerated (and is clearly less than in the US, South Africa, and parts of Latin America), one survey of planning authorities identified around 1,000 gated communities in England (Atkinson *et al.* 2004). Developers spearheading market development in city-centre living in the UK acknowledge that the privatization and gating of communal space has become an accepted design and selling feature (Webster 2001). It is also not restricted to wealthy privately owned enclaves but features in the design and modification of social housing (Blandy 2011). Less dramatic are the potential long-term cultural implications and effects of a defensive mentality which often serves to undermine and obstruct social trust relations and impoverish the public sphere (Crawford 2000).

Situational approaches also raise ethical issues with regard to civil liberties and human rights. Many situational mechanisms are intrusive, entail the collection of personal data, and invade traditional notions of privacy, notably CCTV and identity-based security systems. It is perhaps ironic that in the same country where concerns over civil liberties and fears of intrusive surveillance helped to define a particular vision of prevention and police-work nearly two centuries ago, these arguments largely have been ignored in the proliferation of preventive technology. An exclusionary logic accompanies the instrumental thinking that informs situational approaches. Denying access to, and excluding potential troublemakers from, places where crime opportunities present themselves is likely to be more cost-effective than making goods so hard to get to for 'good consumers' that it would get in the way of business. Exclusion through diverse formal and informal banning orders and private policing strategies are prominent crime prevention strategies (Crawford 2011). Frequently, this entails the use of 'profile-based exclusions' which often target young people (von Hirsch and Shearing 2000).

## SOCIAL–DEVELOPMENTAL CRIME PREVENTION

Social crime prevention primarily centres on interventions that seek to affect and target social processes and collective relations. In contrast to situational prevention, social approaches are concerned with measures aimed at tackling the root causes of crime and the dispositions of individuals to offend (Graham and Bennett 1995). For the purpose of this chapter, we take social crime prevention to include both social influences on individuals and the manner in which social groups foster criminogenic factors and, conversely, generate preventive dimensions of social control. Thus, social crime prevention incorporates interventions aimed at: (i) reducing individual motivations to offend via their social influences and institutions of socialization; and (ii) altering social relations and/or the social environment, through a collective focus on communities, neighbourhoods, or social networks. Elsewhere in the literature (Tonry and Farrington 1995), the former is often referred to as 'developmental' (Tremblay and Craig 1995) or 'risk-focused' prevention (Farrington 2002) and the latter frequently assumes the label 'community crime prevention' or 'community safety' (Hope 1995), to which we return below. Developmental crime prevention has been well covered in a previous edition of this volume (Farrington 2007), what follows is limited to a few critical observations.

Developmental approaches entail intervention early in personal pathways that may result in criminal behaviours and other social problems to prevent the development of criminal potential in individuals. It is based on the idea that offending is determined by behavioural and attitudinal patterns learned and produced over the life-course. It proceeds from the basis that risk factors exist at different ages and that life events yield effects on the course of development. Consequently, developmental prevention concerns the manipulation of multiple risk and protective factors at crucial transition points across a life-time. Hence, it focuses largely on childhood development and the opportunities present at critical junctures across the life-course to prevent the onset of offending in the early years. These developmental stages offer prospects to target prevention resources at those most at risk of offending, where long-term benefits might accrue. This is what van Dijk and de Waard (2009: 137–8) term 'secondary offender-oriented crime prevention', namely early intervention programmes targeted at children and young people (and their parents) identified as 'at risk' of offending. Whilst it is not restricted to interventions with young people, much of the policy focus has been targeted at childhood risk factors (Farrington 2007).

Secondary developmental prevention by identifying 'risk factors' which cluster among groups of known delinquents is premised upon a differentiating logic that focuses upon a targeted group as a sub-population from those who do not occupy the same risk groupings (Homel 2005). This marks it out as distinct from primary situational prevention with its de-differentiating logic and neo-classical influences. Developmental prevention is infused with a heavy dose of positivism drawing causal inferences from assessments of risks. Hence, it is concerned with identifying, classifying, differentiating, and seeking to correct 'risk factors', in much the same way that early positivist criminologists sought to study the pre-dispositional attributes of 'criminality'.

Developmental prevention seeks to highlight risk factors that may signal the future onset of criminality, protective factors that may reduce the likelihood of criminality, and desistance factors which may usher young people out of crime. It is heavily reliant therefore upon predictive tools in assessing the likelihood that a given person with certain risk factors will go on to commit specific crimes (France and Utting 2005). However, calculation of future risks can never be an exact science. There will always be 'false positives', those targeted for intervention, but who would not have gone on to commit crime. There is a financial logic behind this differentiation in that targeting resources at those most 'at risk' rather than providing universal services is considered more cost-effective. However, another implication of differential treatment is the possibility of stigmatization by association and inadvertent labelling (Bernburg and Krohn 2003).

One problem with developmental approaches is to establish which risk factors are causes and which are merely markers or correlated with causes; correlation itself is not the same as causation. Most knowledge about risk factors is based on variation between individuals, whereas prevention requires variation (change) within individuals (Thornberry and Krohn 2005). It is not always clear that findings within individuals are the same as findings between individuals. Ideas of 'nipping crime in the bud' have pushed criminological concern further and earlier into child—and even foetal—development, elaborating more complex chains of causation. The impact of this logic is to expand the range and reach of state interventions deeper into the social fabric. These may be in the interests of the individuals concerned and society more generally, in terms of reductions in crime, but raise ethical issues about the appropriate limits of government intervention, the balance between potential crime preventive benefits and other social goods and the impact on those targeted who might never have developed into criminality. This begs the question, where does social policy end and criminal policy begin? Targeting those 'at risk' for special services may be more politically acceptable than providing these services to people who have offended, which raises objections—of 'less eligibility—that those who do wrong should not benefit from their misdeeds. Nevertheless, a weaker version of this objection may come into play. Why should those who may be teetering on the edge of criminality, whose behaviour may be problematic but not yet criminal, be given resources unavailable to their well-behaved peers?

More generally, developmental prevention is an example of 'risk-thinking' that has become more pervasive and is associated with the rise of 'actuarial justice' with an emphasis upon risk assessment techniques and the elaboration of insurance-based technologies (Feeley and Simon 1994). However, the distinction between 'old' needs-based interventions and the 'new' language of risk-based programmes is not as marked as some critics suggest (Hannah-Moffat 2005). O'Malley notes that 'much developmental crime prevention of late has begun explicitly to identify as risk factors the kinds of "social conditions" previously identified under welfare programmes' (2001: 97–8).

Nevertheless, risk assessment, risk classification, and actuarial profiling have undoubtedly become increasingly influential aspects of contemporary criminal (notably youth) justice systems (see Morgan and Newburn, this volume). Despite the possible preventive benefits and cost savings of targeting resources at 'high-risk' groups, such early intervention schemes raise crucial normative and ethical concerns. Gatti notes the right of children and young people not to be classified as future delinquents, whether they go on to become delinquents or not, as representing 'one of the greatest ethical problems raised by early prevention programmes' (1998. 120). Furthermore, the inaccuracy of predictive knowledge prompts caution. In the conclusion to a major report for the British Government on working with young people and their families to reduce risks of crime, Utting sagely warned:

> [A]ny notion that better screening can enable policy makers to identify young children destined to join the 5 per cent of offenders responsible for 50–60 per cent of crime is fanciful. Even if there were no ethical objections to putting 'potential delinquent' labels round the necks of young children, there would continue to be statistical barriers... [Research] shows substantial flows *out of* as well as *in to* the pool of children who develop chronic conduct problems. As such [there are] dangers of assuming that anti-social five-year olds are the criminals or drug abusers of tomorrow, as well as the undoubted opportunities that exist for prevention. Since the experience of service providers suggests that labelling children would also [be] counter-productive to gaining the trust and participation of parents, there must be a strong presumption in favour of preventive services presenting and justifying themselves in terms of children's existing needs and problems, rather than future risks of criminality. (Utting 2004: 99, emphasis in original)

Consequently, many practitioners prefer universal (i.e. primary prevention) programmes over targeted (i.e. secondary prevention) ones, despite their obvious resource implications.

## COMMUNITY CRIME PREVENTION

Community crime prevention, by contrast, refers to interventions designed to change or alter the social conditions, institutions, and relations that influence offending among social groups and residential communities. In so doing, it seeks to increase the crime preventive capacity and often the informal social control of communities and social groupings; it concerns communal interpersonal relations, values, and norms rather than questions of individual propensities and motivations. Nevertheless, the conceptual boundaries between developmental and community crime prevention are porous. Whilst developmental approaches have largely focused on individual level risk factors, including those expressed in the interactions that individuals have with others—be they in families, kinship relations, peer groups, or school settings—community level factors have also been drawn into these analyses. One example of this, first implemented in the mid-1990s, is the *Communities That Care* (CTC) programme which aimed at working with all young people in targeted areas. The theoretical basis for CTC was what Catalano and Hawkins (1996) named a 'social development model', which purports that child development is influenced by the quality of the interaction between children and adults. Echoing Hirschi's (1969) ideas about the role of social bonds in encouraging individuals to forego their selfish motivations and conform to rules, the project based its intervention on the belief that children who are given clear standards of behaviour and positive social bonding with adults are less likely to get involved in crime. The development of pro-social factors is seen as a means of protecting children from the consequences of risk factors. Importantly, these protective factors do not merely rest in individuals but in social interactions.

Other community-based strategies also assume a developmental logic that underpins both the factors that render certain communities high crime places and those that foster the crime preventive capacities of certain communities. Such approaches are influenced heavily by Wilson and Kelling's (1982) 'broken windows' thesis, which posits a causal (developmental) connection between, on the one hand, incivilities, disorder, and anti-social behaviour, given the fears, anxieties, and perceptions of insecurity that these promote and, on the other hand, subsequent crime. Hence, interventions to halt communities from 'spiralling into crime' necessitate a focus on low-level disorderly 'pre-crimes' (Zedner 2007). In Britain developmental and community-based approaches have increasingly merged around a political agenda focused on 'anti-social behaviour', which has prioritized forms of 'secondary' prevention targeted at individuals, families, and neighbourhoods.

Targeting a community or neighbourhood with high aggregate risk factors avoids the aforementioned objections concerning special resources being given to those perceived to be undeserving because of their association with criminality. Because high levels of criminality often co-exist alongside high levels of victimization, such programmes can be justified as targeting the most vulnerable social groups, rather like crime prevention focused on 'repeat victimization'. This may deflect charges of favouritism, but does not necessarily eliminate the stigmatizing potential of such programmes. Communities may develop reputations which can be hard to shed, with consequent implications for their attractiveness as a place to live. However, much that passes as community crime prevention has little to do with communities as collective entities, but rather deploys a community focus in order to reach individuals or households. Community-based interventions frequently lack a clear sense of purpose or a theory of how change is achieved beyond improving the locality and the well-being of residents. Various forms of community crime prevention might better be interpreted 'not only as applications of criminological theory, but also as complex pieces of socio-political action that also have a defining ideological and ethical character' (Hope 1995: 22). Implicitly, community crime prevention seeks to strengthen latent social control mechanisms and/or provide people with a stake in their own conformity through a diverse array of interventions (Crawford 1998: 124).

One factor that informs much of the community-based prevention is the assumption that the rise in crime since the 1960s is attributable, in part, to the breakdown in traditional social ties and the obligations that derive from them. From an American context, Putnam (2000) has sought to demonstrate declining 'civic engagement' and social capital as symptoms and causes of impoverished democracy and social breakdown. He defines social capital as the 'connections among individuals—social networks and the norms of reciprocity and trustworthiness that arise from them' (2000: 19). This definition emphasizes the norms and networks that enable people to act collectively. Unlike some other forms of economic or human capital, social capital lies between individuals and organizations in relationships. It is not reducible to individual possession. This relational quality means that social capital is believed to operate as a form of social glue that fosters integration, cohesion, and order. It provides a conceptual tool that policy-makers can deploy in promoting strong communities.[3]

However, in much of the policy debate, the linkages between social capital and economic and human capital are often left under developed. Extra-community (top-down) resources and bottom-up capacity building are often entwined. The sources of social capital are frequently confused with the benefits or assets that are believed to derive from them. Some disadvantaged neighbourhoods have high levels of sociability but are unable to utilize or exploit this in ways that produce tangible benefits that address their deprivation. As Sampson and colleagues (1999) suggest, the concentration of multiple forms of disadvantage tend to depress shared expectations for collective action, particularly regarding children. Furthermore, by creating strong in-group loyalty and affective relations, strong bonds of social capital may also foster out-group antagonism between local communities.

## BROKEN WINDOWS, FEAR, AND DISORDER

Possibly the most influential contribution to debates about communities, informal social control and crime prevention is Wilson and Kelling's (1982) 'broken windows' thesis. They argue that minor incivilities—such as vandalism, graffiti, rowdy behaviour, drunkenness, begging—if unchecked and uncontrolled will set in train a series

---

[3] Understandings of social capital have significantly influenced New Labour thinking and policy initiatives, especially within the Civil Renewal Unit in the Home Office and the Neighbourhood Renewal Unit in the Office of the Deputy Prime Minister.

of linked social responses, as a result of which 'decent' neighbourhoods can tip into fearful ghettos of crime. Untended property and unchecked behaviour, they argue, produce a breakdown of community controls, through a spiralling process, whereby: incivilities lead to fear which promotes avoidance, withdrawal, and flight by local residents which, in turn, leads to reduced informal social control which results in more serious crime, which leads to increased fear and so on. As the neighbourhood declines, so disorder, fear, and crime spiral upwards. The 'broken window' is a powerful metaphor for the absence of order and control.

The proposed solution is to stop and reverse the 'cycle of decline' in its earliest stages by focusing upon 'order maintenance' through the policing of incivilities and other 'signs of crime' (Kelling and Coles 1996). What is deemed necessary is for the community to reassert its 'natural forces' of moral authority and control through early intervention in disorderly conduct. The logic is that if one tackles low-level disorders, it is possible to impact upon more serious types of crime. Implicit is the belief that the police have neglected their order maintenance functions in preference for their crime fighting tasks. These ideas have found particular favour with communitarians, such as Etzioni (1993), who articulate a need to revive the moral authority of communities and call for a greater emphasis on social responsibilities rather than individual rights. Strong communities, it is argued, can speak to us in moral voices. They allow the policing *by* communities rather than the policing *of* communities.

However, Wilson and Kelling offer little empirical support for their claims regarding a causal relationship between disorder, fear, and increased crime (Harcourt and Ludwig 2006). Taylor's (2001) findings challenge the assumption that signs of incivility (particularly physical signs) influence crime and fear of crime in any simplistic manner. What is more, 'broken windows' and disorder do not necessarily have the same effects or meanings in different neighbourhoods. They may be interpreted in different ways. Taylor shows how 'fear of crime' differences are greater between individuals than between neighbourhoods. In most cases, fear arises because of differences between residents responding to roughly comparable ecological conditions. Levels of disorder tend to be highest in areas with high poverty, as well as heterogeneous and transient populations (Skogan 1990). Sampson and Raudenbusch (1999) argue that disorder and crime both stem from certain neighbourhood structural qualities, notably concentrated poverty. Disorder does not directly promote crime. Rather, they both stem from a lack of 'collective efficacy', defined as the presence or absence of social cohesion, mutual trust, and a willingness to intervene in support of informal social control, which is itself conditioned by the structural characteristics of neighbourhoods. Interestingly, in 2004, James Q. Wilson, himself, observed that: 'I still to this day do not know if improving order will or will not reduce crime... People have not understood that this was a speculation' (cited in Hurley 2004: 3). Nevertheless, the 'broken windows' thesis has become unchallenged 'orthodoxy' within British government policy, regularly cited in documentation in support of new initiatives (Innes and Jones 2006).[4]

---

[4] This includes the most recent consultation paper produced by the Coalition Government in February 2011 (Home Office 2011) which asserts that: 'Unchecked, anti-social behaviour can be linked to increased disorder, low-level crime and fear of crime in a neighbourhood—the so-called "broken windows" effect' (ibid.: 5).

## LIMITATIONS OF COMMUNITY

In essence, 'broken windows' thesis and 'defensible space' theory, as well as the policies to which they give rise, are premised on a notion of 'community defence' in that they envisage the community to be under attack, notably from 'outsiders'. There is little sense in which offenders are understood as members of, and belonging to, communities—as neighbours, husbands, or sons (Currie 1988). Hence, they have little to say about crimes involving intimate insiders, such as domestic violence and corporate crime. There is an assumption that community members share moral values and conceptions of order, thus marginalizing intra-communal differences. The reality, in many urban areas, is not the homogenous communities of nostalgia but a cosmopolitan mix of age groups, ethnicities, cultures, and social identities. Here, (dis)orderly behaviour itself may be differently interpreted and experienced.

Contrary to communitarian assumptions, 'more community' does not equate in any simple way with 'less crime' (Walklate and Evans 1999). Community and its shared normative values may well be criminogenic. Strong social ties, networks, and mutual trust all sustain organized crime, gang cultures, and hate crime. Deviant social networks can foster anti-social behaviour, transmitting values, skills, and knowledge that constitute 'criminal capital'. Inversely, a lack of strong social ties and bonds of community does not inevitably promote disorder. Affluent, low-crime areas that may display an appearance of civility do not always exhibit characteristics of intimacy, connectedness, and mutual support, as Baumgartner's (1988) research on the moral order of American suburbs testifies. Rather than rely on informal control, suburbanites are likely to call rapidly upon the intervention of formal mechanisms to which they have greater access and which respond to them more readily than more deprived areas. Middle-class suburbs may be lacking in community ties and yet orderly. By contrast, informal control mechanisms are not necessarily absent in all high crime areas (Hope and Foster 1992). The structural attributes of communities—the manner in which they connect with, and are situated within, sources of power and resources in the wider environment—may be more important than community as a sense of belonging.

Assumptions about the nature of community and the relations between communities and offenders produce dilemmas for implementation. Strategies are more likely to be successful in low crime, organized, and homogenous communities that perceive themselves under threat from 'outsiders'. Research confirms, for example, that it is easiest to establish Neighbourhood Watch in affluent, suburban areas with low crime rates involving people who hold favourable attitudes towards the police rather than in inner city, crime-prone public sector housing estates with heterogeneous populations (Hope 2000). This reflects a more general observation that there is generally an inverse relationship between prevention activity and need (Rosenbaum 1988). Many community-based schemes rather than simply relieving the police of burdens can generate new demands. Hence, community-based prevention can have the perverse effect of skewing public resources towards those places which may least need them and those people most capable of protecting themselves.

Paradoxically, the contemporary focus on communities has emerged at an historic time at which empirically communities may be declining in relevance as a source of strong bonds. In much of the policy rhetoric around community crime prevention there is often a slippage between community as a sense of something lost and community as a focus for building modern democratic institutions. The ideals of community—reciprocity, intimacy, and trustworthiness—sit awkwardly with contemporary concerns for individuality, freedom, and mobility. Accordingly, community-based initiatives tend to hold unrealistic expectations of what communities can do to reduce crime. There is a danger that communities have become a site around which individuals and groups can be mobilized to take on board greater responsibility for their own well-being and security. This shedding of responsibility from the state has implications for where the cost for providing security should lie as well as the blame for failure. With a burgeoning security market and the growing purchase by communities of additional security patrols (Crawford *et al.* 2005), the worry is that some communities are better able to carry this burden, whilst others might become blamed for their incapacity to prevent crime.

The focus on community-level governance begs a more fundamental question: to what extent are the 'community' and the 'social' complementary aspects of the same broad rationality of government or different and potentially competing levels of government? Community justice, after all, is not the same as social justice. Community-based solutions tend to be particularistic and parochial, with little concern for externalities and wider social ramifications. Well-defended communities may serve to displace crime onto less well-defended residential areas. Hence, one community's safety may come at the expense of others'. Is it desirable that safety as a public good is transformed into a parochial or quasi-exclusive good?

## THE RISE OF PREVENTIVE GOVERNANCE IN THE UK

As an adaptation to the crisis within criminal justice, crime prevention thinking heralded a fundamental shift in the object of enquiry, ways of conceiving, and methods of responding to the threat of crime. A major declaration of the shift to a preventive mentality within government came with the publication of interdepartmental circular 8/1984. It constituted a decisive statement of the new philosophy, declaring that 'preventing crime is a task for the whole community'. The vehicle to deliver this new message was the Safer Cities Programme and its predecessor the Five Towns Initiative which together ran from the mid-1980s to the mid-1990s. By providing limited short-term funding and a coordinator these local projects sought to draw together emergent partnerships and ignite crime prevention activities across the private and public sectors. The intention was to incorporate a wide range of organizations and interests including representatives of businesses, the voluntary sector, and public sector to consider local crime problems and preventive measures. The symbolic ownership of, and dominant voice within, these partnerships lay with the police and the types of crime prevention promoted tended to be of a police-led situational kind.

The Morgan Committee, established in 1990 to review developments since circular 8/84, fostered a significant shift in the emerging discourse. It advanced a series of key recommendations (Morgan 1991). The two most important were conceptual and institutional. Conceptually, it suggested that the term 'community safety' be preferred to 'crime prevention'. The latter was seen to be too narrow and too closely associated with police-related responsibilities. Community safety, by contrast, was perceived to be open to wider interpretation which could encourage 'greater participation from all sections of the community in the fight against crime' (ibid.: 13). Community safety was also seen as an umbrella term under which situational and social approaches could be combined rather than juxtaposed. Institutionally, the Morgan Report recommended that local authorities should be given 'statutory responsibility' for the prevention of crime, working *with* the police, for the development and promotion of community safety. The Morgan Report also highlighted the lack of central government coordination around crime prevention.

As the Morgan Report noted, crime prevention and community safety were peripheral concerns of diverse agencies but 'a truly core activity of none of them' (ibid.: 15). In response, it articulated and advanced a partnership approach that advocated the co-production of community safety. Prevention demanded a novel holistic approach transcending the competencies of specific professional groups and associations and cutting across disciplinary boundaries. In theory, if not in practice, this new politics:

- recognized that the levels and causes of crime lie far from the traditional reach of the criminal justice system;
- acknowledged that there is no single agency solution to crime and disorder—it is multifaceted in both its causes and effects;
- recognized the need for social responses to crime which reflect the nature of the phenomenon itself and its multiple aetiology;
- allowed for an holistic approach to crime, community safety, and associated issues which is 'problem-focused' rather than 'bureaucracy-premised'; and
- afforded the potential coordination and pooling of knowledge, capacity, and resources.

Pease has argued that community safety is something of a misnomer (2002: 948). Safety, he notes, incorporates harms that extend far beyond crime; including traffic, health, food, pollution, product-design, planning, and so on. A pan-hazard approach would see crime as only a small element of harm-reduction. From this perspective, placing community safety in the context of crime and disorder legislation is rather like the tail wagging the dog. Seeing harm through a crime lens undoubtedly skews the notion of safety by its implications with crime. It fuels an unhelpful focus upon crime-related risks—such as those presented by predatory strangers—at the expense of more immanent yet mundane risks such as those presented by traffic and pollution. Regardless, community safety came to be the defining discourse within which much of contemporary policy in the UK was couched.

The move to 'community safety' was always double-edged. On the one hand, it took the consideration of crime prevention away from being the sole reserve of the police and thereby afforded it the chance to become something more progressive and socially-oriented than it had previously been. On the other hand, it was used as part of the Conservative Government's move to 'responsibilize' (Garland 2001) individuals and their families and to take crime prevention out of the remit of the central state and local government. After all, this was a government committed to rolling back state and welfare provision and to cutting back on public services wherever possible. Nevertheless, the Conservative Government refused to implement many of the Report's recommendations, especially any which would strengthen local authorities. Instead it concentrated on promoting active citizenship through the special constabulary, Neighbourhood Watch, and sponsoring the expansion of CCTV across the country.[5]

The dramatic expansion of CCTV was initially rooted in a political ideology that favoured a situational approach and technological solutions whilst visibly demonstrating that (local and national) government was 'doing something' about crime. However, it also reflected a deeper cultural attraction in that CCTV cameras not only evoke symbols of security by appearing to perform preventive tasks, but also facilitate the acting out of more traditional expressive and punitive sentiments provoked by the footage derived from CCTV cameras where criminal acts and disorder are captured on film. In this manner, CCTV straddles both a preventive logic and a punitive one (Norris and McCahill 2006). It enables both a governance of the present and future through surveillance and deterrence and a reordering of the past by witnessing and recording events. CCTV cameras are tangible reminders that someone is trying to secure personal safety *and* serve to prompt moral indignation at the acts they portray. As town centres, shopping malls, and other locations have increasingly vied to present themselves as safe havens to attract mobile populations to visit, use, or shop, CCTV now constitutes an indispensable symbol of security. Furthermore, it is a field in which the UK is a global leader, with an estimated 20 per cent of the world's CCTVs (but only less than 1 per cent of the world's population).

## COMMUNITY SAFETY PARTNERSHIPS—THE INFRASTRUCTURE

The election of a Labour Government in 1997 provided an eagerly awaited hiatus in crime prevention policy. The 1998 Crime and Disorder Act put in place a new institutional framework for implementing a partnership approach to the prevention of crime and disorder and for working with young offenders. Less focused on individual action, the Act placed a joint duty on local councils and the police to work together with a wide range of other agencies from the public, private, voluntary, and community sectors to develop and implement strategies to reduce crime and disorder. A network of Crime and Disorder Reduction Partnerships (CDRPs)—renamed 'community safety partnerships' in 2010—based in local authority areas across England and Wales were set up to deliver the strategy.[6] Each CDRP was required to conduct a triennial audit

[5] In 1994, the first of four CCTV Challenge Competitions was launched to support the expansion of city-centre CCTV. It is estimated that in the mid-1990s in England some 78% of the Home Office's crime prevention budget was being spent on CCTV systems alone (Koch 1998). This growth has continued with Britain leading the world in the installation of CCTV. According to the British Security Industry Association (BSIA), by 2004 there were over 4.25 million CCTV cameras installed in the UK.

[6] The discussion that follows applies primarily to England and Wales. Obligations set out in the Crime and Disorder Act 1998 do not apply to Scotland, where a voluntaristic approach to partnerships has

of crime and disorder within its area, to consult the local community on the findings, and to deliver a strategic response (Home Office 1998). The Act also provided a power to partners to disclose information for the purposes of preventing crime and disorder (section 15). While stepping back from Morgan's proposal to give local authorities the main responsibility for ensuring the safety of citizens it nonetheless removed the idea that the police were solely responsible and allowed a fundamental realignment of professional expertise in the area of crime prevention paving the way for much greater involvement of the private sector, individuals, and voluntary organizations in crime prevention work.

Section 17 of the 1998 Act also imposed a duty on local authorities, in exercising their various functions, to consider the crime and disorder implications of any new policies and the need to do all that they reasonably could to prevent crime and disorder in their area. The purpose of the duty was to 'give the vital work of preventing crime a new focus across a very wide range of local services... putting crime and disorder considerations at the very heart of decision making, where they have always belonged' (Home Office 1997: para. 33). It was intended as an 'enabling device' to promote the embedding of a crime prevention mentality in the everyday activities of the police and local authorities. Some commentators saw this as the most radical element of the 1998 Act, as anticipating crime could pervade 'every aspect of local authority responsibility, it is difficult to conceive of any decision which will remain untouched by s.17 considerations' (Moss and Pease 1999: 16),

The 1998 Act added 'disorder' to the 'problem' of crime thus casting wider the crime prevention net. It was now not only the breaking of criminal laws to which the Government was addressing its attention but also the wider problem of disruptive and troublesome behaviour. Just what was meant by 'disorder' and by whom it might be considered a nuisance was not addressed. Nevertheless it is not surprising that the problem of 'youth disorder' was incorporated into the legislation. As McLaughlin (2002: 85–8) has outlined it was widely considered that in previous decades there had been a breakdown of community and a 'crisis of the social' across Britain through which lawlessness, criminality, and anti-social behaviour had become normalized within many communities peopled by 'the underclass'. This belief in the need to curb behaviour seen as troublesome (influenced by 'broken windows') had become so ingrained in popular thinking and in political rhetoric (by both Conservative and Labour politicians) that this had become 'the dominant discourse' (Hughes 2007: 112) and would have to be seen to be dealt with. A new infrastructure of local multidisciplinary Youth Offending Teams (YOTS) was established throughout England and Wales with a new principal aim to prevent youthful offending and disorderly behaviour, although the latter remained loosely defined. The 1998 Act introduced a whole raft of new 'orders' (such as ASBOs and curfews) by which young people seen as problematic, and their parents, could be managed, adding significantly to the powers of police and local authorities to restrict the movement and behaviour of individuals

prevailed (see Henry 2009). Whilst the 1998 Act applies to Wales (where CDRPs have always been referred to as 'community safety partnerships'), a slightly different path of development has unfolded in the light of devolved government, given the Welsh Assembly's limited community safety powers (see Edwards and Hughes 2009).

and groups of young people. The then Home Secretary, Jack Straw's, insistence there should be 'no more excuses' given for youth crime betrayed the Government's tough approach to dealing with offenders (see Morgan and Newburn, this volume).

Accompanying this more punitive and controlling agenda, however, was the work of the Government's Social Exclusion Unit (SEU). Set up less than four months into the new Labour administration this innovative government body was seen as defining the difference between Conservative and Labour. 18 Policy Action Teams were formed (including a variety of voices from academics to experts from the voluntary sector) to find solutions to diverse social problems of social polarization which had built up over 17 years of Conservative government. One of the Policy Action Teams was explicitly dedicated to address concerns about 'anti-social behaviour', which in its inception was linked closely to the concentration of social problems within social housing that had occurred during this period. The eventual report specifically argued that anti-social behaviour matters because 'if left unchecked, can lead to neighbourhood decline, with people moving away and tenants abandoning housing' (Home Office, 2000: 7). This overtly interventionist approach seemed to promise a return to a more welfare-oriented stance. As Jack Straw outlined to the New Statesman magazine:

> I think there's a good chance that there will emerge from all this in 10 years' time a society in which class divisions are much less marked. We will hopefully have a combination of the best of the States and the Netherlands, where the searing class divisions in our society are no longer noticeable. You won't have these estates where the casualties of the past 18 years have been dumped... (New Statesman 1998).

However, New Labour's approach to crime prevention and community safety became entangled with stronger influences on public policy promoted in the name of a 'modernization agenda':

- A managerialist impulse to measure performance by results set against clear objectives.
- A rhetorical emphasis on 'evidence-based policy' and the promotion of 'what works' in the rational and cost-effective use of resources.
- Neo-liberal inspired reforms to the public sector through the contracting out of service delivery to the private sector, the separation of purchaser/provider roles, the introduction of internal markets and competition, and the incorporation of private sector management methods into the public sector.

The work of the SEU was wound down from 2002 and the wide-ranging and progressive perspective initially adopted which expressly acknowledged the deep-seated and damaging effects of poverty on a generation of UK citizens, was replaced by a narrower focus on particular 'problem groups', demonstrating a shift away from the collective and social and towards an individualized and privatized route out of exclusion.

## ASSESSING COMMUNITY SAFETY PARTNERSHIPS

Despite their initial promise, the 'honeymoon' period of CDRPs was also short-lived (Phillips 2002) and they did not live up to early expectations. The main barriers to successful partnership included a reluctance of some agencies to participate (especially health, education, and social services); the dominance of a policing agenda; unwillingness to share information; conflicting interests, priorities and cultural assumptions on the part of different agencies; local political differences; lack of inter-organizational trust; desire to protect budgets; lack of capacity and expertise; and over-reliance on informal contacts and networks which lapsed if key individuals moved on (Hughes 2007). The involvement of the private sector has often been patchy and the role of the voluntary sector frequently marginalized. In practice, partnerships experienced considerable problems in reaching agreements or protocols about what data they could legitimately share and on what basis. As a result, concerns over confidentiality often stymied partnership working and problematized inter-organizational trust relations.

Central government responded to the perceived unwillingness of some key agencies to participate actively in CDRPs by expanding the list of organizations under a legal duty to participate. A similar statutory responsibility was extended to police authorities and fire authorities as of April 2003 and Primary Care Trusts (representing the health service) a year later.[7] Demands for such legislative obligations emerged largely because these partners were not deemed to be contributing to partnerships around the country.

In practice, the focus of many partnerships has been compliance with national performance indicators, notwithstanding the requirement upon them to identify and pursue local priorities (Audit Commission 2002). Despite the rhetoric of localism, central government appears to have been unable and unwilling to adopt a more 'hands off' approach to local partnerships. In the politically sensitive arena of crime and disorder, government desires to be seen to be responding to immediate problems encouraged organizational micro-management. A notable example was the Street Crime Initiative. In response to a rise in street robbery, a centrally directed initiative was set up, challenging 10 police forces with short-term reduction targets. This ambiguous stance of central government reflected the dilemma of government pertaining to govern at 'arm's length' but ending up 'hands on' (Crawford 2001).

Such has been the political disappointment with community safety partnerships—despite the steady decline of aggregate crime rates since the mid-1990s—that in late 2004, the Government announced a major review of their activities, governance, and accountability, acknowledging that: 'a significant number of partnerships struggle to maintain a full contribution from key agencies and even successful ones are not sufficiently visible, nor we think accountable, to the public as they should be' (Home Office 2004: 123). The review prompted two developments focused respectively around the role of central government and of local partnerships in delivering community safety. First, the Government published a National Community Safety Plan (Home Office 2005), which incorporated the National Policing Plan within a wider community safety agenda. In the plan, the Government committed itself to deliver a more coordinated national approach by requiring ministers to prioritize community safety policies and consider community safety dimensions of new and existing policies (ibid.: 15). However, the plan created no new obligations and fell considerably short of the

---

[7] Under the Police Reform Act 2002.

proposals put forward in the Morgan Report for government to provide 'a community safety impact statement' for all new legislation and major policy initiatives. Secondly, in 2006, the Government made a number of proposals for the future development of CDRPs (Home Office 2006b) designed to strengthen and streamline their work and require the sharing of data between partners but only appeared to offer 'more of the same' with regard to central steering of local partnerships, propped up by statutory duties.

Similarly, the implementation of section 17 has fallen considerably below expectations. One area where it might have had direct and immediate implications was in the realm of planning applications, where police and councils might have been able to use it as a lever into planning decisions, notably those associated with the expansion of the night-time economy. Despite the well-documented attendant crime and disorder implications of large numbers of alcohol outlets in city centres, the Planning Inspectorate has been largely unwilling to uphold decisions to reject applications on the grounds of section 17 where these had been made by local authorities (Moss 2006). As a branch of central government rather than the local council, the Planning Inspectorate has not felt itself bound by the legislation which applies to local authorities alone; thus reflecting more general tensions between responsibilities of central and local government.

## CONTROLLING DISORDER AND ANTI-SOCIAL BEHAVIOUR

As New Labour's approach to the prevention of crime rolled out it became increasingly top-down and managerial in its emphasis. The early promises to combat the effects of social exclusion using community expertise and commitment co-existed with a clear agenda to enforce a particular way of reading and dealing with the problem of crime. As their second term of office from June 2001 began to unfold, the Government's fervour in this area only increased. New Labour appeared to be less concerned with exclusion and to become more fixated on problems of the 'anti-social' individual and neighbourhood.

By introducing the term 'anti-social behaviour', the 1998 Act and the work of the SEU laid the terrain for the subsequent anti-social behaviour agenda. The legislation defined 'anti-social behaviour' as 'behaviour which causes or is likely to cause harassment, alarm or distress to one or more people who are not in the same household as the perpetrator' (section 1). Its meaning derives less from what it is than from what its consequences are or might be. Distinctive to this definition are: first, that it focuses on the importance of public space and sensibilities about local social order; secondly, it highlights the cumulative effects of persistent behaviour; and thirdly, it accentuates the differential interpretation and meaning of certain local social problems—such as groups of loitering youths, graffiti, and vandalism—and offers an explanation for why perceptions of such problems have a disproportionate impact on people's sense of (in)security (Innes 2004). As such, it foregrounds the dimension of 'public perceptions' into issues of wrongdoing and the governance of local safety. In part, the anti-social behaviour agenda was an attempt to respond to the fact that while rates of recorded crime were falling and police officer numbers were at an all-time high with more civilian staff than ever, public insecurity and fear of crime remained stubbornly unaffected—the so-called 'reassurance paradox'. In talking up law and order concerns, the Government's successive campaigns against anti-social behaviour appeared to have fanned public fears rather than reduced them. With the launch of the 'reassurance policing' programme and the commitment to deliver dedicated 'neighbourhood policing teams' (Home Office 2004), fear reduction moved centre stage, not only within policing but community safety more generally. Consequently public anxieties and community well-being became prominent policy concerns in their own right (Innes 2007).

Labour built further on its anti-social behaviour edifice with the Anti-Social Behaviour Act 2003, which strengthened existing powers and conferred even more powers on police and local authorities and social landlords. The anti-social behaviour agenda was made central to the work of CDRPs and rolled out to further key agencies with initiatives such as the *Together Action Plan* and Nuisance Neighbour Panels. The agenda was enforced through the establishment of the Anti-Social Behaviour Unit, which audited and monitored action in this area and rewarded 'good performance' with additional resource allocation and shamed those partnerships which were seen not to come up to scratch. In early 2006, with much fanfare, Blair launched his *Respect Action Plan* (Home Office 2006a)—its language was particularly condemnatory of anti-social behaviour and petty offending and drove a clear line between the law-abiding and the troublesome. Blair promised: 'tough action so that the majority of law-abiding, decent people no longer have to tolerate the behaviour of the few individuals and families that think they do not have to show respect to others' (2006: 3).

The Plan's 'new approach' to 'problem families' was described as '...challenging them to accept support to change their behaviour, backed up by enforcement measures' (Blair 2006: 3). In its zeal to take action to protect the 'law-abiding' and the vulnerable majority from a troublesome minority, the Respect Action Plan proclaimed the Government's intention to move away from existing judicial measures and a centuries' old rule of law. These were to be replaced by a much greater reliance on the use of out-of-court, summary powers to manage and to punish offending behaviour (see Padmore, Morgan, and Maguire, this volume). Rather than relying on the court process to test an individual's innocence or guilt and allowing a right to defend one's actions before magistrates, more out-of-court measures such as Fixed Penalty Notices for offences such as graffiti and fly-posting and Penalty Notices for Disorder were to be administered. The use of civil orders and injunctions to close premises or curtail the activities of those seen to be causing a nuisance were also extended. While these measures were lauded as cheaper, speedier, and less bureaucratic methods of justice, they also require lower levels of proof, can be more easily misused, and rest on subjective judgement. The Respect Action Plan by-passes the professionals involved in the court process, the magistrates and judges trained in the complexities of the legal code, and hands discretion to a police service which has been heavily criticized in the past for holding prejudicial positions against particular social groups. The Respect Agenda has been criticized for its 'penal populism' (Jamieson 2005: 189); its punitive emphasis which may be satisfying in the short-term but offers little, if any, solution to the social and economic problems which underlie the behaviour of troubled young people and adults (Burney 2009); its promotion, not of tolerance and understanding but of vilification and negative portrayals of many social groups (Squires and Stephen 2005); and its emphasis upon and enforcement of individual responsibility which obscures the Government's role in perpetuating the conditions in which 'anti-social' and 'criminal' behaviour can take hold (Hudson 2003).

As a capacious umbrella term, the anti-social behaviour agenda has come to demarcate a distinct policy field that blurs traditional distinctions between crime and disorder, whilst refiguring the use of civil and criminal, as well as formal and informal, regulatory responses. As such, it represents a major challenge to, and assault upon, traditional conceptions of criminal justice, circumventing established principles of due process, proportionality, and special protections traditionally afforded to young people (Ashworth 2005; Ashworth and Zedner 2008; Crawford 2009b). Perversely, however, the new hybrid tools of regulation that have been spawned over the past decade, in a period of regulatory hyperactivity, have extended rather than undermined the place of criminalization and punishment at the heart of behavioural regulation.

In the Labour administration's later years, notably under Gordon Brown's leadership, there was a softening in the enforcement approach and the use of ASBOs declined. However, a 'new orthodoxy' (Farrington and Welsh 2007) had emerged in which individuals (mainly young people) are risk assessed, profiled, and classified and those deemed at highest risk of offending are brought to the attention of the authorities and subject to early interventions. Youth Inclusion Programmes and Junior Youth Inclusion Programmes, established in 2000 and 2003 respectively, targeted the most marginalized young people with the aim of identifying the 50 most at risk in any given area (see also Morgan and Newburn, this volume). Family Intervention Projects rolled out nationally from 2006 offered intensive support on a wide range of issues to the most vulnerable families. While such interventions *may* prove positive to many of those targeted they symbolize a shift away from improving conditions for the many and towards the identification of the problem as situated within a few, dysfunctional individuals and family groups. There is evidence to suggest that the Conservative-Liberal Democrat Coalition which replaced Labour in government in 2010 will continue along this particular policy trajectory.

## NEW LABOUR AND COMMUNITARIANISM

Labour brought a particular commitment to community involvement in crime prevention, drawing inspiration from the communitarian philosophy espoused by Amitai Etzioni (1993). Again on initial glance, it appeared as though the communitarian perspective might offer more of a progressive than punitive approach when applied to local crime control, however this too took on a 'moralistic and rightist' tone (Hughes 2007: 15). A series of initiatives was designed to re-embed community values and organization at neighbourhood level envisioning neighbourhoods which were largely self-regulating, held in check through informal social controls, and to some degree independent of the state, requiring minimal intervention from above (Evans 2011). It was hoped that building up strong civic institutions, from the more personally oriented such as the family and neighbourhood associations, through to functioning and effective local governance at the micro-level linked to local state providers in education, housing, and health among others, would lead to a resurgence of civic feeling and belonging, a new-found confidence in community and a re-connection to lost moral values flowing from a more collective consciousness, shared understandings, and future goals.

As Hughes has outlined, however, communitarianism places '[a] strong and recurrent emphasis... on duties and responsibilities to the wider society rather than freedoms and rights for the individual' (2007: 20). So, while distinguishing Labour from the hyper-individualism of neo-liberalism, and appealing to social and collaborative measures, it was clearly intended that rights were to be conditional on the exercise of responsibility—in what New Labour defined as the 'something for something society' (Home Office 2003: 3)—a better life was to be achieved through participation not through expectation. This 'moral authoritarian communitarianist' stance (Hughes 1996) set certain approved expectations, standards, and moral values for individuals to follow. Government documents driving and guiding work with local communities were riven with contradictions, on the one hand celebrating the expertise and abilities of those outside government and pushing for the building of ever stronger community organizations with the powers to govern locally, whilst at the same time they allowed only the narrowest of spaces within which these communities could operate. The *Guidance for Crime and Disorder Reduction Partnerships and Community Safety Partnerships* published in 2007 stands as an example of this approach which was replicated across so many documents produced by government departments. In the interests of improving performance and increasing effectiveness of CDRPs the guidance required a whole host of structures to be set up, conditions to be met, and objectives to be aimed for. Then, somewhat naively or disingenuously it suggests that 'Beyond the statutory requirements, partnerships have the flexibility to deliver in their own way' (Home Office 2007: 4).

The police, the other 'responsible authority' within the partnership, were equally subject to the increasing managerialization of public services (McLaughlin 2007: 182–7). They too were now subject to performance targets and were more closely managed from the Home Office. After 1997, McLaughlin argues:

> The first new Labour administration (1997 to 2001) refined the centralizing logics of the existing legislative framework to ensure that police force and police authority efforts were directed to realizing both Whitehall defined 'best value' and crime reduction targets (2007: 184).

Hughes has noted a tendency for communities to be framed in both negative and positive terms—as he puts it as both the breeders of and the prophylactic against crime and disorder (Hughes 2007. 110). Civil and community renewal under New Labour was directly linked to law and order issues. Blunkett, when Home Secretary, suggested that the active citizen would be involved in their local Neighbourhood Watch scheme, a Special Constable, and/or engaged with systems of community-based criminal justice. In the end, the Government's view of communities as fragmented, mistrusting, and crime-ridden severely impinged on their promise to deliver on a vision of positive, community-centred, and local, governance.

## NEW GOVERNMENT, NEW DIRECTION?

There is little evidence that the Coalition Government elected in May 2010 is likely to depart dramatically from the general direction of developments set out by the previous governments. The focus on young people and families is set to continue as is the preoccupation with anti-social behaviour. Whilst the Coalition Government has proposed abolishing the ASBO, it intends to replace this with two new powers—the Criminal Behaviour Order and the Crime Prevention Injunction (the former is a criminal and the latter a civil power)—both of which share many similarities with variants of the ASBO.[8] Interestingly, the proposed new Crime Prevention Injunction, according to the Government, is intended to 'bring together restrictions on future behaviour and support to address underlying problems...that can quickly stop anti-social behaviour before it escalates' (Home Office 2011: 5). In many senses, the new orders represent a 'rebranding' of past tools rather than a change in trajectory or of substance. Early intervention with young people and families at risk has secured a prominent place in the new Government's strategies (Allen 2011). Yet, there remains something of an ideological tension within the Coalition (and within Conservative politics more generally) which plays itself out in the field of anti-social behaviour interventions, between the civil libertarians with their emphasis on a liberal rights discourse, on the one hand, and the more moral authoritarian conservatives with their appeal to a populist and popular punitiveness reflecting a 'responsibilization' rhetoric, on the other hand. This ambiguity has expressed itself in uncertain and hesitant critiques of the use of ASBOs, and other powers introduced under New Labour administrations, and is also evident in the tentative nature of the proposed reforms.

However, there are at least three fault-lines around which we might see future shifts in the organization and mode of delivery of crime prevention and community safety in England and Wales. First, the new Government has promoted its 'localism' agenda, in which it claims it will depart from the perceived failure of centralized state authority associated with New Labour: 'centralisation and top-down control have proved a failure' (HM Government 2010: 7). There is a commitment to lessen the culture of performance measurement and reduce the national targets which for years have constrained local practitioners' discretion. The anti-social behaviour consultation paper, for example, argues forcefully for a 'transformation in the way agencies deal with it, stripping away central initiatives, targets and diktats, and empowering the professionals and communities to join forces to beat this problem' (Home Office 2011: 8). The extent to which this will be realized in practice remains to be seen.

Second, fuelled by the financial and banking crisis, we are witnessing a considerable tightening of the public purse with dramatic cuts in funding across much of the public (and voluntary) sector, including the police and local authorities. According to the new Government: 'the days of big government are over' (HM Government 2010: 7). Reductions in public resources are likely to impact on the capacity of front-line agencies to deliver social crime prevention work through partnerships. There is a genuine concern that fiscal restrictions will cause key public sector organizations to focus on their primary tasks (at the expense of secondary functions) and look to meet their own internal goals rather than partnership goals that link their activities with other services providers. It is also unclear what the impact of reductions to police numbers will be on public perceptions of security and confidence in policing authorities. The projected decline will come as a stark turn-around against the background of a long and sustained period in which

---

[8] In both its criminal and civil guises.

police numbers increased significantly, especially with the introduction of new front-line patrol personnel in the form of Police Community Support Officers (PCSOs).[9]

Third, in place of state provision there is now an appeal to social entrepreneurs in the private and voluntary sectors, as well as active citizens, to take over responsibility for providing social goods, in what the Prime Minister David Cameron has described as the 'Big Society':

> The Big Society is about a huge culture change…where people, in their everyday lives, in their homes, in their neighbourhoods, in their workplace…don't always turn to officials, local authorities or central government for answers to the problems they face…but instead feel both free and powerful enough to help themselves and their own communities. (Cameron 2010)

The small state/big society vision chimes well with the wider critique of the over-interventionist, 'nanny state' of the New Labour era, but leaves unanswered crucial questions about how it will be achieved, especially in a climate of fiscal stringencies. Furthermore, the extent to which the 'Big Society' will be capable of filling the spaces left by the withdrawal of local public services remains a subject of much debate, particularly in areas of high social deprivation where crime and anti-social behaviour thrive. More broadly, this approach—in line with the appeal to localism—implies a critique of the ambitious state-centred, command-and-control style interventionism and social engineering which came to represent the New Labour political legacy. Regardless of the genuine nature of government's desire to draw back and adopt a 'hands off' approach to allow 'local solutions to local problems', it is likely only to take a few high-profile cases—like the tragic Pilkington case in 2007—to ignite demands for government to intervene more and ensure standardized policy delivery.[10]

In a context in which the cultural salience of crime is prominent and crime-related anxieties dominate public debate, governments are caught in something of a *Catch 22*: simultaneously needing to be seen to be doing something about something over which they have little control. More often than not, 'doing something' is translated as reasserting state authority, or at least attempting to do so by invoking 'more law' and, frequently, more criminal law. The number and range of new laws that were created over the course of recent administrations is testimony to their enduring recourse to sovereign command. The politics of crime prevention and community safety over the past decade reflected 'hyper-innovation' in a context of 'hyper-politicization'. We have seen the 'frenetic selection of new institutional modes, and their equally frenetic replacement by alternatives' (Moran 2003: 26). This frantic quest for diverse ways of regulating social life has been premised upon an incoherent conception of 'state craft' embedded in a clash between ambitious central state interventionism and limited capacities. The resultant developments have been both contradictory and volatile as the preventive face of government jostles with its punitive counterpart (O'Malley 1999).

---

[9] First introduced in 2002, there were nearly 17,000 PCSOs across England and Wales by March 2010. By March 2011, this number had declined by about 1,100 (some 6.5%).

[10] Fiona Pilkington was driven to kill herself and her disabled daughter after being terrorized by a local gang. The inquest heard that the 38-year-old rang police 33 times in 10 years over the bullying (13 times in the year of her death). The then Home Secretary Alan Johnson publicly criticized the senior Leicestershire police officer at the Pilkington inquest, who said that dealing with low-level anti-social behaviour was no longer a police matter but should be dealt with by local authorities.

## BLIND SPOTS

The preceding discussions have largely focused upon the principal areas of governmental activity, namely the prevention of crimes and disorder which occur in public places rather than corporate or white-collar crime. This is not to suggest that crime prevention has little to say about such crime. It does, notably in the fields of fraud, money laundering, and cybercrime. Nevertheless, crime prevention in relation to corporate crime raises different questions about appropriate responsibility and competence. For example, the New Zealand Government identified 'white-collar crime' as one of seven priorities in its crime prevention strategy published in 1994 (Department of the Prime Minister and Cabinet 1994). However, when the New Zealand Government tasked its local partnerships, the Safer Community Councils, with the responsibility for implementing the strategy, it became apparent that most local practitioners found it very difficult to generate much interest or activity around 'white-collar crime'. This demonstrated less a lack of will and more a lack of competency on their part (Crawford 1997b). Some elements of crime prevention may be better served by specialist and centralized authorities, than dispersed to local communities.

Likewise, the implications of gender for crime prevention remain largely under-developed (Shaw 2009). Much of the preventive focus has been restricted to the prevention of violence against women, largely in public spaces (Stanko 1990). Shaw and Andrew have noted that '[c]rime prevention in general continues to pay little attention to the significance of gender in the behaviours of potential or actual offenders or victims' (2005: 302). Where the prevention of crime is perceived as the responsibility of the individual this creates its own inequalities as those groups most vulnerable to victimization have had to take on the burden of protecting themselves from harm. Women, for example, have long curtailed their own freedoms in order to protect themselves from personal assaults and harm. Other groups, however, owing to their vulnerable position in society may be unable to take their own preventative measures and may be victimized by the very people who are expected to be their protectors. Children in particular are placed in an ambivalent position; on the one hand, it has been assumed that as especially vulnerable they would enjoy the protection of adults and indeed very little advice has historically been offered to children and young people on how to keep themselves safe. Crime, responsibility, and avoidance all have different implications in private spaces where crime occurs within relations that are familiar or familial. The event-orientation of situational crime sits less well with relational crimes, notably those perpetrated against children. On the other hand, young people have been considered the perpetrators of much harm and the phrase 'young people at risk' has come to suggest to the majority that they are at risk of becoming offenders rather than victims.

## CONCLUSIONS

The last quarter of the twentieth century saw crime prevention emerge 'as a major focus of public policy and criminological research' (Tilley 2002: 13). There is little evidence to demonstrate that this shift will be abandoned or reversed at any time in the near future. However, the move to preventive mentalities in government has not been straightforward, linear, or forged in a constant direction and, as we have seen, approaches to the prevention of crime have remained riven by contradiction and inconsistency. Despite the ideological tensions within the current Coalition Government, the recent discussion around the 2010 White Paper (Ministry of Justice 2010), and furore over Justice Minister Ken Clarke's proposals on reducing sentencing show the populist and punitive rhetoric of old remains alive and well and continuing to shape government thinking. Cameron's continued championing of the 'Big Society' further entrenches the privatization of public services and the responsibilizing of individuals at the heart of political endeavours.

Despite the twists and turns of government policy, Tilley (2002) nevertheless identifies three distinctive, but overlapping periods through which crime prevention has developed. In the first period, 1975–90, crime prevention initiatives and activities were acknowledged as a valid and serious endeavour, in the second, 1985–2000, an accepted body of crime prevention knowledge gained institutional recognition and was co-opted wholesale into mainstream practice and crime prevention became a largely technical and professional affair. In the third phase, 1995–2010 the newly established ways of working to reduce crime were cut free from the largely public institutions which had previously made them their own and crime prevention practice was thrown up in the air once again to find a new balance and focus under a myriad of 'owners' which have turned out to be public, private, voluntary, and commercial. In these latter changes, various commentators have identified what Hughes has termed an 'epochal shift' (2007: 8) taking place in considerations of what to do about the problem of crime.

In the current financial climate with increasing unemployment and precarious existence it is likely that crime will remain high on the political agenda. Crime prevention will remain an important area to study not least because the techniques of prevention are no longer utilized only by public bodies for the limitation of crime but also to inform other aspects of social control and to exclude and contain 'risky' populations and in the avoidance of 'bad risks'. As Crawford and Traynor warn: '[P]eople are increasingly judged in terms of what they *might* do. Anticipating and forestalling potential harm in a risk-averse culture of insecurity implies erring on the side of precaution' (2012, emphasis in original). If this analysis is correct, then the dominant individualizing discourses of risk, prevention, and demonization of the few looks set to continue into the future.

## ■ SELECTED FURTHER READING

The literature on crime prevention and community safety, like the topic itself, continues to expand. Good overviews are available in Crawford (1998), *Crime Prevention and Community Safety*, Hughes (1998), *Understanding Crime Prevention*, Gilling (2007), *Crime Reduction and Community Safety*, and Tilley (2009), *Crime Prevention*. By contrast, Sutton *et al.* (2008), *Crime Prevention: Principles, Perspectives and Practices* offer an Australian perspective on contemporary debates. These texts all situate crime prevention within a broader political and theoretical backdrop. Policy developments are well covered in Hughes (2007), *The Politics of Crime and Community* and Evans (2011), *Crime Prevention: A critical introduction*. Tilley's edited (2005), *Handbook of Crime Prevention and Community Safety* is a useful collection of essays covering a wide range of subjects and includes contributions from many key proponents in contemporary debates. The volume edited by Von Hirsch and colleagues (2000), *Ethical and Social Perspectives on Situational Crime Prevention* presents a wide-ranging critical analysis of situational crime prevention, particularly with regard to its normative implications. The collection of essays in *Crime Prevention Policies in Comparative Perspective* (2009) edited by Crawford offers valuable insights into comparative developments across Europe and beyond, as does Baillergeau and Hebberecht's edited volume *Social Crime Prevention in Late Modern Europe* (2012).

## ■ REFERENCES

ALLEN, G. (2011), *Early Intervention: The Next Steps*, London: Cabinet Office.

ASHWORTH, A. (2004), 'Social Control and ASB: the subversion of human rights', *Law Quarterly Review*, 120: 263–91.

—— and ZEDNER, L. (2008), 'Defending the Criminal Law: Reflections on the changing character of crime, procedure, and sanctions', *Journal of Criminal Law and Philosophy*, 2: 21–51.

ATKINSON, R., BLANDY, S., FLINT, J., and LISTER, D. (2004), *Gated Communities in England*, London: ODPM.

AUDIT COMMISSION (2002), *Community Safety Partnerships*, London: Audit Commission.

BARR, R. and PEASE, K. (1990), 'Crime Placement, Displacement and Deflection', *Crime and Justice*, 12: 277–318.

BAUMGARTNER, M. (1988), *The Moral Order of the Suburbs*, Oxford: Oxford University Press.

BERNBURG, J. G. and KROHN, M. D. (2003), 'Labeling, life chances, and adult crime', *Criminology*, 41: 1287–318.

BLANDY, S. (2011), 'Gating as governance: the boundaries spectrum in social and situational crime prevention', in A. Crawford (ed.), *International and Comparative Criminal Justice and Urban Governance*, Cambridge: Cambridge University Press: 519–44.

BOTTOMS, A. E. and WILES, P. (1986), 'Housing Tenure and Residential Community Crime Careers in Britain', *Crime and Justice*, 8: 101–62.

BRANTINGHAM, P. L., BRANTINGHAM, P. J., and TAYLOR, W. (2005), 'Situational Crime Prevention as a Key Component in Embedded Crime Prevention', *Canadian Journal of Criminology and Criminal Justice*, 47(2): 271–92.

BRANTINGHAM, P. J. and FAUST, L. (1976), 'A Conceptual Model of Crime Prevention', *Crime and Delinquency*, 22: 284–96.

BURNEY, E. (2009), *Making People Behave*, 2nd edn, Cullompton: Willan.

CAMERON, D. (2010), Big Society Speech, 19 July 2010. Available at: http://www.number10.gov. uk/news/speeches-and-transcripts/2010/07/big-society-speech-53572.

CATALANO, R. and HAWKINS, J. D. (1996), 'The Social Development Model: a theory of antisocial behaviour', in J. D. Hawkins (ed.), *Delinquency and Crime*, Cambridge: Cambridge University Press, 149–97.

CLARKE, R. V. (1995), 'Situational Crime Prevention', *Crime and Justice*, 19: 91–150.

—— (2000), 'Situational Prevention, Criminology and Social Values', in A. Von Hirsch, D. Garland, and A. Wakefield (eds), *Ethical and Social Perspectives on Situational Crime Prevention*, Oxford: Hart Publishing.

—— and CORNISH, D. B. (1985), 'Modelling Offenders' Decisions', *Crime and Justice*, 6: 147–85.

—— and WEISBURD, D. (1994), 'Diffusion of Crime Control Benefits', *Crime Prevention Studies*, 2: 165–83.

COHEN, L. and FELSON, M. (1979), 'Social Change and Crime Rate Trends: A Routine Activity Approach', *American Sociological Review*, 44: 588–608.

COLEMAN, A. (1985), *Utopia on Trial*, London: Hilary Shipman.

—— (1989), 'Disposition and Situation: Two Sides of the Same Crime', in D. J. Evans and D. T. Herbert (eds), *The Geography of Crime*, London: Routledge.

CORNISH, D. B. and CLARKE, R. V. (1987), 'Understanding Crime Displacement', *Criminology*, 25(4): 933–47.

—— and —— (2003), 'Opportunities, precipitators and criminal decision', *Crime Prevention Studies*, 16: 41–96.

CRAWFORD, A. (1997a), *The Local Governance of Crime*, Oxford: Clarendon Press.

—— (1997b), *A Report on the New Zealand Safer Community Councils*, Wellington: Ministry of Justice.

—— (1998), *Crime Prevention and Community Safety: Politics, Policies and Practices*, Harlow: Longman.

—— (2000), 'Situational Crime Prevention, Urban Governance and Trust Relations', in A. Von Hirsch, D. Garland, and A. Wakefield (eds), *Ethical and*

*Social Perspectives on Situational Crime Prevention*, Oxford: Hart Publishing, 193–213.

—— (2001), 'Joined-Up but Fragmented', in R. Matthews and J. Pitts (eds), *Crime, Disorder and Community Safety: A New Agenda?*, London: Routledge, 54–80.

—— (2003), 'Contractual Governance of Deviant Behaviour', *Journal of Law and Society*, 30(4): 479–505.

—— (ed.) (2009a), *Crime Prevention Policies in Comparative Perspective*, Cullompton: Willan.

—— (2009b), 'Governing through Anti-Social Behaviour: Regulatory Challenges to Criminal Justice', *British Journal of Criminology*, 49(6): 810–31.

—— (2011), 'From the shopping mall to the street corner: dynamics of exclusion in the governance of public space', in A. Crawford (ed.), *International and Comparative Criminal Justice and Urban Governance*, Cambridge: Cambridge University Press.

——, LISTER, S., BLACKBURN, S., and BUNRETT, J. (2005), *Plural Policing*, Bristol: Policy Press.

—— and TRAYNOR, P. (2012), 'La Prévention de la Délinquance chez les Anglais: From community-based strategies to early interventions with young people', in E. Baillergeau and P. Hebberecht (eds), *Social Crime Prevention in Late Modern Europe*, Brussels: VUB Press.

CURRIE, E. (1988), 'Two Visions of Community Crime Prevention', in T. Hope and M. Shaw (eds), *Communities and Crime Reduction*, London: HMSO.

DEPARTMENT OF THE PRIME MINISTER AND CABINET (1994), *The New Zealand Crime Prevention Strategy*, Wellington: Department of the Prime Minister and Cabinet.

EDWARDS, A. and HUGHES, G. (2009), 'The preventive turn and the promotion of safer communities in England and Wales', in A. Crawford (ed.), *Crime Prevention Policies in Comparative Perspective*, Cullompton: Willan.

EKBLOM, P. (1995), 'Less Crime By Design', *The Annals*, 539: 114–29.

—— (2000), 'The Conjunction of Criminal Opportunity', in S. Ballintyne, K. Pease, and V. McLaren (eds), *Secure Foundations*, London: IPPR, 30–66.

—— (2005), 'Designing Products Against Crime', in N. Tilley (ed.), *Handbook of Crime Prevention and Community Safety*, Cullompton: Willan.

ETZIONI, A. (1993), *The Spirit of Community*, New York: Simon Schuster.

EVANS, K. (2011), *Crime Prevention: A critical introduction*, London: Sage.

FARRINGTON, D. (2000), 'Explaining and Preventing Crime: The Globalization of Knowledge', *Criminology*, 38(1): 1–24.

—— (2002), 'Developmental Criminology and Risk-Focused Prevention', in M. Maguire, R. Morgan, and R. Reiner (eds), *The Oxford Handbook of Criminology*, 3rd edn, Oxford: Oxford University Press.

—— (2007), 'Childhood Risk Factors and Risk-Focused Prevention', in M. Maguire, R. Morgan, and R. Reiner (eds), *The Oxford Handbook of Criminology*, 4th edn, Oxford: Oxford University Press.

—— and WELSH, B. C. (2007), *Saving Children from a Life of Crime: Early Risk Factors and Effective Intervention*, Oxford: Oxford University Press.

FEELEY, M. and SIMON, J. (1994), 'Actuarial Justice', in D. Nelken (ed.), *The Futures of Criminology*, London: Sage.

FELSON, M. (1998), *Crime and Everyday Life*, 2nd edn, London: Sage.

—— and CLARKE, R.V. (1998), *Opportunity Makes the Thief: Practical Theory for Crime Prevention*, London: Home Office.

FRANCE, A. and UTTING, D. (2005), 'The Paradigm of "Risk and Protection-Focused Prevention" and its Impact on Services for Children and Families', *Children and Society*, 29: 77–90.

GARLAND, D. (1996), 'The Limits of the Sovereign State', *British Journal of Criminology*, 36(4): 445–71.

—— (2000), 'Ideas, Institutions and Situational Crime Prevention', in A. Von Hirsch, D. Garland, and A. Wakefield (eds), *Ethical and Social Perspectives on Situational Crime Prevention*, Oxford: Hart Publishing, 1–16.

—— (2001), *The Culture of Control*, Oxford: Oxford University Press.

GATTI, U. (1998), 'Ethical issues raised when early intervention is used to prevent crime', *European Journal on Criminal Policy and Research*, 6: 113–32.

GOLDBLATT, P. and LEWIS, C. (eds) (1998), *Reducing Offending*, London: Home Office.

GRAHAM, J. and BENNETT, T. (1995), *Crime Prevention Strategies in Europe and North America*, Helsinki: HEUNI.

GUERETTE, R. T. and BOWERS, K. (2009), 'Assessing the extent of crime displacement and diffusion of benefit', *Criminology*, 47(4): 1331–68.

HAKIM, S. and RENGERT, G. F. (1981), *Crime Spillover*, Beverly Hills, California: Sage.

HANNAH-MOFFAT, K. (2005), 'Criminogenic needs and the transformative risk subject: Hybridizations of risk/need in penalty', *Punishment and Society*, 7(1): 29–51.

HARCOURT, B. E. and LUDWIG, J. (2006), 'Broken windows: New evidence from New York City and a five city social experiment', *University of Chicago Law Review*, 73: 271–320.

HENRY, A. (2009), 'The development of community safety in Scotland: a different path?', in A. Crawford (ed.), *Crime Prevention Policies in Comparative Perspective*, Cullompton: Willan, 38–61.

HILLIER, B. and SHU, S. (2000), 'Crime and Urban Layout: the need for evidence', in S. Ballintyne, K. Pease, and V. McLaren (eds), *Secure Foundations*, London: IPPR, 224–48.

HIRSCHI, T. (1969), *Causes of Delinquency*, Berkeley, CA: University of California Press.

HM GOVERNMENT (2010), *The Coalition: Our Programme for Government*, London: Cabinet Office.

HOMEL, R. (2005), 'Developmental Crime Prevention', in N. Tilley (ed.), *Handbook of Crime Prevention and Community Safety*, Cullompton: Willan, 71–106.

HOME OFFICE (1997), *Getting to Grips with Crime: A New Framework for Local Action*, London: Home Office.

—— (2000), *Anti-Social Behaviour*, Report of Policy Action Team 8, National Strategy for Neighbourhood Renewal, London: Home Office.

—— (2003), *Respect and Responsibility—Taking a Stand Against Anti-Social Behaviour*, London: Home Office.

—— (2004), *Building Communities, Beating Crime*, London: Home Office.

—— (2005), *National Community Safety Plan 2006– 2009*, London: Home Office.

—— (2006a), *Respect Action Plan*, London: Home Office.

—— (2006b), *Review of Partnership Provisions of the Crime and Disorder Act 1998, Report of Findings*, London: Home Office.

—— (2007), *Delivering Community Safety: A guide to effective partnership working*, London: Home Office.

—— (2011), *More Effective Responses to Anti-Social Behaviour*, London: Home Office.

HOPE, T. (1995), 'Community Crime Prevention', *Crime and Justice*, 19: 21–89.

—— (2000), 'Inequality and the Clubbing of Private Security', in T. Hope and R. Sparks (eds), *Crime, Risk and Insecurity*, London: Routledge, 83–106.

—— and FOSTER, J. (1992), 'Conflicting Forces: Changing the dynamics of crime and community', *British Journal of Criminology*, 32: 488–504.

HUDSON, B. (2003), *Justice in the Risk Society: Challenging and Re-affirming Justice in Late Modernity*, London: Sage.

HUGHES, G. (1996), 'Communitarianism and law and order', *Critical Social Policy*, 16: 17–41.

—— (2007), *The Politics of Crime and Community*, Basingstoke: Palgrave.

——, MCLAUGHLIN, E., and MUNCIE, J. (eds) (2002), *Crime Prevention and Community Safety: New Directions*, London: Sage.

HURLEY, D. (2004), 'On Crime as Science (a neighbor at a time)'. Available at: www.ctdatahaven.org/know/images/6/6c/On_Crime_As_Science.pdf.

INNES, M. (2004), 'Reinventing Tradition? Reassurance, neighbourhood security and policing', *Criminal Justice*, 4(2): 151–71.

—— (2007), 'The Reassurance Function', *Policing*, 1(2): 132–47.

—— and JONES, V. (2006), *Neighbourhood Security and Urban Change*, York: JRF.

JACOBS, J. (1961), *The Death and Life of Great American Cities*, New York: Random House.

JAMIESON, J. (2005), 'New Labour, Youth Justice and "Respect"', *Youth Justice*, 5(3): 180–93.

JEFFERY, C. R. (1971), *Crime Prevention Through Environmental Design*, Beverly Hills, California: Sage.

JOHNSTON, L. and SHEARING, C. (2003), *Governing Security*, London: Routledge.

KELLING, G. and COLES, C. M. (1996), *Fixing Broken Windows*, New York: Touchstone.

KING, M. (1989), 'Social Crime Prevention à la Thatcher', *Howard Journal*, 28(4): 291–312.

KOCH, B. (1998), *The Politics of Crime Prevention*, Aldershot: Ashgate.

LAYCOCK, G. (2005), 'Defining Crime Science', in M. J. Smith and N. Tilley (eds), *Crime Science: New Approaches to Preventing and Detecting Crime*, Cullompton: Willan.

MCLAUGHLIN, E. (2002), 'The crisis of the social and the political materialization of community safety', in G. Hughes, E. McLaughlin, and J. Muncie (eds), *Crime Prevention and Community Safety. New Directions*, London: Sage.

MARTINSON, R. (1974), 'What Works?—Questions and Answers about Prison Reform', *The Public Interest*, 35(1): 22–54.

MATTHEWS, R. (1992), 'Developing More Effective Strategies for Curbing Prostitution', in R.V. Clarke (ed.), *Situational Crime Prevention: Successful Case Studies*, Albany, NY: Harrow and Heston.

MINISTRY OF JUSTICE (2010), *Breaking the Cycle: Effective Punishment, Rehabilitation and Sentencing of Offenders*, London: Ministry of Justice.

MORAN, M. (2003), *The British Regulatory State*, Oxford: Oxford University Press.

MORGAN, J. (1991), *Safer Communities: The Local Delivery of Crime Prevention Through the Partnership Approach*, London: Home Office.

MOSS, K. (2006), 'Crime Prevention as Law', in K. Moss and M. Stephens (eds), *Crime Reduction and the Law*, London: Routledge, 1–13.

—— and PEASE, K. (1999), 'Crime and Disorder Act 1998: Section 17 a Wolf in Sheep's Clothing?', *Crime Prevention and Community Safety*, 1(4): 15–19.

NEW STATESMAN (1998), 'Interview of Jack Straw by Steve Richards', *New Statesman*, 3 April, 127(4379), 14–16.

NEWMAN, O. (1972), *Defensible Space: People and Design in the Violent City*, London: Architectural Press.

NORRIS, C. and MCCAHILL, M. (2006), 'CCTV: Beyond Penal Modernism', *British Journal of Criminology*, 46(1): 97–118.

O'MALLEY, P. (1992), 'Risk, Power and Crime Prevention', *Economy and Society*, 21(3): 252–75.

—— (1999), 'Volatile and Contradictory Punishment', *Theoretical Criminology*, 3(2): 175–96.

—— (2001), 'Risk Crime and Prudentialism Revisited', in K. Stenson and R. Sullivan (eds), *Crime, Risk and Justice: The politics of crime control in liberal democracies*, Cullompton: Willan.

PEASE, K. (2002), 'Crime Reduction', in M. Maguire, R. Morgan, and R. Reiner (eds), *The Oxford Handbook of Criminology*, 3rd edn, Oxford: Oxford University Press.

PHILLIPS, C. (2002), 'From Voluntary to Statutory Status', in G. Hughes, E. McLaughlin, and J. Muncie (eds), *Crime Prevention and Community Safety: New Directions*, London: Sage.

POYNER, B. (1992), 'Situational Crime Prevention in Two Parking Facilities', in R.V. Clarke (ed.), *Situational Crime Prevention: Successful Case Studies*, Albany, NY: Harrow and Heston.

PUTNAM, R. (2000), *Bowling Alone: The Collapse and Revival of American Community*, New York: Simon and Schuster.

ROSENBAUM, D. P. (1988), 'Community Crime Prevention: A Review and Synthesis of the Literature', *Justice Quarterly*, 5(3): 323–93.

SAMPSON, R. J., MORENOFF, J., and EARLS, F. (1999), 'Beyond Social Capital', *American Sociological Review*, 64(5): 633–60.

—— and RAUDENBUSH, S. (1999), 'Systematic Social Observations of Public Spaces: A New Look at Disorder in Urban Neighborhoods', *American Journal of Sociology*, 105(3).

SHAPLAND, J. (2000), 'Situational Prevention: Social Values and Social Viewpoints', in A. Von Hirsch, D. Garland, and A. Wakefield (eds), *Ethical and Social Perspectives on Situational Crime Prevention*, Oxford: Hart.

SHAW, M. (2009), 'International Models of Crime Prevention', in A. Crawford (ed.), *Crime Prevention Policies in Comparative Perspective*, Cullompton: Willan.

—— and ANDREWS, C. (2005), 'Engendering Crime Prevention', *Canadian Journal of Criminology and Criminal Justice*, 47(2): 293–316.

SHERMAN, L. W., GARTIN, P. R., and BUERGER, M. E. (1989), 'Hot Spots of Predatory Crime', *Criminology*, 27(1): 27–55.

SIMON, J. (2007), *Governing Through Crime*, Oxford: Oxford University Press.

SKOGAN, W. (1990), *Disorder and Decline*, New York: Free Press.

SQUIRES, P. and STEPHEN, D. (2005), *Rougher Justice: Young People and Anti-social Behaviour*, Cullompton: Willan.

STANKO, E. (1990), 'When Precaution is Normal: A Feminist Critique of Crime Prevention', in L. Gelsthorpe and A. Morris (eds), *Feminist Perspectives in Criminology*, Milton Keynes: Open University Press.

TAYLOR, R. B. (2001), *Breaking Away from Broken Windows*, Colorado: West View Press.

THALER, R. H. and SUNSTEIN, C. R. (2008), *Nudge: Improving Decisions About Health, Wealth, and Happiness*, New Haven: Yale University Press.

THORNBERRY, T. P. and KROHN, M. D. (2005), 'Applying interactional theory to the explanation of continuity and change in antisocial behavior', in D. P. Farrington (ed.), *Integrated Developmental and Life-Course Theories of Offending*, New Brunswick, NJ: Transaction.

TILLEY, N. (2002), 'Introduction: Analysis for crime prevention', in N. Tilley (ed.), *Analysis for Crime Prevention*, Monsey, NY: Criminal Justice Press, 1–13.

TONRY, M. and FARRINGTON, D. (1995), 'Strategic Approaches to Crime Prevention', *Crime and Justice*, 19: 1–20.

TREMBLAY, R. and CRAIG, W. (1995), 'Developmental Crime Prevention', *Crime and Justice*, 19: 151–237.

TUCK, M. (1988), 'Crime Prevention: A Shift in Concept', *Home Office Research and Planning Unit Research Bulletin, No. 24*, London: Home Office.

UTTING, D. (2004), 'Overview and Conclusion', in C. Sutton, D. Utting, and D. Farrington (eds), *Support from the Start: Working with Young Children and their Families to Reduce the Risks of Crime and Anti-Social Behaviour*, London: Department for Education and Skills, 89–100.

VAN DIJK, J. and DE WAARD, J. (2009), 'Forty years of crime prevention in the Dutch polder', in A. Crawford (ed.), *Crime Prevention Policies in Comparative Perspective*. Cullompton: Willan.

VON HIRSCH, A. and SHEARING, C. (2000), 'Exclusion from Public Space', in A. Von Hirsch, D. Garland, and A. Wakefield (eds), *Ethical and Social Perspectives on Situational Crime Prevention*, Oxford: Hart.

WALKLATE, S. and EVANS, K. (1999), *Zero Tolerance or Community Tolerance? Managing Crime in High Crime Areas*, Aldershot: Ashgate.

WEATHERITT, M. (1986), *Innovations in Policing*, London: Croom Helm.

WEBB, B. (2005), 'Preventing vehicle crime', in N. Tilley (ed.), *Handbook of Crime Prevention and Community Safety*, Cullompton: Willan.

WEBSTER, C. (2001), 'Gated Cities of Tomorrow', *Town Planning Review*, 72(2): 149–69.

WILSON, J. Q. (1975), *Thinking About Crime*, New York: Vintage.

—— and KELLING, G. (1982), 'Broken Windows', *The Atlantic Monthly*, March: 29–37.

ZEDNER, L. (2006), 'Policing before and after the Police: the historical antecedents of contemporary crime control', *British Journal of Criminology*, 46: 78–96.

—— (2007), 'Pre-Crime and Post-Criminology', *Theoretical Criminology*, 11(2): 261–81.

# 27

# POLICING AND THE POLICE

*Tim Newburn and Robert Reiner*

## INTRODUCTION: CRIMINOLOGY AND POLICING

Public and political discourse assumes that police are the primary source of security. If crime falls, cops claim the credit; 'Crime is down...blame the police' in the vainglorious boast of David Cameron's new hero William Bratton, former Chief of the NYPD (Bratton 1998). And if crime rises politicians usually call for more police.

Criminology has become increasingly focused on police research. At the 2011 British Criminology Conference, for example, about one out of every six papers was on policing. Yet for most of the history of criminology policing did not figure at all in its research or theoretical agendas.

This is a little curious in that one root of criminology is the eighteenth century 'science of police', although the term 'police' was used then in a much broader way to connote the whole craft of governing a social order (Neocleous 2000; Dubber 2005; Zedner 2006; Reiner, this volume).

This chapter will review the development and findings of police research. The next section explores the growth of research on the police over the last half-century. The third section addresses the fundamental conceptual questions: What is policing and who are the police? The fourth section analyses police discretion, how the 'law in the books' gets translated into the 'law in action' of policing practice. The fifth section assesses the emergence in the last 20 years of new, innovative policing tactics. The sixth section examines the pluralization of policing, the proliferation of forms of policing beyond the police. The penultimate section charts the growing internationalization of policing in an era of globalization. The conclusion considers possible future trends in policing.

## THE DEVELOPMENT OF POLICE RESEARCH

Systematic research on the police developed at roughly the same time, the early 1960s, on both sides of the Atlantic (for a fuller analysis see Reiner and Newburn

2007). In both Britain and the USA changes in the focal concerns of police research have been shaped by the shifting politics of law and order at least as much as by the immanent dynamic of intellectual unfolding that appears on the surface of academic discourse.

In the USA the key motor driving early police research was concern that police practice often violated civil rights, highlighted by controversial Supreme Court decisions that sought to regulate policing through tighter specification of due process legality (Sklansky 2008: ch. 2). Socio-legal researchers began to analyse how the police role, organization, and culture structured malpractices. In 1968 'law and order' displaced 'civil rights' as the key domestic political issue in the USA (Beckett 1997). The civil libertarian impulses that had given birth to police research were largely eclipsed by policy-oriented, managerial work on police effectiveness in controlling crime and disorder.

The development of British police research also reflected the politics of law and order as much as theoretical developments in criminology. The 1950s were the heyday of cross-party consensus on law and order (Downes and Morgan, this volume). The pedestal on which the police then stood was illustrated by the popularity of the TV series *Dixon of Dock Green*, encapsulating the cosy stereotype of the British bobby (Sydney-Smith 2002; Leishman and Mason 2003; McLaughlin 2007: ch. 1; Reiner 2008). In the late 1950s a series of scandals indicated the stirrings of controversy about policing, and culminated in a Royal Commission examining the role, organization, and accountability of the police (Royal Commission 1962).

Research on the police in Britain developed in this context. Banton's pioneering empirical study (Banton 1964) found the police role was primarily 'peace-keeping', not law enforcement. Banton's key analytic theme, the dependence of formal or informal social control, has often been re-discovered, as in much current discussion about partnership and pluralization. Despite eschewing any concerns with scandal, Banton was acutely aware that there were severe threats to the benign and consensual mode of policing he described.

These themes were developed by a number of young British researchers in the early 1970s (Holdaway 1979). Their observations found that the backstage life of the police—apparently the acme of a bureaucratic, rule-bound organization, disciplined to discipline others—was in fact a fluid world, seething with tensions, spontaneity, and deviance.

In the later 1970s 'law and order' became a central political issue, and was crucial to the 1979 Conservative General Election victory. The police themselves became an overt pressure group on the political stage (Reiner 1978). The politicization of policing stimulated two new strands of research. In the academic and political worlds overtly critical or Marxist work on the police proliferated (e.g. Hall *et al.* 1978; Hain 1979, 1980; Brogden 1982; Scraton 1985; Grimshaw and Jefferson 1987). The other new strand of police research in the late 1970s was policy-oriented research commissioned by government bodies. Official policy-oriented research is not necessarily uncritical, but the fastest growth since the mid-1980s has been in managerialist studies of immediate practical relevance, often conducted by the police themselves (Brown 1996).

# 'POLICE' AND 'POLICING'

Understanding the nature of *policing* requires conceptual deconstruction of the idea of *the police*. Policing refers to 'organised forms of order-maintenance, peace-keeping, rule or law enforcement, crime investigation and prevention and other forms of investigation and information-brokering' (Jones and Newburn 1998: 18; Reiner 2010: ch. 1). Diverse policing strategies are proliferating today (see the section on pluralization below), even though it is only the state agency with the omnibus mandate that is popularly understood by the label *the* police.

Until modern times policing functions were primarily carried out as a by-product of other social relationships. Anthropological studies show that many pre-literate societies have existed without any formalized system of policing. Policing originated in collective and communal processes of social control, but specialized police forces developed only with the emergence of social inequality, hierarchy, and more centralized, dominant state systems (Robinson and Scaglion 1987: 109). During this transition communal policing forms were converted in incremental stages to state-dominated ones, which functioned as agents of class control rather than impartial protection. The complex and contradictory function of contemporary police, as simultaneously embodying the quest for general and stratified order—'parking tickets' as well as 'class repression' (Marenin 1983)—is inscribed in their origins.

Conventional histories of the British police purport to trace a direct lineage between ancient tribal forms of collective self-policing and the contemporary Bobby (Reith 1956). Such claims have been characterized aptly as 'ideology as history' (Robinson 1979). Many European systems of police developed overtly as instruments of state control, but police development in Britain and the USA was also shaped by class and state structures and strategies (Silver 1967; Storch 1975; Miller 1977; Emsley 2008, 2009; Reiner 2010: chs 2 and 3). The supposedly benign 'British' model was in any case for home consumption only. A more militaristic and coercive model was exported to colonial situations (Brogden 1987). The more coercive face of policing has always been played down in the construction of the public image of British policing, and in the more consensual decades of the middle of the twentieth century largely disappeared from view. But as social and political conflict has become more pronounced since the 1970s there has been a highly visible and controversial militarization of tactics especially in relation to public order (Waddington and Wright 2008; Reiner 2010: ch. 3). The return of rioting to the British mainland, in the 1980s and again in 2011, has once more brought this to the forefront of debate.

Although contemporary patterns of police vary in detail, they have converged increasingly around fundamentally similar organizational and cultural lines, without the qualitative distinctions of the kind implied in traditional British police ideology (Bayley 1985; Brodeur 1995; Mawby 2008). This is accentuated by the emergence of a new international cadre of experts who facilitate the diffusion of fashions in police thinking around the globe (Newburn and Sparks 2004).

The police are called upon routinely to perform a bewildering miscellany of tasks, from traffic control to terrorism. The uniting feature of police work is not a particular social function, whether it be crime control, social service, order maintenance, or political repression. Rather, it is that all demands on the police involve 'something that ought not to be happening and about which someone had better do something **now!**' (Bittner 1974: 30, emphasis in original). In other words, policing tasks arise in emergency situations, usually with an element of social conflict (Brodeur 2007).

The police normally resort to a variety of ways and means to keep the peace without initiating legal proceedings. But underlying their tactics is the bottom-line power to wield legal sanctions, ultimately the use of legitimate force (Bittner 1970, 1974: 35; Brodeur 2010). In performing these tasks the police necessarily operate with a considerable measure of discretion.

## POLICE DISCRETION: ITS NATURE, OPERATION, AND CONTROL

Although many jurisdictions have denied the legitimacy of police discretion, it is both routine and inevitable. Breaches of the law outstrip police capacity to process them, so choices about priorities are inescapable. Discretion is also logically necessary as legal rules require interpretation in unpredictable fact situations. Discretion could also be desirable to avoid oppressiveness, as British law has long claimed (Reiner and Leigh 1992).

The recognition that the police do not adhere mechanistically to the rule of law raises the prospect of discrimination and malpractice. Police discretion is hard to regulate, however, because the dispersed character of routine police work gives it 'low visibility' (Goldstein 1960). Thus 'the police department has the special property . . . that within it discretion increases as one moves down the hierarchy' (Wilson 1968: 7). There is a gulf between 'street' and 'management' cops, and the culture of the former informs practice (Ianni and Ianni 1983).

In the late 1970s a structuralist critique (McBarnet 1978, 1979) argued that although a degree of discretion was inevitable, British law took an unnecessarily permissive stance to police powers by formulating elastic and vague rules. This paved the way for more detailed studies of the interaction between legal rules and police practice (Dixon 1997; Sanders and Young 2008; Reiner 2010: ch. 7).

### THE OPERATION OF POLICE DISCRETION

The Scarman Report on the 1981 Brixton disorders (Scarman 1981) influentially argued that public tranquillity should have priority over law enforcement. Discretion was the better part of police valour. But police discretion is not an equal opportunity phenomenon. It disguises the disproportionate use of police powers against unpopular and powerless minorities, 'police property' (Lee 1981: 53–4). The police also tend to neglect the victimization of the powerless, who are over-policed *and* under-protected.

The characteristic deployment of the police underpins this practical concentration on policing the underclass. Most police resources are devoted to uniformed patrol of public space, but privacy has a class dimension (Stinchcombe 1963). The lower the social class of a person, the more their social lives take place in public space, and the more 'available' they are to come to police attention (Fitzgerald 1999; Quinton *et al.* 2000; Waddington *et al.* 2004). Adversarial policing falls disproportionately on young men in the lowest socio-economic groups.

### Racial discrimination

Numerous studies have shown that the police disproportionately exercise their powers against black people (Bowling and Phillips 2002, 2007, 2008; Rowe 2004; Delsol and Shiner 2006; Phillips and Bowling, this volume). This results from a complex interaction between police discrimination, and social pressures that generate disproportionate offending by young black men (Reiner 1993, 2010: 159–75).

It is also widely documented that ethnic minorities are disproportionately victimized by crime of all kinds, and that they often perceive the police response as inadequate (Bowling 1999; Foster *et al.* 2005). These problems are related to the issue of racial discrimination within the police force in the treatment of ethnic minority officers (Holdaway 2009).

### Gender and policing

The very small proportion of female suspects at every stage of the process is probably the most consistent pattern in criminal justice (see Heidensohn and Silvestri, this volume). The low rate of formal processing of women as suspects masks a complex web of discrimination. Some women escape suspicion because 'chivalry' places them outside the frame of likely offenders in the stereotypes of investigating officers. Yet others, such as teenage girls behaving in sexually precocious or deviant ways, or prostitutes, may be dealt with by the police at a lower threshold of entry into the system because they violate the officers' codes of acceptable behaviour, or may be seen paternalistically as in need of 'protection' from themselves.

There is much clearer evidence of discrimination against women in their treatment by the police as victims. Calls to domestic disturbances have always been a significant part of the police workload, but tended to be treated by officers without recourse to criminal proceedings even where evidence of assault is present. 'Domestics' are seen as messy, unproductive, and not 'real' police work in traditional cop culture. This issue has become highly charged in the last three decades around the world, and police forces have attempted to improve their response to domestic assaults, with debatable results (Hoyle 1998). There has also been much concern about insensitive or even hostile treatment of rape victims, an issue dramatically highlighted 25 years ago by Roger Graef's TV documentary on the Thames Valley Police which filmed the interrogation of a rape victim (BBC 1, 18 January 1982). Despite considerable improvements since then, the treatment of rape victims by police remains problematic (Horvath and Brown 2010).

Women are also discriminated against as police officers. Until 35 years ago discrimination within police forces was institutionalized: separate women's divisions carried out radically different functions. The Sex Discrimination Act 1975 formally integrated women into the same units as male officers, but discrimination survived in a variety of ways. Although the recruitment of women officers has increased over time, as has their presence in senior ranks (several women chief constables have been appointed in the last ten years), the continuation of discrimination has been documented by numerous studies (Heidensohn 1992, 2008; Brown and Heidensohn 2000; Silvestri 2003, 2007).

## THE EXPLANATION OF POLICE DISCRETION

Three broad approaches to explaining how police discretion operates can be distinguished: individualistic, cultural, and structural.

### Individualistic explanations

It has frequently been alleged that police work attracts people with distinctive personalities, in particular authoritarianism. Most research does not support the view that police recruits are more authoritarian than comparable civilian samples (Waddington 1999a). Studies of the socialization of recruits suggest that training has a temporary liberalizing effect (Brown and Willis 1985; Fielding 1988), but exposure to practical policing results in a more authoritarian perspective. This is better understood as a cultural adaptation to the exigencies of police work than the unfolding of a set of basic personality traits, and anyway is not necessarily translated into policing practice.

### Cultural explanations

The impact of the informal culture of the rank and file is the most common explanation of police working practices found in the research literature. In Skolnick's classic formulation, police in a liberal democracy are faced with a basic dilemma: they are under pressure to achieve results in the form of law enforcement, but the rule of law restricts the methods they can use (Skolnick 1966: ch. 3). They are also visible embodiments of social authority, exposing them to danger from deviants, and creating tensions in all their social relationships. These pressures of the police condition are coped with by the development of a set of informal rules, rites, and recipes, a subculture that is transmitted by storytelling, a toolkit of examples for dealing with police work (Shearing and Ericson 1991).

Skolnick identified three main aspects of cop culture: suspiciousness, internal solidarity coupled with social isolation, and conservatism. Suspiciousness arises from the pressure to achieve results by catching offenders, and the concern with danger: people and places are constantly scrutinized for signs of crime or risk. Suspiciousness makes the police prone to operate with prejudiced stereotypes of potential 'villains' and 'troublemakers'. Internal solidarity and social isolation are mutually reinforcing. Solidarity is knitted from the intense experience of confronting shared dangers, and the need to be able to rely on colleagues in tight spots. Isolation is the product of organizational aspects of the work such as the shift system, and people's wariness in interacting with authority figures.

Solidarity can become a device for shielding wrongdoing, whilst isolation may exacerbate prejudiced stereotypes. Moral and social conservatism is inherently related to the core police function of symbolizing and safeguarding authority. Charged with upholding law and maintaining order, police are likely to have an elective affinity with the values underpinning them. Many studies have observed racism and machismo in police culture (Graef 1989; Young 1991; Westmarland 2001, 2008). Others have emphasized officers' strong commitment to what they see as 'real' policing—fighting crime and catching criminals.

Many reforms in the last 20 years, primarily stemming from the Scarman and the Macpherson reports have aimed at reducing if not eliminating these characteristic traits of traditional rank-and-file police culture (Henry and Smith 2007; Rowe 2007). There does appear to be some progress in controlling the overt display of prejudice (Foster *et al.* 2005). However, recent ethnographic and other research suggests that the traditional police culture remains largely resilient in the face of these reforms (O'Neill *et al.* 2007; Loftus 2008, 2009, 2010). This is also indicated by such scandals as the covert filming of police recruits for the BBC documentary *The Secret Policeman*, which revealed the continuation of virulent racial prejudice (McLaughlin 2007: ch. 6).

Studies of police culture have been attacked for presenting a monolithic picture, overlooking differences between and within forces (Chan 1997; Foster 2003). However, many researchers since Skolnick have analysed such variations (Reiner 2010: ch. 4).

### Cultural variations within forces

The rank hierarchy and division of labour within police organizations structure different subcultures. There are also variations due to age, gender, ethnic group, educational and social background, as well as individual personality and choice.

The most obvious cultural gulf is between the street level and the management ranks, with conflicting interests and perspectives (Ianni and Ianni 1983; Punch 1983). Senior ranks are mainly concerned with administration, and with presenting a public face of acceptable conduct to external audiences. Senior officers will often be in an adversarial role vis-à-vis the rank and file, who tend to hold derogatory images of the managerial levels as parasitic pen-pushers rather than 'real' police.

Nonetheless it is important not to lose sight of the common interests uniting all ranks. They share a stake in the status, reputation, and resources of the organization. The cultural gulf between street and management cops may be analysed as something of a cynical, Faustian bargain. It allows management cops to present acceptable glosses of police practice to influential public audiences whilst being shielded from the more sordid aspects of street policing.

The organizational division of labour also produces systematic differences in the subcultures associated with specialisms. The most hallowed is the perennial rivalry between uniform and detective branches. Uniform branches will often see themselves as the bedrock of the organization, and argue that contrary to public impressions they apprehend the majority of offenders. The CID will be resented for taking over cases for court processing after the hard work of capture has already been accomplished, grabbing the glamour and the glory. For their part detectives pride themselves on being dedicated to 'real' policing, dealing with crime and criminals, in particular the more serious cases (Hobbs 1988: chs 4, 8; Innes 2003, 2007; Maguire 2008).

### Cultural variations between forces

The cultures of different forces vary over time and between places. They are shaped by law, external social contexts, management strategies, and government policy.

James Q. Wilson's comparative research on eight US forces (Wilson 1968) distinguished three departmental cultures, the 'watchman', 'legalistic', and 'service' styles, related to departmental policy choices, and varying social and political contexts. Cultural variations between forces have been demonstrated by several subsequent US studies, related to social context and political choices (Skogan and Frydl 2004: ch. 5).

British research has also identified cultural variations between forces. Numerous studies over 40 years have found differences in the cultures of rural and city forces. Rural police generally are more strongly integrated into their communities, city officers more alienated (Cain 1973; Jones and Levi 1983; Young 1993; Loftus 2009).

Thus although there are common tendencies generated by the basic features of police work in any contemporary industrial society, their cultural expression can differ. This is partly because of varying social and political contexts, partly because of management philosophies. Police culture is neither monolithic nor invariant, but responsive to social structure and official policy (Foster 1989, 2003).

### Structural explanations

Structural explanations of policing supplement rather than supplant cultural accounts. The major analyses of police culture do not portray it as a freestanding phenomenon into which successive generations of police are socialized as passive cultural dopes. The culture is generated and sustained by the problems and tensions of the police role, structured by legal and social pressures.

Culture does not determine practice, but is enacted in concrete situations where other pressures have to be taken account of. For example, officers who are racially prejudiced may nonetheless be restrained from acting in overtly discriminatory ways by clear and effectively sanctioned rules (Waddington 1999b).

Police practice is structured by the legal and social institution of privacy, patterned by class, race, and gender. There is an isomorphism between the structure of social power and the mapping of the population as potential trouble and hence suspicious in police culture (Reiner 2010: 122–5). The racism, sexism, impatience with legal formality, and other characteristics of police culture that have alarmed liberal critics are not simply manifestations of pathological authoritarian personalities, excessive exposure to *The Sun*, or a self-sustaining canteen cowboy ethos. The basic determinant is the role the police are assigned in the social order: moral street-sweeping. Their control powers are primarily directed against the young, male, disproportionately black, economically marginal, street population who threaten the tranquillity of public space as defined by dominant groups.

## THE CONTROL OF POLICE DISCRETION

The formal control of police discretion in Britain is limited by the common law doctrine of constabulary independence. As stated by Lord Denning, this holds that a 'constable . . . is not the servant of anyone, save of the law itself. No Minister of the Crown can tell him that he must, or must not, keep observation on this place or that; or that he must, or must not, prosecute this man or that one. Nor can any police authority tell him so. The responsibility for law enforcement lies on him.' (*R v Metropolitan Police Commissioner, ex p. Blackburn* [1968] 2 QB 136)

### Individual accountability

There are two principal channels for holding individual officers to account for alleged wrongdoing: the courts and the complaints process.

## Legal accountability

Statute and common law provide powers to the police to accomplish their duties, but also set limits to their legitimate use. The main statutory powers of the police are codified in the Police and Criminal Evidence Act 1984 (PACE), although they have been expanded since.

PACE attempted for the first time to develop a comprehensive set of police powers and safeguards for suspects, aiming to achieve a 'fundamental balance' between them (this was the axiom of the 1981 Royal Commission on Criminal Procedure (RCCP) Report which led to PACE). The safeguards are set out partly in the Act itself, partly in Codes of Practice accompanying it. PACE sought to overcome the perennial problem of the low visibility of police work by requiring that each exercise of a power had to be recorded contemporaneously. For example, section 1 extended the power to stop and search, but this must be grounded in 'reasonable suspicion', with a record written as soon as possible, and made available to the suspect. All the safeguards are underpinned by section 67 of PACE, which makes failure to comply with them a disciplinary offence. Judges were given a broad discretion to exclude evidence gathered in ways that would render the proceedings as a whole unfair (section 78). In addition, PACE includes sections purporting to enhance police accountability more generally, for example through the complaints process and by community consultation.

During its protracted parliamentary passage critics of PACE were particularly vexed about its reliance on internal police recording and discipline. But after the Act came into operation criticism came primarily from the police, who complained that the recording and other procedural requirements hampered effective investigation.

In the decade following PACE there was extensive research evaluating the impact of PACE on police practice (for summaries see Dixon 1997; Brown 1997; Reiner 2010: ch. 7). Some studies suggested that suspects systematically fail to receive their rights (McConville *et al.* 1991; Choongh 1997). They argued that the Act did not fundamentally erode the structural advantage the police have in the investigation process, especially after a suspect is in police custody. Most commentators found, however, that the new procedures achieved some improvements in the treatment of suspects, although since the mid-1990s there has been a clear trend to extending powers without balancing safeguards (Cape and Young 2008). It also appears to be the case that the courts in general were initially more vigorous in excluding evidence gathered in violation of PACE procedures than they were under the old Judges' Rules (Feldman 1990).

When the government was forced to establish the Royal Commission on Criminal Justice in 1991 in the wake of the successful appeals by the Birmingham Six and Guildford Four, it was hoped by civil libertarians that the protection of suspects would be boosted even further. In the event its recommendations on police powers and safeguards (Royal Commission 1993) amounted only to detailed footnotes to PACE, and they were implemented in an unbalanced way. Most of the new powers recommended by the 1993 Royal Commission Report were incorporated into the Criminal Justice and Public Order Act 1994. The Act extended stop and search powers (section 60), and gave new powers to control trespassers and raves. Most fundamentally, it introduced the right for the prosecution to comment adversely on a suspect's exercise of the right to silence in police interviews, with a corresponding change in the caution given beforehand. This overturned the recommendations of both the Royal Commissions on Criminal Procedure (1981) and Criminal Justice (1993), which had seen the right to silence as a cornerstone safeguard for suspects. It resulted in a decline in the proportion of suspects exercising their right of silence in relation to some or all questions (Bucke *et al.* 2000).

Since then expansion of police powers has accelerated. New powers to intercept communications, conduct covert operations, stop and search and arrest, and new public order offences were created by the Police Act 1997, the Crime and Disorder Act 1998, the Regulation of Investigatory Powers Act 2000, the Terrorism Act 2000, and the Criminal Justice and Public Order Act 2001.

In 2002 the Home Office conducted a review of PACE, premised on the view that the regime of safeguards it had instituted created a regime of procedures adequately protecting suspects. Accordingly the Review floated a number of proposals to dilute the safeguards of PACE, which have been partly implemented in subsequent legislation. The Criminal Justice Act 2003 authorized detention for 36 hours for all (not just 'serious') arrestable offences. The Serious Organised Crime and Police Act 2005 created a power of arrest for *all* offences, not just the more serious ones hitherto deemed 'arrestable'. It also allowed for the creation of civilian custody officers, overturning the PACE requirement that they should normally be police sergeants (Binns 2011). The clear trend is for enhanced powers and reduced safeguards, reflecting the law and order politics that have prevailed since the early 1990s.

Initially in 2010 the Conservative-led Coalition Government appeared as if it might reverse this trend. Home Secretary Theresa May announced on 8 July 2010 that section 44 of the Terrorism Act 2000, empowering officers to stop and search anyone in a designated area without having to show reasonable suspicion, was suspended. This followed a ruling by the European Court of Human Rights that the powers were unlawful because they were too broadly drawn and lacked sufficient safeguards to protect civil liberties. However, the ensuing Terrorism Act 2000 (Remedial) Order of March 2011 merely tightens the procedure and criteria for declaring a designated area *but* retains the power to stop/search in the absence of reasonable suspicion. Furthermore, the recording requirements under Code 1 of PACE were reduced (partly because mobile technology supplants it by automatic recording of location, time, date). The requirement to record 'stop and account' actions (not based on any legal power but common practice legitimized paradoxically by the Macpherson Report recommendation that as it occurred anyway it should be recorded) was abolished.

### The complaints process

A statutory procedure for handling complaints against the police was first established by the Police Act 1964. It relied on police investigation and adjudication, but since then independent elements have been introduced. The Police Act 1976 established an independent Police Complaints Board (PCB) to adjudicate complaints. An element of independence in the investigation of complaints was initiated by PACE in 1984, replacing the PCB by the Police Complaints Authority (PCA), with powers to supervise some police investigations.

The Police Reform Act 2002 established an independent body empowered to investigate complaints against the police, the Independent Police Complaints Commission. This achieved a long-standing central demand of civil libertarians, but it has not, as yet, achieved public confidence in the system (Smith 2009). Experience in other countries suggests independent investigation of complaints is not a panacea for regulating police misconduct (Goldsmith and Lewis 2000). No matter who does the investigating, complaints against the police are hard to sustain, because of the low visibility of most encounters. This turns most cases into a head-on collision of testimony in which the complained-against police officer usually has the advantage.

### Policy accountability

What avenues are there for the public accountability of police policy decisions? The present formal structure of police governance in England and Wales is set out in the Police Act 1964 and the Police and Magistrates' Court Act 1994, consolidated as the Police Act 1996. The 1964 Act enshrined the so-called 'tripartite' system of accountability for the (currently 41) provincial forces in England and Wales, comprising local police authorities, the Home Secretary, and chief constables.

The two London forces differed from this pattern. The Metropolitan Police had the Home Secretary as their police authority from 1829 until 1999, when the Greater London Authority Act created a police authority for the Met. The City of London force is accountable to the Common Council of the City of London (the Aldermen and Mayor), as well as the Home Secretary.

The 1964 Police Act divided accountability for provincial policing between chief constables, responsible for 'direction and control' of their forces; local police authorities, with the duty of 'maintenance of an adequate and efficient police force for the area' (section 4); and the Home Secretary, who was expected to use a variety of powers to further the efficiency of policing throughout the country. Under the 1964 Act police authorities consisted two-thirds of elected local councillors, and one-third of JPs (Lustgarten 1986; Walker 2000). Until the late 1970s it seemed to be accepted that the role of the police authority was as a sounding board for the professional expert, the chief constable. The Home Secretary's powers remained dormant.

This cosy consensus was shattered by the politicization of policing issues in the late 1970s. In 1981 radical Labour councils were elected in most large cities, and the metropolitan police authorities began to try and influence policing policy in controversial areas, notably public order tactics, especially during the 1984–5 miners' strike. The clashes underlined the impotence of local police authorities. Home Secretaries invariably supported the chief constables against police authority attempts to influence 'operational' matters. In the late 1980s the almost complete powerlessness of the local authority leg of the tripartite structure was highlighted by legal developments (Reiner 1991: ch. 2).

A centralizing trend became more apparent following subsequent reforms of police governance. The Police and Magistrates' Courts Act 1994 subtly altered the functions of police authorities from 'maintenance of an adequate and efficient' force to 'efficient and effective' (Police Act 1996, section 6). The precise scope of this responsibility remains as gnomic as in the 1964 version, but the symbolism is obvious. The prime purpose of the new-fangled police authorities is to be local watchdogs of the managerialist, value-for-money ethos that successive governments have injected into the whole public sector (McLaughlin 2007: ch. 7; Savage 2007).

The most controversial changes were to the structure of police authorities. The democratically elected councillor component of police authorities was reduced from two-thirds to just over a half (nine out of the normal total of 17 members: Police Act, 1996 Schedule 2, para. 1(1)(a)). Three members are magistrates (i.e. just over one-sixth instead of one-third: para. 1(1)(b)). The remaining five members are appointed under complex and arcane procedures detailed in Schedule 3 to the 1996 Act. Overall the Act left police authorities with a slight preponderance of elected members, as a fig leaf to hide growing centralization.

The explicit intention was to make police authorities more 'businesslike'. They acquired new duties to issue an annual policing plan for their area (Police Act 1996, section 8) and local policing objectives (section 7). The chief constable has the same general function of 'direction and control' of the force as in the 1964 Act, but this must be exercised with regard to the local policing plan and objectives which the authority draws up in liaison with him (section 10).

The changes in governance must be considered in the context of other elements of successive governments' police reforms. The 1993 Sheehy Inquiry into Police Responsibilities and Rewards recommended changes in pay and conditions that would have given governments considerable economic leverage. The toughest aspects of Sheehy were defeated by a storm of opposition from police representative associations. But arguably enough remained (short-term contracts and performance-related pay for senior ranks) so that, without formally abandoning the constabulary independence, the Home Secretary could colour the use of discretion by constables. The police would no longer be accountable in the gentlemanly 'explanatory and co-operative' style which (in Geoffrey Marshall's words) characterized the impact of the 1964 Police Act (Marshall 1978). Nor would they be subject to the 'subordinate and obedient' style of accountability to democratically elected local authorities that had been demanded by the Act's radical critics. Instead they would be subject to a new market-style 'calculative and contractual' discipline (Reiner and Spencer 1993), capable of penetrating the parts of policing which earlier models could not reach, the day-to-day operation of discretion.

The centralizing trend continued with the Police Reform Act 2002. This required the Home Secretary to issue an annual National Policing Plan and objectives. A Home Office 'Police Standards Unit' was established to improve the performance of all basic command units across the country. This process was consolidated by the creation of the National Policing Improvement Agency, although this has now been abolished by the Coalition Government. The Labour Government had also planned a sweeping amalgamation programme (HMIC 2005; Loveday 2006), but the plans were frustrated by opposition (McLaughlin 2007: ch. 7).

There has certainly been a profound transformation in the formal organization of police governance in the years since 1994, with a clear trend to enhancing central control. In the last few years this has been called into question by a growing cross-party consensus about the need to invigorate local input into shaping policing. In the 2010 General Election all the party manifestos offered proposals for this.

The victorious Conservative-led coalition introduced a Police Reform and Social Responsibility Bill on 30 November 2010. Seemingly influenced by aspects of American urban police governance (Newburn 2012), it will abolish Police Authorities and replace them with directly elected Police and Crime Commissioners serving four-year terms. The elected Commissioners will have a broad range of powers, subject only to limited scrutiny by newly created Police and Crime Panels. The Commissioners will be responsible for securing the maintenance of the police force, setting the local area policing plan and budget, and will have the power to hire and fire the Chief Constable.

The Bill claims to make police more accountable to the people. It places a huge amount of power in one place, subject only to the electoral process, with the risk of producing a local tyranny of the majority. The proposals endanger the centuries old pillars of police independence and tripartite checks and balances.

The developments in governance since 1994 have all been predicated on a clear but contentious conceptualization of the police role as being primarily 'catching criminals' (para. 2.2 of the 1993 White Paper, *Police Reform*). In theory and practice the police mandate had traditionally encompassed a much broader spectrum of concerns, including crime prevention and management, order maintenance and peace-keeping, emergency and other services . The police capacity to control crime is inherently limited by the deep roots of policing problems in wider social, political-economic, and cultural processes (Reiner 2010: ch. 5). The current coalition legislation continues this trend, whilst purporting to shift power to local people. This is indicated by the title 'Police and Crime Commissioners'.

## 'NEW TRICKS': INNOVATIVE POLICING STRATEGIES

The original mandate of Peel's Metropolitan Police placed greatest emphasis on the prevention of crime (Emsley 2009). This was to be achieved primarily through visible patrol. During the course of the nineteenth century a detective function was added and these two strategies—preventive patrol and criminal investigation—have continued to form the core of policing over the past century or more. Nevertheless, recent decades have witnessed some important developments in policing, many prompted by the pressures under which all criminal justice agencies were placed by governments increasingly concerned to secure 'value for money' and 'economy, efficiency and effectiveness' in public services (Savage 2007). They were also partly a reaction against the 'nothing works' penal pessimism of the 1970s and the apparently precipitous decline in public confidence in policing during roughly the same period. New developments in policing are almost always as much about police legitimation as they are about police effectiveness (Henry and Smith 2007; Reiner 2010).

From the 1970s research, primarily in the USA, had begun seriously to question the efficacy of patrol (for a summary of contemporary British research see Clarke and Hough 1984). The Kansas City experimental study of preventive patrol found little impact on reported crime, fear of crime, or confidence in the police (Kelling *et al.* 1974). One response to the Kansas City findings—which were a study of car patrol—was to reaffirm faith in some quarters in the perceived benefits of foot patrol, and subsequent large-scale research in Newark in the USA found some evidence of impact on fear of crime, and ratings of the police, though not on crime levels (Pate and Skogan 1985). Through its influence on Wilson and Kelling's much-cited (1982) 'Broken Windows' article, which argued strongly that police action against minor incivilities and nuisances was an important factor in preventing the development of more significant and less tractable problems, the Newark study played a significant role in maintaining faith in routine visible patrol as a cornerstone of contemporary policing (for a thorough critique, see Harcourt 2001).

In recent years policing has seen the regular appearance of what are alleged to be new 'models' of police work, each claiming to reorient and refashion policing in ways that represent a more or less radical departure from traditional methods. Many have been nothing more than fancy labels and promotional devices rather than genuine developments in policing styles and tactics. However, from among the morass it is possible to identify a number of developments in policing that are worthy of more sustained analysis. Weisburd and Eck (2004), focusing primarily on American developments, draw attention to three community policing, problem-oriented policing, and hotspots policing—to which a fourth, British, variant might be added—intelligence-led policing. What links all these innovations is the diagnosis that policing hitherto has been too reactive and should become more proactive (Tilley 2003).

## COMMUNITY POLICING

Of the various innovations it is undoubtedly community policing that has spread the furthest or, at least, is the most frequently and prominently talked about. Although the precise characteristics of community policing are often rather difficult to pin down (Klockars 1988), broadly speaking such approaches propose that there be greater citizen involvement in the identification of the problems that should form priorities for police attention as well as in the responses to those problems (Trojanowicz and Bucqueroux 1990). Community policing emerged from the growing acceptance that at best the police could often only offer a very partial solution to the difficulties they confronted (Morgan and Newburn 1997). In both the USA and the UK community policing emerged from the recognition that police-community relations had deteriorated significantly, particularly with some minority ethnic communities (Skogan and Hartnett 1997). Community policing initiatives proliferated in the 1980s, though the available evidence suggests many were of very limited if any impact. Nevertheless, in the UK in the aftermath of the urban riots of the early 1980s, and Lord Scarman's plea for greater police-community consultation, ideas associated with community policing became the accepted policing orthodoxy, at least amongst senior officers (Reiner 1991) and policy-makers. Indeed, continuing senior police scepticism about aggressive police patrol tactics was a very significant stumbling block when politicians began extolling the virtues of 'zero tolerance policing' in the mid-to late 1990s (Jones and Newburn 2007). So well established has community policing become in the USA that it has been described as the 'national mantra of the American police' (Greene 2000: 301).

The major difficulties with community policing are contained in the term itself. It is sufficiently awkward to define to allow for almost any policing activity to be included under its rubric (Bayley 1994). Moreover, with its connotations of inclusiveness,

consensus, communication, and consultation, an idea such as community policing, however difficult to pin down, is almost impossibly seductive (Brogden 1999).
Nevertheless, there have been numerous attempts both to define, and to evaluate,
community policing. Skogan (2009: 43) describes it as 'an organizational strategy
which supplements traditional crime fighting with problem-solving and prevention-
oriented programmes that emphasize new roles for the public'. It is clear that the
intention behind community policing is that it should be geared to locally identified
priorities and, moreover, that it should adopt tactics and styles that are appropriate to
local needs. Consequently, it is a model of policing in which there is expected to be a
wide array of approaches and which is therefore very distinct from the more uniform
policing styles that dominated much of the twentieth century. Such variety is partly
what makes it difficult to define and contributes to difficulties in evaluation.

The largest and arguably most successful community policing experiment to date
has been the Chicago Alternative Policing Strategy (CAPS). This programme, carried
out in five experimental districts, involved all elements of the police department in
community policing—not just patrol officers—and aimed to reduce officer resistance
to such approaches. It sought to stimulate citizen involvement through 'beat meetings',
and to solve the twin problems of only attracting the 'usual suspects' to community
meetings and police domination of the problem-solving elements of such meetings.
Finally, it endeavoured to integrate policing with other city services in order that
local problem-solving was not undermined by the ability to act across institutional
boundaries. The results in Chicago, as in many other evaluated community policing
initiatives, have been mixed. According to Skogan and Hartnett (1997) elements of
the CAPS initiative, as with others, were found in the aggregate to have succeeded
about half the time. A more recent review of community policing in seven American
cities found that police departments generally remained poor at problem-solving and
inconsistent in relation to community engagement (Maguire and Wells 2009). The
significance of CAPS undoubtedly lies in its scale. Whereas the majority of other community policing evaluations have been based on relatively small-scale experiments,
the CAPS experiment has been both sizeable and ongoing. The tension in community policing lies in the danger that even the most well-meaning community-oriented
programmes may easily revert to more classic police approaches which use them as a
means either of securing legitimacy for police actions or of increasing police information and intelligence (Mastrofski 2006).

## PROBLEM-ORIENTED POLICING

At the heart of many community policing initiatives is the idea of police as 'problem-
solvers' (Eck and Spelman 1987). Often considered a variant of community policing,
'problem-oriented policing' is somewhat easier to describe. Emanating from the work
of Herman Goldstein (1990), problem-oriented policing (POP) is an explicit attempt
to make police work more analytical in the identification of the 'problems' to be
addressed, and constructive in the solutions applied to the problems identified. The
underlying assumption is that much policing treats incidents brought to its attention
as if they were discrete—having no connection or pattern. By contrast, POP looks
for connections and patterns, with the aim of finding lasting solutions to ongoing

problems (Moore 1992). As a consequence a number of 'tools' have come to be associated with this approach, notably the problem analysis triangle (the PAT, consisting of the offender, the victim, and the location) and the SARA process in which four sequenced stages—scanning, analysis, response, and assessment—form the basis for problem-solving (Tilley 2008).

A focus on problem-solving has given rise to a number of linked policing strategies concentrating on such patterning as repeat or prolific offenders (Everson and Pease 2001), repeat victimization (Farrell and Pease 2001), and hotspots (Sherman 1990) among others. Indeed, there is a growing literature particularly around 'hotspots policing'. There have been a number of experimental studies in which focused and increased police patrols in areas where there are particular problems have had a measurable impact on levels of crime and disorder (Sherman and Weisburd 1995; Braga *et al.* 1999; Weisburd *et al.* 2010). However, as with community policing, there has also been considerable cultural resistance within the police to POP (Read and Tilley 2000; Scott 2000). There remains a very strong enforcement orientation in policing and an attachment to the excitement and glamour of the flashing blue lights of emergency response. The potentially more sedate world of data collection and analysis holds fewer attractions. It is also something that few police departments are well equipped to deal with. Although the police are increasingly concerned with information brokerage and knowledge production (Ericson and Haggerty 1997), they tend still to be short on those skills that would make for successful problem-solving (Bullock and Tilley 2003), meaning that much policing practice falls well short of the ideals espoused by Goldstein (Eck 2006).

## INTELLIGENCE-LED POLICING

Arguably, it is precisely the identification of such limitations that lay behind the emergence of a further variation—so-called 'intelligence-led policing' (ILP). This approach departs somewhat from problem-oriented and community policing in its tendency to privilege crime fighting and enforcement over other policing functions. Moreover, its underlying assumption is that these functions can be performed more efficiently and effectively through greater stimulation and use of intelligence. The link with POP lies in its emphasis upon the search for patterns in offending and victimization.

One of the most recent variants on the community policing and intelligence-led policing theme in Britain is the development of 'reassurance policing' (Dalgleish and Myhill 2004). A significant programme was established under this rubric between 2003 and 2005, arising in part from survey research which showed that despite year-on-year falls in crime since the mid-1990s a significant proportion of the public continued to believe that crime was still rising. In government circles this became known as the 'reassurance gap'. The idea of 'signal crimes' was the intellectual glue that allowed concerns about the 'reassurance gap' to be linked with the antisocial behaviour agenda (Innes and Fielding 2002; Innes 2006). At the core of the signal crimes idea is that there are particular crimes and disorders that act as warning signals to people about the nature of risk. One highlights the signal that disorder sends to potential offenders, the other the signal it sends to local citizens. Though talk of reassurance policing has been largely replaced in England and Wales by a series of other initiatives, including Citizen-Focused

Policing (Home Office 2006) and Neighbourhood Policing (Home Office 2005), most such approaches represent some form of amalgam of elements of community policing and POP. Central to each of them is the assumption that a visible presence is important to local feelings of security, that the community should be involved in both the identification of local problems and the action taken in response, and, centrally, that policing activity should be targeted at those problems that appear to matter most.

## PLURALIZATION

It is no longer possible to argue or imagine that policing and the police are largely synonymous. Liberal democracies in the twenty-first century are policed by what often appears to be a bewildering array of organizations (Crawford 2008; Walker 2008; Jones and Newburn 2006a). Such has been the pace and extent of change in this area that two leading commentators have argued that 'future generations will look back on our era as a time when one system of policing ended and another took its place' (Bayley and Shearing 1996: 585). The period since the mid-1960s they argue has seen the 'end of a monopoly' by the public police (though see Jones and Newburn 2002) and the emergence of what they call a 'multilateralized' system of security provision (Bayley and Shearing 2001). Through this term they seek to draw attention to the increasing complexity of policing, in terms not just of its provision, but also of its authorization or governance (Shearing 2006; Jones, this volume). One of the consequences of these changes to the landscape of policing is that a number of observers have increasingly come to talk of policing as having become 'pluralized' (Crawford *et al.* 2005; Jones and Newburn 2006a) and others have argued for the use of the term 'governance of security' in preference to the term 'policing' (Johnston and Shearing 2002; Wood and Dupont 2006).

In essence 'pluralization' may be taken to refer to three related sets of developments. First, the increasing size and pervasiveness of the commercial security sector that is visible in many countries (see the contributions in Jones and Newburn 2006c). Secondly, there has been the growing 'commodification' of public policing. Commodification itself may be broken down into three distinct processes (Loader 1999): 'managerialism' (becoming more 'business-like'); 'consumerism' (the re-presentation of public policing as a 'service' and of the public as 'consumers'); and 'promotionalism' (the increasingly professional promotion of the 'product'). Relatedly, from the 1980s onwards we have seen successive waves of 'civilianization' and the beginning of discussions about possibilities of privatization. In addition, many countries have seen the emergence of forms of policing provision that can be distinguished both from commercial security and from traditional state constabularies. Key examples include the recent introduction of '(police) community support officers' and 'neighbourhood wardens' in the UK (Crawford 2003), the establishment of local municipal police organizations in France (Roche 2002), and the introduction of police auxiliaries (*politie-surveillanten*) and 'city guards' (*stadswachten*) in the Netherlands (Jones *et al.*

2009). Finally, criminologists in some countries have come to pay increasing attention to the activities of a range of governmental regulatory and investigatory agencies undertaking important 'policing' tasks (e.g. Hutter 1988). However, undoubtedly the most visible manifestation of pluralization has been the growing visibility and variety of private, municipal, and civilian guards, officers, and wardens on the streets of every major city and many smaller communities.

## PRIVATE SECURITY

In recent decades an increasingly complex division of labour has emerged in which private security personnel far outstrip police in numerical terms (Jones and Newburn 1998, 2006b)—and have access to increased powers in some cases—in which civilian employees and auxiliaries have become an accepted part of state policing, and in which the police and numerous other agencies—public, private, and voluntary—work in 'partnership' (Button 2007).

The proliferation of private security has involved the spread of new technologies, such as closed-circuit television (CCTV) (Lyon 2001), and the growing incursion of the private sector into forms of work, or areas of activity, more usually associated with public policing such as the enforcement of parking and traffic regulations, the transport and guarding of prisoners, and most importantly—certainly for the way we view policing—the patrolling of public streets. Though some of these are relatively recent developments, a degree of caution has to be exercised when discussing the degree to which this is a departure from previous arrangements (Zedner 2006). In fact, there is good evidence to suggest that by the late 1950s/early 1960s the numbers employed in the private security industry already exceeded the number of police officers (Jones and Newburn 1998). Despite this, it is arguably only in the last two decades that the police service's dominant position in the public mind as the 'thin blue line' protecting the public from crime and lawlessness has come under successful challenge.

The private security sector includes staffed services, security equipment, and investigation. However, the most significant growth area in recent times has been in the proliferation of security hardware and, in particular, the expansion of the use of CCTV (McCahill and Norris 2002 ). The first major city-centre CCTV systems were introduced as part of the 'Safer Cities' initiative in the mid-1980s and a small number of towns went ahead with such installations at around the same time using local authority rather than central government funding. By the mid-1990s fewer than 80 towns and cities had CCTV schemes (Fyfe and Bannister 1996). By May 1999 there were over 530 town and city-centre CCTV systems in operation and further government funding since then has further fuelled expansion, with the latest estimates suggesting that there are now in excess of four million cameras in operation in Britain (Norris *et al.* 2004; though for a corrective to some of the more extreme claims about the numbers of cameras see Tarleton 2009). It is extremely difficult to provide accurate estimates of the size of the private security sector (Jones and Newburn 2006b). Research (Crawford *et al.* 2005) using industry data suggests the turnover in the sector had reached close to £2 billion by 2003 and subsequent work (Keynote Report 2004) estimates that the figure may be closer to £5 billion.

## EXPLAINING THE GROWTH OF PRIVATE SECURITY

Explanations vary, some arguing that the growth of private security is the result of increasing financial constraints on the police who, as a consequence, are unable to meet the demands placed upon them (Spitzer and Scull 1977). Despite generally increasing expenditure on public policing in recent decades, it is clear that a 'demand gap' exists (Morgan and Newburn 1997). Despite recent downward trends in crime, public perceptions of safety and security have not followed suit and demands for increased policing provision continue. Another factor is undoubtedly the growing privatization of urban space, notably the growth of 'mass private property' (Shearing and Stenning 1981; though see Jones and Newburn 1999) and the gradual emergence of gated residential communities—though these remain less in the UK than in the USA and Canada (Blakely and Snyder 1997; Atkinson and Flint 2004).

A third factor is the direct privatization of public functions by government. Although the private security sector was a very substantial presence much earlier, it was not until the 1980s that privatization emerged as a formal element of government policy and began to have an effect on the police. The initial battleground was police funding. From 1982/3 onwards the government began vigorously to pursue its 'Financial Management Initiative' (FMI), designed to encourage efficiency and cost savings by applying private- sector management methods to the public sector, and imposing market disciplines on them (Rawlings 1991). As we described earlier, the pace of change really picked up in the 1990s, with the subsequent Police and Magistrates' Courts Act 1994 and the Sheehy Inquiry introducing a range of managerialist initiatives.

Privatization—directly or by contracting out—has been a minor factor in the changing face of policing in contemporary Britain than appeared likely in the early 1990s. Some functions have been transferred entirely to the private sector. Starting in 1991, the Criminal Justice Act 1991 transferred responsibility for security arrangements for prisoners in transit from the police and prison service to private contractors, and also (section 76) made provision for magistrates' courts to contract-in security officers to maintain order. Subsequent reforms have enabled the contracting out of the construction and management of custody centres, reception duties, and post-charge administration—including the taking of fingerprints, photographs, DNA samples, and PNC checks. Current pressure on budgets, and a desire to protect 'frontline' policing may lead to further contracting out in due course (Neyroud 2010). Nevertheless, rather than direct privatization, it has been growing civilianization, including that of the custody officer role (section 120 of the Serious Organised Crime and Policing Act 2005), the encouragement of police partnership with other providers such as the Highways Agency in traffic policing, and most recently the introduction of a new tier of auxiliaries, that has had the greatest impact on the contemporary policing landscape.

## CIVILIANIZATION AND THE 'NEW AUXILIARIES'

The police have long been encouraged to 'civilianize' posts that do not require the training and legal powers of a police officer. The significant drive to civilianize began during the 1980s (Jones et al. 1994) with the Home Office encouraging forces to recruit civilian staff into financial management, legal services, research, forensics, and human resources jobs within the police service (Mawby and Wright 2003). Some are now employed at senior levels (ACPO rank) and are part of force management teams and civilians make up over a third of the total police workforce. The last decade has seen the mushrooming of what has been the termed the 'new public auxiliaries' (Crawford and Lister 2004).

Directly and indirectly, through a number of measures, successive governments have stimulated further moves in the direction of a more complex and fragmented policing division of labour. The Police Reform Act 2002, via the creation of community support officers and the accreditation of extended police family members, is the most visible of the recent measures, though the neighbourhood policing programme launched in 2005 subsequently placed the new auxiliaries at the heart of all neighbourhood policing teams. Introduced only a few years ago there are now approximately 16,000 PCSOs in England and Wales (Dhani and Kaiza 2011) out of a total workforce of 230,000.

How plural policing arrangements are to be governed is an issue that remains not only unresolved but largely ignored (for exceptions see Crawford 2003; Stenning 2009; Jones, this volume). Of all the recent inquiries into policing, the most explicit recognition of the increasingly 'plural' nature of policing and security provision was contained in the proposals advanced by The Independent Commission on Policing in Northern Ireland (the Patten Inquiry) which was set up as part of the Good Friday Agreement (10 April 1998) (Patten 1999). It recommended a radical overhaul of accountability structures, including the introduction of a Police Ombudsman and a new Policing Board (not Police Board) to replace the largely discredited Police Authority. Beneath the Policing Board it recommended the establishment of District Policing Partnership Boards (DPPB) as a committee of district councils with a majority elected membership. In particular, it was envisaged that these boards would have responsibility for promoting partnership of community and police in the collective delivery of community safety. Perhaps most radically in this regard the Inquiry recommended that district councils should have the power to contribute financially towards the improved policing of the district. This could enable DPPBs to purchase additional services from the police or other statutory agencies, or indeed from the private sector. Though these proposals were by no means enacted in full in Northern Ireland (McEvoy et al. 2002; Mulcahy 2006), nor similar ones in Canada (Law Commission of Canada 2006) they are considered by a number of commentators to have considerable potential (Neyroud 2001; Stenning 2009).

## INTERNATIONALIZATION

The bulk of criminological literature focuses on policing as a set of domestic activities undertaken by agents of the state within particular national boundaries. This is hardly surprising given that the maintenance of internal order by the police is generally viewed as one of the defining characteristics of the modern nation state. However, if the rise of the police was paradigmatic of the modern then the changing socio-political conditions characteristic of globalization are slowly making such a conception appear increasingly anachronistic. That this is so can be seen in the gradual pluralizing of policing already described, and also in the increasing visibility of what is now generally referred to as 'transnational policing' (Sheptycki 2000a)—activities undertaken by policing bodies that draw their authority from polities that lie beyond individual nation states.

## EUROPEAN DEVELOPMENTS

Early European initiatives in transnational policing activity date back to the late nineteenth century (Deflem 2002). The first permanent body was the International Criminal Police Commission established in Vienna in 1923, succeeded after the Second World War by the International Criminal Police Office or Interpol (Walker 2000). From small and informal beginnings Interpol has expanded significantly and has participating bureaux in nearly two hundred countries. Despite this, and its widening functional remit (Cameron-Waller 2008; Ling 2010), Interpol is no longer the primary site of transnational policing activity. In particular European countries began making other arrangements because of Interpol's perceived shortcomings in relation to anti-terrorist policing, as well as concerns about the security of its communications network (House of Commons 1990). Very significant expansions in the area of European transnational police cooperation have taken place in the last two decades. A number of factors have been important in stimulating such activity, notably the growing international reach of US law-enforcement activities (Nadelmann 1993) and the growing visibility and power of the European Union (Anderson *et al.* 1995). The internationalization of policing was given particular impetus by America's 'War on Drugs' and its use of the military as well as its Drug Enforcement Agency and the FBI in its interdiction efforts (Nadelmann 1993), though non-state actors also appear to have played an important role (Sheptycki 2000b). As part of this effort a series of Mutual Legal Assistance Treaties were signed providing a legal basis for cross-border police activity, particularly covert activity (Manning 2000).

According to Bigo (2000) the 1970s were the watershed in the process of Europeanization of crime and policing issues. The establishment of TREVI in 1976 was followed by the initial Schengen Agreement in 1985, comprising five member states, and a more extensive Implementation Agreement in 1990 which established the computerized Schengen Information System and police cooperation in activities such as 'hot pursuit' (Walker 2000).

Following the signing of the Maastricht Treaty in 1992 Europol has been established as the Europe-wide police intelligence agency that would receive and supply information to the police forces of member states, though it did not become fully operational until 1999 (Walker 2003). There has been significant expansion of European policing activity since that point, not least as the repercussions of the attacks in the United States on 11 September 2001 were felt across the Atlantic (Andreas and Nadelmann 2006). The European security agenda which is driving such developments is now focused primarily on transnational organized crime (Dorn and Levi 2007) and the threat of international terrorism. In particular, the scale of the terrorist threat seems to have overcome the majority of remaining national concerns about the growing power of Europol and related EU institutional arrangements. Moreover, the post-9/11 security agenda has vastly increased EU cooperation with the USA in relation to the exchange of intelligence and personal data and significantly enhanced US involvement in EU border policing and security planning (Den Boer and Monar 2002).

In the last five years Europol's mandate has been extended to allow it to investigate murder, kidnapping, hostage-taking, racism, corruption, unlawful drug-trafficking, people-smuggling, and motor vehicle crime (Lavranos 2003). European Union sharing of information and intelligence with the USA has occurred primarily through Europol, but also through the establishment of Eurojust—the EU inter-governmental institution responsible for judicial cooperation around crime (Dubois 2002). The European arrest warrant came into force in 15 member states in January 2004 enabling the transnational transfer of accused persons (Walker 2003). It is important, however, not to exaggerate the nature and reach of such policing initiatives:

> Europol cannot yet compare to the federal police agencies and multiagency task forces that have proliferated in the United States, and the prospect of supranational police agencies with international arrest powers still seems chimerical. (Andreas and Nadelmann 2006: 238)

Although current European developments fall some way short of the emergence of a transnational FBI, domestic reforms suggest that this is the direction in which European policing is heading even though they may take a couple of decades or more to reach that stage.

## SERIOUS AND ORGANIZED CRIME

The transnationalizing effects of the twin concerns of international terrorism and global organized crime can also be seen in domestic developments in British policing organization and activity (Edwards and Gill 2003; Hobbs 1998; Levi 2003; Matassa and Newburn 2003). There has been a gradual centralization of serious and organized crime policing in the UK culminating in 2005 with the creation of the Serious and Organised Crime Agency (SOCA), subsequently to be replaced by the National Crime Agency. This body will report directly to the Home Secretary and will incorporate a range of investigative and law enforcement responsibilities covering those otherwise held by the police, UK Border Agency, and HM Revenue & Customs (Home Office 2011).

## TRANSNATIONAL PRIVATE SECURITY

It is not only public policing but also commercial security that can increasingly be found operating transnationally. Indeed, this trend is arguably clearer in relation to private policing. By the turn of the century Johnston (2000: 22) was able to note that 'While transnational public policing is a relatively new phenomenon, the commercial security market is already dominated by a small number of transnational companies'. This includes traditional contract security operations but also less frequently studied areas such as risk management, business intelligence, and military services (Johnston 2006). Such companies, he suggests, are able to generate high revenues, high rates of growth, and huge profits. Group 4 Securicor is a good example. It currently employs over 400,000 people and operates in over 100 countries, describing itself as having an 'unrivalled geographic footprint'. Its activity is divided among three sectors: what it calls 'security services', which includes manned guarding and other activities relating to justice systems such as running custodial institutions, immigration detention, prisoner transfer, and electronic monitoring; security systems including alarms, entry systems, CCTV, and biometrics; and the guarding and transfer of cash and other valuables. Its turnover in 2010 was £7.3 billion (of which £6.2 billion was non-UK turnover), making it one of the world's largest security companies.

The end of the Cold War and more recently the growing impact of the 'War on Terror' have progressively blurred the boundary between internal and external threats. One of the more significant consequences of these developments has been the growth of the private military industry. It is generally held to consist of three main sectors (Singer 2003): 'military support firms' which provide logistical and intelligence services; 'military consulting firms' that provide strategic advice and training; and 'military provider firms' which offer tactical military assistance including the defence of key installations and individuals together with combat services. To the extent that it is possible to identify the emergence of a 'new structure' of 'multilateralized' policing (Bayley and Shearing 2001), it is clear that this encompasses 'high' as well as 'low' policing activities (Bowling and Newburn forthcoming).

Transnational policing is undoubtedly set to increase markedly and the growth and spread of private and public transnational policing bodies inevitably raises questions of governance. There is an emerging debate in academic criminology over how best to imagine—practically and normatively—what appropriate structures for the governance of transnational security might look like and, more particularly, within this what the role of the nation state should be (Johnston and Shearing 2002; Loader and Walker 2006; Johnston 2006; Cutler 2010).

## CONCLUSION: FUTURES OF POLICING

The modern British police were established during the first half of the nineteenth century against widespread opposition across the social and political spectrum (Emsley 2008, 2009; Rawlings 2008). As a way of overcoming this, the architects of the British police tradition strove to construct a distinctive organizational style and image (Miller 1977; Reiner 2010: chs 2, 3). This emphasized the idea of the police as an essentially civilian body, minimally armed, relying primarily on the same legal powers to deal with crime as all citizens shared, strictly subject to the rule of law, insulated from governmental control, and drawn from a representative range of working-class backgrounds to facilitate popular identification. The pacific image of the British bobby was a myth deliberately constructed in order to defuse the virulent opposition which existed to the very idea of police in early nineteenth century Britain. That it succeeded owed at least as much to the long-term process of greater social integration and consensus over the century between the 1850s and the 1950s as to any actions of the police themselves.

By the mid-1950s, however, the police had negotiated a huge degree of public support and they stood as symbols of the nation. Behind this facade there is much evidence from oral histories and memoirs that in the 'Golden Age' of consent to policing, the treatment of the 'police property' groups at the base of the social hierarchy was rough, ready, and uninhibited by notions of legality or justice (Mark 1978: chs 2–4; Young 1991; Weinberger 1995).

In the last 40 years the process of growing acceptance of the police in Britain has been reversed, although the police still remain central symbols of security (Loader and Mulcahy 2003). A number of changes have plunged them into acute controversy and conflict: corruption and miscarriage of justice scandals; accusations of race and sex discrimination; increasing public disorder and the militarization of police tactics; rising crime and an apparently declining police ability to deal with it (Morgan and Newburn 1997); decreasing public accountability as forces have grown larger, more centralized, and more reliant on technology. Police leaders recognized this problem and introduced reforms to deal with it, professionalizing management, improving training, streamlining working procedures, and becoming more open to the public through consultation of various kinds. None of this self-engineered change has been sufficient to satisfy recent governments.

In recent times the police have been widely perceived as guilty of systematic malpractice as well as falling down on the job. The prospects for reversing this by recent governments' reform agendas are doubtful. Their strategy rests upon a fundamental misconception of policing, which whilst commonly shared, has for many years been called into question by research. The premise underlying current initiatives is that—if properly organized  policing *can* have a significant impact on crime levels, deterring crime in the first place by uniform patrol, and detecting criminals efficiently after the event if crimes do occur. This can be referred to as the rational deterrent model of policing.

By this standard it certainly seems at first sight that the police in Britain are far less efficient and effective than they used to be, despite large increases in resources. In the period since the Second World War recorded crime levels have increased inexorably, albeit with some decline in recent years. The proportion of crimes cleared up by the police has fallen dramatically over the same period. Whilst the clear-up rate is a notoriously inadequate measure of police performance, the decline in it has been politically damaging for the police, and exposed them to the government's current policing initiatives.

There is, however, a substantial body of research evidence suggesting that policing resources and tactics have a tenuous relationship to levels of crime or the clear-up rate (Clarke and Hough 1980, 1984; Bayley 1994; Morgan and Newburn 1997; Reiner 2010: ch. 5). Innovative strategies may have some impact, as reviewed earlier, but are generally held to be unlikely to have a major effect on the overall levels of crime. That said, there is a major debate underway, especially in the United States, exploring the role of major urban police departments on the very substantial crime declines visible in the past decade or more (Blumstein and Wallman 2006; Zimring 2011). Nevertheless, the police are primarily managers of crime and keepers of the peace, not a vehicle for reducing crime substantially. Crime is the product of deeper social forces, largely beyond the ambit of any policing tactics, and the clear-up rate is a function of crime levels and other aspects of workload rather than police efficiency.

Underlying the many specific causes of controversy over policing, such as malpractice, militarization, or apparently declining effectiveness, there are deeper and more fundamental changes in contemporary society. We saw earlier that the rise of a specific organization specializing in policing functions coincided with the development of modern nation states, and was an aspect of the process by which they sought to gain centralized control over a particular territory. This was especially true of the British case where bureaucratic police organizations came into being comparatively late by European standards and coincided with the historical trajectory towards greater social integration after the initial impact of the Industrial Revolution. In all societies the symbolic functions of the police are at least as important as their direct instrumental effectiveness in dealing with crime and disorder. This is particularly true in Britain, where the police came to stand—together with the monarchy whose peace they are sworn to protect—as symbols of consensual and legitimate order.

The position of the police as an organization symbolizing national unity and order is threatened by social changes transforming the modern world economically, socially, politically, and culturally. Consumerism becomes the driving force of action, and the social structure follows a dynamic of fragmentation, dis-organization, pluralism, and de-centring. Economic changes have transformed the economic and social framework, dispersing and globalizing the centralized 'Fordist' production systems of modern times, and increasing economic inequality. Whilst the majority participate, albeit very unevenly and insecurely, in unprecedented levels of consumption, a substantial and growing 'underclass' is permanently and hopelessly excluded (Taylor 1999; Young 1999; Reiner 2007). Certainly with the political dominance of free-market economic policies there is no prospect at all of their incorporation into the general social order. In other words, the 'police property' group grow far larger than ever before, and more fundamentally alienated. This economic fragmentation interacts with a long and complex process of cultural diversification, declining deference, erosion of moral absolutes, 'desubordination' (Miliband 1978), and growing anomie to create a more turbulent, disorderly social world.

In this context, the British conception of the police as a body with an omnibus mandate, symbolizing order and harmony, becomes increasingly anachronistic but also more vital to many as the sole remaining national symbol (Loader and Mulcahy 2003). The British police are likely to move more towards the international pattern of specialist national units for serious crime, terrorism, public order, large-scale fraud, and other national or international problems. Local police providing services to particular communities will remain, but with sharp differences between 'service'-style organizations in stable suburban areas, and 'watchman' bodies with the rump duties of the present police, keeping the lid on underclass crime in symbolic locations.

For those in society who can afford it, provision of security will be increasingly privatized, either in residential areas or in the 'mass private property' sector where more and more middle-class leisure and work takes place (Shearing and Stenning 1983; South 1988; Johnston 1992, 2000; Jones and Newburn 1998; Button 2007). Specialized human policing in any form, however, will become a smaller part of an array of impersonal control processes built into the environment, technological control, and surveillance devices, and the guarding and self-policing activities of ordinary citizens. *The police will be replaced by a pluralized assortment of bodies with policing functions,* and a more diffuse array of policing processes, as discussed above. The extent to which this represents a qualitative transformation to a fundamentally new mode of policing can be debated (Bayley and Shearing 1996; Jones and Newburn 2002; Johnston and Shearing 2002; Reiner 2011: pt I). But the profound changes in social structure, culture, crime, and order in an age of increasing global interdependence and insecurity are bound to have momentous implications for the policing that seeks to regulate them.

## ■ SELECTED FURTHER READING

The most comprehensive coverage of policing issues is in the *Handbook of Policing* edited by Tim Newburn (Cullompton: Willan, 2nd edn, 2008), its accompanying reader, *Policing: Key Readings* (Cullompton: Willan, 2005), and the fourth edition of Robert Reiner's, *The Politics of the Police* (Oxford: Oxford University Press, 2010). Other single authored overviews include N. Fielding, *The Police and Social Conflict*, 2nd edn (London: Glasshouse, 2005); P. A. J. Waddington, *Policing Citizens* (London: UCL Press, 1999), and L. Johnston, *Policing Britain: Risk, Security and Governance* (London: Longman, 2000).

## ■ REFERENCES

ANDERSON, M., DEN BOER, M., CULLEN, P., WILLMORE, W., RAAB, C., and WALKER, N. (1995), *Policing the European Union*, Oxford: Oxford University Press.

ANDREAS, P. AND NADELMANN, E. (2006), *Policing the Globe*, New York: Oxford University Press.

ATKINSON, R. AND FLINT, J. (2004), 'Fortress UK? 'Gated communities, the spatial revolt of the elites and time-space trajectories of segregation', *Housing Studies,* 19(6): 875–892.

BANTON, M. (1964), *The Policeman in the Community*, London: Tavistock.

BAYLEY, D. (1985), *Patterns of Policing*, New Brunswick, N.J.: Rutgers University Press.

—— (1994), *Police For The Future*, New York: Oxford University Press.

—— and SHEARING, C. (1996), 'The Future of Policing', *Law and Society Review*, 30(3): 586–606

—— and —— (2001), *The Worldwide Restructuring of the Police*, Washington DC: National Institute of Justice.

BECKETT, K. (1997), *Making Crime Pay*, New York: Oxford University Press.

BIGO, D. (2000), 'Liaison Officers in Europe: New Officers in the European Security Field', in J. W. E. Sheptycki, *Issues in Transnational Policing*, London: Routledge.

BITTNER, E. (1974), 'Florence Nightingale in Pursuit of Willie Sutton: A Theory of the Police', in H. Jacob (ed.), *The Potential for Reform of Criminal Justice*, Beverly Hills Cal.: Sage.

—— (1970), *The Functions of the Police in Modern Society*, Chevy Chase, Md.: National Institute of Mental Health.

BLAKELY, E. J. and SNYDER, M. G. (1997), *Fortress America: Gated Communities in the United States*, Washington DC: Brookings Institution.

BLUMSTEIN, A. and WALLMAN, J. (2006) (eds), *The Crime Drop in America*, 2nd edn, Cambridge: Cambridge University Press.

BOBBITT, P. (2002), *The Shield of Achilles*, London: Penguin.

BOWLING, B. (1999a), 'The Rise and Fall of New York Murder', *British Journal of Criminology*, 39(4): 531–54.

—— (1999b), *Violent Racism*, Oxford: Oxford University Press.

—— (2008), 'Policing Ethnic Minority Communities', in T. Newburn (ed.), *Handbook of Policing*, Cullompton, Devon: Willan.

BRAGA, A. A., WEISBURD, D., WARING, E. J., MAZEROLLE, L., SPELMAN, W., and GAJEWSKI, F. (1999), 'Problem-oriented policing in violent crime/places: A randomized controlled experiment', *Criminology*, 37(3): 541–80.

BRODEUR, J. -P. (ed.) (1995), *Comparisons in Policing*, Aldershot: Avebury

—— (ed.) (1998), *How to Recognise Good Policing*, Thousand Oaks, Cal.: Sage.

BROGDEN, M. (1982), *The Police: Autonomy and Consent*, London: Academic Press.

—— (1987), 'The Emergence of the Police: The Colonial Dimension', *British Journal of Criminology*, 27(1): 4–14.

—— (1999), 'Community Policing As Cherry Pie', in R. Mawby (ed.), *Policing Across the World*, London: UCL Press.

BROWN, D. (1997), *PACE Ten Years On: A Review of the Research*, Home Office Research Study 155, London: HMSO.

BROWN, J. (1996), 'Police Research: Some Critical Issues', in F. Leishman, B. Loveday, and S. Savage (eds) *Core Issues in Policing*, London: Longman.

BROWN, J. and HORVATH, M. (2010), *Rape: Challenging Contemporary Thinking,* Cullompton: Willan.

—— and HEIDENSOHN, F. (2000), *Gender and Policing: Comparative Perspectives,* London: Macmillan.

BROWN, L. and WILLIS, A. (1985), 'Authoritarianism in British Police Recruits: Importation, Socialisation or Myth?', *Journal of Occupational Psychology,* 58(1): 97–108.

BUCKE, T., STREET, R., and BROWN, D. (2000), *The Right of Silence: The Impact of the CJPO 1994,* Home Office Research Study 199, London: HMSO.

BULLOCK, K. and TILLEY, N. (eds) (2003), *Crime Reduction and Problem-Oriented Policing,* Cullompton, Devon: Willan.

BUTTON, M. (2002), *Private Policing,* Cullompton, Devon: Willan.

—— (2007), *Security Officers and Policing,* Aldershot: Avebury.

CAIN, M. (1973), *Society and the Policeman's Role,* London: Routledge.

CAMERON-WALLER, S. (2008), 'Interpol: a global service provider', in S. D. Brown, *Combating International Crime: The Longer Arm of the Law,* London: Routledge Cavendish.

CAPE, E. and YOUNG, R. (eds) (2008), *Regulating Policing: The Police and Criminal Evidence Act 1984 – Past, Present and Future,* Oxford: Hart.

CASSELS, J. (1994), *The Role and Responsibilities of the Police: Report of an Independent Inquiry,* London: Police Foundation/Policy Studies Institute.

CHAN, J. (1997), *Changing Police Culture,* Cambridge: Cambridge University Press.

CHOONGH, S. (1997), *Policing as Social Discipline,* Oxford: Oxford University Press.

CLARKE, R. and HOUGH, M. (eds) (1980), *The Effectiveness of Policing,* Farnborough: Gower.

—— and —— (1984), *Crime and Police Effectiveness,* London: Home Office Research Unit.

COLEMAN, R. (2004), *Reclaiming the Streets,* Cullompton, Devon: Willan.

CRAWFORD, A. (2003), 'The Pattern of Policing in the UK: Policing Beyond the Police', in T. Newburn, *Handbook of Policing,* Cullompton, Devon: Willan.

—— and LISTER, S. (2004), *The Extended Policing Family,* York: Joseph Rowntree Trust.

——, ——, BLACKBURN, S., and BURNETT, J. (2005), *Plural Policing: The Mixed Economy of Visible Patrols in England and Wales,* Bristol: Policy Press.

CUTLER, A. C. (2010), 'The legitimacy of private transnational governance: experts and the transnational market for force', *Socio-Economic Review,* 8(1): 157–85.

DALGLEISH, D. and MYHILL, A. (2004), *Reassuring the Public: A review of international policing interventions,* London: Home Office.

DEFLEM, M. (2002), *Policing World Society: Historical Foundations of International Police Co-operation,* Oxford: Clarendon Press.

DELSOL, R. and SHINER, M. (2006), 'Regulating Stop and Search: A Challenge for Police and Community

Relations in England and Wales', *Critical Criminology,* 14: 241–63.

DEN BOER, M. and MONAR, J. (2002), '11 September and the Challenge of Global Terrorism to the EU as a Security Actor', *Journal of Common Market Studies,* 40(1): 11–28.

DHANI, A. AND KAIZA, P. (2011), *Police Service Strength England and Wales,* 31 March 2011, Home Office Statistical Bulletin, 13/11.

DIXON, B. and SMITH, G. (1998), 'Laying Down the Law: The Police, The Courts and Legal Accountability', *International Journal of the Sociology of Law,* 26: 419–35.

DIXON, D, (1997), *Law in Policing,* Oxford: Oxford University Press.

DORN, N. and LEVI, M. (2007), 'European Private Security, Corporate Investigation and Military Services: Collective Security, Market Regulation and Structuring the Public Sphere', *Policing and Society,* 17(3): 213–38.

DUBBER, M. (2005), *The Police Power,* New York: Columbia University Press.

DUBOIS, D. (2002), 'The attacks of 11 September: EU-US cooperation against terrorism in the field of justice and home affairs', *European Foreign Affairs Review,* 7: 317–35.

ECK, J. (2006), 'Science, values and problem-oriented policing: why problem-oriented policing?', in D. Weisburd and A. A. Braga (eds), *Police Innovation: Contrasting Perspectives,* Cambridge: Cambridge University Press.

—— and SPELMAN, W. (1987), 'Who ya gonna call? The police as problem-busters', *Crime and Delinquency* January, 31–52.

EDWARDS, A. and GILL, P. (2003), *Transnational Organised Crime,* London: Routledge.

EMSLEY, C. (2008), 'The Birth and Development of the Police', in T. Newburn (ed.), *Handbook of Policing* Cullompton, Devon: Willan.

—— (2009), *The Great British Bobby,* London: Quercus.

ERICSON, R. and HAGGERTY, K. (1997), *Policing Risk Society,* Oxford: Oxford University Press.

EVERSON, S. and PEASE, K. (2001), 'Crime against the same person and place: detection, opportunity and offender targeting', in G. Farrell and K. Pease (eds), *Repeat Victimization: Crime Prevention Studies Series 12,* Monsey, N.Y.: Criminal Justice Press.

FARRELL, G. and PEASE, K. (eds) (2001), *Repeat Victimization: Crime Prevention Studies Series 12,* Monsey, N.Y.: Criminal Justice Press.

FELDMAN, D. (1990), 'Regulating Treatment of Suspects in Police Stations: Judicial Interpretation of Detention Provisions in the Police and Criminal Evidence Act 1984', *Criminal Law Review,* 452–571.

FIELDING, N. (1988), *Joining Forces,* London: Routledge.

—— (2005), *The Police and Social Conflict,* 2nd edn, London: Glasshouse.

FITZGERALD, M. (1999), *Searches in London Under Section 1 of the Police and Criminal Evidence Act,* London: Metropolitan Police.

FOSTER, J. (1989), 'Two Stations: An Ethnographic Analysis of Policing in the Inner City', in D. Downes (ed.), *Crime and the City*, London: Macmillan.

—— (2003), 'Police Cultures', in T. Newburn (ed.), *Handbook of Policing*, Cullompton, Devon: Willan.

——, NEWBURN, T., and SOUHAMI, A. (2005), *Assessing the Impact of the Stephen Lawrence Enquiry*, London: Home Office.

FYFE, N. R. and BANNISTER, J. (1996), 'City watching: closed circuit television in public spaces', *Area*, 28(1): 37–46.

GOLDSMITH, A. and LEWIS, C. (2000), *Civilian Oversight of Policing*, Oxford: Hart.

GOLDSTEIN, H. (1990), *Problem-Oriented Policing*, New York: McGraw Hill.

GOLDSTEIN, J. (1960), 'Police Discretion Not To Invoke the Criminal Process: Low Visibility Decisions in the Administration of Justice', *Yale Law Journal*, 69, March: 543–94.

GRAEF, R. (1989), *Talking Blues*, London: Collins.

GREENE, J. (2000), 'Community Policing in America', in J. Horney (ed.), *Criminal Justice 2000 Vol. 3: Policies, Processes and Decisions of the Criminal Justice System*, Washington, DC: National Institute of Justice.

GRIMSHAW, R. and JEFFERSON, T. (1987), *Interpreting Policework*, London: Unwin.

HAIN, P. (ed.) (1979), *Policing the Police*, London: Calder.

—— (ed.) (1980), *Policing the Police 2*, London: Calder.

HALL, S., CRITCHER, C., JEFFERSON, T., CLARKE, J., and ROBERTS, B. (1978), *Policing the Crisis*, London: Macmillan.

HARCOURT, B. (2001), *Illusion of Order: The False Promise of Broken Windows Policing*, Cambridge, Mass.: Harvard University Press.

HEIDENSOHN, F. (1985), *Women and Crime*, London: Macmillan.

—— (1992), *Women in Control? The Role of Women in Law Enforcement*, Oxford: Oxford University Press.

—— (2008), 'Gender and Policing', in T. Newburn (ed.), *Handbook of Policing*, Cullompton, Devon: Willan.

HENRY, A. and SMITH, D. J. (eds), *Transformations of Policing*, Aldershot: Ashgate.

HER MAJESTY'S INSPECTORATE OF CONSTABULARY (2004), *Modernising the Police Service*, London: HMIC.

—— (2005), *Closing the Gap*, London: HMIC.

HOBBS, D. (1988), *Doing the Business: Entrepreneurship, The Working Class and detectives in the East End of London*, Oxford: Oxford University Press.

—— (1998), 'Going down the Glocal: the local context of organized crime', *Howard Journal of Criminal Justice*, 37(4): 407–22.

HOLDAWAY, S. (ed.) (1979), *The British Police*, London: Edward Arnold.

—— (1983), *Inside the British Police*, Oxford: Blackwell.

—— (2009) *Black Police Associations*, Oxford: Oxford University Press.

HOME OFFICE (1993), *Police Reform White Paper*, London: Home Office.

—— (2001), *Secure Borders, Safe Haven: Integration with diversity in modern Britain*, London: Home Office.

—— (2005), *Neighbourhood Policing—Your Police, Your Community, Our Commitment*, London: Home Office.

—— (2006), *Citizen Focus: Good Practice Guide*, London: Home Office.

—— (2011), *Law enforcement agencies including the police*, UK Border Agency, HM Revenue & Customs, Cm 8097, London: Home Office.

HOUSE OF COMMONS (1990), *Practical Police Cooperation in the European Community*, Home Affairs Committee (7th Report), Session 1989–90, London: HMSO.

HOYLE, C. (1998), *Negotiating Domestic Violence: Police, Criminal Justice and Victims*, Oxford: Oxford University Press.

HUTTER, B. (1988), *The Reasonable Arm of the Law? Law Enforcement Procedures of Environmental Health Officers*, Oxford: Oxford University Press.

IANNI, E. R. and IANNI, F. (1983), 'Street Cops and Management Cops: The Two Cultures of Policing', in M. Punch (ed.), *Control in the Police Organisation*, Cambridge, Mass.: MIT Press.

INNES, M. (2003), *Investigating Murder: Detective Work and The Police Response to Criminal Homicide*, Oxford: Oxford University Press.

—— (ed.) (2006), 'Reassurance and the "New" Community Policing', Special Issue, *Policing and Society*, 16(2).

—— (2007), 'Investigation and Major Crime Enquiries', in T. Newburn, T. Williamson, and A Wright (eds), *Handbook of Criminal Investigation*, Cullompton: Willan.

—— and FIELDING, N. (2002), 'From Community to Communication Policing: "Signal Crimes" and the Problem of Public Reassurance', *Sociological Research Online*, 7(2)

JOHNSTON, L. (1992), *The Rebirth of Private Policing*, London: Routledge.

—— (2000), *Policing Britain*, London: Longman.

—— (2006), 'Transnational security governance', in J. Wood and B. Dupont (eds), *Democracy, Society and the Governance of Security*, Cambridge: Cambridge University Press.

—— and SHEARING, C. (2002), *Governing Security*, London: Routledge.

JONES, S. and LEVI, M. (1983), 'The Police and the Majority: The Neglect of the Obvious', *Police Journal*, 56(4): 351–64.

JONES, T. and NEWBURN, T. (1998), *Private Security and Public Policing*, Oxford: Oxford University Press.

—— and —— (1999), 'Urban Change and Policing: Mass Private Property Reconsidered', *European Journal of Criminal Policy and Research*, 7(2): 225–44.

—— and —— (2002), 'The Transformation of Policing? Understanding Current Trends in Policing Systems', *British Journal of Criminology*, 42(1): 129–46.

—— and —— (2006a), 'Understanding plural policing', in T. Jones and T. Newburn (eds), *Plural Policing: A Comparative Perspective*, London: Routledge.

—— and —— (2006b), 'The United Kingdom', in T. Jones and T. Newburn (eds), *Plural Policing: A Comparative Perspective*, London: Routledge.

—— and —— (2007), *Policy Transfer and Criminal Justice*, Buckingham: Open University.

——, ——, and SMITH, D. (1994), *Democracy and Policing*, London: Policy Studies Institute.

——, VAN STEDEN, R., and BOUTELLIER, H. (2009), 'Pluralisation of policing in England & Wales and the Netherlands: exploring similarity and difference', *Policing and Society*, 19(3): 282–99.

KARMEN, A. (2000), *New York Murder Mystery*, New York: New York University Press.

KELLING, G. *et al.* (1974), *The Kansas City Preventive Patrol Experiment*, Washington, DC: Police Foundation.

KEYNOTE REPORT (2004), *The Security Industry: Industry Report*, September 2004 (see also www.keynote.co.uk).

KLOCKARS, C. (1988), 'The Rhetoric of Community Policing', in J. R. Greene and S. D. Mastrofski (eds), *Community Policing: Rhetoric or Reality?*, New York: Praeger.

LAVRANOS, N. (2003), 'Europol and the fight against terrorism', *European Foreign Affairs Review*, 8: 259–75.

LAW COMMISSION OF CANADA (2006), *In Search of Security: The Future of Policing in Canada*, Ottawa: Minister of Public Works and Government Services.

LEE, J. A. (1981), 'Some Structural aspects of Police Deviance in Relations With Minority Groups', in C. Shearing (ed.), *Organisational Police Deviance*, Toronto: Butterworth.

LEISHMAN, F. and MASON, P. (2003), *Policing and the Media*, Cullompton, Devon: Willan.

LEVI, M. (2003), 'Organised and Financial Crime', in T. Newburn (ed.), *Handbook of Policing*, Cullompton, Devon: Willan.

LING, C. W. (2010), 'Mapping Interpol's Evolution: Functional Expansion and the Move to Legalization', *Policing*, 28–37.

LOADER, I. (1999), 'Consumer Culture and the Commodification of Policing and Security', *Sociology*, 33(2): 373–92.

—— and MULCAHY, A. (2003), *Policing and the Condition of England*, Oxford: Oxford University Press.

—— and WALKER, N. (2006), 'Necessary virtues: the legitimate place of the state in the governance of security', in J. Wood and B. Dupont (eds), *Democracy, Society and the Governance of Security*, Cambridge: Cambridge University Press.

LOFTUS, B. (2008), 'Dominant Culture Interrupted: Recognition, Resentment and the Politics of Change in an English Police Force', *British Journal of Criminology*, 48/6: 778–797.

—— (2009), *Police Culture in a Changing World*, Oxford: Oxford University Press.

—— (2010), 'Police Occupational Culture: Classic Themes, Altered Times', *Policing and Society*, 20(1): 1–22.

LUSTGARTEN, L. (1986), *The Governance of the Police*, London: Sweet & Maxwell.

LYON, D. (2001), *Surveillance Society*, Maidenhead: Open University Press.

MCBARNET, D. (1978), 'The Police and the State', in G. Littlejohn, B. Smart, J. Wakeford, and N. Yuval-Davis (eds), *Power and the State*, London: Croom Helm.

—— (1979), 'Arrest: The Legal Context of Policing', in S. Holdaway (ed.), *The British Police*, London: Edward Arnold.

MCCAHILL, M. and NORRIS, C. (2002), 'CCTV in Britain', Urban Eye Working Paper No.3. www.urbaneye.net/results/ue_wp3.pdf.

MCCONVILLE, M., SANDERS, A., and LENG, R. (1991), *The Case for the Prosecution: Police Suspects and the Construction of Criminality*, London: Routledge.

MCEVOY, K., GORMALLY, B., and MIKA, H. (2002), 'Conflict, crime control and the "re"-constitution of state-community relations in Northern Ireland', in G. Hughes, E. McLaughlin, and J. Muncie (eds), *Crime Prevention and Community Safety: New Directions*, London: Sage.

MCLAUGHLIN, E. (1992), 'The Democratic Deficit: European Unity and the Accountability of the British Police', *British Journal of Criminology*, 32(4): 473–87.

—— (2007), *The New Policing*, London: Sage.

MAGUIRE, E. and WELLS, W. (eds) (2009), *Implementing Community Policing: Lessons from 12 Agencies*, Washington DC: Department of Justice/Community Oriented Policing Services.

MAGUIRE, M. (2000), 'Policing By Risks And Targets: Some Dimensions and Implications of Intelligence-led Crime Control', *Policing and Society*, 9: 315–36.

—— (2008), 'Criminal Investigation and Crime Control', in T. Newburn, *Handbook of Policing*, Cullompton, Devon: Willan.

MANNING, P. K. (2000), 'Policing new social spaces', in Sheptycki, J. W. E. (ed.), *Issues in Transnational Policing*, London: Routledge.

MARENIN, O. (1983), 'Parking Tickets and Class Repression: The Concept of Policing in Critical Theories of Criminal Justice', *Contemporary Crises*, 6(2): 241–66.

MARK, R. (1978), *In the Office of Constable*, London: Collins.

MARSHALL, G. (1978), 'Police Accountability Revisited', in D. Butler and A. H. Halsey (eds), *Policy and Politics*, London: Macmillan.

MASTROFSKI, S. (2006), 'Community policing: A sceptical view', in D. Weisburd and A. A. Braga (eds), *Police Innovation: Contrasting Perspectives*, Cambridge: Cambridge University Press.

MATASSA, M. and NEWBURN, T. (2003), 'Policing and Terrorism', in T. Newburn (ed.), *Handbook of Policing*, Cullompton, Devon: Willan.

MAWBY, R. I. (1991), *Comparative Policing Issues*, London: Unwin.

—— (2003), 'Models of Policing', in T. Newburn (ed.), *Handbook of Policing*, Cullompton, Devon: Willan.

—— and WRIGHT, A. (2003), 'The Police Organisation', in T. Newburn (ed.), *Handbook of Policing*, Cullompton, Devon: Willan.

MILIBAND, R. (1978), 'A State of Desubordination', *British Journal of Sociology*, 29(4): 399–409.

MILLER, W. (1977), *Cops and Bobbies*, Chicago: Chicago University Press.

MOORE, M. (1992), 'Problem-Solving and Community Policing', in M. Tonry and N. Morris (eds), *Modern Policing*, Chicago: Chicago University Press.

MORGAN, R. and NEWBURN, T. (1997), *The Future of Policing*, Oxford: Oxford University Press.

MUIR, W. K. (1977), *The Police: Streetcorner Politicians*, Chicago: Chicago University Press.

MULCAHY, A. (2006), *Policing Northern Ireland: Conflict, legitimacy and reform*, Cullompton, Devon: Willan.

NADELMANN, E. (1993), *Cops Across Borders: The internationalization of U.S. criminal law enforcement*, University Park, Pa.: Penn State Press.

NEOCLEOUS, M. (2000), *The Fabrication of Social Order*, London: Pluto.

NEWBURN, T. (ed.) (2008), *Handbook of Policing*, 2nd edn, Cullompton, Devon: Willan.

—— (ed.) (2005), *Policing: Key Readings*. Cullompton, Devon: Willan.

—— (2012), 'Police and crime commissioners: The Americanization of policing or a very British reform?', *International Journal of Law, Crime and Justice*, forthcoming.

—— and JONES, T. (1996), 'Police Accountability', in W. Saulsbury, J. Mott, and T. Newburn (eds), *Themes in Contemporary Policing*, London: Police Foundation: Policy Studies Institute.

—— and SPARKS, R. (eds) (2004), *Criminal Justice and Political Cultures*, Cullompton, Devon: Willan.

NEYROUD, P. (2001), *Public Participation in Policing*, London: Institute for Public Policy Research.

—— (2010), 'Protecting the frontline: a recessionary dilemma, *Policing*, 44(1): 1–3.

—— and BECKLEY, A. (2001), *Policing, Ethics and Human Rights*, Cullompton, Devon: Willan.

NORRIS, C., MCCAHILL, M., and WOOD, D. (2004), 'The growth of CCTV: a global perspective on the international diffusion of video surveillance in publicly accessible space', *Surveillance and Society*, 2(2/3): 111–35.

O'NEILL, M., MARKS, M., and SINGH, A-M. (eds) (2007), *Police Occupational Cultures*, Oxford: JAI.

PACKER, H. (1968), *The Limits of the Criminal Sanction*, Stanford, Cal.: Stanford University Press and Oxford University Press.

PATE, A. M. and SKOGAN, W. G. (1985), *Coordinated community policing: The Newark experience. Technical report*, Washington, DC: Police Foundation.

PATTEN, C. (1999), *A New Beginning: Policing Northern Ireland*, The Report of the Independent Commission on Policing For Northern Ireland, Norwich: HMSO.

POSEN, I. (1995), *Review of Police Core and Ancillary Tasks*, London: HMSO.

PUNCH, M. (1979), 'The Secret Social Service', in S. Holdaway (ed.), *The British Police*, London: Edward: Arnold.

—— (1983), 'Officers and Men', in M. Punch (ed.), *Control in the Police Organisation*, Cambridge, Mass.: MIT Press.

QUINTON, P., BLAND, N., and MILLER, J. (2000), Police Stops, Decision-Making and Practice, *Police Research Paper 130*, London: Home Office.

RAWLINGS, P. (2008), 'Policing before the Police', in T. Newburn (ed.), *Handbook of Policing*, Cullompton, Devon: Willan.

READ, T. and TILLEY, N. (2000), *Not Rocket Science: Problem-solving and Crime Reduction*, Crime Reduction Series Paper No. 6, London: Home Office.

REINER, R. (1978), *The Blue-Coated Worker*, Cambridge: Cambridge University Press.

—— (1991), *Chief Constables*, Oxford: Oxford University Press.

—— (1993), 'Race, Crime and Justice: Models of Interpretation', in L. Gelsthorpe and W. McWilliams (eds), *Minority Ethnic Groups and the Criminal Justice System*, Cambridge: Institute of Criminology.

—— (2007), *Law and Order: An Honest Citizen's Guide to Crime and Control*, Cambridge: Polity

—— (2010), *The Politics of the Police*, 4th edn, Oxford: Oxford University Press.

—— (2011), *Policing, Popular Culture and Political Economy: Towards a Social Democratic Criminology*, London: Ashgate.

—— and LEIGH, L. (1992), 'Police Power', in G. Chambers and C. McCrudden (eds), *Individual Rights in the UK Since 1945*, Oxford: Oxford University Press/Law Society.

—— and NEWBURN, T. (2007), 'Police Research', in R. King and E. Wincup (eds), *Doing Research on Crime and Justice*, 2nd edn, Oxford: Oxford University Press.

—— and SPENCER, S. (eds) (1993), *Accountable Policing: Effectiveness, Empowerment and Equity*, London: Institute for Public Policy Research.

REITH, C. (1956), *A New Study of Police History*, London: Oliver and Boyd.

ROBINSON, C. D. (1979), 'Ideology As History', *Police Studies*, 2(2): 35–49.

—— and SCAGLION, R. (1987), 'The Origin and Evolution of the Police Function in Society', *Law and Society Review*, 21(1): 109–53.

ROCHE, S. (2002), 'Towards a new governance of crime and insecurity in France', in A. Crawford (ed.), *Crime and Insecurity: The governance of safety in Europe*, Cullompton, Devon: Willan.

ROWE, M. (2004), *Policing, Race and Racism* Cullompton: Willan.

—— (ed.) 2007), *Policing Beyond Macpherson* Cullompton: Willan.

ROYAL COMMISSION ON CRIMINAL JUSTICE (1993), *Report*, Cm. 2263, London: HMSO.

ROYAL COMMISSION ON THE POLICE (1962), *Final Report*, Cmnd. 1728, London: HMSO.

SANDERS, A. and YOUNG, R. (2008), 'Police Powers', in T. Newburn (ed.), *Handbook of Policing*, Cullompton, Devon: Willan.

SAVAGE, S. (2007), *Police Reform*, Oxford: Oxford University Press.

SCARMAN, LORD (1981), *The Brixton Disorders*, Cmnd. 8427, London: HMSO.

SCOTT, M. (2000), *Problem-oriented Policing: Reflections on the First 20 Years*, Washington, DC: Department of Justice.

SCRATON, P. (1985), *The State of the Police*, London: Pluto.

SHEARING, C. (1996), 'Reinventing Policing: Policing as Governance', in O. Marenin (ed.), *Policing Change, Changing Police*, New York: Garland.

—— and ERICSON, R. (1991), 'Culture As Figurative Action', *British Journal of Sociology*, 42: 481–506.

—— and STENNING, P. (1981), 'Modern Private Security: Its Growth and Implication', in M. Tonry and N. Morris (eds), *Crime and Justice 3*, Chicago: Chicago University Press.

——and—— (1983), 'Private Security: Implications for Social Control', *Social Problems*, 30(5): 493–506.

SHEEHY, P. (1993), *Inquiry Into Police Responsibilities and Rewards*, London: Home Office (the Sheehy Report).

SHEPTYCKI, J. (ed.) (2000a), *Issues in Transnational Policing*, London: Routledge.

—— (2000b), 'Policing the virtual launderette: money laundering and global governance', in J. Sheptycki (ed.), *Issues in Transnational Policing*, London: Routledge.

SHERMAN, L. W. (1990), 'Police crackdowns: Initial and residual deterrence', in M. Tonry and N. Morris (eds), *Crime and justice: A review of research*, Vol. 12, Chicago: University of Chicago Press.

—— and WEISBURD, D. (1995), 'General deterrent effects of police patrol in crime "hot spots": A randomized, controlled trial', *Justice Quarterly*, 12(4): 625–48.

SILVER, A. (1967), 'The Demand For Order in Civil Society', in D. Bordua (ed.), *The Police*, New York: Wiley.

SINGER, P. W. (2003), *Corporate Warriors, The Rise of the Privatized Military Industry*, Ithaca, N.Y.: Cornell University Press.

SKINNS, L. (2010), *Police custody: governance, legitimacy and reform in the criminal justice process*, Cullompton: Willan.

SKLANSKY, D. (2008), *Democracy and the Police*, Stanford: Stanford University Press.

SKOGAN, W. (2006), 'The promise of community policing', in D. Weisburd and A. A. Braga (eds), *Police Innovation: Contrasting Perspectives*, Cambridge: Cambridge University Press.

—— (2009), 'An overview of community policing: Origins, concepts and implementation', in T. Williamson (ed.), *The Handbook of Knowledge-Based Policing*, Chichester: Wiley.

—— and FRYDL, K. (eds) (2004), *Fairness and Effectiveness in Policing: The Evidence*, Washington, D. C., National Research Council: National Academies Press.

—— and HARTNETT, S. (1997), *Community Policing, Chicago Style*, New York: Oxford University Press.

SKOLNICK, J. (1966), *Justice Without Trial*, New York: Wiley.

—— and BAYLEY, D. (1986), *The New Blue Line*, New York: Free Press.

—— and —— (1988), *Community Policing: Issues and Practices Around the World*, Washington, DC: National Institute of Justice.

SMITH, D., GRAY, J., and SMALL, S. (1983), *Police and People in London*, London: Policy Studies Institute.

SMITH, G. (2009), 'Why Don't More People Complain Against the Police?', *European Journal of Criminology*, 6(3): 249–66.

SOUTH, N. (1988), *Policing For Profit*, London: Sage.

SPITZER, S. and SCULL, A. (1977), 'Social Control in Historical Perspective', in D. Greenberg (ed.), *Corrections and Punishment*, Beverly Hills Cal.: Sage.

STINCHCOMBE, A. (1963), 'Institutions of Privacy in the Determination of Police Administrative Practice', *American Journal of Sociology*, 69(2): 150–60.

STORCH, R. (1975), 'The Plague of Blue Locusts: Police reform and Popular resistance in northern England 1840–1857', *International Review of Social History*, 20(1): 61–90.

—— (1976), 'The Policeman as Domestic Missionary', *Journal of Social History*, 9(4): 481–509.

SYDNEY-SMITH, S. (2002), *Beyond Dixon of Dock Green*, London: I.B. Taurus.

TARLETON, A. (2009), 'Factcheck: How many CCTV cameras?', *Significance*, December, 191–2.

TAYLOR, I. (1999), *Crime in Context*, Cambridge: Polity.

——, WALTON, P., and YOUNG, J. (1973), *The New Criminology*, London: Routledge.

TILLEY, N. (2003), 'Community Policing, Problem-Oriented Policing and Intelligence-Led Policing', in T. Newburn (ed.), *Handbook of Policing*, Cullompton, Devon: Willan.

TROJANOWICZ, R. and BUCQUEROUX, B. (1990), *Community Policing*, Cincinnati, Ohio: Anderson Publishing.

TUFFIN, R., MORRIS, J., and POOLE, A. (2006), *An Evaluation of the Impact of the National Reassurance Policing Programme*, London: Home Office.

VAN STEDEN, R. and HUBERTS, L. (2006), 'The Netherlands', in T. Jones and T. Newburn (eds), *Plural Policing: A Comparative Perspective*, London: Routledge.

WADDINGTON, P. A. J. (1999a), *Policing Citizens*, London: UCL Press.

—— (1999b), 'Police (Canteen) Sub-culture: An Appreciation', *British Journal of Criminology*, 39(2): 287–309.

—— and WRIGHT, M. (2008), 'Police Use of Force, Firearms and Riot-Control', in T. Newburn (ed.), *Handbook of Policing*, Cullompton, Devon: Willan.

—— , STENSON, K., and DON, D. (2004), 'In Proportion: Race and Police Stop and Search', *British Journal of Criminology*, 44(6): 889–914.

WAKEFIELD, A. (2003), *Selling Security*, Cullompton, Devon: Willan.

WALKER, N. (2000), *Policing in a Changing Constitutional Order*, London: Sweet & Maxwell.

—— (2003), 'The Pattern of Transnational Policing', in T. Newburn (ed.), *Handbook of Policing*, Cullompton, Devon: Willan.

WALL, D. (1998), The Chief Constables of England and Wales, Aldershot: Avebury.

WEINBERGER, B. (1995), *The Best Police in the World*, London: Scolar.

WEISBURD, D. and ECK, J. E. (2004), 'What can the police do to reduce crime, disorder and fear?', *The Annals*, 593, (May): 42–65.

—— , TELEP, C., HINKLE, J., and ECK, J. (2010), 'Is problem-oriented policing effective in reducing crime and disorder?', *Criminology and Public Policy*, 9(1): 139–72.

WESTLEY, W. (1970), *Violence and the Police*, Cambridge, Mass.: MIT Press.

WESTMARLAND, L. (2001), *Gender and Policing: Sex, Power and Police Culture*, Cullompton: Willan.

WILLIAMS, J. W. (2005), 'Reflections of the private versus public policing of economic crime', *British Journal of Criminology*, 45(3): 316–39.

WILSON, J. Q. (1968), *Varieties of Police Behaviour*, Cambridge, Mass.: Harvard University Press.

—— and KELLING, G. (1982), 'Broken Windows', *Atlantic Monthly*, 249(3): 29–42.

WOOD, J. AND DUPONT, B. (eds) (2006), *Democracy, Society and the Governance of Security*, Cambridge: Cambridge University Press.

YOUNG, J. (1999), *The Exclusive Society*, London: Sage.

YOUNG, M. (1991), *An Inside Job*, Oxford: Oxford University Press.

—— (1993), *In the Sticks: An Anthropologist in a Shire Force*, Oxford: Oxford University Press.

ZEDNER, L. (2006), 'Policing Before the Police', *British Journal of Criminology*, 46(1): 78–96.

ZIMRING, F. (2011), *How New York beat crime, Scientific American*, August, 75–9.

# 28

# FROM SUSPECT TO TRIAL

*Andrew Sanders and Richard Young*

This chapter looks at the use of legal powers in the criminal justice system of England and Wales. The principles underlying different criminal justice systems vary according to history, culture, and ideology. The adversary principle underpins the English system, other common law systems such as those of Australia, Canada, and the United States, and 'hybrid' systems such as in Scotland. Thus, much of what follows draws upon what we know of, and applies to, these other systems, although the focus is domestic.

We examine various models of criminal justice, police decisions 'on the street', aspects of police station detention, decisions to prosecute and caution, and the pre-trial process. Although we do not look at trials as such, most cases end in guilty pleas or (less frequently) are dropped by the Crown Prosecution Service (CPS). We contrast the police with other enforcement agencies, and compare the 'law in the books' with what really happens. While space constraints require us to present 'the police' as if it was a unitary or fairly homogenous body, much of what we say would require some modification when applied to specialist agencies or squads such as Special Branch (on which see Lowe 2011). Sentencing and the enforcement of penalties is discussed in Ashworth and Roberts, this volume.

Most police actions and court cases are in all probability unproblematic. Inevitably, though, this chapter highlights the problems—for it is little consolation to someone who is constantly stop-searched, or to an innocent person who is found guilty, that they are unusual and that the system generally works well. Unfortunately we only have space to barely mention appeals and remedies for police malpractice although these are covered in Sanders *et al.* (2010: chs. 11 and 12).

## MODELS OF CRIMINAL JUSTICE

The adversary principle is often characterized as embodying the search for 'proof' rather than 'truth'. The search for 'truth' is usually said to be embodied in 'civil law' systems (such as the French), which are 'inquisitorial'. It would be nice if 'proof' and 'truth' were synonymous and sought with equal vigour. But, using the 'due process' and 'crime control' models developed by Packer (1968), we will see that this is unrealistic. Although in some respects these models are now dated, they remain starting-points for much discussion about criminal justice (e.g. MacDonald 2008; Aviram 2011).

'Due process' values prioritize civil liberties in order to secure the maximal acquittal of the innocent, risking acquittal of many guilty people. 'Crime control' values prioritize the conviction of the guilty, risking the conviction of some (fewer) innocents and infringement of the liberties of some citizens to achieve the system's goals. Due process-based systems tightly control the actions and effects of crime-control agencies, while crime-control-based systems, with their concern for convictions, do not. No system corresponds exactly with either model (just as no system is entirely adversarial or entirely inquisitorial), but in most systems the values of one or the other model appear to predominate.

As soon as the police challenge any individual whom they have any reason to suspect, an adversarial relationship is formed. In Britain, this triggers due process protections, such as the caution against self-incrimination and the usual requirement of 'reasonable' suspicion for the exercise of coercive powers. On arrest the suspect is generally taken to a police station and detained. This triggers further due process protections, such as a right of access to lawyers, as civil liberties are further eroded by detention, interrogation, search of the suspect's home, fingerprinting, and so forth. At the prosecution stage, further evidence is required and further protections are provided: the CPS to vet the case and legal aid to prepare a defence. In order to convict there must be yet more evidence. So, due process requirements become more stringent at each stage, in parallel with the increased coerciveness of suspicion, accusation, and trial. Suspects may be believed to be guilty by the police, and may indeed be guilty 'in truth'. But in the absence of sufficient evidence (i.e. sufficient proof) due process requires that they be exonerated. At the final stage proof need not be absolute, but only 'beyond reasonable doubt'. Legal guilt and actual guilt are therefore not synonymous. Even in a due process system there will occasionally be legally guilty persons who are not 'actually' guilty, and many actually guilty persons who are not legally guilty. This means that all systems will produce some cases like the Birmingham Six, Guildford Four, Cardiff Three, and so forth. Whether or not miscarriages of justice like these are evidence of system failure depends on how often they occur, why they occur, and whether there are adequate systems of review and appeal.

The models differ in the way they seek the truth and their degrees of success. Adversarial systems lack 'transparency' because each side guards 'its' evidence, but inquisitorial systems lack impartiality because too much trust is placed in investigators (Hodgson 2010). Similarly, doubts about police efficiency and propriety on the part of advocates of due process lead them to argue for the process of legal proof; while advocates of crime control argue that court processes and legal protections obstruct truth discovery.

But Packer's models are limited. They do not attempt to prescribe what the goals of the criminal process should be. Ashworth and Redmayne (2010) try to do this by developing a framework of ethical principles derived from the European Convention on Human Rights (ECHR)—which, through the Human Rights Act 1998, is applicable to all areas of UK law. But it creates as many problems as it solves. For example,

Ashworth and Redmayne's principles include rights for victims ('to respect' and 'to compensation') that are major lacunae in Packer's models, but little guidance is provided on how to reconcile these rights with those of suspects and defendants when conflicts occur (Cape 2004). Other rights are reformulations of key due process principles. Many of them are vague, such as 'to be treated fairly and without discrimination' and 'reasonable grounds for arrest and detention'. Those that are precise, such as the 'right of innocent persons not to be convicted', are not absolute, but may be undercut by the kinds of considerations one finds in the crime-control model.

Another promising framework is that of social integration and exclusion. Faulkner (1996) characterizes the 'exclusion' approach as one whereby 'crime is to be prevented by efficiency of detection, certainty of conviction and severity of punishment.... "criminals" are to be seen as an "enemy" to be defeated and humiliated, in a "war" in which the police are seen as the "front line"'. He contrasts this with Locke's view, that 'the end of law is not to abolish or restrain but to preserve and enlarge freedom'. On this inclusionary approach, 'authority will not be respected if it is simply imposed: it has to be accountable and it has to be legitimate... solutions to the problem of crime have to be sought by inclusion within the community itself' (ibid.: 6). This position is compatible with forms of 'restorative justice' that bring together 'stakeholders' in offences (including victims) to try to repair the harm caused by the offender (see Hoyle; Morgan and Newburn, this volume).

One specific inclusionary approach is our own 'freedom model'. It recognizes conflicting values, aims, and interests in the criminal process, such as: convicting the guilty; protecting the innocent from wrongful conviction; protecting human rights by guarding against arbitrary or oppressive treatment; protecting victims; maintaining order; securing public confidence in, and cooperation with, policing and prosecution; and achieving these goals without disproportionate cost and consequent harm to other public services. Whilst politicians often pretend that these goals are all equally achievable, in reality we have to decide which to prioritize.

We do this by making freedom the overriding purpose of the criminal justice system. All the interests and goals of criminal justice in a liberal democracy can be seen as connected to this underlying goal. Prosecution is not a valuable activity in itself: by censuring wrongdoing it should reinforce law-abiding instincts and habits, and the punishment or treatment of offenders aims to reduce their propensity to commit crime. Either way, the freedom of past and potential future victims should be enhanced through having their fear of crime reduced. Similarly we expect prosecutors to respect the rights of suspects and defendants not because protection is a goal in itself but to promote their freedom. And prosecutions are brought as one method of upholding order not because an orderly society is desirable in itself but because a degree of order is needed to enable individuals and communities to pursue their own ends. Whilst the various interests described will still come into conflict, at least under this model we keep in focus the ultimate aim of the system and can opt for compromises that are likely to maximize overall freedom. 'Freedom' is, of course, highly contestable. We use the term loosely in order to concentrate attention on the need for change, and discuss elsewhere what some of those changes should be (e.g. Young and Sanders 2004; Sanders *et al*. 2010; and Sanders 2010).

# POLICE DECISIONS 'ON THE STREET'

The due process origins of our system can be seen in the fact that, in the first decades after the establishment of the modern police in the nineteenth century, sufficient evidence to prosecute was needed before street powers could be exercised. Arrested persons had to be taken directly before the magistrates, who decided whether to prosecute. In theory, then, police investigation had to take place *before* arrest, although in reality many people used to be held by the police without formal arrest (supposedly 'helping the police with their enquiries'). Arrests are now often made to *facilitate* investigation, bringing the formal rules into line with a crime-control reality. Moreover, the police now have stop-search and other street-based powers (for details see Sanders *et al.* 2010: chs 2–3).

The current legal position is now somewhere between the crime-control and due process polarities but heading firmly in the direction of crime control. Stop and search without judicial warrant is allowed for most 'normal' crimes (theft, drugs offences, criminal damage, possession of offensive weapons, etc.), and the Serious Organised Crime and Police Act 2005 abolished the concept of an 'arrestable' (i.e. serious) offence by giving the police the power to arrest for *any* offence (again, without judicial warrant). Most of these powers require 'reasonable suspicion' of a specific offence. The Code of Practice on stop and search (Code A) issued by the Home Office to accompany the Police and Criminal Evidence Act 1984 (PACE) states that this must have 'an objective basis', adding: '[r]easonable suspicion can never be supported on the basis of personal factors. It must rely on intelligence or information about, or some specific behaviour by, the person concerned' (paragraph 2.2). The Code has been tightened up in successive editions since 1984 in an attempt to deal with the problem of the police stereotyping some types of people (especially young ethnic minority males) as pre-disposed to engage in crime, but the problem remains that the police have a wide latitude in deciding what counts as sufficient 'intelligence' and in interpreting 'specific behaviour' as suspicious. There are now over 1 million PACE stop-searches per annum (Povey *et al.* 2011: 33).

Under section 60 of the Criminal Justice and Public Order Act 1994 officers can stop-search for weapons in areas designated by an inspector, and section 44 of the Terrorism Act 2000 allows stop-search in relation to suspected terrorism. In 2009/10 there were 118,446 section 60 special weapons searches and 91,568 section 44 searches (Povey *et al.* 2011: 33). These powers can be exercised without reasonable suspicion. It emerged in *Gillan & Anr v Commissioner of Police of the Metropolis & Anr* [2004] EWCA Civ 1067 that rolling (successive) authorizations allowing section 44 searches over the whole of London had been made by the police and approved by the Home Secretary since section 44 came into force. The UK courts saw nothing wrong with this but the European Court of Human Rights subsequently ruled that section 44 searches breached Article 8 of the European Convention on Human Rights, in part because the powers of authorization and confirmation, as well as the powers of stop-search themselves, were 'neither sufficiently circumscribed nor subject to adequate legal safeguards against abuse' (*Gillan and Quinton v the UK* (4158/05) [2010] ECHR 28 [87]). The Coalition Government elected in 2010 accordingly directed police forces not to use section 44. A 'remedial order' substitutes a more restricted power pending statutory reform through clause 60 of the Protection of Freedoms Bill (Povey *et al.* 2011: 39). This power will still allow searches by individual officers who lack reasonable suspicion so both these and special weapons searches will continue to reflect crime control values.

Another form of police street power is the 'penalty notice for disorder' (PND) introduced by the Criminal Justice and Police Act 2001. This extends the idea of fixed penalty notices for motoring offences to some fairly serious non-motoring offences (e.g. public order offences, criminal damage, possession of cannabis, and theft). Most fixed penalties are for £80. There is no prosecution, and no conviction is recorded, if it is paid within 21 days. The person fined can request that the matter be prosecuted as a normal charge, but this may result in a criminal conviction and higher penalty, so only 1 in a 100 persons challenges their PND. 86,076 PNDs were issued in 2010–11 (less than 10 per cent of all cases prosecuted or diverted) a drop in their use from a high in 2007/9 of over 129,018 per annum (Taylor and Chaplin 2011: Table 3). While the PND scheme does not serve the crime control goal of maximizing convictions directly, it is aligned with such crime control stances as maximizing efficiency, reducing the opportunities for challenge, and trusting the police to distinguish between the innocent and guilty fairly. It is, in short, a further step away from court-based adversarial justice towards police-imposed summary justice (Young 2008; and Padfield, Morgan, and Maguire, this volume).

### DISCRETION

Discretion is at the root of criminal justice practice. Police officers necessarily exercise discretion in deciding whether to issue a PND, stop and search or arrest. Some people look less 'suspicious' than others, and possible offences have to be prioritized. Arrest is less frequent than informal action even for relatively serious violence (Paradine and Wilkinson 2004). Similarly, when officers are able to be proactive (as compared to their usual reactive mode) they have to use discretion about the offences or offenders in which to invest scarce time. Discretion is also created as a consequence of the way offences are defined. Most offences require *mens rea* (a 'guilty mind') that, broadly, amounts to intent or advertent recklessness. Thus knocking someone to the ground would be a crime if done deliberately, but not if done accidentally or in self-defence. Since *mens rea* is so difficult to assess, officers have ample scope to arrest or not according to their preference. Moreover, the definition of many offences, particularly in the realms of public order and terrorism, are inherently vague and broad. So, PND, stop and search and arrest decisions are constrained only loosely by law.

Discretion is structured by 'cop culture' (see Loftus 2009). Its elements of sexism and racism, and its stereotyping of people and groups of certain types (on 'rough' estates, with certain lifestyles, etc.) affect the way officers view society. Take the Code of Practice's reference (para. 2.3) to 'specific behaviour' such as 'obviously trying to hide something'. To many marginalized youths spending much of their lives on the street, hooded clothing may be a fashion choice or simply a way of keeping warm. To police officers, 'hoodies' may be perceived as 'obviously trying to hide something', particularly following the English riots of August 2011 in which many looters wore hooded clothing in an attempt to mask their identity. Police officers are not representative of the population. They tend to be disproportionately white, male, and conservative. The homogeneity of this group, coupled with police training and socialization processes, enables 'cop culture' to be easily reproduced (Reiner 2010: esp ch. 4).

## PATTERNS OF BIAS AND POLICE WORKING RULES

Research prior to the implementation of PACE in the mid-1980s found that the weak constraints imposed on discretion by law allowed huge bias in policing. Stops were often based on classic stereotypes leading to patterns of bias on lines of class, gender, and race (see Sanders *et al.* 2010: ch. 2 for details). PACE was intended to make some difference. For although PACE gave more, not less, power to the police, it also incorporated more controls than before. These include requirements to tell suspects why they are being arrested or stop-searched and to make records of the incident. However, stop and search and arrest decisions are of intrinsically low visibility. Widespread use of mobile phone cameras and the sharing of images of police deviance across the Internet (Goldsmith 2010) may expose examples of excessive force (as in the death of Ian Tomlinson at the G20 protest in 2009), but this cannot expose systematic low-level malpractice. Thus written records can be constructed after the event. As one officer put it to McConville *et al.* (1991), he would stop a suspect 'instinctively and then think about how he would satisfy a disinterested third party' (field notes).

This suggests improvements in the way officers *account* for their exercise of discretion, but not in how they *actually* exercise it. Thus formulaic wording is routinely used to cloak stop-searches in apparent legality (Fitzgerald 1999). It is hardly realistic to expect an officer to record on his stop-search form that his reason for exercising a power was that he had come across a 'Rastafarian out at night', or 'because he's a fucking paki' (BBC 2003) yet we know that such reasoning does take place (see below). On the other hand, at least the requirement to record has the *potential* to focus officers' minds on the limits of their legal powers. However, the reasons for searches sometimes recorded on the forms are so vague (e.g. 'drugs search', 'info received', 'acting furtively': Bland *et al.* 2000: 44) that one doubts the extent to which there has been a genuine shift in police reasoning. Thus recent emphasis on requiring supervisors to scrutinize patrol officers' records and patterns of decision-making more carefully (Code A, para 5.1) is also likely to have limited effect.

In 2008/9 police records showed that a black person was over seven times, and an Asian person over two times, more likely to be stop-searched than a white person (Ministry of Justice 2010). Some researchers argue that when statistics on recorded stops and searches are compared with the population 'available' to be stopped and searched (i.e., those who use public places when and where stops take place) no *general* pattern of bias against those from ethnic minorities is evident (MVA and Miller 2000; cf. Hallsworth 2006: 301–2). However, findings based on *recorded* stop-searches is flawed as both stops and searches are substantially under-recorded (Bland *et al.* 2000; Home Office 2005: 39). In addition, these studies did not examine: whether ethnic minorities suffered more often than did whites from stops and searches that were not legally justified (i.e., no reasonable suspicion); whether the use of stop-search powers resulted in an arrest (i.e., whites may have been less often drawn further into the system); and whether the use of stop-search powers was accompanied by differing degrees of respectful treatment according to the colour of the suspect's skin. Finally, MVA and Miller acknowledge that black and Asian people are over-represented in the stop-search figures relative to their presence in the overall population and that this remains 'an important indicator of the actual experience of different ethnic groups' (2000: 88). Black people, Brown concluded in a review of PACE research, are more likely to be stopped than white people or Asians, more likely to be repeatedly stopped, more likely (if stopped) to be searched, and more likely to be arrested (1997: chs 2 and 4).

Statistics will only ever give senior officers a partial picture, however. This is not just due to the problem of under-recording, or widespread failure to record the ethnicity of those who attract police attention, as happens in the case of PNDs (Young 2010), or abolition of the recording requirement (as has happened in the case of 'simple' stops) but also because statistics can never convey the experience of an abusive or disrespectful encounter with the police. 'It's not what they say, it's how they say it'. Offensive and racist language is particularly resented: 'their exact words were, yeah (and I've got witnesses because I was with two other people, yeah) was: "Don't fuck me about right, and I won't fuck you about, where have you got your drugs?"' (Bland *et al.* 2000: 87, 83). Black people were far less likely than Asian or white people to report any positive experiences of respectful treatment by the police. Despite (or perhaps partly because of) the strongest possible exhortations from the Government for stop-search to be deployed in an 'intelligence-led' way, under which the police are meant to focus on crime 'hot spots' and 'persistent offenders', and despite its angst about racial disproportionality, racial disparities continue to disfigure the criminal justice system, and are getting worse (Ministry of Justice 2010: 9; Miller 2010) because of indirect discrimination (arising through the targeting of 'available' young males), direct prejudice, and even naked racist hostility (BBC 2003).

Stop-search is a crude instrument of crime-control. Although more stops generally lead to more arrests, the proportion of stops that lead to arrest decreases as the number of stops rises. Since 1984 the number of recorded PACE stops has increased tenfold yet the proportion leading to arrest declined from 17 per cent to 9 per cent in 2008/9 (Povey *et al.* 2011). In other words, it is only in a small minority of stop-searches that police suspicions are borne out by evidence on which to base an arrest. Section 44 and section 60 searches are even more 'inefficient', with 0.5 per cent and 2 per cent chances, respectively, of arrests (Povey *et al.* 2011). A low arrest rate is not inconsistent with crime-control goals, however. Stop and search is increasingly used for intelligence gathering and in 'reassurance policing' (i.e. providing highly visible policing to reassure 'the public' that 'law and order' is being maintained):

> In a number of forces stop and search was used as a tool for public reassurance and to prevent people who were seen as creating a public nuisance from gathering in certain places, although there was no reasonable suspicion of a crime (Home Office 2005: 38).

Whether these crime control practices are effective is another matter. Police searches in 1997 probably reduced the number of crimes susceptible to this tactic by just 0.2 per cent (Miller *et al.* 2000: 28), while much 'intelligence gathering' is valueless or even counterproductive in creating a blizzard of information 'that's actually going to make any intelligence picture even harder to understand' (front-line officer quoted in Shiner 2010: 949).

Several 'working rules' structure police decision-making. The first is 'previous' (i.e. being known to the police). As an arresting officer told McConville *et al.*: 'When you get to know an area, and see a villain about at 2.00 a.m. in the morning, you will always stop him to see what he is about' (1991: 24). This focus on the 'usual suspects' (McAra and McVie 2005) also finds expression in police briefings (Quinton *et al.* 2000) and the Government's emphasis on targeting known and persistent offenders (Home Office 2005). The second concerns disorder and police authority. Dealing with disorder is a prime police task. Unless the use of the arrest power would exacerbate disorder (e.g. Hoggett and Stott 2010), the police arrest people who do not cease their disorderly behaviour even when it is trivial (Brown and Ellis 1994). This is in part because of the challenge thereby presented to police authority, even if no specific charge fits the facts or if the offence—such as cannabis possession—is trivial (Warburton *et al.* 2005). Police cautions and PNDs eliminate independent oversight in many of these cases.

Other working rules include consideration of victims and their wishes, 'information received', workload and 'suspiciousness' ('something undefinable': McConville *et al.* 1991: 26–8). Studies carried out in the wake of the Stephen Lawrence Inquiry (Macpherson 1999) have confirmed the continuing purchase of all of these working rules (Quinton *et al.* 2000: 19–52; Loftus 2009).

Changes in formal rules are not always completely ineffective. Studies of domestic violence assessed the impact of Home Office policies that encouraged arrest wherever there was evidence of an offence. Arrests rose significantly as a result, although not to the extent that full compliance would have produced (e.g. Paradine and Wilkinson 2004). The perception by 'cop culture' of domestic assaults as 'rubbish' can, it seems, be *partially* overcome. Police culture is not independent of societal pressures and legal rules. Indeed, Rowe (2007) found that computerized call handling led to full compliance by patrol officers with the pro-arrest policy, even in cases where arrest was seen by them as clearly counterproductive and contrary to the victim's wishes and interests, largely to avoid criticism from supervising officers. It will be harder, however, to change police practice in the direction of *less* frequent use of their power, or more frequent *compliance with safeguards* as can be seen by the minimal impact on street-level policing of the high-profile Macpherson Report (1999) on the reasons for an inadequate police response to the murder of a young black man (see further Shiner 2010; Miller 2010).

## STOP-SEARCH AND ARREST: INCLUSIONARY OR EXCLUSIONARY?

Although arrests usually follow information from, and complaints by, victims or witnesses (despite a revival of proactive policing in the late 1990s) discretion, and the patterns of bias that are reflected by it, still shape the official suspect population. For citizen initiation rarely takes the form of citizen arrest. More usually it is the transmission of often sketchy and sometimes unreliable information to the police (Quinton *et al.* 2000: 31–33). That information has to be sifted, evaluated, and acted upon (or not) by the police. The police record, at most, three-quarters of the crime reported to them (Nicholas *et al.* 2005: 36). In other words, police discretion and the exercise of judgement are still operative even when arrests are citizen-initiated. The same is true of information from informants, on which the police increasingly depend (Maguire and Norris 1992). Information from the public is one resource among many which the police use in exercising discretion on the street according to their own priorities, and so the community is harnessed by the police in an inclusionary way, but only where doing so is consistent with police working rules.

Increases in the formal powers of stop-search, arrest, and disposition (through PNDs), together with the ability of the police to use these powers largely when they want to on the basis of broad intangible suspicion, have led to greater intrusive police activity since PACE was enacted. PND and arrest powers have been increasingly provided for trivial offences that the police use extensively to bolster their authority (Brown and Ellis 1994; Young 2008). Young males, especially from poor and minority sections of the community, bear the brunt of all this power and feel—with some justification—discriminated against (Sharp and Atherton 2007). The consequent social unrest creates a vicious spiral of yet more policing and more unrest (Macpherson 1999)—and that spiral looks set to become still more vicious following the riots in London and elsewhere of August 2011. The police sometimes use arrest powers to stamp their authority on challengers, often without any intention of prosecuting (Choongh 1997; Warburton et al. 2005). In these circumstances, the poor and underprivileged are treated dismissively as part of, and in order to emphasize, their exclusion from normal standards of protection. If our 'freedom' approach underlay the criminal justice system, arrest and stop-search powers would be used very differently and with restraint.

## DETENTION IN THE POLICE STATION

We have seen that in relatively recent times the law moved in a crime-control direction by allowing interference in the liberty of the citizen without sufficient evidence to prosecute. This was initially unplanned, *ad hoc*, and imprecise, giving rise to legal 'fudges' like 'helping police with their enquiries'. The Royal Commission on Criminal Procedure (RCCP) (1981) was therefore urged, on the one hand, to prohibit pre-charge detention (the due process position) and on the other to extend it (the crime-control position). The Royal Commission decided that pre-charge detention should be reduced, and allowed only when it was 'necessary'. In this and other ways the Royal Commission attempted to satisfy both due process and crime-control lobbies, but we shall see in this section that PACE and subsequent legislation has increasingly moved the system in a crime control direction (see Sanders et al. 2010: ch. 1 for a brief recent history).

### DETENTION WITHOUT CHARGE

Anyone at a police station is either free to leave or is under arrest (PACE section 29). If the latter, there are clear time limits on how long a suspect can be held: up to 36 hours; or even 96 hours with the leave of the magistrates (sections 41–44). On arrest, all suspects, except in exceptional cases, should be taken directly to a police station (section 30). It is then for the 'custody officer' (the old station sergeant, with an enhanced role and training) to decide whether or not the suspect should be detained. There are only two grounds for detention: in order to charge or caution (warn) the suspect, or to secure the evidence to charge or caution, but only where detention is *necessary* for that purpose (section 37), and only for as long as it is necessary; senior officers are supposed periodically to review detention to ascertain this.

Although 'independent' custody officers have to complete 'custody sheets' on all suspects that record the particulars of their detention, and so forth, this 'evidence' is written by the police against whom this is supposed to be a protection for suspects—like records of stop and search. It is not surprising to find that 'helping with enquiries' has not been eliminated, detention is hardly ever refused, and detention is continued for as long as investigating officers wish (subject to the time limits in PACE) by custody officers in the same routinized way that it is authorized in the first place (McConville *et al.* 1991; Phillips and Brown 1998).

### ACCESS TO LEGAL ADVICE

The most striking due process aspect of PACE is the provision, under sections 58–59, of free legal advice to all suspects who request it. Information about this unambiguous right has to be provided by the custody officer to the suspect. Advice may be delayed in exceptional cases but not denied outright. Custody records state whether or not suspects were informed of their rights, whether or not suspects requested advice, and what (if anything) happened then. Request rates have risen to around 45 per cent and actual advice rates to around 35 per cent (Pleasance *et al.* 2011). This is a massive increase over the pre-PACE situation, but it is still lower than one might have expected. Why should more than half of suspects reject an entirely free service? Why do so many requests fail?

First, some suspects do not request advice because they are not informed (wholly or partly) of their rights. Secondly, some suspects' requests are denied, ignored, or simply not acted upon, custody records recording only some of these malpractices. This underlines the point made earlier about police-created records. Thirdly, the police often use 'ploys' to attempt to dissuade suspects from seeking advice and to persuade them to cancel their requests. These ploys range from the incomprehensible reading of rights to scare stories, such as 'You'll have to wait in the cells until the solicitor gets here' (Kemp and Balmer 2008; Skinns 2011).

The problem does not lie wholly with the police. Many suspects have negative attitudes towards solicitors (Kemp and Balmer 2008). This is not surprising: advice is frequently provided by telephone, rather than in person; in many cases solicitors do not attend interrogations; and when they do they are usually passive. Legal aid lawyers have a generally non-adversarial stance, at least so far as their actions are concerned (Newman 2011), and take their lead from the police. They routinely allow the police to use overbearing tactics, such that in one notorious case the suspect's lawyer had not objected to intimidation that the Court of Appeal condemned without hesitation (the Cardiff Three case, discussed by Sanders *et al.* 2010: ch. 5). The net result is that the possibility of help from a solicitor is one thing among many that suspects must weigh up when detained. Belatedly, police station legal advice and assistance is now regulated more rigorously, but the effect of this is undermined by changes to the right of silence and several criminal evidence rules (see below). Clause 12 of the Legal Aid and Sentencing Bill 2011, if implemented, will take us another step backwards as it is proposed to means test suspects and provide free advice only to those who cannot afford it.

## POLICE INTERROGATION

Interrogation has assumed ever greater importance in police investigation over the years. Nearly half of all detained suspects are interrogated. In part this is because, as we have seen, investigation now usually takes place after, rather than before, arrest. It is also a product of the *mens rea* requirements of substantive criminal law. It is usually necessary to prove that the suspect intended the offences or was reckless. Since these are features of the suspect's mental state the best evidence is a confession. Even when other ways of securing evidence are available, interrogation often serves as a 'short cut' and produces information about other offences and other offenders (Phillips and Brown 1998: 73). The PACE Code of Practice on Detention and Questioning (Code C) sets out basic standards for interrogation (the provision of proper heating, ventilation, breaks, access to solicitors and others, and so forth), but also states that the police may persist in interrogating non-cooperative or silent suspects (para. 12.5). So, police officers may attempt to persuade suspects to change their minds about speaking and hold them, subject to the time limits, for as long as that takes. Detention is experienced as *coercive* by suspects as, for example, time passes 'exceedingly slowly in the cells' (Newburn and Hayman 2002: 97). Given the importance attached by most suspects to the shortest detention possible (Skinns 2011), and recent changes to the right of silence (see below) the pressures on suspects to speak are considerable (see e.g. Hillyard 1993).

How is evidence of guilt secured? First there are those many suspects who simply and speedily acquiesce, against whom there would often be plenty of evidence anyway. Secondly, many suspects are susceptible to 'deals' (confessions or information in exchange for favours or reduced charges). Suspects are in a relatively weak position in these negotiations—they want to strike deals because of the coercive setting in which they find themselves, and the police use this to their advantage (Dunninghan and Norris 1996). Then there are those who are intimidated by being held against their will in 'police territory' where the environment is deliberately denuded of psychological supports, by being in fear of spending the night in the cells, or by the employment of any number of 'tactics' against them including offering inducements such as bail, keeping suspects off-balance by selective or gradual disclosure of the evidence against them, claiming that there is overwhelming evidence against the suspect, using custodial conditions such as return to the cells, and so forth (see e.g. Cape 2003: 264; Quinn and Jackson 2007; Skinns 2011). The key to understanding this is the nature of the typical police cell: 'The [integral] toilets have no separate seat.... They have no lids and the cells sometimes smell fetid. Toilet paper is provided on request, but in limited amounts because of fears that a detainee will attempt to block the system. There is no hand basin and drinking water has to be requested.' (Newburn and Hayman 2002). Moreover, detainees can be observed whilst going to the toilet. If a tactic does not work in the initial interrogation, 36 hours allows ample time for the suspect to be psychologically 'softened up' for further interrogation.

Extreme tactics (such as violence, or blatant lies about the strength of the evidence against a suspect) are now rare in formal interrogations since they are audio recorded. This gives rise to a fourth way of securing confession: through informal interrogation. The extent of this is controversial but its existence is not. Informal interrogation occurs on the way to the police station (the 'scenic route'), before and after formal interrogations, in the cells under the guise of 'welfare visits', and in police station exercise yards (Dixon 2005; Skinns 2011). It is precisely on confessions allegedly made 'informally' (but not repeated 'formally') that so many appeals have turned. To the extent that 'tactics' are now used less frequently in formal interrogations than they were before PACE, it is likely that they are now simply being used more under 'low visibility' conditions (Maguire and Norris 1992). The low visibility of informal interviews provides the opportunity to officers to 'gild the lily'. As one officer told Maguire and Norris (1992: 46–7), there was nothing to prevent him from distorting the contents of informal conversations 'if I was dishonest'.

Coercion may occur too, in both informal and formal interrogations. This is inevitable under English law, for the job of the police interrogator is to elicit answers even from suspects who have declared a refusal to provide answers. Even interrogation practices which would be innocuous to most people are coercive to vulnerable people (Gudjonsson and MacKeith 1982). Procedures for identifying, and making allowances for, vulnerable people in police custody (such as requiring the attendance of a supportive 'appropriate adult') are inadequate (Phillips and Brown 1998; Young 2002; Pierpoint 2008). And even supposedly non-vulnerable people often make 'coerced-passive' confessions (McConville et al. 1991: 4). Finally, there are false confessions. These are sometimes (Gudjonsson and MacKeith 1988), but not always, a result of coercion. Questioning taking the form of a supported direct accusation (i.e. an accusation with details of the crime itself) can lead to internalization by suggestible suspects whose subsequent 'confessions' will contain details provided by the police themselves (Moston and Engelberg 1993). Many people who are apparently robust are vulnerable to police tactics and the sheer fear of being cut off and confined for a period of time beyond one's own control. As one of the authors of a false confession in the 'Kerry Babies' case put it, 'I didn't think my mind was my own' (O'Mahony 1992).

Whilst false confessions arising from disorientation are doubtless rare, falsity can be a matter of interpretation and degree for interrogation is a process of construction whereby facts are made and not discovered. An example is given by Maguire and Norris (1992: 4), who report a CID sergeant saying that he had been taught to induce people found carrying knives to say that they were for their own protection. This, unknown to the suspect, constitutes admission of the crime of carrying an 'offensive weapon'. Moston and Engelberg (1993) argue that police failure to verify confessions and avoid leading questions is simply a matter of technical competence, a failure of training, and the decision to adopt adversarial styles. Thus new guidelines and training packages, incorporating inquisitorial styles, were devised in the 1990s. Code C (note 11B) now calls on interviewers to engage in 'investigative' or 'ethical' interviewing, pursuing all lines of enquiry whether they point towards or away from the suspect in front of them. But while there is less use of leading questions, and information such as the right to legal advice is provided more readily, police behaviour has not radically changed. For example, listening skills remain poor, interviews are dominated by the use of closed and leading questions, and many interviews breach PACE. Interviewers avoid exculpatory lines of enquiry, frequently look to interviewees to confirm police suspicions rather than provide their own accounts, and tactics are deployed when suspects do not confess readily (Taylor 2006: 147–9; Soukara *et al.* 2009; Walsh and Milne 2007). There is little effective supervision of interviewing and scant interest is shown by police leaders in ensuring that their officers actually use the skills taught in training. This complacency reflects police confidence that they are good at distinguishing truth from falsehood in interview, even though, according to Vrij (2008), they are quite wrong about this.

Technical solutions to problematic interviewing styles, such as better training or video-recording (Dixon 2006), imply a bureaucratic explanation for false confessions and coercion that presupposes that due process is achievable in interrogation. But arguably the search for 'better' or more 'objective' interrogation is naïve, because the job of the police is to build a case, not to identify verifiable facts. So while the (slow) shift towards investigative interviewing is welcome, miscarriages of justice arising from coercion and false confessions would be more effectively reduced by preventing confession evidence forming the sole basis of convictions, and by providing the defence with the same resources as are provided to the prosecution. But that is simply not on the agenda. Instead, in the context of custodial interrogation, blatant police oppression and trickery is being replaced by latent police power and control. The attenuation of the right to silence brought about by the Criminal Justice and Public Order Act 1994 is one clear example of that (see below), and the increase in the length of police-authorized custody for all indictable offences from 24 hours to 36 hours (section 43(7), Schedule 7 of the Serious Organised Crime and Police Act 2005) is another. And then there are the increases in detention time limits for terrorism-related arrests from seven to 14 days (section 306, Criminal Justice Act 2003), and then from 14 to 28 days (section 23, Terrorism Act 2006) (soon to revert to 14 days except in 'emergencies', according to the Coalition Government). This provides plenty of scope for the psychological vulnerabilities of suspects to be exploited under the pretext that the complexity of an investigation requires such lengthy detention (Sidhu 2010). Against this background of increasing police power, ethical custodial interrogation looks increasingly like a contradiction in terms.

## THE RIGHT OF SILENCE

Over half of all suspects who are interrogated either confess or make incriminating statements to the police (Bucke *et al.* 2000). We have seen that the police have various methods of securing confessions, but these do not always work. When suspects exercise their 'right to remain silent' are the police unjustifiably impeded? The answer turns principally on four things: what, precisely, 'silence' means in this context; what the association is between silence and outcome; in what ways the police are obstructed by silence; and what are the arguments of principle. Only 2–4 per cent of suspects in the post-PACE studies exercise absolute silence although a further 5 per cent or so simply make flat denials, while 8–15 per cent answer some questions but not others, and some suspects are silent at the start but then answer questions later (or vice versa). Leng (1992) estimates a 'true' silence rate of 4.5 per cent. He found that in only a small percentage of 'no further actions' or acquittals was silence exercised, and that these outcomes rarely seemed to be a product of silence. Leng found that 'ambush' defences (not disclosed until trial) were rare. When they were used, they were unsuccessful. Most acquittals were the result of unforeseen, but not unforeseeable, defences—sometimes they mirrored exculpatory statements to which the police would not listen in interrogation.

The Royal Commission on Criminal Justice (RCCJ) therefore concluded in 1993 that the right to silence should be retained, as abolition would benefit the police in few cases, and would put pressure on innocent people instead of experienced criminals. Despite this, the government enacted the Criminal Justice and Public Order Act 1994. This provides that, when someone relies in court on a fact which s/he could have been reasonably expected to mention when questioned by the police, the court can draw an adverse inference from this silence. Similarly, courts can draw adverse inferences from failures to answer questions in court. Exactly what inferences a court should draw from silence is a matter of debate. Despite Art 6 of the ECHR proclaiming that 'Everyone...shall be presumed innocent until proved guilty by law', the European Court of Human Rights accepted the lawfulness, with caveats, of these provisions (Sanders *et al.* 2010: ch. 5). As might be expected, the effect of the new provisions is to lower the use of the right of silence, probably because lawyers, who were becoming more adversarial in the early to mid-1990s, became more circumspect again about advising silence. Interestingly, these changes made little difference to admission and conviction rates (Bucke *et al.* 2000: 34 and 66–7). While they may have greater symbolic-electoral value than instrumental use, they support the broader purposes of interrogation, such as gaining general criminal intelligence and exercising disciplinary power over suspects. The conviction rate may not have increased, but the erosion of the privacy and freedom of the citizen certainly has.

## A SEA CHANGE IN THE NATURE OF DETENTION?

Rather than leading to less pre-charge detention, the RCCP's scheme (enacted in PACE) led to more. The formalization of pre-charge procedures was intended to protect suspects, and it doubtless does so to some extent. But detention can still be lengthy and intimidating, access to lawyers can be obstructed and is often of little value (particularly now that the right of silence has been further restricted), and the police have learnt to substitute psychological pressure for physical pressure. On the broader impact of PACE on policing, researchers have reached different conclusions. As part of a critique of *The Case for the Prosecution* (McConville *et al.* 1991) Dixon (1992) divides criminal justice researchers into two main camps: the 'sea change theorists' who argue that PACE significantly obstructed the police and enhanced protections for suspects; and 'new left pessimists' who argue that the changes are largely cosmetic.

It seems that PACE has changed practices, but largely by *shifting* the unwanted behaviour instead of eradicating or even reducing it. Thus there is little violence now, although deaths in custody are still deeply troubling (Sanders *et al.* 2010: ch. 4). But there is more use of other tactics and pressures, and of deceptive covert policing (see later); and confessions purportedly given in 'informal' interrogations are still admissible. The PACE framework is like the post-*Miranda* approach in the United States, where interrogation has similarly shifted from physical to psychological strategies. As Leo puts it, '[t]he law has also empowered the police to create more specialised and seemingly more effective interrogation strategies...they can lie, they can cajole, and they can manipulate' (1994: 116). The new rules and constraints that are implicitly relied upon by Dixon are access to lawyers, tape recording of interrogation, custody records, and the general supervisory role of the custody officer. We have seen that these developments hardly represent a 'sea change' in policing.

PACE only appears to provide a 'balance' between due process and crime control because we now unquestioningly accept the right of the police to use coercive powers. But why do suspects not want to wait for a lawyer or appropriate adult to come to the station? Why are so many people so vulnerable that PACE has to establish elaborate codes and protections? Why do suspects 'voluntarily' answer police questions? Only because they are in the police station against their will in the first place. So, for example, most suspects do want lawyers, but the desire to get out of the station quickly is stronger. And why is police station legal work so poor so often? Again, largely because the police have the power to create the forces that so shape it. Solicitors send unqualified staff, give telephone advice, or miss interrogations largely because of all the time they would otherwise waste—time for which they no longer get paid following the introduction of fixed fees for police station work. But it is the police who control and exploit the time frame (Kemp and Balmer 2008). And the legal 'trading' which undermines adversarialism is forced onto lawyers—who, it has to be admitted, usually need little persuading—because the police are in control. Once the police are given the right to detain, the rule of law is jeopardized, due process is made unviable, and human rights norms are tested to their limit. Thus PACE does not merely 'balance' rights and powers poorly, but, in providing the right to detain in such broad circumstances, it cedes most practical power to the police (Sanders and Young 1994). The 'sea change', if there has been one, has been in favour of the police and subsequent legislative changes reinforced this.

Why do we put up with this? Is it because it is not 'we' who bear the brunt of these powers? Most people who are stopped, searched, arrested, detained, and interrogated are young working-class men, especially in ethnic minorities. The treatment they are given is frequently humiliating—and deliberately so (Choongh 1997). These groups are also treated worse than others when in custody, being more than twice as likely to be strip-searched, for example (Newburn *et al.* 2004). Opinion-formers, lawyers, and legislators, on the other hand (older middle-class white men in the main), are very rarely subjected to such exclusionary processes. It is true that over one-third of men will have been convicted of at least one non-motoring offence before they reach the age of 40, which means that many more than this will have been stopped, arrested, and/or reported for motoring offences. But the way in which police power is exercised and its frequency are as important as outcome (Tyler 1990), and this bears down far more heavily on the poor than on the wealthy. Of course some middle-class people are roughly treated and some poor people are not. But the contrast between the integrated and the excluded is as striking in the field of criminal justice as in other fields of social policy (Dorling 2011). Arguably, major advances in liberty are only ever secured in the United Kingdom when the middle classes are threatened by police actions. If so, we can expect this divided society to manifest these exclusionary processes for a long time to come and for 'freedom' in the sense we use it here to be given little weight by policy makers and practitioners.

## WHETHER OR NOT TO PROSECUTE

When the police were first established they gradually took over responsibility for prosecution in the absence of any specific or exclusive prosecution powers or controls over their discretion. As arrest turned into a tool for (rather than the culmination of) investigation, pre-charge detention increased and the police developed various non-prosecution dispositions. To secure consistency of decision-making, and to counterbalance extra police powers, the RCCP recommended establishing the CPS. Apart from organizational and accountability matters with which we shall not be concerned here (on which see Sanders *et al.* 2010: ch. 7), the Government followed the Royal Commission's recommendations in the Prosecution of Offences Act 1985. The CPS is built around the pre-existing system, and is headed by the Director of Public Prosecutions (DPP), whose office had previously been responsible for prosecutions of particular importance and for the prosecution of police officers. The police continued to charge, summons, caution, and take NFA in the same way as before, simply handing prosecutions over to the CPS. As this made little difference, most prosecution decisions were transferred to the CPS by the 'statutory charging scheme' in the Criminal Justice Act 2003. However, this was seen by the Coalition Government elected in 2010 as unnecessary 'bureaucracy'. It plans to transfer 80 per cent of charging decisions back to the police (*Guardian*, 9 May 2011) though no specific legislation had been drafted at the time of writing (August 2011).

### NO FURTHER ACTION (NFA)

Around one in four suspects are released from pre-charge detention with no further action. Police officers make release decisions themselves on the basis of their own criteria and on evidence collected and evaluated by themselves. Many NFAs are of cases with strong evidence where the police were always reluctant to arrest but did so under pressure from victims or other members of the public and where they do 'deals' with suspects, especially informants. And just as prosecution is sometimes used to protect the police against allegations of malpractice, so in some circumstances NFA prevents the airing in public of events about which the police prefer to keep quiet. Some NFAs, of course, are simply cases in which the police would have liked to prosecute had they had more evidence. The obstacle here is rarely physical or legal, but simply one of resources. Cases are a product of police work, and so the absence of a case is also a police product. On the other hand, many NFAs are a product of purely speculative arrests (McConville *et al.* 1991: 2, 6, 111). Often the police accept that the suspect did not commit the offence or that there is no evidence: for instance, where the police 'trawl' local people with relevant previous convictions simply to eliminate them from a major rape enquiry; where suspects are arrested so that they can be held pending their questioning as witnesses; and where *all* inhabitants of, and visitors to, a building where there has been a drugs raid are arrested, even though the building consists of several self-contained flats (Leng 1992).

Arrest and detention is not always geared to prosecution. If the police arrest in furtherance of the 'assertion of authority' working rule, for instance, the arrestee may be detained in order to be humbled. The exercise of power is sometimes used to intimidate sections of the population such as the Irish (Hillyard 1993) or other ethnic minorities (Choongh 1997). NFAs would have been anticipated even at the moment of arrest. In these types of case, and in many of those discussed earlier, no due process standards, substantive or procedural, are adhered to. This is all consistent with the 'new left pessimist' argument that the 'PACE regime' facilitates the 'crime-control' drift.

## DIVERSION FROM PROSECUTION

The ratio of police prosecutions to police cautions has been about 2:1 over the past decade, with the percentage cautioned peaking between 2005 and 2008 (Taylor and Chaplin 2011: Table 3). This reflects a massive increase in cautioning since the 1970s. The RCCP (1981: Table 23.4) noted considerable variations in cautioning rates among police forces that could not be explained solely by offence variations. The Home Office guidelines tried to establish clearer criteria for prosecution and caution: offence seriousness, previous convictions, dramatic mitigating circumstances, wishes of the victim, and so forth. However, both inter-force and intra-force disparities continue, partly because the guidelines are vague (how serious an offence or record? what kinds of personal circumstance should be taken into account?), manipulable (the police themselves sometimes influence the wishes of victims), and largely non-prioritized (though now offence seriousness predominates). Diversion is encouraged in many cases which would once have been prosecuted, because it is cheaper than prosecution and because it is thought to avoid stigmatizing offenders. It was generally accepted in the 1980s and early 1990s that prosecution and punishment can exaggerate criminal self-identity. Thus cautioning has always been used more for young people than adults. But now the Crime and Disorder Act 1998 (which put cautioning for youths on a statutory basis) specifies that a maximum of two cautions (save in exceptional circumstances) can be offered to youths in the form of 'reprimands' for minor offences, or 'warnings' for more serious or repeat offending (see Morgan and Newburn, this volume, for discussion of this punitive approach). Warnings are supposed to be accompanied by 'action plans' drawn up by the multi-agency Youth Offender Teams created under the 1998 Act and the emphasis is now on 'early intervention', 'nipping crime in the bud', and restorative justice, although cost-reduction, punitive, and stigma-avoidance aims have not been entirely dispensed with (for discussion of some of the problems see Gray 2005).

The various objectives of cautioning would be undermined if cautions, reprimands, and warnings were used in cases that would not otherwise be prosecuted. This 'net widening' undoubtedly occurs, but it is difficult to assess its extent (Warburton *et al.* 2005). Preconditions for caution are that there is sufficient evidence to prosecute and that the suspect admits the offence and accepts the caution (the requirement of consent was removed in the case of youths by the 1998 Act). But these preconditions are often ignored (Gillespie 2005). Indeed, some suspects are cautioned precisely *because* there is insufficient evidence to prosecute. The low-visibility nature of caution decisions, and the fact that the police should, but need not, seek CPS advice on cautioning in difficult cases, also enables the police to use cautions as bargaining tools with suspects who would normally be prosecuted and to deal inappropriately with people with learning disabilities and mental health problems (Young 2002). The Criminal Justice Act 2003 gave the CPS a power to 'conditionally caution'. But this is little used (less than 20 per cent of all CPS disposals), and—like all diversionary measures—has been falling recently (CPS 2011). PNDs, on the other hand, were intended to 'net-widen' ('cost-effectively') so cannot really be seen as 'diversion'.

## PROSECUTION

There are now over 1.5 million police prosecutions per year. Police and CPS decision-making should be based on the Code for Crown Prosecutors, the latest edition of which was published in 2010. In order to prosecute there should be a 'realistic prospect of conviction' and it should be in the 'public interest' (otherwise the case should be diverted as discussed above). Under the statutory charging scheme, prosecutors decide whether or not to prosecute all non-trivial cases. To prevent delays and/or unnecessary time in custody, and to increase the efficiency and quality of decision-making, prosecutors are increasingly being sited in police stations and working with police officers on these decisions. Where appropriate, the police will be told they need to secure more evidence, and suspects are sometimes released on bail for this purpose.

But the police follow their working rules when making charge decisions, and use prosecutions (like stop and search, arrest, interrogation, and caution) as a policing resource. They do this by constructing cases to appear strong, in accordance with adversarial principles. Since the system is concerned more with legal truth than with actual truth, the police are also more concerned with the former, selecting, interpreting, and sometimes even 'creating' facts which bear little relation to any reality which the suspect might recognize (McBarnet 1981; Taylor 2006). It follows that, just as officers can often secure cautions when NFA would be more in keeping with the rules, so they can often secure charges when cautions would be more appropriate (and vice versa). The police 'overcharging' that this leads to was castigated by, for example, HM Crown Prosecution Service Inspectorate (2003). McConville *et al.* (1991) found that the CPS rarely dropped cases that were evidentially weak and never dropped cautionable cases. There were three main reasons for this: policy (the furtherance of police working rules, shared by both prosecutors and police officers); the chance of a freak conviction (because verdicts are so hard to predict); and guilty pleas (just because a case is evidentially weak it does not follow that the defendant will contest the case; weak cases are continued in the often correct expectation of a guilty plea). Cretney and Davis (1996) found, for example, that the police and CPS prosecute weak cases with victims of domestic violence and with vulnerable victims because they believe in the guilt of the suspect, ignoring the probability that problems concerning the victims' testimony will lead to acquittal. In these and other sensitive cases, such as sexual offences, this is urged on the police and CPS. If this leads to innovative ways of securing successful prosecutions of those who are factually guilty, this is commendable, but not if the 'public interest' in such cases simply trumps the 'evidential' test.

In recent years discontinuances have risen, particularly on evidential grounds, but there are still many Crown Court acquittals in cases that were obviously weak from the outset (Sanders *et al.* 2010: ch. 10). Many 'public interest' discontinuances are of trivial cases, and are made on cost grounds. A revealing case involved over 150 activists who occupied a department store in March 2011. The police officer in charge of the policing operation described the occupation as non-violent and 'sensible' and told the activists that if they left peacefully they would be free to go. In fact they were all arrested and charged with aggravated trespass. The CPS allowed these charges to continue for four months until, in July, they dropped them against 109 of the defendants. This meant that those concerned had charges hanging over their heads for months on end having been initially handcuffed and held in cells overnight all over London. Five of these were under-18s (*Guardian*, 19 July 2011). While the formal independence of the CPS from the police ultimately resulted in a large-scale termination of prosecutions, a 'back the police' mentality can nonetheless be inferred.

Ethnic minority defendants have their cases disproportionately discontinued by the CPS *and* dismissed in court (Mhlanga 2000). This suggests that the CPS counters some of the race bias produced by the police discussed earlier in this chapter, but not all. The CPS is in a structurally weak position to carry out its ostensible aims primarily because of police case construction. The CPS reviews the quality of police cases on the basis of evidence provided solely by the police. This is like the problem of written records, where those who are being evaluated write their own reports. Cases being prosecuted are usually presented as prosecutable; the facts to support this are selected, while less helpful facts are ignored, hidden, or undermined. Thus weaknesses or cautionable factors, whether known by the police or not, often emerge only in or after trial (Leng 1992). This situation is exacerbated when the CPS relies on police summaries, which are very selective indeed. But the statutory charging scheme *requires* prosecutors to rely on police summaries (often oral), if only so that most suspects can be released from custody in a reasonable time; and it allows the police or CPS to make an initial charge based on a very low evidential threshold in serious cases. Thus the CPS remains structurally weak. That the CPS is primarily a police prosecution agency is hardly surprising in an adversarial system, but it does suggest that suspects cannot rely on the CPS, as presently constituted, to protect them. Prosecutors could become adequate reviewers of either evidence or public interest only if placed in a different structural relationship with the police. This would require fundamental changes in the adversarial system, and might well then be unsuccessful, if the evidence we have of continental systems is anything to go by (Hodgson 2010). It would be better to strengthen the position of the defence in the adversarial system, but the new 'Criminal Defence' service, including a 'Public Defender' service on US lines, is likely to take us further in the crime control direction (see Goriely 2003, on a Scottish experiment; and Sanders *et al.* 2010: chs 7 and 9 for general discussion).

## NON-POLICE AGENCIES

Many other agencies also prosecute. These include Department of Social Security (DSS), Health and Safety Inspectorate, and so forth. Although these agencies follow a diversity of policies and procedures they all share a propensity not to prosecute, attempting to secure compliance with the law and/or to secure financial compensation primarily through informal negotiation. Whether their approach is so different from that of the police because the offences with which they deal are viewed differently by 'society', or whether the causal effect is in the other direction, is not clear (see Nelken: Chapter 21, this volume). Hawkins titled his study of the Health and Safety Inspectorate *Law as Last Resort* appropriately. He says 'prosecution tends to be used in those cases which have something special about them' (2002: xii). Even the treatment by the police of people who are unlawfully killed is completely different from that of non-police agencies, which virtually never consider prosecuting for manslaughter in circumstances where this would be viable and, arguably, desirable.

The patterns of bias identified in street policing (race, class, and so forth) may also be evident in prosecution and diversion decisions, but the greater class bias is between police-enforced and other crime. The police overwhelmingly prosecute instead of cautioning. Both the police and other types of agency have near-absolute discretion. The police (dealing with mainly working-class crime) use it one way, while most other agencies (dealing with mainly middle-class crime) use it in another. Indeed, non-police agencies that deal with poor people (such as the DSS) behave much more like the police than like the Inland Revenue or HSE (Walker and Wall 1997). It is difficult to see how this can be justified in terms of offence seriousness, previous criminality, and so forth except, perhaps, in terms of a narrowly defined 'efficiency' (Middleton 2005). Thus the dispositions of both police and non-police agencies serve to further the different working rules of those different agencies. And the stigmatizing and exclusionary process of prosecution is used routinely against the poor but rarely against the wealthy. The Coalition Government's crackdown on benefit fraudsters (Tunley 2011) is merely the latest example of hitting the poor as a cynical way of diverting attention from the (sometimes criminal) responsibility of the rich and powerful for producing the inequality that generates crime in the first place.

# PRE-TRIAL PROCESSES

## POLICE BAIL

After charge, the custody officer decides whether to release on bail or to hold the suspect in custody pending the next magistrates' court hearing (usually the next morning). Detention is allowed only if the suspect's real name and address cannot be ascertained, if he is unlikely to appear in court to answer the charge, if he is likely to interfere with witnesses or police investigations, or if he is likely to commit a significant crime. These reasons should be based on evidence, not speculation, but this is both unrealistic and inconsistent with the crime control elements of English law and practice: most of these provisions require custody officers to predict what might happen if the suspects were released, relying primarily on what investigating officers say. Also, suspects cannot prove that they would not do something wrong if they are given the opportunity to do it. Thus decisions are taken quickly on the basis of inadequate information; although decisions are taken by theoretically independent custody officers to protect suspects from the partisanship of arresting/investigating officers, most of the information used will come from the very officers against whom protection is provided; and assessment of the quality of decision-making is almost impossible.

Bail gives the police a powerful bargaining tool in interrogation. Although they should not offer 'inducements' (of which bail is one), this is a recognized interrogation 'tactic': 'They [the police] said if I cough I'll get bail; if not then I'll be in court tomorrow' (McConville and Hodgson 1992: 79). The opportunity for informal 'chats' discussed above ensures that such negotiations need never take place in front of tape recorders, researchers, or solicitors, and most suspects know or think they know that they can make deals on these lines. For bail bargaining is 'all part of the relationship' (detective, quoted in McConville *et al.* 1991: 63). The power of the police to deny bail is enhanced by the suspect's fear of being held overnight and by the failure of many solicitors to attend the station either at all or for a sufficient time. However, victims also sometimes have an interest in whether alleged offenders secure bail or the terms on which they get bail. Victims of violence, for example, may want a 'no contact' condition. Courts have for many years been able to grant conditional, as well as unconditional, bail (see later). The police were given the power to set conditions in the mid-1990s because it was believed that the police were refusing bail to some suspects in order to encourage the court to set conditions which the police (often justifiably) thought were appropriate. The result has been an increase in the percentage of defendants being granted bail (now around 80 per cent), but a reduction in the percentage of suspects given unconditional bail (Hucklesby 2001).

## COURT BAIL

Court bail may or may not be opposed by the police (through the CPS), and may or may not be requested by the defendant (usually through a solicitor). But magistrates usually reach the same conclusions as the police and CPS, for they consider similar criteria and similar information. This is often 'incomplete and for that and other reasons inaccurate' (Auld 2001: 428).

Bail is refused in about 11–13 per cent of magistrates' cases each year. Though a small (but rising) percentage of all cases, remand prisoners form a substantial percentage of people in prison, greatly contributing to overcrowding and the huge cost of criminal justice. Most hearings seem to take less than 10 minutes (Dhami and Ayton 2001). When information from more diverse sources is presented, bail is less frequently opposed by the CPS and more frequently granted. Bail information schemes, organized by local probation services, lead to the release of higher proportions of defendants than normal, demonstrating the partial (i.e. adversarial) approach of the police and the over-cautious approach of many courts. As with schemes to encourage more diversion from prosecution, this shows the potential in the CPS for more independence if independent information is provided to it.

A suspect's remand in custody can obstruct defence work (including preparation of bail applications): defendants remanded in custody are, all other things being equal, more likely to be convicted and, if convicted, to be given custodial sentences than those given bail. But since not all defendants remanded in custody are convicted and given custodial sentences, some defendants who are legally innocent are held in custody, and some whose offence or circumstances do not warrant custodial sentences, are also held in custody before sentence (this is true of nearly half of all male remand prisoners, many of whom are in custody for over three months: see Liebling and Crewe, this volume). On the other hand, 10–17 per cent of all persons released on bail commit an offence while at liberty (Hucklesby and Marshall 2000). Clearly magistrates have inadequate information on which to make confident decisions, yet the stakes are high. Offending on bail is undesirable; yet so, in a supposedly due process-based system, is pre-trial imprisonment of innocent people and minor offenders. Magistrates seem to cope by over-using conditions when they do grant bail and by developing an 'unquestioning culture' whereby information from the CPS is seen as factual but information from the defence is seen as partial. This is a problem in relation to all magistrates' decisions, such as applications for search warrants (Sanders *et al.* 2010: ch. 6). Magistrates even sometimes refer to prosecutors as 'our solicitor' (Hucklesby 1996: 218–19, 224).

## DISCLOSURE OF EVIDENCE

The failure of the police to disclose information helpful to the defence can not only make cases appear strong to prosecutors, but actually to be strong in court—often leading to wrongful convictions. The types of evidence in question are almost infinite, but include scientific tests and identification evidence that point to suspects other than the defendant, and witness evidence that suggested the suspect was somewhere else when the crime occurred or acted in self-defence.

In an attempt to secure some limited balance of crime control and due process considerations, the Criminal Procedure and Investigations Act 1996 created a three-stage process for disclosure, preceded by the police sending the CPS two schedules of material: 'non-sensitive' (that can, in principle, be seen by the defence) and 'sensitive' (for which a court order would have to be obtained—such as relating to state secrets, informers, or other covert methods of collecting intelligence). The three stages are: the CPS send the defence all material that might undermine the prosecution case; the defence send the CPS an outline of its case; the CPS then sends additional material that might assist that case. Leaving aside the issue of 'sensitive' material, the problems with this scheme include: the police often have little time, training, or inclination to do the job adequately; the CPS, as seen earlier, are adversarial and also are often disinclined to undermine their own cases; even were they more inclined to be objective, they are entirely reliant on the police for the information and how it is described in the schedules; and the system was in principle unfair in holding back material that could shed light on a claim of innocence (HMCPSI 2000; Plotnikoff and Woolfson 2001; Taylor 2006).

The Criminal Cases Review Commission identified non-disclosure as the third most common reason for referring convictions to the Court of Appeal in its Annual Report for 1999–2000, and it identified this as a problem again four years later. The Criminal Justice Act 2003 attempts to deal with some of these problems by requiring disclosure of material possibly helpful to the defence at the first stage, but this leaves all the other problems unchanged (for background to the problem, see Leng 2002; for a fuller discussion see Sanders *et al.* 2010: ch. 7). A particularly dramatic example is the case of environmental activists charged with breaking into a power station. Surveillance tapes that could have shed light on the defendants' actions were not disclosed to them, probably because they would have exposed the undercover officer, Mark Kennedy, who had infiltrated them. This was only discovered because he 'blew the whistle'. This case then triggered revelations that the CPS lawyer involved had failed to disclose exculpatory evidence in completely unrelated fraud and drugs cases. A Court of Appeal judge is now conducting a judicial inquiry (*Guardian*, 19 July 2011).

### GUILTY PLEAS

Most defendants (around 60 per cent in the Crown Court and 92 per cent in the magistrates' courts) either plead guilty or fail to appear and are found guilty in their absence (Sanders *et al.* 2010: ch. 8). This is what police and prosecutorial pre-trial practices are geared to. Suspects who confess, for example, find it almost impossible to contest the guilt that they admitted to the police earlier.

The system has increasingly encouraged overt bargaining to secure guilty pleas in recent years. The decision in *Goodyear* [2005] EWCA Crim 888 allows judges to indicate (on a request from the defendant) the maximum sentence they would impose if a guilty plea were to be entered, and the Criminal Justice Act 2003 allows a defendant in the magistrates' courts to ask whether a custodial or non-custodial penalty would be more likely if they pleaded guilty. These bargaining practices are underpinned by the incentive to plead guilty provided by sentence discounts (section 48 Criminal Justice and Public Order Act 1994). This puts immense pressure on defendants (some of whom will be innocent) to admit guilt in order to avoid prison. Bargaining also takes place between defence and prosecution over the seriousness of the charge.

We have seen that defence lawyers often fail to attend interrogations. This sends suspects the due process message that it is the court, not police questioning, which is important. However, this facilitates crime-control practices at the police station, and hence confessions, leaving little for the defence lawyer to do in court other than to mitigate on a guilty plea and to bargain, which they often do half-heartedly, seeing their clients in the same light as do the police (McConville *et al.* 1991; Newman 2011). The result is a remarkably high guilty plea rate. Inevitably, some innocent people plead guilty: over 10 per cent of guilty pleaders in the Crown Court claim to be innocent, in a similar number of cases the CPS believe there would have been a reasonable chance of acquittal, and in around half of these cases—some 1,400 each year—claims of innocence are believed by their barristers (Zander and Henderson 1993). Coalition Government proposals to increase the standard sentence discount for an early guilty plea from one-third to one-half produced a storm of protest in June 2011 about 'offenders escaping their just deserts', but there was little concern that such a huge discount would generate more miscarriages of justice. The proposals have now been scrapped.

## CONCLUSION

Criminal justice continually evolves in response to new ideas, new pressures, new scandals, and deeper socio-economic and political changes. No system corresponds exactly with any one theoretical model, and there are always gaps between rhetoric, rules, and reality. Thus we have seen a largely due process-based rhetoric (increasingly infused with crime-control rhetoric), rules which (often incoherently) combine both crime control and due process, and a largely crime-control reality. Even in court the presumption of innocence is compromised by the erosion of the right of silence, the guilty plea system, and bail systems whereby most decisions are made on the basis of police information.

The gap between many legal rules and the working rules of the police shows that the law appears to exert little moral force on the police. If due process rules were enforced rigorously it is not clear whether crime would be less well controlled. It depends on how successful the police (and associated agencies) are in establishing actual guilt and innocence. Miscarriages of justice, the abuse of powers of stop, arrest and surveillance, attempted cover-ups of police violence (as with the death of Ian Tomlinson mentioned earlier), police inability to detect when suspects are telling the truth, and questionable cautioning and PND decisions, are just some of the reasons to doubt this. Just because due process is a suspect-orientated way of establishing 'truth' it does not follow that it is a less effective one. As it is, law-breaking by the police and lesser failures of due process are tolerated by a system which fails to punish and deter the police or to compensate most victims of those practices (despite a new police complaints body (the IPCC) that leaves most of the police complaints investigation system untouched: Sanders *et al.* 2010: ch. 12). It is argued by some (such as Dixon 1992) that changes to legal rules can radically change police practices rather than simply do so at the margin. These critics see PACE as having changed interrogations, leading to more 'ethical interviewing', less informal interviewing, fewer confessions, and a drop in convictions. There is some truth in this. However, the effect is, first, seen in the speedy response of government to emasculate the right of silence, thus returning to the police their eroded interrogation power; and, secondly, to displace crime-control activity to another part of the system. Proactive policing—including the use of informants, surveillance, and bugging—is an increasingly important part of the police armoury. This is even less controllable and of less *external* visibility (cf Lowe 2011) than interrogation (Sanders *et al.* 2010: ch. 6). The infiltration of Mark Kennedy into environmental activist circles discussed earlier is an example of gross misuse of public money if nothing else. Patterns of bias on the street particularly concerning class and race are reproduced throughout the system, so that in the prisons black and working-class people in particular are vastly over-represented (Ministry of Justice 2010; see also Liebling and Crewe, this volume).

The criminal justice system is not geared solely to detecting and punishing criminal activity. It—and its modern arm, the police—have always been at least as concerned with high-level politics and low-level disorder: that is, with the control of the less powerful. It follows that the interests of victims (especially less powerful victims) are furthered where this fits in with broader working rules, but not necessarily otherwise (Roach 1999). The exclusionary model helps us to understand these processes, showing how the system prioritizes authority and control over the less powerful above justice, the rule of law, and the interests of victims—for victims can be the victims of exclusionary criminal justice practices as much as of criminal practices (Sanders 2002). This is especially true of ethnic minority victims (see Phillips and Bowling, this volume).

Prospects for change depend in part on one's view of the reasons why criminal justice operates as it does. Bureaucratic explanations, which focus on the values of particular institutions, produce more optimistic scenarios than do societal ones. They also depend on the impact of changes to criminal justice processes, about which we know too little. There has been an explosion of criminal justice research in the last 30 years, but most of it is 'top-down', trying to solve the system's problems; very little has been 'bottom-up', asking what it feels like for suspects and defendants. Research should pay more attention to the experiences of suspects, to the lessons to be drawn from Northern Ireland, and to the linking of theoretical, policy, and empirical questions as in the few, but notable, examples of Hillyard 1993; Carlen 1996; Loader 1996; Choongh 1997; and McConville and Mirsky 2005.

Only rarely is the fundamental question 'why prosecute?' asked in relation to the police and CPS. Prosecution often does too much and too little: in many cases it does too much by stigmatizing offenders and driving a wedge between them and their victims; and it does too little to protect victims from re-offending. In other cases it does too much by putting the victim through the ordeal of the court process and too little by allowing a plea bargain, discontinuance, or acquittal which minimizes the harm done to the victim. For victims and defendants alike an inclusionary approach would often be more effective and less alienating than the exclusionary approach embodied in prosecution. Victims are generally less punitive than the tabloid media would have us believe (see Hough and Roberts, this volume). So the limited moves towards 'restorative' and conditional cautioning are welcome, but traditional police agendas still dominate some restorative encounters, leaving offenders and victims sometimes as marginalized as before (Young 2001). The question 'why prosecute?' could only be asked from an inclusionary perspective. It is at least implicitly asked in one sphere of criminal justice: 'white-collar' law enforcement. Here, inclusionary policies are adopted by non-police agencies. They avoid prosecution and the other trappings of crime control such as arrest, detention, oppressive interrogation, and so forth. Instead they use techniques of 'compliance'. It is hardly credible that these differences are the product of bureaucratic pressures or accident. Present practice reflects processes of inclusion for 'white-collar criminals' and processes of exclusion for the poor, deprived, and powerless. This is a society in which some of the most damaging criminals are treated in the most humane ways while those who are arguably society's victims are treated as society's enemies so that, in time, they live up to their labels. The increasingly fuzzy boundary between civil and criminal processes, regarding anti-social behaviour, for example (Crawford 2009; and Crawford and Evans, this volume), exacerbates this problem. It remains to be seen whether the recent enthusiasm for restorative justice will result in more inclusionary freedom-enhancing ways of responding to street-level crime or simply create new sites for unaccountable extensions of state power wielded to exclusionary ends (see also Chapter 14, this volume).

### ■ SELECTED FURTHER READING

Several texts on criminal justice cover sentencing and penal policy as well as the earlier stages discussed in this chapter; the pick of the bunch is L. Zedner, *Criminal Justice* (2004), Oxford: OUP. Most textbooks take either a 'legal' or a 'social policy' approach. Two texts which integrate legal and sociological material, and which do not discuss sentencing and penal policy, are A. Ashworth and M. Redmayne (2010), *The Criminal Process*, 4th edn, Oxford: Oxford University Press and A. Sanders, R. Young, and M. Burton (2010), *Criminal Justice*, 4th edn, Oxford: OUP. Ashworth and Redmayne adopt a human rights approach, while Sanders, Young, and Burton use Packer's crime-control and due process models for descriptive purposes and the freedom perspective as a prescriptive guide.

Among the 'classics' in this area of work, D. McBarnet (1981), *Conviction*, London: Macmillan, is still well worth reading for its analysis of the relationship between legal rules and the reality of the criminal justice system, as is C. Walker and K. Starmer (eds) (1999), *Miscarriages of Justice: A Review of Justice in Error*, London: Blackstone. The role of victims is central to J. Doak (2008), *Victims' Rights, Human Rights and Criminal Justice*, Oxford: Hart. Lawyers receive searching empirical scrutiny from M. McConville, J. Hodgson, L. Bridges, and A. Pavlovic (1994), *Standing Accused*, Oxford: Oxford University Press, as do the police in B. Loftus, *Police Culture in a Changing World* (2009), Oxford: OUP, and L. Skinns (2010), *Police custody: governance, legitimacy and reform in the criminal justice process*, Cullompton: Willan. High-quality monographs which blend theory with strong empirical analysis include I. Loader, *Youth, Policing and Democracy* (1996), Basingstoke: Macmillan Press and K. Hawkins (2002), *Law as Last Resort*, Oxford: OUP.

## ■ REFERENCES

AULD, LJ (2001), *Review of the Criminal Courts of England and Wales*, London: TSO.

AVIRAM, H. (2011), 'Packer in Context: Formalism and Fairness in the Due Process Model', *Law & Social Inquiry*, 36: 237.

ASHWORTH, A. and REDMAYNE, M. (2010), *The Criminal Process*, 4th edn, Oxford: Oxford University Press.

BALDWIN, J. and McCONVILLE, M. (1977), *Negotiated Justice*, Oxford: Martin Robertson.

BBC (2003), *The Secret Policeman*, documentary first broadcast on 21 October 2003.

BLAND, N., MILLER, J., AND QUINTON, P. (2000), *Upping the PACE? An evaluation of the recommendations of the Stephen Lawrence Inquiry on stops and searches*, Police Research Series Paper 128, London: Home Office.

BROWN, D. (1997), *PACE Ten Years On: A Review of the Research*, Home Office Research Study No. 155, London: HMSO.

—— and ELLIS, T. (1994), *Policing Low Level Disorder*, Home Office Research Study No. 135, London: HMSO.

BUCKE, T., STREET, R., and BROWN, D. (2000), *The Right of Silence: The Impact of the CJPO 1994*, Home Office Research Study No. 199, London: HMSO.

CAPE, E. (2003), *Defending Suspects at Police Stations* 4th edn, London: LAG.

—— (ed.) (2004), *Reconcilable Rights? Analysing the Tension Between Victims and Defendants*, London: LAG.

CARLEN, P. (1996), *Jigsaw: A Political Criminology of Youth Homelessness*, Buckingham: Open University Press.

CHOONGH, S. (1997), *Policing as Social Discipline*, Oxford: Clarendon Press.

CRAWFORD, A. (2009), 'Governing through anti-social behaviour', *British Journal of Criminology*, 49(6): 810.

CRETNEY, A. and DAVIS, G. (1996), 'Prosecuting Domestic Assault', *Criminal Law Review*, 162.

CROWN PROSECUTION SERVICE (2011), *Annual Report, 2010–11*, London: CPS.

DHAMI, M. and AYTON, P. (2001), 'Bailing and Jailing the Fast and Frugal Way', *Journal of Behavioural Decision Making*, 14: 141.

DIXON, D. (1992), 'Legal Regulation and Policing Practice', *Social and Legal Studies*, 1: 515.

—— (2005), 'Regulating Police Interrogation', in T. Williamson (ed.), *Investigative Interviewing: Rights, research, regulation*, Cullompton: Willan.

—— (2006), ' "A Window Into the Interviewing Process?" The Audio-visual Recording of Police Interrogation in New South Wales, Australia', *Policing and Society*, 16(4): 323.

DORLING, D. (2011), *Injustice: Why Social Inequality Persists*, Bristol: Policy Press.

FAULKNER, D. (1996), *Darkness and Light*, London: Howard League.

FITZGERALD, M. (1999), *Stop and Search: Final Report*, London: Metropolitan Police.

GILLESPIE, A. (2005), 'Reprimanding Juveniles and the Right to Due Process', *Modern Law Review*, 68: 1006.

GOLDSMITH, A. (2010), 'Policing's New Visibility', *British Journal of Criminology*, 50(5): 914.

GORIELY, T. (2003), 'Evaluating the Scottish Public Defence Solicitors' Office', *Journal of Law and Society,* 30: 84.

GRAY, P. (2005), 'The Politics of Risk and Young Offenders' Experiences of Social Exclusion and Restorative Justice', *British Journal of Criminology,* 45: 938.

GUDJONSSON, G. and MACKEITH, J. (1982), 'False Confessions', in A. Trankell (ed.), *Reconstructing the Past,* Deventer: Kluwer.

—— and —— (1988), 'Retracted Confessions: Legal, Psychological and Psychiatric Aspects', *Medicine, Science, and the Law,* 28: 187.

HALLSWORTH, S. (2006), 'Racial Targeting and Social Control: Looking Behind the Police', *Critical Criminology,* 14: 293.

HAWKINS, K. (2002), *Law as Last Resort,* Oxford: Oxford University Press.

HILLYARD, P. (1993), *Suspect Community,* London: Pluto.

HM CPSI (2000), *Thematic Review of the Disclosure of Unused Material,* London: CPSI.

—— (2003), *Thematic review of attrition in the prosecution process (the Justice Gap),* London: CPSI.

HODGSON, J. (2010), 'The French Prosecutor in Question', *Washington and Lee Law Journal,* 67(4): 1361.

HOGGETT, J. AND STOTT, C. (2010), 'The role of crowd theory in determining the use of force in public order policing', *Policing & Society,* 20(2): 223.

HOME OFFICE (2005), 'Stop & Search Manual', London: Home Office.

HUCKLESBY, A. (1996), 'Bail or Jail', *Journal of Law and Society,* 23: 213.

—— (2001), 'Police Bail and the Use of Conditions', *Criminal Justice,* 1: 441.

—— and MARSHALL, E. (2000), 'Tackling Offending on Bail', *Howard Journal,* 39: 150.

KEMP, V. and BALMER, N. (2008), *Criminal Defence Services: User's Perspectives,* Research Paper No. 21, London: Legal Services Research Centre.

LENG, R. (1992), 'The Right to Silence in Police Interrogation', RCCJ Research Study No. 10. London: HMSO.

—— (2002), 'The Exchange of Information and Disclosure', in M. McConville. and G. Wilson (eds), *Handbook of the Criminal Justice Process,* Oxford: Oxford University Press.

LEO, R. (1994), 'Police Interrogation and Social Control', *Social and Legal Studies,* 3: 93.

LOADER, I. (1996), *Youth, Policing and Democracy,* Basingstoke: Macmillan Press.

LOFTUS, B. (2009), *Police Culture in a Changing World,* Oxford: Oxford University Press.

LOWE, D. (2011), 'The lack of discretion in high policing', *Policing & Society,* 21(2): 233.

MACDONALD, S. (2008), 'Constructing a Framework for Criminal Justice Research: Learning from Packer's Mistakes', *New Criminal Law Review,* 11(2): 257.

MACPHERSON, SIR WILLIAM (1999), *The Stephen Lawrence Inquiry,* Cm 4262-I, London: SO.

MCARA, L. and MCVIE, S. (2005), 'The Usual Suspects? Street-Life, Young People and the Police', *Criminal Justice,* 5(1): 5.

MCBARNET, D. (1981), *Conviction,* London: Macmillan.

MCCONVILLE, M. and HODGSON, J. (1992), 'Custodial Legal Advice and the Right to Silence', RCCJ Research Study No. 16. London: HMSO.

—— and MIRSKY, C. (2005), *Jury Trials and Plea Bargaining: A True History,* Oxford: Hart.

——, SANDERS, A., and LENG, R. (1991), *The Case for the Prosecution,* London: Routledge.

MAGUIRE, M. and NORRIS, C. (1992), *The Conduct and Supervision of Criminal Investigations,* RCCJ Research Study No. 5, London: HMSO.

MHLANGA, B. (2000), *Race and the CPS,* London: SO.

MIDDLETON, D. (2005), 'The Legal and Regulatory Response to Solicitors Involved in Serious Fraud: Is Regulatory Action More Effective than Criminal Prosecution?', *British Journal of Criminology,* 45: 810.

MILLER, J. (2010), 'Stop and Search in England: A Reformed Tactic or Business as Usual?', *British Journal of Criminology,* 50(5): 954.

MILLER, J., BLAND, N., AND QUINTON, P. (2000), *The Impact of Stops and Searches on Crime and the Community* Police Research Series Paper 127, London: Home Office.

MINISTRY OF JUSTICE (2010), *Statistics on Race and the Criminal Justice System 2008/09,* London: Ministry of Justice.

MOSTON, S. and ENGELBERG, T. (1993), 'Police Questioning Techniques in Tape Recorded Interviews with Criminal Suspects', *Policing and Society,* 3(3): 223.

NEWBURN, T., SHINER, M., and HAYMAN, S. (2004), 'Race, crime and injustice? Strip-search and the treatment of suspects in custody', *British Journal of Criminology,* 44: 677.

——. and HAYMAN, S. (2002), *Policing, Surveillance and Social Control,* Cullompton: Willan.

NEWMAN, D. (2011), 'Access to Justice and the Practitioner-Client Relationship: An Ethnographic Investigation into the World of Criminal Legal Aid', Unpublished PhD (University of Bristol).

NICHOLAS S., POVEY D., WALKER A., and KERSHAW C. (2005), *Crime in England and Wales 2004/2005* (Home Office Statistical Bulletin 11/05), London: Home Office.

O'MAHONEY, P. (1992), 'The Kerry Babies Case: Towards a Social Psychological Analysis', *Irish Journal of Psychology,* 13: 223.

PACKER, H. (1968), *The Limits of the Criminal Sanction,* Stanford, Cal.: Stanford University Press.

PARADINE, K. and WILKINSON, J. (2004), *Protection and Accountability: The Reporting, Investigation and Prosecution of Domestic Violence Cases,* London: HMIC and HMCPSI.

PHILLIPS, C. and BROWN, D. (1998), *Entry into the Criminal Justice System,* HORS No 185, London.

PIERPOINT, H. (2008), 'Quickening the PACE: The Use of Volunteers as Appropriate Adults', *Policing and Society: An International Journal,* 18(4): 397.

PLEASENCE, P., KEMP, V., and BALMER, N. (2011), 'The Justice Lottery: Police Station Advice 25 Years on from PACE', *Criminal Law Review*, 3.

PLOTNIKOFF, J. and WOOLFSON, R. (2001), *'A Fair Balance'? Evaluation of the Operation of Disclosure Law*, London: Home Office.

POVEY, D. (ed), MULCHANDANI, R., HAND, T., and PANESAR, L. K. (2011), 'Police Powers and Procedures England and Wales, 2009/10', Home Office Statistical Bulletin 07/11, London: Home Office.

QUINN, K. and JACKSON, J. (2007), 'Of Rights and Roles: Police Interviews with Young Suspects in Northern Ireland', *British Journal of Criminology*, 47: 234.

QUINTON, P., BLAND, N., and MILLER, J. (2000), *Police Stops, Decision-making and Practice*, Police Research Series Paper 130, London: Home Office.

REINER, R. (2010), *The Politics of the Police*, 4th edn, Oxford: Oxford University Press.

ROACH, K. (1999), *Due Process and Victim's Rights*, Toronto: Toronto UP.

ROWE, M. (2007), 'Rendering Visible the Invisible: Police Discretion, Professionalism and Decision-making', *Policing & Society*, 17(3): 279.

ROYAL COMMISSION ON CRIMINAL JUSTICE (1993), *Report*, London: HMSO.

ROYAL COMMISSION ON CRIMINAL PROCEDURE (1981), *Report*, London: HMSO.

SANDERS, A. (2002), 'Victim Participation in Criminal Justice and Social Exclusion', in C. Hoyle and R. Young (eds), *New Visions of Crime Victims*, Oxford: Hart.

SANDERS, A. (2010), 'The nature and purposes of criminal justice: the 'freedom' approach', in T. Seddon and G. Smith (eds), *Regulation and Criminal Justice* Cambridge, Cambridge University Press.

——, and YOUNG, R. (1994), 'The Rule of Law, Due Process and Pre-trial Criminal Justice', *Current Legal Problems*, 47: 125.

—— YOUNG, R., and BURTON, M. (2010), *Criminal Justice*, 4th edn, Oxford: Oxford University Press.

SHARP, D. and ATHERTON, S. (2007), 'To Serve and Protect? The Experiences of Policing in the Community of Young People from Black and Other Ethnic Minority Groups', *British Journal of Criminology*, 47(5): 746.

SHINER, M. (2010) 'Post-Lawrence Policing in England and Wales', *British Journal of Criminology*, 50(5): 935.

SIDHU, J. (2010), 'Twenty-eight Days—What's the Verdict?,' *Criminal Law & Justice Weekly* (20th February), 103.

SKINNS, L. (2011), 'The Right to Legal Advice in the Police Station: past, present and future', *Criminal Law Review*, 19.

SOUKARA, S., BULL R., VRIJ, A., and TURNER, M. (2009), 'What really happens in police interviews of suspects', *Psychology, Crime and Law*, 15(6): 493.

TAYLOR, C. (2006), *Criminal Investigation and Pre-Trial Disclosure in the United Kingdom: How Detectives Put Together a Case*, Lampeter: Edwin Mellen Press.

TAYLOR, P. and CHAPLIN, R. (2011), *Crimes Detected in England and Wales, 2010–11* HOSB 11/11, London: Home Office.

TUNLEY, M. (2011), 'Another Case of Old Wine in New Bottles?: The Coalition Government's Misguided Strategy to Reduce Benefit Fraud', *Howard Journal of Criminal Justice*, 50(3): 314.

TYLER, R. T. (1990), *Why Do People Obey the Law?*, New Haven, Conn., and London: Yale University Press.

VRIJ, A. (2008), *Detecting Lies and Deceit*, 2nd edn, Chichester: Wiley.

WALKER, C. and WALL, D. (1997), 'Imprisoning the Poor: TV Licence Evaders and the Criminal Justice System', *Criminal Law Review*, 173.

WALSH, D. and MILNE, R. (2007), 'Giving P.E.A.C.E. a Chance: A study of DWP's investigators perceptions of their interviewing practices', *Public Administration*, 85: 525.

WARBURTON, H. MAY, T., and HOUGH, M., (2005), 'Looking the Other Way: The Impact of Reclassifying Cannabis on Police Warnings, Arrests and Informal Action in England and Wales', *British Journal of Criminology*, 45: 113.

YOUNG, H. (2002), 'Securing Fair Treatment: An Examination of the Diversion of Mentally Disordered Offenders from Police Custody, Unpublished PhD, (Birmingham University).

YOUNG, R. (2001), 'Just Cops Doing "Shameful" Business: Police-Led Restorative Justice and the Lessons of Research', in A. Morris and G. Maxwell (eds), *Restorative Justice for Juveniles*, Oxford: Hart.

—— (2008), 'Street Policing after PACE: The Drift to Summary Justice', in E. Cape and R. Young. (eds), *Regulating Policing*, Oxford: Hart.

—— (2010), 'Ethnic Profiling and Summary Justice—An Ominous Silence', in K. Sveinsson (ed.), *Ethnic Profiling: The Use of 'Race' in UK Law Enforcement*, London: Runnymede Trust.

—— and SANDERS, A. (1994), 'The Royal Commission on Criminal Justice: A confidence trick?', *Oxford Journal of Legal Studies*, 14: 435.

—— and —— (2004), 'The Ethics of Prosecution Lawyers', *Legal Ethics*, 7(2): 190.

ZANDER, M. and HENDERSON, P. (1993), 'Crown Court Study', Royal Commission on Criminal Justice, Research Study No. 19, London: HMSO.

# 29

# SENTENCING: THEORY, PRINCIPLE, AND PRACTICE

## Andrew Ashworth and Julian Roberts

The passing of a sentence on an offender is the most public stage of the criminal justice process. Sentencing attracts widespread media coverage, intense public interest—and much public criticism. Selective news coverage, populist journalism, and the complexities of sentencing help to explain why polls conducted in all western nations routinely demonstrate that most people believe their courts to be too lenient[1] (see Hough and Roberts, this volume). When researchers provide sufficient information about sentencing decisions, the 'punitiveness gap' between the public and the courts diminishes greatly—but it is the polls that attract headlines.

This chapter begins by examining the various rationales for sentencing and then explores sentencing procedures and practices, including both custodial and non-custodial sentencing. We also discuss the sentencing guidelines that have been issued over the past decade in England and Wales. Throughout the chapter our focus is upon sentencing in England and Wales. However, since many of the problems confronting sentencing and indeed the solutions to those problems are shared by many countries, we also periodically provide illustrations from other common law jurisdictions.

## RATIONALES FOR SENTENCING

When a court passes sentence, it authorizes the use of state coercion against a person for committing an offence. The sanction may take the form of some deprivation, restriction, or positive obligation. Deprivations and obligations are fairly widespread in social contexts—e.g. duties to pay taxes, to complete various official forms, etc. But when imposed as a sentence, there is the added element of condemnation, labelling, and censure of the offender for the offence. In view of the direct personal and indirect

---

[1] Thus in 2011, three-quarters of the polled public in England and Wales expressed the view that sentencing was too lenient (see Ashcroft 2011 and Hough and Roberts, this volume).

social effects this can have, punishment requires justification. In order to understand punishment as a social institution and to understand the tensions inherent in any given 'system', there is benefit in identifying the principal approaches to sentencing. Among the issues to be considered are the behavioural and the political premises of each approach, its empirical claims, and its practical influence.

## DESERT THEORIES

Retributive theories of punishment have a long history, going back to the writings of Kant and Hegel. In their modern guise as the 'just deserts' perspective, they came to prominence in the 1970s, propelled by the alleged excesses and failures of rehabilitative ideals (von Hirsch 1976). Desert theorists argue that punishment is justified as the morally appropriate response to crime: those who culpably commit offences deserve censure; this censure should be conveyed through some 'hard treatment' that prompts the offender to take the censure seriously, but the amount of hard treatment should remain proportionate to the degree of wrongdoing, respecting the offender as a moral agent (see von Hirsch and Ashworth 2005).

The justification for the institution of state punishment also incorporates the consequentialist element of underlying general deterrence: without the restraining effect of a system of state punishment, anarchy might well ensue. Some, notably Duff (2000), tie further consequentialist aims into a fundamentally retributivist justification, arguing that punishment ought not only to communicate justified censure but also to persuade offenders to repentance, self-reform, and reconciliation. The behavioural premise of desert is that individuals are and should be treated as responsible (though occasionally fallible) moral agents. The political premise is that all individuals should be respected as moral agents: an offender deserves punishment, but does not forfeit all rights on conviction, and has a right not to be punished disproportionately to the crime committed.

Proportionality is the key concept in desert theory. There are two forms of proportionality. *Cardinal proportionality* concerns the magnitude of the penalty, requiring that it not be out of proportion to the gravity of the conduct: five years' imprisonment for theft from a shop would clearly breach that, as would the imposition of a trivial penalty for a very serious offence. *Ordinal proportionality* concerns the ranking of the relative seriousness of different offences: to what degree is rape more serious than robbery, for example? In practice, much depends on the evaluation of conduct, especially by sentencers, and on social assumptions about traditional (e.g. street crime) compared with new types of offence (e.g. commercial fraud, pollution). In theory, ordinal proportionality requires the creation of a scale of values which can be used to assess the gravity of each type of offence: culpability, together with aggravating and mitigating factors, must then be assimilated into the scale. This task, which is vital to any approach in which proportionality plays a part, makes considerable demands on theory (see von Hirsch and Ashworth 2005: Appendix 3; Ashworth 2010: ch. 4); some would say that decisions on relative offence-seriousness can never be more than contingent judgements which bear the marks of the prevailing power structure.

## DETERRENCE THEORIES

Deterrence theories regard the prevention of further offences through the threat of legal sanctions as the rationale for punishing. There is little modern literature on individual deterrence, which sees the deterrence of further offences by the particular offender as the measure of punishment. A first offender may require little or no punishment, while a recidivist might be thought to require an escalation of penalties. The seriousness of the offence becomes less important than the prevention of repetition. Traces of this approach can certainly be detected in the treatment of persistent offenders and so-called 'dangerous offenders' in contemporary sentencing, as noted below.

More attention has been devoted to general deterrence, which involves calculating the penalty on the basis of what will deter others from committing a similar offence. Leading utilitarian writers such as Bentham (1789; cf. Walker 1991) and economic theorists such as Posner (1985) develop the notion of setting penalties at levels sufficiently severe to outweigh the likely benefits of offending. The behavioural premise is that offenders are predominantly rational, calculating individuals—a premise that criminologists may call into question. The political premise is that the greatest good for the greatest number represents the supreme value, and that the individual counts only for one: it may therefore be justifiable to punish one person severely in order to deter others effectively, thereby overriding the claims of proportionality. This reasoning depends on convincing empirical evidence of the effect of deterrent sentencing on individual behaviour. This requires, among other things, demonstration that people are aware of the level of likely sentences; and that they desist from offending largely because of that sentence level and not for other reasons. A careful analysis of the general deterrence research by von Hirsch *et al.* (1999) found that there is evidence of a link between the *certainty* of punishment and crime rates, but considerably weaker evidence of a link between the *severity* of sentences and crime rates (see also Doob and Webster 2003; Bottoms and von Hirsch 2011).

## REHABILITATION

The rationale here is to prevent further offending by the individual through rehabilitation, which may involve therapy, counselling, cognitive-behavioural programmes, skills training, etc. Still a leading rationale in many European countries, it reached its zenith in the United States in the 1960s, declined in the 1970s, and then began to regain ground in the 1990s (see von Hirsch, Ashworth, and Roberts 2009: ch. 1). A humanitarian desire to help those with obvious behavioural problems has ensured that various treatment programmes continue to be developed. The key issue is the effectiveness of various interventions, and there is a long-running debate about the concept and the measurement of effectiveness (e.g. Lloyd *et al.* 1994). The reality is that certain rehabilitative programmes are likely to work for some types of offender in some circumstances. The 'What Works?' movement rekindled interest in various programmes for behaviour modification, with the development of 'accredited' programmes in prisons and as part of community sentences (see McGuire 2002; Harper and Chitty 2005), but a sober assessment of the available results demonstrated that the claims made by the Home Office and other protagonists have not been translated into practice (Bottoms 2004).

The behavioural premise of rehabilitative theory is that criminal offences are to a large extent determined by social pressures, psychological difficulties, or situational problems of various kinds. The political premise is that offenders are seen as unable to cope in certain situations and in need of help from experts, and therefore (perhaps) as less than fully responsible individuals. The rehabilitative approach advocates that sentences should be tailored to the needs of the particular offenders: in so far as this needs-based approach places no limits on the extent of the intervention, it conflicts with the idea of a right not to be punished disproportionately. Its focus instead is upon the diagnosis, treatment, and completion of accredited programmes. 'Diagnostic' tools such as the pre-sentence report are seen as essential to this approach to sentencing (see Raynor, this volume).

## INCAPACITATION

The incapacitative approach is to identify offenders or groups of offenders who are likely to do such harm in the future that special protective measures (usually in the form of lengthy incarceration) are warranted. The primary example of this in England and Wales, originally introduced by the *Criminal Justice Act 2003*, is the IPP sentence (Imprisonment for Public Protection), prescribed for certain offenders classified as dangerous. The nature of this sentence is discussed later in this chapter. Incapacitation has no behavioural premise. It is neither linked with any particular causes of offending nor dependent on changing the behaviour of offenders: it looks chiefly to predicted risk and to the protection of potential victims. The political premise is often presented as utilitarian, justifying incapacitation by reference to the greater aggregate social benefit and therefore sacrificing the individual's right not to be punished disproportionately to the wrongdoing. The repeatedly confirmed fallibility of predictive judgements (e.g. Monahan 2004) calls into question the justification for any lengthening of sentences on grounds of public protection, and yet the political pressure to have some form(s) of incapacitative sentence available to the courts has been felt in most countries. If this is the reality of penal politics then there is surely a strong case for procedural safeguards to ensure that the predictive judgements are soundly based and open to thorough challenge.

## RESTORATIVE AND REPARATIVE THEORIES

These are not regarded as theories of punishment. Rather, their argument is that sentences should move away from punishment towards restitution and reparation, aimed at restoring the harm done to the victim and to the community (see Hoyle, this volume). Restorative theories emphasize the significance of stakeholders in the offence (not just the state and the offender, but also the victim and the community), the importance of process (bringing the stakeholders together in order to decide on the response to the offence), and restorative goals (usually some form of reparation to the victim and 'restoration' of the community). There are many variations of restorative justice in different countries, some established in law and others at an experimental stage, and an assessment cannot be given here (see Dignan 2005). They are often based on a behavioural premise similar to rehabilitation for the offender, and also on the premise that the processes help to restore the victim; their political premise is that the response to an offence should not be dictated by the state but determined by all the interested parties, placing compensation and restoration ahead of mere punishment of the offender, and encouraging maximum participation in the processes so as to bring about social reintegration.

### Victim personal (impact) statements

There are other victim-oriented initiatives at sentencing. One that is widespread in both European and common law countries is to allow victims to submit a 'victim impact statement' (VIS) to the court, detailing the effects of the crime from their point of view. In England and Wales this is known as a 'victim personal statement' and may be submitted to any sentencing court. The VPS has been a feature of sentencing in this jurisdiction since 2001 but has been used in US jurisdictions, Canada, Australia, and New Zealand for many years now (Roberts 2009). The VIS has generated considerable research, and has spawned much heated debate as to whether it is either appropriate in principle or desirable in practice, and whether there are benefits associated with victim impact statements (see Erez 1999; Sanders *et al.* 2001; Chalmers et al. 2007; Edwards 2004). It is worth distinguishing between jurisdictions which allow a victim to provide only a description of the harm and others where the statement may also include the victim's opinion on the appropriate sentence. Criticism of the victim impact statement has focused on the latter form of victim participation. Allowing victims to make specific recommendations for sentence raises deep questions about crimes as public and/or private wrongs (see Ashworth 2010: 382–7).

### SOCIAL THEORIES

There has been a resurgence of writings which emphasize the social and political context of sentencing (see Duff and Garland 1994: ch. 1). Important in this respect are Garland's (1990) analysis of the theoretical underpinnings of historical trends in punishment, and Hudson's arguments (1993) in favour of a shift towards a more supportive social policy as the principal response to the problem of crime. Those who have been influenced by Hart's distinction (1968) between the general justifying aim of punishment (in his view, utilitarian or deterrent) and the principles for distribution of punishment (in his view, retribution or desert) should consider the challenge to this dichotomy in Lacey (1988). She argues that both these issues raise questions of individual autonomy and of collective welfare and we should address this conflict and strive to ensure that neither value is sacrificed entirely at either stage. In developing this view she explores the political values involved in state punishment and argues for a clearer view of the social function of punishing.

### Sentencing rationales in practice

It will be evident from the foregoing discussion that the various objectives for sentencing point in different directions. Despite this obvious conclusion, in 2003 the then government proclaimed that it was taking a significant step towards consistency in English sentencing by enacting section 142 of the Criminal Justice Act 2003, which provides:

(1) Any court dealing with an offender in respect of his offence must have regard to the following purposes of sentencing—

  (a)  the punishment of offenders,
  (b)  the reduction of crime (including its reduction by deterrence),
  (c)  the reform and rehabilitation of offenders,
  (d)  the protection of the public, and
  (e)  the making of reparation by offenders to persons affected by their offences.

Three difficulties arise with lists of purposes such as that found in section 142. First, the objectives are potentially conflicting (except for reparation which can sometimes be achieved alongside another purpose). Second, no direction is provided as to whether one objective is particularly appropriate for certain cases—whether, for example, deterrence should be uppermost in a court's mind when sentencing corporate offending. Third, as the Home Office Sentencing Review (2001) pointed out, the evidence for (b), (c), and (d) is weak. It is therefore unclear on what evidence an individual sentencer could make a rational choice among the various purposes. For these reasons, lists of this kind have been criticized in the academic literature. England and Wales is not alone in taking this approach to providing guidance regarding sentencing objectives. Similar lists of objectives have been placed on a statutory footing in New Zealand and Canada, and the US guidelines manuals provide a similar range of options for sentencers in the US jurisdictions (e.g. Minnesota Sentencing Guidelines Commission 2010).

However, the Criminal Justice Act 2003 contains other provisions that may be used to clarify matters. Section 143(1) states that:

> In considering the seriousness of any offence, the court must consider the offender's culpability in committing the offence and any harm which the offence caused or was intended to cause or might foreseeably have caused.

Further, when the Act sets the threshold for community sentences and for custody, and the standard for the length of custodial sentences, it uses 'the seriousness of the offence' as the key indicator. On this basis the Sentencing Guidelines Council (now the Sentencing Council) issued a guideline entitled *Overarching Principles—Seriousness*[2] to the effect that the proportionality principle enshrined in section 143(1) should be used by sentencers as the touchstone. That is fully consistent with the thresholds set by the 2003 Act, but leaves the 'pick and mix' approach of section 142 somewhat in limbo.

It is hard to know how the various rationales for sentencing affect sentencing practice. Judges often refer to general deterrence, most notoriously in the judgment in *Blackshaw* [2011] EWCA Crim 2312, where sentences significantly above the guidelines were approved for offenders involved in the riots of August 2011, on grounds of general deterrence. There was no recognition of the weakness of the evidence for general deterrence, or other objections. Parliament too has legislated for mandatory sentences—for example the mandatory minimum of five years for possession of certain firearms, in section 287 of the Criminal Justice Act 2003—based on a deterrent rationale.

---

[2] All guidelines referred to in this chapter are available at: www.sentencingcouncil.org.uk.

Protection of the public (incapacitation) remains as an exception to the proportionality principle when dealing with so-called dangerous offenders, and those provisions of the 2003 Act are discussed below.

The reform and rehabilitation of offenders is a relevant purpose once the court has decided that a community sentence of a particular level is justified by the seriousness of the offence: in those cases, therefore, the proportionality principle must be applied first, and once the threshold is passed, the possibility of achieving a rehabilitative purpose enters the equation. All these points will be taken further below. What they suggest, and as the seriousness guideline states, is that proportionality should be the sentencer's guide, except in dangerousness cases, but that within the framework of a proportionate sentence it may be desirable to aim for rehabilitation. A reparative measure may also be possible.

In so far as the proportionality principle holds sway, it places some limits on the use of state power over those who offend. Even approaches that are critical of desert theory, such as the republicanism of Braithwaite and Pettit (1990) and the communitarianism of Lacey (1988), recognize some limits to state power at the sentencing stage. The argument that desert theory leads to harsh penalties is not sustainable by reference to international comparisons (von Hirsch and Ashworth 2005: ch. 6), although it does need to be combined with the principle of penal parsimony to ensure that a movement towards punitiveness is avoided.

# THE MECHANICS OF SENTENCING IN ENGLAND AND WALES

In this part of the chapter some basic elements of the law and practice of sentencing are set out. The various stages of a criminal case are discussed, together with the procedures which surround the sentencing stage itself.

### THE SELECTION OF CASES FOR SENTENCE

Courts pass sentence in only a small proportion of the crimes committed in any one year. The explanation for this is to be found in the concept of 'case attrition' in the process from the commission of the offence through to the imposition of a sanction in cases which proceed that far. As Maguire demonstrates in Chapter 8 of this volume, the attrition rate in England and Wales comes about because only a small minority of all crimes committed are reported, recorded, detected, and prosecuted to conviction.

The most recent statistics illustrate the phenomenon. In 2009 approximately 9.5 million crimes were reported to the British Crime Survey (Ministry of Justice 2010b: Table 1A). A total of 4,338,604 crimes were recorded by the police and a sentence was imposed in 13 per cent of these cases (Home Office 2010a: Figure 1.1). However, since a large proportion of crimes are not reported to the BCS, it is likely that only approximately 3 per cent of all offences in any given year result in court sentences. This is not to suggest that sentencing is unimportant, for it may have a social or symbolic importance considerably in excess of the small proportion of crimes resulting in a sentence. But these statistics do suggest the need for caution in assessing the crime-preventive effects of sentencing. Theoretical rationales which look to the consequences of sentencing may over-estimate its potential for reducing overall rates of criminal behaviour.

The selection of cases for sentence is not merely a quantitative filtering process. There are also various filters of a qualitative kind, some formal, some informal. The role of the regulatory agencies is significant: the Health and Safety Executive, the Environment Agency, and various other regulatory bodies tend to regard prosecution as a last resort (see, e.g., Hawkins 2003). These and other agencies, such as HM Revenue and Customs, also have various means of enforcing compliance without resort to prosecution, such as warning notices or the 'compounding' of evaded tax and duty. Even though the orientation of the police and the Crown Prosecution Service is more towards prosecutions in court, they have various out-of-court disposals which are being used increasingly. When an offence is reported to the police, the choice among alternative courses (e.g. no further action; informal warning; Penalty Notice for Disorder; cannabis warning; fixed penalty notice; or passing the case to the Crown Prosecution Service with a view to prosecution) has relatively low visibility (see further on these issues Padfield, Morgan, and Maguire, this volume). If the CPS take over the case, they too have the alternatives of offering a conditional caution (specifying certain conditions, compliance with which will lead to the dropping of the charge) or of returning the case to the police with a view to a simple caution.

The Code for Crown Prosecutors (2010) states that a prosecution should not be brought unless there is a realistic prospect of conviction on the charge, but allows the CPS not to prosecute if to do so would not be in the public interest. At the stage of plea the system contains strong incentives to plead guilty, and there is no shortage of empirical evidence that negotiation is a familiar part of justice in magistrates' courts and in the Crown Court (see Ashworth and Redmayne 2010: ch. 10). In summary, therefore, the offences for which the courts have to pass sentence are both quantitatively and qualitatively different from what might be described as the social reality of crime. The courts see only a small percentage of cases. Even if it may be assumed that these are generally the more serious offences, how they are presented in court may be shaped as much by the systemic drivers towards guilty pleas, and by the working practices and priorities of the police, prosecutors, and defence lawyers as by any objective conception of 'the facts of the case' (see further Sanders and Young, this volume).

## CROWN COURT AND MAGISTRATES' COURT

In most jurisdictions there are two or three levels of criminal courts. In England and Wales there are two levels: the Crown Court deals with the more serious cases and the magistrates' courts with the less serious. The Crown Court sits as a trial court with judge and jury. Some two-thirds of Crown Court cases involve a guilty plea, and these are dealt with by judge alone—juries play no part in sentencing in this jurisdiction.

In almost all other common law jurisdictions sentencing is conducted by professional judges; England and Wales is almost unique in using lay adjudicators (members of the public who have been appointed magistrates). The lay magistracy has existed for over six centuries in this jurisdiction. There are approximately 28,000 lay magistrates in England and Wales, and they usually sit in benches of three, assisted by a legally-trained adviser. Alternatively some magistrates' courts, particularly in large cities, have a professional District Judge. The maximum sentence in a magistrates' court is six months' imprisonment or a total of 12 months' imprisonment if there are two or more convictions. In 2009, fully 93 per cent of all offenders sentenced were disposed of in the magistrates' courts (Ministry of Justice 2010a).

For many offences a magistrates' court has the power to commit an offender to the Crown Court for sentence if it believes that its own sentencing powers are inadequate. Finally, it should be mentioned that the number of offenders dealt with in the magistrates' courts has declined in recent years, as a result of the greater use of out-of-court penalties: this raises serious questions of principle about the quasi-sentencing powers given to the police and prosecutors (out-of-court penalties, conditional cautions), and about the proper functions of a criminal court (see Padfield, Morgan, and Maguire, this volume).

## COURT OF APPEAL OF ENGLAND AND WALES

There is the possibility of appeal against sentence, from magistrates' court to Crown Court, or from Crown Court to the Court of Appeal. The Court of Appeal, Criminal Division, presided over by the Lord Chief Justice and the Vice President of the Criminal Division, hears all appeals in criminal matters from the Crown Court. The sentencing caseload of the criminal division has increased in recent years. In 2009, there were 7,195 applications for leave to appeal, and of these fully three-quarters were sentence appeals (Ministry of Justice 2010d: 156). Of the 2,136 appeals involving sentence heard in that year 1,484 or 73 per cent were allowed (Ministry of Justice 2010d: Table 7.7).

## MAXIMUM PENALTIES

In most countries the legislature sets the maximum sentence for each offence. This is the position in England and Wales, except that there remain a few common law offences which have no fixed maximum (e.g. manslaughter, conspiracy to outrage public decency). Parliament has set the maxima at different times, in different social circumstances, and without any overall plan, often based on the number of years for which offenders were transported to Australia in earlier centuries (Radzinowicz and Hood 1990: ch. 15). The legislature in this country (and most other common law countries) continues to assign and revise maximum penalties on a piecemeal basis. For example, in England the Criminal Justice Act 2003 raised the maxima for many summary offences, and the maximum for causing death by dangerous driving was increased from 10 to 14 years. As we shall see below, a small number of offences have a mandatory sentence or a mandatory minimum sentence.

## THE RANGE OF AVAILABLE SENTENCES

In this section we will begin by summarizing the principal disposals available to a sentencing court in England and Wales, after which we shall discuss the relative use of these disposals over the past decade.

Beneath the maximum penalty for the offence, the court usually has discretion to choose among alternative disposals. In England and Wales the available sentences may be represented in terms of three tiers. At the lowest level are the so-called 'first tier' sentences. These include the *absolute discharge*, usually reserved for a small number of cases of very low culpability; the *conditional discharge*, where the condition is that the offender does not re-offend within a specified time (one, two, or three years), and breach of which condition means that the offender will be sentenced for the original offence as well as the new offence; and the *fine*, still much used for summary offences (the least serious) but declining in use for other offences.

Courts are required to take account of the means of the offender when calculating a fine, but there has been resistance to the adoption of the kind of 'day fine' system operating in many other European countries. The day fine permits courts to ensure that the magnitude of the imposed fine reflects the offender's ability to pay (Ashworth 2010: 327–38). The Carter Review (2003: 27) argued that 'fines should replace community sentences for low-risk offenders', suggesting that some 30 per cent of community sentences ought to be replaced by fines, but no formal steps have been taken to bring that about.

The second tier of sentencing is occupied by *community sentences*. For the last 30 years it has been official policy that the courts should use community sentences instead of some shorter custodial sentences; in practice the use of community sentences has increased, but the numbers of short custodial sentences have also increased, albeit at a slower rate than other prison sentences. The 2003 Act retained the requirement that a court should not impose any community sentence unless satisfied that the offence is serious enough to warrant it; and also the requirement that, if the court decides that the case is serious enough, it should ensure that the community order (a) is the most suitable for the offender, and (b) imposes restrictions on liberty which are commensurate with the seriousness of the offence (Criminal Justice Act 2003, section 148(2)). In many such cases a 'pre-sentence report' will have been prepared by the Probation Service to 'assist' the court. The theory and practice of community sentences are discussed by Raynor in this volume, and the 12 possible requirements (including supervision, unpaid work, drug rehabilitation, and so on) are set out there. The legislation provides for the possibility of imprisonment on breach. However, the relevant guideline states that 'custody should be the last resort, reserved for those cases of deliberate and repeated breach where all reasonable efforts to ensure that the offender complies have failed' (Sentencing Guidelines Council 2004: para. 1.1.47[3]).

Finally, there are the third tier sentences. A *suspended sentence order* should only be imposed when the court is satisfied that a custodial sentence is unavoidable, and that the court would have imposed imprisonment if the power to suspend had not been available. A court is empowered to suspend a sentence of imprisonment of up to 12 months for a period of up to two years, and the court may add to the order one or more of the same 12 requirements that apply to community sentences (see above). On breach of a suspended sentence order the court must activate the prison sentence unless it is unjust to do so. The other third tier sentence is *immediate imprisonment*,

---

[3] Available at: www.sentencingcouncil.org.uk.

and this will be discussed in detail in the paragraphs below. At all three tiers there are separate orders for young offenders (see Morgan and Newburn, this volume), and also some separate orders for mentally disordered offenders (see Peay, this volume).

In all cases involving death or injury, loss or damage, the court must consider making a *compensation order*, requiring the offender to make compensatory payments to the victim according to the offender's ability to pay. The court may also, where appropriate, impose one of several preventive orders—for example, an anti-social behaviour order, a sexual offences prevention order, a serious crime prevention order, and so on. In drug trafficking cases there are mandatory provisions requiring the judge to consider making a *confiscation order*, requiring the offender to yield certain assets to the court, and the Proceeds of Crime Act 2002 (UK) makes confiscation orders available in other serious cases too.

## SENTENCING PATTERNS IN ENGLAND AND WALES

Figures 29.1 and 29.2 reveal sentencing patterns for indictable offences in the magistrates' and Crown Courts in 2009. As can be seen, community orders are the most frequent disposal for indictable offences in the magistrates' courts (accounting for 39 per cent of all cases), followed by fines (23 per cent), suspended sentences (20 per cent and custody (13 per cent; see Figure 29.1). Reflecting their more serious caseload, in the Crown Court immediate custody was imposed in over half the cases (57 per cent), followed in frequency by suspended sentences (21 per cent) and community orders (16 per cent). Fines accounted for only 2 per cent of cases (see Figure 29.2).

Table 29.1 summarizes trends for the principal sentences imposed for indictable offences over the last decade (2000–9). Several important trends are worth noting. First, the volume of cases sentenced changed little during this time, increasing by only

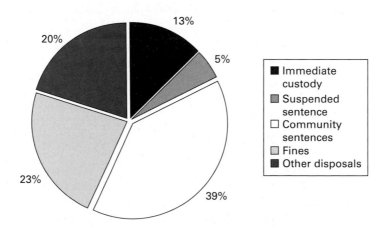

**Figure 29.1** Sentences imposed, indictable offences, magistrates' courts, 2009
*Source*: Ministry of Justice (2010b).

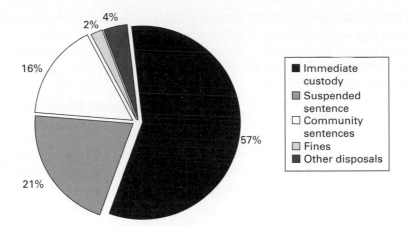

**Figure 29.2** Sentences imposed, indictable offences, Crown Courts, 2009
*Source:* Ministry of Justice (2010b).

1 per cent. Second, the proportionate use of immediate custody remained stable at one quarter of all cases; this explains the fact that the number of prison sentences, which had increased from 1993–2000,[4] levelled out over the most recent decade. Third, following the re-introduction of the suspended sentence in 2005, the use of immediate custody fell only slightly (see Table 29.1). This suggests that courts sometimes use suspended sentences where they would otherwise impose a community sentence, not an immediate custodial sentence.

Fourth, the proportionate use of fines declined—from 25 per cent to 17 per cent of all cases from the beginning to the end of the decade. A fine was the most severe sanction in 82,110 cases in 2000, declining to 56,029 in 2009. Where did these cases which previously resulted in a fine go? As can be seen in Table 29.1, the decline in fines was accompanied by a dramatic increase in the use of suspended sentences of imprisonment due to their revival in 2005 (see above). This may be described as 'uptariffing' —by which we mean the increasing tendency to impose a more severe sanction. Suspended sentences accounted for less than 1 per cent of cases in 2000, but 10 per cent in 2009, while community orders rose to account for 33 per cent of cases in 2009 from 30 per cent in 2000 (see Table 29.1).

## VARIATION IN SENTENCING OUTCOMES

Alleged inconsistencies in sentencing have been a cause for concern the world over—ever since the first scientific analysis was published in 1932 (Gaudet, Harris, and St. John 1932). Since then, empirical research in the United States, Canada, and other countries has repeatedly demonstrated variability in sentencing, across a range of different methodologies (e.g. Austin and Williams 1977; Palys and Divorski 1987).[5]

---

[4] Over the period 1995–2002, the custody rate for indictable offences increased from 22% to 28% (Ministry of Justice 2009: 6).

[5] Where there are fairly high maximum penalties and a wide range of available sentences, inconsistency might appear to be an obvious consequence. Yet even before there were many statutory restrictions and

**Table 29.1** Sentences imposed, all indictable offences, 2000–2009, number of cases and percentage of all cases

|  | Immediate Custody | Suspended Sentence | Community Order | Fine | Other Disposals | Total cases sentenced |
|---|---|---|---|---|---|---|
| 2000 | 80,784 | 2,453 | 97,948 | 82,110 | 65,368 | 326,210 |
|  | *25%* | *<1%* | *30%* | *25%* | *20%* | *(100%)* |
| 2001 | 80,273 | 2,139 | 102,063 | 77,466 | 63,401 | 323,203 |
| 2002 | 85,151 | 1,963 | 110,768 | 78,470 | 62,355 | 336,744 |
| 2003 | 80,794 | 2,055 | 109,648 | 78,250 | 65,238 | 333,930 |
| 2004 | 79,938 | 2,143 | 111,784 | 65,095 | 60,120 | 316,937 |
| 2005 | 76,291 | 5,610 | 111,724 | 58,433 | 60,150 | 306,598 |
| 2006 | 73,532 | 20,799 | 102,971 | 51,628 | 53,607 | 302,537 |
| 2007 | 74,037 | 27,254 | 105,142 | 49,463 | 56,362 | 312,258 |
| 2008 | 79,058 | 28,455 | 102,782 | 49,646 | 55,959 | 315,900 |
| 2009 | 80,239 | 31,119 | 107,852 | 56,029 | 51,907 | 327,146 |
|  | *25%* | *10%* | *33%* | *17%* | *16%* | *(100%)* |
| *change 2000–09* | *<1%* | *+1,200%* | *+10%* | *-32%* | *-21%* | *<1%* |

*Notes:* row percentages rounded.
*Source:* Ministry of Justice (2010b).

In magistrates' courts, where most sentencing takes place, local variation is a long-standing phenomenon. Hood (1962) showed that some courts in England are 'probation-minded' and others are not, while Tarling demonstrated that much variation in outcomes remained even after accounting for the different 'mix' of offences coming before the courts (Tarling *et al.* 1985). The latest statistics show that the immediate custody rate for indictable offences in the magistrates' courts varied from a low of 5 per cent in Wiltshire to 18 per cent in the West Midlands (Ministry of Justice 2010a: Table 5(ii)).

Variations are also to be found in the Crown Court. In 2009 the custody rate for indictable offences in the Crown Court varied from 44 per cent in Durham to 64 per cent in Kent (Ministry of Justice 2010a: Table 5(ii)). The average custodial sentence imposed also varied significantly—from a low of 20 months in Norfolk to a high of 31 months in Sussex (Ministry of Justice 2010a: Table 5.2). In their survey of sentencing in both levels of courts in the mid-1990s, Flood-Page and Mackie (1998) found that 'attempts to predict sentences on the basis of case factors were not particularly successful', indicating wide differences in the way that community sentences, in particular, were used. More recently, Mason *et al.* attempted to explain variation in sentencing practices by differences in the seriousness of cases and characteristics of offenders appearing for sentence but concluded that these factors were insufficient. They note that 'some kind of local "court culture" is at work which perpetuates differences in sentencing outcomes for comparable cases' (2007: 26).

guidelines, judges expressed themselves as having little choice in the sentences they passed: 'the least possible sentence I can pass…' 'I have no alternative but to …' (Ashworth *et al.* 1984: 53–4); 20 years later the sentencers interviewed by Hough *et al.* (2003: 38) expressed themselves similarly.

While discretion is important to enable sentencers to take account of the wide range of factors that might be relevant, it does leave decision-making open to factors irrelevant to sentencing. For example, Hood's (1992) study showed that at some courts black offenders were significantly more likely to receive custody than similarly situated white offenders. Hedderman and Gelsthorpe (1997) found variations in the sentencing of men and women that cannot be explained by case factors, and showed that sentencers' attitudes may explain why women are fined less frequently and given certain community sentences more frequently than men. Judges tend to argue strongly against any curtailment of 'their' discretion, but rarely acknowledge the risks of discrimination, individual idiosyncrasy, and other irrelevant influences which accompany discretion that is not well structured or well monitored (see Hudson 1998).

## INFORMATION ABOUT THE OFFENCE AND THE OFFENDER

Courts depend for their information on what they hear or what they are told. Since over 90 per cent of cases in magistrates' courts and almost three-quarters of cases in the Crown Court (see below) involve guilty pleas, the main source of information about the offence is likely to be the statement of facts which the prosecutor reads out. It will usually have been compiled by the police, and the way in which it describes or omits certain factors may reflect a particular view of the offence, or perhaps a 'charge-bargain' struck with the police (see Sanders and Young, this volume).

In addition to the prosecution statement of facts, the court may acquire further perspectives on the crime from the defence plea in mitigation, and from a pre-sentence report (if available). Any account of 'the facts' is likely to be selective, determined to some extent by the compiler's preconceptions. It is likely that judges and magistrates will be influenced by the selections made by those who inform them, as well as by their own perspectives. The prosecution's account of the facts may be disputed by the defence. In a trial there is usually an opportunity to resolve these matters, but this is not always so: some facts relevant to sentencing are irrelevant to criminal guilt. The greatest difficulty arises where the defendant pleads guilty but only on a 'basis of plea' more favourable than the version presented by the prosecution. The courts have developed a procedure for resolving most such issues by means of a pre-sentence hearing, known as a '*Newton* hearing' at which evidence is presented and witnesses may be heard [6] Since the outcome can have a considerable effect on the length of a custodial sentence, procedural fairness at this stage is important.

In England and Wales a court may obtain information about the offender from at least five sources: the police antecedents statement; the defence plea in mitigation; a pre-sentence report; a medical report; and the offender's own statements in court.

The contents of the *antecedents statement* are regulated by the Consolidated Practice Direction (Ministry of Justice 2010e: III.27). They are compiled by the police from the Police National Computer, and should always contain personal details and information about previous convictions and previous cautions. The purpose of a *defence plea in mitigation* is to show the offender and offence in the best light. The purpose of a *pre-sentence report* is to assist the sentencer by providing information regarding

---

[6] After the leading case of *Newton* (1982) 4 Cr App R (S) 388.

the offence, the offender, and related matters. The form of the report is regulated by National Standards for the Management of Offenders (2007): the report should focus on 'the risk of serious harm posed by the offender, the likelihood of reoffending, and factors that need to be addressed to support desistance from further offending'. A *psychiatric report* is relatively rare, but a court may decide to call for one, and is obliged to obtain one before passing a custodial sentence if the defendant is or appears to be mentally disordered (see further Peay, this volume). The impact of the offender's demeanour and conduct in court is difficult to gauge, but judges recognize that they take account of it and tend to feel that sentencing would be even more difficult if they did not see the offender in person (Cooke 1987: 58; Ashworth *et al.* 1984: ch. 3). This fifth source of influence serves to demonstrate that the impact of information received by a court may be mediated by the attitudes of the sentencer (Shapland 1987).

### REPRESENTATION AT SENTENCING: ROLE OF ADVOCATES

In most common law jurisdictions prosecutors take an active role at the sentencing hearing, usually placing a specific sentence recommendation before the court. Sometimes the prosecutor and defence advocate submit a 'joint submission' at sentencing, usually following plea discussions. Traditionally, English prosecutors make no such sentence recommendation. This practice is changing; prosecutors are now encouraged to be more active at the sentencing stage. The Code for Crown Prosecutors (Crown Prosecution Service 2010: 11.1) states that the prosecutor should draw the court's attention to aggravating and mitigating factors disclosed by the prosecution case, to any statutory provisions or relevant guidelines, to any victim personal statement, and (where appropriate) to the 'impact of the offending on the community'. Some of what is said by an advocate making a defence plea in mitigation will bear directly on the sentence, and the advocate may propose a particular course to the sentencer. However, both prosecution and defence advocates have a duty to prevent the judge from passing an unlawful sentence, and to remind the judge of any relevant sentencing guidelines.

### THE EVOLUTION OF A CUSTODIAL 'TARIFF'

Apart from the few mandatory and minimum sentences, discussed below, the general English approach is to set a fairly high maximum sentence for each offence. One consequence is that most day-to-day sentencing practices are little affected by legislative constraints. For Crown Court sentencing, some normal ranges or starting points have developed over the years, often termed 'the going rate' by judges and 'the tariff' by others. Historically the idea of 'normal' sentences can be traced back at least as far as the 'Memorandum of Normal Punishments' drawn up by Lord Alverstone, the Lord Chief Justice, in 1901 (Radzinowicz and Hood 1990: 755–8). Since 1907 the Court of Criminal Appeal, and since 1966 its successor the Court of Appeal (Criminal Division), has shaped aspects of the tariff. Increased reporting of Court of Appeal judgments on sentencing assisted the concretization of sentencing principles, and the publication of the first edition of Thomas's *Principles of Sentencing* (1970) was a landmark in the development of a common law of sentencing.

The evolution of the custodial tariff was largely driven by the judges, and in the 1980s the Court of Appeal began to issue a few 'guideline judgments' which formalized the 'going rate' for certain offences. Lord Lane, the then Lord Chief Justice, would occasionally take a particular case and, rather than giving a judgment on the facts alone, would construct a judgment dealing with sentencing for all the main varieties of that particular crime. The first of these was in the case of *Aramah*,[7] where guidance was given on sentencing levels for the whole range of drugs offences.[8]

## SENTENCING GUIDELINES

Sentencing guidelines now exist in many jurisdictions. The oldest—and the most researched—are found in the United States, where guidelines originated in the 1970s. Many US states use two dimensional sentencing grids. One dimension is the seriousness of the crime and the other the offender's criminal history. For any given offence, the guidelines will specify a sentence length range for each of a number of categories of criminal history. A sentencing court in a state like Minnesota must impose a sentence within a relatively narrow range. If it wishes to impose a less or more severe sentence the court must find 'substantial and compelling' reasons why the guideline sentence is not appropriate (see Frase 2005 for discussion).

The US-style systems have been rejected by many other jurisdictions. The guideline system in England and Wales, and proposals made in New Zealand, for example, aim to structure sentencers' discretion yet allow more flexibility than the US grid-based schemes (see Young and Browning 2008 and, generally, von Hirsch *et al.* 2009: ch. 6). Other countries such as Sweden have developed what may be described as 'guidance by words'—instead of numerical guidelines the Swedish system articulates principles with which to guide sentencers (see Jareborg 1995). Finally, a number of other countries such as South Africa and Canada have resisted calls to develop sentencing guidelines, and judges in these jurisdictions continue to sentence as they have for decades, enjoying wide discretion and guided only by appellate review (see von Hirsch *et al.* 2009: ch. 6).

### EVOLUTION OF STRUCTURED SENTENCING IN ENGLAND AND WALES

The process of formalizing the tariff through occasional guideline judgments (see above) may be seen as the first phase of the 'guideline movement' in England and Wales. The second phase was initiated by the Crime and Disorder Act 1998, which created the Sentencing Advisory Panel. The Panel drafted possible guidelines for

---

[7] (1982) 4 Cr App R (S) 407.

[8] This judgment was subsequently revised (in *Aroyewumi* (1995) 16 Cr App R (S) 211) so that its guidance is calibrated according to weight and purity level rather than estimates of 'street value', and parallel guidance for newer drugs was added in other judgments (e.g. for 'Ecstasy' in *Warren and Beeley* [1996] 1 Cr App R (S) 233).

sentencing particular offences, conducted public and professional consultations, and then sent its 'advice' to the Court of Appeal. The court was then free to adopt the proposals, or to amend or reject them.[9]

A new phase in the development of guidelines was ushered in by the Criminal Justice Act 2003. The Panel still operated in a similar fashion, but its function was to formulate advice for a body called the Sentencing Guidelines Council. The Council received the Panel's advice (draft guideline), discussed it, issued its own draft guideline for consideration by the Minister for Justice and the Justice Committee of the House of Commons, received their comments, and then formulated what is termed a 'definitive guideline'. Courts were required to have regard to such guidelines and to give reasons if they wished to depart from an applicable guideline. During this period the guideline movement surged forwards, with the result that most cases in the lower courts were covered by the Magistrates' Court Sentencing Guidelines (2008), and in the Crown Court the bulk of cases now fall within guidelines.

In 2010, sentencing in this jurisdiction entered a new era (for a history of the guidelines to that point see Ashworth and Wasik 2010). The Coroners and Justice Act 2009 introduced a number of important changes to the sentencing environment. The reforms introduced by the Coroners Act may be traced to two significant developments. The first was a review of the use of imprisonment conducted by Lord Carter in response to the high and rising prison population in this jurisdiction. In his report Lord Carter proposed a Working Group to consider the utility of a sentencing commission for England and Wales (Carter 2007) and one was duly created by the government in the spring of 2008. The Sentencing Commission Working Group conducted a limited review of sentencing guidelines in other jurisdictions and issued a public consultation document which attracted considerable response from the judiciary and other stakeholders in the sentencing process. A consensus emerged from respondents that a grid-based guidelines system such as that found in Minnesota and other US jurisdictions was not an appropriate model for England and Wales. The Working Group recommended a revamp of the current arrangements rather than adoption of a completely new system of guidelines (Sentencing Commission Working Group 2008).

These developments resulted in the Coroners and Justice Act 2009. This legislation introduced a number of changes to the sentencing guidelines in England and Wales (see Roberts 2011a). First, it amended the duty of a court to comply with the guidelines. Under the previous regime the statute stated that courts 'must have regard' to any relevant guidelines. Section 125 of the new Act states that:

(1) Every court—
   (a) must, in sentencing an offender, follow any sentencing guidelines which are relevant to the offender's case, and
   (b) must, in exercising any other function relating to the sentencing of offenders, follow any sentencing guidelines which are relevant to the exercise of that function,

unless the court is satisfied that it would be contrary to the interests of justice to do so.

---

[9] Usually the Panel's proposals were accepted in most respects, and found their way into a guideline judgment delivered by the Court of Appeal (on, e.g., racially aggravated offences, child pornography, handling stolen goods, and burglary).

Second, the previous statutory bodies have been replaced by a single authority, the *Sentencing Council of England and Wales*. The new Council retains a judicial majority among its 14 members. Before being replaced by the Sentencing Council in 2010, the Sentencing Guidelines Council had issued definitive guidelines for a range of offences. These guidelines remain in force until such time as the Sentencing Council revises and re-issues them—a task which will take several years to complete. In the meantime, the new Council has started issuing its own guidelines. These assume a rather different structure than the SGC Guidelines. The first new guideline—which came into effect in June 2011—relates to the assault offences (see sentencingcouncil.org.uk).

### EXAMPLE OF ENGLISH GUIDELINES

The new format of guideline requires a sentencing court to follow a clear methodology in determining sentence (see Roberts and Rafferty 2011 for further discussion). Let us consider a specific offence to illustrate how the guidelines function. The definitive guideline for causing grievous bodily harm (Offences Against the Person Act 1861, section 18) identifies three overlapping ranges of sentence length, each range relating to a separate category of seriousness. The ranges are: 9–16 years' custody for the most serious assaults; 5–9 years' custody for cases of intermediate seriousness, and a 3–5 years' custody the least serious forms of causing grievous bodily harm.

As a court moves towards determining the sentence to be imposed it will follow the guideline which identifies a series of nine steps. The first task is to determine which of the three levels of seriousness is appropriate for the case appearing for sentencing. The court takes into account the principal elements of the case to be sentenced—for example the degree of premeditation and whether a vulnerable victim was deliberately targeted—to determine which of the three ranges is most appropriate. Thus the most serious cases which involve a high level of harm and a high level of culpability on the part of the offender will fall into the category with the longest sentence length range (9–16 years). Once a court has determined which category range is appropriate it will use the starting point sentence within the range as a point of departure. For the most serious category the starting point—from which a court will calculate a provisional sentence—is 12 years' custody.

The second step is to 'fine tune' the sentence within the chosen range by considering other, less important factors which relate to the seriousness of the crime as well as personal mitigation. These factors include circumstances such as an abuse of power by the offender, any attempt to conceal evidence, or the fact that the crime was committed while the offender was on licence. Personal mitigation includes factors such as an absence of prior convictions, remorse, and any attempts by the offender to address addictions or other problems associated with offending. Having completed this, the court then follows a series of seven other steps to determine the final sentence. For example, step 4 requires a court to take into account whether (and when) the offender entered a guilty plea (see below for further discussion). Figure 29.3 provides a summary of the steps contained in the sentencing guideline for the offence of causing grievous bodily harm with intent.

**Figure 29.3** Summary of Sentencing Guideline Structure in England and Wales[1]

*Offence: Causing Grievous Bodily Harm with intent*[2]

*Total Offence Range: 3–16 years' custody*

*Step 1:* Use the factors provided in the guideline which comprise the principal elements of the offence[3] to determine the offence category which is appropriate:

Category 1:  Greater harm[4] *and* high culpability

Category 2:  Greater harm and lower culpability *or* lesser harm *and* higher culpability

Category 3:  Lesser harm *and* lower culpability

*Step 2:* Use the *starting point* from the appropriate *offence category* to generate a provisional sentence within the *category range.* The *starting point* applies to all offenders irrespective of plea and previous convictions. The guideline contains a list of additional aggravating and mitigating factors. These factors affect crime seriousness[5] or relate to personal mitigation[6] and should result in upward or downward adjustment from the *starting point.*

| Offence category | Starting point | Category sentence range |
|---|---|---|
| 1 | 12 years | 9–16 years |
| 2 | 6 | 5–9 |
| 3 | 4 | 3–5 |

*Step 3:* Consider if any reduction in the provisional sentence should be made to reflect assistance offered or provided to the prosecution.

*Step 4:* Consider the level of reduction appropriate to reflect a guilty plea.[7]

*Step 5:* Consider whether the offender meets dangerousness criteria necessary for imposition of an indeterminate or extended sentence.[8]

*Step 6:* If sentencing for more than one offence apply the totality principle to ensure that the total sentence is just and proportionate to the total offending behaviour.

*Step 7:* Consider whether to make a compensation order and/or other orders.

*Step 8:* Give reasons for and explain the effect of the sentence on the offender.

*Step 9:* Consider whether to give credit for time on remand or bail.

---

[1] Note: complete guideline available at: www.sentencingcouncil.gov.uk
[2] Section 18 Offences against the Person Act 1861; maximum penalty: life imprisonment.
[3] E.g., victim was particularly vulnerable; offender played a leading role in a gang; premeditation.
[4] Greater harm means that serious injury must normally be present.
[5] E.g., victim forced to leave her home; offence committed while offender on bail.
[6] E.g., remorse; no previous convictions; offender is sole provider for dependent relatives.
[7] To a maximum of one third if plea entered at first possible opportunity.
[8] E.g., a life sentence; imprisonment for public protection (IPP) or an extended sentence.

The English sentencing guidelines allow courts considerable variation when determining sentence and are more flexible than the two-dimensional sentencing grids found in states such as Minnesota. What remains unclear for the present at least is the extent to which the guidelines have promoted consistency in sentencing— one of the primary objectives of any sentencing guidelines system. Although the US sentencing commissions routinely collect data showing the proportion of sentences imposed outside the guidelines, this has not been the case in England. However, one of the statutory duties of the Sentencing Council is to monitor the impact of its guidelines, so more comperhensive information will become available as the Council fulfils this duty (see Sentencing Council 2011).

# LEGISLATIVE REQUIREMENTS FOR CUSTODIAL SENTENCES

Legislatures generally set the maximum sentence for each offence, but in some systems they go further. In England and Wales three further forms of legislative intervention may be identified.

## MANDATORY SENTENCES

There has long been a minimum sentence of disqualification from driving for 12 months on conviction for drunk driving. Mandatory minimum prison sentences were introduced in 1997 following a fierce battle between the Home Secretary and the senior judiciary (see Dunbar and Langdon 1998: ch. 10; Ashworth 2001).

One provision requires a court to impose a minimum sentence of seven years for the third Class A drug trafficking offence, unless it would be 'unjust to do so in all the circumstances'. In fact most such offenders would receive at least seven years anyway, and therefore this minimum sentence has impinged little on sentencing practice. A second provision requires a court to impose a minimum sentence of three years for the third domestic burglary conviction, so long as the offender is aged at least 18 and each burglary was committed after the previous conviction for burglary. A court is not bound to impose the minimum if it would be 'unjust to do so in all the circumstances'. It is not clear to which extent this minimum sentence has deflected courts from their normal approach.

The Criminal Justice Act 2003 introduced a further mandatory minimum sentence: for possession of prohibited firearms a court is required to impose at least five years' imprisonment (three years' if the offender is under 18). This is a much stronger provision than the others just discussed, since it applies to a first offence and courts may impose a lesser sentence only in 'exceptional circumstances.'

## SENTENCING FOR MURDER

The 2003 Act also altered the sentencing approach for murder. Since 1965 a court sentencing an offender for murder has been bound to impose life imprisonment. The trial judge would propose a minimum term, reviewed by the Lord Chief Justice, but the final decision would be that of the Home Secretary. On expiry of the minimum term, the murderer would remain in prison until deemed not to present a risk to the public, and would then be released on licence (and subject to recall) for the rest of his life. Following judgments of the European Court of Human Rights and the House of Lords in 2002 that fixing the minimum term for a life sentence is a sentencing decision and must be carried out by a court, the Home Secretary relinquished his jurisdiction but Parliament introduced statutory restrictions on the court's powers. Section 269 of the Criminal Justice Act 2003 requires a court, when setting the minimum term to be served by a person convicted of murder, to have regard to the principles set out in Schedule 21 to the Act. The Schedule indicates three starting points:

- a whole life minimum term for exceptionally serious cases, such as premeditated killings of two people, sexual or sadistic child murders, or political murders;
- 30 years for the most serious cases such as murders of police or prison officers, murders involving firearms, sexual or sadistic killings, or murders aggravated by racial or sexual orientation; and
- 15 years for other murders not falling within either of the higher categories.

In 2009 the Minister of Justice added a further starting point, one of 25 years for murder with a knife carried to the scene. However, the language in Schedule 21 is not constraining, and judges may take account of aggravating and mitigating factors when calculating the minimum term.[10] It remains controversial whether it is right to have a mandatory sentence for murder,[11] in view of the considerable variations in the gravity of the offence; and, if so, whether the minimum terms are too high. The current Coalition Government has described Schedule 21 as 'ill thought-out and overly prescriptive' (Ministry of Justice 2010c: para. 170), and so some loosening of Schedule 21 in favour of guidelines seems likely.

## STATUTORY RESTRICTIONS ON CUSTODIAL SENTENCES

Most jurisdictions attempt to regulate the use of custody by the courts, often by means of statutory restrictions on the imposition of custody. In states with sentencing guidelines the location of an offence within the sentencing grid determines whether custody is an option for the court. In jurisdictions without guidelines there is often a statutory restriction, or direction to courts to use custody only as a last resort, or only when no other sanction is sufficient to achieve the objectives of sentencing.

The Criminal Justice Act 2003 established two significant principles: by section 152(2) a custodial sentence should not be imposed unless the offence is too serious for a community sentence or fine, and by section 153(2) any custodial sentence must be 'for the shortest term...commensurate with the seriousness of the offence'.

---

[10]  *Sullivan* [2005] 1 Cr App R (S) 308.

[11]  Advocates of the mandatory life sentence for murder frequently cite public opinion as a justification for this sanction. However, in the only empirical test of public attitudes, researchers found that the public were not strongly attached to the mandatory life sentence. When asked to sentence cases of murder members of the public often favoured definite terms of imprisonment (see Mitchell and Roberts 2011).

These judgments depend on proportionality, as mentioned earlier. The Sentencing Guidelines Council established guidelines on the application of the custody threshold, stating that its clear intention 'is to reserve prison as a punishment for the most serious offences' and that 'passing the custody threshold does not mean that a custodial sentence should be deemed inevitable', since there may be personal mitigation or 'a suitable intervention in the community which provides sufficient restriction (by way of punishment) while addressing the rehabilitation of the offender to prevent future crime' (SGC, *Overarching Principles—Seriousness* 2004).

## AGGRAVATION AND MITIGATION AT SENTENCING

When courts are determining the seriousness of an offence—the harm caused or threatened and the offender's culpability—they should have regard to its aggravating and mitigating features. Among the mitigating factors listed by the SGC (*Overarching Principles – Seriousness*) are various forms of reduced culpability (e.g. mental disorder, financial pressures) and a good previous record. Courts also recognize mitigating factors that have no bearing on the offence or the offender's culpability—the impact of the sentence on others, an act of heroism by the offender, the payment of compensation to the victim, or assisting the state in prosecuting other offenders (Ashworth 2010: ch. 5.4). The interplay of these factors is critical where a case is 'on the cusp' of custody: in such cases Hough *et al.* (2003: 36–8) found that in custody cases sentencers placed more emphasis on the nature of the offence or the criminal record, whereas in the non-custodial cases the emphasis was on factors personal to the offender. Subsequent research by Jacobson and Hough (2007) involving court observations and interviews with sentencers has demonstrated the importance of personal mitigation; in approximately a third of cases personal mitigation was the major factor reducing the sentence from immediate custody to a community penalty (see Roberts 2011b for further discussion of sentencing factors).

### PREVIOUS CONVICTIONS

How significant should a bad criminal record be in sentencing? The common law principle was the 'progressive loss of mitigation': a first offender received substantial mitigation, which would be lost after the second or third conviction, but it would not be right to 'sentence on the record' and to impose a penalty disproportionate to the seriousness of the offence committed (Ashworth 2010: ch. 6). This principle succumbed to a silent eclipse during the 1990s, and section 143(2) of the Criminal Justice Act 2003 now proclaims an entirely different approach—that a court must treat each previous conviction as an aggravating factor if its relevance to the current offence, and the time that has elapsed since that conviction, make it reasonable to do so. This section suggests a recidivist premium and is reminiscent of the US guidelines where sentence lengths are progressively increased to reflect higher numbers of prior convictions (see Roberts 2008 and von Hirsch *et al.* 2009: 148–62).

## GUILTY PLEA DISCOUNT

Perhaps the most significant mitigating factor is the guilty plea. Well established at common law, the 'discount' is set out in section 144 of the Criminal Justice Act 2003. The guilty plea rate has steadily increased from 63 per cent in 2005 to 71 per cent in 2009 (Ministry of Justice 2010d: 98). The Sentencing Guidelines Council issued a definitive guideline on *Reduction of Sentence for a Guilty Plea* (2007), which recognizes various pragmatic reasons for the discount—saving cost, avoiding trials, reducing anxiety among victims and witnesses. Despite the existence of a definitive guideline regarding the guilty plea discount, the Coroners and Justice Act 2009 explicitly directed the Sentencing Council to produce a guideline on this matter, and one is scheduled to be issued at some future date.

The current guideline establishes a sliding scale, with a maximum reduction of one-third for a guilty plea indicated at the earliest opportunity, reducing to one-tenth if the guilty plea is tendered 'at the door of the court'. The guideline also states that 'the reduction principle may properly form the basis for imposing…an alternative to an immediate custodial sentence'. Thus the guilty plea discount may well make the difference between prison or not, and the statistics bear this out —for example, the custody rate was significantly higher for offenders who pleaded not guilty (69 per cent vs. 55 per cent; Ministry of Justice 2010a: Table 2p). In addition, the average sentence length for offenders convicted on a not guilty plea in 2009 was more than double the length for those who pleaded guilty (47 months vs 22 months; Ministry of Justice 2010a: Table 2p).

Such substantial discounts create considerable pressure on defendants to forgo the right to trial which goes with the presumption of innocence. Where defendants are advised that the discount may make the difference between a custodial and a non-custodial sentence, the risk of innocent people pleading guilty is particularly high.[12] Finally, a very substantial discount for a guilty plea may also have adverse effects on principled sentencing. If the primary determinants of sentence are crime seriousness and culpability, allowing a large discount for a guilty plea will undermine these considerations. After all, even though a guilty plea saves the state's resources and spares victims and witnesses from having to testify, the plea is unrelated to the seriousness of the offence or the offender's level of culpability.

## 'DANGEROUSNESS' SENTENCES

Despite the poor prospects of accurate prediction, governments in many countries regard it as politically necessary to have some kind of 'dangerousness' statute,

---

[12] A further development heightens this risk. The Court of Appeal has altered its position on judges giving indications of sentence, and it is now possible for a defendant who has pleaded not guilty to ask the judge what would be the maximum sentence imposed if the defendant were to change the plea to guilty at this stage (*Goodyear* [2005] Crim LR 659). If the judge indicates a community sentence, and counsel suggests that it would be custody if the defendant persisted in pleading not guilty and were convicted, then the pressure on the defendant would be enormous. (A similar procedure of advance indication of sentence is available in magistrates' courts.)

proclaiming greater public protection from sexual and violent predators. In England and Wales the Criminal Justice Act 2003 adopted this approach and introduced a three-pronged strategy against 'dangerous' offenders. Thus, where the offence had a maximum of life imprisonment, the court was required to impose life imprisonment if the court found that the current offence was serious enough to justify a life sentence, and if the offender was 'dangerous'. If the offence was 'serious' but either did not carry life imprisonment or was not sufficiently serious, the court was required to impose a sentence of imprisonment for public protection. The Imprisonment for Public Protection (IPP) sentence is hardly less constraining than life imprisonment, in the sense that the court sets a minimum term, after which release is only when the Parole Board thinks the risk to the public no longer justifies imprisonment, and release is on licence indefinitely. Then there is the third form of sentence, the extended sentence, composed of the proportionate sentence for the offence, plus an extension period (on licence with conditions) for a violent offence or a sexual offence.

The condition that must be fulfilled before a court imposes any of these sentences is a finding that 'there is a significant risk to members of the public of serious harm occasioned by the commission by him of further specified offences'. The Court of Appeal delivered a 'guidance' judgment on the 'dangerousness' provisions which identified three separate issues.[13] First, the 2003 Act leaves the key term 'significant risk' undefined: the choice of 'significant' rather than 'substantial' may suggest a widening of the net, but the Court of Appeal requires a risk that is 'of considerable amount or importance'. Secondly, there must be a significant risk of this offender committing further 'specified' offences. And thirdly, those offences must be such as to put members of the public at significant risk of serious harm. 'Serious harm' means 'death or serious personal injury, whether physical or psychological'. However, a court was required to have regard to section 229, which created the presumption of significant risk of serious harm where an offender over 18 has been convicted of another such offence; a court should assume this unless, having considered the nature of the offences and any reports about the offender, it considers that it would be unreasonable to regard the risk as significant.

The 'dangerousness' provisions in the 2003 Act were a penological disaster. They were mandatory, and they spread the net so widely as to perpetrate real injustice by subjecting relatively low level offenders to indefinite imprisonment. Moreover, the planning was so poor that the prisons were unable to provide sufficient courses for IPP prisoners to complete in order to secure their release (see, e.g., House of Commons 2008: paras 39–85). The Government recognized some of these criticisms, and in 2008 the mandatory element of the 'dangerousness' sentences described above was removed, and the threshold for imposing such a sentence was increased to crimes 'worth' four years' imprisonment. However, a recent government document refers openly to 'the limitations in our ability to predict future serious offending [that] call into question the whole basis on which many offenders are sentenced to IPP' (Ministry of Justice 2010c: para. 186). The current proposal is to abolish IPP sentences in favour of automatic life

---

[13] *Lang* [2006] Crim LR 174.

imprisonment for the second serious offence, provided that the offences reach a high threshold of seriousness. There remains an urgent need to reconsider the cases of the many people subjected to IPP sentences between 2003 and 2008 and still imprisoned.

## CUSTODIAL SENTENCES AND EXECUTIVE RELEASE

The practical meaning of a prison sentence varies from country to country depending upon the nature of early release provisions. The current situation in England and Wales is that all prisoners serving determinate sentences are released after serving one-half, and are then on licence under supervision (with requirements) until the end of their sentence. Release at an earlier point is possible through the operation of Home Detention Curfew (see Padfield, Morgan, and Maguire, this volume). Decisions on release from sentences of imprisonment for life or imprisonment for public protection, imposed under the 'dangerousness' provisions of the 2003 Act, continue to be made by the Parole Board. Research has shown the risk assessments made by the Parole Board to be unduly conservative in many cases (Hood and Shute 2000).

Release policies are one of the factors that impact on the size of the prison population. Between 1995 and 2009 the English prison population grew by 32,500 inmates or 66 per cent (Ministry of Justice 2010a: 2; see further Liebling and Crewe, this volume). The judiciary and the magistracy tend to explain this as a response to what they regard as the climate of opinion in society, fuelled largely by political and media rhetoric. Despite strong evidence of widespread public misunderstanding about sentencing levels (see Roberts and Hough 2005: 69–71), politicians and the media continue to press for severity. An escalating response to previous convictions and to breaches of court orders has also played a major part in the trend to severity.

Some mandatory or minimum sentences exist, opposed by the judges who point to the need for discretion in sentencing. However, to follow up the earlier discussion, discretion has its disadvantages as well as its advantages. It is a good thing to avoid mechanical sentencing and rigid controls which prevent courts from taking account of particular factors in individual cases. But it is undesirable to allow different approaches that may result in discrimination on grounds of race (Hood 1992) or gender (Hedderman and Gelsthorpe 1997), or allow individual judges to pursue their own policies, or local courts to follow local traditions. There is an urgent need for research to assess the effectiveness of guidelines in terms of shaping the decisions of the courts.

Vital to the success of the 2003 Act in moderating levels of custodial sentencing are decisions around the custody threshold. Where sentences have tended to be ratcheted up, they need to be brought down again. The previous Government considered bringing forward legislation on unit fines, as part of a strategy to revive the use of financial penalties, but nothing happened. Both the 2003 Act and the Council's guideline makes it clear that substantial fines may be used for fairly serious offences, as an alternative to a community sentence, but the real issues are at the other end of the scale. Courts, politicians, and newspaper editors must be persuaded that what appears to them to be a low or 'derisory' fine may make considerable demands on the financial resources of an offender on state benefits. Unless this bridge is crossed, there is little prospect of reducing the number of less serious offenders receiving community sentences.

Where cases are serious enough to justify the imposition of a community sentence, courts must follow the guidelines in distinguishing between the three levels of community sentence (low, medium, and high) and in ensuring that the resulting order is proportionate to the seriousness of the offence. In effect, courts must be prepared to give another community sentence after one has failed: the penal ladder should not be shortened because there is only one form of community sentence, but rather courts must try different programmes and requirements if the offence(s) fall(s) short of justifying imprisonment.

Likewise, the malfunctioning of the suspended sentence must be avoided: exactly how the courts locate it in their sentencing practice will determine whether it is applied to offenders who would otherwise have received an immediate prison sentence (as it should be) or to offenders who might hitherto have been given a community sentence. In the training of magistrates and of judges, this will be a key issue. There is much that is positive in community sentences, with evidence of a determination to reduce re-offending through some imaginative programmes, but the underlying framework remains strongly punitive and the various malfunctions described above might operate so as to increase rather than to decrease the punitiveness of the whole system.

Finally, the role of previous convictions and sentencing for breach must be highlighted. The 2003 Act's provision on previous convictions appears to endorse the 'cumulative' sentencing of repeat offenders,[14] but also there is a growing number of preventive orders imposed on offenders, which may then lead to breach. The rise of the preventive order is evident from provisions in the Sexual Offences Act 2003 for sexual offences prevention orders and risk of sexual harm orders, which join other preventive orders such as travel restriction orders, football spectator banning orders, and exclusion from licensed premises orders. Breach of any such order is an offence carrying imprisonment.

## CONCLUSIONS

Over the past decade, sentencing has evolved more rapidly in England and Wales than any other common law jurisdiction. In addition to the proliferation of definitive guidelines, Parliament has introduced a series of legislative amendments affecting sentencing and early release from prison. In 2010 the current Coalition Government issued a Green Paper entitled *Breaking the Cycle: Effective Punishment, Rehabilitation and Sentencing of Offenders*. Consistent with the general intent of the Government to reduce the costs of public services, the Green Paper proposed to increase the extent to which offenders make financial reparation to 'victims and the taxpayer' (Ministry

---

[14] Section 142 of the Act states that courts should consider each prior conviction to aggravate the seriousness of the offence (and thus the severity of the sentence) in the event that it is reasonable to do so.

of Justice 2010c: 20). At the time of writing (July 2011), the Government has just published its response to the Green Paper. In that response the Government has expressed an intention to work with the Sentencing Council to promote the greater use of financial penalties; to review current arrangements regarding the sentencing for serious sexual and violent offenders; and to simplify a number of elements of sentencing law. It is anticipated that Parliament will put forward a reform Bill late in 2011 (Ministry of Justice 2011).

Sentencing has changed significantly in England and Wales over the last decade. Of all developments, the most promising would appear to be the evolution of sentencing guidelines. The Sentencing Council of England and Wales has, as noted, issued a new format of sentencing guidelines and will continue to issue additional guidelines over the next few years. Sentencers in this jurisdiction now have more structure and guidance than at any previous time, and the benefits in terms of fairer and more principled sentencing cannot be under-estimated.

## ■ SELECTED FURTHER READING

Readings on rationales for sentencing and related issues may be found in: A. von Hirsch, A. Ashworth, and J. V. Roberts (eds) (2009), *Principled Sentencing: Readings in Theory and Policy*, 3rd edn, Oxford: Hart Publishing; M. Tonry (ed.) (2011), *Why Punish, How Much? A Reader on Punishment*, Oxford: Oxford University Press; R. A. Duff and D. Garland (eds) (1994), *A Reader on Punishment*, Oxford: Oxford University Press. See also A. Ashworth and M. Wasik (eds) (1988), *Fundamentals of Sentencing Theory*, Oxford: Oxford University Press. Monographs on sentencing theory include: N. Lacey (1988), *State Punishment*, London: Routledge; R. Duff (2000), *Punishment, Communication and Community*, New York: Oxford University Press; and A. von Hirsch and A. Ashworth (2005), *Proportionate Sentencing*, Oxford: Oxford University Press.

Sentencing texts include: A. Ashworth (2010), *Sentencing and Criminal Justice*, 5th edn, Cambridge: Cambridge University Press; and S. Easton and C. Piper (2008), *Sentencing and Punishment: The Quest for Justice*, 2nd edn, Oxford: Oxford University Press. The website of the Sentencing Council of England and Wales also provides a wealth of material about sentencing and sentencing guidelines in this country: www.sentencingcouncil.co.uk.

For international sentencing see the special issue of the *Federal Sentencing Reporter* published in April 2010; A. Freiberg and K. Gelb (eds) (2008), *Penal Populism, Sentencing Councils and Sentencing Policy*, Cullompton: Willan; C. Tata and N. Hutton (eds) (2002), *Sentencing and Society: International Perspectives*, Aldershot: Ashgate Publishing; M. Tonry and R. Frase (eds) (2001), *Sentencing and Sanctions in Western Countries*, New York: Oxford University Press.

## ■ REFERENCES

Ashcroft, Lord (2011), *Crime, Punishment and the People*, London: House of Lords.

Ashworth, A. (2001), 'The Decline of English Sentencing', in M. Tonry and R. Frase (eds), *Sentencing and Sanctions in Western Countries*, New York: Oxford University Press.

—— (2010), *Sentencing and Criminal Justice*, 5th edn, Cambridge: Cambridge University Press.

—— *et al.* (1984), *Sentencing in the Crown Court*, Oxford: Centre for Criminology, University of Oxford.

—— and Redmayne, M. (2010), *The Criminal Process*, 4th edn, Oxford: Oxford University Press.

——and Wasik, M. (2010), 'Ten years of the Sentencing Advisory Panel', in: Sentencing Guidelines Council and Sentencing Advisory Panel. *Annual Report*. Available at: www.sentencing.council.org.

Austin, W. and Williams, T. (1977), 'A Survey of Responses to Simulated Legal Cases: Research Note on Sentencing Disparity', *Journal of Criminal Law and Criminology*, 68: 305–10.

Bentham, J. (1789), *Principles of Morals and Legislation*, London: W. Pickering.

Bottoms, A. (2004), 'Empirical Research relevant to Sentencing Frameworks', in A. Bottoms, S. Rex, and G. Robinson (eds), *Alternatives to Prison: Options for an Insecure Society*, Cullompton, Devon: Willan.

——, Gelsthorpe, L. and Rex, S. (eds) (2001), *Community Penalties: change and challenges*, Cullompton, Devon: Willan.

——and Von Hirsch, A. (2011), 'The Crime Preventive Impact of Penal Sanctions', in P. Cane and H. Kritzer (eds), *The Oxford Handbook of Empirical Legal Research*, Oxford: Oxford University Press.

Braithwaite, J. and Pettit, P. (1990), *Not Just Deserts*, Oxford: Oxford University Press.

Carter, Lord (2007), *Securing the Future*, London: Ministry of Justice.

Carter Review (2003), *Managing Offenders, Reducing Crime*, London: The Strategy Unit.

Chalmers, J., Duff, P., and Leverick, F. (2007), 'Victim Impact Statements: Can work, Do work (for those who bother to make them)', *Criminal Law Review*, (May) 360–79.

Cooke, R. (1987), 'The Practical Problems of the Sentencer', in D. Pennington and S. Lloyd-Bostock (eds), *The Psychology of Sentencing*, Oxford: Centre for Socio-Legal Studies, University of Oxford.

Crown Prosecution Service (2010), *Code for Crown Prosecutors*, 2010. Available at: www.cps.gov.uk/.

Dignan, J. (2005), *Understanding Victims and Restorative Justice*, Maidenhead: Open University Press.

Doob, A. and Webster, C. (2003), 'Sentence Severity and Crime: Accepting the Null Hypothesis', *Crime and Justice: a Review of Research*, 30: 143.

Duff, R. A. (2000), *Punishment, Communication and Community*, New York: Oxford University Press.

——and Garland, D. (eds) (1994), *A Reader on Punishment*, Oxford: Oxford University Press.

Dunbar, T. and Langdon, A. (1998), *Tough Justice: Sentencing and Penal Policies in the 1990s*, London: Blackstone Press.

Edwards, I. (2004), 'An Ambiguous Participant: The Crime Victim and Criminal Justice Decision-Making', *British Journal of Criminology*, 44: 967–82.

Erez, E. (1999), 'Who's Afraid of the Big, Bad Victim', *Criminal Law Review*, 545–56.

Flood-Page, C. and Mackie, A. (1998), *Sentencing Practice: an examination of decisions in magistrates' courts and the Crown Court in the mid-1990s*, Home Office Research Study No. 180, London: Home Office.

Frase, R. (2005), 'Sentencing Guidelines in Minnesota, 1978–2003', in M. Tonry (ed.), *Crime and Justice*, Chicago: University of Chicago Press.

Garland, D. (1990), *Punishment and Modern Society*, Oxford: Oxford University Press.

Gaudet, F., Harris, G., and St. John, C. (1932), 'Individual Differences in the Sentencing Tendencies of Judges', *International Journal of Criminal Law, Criminology and Political Science*, 23: 811–18.

Harper, G. and Chitty, C. (eds) (2005), *The Impact of Corrections on Re-offending: a review of 'what works'*, Home Office Research Study 291, London: Home Office.

Hart, H. L. A. (1968), *Punishment and Responsibility*, Oxford: Oxford University Press.

Hawkins, K. (ed.) (1992), *Discretion*, Oxford: Oxford University Press.

—— (2003), *Law as Last Resort*, Oxford: Oxford University Press.

Hedderman, C. and Gelsthorpe, L. (1997), *Understanding the Sentencing of Women*, Home Office Research Study No. 170, London: Home Office.

Home Office 2000), *National Standards for the Supervision of Offenders in the Community*, 3rd edn, London: Home Office.

—— (2001), *Making Punishments Work*, London: Home Office.

Hood, R. (1962), *Sentencing in Magistrates' Courts*, London: Tavistock.

—— (1992), *Race and Sentencing*, Oxford: Oxford University Press.

——and Shute, S. (2000), *The Parole System at Work*, Home Office Research Study No. 202, London: Home Office.

Hough, M., Jacobson, J., and Millie, A. (2003), *The Decision to Imprison*, London: Prison Reform Trust.

Hudson, B. (1993), *Penal Policy and Social Justice*, London: Macmillan.

—— (1998), 'Doing Justice to Difference', in A Ashworth and M. Wasik (eds), *Fundamentals of Sentencing Theory*, Oxford: Oxford University Press.

Jacobson, J. and Hough, M. (2007), *Mitigation: The role of personal factors in sentencing*, London: Prison Reform Trust.

Lacey, N. (1988), *State Punishment*, London: Routledge.

Lloyd, C., Mair, G., and Hough, M. (1994), *Explaining Reconviction Rates: a critical analysis*, Home Office Research Study No. 135, London: HMSO.

McGuire, J. (ed.) (2002), *Offender Rehabilitation and Treatment: Effective Programmes and Policies to Reduce Re-Offending*, New York: John Wiley.

Mason, T. et al. (2007), *Local Variation in Sentencing in England and Wales*, London: Ministry of Justice.

Ministry Of Justice (2009), *Story of the prison population 1995–2009. England and Wales*. Available at: www.justice.gov.uk.

—— (2010a), *Sentencing Statistics: England and Wales 2009*. Available at: www.justice.gov.uk.

—— (2010b), *Criminal Statistics: England and Wales 2009*. Available at: www.justice.gov.uk.

—— (2010c), *Breaking the Cycle: Effective Punishment, Rehabilitation and Sentencing of Offenders*. Available at: www.justice.gov.uk.

—— (2010d), *Judicial and Court Statistics 2009*. Available at: www.justice.gov.uk.

—— (2011), *Breaking the Cycle: Government Response*. Available at: www.justice.gov.uk.

MINNESOTA SENTENCING GUIDELINES COMMISSION (2010), *Sentencing Guidelines and Commentary*. Available at: www.msgc.state.mn.us/.

MITCHELL, B. and ROBERTS, J. V. (2011), 'Public Attitudes Towards the Mandatory Life Sentence for Murder: Putting Received Wisdom to the Empirical Test', *Criminal Law Review*, 6: 456–65.

MONAHAN, J. (2004), 'The Future of Violence Risk Management', in M. Tonry (ed.), *The Future of Imprisonment*, New York: Oxford University Press.

PALYS, T. and DIVORSKI, S. (1987), 'Explaining Sentence Disparity', *Canadian Journal of Criminology*, 28: 347–62.

POSNER, R. (1985), 'An Economic Theory of the Criminal Law', *Columbia Law Review*, 85: 1193–231.

RADZINOWICZ, L. and HOOD, R. (1990), *The Emergence of Penal Policy in Victorian and Edwardian England*, Oxford: Oxford University Press.

ROBERTS, J. V. (2008), *Punishing Persistent Offenders*, Oxford: Oxford University Press.

—— (2009), 'Listening to the Crime Victim: Evaluating Victim Input at Sentencing and Parole', in M. Tonry (ed.), *Crime and Justice*, Vol. 38, Chicago: University of Chicago Press.

—— (2011a), 'Sentencing Guidelines and Judicial Discretion: Evolution of the Duty of Courts to Comply in England and Wales', *British Journal of Criminology*, 51: 997—1013.

—— (ed.) (2011b), *Aggravation and Mitigation at Sentencing*, Cambridge: Cambridge University Press.

—— and HOUGH, M. (2005), *Public Attitudes to Criminal Justice*, Maidenhead: Open University Press.

—— and RAFFERTY, A. (2011), 'Structured Sentencing in England and Wales: Exploring the new Guideline Format', *Criminal Law Review*, in press.

SANDERS, A., HOYLE, C., MORGAN, R., and CAPE, E. (2001), 'Victim Impact Statements: Don't Work, Can't Work', *Criminal Law Review*, 447–58.

SENTENCING COMMISSION WORKING GROUP (2008), *Sentencing Guidelines in England and Wales: An Evolutionary Approach*, London: SCWG.

SENTENCING COUNCIL (2011), Crown Court Sentencing Survey: Experimental Statistics, London: Sentencing Council.

SHAPLAND, J. (1987), 'Who Controls Sentencing? Influences on the Sentencer', in D. Pennington and S. Lloyd-Bostock (eds), *The Psychology of Sentencing*, Oxford: Centre for Socio-Legal Studies, University of Oxford.

SHUTE, S. (1999), 'Who Passes Unduly Lenient Sentences?', *Criminal Law Review*: 603.

TARLING, R., MOXON, D., and JONES, P. (1985), 'Sentencing of Adults and Juveniles in Magistrates' Courts', in D. Moxon (ed.), *Managing Criminal Justice*, London: HMSO.

THOMAS, D. (1970), *Principles of Sentencing*, London: Heinemann.

VON HIRSCH, A. (1976), *Doing Justice*, New York: Hill and Wang.

—— and ASHWORTH, A. (2005), *Proportionate Sentencing*, Oxford: Oxford University Press.

——, ASHWORTH, A., and ROBERTS, J. V. (eds) (2009), *Principled Sentencing: Readings in Theory and Policy*, 3rd edn, Oxford: Hart.

——, BOTTOMS, A., BURNEY, E., and WIKSTRÖM, P-O. (1999), *Criminal Deterrence: an Analysis of Recent Research*, Oxford: Hart.

WALKER, N. (1991), *Why Punish?*, Oxford: Oxford University Press.

WASIK, M. (1985), 'The Grant of an Absolute Discharge', *Oxford Journal of Legal Studies*, 5: 211.

YOUNG, W. and BROWNING, C. (2008), 'New Zealand's Sentencing Council', *Criminal Law Review*, April, 287–98.

# 30

# PRISON LIFE, PENAL POWER, AND PRISON EFFECTS

*Alison Liebling and Ben Crewe*

[Prisons] are places where relationships, and the treatment of one party by another, really matter. They raise questions of fairness, order and authority (others might say legitimacy), but also some other questions about trust, respect and well-being in an exceptionally palpable way. [Liebling, assisted by Arnold 2004: xviii]

## INTRODUCTION

Prisons have long been considered exemplary sites for the study of power (see *inter alia* Sykes 1958; Sparks *et al.* 1996; Carrabine 2004). They are places where distinct forms of power flow, sometimes unobtrusively, and sometimes starkly. Writing in the years following the Second World War, Sykes (1958) directly compared the penitentiary with the concentration camp and the labour colony, noting that each was 'a social system in which an attempt is made to create and maintain total or almost total social control' (Sykes 1958: xiv). The results of the notorious Stanford Prison experiment (Haney *et al.* 1973), in which a simulated prison populated by students who had been assigned the role of either prisoner or guard soon descended into mistreatment and abuse, still provides a compelling critique both of the prison as an institution and the brutalizing tendencies of power. Foucault (1977) considered the prison to be the archetypal institution of modern society. By describing the workings of the 'Panopticon', in which (in theory) the perpetual awareness of prisoners that they might be under staff surveillance led them to internalize the external 'gaze' and become docile, self-regulating subjects, Foucault sought to demonstrate wider shifts in the nature of power, governance, and control. Certainly, as a place where there are such stark differentials in power, where the coercive potential of the state is at its most apparent, and where individuals are stripped of many conventional forms of autonomy and control, the prison represents a relatively unique social domain.

Prisons are ultimately coercive environments, but they vary significantly in their power configurations. These variations lead to differences in their moral and emotional climates and result in different types of social order—both between jurisdictions, and within single jurisdictions—some of which are more durable and legitimate than others (Sparks *et al.* 1996). They are special communities (but communities nevertheless), whose form is shaped by social and political ideas held about crime, punishment, social order, and human nature. They are susceptible to abuses of power and to breakdowns in order, and they are marked by inherent legitimacy deficits, not least (but not only) because prisoners are almost always held against their will. They are volatile places, where values are always in tension, respect is always under threat, and compliance has to be constantly worked at, but, for the most part, they are places of order and routine. They are environments where (except in a very few cases, such as some segregation units in some super-maximum prisons (King 1999) relationships exist, and constitute the 'oil' keeping routines flowing (Liebling, Price, and Shefer 2010). Many of the issues addressed in this chapter relate to these matters of power, morality, relationships, and order, seeking to link these 'interior' matters of what prisons are *like* to 'exterior' issues of what prisons are *for* (Carrabine 2004).

## PRISON USE, POLITICAL ECONOMY, AND PENAL POLICY[1]

There were, on 2 September 2011, an unprecedented 88,554 people held in 135 prisons and three Immigration Removal Centres in England and Wales, just under five per cent of whom (4,225) were women.[2] This was substantially over 'useable operational capacity', in itself a 'safe overcrowded' figure, meaning that prisoners are routinely 'doubled up' in cells designed for one to an officially 'safe' level. 80 prisons were overcrowded at May 2011, resulting in a system 'buckling under the strain' (Loader 2001: 351). A further 2,783 offenders (who would otherwise be in prison) were on Home Detention Curfew (Ministry of Justice 2011). 15 per cent of the prison population are on remand, awaiting trial or sentence. The prison population was considerably lower in 1992, at 42,000, and so has more than doubled in two decades. New indeterminate sentences for public protection (IPP), lengthening sentences, and increasing breach of licence proceedings leading to recall to prison, account for much of the increase. Twenty nine per cent of the prison population are serving sentences of four years or longer. An additional 13,644 prisoners (16 per cent) are serving indeterminate sentences. This means almost half of all prisoners are serving sentences of four years or longer, including life (compared to 23 per cent in 1985). The average term served

---

[1] As this chapter has been substantially reshaped since the previous edition of the *Handbook*, some readers may wish to consult earlier editions for a more detailed account of the history and legal organization of prisons. We have also, for reasons of space, restrained from writing in this chapter about prison staff and management, but have done so elsewhere; see Liebling and Crewe, forthcoming.

[2] The number of women in prison has increased by 114% over the past 15 years (see *Bromley Briefings*, June 2011). For up to date facts and figures on the nature, size, and characteristics of the prison population, there is no better source than recent editions of the Prison Reform Trust's *Bromley Briefings*.

by life sentence prisoners has increased from 10.7 years in 1985 to 13.8 years in 1995 and 16.5 years in 2011. Twenty-two prisoners are serving 'whole life' terms, meaning they will never be released. Seven per cent of current prisoners (5,646) are recalls to prison (Ministry of Justice 2011). The sentencing rate has remained stable, but the trend is towards longer sentences and restricted use of parole. IPP prisoners in particular tend to serve well beyond their tariff expiry date. The only population to fall during this period has been the under-18 age group (see Morgon and Newburn, this volume). 26 per cent of the prison population are from a minority ethnic group, and 13 per cent are foreign national prisoners. Sixty eight per cent of prisoners are at, or below, the level expected of an 11-year old in reading (see *Bromley Briefing*, June 2011: 7, and more generally).

England and Wales has the highest imprisonment rate in 'old' Europe (at 154 per 100,000 prisoners), beating Spain and Turkey by a small margin and France, Germany, and especially Nordic countries by a large margin (see ICPS World Prison Brief 2011). Figures from many countries confirm that there is no simple relationship between crime and punishment. Some non-European countries, such as the USA, South Africa, and New Zealand are also 'punitive outliers' (Loader 2011) with imprisonment rates of 743, 316, and 199 per 100,000 respectively. Other countries, such as Finland, have decarcerated in recent years without leading to huge rises in crime relative to comparable nations (Lappi-Seppälä 2006). Imprisonment rates have grown enormously in some countries traditionally regarded as tolerant (for example, the Netherlands, at 319 per 100,000 in 2011). The use of imprisonment is less a reflection of crime rates (which have generally been falling or stable in recent years) than an outcome of a country's political, economic, and institutional conditions (see, e.g., Lacey 2008; Lappi-Seppälä 2011). Cavadino and Dignan (2006) argue that 'there are almost watertight dividing lines between the different types of political economy as regards imprisonment rates in these countries'. That is, neo-liberal nations (e.g. the US, the UK, Australia), where there are limited welfare states, high levels of economic inequality, and relatively individualistic cultures, imprison at much higher rates than countries where there is a more egalitarian culture, and where the state is more committed to providing welfare for all of its citizens (e.g. Denmark, Norway, and Sweden). As well as protecting the poor from poverty and crime, welfare spending reduces the social and symbolic distance between rich and poor, reflecting and reinforcing societal attitudes towards offenders that are more forgiving and inclusive (see also Downes and Hansen 2006; Lappi-Seppälä 2011). Wacquant (2000, 2001, 2009) makes a similar case about the US, arguing that the real function of the prison is to manage social insecurity and penalize poverty. The downsizing of welfare and increase in the use of imprisonment constitute a continuum of interventions designed to manage the urban (sub)proletariat at the margins of (or superfluous to) the neo-liberal economy. The prison and the ghetto thus serve almost identical functions, and are increasingly similar as dilapidated, workless, 'dark' environments aimed mainly at encaging and neutralizing an irredeemable underclass from the surrounding society. The links between political-economy, penal severity, and prison populations are complex (see Lacey 2008), but it is no coincidence that prisoners are disproportionately poor and socially excluded, with multiple disadvantages in terms of education, housing, employment, and mental health

(Social Exclusion Unit 2002). Scholars in the UK have called for penal restraint, or moderation, arguing that the prison is being used excessively for cynical purposes such as short-term political advantage (see Loader 2011).

# THE AIMS, EFFECTIVENESS, AND RECENT HISTORY OF IMPRISONMENT

Politicians, the public, and policy-makers have increasing expectations of the prison. It is used as a means to various ends, including political credibility, and more narrowly, public protection, with high stakes (for example, the ending of political and public office) when it fails to achieve these ends. But outside a small group of specialists and practitioners, few of those with stakes in the prison's effectiveness have a clear understanding of how, or whether, prisons 'work'. The prison is beyond visibility: a symbolic as well as a starkly physical and imposing institution, or 'black box'—a term used in criticisms of evaluation research, which often takes before-after measures (or outcomes) at face value. The effectiveness or otherwise of the prison tends to be judged using reconviction rates following release, but with little explanatory theorizing about the mechanisms or contexts at play in producing these rates. It is difficult to build theories about how specific penal strategies work (or why they don't) without a deeper understanding of what shapes prison life. There are several competing hypotheses about what might be going on, including a deterrence hypothesis (where the effects on recidivism are positive due to unpleasant and unhelpful experiences), a 'damage' hypothesis (where the effects on recidivism are negative, due to unpleasant or unhelpful experiences); and a resocialization hypothesis (where the effects are positive, for the opposite reason to the deterrence hypothesis: due to constructive experiences). These mechanisms may be complementary (that is, they can increase together), or they may be in conflict. There is little evidence for the effectiveness of deterrence or reform at a general level, although certain programs, and certain individuals, sometimes show positive effects.[3] The prison has been found to have an overall criminogenic (that is, negative) effect (see Nagin *et al.* 2009)—destabilizing family ties, disrupting employment opportunities, and stigmatizing and otherwise deskilling its population (Sampson and Laub 1993). As Gallo and Ruggiero propose, the prison may best be seen as a 'factory for the manufacture of handicaps' (1991).

Around 50 per cent of the adult male population released from prison each year are reconvicted within two years (the standard follow-up period; see Ministry of Justice figures released each year). Rates are higher for the young (at 75 per cent), and slightly, although decreasingly, lower for women. Thirty to 35 per cent of adult males

---

[3] There is marginally more support for the effectiveness of rehabilitation than for deterrence. A German longitudinal study has identified two types of offenders in prison: the hedonistic, rational choice group, and the 'neurotic' or 'irrational' group, who suffer more from the pains of imprisonment but return with greatest frequency; see the Hanover Prison project on the Developmental Consequences of Imprisonment, led by Daniela Hosser; see, e.g., Windzio 2006; and www.kfn.de/Research_areas_and_projects/Past_Projects/Developmental_Consequences_of_Incarceration.htm?lang=en.

are recommitted to prison within two years. Because of the 'black box' problem, it is impossible to establish whether those who were not reconvicted just escaped detection, were effectively deterred, or effectively rehabilitated. Reconviction rates tend to be higher when the prison population grows, and lower when the prison population falls (this might be an artefact of length of stay). There are other reasons to believe that as the prison is used more, it becomes less effective. More marginal or low-risk offenders are brought into the 'net' and fewer prisoners have access to the resources they need to work their way out successfully.

So the question of whether prisons are effective is complex. Some observers have noted that what happens in prison has little impact on what happens after release: what shapes behaviour is the current environment (Haines 1997). Sociologists have suggested that to conceive of the prison in terms of 'effectiveness'—an instrumental or technical purpose—is to misunderstand the prison's true function, which is unrelated to its impact on the individual offender. Prisons exist to express public sentiment, articulate moral boundaries, and shore up the power of the state. In other words, punishment, whether in prison or out of it, has deeply social meanings and expressive functions (Garland 1990). As Rod Morgan put it, confined to its 'instrumental crime-control pretensions', the prison is 'not comprehensible, not least because, considered within these limited technical horizons, it does not work' (Morgan 1994). It is possible that the prison is more effective in these wider social and symbolic tasks than in any of its instrumental aims. These functions may explain the prison's continuing appeal, despite its many failings as an institution of social and individual reform.

Many scholars and practitioners have argued that whatever the effectiveness of the prison in instrumental terms, its inner life should be shaped by moral aspirations and values (Stern 1983; Bottoms 1990; Woolf 1991). Without a moral purpose, prisons easily become the abusive and destructive institutions illustrated by Zimbardo (and replicated in countless non-experimental penal settings: most notably the abuses and tortures that took place at Abu Ghraib, and Guantanamo Bay; see Zimbardo 2007). Managerialists (see further below) argue that prisons should be managed according to clearly specified goals. That these goals are, or should be, derived from higher order ends is a test few prisons would pass, theoretically or empirically. The higher order ends (e.g. social utility or social justice) are contested, as are the means by which they might be accomplished. These are political and ideological matters (or choices, see Christie 1993). Prisons are historically a Western development (and notion), so these questions of purpose and value are even harder to address in countries where 'the prison' has been planted by colonial rulers against the grain of local cultures and values (see Jefferson 2010; Cuneen 2011; Akoensi 2011). The links between economic exploitation and slavery in settler societies and the over-representation of impoverished minorities in criminal justice have been noted by many scholars of the prison (e.g. Cuneen 2011, Hallett 2000; Wacquant 2001; and see Bowling and Phillips 2002). In a more general sense, the prison could be said to represent dominance: a basic fact that makes questions of its *legitimacy* always problematic.

The deeper meaning (as well as internal structure) of prisons changes over time as different stakeholders (politicians, the public, campaigning organizations, and the media) demand different functions of it. Ministers and managers have discovered the tools necessary to shape prison life (information technology, performance targets, and management accountability), and therefore the oscillations between security-oriented and punitive sentiments and justice or rehabilitative sentiments noted by Sparks (1998) and others seem to occur with ever-greater speed. These changes in the emotional and political tone of penal policy have deep effects on prison life, as does the language used to define penal ends. Indeed, the recent history of prisons in England and Wales has been profoundly shaped by such shifts in penal sensibilities and language, which are often magnified in their significance in prison, where apparently small differences (for example, between the existence of some trust between staff and prisoners, and none at all) have major implications for prison life (see further, Liebling, assisted by Arnold 2004, and below). This is morally, managerially, and personally challenging for those operating prisons, who have to get right the complex and precarious balance between the imposition of order, and the respectful and legitimate treatment of individual prisoners.

The period 1990–92, for example, was, in hindsight, a period of liberal optimism: prison populations were declining, Lord Justice Woolf had written his 456-page analysis of the importance of justice in prison, following the most serious prison disturbances the UK had ever seen (Woolf 1991). The Conservative Home Secretary Douglas Hurd (later, incidentally, the Chairman of the Prison Reform Trust) had declared that prisons were 'an expensive way of making bad people worse'. Prison officers understood, following Woolf, that one way of improving order in prisons was to treat prisoners more carefully. But Woolf's careful concept of justice was translated into the slippery concept of 'care'. His report's sub-title was 'Security, control and justice', but the White Paper to follow had the title, 'Custody, *care* and justice'. Serious and unforeseen consequences followed. In the interests of good relationships with prisoners, and influenced by an ideology that associated collective disorder with a sense of unfairness, prison officers under-enforced certain security procedures. Two sets of escapes from maximum security prisons in 1994 and 1995 followed, and were directly linked to these practices. In the interest of 'fairness', 'care', and order, prison staff had, in effect, allowed one prisoner to accumulate 84 boxes of property, a small amount of semtex and a bicycle (Home Office 1994).[4]

The response to Sir John Learmont's scathing report on Whitemoor's Special Security Unit by a then Conservative Government was to demand stricter restrictions on prisoners' property (volumetric control), and to insist that prisoners earned their privileges by 'good behaviour and hard work' (Bottoms 2003). The Director General (or Chief Executive) of the Prison Service was sacked (see Lewis 1997) and the Prison Service was berated and instructed to follow its own procedures more carefully in future. Following two years of 'liberal consensus' and progressive reforms, including the introduction of a Prisons Ombudsman, new grievance procedures, more time

---

[4] There were reasons for this slow accumulation of property by highly knowledgeable and organized prisoners, as well as for the gradual pushing back of prison officers on matters of detail over time. The practice (known as 'conditioning' since the escapes, but having many other explanations) is characteristic of prisons in many different places, so that prison sociologists (and psychologists) have written of the precarious balance of power, the inroads prisoners make, the pressure on staff to give away some of their power, and the compromises, accommodations or corruptions necessary to getting through the day peacefully (see, in particular, Sykes 1958).

out of cell, and better access to families, prisoners were portrayed in media headlines as living in luxury, sending prison officers to the shops for cooking ingredients (one officer was sent out twice because he brought back 'the wrong sized potatoes' (Home Office 1994), and causing instability, as drug taking and assault rates increased. If this was justice, the then Home Secretary Michael Howard declared, then the Prison Service should be wary of it. Our point is that this model was not justice, but laxity (or what we would call 'under-policing'). Practitioners had been right to think that fairness and care led to order (see below), but they did not understand how fairness operated in prison. Although prisoners often experience fairness as a *form* of care, the two are not synonymous, and care is not the same as indulgence or laissez-faire management. There is more to be said about the under-use of power by prison staff, as well as its over-use, and we return to this theme later. But, at the time, little attention was paid to finding an explanation for this common prison practice, or to exploring and defining the meaning of critical terms, like justice and humanity, lying at the heart of penal policy.

The political backlash that followed constituted one of the most dramatic transformations of the inner life of prisons witnessed in the UK. The term 'decent but austere' was used to communicate a more restricted and individually earned quality of life for prisoners. Their material lives were completely redrawn (see Liebling 1999 for an account). From 1995, prisoners' perceptions of relationships between staff and prisoners declined, suicide rates went up, and instances of staff violence against prisoners began to reappear, following a marked decrease in the period immediately after Woolf (Liebling, assisted by Arnold 2004). This reassertion of penal authority coincided with a redrawing of the boundaries of tolerance towards offenders in general (see Sparks 1996). The moral status of prisoners declined and there was a marked harshening of the emotional tone of penal policy. This led to a deepening of the prison experience: both a rise in the prison population, and a feeling among prisoners that the 'weight' or psychological burden of imprisonment was increasingly acute. There were some specific policies that contributed to this transformation (the introduction of earned privileges, mandatory drug testing, the control of prisoners' personal possessions, the use of CCTV, and so on), but significant changes in the tone of prison life were also brought about simply through a transformation in the wider moral status of prisoners—changing ideas about who prisoners are and their claims to rights and freedoms.

One of the explanations for the significance of *ideas* in shaping prison life is that policies and official reports often live on shelves, and what takes place 'out there on the landing' is a *popular conception* of what the policy or the report is all about. Prison officers are members of the public, and (especially given the relatively brief training of new entrant officers in England and Wales) their understanding of who prisoners are or what they deserve is influenced by shifting public perceptions, as well as by policy instructions, which hardly any prison officer ever manages to read. Changes in the popular meaning of imprisonment can also influence prisoners directly. Psychological experiments have shown that placing volunteers in isolation has different effects depending on whether or not the volunteers are told that the isolation experience is *intended* to be punishing (Orne 1968).

## LEGITIMACY AND ORDER IN PRISON

The first prison scholars to address seriously and empirically the concept of legitimacy and its application to daily prison life were Richard Sparks, Tony Bottoms, and Will Hay. At the heart of their book, *Prisons and the Problem of Order* (Sparks *et al.* 1996) is a detailed comparison of two English high-security prisons and the contrasting ways in which they sought and maintained order. The two prisons (Albany and Long Lartin) differed in terms of their regimes and institutional 'climates', so that Albany operated a stringently controlled regime (relative to other English long-term prisons) involving restrictions on association and movement within the prison, and stricter rule enforcement, while Long Lartin operated a more 'liberal' regime, where prisoners had more time out of cell, more freedom of movement, a lighter supervisory style, and a more relaxed ethos of staff-prisoner relationships, in which staff sought to manage the prison 'without formally sanctioning every small infraction of the rules' (Sparks and Bottoms 2008: 94).

When the authors reflected on the question of which regime was perceived as more legitimate by prisoners, it transpired that the prisons offered different advantages, and had competing strengths and weaknesses. Albany looked more conflict-ridden on the surface. Numerous rubbing points with staff led to high rates of disciplinary infractions (e.g. refusals to work, disobedience, and fighting).[5] However, for most prisoners, it was quite safe: because it was closely policed, prisoners could collect their meals, return to their cells and eat them, untroubled by others, which they appreciated, and some older prisoners welcomed the restraining effect of the regime on younger, more boisterous prisoners. The regime had other strengths, in that it was 'quite highly procedurally explicit and relatively consistent in its operation, and emphasised good "service delivery" in matters such as food and pre-release programmes' (Sparks and Bottoms 2008: 94). Moreover, prisoners drew a sharp distinction between the regime and the staff who administered it, whom they considered to be 'largely reasonable, fair, and just doing their job'. Other scholars have found this distinction between the demeanour of staff and the material properties of the regime (e.g. Ahmad 1996; Bottoms and Rose 1998; Liebling, assisted by Arnold 2004; Liebling, Price and Shefer 2010), confirming the argument that prison staff 'actually embody' a prison's regime: their attitude, approach to their work, and treatment of prisoners define and shape a prison's quality, and prisoners' experience of it.

Although prisoners were generally more approving of the more liberal regime at Long Lartin, there were two kinds of objections against its 'social' rather than 'situational' model of order: first, staff had too much procedural discretion at their disposal, leading to inconsistency; second, because of its more hands-off supervisory style, it offered more opportunities for predation and violence, and therefore provided a less safe form of custody:

---

[5] This gave rise to 'a working theory that over attending to the risk of disorder in one way might serve to exacerbate it on another' (Sparks and Bottoms 2008).

The level of *sub rosa* economic activity (for example, the supply of drugs, and gambling) was high; there was evidence from hospital records and numbers of alarm bells to suggest that the level of back-stage violence might have been much greater than the official picture of calm would indicate; and when incidents did occur those within our sample were more likely than at Albany to involve numerous people and the use of weapons. (Sparks and Bottoms 2008)

The study has a number of implications. First, prisons vary in their approaches to and visions of order, and this has consequences for the prisoner experience. Second, some prisons are more legitimate than others, but legitimacy has a number of components, and there may be trade-offs between the over-enforcement and under-enforcement of rules. Third, legitimacy is not just about 'pleasing the prisoners'. The criteria for legitimacy are based on more than assent—they are also based on shifting standards of fairness generally accepted in society at large (see further Bottoms and Tankebe 2011). Fourth, differences in the legitimacy of prison regimes relate to the ways in which members of staff use their power:

> What...becomes crucial is *the way* that that power is exercised. Some regime conditions can seem to prisoners to be deeply unfair (as the restricted regime at Albany did), and some decisions made by prison staff can seem, for example, capricious in outcome, or arrived at without properly listening to the prisoner, and in either case unfair. To the extent that such situations are ameliorated, however, prisoners are normally willing to admit that particular regimes, or particular kinds of staff behaviour, are *fair* rather than unfair. In such contexts, we argued, prisons can indeed appear legitimate to prisoners. (Sparks and Bottoms 2008: 98)

This analysis has changed the terms on which prisons are studied, and has shaped subsequent approaches to the sociology of prison life. Whilst much of the interest in legitimacy has been linked to the matter of compliance (prisoners comply with regimes, at least in part, because of their perception of the legitimacy or otherwise of specific regimes and practices) this type of analysis of the inner life of prison has also been found to be relevant to prisoner *well-being* (see further below). It also draws attention to the importance in prisons of *non*-coercive forms of power.

## POWER, COERCION, AND THE CHANGING SHAPE OF PRISON LIFE

Coercion is often regarded as the prison's essential mode of power. As Cover (1986: 1607) notes, 'most prisoners walk into prison because they know they will be dragged or beaten into prison if they do not walk'. Some prisons, such as 'supermax' institutions, are defined almost entirely by coercive forms of power (see Rhodes 2004; King 1991, 2005). But, as Sykes (1958) noted, and as our account of legitimacy suggests, coercion is an inefficient and dangerous basis on which to run a prison. It is time-consuming to apply ankle-locks and handcuffs, and it is provocative to rely on threats in order to get things done. In the UK, only a very small number of prisoners held in 'special security units' or the segregation sections of 'close supervision centres' are subjected to a regime that is comparable to the supermax, and even in these units efforts are made to engage with prisoners. In the majority of prisons in England and Wales, a casual visitor might be surprised by how rarely direct force is used. But the fact that naked coercion is employed relatively infrequently inside most prisons in the UK does not mean that its presence has no impact, for the threat of force often works as a 'final persuader' (Wrong 2002: 26). Prisoners are aware that the coercive potential of the institution is considerable, and daily life in prison is defined by a set of tacit, ritualized warnings that the authorities have a range of coercive measures (e.g. segregation, transfer, direct force) at their disposal, or held in reserve. Further, the prison's locks, gates, and walls – its 'situational control measures'—directly constrain movements in all manner of ways.

These measures become part of a wider psychological architecture that generates compliance, or shapes behaviour, through habit and a sentiment of resignation. As Foucault (1977) argued, through the prison's rigid timetable and regimentation of daily activity, prisoners become 'trained' or 'habituated' into certain patterns of behaviour. As in society outside, they become accustomed to a daily set of rituals and routines and begin to take for granted their predicament. Compliance becomes almost automatic, a result of the 'dull compulsion' of penal subsistence (cf. Abercrombie et al. 1980). Meanwhile, the endemic symbols of institutional power (uniforms, fences, security cameras, and so on) reinforce to prisoners the sense that there is little alternative but to comply. From the time they enter the institution, prisoners undergo a set of rites and degradations which reiterate to them their powerless status. These range from breaches of personal and bodily boundaries (e.g. strip-searches; and the use of personal files to which they have no access), to directives on how they must dress, organize their living spaces, and address their captors (Garfinkel 1956; Goffman 1961). Any explanation of prisoner compliance needs to take into consideration the fact that, as a result of these processes—and, as most prisoner typologies emphasize (e.g. Goffman 1961; Morris and Morris 1963; Cohen and Taylor 1972)—most prisoners see little alternative but to 'make do', 'get their head down' (see Carrabine 2004), and get on with the sentence with a general attitude of unenthusiastic conformity. This does not mean that they are reconciled to their situation, or approving of it.

Order and compliance are also maintained through incentives and disincentives, although their power is often exaggerated relative to normative factors (Bottoms 2003). First, exploiting the fact that imprisonment is inherently depriving, prisons offer a number of inducements to behave. Divested of personal possessions and normal sources of identity, activity, and comfort, most prisoners are willing to comply with the regime in order to improve their daily quality of life. Rights and rewards that may seem trivial, such as the opportunity to watch television or have extra use of the prison gym, become institutional levers to regulate behaviour (Goffman 1961; Mathiesen 1965). In the American penitentiary described in Sykes's classic study, *The Society of Captives*, power flowed through an illicit negotiation between staff and prisoners, with the former dispensing privileges to inmate leaders in order to keep the peace. Sykes believed that the official rewards that the institution could offer had less traction than informal perks such as a desirable job or material goods, even if (as later scholars illustrated—see Jacobs 1977), mutual self-interest was an insecure basis for order and compliance.

In prisons in England and Wales, the appeal to prisoner self-interest was formalized from 1995 onwards through an official incentives and earned privileges (IEP) scheme, which offers prisoners extra or longer visits, an additional spending allowance, and other such benefits, providing that they behave in an institutionally desirable way. Prisoners on 'basic', the lowest tier of the IEP scheme, are subject to a regime that is considerably more austere: for example, their in-cell television is removed, they are given reduced opportunities to mix with other prisoners, and they are obliged to wear prison uniform (the precise details of each prison's scheme varies, within parameters). Although the introduction of the IEP scheme was beset with difficulties (see Liebling *et al.* 1999) and the effects on behaviour are mixed (Bottoms 2003; Liebling 2008) the appeal of privileges and (perhaps more importantly) the threat of having them withdrawn mean that the policy exerts considerable influence on most prisoners, especially those who fear that they would cope poorly on a restricted regime (see Crewe 2009). Private prisons in particular rely on a consumerist model of prisoner compliance, generally providing higher wages and better material conditions than their public sector counterparts. In both sectors, even greater leverage is produced by the promise of freedom, i.e. temporary leave and early release schemes. Many prisoners claim that it is the prospect of release, rather than immediate material conditions, which motivates them to comply.

The problem with many of these schemes in practice is the difficulty of administering them fairly (or legitimately) in the eyes of prisoners. Giving prison officers wide-ranging discretionary power to form judgments with effects on prisoners' quality of life in prison, and their prospects of release, can be fraught with dangers. How do officers judge prisoners' 'deservingness', or 'riskiness', without the risk of discrimination? Prisoners tend to agree with the *principles* of earned privileges, and earned freedom (see Liebling *et al.* 1997), but they rarely agree with its execution in practice. The 'justice safeguards' documented the policy (appeals procedures, criteria for decision-making, and the existence of a formal board) are, like many prison practices, honoured more in the breach.

Critical penologists more often highlight the 'harder', more coercive components of prison life than the 'softer' and more varied forms of practice observable in ordinary prisons. In doing so, they emphasize the fundamental disparity in power between staff and prisoners. This imbalance is brought into particular relief when abuses are exposed, such as systematic staff brutality in the segregation unit of HMP Wormwood Scrubs in the 1990s. The picture painted by Sykes (1958) of a necessary compromise between prisoners and staff implies a rather different balance of power. Sykes argued that a number of factors militated against officials being the 'omnipotent rulers' that they appear to be (Sykes 1958: 42). Among the many 'defects' in their power, they were outnumbered by and reliant upon prisoners who were hostile to institutional authority, leading them to cede power to influential prisoners, and to turn a blind eye to some rule infractions in return for peace. Here, then, the emphasis is on the relative powerlessness of staff, and the capacity for prisoners to exert considerable 'upward' influence upon them. It is significant, for example, that the highest proportion of prisoners 'on basic' tend to be found in young offender institutions and (during its early implementation, at least) in women's prisons, and the lowest proportion in high security prisons, where 'misbehaviour' (where it occurs) can be of a more serious nature. Prisoners manage the way staff use their power 'from below' (see Liebling *et al.* 1997).

The idea that prisons should be run on the basis of this kind of compromise or accommodation between staff and prisoners has become unfashionable, though until the period of the escapes, it was relatively widespread in the UK. The delegation of too much power to prisoners risks creating an illegitimate tyranny. The under-use of staff authority may be as dangerous as its over-use, if it leads to regimes which are under-policed and disordered (and therefore experienced as unsafe). Getting this balance of power right is the key task of prison management. Prisoners do not like to be restricted unduly, but they want restrictions to be placed on the activities of their peers (whether in relation to noise or the potential for victimization, as Sparks *et al.* noted, above). When excessive power is granted to prisoners, or staff under-police the wings, prisoners are exposed to 'exploitation, wheeler-dealing and strong-arming of various kinds' (McDermott and King 1988: 364). Moreover, many prisoners complain that, in under-regulated environments, it is hard not to 'get into trouble' (Crewe *et al.* 2011) and easy to feel that staff are indifferent to one's concerns and development. In other words, a certain amount of power, or 'supportive limit-setting' (Wachtel and McCold 2001), is generally welcomed by prisoners (and may be a moral requirement), for it can indicate care, provide reassurance, generate fairness and 'save you from yourself'. Prisoners certainly include consistency and 'policing' in their discussions of the fairness of a prison regime (as we suggested above; see also Liebling, assisted by Arnold 2004; Liebling *et al.* 2011). Nonetheless, it is worth noting how frequently staff and prisoners alike recognize two of Sykes's key observations: first, unless prisons are to be inhumane, a certain amount of low-level compromise and under-enforcement is necessary for staff and prisoners to get through the day; second, prisons run only with the 'permission' (expressed consent) of their captives (see further Bottoms and Tankebe 2011).

Important shifts have undoubtedly occurred in the forms of power found in prisons in England and Wales in recent decades. Describing prisons of the 1970s and 80s, prison scholars consistently documented a system that, while harbouring pockets of liberal-humanitarianism in special places (therapeutic communities, or special purpose wings), was primarily characterized by coercive control and punitive neglect (Stern 1983; Scraton *et al.* 1991). In many prisons, intimidation and unprovoked aggression were used to humiliate prisoners and threaten them into compliance, while prisoners' rights were routinely and callously neglected (Scraton *et al.* 1987; Scraton *et al.* 1991; McDermott and King 1988; King and McDermott 1990; Jameson and Allison 1995; Smith 2004; Sim 2008). Staff-prisoner relationships were, as a result, defined by 'toxic hostility' (Sim 2008) and mutual contempt (McDermott and King 1988).

Based on research in a medium-security men's training prison, Crewe (2009, 2011) argues that penal power has been re-shaped extensively, with 'softer' modes of power having superseded (but not replaced) 'harder' and more punitive mechanisms (see also Carlen and Tombs 2006; Sim 2009). In most prisons, staff-prisoner relationships are reasonably positive, and the tone on the landings is less tense and authoritarian than in the past. The prison is coercive mainly as a last resort, when other measures fail. Most prisoners fear physical violence less than 'the power of the pen'—the potential for comments written in wing files and reports by prison psychologists to impact negatively on their conditions and future prospects. Prisoners can no longer move through their sentences passively, but must instead 'engage' with staff, actively address their offending behaviour, and self-regulate. Many feel they have to re-form their identities in narrowly prescribed ways in order to meet the demands of the system. If they want to improve their living conditions and expedite their progression through the system, they have to exercise their autonomy in specific ways. This analysis is consistent with the literature on 'governmentality' (see Garland 1997), and suggests that Foucault's (1977) notion of panoptical power has considerable value for thinking about modern imprisonment in England and Wales. New sentence conditions and highly demanding forms of psychological power mean that power is less directly oppressive than in the past, but is highly demanding and invasive. Under this form of 'neo-paternalism' (Crewe 2009, 2011), the prison experience is defined by 'tightness' (ibid.; Crewe 2010) as well as 'depth' (Downes 1988) and 'weight' (King and McDermott 1995), the former referring to the impact of security and control measures, and the latter to the onerousness of the prison experience i.e. the degree to which prison life is 'an ordeal, an assault on the self' (Downes 1988: 179).

The balance between these qualities depends on the culture of an establishment and its role within the prison system. In higher-security prisons, the prisoner experience is tighter, deeper, and altogether heavier than in medium-security conditions (Liebling *et al.*, in press). The institution is preoccupied with security and risk assessment, and prisoners are either resigned to or struggling to come to terms with increasingly long sentences. Staff are not physically brutal towards prisoners, but many are indifferent to and suspicious of them, and relationships are defined by a lack of trust. In stark contrast, research in HMP Grendon, a prison which operates as a therapeutic-community, documents an altogether more positive culture, in which prisoners engage openly with staff and describe a regime that recognizes their humanity and treats them with high levels of respect (Shuker and Sullivan 2010; see also Cooke 1989; Genders and Player 1995). Prisoners rate Grendon highest on MQPL—the prisoner quality of life survey originating in the Liebling *et al.* research (see, e.g., 2011). Even here, though, there is plenty of power 'flowing', not least through the colonizing framework of therapeutic ideology, and through the implicit threat to prisoners that they can easily be returned to the mainstream prison system should they not comply.

However penal power is organized, it is likely to generate some level of resistance precisely because prisons confine people against their will and impose upon them a range of behavioural obligations. Even if prisoners can do little to alter their general predicament, it is rare that they do not seek to counteract and contest some aspects of authority and its manifold intrusions. The most extreme manifestations of resistance are prison riots, which seek to disrupt or overturn the core functions of the institution (Useem and Kimball 1989; Scraton *et al.* 1991; Colvin 1992; Carrabine 2004). But just as institutional coercion is observed more often through threat than direct action, so too is prisoner resistance more often expressed in forms other than open, violent rebellion. Instead, it is the *risk* of collective defiance and the perpetual push-back against institutional power that exert more 'upwards' force on the institution. Collective (or subgroup) influence is enhanced when prisoners can draw upon resources outside prison to negotiate with the authorities. These can include gang structures, political ideologies, legal resources, and external sensibilities based around faith and ethnicity

(Jacobs 1977; Buntman 2003). McEvoy's (2000) study of paramilitary imprisonment in Northern Ireland illustrates the galvanizing potential of political-religious conviction, especially when backed by a wider community providing ideological support, political influence, and a real external threat to prison managers. In the wings within The Maze prison, highly disciplined prisoner groups gained incremental control over institutional space by constantly pushing at boundaries, using external contacts to intimidate staff. They also resorted to extreme challenges such as escape attempts, hunger strikes, and 'dirty protests' (the desecration of cells using excrement) to impress upon the authorities their resistance to its claims to legitimacy. Less confrontational forms of politically-inspired collective action include self-education and 'go-slows' (see Buntman 2003).

The will and solidarity required to maintain such challenges is uncommon in prisons in England and Wales (although see Liebling *et al.*, in press). Prisoners rarely act against the prison on the basis of a collective 'convict' identity (although minor collective action—sit down protests or refusals to come in from the exercise yard—are not so unusual). However, individual prisoners who make use of the law can alter penal practices significantly; threats to resort to the law can shape staff behaviour, and organizational concerns with the risk of legal challenge can force the hands of reform (Whitty 2010). Everyday negotiations between staff and prisoners are increasingly animated by factional assertions of religious rights and ethnic identities (Phillips 2011; Liebling *et al.*, in press). Even when prisoners are needy, divided, and highly dependent on staff, they can exert influence through what Mathiesen (1965) called 'censoriousness'—chastising officials for not conforming to their own rules (the strategy of the 'barrack-room lawyer'). This strategy has the advantage of challenging the authorities on terms that they cannot easily dismiss. As a form of resistance and self-assertion, it is therefore both prudent and effective.

Acts and gestures that are apparently trivial (e.g. the use of indecipherable language, specific forms of dress, choosing to close one's cell door rather than let it be closed by staff) represent refusals to allow the institution to swamp one's identity, impose its definitions, or extinguish feelings of dignity and control (Bosworth 1999; Bosworth and Carrabine 2001; Rowe 2011). Some prisoners use religious and spiritual practices, or activities such as body-building or art, to escape temporarily the grasp of power (Cohen and Taylor 1972). Whether such acts constitute resistance—the attempt to 'dilute, circumvent, or eliminate the imposition of unwelcome power' (Buntman 2003: 37)—rather than psychological survival or coping, or whether these motives are related, is arguable. The point is that resistance is not limited to its most explosive and organized manifestations, nor is the absence of such manifestations an indication that prisoners are content. Since open defiance is risky, most prisoners limit their dissent to minor rule-breaking or to backstage areas where they can expel their frustrations without repercussions.

As we outlined above, some prisons are more legitimate or less coercive than others, and this helps shape the terms of resistance and compliance, as well as the coping strategies available for use. Prisoner autobiographies provide powerful evidence that authoritarian regimes produce anger, resentment, and sometimes violent retribution (McVicar 1974; Smith 2004). They also illustrate that, when exposed to more decent environments or inspiring individuals, the behaviour of people previously considered to be pathologically violent can be transformed (Boyle 1984; and see Cooke 1989; Sparks 2002; Bottomley *et al.* 2004). These prisons are certainly more psychologically survivable (Liebling 2005a). When institutions are more 'hard-line', they tend to set the tone for harder and more violent reactions among prisoners as well as higher numbers of suicides (see Jacobs 1977; McEvoy 2001; Liebling 2007). Harsh treatment produces defiance and distress (Mandaraka-Sheppard 1986). Softer forms of power seem to generate softer forms of resistance: under conditions of 'tightness' (a significant, but still 'soft' form of power), there are few obvious targets for frustration, and violence is neither justified (or provoked) by the nature of staff treatment nor a prudent way to vent one's feelings (see Crewe 2009). The arrangements of power give shape to different forms of response.

Within any one prison, different prisoners will be addressed, engaged, and provoked by different components and combinations of power. 'Some may obey rules from fear, while others might support them out of habit or loyalty. They may even be obedient because they believe in the legitimacy of regulations in their own right' (Bosworth and Carrabine 2005: 506). Crewe (2009) illustrates how the fear of coercion, feelings of helplessness, the pull of incentives, and the assessment of institutional decency depend on such factors as a prisoner's material needs, their experiences of authority, and their sentence type (see also Wheeler 1961). Some prisoners, mainly former drug addicts who are ashamed of their past, may side with the prison morally, and comply out of genuine normative commitment. Other prisoners are more pragmatic, complying either because they want to enhance their material conditions, or because, over long periods of incarceration, and despite high levels of frustration, they have developed an ethos of fatalistic stoicism. Other prisoners comply in highly superficial ways, consciously constructing themselves to 'look good on paper', appearing compliant to staff, and feigning reform, while engaging in all manner of backstage subversion, including drug dealing. Evidence suggests that increasingly restrictive sentences and (post-)release conditions have unintended effects, inciting new kinds of 'master identities' (Lacombe 2008), and encouraging some prisoners to 'max out' their sentence rather than apply for parole (Ostermann 2011; Robert 2012, forthcoming).

## PRISON SOCIAL LIFE AND CULTURE

In the post-war years, in the US in particular, detailed studies of the ordinary life of prisons were common (e.g. Sykes 1958; Irwin and Cressey 1962; Irwin 1970; see also Morris and Morris 1963). In recent years, however, fine-grained accounts of the prisoner social world have largely been displaced by analyses of 'mass imprisonment' (Garland 2001; Wacquant 2009) and what Sim (2009) labels 'top-down' accounts of penal policy. As Wacquant (2002: 385) summarizes, at a time when it is vital to understand what increasing numbers of people are subjected to, prison ethnography 'is not merely an endangered species but a virtually extinct one'.

Because studies of the inner life of prisons are rare and dispersed, it is difficult to talk in general terms about prison social life and culture. Nonetheless, some basic features can be outlined. Most accounts of prisoner social relations have depicted a world of social caution and wariness, lacking in 'basic cohesion' (Clemmer 1958: 129; see also Mathieson 1965). Prisons are difficult places in which to evaluate character, and risky places in which to extend trust. Kindness is often 'taken for weakness', and vulnerabilities can be easily exploited. As Sykes (1958) highlighted, prisoners are acutely aware that their criminal peers may be dangerous, exploitative, or unreliable. Most friendships are therefore reserved and pragmatic (Clemmer 1940/1958; Morris and Morris 1963; Cohen and Taylor 1972), based on defensive needs to prevent exploitation rather than affection. Prisoners who know each other prior to imprisonment, or from previous sentences, are more likely to trust each other. Place is a central component of prisoner social life (far from the abstract entity described in some social theory, e.g. Giddens 1991). Prisoners who come from the same towns or cities are bound together by shared reference points and external networks which mean that in-prison behaviour has consequences for a prisoner's reputation both inside and outside prison (Crewe 2009).

In North America, in men's prisons, the social system is structured primarily around ethnicity and religion, often with high levels of conflict between different social groups (Jacobs 1983; Wacquant 2000; Irwin 2005). In the UK, factors such as age, lifestyle, and criminal identity contribute to a complex set of social relations, in which there is considerable fluidity between small prisoner cliques. Relations between prisoners from different ethnic and religious groups are generally relatively harmonious (Genders and Player 1989; Phillips 2008; Crewe 2009) but there is evidence that this may be changing (Phillips 2011; Liebling *et al.* 2011). Minority ethnic prisoners tend to stress that their preference for socializing with people of the same race or ethnicity is linked to commonalities of experience, and shared values, rather than a statement of hostility towards majority ethnic groups. Affiliations based around race, religion, and ethnicity often provide secondary support in times of need or crisis (see Wilson 2003). Yet the negotiation of race is 'difficult terrain' (Phillips 2008: 322). Social fissures are made visible when disputes between prisoners relate in any way to race or religion (see Edgar *et al.* 2003; Owen 1998), and beneath a public culture of 'constrained conviviality', private views are often more hostile (see also Genders and Player 1989). In particular, the growing presence of highly cohesive and relatively politicized Muslim prisoners, especially in some male prisons, is generating considerable tension with other prisoners, who both admire and resent their in-group loyalty and collective power (Crewe 2009; Liebling *et al.*, forthcoming; Phillips 2011).

A second important component of prisoner social life is power relations between prisoners. The power that prisoners exert over each other, and the allocation of status and stigma, shape the experience of imprisonment alongside the power that is exercised by the institution. Identifying prisoners who are at the base of the status system is easier than those who are at its apex. Sex offenders are almost universally reviled by 'mainstream' prisoners (Akerstrom 1986; Winfree *et al.* 2002), who regard themselves as completely distinct, both socially and morally. Prisoners who inform on their peers are, at best, ostracized, and those who develop close relationships with staff are often derided. Other low status prisoners include drug users and addicts (see below), and prisoners who struggle to cope with the daily demands of imprisonment (Liebling 1992).

High status is a more complex matter. In most prisons, there are few visible 'kingpins' who run the wings (although they can be found in some). Some prisoners actively seek to acquire power—often young, short-sentenced, 'state-raised youth', whose horizons are relatively restricted (Irwin and Cressey 1962; Irwin 1970; King and Elliot 1977)—but the risks of doing so are considerable: other prisoners might want to displace you, and there is much to lose if the institution regards you as influential. For most prisoners, it is sufficient to be 'above the line', since this allows life to be lived with a minimum of risk and interference. In order to achieve this, it is helpful to hold a credible threat of violence or to have a 'reputation' based on activities and networks outside prison. Offence type contributes in some respects to status and reputation: life-sentence prisoners are generally both feared (because of the enormity of their offence) and admired (because, as experienced prisoners, they tend to conduct themselves honourably), and prisoners whose crimes involve sophisticated planning or have generated significant wealth are generally acclaimed. High-level drug dealers and organized criminals are therefore granted a certain level of respect. However, few offences 'carry an automatic bonus of prestige' (Morris and Morris 1963: 226). Petty criminals often express moral revulsion about the offences of murderers, drug dealers, and armed robbers (Crewe 2009), and most prisoners distinguish between different forms of a particular offence (for example, between the murder of a spouse and a contract killing). Terrorist prisoners may be admired in some political contexts and despised in others (see Liebling *et al.*, in press). When prisoners talk of having 'respect' for someone, they often mean fear rather than admiration. Meanwhile, there are alternative means of acquiring kudos: through one's intelligence or capacity to 'work the system', or through specific skills such as art, education, or sporting prowess.

Third, in almost all prisons, there is an 'inmate code' which exerts some control over prisoner behaviour (Clemmer 1940/1968; McCorkle and Korn 1954; Sykes 1958). In its most rudimentary form, this code promotes mutual loyalty between prisoners, discouraging them from betraying their peers ('don't inform') or siding with the authorities. According to this value system, attitudes towards the institution should be cynical and opportunistic, and prisoners should show stoicism and resilience in the face of frustration. They should not show weakness or vulnerability. In most prisons, bullying and exploitation are disapproved of, as is getting involved in another prisoner's business. Prisoners should not get involved with drugs, borrowing, or trade unless they can deal with the consequences; should be hygienic and take care of their appearance; and be respectful of old people, mothers, and children (Crewe 2009; Liebling, assisted by Arnold 2004: 359).

The pioneers of prison sociology were primarily interested in how what appeared to be oppositional values and 'criminalistic ideologies' might hinder attempts at rehabilitation. Initial assumptions that increased exposure to this culture would lead to a deeper internalization of its norms were not supported by empirical research. 'Prisonization' is not a simple or linear process; rather, prisoners might be most committed to these values at the 'deepest' point of their imprisonment, when they are most dependent on other prisoners for status, identity, and other forms of psychological and practical support (Wheeler 1961). Certainly, many prisoners explain that they deliberately withdraw from the hazards of the prisoner world as they approach release, because the need for involvement becomes less powerful while the risks become more tangible. In any case, the inmate code is not uniformly 'anti-social'. In many respects, it has a positive normative quality, in that it discourages exploitative behaviour and prevents the prison from descending into brutal anarchism. For example, violence is not celebrated uncritically (Edgar *et al.* 2003).

Most prisoners do not conform to the prisoner code in practice. Dominant norms and values are not universally accepted and are 'subject to different interpretations' (Clemmer 1958: 155). Prisoners hold different views about the degree to which one should share a joke with staff, whether it is fair to make profit by trading on another prisoner's needs (e.g. by charging interest on the loan of tobacco), and the circumstances which excuse informing on their peers. 'Grassing' is deemed by many prisoners to be both legitimate and morally righteous if someone is at risk of serious harm, or if a prisoner is dealing drugs on the wing. Other prisoners inform upon their peers to settle scores or obtain favours from staff. Meanwhile, many of the core tenets of the inmate code are contradictory—for example, prisoners are expected to be loyal to their peers, but not to get involved in disputes that are not their direct concern; they must be authentic but must not show weakness. Navigating such injunctions successfully requires prisoners to walk a perilous tightrope of acceptable behaviour. For some prisoners, rules such as 'don't show emotion or vulnerability' are themselves a source of distress (Gallo and Ruggiero 1991).

Fourth, the widespread presence of hard drugs within prisons—primarily heroin—since the late 1980s has altered the prisoner society in a number of ways (Crewe 2005a, 2005b). Heroin use in prison is common but is highly stigmatized, in part because most users breach a number of the tenets of the 'inmate code'. They often steal from other prisoners; they are considered untrustworthy and undignified, and—unless they handle their habit carefully—they are disdained for being incapable of coping with imprisonment without a narcotic crutch. Their moods are volatile and unpredictable, generating low-level conflict and tension. The debts that they incur often lead to violence, or result in them informing upon other prisoners in order to escape the wings (and therefore their creditors). As a result of developing a noticeable drug habit, a prisoner can slide down the status hierarchy. Meanwhile, drugs and power are interlinked: prisoners who control the internal drugs trade are able to build up a considerable degree of wealth, clout, and 'respect'.[6]

The problem with presenting this kind of digest of prison social life and culture is threefold. First, within any one prison, there are areas where normal rules are suspended or modified. There are semi-private spaces, such as cells, where acts of kindness and selflessness are common (see Harvey 2007). Likewise, there are 'emotion zones', such as education classes, faith centres, and visits rooms, where prisoners are able to express themselves more openly and mentally escape the prison.[7] Second, it makes little sense to think of the prison as a uniform community. There are often cultural differences between wings—for example, between voluntary drug-testing units and induction wings, or between those holding sex offenders compared to 'mainstream prisoners' (Sparks *et al.* 1996). Even within wings, there are a number of coexisting

---

[6] This 'powder power' has a distinctive quality, in that it is partly dependent on the drugs themselves and is therefore rather ephemeral.

[7] Toch (1992) describes these places as 'niches', where prisoners are able to survive or even flourish (see Bottoms 1990 on the importance of this possibility).

sub-worlds. Third, there is considerable variation between prisons in terms of prison social life and culture.

To explain both variation and consistency requires a detour into the history of prison sociology. Writing in its early years, 'deprivation theorists', such as Gresham Sykes and Erving Goffman, argued that prison social life and culture were outcomes of the inherent qualities of institutional life. Sykes (1956, 1958) had noted that the internal cultures of prisons were essentially alike, and claimed that the existence of a 'strikingly pervasive value system' among prisoners reflected the fact that certain kinds of pains and deprivations were intrinsic features of incarceration (Sykes 1960: 5; see also Sykes and Messinger 1960; Cloward *et al.* 1960). The inmate code was thus explained as a collective attempt to mitigate the indignities, dispossessions, and assaults on personal identity that imprisonment entailed. The more that prisoners acted in solidarity with each other, shared their goods, suppressed their irritations, exhibited masculine courage, and presented a positive group identity, the more they could offset feelings of insecurity, material deficiencies, and the threats to adult, masculine identity that imprisonment produced (Sykes and Messinger 1960: 16). The stance of opposition to the institution was a 'functional response' to moral denunciation, a way to 'reject the rejecters' (McCorkle and Korn 1954). Yet, only a minority of prisoners truly embodied and enacted this code. Faced with a range of frustrations and unmet needs, the vast majority chose to alleviate their predicament and re-coup some sense of status and masculine esteem not by binding together with their peers but exploiting, assaulting, or betraying them in some way.

Subsequent studies disputed this 'deprivation' thesis, noting that the norms and values of the prison resembled those found in criminal and lower-class subcultures outside it.[8] Sykes and Goffman had documented a bewilderingly distinctive prison world, detached from wider society, which stripped inmates of their previous identities and severed them from their pre-custodial relationships and assumptions. In contrast, 'importation' theorists (see, e.g., Irwin and Cressey 1962; Irwin 1970, 1980; Jacobs 1977) emphasized that the prison walls were porous and permeable (increasingly so, as prisons became accountable to the courts, and actively sought to maintain rather than sever prisoners' relationships with external parties). Prisoners navigated and negotiated the demands of the environment by drawing on values, resources, and patterns of behaviour that they held prior to entering it. Their pre-prison identities were not entirely overwhelmed by the rigours and degradations of the environment—indeed, as Jacobs (1974) noted, on entering the environment, the experience of many prisoners was virtually a 'homecoming ceremony', as they were received by associates from the streets. Events on the streets had direct repercussions within the prison. Status and social relations likewise reflected external social structures: men who were high-up in criminal or gang hierarchies outside prison took up positions of power

---

[8] It also seems plausible that attitudes towards bullying, sensitivities about peer disloyalty, protective attitudes towards female officers, and the contempt expressed towards sex offenders are shaped by specific life experiences (Crewe and Maruna 2006; Crewe 2009). Very little research has taken seriously this possibility that biographical and psycho-social factors might contribute to the terms of prisoner culture, despite the fact that prisoners' life stories very often include accounts of childhood victimization, betrayals of trust, domestic abuse between parents, and sexual abuse.

almost as soon as they entered it. Meanwhile, the increasingly hostile divisions between prisoners reflected social and ethnic divisions in the urban communities from which most prisoners were drawn.

The evidence for both importation and deprivation perspectives is compelling, and there is a consensus that studies of prison life need to integrate both explanatory positions.[9] That there are some recurring traits of prison life is testament to the essential facts of imprisonment: at their barest, the confinement of people, against their will, with many people they do not know. However, the variance in culture and social life between different prisons exposes a limitation of a strict interpretation of the deprivation position. It is difficult to account for the absence, in the UK, of the kinds of organized prison gangs which dominate many American establishments without reference to the features of external society (Morgan 2002). Similarly, it is hard to explain the predatory culture of Young Offender Institutions, where violence and victimization are pervasive compared to adult prisons (Edgar *et al.*, 2003; HMCIP 2001), without recognizing some of the imported differences between young offenders and adult males.

As Sparks *et al.* (1996) illustrated (see above), variations between prisons are the outcomes of institutional as well as imported characteristics—and it is perhaps these variations between prisons which are of most interest to prison scholars. Here, the deprivation perspective remains valuable in highlighting the connections between the particular set of needs and frustrations that a prison produces and the responses it generates: in prisons where there are few opportunities to alleviate material deficits through official channels (e.g. work; incentive schemes), prisoners are more likely to turn to drugs, trade, or theft in order to make life more bearable. Power accrues to those who can provide the services that their peers desire—hence the currency of drugs, which help users cope with boredom and distress, while enabling dealers to address subjective deficits in wealth and masculine status. In an establishment where warmth and hope are scarce, religious faith becomes especially attractive as a means of providing emotional sustenance and a positive self-narrative (Liebling *et al.*, in press).

Links of this kind were first demonstrated in what Kruttschnitt and Gartner (2005: 3) call 'situational functionalist' tests of the deprivation model (e.g. Grusky 1959; Street 1965; Berk 1966). Street (1965) delineated two variables which linked institutional practices with the contours of the prisoner society: first, variations in levels of degradation (the degree to which prisoners needed to offset deprivations and the opportunities for them to do so); second, variations in the ways in which staff exercised authority and control (formal or informal measures; severe or less severe sanctions). In more custody-oriented institutions, prisoners confronted a more acute set of problems—greater deprivation and greater control—which they blamed upon the institution, leading to a culture of 'solidary opposition' to the authorities. However, the restrictions on their freedoms meant that there were few opportunities for prisoners to alleviate their deprivations through collective solutions and fewer possibilities for group formation. In treatment-oriented settings, the psychological pains of imprisonment were

---

[9] In the US, attention seems to have turned away from the interior life of prisons to the collective impact of 'mass incarceration' on children, communities, and wider socio-political structures (Garland 2001), and the processes by which prison culture has been exported to, or merged with, the culture of the streets (Wacquant 2001). This might be thought of as an 'exportation' perspective on prison culture.

less severe, in part because staff were less rule-oriented. Efforts made by the institution to rehabilitate prisoners meant that less resentment was directed against it. Because prisoners were able to associate with each other, their collective culture was solidary but not anti-institutional, and they were more likely than prisoners in custodial institutions to have strong and relatively open friendships with other prisoners.

In considering how different kinds of regimes and arrangements of power give rise to different social experiences, the concepts of 'depth', 'weight', and 'tightness' can be used and might provide a helpful basis for further research. Prisoners at the 'deep end' of the system (further from release) are more reliant on their peers for status and support, hence the tendency towards elaborate subcultures in high-security prisons. In 'shallower' conditions, i.e. when prisoners are closer to release or in less restrictive conditions, they have more opportunities to form networks and loyalties, but less need to do so and often little inclination, given the risks of being denied parole or early release. Some institutions are more 'total' than others—i.e. more psychologically depriving. Where prisoners are able to maintain better contact with the outside world, where they are called by their first names and allowed to wear their own clothing, it is easier for them to retain their pre-prison personalities and individuality.

Relationships with staff might be said to constitute 'weight'. Where staff are less authoritarian, the injunction against mixing with them is asserted less forcefully and adhered to less strictly. In Grendon, for example, the therapeutic ideology creates a culture in which prisoners develop relationships with officers, tolerate sex offenders, and engage in emotional disclosure (Genders and Player 1989). In terms of prisoner dynamics, the outcomes of weight are more complex (see Liebling, assisted by Arnold, 2004: 364). Where prisons are harsh, the shared predicament of oppression and a common enemy might generate high levels of group solidarity (e.g. McEvoy 2000), but might equally create an environment where prisoners withdraw trust completely and take out their frustrations on each other. Further, as *Prisons and the Problem of Order* documented—and we emphasize—it is a mistake to assume that prisons that are 'light' are always more legitimate than those that are 'heavy'. Where imprisonment feels onerous and depriving, more pressure exists for prisoners to seek solutions to their frustrations through the prisoner subculture. However, the restrictions that create these frustrations also limit the degree to which prisoners can resolve them through exploitation and manipulation. Prisons that are *light* are less depriving, as such, but by giving prisoners more freedom of movement, responsibility, and material possessions, they can 'set the stage for more bitter struggles with higher stakes' (Sykes 1956: 137; Street 1965; Sparks *et al.* 1996). This is often a problem in private sector prisons (see below), where the under-use of staff authority can allow the development of prisoner hierarchies and leave some prisoners feeling unsafe and psychologically insecure (see Crewe *et al.* forthcoming).

In contrast to the prisons studied in the post-war years of prison sociology and the 'warehouse prisons' that now exist in many parts of the US (Irwin 2005; see also Feeley and Simon 1992, Alford 2000), most prisons in England and Wales are now relatively 'tight', and this has implications for the terms of prison social life and culture. The 'Big House' correctional facilities described by Clemmer, Sykes, and Irwin were like self-sufficient cities, in which, within a highly authoritarian system, prisoners were left more or less unhindered to trade with, exploit, and govern each other (see Irwin and Austin 1997; Irwin 2005; Cox 2009). This 'loose' form of power enabled a distinctive pattern of culture and social arrangements: low-level solidarity, born of shared oppression, alongside interpersonal exploitation of various kinds, tolerated or unregulated by staff. In the current context in the UK, both of these states are less probable. Institutional policies and practices permeate the landings, shaping prisoner behaviour in particular ways, and allowing the tentacles of power to extend further. The power of risk assessment practices and wing reports means that prisoners are aware that they can jeopardize their progression by getting involved in 'gang activity' or low-level resistance. By individualizing prisoners and discouraging their involvement in the prisoner social world, these *tight* institutional forces shape all aspects of prison culture, as well as the individual prisoner's experience. It is more difficult than ever to use terms like 'the prisoner community' (Clemmer 1940) almost untouched by the aims and practices of the official administration. At the same time, the conventional pains of imprisonment remain, and some are intensified, so that concerns about material hardship, loneliness, and physical safety push prisoners to form social allegiances which provide the forms of physical back-up, material support, and everyday companionship that make the environment more survivable.

## WOMEN'S IMPRISONMENT AND GENDER

Women have been a peripheral concern in the study of imprisonment, and the relationship between gender and punishment remains under-explored (Howe 1994). Carlen (1998) argued that, women are not seen as 'real prisoners', women's prisons are not seen as 'real prisons', and female prisoners are not seen as 'real women'.

In the 1960s and 70s, a number of studies sought to replicate in women's prisons the kinds of ethnographies that had been undertaken in men's establishments (Ward and Kassebaum 1965; Giallombardo 1966). Using these studies as their benchmark, such works identified a very different pattern of prisoner relationships. Violence was less prevalent, consensual sexual relationships were common, and there were few signs of the code of solidarity that pervaded establishments for men (see also Carlen 1983). Researchers argued that, compared to men, women in effect experienced distinctive pains of imprisonment—in particular, the dispossession of their roles as mothers and care-givers. Thus, the widespread existence in women's prisons of 'pseudo-family' social units and non-sexual dyads was explained as a substitute affective universe: a response to the emotional deprivations that imprisonment entailed and its disruption of family-based identities. As subsequent studies have shown, the separation from children (alongside the high chance of them being taken into care) and the possibility of losing one's fertile years make imprisonment particularly distressing for women, particularly those serving long sentences (Walker and Worrall 2000; Rowe 2011). Further, many of the dynamics of penal power evoke experiences of sexual and psychological abuse, which compound feelings of powerlessness and distress (Carlen 1998; Zaitzow and Thomas 2003). Female prisoners also express greater concern than male prisoners about the loss of control they experience in relation to personal health, matters of privacy, and self-presentation, and about intimate intrusions such as strip-searches.

These differences in the prison experience primarily lend support to importation theories, in that the distinctive pains experienced by female prisoners seem to be reducible to their status *as women* and their socialization into feminine roles and behaviours. But women's imprisonment may be distinctively painful due, in part, to the particular ways in which it is organized. Because there are relatively few women's prisons, women are often confined a long distance from their homes, making it difficult for friends and family to visit. They are also subjected to regimes, security standards, and cognitive programmes that have been developed around the model of the male prisoner (Shaw and Hannah-Moffat 2000). In this respect, most women are often more 'deeply' imprisoned than they merit, especially relative to men who have committed similar offences. Meanwhile, women's confinement has always been shaped by powerful and pervasive ideologies about appropriate femininity and the 'proper place' of women (e.g. Zedner 1991; Bosworth 1999; Carlen 1983, 1988; Rock 1996). Traditionally, women's prisons have served to feminize, domesticize, medicalize, and infantilize their occupants (Carlen *et al.* 1985; Carlen and Worrall 2004), disciplining them in ways that are consistent with gendered norms and sanctions in the outside community (see Howe 1994). Apparently benign intentions to protect women from themselves and teach them virtuous forms of domesticity have resulted in inappropriate regimes that are more punitive and infantilizing than those in men's prisons, with higher expectations about the details of behaviour (Zedner 1991; Carlen 1998). Thus, women's imprisonment has always been 'tight', just as the regulation of women in the wider community has always had a panoptical quality (Howe 1994).

Some of the moralizing discourse has disappeared from women's prisons in recent years. However, the invasive policing of female prisoners remains, in revised forms, and disciplinary proceedings against women in prison are still more common than those against men (Ministry of Justice 2010). Haney (2010) describes how community-based prisons in the US regulate women's needs and emotions through forms of therapeutic governance which widen the 'parameters of vice'. As Liebling (2009: 21) notes, 'the recent emphasis on responsibilisation and self-governance is particularly pertinent to women, given the emphasis in women's lives on self-control'. It is unsurprising, then, that the frustrations of imprisoned women, and their modes of resistance, have tended to focus around matters of agency and identity (Bosworth 1999; Rowe 2011) i.e. as part of a dialectic of aggravation and dissent (see Mandaraka-Sheppard 1986). The historical 'tightness' of women's prisons may be one reason why their subcultures have been less developed, and high levels of distress and intense frustration manifest themselves more in minor forms of destructive 'retreatism', such as self-harm and self-medication, than in group solidarity or collective protest.

The disproportionate emphasis in studies of women's imprisonment on gender-related topics, such as sexuality and motherhood, has led to a neglect of many of the issues most pertinent to incarceration, such as fairness, legitimacy, and order (Liebling 2009). Bosworth (1999) argues that the concept of legitimacy is gender-blind, and that female prisoners grant or withhold it according to distinctive standards, but this remains an empirical question worthy of further exploration. Kruttschnitt and Gartner's (2005) research is therefore significant in three ways (see also Kruttschnitt 2005; Kruttschnitt and Hussemann 2008). It is one of few recent attempts to explore the experience and social structure within women's prisons in what is a much-changed penal context. Second, by comparing contemporary data from one of their two prisons with Ward and Kassebaum's (1965) original material, it shows how institutional practices and women's adaptations have changed over the course of four decades. As women's prisons have become more austere, have prioritized 'personal responsibility' over traditional notions of rehabilitation, and have made fewer concessions to (or assumptions about) the specific needs of women, female prisoners have become more self-reliant, and more socially isolated, with fewer friendships, less peer solidarity, and lower trust in other prisoners and staff (see also Greer 2000). Third, by contrasting two contemporary establishments, Kruttschnitt and Gartner illustrate that 'gendered' responses to confinement are more likely in prisons where traditional assumptions about femininity and women's criminality endure. Thus, in the more gender-neutral prison, fewer women chose to do time by forging close relationships either with staff or with each other.

Research of this kind alerts us to the danger of under-estimating the role of institutions in reproducing certain kinds of gendered behaviours, and of over-stating the role of imported characteristics in shaping differences between the social structures of men's and women's prisons. High levels of 'informing' in women's prisons might be less to do with putatively feminine qualities than the expectation that they inform as a means of showing 'progress' and their limited means of influencing staff decisions in other ways (Ward 1970). Greer (2000) speculates that the decline of pseudo-family structures within women's prisons might reflect the move away from cottage-style accommodation, which encouraged such arrangements. In other words, held in similar conditions, the differences between male and female prisoners might not be so significant. Indeed, many accounts of women's imprisonment have pointed to similarities between the adaptive patterns of male and female prisoners (Heffernan 1972; Owen 1998). Greer's (2000) account of interpersonal relationships in a women's prison in the US is similar in many respects to the way that social relations in men's prisons have been reported: prisoners see most relationships as transient, extend little trust, and differentiate between 'real friends' and associates (see also Rowe 2011). At the same time, the enduring presence in women's prisons of openly practiced same-sex relationships (see Owen 1998; Greer 2000) indicates that differences between male and female prisoners are not just the outcome of differential treatment. The task of future researchers is to explain these patterns and describe undocumented aspects of the social world of women's prisons, such as drug culture and hierarchies, within a wider analysis of penal power (and, ideally, without reprising the prurient moralism of earlier scholarship).

# SUICIDES, SUICIDE ATTEMPTS, AND THE EFFECTS OF IMPRISONMENT

There is no question that prison life is experienced as painful by many prisoners (see, for example, Boyle 1985; Cohen and Taylor 1972; Haney 1972; Liebling 1999). One outcome of the unbearable nature of some prison regimes and experiences is the high rate of prison suicide. Prison suicides tend to fall into distinguishable categories (e.g. the young repeat offender, the mentally ill, and the life sentence or prospective life sentence prisoner) each of which can, like many aspects of prison life, be explained by a distinctive combination of 'imported vulnerability' and experienced 'deprivation' in prison (see Liebling 1999). Whereas, in the community, men are three times more likely than women to take their own lives (with those from low socio-economic groups at particular risk), in prisons, the rates for men and women are the same (see Liebling, assisted by Arnold 2004). The prison population is arguably a careful selection of the most at risk populations in the community (Liebling 1999).

Pains and deprivations are experienced at all stages of life in custody (Liebling and Maruna 2005; Liebling 2011, 2007), but the entry into custody phase is often experienced most intensely (Gibbs 1982; Liebling 1992; Harvey 2007). Half of all prison suicides take place within one month of entering prison. Between 2001 and 2004, Liebling and colleagues evaluated the Prison Service's new suicide prevention strategy, which focused on local prisons with high suicide rates (see Liebling 2009; Liebling et al. 2005). The research showed that 'imported vulnerability' could be measured, indicating how much of the suicide risk in an establishment could be accounted for by variations in the nature of the prison populations. Imported suicide risk varied significantly between prisons of similar types, so that in one women's prison, around 40 per cent of the population had attempted suicide before entering custody, compared to around 12 per cent in one male local prison. Other factors included previous self-harm and previous psychiatric treatment (see Liebling 2007). These factors varied, so that the risk carried by a particular prison's population differed significantly.

Average levels of distress (as measured by a short version of the General Health Questionnaire) were extremely high in all prisons, so that even in those prisons with the least distress, the average measure (12) approached the threshold indicating a need for psychiatric intervention. The authors found a statistically significant relationship between mean levels of distress among prisoners in each prison, and moving average suicide rates for the relevant period (Liebling et al. 2005a). This is important, as it means that instead of relying on variations to and changes in relatively small numbers of suicides in individual prisons, observers can look for more numerous variations or reductions in overall prisoner distress in evaluating suicide prevention (and other) policy and practices. The study found that suicide prevention strategies could work in three ways: reducing distress at a general level by improving regimes, managing distress better at an individual level, and generating less distress in the first place by improving staff culture (see Liebling and Tait 2007).

Drawing on data from all 12 prisons, the authors were also able to model prisoner distress. Differences in feelings of *safety* accounted for a significant proportion (38–40 per cent) of the variation in levels of distress among prisoners. Relational variables (e.g. the extent to which prisoners felt treated with respect) and family contact also mattered. Pre-existing vulnerability added something to the model (8–10 per cent) but these factors tended to interact with environmental variables: so, for example, prisoners who had attempted suicide before entering custody were especially sensitive to fluctuations in safety in prison (Liebling and Tait 2006), and to the quality of relationships (Liebling et al. 2005a). This variation in ontological security is significant, suggesting that prisons pose both general threats to psychological well-being (see, e.g., Cohen and Taylor 1972), and the particular exposure of vulnerability in particular individuals (Liebling 1999). Variations in perceptions of safety in prison were not determined by actual levels of assault (i.e. actual risks) in each prison but by 'relational' variables like the approachability of staff, which created a feeling of 'trust in the environment' (Liebling and Tait 2006; also Bottoms, this volume). Fluctuations in the control of the drug supply were significant.

Interestingly, participation in offending behaviour programmes was significantly associated with decreased levels of distress, suggesting that strategies that help offenders reduce their risk of re-offending (whatever the limitations of this model) might also help reduce suicide risk. This finding is consistent with the desistance literature, suggesting that hope, future orientation, and help with practical and emotional difficulties assist in encouraging better outcomes for individuals (see Lösel, this volume). It is of interest to criminologists that being a persistent offender (especially perhaps in prison) is not psychologically pleasant. Low levels of self-control and affective and social capital, and the pursuit of short-term need gratification, leaves people hugely psychologically vulnerable, and often in an emotional state where they yearn for help (see, e.g., Bottoms and Shapland 2011).

Data collected from staff showed that communication between staff groups, job satisfaction, an appropriate distribution of roles and responsibilities among staff members, and staff-senior management relationships, all mattered a great deal in effective suicide prevention. Significantly different results on a post-hoc measure of 'staff culture' explained much of the variance in levels of prisoner distress as well as the variance in speed and success of the strategy's implementation (Liebling 2007; Arnold, Liebling and Tait 2007). Where there were very small numbers of enthusiastic staff with favourable attitudes towards prisoners and managers, and large numbers who were 'anti-prisoner' and 'anti-management', it was extremely difficult to change culture and practices in the direction of 'care for vulnerable prisoners'. In one of the prisons, despite considerable training and efforts to shape recruitment policies, the proportion of *resistant* staff was reduced by half, but it was not possible to increase the numbers of *positive* staff. This suggests that the two management tasks of reducing staff resistance, and building positive cultures around constructive aims, may be two distinct stages in any cultural change programme in prison. This analysis of the significance of staff and senior management suggest that neither should be overlooked in the sociology of prison life (see Liebling and Crewe, forthcoming).

## PRIVATIZATION

It is impossible to describe contemporary prisons without some reference to private prisons, since there are 11 in England and Wales at the time of writing (and two in Scotland),[10] and more opening in the near future. The first was Wolds, opened in 1992.

---

[10] These prisons are run by three different companies: Serco, G4S, and Kalyx.

Increased emphasis is being placed on 'contestability'—that is competition between different providers, value for money, and innovation – in the management of prisons.

Like managerialism, private sector involvement in prisons can be regarded as an attempt to exert increasing management control over a system that had come to be seen as both delinquent and intransigent. The introduction of private sector competition in England and Wales in 1991 shared many of the aims of managerialism: to reassert management grip, curb the power of the Prison Officers Association and provide a competitive threat to the public sector which would accelerate regime improvement (particularly in local prisons) and the reform of working practices, drive down costs, and although this was not at first the principal goal (Moyle 1995; Harding 1997, 2001; Jones and Newburn 2005) bring about positive changes in staff attitudes and behaviour towards prisoners (Harding 1997). Other motives included the desire to make a strong symbolic gesture about the (Conservative) Government's willingness to confront union power and pursue its agenda of public sector reform, in an area where private sector provision had previously been considered inconceivable (Windlesham 1993; Harding 1997).

Opponents of privatization argue that the deprivation of liberty is a core state function, a responsibility that should not be contracted out to private companies, for them to derive profit. Sparks (1994) notes that, whether or not private prisons provide good conditions for prisoners, by enabling the expansion of prison systems, they offer a weak and dangerous solution to wider legitimation problems. Other concerns include the possibility that private sector companies will lobby for growth in the prison population and the risk of private companies becoming insolvent. Proponents of privatization argue that a distinction can be made between the allocation of punishment (by the courts) and the delivery of punishment (Moyle 1995), and that private prisons in England and Wales are *more* accountable than public sector prisons, in that they are subject to the same oversight mechanisms plus the presence of a state appointed 'Controller' who monitors compliance with the terms of the contract. Harding (1997) sets out the tenets of accountability under which private prisons should operate, and states that, under such conditions, competition offers 'a unique opportunity to raise standards and increase accountability across the total prison system' (Harding 1997: 31). That is, in assessing the benefits of private sector prisons, it is crucial to look at the degree to which *public sector* prisons have become more decent, cheaper, or more innovative as a result of competition.

Most prison governors who initially objected to private sector involvement in the management of prisons are now reluctant converts, recognizing that some privately run establishments have set impressive standards (see Home Affairs Committee 1997, and HMIP reports on Altcourse and Lowdham Grange) and observing that the threat and example provided by private prisons have generated otherwise unlikely improvements in the public sector (see Crewe and Liebling, in press). Private prisons have been instructed and incentivized to outperform the public sector on matters of decency and respectful treatment (James *et al.* 1997). The first private prison senior management team at Wolds drew directly on the liberal recommendations of the Woolf Report in order to develop the establishment's ethos and practices, focusing in particular on seeking to develop 'constructive relationships' and a regime that was less oppressive than public sector comparators. Early evaluations found that the performance of newly opened private prisons was 'at least as good as that of publicly run prisons and in some areas better', and that the cost differential between the sectors was decreasing (Home Affairs Committee 1997: xiv; Woodbridge 1999). Although such evidence is limited—often relying on secondary or official performance data, such as costs, suicide rates, or assaults (Home Affairs Committee 1997; NAO 2003; and Logan 1992)—comparisons of public and private prisons show fairly consistent findings: in privately run prisons, prisoners generally report a more progressive staff culture, in which officers are friendly, courteous, and benign, leading to an experience that feels less 'heavy' and oppressive than the public sector. However, low staffing levels, a less experienced workforce, and relatively high levels of staff turnover—all of which might be seen as structural outcomes of the imperative to make profit—tend to produce weaknesses in the areas of safety, security, and staff professionalism (James *et al.* 1997; NAO 2003; Liebling, assisted by Arnold 2004; HMCIP 2007; see also Liebling and Shefer 2008, Moyle 1995; Rynne *et al.* 2008; Taylor and Cooper 2008).

The degree to which these strengths and weaknesses prevail varies a great deal *within* the private sector. The best private prisons are among the better prisons in the system, providing an environment for prisoners that is safer and more respectful than almost all comparable public sector establishments (Crewe *et al.* 2011; Crewe *et al.* under review). However, the opposite is also true: the least good private prisons are chaotic, dangerous, and disrespectful, even though prisoners describe staff as 'nice people' with positive motivations (Crewe *et al.* 2011; NAO 2003; see also, e.g., HMCIP 2002, 2005, 2007). It is significant too that, regardless of quality, the 'feel' in private prisons tends to be relatively 'light' compared to the public sector. Whereas the problem in many public sector prisons is that staff over-use their authority and have excessive collective power, the opposite is often the case in private prisons, due to the absence of strong unions, low staffing numbers, staff inexperience, and a lack of confidence about the appropriate use of authority (Crewe *et al.* 2011). Thus, a significant weakness of the privatization 'experiment' is that, by deliberately diminishing the power of uniformed staff and exerting greater control over the workforce, it weights the balance of power between prisoners and staff sometimes excessively towards the former. The risks of this imbalance are all the greater if prisons are run at very low cost.

The announcement in July 2011 that a further eight public sector establishments would be market tested, and the opening up in all establishments (as well as probation services) to increasing competition by private and third sector agencies, including work, education, and other rehabilitative interventions, indicate that we are entering a new and accelerated phase of private sector involvement in penal provision. The intensification of the process of market testing appears to be taking place on the ideological belief that private sector management is inherently superior to public sector management. The evidence base on the relative quality and effectiveness of public and private sector prisons is not developed enough to justify such a rapid expansion of private sector involvement (Camp, Gaes, and Saylor 2002; Perrone and Pratt 2003). Opponents of privatization would say that evidence of performance and efficiency cannot settle the most important questions about the legitimacy or wider impact of privatization (Ryan and Ward 1989).

## CONCLUSION

The use of imprisonment has expanded beyond all expectation in recent decades, and the prison has also deepened and tightened in ways that bear heavily on the increasingly individualized and largely 'ghetto-ized' population. The evidence suggests that prisons damage rather than deter, exerting an overall criminogenic influence on those they contain, and that in the UK they are over-used, for example, by comparison with all other European countries. Garland (1990) argued that the prison is a 'tragic' institution, destined to fail at any of its instrumental tasks, but having deeper social and symbolic tasks which, if recognized, may lead to more parsimonious use of it. It is certainly possible to envision a more restrained and constructive approach to prison use, as well as to the shape and purpose of regimes. Although all prisons suffer from an inherent legitimacy-deficit, it is clear, and significant, that some are (internally, at least) more legitimate than others, and that the activities and values of staff and managers contribute to these differences. Without understanding what goes on inside prisons—in particular, the relationships between staff and prisoners, and the realities behind terms such as 'progress', rehabilitation, and 'productive work'—it is impossible to draw conclusions about penal policy.

### ■ SELECTED FURTHER READING

Two good introductions to life in prison are *A Life Inside* by Erwin James (2005) and *The Invisible Crying Tree* by Tom Shannon and Christopher Morgan (1996) (letters between a life-sentence prisoner and his pen-friend). Students may want to read David Ramsbotham's *Prisongate* (he was an ex-Chief Inspector of Prisons) as well as relevant articles in *Punishment and Society: The International Journal of Penology.* The *Handbook on Prisons* (Jewkes 2007) contains many interesting chapters, including a good general introduction to contemporary issues in UK imprisonment by Anne Owers. M. Cavadino and J. Dignan's (2007), 4th edn, *The Penal System: An Introduction* is still a good basic introduction to prisons and their organization and difficulties. Their article on 'Penal policy and political economy', in *Criminology and Criminal Justice*, 6(4) 435–56 is a more considered analysis of some of the themes we touch on under 'prison use and political economy'. Liebling's (2004), *Prisons and their Moral Performance: A Study of Values, Quality and Prison Life* and Crewe's (2009), *The Prisoner Society* are good sources and helpful starting points for further reading on the sociology of prison life. *Prison Readings: A Critical Introduction to Prisons and Imprisonment* by Y. Jewkes and H. Johnston (eds) (2006) provides a broad selection of relevant readings. For further discussion of the philosophy of punishment, see *Why Punish?* by Nigel Walker (1991).

# ■ REFERENCES

ADVISORY COUNCIL ON THE PENAL SYSTEM (1968), *The Regime for Prisoners in Conditions of Maximum Security* (Radzinowicz Report), London: HMSO.

ABERCROMBIE, N., HILL, S., and TURNER, B. (1980), *The Dominant Ideology Thesis*, London: Allen and Unwin.

AHMAD, S. (1996), 'Fairness in Prisons', *Ph.D. thesis*, University of Cambridge.

AKOENSI, T. D. (2011), *So stressful that you hardly have time for your family: Job stress among Prison officers in Ghana–A mixed methods study* (University of Cambridge Ph.D thesis, in progress).

ALARID, L. F. (2000), 'Sexual assault and coercion among incarcerated women prisoners: excerpts from prison letters', *The Prison Journal*, 80(4): 391–406.

BECKETT, K. and SASS, T. (2004), *The politics of injustice: crime and punishment in America*, 2nd edn, Thousand Oaks: Sage Publications.

BERK, B. (1966), 'Organizational goals and inmate organization', *American Journal of Sociology* 71 (March): 522–4.

BOSWORTH, M. (1999), *Engendering Resistance: Agency and Power in Women's Prisons*, Aldershot: Dartmouth.

BOTTOMS, A. E. (1990), 'The aims of imprisonment', in D. Garland (ed.), *Justice, Guilt and Forgiveness in the Penal System*, Edinburgh: University of Edinburgh Centre for Theology and Public Issues, Occasional Paper No. 18.

—— (2003), 'Theoretical Reflections on the Evaluation of a Penal Policy Initiative', in L. Zedner and A. Ashworth (eds), *The Criminological Foundations of Penal Policy : Essays in Honour of Roger Hood*, Oxford: Oxford University Press.

—— and ROSE, G. (1998), 'The Importance of Staff-Prisoner Relationships: Results from a Study in Three Male Prisons', in D. Price and A. Liebling, 'Staff Prisoner Relationships: A Review of the Literature', unpublished report submitted to the Prison Service.

—— and TANKEBE, J. (2011, in preparation), *Legitimacy and Social Order in Criminal Justice*.

BOWLING, B. and PHILLIPS, C. (2002), *Racism, crime and justice*, London: Longman (Pearson).

BOYLE, J. (1984), *The Pain of Confinement: Prison Diaries*, Edinburgh: Canongate.

BUNTMAN, F. L. (2003), *Robben Island and Prisoner Resistance to Apartheid*, Cambridge: Cambridge University Press.

CAMP, S. D., GAES, G. G., and SAYLOR, W. (2002), 'Quality of Prison Operations in the Federal Sector: A Comparison with a Private Prison', *Punishment and Society*, 4(1): 27–53.

CARLEN, P. (1998), *Sledgehammer: Women's Imprisonment at the Millennium*, Basingstoke: Macmillan.

CARRABINE, E. (2004), *Power, Discourse and Resistance: A Genealogy of the Strangeways Prison Riot*, Dartmouth: Ashgate.

—— (2005), 'Prison Riots, Social Order and the Problem of Legitimacy', *British Journal of Criminology*, 45: 896–913.

CAVADINO, M. and DIGNAN, J. (2006), 'Penal policy and political economy', *Criminology and Criminal Justice*, 6(4): 435–56.

CHELIOTIS, L. and LIEBLING, A. (2006), 'Race Matters in British Prisons', *British Journal of Criminology*, 46: 286–317.

CHRISTIE, N. (1993), *Crime Control as Industry: Towards Gulags, Western Style?*, London: Routledge.

CLARE, E., BOTTOMLEY, K., GROUNDS, A., HAMMOND, C. J., LIEBLING, A., and TAYLOR, C. (2001), *Evaluation of Close Supervision Centres*, London: Home Office.

CLEMMER, D. (1940, 1958), 2nd edn, *The Prison Community*, New York: Holt, Rinehart and Winston.

CLOWARD, R., GROSSER, G., MCCLEERY, R., OHLIN, L., SYKES, G., and MESSINGER, S. (1960), *Theoretical Studies in Social Organization of the Prison*. New York: Social Science Research Council.

COHEN, S. and TAYLOR, L. (1972), *Psychological Survival: The Experience of Long-Term Imprisonment*, Harmondsworth: Penguin.

COOKE, D. (1989), 'Containing violent prisoners: an analysis of the Barlinnie Special Unit', *British Journal of Criminology*, 29: 129–43.

COVER, R. M. (1986), 'Violence and the Word', *Yale Law Journal*, 95: 1601–29.

CREWE, B. (2005a), 'Codes and Conventions: The Terms and Conditions of Contemporary Inmate Values', in A. Liebling and S. Maruna (eds), *The Effects of Imprisonment*, 177–208, Cullompton: Willan.

—— (2005b), 'The Prisoner Society in the Era of Hard Drugs', *Punishment and Society*, 7(4): 457–81.

—— (2006), 'Prison Drug Dealing and the Ethnographic Lens', *The Howard Journal of Criminal Justice*, 45(4): 347–68.

—— (2007), 'Power, adaptation and resistance in the late-modern prison', *British Journal of Criminology*, 47(2): 256–275.

—— (2009), *The Prisoner Society: Power, adaptation, and social life in an English prison*, Oxford: Oxford University Press.

—— and MARUNA, S. (2006), 'Self-Narratives and Ethnographic Fieldwork', in D. Hobbs and R. Wright (eds), *The Handbook of Fieldwork*, London: Sage Publishing.

—— LIEBLING, A., HULLEY, S., and MCLEAN, C. (2011), '*Prisoner Quality of Life in Public and Private Sector Prisons* (under review).

CUNEEN, C. (2011), 'Postcolonial Perspectives for Criminology', in M. Bosworth and C. Hoyle (eds), *What is Criminology?*, Oxford: Oxford University Press.

DOWNES, D. (1988), *Contrasts in Tolerance*, Oxford: Clarendon Press.

—— and HANSEN, K. (2006), 'Welfare and punishment: the relationship between welfare spending and imprisonment'. www.crimeandsociety.org.uk .

EDGAR, K., O'DONNELL, I., and MARTIN, C. (2003), *Prison Violence: The Dynamics of Conflict, Fear and Power*, Cullompton: Willan.

FEELEY, M. M. and SIMON, J. (1992), 'The New Penology: Notes on the Emerging Strategy of Corrections and its Implications', *Criminology*, 30(4): 449–74.

FOUCAULT, M. (1977), *Discipline and Punish: The Birth of the Prison*, Harmondsworth: Penguin.

—— (1991), 'Governmentality', in G. Burchell, C. Gordon, and P. Miller (eds), *The Foucault Effect*, Hemel Hempstead: Harvester Wheatsheaf.

GALLO, E. and RUGGIERO, V. (1991), 'The "Immaterial" Prison: Custody as a Factory for the Manufacture of Handicaps', *International Journal of the Sociology of Law*, 19/3: 273–91.

GARFINKEL, H. (1956), 'Conditions of successful degradation ceremonies', *American Journal of Sociology*, 61: 420–4.

GARLAND, D. (1990), *Punishment and Modern Society*, Oxford: Clarendon Press.

—— (1997), ' "Governmentality" and the Problem of Crime: Foucault, Criminology, Sociology', *Theoretical Criminology*, 1: 173–214.

—— (ed.) (2001), *Mass Imprisonment: Social Causes and Consequences*, London: Sage.

GENDERS, F. and PLAYER, E. (1989), *Race Relations in Prisons*, Oxford: OUP.

—— and —— (1995), *Grendon: A Study of a Therapeutic Prison*, Oxford: Clarendon Press.

GIDDENS, A. (1991), *Modernity and Self-Identity: Self and Society in the Late Modern Age*, Stanford University Press.

GOFFMAN, E. (1961), *Asylums: Essays on the Social Situation of Mental Patients and Other Inmates*, Harmondsworth: Penguin.

GREER, K. (2000), 'The changing nature of interpersonal relationships in a women's prison', *The Prison Journal*, 80(4): 442–68.

GRUSKY, O. (1959), 'Organizational goals and the behaviour of informal leaders', *American Journal of Sociology*, 65 (July): 59–67.

HAINES, K. (1990), *After-care services for released prisoners: a review of the literature*. Cambridge: University of Cambridge: Institute of Criminology.

HALLETT, M. A. (2006), *Private Prisons in America: A Critical Race Perspective*, Chicago: University of Illinois Press.

HANEY, C., BANKS, W. C., and ZIMBARDO, P. G. (1973), 'Interpersonal dynamics in a simulated prison', *International Journal of Criminology and Penology*, 1: 69–97.

HARVEY, J. (2007), *Young Men in Prison: Surviving and Adapting to Life Inside*, Cullompton: Willan.

HOME OFFICE (1994), *Report of an Enquiry into the Escape of Six Prisoners from the Special Security Unit at Whitemoor Prison, Cambridgeshire on Friday 9th September 1994 by Sir John Woodcock*, London: HMSO.

HOSSER, D. (2011) www.kfn.de/Research_areas_and_projects/Past_Projects/Developmental_Consequences_of_Incarceration.htm?lang=en.

ICPS (2011), *World population brief* – http://www.prisonstudies.org/info/worldbrief/.

IRWIN, J. (1970), *The Felon*, Englewood Cliffs, NJ: Prentice Hall.

—— (1980), *Prisons in Turmoil*, Chicago, Little Brown.

—— and AUSTIN, J. (1997), *It's About Time: America's Imprisonment Binge*, 2nd edn, Belmont CA: Wadsworth.

—— and CRESSEY, D. (1962), 'Thieves, convicts and the inmate culture', *Social Problems*, 10: 142–55.

JACOBS, J. (1974), 'Street Gangs Behind Bars', *Social Problems*, 21(3): 395–409.

—— (1977), *Stateville: The Penitentiary in Mass Society*, Chicago: University of Chicago Press.

—— (1983), *New Perspectives on Prisons and Imprisonment*, Ithaca: Cornell University Press.

JEFFERSON, A. M. (2010), 'Traversing sites of confinement: Post-prison survival in Sierra Leone', *Theoretical Criminology*, 14(4): 387–406.

KING, R. (1991), 'Maximum-security custody in Britain And The USA: A Study of Gartree and Oak Park Heights', *British Journal of Criminology*, 31: 126–52.

—— (1999), 'The Rise and Rise of Supermax: An American Solution in Search of a Problem?' *Punishment & Society*, 1(2): 163–86.

—— (2005), 'The effects of supermax custody', in A. Liebling and S. Maruna (eds), *The Effects of Imprisonment*, Cullompton: Willan.

—— and ELLIOTT, K. (1977), *Albany: Birth of a Prison, End of an Era*, London: Routledge & Kegan Paul.

—— and MCDERMOTT, K. (1989), 'British Prisons 1970–1987: The ever-deepening crisis', *British Journal of Criminology*, 29: 107–128.

—— and —— (1990), ' "My geranium is subversive": some notes on the management of trouble in prisons', *British Journal of Sociology*, 41(4): 445–471.

—— and —— (1995), *The State of Our Prisons*, Oxford: Clarendon Press.

KRUTTSCHNITT, C. and GARTNER, R. (2005), *Marking Time in the Golden State: Women's Imprisonment in California*, Cambridge: Cambridge University Press.

LACEY, N. (2008), *The Prisoners' Dilemma: political economy and punishment in contemporary democracies*, Cambridge: Cambridge University Press.

LAPPI-SEPPÄLÄ, T. (2011), 'Explaining imprisonment in Europe', *European Journal of Criminology*, July 2011, 8: 286–302.

—— (2006), 'Reducing the prison population: long-term experiences from Finland', in, *Crime Policy in Europe*, Council of Europe, Strasbourg: Council of Europe Publishing.

LEWIS, D. (1997), *Hidden Agendas: Politics, Law and Disorder*, London and New York: Hamish Hamilton, Penguin Books.

LIEBLING, A. (2008), 'Incentives and Earned Privileges Revisited: Fairness, Discretion, and the Quality of Prison Life', in Journal of Scandinavian Studies in Criminology and Crime Prevention, 9: 25–41.

—— (1999), 'Prison suicide and prisoner coping', in M. Tonry and J. Petersilia (eds), Prisons, Crime and Justice: An Annual Review of Research, 26: 283–360.

—— (1992), Suicides in Prison, London: Routledge Press.

——, TAIT, S., DURIE, L., STILES, A., HARVEY, J. (assisted by ROSE, G.) (2005), An Evaluation of the Safer Locals Programme, Final Report (revised June 2005), Cambridge: Cambridge Institute of Criminology, Prisons Research Centre.

—— (assisted by ARNOLD, H.) (2004), Prisons and Their Moral Performance: A Study of Values, Quality, and Prison Life, Oxford: Clarendon Press.

—— and CREWE, B., (2012) 'Prisons beyond the new penology: the shifting moral foundations of prison management', (forthcoming) in R. Sparks and J. Simon, (eds), The SAGE Handbook of Punishment and Society, London: SAGE Publications.

——, PRICE, D., and SHEFER, G. (2010), The Prison Officer, 2nd edn, Cullompton, Devon: Willan Publishing.

——, Arnold, H. and Straub, C. (2011, in press), An Exploration of Staff-Prisoner Relationships at HMP Whitemoor: Twelve Years On, London: Home Office.

——, MUIR, G., ROSE, G., and BOTTOMS, A. E. (1997), 'An Evaluation of Incentives and Earned Privileges: Final Report to the Prison Service', unpublished report to Home Office, London.

——, ——, ——, and —— (1999), 'Incentives and Earned Privileges in Prison. Research Findings 87', London: Home Office Research, Development and Statistics Directorate.

LOADER, I. (2010), 'For Penal Moderation: Notes towards a public philosophy of punishment', Theoretical Criminology, 14(3): 349–367.

MATHIESEN, T. (1965), The Defences of the Weak: A Sociological Study of a Norwegian Correctional Institution, London: Tavistock.

MCCORKLE, L. and KORN, R. (1954), 'Re-socialization within the walls', The Annals of the American Academy of Political and Social Sciences, 293 (May): 88–98.

MCDERMOTT, K. and KING, R. (1988), 'Mind Games: Where the Action is in Prisons', British Journal of Criminology, 28(3): 357–77.

MCEVOY, K. (2001), Paramilitary Imprisonment in Northern Ireland, Oxford: Clarendon Press.

MCVICAR, J. (1974), Mcvicar by Himself, London: Hutchinson.

MINISTRY OF JUSTICE (2010), Statistics on Women and the Criminal Justice System, London: Ministry of Justice.

MORGAN, R. (1994), 'Imprisonment', in M. Maguire, R. Morgan, and R. Reiner (eds), The Oxford Handbook of Criminology, 1st edn, Oxford: Oxford University Press.

—— (2002), Imprisonment: a brief history, the contemporary scene and likely prospects, in M. Maguire, R. Morgan, and R. Reiner (eds), The Oxford Handbook of Criminology, 3rd edn, Oxford: Oxford University Press.

MORRIS, P. and MORRIS, T. (1963), Pentonville: A Sociological Study of an English Prison, London: Routledge.

NAGIN, D. S., CULLEN, F. T., and JONSON, C. L. (2009), 'Imprisonment and Re-offending', in M. Tonry (ed.), Crime and Justice: A Review of Research, Vol. XX, Chicago: University of Chicago Press.

O'DONNELL, I. (2004), 'Prison rape in context', The British Journal of Criminology, 44: 241–55.

—— and EDGAR, K. (1998), 'Routine victimisation in prisons', The Howard Journal, 37(3): 266–79.

—— and —— (1998), Bullying in Prisons, Occasional Paper No. 18, Oxford: Centre for Criminological Research.

ORNE, M. T. (1968), 'On the Social Psychology of the Psychological Experiment', in P. G. Swingle (ed.), Experiments in Social Psychology, New York: Academic Press.

OWEN, B. (1998), In the Mix: Struggle and Survival in a Women's Prison, Albany, NY: State University of New York Press.

PHILLIPS, C. (2008), Negotiating identities: Ethnicity and social relations in a young offenders' institution, Theoretical Criminology, 12(3): 313–31.

PRISON REFORM TRUST (2011), Bromley Briefings www. prisonreformtrust.org.uk/Portals/0/Documents/Fact%20File%20June%202011%20web.pdf.

RHODES, L. (2004), Total Confinement: Madness And Reason In The Maximum Security Prison, California: University of California Press.

RYAN, M. and WARD, T. (1989), Privatization and the penal system: The American experience and the debate in Britain, Milton Keynes: Open University Press.

SAMPSON, R. J. and LAUB, J. H. (1993), Crime in the Making: Pathways and Turning Points through Life, London and Cambridge, Mass.: Harvard University Press.

SCOTT, J. (1990), Domination and the Arts of Resistance: Hidden Transcripts, New Haven and London: Yale University Press.

SCRATON, P. (ed.) (1987), Law, Order and the Authoritarian State, Milton Keynes: Open University Press.

——, SIM, J., and SKIDMORE, P. (1991), Prisons Under Protest, Milton Keynes: Open University Press.

SIMON, J. (1993), Poor Discipline: Parole and the Social Control of the Underclass, 1890–1990, Chicago: University of Chicago Press.

—— (2000), 'The 'society of captives' in the era of hyper-incarceration', Theoretical Criminology, 4(3): 285–308.

—— (2007), Governing Through Crime. How the War on Crime Transformed American Democracy and Created a Culture of Fear, Oxford: Oxford University Press.

SMITH, R. (2004), *A Few Kind Words and a Loaded Gun: The Autobiography of a Career Criminal*, London: Penguin.

SOCIAL EXCLUSION UNIT (2002), *Reducing reoffending by ex-prisoners*, London: Social Exclusion Unit.

SPARKS, R. (1996), 'Penal austerity: the doctrine of less eligibility reborn?', in R. Matthews and P. Francis (eds), *Prisons 2000: An International Perspective on the Current State and Future of Imprisonment*, Basingstoke: Palgrave Macmillan.

—— and BOTTOMS, A. E. (2008), 'Legitimacy and imprisonment revisited: notes on the problem of order ten years after', in J. Byrne, F. Taxman, and D. Hummer (eds), *The Culture of Prison Violence*, Boston: Pearson/Allyn and Bacon.

——, BOTTOMS, A., and HAY, W. (1996), *Prisons and the Problem of Order*. Oxford: Clarendon.

STERN, V. (1983), *Bricks of Shame*, 2nd edn, London: Penguin.

STREET, D., VINTNER, R., and PERROW, C. (1969), *Organization For Treatment*, New York: The Free Press.

SYKES, G. (1956), 'Men, merchants and toughs: a study of reactions to imprisonment', *Social Problems*, 4: 130–38.

—— (1958), *The Society of Captives: A Study of a Maximum-Security Prison*, Princeton, NJ: Princeton University Press.

—— (1995), 'The structural-functional perspective on imprisonment', in T. Blomberg and S. Cohen (eds), *Punishment and Social Control. Essays in Honor of Sheldon L. Messinger*, New York: Aldine de Gruyter.

—— and MESSINGER, S. (1960), 'The Inmate Social System', in R. A. Cloward et al., *Theoretical Studies in the Social Organization of the Prison*. New York: Social Science Research Council.

TOCH, H. (1992), *Living in Prison: The Ecology of Survival*, New York: The Free Press.

—— and ADAMS, K. (1989), *Coping: Maladaptation in prisons*, New Brunswick, NJ: Transaction.

USEEM, B. and KIMBALL, P. (1989), *States of Siege: US Prison Riots, 1971–1986*, Oxford: Oxford University Press.

WACHTEL, T. and MCCOLD, P. (2001), 'Restorative Justice in Everyday Life', in H. Strang and J. Braithwaite (eds), *Restorative Justice and Civil Society*, Cambridge: Cambridge University Press, 114–29.

WACQUANT, L. (2000), 'The new "Peculiar Institution": On the Prison as Surrogate Ghetto', *Theoretical Criminology*, 4(3): 377–89.

—— (2001), 'Deadly Symbiosis: Where Ghetto and Prison Meet and Merge', *Punishment and Society*, 3(1): 95–133.

—— (2002), 'The curious eclipse of prison ethnography in the age of mass incarceration', *Ethnography*, 3(4): 371–98.

—— (2009), *Punishing the Poor: The Neoliberal Government of Social Insecurity*, Durham, NC: Duke University Press.

WALKER, S. and WORRALL, A. (2000), 'Life as a woman: the gendered pains of indeterminate imprisonment', *Prison Service Journal*, 132: 27–37.

WHEELER, S. (1961), 'Socialization in Correctional Communities', *American Sociological Review*, 26: 697–712.

WILSON, D. (2003), ' "Keeping Quiet" or "Going Nuts": Strategies Used by Young, Black, Men in Custody', *The Howard Journal of Criminal Justice*, 43(3): 317–30.

WINDZIO, M. (2006),'Is there a deterrent effect of pains of imprisonment? The impact of "social costs" of first incarceration on the hazard rate of recidivism', *Punishment and Society* 8: 341–64.

WOOLF REPORT (1991), *Prison Disturbances April 1990. Report of an Inquiry by the Rt Hon. Lord Justice Woolf (Part I and II) and his Honour Judge Stephen Tumim (Part II)*, Cm. 1456, London: HMSO.

WRONG, D. (2002), *Power: Its Forms, Bases and Uses*, 3rd edn, New Brunswick, Transaction Publishers.

ZAITZOW, B. and THOMAS, T. (eds) (2003), *Women in Prison: Gender and Social Control*. Boulder, CO: Lynn Rienner Publishers.

ZIMBARDO, P. (2007), *The Lucifer Effect*, London: Rider Publications.

# 31

# COMMUNITY PENALTIES, PROBATION, AND OFFENDER MANAGEMENT

*Peter Raynor*

## INTRODUCTION: SLIPPERY CONCEPTS IN UNSTABLE TIMES

The term 'community penalty' is widely used but not always easy to define. For example, 'community penalty' is not normally used simply to describe forms of punishment imposed in the community, or outside prison. If this were its usual meaning, most discussions of community penalties would probably be about fines, since these are the most widely used non-custodial punishment. Instead, we find that most discussions of community penalties are actually about probation, a penalty which allows the offender to retain his or her liberty by complying with the requirements of a court order and being supervised by an appropriately authorized official employed by, or acting on behalf of, a probation service. In recent years such discussions have also included community service orders (a rather different kind of penalty involving indirect reparation supervised by probation services, more recently rebranded as punitive unpaid work or 'Community Payback') and other forms of supervisory penalty such as electronically monitored curfew orders, which are not necessarily supervised by probation services. On the other hand, discussions of community penalties often exclude a large proportion of the offenders actually supervised by probation services (at least in Britain) because their original sentences are custodial, and they are being supervised under a form of licence or conditional release.

The chapter concentrates mainly on developments in England and Wales. These countries have one of the world's longest histories of probation (though not the longest), and during the period of the development of welfare states in the mid-twentieth century they were routinely placed among the pioneers and world leaders of this kind of work. For example, in 1952 Max Grünhut (a German lawyer and criminologist who, like Hermann Mannheim and Leon Radzinowicz, had escaped from the Nazi regime before the war and helped to found the academic discipline of criminology in Britain) wrote: 'Probation is the great contribution of Britain and the USA to the treatment of offenders. Its strength is due to a combination of two things, conditional suspension of punishment, and personal care and supervision by a court welfare officer. With the growing use of probation, social case work has been introduced into the administration of criminal justice ...' (Grünhut 1952: 168). In a similar vein, in 1958 Leon Radzinowicz wrote: 'If I were asked what was the most significant contribution made by this country [i.e. England] to the new penological theory and practice which struck root in the twentieth century... my answer would be probation' (Radzinowicz 1958: x). As David Garland has pointed out, the rapid development of probation in the period after the Second World War can be understood as part of a process of social reconstruction, increased state responsibility for the welfare of citizens, and confidence in the ability of experts and professionals to ameliorate social problems (Garland 1997). It should also be noted that the popularity of probation during the third quarter of the twentieth century was not mainly based on evidence of effectiveness, which was scarce, but on general support for the principles of the welfare state. Conversely when better evidence did later become available, as described later in this chapter, this did not always help the image and reputation of probation services as much as might have been expected if penal policy were in reality as evidence-based as it sometimes claims to be.

It is also clear that probation in England and Wales is no longer typical: by international standards it is unusual to regard probation as a form of 'punishment in the community', as it has been in England and Wales since the 1991 Criminal Justice Act. However, in spite of all the changes, a number of commentators (for example Vanstone 2004; Deering 2011) still identify strong elements of continuity in the core features of community sentences, and describe them in terms not very different from those used by Grünhut above. These include giving offenders an opportunity to demonstrate that they can avoid further offending, and holding them accountable through a supervision process which combines monitoring with encouragement and assistance—the mixture of supervision and help, which has been probation's preferred style since very early in its evolution. Thus 'community penalties' are usually not purely punitive (like a fine), neither are they based on coercive restriction of liberty like a prison; instead they rely on the cooperation of offenders in accepting the requirements of a court order, and often on the capacity of supervisors to negotiate, motivate, and persuade.

This chapter, then, is mainly about 'community penalties', mainly about England and Wales, and mainly about adults. Some mention will also be made of those aspects of post-custodial supervision which resemble community penalties. The chapter briefly describes the current variety of community penalties and their use in sentencing, outlines the changes in the functions and perception of probation services which have led up to the current pattern of work, and assesses the likely impact of the most recent shifts in policy and practice.

## CURRENT COMMUNITY PENALTIES IN ENGLAND AND WALES

Much of the history of community penalties is about probation orders (requiring an offender to be under the supervision of a probation officer) and community service orders (requiring the performance of supervised unpaid work as a form of reparation to the community), and these terms will be used frequently throughout this chapter. However, in England and Wales these familiar names were replaced in 2000 by 'community rehabilitation orders' and 'community punishment orders' respectively, together with a combination of the two known as a 'community punishment and rehabilitation order'. These cumbersome and not particularly popular redesignations were in their turn replaced by a new 'generic community sentence' under the 2003 Criminal Justice Act, which can be up to three years in length, although shorter terms can be specified. To this order can be attached any of (and most combinations of) 12 different requirements relating to unpaid work, specified activities, accredited programmes, prohibited activities, curfews, exclusions from specified places, residence in specified places, mental health treatment, drug rehabilitation, alcohol treatment, supervision by a responsible officer, and attendance centres for younger offenders. With several of these, electronic monitoring can also be included. Some of these are derivatives of earlier familiar orders (for example, unpaid work is community service, and drug treatment requirements resemble the earlier Drug Treatment and Testing Orders (Turnbull *et al.* 2000)). The details of permitted time limits and combinations are too complex to expound here, and readers seeking this level of detail are referred to one of the legal guides to the Act, such as Gibson (2004). This Act also introduced a new suspended sentence order in which similar requirements could be included. What was much less clear was how these new orders would impact on the sentencing landscape: for example, would sentencers be tempted to combine large numbers of requirements into over-demanding packages which will result in higher breach rates? Early indications are that the new community sentences are mostly not being used in this way, but this could change over time (Mair *et al.* 2007).

For many years the Probation Service has also been responsible for supervising some young offenders on licence after their release from custodial institutions, and adult prisoners on parole and (since the 1991 Criminal Justice Act) on automatic conditional release. This increasingly prevalent pattern of a custodial sentence followed by a period of conditional liberty under supervision came during the late 1990s to be seen as a single 'seamless' sentence to be planned as one continuous process (Maguire and Raynor 1997). The Halliday Report (2001) and the resulting 2003 Criminal Justice Act attempted to introduce a new hybrid sentence known as 'Custody Plus' to provide supervision on release for short sentence prisoners (sentenced to less than one year), but this was never implemented due to lack of money. Instead this particular group of offenders, 61 per cent of whom are reconvicted within one year of release (Ministry of Justice 2010a), remain without any provision for their resettlement other than local experimental projects.

The latest Ministry of Justice annual statistics of Probation Service activities in England and Wales (Ministry of Justice 2010b) show 241,504 people under supervision at the end of 2009, a full 38 per cent higher than in 1999. This total comprised over 140,000 court orders, including the equivalent of the old probation and community service orders and nearly 44,000 suspended sentence orders, which became available on implementation of the 2003 Criminal Justice Act and account for an increasing proportion of the caseload. Most of the remainder is made up of about 100,000 people who are or will be subject to supervision on release from custodial establishments, of whom about two-thirds are not yet released. In addition, probation staff prepared about 218,000 pre-sentence reports for judges and magistrates. The 2010–11 budget for probation services (before the latest cuts took effect) was £884 million (House of Commons Justice Committee 2011), less than a quarter of the cost of the prisons in England and Wales. In addition there is probation-related expenditure within NOMS, the National Offender Management Service, which has since 2004 provided an over-arching central administration for prisons and probation, as described later in this chapter. Adding the NOMS component probably brings the total probation-related expenditure to about one billion pounds per year (Mills *et al.* 2010), although expenditure in NOMS is notoriously difficult to ascertain. In 2008 the full staff complement of probation services was recorded by NOMS as 21,140 full-time equivalent staff (Mills *et al.* 2010); the workforce increased substantially from the late 1990s to 2006, then started to decrease due to public expenditure cuts.

## THE HISTORY: PROBATION AS SOCIAL WORK

Probation had its origins in local court practices in the early nineteenth century, whereby young offenders or those guilty of minor offences could be discharged or bound over if a suitable person offered to take responsibility for supervising their future conduct. In 1876 the Church of England Temperance Society began to maintain an active presence in some city police courts in order to promote the moral reform of offenders and absten-tion from alcohol. Sentencers developed the practice of seeking information from the missionaries about offenders and placing some of them under informal supervision in lieu of other punishment if they seemed likely to reform. This was an opportunity to 'prove' themselves: hence the term 'probation', a proof or test. A similar system had developed in parts of the United States from the 1840s, and seems first to have been formalized in the legal guise of supervision by an officer of the court in Massachusetts in 1869. The Probation of Offenders Act was passed in England and Wales in 1907, but several more decades were to elapse before probation services everywhere in Britain were provided by salaried public officials rather than by a mixed workforce of pro-fessionals and missionaries. By the time that serious research on probation began to be undertaken the emerging professional service had found itself a new theory: like the rest of social work, it had adopted a psychosocial rationale strongly influenced by psychoanalytic ideas about the unconscious and defence mechanisms (see Richmond 1917 for a pre-Freudian model of diagnostic social work, and Hollis 1964 for a more developed and psychoanalytically influenced version). The new theory co-opted the old term 'casework' (which in its original usage by the Charity Organization Society meant simply 'work on cases') and changed its meaning to denote a process of thera-peutic work in which the offender's needs and motivations, characteristically hidden behind a 'presenting problem', could be revealed through a process of insight facilitated by a relationship with a probation officer (see, e.g., Monger 1964). Armed with such theories, the Probation Service could take its place alongside other useful but paternal-istic agencies as a small but significant part of the post-war welfare state.

Early British studies of the effects of probation, such as Wilkins (1958) and Radzinowicz (1958), were clearly located within what subsequently became known as the 'treatment model': in Radzinowicz's formulation, probation was 'a form of social service preventing further crime by a readjustment of the culprit' (Radzinowicz 1958: x), and the studies were designed to measure whether this readjustment had been successfully achieved. Their results were mixed and not particularly favourable to probation. However, from the point of view of this chapter it is more interesting to consider where they directed their attention and where they did not. In line with the 'treatment' model, they looked for effects on offenders' subsequent behaviour; they were not interested in criminal justice system issues such as impacts on sentencing, 'market shares' (i.e. the extent to which probation orders were preferred to other sentences by the courts), or the tariff level of those supervised. ('Tariff level' in this context refers to the severity of sentence an offender might expect if not on probation: prison is high in the sentencing 'tariff', fines are low.) Early researchers also appeared to have little interest in the methods used: probation was regarded as a method in itself, and the package was not unwrapped to see what lay inside.

During the 1960s the Home Office launched an ambitious programme of research aimed at classifying probationers and their problems empirically (e.g. Davies 1969 and 1974). The Probation Service tended to claim that caseloads were too high to allow it to show what it could achieve given better resources, and the eventual response to this was a controlled experiment. The IMPACT study ('Intensive Matched Probation and After-Care Treatment') randomly allocated probationers to normal or 'intensive' caseloads, and compared both the work done and the subsequent offending in these two groups—a classic research design for testing 'treatment'. The results of the study (Folkard *et al.* 1976) were 'small non-significant differences in reconviction in favour of the control cases', and no confirmation that more probation 'treatment' produced better (or any) effects. The one significant exception was that 'the only experimental cases that apparently do much better are those which have been rated as having low criminal tendencies and which perceive themselves as having many problems', a fairly small group and arguably rather untypical of offenders in general. One possible interpretation is that the typical content of probation in the 'treatment' era could be helpful to those who were distressed, anxious to change, and not particularly criminal. The overall conclusion had to be seen as a negative verdict on probation as a general-purpose 'treatment' for crime.

By the end of the 1970s the 'treatment model' was being strongly criticized on a number of empirical and ethical grounds. Empirically, studies of the effectiveness of penal sanctions of all kinds had produced generally discouraging results, and while this was not true of all studies, the general impression that 'nothing works' was reinforced by journalistic summaries (Martinson 1974) and by the overall conclusions of wide-ranging research reviews (Lipton *et al.* 1975; Brody 1976). These findings also gained strength from what were essentially moral or philosophical arguments against 'treatment', such as that it objectified or dehumanized its subjects, or that it rested on unsubstantiated claims of superior professional wisdom (Bottoms and McWilliams 1979). Legal scholars were increasingly questioning whether unreliable predictions about future behaviour should continue to influence sentencing and argued instead for proportionate 'justice' based on the seriousness of the offence (Hood 1974; von

Hirsch 1976). The limitations of the 'nothing works' research and the emergence of other, more positive sources of evidence about effective rehabilitation are covered in detail by Lösel's chapter in this volume. Its specific impact on probation services was complex, leading first to a focus on diversion from custody and later to a focus on 'punishment in the community', modified in due course by a developing knowledge base about 'what works'. The next part of this chapter traces each of these developments in turn.

## ALTERNATIVES TO CUSTODY: PROBATION AS DIVERSION

If the emphasis of the 1970s had been on doing good, without much success in demonstrating that good was being done, the 1980s were to be about avoiding harm, in particular by reducing unnecessary incarceration. This seemed a more achievable aim and one which might commend itself on the grounds of economy even to communities or politicians who were not in sympathy with the underlying humanitarian aim. If nothing works, cheaper is better. Probation now entered the era of 'alternatives to custody': it was to be a non-custodial penalty aiming to increase its market share and reduce imprisonment, rather than a 'treatment' aiming to change people. Community service, introduced by the 1972 Criminal Justice Act, was initially implemented on an experimental basis in a number of pilot areas, and the associated Home Office research was primarily concerned with whether it was feasible to implement it; whether courts were using it; and how far it was being used for offenders who would otherwise be sent to prison (Pease *et al.* 1977; Pease and McWilliams 1980). In other words, the community service research agenda was about effects on systems rather than people, and a departure from the 'treatment' agenda. Other more rehabilitation-oriented innovations, such as the day training centres, received far less official research attention (Vanstone and Raynor 1981). Although activities such as social enquiry reports (reports to sentencers by probation officers about offenders prior to sentence, now known as pre-sentence reports) continued to attract interest (Thorpe 1979), government sponsored research on the effectiveness of probation virtually ceased after IMPACT.

The dominance of new post-treatment, system-centred aims was underlined by the publication in 1984 of a *Statement of National Objectives and Priorities* for probation services in England and Wales (Home Office 1984, usually known as SNOP). This document, the first attempt at a national statement of the Probation Service's purpose, was clearly informed by the intention to develop community-based supervision in such a way as to reduce custodial sentencing. Social enquiry reports were to be a high priority 'where the court may be prepared to divert an offender from what would otherwise be a custodial sentence', and probation and community service orders were desirable 'especially in cases where custodial sentences would otherwise be imposed'. When, later on, policy moved away from a focus on diversion, this was not because diversion had failed: on the contrary, among juveniles in particular it succeeded quite well, with very substantial reductions in custodial sentencing and the almost complete disappearance of residential care for juvenile offenders during the 1980s (Smith 2007). Although concentrating too exclusively on diversion may involve doing too little about some persistent offenders, in its own terms the policy of 'alternatives to custody' for juvenile offenders succeeded until public and political opinion in the 1990s began to favour a more punitive approach and the numbers of juvenile offenders in custody began to rise again.

It has sometimes been argued that the creation of 'alternatives to custody' is a self-defeating strategy which has the unintended effect of increasing recruitment to the custodial part of the system. Several commentators, most notably Cohen (1985), have argued that the creation of less severe sentencing options often serves simply to draw more people into the net of social control measures ('net-widening') and that this exposes them to more severe sanctions when lower-tariff measures 'fail' (a process known in youth justice circles as 'tariff escalation'). There was clear evidence that suspended sentences, for example, had contributed to more imprisonment rather than less (Bottoms 1980). However, there was not much evidence of a general tendency towards tariff escalation resulting from community sentences in the 1980s. Among adults, probation orders successfully moved 'up-tariff' to accommodate a more heavily convicted group of offenders: the proportion of new probationers who had no previous convictions fell from 23 per cent in 1981 to 11 per cent in 1991 (Home Office 1992. Later it was to rise again to 27 per cent by 2001 [Home Office 2002] but that was after diversion ceased to be a primary goal for probation, as explained below). Studies of successful 'alternative' projects emphasized appropriate targeting to ensure that only those genuinely at risk of custodial sentences became involved, and appropriate enforcement strategies, agreed with the courts, to ensure that the outcome of enforcement action would be a return to the project in as many cases as possible. For example, seven out of ten breach cases in one successful project (Raynor 1988) resulted in returns to the project rather than custodial sentences, despite the 'high-tariff' nature of the offenders concerned.

Given such safeguards, the existence of additional sentencing options can be advantageous, and appropriate targeting is quite feasible: for instance, it appeared to be achieved in several early 'intensive probation' experiments (Mair et al. 1994) which recruited offenders clearly at risk of custodial sentences. Early studies of community service also found that 45–50 per cent of such orders appeared to be made instead of prison (Pease et al. 1977). However, it is also clear that the development of alternatives to custody has had limited long-term impact on the use of imprisonment. The best and most effective practices are by definition not universal, and in the absence of political commitment to send fewer people to prison, it seems unrealistic to expect the Probation Service to achieve this by stealth through the marketing of alternatives (see Mair 2011; Mills and Roberts 2011).

Overall the 1980s were a period of rapid and varied development for the Probation Service. Community service seemed to be a marketing success, but the market share of probation orders had been falling through most of the 1970s. A search for more substantial and effective programmes of supervision produced many unevaluated innovations, and also a handful of better documented and more successful examples (such as Raynor 1988 and Roberts 1989). At the end of the decade the Probation Service found itself in a confusing situation, expected by the Home Office to facilitate diversion from custody but retaining, within the Service itself, a considerable measure of belief in the possibility of effective rehabilitation, without much evidence to support it. Wider policy, meanwhile, was moving in a different direction: as the next section describes, the Government was beginning to outline a new 'centre stage' role for the Service as a provider of punishments in the community.

## JUST DESERTS AND 'PUNISHMENT IN THE COMMUNITY'

The 1991 Criminal Justice Act was a rare attempt to move beyond pragmatism towards a philosophically coherent sentencing system and penal policy. Bringing together much of the thinking and experience of the long period of Conservative government since 1979, it reflected the 'back to justice' movement of the late 1970s (Von Hirsch 1976; Hood 1974) by emphasizing the individual moral responsibility of offenders, and sentencing them for what they had done ('just deserts') rather than for their individual characteristics, their treatment needs or their expected future behaviour. The Act was preceded by several Green and White Papers (Home Office 1988, 1990a, 1990b) and accompanied by a comprehensive training programme for sentencers and probation staff. It also aimed to bring about a significant shift in probation and related non-custodial penalties which had previously been seen as orders made 'instead of sentence'. In future, they were to be part of the sentencing tariff, 'community sentences' to be imposed if the offence was 'serious enough', but not 'so serious' that only a custodial sentence could be justified. This redefinition of probation as a 'punishment in the community' (Home Office 1990a) was initially resisted by probation staff, and some commentators (e.g. Rumgay 1989) warned that what was presented primarily as a change of language, intended to sell a reform package to a sceptical electorate, could eventually influence the nature of the activity to which it was applied. On the other hand, for those who had been campaigning against excessive use of imprisonment it was enormously encouraging to see a White Paper stating that imprisonment 'can be an expensive way of making bad people worse' (Home Office 1990b: 6).

At the same time, paradoxically, probation services were suddenly discouraged by Home Office officials from using the language of 'alternatives to custody': community sentences and prisons were no longer to be in competition but were targeting different levels of seriousness. The two services were meant to be cooperating in new forms of throughcare for prisoners (Maguire and Raynor 1997), and this process would not be helped if one service continued to define its mission as saving people from the other. In practice, the 1991 Act turned out to be genuinely decarcerative: there were very substantial reductions in the use of custodial sentences during the few months of 1992 and 1993 in which the Act was allowed to operate as intended, before politicians shifted their stance and repealed key sections of it. However, the decisive shift away from the language of 'alternatives to custody' and its replacement by the language of punishment turned out to be one of the more enduring legacies of the 1991 Act, to the extent that much of what was learned from successful diversionary research and practice in the 1980s is seldom now discussed.

In 1993, the policy context suddenly and dramatically changed. As part of an unprecedented package of populist 'Law and Order' initiatives, the recently appointed Conservative Home Secretary Michael Howard announced that 'prison works' (Howard 1993). Before long he was proposing a series of changes to the Probation Service which were intended to constitute a definitive break with its former 'social work' identity. Howard's populist stance did not save the unpopular Government in which he served from comprehensive defeat in the General Election of 1997; however, his criminal justice policies have had profound consequences for the prison population, rising almost continuously since his 1993 speech, and for the Probation Service, which needed urgently to find a new mission around which to build a case for survival. This new mission became the 'What Works' movement.

## COMMUNITY PENALTIES AND CRIME REDUCTION: THE REDISCOVERY OF REHABILITATION

The origins of this movement and the theories behind it have been thoroughly reviewed elsewhere (for example, Raynor and Vanstone 2002; Raynor and Robinson 2009a; from a more sceptical stance Mair 2004; and see also chapters by Hollin and Lösel in this volume). Readers interested in the full detail and psychological background are referred to these sources. In brief, awareness of a body of research pointing to effective methods of work with offenders was already entering the British probation world in the late 1980s, not from the Home Office (where such research was still paralysed by the legacy of Martinson) but largely from other countries where reputable research on effective methods had continued. Work carried out in Canada and the USA was drawn to the attention of British audiences by the early 'What Works' conferences, in which James McGuire played a leading role (McGuire 1995); by a research review funded by the Scottish Office, which had never lost its commitment to rehabilitative penal methods (McIvor 1990); and by many other contributions.

Particularly influential were two large meta-analyses of service and project evaluations which supported the argument that the right kind of intervention with offenders under supervision could make a significant difference to levels of re-offending (Andrews *et al.* 1990; Lipsey 1992). These meta-analyses tended to favour methods which were based on the now familiar principles of risk, need and responsivity (i.e. that services should target higher risk offenders, should focus on areas of need which contribute to offending, known as 'criminogenic' needs, and should be delivered in a way which suits the circumstances and learning style of the offender). They also favoured the use of cognitive-behavioural methods designed to help offenders to change anti-social beliefs and attitudes and acquire new skills for dealing with problems. A local experiment involving the delivery of a cognitive-behavioural programme by probation officers was evaluated in South Wales (the STOP programme: see Raynor and Vanstone 1996, 1997).

In 1995 the Home Office issued a circular (Home Office 1995) encouraging (or requiring) probation services to adopt effective methods and promising a follow-up inspection by Her Majesty's Inspectorate of Probation (HMIP). Instead of a simple inspection to follow up the 1995 circular, a research exercise was set up involving a detailed survey of probation areas by Andrew Underdown, a senior probation manager who was already closely involved in issues around effective practice. The results, eventually published in 1998 (Underdown 1998), after the election of a Labour Government expected to be better disposed towards the Probation Service, were alarming. Of the 267 programmes which probation areas claimed they were running based on the principles of effective practice set out in the 1995 Circular, evidence of actual effectiveness based on reasonably convincing evaluation was available only for four (Ellis and Winstone 2002).

The poor results of the Inspectorate's survey of current practice pointed to the need for a centrally-managed initiative to introduce more effective forms of supervision. The Home Office's Probation Unit worked closely with the Inspectorate to develop the 'What Works initiative'; publications were issued to provide guidance (Chapman and Hough 1998; McGuire 2000) and a number of promising programmes were identified for piloting and evaluation as 'pathfinder' programmes, with support in due course from the Government's Crime Reduction Programme (CRP). The pathfinders included several cognitive-behavioural programmes (Hollin et al. 2004) but also included work on basic skills (improving literacy and numeracy to improve chances of employment (McMahon et al. 2004; Haslewood-Poszik et al. 2004)), pro-social approaches to supervision in Community Service (Rex and Gelsthorpe 2002; Rex et al. 2003), and a number of joint projects run by probation services with prisons and in some cases voluntary organizations working on the resettlement of short-term prisoners after release (Lewis et al. 2003; Clancy et al. 2006).

In the meantime a new probation service was taking shape, to come formally into existence as the National Probation Service (NPS) for England and Wales in April 2001, replacing the old separate area probation services and explicitly committed to public protection and crime reduction. Instead of 54 separate probation services, each responsible to and employed by a local Probation Committee consisting largely of local magistrates, the National Probation Service (NPS) was a single organization run by a Director with a substantial central staff located in the Home Office (the National Probation Directorate). The main aim of the changes was to create an organization which could be more effectively managed and directed from the centre. Detailed national policies and targets were published in a document intriguingly entitled 'A New Choreography' (NPS 2001) incorporating 'stretch objectives' designed to produce change, and performance was monitored. All this represented a considerable transformation over a very short period of time, and the new organization was faced with the problem of how to maintain a sense of involvement among those groups which had less influence in the new structure than they had in the past. These groups included the magistrates who passed most of the community sentences, and some of the Service's own staff, who found their traditional autonomy reduced by a more managerial regime. At the same time, the Service's new Director chose to emphasize a decisive shift in direction by adopting the slogan 'Enforcement, rehabilitation and public protection' (NPS 2001).

## WHAT WORKED AND WHAT DIDN'T?

The end of the twentieth century marked the high point of optimism for the 'What Works' movement in the Probation Service of England and Wales. Promising programmes were identified and being piloted; the Joint Prisons and Probation Accreditation Panel (later Correctional Services Accreditation Panel) was set up in 1999 to apply some independent quality control to the programmes adopted by prisons and probation services (for an appraisal of its work see Maguire *et al.* 2010) and substantial funding was attracted from the Treasury to finance programme implementation and research (though not without strings, such as hugely ambitious target numbers for programme completions and an unrealistically short period during which evaluations were to be completed: for fuller discussion of the problems of the Crime Reduction Programme see Hough 2004; Homel *et al.* 2005). A good example of the general optimism was provided by John Halliday in his influential review of sentencing (Halliday 2001) which became the underpinning rationale for most of the 2003 Criminal Justice Act: '...if the programmes are developed and applied as intended...reconviction rates might be reduced by 5–15 percentage points (i.e. from the present level of 56% within two years, to (perhaps) 40%)' (Halliday 2001: 7). It is not clear how Halliday arrived at this remarkable example of a 'best case' scenario, but presumably he had been talking with the Home Office and probation staff who were pressing ahead with 'What Works'.

More difficult times lay ahead. No correctional service anywhere in the world had tried to implement 'What Works' principles on such a scale, at such a speed, and subject to such comprehensive scrutiny and evaluation. This inevitably led to a number of short cuts, sometimes running well ahead of or even contrary to the available evidence. For example, the targets for accredited programme completions set in 1999, which drove the pace of the roll-out of offending behaviour programmes, had been negotiated with Treasury officials without any systematic prior assessment of the characteristics of offenders under supervision and their suitability for programmes (Raynor 2007). After experiments with other simpler risk and need assessment instruments (Raynor *et al.* 2001), a new assessment instrument was developed known as the Offender Assessment System (OASys). This was originally promised for August 2000, but was not available to inform the target-setting process. (Since then it has proved to be a reasonably good predictor, comparable to other established instruments, but cumbersome and unpopular in practice, so that it is now not used, or not used in full, for several categories of offenders, and reassessments are sometimes not carried out so that a good deal of data is missing—see Debidin 2009.) The targets quickly proved too high for most probation areas to achieve and were eventually reduced, but not before consuming much time and effort and causing many problems for staff and managers.

Within the pathfinders themselves, researchers noted a large number of implementation difficulties: projects were often not running in a fully developed form when the evidence which would be used to measure their effectiveness was collected. The very mixed results of the pathfinder evaluations have been reviewed elsewhere (for example Raynor 2004a, b; Roberts 2004a, b; Harper and Chitty 2004). For the purposes of this chapter, it is sufficient to note that, for a variety of reasons, they fell short of a clear demonstration of the effectiveness of the pathfinder projects. Often, as in the resettlement study, local projects depended on small numbers of staff and were vulnerable to staff sickness or communication problems (Lewis *et al.* 2003). In all the pathfinder studies, projects tended to make a slow start and not to achieve their target numbers; in the 'basic skills' and 'employment' pathfinders (McMahon *et al.* 2004; Haslewood-Pocsik *et al.* 2004) numbers completing were so small that the evaluation could not be carried out as intended. In the 'offending behaviour' pathfinders (e.g. Roberts 2004a; Hollin *et al.* 2004) the high levels of attrition, due in large part to enforcement action leading to the termination of orders for non-compliance, led to difficulties in interpreting evidence. (Outcomes based on programme completers, when these are only a small proportion of those who start the programme, may show effects of the programme or may show simply the effects of whatever selection or self-selection processes led to those people, rather than others, completing it.) In addition, the top-down management style which was seen as necessary to drive implementation forward within the prescribed time-scale (Blumsom 2004) alienated parts of the workforce, particularly probation officers who were used to a high degree of autonomy. The probation officers' union NAPO expressed its concern in conference resolutions which rejected aspects of the 'What Works' approach (National Association of Probation Officers 2001). In such circumstances researchers could hardly be surprised if some of the data quality was poor.

Some warning notes might also have been sounded by an American study (Lipsey 1999) of differences between 'demonstration' and 'practical' interventions. The former are the special pilot projects which are often the source of the research covered in systematic reviews, and the latter are the routine implementations which follow organizational decisions to adopt new methods, as in the rapid roll-out of the Probation Service's new programmes. Better results are more commonly found among the 'demonstration' projects: in Lipsey's study the 196 'practical' programmes reviewed were on average half as effective as the 205 'demonstration' programmes. (Even this level of effectiveness depended heavily on a few programmes, as 57 per cent of the 'practical' programmes had no appreciable effect.) As he points out, 'rehabilitative programmes of a practical "real world" sort clearly can be effective; the challenge is to design and implement them so that they, in fact, are effective' (Lipsey 1999: 641). Problems also arose from a tendency to be preoccupied with implementing programmes or 'interventions' rather than with providing an experience of supervision which would be effective as a whole. Although this had been pointed out by earlier British research (Raynor and Vanstone 1997), by Rod Morgan when, as Chief Inspector of Probation, he warned against 'programme fetishism' (Morgan 2003) and by the Correctional Services Accreditation Panel which insisted on continuity as one of its accreditation criteria (Correctional Services Accreditation Panel 2003), little attention was paid to the need for effective case management until attrition rates started to cause concern.

The early 'What Works' years in England and Wales have also been criticized for their lack of a clear penal strategy. In other words, there does not seem to have been any clear shared vision of the pattern of sentencing which was intended to result from the initiative, or any clear policy regarding the functions and desirable levels of custodial and community sentencing. Although efforts were made, with only partial success, to ensure that programmes were not used for low-risk offenders, little else was done to eliminate the down-tariff drift of community sentences which had been going on throughout the 1990s. As already noted, the proportion of those sentenced to community sentences who were first offenders, which fell overall during the 1980s, rose again during the 1990s, while the proportion of orders passed for less serious or summary offences also rose (Home Office 2002). The down-tariff drift of probation also coincided with increased imprisonment and a reduction in the use of fines. However, in a remarkable act of collective amnesia, probation's leaders made no connection between the 'What Works' agenda and their earlier strategy of reducing reliance on custodial sentences. There was little attempt to promote programmes as an alternative to short custodial sentences, until the announcement several years later, in January 2008, of a programme of 'Intensive Alternatives to Custody' (Ministry of Justice 2008). The potential impact of the 'What Works' initiative on the wider penal system was probably diminished as a result.

During this period several other developmental issues attracted attention in the form of special projects and research, and space does not allow a full exploration of them here. The 'What Works' initiative was criticized for over-generalizing from research on white men, leading to research on minority ethnic offenders (Lewis et al. 2006) and to proposals for distinctive provision for women offenders (Shaw and Hannah-Moffatt 2004; Sheehan et al. 2007; Fawcett Society 2009). The assessment and management of risk attracted two kinds of attention based on two meanings of risk, perhaps better understood as risk and danger respectively. Risk-need assessment (Raynor et al. 2000; OASys Development Team 2001; Bonta and Wormith 2007), based on assessing levels of criminogenic need or dynamic risk factors, became the dominant method for assessing the risk of re-offending and developing supervision plans to reduce it, while the risk of harm to the public from dangerous violent or sexual offences was assessed in other ways geared to the identification of triggers and the development of methods of control and surveillance to protect potential victims through multi-agency public protection arrangements (MAPPA: see Kemshall and Maguire 2001; Kemshall et al. 2005; Kemshall 2008). The work of the panels set up under these arrangements represents, in fact, one of the more successful recent developments in offender management and was commended by the outgoing Chief Inspector of Probation in his retirement lecture (Bridges 2011). However, they also represent a reputational hazard, since they supervise at any given time such a high proportion of the dangerous offenders who are at liberty in the community that occasional serious re-offending by people under supervision is unavoidable. Whenever this occurs it leads to public concern and alarm, and often to official enquiries or special inspections. Some of these point to avoidable errors (e.g. Her Majesty's Inspectorate of Probation 2006a, b) while others confirm that the quality of supervision was reasonable in the circumstances (e.g. Omand 2010). However, none of these seem completely to allay public and media concern, which appears to be based on an unrealistic picture of what being under supervision in the community actually involves.

Overall, in spite of the hard work and undeniable achievements of many very able and dedicated staff, it is clear that the early results of the 'What Works' initiative were not impressive enough to bring about the radical change in the Probation Service's standing and prospects anticipated by 1990s pioneers such as its Chief Inspector, Graphm Smith. With hindsight, it is also clear that a three-year implementation time-scale, with a major reorganization in the middle, was never likely to be long enough to show significant benefit from such a complex process of change.

## AFTER 'WHAT WORKS', WHAT NEXT? MANAGERIALISM, POLITICS, AND NOMS

In the winter of 2003–4 the National Probation Service received a severe shock, in the form of a proposal to bring the prison and probation services together under the single organizational umbrella of a National Offender Management Service (NOMS). The threat which seemed to have been seen off in 1998 was suddenly revived. Briefly, this proposal arose from a review of correctional services carried out by Patrick Carter, a businessman with experience of the private health-care sector and highly regarded in Downing Street. His report (Carter 2003) offered a diagnosis of the system's problems with which few specialists would disagree, pointing to prison overcrowding, failure to help short-term prisoners, and the fact that for persistent offenders who passed repeatedly through the custodial and community systems, no one agency had the clear responsibility for managing the sentence as a whole in the way that offered the best prospect of reducing re-offending. The proposed alternative, known as 'end-to-end offender management', required, in Carter's view, a single agency to run it, namely NOMS. Under a Chief Executive and a National Offender Manager, 10 Regional Offender Managers (ROMs) would 'commission' the services required, whether custodial or non-custodial, for the management of offenders in their region. Even more controversial was Carter's proposal that the best way to improve the effectiveness of services in the community was to introduce contestability or market testing, in order to bring in other providers from the voluntary sector and particularly the private sector.

It is difficult to take issue with the argument that probation services needed to work more in partnership with other organizations. The range of services needed by offenders greatly exceeds what the Probation Service itself is equipped to supply. The 'Reducing Re-offending Action Plan' (Home Office 2004), based partly on work by the Social Exclusion Unit (2002) and others on the resettlement needs of prisoners, identified seven 'pathways' for the development of services to support resettlement and rehabilitation. These were accommodation; education, training and employment; mental and physical health; drugs and alcohol; finance, benefits and debt; children and families of offenders; and attitudes, thinking, and behaviour. Intervention in relation to almost all of these would require collaboration with other organizations. However, it was much harder to see how the core of offender management, which coordinates these other elements and provides continuity and structure for the offender, could benefit from the fragmentation implied by contestability. This aspect of the proposals was widely criticized (see, e.g. Hough, Allen, and Padel 2006). For the purposes of this chapter, it is also important to note that the Carter proposals actually constituted a significant rupture in the 'What Works' project as it developed up to 2003. Instead of a process of evidence-based change driven by piloting and evaluation, the Carter review offered the market solution of contestability as if this guaranteed better results. Commissioning, a purchaser-provider split, contestability, and a greater role for the private sector were becoming standard ingredients in New Labour's 'reform' programme for public services. In other ways, however, the National Probation Service itself may have unwittingly paved the way for NOMS. The nationalization of a service which was formerly rooted in localities and at least to some degree in a sense of ownership by local sentencers may have made it more vulnerable to politically-driven change: a single service based in London under the eye of the Home Office was arguably a more obvious focus of political awareness and target for political gestures than 54 locally based services involving hundreds of influential magistrates, particularly when the single service was criticized as slow to meet targets and prone to overspend its budget.

Two aspects of the Carter proposals and the NOMS 'reform' package which attracted wide-ranging support were the end-to-end offender management model and the underpinning aim of controlling the growth of imprisonment. The importance of continuity in offender management had been strongly indicated by a series of studies of the resettlement of prisoners (Maguire, Perroud, and Raynor 1996; Maguire *et al.* 2000; Lewis *et al.* 2003; Clancy *et al.* 2006) and was also supported by a Home Office study of case management practice in the Probation Service (Partridge 2004; see also Robinson 2005) and in due course by a practical pilot study (PA Consulting Group 2005). What eventually emerged was the National Offender Management Model (NOMM: Home Office 2005) which emphasized that a named 'offender manager' should be responsible for each offender throughout a sentence, including both custodial and community components, in order to ensure consistent assessment, planning, and intervention. However, the NOMM is also seen as combining three separate processes of 'management', 'supervision', and 'administration' which may be carried out by different individuals, so that the actual experience of being supervised may be less seamless than the model implies. There is also provision for four 'tiers' of cases: all offenders will undergo 'punishment', but only some will also require help. Of these, only some will also require change efforts such as programmes, and even fewer will require active measures of control to reduce risks of serious harm to the public. The four-tier model can therefore be summed up, in ascending order of resource commitment, as punishment only (Tier 1); punishment plus help (Tier 2); punishment plus help plus change (Tier 3); and punishment plus help plus change plus control (Tier 4). It should also be noted that the strong emphasis on punishment as a part of probation is out of tune with the history of probation and with practice in most other jurisdictions, where probation is still seen as a conditional suspension of punishment (Vanstone and Raynor 2010; Raynor, forthcoming).

The allocation of offenders to tiers in theory depends on the levels of assessed risk and need, though inevitably the perceived seriousness of the offence and consequent severity of the sentence also play a part. In short, the model offers a comprehensive typology of approaches to case management, but can accommodate a variety of approaches and some degree of fragmentation in practice, depending on resources and on how well it is implemented. If resource constraints dictate that only the upper tiers will receive attention from trained and experienced staff, the work done with lower-tier offenders may be somewhat tokenistic, and recent evidence to the Justice Committee of the House of Commons suggests that this is indeed the case (House of Commons 2011). In addition, it is never easy to reconcile tidy models with the unpredictable day-to-day reality of supervising people who are often disorganized, distressed or difficult, and beset by unpredictable or at least unforeseen practical problems. If offenders had tidy and predictable lives they would not need supervision.

Carter's other central aim, to control the use of imprisonment, was widely welcomed but has simply not been achieved. Instead, within a few years Carter was producing another report (Carter 2007) on how to accommodate continuing growth in the number of prisoners. His 2007 report contains no assessment of progress made, or not made, in implementing his earlier report. NOMS itself has yet to assume a stable form: Judy McKnight, who was General Secretary of NAPO from 1993 to 2008, has described the constant frantic reorganization and the series of barely comprehensible 'organograms' (McKnight 2009), in which key posts such as National Offender Manager could appear and disappear without any obvious explanation. Both NOMS and its predecessor the National Probation Directorate have been criticized for over-centralization, target-driven managerialism and poor control of growth in staff and expenditure at the centre.

A recent Parliamentary Select Committee report has taken NOMS to task for creating a culture of micromanagement which leads to probation officers spending far more time filling in forms on computer screens than working with offenders; for wasting money on badly handled procurements such as the computerized case management system C-NOMIS which was eventually abandoned; and for operating a command-and-control management structure, based on the Prison Service model, which is said to be insensitive to local needs and to the requirements of offender supervision in the community. The Committee's overall conclusion is that 'the Ministry of Justice should commission an externally-led review of the operation of NOMS to assess whether it is: delivering value for money; giving trusts' (Probation Trusts—see below) 'the appropriate levels of support and autonomy they require; and integrating the supervision of offenders in prison and the community effectively. Our evidence suggests that it is not doing these things well. Should the review reach similar conclusions the Department should be prepared to take radical steps to redesign the structure and operation of NOMS.' (House of Commons 2011, para. 114.) In the meantime the Probation Service has undergone yet another reorganization, announced by the Labour Home Secretary Charles Clarke in 2005 and incorporated in the Management of Offenders Act 2007. Central government arrangements also changed in 2007, with responsibility for probation and prisons transferring from the Home Office to a new Ministry of Justice.

At the time of writing (but who knows for how long?) probation services are delivered by 35 Probation Trusts, replacing 42 Probation Boards and intended to operate in a more business-like way in the context of 'contestability'. On the one hand, Trusts may restore some of the local dimension to the management and development of probation:

certainly they seem to want to do so. On the other had they are currently faced, like the whole of the public sector, with the need to implement a programme of cuts. One consolation may be that cuts are also occurring at the centre, and the Ministry of Justice may no longer be able to afford top-down micromanagement.

Overall, it has to be recognized that the impact of the New Labour Governments of 1997–2010 on the Probation Service was at best mixed. Welcomed initially as saviours of a threatened service, they increased expenditure and initiated a process of evidence-based change; however, by 2003 leading politicians seemed disillusioned with what was being achieved and began to seek market-based solutions instead, preferring to take advice from businessmen about how to manage public services. Much of the new money went on central management and administration costs which did not necessarily improve effectiveness, and attempts to reorganize in the direction of contestability led to prolonged and sometimes bitter conflict with probation staff. The prison population continued to increase, and ministers seemed increasingly preoccupied with the need to appear tough in the eyes of the electorate and the popular media. There was direct ministerial involvement in the drafting of the 2000 National Standards to make enforcement tougher (Home Office 2000) and in the later years of the New Labour governments a Home Secretary who liked to be known as 'the Enforcer' made a speech to prisoners in which he told them that the Probation Service which would be supervising them on their release was 'not working as well as it should' and needed 'fundamental reform' (mostly meaning different providers: Reid 2006). In another bizarre episode, a Labour Justice Minister used a lecture at the Royal Society of Arts to announce that he was 'driven nuts' when the 'penal reform lobby' talked about 'the criminogenic needs of offenders', as if offenders' needs were equivalent to those of other people (Straw 2008). It is not surprising that many probation practitioners came to feel that the Government was not on their side. Meanwhile tougher enforcement of community sentences actually increased the prison population: by 2004 nearly 9,000 people per year were being imprisoned as a result of enforcement of community sentences (Home Office RDS NOMS 2005).

## CONCLUSION: THE END OF PROBATION, OR A 'REHABILITATION REVOLUTION'?

In 1997 at the Probation Studies Unit colloquium in Oxford, David Garland argued that trends towards toughness and punitiveness in the world of probation were an example of a wider trend in the penal systems of many countries (Garland 1997). As in his influential book *The Culture of Control* (Garland 2001) he attributed this to broad social and cultural changes characteristic of late modern societies. Some of the recent changes in British probation are clearly in line with these arguments: for example, a preoccupation with risk and the technology of risk management recalls the arguments of Giddens (1990) and Beck (1992). Some of the uses of risk assessment, and in particular the re-emergence of sentencing according to risk rather than desert, are consistent with the critique developed by Feeley and Simon (1992) and Hudson (2003), although other uses are more consistent with rehabilitative aims (Raynor 2007, 2010). The globalization of capital and the colonization of public life and public services by commercial business models and economic rationality (Christie 1993, 2004) define the context for privatization and 'contestability', whilst developments in information and communication technology (ICT) transform the possibilities for impersonal supervision of offenders by ever more sophisticated forms of tagging (Nellis 2004a). More detailed attempts to extrapolate from recent developments in probation to predict the future form and effectiveness of probation services are hazardous. Some commentators see 'the end of Probation' (Nellis 2004b) or argue that it has already died (Mantle 2006). On the other hand, the Conservative-led Coalition Government elected in 2010 quickly produced a Green Paper (Ministry of Justice 2010c) promising a 'rehabilitation revolution' which would focus the entire penal system on a primary goal of reducing re-offending, but underpinned by a system of payment-by-results drawing extensively on the private sector and voluntary organizations. In short, probation is not in control of its own destiny: like any other social institution it is both constituent and product of the wider society, and the political and ideological developments which influence its role and resources are not necessarily congruent with internal developments in its methods or its potential effectiveness.

This does not mean that internal developments are unimportant. Both the achievements and the evolving capacities of probation services help to form official perceptions of what is feasible. Any picture derived from these components must, at the present time, be mixed. If we consider probation's two long-established aims of reducing re-offending and reducing reliance on custodial sentencing, the latter has clearly not happened. Sentencing trends show that the proportionate use of both imprisonment and community sentences has increased since the mid-1990s while the use of fines has decreased (Ministry of Justice 2011). In other words, diversion has been from fines rather than prison. This is a worrying pattern, partly for financial reasons and partly because available evidence suggests that applying more intrusive penalties to lower-risk offenders is counterproductive (Andrews et al. 1990). At least one study in Britain showed some years ago that first offenders were about twice as likely to be reconvicted after a probation order than after a fine (Walker et al. 1981). However, even allowing for the probability that some community sentences are inappropriate, recent research consistently shows that known re-offending after a community sentence is lower than for similar offenders who have received short (under one year) custodial sentences, and a compendium of information to this effect was produced to accompany the Green Paper (Ministry of Justice 2010a). Whilst the difference in reconviction rates is not huge (typically around seven percentage points after controlling for differences between offenders) and is smaller than the differences reported from some early programme evaluations (such as Raynor and Vanstone 1997), nevertheless there is increasingly persuasive evidence that the impact of community sentences is generally positive, and potentially still more positive. For example, Hollis (2007) found that people who completed programmes in 2004 were reconvicted at 25.8 per cent less than the expected rate, and if all who started programmes were counted (including those who failed to complete) the difference was still 10.3 per cent.

In addition, there are signs that the impact of individual supervision, which tended to be discounted or overlooked when the early stages of the 'What Works' developments concentrated on programmes, is now receiving more attention. There are both theoretical and empirical reasons for this. The 'Carter Report' of 2003 distinguished between 'interventions' such as programmes, which were meant to produce change, and 'offender management' which was a form of oversight, not necessarily the same as supervision, designed mainly to ensure appropriate assessment and referral to 'interventions'. However, as NOMS began to develop the National Offender Management Model, the available evidence included emerging findings about the contribution to effectiveness made by the skills used in individual supervision, or 'Core Correctional Practices' (Dowden and Andrews 2004; Raynor *et al.* 2010). ('Core Correctional Practices' was a term coined in Canada to denote skills such as effective use of authority, pro-social modelling, teaching problem-solving skills, using community resources effectively, and maintaining positive, optimistic, understanding, cooperative, and respectful relationships.) In this way what began as a rather managerial exercise in allocating resources according to risk levels gradually became a focus for interest in the processes and skills of individual supervision.

These developments also benefited from new international work on individual engagement with offenders. Criminological interest in the process of desistance from crime sometimes highlighted the importance of changes in self-concept and life-plan (for example, Maruna 2001; Farrall and Calverley 2006), and this led to the idea that work with offenders in the criminal justice system should try to support and facilitate such changes (McNeill 2006). At the same time many practitioners were encouraged by the emergence of the 'Good Lives' model of work with offenders (McMurran and Ward 2004; Ward and Maruna 2007) which criticized the Risk/Need/Responsivity model of rehabilitation ('RNR'; Andrews *et al.* 1990) for its supposed focus on deficits rather than strengths, and advocated working with offenders to achieve their own visions of a 'good life' without offending. Whilst it can be argued that these criticisms of the RNR model are exaggerated, and there is little doubt that a wide range of positive empirical findings have emerged from the RNR tradition (Andrews and Bonta 2010; Andrews *et al.* 2011), the emergence of new 'creative' approaches to supervision has helped to stimulate international research interest (see McNeill *et al.* 2010; Brayford *et al.* 2010). A recent development within NOMS itself is the Offender Engagement Programme, which includes a project designed to train probation officers in the skills of effective individual supervision and to find out if the offenders they supervise make better progress as a result. Studies in other jurisdictions, including Canada (Bonta *et al.* 2010), the USA (Taxman *et al.* 2006), Australia (Trotter and Evans 2010), and the British Channel Islands (Raynor *et al.* 2010; Raynor 2011) have produced interesting results: for example, in the Canadian study, which was firmly based in the RNR tradition, a random allocation controlled experiment showed significantly lower recidivism rates in the caseloads of officers trained in effective supervision skills than in the caseloads of similar officers who had not received this training. Within NOMS itself it is clear that some staff see the Offender Engagement Programme as part of a cultural change away from centralized over-management towards greater reliance on practitioners' discretion, professional supervision, and less prescriptive National Standards—to which the most obvious response is: better late than never.

Such developments offer some encouragement to those who welcome continuity with traditional Probation Service values and practices. Robinson (2008) and others (such as Priestley and Vanstone 2010) have drawn attention to the manner in which the rehabilitation of offenders becomes redefined to fit different social and political circumstances: a major shift in recent times, as Garland (2001) points out, is from a focus on offenders' welfare to a focus on reducing re-offending in the interests of the potential future victim. The desistance perspective, with its emphasis on how offenders can turn their lives around through the use of internal and external resources (personal and social capital) offers a possible middle way or reconciling position between the interests of offender and victim, as does the continuing international development of theory and practice in restorative justice. However, other political developments within the next few years may bring about more fundamental changes in the nature and purposes of probation, and these are more likely to be driven by politics and ideology than by internal developments, however promising, in the theory and practice of offender supervision. The rebranding of probation has discarded probation orders in favour of community sentences and transformed probation officers into 'offender managers': in fact the term 'probation' survives only in the titles of organizations such as Probation Trusts, the Probation Association, or the National Association of Probation Officers. National governments in a globalized economy have limited control over many events, but can put on a show of power in areas such as criminal justice which are nationally administered and, at least in theory, more under their control. Similarly, economic pressure to reduce state expenditure reduces investment in welfare states, and recipients of welfare are more likely to be seen as individually responsible for their predicament and for getting themselves out of it (Rose 2000). This process of 'responsibilization' creates a climate in which the welfare of offenders is not a priority, and makes society less receptive to the idea than responsibility for social problems is shared between individuals and society, or that people can find themselves in trouble for reasons largely outside their own control.

Another modern political development with implications for the delivery of community sanctions is the continuing tendency for governments to withdraw from direct service provision in favour of some degree of marketization or privatization. The attempt to introduce this in the Carter Report of 2003 has already been described, and the process has been taken further by the authors of the 2010 Green Paper who argue that bringing a diversity of service providers into criminal justice will encourage innovation and effectiveness by making payment conditional on meeting targets—'payment by results'. They also point to the relatively long-standing use of the private sector to build and run prisons and to operate electronic monitoring (which in England and Wales has been developed mainly as a stand-alone provision rather than as an adjunct to personal supervision, as in most European countries). Opponents question whether real long-term savings can be made by contracting with private companies which have to make a profit for shareholders (though there is less opposition to using the specialist skills of voluntary organizations in what is known as the 'third sector'). It can also be argued that criminal justice is not a commodity or a service but a transaction between the state and the citizen, best managed through public servants who do not need to serve shareholder interests in addition to the public interest. These considerations point to a supporting role for the private sector, with control and accountability maintained through commissioning by public sector organizations; however, there is also some political support for more far-reaching replacement of public sector providers. The current tendering exercise to engage the private sector in the provision of Community Payback (formerly Community Service) will be an interesting indicator of likely future trends, as will the progress of the Peterborough Prison project. This draws its funding from investors and trusts through a financial instrument known as a Social Impact Bond, with profits to be made only if the project succeeds in reducing re-offending by providing effective resettlement services for short-sentence prisoners. The direct work with offenders is in turn subcontracted to experienced third-sector providers (Directgov 2010).

All this takes us a long way from the twentieth century development of probation as part of the welfare state, supporting the legitimacy of government through a social contract with citizens which was meant to provide social support in return for adherence to social norms. The development of community sentences depends on wider penal policy, which in turn depends on social policy and the wider political climate. The 2010 Green Paper's aim to stem the rise in the adult prison population was quickly undermined by criticisms of 'soft justice' from right wing politicians and the right wing newspapers even before the urban riots of August 2011 in England gave a sudden boost to prison numbers, but neo-liberalism has yet to resolve the dilemma of how to be 'tough on crime' while also saving money from the criminal justice budget. The relative priority given to these aims will be a major influence on the future of community sentences and probation in England and Wales. By way of contrast, the use of custody for young offenders fell by 30 per cent between 2008 and 2011 (Allen 2011) until the riots increased it again.

This chapter, in keeping with the focus of this book, has concentrated on England and Wales, but it is important to be aware of developments in some other jurisdictions. One lesson from international studies of probation is that the direction taken in England and Wales, and particularly the emphasis on community sentences as punishment, is not inevitable. For example, much of Europe still requires the probationers' consent to a probation order (van Kalmthout and Derks 2000) which was abolished in England and Wales in 1997. Although France appears to be experiencing political pressure to toughen probation and to subordinate it to Prison Service management (Herzog-Evans 2011), other countries continue to take a less punitive and more rehabilitative approach: for example, the head of the Belgian 'Houses of Justice' recently described probation's task as 'social work under judicial mandate' (Devos 2009), and in Italy probation is described as 'affidamento in prova ai servizi sociali' (Ravagnani 2011), roughly meaning 'entrusting to the social services as a proof or test'. Nearer home, Scotland has retained a more welfare-centred approach to supervising offenders as well as to many other areas of social policy, and the Scottish Prisons Commission's report 'Scotland's Choice' includes the memorable statement that '[u]ltimately, one of the best ways for offenders to pay back is to turn their lives around' (Scottish Prisons Commission 2008: 27). Northern Ireland has rebuilt its system for dealing with young offenders on a foundation of restorative justice (Jacobson and Gibbs 2009) and its Probation Service's approach emphasizes rehabilitation and reintegration rather than punishment (Probation Board for Northern Ireland 2011). The Channel Island probation services retain many traditional features, remaining responsible to the courts (Raynor and Miles 2007). Wales is also uncomfortable with neo-liberalism but lacks, as yet, sufficient devolved powers to take criminal justice in a radically different direction from that laid down by England. In addition, the theories of social contract which underpinned the development of welfare states reappear as part of the theory of 'state-obligated rehabilitation' (Rotman 1990), which is one of the more convincing recent rationales for rehabilitation as a penal strategy (Raynor and Robinson 2009b): the argument is that if the state expects persistent offenders to stop offending, it also has an obligation to help them to access some of the opportunities and support which would make this possible. Some governments recognize this obligation more than others. If current trends in England and Wales continue, we can expect to see more diversity and variation in the provision of community sentences, with both good and bad results. These developments, however, seem likely to be driven more by political ideologies and expediency than by the needs of courts, victims, or offenders.

## ■ SELECTED FURTHER READING

General texts on probation and community penalties quite quickly become dated. Among the most useful at the moment are Worrall and Hoy's (2005), *Punishment in the Community* (Cullompton: Willan), Raynor and Robinson's (2009), *Rehabilitation, Crime and Justice*, 2nd edn (Basingstoke: Palgrave), Canton's (2011), *Probation—Working with Offenders* (Willan), and Mair and Burke's (2011), *Redemption, Rehabilitation and Risk Management—A History of Probation* (Routledge). Good edited collections are Bottoms, Rex, and Robinson's (2004), *Alternatives to Prison* (Cullompton: Willan) and Gelsthorpe and Morgan's (2007), *Handbook of Probation* (Cullompton: Willan). A good history of the Probation Service can be found in Vanstone's (2004), *Supervising Offenders in the Community: a history of probation theory and practice* (Aldershot: Ashgate). For the origins of NOMS, see *Reshaping Probation and Prisons* edited by Hough, Allen, and Padel (2006) (Bristol: Policy Press).

Other useful texts on particular aspects of Probation Service practice include Trotter's (1999), *Working with Involuntary Clients* (London: Sage) and the recent edited collection *Offender Supervision* (edited by McNeill, Raynor, and Trotter) (2010) (Cullompton: Willan). Community service orders (later community punishment orders, now 'unpaid work') were well covered in their early days by texts such as Pease and McWilliams' (1980) edited collection *Community Service by Order* (Edinburgh: Scottish Academic Press) and, more recently, by McIvor's (1992) Scottish evaluative study *Sentenced to Serve* (Aldershot: Avebury).

The resettlement of prisoners is addressed in a seminal report by the Social Exclusion Unit (2002), *Reducing Re-offending by Ex-Prisoners* (London: SEU), in Clancy *et al.* (2006), *Getting out and Staying Out* (Bristol: Policy Press) and in Hucklesby and Hagley-Dickinson's (2007), *Prisoner Resettlement* (Cullompton: Willan). On risk, Kemshall's (2005), *Understanding Risk in Criminal Justice* (Buckingham: Open University Press) and (2008), *Understanding the Community Management of High Risk Offenders* (Maidenhead: Open University Press) are very useful.

Lastly, the recent literature on 'What Works' in and around probation includes some useful edited collections, such as McGuire's (2002), *Offender Rehabilitation and Treatment* (Chichester: Wiley), and Hollin and Palmer's (2006), *Offending Behaviour Programmes* (Chichester: Wiley).

# ■ REFERENCES

ALLEN, R. (2011), *Last resort? Exploring the reduction in child imprisonment 2008–2011*, London: Prison Reform Trust.

ANDREWS, D. A. and BONTA, J. (2010), *The Psychology of Criminal Conduct*, New Providence, NJ: Anderson Publishing.

——, —— and WORMITH, J. S. (2011), 'The Risk-Need-Responsivity (RNR) model: does adding the Good Lives Model contribute to effective crime prevention?', *Criminal Justice and Behavior* 38(7): 735–55.

——, ZINGER, I., HOGE, R. D., BONTA, J., GENDREAU, P., and CULLEN, F. T. (1990) 'Does Correctional Treatment Work? A Clinically Relevant and Psychologically Informed Meta-Analysis', *Criminology*, 28: 369–404.

BECK, U. (1992), *Risk Society: Towards a New Modernity*, London: Sage.

BLUMSON, M. (2004), 'First steps and beyond: the pathway to our knowledge of delivering programmes', *VISTA* 8: 171–6.

BONTA, J. and WORMITH, J. S. (2007), 'Risk and need assessment', in G. McIvor and P. Raynor (eds), *Developments in Social Work with Offenders*, London: Jessica Kingsley.

BONTA, J., BOURGON, G., RUGGE, T., SCOTT, T., YESSINE, A., GUTIERREZ, L., and LI, J. (2010), *The Strategic Training Initiative in Community Supervision: risk-need-responsivity in the real world*, Corrections Research User Report 2010–1, Ottawa: Public Safety Canada.

BOTTOMS, A. E. (1980), *The Suspended Sentence after Ten Years*, Leeds: Centre for Social Work and Applied Social Studies, University of Leeds.

—— and MCWILLIAMS, W. (1979), 'A non-treatment paradigm for probation practice', *British Journal of Social Work*, 9: 159–202.

BRAYFORD, J., COWE, F., and DEERING, J. (eds), (2010), *What else works? Creative work with offenders*, Cullompton: Willan.

BRIDGES, A. (2011), *Probation and Youth Offending work: a tribute to those who do it well*, London: HM Inspectorate of Probation.

BRODY, S. R. (1976), *The Effectiveness of Sentencing*, Home Office Research Study 35, London: HMSO.

CARTER, P. (2003), *Managing Offenders, Reducing Crime: A New Approach*, (Correctional Services Review), London: Home Office.

—— (2007), *Securing the Future: proposals for the efficient and sustainable use of custody in England and Wales*, London: Ministry of Justice.

CHAPMAN, T. and HOUGH, M. (1998), *Evidence-Based Practice*, London: Home Office.

CHRISTIE, N. (1993), *Crime Control as Industry*, London: Routledge.

—— (2004), *A Suitable Amount of Crime*, London: Routledge.

CLANCY, A., HUDSON, K., MAGUIRE, M., PEAKE, R., RAYNOR, P., VANSTONE, M., and KYNCH, J. (2006), *Getting Out and Staying Out: results of the prisoner resettlement Pathfinders*, Bristol: Policy Press.

COHEN, S. (1985), *Visions of Social Control*, Cambridge: Polity Press.

CORRECTIONAL SERVICES ACCREDITATION PANEL (2003), *Report 2002–2003*, London: CSAP.

DAVIES, M. (1969), *Probationers in their Social Environment*, Research Study 2, London: HMSO.

—— (1974), *Social Work in the Environment*, Research Study 21, London: HMSO.

DEBIDIN, M. (ed.) (2009), *A compendium of research and analysis on the Offender Assessment System (OASys) 2006–2009*, Ministry of Justice Research Series 16/09, London: Ministry of Justice.

DEERING, J. (2011), *Probation practice and the new penology: practitioner reflections*, Farnham: Ashgate.

DEVOS, A. (2009), address to 10-year Conference of Houses of Justice, Belgium, 2 December.

DIRECTGOV (2010), 'Investors in rehabilitation: social impact bond launched'. www.direct.gov.uk.

DOWDEN, C. and ANDREWS, D. (2004), 'The importance of staff practice in delivering effective correctional treatment: a meta-analysis', *International Journal of Offender Therapy and Comparative Criminology* 48: 203–214.

ELLIS, T. and WINSTONE, J. (2002), 'The policy impact of a survey of programme evaluations in Britain', in J. McGuire. (ed.), *Offender Rehabilitation and Treatment: Effective Programmes and Policies to Reduce Re-offending*, Chichester: Wiley.

FARRALL, S. and CALVERLEY, A. (2006), *Understanding desistance from crime*, Maidenhead: Open University Press.

FAWCETT SOCIETY (2009), *Engendering Justice—from Policy to Practice. Final report of the Commission on Women and the Criminal Justice System*, London: Fawcett Society.

FEELEY, M. and SIMON, J. (1992), 'The new penology: notes on the emerging strategy of corrections and its implications', *Criminology*, 30: 449–74.

FOLKARD, M. S., SMITH, D. E., and SMITH, D. D. (1976), *IMPACT Volume II: The results of the experiment*, Home Office Research Study 36, London: HMSO.

GARLAND, D. (1997), 'Probation and the reconfiguration of crime control', in R. Burnett (ed.) *The Probation Service: Responding to Change* (Proceedings of the Probation Studies Unit First Colloquium: Probation Studies Unit Report No. 3), Oxford: University of Oxford Centre for Criminological Research.

—— (2001), *The Culture of Control*, Oxford: Oxford University Press.

GIBSON, B. (2004), *Criminal Justice Act 2003: a guide to the new procedures and sentencing*, Winchester: Waterside Press.

GIDDENS, A. (1990), *The Consequences of Modernity*, Cambridge: Polity Press.

GRÜNHUT, M. (1952), 'Probation in Germany', *Howard Journal*, 8: 168–74.

HALLIDAY, J. (2001), *Making Punishments Work: Report of a Review of the Sentencing Framework for England and Wales*, London: Home Office.

HARPER, G. and CHITTY, C. (2004), *The impact of corrections on re-offending: a review of 'what works'*, Home Office Research Study 291, London: Home Office.

HASLEWOOD-POCSIK, I., MERONE, L., and ROBERTS, C. (2004), *The evaluation of the Employment Pathfinder: lessons from Phase 1 and a survey for Phase 2*, Online Report 22/04, London: Home Office.

HER MAJESTY'S INSPECTORATE OF PROBATION (2006a), *An Independent Review of a Serious Further Offence case: Damien Hanson and Elliot White*. London: HMIP.

—— (2006b), *An Independent Review of a Serious Further Offence case: Anthony Rice*. London: HMIP.

HERZOG-EVANS, M. (2011), 'French probation virtually destroyed', Personal communication.

HOLLIN, C., PALMER, E., MCGUIRE, J., HOUNSOME, J., HATCHER, R., BILBY, C., and CLARK, C. (2004), *Pathfinder Programmes in the Probation Service: a retrospective analysis*, Home Office Online Report 66/04, London: Home Office.

HOLLIS, F. (1964), *Casework: a Psychosocial Therapy*, New York: Random House.

HOLLIS, V. (2007), *Reconviction Analysis of Programme Data Using Interim Accredited Programmes Software (IAPS)*, London: National Offender Management Service.

HOME OFFICE (1984), *Probation Service in England and Wales. Statement of National Objectives and Priorities*, London: Home Office.

—— (1988), *Punishment, Custody and the Community*, Cm 424, London: HMSO.

—— (1990a), *Supervision and Punishment in the Community*, Cm 966, London: HMSO.

—— (1990b), *Crime, Justice and Protecting the Public*, Cm 965, London: HMSO.

—— (1992), *Probation Statistics England and Wales 1991*, London: Home Office.

—— (1995), *Managing What Works: Conference Report and Guidance on Critical Success Factors for Probation Supervision Programmes*, Probation Circular 77/1995, London: Home Office.

—— (2000), *The National Standards for the Supervision of Offenders in the Community*, London: Home Office.

—— (2002), *Probation Statistics England and Wales 2001*, London: Home Office.

—— (2004), *Reducing Re-offending National Action Plan*, London: Home Office.

—— (2005), *The NOMS Offender Management Model*, London: Home Office, www.noms. homeoffice.gov.uk/downloads/NOMS_Offender_ Management_Model.pdf.

HOME OFFICE RDS NOMS (2005), *Offender Management Statistics 2004*, London: Home Office.

HOMEL, P., NUTLEY, S., WEBB, B., and TILLEY, N. (2005), *Investing to Deliver: reviewing the implementation of the UK Crime Reduction Programme*, Home Office Research Study 281, London: Home Office.

HOOD, R. (1974), *Tolerance and the Tariff*, London: NACRO.

HOUGH, M. (ed.) (2004), *Criminal Justice* 4, 3. Special Issue: *Evaluating the Crime Reduction Programme in England and Wales*.

——, ALLEN, R., and PADEL, U. (eds) (2006), *Reshaping Probation and Prisons: the new offender management framework*, Bristol: Policy Press.

HOUSE OF COMMONS (2011), *The Role of the Probation Service*, Justice Committee report, London: House of Commons.

HOWARD, M. (1993), speech to Conservative Party conference, October.

HUDSON, B. (2003), *Justice in the Risk Society*, London: Sage.

JACOBSON, J. and GIBBS, P. (2009), *Making Amends: restorative youth justice in Northern Ireland*, London: Prison Reform Trust.

KEMSHALL, H. (2008), *Understanding the Community Management of High Risk Offenders*, Maidenhead: Open University Press.

—— and MAGUIRE, M. (2001), 'Public protection, partnership and risk penality: the multi-agency risk management of sexual and violent offenders', *Punishment and Society* 3. 237–64.

KEMSHALL, H., MACKENZIE, G., WOOD, J., BAILEY, R., and YATES, J. (2005), *Strengthening Multi-Agency Public Protection Arrangements*, Home Office Development and Practice Report 45, London: Home Office.

LEWIS, S., RAYNOR, P., SMITH, D., and WARDAK, A. (eds) (2006), *Race and Probation*, Cullompton: Willan.

LEWIS, S., VENNARD, J., MAGUIRE, M., RAYNOR, P., VANSTONE, M., RAYBOULD, S., and RIX, A. (2003), *The Resettlement of Short-term Prisoners: An Evaluation of Seven Pathfinders*, RDS Occasional Paper No. 83, London: Home Office.

LIPSEY, M. (1992), 'Juvenile delinquency treatment: a meta-analytic enquiry into the variability of effects', in T. Cook, H. Cooper, D. S. Cordray, H. Hartmann, L. V. Hedges, R. L. Light, J. A. Louis, and F. Mosteller (eds), *Meta-Analysis for Explanation: a case-book*, New York: Russell Sage.

—— (1999), 'Can rehabilitative programs reduce the recidivism of juvenile offenders? An inquiry into the effectiveness of practical programs', *Virginia Journal of Social Policy and the Law*, 6: 611–41.

LIPTON, D., MARTINSON, R., and WILKS, J. (1975), *The Effectiveness of Correctional Treatment*, New York: Praeger.

MCGUIRE, J. (2000), *Cognitive-Behavioural Approaches*, London: Home Office.

—— (ed.) (1995), *What Works: Reducing Reoffending*, Chichester: Wiley.

MCIVOR, G. (1990), *Sanctions for Serious or Persistent Offenders*, Stirling: Social Work Research Centre.

McKNIGHT, J. (2009), 'Speaking up for probation', *Howard Journal of Criminal Justice,* 48(4): 327–43.

McMAHON, G., HALL, A., HAYWARD, G., HUDSON, C., and ROBERTS, C. (2004), *Basic Skills Programmes in the Probation Service: an Evaluation of the Basic Skills Pathfinder,* Home Office Research Findings 203, London: Home Office.

McMURRAN, M. and WARD, T. (2004), 'Motivating offenders to change in therapy: an organising framework', *Legal and Clinical Psychology,* 9: 295–311.

McNEILL, F. (2006), 'A desistance paradigm for offender management', *Criminology and Criminal Justice,* 6(1): 39–62.

——, RAYNOR, P., and TROTTER, C. (eds) (2010), *Offender Supervision: new directions in theory, research and practice,* Abingdon: Willan.

MAGUIRE, M. and RAYNOR, P. (1997), 'The revival of throughcare: rhetoric and reality in Automatic Conditional Release', *British Journal of Criminology,* 37(1): 1–14.

——, PERROUD, B., and RAYNOR, P. (1996), *Automatic Conditional Release: the first two years,* Research Study 156, London: Home Office.

——, GRUBIN, D., LÖSEL, F., and RAYNOR, P. (2010), '"What Works" and the Correctional Services Accreditation Panel: taking stock from an insider perspective', *Criminology and Criminal Justice* 10(1): 37–58.

——, RAYNOR, P., VANSTONE, M. and KYNCH, J. (2000), 'Voluntary after-care and the Probation Service: a case of diminishing responsibility', *Howard Journal of Criminal Justice,* 39: 234–48.

MAIR, G. (ed.) (2004), *What Matters in Probation.* Cullompton: Willan.

—— (2011), 'To keep going back to a policy that has consistently failed shows only a failure to learn from mistakes and a lack of creativity', *Criminal Justice Matters,* 84: 41.

——, LLOYD, C., NEE, C., and SIBBITT, R. (1994), *Intensive Probation in England and Wales: an evaluation,* London: HMSO.

——, CROSS, N., and TAYLOR, S. (2007), *The use and impact of the Community Order and the Suspended Sentence Order,* London: Centre for Crime and Justice Studies.

MANTLE, G. (2006), 'Probation: dead, dying or poorly?', *Howard Journal of Criminal Justice,* 45(3): 321–24.

MARTINSON, R. (1974), 'What works? Questions and answers about prison reform', *The Public Interest,* 35: 22–54.

MARUNA, S. (2001), *Making Good,* Washington: American Psychological Association.

MILLS, H. and ROBERTS, R. (2011), 'Is penal reform working? Community sentences and reform sector strategies', *Criminal Justice Matters,* 84: 38–9.

MILLS, H., SILVESTRI, A., and GRIMSHAW, R. with SILBERHORN-ARMANTRADING, F. (2010), *Prison and Probation Expenditure 1999–2009,* London: Centre for Crime and Justice Studies.

MINISTRY OF JUSTICE (2008), *Prison Policy Update,* London: Ministry of Justice.

—— (2010a), *Green Paper Evidence Report,* London: Ministry of Justice.

—— (2010b), *Offender Management Caseload Statistics 2009,* London: Ministry of Justice.

—— (2010c), *Breaking the Cycle: effective punishment, rehabilitation and sentencing of offenders,* Cm 7972, London: Ministry of Justice.

—— (2011), *Criminal justice statistics quarterly update to December 2010,* London: Ministry of Justice.

MONGER, M. (1964), *Casework in Probation,* London: Butterworth.

MORGAN, R. (2002), 'Something has got to give', *HLM—the Howard League Magazine,* 20(4): 7–8.

—— (2003), 'Foreword', *Her Majesty's Inspectorate of Probation Annual Report 2002/2003,* London: Home Office.

NATIONAL ASSOCIATION OF PROBATION OFFICERS (2001), 'AGM resolutions 2001', *NAPO News,* 134: 10–15.

NATIONAL PROBATION SERVICE (2001), *A New Choreography,* London: Home Office.

NELLIS, M. (2004a), 'The Electronic monitoring of Offenders in Britain: a critical overview', in S. Collett (ed.), *Electronic Monitoring of Offenders: Key Developments,* ICCJ Monograph 5, London: NAPO.

—— (2004b), 'Into the Field of Corrections: the end of English probation in the early 21st century?', *Cambrian Law Review,* 35: 115–34.

OASYS DEVELOPMENT TEAM (2001), *Offender Assessment System User Manual,* London: Home Office.

OMAND, D. (2010), *Independent Serious Further Offence Review: the case of John Venables,* London: Ministry of Justice.

PA CONSULTING GROUP (2005), *Action Research Study of the Implementation of the National Offender Management Model in the North West Pathfinder,* London: PA Consulting Group.

PARTRIDGE, S. (2004), *Examining Case Management Models for Community Sentences,* Home Office Online Report 17/04, London: Home Office.

PEASE, K. and McWILLIAMS W. (eds) (1980), *Community Service by Order,* Edinburgh: Scottish Academic Press.

PEASE, K., BILLINGHAM, S., and EARNSHAW, I. (1977), *Community Service Assessed in 1976,* Home Office Research Study No. 39, London: HMSO.

PRIESTLEY, P. and VANSTONE, M. (eds) (2010), *Offenders or Citizens: readings in rehabilitation,* Cullompton: Willan.

PROBATION BOARD FOR NORTHERN IRELAND (2011). http://www.pbni.org.uk.

RADZINOWICZ, L. (ed). (1958), *The Results of Probation,* A Report of the Cambridge Department of Criminal Science, London: Macmillan.

RAVAGNANI, L. (2011), 'PO labelling III'. Personal communication.

RAYNOR, P. (1988), *Probation as an Alternative to Custody,* Aldershot: Avebury.

—— (1998), 'Reading Probation Statistics: a Critical Comment', *VISTA* 3: 181–185.

—— (2004a), 'Rehabilitative and reintegrative approaches', in A. Bottoms, S. Rex, and G. Robinson (eds), *Alternatives to Prison*, Cullompton: Willan.

—— (2004b), 'The probation service "pathfinders": finding the path and losing the way?', *Criminal Justice*, 4: 309–25.

—— (2007), 'Risk and need in British probation: the contribution of LSI-R', *Psychology, Crime and Law*, 13(2): 125–38.

—— (2010), 'Usages et abus du risque dans la justice pénale britannique', *Déviance et Société*, 34(4): 671–88.

—— (2011), *The Jersey Supervision Skills Study*, Offender Engagement Research Bulletin, London: Ministry of Justice.

—— (forthcoming), 'Is probation still possible?', the Bill McWilliams Memorial Lecture 2011, *Howard Journal of Criminal Justice*.

—— and MILES, H. (2007), 'Evidence-based probation in a microstate: the British Channel Island of Jersey', *European Journal of Criminology*, 4(3): 299–313.

—— and ROBINSON, G. (2009a), *Rehabilitation, Crime and Justice*, 2nd edn, Basingstoke: Palgrave Macmillan.

—— and —— (2009b), 'Why help offenders? Arguments for rehabilitation as a penal strategy', *European Journal of Probation*, 1(1): 3–20.

—— and VANSTONE, M. (1996) 'Reasoning and Rehabilitation in Britain: the results of the Straight Thinking On Probation (STOP) programme', *International Journal of Offender Therapy and Comparative Criminology*, 40: 272–84.

—— and —— (1997), *Straight Thinking On Probation (STOP): The Mid Glamorgan Experiment*. Probation Studies Unit Report No. 4, Oxford: University of Oxford Centre for Criminological Research.

—— and —— (2002), *Understanding Community Penalties*, Buckingham: Open University Press.

——, UGWUDIKE, P., and VANSTONE, M. (2010), 'Skills and strategies in probation supervision: the Jersey study', in F. McNeill, P. Raynor, and C. Trotter (eds), *Offender Supervision: new directions in theory, research and practice*, Abingdon: Willan.

——, KYNCH, J., ROBERTS, C., and MERRINGTON, M. (2000), *Risk and Need Assessment in Probation Services: an Evaluation*. Research Study 211, London: Home Office.

REID, J. (2006) speech to Wormwood Scrubs Prison, 7 November.

REX, S. and GELSTHORPE, L. (2002), 'The role of Community Service in reducing offending: evaluating pathfinder projects in the UK', *Howard Journal*, 41: 311–25.

REX, S., GELSTHORPE, L., ROBERTS, C., and JORDAN, P. (2003), *Crime Reduction Programme: an Evaluation of Community Service Pathfinder Projects: Final Report 2002*, RDS Occasional Paper 87, London: Home Office.

RICHMOND, M. (1917), *Social Diagnosis*, New York: Russell Sage Foundation.

ROBERTS, C. (1989), *Hereford and Worcester Probation Service Young Offender Project: first evaluation report*, Oxford: Department of Social and Administrative Studies.

—— (2004a), 'An early evaluation of a cognitive offending behaviour programme ("Think First") in probation areas', *VISTA* 8: 137–45.

—— (2004b), 'Offending behaviour programmes: emerging evidence and implications for research', in R. Burnett and C. Roberts (eds), *What Works in Probation and Youth Justice*, Cullompton: Willan.

ROBINSON, G. (2005), 'What works in offender management?', *Howard Journal*, 44: 307–18.

—— (2008), 'Late-modern rehabilitation: the evolution of a penal strategy', *Punishment and Society*, 10(4): 429–45.

ROSE, N. (2000), 'Government and control', *British Journal of Criminology*, 40: 321–39.

ROTMAN, E. (1990), *Beyond Punishment: A New View of the Rehabilitation of Offenders*, Westport, Conn.: Greenwood Press.

RUMGAY, J. (1989), 'Talking tough: empty threats in probation practice', *Howard Journal*, 28: 177–86.

SCOTTISH PRISONS COMMISSION (2008), *Scotland's Choice*, Edinburgh: Scottish Prisons Commission.

SHAW, M. (1974), *Social Work in Prisons*, Home Office Research Study 22, London: HMSO.

—— and HANNAH-MOFFATT, K. (2004), 'How cognitive skills forgot about gender and diversity', in G. Mair (ed.), *What Matters In Probation*, Cullompton: Willan.

SHEEHAN, R., MCIVOR G., and TROTTER, C. (eds) (2007), *What Works with Women Offenders*, Cullompton: Willan.

SMITH, R. (2007), *Youth Justice: Ideas, Policy, Practice*, Cullompton: Willan.

SOCIAL EXCLUSIVE UNIT (2002), *Reducing Re-offending by Ex-prisoners*, London: Office of the Deputy Prime Minister.

STRAW, J. (2008), speech to Royal Society of Arts, 27 October.

TAXMAN, F., YANCEY, C., and BILANIN, J. (2006), *Proactive Community Supervision in Maryland: changing offender outcomes*, Virginia Commonwealth University and University of Maryland.

THORPE, J. (1979), *Social Inquiry Reports: a survey*, Home Office Research Study 48, London: HMSO.

TROTTER, C. and EVANS, P. (2010), 'Supervision skills in juvenile justice', in F. McNeill, P. Raynor, and C. Trotter (eds), *Offender Supervision: new directions in theory, research and practice*, Abingdon: Willan.

TURNBULL, P., MCSWEENEY, T., WEBSTER, R., EDMUNDS, M., and HOUGH, M. (2000), *Drug Treatment and Testing Orders: final evaluation report*, Home Office Research Study 212, London: Home Office.

UNDERDOWN, A. (1998), *Strategies for Effective Supervision: Report of the HMIP What Works Project*, London: Home Office.

VAN KALMTHOUT, A. and DERKS, J. (2000), *Probation and Probation Services: a European perspective*, Nijmegen: Wolf Legal Publishers.

Vanstone, M. (2004), *Supervising Offenders in the Community: A History of Probation Theory and Practice,* Aldershot: Ashgate.

—— and Raynor, P. (1981), 'Diversion from prison—a partial success and a missed opportunity', *Probation Journal,* 28: 85–9.

—— and —— (2010), 'Supervising Freedom: the philosophy, values and historical origins of probation', in M. Herzog-Evans (ed.), *Transnational Criminology Manual,* Vol. 3, Nijmegen: Wolf Legal Publishers.

Von Hirsch, A. (1976), *Doing Justice: The Choice of Punishments,* Report of the Committee for the Study of Incarceration, New York: Hill and Wang.

Walker, N., Farrington, D., and Tucker, G. (1981), 'Reconviction rates of adult males after different sentences', *British Journal of Criminology,* 21: 357–60.

Ward, T. and Maruna, S. (2007), *Rehabilitation,* London: Routledge.

Wilkins, L. T. (1958), 'A small comparative study of the results of probation', *British Journal of Delinquency,* 8: 201–9.

# 32

# OUT OF COURT, OUT OF SIGHT? CRIMINAL SANCTIONS AND NON-JUDICIAL DECISION-MAKING

*Nicola Padfield, Rod Morgan, and Mike Maguire*

## INTRODUCTION

The allocation of criminal sanctions, traditionally referred to as sentencing, has generally been thought of as something for which judges and magistrates in the criminal courts are responsible, and this *Handbook* has always had, and continues to have, a chapter devoted to that topic (see Ashworth and Roberts, this volume). But the system for determining sanctions has, almost by stealth, been stretched: key elements of decision-making have been moved upstream and downstream of the courts, thereby falling largely outside judicial control. On the one hand, a significant number and proportion of criminal sanctions (mainly, but not exclusively, financial penalties) are today imposed out of court, administratively, by the police, the Crown Prosecution Service (CPS), and many other bodies. At the other end of the spectrum, decisions about whether and when to release the fast growing numbers of prisoners serving indeterminate custodial sentences lie in the hands of the Parole Board.

Actions relating to the *implementation and enforcement* of sanctions also have significant consequences for offenders. In particular, 'breach' decisions by probation officers—themselves constrained by stricter administrative rules—led during the 1990s and 2000s to major increases in the numbers of offenders under supervision in the community who were subsequently sent to prison or otherwise punished, not for committing further offences but for failing to comply with sentence or licence conditions. Although recent efforts have been made to reverse this trend, the numbers remain historically high.

These developments in out-of-court decision-making are now significant enough for the subject to merit a *Handbook* chapter in its own right. It is no longer sufficient, if it ever was, to make only passing reference to fixed penalty notices, police cautioning, or release on licence. Such topics raise important questions about the transparency, fairness, and accountability of the quasi-judicial decisions that significantly affect the lives of both offenders and victims. They also raise questions about the extent to which different kinds of offence, suspect, or offender are, or should be, treated differently in terms of the locus of decisions made about them and the safeguards that surround the process. In this chapter we shall explore these issues through analysis of the recent history of Anglo-Welsh policy and practice around key decisions at each end of the sanctioning process: first, the imposition of criminal sanctions by the police and CPS and secondly, decisions relating to the release (or not) of prisoners by the Parole Board, and to subsequent recalls to custody. We conclude by pointing out the relevance of this discussion for criminal justice and criminological scholarship.

## OUT-OF-COURT SANCTIONS

### THEORY AND PRINCIPLES

In an ideal world, criminal justice systems safeguard the public interest, achieve justice for victims, and maintain legitimacy, through effective procedures to maximize the chances of genuine law-breakers being 'brought to justice', while at the same time ensuring that all accused persons are granted full rights and assistance to defend themselves, treated with integrity, and not wrongly convicted. Thus evidence of guilt should be presented and tested in open court. However, in reality all criminal justice systems put a price on justice. 'Law and order' expenditure has to compete with that for other public services, with inevitable implications for the quality of justice—at least in a proportion of cases. In setting boundaries for entry to the criminal justice system, decisions on priorities have to be made and, within systems, different cases are responded to differentially according to their perceived importance. Contested trials have become the exception rather than the norm, and it has been argued that the trial itself is becoming side-lined (see Duff *et al.* 2007).

If, out of practical necessity, different standards have to be applied to different types of case, there are a number of defensible ways of organizing this. Thus the principle of *proportionality* requires that criminal justice goals be pursued efficiently and effectively without disproportionate cost and consequent harm to other public services (Sanders, Young, and Burton 2010; Ashworth and Redmayne 2010: 57–8). That is, the level of criminal justice intervention, both the process and the sanction, must be proportionate to the seriousness of the offence and/or the culpability of (or in some cases the threat of future harm posed by) the offender. Adherence to this principle suggests that more serious offences deserve both more onerous sanctions, and greater procedural safeguards to ensure that individuals' rights are protected and miscarriages of justice avoided. Conversely, minor offences, and offenders not deemed seriously culpable (e.g., young or first-time offenders), become candidates for diversion from the system or, if brought within its ambit, dealt with leniently following a simplified procedure. However, as we shall see, there are serious questions to be asked about the selection of cases for diversion, and whether the system of allocation works openly and fairly.

All criminal justice systems adhere to the proportionality principle to some degree, and most criminal court systems have two or more tiers. In England and Wales the Crown Court deals with the most serious cases, for which the most severe penalties are available, and determinations of guilt and levels of punishment are made by juries and judges. The lower courts, by contrast, have limited powers of punishment and are usually presided over by lay magistrates. The latter system is widely agreed to offer less robust safeguards to the accused than the option of trial by jury under the guidance of a judge (though both systems have critics: see Sanders and Young; Ashworth and Roberts, this volume). The traditional lauding of the jury trial explains why, until relatively recently, discussions of 'summary justice' generally focused on the question of which offences should automatically be dealt with in the magistrates' courts and hence denied the highest level of justice[1] (see, e.g., Royal Commission 1993). However, the sphere of *out-of-court* summary justice, whereby cases are dealt with administratively by the police and CPS, coming before the courts only if guilt is contested, has grown hugely in recent years. It raises a number of specific concerns.

First is the standard of proof required to establish guilt. A basic principle of criminal law is that citizens should only be convicted if guilt is proven 'beyond reasonable doubt'. This is a high certainty threshold which applies—in theory at least—in the criminal courts at all levels. However, when it comes to some out-of-court penalties there is arguably a lower test of certainty applied by police officers or prosecutors. Moreover, while such decisions can be challenged in court, this is seldom done: the accused may decide it is not worth the candle, or that the risk of a more severe sanction is too great (see Sanders and Young, this volume).

Some commentators find such differences in standards of proof perfectly acceptable and propose a fundamental differential. Halpern, for example (2010. 69), proposes application of a utilitarian *graduated certainty of conviction* principle whereby serious cases, where the consequences of conviction for the accused are grave, would have to be proved 'beyond reasonable doubt', but relatively minor cases, carrying low penalties, would have a lesser standard of proof, such as the 'balance of probabilities' test employed in civil cases. Application of this principle would undoubtedly be met with fierce resistance; opponents would argue that, no matter how minor the offence or sanction, a criminal conviction puts a stain on a citizen's character and reputation and should not be imposed without a high degree of certainty of their guilt (Morgan 2008; Young 2008).

Related concerns about out-of-court 'sentencing' include lack of transparency of and accountability for decisions. Where a personal victim is involved, there are further

---

[1] There have always been hotly contested debates on this issue. There is no right to trial by jury enshrined in English law (Darbyshire 1991) and the list of offences for which defendants can elect trial by jury has been subject to periodic adjustment, not least because of workload and cost implications.

concerns about justice not being 'seen to be done': punishment, imposed in the name of the public, should be imposed in public.

Why has there been so little critical attention paid to this development in policy? Part of the answer lies in the fact that the granting of powers to executive bodies to impose penalties for what are essentially 'criminal' offences is not a new phenomenon. Other long-existing forms of 'administrative' sanctions have become widely accepted as legitimate, especially those imposed by bodies such as Her Majesty's Revenue and Customs (HMRC) and a variety of social benefit agencies. These bodies deal with numerous cases of alleged fraud, some very serious, but bring court prosecutions in only a small proportion, preferring instead to levy financial penalties using so-called administrative powers. Benefits agencies are more likely to prosecute than HMRC, a tendency which has been interpreted as evidence of differing kinds of justice for the rich and the poor (see, e.g., Cook 1989, 2006). Many other government and non-governmental agencies make decisions to prosecute, or not. Padfield (2008) uses data published by the Environment Agency and the Health and Safety Executive to explore their policies on prosecutions. Other bodies, such as the RSPCA, bring 'private' prosecutions. Decisions in many cases are made in a routine, bureaucratic fashion, without the need for robust proof of guilt, and there are limited opportunities for the 'offender' to challenge them. Yet we have become so used to the exercise of these powers by non-judicial bodies that few challenges are made to the assumption that they should possess them.

The growing importance of EU criminal law has been widely noted (see, e.g., Klip 2009; Mitsilegas 2009). Common minimum rules on the definition of criminal offences and sanctions may now be adopted if they are essential for ensuring the effectiveness of a harmonized EU policy. But there has been little discussion of the appropriate boundaries between criminal and non-criminal sanctions: whether the large fines which are frequently imposed for breaches of consumer protection rules or unfair commercial practices should be subject to criminal law protections, for example. Nor have there been many academic studies of discretionary decision-making within the EU (though Boekhout van Solinge (2002) provides a critical anthropological analysis of what he calls 'inscrutable' EU drugs policy decision-making).

Finally, the example of 'administratively' imposed fines (e.g. by HMRC) draws attention to the important issue of the impact of sanctions on a person's reputation, and the social consequences which may follow. Most tax evaders presumably prefer the relative anonymity, and lack of stigmatization, which characterizes an 'administrative' fine, as opposed to a court case and possible attendant publicity. Further, the acquisition of a criminal record can have a major impact on an individual's future employment opportunities, so there are advantages in being offered a way of atoning for the offence which avoids this. One question to consider in relation to the new forms of out-of-court sanction, is the extent to which offenders' anonymity is protected, in terms of avoiding both press publicity and official recording systems, most importantly entries on the Police National Computer (PNC). We return to this blurred boundary between 'out-of-court' administrative and criminal penalties, which raises important issues about the nature and scale of the safeguards that should protect the rights of both offenders and victims, in our conclusions.

## HISTORY AND CURRENT PROVISION

### Police prosecutions and cautions

Until 1986 the prosecutorial function lay largely in the hands of the police (see Sanders and Young, this volume). Although the Director of Public Prosecutions' consent was required before the prosecution of certain serious or sensitive cases could proceed, the majority of criminal cases were either prosecuted by the police themselves or by solicitors or barristers employed by them. When the CPS took over the prosecutorial function in 1986, the police retained a discretion, which they had had from the birth of modern policing, to caution, either informally or formally (Steer 1970).

Little is known even today about informal 'off the record' cautions. From the 1960s use of formal, recorded cautions by the police (a precondition for which was an admission of guilt by the offender) was officially encouraged, in a number of Home Office Circulars, particularly for children and young people. These also began to be enumerated in Home Office statistics. By the early 1990s, 17 per cent of all persons found guilty or cautioned were formally cautioned. In the case of juveniles this figure reached 52 per cent. In the mid-1990s, however, the Audit Commission severely criticized use of repeat cautions for juveniles and following New Labour's victory in the 1997 General Election, a new policy began to be enunciated.

The first step was tighter regulation of cautions for juveniles. Henceforth, following the Crime and Disorder Act 1998, cautions for juveniles were replaced with reprimands and final warnings, after which, no matter how trivial any further offence, the child or young person had to be brought before the youth court (see Morgan and Newburn, this volume). Cautions for adults remain very common. In 2009 the cautioning rate (including conditional cautions, see below) for all offences excluding motoring offences was 26 per cent: 159,300 cautions were administered for indictable (including triable-either-way) offences and 131,100 for summary offences. The most frequently administered caution for indictable offences, 38 per cent, was for 'theft and handling stolen goods' and almost half of those for summary offences were for common assault. Twenty-two cautions were given for rape (see Ministry of Justice 2010). Beyond these statistics, very little is known about the reality of how these important decisions are reached.

### New out-of-court penalties: FPNs, PNDs, and cannabis warnings

Fixed penalty notices (FPNs) were introduced for parking offences in the 1950s and their use was gradually extended in subsequent decades for a variety of motoring offences relating both to driving (most commonly speeding) and construction (having a defective brake light or a bald tyre, for example). In 1990 their use was extended to environmental abuses such as littering. It was under New Labour, however, that the use of out-of-court penalties took off, particularly with the introduction of Penalty Notices for Disorder (PNDs). Though issued administratively, the range of offences for which these could be and were used included some that were unequivocally serious, accompanied by consequences that were often not appreciated.

Prime Minister Blair's proposition that in 2000 'young thugs' be given on-the-spot fines by being 'marched to a cash machine' (Blair 2010: 287) was initially dismissed as an unfeasible political gimmick. But it soon became clear that the basic idea was taken seriously by the Government and envisaged as far-reaching. The case for out-of-court criminal sanctions was later set out by then Lord Chancellor, Lord Falconer:

> Some anti-social behaviour and other less serious crimes, such as certain cases of criminal damage, theft or public order offences, do not need to come to court if the defendant admits guilt and is willing to make reparation to the victim, accept a fine, pay compensation, go for drug treatment or carry out unpaid work. Many cases can be diverted out of court and dealt with by the use of fixed-penalty notices or Conditional Cautions. (Falconer 2006: 10)

The Government argued that where appropriate these pre-court interventions could be accompanied by 'work to support individuals and prevent such behaviour from arising'. Victims were more likely to be satisfied because 'the visible punishment... sends a signal to the wider community that the behaviour is being tackled and not tolerated' thereby increasing public confidence in the criminal justice system generally (Home Office 2006a: 6). Anticipating civil libertarian objections, the Home Office argued that appropriate safeguards were in place. If the pre-court sanction or condition was not agreed by the offender or, in the case of children and young people, the offender's parent or guardian, they had the right to challenge the decision—in which case the relevant authorities must either drop the matter or charge the offender and bring the case before the court to determine. The balance between these considerations within the criminal justice system was that:

> The defendant needs proper protection against injustice within the system, but our aim should be a system that will allow the court to know what happened and a process that will be driven by the substantive merits of the case, not the exploitation of safeguards. If the case is to proceed to trial, courts have a proactive role to ensure the prosecution and defence have the case ready in a timely fashion. The defendant should not have pressure put on them but, where the weight of evidence is against him or her, they should be given every opportunity to admit their guilt and allow the matter to be resolved quickly' (Falconer 2006: 10).

The number of out-of-court sanctions for criminal offences proliferated under New Labour, as did their aggregate use as a proportion of all detected offending. The scale of the increase is apparent from Figure 32.1.[2]

The total number of court convictions in 2006/7 (the numerical high point during the period) was almost the same as in 1998/9, though the aggregate number of what New Labour termed 'offenders brought to justice' (OBTJ) was 300,000 greater. The latter increase, as Figure 32.2 shows, resulted almost entirely from the increased use of cautions (including reprimands and final warnings for juveniles) and the introduction in 2004 of penalty notices for disorder (PNDs) and warnings of adults for possession of cannabis.

As Morgan (2008: 26) noted, though the majority of violent offenders continued to be dealt with through conviction in the courts, the proportion dealt with by means of cautions, both those committing more and less serious offences, increased very substantially up to 2006. After 2006/7 there was a sharp contraction in the

---

[2] The figures shown exclude two to three million FPNs, mainly for traffic-related offences, the numbers of which rose and fell substantially during the period (see Povey *et al.* 2010: ch. 3).

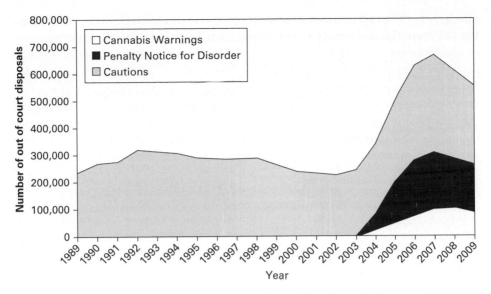

**Figure 32.1** Number of offenders who received an out-of-court penalty by type 1999–2009
*Source:* Ministry of Justice 2010: Figure 2.2

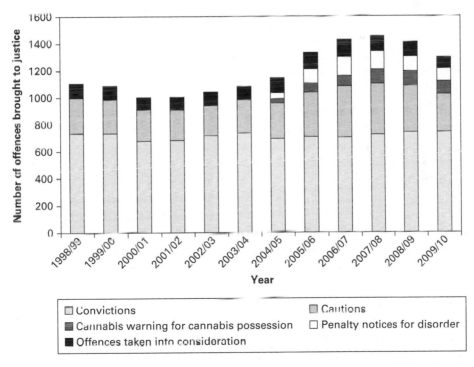

**Figure 32.2** Number of Offences Brought to Justice by outcome 1998/99–2009/10 (thousands)
*Source:* Ministry of Justice 2010: Figure 2.3

number of OBTJs, albeit the total number remained substantially higher than when the new out-of-court penalties were introduced. The reason for this contraction is straightforward. In 2007 the Government abandoned its global target for OBTJs, determining that the police should in future concentrate on bringing to justice relatively serious offences ('serious, violent, sexual and acquisitive offences'). The police were no longer to be rewarded for picking what some commentators referred to as the 'low hanging fruit' of minor (and often very young) offenders. Given that the incoming Coalition administration in 2010 abandoned this OBTJ target entirely and announced substantial cuts to police budgets, it is unsurprising that the aggregate number of individuals given either an out-of-court disposal or proceeded against at court is now falling significantly. Compared with the 12 months to March 2010, there was a 13.3 per cent fall in the use of out-of-court disposals from 522,100 to 452,700 and a 3 per cent fall in the number of defendants proceeded against at court (Ministry of Justice 2011).

New Labour's principal innovation was the PND, use of which, contrary to the title, is not restricted to disorderly behaviour. Introduced in the Criminal Justice and Police Act 2001, PNDs were part of a portfolio of measures for tackling anti-social behaviour (ASB) about which, as successive sweeps of the British Crime Survey showed, there was widespread public concern (see Maguire, this volume). Unlike the anti-social behaviour order (ASBO: see Morgan and Newburn, this volume), however, PNDs initially attracted little attention or controversy.

PNDs work as follows. They can be issued on the spot as well as following arrest for disorderly behaviour ranging from drunken or threatening behaviour to throwing fireworks. They may also be issued for behaviour which may or may not be disorderly (wasting police time or criminal damage up to £500, for example) or which is generally unrelated to disorder (retail theft up to a value of £200, for example). PNDs can be issued by police community support officers (PCSOs) granted designated powers, as well as by sworn police officers. The offender receives an immediate fine of either £50 or £80, depending on the offence, to be paid within 21 days. If the fine is not paid, it is increased by one and a half times. Unpaid PNDs are lodged with the court and thereafter enforced as if they were court-imposed fines. Only if the recipient denies the offence do the police refer the case to the courts for hearing.

Although PNDs (unlike a formal caution) do not involve a formal admission of guilt or the acquisition of a criminal record, the offences for which they are most commonly used—retail theft, drunk and disorderly, behaviour likely to cause harassment, alarm and distress and criminal damage (together accounting for 85 per cent of all PNDs issued: see Ministry of Justice 2010: 21)—are recordable and notifiable. That is, they count as police 'sanction detections' and are recorded on the PNC for what are described as *administrative purposes* (so that the police can decide, for example, whether or not it would be appropriate to impose a PND on a future occasion). This is critical. It means that though the culprit does not formally have a criminal record, his or her receipt of a PND can, if deemed relevant, be cited on future occasions. Thus, PNDs are more than mere penalties designed to ensure compliance, as is the case with, say, parking fines: in this respect, they are on a par with minor court convictions. This explains why concerns have been expressed about the fact that there is no requirement placed on the police to advise PND recipients, who include 16- and 17-year-olds, that they may wish to seek legal advice. Home Office guidance suggests that the 21 days allowed for payment gives ample opportunity for recipients to consult whomsoever they choose. It seems unlikely that most 16- and 17-year-olds, or their parents, or indeed most young adults, will consult persons who understand these ramifications. Faced with the real prospect that by paying £80 they will not have to go to court and apparently hear nothing more of the matter, it is perhaps not surprising that a mere 1 per cent of PND recipients challenge their PND (ibid.: 23). PNDs for notifiable offences are not covered by the Rehabilitation of Offenders Act 1974 which means that they are *never spent*: they can be cited in court following a further conviction for ever after.

### Formal warnings, conditional cautions, and youth restorative disposals

In 2004 formal warnings were introduced for possession of cannabis, an offence which previously often resulted in a police caution. This measure accompanied the downgrading of cannabis from Class B to C (a decision reversed in 2010 when possession of cannabis also became an offence for which a PND could be issued: see Measham and South, this volume). Cannabis warnings, which are not available for juveniles, can, like PNDs, be issued on the street and, unlike PNDs, usually are. As the data in Figures 32.1 and 32.2 indicate, cannabis warnings are used extensively and remain available for first time offenders. The New Labour Government added a further out-of-court option for the police to employ and piloted two more.

Conditional cautions, first introduced by the Criminal Justice Act 2003, were made available for adults in circumstances the same as for simple cautions: the case must pass the 'evidential sufficiency test' for prosecution (i.e. there must be evidence of the offender's guilt 'sufficient to give a realistic prospect of conviction'); the offender must admit the offence; and the offender must understand the significance of the caution and give his/her informed consent (Blackborough and Pierpoint 2007). A conditional caution must be authorized by a Crown prosecutor, and involve a rehabilitative or reparative condition (participation in substance misuse treatment, or compensating a victim, for example). The Police and Justice Act 2006 toughened the option by allowing conditions of an explicitly punitive nature. These include payment of a financial penalty and attendance at a specified place at specified times for up to 20 hours, not including any attendance required for the purposes of rehabilitation. This means that offenders may now be required to undertake up to 20 hours' unpaid work. If the condition set is not complied with, the CPS will normally prosecute.

Proposals for an extension of the conditional caution to juveniles and the introduction of a further option for young people, the youth restorative disposal (YRD), are still under consideration at the time of writing: both have been piloted and evaluated, though the evaluations have yet to be published. The YRD allows the victim and offender, if they both agree, to be brought together for a restorative conference, a procedure which advocates of the YRD reasonably hope will satisfy victims, reduce the likelihood of reoffending, and save a great deal of administrative time and expense. The new Government now also proposes to test an approach using Neighbourhood Justice Panels or Neigbourhood Resolution Panels as a new form of out-of-court process to tackle low-level crime.

## DISCUSSION

It was Prime Minister Blair's boast that the criminal justice reforms in which he took pride had one thing in common: 'they bypass the traditional way the criminal justice system used to work ... the rules of the game have changed' (Blair 2005). If that meant curtailing traditional liberties then, he argued, this was necessary to protect the interests of the 'law-abiding majority'. It would not wash, he asserted, to say that the liberties of victims and offenders are not in conflict. They are. And 'every day we don't resolve [that conflict] by rebalancing the system, the consequence is not abstract, it is out there, very real on our streets'. 'Rebalancing' in this context meant greater use of summary justice, without which the new threats the country was said to be facing would not be beaten, the interests of the law-abiding majority would not be protected (Blair 2006).

The consequencs of this policy shift remains sifnificant. As we have seen, in 2009/10, 38 per cent of the 1.29 million offences brought to justice by the police were dealt with outside the court system (Her Majesty's Inspectorate of Constabulary 2011). How satisfactory are the current arrangements?

The first point to make is that all criminal justice systems of which we are aware involve the use of 'administrative' penalties for common, minor offences and offenders who have not previously been convicted or become known to the police (Tak 1983). This is sensible given that, all other things being equal, indelible criminalization is criminogenic, particularly for young people (see Morgan and Newburn; McAra and McVie, this volume): the available evidence suggests that diversion from criminal court appearance and judicial punishment is likely to be cost effective if operational practice satisfies certain tests—of proportionality, fairness, efficiency, and effectiveness—which meet public expectations of justice and inspire public confidence. It is the empirical evidence and these tests to which we now turn although, as will become clear, much of what follows is necessarily tentative or speculative because the available data are few and those there are have been subject to virtually no published analysis.

### Proportionality

Competing claims have been made that serious cases are inappropriately being dealt with out of court and that significant numbers of minor offences or offenders continue to be prosecuted who would more appropriately be dealt with out of court (see Morgan 2008). There have been serious criticisms of out-of-court solutions in the courts, where both victims and offenders have successfully challenged police and CPS decisions: see, for example, *R (Guest) v DPP* [2009] EWHC 594 (Admin), where Goldring LJ said:

> It seems to me astonishing, as it would no doubt to many members of the public, that the CPS could seriously contemplate not prosecuting someone who, it was alleged, deliberately went to a person's house at night, attacked him inside that house with some ferocity (including kicking him) in the presence of his (obviously very frightened) partner. I very much hope that this was a one-off aberration and not typical of the manner in which the CPS discharges its heavy responsibilities in respect of conditional cautioning (at para 56–57).

Other hints of dissatisfaction appear in reports of independent CPS Hate Crime Scrutiny Panels (many of which are on-line). In 2010 these various criticisms prompted a thematic inspection jointly undertaken by the constabulary and CPS inspectorates. This review produced some disquieting findings, albeit based on a very small sample of cases.

The inspectors found that one-third of the various out-of-court disposal cases they scrutinized were applied inappropriately, that is, contrary to the rules and guidance. The most common non-compliance related to offenders' offending history (out-of-court penalties should 'not normally be considered for those who offend repeatedly') and, second, offence gravity (in one case a caution was administered to an offender who had stolen £5,000, of which very little had been recovered, from his employer). Further, the rationale in particular cases for using the out-of-court disposals was rarely recorded (even though force policies required it) and oversight of decision-making by 'evidence review officers' did not extend to disposals issued on the street (HMIC/CPSI 2011: 23–4). Not only were many of the decisions not made according to the current rules but there was a lack of transparency and quality assurance. A substantial question mark hangs over the integrity of allocational decisions by both the police and the CPS to out-of-court disposals with regard to the *proportionality of imposition* principle. Some relatively serious offences and offenders who arguably should be brought before the courts are being dealt with out of court. The inspectorates recommended that the Ministry of Justice produce 'a clear and consolidated set of guidance for all out-of-court disposals based on a proportionate response to the level of offending and the nature of the offender' (ibid.: 37). Almost all prosecuted cases considered by the inspectors were correctly prosecuted according to the current guidance, but that issue, many practitioners contend, needs revisiting (see Morgan and Newburn, this volume).

### Fairness

That like cases be treated alike is fundamental to justice and the rule of law. The use of discretion which comprises no more than the expression of preference by decision-makers, as opposed to judgment exercised according to law, can be damaging to the rule of law since it can be used to undermine or distort the law, (Bingham 2010. ch. 4). Here we have wide discretionary powers exercised on a day-to-day basis, largely invisibly, by police officers (and prosecutors), decisions which are the 'stuff of justice' and which make for justice or injustice (Gelsthorpe and Padfield 2003). Major apparent[3] differences between police forces, which have continued for many years, with regard to prosecution policy, must be a matter of concern. 'Post-code justice' is unlikely to command public confidence. In 2009 the use of out-of-court disposals ranged in the 43 police force areas in England and Wales from 26 to 49 per cent of all offences brought to justice. Dyfed-Powys had a 50 per cent cautioning rate for indictable offences, Greater Manchester 20 per cent. The inspectorates unequivocally found that differences in local crime and offending patterns 'do not fully explain the scale of the variation' (HMIC/CPSI 2011: 5).

---

[3] We say *apparent* because there may be differences in the offence and offender characteristic mix between police areas that are not evident from the published data. Further, when new disposals are being introduced, often using pilot or phased introductions, it necessarily takes time for operational practice to settle down in a consistent manner across the country.

### Effectiveness and costs

Even if justice considerations are satisfied, various cost-effectiveness tests can and arguably should be applied when considering the sort of major policy shift which has characterized the use of out-of-court disposals in recent years. Are offenders more or less likely, *ceteris paribus,* to comply with the sanction (pay the fine or make reparation, for example) if they are dealt with out of court as opposed to prosecuted? Are they more or less likely to re-offend? And, heavily dependent on the answers to those two questions, does the criminal justice system and society at large save money from the use of such measures?

The published data currently available do not enable these questions to be answered. They permit, at best, indications. Taking the third question first, 39 per cent of offenders given a PND pay in full within 21 days and a further 14 per cent pay in full after 21 days but before the penalty is registered with the court for enforcement.[4] This means that 47 per cent of all PNDs end up in the courts for enforcement, though what happens thereafter is unknown because no statistics are kept distinguishing court enforcement of PNDs as opposed to court-imposed fines. Even if out-of-court penalties displace some minor court business, a high proportion re-enter court caseloads by the back door for enforcement, which, given that out-of-court penalties have undoubtedly net-widened the criminal justice system, may mean that overall costs have increased.

As far as the initial work of front-line police officers is concerned the inspectorates have estimated the benefits of out-of-court penalties. A PND issued on the street takes an average 3 hours 31 minutes to administer compared to 8 hours 45 minutes for bringing an equivalent charge (though any savings in police time make little sense if out-of-court penalties subsequently have to be enforced). A conditional caution on the other hand takes almost as long as bringing a charge (HMIC/HMCPSI 2011: 29).

Reconviction estimates suggest that offenders who are conditionally discharged or fined in court are slightly more likely to be reconvicted than offenders who are cautioned (Ministry of Justice 2010), but the differences are small and unreliable. Offenders who subsequently received a PND were not included in the analysis, a factor that rendered the estimates of even more questionable value. As far as public confidence in the use of out-of-court penalties is concerned the inspectorates found, albeit on the basis of very few cases indeed, that there was least satisfaction among victims of cases that went to court. This had more to do with whether victims were consulted and kept informed about what actions had been taken than the character of the disposal (HMIC/HMCPSI 2011: 27).

### CONCLUSION

The case for using out-of-court penalties to divert minor offenders who admit their offences from appearing in court and acquiring a more serious stain on their character is a powerful one. Such arrangements are capable of being entirely consistent with the principle of *proportionality.* However, the New Labour Government greatly expanded the use of these penalties without adequate safeguards and in a manner which could

---

[4] Hansard, written answer, 29 June 2011.

lead to abuse. Setting numerical targets for OBTJs, for which out-of-court penalties contributed, was not, as the inspectorates concluded, 'conducive to the effective exercise of discretion' (HMIC/HMCPSI 2011: 5). It resulted, as Sir Ronnie Flanagan's review of policing concluded, in minor offenders, particularly children, being criminalized when it was not in the public interest (Flanagan Report 2008: 10).

The result has been a good deal of mistrust, particularly among sentencers, who believe that serious cases which should be brought to court are being dealt with inappropriately and without proper accountability. This is an issue which might be addressed were the Ministry of Justice to undertake the review and issue fresh, comprehensive guidance for which the inspectorates have called. There is also a case for giving the lay magistracy an accountability role overseeing police and CPS use of out-of-court penalties (see Judge 2011).

# 'BACK DOOR' SENTENCING?[5] EARLY RELEASE, PAROLE, AND INDETERMINATE SENTENCES

The discussion so far has focused on out-of-court decisions which may be financially damaging to those on the receiving end, or may harm their reputation through the acquisition of a 'record'. However, although failure to comply with a PND can ultimately result in imprisonment as a fine defaulter, such penalties do not directly affect people's liberty. By contrast, there are major decision-making processes operated outside the control of the criminal courts, which (within some court-determined parameters) determine how long those sentenced to imprisonment actually spend in custody. These include discretionary decisions on the early release of determinate sentence prisoners and decisions as to whether and when those given 'life' or other indeterminate sentences are to be released. In this section we outline how these processes work, raising questions about their justifiability, fairness, transparency, and accountability.

### EARLY RELEASE FROM PRISON

Few, if any, criminal justice systems stipulate that those sent to prison will serve every day of the sentence passed by the judge. Even under the severe 'truth in sentencing' provisions introduced in many states in the USA during the late 1990s most states set the minimum term to be served at 85 rather than 100 per cent.[6] However, there has been much dispute about how much of a 'discount' on sentences is acceptable, for whom, and on what grounds. Concerns have focused on the fairness and consistency

---

[5] This phrase was adopted by the House of Commons Justice Committee (2008) at para 160.

[6] These provisions were introduced in a climate of hardening attitudes to crime, in response to strong political lobbying against parole and claims that the public was being 'deceived' by the fact that most prisoners served less than half their sentence in custody. National legislation in 1994 offered financial incentives to any US state that set the minimum period to be served at 85 per cent of the sentence passed by the judge (Ditton and Wilson 1999; Wood and Dunaway 2003).

of the decision-making processes involved, and on who should control and administer them (Padfield 2007; Padfield, Van Zyl Smit, and Dünkel 2010).

A number of reasons can be advanced for affording prisoners the possibility of early release. One is simply that it injects some humanity into an otherwise harsh penal system and offers them a ray of hope; there may also be times, such as in the case of terminal illness or old age, when the authorities consider it right to show mercy to individuals. A more pragmatic reason is that the lure of early release is valuable to prison staff as a carrot to encourage compliance from inmates. Cynically, too, it can be argued that it provides a useful tool with which governments can save money or ease problems of prison overcrowding by letting inmates out quietly by the 'back door', rather than being seen to interfere directly in judicial decision-making (or to appear 'soft on crime') by advocating or legislating shorter sentences. A quite different kind of argument—and perhaps the most commonly deployed in public debate—is that, if the transition from custody to community is skilfully managed, early release can assist rehabilitation, help to manage risk, and bring about reductions in reoffending. In some penal systems this is reinforced by a constitutional right to rehabilitation (van Zyl Smit and Snacken 2010).

Early release mechanisms come in a variety of forms, ranging from the fully automatic to the highly selective. At one end of the scale are those in which early release is treated essentially as an entitlement, and granted in routine fashion to all prisoners who fall into a particular category or meet certain well-defined criteria. At the other end of the scale are systems in which decisions are taken on an individual basis, allowing a significant amount of discretion by those considering the case.

Perhaps the most common type of early release mechanism around the world has been remission of part of the sentence for 'good behaviour' (often referred to as 'good time' in the USA). Designed originally to aid the maintenance of order in prisons, in many jurisdictions this began as a privilege that had to be 'earned' through co-operation with the regime. As such, it allowed the use of discretion by prison staff, for example in awarding 'marks' for good behaviour. However, in most cases, such practices were eventually replaced by arrangements in which remission of a set proportion of the sentence was treated as a right which could be forfeited only under specified circumstances—thus locating them towards the 'automatic' end of the scale (see Hood 1965, for example, for a discussion of the development of the Borstal system for young offenders; Padfield, Van Zyl Smit, and Dünkel 2010, for modern European examples). In England and Wales, for most of the second half of the twentieth century, all determinate sentence prisoners had to be granted unconditional release after serving a maximum of two-thirds of their sentence.[7] Many significant changes to these rules and terminology took place during the 1990s and early 2000s, the concept of 'remission' ultimately giving way to a new view of determinate sentences as incorporating a custody *and* a community element, each of equal length.

Another mechanism in which release tends to be granted *en bloc* to all those who meet certain specified criteria (although determining precisely who meets them may involve subjective judgements on the part of staff) is the use of short-term or emergency

---

[7] That is, unless they were formally awarded 'loss of remission' (expressed as a number of days) at a disciplinary adjudication.

measures to reduce prison overcrowding. These can range from mass releases under amnesties, to systems such as the End of Custody Licence (ECL) system in operation in England and Wales between 2007 and 2010, whereby large numbers of low-risk prisoners were released up to 18 days early. Interestingly, when the ECL scheme was discontinued—partly owing to pressure from political opponents who portrayed it as 'soft' on offenders—the Ministry of Justice wrote to all potentially eligible prisoners to remind them that they could apply for an alternative form of early release, Home Detention Curfew (HDC). HDC, introduced in 1999, allows some prisoners to be released up to 135 days early on an electronic 'tag', which monitors a curfew at set times.[8] It had hitherto been presented as a rehabilitative measure to enhance the resettlement of prisoners and reduce reoffending (Marie *et al.* 2011). However, the Ministry of Justice letter was seized on by critics as simply another attempt by the Minister to reduce the prison population by letting more inmates out through the 'back door', while at the same time appearing to be acting tough by ending ECL.[9] This episode nicely illustrates the highly political nature of early release in a punitive climate where those in government are unwilling to leave themselves open to charges of excessive leniency, yet at the same time are faced with major practical problems and financial costs caused by prison overcrowding.

While release systems like those described above sometimes provoke debates about 'truth in sentencing' and the appropriate size of any 'discount' to be allowed, most of them arouse relatively few concerns in terms of the fair treatment of offenders. Prisoners know where they stand and are broadly treated alike.[10] By contrast, release arrangements in which decisions are made on an individual basis by executive bodies with substantial discretionary powers, have frequently attracted criticism and concern in relation to issues of human rights, fairness, openness and accountability. These tend to be systems in which the central aims are expressed in terms of the reduction of reoffending and/or the protection of the public, and the task of the decision-making body is to weigh up the risks and benefits of releasing each individual prisoner: parole systems being the prime example. The kinds of concerns that they raise are further magnified in the case of prisoners with *indeterminate* sentences—i.e. where the court has stipulated no maximum time to be served, short of the prisoner's death. Clearly, in these cases, the parole authorities perform a very significant quasi-sentencing role.

The following section addresses such issues primarily through a discussion of the work of the Parole Board in England and Wales. We begin with a brief outline of

---

[8] About 50,000 prisoners a year are eligible for HDC. In 2004, almost one in three were granted it, but the proportion fell in subsequent years, to around one in five between 2007 and 2009 when ECL was in operation. With the discontinuation of ECL there are signs of an increase in the use of HDC: in 2010, 12,250 (26%) of 46,500 eligible prisoners were granted it (Ministry of Justice 2011c).

[9] See, e.g., 'Prison officials urging inmates to apply for early release' by Tom Whitehead, Home Affairs Editor, *The Telegraph*, 1 March 2010. www.telegraph.co.uk/news/uknews/law-and-order/7337649/Prison-officials-urging-inmates-to-apply-for-early-release.html.

[10] There is, of course, significantly more risk of unfairness in the HDC process, which involves interpretation by prison governors of evidence about inmates' eligibility and suitability, than in those such as automatic remission, where no decision-making is involved. However, governors' decisions are guided by a fairly prescriptive set of rules and are also open to appeal (see House of Commons Committee of Public Accounts 2006; and www.prisonersadvice.org.uk/DOCS/INFORMATION/HDC.pdf).

its history, which reflects the shifting views about the role of non-judicial bodies in decisions about imprisonment. The focus then moves to particular concerns arising from the startling growth over the past decade in the numbers of prisoners serving indeterminate sentences, particularly so-called IPPs (those sentenced to open-ended 'life' terms of imprisonment for public protection), and the part played by the Parole Board in deciding their fate, as well as the fate of the fast growing numbers of prisoners recalled to prison during the second or community-based part of their sentence.

## THE CHANGING ROLE OF THE PAROLE BOARD

In the USA, parole has a long history, with locally managed experiments dating back to the nineteenth century. Legislation to establish a national Board of Parole in the federal system was passed in 1930, and most states had established formal parole systems by the 1940s (Fulwood 2003; Abadinsky 2008). In many cases, these operated in a context of sentencing systems which allowed wide leeway for executive discretion on release, whereby judges could pass sentences such as '10–20 years', leaving determination of the actual date of release to the parole authorities.

In England and Wales, by contrast, with its strong tradition of fixed term sentencing, parole was not introduced until 1968, in the Criminal Justice Act 1967. Penal thinking at the time was infused by what has been referred to as the 'rehabilitative ideal'—i.e. the notion that one of the main aims of the criminal justice system should be to prevent future re-offending, even if this violated to some extent the principle of appropriate punishment for the offence. Strong claims were also made for the ability of 'experts' such as criminologists and psychologists to understand and predict the behaviour of offenders and to devise interventions to change it. Thus the publicly stated rationale for parole was that if the 'right' people were selected for early release at the 'right' time and given the appropriate support and supervision, they would be less likely to reoffend. The White Paper which preceded the Act (Home Office 1965) included an assertion that there is an identifiable 'peak in training' experienced by many prisoners—i.e. a point at which they have obtained maximum benefit from rehabilitative interventions received in prison— and that if they are released under probation supervision at this time, their chances of avoiding re-offending will be maximized. To achieve this, it was proposed to set up a Parole Board populated by a variety of experts and with the power to recommend release, without reference to the courts, as early as the one-third point in an individual's sentence. At the time there was surprisingly little opposition to these proposals, despite some concerns being expressed that it was in effect allowing what amounted to a 'sentencing' function to be performed, without judicial oversight, by an unaccountable executive board—albeit that its decisions had to be approved by the Home Secretary.[11]

---

[11] The Home Secretary retained a 'veto' over recommended releases, but could not grant parole without the Board first recommending it. Of course, constitutional questions remain about the extent to which members of the government should themselves be permitted to 'interfere' with sentences of the courts (beyond, for example, exercise of the prerogative of mercy in exceptional cases).

Initially, the Parole Board—made up of judges, psychiatrists, psychologists, criminologists, senior probation managers, and independent members—could recommend release on licence at any time between the one-third and two-thirds points in the sentence, provided that the prisoner had already spent a minimum of 12 months in custody. The first few years saw a cautious approach, in which the first Chairman stressed that parole should be regarded as a 'privilege not a right' and only a small minority of those eligible were recommended for release. However, in 1975 the then Home Secretary, Roy Jenkins, concluded that there was sufficient public confidence in the parole system to allow him to encourage a less cautious approach, and made significant changes to the rules and guidelines with the explicit intention of increasing the numbers released. As a result, the proportion of eligible prisoners granted parole rose rapidly towards 50 per cent (Maguire 1992: 182–5). Further rule changes implemented by Leon Brittan in 1984 pushed this higher, as well as bringing many shorter-term prisoners within the scope of parole.[12]

Paradoxically, just as the use of parole was expanding, the penal climate was beginning to turn against it. For some commentators, the Jenkins changes simply increased suspicions that, despite its rehabilitative rhetoric, parole was in reality driven mainly by the pragmatic aim of keeping prison numbers down (see, for example, Morgan 1983). At a broader political level, particularly in the USA, parole was coming under attack from both right and left: it was portrayed, on the one hand, as a tool for over-lenient treatment of offenders and, on the other, as a vehicle for racial discrimination and serious violations of prisoners' rights.[13] Academics also began to question both the empirical base and the fundamental assumptions that underpinned the whole concept of selective release by an expert panel. For example, Hood (1974; see also Nuttall 1977) pointed out that there was no conclusive evidence that the system as a whole reduced reoffending, nor, that the so-called 'peak in training' existed or that it could be identified by members of the Parole Board or those who provided it with reports. This accorded with research in the USA suggesting that expert judgement was no better at predicting reconviction than statistical models (Wilkins 1969; see also Carroll et al. 1982; Shute 2004). Such findings clearly undermined some of the utilitarian justifications for parole and brought into sharper relief arguments that it violated fundamental principles of justice by allowing the executive to usurp core judicial functions. In this view, parole decisions amounted to an unfair and secretive form of 're-sentencing' by an unaccountable non-judicial body (Hood 1975). It was seen as particularly unfair that the Parole Board, often on the basis of little more information than had been available to the trial judge, tended to grant release to prisoners who had

---

[12] The main changes introduced by Jenkins were (a) to encourage more release recommendations for minor property offenders who were unlikely to commit a serious crime, even if there was a sizeable risk of further minor offending; and (b) to allow Local Review Committees, who 'sifted' cases for presentation to the main Parole Board, to recommend release directly to the Home Secretary in low-risk cases. Brittan lowered the threshold of eligibility, requiring prisoners to have served a minimum of only 6 months, rather than 12 months, before becoming eligible for consideration by the Board. This brought large numbers of prisoners with sentences as low as 14 months within the scope of parole.

[13] For example, it was claimed that black prisoners, especially those involved in protest movements, were often kept in prison for political and other reasons unrelated to rehabilitation (American Friends Service Committee 1971).

committed relatively minor crimes while refusing it to more serious offenders, thus in effect widening the differentials in sentence length judged appropriate by the courts: a form of 'double sentencing' for the long-termers. Perhaps the most influential critique of parole as a concept came from Von Hirsch (1976), who argued from first principles that responses to crime should be based on retributivist principles and aim to deliver *just deserts*, using a scale of punishments which reflect the seriousness of the offence committed: it was wrong even for judges to stray significantly from the appropriate punishment for the crime, let alone for parole boards meeting in secret to change the differentials between sentences passed in open court.

Over the following years, in the US and the UK, as the language of rehabilitation rapidly gave way to that of 'nothing works' and 'just deserts', these kinds of views found growing support among academics, politicians, and policy-makers and, together with successful legal challenges by prisoners to parole decisions and procedures, paved the way for major changes. In the United States, during the 1980s and 1990s many states adopted 'just deserts' and 'truth in sentencing' policies and abolished parole entirely except for life sentence prisoners (many of whom were also excluded by the growing use of sentences of 'life without the possibility of parole'[14]). In England and Wales, the parole system underwent a series of significant reforms, particularly during the 1990s and early 2000s, culminating in a situation in which the Parole Board now performs a very different function to that envisaged at the time of its birth in the late 1960s.

The changes in England and Wales led in three main directions. First, as court judgments recognized the human rights failings of the system, the Board's procedures were incrementally reformed to make them more 'court-like' and bring them more into line with the principles of natural justice and of the European Convention on Human Rights (e.g. in terms of giving reasons for decisions, allowing prisoners to see their dossiers, legal representation, and attendance at hearings). The Criminal Justice Act 1991 created 'Discretionary Lifer Panels', which allowed prisoners serving life sentences (other than for murder) an oral hearing before a panel of the Board. This right was slowly extended to those convicted of murder when children (HMP prisoners), and then to mandatory lifers (see Padfield 2002). For similar reasons, efforts were made to distance the Parole Board from the executive and to increase its formal independence. In 1996 its status changed from an advisory board to an Independent Non-Departmental Public Body, and it gradually acquired powers to make final decisions, rather than simply recommendations to the Home Secretary. However, this incremental change has not transformed the Board into a court-like body sufficient to satisfy the requirements of Article 5(4) of the European Convention on Human Rights (see the decision of the Court of Appeal in *R (Brooke) v Parole Board* [2008] EWCA Civ 29). This led to a Ministry of Justice consultation on the *Future of the Parole Board* in 2009, but no further steps have been initiated to secure the independence of the Parole Board from executive control.

Secondly, parole has been replaced by automatic release for more categories of determinate sentence prisoners. After 1992, prisoners sentenced to under four years were

[14] In 2004, it was estimated that 28 per cent of US lifers had no hope of release ('To More Inmates, Life Term Means Dying Behind Bars', *New York Times*, 2 October 2005).

excluded from parole entirely, instead being released automatically at the half-way point in their sentence, and in 2005, release at the half-way point was extended to prisoners given determinate sentences of any length.[15] These changes should not be interpreted simply as an extension of 'remission' as previously understood: the move to automatic release from custody has been offset by longer and more strictly enforced license conditions after release. Indeed, in line with the philosophy of the Halliday Report (2001) which underpinned some of the changes, determinate sentences are officially portrayed as 'seamless': i.e. comprised of two 'halves', one served in custody and the other in the community (see Hudson, Maguire and Raynor 2007).[16] The role in this system of the 'offender manager'—normally a probation officer based in the offender's home area—is crucial (see Raynor, this volume).

Thirdly, and most importantly for our purposes, the focus of Parole Board activity shifted sharply away from rehabilitation to the *management of risk*, particularly in relation to decisions about two growing categories of prisoners: those serving *indeterminate sentences* and those *recalled to prison* subsequent to release. It is to this last set of developments that we now turn, arguing that they raise perhaps the greatest concerns of all in relation to the growing trend towards 'out-of-court justice'.

## RISK AND PUBLIC PROTECTION: TAKING OUT-OF-COURT JUSTICE TOO FAR?

It is somewhat ironic that, while all determinate sentences passed in England and Wales now result in automatic rather than discretionary release, the Parole Board is busier than ever and has many more members than it did in the 1980s, when it was making decisions about most medium- and long-term prisoners. Indeed, the workload expanded so quickly in the late 2000s that major backlogs of cases built up and the Board had to pay compensation for delays to increasing numbers of prisoners.[17] The scale of the problem can be gauged from the fact that in 2010/11 the Board expanded its membership by almost 100, to a total in excess of 230 (Parole Board 2011a); this compares with around 90 in the late 1980s.[18] The main factors behind this situation were a huge increase in the numbers of indeterminate sentence prisoners

---

[15] Changes enacted in the Criminal Justice Act 2003, and brought into force in 2005. The only exception was Extended Sentences for Public Protection, aimed at serious violent and sexual offenders, who were not released early except on the recommendation of the Parole Board. This exception was removed in 2008 (Criminal Justice and Immigration Act).

[16] Despite their relatively high needs and risks of reconviction, the one group excluded from post-release supervision requirements is adult prisoners sentenced to less than 12 months. Their inclusion has often been mooted, especially via implementation of the 'seamless' sentence of 'Custody Plus' proposed by Halliday (Hudson *et al.* 2007). The main obstacle remains the prohibitive costs involved

[17] Recent Annual Reports contain frank recognition of the validity of legal challenges by prisoners under Art. 5(4) of the European Convention on Human Rights, which deals with rights to timely justice. It is readily admitted that, even after substantial increases in membership, the Board cannot keep pace with its expanding workload, and hence that it has to be prepared to pay significant amounts of compensation (Parole Board 2010, 2011a).

[18] We should note not only the expanded membership but the changing nature of that membership: a decline in use of full-time members, a declining number of criminologists, had the use of 'independent' non-lawyer members to chair panels.

and, closely linked to this, major changes in the nature of the Parole Board's work—most obviously, the expansion of oral hearings rather than 'paper panels'. Both developments are clearly pertinent to debates about one of the central issues of this chapter: the justifiability of giving major decisions about the liberty of individuals to a 'non-judicial' or 'non-court' body.

### 'Bifurcation' and the expansion in indeterminate sentencing

Whilst the 1980s and early 1990s saw a shift in penal thought and practice away from the 'rehabilitative ideal' towards policies built around the concept of 'just deserts', the last 20 years have seen an equally striking transformation of social and political attitudes towards crime and justice that has both magnified the focus on punishment and at the same time afforded a dominant place to concerns about 'risk' and 'public protection' (Feeley and Simon 1992; Garland 2001). One manifestation of this has been an increasing bifurcation (Bottoms 1977) in responses to offenders, whereby those considered to be 'high risk' or 'dangerous' are treated very differently to the rest. Put broadly, it might be said that, while the majority are dealt with primarily in accord with a traditional retributive model of justice (i.e. they receive punishment from the courts roughly proportionate to the seriousness of the offences they have committed—albeit tempered in some cases by rehabilitative considerations), responses to those labelled 'high risk' or 'dangerous' are driven largely by a preventive/incapacitative philosophy, in which more attention is given to the risk of future offending than to the nature of the current offence. In England and Wales, this is reflected especially in the growth of indeterminate sentences for 'public protection' and in the increased emphasis on licence conditions monitored in the community. Unlike mandatory life sentences for murder, these sentences are not primarily aimed at marking the gravity of the current offence: indeed, in many cases, the minimum tariff set by the judge to reflect this has been short. Rather, the aim is to allow the Parole Board to keep the offender in custody beyond the tariff date, for as long as it feels that he or she poses a sufficient risk of harm to the community. In short, for the 'mainstream majority' of prisoners, the actual length of time they will spend in custody is now once again determined principally by the judiciary and (apart from the automatic release rules), is open to only limited executive alteration—for example by earlier release on HDC or compassionate grounds. By contrast, for the fast-increasing numbers who are deemed 'dangerous', responsibility for decisions about how long they will spend in custody has substantially been transferred from the courts to the Parole Board. As we shall see, Offender Managers, too, play a critical part in these decision-making processes.

Imprisonment for Public Protection (IPP) was introduced in the Criminal Justice Act 2003.[19] The speed and scale of the increase can be illustrated by prison population figures which show that in June 2002, the total indeterminate sentenced population

---

[19] An earlier attempt to increase the use of indeterminate sentences was the 'Two strikes and you're out' rule, introduced under the Crime (Sentences) Act 1997, which required judges to pass a life sentence in the case of a second grave sexual or violent offence. However, the requirement was effectively neutralized by a Court of Appeal ruling which allowed judges to treat their own judgment that the offender was not dangerous as 'exceptional circumstances'. For an account of the origins of this kind of legislation in the USA and of how the idea was transferred to the UK, see Jones and Newburn 2007.

(mainly 'lifers') was 5,147, but increased to 9,481 by 2007 and 13,587 in March 2011, a rise over nine years of 164 per cent (Ministry of Justice 2011b: see also Liebling and Crewe, this volume). At this point, indeterminate sentence prisoners made up almost 19 per cent of the total sentenced population. By March 2011, on a provisional count, there were 6,550 IPPs among the sentenced population, 150 of them female (Ministry of Justice 2011a). The speed of arrival of IPP prisoners has now slowed (the criteria were tightened in the Criminal Justice and Immigration Act 2008, and the sentencing judiciary was given more discretion not to impose IPP on those deemed 'dangerous'), but the numbers are unlikely to decline, given the very low proportion being released by the Parole Board (see below).

Oral hearings have taken on an increasingly 'court-like' character with close attention to procedural detail (Parole Board 2010, 2011b; Arnott and Creighton 2010). This is a far cry from the 1980s, when it was standard practice for panels to decide 32 determinate sentence cases in one day, based on consideration only of written reports and representations. These 'paper panels' (often now made up of one member) continue to decide the majority of the remaining determinate sentence prisoners who were sentenced before 2005 under the old rules and the fast-increasing number of recalled prisoners, only some of whom are able to convince the Board of their right to an oral hearing. We return to the sharp contrast between oral hearings and paper panels below.

### Indeterminate sentences and Parole Board decision-making

In assessing the role of the Parole Board in relation to indeterminate sentence cases, it is important to note that the majority of IPPs currently in prison have short tariffs.[20] As Table 32.1 shows, over two-thirds of those in custody in March 2011 had a tariff of four years or under and close to a quarter less than two years (some, indeed, only a few weeks); by comparison, almost two-thirds of 'lifers' had tariffs of over ten years. At least in its early years, the IPP system caught in its net large numbers of offenders whose offences fell far below the level of seriousness that would be required to qualify for a life sentence (see also Prison Reform Trust 2007; Justice 2009). This raises serious questions about the justifiability of a sentence which departs so far from normal considerations of proportionality in sentencing. The changes of the Criminal Justice and Immigration Act 2008 significantly reduced the number of IPP sentences being imposed. However, these changes were driven as much by concerns about the resource implications of the unexpected flood of prisoners (neither the high numbers of IPPs nor the predominance of low tariffs had been predicted when the 2003 Act was drafted) as by concerns for justice and proportionality. The drop in the number of IPPs has also led to a large increase in the number of extended sentences, another development which needs careful monitoring (see Ashworth and Roberts, this volume).

---

[20] The tariff refers to the judge's declaration of the minimum period of time that has to be served before the Parole Board can consider the prisoner for release. The tariff is half the determinate sentence that would be imposed for the offence, were a determinate sentence to be passed (see Ashworth and Roberts, this volume).

**Table 32.1** Provisional figures on tariff lengths of offenders serving life sentences and indeterminate sentences of imprisonment for public protection (IPPs) at March 2011

| IPP population by tariff, March 2011 | |
| --- | --- |
| Less than 2 years | 1,550 |
| 2 years–4 years | 3,200 |
| Over 4 years–6 years | 1,200 |
| Over 6 years–10 years | 500 |
| More than 10 years | 50 |
| Tariff unavailable | 50 |
| Total | 6,550 |
| **Lifer population by tariff, March 2011** | |
| Up to 10 years | 2,650 |
| Over 10 and up to 20 years | 4,350 |
| 20 years or more | 850 |
| Whole life | 41 |
| Tariff unavailable | 250 |
| Total | 8,141 |

*Source*: Ministry of Justice (2011a)

*Note*: These figures are labelled by the MoJ as provisional. They are not fully reliable, as the two totals sum to 14,691, which is considerably higher than the official number of indeterminate sentence prisoners (13,587) presented in the official MoJ statistics on the prison population (Ministry of Justice 2011b). The latter, however, do not break this figure down into IPPs and lifers.

Despite the relatively low tariffs set for most IPPs, the Parole Board has so far shown considerable reluctance to release them. Table 32.2 shows the proportions of 'on or post' tariff IPP hearings (including paper panels) in each year which have resulted in release being directed. As can be seen, these have fluctuated between the strikingly low rates of 5 and 8 per cent.

The total number of releases granted during the first six years of the IPP sentence (under 300) can be contrasted with the numbers of IPP prisoners who remain in prison beyond their tariff, often for several years. As at March 2011, this already amounted to well over half (3,500) of all those sentenced to date (Ministry of Justice 2011a). Moreover, over 1,500 of these were prisoners with tariffs of less than two years who had been sentenced prior to the 2008 Act which raised the minimum threshold to two years. In other words, had they been convicted at any other time than between 2005 and 2008, they would have received a relatively short determinate sentence, whereas they now face uncertainty about when, if ever, they will be released—a situation widely viewed as exceptionally disproportionate and particularly unjust (Jacobson and Hough 2010; and Ashworth and Roberts, this volume). While it is too early to know what will eventually turn out to be the average length of time for which IPP prisoners are kept in custody beyond their tariff, Ministry of Justice prison population

**Table 32.2** Summary of decisions in on/post tariff and recall IPP cases considered 2006/07–2010/11

|  | 2006/07 | 2007/08 | 2008/09 | 2009/10 | 2010/11 |
| --- | --- | --- | --- | --- | --- |
| Cases considered | 74 | 253 | 556 | 1423 | 2,261 |
| Release directed | 6 | 17 | 43 | 68 | 140 |
|  | 8% | 7% | 8% | 5% | 6% |
| Not directed | 44 | 192 | 390 | 1,197 | 1,901 |
|  | 59% | 76% | 70% | 83% | 84% |
| Adjourned/deferred | 24 | 44 | 123 | 167 | 220 |
|  | 32% | 17% | 22% | 17% | 17% |

*Source*: Parole Board (2011a)

*Note*: The figures shown do not reflect the total number of IPP prisoners considered for release, as some will have been considered at more than one hearing or panel.

projections published in 2009 estimated it at four and a half years (Ministry of Justice 2009a: Appendix Table B1).

Jacobson and Hough (2010) put forward a number of reasons for the apparently over-cautious approach to decision-making so far adopted by the Parole Board·

> First, the Parole Board is clearly overstretched and, in addition, its decision-making is highly risk averse, as reflected in its low release rates. Secondly, offending behaviour programmes—completion of which is viewed as essential for people's readiness for release—are limited in their availability and also, even more importantly, in their scope and effectiveness. Thirdly, it is inherently extremely difficult for someone to demonstrate their reduced dangerousness, given that the converse of the low dangerousness threshold set by the IPP sentence is a high 'safety' threshold for release.

On the last point, the Parole Board is not helped by the lack of guidance in law on the level of assessed risk at which release should be granted. The Crime (Sentences) Act 1997 simply states that 'an indeterminate sentenced prisoner can be released if the Parole Board is satisfied that it is no longer necessary for the protection of the public that he be confined' (section 28(6)(b)). They receive some assistance from pre-diction tools, which calculate 'risk of re-offending' or 'risk of harm' scores for each individual,[21] but these are by no means reliable predictors of whether a specific individual will or will not reoffend, and are less reliable in predicting serious re-offending (Kemshall 2003; Crassiati and Sindall 2009; see also Hollin; Raynor, this volume).[22]

---

[21] For example, risk of reoffending can be calculated using OGRS3, which is based on 'static' risk factors such as age and previous convictions, or the more recently devised OGP, which includes 'dynamic' factors such as substance abuse. Risk of harm is usually assessed with the help of instruments (such as Risk Matrix 2000) which incorporate clinical judgement into the scoring.

[22] Nor is completion or not of offending behaviour programmes in itself a proven indicator of risk: in any case there are currently insufficient programmes available for all prisoners to be able to undertake them before their first parole review (and since prisoners with low IQs are deemed ineligible to participate, the test is discriminatory).

Perhaps of more relevance in practice is the knowledge of Parole Board members that if a prisoner they have released commits a serious further offence, they may face a storm of public anger from politicians and the media. It would be surprising if this had not contributed to their highly risk averse approach.[23]

### Recall and re-release

Not only has the Parole Board become more cautious about release decisions, but the numbers of offenders recalled to prison subsequent to release have been rising fast for several years (Padfield and Maruna 2006). According to the Ministry of Justice the recall population rose by 5,300 between 1995 and 2009, and this increase accounted for 16 per cent of the overall increase in prison population over the period. It explains this as follows:

> Changes to the law have meant that more offenders are liable to be recalled, and to spend longer in custody having been recalled. Growth in the recall population began in 1999, reflecting changes introduced under the Crime and Disorder Act 1998 which extended executive recall to medium-term sentences of 12 months to less than 4 years, making it easier to recall these prisoners (previously they could only be recalled by the Probation Service through the courts). The Criminal Justice Act 2003 (CJA03), introduced in April 2005, included changes to the recall process. The licence period for determinate sentences of 12 months or more was extended to the end of sentence, whereas previously it had ended at the three quarters point. Similarly, recalled offenders were now liable to serve 100% of their original custodial sentence (previously this had been 75%). In addition, the CJA03 introduced a requirement for the Parole Board to review all recall cases, resulting in low rate of re-release. These changes contributed to increases in the average length of time spent in prison on recall. (Ministry of Justice 2009: 7)

The scale of change involved is evident in the growth in recalls from 1,272 in 1999/2000 to 11,171 in 2004/5 and 15,631 in 2010/11 (Ministry of Justice 2011c). Some are HDC recalls, but most involve breaches of standard licences from determinate sentences. Recalls of indeterminate sentence prisoners have also risen (see Table 32.3): indeed, nearly as many lifers are now being recalled each year as are being granted first release, and in 2006, *more* lifers were recalled than were released (Appleton 2009). Moreover, the majority are recalled not for re-offending, but because of 'deterioration' in their behaviour, which raises questions about the degree of executive discretion being exercised in decisions which can have huge consequences for individuals.

The decision to recall is now taken purely administratively. It is initiated by an Offender Manager and endorsed by a senior probation manager. A report is then sent to the Public Protection Unit (PPU) in the Ministry of Justice, who authorize the police to arrest the offender. Some recalls are for a fixed term of 28 days, but most stipulate that the offender will serve his or her full sentence unless re-release is granted.

Re-release decisions remain mainly in the hands of the Parole Board (the Ministry of Justice may also order re-release). A recalled prisoner serving a determinate

[23] Two of the most prominent are the cases of Damian Hanson and Anthony Rice, both of whom committed murder, in 2004 and 2005 respectively, after having been released by the Parole Board.

**Table 32.3** Life licensees recalled to prison, 2003/4 to 2010/11

|                 | 2003/4 | 2004/5 | 2005/6 | 2006/7 | 2007/8 | 2008/9 | 2009/10 | 2010/11 |
|-----------------|--------|--------|--------|--------|--------|--------|---------|---------|
| Number recalled | 52     | 90     | 140    | 178    | 114    | 89     | 90      | 111     |

*Source*: Parole Board Annual Reports

sentence may apply for an oral hearing, but these are rarely granted. Delays awaiting Parole Board reviews compound the problems facing prisoners seeking re-release, with the result that many will serve lengthy periods in prison on recall. Even at an oral hearing (to which indeterminate sentence prisoners are entitled), a crucial factor which will affect the Board's decision will be the strength of the support of the Offender Manager. Here is not the place to discuss in detail Parole Board decision-making, save to say that their powers are severely constrained by the decisions taken by others (Hood and Shute 2000; Padfield and Liebling 2002).

### Possible alternatives to the Parole Board

Given the gravity of decisions taken by the Parole Board, the heightened media responses to any which 'go wrong', the injustices and legal actions arising from delays in the system (e.g. access to offending behaviour programmes), the inexactness of the 'science' of predicting reoffending, the limited degree to which prisoners can refute assumptions about their levels of risk or challenge decisions, and so on—it has to be asked what might be done either to improve the current system, or even replace it. The Lord Chief Justice concluded in *Brooke* (above):

> Neither the Secretary of State nor his Department has adequately addressed the need for the Parole Board to be and to be seen to be free of influence in relation to the performance of its judicial functions. Both by Directions and by the use of his control over the appointment of members of the Board the Secretary of State has sought to influence the manner in which the Board carries out its risk assessment. The close working relationship between the Board and the unit acting as its sponsor has tended to blur the distinction between the executive role of the former and the judicial role of the latter (para 78).

He was also critical of the funding restriction which stopped the Board from interviewing prisoners, contrary to its wishes:

> While this did not threaten the Board's impartiality it was interference that exceeded what could properly be justified by the role of sponsor (para 80).

The Ministry of Justice's Consultation paper *The Future of Parole* (Consultation Paper 14/09) set out options for the future status and functions of the Parole Board. Acknowledging that the Board is no longer just a body advising the Crown on the exercise of its prerogative, but has evolved into a more court-like body that makes decisions about the safe release of offenders back into the community, it asked whether the Board should be a court, a tribunal or hold some other status. Sadly, the debate seems to have frozen with the 2010 General Election.

Should serious consideration be given to the creation of a formal court with the legal duty to supervise the implementation and progress of all sentences? Halliday (2001: vii) suggested:

> Sentence management issues—such as sentence calculation and enforcement—have been the source of many difficulties. Enforcement mechanisms, in particular, are complicated and not transparent. Procedures for enforcing sentences, and penalties for breach of conditions vary greatly. There is also a sharp division of roles between sentencers who confine themselves to the immediate offences and the sentencing decision, and the prison and probation services who implement the sentences passed. Unless sentencers request progress reports, there is no procedure through which sentencers can receive feed-back from the outcomes and implications of their decisions, or take account of an offender's progress or otherwise, during the sentence—other than for drug treatment and testing orders....
>
> In order to enable courts to have a more active role in determining what is needed, not just at the point of sentence but during its course, and with better information about the outcomes of their decisions, the courts would develop and provide a 'sentence review' capacity. This new function would deal with breaches of community sentences, hear appeals against recall to prison, authorise pre-release plans, and review progress during community sentences or the community part of custodial sentences. Visible involvement of the court for the duration of the sentence would exert additional leverage over the sentenced offender, especially at the crucial stage of release from prison, but also during periods in the community, whether after release from prison, or under a community sentence. Offenders would realise that when they were under sentence in the community, whether they stayed there or faced return to prison would depend on their own good behaviour and compliance. This would also be transparent to the public. Services with an interest in the behaviour of offenders under sentence in the community—the probation and police services, and providers of electronic monitoring services—should be under explicit obligations to co-operate in the prevention of re-offending and protection of the public through work with offenders under sentence. The Parole Board would continue to operate in respect of life sentences, and the new special sentence for 'dangerous' offenders, leaving review hearings to deal with community and custodial sentences.

We would encourage further research to look at practices in other European states, particularly the increasing judicialization of the implementation of sanctions in France, with the strengthening of the position of the *juge de l'application des peines*, particularly in the last 10 years (Herzog-Evens 2012). The French expression *aménagement des peines* is difficult to translate, but in practice the courts are heavily involved in the execution of sentences, and have powers to vary their original conditions, including the length of prison terms (see Padfield 2011). *Aménagement* may take place *ab initio*, or later, when decisions will be made by a separate judicial authority: the *juge d'application des peines* or the *Tribunal de l'application des peines*, made up of three judges. The key difference between the English and French system of sentence implementation is the role given to the *juge* in France. There have, of course, been many experiments with involving judges in sentence enforcement in England: such as the short-lived drug treatment and testing orders, abolished by the Criminal Justice Act 2003, and more recent experiments with community justice courts and dedicated drugs courts (McKenna 2007). Those who breach community sentences may well be brought back to court for re-sentencing. But these various initiatives have not been developed into a coherent judicial system of sentence management or enforcement (on the advantages of which see Samuels 2004).

## CONCLUDING THOUGHTS

This chapter has looked at 'out-of-court' sanctions in order to raise some fundamental questions about current trends in criminal justice practice and therefore to point the direction for future scholarship.

The criminal justice process does not simply concern court decision-making. Many offenders do not reach a court: they are cautioned or punished by an out-of-court solution. This itself raises fundamental questions about the nature of 'criminal justice'. When criminologists discuss the extent of the criminal law, they often point out the political nature of the debate: 'tough' politicians talking up crime, and creating more criminal offences (see Downes and Morgan, this volume). There is theoretical and jurisprudential debate on the proper limits of the criminal law (see Simester and von Hirsch 2011, for example). But what is missing is the wider application of that debate. When are waste management laws, or laws against dropping litter, or EU laws against unfair competition simply 'administrative' and not 'truly' criminal? When we discuss 'administrative penalties', we must be careful to distinguish the administrative imposition of criminal sanctions from purely administrative regulation. We would suggest that the difference, whilst difficult to identify, is important.

So, first, we have to decide what is 'truly' criminal. Cautions and PNDs are very clearly imposed for criminal offences. We would suggest that to call PNDs, for example, 'administrative' penalties is misleading: these are sanctions for truly criminal offences. When they are imposed administratively, extra vigilance is necessary to ensure that they are properly imposed, respecting the procedural rights of all parties. Not only should the suspect enjoy 'normal' due process safeguards against abuse of power, but victims, too, should be informed about the outcome of proceedings. The rights of offenders to fair treatment and due process should be respected throughout the criminal justice process, including during the implementation of the sanction.

Sanctions, especially increases in the burdens of a sanction, must be appropriate and proportionate. We have in this chapter asked many questions about the out-of-court sanctions which divert people from the court system (FPNs, PNDs, cautions, and conditional cautions) as well as the 'out-of-court' release and recall processes applied to prisoners. The Parole Board—still a non-judicial body, albeit often acting in a more 'court-like' fashion than in the past—has come to occupy a central role in major quasi-sentencing decisions about a large and rapidly growing number of offenders defined as 'dangerous' or 'risky'. These decisions, often based on decisions taken 'administratively' earlier in the sentence by prison or probation staff, must be made in ways which are transparent and accountable.

This raises another question we have not discussed: what constitutes a court? And why are courts important? What is 'wrong' with the Parole Board? Constitutional theory and practice require the judiciary to maintain an oversight of the executive for good reasons concerned with good governance, the rule of law, and the separation of powers. In this area, we suggest that the longstop of judicial review is an inadequate check on the abuse of executive power, and an independent court or tribunal should have regular review of all criminal justice decisions.

The debate should not stop with the examples raised in this chapter. For example, the role of the Youth Offending Panels (YOPs, see Morgan and Newburn, this volume) could as easily have formed part of our discussion. Why have YOPs replaced the magistrates as the principal decision-making body for many offences committed by children? It may well be that the magistrates' court had become a body which the new Labour Government in 1997 did not trust with its new crime policies for young people, but we need to question whether there is enough judicial oversight of these 'out-of-court' solutions. Is the YOP adequately accountable for its decisions? Why was the magistrates' court not reformed, rather than this invention of another out-of-court arrangement?

Another example: MAPPA (Multi-Agency Public Protection Arrangements) are 'statutory arrangements for managing all sexual and some violent offenders. MAPPA is not a statutory body in itself but is a mechanism through which the police, prison and probation services can better discharge their statutory responsibilities and protect the public in a co-ordinated manner with co-operation from other statutory agencies, including local authorities, health, housing authorities and education authorities' (House of Commons Justice Committee 2011: para. 157). MAPPAs exercise significant powers and have an enormous impact on people's lives (see Hoyle, this volume; Wood and Kemshall 2007). One of the functions of this chapter is to question whether this form of non-court decision-making is adequately transparent.

Of course, we are not suggesting that courts are the solutions to many of the problems faced by a criminal justice system. Courts are reliant upon the decisions of others made earlier in the process: the police to arrest, the probation officer to initiate breach proceedings or to recall a prisoner to prison. We argue simply that criminologists and criminal justice scholars should keep their eyes on the less visible criminal justice processes as well the more open and transparent. Out of court should not be out of sight.

### ■ SELECTED FURTHER READING

Regarding the growth and nature of out-of-court penalties there is as yet little material and no substitute for study of the most recent Ministry of Justice *Criminal Statistics* and *Offender Management Caseload Statistics*, though Morgan's (2008), *Summary justice: Fast—but Fair?* (accessible from the Centre for Crime and Justice Studies website) remains a useful introduction alongside Lord Falconer's (2006), *Doing Law Differently*, which sets out the Labour Government's rationale for their development. Regarding executive release and recall the annual reports of the Parole Board provide an essential reference point and Arnott and Creighton's (2010), *Parole Board Hearings Law and Practice* is the best legal guide. Hood's 1975 article 'The case against executive control over time in custody', Hood and Shute's 2000 study, *The parole system at work: a study of risk based decision-making*, and Padfield's 2007 edited collection of essays, *Who to Release? Parole, Fairness and Criminal Justice*, all provide valuable critical appraisals.

# ■ REFERENCES

ABADINSKY, H. (2008), *Probation and Parole: Theory and Practice,* 10th ed, New York: Prentice Hall.

AMERICAN FRIENDS SERVICE COMMITTEE (1971), *Struggle for Justice: A Report on Crime and Punishment in America*, New York: Farrar Straus & Giroux.

APPLETON, C. (2010), *Life after Life Imprisonment*, Oxford: Oxford University Press.

ARNOTT, H. and CREIGHTON, S. (2010), *Parole Board Hearings Law and Practice*, 2nd edn, London: LAG.

ASHWORTH, A. (2010), *Principles of Criminal Law*, Oxford: Oxford University Press.

—— and REDMAYNE, M. (2010), *The Criminal Process*, 4th edn, Oxford: Oxford University Press.

BOEKHOUT VAN SOLINGE, T. (2002), *Drugs and Decision-Making in the European Union*, Amsterdam: CEDRO/Mets en Schilt.

BINGHAM, T. (2010), *The Rule of Law*, London: Allen Lane.

BLAIR, T. (2005), Speech to launch a Respect and Parenting Order Task Force, Hertfordshire, 2 September.

—— (2006), 'Our Nation's Future: Criminal Justice', Speech delivered at University of Bristol, 23 June.

—— (2010), *A Journey,* London: Hutchinson.

BLAKEBOROUGH, L. and PIERPOINT, H. (2007), *Conditional Cautions: An Examination of the Early Implementation of the Scheme*, Ministry of Justice Research Summary 7, London: Ministry of Justice.

BOTTOMS, A. E. (1977), 'Reflections on the Renaissance of Dangerousness', *Howard Journal*, Vol. 16, 2: 70-96.

CARROLL, J., WIENER, R., COATES, D., GALEGHER, J., and ALIBRIO, J. (1982), 'Evaluation, Diagnosis and Prediction in Parole Decision-making', *Law and Society Review*, 17(1): 199–228.

COLLINS, H. (2007), 'A Consideration of Discretion, Offender Attributes and the Process of Recall', in N. Padfield (ed.), *Who to Release? Parole, Fairness and Criminal Justice*, Cullompton: Willan Publishing.

COOK, D. (1989), *Rich Law, Poor law*, Milton Keynes: Open University Press.

—— (2006), *Criminal and Social Justice*, London: Sage.

CRASSIATI, J. and SINDALL, O. (2009), 'Serious Further Offences: an exploration of risk and typologies', *Probation Journal*, 56:9.

CRIMINAL JUSTICE SYSTEM (2002), *Justice for All*, Cm 5563, London: Her Majesty's Stationery Office. Available at www.cps.gov.uk/publications/docs/jfawhitepaper.pdf.

DARBYSHIRE, P. (1991), 'The Lamp that Shows that Freedom Lives: is it worth the candle?', *Criminal Law Review*, 740.

DIGARD, L. (2010), 'When legitimacy is denied: Offender perceptions of the prison recall system', *Probation Journal*, 57: 43.

DINGWALL, G. and HARDING, C. (1998), *Diversion in the Criminal Process*, London: Sweet and Maxwell.

DITTON, P. and WILSON, D. (1999), *Truth in Sentencing in State Prisons*, Bureau of Statistics Special Report, Washington, DC: US Department of Statistics.

FALCONER, LORD (2006), *Doing Law Differently*, London: DCA.

FLANAGAN REPORT (2008), *The Review of Policing by Sir Ronnie Flanagan: Final Report*, London: HMIC.

FULWOOD, I. (2003), *History of the Federal Parole System*, Washington, DC: US Department of Justice. www.justice.gov/uspc/history.pdf.

HALPERN, D. (2010), *The Hidden Wealth of Nations*, Cambridge: Polity.

HALLIDAY, J. (2001), *Making Punishments Work: Report of a Review of the Sentencing Framework for England and Wales*, London: Home Office. http://webarchive. nationalarchives.gov.uk/+/http://www.homeoffice. gov.uk/documents/halliday-report-sppu/.

HAWKINS, K. (2003), *Law as Last Resort*, Oxford: Oxford University Press.

HM INSPECTORATE OF CONSTABULARY/HM INSPECTORATE OF THE CPS (2011), *Exercising Discretion: the Gateway to Justice*, London: Criminal Justice Joint Inspection.

HM INSPECTORATE OF PRISONS (2005), *Recalled Prisoners: A Short Review of Recalled Adult Male Determinate-sentenced Prisoners*.

HERZOG-EVANS, M. (2012), *Droit de l'Exécution des Peines*, Paris: Dalloz.

HOME OFFICE (1965), *The Adult Offender*, Cmnd. 2852, London: Her Majesty's Stationery Office.

—— (2006), *Strengthening Powers to Tackle Anti-Social Behaviour: Consultation Paper*, London: Home Office.

HOOD, R. (1974), 'Some fundamental dilemmas of the English Parole System', in D. A. Thomas (ed.), *Parole: Its Implications for the Penal and Criminal Justice System*, Cambridge: Institute of Criminology.

—— (1975), 'The case against executive control over time in custody', *Criminal Law Review*, 33: 545–52.

—— and SHUTE, S. (2000), 'The parole system at work: a study of risk based decision-making', Home Office Research Study No. 202.

——, ——, FEILZER, M., and WILCOX, A. (2002), 'Sex offenders emerging from long-term imprisonment', *British Journal of Criminology*, [42]: 371–94.

HOUSE OF COMMONS COMMITTEE OF PUBLIC ACCOUNTS (2006), *The Electronic Monitoring of Adult Offenders* (HC 997), London: Stationery Office.

HOUSE OF COMMONS JUSTICE COMMITTEE (2008), *Towards Effective Sentencing* (HC 184), London: Stationery Office.

HUDSON, K., MAGUIRE, M., and RAYNOR, P. (2007), 'Through the Prison Gate: Resettlement,' 'Offender Management and the Birth of the "Seamless

Sentence'", in Y. Jewkes, *Handbook of Prisons*, Devon: Willan.

JACOBSON, J. and HOUGH, M. (2010), *Unjust Deserts: Imprisonment for Public Protection*, London: Prison Reform Trust.

JANSSON, K., BUDD, S., LOVBAKKE, J., MOLEY, S., and THORPE, S. (2007), *Attitudes, perceptions and risks of crime: Supplementary Volume 1 to Crime in England and Wales 2006/7*, Home Office Statistical Bulletin 19/07, London: Home Office.

JONES, T. and NEWBURN, T. (2007), *Policy Transfer and Criminal Justice*, Maidenhead: Open University Press.

JUDGE, Lord (2011), 'Summary Justice in and out of court', The Police Foundation's John Harris Memorial Lecture. www.judiciary.gov.uk/Resources/JCO/Documents/Speeches/lcj-speech-john-harris-lecture.pdf.

JUSTICE (2009), *A New Parole System for England and Wales*. www.justice.org.uk.

KLIP, A. (2009), *European Criminal Law: An Integrative Approach*, Antwerp: Intersentia.

MAGUIRE, M. (1988), 'Parole', in E. Stockdale and S. Casale (eds), *Criminal Justice Under Stress*, London: Blackstone Press.

MARIE, O., MORETON, K., and GONCALVES, M. (2011), *The effect of early release of prisoners on Home Detention Curfew (HDC) on recidivism*, Research Summary No. 11, London: Ministry of Justice. www.justice.gov.uk/downloads/publications/research-and-analysis/moj-research/effect-early-release-hdc-recidivism.pdf.

MINISTRY OF JUSTICE (2009a), *Prison Population Projections 2009–2015*, Ministry of Justice Statistics bulletin, London: Ministry of Justice.

—— (2009), *Story of the prison population 1995–2009 England and Wales*, Ministry of Justice Statistics bulletin, London: Ministry of Justice.

—— (2009b), *The Future of the Parole Board*, Consultation Paper 14/09, London: Ministry of Justice.

—— (2010), *Criminal Statistics 2009: England and Wales*, London: National Statistics.

—— (2011a), *Criminal Justice Statistics Quarterly Update to March 2011*, Ministry of Justice.

—— (2011b), *Provisional figures relating to offenders serving indeterminate sentence of imprisonment for public protection (IPPs)*, London: Ministry of Justice. www.justice.gov.uk/downloads/publica-tions/statistics-and-data/mojstats/provisional-ipp-figures.pdf.

—— (2011c), *Offender Management Caseload Statistics, 2010 Tables*, London: Ministry of Justice. www.justice.gov.uk/publications/statistics-and-data/prisons-and-probation/oms-quarterly.htm.

MITSILEGAS, V. (2009), *EU Criminal Law*, Oxford: Hart Publishing.

MORGAN, N. (1983), 'The shaping of parole in England and Wales', *Criminal Law Review*, 131–51.

MORGAN, R. (2008), *Summary justice: Fast—but Fair?*, London: Kings College Centre for Crime and Justice Studies.

NUTTALL, C. *et al.* (1977), *Parole in England and Wales*, Home Office Research Study No. 38, London: Her Majesty's Stationery Office.

PADFIELD, N. (2002), *Beyond the Tariff: Human rights and the release of life sentence prisoners*, Devon: Willan.

—— (ed.) (2007), *Who to release? Parole, fairness and criminal justice*, Devon: Willan.

—— (2008), *Text and Materials on the Criminal Justice Process*, 4th edn, Oxford: Oxford University Press.

—— (2011), 'An Entente Cordiale in Sentencing?', *Criminal Law and Justice Weekly*, 175: 239, 256, 271, and 290.

—— and LIEBLING, A. (2000), *An Exploration of Decision-Making at Discretionary Lifer Panels*, Home Office Research Study No. 213, London: Home Office.

—— and MARUNA, S. (2006), 'The Revolving Door at the Prison Gate: Exploring the Dramatic Increase in Recalls to Prison', *Criminology and Criminal Justice*, 6: 329.

——, VAN ZYL SMIT, D., and DÜNKEL, F. (eds) (2010), *Release from prison—European policy and practice*, Devon: Willan.

PAROLE BOARD (2007), *Annual Report and Accounts 2006/07, the Parole Board for England and Wales*, HC 1022, London: The Stationery Office.

—— (2010), *Annual Report and Accounts 2009/10, the Parole Board for England and Wales*, HC 162, London: The Stationery Office.

—— (2011a), *Annual Report and Accounts 2010/11, the Parole Board for England and Wales*, HC 1363, London: The Stationery Office.

—— (2011b), *The Parole Board for England and Wales: Practice Guidance for Oral Hearings*, London: Justice website. www.justice.gov.uk/guidance/prison-probation-and-rehabilitation/parole-board/oral-hearings.htm.

POVEY D., HAND, T., RISHARAJ A., and MULCHANDANI, R. (2010), *Police Powers and Procedure, England and Wales 2008/09*, Home Office Statistical Bulletin, London: National Statistics.

PRISON REFORM TRUST (2005), *Recycling Offenders through Prison*, Prison Reform Trust.

—— (2007), *Indefinitely Maybe? How the Indeterminate Sentence for Public Protection is Unjust and Unsustainable*, London: Prison Reform Trust. www.prisonreformtrust.org.uk/Portals/0/Documents/Indefinitely Maybe—IPP briefing.pdf.

ROYAL COMMISSION ON CRIMINAL JUSTICE (chair, Viscount Runciman) (1993), *Report*, Cmnd. 2263, London: Her Majesty's Stationery Office.

SAMUELS, H. H., JUDGE, J. (2004), 'Judicial Sentence Review: a "carrot and stick" approach to rehabilita-tion', *Criminal Justice Matters*, 32: 32.

SANDERS, A. and YOUNG, R. (2010), *Criminal Justice*, 4th edn, London: Butterworths.

SHUTE, S. (2004), 'Does parole work? The empirical evidence from England and Wales', *Ohio State Journal of Criminal Law*, 2: 315–31.

SIMESTER, A. and von Hirsch, A. (2011), *Crimes, Harms and Wrongs*, Oxford: Hart.

STEER, D. (1970), *Police Cautions—a Study in the Exercise of Police Discretion*, Oxford University Penal Research Unit, Occasional Paper No. 2, Oxford: Basil Blackwell.

TAK, P. J. P. (1983), *The Legal Scope for Non-Prosecution in Europe*, Helsinki: HEUNI.

TYLER, T. R. (1990), *Why People Obey the Law*, New Haven: Yale University Press.

—— (2010), 'Legitimacy in Corrections: Policy Implications', *Criminology and Public Policy*, 9: 127.

VAN ZYL SMIT, D. and SNACKEN, S. (2009), *Principles of European Prison Law and Policy: Penology and Human Rights*, Oxford: Oxford University Press.

VON HIRSCH, A. (1976), *Doing Justice*, New York: Hill and Wang.

WILKINS, L. (1969), *Evaluation of Penal Measures*, New York: Random House.

WOOD, P. B. and DUNAWAY, R. G. (2003), 'Consequences of Truth in Sentencing: The Mississippi Case', *Punishment and Society*, 5(3): 139–54.

YOUNG, R. (2008), 'Street Policing after PACE: The Drift to Summary Justice', in E. Cape and R. Young (eds), *Regulating Policing*, Oxford: Hart.

# 33

# OFFENDER TREATMENT AND REHABILITATION: WHAT WORKS?

*Friedrich Lösel*

Offender rehabilitation is very much a live topic in many Western countries. In the United Kingdom, for example, the current government has announced a 'revolution in the rehabilitation of offenders' as a crime policy priority (Ministry of Justice 2010), even though revolutions are normally feared by political leaders. However, the UK Government wants only to express new ambitious aims with regard to effectiveness and cost-benefit going beyond the existing Crime Reduction Programme of the previous Labour regime (Carter 2003; Maguire 2004). The topic of rehabilitation is not just current: it has a long history. Nearly 300 years ago, one of the pioneers of criminology pleaded for the abolition of torture, cruel punishment, and the death penalty and also for more specific deterrence instead of retribution (Beccaria 1764; see also the utilitarian concept of Bentham 1830). In the late nineteenth century the future orientation of criminal law was particularly emphasized by von Liszt (1882/83). He differentiated between three groups of offenders. The first group do not need a basic change; for them deterrence by routine sanctions is appropriate. The second group is not willing and able to improve their behaviour, and should therefore be rendered innocuous by long-term or lifetime incarceration. The third group is able to change, but need reformative treatment and education to desist from crime. More than a century later, such concepts remained current (Walker 1991) and today incorrigible offenders may be subsumed under labels such as 'psychopathy', whereas the third group is the main target of rehabilitation, re-socialization, or correctional treatment measures which are the topic of this chapter.

This chapter will focus on empirical research that plays a vital role for penal policy (Hood 2002). There is no space to discuss terminological details of the above-mentioned and related terms such as resettlement or reintegration (see Morgan and Owers 2001; Raynor and Robinson 2005). Traditionally, 'rehabilitation' refers to regeneration of a previous state. This can be seen as reintegration into society, although one may ask whether offenders from deprived backgrounds have ever been integrated and whether modern societies are characterized more by individualization and subcultures. Similar issues apply to the term 're-socialization'. Here one must be aware that socialization is not a one-way process, but indicates an interaction between individuals and their social context. Other terms such as 'correctional treatment' or 'offender treatment' sound more medical or psychological. However, they do not imply that the offender needs to be cured of a mental health problem; the respective interventions may include psychotherapy or medical treatment as well as, for example, education, vocational training, and supervision. Pragmatically, all these terms have in common reference to measures and processes that aim to reduce reoffending. In different countries this basic aim may be complemented by broader objectives such as regular employment, positive social relations, adequate accommodation, mental health, and other indicators of a 'good life' (e.g. Ward and Brown 2004).

Most civilized societies include the reduction of reoffending among their penal aims. In practice this objective varies according to the emphasis given to the aims of protection of the public, positive and negative general deterrence, and retribution. These differences and related variations in criminal laws, sentencing practices, criminal justice system structures, financial resources, staff attitudes, and general public opinion suggest caution in generalizing empirical findings with regard to offender rehabilitation across countries and cultures. Bearing that in mind, the chapter will give a brief overview of what works in this field. It will first address the development from 'nothing works' to 'what works'. Then the main findings from evaluations of correctional treatment will be presented with regard to types of programmes and many other influences on outcome. There then follows a discussion of current controversies about the 'what works' movement. The chapter will end with conclusions and recommendations for future policy, practice, and research.

## FROM 'NOTHING WORKS' TO 'WHAT WORKS'

After mainly psychodynamic approaches to offender treatment in the first decades of the twentieth century (Aichhorn 1925; Healy and Bronner 1936), there was a strong increase of rehabilitation programmes from the 1960s onwards (Palmer 1992). The development was related to the widespread belief in the potential of social programmes that emerged during the Kennedy era in the United States. California was in the forefront of states which implemented a range of custodial and community rehabilitation programmes. There was also great optimism about offender treatment in European countries. These positive expectations came to an abrupt halt when Lipton, Martinson, and Wilks (1975) carried out a comprehensive review of 231 evaluations of correctional treatment programmes. Martinson's (1974) pre-publication of this review led to the widely cited doctrine of 'nothing works'. However, the real message was the lack of methodologically sound evaluations that did not allow a definite answer on the effects of offender rehabilitation. Although the review contained thorough analyses it suffered from mere counting of significant versus non-significant results ('vote counting'). As the statistical power of evaluations depends on the sample size, many small-scale studies could show positive non-significant effects, whereas their integration would have led to a large total sample and a highly significant effect.

The article of Martinson was both criticized (Gendreau 1981; Palmer 1975) and supported by other data (Sechrest *et al.* 1979). Its widespread influence was probably not primarily due to the presented facts, but to their fit to various political orientations. For example, it offered comfort to heterogeneous groups who: advocated a policy of tough punishment; wanted to avoid the costs of rehabilitation programmes; feared the forced personality change of offenders; were against an increase in informal decisions; or saw the primary aim of criminal justice as 'just deserts' punishment (von Hirsch 1976). However, although offender rehabilitation ranked temporarily low on the list of crime policies, there was less change in daily practice. Some time later correctional treatment enjoyed a renaissance (Hood 1993; Lösel 1993; Palmer 1992). This was partially due to new evidence resulting from more sound evaluation studies and, in particular, the emergence of systematic reviews and meta-analyses that replaced vote counting by integrative computations of effect size (Andrews *et al.* 1990; Garrett 1985; Lösel and Köferl 1989; Lipsey 1992a). These more adequate research syntheses generally showed positive treatment effects. Over time, this finding has been replicated by numerous meta-analyses on more than 600 evaluations. Figure 33.1 contains some examples.

Although the characteristics of the studies included in these reviews varied substantially, the positive effect remained (Lipsey and Cullen 2007; Lösel 1995a; McGuire 2002a). The typical mean effects of correctional interventions vary between *d*-coefficients of approximately 0.10 and 0.30 with an estimated mean of $d = 0.20$ plus/minus 0.05. This positive effect is small, but by no means trivial. If, for example, the recidivism rate in the control group is 50 per cent, the respective rate in the treated group would be 40 per cent, a reduction of 10 percentage points.

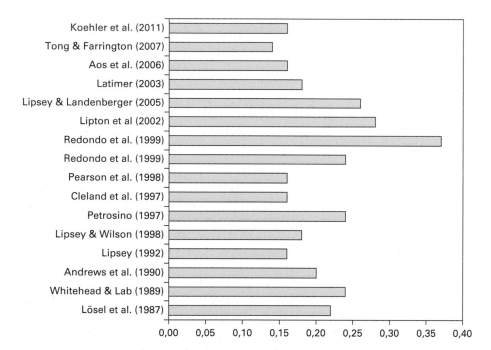

**Figure 33.1** Average effect sizes of various meta-analyses on correctional treatment
*Source*: Lösel (2011)

Such mean effect sizes are rather small in comparison to psychotherapy in general (Lipsey and Wilson 1993; Smith *et al.* 1980). However, whereas patients with anxieties or depression, for example, often have a strong motivation to change and are treated in supportive contexts, offender treatment is more or less coerced and frequently embedded in a non-therapeutic milieu. Further, many offenders have problems of substance misuse and are not well educated or verbally skilled. The main outcome measure is objective recidivism after several years, whereas general psychotherapy research often uses subjective indicators after shorter time periods.

The overall encouraging results of early meta-analyses on correctional treatment led to the question of what is more or less, or not at all, effective. This 'what works' movement was triggered by more than empirical research. In accordance with theories of policy diffusion and agenda setting (Kingdon 2003; Windlesham 1998) there was awareness of existing problems, not the least of which was the growing cost of failing penal policies. Particularly relevant were media reports of extreme cases of sexual and violent offending that led to serious concerns among the general public and policy makers. More punitive policies increased incarceration rates in many countries (Walmsley 2008), and California, the former pioneer state in rehabilitation, even introduced the 'three strikes' rule. On the other hand, expensive incarceration policies did not solve the problem of frequent reoffending and 'what works' thinking therefore attracted active interest groups and policy-makers.

## VARIOUS TYPES OF CORRECTIONAL PROGRAMMES

Space considerations dictate that in what follows some types of interventions must be lumped together and can be addressed only briefly. The focus is on measures for which at least a few controlled evaluations of reoffending are available. Other approaches such as faith-based programmes (Boddie and Cnaan 2006) require more sound evaluations (Aos *et al.* 2006).

### PUNISHMMENT, DETERRENCE, AND INTENSIVE SUPERVISION

Nearly all modes of offender treatment are embedded in or linked to the basically punitive measures of criminal justice. One must therefore begin by asking whether punishment, deterrence, and intensive control of criminals is not sufficient or perhaps more effective than the treatment measures that have the incorrect image of being softer? Punishment is popular among the general public and policy-makers who want to demonstrate they are tough on crime. However, although punishment is the most traditional reaction to offending, its empirical effects are not well-known. This is partly due to the legal difficulty attending controlled evaluations with groups who have carried out similar offences, but who, for research purposes, have been differentially sentenced.

Various studies have addressed the effects of imprisonment. Using matching procedures, Wermink *et al.* (2010) showed that first-time imprisonment may even have a criminogenic effect compared to community sanctions. Gaes and Camp (2009) came to similar conclusions in an experimental study of security level placements. Systematic reviews have revealed that custodial instead of community sanctions or longer instead of shorter prison sentences lead to slightly higher reoffending rates or at least non-significant differences (Killias *et al.* 2006; Pearson *et al.* 1997; Smith *et al.* 2002). In a recent comprehensive literature review Durlauf and Nagin (2011) found that imprisonment has no deterrent but a small criminogenic effect. The authors did not address the combined impact of custodial treatment programmes, but research in the latter field also showed some advantage of community programmes (Lipsey and Cullen 2007; Lösel and Schmucker 2005).

Of course, the function of custody goes beyond the target of reducing reoffending (see above) and significant numbers of ex-inmates do not reoffend: this may be due to self-critical reflection, protection from criminogenic networks in the community, or merely getting older. However, we must be aware that some undesirable consequences of incarceration are not only relevant for 'pure punishment', but also for rehabilitation-oriented custody (e.g. contamination effects, identification with subcultures, break-up of social relations, and stigmatization after release).

The finding that first-time imprisonment fails to deter is consistent with evaluations of 'shock incarceration' or 'scared straight' programmes. Here, juvenile offenders make visits to, or have short stays in, prisons with particularly tough regimes and housing many prolific offenders exhibiting intimidating behaviour. In contrast to the expectation of a negative reinforcement or deterrent effect, systematic reviews demonstrate higher instead of lower reoffending among participants of such programmes (Lipsey and Wilson 1998; Petrosino *et al.* 2003). Perhaps, the young men are impressed and attracted by the macho subculture.

Deterrence is also one underlying rationale for boot camps for juvenile or adult offenders. These institutions have tough regimes similar to basic military training camps (e.g. strict execution of command and obedience, challenging physical exercise, and immediate punishment for misbehaviour). Boot camp programmes vary widely and their tough regimes are sometimes combined with psychosocial treatment and education. Yet despite the common sense attractiveness of the concept (particularly in the United States), systematic reviews have revealed no effect (Aos *et al.* 2001; MacKenzie *et al.* 2001). The mean effect size is around zero, with a large variation from positive to negative outcomes in single studies. There is some indication that only boot camps with educational and treatment components may have a rehabilitative effect (MacKenzie 2006). As the classic boot camps reduced neither reoffending nor prison crowding or saved public money, a dozen of US states have abolished them since the late 1990s (Bergin 2011).

The findings on intensive supervision, intermediate sanctions, or 'smart punishment' programmes in the community are similar. Some reviews have revealed zero to small positive effects of such measures in comparison to routine parole, probation, fines, or diversion (Aos *et al.* 2001, 2006; Lipsey and Wilson 1998; Pearson *et al.* 1997; Smith *et al.* 2002). However, criminogenic effects have also been recorded

(Andrews *et al.* 1990a; Gendreau *et al.* 2000). Intensive community supervision (i.e. a reduced caseload for probation officers) only seems to be effective when accompanied by some form of treatment (Aos *et al.* 2006). Potentially positive effects of intensive supervision may also be counteracted by an enhanced risk of failure due to the closer monitoring and violation of licensing orders. The same applies to the popular measures of electronic monitoring. Although there are some promising findings, better controlled studies are needed (Renzema and Mayo-Wilson 2005). The mean effect size in the meta-analysis of Aos *et al.* (2006) was zero.

As mentioned above, all these measures of mere punishment, deterrence, and control can be justified for various penal reasons. However, as stand-alone interventions they do not reduce reoffending. We need to ask what more rehabilitative measures can achieve, therefore.

## EDUCATIONAL AND VOCATIONAL TRAINING

A substantial proportion of offenders have a background of low school achievement, early school dropout and problems in reading, writing, and numeracy. As a result of these deficits and accompanying motivation problems, alcohol misuse, and juvenile delinquency, many repeat offenders have few, if any, vocational qualifications and frequent histories of unemployment. Employment and stable integration in the labour market are important factors for desistance from crime (Farrall 2002; Maruna 2001; Sampson and Laub 1993). For these and other reasons, basic education and vocational training programmes are core elements of offender rehabilitation. Yet there is surprisingly little well-controlled evaluation on these measures. The few systematic reviews show that academic education and vocational training programmes make a significant contribution to reducing reoffending (MacKenzie 2006; Wilson *et al.* 2000). However, there is not yet consistent evidence for a rehabilitative effect of prison work and non-custodial employment programmes (MacKenzie 2006; Visher *et al.* 2006; Wilson *et al.* 2000). More controlled evaluations and differentiated analyses of essential programme features are needed. Employment and work programmes may be successful only if the respective qualifications are valued by the labour market and accompanied by the personal skills necessary to retain a job (Romig 1978). Such measures should not be seen in isolation, therefore, but in combination with psychosocial treatment programmes and motivational modules.

## COGNITIVE-BEHAVIOURAL TREATMENT

The best replicated findings from the 'what works' research refer to cognitive-behavioural treatment (CBT). Such programmes are based on theories of social learning, information processing, action, and moral reasoning and contain sessions on self-reflection, anger management, self-control, social skills training, interpersonal problem solving, considering action alternatives, value-orientation, perspective taking/empathy, and pro-social roles (Andrews and Bonta 2010; Bandura 1973; Hollin and Palmer 2009). CBT programmes vary with regard to structure, content, and intensity (e.g. between 20 and 200 sessions). Typical examples are Reasoning and Rehabilitation

(Ross and Ross 1995), Aggression Replacement Training (Goldstein, Glick, and Gibbs 1988), the Enhanced Thinking Skills, and the more recent integrated Thinking Skills Programme of the National Offender Management Service (NOMS).

Meta-analyses have shown that CBT programmes are successful (Andrews *et al.* 1990; Aos *et al.* 2006; Garrett 1985; Koehler *et al.* 2011a; Landenberger and Lipsey 2005; Lipsey and Cullen 2007; Lipsey and Wilson 1998; Pearson *et al.* 2002; Redondo *et al.* 2002; Tong and Farrington 2006). Depending on the specific programme, target groups, research design, and many other variables, CBT programmes can reduce reoffending by between approximately 10 and 30 per cent. Although some developers advertise their own programmes as if they were magic bullets, no single concept has proved clearly superior. However, specific CBT components seem to be more important for a positive effect than others, in particular modules on anger control, interpersonal problem solving, and cognitive skills training (Jolliffe and Farrington 2009; Landenberger and Lipsey 2005). Programmes also differ in how much they focus on cognitive aspects, concrete social skills, or basic behaviour modification techniques. The latter approach is controversial because reinforcement of positive behaviour may not last beyond the specific context and aversive techniques can have negative side effects. However, systematic reviews suggest that behavioural methods such as reinforcement and contingency management are effective, particularly in the treatment of young offenders (Koehler *et al.* 2011a; Lipsey 2009; Lipsey and Wilson 1998).

CBT has shown positive effects with a broad range of target groups and problems. For example, the above-mentioned meta-analyses covered both juvenile and adult offenders. Female offenders also benefit from CBT programmes (Dowden and Andrews 1999). Although most research has addressed general and violent offenders, meta-analyses have revealed positive outcomes for drug or alcohol-addicted offenders (Holloway *et al.* 2008; Lipsey and Wilson 1998; Mitchell *et al.* 2007; Pearson and Lipton 1999) as have evaluations of drug courts, which often combine judicial action and intensive supervision with CBT elements (Wilson *et al.* 2006; Lowenkamp *et al.* 2005). However, most evaluations of CBT programmes for drug-addicted offenders have been carried out in North America and though such interventions are widespread in Europe, few sound studies have been undertaken on this side of the Atlantic (Hamilton *et al.* 2011). Meta-analyses have further demonstrated that CBT is effective for sexual offenders (Hanson *et al.* 2002; Lösel and Schmucker 2005; Schmucker and Lösel 2009) and this holds true when other study characteristics are controlled for.

## THERAPEUTIC COMMUNITIES, MILIEU THERAPY, AND SOCIAL THERAPEUTIC PRISONS

Therapeutic communities (TCs) and milieu therapy aim for a more comprehensive approach to rehabilitation than circumscribed offending behaviour programmes. They can be implemented in custody as well as in community residential care institutions (Cullen and Woodward 1997). There are various TC models (Roberts 1997). Typically: people live together; have informal non-hierarchical relationships; share information; are committed to the goal of learning; strive for an open resolution of problems; are sensitive to the psychodynamic of individual and group processes; and follow a basic set of boundaries concerning roles, time, and place (Kennard 1994). TCs originally placed particular emphasis on democratic processes and inmates' self-governing, but various TCs are now more hierarchic and structured. They contain a therapeutic social climate and regime, intensive contact between staff and inmates, relatively large numbers of therapeutic staff, sensitivity to group dynamics, various modes of therapy, appropriate responsibilities, control and reward systems, and a graduated opening to the world outside. The specific form of social-therapeutic prisons in Germany is similar to hierarchical TCs, but shares basic organizational structures with regular custody (Lösel and Egg 1997). In both concepts, manual-based offending behaviour programmes can be integrated as one element of treatment among others.

TCs and milieu-oriented approaches are particularly appropriate for offenders with personality disorders and accumulated other problems. Systematic reviews have shown overall positive effects (Lösel 1995b; Lees et al. 1999; Lipton et al. 2002). The mean effect sizes are smaller than those of sound CBT programmes (Aos et al. 2001), but one must also take the often rather difficult target groups into account. TCs and social-therapeutic prisons seem to work not only for groups of general and violent offenders but also with drug-addicted delinquents (Holloway et al. 2008; Mitchell et al. 2007; Pearson and Lipton 1999). They can provide a therapeutic environment for sexual offenders though targeted programmes for these groups need to be included as well (Lösel 2000; Lösel and Schmucker 2005).

## MULTISYSTEMIC THERAPY (MST) AND FAMILY-ORIENTED PROGRAMMES

MST and similar programmes are intensive, short term, family- and community-based interventions for juvenile offenders (Henggeler et al. 2009; Borduin et al. 1995) which are now more broadly used for both treatment and preventive purposes. MST aims to reduce reoffending, drug misuse, out-of-home placements, school failure, and other problems. It works with the young people and their family, but also with peer groups, schools, extended families, neighbourhoods, community services, healthcare, and juvenile justice. Similar to milieu therapy it requires qualified therapeutic staff, although the focus is the youths' social system. The approach is structured and manual-based, but not as standardized as CBT programmes. It uses broader therapeutic principles: match the youngster's problems and his/her systemic context; focus on strengths as well as deficits; increase responsibility; present- and action-oriented; target behavioural sequences in the system; develop appropriate behaviour; promote continuity in effort; ensure evaluation and accountability; and generalize application. The concrete interventions depend on the respective case.

Evaluations have demonstrated positive effects of MST on delinquency, violence, substance abuse, and school achievement (Borduin et al. 1995; Henggeler et al. 2009; Ogden and Hagen 2006). Meta-analyses have revealed significant reductions in recidivism for MST and similar family-based approaches (Aos et al. 2001; Curtis et al, 2004; Farrington and Welsh 2007; Latimer 2001; Lipsey and Wilson 1998; Schmucker and Lösel 2009). However, some primary studies have generated less positive findings (Leschied and Cunningham 2002; Sundell et al. 2008) and others have contained design problems or were carried out by the programme developers themselves (Littell 2006). These shortcomings are not specific for MST and suggest the need for further research.

## LOW-STRUCTURED COUNSELLING AND THERAPEUTIC APPROACHES

Although manual-based CBT programmes are now widely used in offender rehabilitation, there are also less structured interventions. These contain counselling and therapeutic approaches based on theoretically unspecific concepts of traditional case work or psychodynamic and humanistic concepts of psychotherapy. They aim to realize basic therapeutic principles such as emotional acceptance, empathy, openness, mutual bonding, and support between clients and professionals or within treatment groups. Psychodynamic approaches in particular may address core conflicts and defence mechanisms, however, this is normally done in a more structured and educative format. Sigmund Freud and early psychoanalysts already maintained that anti-social clients often lack bonding and emotional transference as well as ego strengths that hinder the classical 'talking cure' (Aichhorn 1925).

Early meta-analyses did not support low-structured counselling and non-cognitive behavioural concepts of therapy (Andrews *et al.* 1990; Garrett 1985; Lipsey 1992a). Other reviews have painted a more favourable picture, although effects are smaller than for CBT (Koehler *et al.* 2011a; Lipsey and Wilson 1998; Pearson *et al.* 1997; Redondo *et al.* 1999). The mixed results may be partially due to the heterogeneity and more individualized content of such approaches that lead to lower programme integrity. The relationship and interaction characteristics that play a key role in these approaches (e.g. basic acceptance, cooperation, and empathy) are important in all kinds of psychotherapy (Orlinsky *et al.* 1994). They are essential in therapeutic communities and systemic approaches and may provide value in addition to fully structured programmes. A basic therapeutic philosophy is also relevant for interventions with juvenile offenders (Lipsey 2009). Although the evidence does not suggest psychodynamic and humanistic models as the main approach in offender rehabilitation, the 'what works' movement should not ignore relevant issues from outside the CBT mainstream. Some 'psychodynamic' concepts such as Adler's individual psychology also have much in common with goal-directed CBT and systems-oriented family approaches. More systematic evaluations on counselling and non-behavioural treatment are needed.

## MENTORING PROGRAMMES

Elements of low-structured counselling and treatment are also contained in mentoring programmes for young offenders. These interventions typically involve a helping, non-deviant reference person who forms a relationship with the offender, gives advice, and functions as a role model. Meta-analyses on mentoring programmes for young offenders or at-risk groups show small positive effects on aggression and delinquency (DuBois *et al.* 2002; Tolan *et al.* 2008), but there is not yet sound evidence that they reduce reoffending in the longer term (Jolliffe and Farrington 2008). Mentoring seems to be primarily of worth as part of more comprehensive and intensive interventions.

It is most promising for those young offenders who have no protective reference persons in their natural social network. Practical implementation must ensure sufficient continuity with messages communicated by mentors being consistent with the aims of other programmes in which offenders participate.

## RESTORATIVE JUSTICE (RJ) PROGRAMMES

Following ethnographic work by Braithwaite (1989), RJ has become an element in the criminal justice systems in many Western countries. Its principles are also applied in business, schools and other contexts (Dussich and Schellenberg 2010). The aim is not punishment, but conflict resolution and reparation of the harm caused to victims and other stakeholders. This implies, for example, that the offenders show insight into the harm they have done, truly regret, and, where appropriate, are willing to compensate. The respective programmes must involve all stakeholders, promote their readiness for an RJ procedure, identify the harm, and take concrete steps to repair it. RJ programmes range from victim-offender-mediation and conferencing to restitution and community services (Ahmed *et al.* 2001; Sherman and Strang 2007).

Although RJ aims extend beyond reducing reoffending (they include, for example, victim satisfaction and cost reduction) systematic reviews show desirable effects on recidivism (Nugent *et al.* 2003; Sherman and Strang 2007). This is particularly the case for face-to-face conferences convened by professionals (e.g. police officers or youth justice workers) involving offenders, victims, family members, and other stakeholders. Well controlled British trials of three RJ schemes that applied direct and/or indirect mediation resulted in a significant reduction in the frequency of re offending and no significant effect on seriousness of repeat offending (Shapland *et al.* 2008). There was also a financial payoff and no differential impact in various offender groups. Some studies suggest that offender-victim mediation may be less effective with juvenile property offenders, drunk drivers, and, in particular, aborigines in Australia (Sherman and Strang 2007). RJ is limited by the requirement of mutual agreement and one should not expect serious and substance abusing offenders to desist from crime simply because of brief conferences with victims. However, successful RJ programmes contain elements such as perspective taking, cognitive restructuring, and motivation to change that are similar to what more intensive CBT offending behaviour programmes are aiming for. More integration between correctional treatment and RJ programmes is therefore worthwhile.

## MODERATORS OF TREATMENT EFFECTS

Although the last section has shown that various approaches to offender rehabilitation differ in their effectiveness, this message is only a part of the story on 'what works'. As in medicine or general psychotherapy (Chambless and Ollendick 2001) evaluators ask whether there are at least a few well-controlled studies with a significantly positive effect (not contradicted by negative other results). Then programmes may get labels such as 'works', 'promising', or 'does not work' (Sherman *et al.* 1997). Although this approach is important for a basic orientation, it does not sufficiently represent the complexity of research findings. Most meta-analyses of correctional programmes have shown large variations in the outcomes of similar or even one and the same programme (Lipsey and Wilson 1998; Schmucker and Lösel 2009; Tong and Farrington 2006). They have also revealed that the different types of interventions do not explain the major part of outcome variance. Therefore, both research and practice need a broader view on what does and does not lead to a positive effect (see also Palmer 1995). This is the question posed by moderators of programme effects: What factors beyond the content of a programme may have an impact on the outcome?

In the following, a selection of such factors will be briefly discussed. Figure 33.2 contains an overview. Some of the factors are well replicated, whereas others require more research.

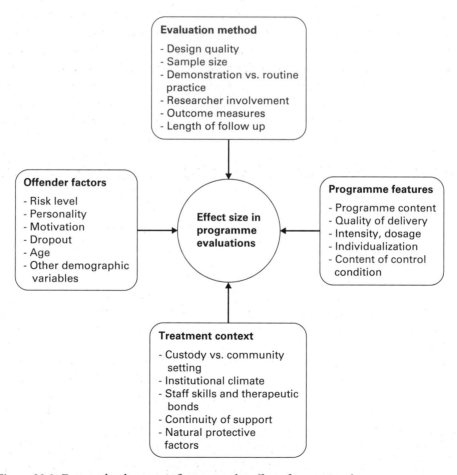

**Figure 33.2** Factors that have an influence on the effect of correctional programmes

## EVALUATION METHOD

1. *Quality of the research design*: Internal validity of the evaluation is necessary for drawing causal inferences. The design quality is often rated on summary scales such as the Maryland Scale of Methodological Rigour (Sherman *et al.* 1997) and some criminological reviews suggest smaller effects in more valid studies (Weisburd *et al.* 2011; Welsh *et al.* 2011). However, reviews on offender rehabilitation do not yet reveal a consistent pattern. They have found slightly negative as well as positive or zero correlations between design quality and effect sizes (Jolliffe and Farrington 2009; Koehler *et al.* 2011a; Lipsey and Cullen 2007; Lösel 1995a). There is also no clear difference in the outcomes of randomized controlled trials (RCTs) versus quasi-experimental designs (Lipsey and Wilson 1998; Lösel and Schmucker 2005). The mixed findings may be due to the influence of other moderator variables (Lipsey 2003) and confounded methodological issues (Lösel 2007). For example, differences in outcome measures or length of follow up can have more influence on the effect than the evaluation design alone. Therefore, design quality ratings should be complemented by more differentiated assessments of internal, statistical, construct, external, and descriptive validity (Farrington 2006; Lösel and Köferl 1989).

2. *Sample size*: Meta-analyses of correctional treatment regularly show stronger effects in small than in large samples (Koehler *et al.* 2011a; Lipsey *et al.* 2007; Lipsey and Wilson 1998; Lösel and Schmucker 2005). This may be due to a publication bias (i.e. a preference of authors, reviewers, or editors for significant findings), because effects in small samples must be larger to become statistically significant. However, similar relations among unpublished studies and sensitivity analyses suggest that this explanation is not sufficient. Therefore, one must also assume that the difference may be due to better programme integrity in smaller studies (Lösel and Beelmann 2003).

3. *Demonstration projects versus routine practice*: The latter explanation is indirectly supported by the finding of much larger effects in demonstration projects ('efficacy') than in evaluations of routine practice ('effectiveness'; Andrews and Bonta 2010; Koehler *et al.* 2011a; Lipsey and Landenberger 2006; Lipsey and Wilson 1998; Lösel and Schmucker 2005). Demonstration projects are often carried out in collaboration with universities, have highly motivated staff, contain a careful selection of participants, and apply systematic methods of monitoring. Such procedures are more feasible in smaller studies and may lead to better implementation quality.

4. *Involvement of programme developers in evaluation*: This issue is also related to the previous ones. Evaluations carried out by programme developers repeatedly showed larger effects than those by independent researchers (Lipsey and Landenberger 2006; Lipsey and Wilson 1998; Lösel and Schmucker 2005). This is in accordance with evaluations in other fields (Eisner 2009; Petrosino and Soydan 2005). One must not assume intentional faking, but data grouping and analyses contain many decisions that may favour one's own programme. Furthermore, researchers who evaluate their own programme may be particularly interested in

high-quality implementation and thus reach better effects (Lösel and Beelmann 2003; Sherman and Strang 2009).

5. *Type of outcome measures*: Although official recidivism data, such as arrest or reconviction, contain problems (Lloyd *et al*. 1994; Maguire, this volume), they are most important for policy and practice. Some reviews suggest larger treatment effects for more serious offences (Morales *et al*. 2010) or non-official indicators of success (Lösel and Schmucker 2005). Psychometric measures of personality factors or skills also reveal positive outcomes (Lipsey 1992b; McDougall *et al*. 2009). Such constructs are directly related to programme content (e.g. hostility, impulsivity, deviant attitudes), but biased towards social desirability and other response sets. Both issues may account for the often low correlations between intermediate outcomes in psychometrics and later recidivism (Barnett *et al*. 2010; Lipsey 1992b).

6. *Length of follow up*: The length of follow up is also relevant. Programme effects often decrease over time (Lösel 1995a; Lösel and Schmucker 2005). This can be due to the deteriorating impact of what was learned in programmes, termination of aftercare, new stressors over time, more desistance in the control groups, and other factors. Although, programme effects could also increase over time, such 'sleeper effects' are rarely analysed in rehabilitation studies.

## PROGRAMME FEATURES

1. *Content*: The concept of a programme in manuals is not necessarily the same as that delivered. This issue refers to programme integrity and requires careful monitoring and process evaluation. With regard to more complex programmes there are often not enough reported details to evaluate what components are most relevant for effectiveness (Shaffer and Pratt 2009; Lösel 1995a). This is particularly relevant when programmes fail: one does not know which parts need to be improved and which worked well. The descriptive validity of evaluations (Farrington 2006; Lösel and Köferl 1989) correlates positively with effect size (Lösel and Schmucker 2005; Schmucker and Lösel 2009).

2. *Quality of implementation*: Integrity is a summary label for the reliability of programme implementation (Lösel and Wittmann 1989). It is related to quality features such as staff competence, motivation, and programme monitoring (Hollin 1995). When programmes are not reliably implemented, positive effects may be due, for example, to individual staff competences but not the programme itself. On the other hand, even a good programme can fail because of inappropriate implementation. Systematic reviews show larger effect sizes for high quality programme implementations (Andrews and Dowden 2005; Gendreau *et al*. 1999; Goggin and Gendreau 2006; Lipsey *et al*. 2007).

3. *Intensity*: Intensity refers to dosage issues: overall duration, number of sessions, frequency per week, etc. Intensive programmes tend to have larger effects (Lipsey *et al*. 2007). However, treatment dosage should not be evaluated in absolute terms but with regard to its fit with the offenders' risk level and specific needs (Andrews and Bonta 2010).

4. *Individualization*: Many offending behaviour programmes are standardized. The contents, modes of delivery, assessment and management procedures are prescribed in manuals. This should ensure programme integrity and enable replication across different sites and countries. However, there is a question mark over whether fully structured, manual-based programmes meet the more specific needs of individual offenders, particularly in a group format. There are different views on this issue. In the field of sexual offender treatment; for example, Ware *et al.* (2009) plausibly argue for group treatment, whereas a recent systematic review shows better effects for programmes with some degree of individualization (Schmucker and Lösel 2009). The latter finding is consistent with the results of approaches such as MST. There is need for careful investigation of the strengths and weaknesses of both concepts.

5. *Control group context*: Evaluations typically focus on the programme content. However, the characteristics of the control group context—imprisonment or probation delivered as usual—can be as important as the treatment itself (Lösel and Egg 1997). When the control group receives no rehabilitative measures at all, the outcome of a programme may look particularly strong. In contrast, some other kind of treatment in the control group may lower effect sizes (Holloway *et al.* 2008). Although correctional programmes are often continuously improved, a transfer of the 'what works' knowledge into 'practice as usual' could similarly enhance the situation of the control groups. Changes in control group conditions and more rigorous research designs may have contributed to reduced effects in recent studies (Jolliffe and Farrington 2009; Lösel and Schmucker 2005; Tong and Farrington 2006).

## TREATMENT CONTEXT

1. *Custodial versus community settings*: On average, evaluations of community-based programmes reveal larger effects than prison-based interventions (Andrews and Bonta 2010; Koehler *et al.* 2011a; Lipsey and Cullen 2007; Schmucker and Lösel 2009). This may be due to iatrogenic 'contamination effects' when offenders are concentrated in groups (Gatti *et al.* 2009), the deferred transfer of learned contents to the world outside, difficulties during resettlement, and other influences. However, one must bear in mind that most evaluation studies comprise comparisons with same-setting control groups and not between custodial and community measures: part of the difference in effect size may be due to differences in the respective clienteles.

2. *Institutional climate*: Since the pioneering work of Moos (1975) on institutional climate, research suggests that mutual respect, humanity, support, relationship-orientation, and trust play an important role for the prevention of conflicts, suicides, and other problems (Liebling and Arnold 2002, 2005). Similarly, thorough assessment and management of situational risk factors is relevant for reducing violence in custodial settings (Cooke *et al.* 2008; Cooke and Johnstone 2010). Although aspects of institutional climate are targeted in therapeutic

communities, they are also important framing conditions for specific offending behaviour programmes.

3. *Staff competences and relationship skills*: In psychotherapy research it is well documented that therapeutic alliances and emotional bonds between clients and therapists are as important as specific therapeutic techniques (Orlinsky *et al.* 1994). This has also been emphasized repeatedly with regard to correctional treatment (Lösel 1995a; Ward and Maruna 2007). Research and practical experience suggests that programme effects are larger when staff have good relationship and problem-solving skills, reinforce offenders' desirable behaviour, and are generally socially competent (Dowden and Andrews 2004; Goggin and Gendreau 2006). Accordingly, it is important that programme deliverers are well selected, trained, and regularly supervised (Antonowizc and Ross 1994; Gendreau *et al.* 1999).

4. *Continuity of care*: Even the best custodial treatment programme is often only an island of structure and support in a stream of instability and deprivation during life. Institutional programme effects also depend on appropriate throughcare, aftercare, and relapse prevention measures (Farrall and Calverly 2006; Maguire and Raynor 2006; MacKenzie, 2006). This is particularly relevant for drug-addicted and sexual offenders vulnerable to relapse triggers. For these groups, relapse prevention measures are often an integrated part of rehabilitation programmes. But resettlement and relapse prevention are also important for other offender groups, and there is a lack of research on their additional effects. The same applies to combinations of community treatment programmes with employment, education, or family support measures.

5. *Natural protective factors*: The 'what works' literature focuses on programmes within the criminal justice system, private institutions, or the third sector. Only approaches such as milieu and multisystemic therapy make intensive use of the fact that the offender's natural environment is highly relevant for whether a programme reduces reoffending or not. This view is clearly supported by the research on protective factors and desistance (Farrall 2002; Lösel and Bender 2003; Maruna 2001; Sampson and Laub 1993). The findings on the protective functions of marriage, employment, and other factors are 'only' correlative in nature. However, they suggest an important mediating role in those programme participants who do not reoffend.

## OFFENDER CHARACTERISTICS

1. *Risk level of offenders*: Meta-analyses of correctional treatment show larger effects in high or medium-risk offenders than in low-risk groups (Andrews and Bonta 2010; Andrews and Dowden 2006; Lipsey 2009; Lipsey *et al.* 2007; Lipsey and Wilson 1998; Lösel and Schmucker 2005). This is plausible insofar as the first groups have a higher base rate of reoffending and therefore offer a larger impact range for effective programmes. By contrast, the vast majority of low-risk offenders do not reoffend and therefore the difference with

untreated control groups can only be small ('floor effect'). Low-risk offenders often have access to natural resources and do not need intensive treatment: they can be diverted from the criminal justice system and incarceration. Although larger effects for high-risk offenders have been replicated, one should not generally expect the best effects in very high-risk groups. Because of the particular difficulties with psychopathic offenders and similar cases, an inverted U-shaped relationship between risk level and effect size may be realistic (Lösel 1996).

2. *Personality factors*: Risk assessment in treatment programmes normally includes static risks (e.g. offence history) *and* dynamic factors such as lack of self-control or crime-prone attitudes. The moderator effect of risk level is partially due to differences in offenders' personalities. However, these are also more directly relevant for rehabilitation outcomes. For example, offenders with psychopathic traits are particularly difficult to manage (Lösel 1998; Salekin *et al.* 2010) and, therefore, are often excluded. Inadequate programmes may even lead to negative effects in this group (Rice *et al.* 1992). In addition to temperament and attitudes, mental health problems, intelligence, and other variables may have an impact on treatment effects. Such characteristics require individual adaptations adhering to the 'Risk, Need, and Responsivity' (RNR) model (see below).

3. *Offender motivation*: Offenders' motivation and engagement in a treatment programme are a prerequisite for its success (McMurran 2002). Older therapeutic models assumed that clients must have developed a genuine wish to change before participating in treatment. Current approaches, however, see treatment motivation as a more dynamic and interactive process (Porporino 2010; Prochaska and Levesque 2002; Wormith *et al.* 2007) regarding aspects of willingness, readiness, and ability to change. Many programmes make use of modules on motivational interviewing (Miller and Rollnick 2002) or coping with lapse and relapse (Prochaska and Levesque 2002). It is therefore plausible that some reviews have not found outcome differences between voluntary and mandatory participation (Koehler *et al.* 2011a; Schmucker and Lösel 2009).

4. *Treatment dropout*: This relates to characteristics of the offender, programme, and evaluation method. Programme dropouts typically are more recidivist than completers (Lösel 1995a, Lipsey and Cullen 2007) and their recidivism rate is often higher than that in untreated control groups. This may be due to lower motivation, problematic personality characteristics, or later stigmatization of dropouts. A high dropout rate may also indicate programme implementation problems. For these reasons it is plausible that programmes with very low dropout rates show larger effects (Koehler *et al.* 2011a). On the other hand, intent-to-treat analyses which allocate dropouts to the treatment group reveal smaller effects (Jolliffe and Farrington 2009; Lipsey and Wilson 1998).

5. *Age of offenders*: The relationship between offender age and programme effects is complicated. First, programmes for juveniles may differ in content and context from those for adults. Second, analyses of different age groups are rare,

particularly in studies of adults. Third, with increasing age potential programme effects get more confounded with natural desistance according to the
age-crime curve. Programmes for juvenile offenders tend to show slightly larger effects than those only for adults (Lipsey and Cullen 2007; Redondo *et al.*
2002). This could be due to less consolidated criminal dispositions in younger
people, or a higher base rate of reoffending that goes along with larger effects
(Lösel 2007).

6. *Other biographical factors*: Gender may be relevant for programme effects. Although
most research focuses on males, sound treatment programmes work similarly well
for women (Andrews and Bonta 2010; Dowden and Andrews 1999; Landenberger
and Lipsey 2005; Zahn *et al.* 2009). However, this does not mean that females have
the same treatment needs. Both sexes have many risk factors in common, but female
delinquency seems to be more related to abusive close relationships, mental health
problems, and social marginalization (Moffitt *et al.* 2001; Odgers and Moretti
2002). Rehabilitation programmes for women therefore need to pay attention to
gender-specific pathways to reducing reoffending. Similar issues arise with regard
to ethnicity. North-American research shows that black or other minorities can
benefit from the same programmes as white offenders (Landenberger and Lipsey
2005; Wilson *et al.* 2003), but this does not imply that ethnic issues are irrelevant
for programme implementation and outcomes. This is reflected in RJ measures for
aborigines (see above) in programmes for sexual or domestic violence offenders
that are less suitable for minorities with different value systems.

Many moderators are confounded and there are not enough studies on specific combinations of them (see Lipsey 2003). Despite such problems, Figure 33.2 clearly shows
that the 'what works' question cannot simply be reduced to one or the other type of
programme.

# BROADER APPROACHES TO 'WHAT WORKS' IN PRACTICE

Taking the above findings into account, research and practice have developed concepts
going beyond the content of specific offending behaviour programmes. Broader perspectives are obvious in systems-oriented approaches and they are also supported by
the Risk-Need-Responsivity (RNR) model of Andrews *et al.* (1990). These authors
applied evidence-based social-cognitive learning and personality theories to establish basic criteria for clinically meaningful rehabilitation programmes. 'Appropriate'
treatment must match the offender's risk for reoffending (R), address his/her specific
criminogenic needs (N), and use methods that fit the individual's learning style (R).
Andrews *et al.* (1990) found that appropriate programmes reduced reoffending by up
to 60 per cent. More recent and perhaps more realistic data suggest 20–30 per cent
less (Andrews and Bonta 2010). Programme effects systematically increased with
the number of principles realized. Appropriate treatment (all three) led to roughly

one quarter less reoffending whereas inappropriate treatment (no criterion satisfied) even had a slightly negative effect. A similar relationship between RNR and effect size was reported for sexual offender treatment (Hanson *et al.* 2009). The RNR model was also confirmed in a meta-analysis of young offender treatment in Europe (Koehler *et al.* 2011a): adherence to RNR showed 18 per centage points less recidivism; lack of adherence resulted in no significant effects.

Although the social learning theory background of the RNR model particularly supports CBT programmes, it is not limited to these. This avoids the often unfruitful controversies between traditional 'schools' of psychotherapy. Another strength of the model is the emphasis on structured assessment of risks/needs (e.g. previous delinquency, criminogenic personality traits, anti-social cognitions, deviant peers, problems in the family/partnership, at school/work, in leisure, and substance misuse). As in any treatment concept there are some problems. For example, risks and needs are partially confounded categories and responsivity may sometimes be inferred from a good outcome. In most studies there was less differentiation than in theory and RNR-oriented programmes addressed broadly defined groups. However, typing of individual cases is a necessity of science and the authors differentiated between general and specific (more individualized) responsivity. They also widened the concept by including organizational factors, staff skills, therapeutic relationships, offenders' strengths, and community linkages (Andrews and Bonta 2010). These broader views have been suggested within the RNR model (Andrews 1995) and by authors with a social-therapeutic background (Lösel 1995a).

The more general perspectives on effective rehabilitation were transformed into detailed criteria for programme accreditation that have been introduced in countries such as England and Wales, Netherlands, Norway, Scotland, Sweden, various US states, and (temporarily) Canada. The Correctional Services Accreditation Panel of England and Wales, for example, applies the following criteria (see Maguire *et al.* 2010):

1. clear model of change;
2. thorough selection of offenders;
3. targeting a range of dynamic risk factors;
4. effective learning and teaching methods;
5. skill-orientation;
6. adequate sequence and duration;
7. promotion of offender motivation;
8. continuity of services;
9. ensuring programme integrity; and
10. ongoing evaluation.

As part of the Crime Reduction Programme (Maguire 2004), England and Wales developed a policy that was probably the world's most ambitious transfer of the 'what works' research into practice. Within a decade more than 40 community and custodial programmes for general, violent, sexual, alcohol-misusing, drug-addicted, domestic violence, and other offender groups have been accredited. Participation rates quickly increased from a few hundred to more than 25,000 per annum. There was also a strong investment in quality management through systematic offender assessment, staff training, supervision, and auditing. The Government's dedication to reducing reoffending was also indicated by the establishment of NOMS and the aim of integrating the prison and probation services leading to more effective end-to-end management of offenders (see Raynor, this volume). The expansion of mostly structured offending behaviour programmes was only one part of a range of NOMS's pathways to reduce reoffending that comprised: accommodation; education, training and employment; mental and physical health; drugs and alcohol; finance and debts; children and families; and attitudes, thinking, and behaviour; plus support in cases of sexual abuse/rape and prostitution for female offenders.

The fast and large-scale roll-out of correctional programmes inevitably led to some problems, for example, high staff turnover, partial violation of eligibility criteria, dropouts, and a lack of audit in the community (Maguire *et al.* 2010). Major organizational changes (decentralization, contestability, privatization, and formation of probation trusts) led to unstable framing conditions, particularly for community interventions (Morgan 2007). There was also insufficient evaluation. For some programmes the results of North-American studies were taken for granted, although these came from a different culture and from demonstration projects rather than routine practice. Many programmes that were developed in Britain underwent no outcome evaluation at all. Quasi-experimental evaluations of the frequently applied cognitive skills programmes showed mixed results (Cann *et al.* 2003; Friendship *et al.* 2002; Hollin *et al.* 2004). Overall, there were some encouraging findings for well-implemented CBT programmes for medium- to high-risk offenders, aggression replacement training in probation, sex offender treatment, and drug treatment programmes (Harper and Chitty 2005). However, a clearer evaluation of outcome of the ambitious correctional policy was hindered by lack of research and methodological controversies (Hollin 2008; Maguire *et al.* 2010).

Although more sound evaluations are needed, there are indirect indicators of success. For example, from 2000 to 2006 the rate of reoffending within one year of discharge from prison or commencement of probation decreased by 11 per cent. From 2000 to 2004 reconviction rates dropped by between 6 and 13 per cent for those offenders with prison sentences of more than one year (HMPS 2007) who are the typical recipients of programmes. Comparisons between actual and expected reconviction rates for community treatment programmes are also promising (Hollis 2007), although they are weakened by incomplete data. Most recently, Travers *et al.* (2011) compared more than 17,000 participants of the custodial Enhanced Thinking Skills programme with offenders from a national cohort who were matched for risk level and sentence length. There was an overall reduction in reoffending of more than 12 per cent and consistency across risk levels. Similarly positive results were observed in a smaller study with propensity score matching (Sadlier 2010). Comparisons between a large sample of treated sexual offenders with a national cohort of untreated sexual offenders also revealed positive outcomes (4.5 versus 8.2 per cent sexual reconvictions within two years; Wakeling *et al.* 2011). Although such quasi-experimental studies contain threats to validity, they are valuable because they address large samples in routine practice.

# CONTROVERSIES ABOUT 'WHAT WORKS'

In spite of encouraging findings, the 'what works' movement has been questioned (Brayford *et al.* 2010; McNeill 2006; Ward and Maruna 2007). Unrealistic expectations with regard to effect sizes may have contributed to critical views, but other issues are more relevant. For example, it has been criticized that the prevailing 'what works' approaches: promote too much centralization and top-down administration; contain demanding procedures of accreditation and audit; reduce diversity and creativity in practice; place too much emphasis on quantitative data; give too much weight to standardized CBT and RNR-oriented programmes; focus primarily on characteristics of the individual; ignore systems and institutional issues, and adhere to a risk and deficit-oriented image of the offender. None of these arguments is totally wrong; however, they exaggerate and stereotype issues. The first four arguments are part of a frequent reaction to the implementation of evidence-oriented policies, accreditation and quality management (Maguire *et al.* 2010). Similar discussions took place in the general field of empirically supported psychotherapy (Chambless and Ollendick 2001). The last four arguments do not adequately acknowledge the diversity of rehabilitation programmes or expansions of the RNR model (Andrews *et al.* 2011; Lipsey and Cullen 2007; Lösel 2011). The overarching message in these and other arguments is that the criminal justice system must keep an adequate balance between an effective organizational management and the humane and relationship aspects of working with individuals.

As an alternative to the typical 'what works' literature and particularly the RNR model the Good Lives Model (GLM) has been proposed (Ward and Brown 2004; Ward and Maruna 2007). Although the authors acknowledge that CBT and RNR-oriented programmes are based on replicated research findings, they emphasize a number of shortcomings. They criticize prevailing programmes on the grounds that they: do not inform offenders about the positive rewards of desisting from crime; neglect the role of the offender's identity and self-directed actions; ignore offenders' need for specific experiences; use a psychometric model; do not address the role of treatment alliances; and often contain a one-size fits all approach (Ward and Brown 2004). The range of rehabilitation measures in this chapter and the various pathways to rehabilitation suggest that this view is rather selective. However, as mentioned, the large-scale role out of standardized programmes was indeed at risk of not giving enough attention to therapeutic relationships, differential indication, and specific experiences.

The GLM integrates a mix of ideas from positive psychology, humanistic therapy, social learning, and strain theory. It assumes that offenders—like all human beings—want to achieve legitimate goals. Therefore they need competences and resources to reach basic goods, i.e. healthy functioning, knowledge, excellence in work and play, autonomy and self-directedness, inner peace and freedom of stress, friendship and community, spirituality, happiness, and creativity. The acceptance of the GLM by many practitioners has benefited from the 'positive language' that similarly impressed me when I began research on resilience (Lösel and Bliesener 1990). However, one should not polarize deficit-oriented and strength-oriented perspectives; both are needed for an adequate explanation of behavioural outcomes (Lösel and Bender 2003).

Parts of the GLM are compatible to the broad empirical research on protective factors in human development (Lösel and Bender 2003; Werner and Smith 1992).

In an analysis of the GLM, Andrews *et al.* (2011) found overlap with their expanded RNR model, but also assumptions about human motivation and self-direction that are problematic with regard to the origins of reoffending. The latter is in accordance with psychotherapy research that does not suggest non-directive approaches as the best choice for cases of high impulsivity and aggression (Beutler and Harwood 2000). In addition to other arguments against the GLM (see Andrews *et al.* 2011; Ogloff and Davis 2004) it should be noted that there are very few, and mainly case-oriented, studies on its effectiveness (e.g. Whitehead *et al.* 2007). The arguments need to be resolved through systematic research.

In another current discussion authors propose a shift from the 'what works' to a 'desistance paradigm' (Brayford *et al.* 2010; McNeill 2006). Here, the focus switches from specific programmes to social institutions and protective factors in offenders' natural development. Marriage to a non-deviant partner or stable employment are typical examples of such turning points in life, but many other personal and social resources can contribute to desistance (Bottoms and Shapland 2011; Farrall *et al.* 2011; Farrington 2007; Laub and Sampson 2007; Lösel and Bender 2003; Maruna 2001; Sampson and Laub 1993; Theobald and Farrington 2009). The focus on desistance is not in conflict with the 'what works' movement. Although more weight is given to community services (including probation), social resources, and individual strengths, 'what works in reducing reoffending' can easily be translated into 'what works in promoting desistance' (Lösel 2011; Porporino 2010). In both perspectives correctional treatment programmes may contribute to a desirable outcome, but do not determine it.

In contrast to (quasi-) experimental research on programme evaluation, desistance research is based on correlation designs that contain methodological difficulties (Loeber *et al.* 2008; Lösel and Farrington 2010). Although most offenders desist from crime at some time in their life (Laub and Sampson 2007), at younger ages 70 per cent may reoffend. Good intentions and first steps to desist are often counteracted by personal and social obstacles (Bottoms and Shapland 2011). Such problems are targeted by motivational modules, cognitive interviewing, or applications of the cycle of change in correctional programmes (McMurran 2002). Many rehabilitation programmes also contain elements to support protective mechanisms.

## CONCLUSIONS AND PERSPECTIVES

The above analyses show evidence that various measures from the 'what works' literature are effective. Typical effect sizes range somewhere between 10 and 20 per cent less reoffending in treated than in control groups, but there are also larger or smaller effects. Desirable outcomes have been found for cognitive-behavioural programmes, therapeutic communities, social-therapeutic prisons, milieu therapy, multisystemic treatment, RJ measures, education and vocational programmes. Approaches based on the RNR model are particularly effective, whereas low-structured case work, counselling, and therapy have somewhat weaker effects. Purely punitive, deterrent, and intensive supervision measures show no or even slightly negative effects.

Although the type of correctional rehabilitation has proved to be important, there are many moderators of outcome. Effect sizes depend on numerous programme characteristics, the context, the offender, and the respective evaluation methods. It follows that the 'what works' question extends beyond the content of programmes. Broad implementations of the 'what works' research into policy and practice as in the UK have had to cope with many problems and suffered from a lack of sound evaluation, but are overall encouraging. Although critiques of the 'what works' movement by advocates of the Good Lives Model or a new 'desistance paradigm' contain helpful arguments, the empirical evidence supports a continuous development of 'what works' instead of a paradigm shift. Unintentionally, the latter could increase the risk of lowering rehabilitation quality in the current times of financial strain, staff cuts, and outsourcing. Without doubt, there are many creative activities that go beyond the mainstream of 'what works' and may have an impact on the culture within the criminal justice system (e.g. Brayford *et al.* 2010). However, we know little about their effects on reoffending and should therefore systematically investigate 'what else works'.

As the analysis of moderators of outcome has shown, we need much more research on 'what works' with whom, in what contexts, under what conditions and with regard to what outcomes. To progress in this direction, I propose the following strategies:

1. *More 'systems' instead of silo' approaches*: In the prevailing 'what works' literature programmes are seen as isolated entities. However, in practice offenders may not only participate in a specific CBT programme but also get education, vocational training, social services in the community, and other measures. These interventions are not randomly allocated and may not exert simple additive effects. As clinical pharmacology and technology show, the effects of one specific measure can strongly increase or decrease depending on the context of others. Similar thoughts underlie multimodal treatments such as therapeutic communities or multisystemic therapy. A broad systems-oriented concept is followed in NOMS's seven pathways to reducing reoffending and such patterns of interventions require flexible evaluation strategies.

2. *More controlled evaluations of routine practice*: The above-mentioned systems- and multi-agency approaches are less suitable for standard (quasi-) experimental evaluations of single programmes. This should not lead to a fall-back into non-interpretable research designs. On the one hand, experimental designs can address systematic combinations of different intervention elements. On the other hand, large-scale cohort studies with matching procedures can be used to evaluate patterns of interventions. Such studies would better connect the efficacy findings from demonstration projects to the effectiveness in routine practice.

3. *More systematic process evaluation*: In addition to programme content, quality of implementation is highly relevant for effectiveness (Goggin and Gendreau 2006; Shaffer and Pratt 2009). This sounds trivial, but most outcome studies

provide no or only rudimentary data on integrity. Audit systems have limited value for this purpose because they often address organizational features and reveal not much differentiation between institutions. Evaluations should place more emphasis on treatment implementation and descriptive validity (Lösel 2007). Regular combinations of programme and outcome evaluation are also necessary to answer detailed practical questions such as the impact of fixed groups versus a rolling format.

4. *More links between programmes and the institutional context*: Institutional climate is important for the well-being and behaviour of clients. Such factors are, for example, related to prison suicides (Liebling and Arnold 2005) or institutional violence (Cooke and Johnstone 2010). We need more research on the moderating or mediating effects of institutional contexts on treatment programmes.

5. *More emphasis on relationship issues*: In psychotherapy mutual cooperation, reinforcement, and bonding between client and therapist are very important for the outcome (Orlinsky *et al.* 1994). Although correctional programmes are often more structured and educative, Ward's plea for more attention to therapeutic alliances is appropriate. Such factors should be addressed in programme designs, staff selection and training and process evaluation. This does not mean that 'what works' is replaced by 'who works' (as is sometimes suggested); unstructured case work has not been particularly effective (Andrews and Bonta 2010; Lipsey and Cullen 2007).

6. *More differentiation and individualization*: Many current offending behaviour programmes are standardized. There is not much evidence on this issue, but some results (Schmucker and Lösel 2009) and the concept of specific responsivity suggest that partially individualized programmes seem to be more effective. Correctional programmes should not move too far towards individual delivery: this would be expensive and abandon the strengths of learning in groups. However, rehabilitation programmes should provide free space to deal with intimate family problems, personal difficulties, or ethnic minority issues that are not sufficiently addressed in standard programmes.

7. *More integration of natural protective factors*: The RNR concept focuses on dynamic risk factors and its expansions also include the assessment of strengths (Andrews *et al.* 2011). Following desistance studies, the GLM, and the broader field of resilience research, the relation of rehabilitation programmes and natural protective factors should be intensified. Most protective factors are only the opposite pole of risk factors and many offenders show an accumulation of the latter. This requires sophisticated modelling of dose-response functions of risk and protective effects (Lösel and Bender 2003; Lösel and Farrington 2011).

8. *More theoretical foundation*: One reason why CBT programmes are particularly effective can be seen in their sound theoretical basis in social-cognitive learning theories. Various correctional programmes rely more on common sense than on empirically validated theories. We need more connections between basic research of the origins of crime and measures to prevent it. However, adequate

theories on the causes are not sufficient because effective interventions also require valid theories of programming and of the change process (Chen 1989). The latter is particularly relevant for the transfer of research on desistance into measures that promote such processes.

9. *More links with neurobiology*: Neurobiological research on personality-disordered offenders has made substantial progress (Glenn and Raine 2008). This field should receive more attention in offender treatment. Currently, the most widespread (and moderately effective) use of medication is in substitution programmes for drug-addicted offenders (Koehler *et al.* 2011b). However, there are also some promising findings on anti-androgen treatment for specific groups of sexual offenders (Lösel and Schmucker 2005) and on selective serotonin re-uptake inhibitors (SSRIs) for subgroups of personality-disordered clients (Bellino *et al.* 2011). In both fields more controlled evaluation is needed (also on negative side-effects). One could follow the model of treating serious depression by combinations of CBT and medication. Integrations of neurobiological findings will not necessarily result in more pharmacotherapy but can support differentiations of psychosocial intervention.

10. *More direct comparisons of custodial and community measures*: Research suggests that imprisonment has no deterrent but even a criminogenic effect (Durlauf and Nagin 2011). However, there is a lack of direct experimental comparisons of custody and community-based sanctions and treatment. For reasons of public security and cost-effectiveness, more studies should investigate what levels of offender risk and harm can be most effectively addressed in both contexts.

11. *More attention to cost-benefit issues*: Custodial versus community intervention is not just a proportionality issue but also one of cost-benefit. Persistent criminal behaviour leads to immense costs for society (Cohen and Piquero 2009) and some rehabilitation programmes have a better payoff than others (Welsh and Farrington 2000). Cost-effectiveness and cost-benefit analyses need more often to be part of outcome evaluations. Although this is in accordance with the British Government's aim to get the best value for money (Ministry of Justice 2010), the respective calculations and reward systems must be sufficiently complex. For example, programmes or institutions that are already doing well have a lower chance of further improvement than those that are less successful in reducing reoffending. One must also take adequately into account the many outcome moderators.

12. *More attention to national and cultural differences*: The current evidence on 'what works' is mainly based on North-American studies. Systematic reviews of controlled research in Asia, South America, and Africa are lacking, but also in many European countries (Koehler *et al.* 2011a, b). Research and practice needs to address in more detail the problems of transferring and adapting Anglo-American correctional programmes to other justice systems and local needs. Such an improved evidence base would make less likely unnecessary pendulum swings in crime policy.

## ■ SELECTED FURTHER READING

*Offender rehabilitation and treatment* edited by McGuire (2002) gives a good overview on effective programmes and policies. Andrews and Bonta's (2010) volume, *Psychology of criminal conduct,* describes important theoretical concepts of correctional treatment and provides information about assessment, treatment methods, and empirical results (with a focus on the RNR model). Lipsey and Cullen's (2007) article, *The effectiveness of correctional rehabilitation: A review of systematic reviews,* summarizes the main findings from meta-analyses and thus presents the evidence base of 'what works' in a nutshell. Ward and Maruna's (2007), *Rehabilitation: Beyond the risk paradigm* contains a critical discussion of parts of the 'what works' literature. Its reading is complemented by evidence-based counter-arguments in *The Risk-Need-Responsivity (RNR) Model: Does adding the Good Lives Model contribute to effective crime prevention?* by Andrews, Bonta, and Wormith (2011). The paper *'What works' and the Correctional Services Accreditation Panel: Taking stock from an inside perspective* by Maguire, Grubin, Lösel, and Raynor (2010) briefly sets out the challenges involved in transforming the research on offender rehabilitation into policy and practice.

## ■ REFERENCES

AHMED, E., HARRIS, N., BRAITHWAITE, J., and BRAITHWAITE, V. (eds) (2001), *Shame management through integration,* Cambridge: Cambridge University Press.

AICHHORN, A. (1925), *Verwahrloste Jugend: Die Psychoanalyse in der Fürsorgerziehung* [*Wayward youth: Psychoanalysis in correctional education*], Vienna, Austria: Internationaler Psychoanalytischer Verlag.

ANDREWS, D. A. (1995), 'The psychology of criminal conduct and effective treatment', in J. McGuire (ed.), *What Works: Reducing reoffending.* New York: Wiley.

—— and BONTA, J. (2010), *The psychology of criminal conduct,* 5th edn, Cincinatti, OH: Anderson.

——, ——, and WORMITH, S. (2011), 'The Risk-Need-Responsivity (RNR) model: Does adding the Good Lives Model contribute to effective crime prevention?', *Criminal Justice and Behavior,* 38: 735–55.

——, ZINGER, I., HOGE, R. D., BONTA, J., GENDREAU, P., and CULLEN, F. T. (1990), 'Does correctional treatment work? A clinically relevant and psychologically informed meta-analysis', *Criminology,* 28: 369–404.

—— and DOWDEN, C. (2006), 'Risk principle of case classification in correctional treatment: a meta-analytic investigation', *International Journal of Offender Therapy and Comparative Criminology,* 50: 88–100.

ANTONWICZ, D. H. and ROSS, R. R. (1994), 'Essential components of successful rehabilitation programs for offenders', *International Journal of Offender Therapy and Comparative Criminology,* 38: 97–104.

AOS, S., PHIPPS, P., BARNOSKI, R., and LIEB, R. (2001), *The comparative costs and benefits of programs to reduce crime,* Olympia, WA: Washington State Institute of Public Policy.

——, MILLER, M., and DRAKE, E. (2006), *Evidence-based adult corrections programs: What works and what does not,* Olympia, WA: Washington State Institute of Public Policy.

BANDURA, A. (1973), *Aggression: A social learning analysis,* New York: Prentice Hall.

BARNETT, G. D., WAKELING, H. C., MANDEVILLE-NORDEN, R., and RAKESTROW, J. (2010), *What does change in psychometric test scores tell us about risk of reconviction in sexual offenders?* Unpublished manuscript, London: NOMS.

BECCARIA, C. (1764), *Dei delitti e delle pene [Of crimes and punishments],* Livorno: Marco Coltellini.

BELLINO, S., RINALDI, C., BOZZATELLO, P., and BOGETTO, F. (2011), 'Recent approaches to pharmacotherapy of personality disorders', *Neuropsychiatry,* 1: 259–73.

BENTHAM, J. (1830), *The rationale of punishment, London:* Robert Howard.

BERGIN, T. (2011), *Criminal justice policy diffusion: An examination of the spread and contraction of correctional boot camps in the United States,* Doctoral dissertation, University of Cambridge: Institute of Criminology.

BEUTLER, L. E. and HARWOOD, T. M. (2000), *Prescriptive psychotherapy: A practical guide to systematic treatment selection,* New York: Oxford University Press.

BODDIE, S. C. and CNAAN, R. A. (2006), 'Setting the context: Assessing the effectiveness of faith-based social services', *Journal of Religion and Spirituality in Social Work,* 25(3–4): 5–18.

BORDUIN, C. M., MANN, B. J., CONE, L. T., HENGGELER, S. W., FUCCI, B. R., BLASKE, D. M., and WILLIAMS, R. A. (1995), 'Multisystemic treatment of serious juvenile offenders: Long-term prevention of criminality and violence', *Journal of Consulting and Clinical Psychology,* 63: 560–78.

BOTTOMS, A. and SHAPLAND, J. (2011), 'Steps towards desistance among young male adult offenders', in

S. Farrall, M. Hough, S. Maruna, and R. Sparks (eds), *Escape routes: Contemporary perspectives on life after punishment*, Milton Park, UK: Routledge.

BRAITHWAITE, J. (1989), *Crime, shame and reintegration*, Cambridge: Cambridge University Press.

BRAYFORD, J., COWE, F., and DEERING, J. (eds) (2010), *What else works? Creative work with offenders*, Cullompton, UK: Willan.

CANN, J., FALSHAW, L., NUGENT, F., and FRIENDSHIP, C. (2003), *Understanding what works: accredited cognitive skills programmes for adult men and young offenders*, Home Office Research Findings No. 226, London: Home Office.

CARTER, P. (2003), *Managing offenders, reducing crime: a new approach*, London: Strategy Unit.

CHAMBLESS, D. L. and OLLENDICK, T. H. (2001), 'Empirically supported psychological interventions: Controversies and evidence', *Annual Review of Psychology*, 52: 685–716.

CHEN, H. T. (1989), *Theory-driven evaluation*, Newbury Park, CA: Sage.

COHEN, M. A. and PIQUERO, A. R. (2009), 'New evidence on the monetary value of saving a high risk youth', *Journal of Quantitative Criminology*, 25: 25–49.

COOKE, D. J. and JOHNSTONE, L. (2010), 'Somewhere over the rainbow: Improving violence risk management in institutional settings', *International Journal of Forensic Mental Health*, 9: 150–58.

COOKE, D. J., WOZNIAK, E., and JOHNSTONE, L. (2008), 'Casting light on prison violence in Scotland: Evaluating the impact of situational risk factors', *Criminal Justice and Behavior*, 35: 1065–78.

CULLEN, E., JONES, L., and WOODWARD, R. (eds) (1997), *Therapeutic communities for offenders*, Chichester, UK: Wiley.

CURTIS, N. M., RONAN, K. R., and BORDUIN, C. M. (2004), 'Multisystematic treatment: a meta-analysis of outcome studies', *Journal of Family Psychology*, 18: 411–19.

DOWDEN, C. and ANDREWS, D. A. (1999), 'What works for female offenders: A meta-analytic review', *Crime and Delinquency*, 45: 438–52.

—— and —— (2004), 'The importance of staff practices in delivering effective correctional treatment: A meta-analysis of core correctional practices', *International Journal of Offender Therapy and Comparative Criminology*, 48: 203–14.

DUBOIS, D. L., HOLLOWAY, B. E., VALENTINE, J. C., and COOPER, H. M. (2002), 'Effectiveness of mentoring programs for youth: A meta-analytic review', *American Journal of Community Psychology*, 30: 157–97.

DURLAUF, S. N. and NAGIN, D. S. (2011), 'Imprisonment and crime: Can both be reduced?', *Criminology & Public Policy*, 10: 13–54.

DUSSICH, J. P. J. and SCHELLENBERG, J. (2010) (eds), *The promise of restorative justice: New approaches for criminal justice and beyond*, Boulder, CO: Lynne Rienner Publishers.

EISNER, M. (2009), 'No effects in independent prevention trials: Can we reject the cynical view?', *Journal of Experimental Criminology*, 5: 163–83.

FARRALL, S. (2002), *Rethinking what works with offenders: Probation, social context and desistance from crime*, Cullompton, UK: Willan.

—— and CALVERLEY, A. (2006), *Understanding desistance from crime: Theoretical directions in resettlement and rehabilitation*, Maidenhead, UK: Open University Press.

——, HOUGH, M., MARUNA, S., and SPARKS, R. (eds) (2011), *Escape routes: Contemporary perspectives on life after punishment*, Milton Park, UK: Routledge.

FARRINGTON, D. P. (2006), 'Methodological quality and the evaluation of anticrime programmes', *Journal of Experimental Criminology*, 2: 329–37.

—— (2007), 'Advancing knowledge about desistance'. *Journal of Contemporary Criminal Justice*, 23: 125–34.

—— and WELSH, B. C. (2007), *Saving children from a life of crime: Early risk factors and effective interventions*, New York: Oxford University Press.

FRIENDSHIP, C., BLUD, L., ERIKSON, M., and TRAVERS, R. (2002), *An evaluation of cognitive behavioural treatment for prisoners*, Home Office Research Findings No. 161, London: Home Office.

GAES, G. G. and CAMP, P. S. D. (2009), 'Unintended consequences: experimental evidence for the criminogenic effect of prison security level placement on post-release recidivism', *Journal of Experimental Criminology*, 5: 139–62.

GARRETT, C. J. (1985), 'Effects of residential treatment on adjudicated delinquents: a meta-analysis', *Journal of Research on Crime and Delinquency*, 22: 287–308.

GATTI, U., TREMBLAY, R. E., and VITARO, F. (2009), 'Iatrogenic effects of juvenile justice', *Journal of Child Psychology and Psychiatry*, 50: 991–8.

GENDREAU, P. (1981), 'Treatment in corrections: Martinson was wrong', *Canadian Psychology*, 22, 332–38.

——, GOGGIN, C., CULLEN, F. T., and ANDREWS, D. A. (2000), 'Does "getting tough" with offenders work? The effects of community sanctions and incarceration', *Forum on Corrections Research*, 12: 10–13.

——, GOGGIN, C., and SMITH, P. (1999), 'The forgotten issue in effective correctional treatment: Program implementation', *International Journal of Offender Therapy and Comparative Criminology*, 43, 180–87.

GLENN, A. L. and RAINE, A. (2008), 'The neurobiology of psychopathy', *Psychiatric Clinics of North America*, 31: 463–75.

GOGGIN, C. and GENDREAU, P. (2006), 'The implementation and maintenance of quality services in offender rehabilitation programmes', in C. Hollin and E. Palmer (eds), *Offending behaviour programmes*, Chichester, UK: Wiley.

GOLDSTEIN, A. P., GLICK, B., and GIBBS, J. C. (1998), *Aggression Replacement Training: A comprehensive intervention for aggressive youth*, rev edn, Champaign, Il, US: Research Press.

HAMILTON, L., KOEHLER, J. A., and LÖSEL, F. (2011), *Programmes to reduce reoffending throughout Europe: Three surveys of current practice*,

Research report of the STARR Project, University of Cambridge: Institute of Criminology.

HANSON, K., BURGON, G., HELMUS, L., and HODGSON, S. (2009), 'The principles of effective correctional treatment also apply to sexual offenders: A meta-analysis', *Criminal Justice and Behavior*, 36: 865–91.

HANSON, R. K., GORDON, A., HARRIS, A. J. R., MARQUES, J. K., MURPHY, W., *et al.* (2002), 'First report of the collaborative outcome data project on the effectiveness of psychological treatment for sex offenders', *Sexual Abuse: A Journal of Research and Treatment*, 14: 169–94.

HARPER, G. and CHITTY, C. (eds) (2005), *The impact of corrections on re-offending: a review of 'what works'*, Home Office Research Study 291, London: Home Office.

HEALY, W. and BRONNER, A. (1936), *New light on delinquency and its treatment*, New Haven, CT: Yale University Press.

HENGGELER, S. W., SCHOENWALD, S. K., BORDUIN, C. M., ROWLAND, M. D., and CUNNINGHAM, P. B. (2009), *Multisystemic treatment of antisocial behavior in children and adolescents*, 2nd edn, New York: Guilford Press.

HOLLIN, C. R. (1995), 'The meaning and implications for programme integrity', in J. McGuire (ed.), *What works: Reducing re-offending*, Chichester, UK: Wiley.

—— (2008), 'Evaluating offending behaviour programmes: Does only randomization glister?', *Criminology and Criminal Justice*, 8: 89–106.

—— and PALMER, E. J. (2009), 'Cognitive skills programmes for offenders', *Psychology Crime and Law*, 15: 147–64.

——, PALMER, E., MCGUIRE, J., HOUNSOME, J., HATCHER, R., BILBY, C., and CLARK, C. (2004), *Pathfinder Programmes in the Probation Service: a retrospective analysis*, Home Office Online Report 66/04, London: Home Office.

HOLLIS, V. (2007), *Reconviction analysis of interim accredited programmes software (IAPS) data*, London: NOMS.

HOLLOWAY, K., BENNETT T. H., and FARRINGTON, D. P. (2008), *Effectiveness of treatment in reducing drug-related crime*, Stockholm: Swedish National Council for Crime Prevention.

HOOD, R. (ed.) (1993), *Psychosocial interventions in the criminal justice system. Proceedings of the 20th Criminological Research Conference*, Strasbourg: Council of Europe.

—— (2002), 'Criminology and penal policy: The vital role of empirical research', in A. Bottoms and M. Tonry (eds), *Ideology, crime and criminal justice: a symposium in honour of Sir Leon Radzinowicz*, Cullompton, UK: Willan.

JOLLIFFE, D. and FARRINGTON, D. P. (2008), *The influence of mentoring on reoffending*, Stockholm: Swedish National Council for Crime Prevention.

—— and —— (2009), *Effectiveness of interventions with adult male violent offenders*, Stockholm: Swedish National Council for Crime Prevention.

KENNARD, D. (1994), 'The future revisited: New frontiers for therapeutic communities', *Therapeutic Communities*, 15: 107–13.

KILLIAS, M., VILLETTAZ, P., and ZODER, I. (2006), *The effects of custodial vs. non-custodial sentences on reoffending: A systematic review of the state of knowledge*. www.campbellcollaboration.org/reviews_crime_justice/index.php.

KINGDON, J. (2003), *Agendas, alternatives, and public policies*, 3rd edn, New York: Longman.

KOEHLER, J., LÖSEL, F., AKOENSI, T., and HUMPHRIES, D. (2011a), *A systematic review and meta-analysis on the effects of young offender treatment programmes in Europe*, Research report of the STARR Project, Cambridge: Institute of Criminology.

——, HUMPHREYS, D. K., AKOENSI, T. D., SÁNCHEZ DE RIBERA, O., and LÖSEL, F. (2011b), *A systematic review and meta-analysis on the effects of drug treatment programmes to reduce reoffending in Europe*, Research report of the STARR Project, University of Cambridge: Institute of Criminology.

LANDENBERGER, N. A. and LIPSEY, M. W. (2005), 'The positive effects of cognitive-behavioral programs for offenders: a meta-analysis of factors associated with effective treatment', *Journal of Experimental Criminology*, 1: 451–76.

LATIMER, J. (2001), 'A meta-analytic examination of youth delinquency, family treatment, and recidivism', *Canadian Journal of Criminology*, 43: 237–53.

LAUB, J. H. and SAMPSON, R. J. (2007), *Shared beginnings, divergent lives: Delinquent boys to age 70*, Cambridge, MA: Harvard University Press.

LEES, J., MANNING, N., and RAWLING, B. (1999), *Therapeutic community effectiveness: A systematic international review of therapeutic community treatment for people with personality disorders and mentally disordered offenders*, University of York, UK: Centre for Research and Dissemination.

LESCHIED, A. W. and CUNNINGHAM, A., (2002), *Seeking effective interventions for serious young offenders: Interim results of a four-year randomized study of multisystemic therapy in Ontario, Canada*, London, CAN: Centre for Children & Families in Justice.

LIEBLING, A. and ARNOLD, H. (2002), 'Measuring the quality of prison life', *Research Findings 174*, London: Home Office.

—— (2005), *Prisons and their moral performance: a study of values, quality, and prison life*, Oxford: Oxford University Press.

LIPSEY, M. W. (1992a), 'Juvenile delinquency treatment: A meta-analytic inquiry into variability of effects', in T. D. Cook, H. Cooper, D. S. Cordray, H. Hartmann, L. V. Hedges, R. L. Light, T. A. Louis, and F. Mosteller (eds), *Meta-analysis for explanation*, New York: Russell Sage Foundation.

—— (1992b), 'The effect of treatment on juvenile delinquents: Results from meta-analysis', in F. Lösel, D. Bender, and T. Bliesener (eds), *Psychology and law: International perspectives*, Berlin: de Gruyter.

—— (2003), 'Those confounded moderators in meta-analysis: Good, bad, and ugly', *Annals of the*

*American Academy of Political and Social Science*, 587: 69–81.

—— (2009), 'The primary factors that characterize effective interventions with juvenile offenders', *Victims and Offenders*, 4: 124–47.

—— and CULLEN, F. T. (2007), 'The effectiveness of correctional rehabilitation: A review of systematic reviews', *Annual Review of Law and Social Science*, 3: 297–320.

—— and LANDENBERGER, N. A. (2006), 'Cognitive-behavioral interventions', in B. C. Welsh and D. P. Farrington (eds), *Preventing crime: What works for children, offenders, victims, and places*, Dordrecht, NL: Springer.

——, LANDENBERGER, N. A., and WILSON, S. (2007), *Effects of cognitive-behavioral programs for criminal offenders*, Systematic review for the Campbell Collaboration: www.campbellcollaboration.org/reviews_crime_justice/index.php.

—— and WILSON, D. B. (1993), 'The efficacy of psychological, educational, and behavioral treatment: Confirmation from meta-analysis', *American Psychologist*, 48: 1181–209.

—— and —— (1998), 'Effective intervention for serious juvenile offenders', in R. Loeber and D. P. Farrington (eds), *Serious and violent juvenile offenders*, Thousand Oaks, CA: Sage.

LIPTON D. S., MARTINSON R., and WILKS, J. (1975), *The effectiveness of correctional treatment*, New York: Praeger.

——, PEARSON, F. S., CLELAND C. M., and YEE, D. (2002), 'The effects of therapeutic communities and milieu therapy on recidivism', in J. McGuire (ed.), *Offender rehabilitation and treatment*, Chichester, UK: Wiley.

LITTELL, J. H. (2006), 'The case for Multisystemic Therapy: Evidence or orthodoxy?', *Children and Youth Services Review*, 28: 458–72.

LLOYD, C., MAIR G., and HOUGH, M. (1994), *Explaining reconviction rates: A critical analysis*, Home Office Research Study, 136, London, UK: HMSO.

LOEBER, R., FARRINGTON, D. P., STOUTHAMER LOEBER, M., and WHITE, H. R. (2008), *Violence and serious theft: Development and prediction from childhood to adulthood*, New York: Routledge.

LÖSEL, F. (1993), 'The effectiveness of treatment in institutional and community settings', *Criminal Behaviour and Mental Health*, 3: 416–37.

—— (1995a), 'The efficacy of correctional treatment: A review and synthesis of meta-evaluations', in J. McGuire (ed.), *What works: Reducing reoffending*, Chichester, UK: Wiley.

—— (1995b), 'Increasing consensus in the evaluation of offender rehabilitation? Lessons from research syntheses', *Psychology, Crime and Law*, 2: 10–30.

—— (1996), 'Changing patterns in the use of prisons: An evidence-based perspective', *European Journal on Criminal Policy and Research*, 4: 108–27.

—— (1998), 'Treatment and management of psychopaths', in D. J. Cooke, A. E. Forth, and R. B. Hare (eds), *Psychopathy: Theory, research and implications for society*, Dordrecht: Kluwer Academic Publishers.

—— (2000), 'The efficacy of sexual offender treatment: A review of German and international evaluations', in P. J. van Koppen and N. H. M. Roos (eds), *Rationality, information and progress in psychology and law*, Maastricht, NL: Metajuridica Publications.

—— (2007), 'Doing evaluation in criminology: Balancing scientific and practical demands', in R. D. King and E. Wincup (eds), *Doing research on crime and justice*, 2nd edn, Oxford: Oxford University Press.

—— (2011), 'What works in correctional treatment and rehabilitation for young adults?', in F. Lösel, A. E. Bottoms, and D. P. Farrington (eds), *Young adult offenders: Lost in transition?*, Milton Park, UK: Routledge (in press).

—— and BEELMANN, A. (2003), 'Effects of child skills training in preventing antisocial behavior: A systematic review of randomized experiments', *Annals of the American Academy of Political and Social Science*, 587: 84–109.

—— and BENDER, D. (2003), 'Protective factors and resilience', in D. P. Farrington and J. Coid (eds), *Prevention of adult antisocial behaviour*, Cambridge: Cambridge University Press.

—— and BLIESENER, T. (1990), 'Resilience in adolescence: A study on the generalizability of protective factors', in K. Hurrelmann and F. Lösel (eds), *Health hazards in adolescence*, Berlin: De Gruyter.

—— and EGG, R. (1997), 'Social-therapeutic institutions in Germany: Description and evaluation', in E. Cullen, L. Jones, and R. Woodward (eds), *Therapeutic communities in prisons*, Chichester: Wiley.

—— and FARRINGTON, D. F. (2010), *Promotive and protective factors in the development of youth violence*, Paper for the U.S. Centres of Disease Control and Prevention, Atlanta, GA: CDC.

—— and KÖFERL, P. (1989), 'Evaluation research on correctional treatment in West Germany: A meta-analysis', in H. Wegener, F. Lösel, and J. Haisch (eds), *Criminal behavior and the justice system*, New York: Springer.

—— and SCHMUCKER, M. (2005), 'The effectiveness of treatment for sexual offenders: A comprehensive meta-analysis', *Journal of Experimental Criminology*, 1: 117–46.

—— and WITTMANN, W. (1989), 'The relationship of treatment integrity and intensity to outcome criteria', *New Directions for Program Evaluation*, 42: 97–107.

LOWENKAMP, C. T., HOLSINGER, A. M., and LATESSA, E. J. (2005), 'Are drug courts effective?' A meta-analytic review', *Journal of Community Corrections*, 28: 5–10.

MACKENZIE, D. L. (2006), *What works in corrections? Reducing the criminal activities of offenders and delinquents*, Cambridge: Cambridge University Press.

——, WILSON, D. B., and KIDER, S. B. (2001), 'Effects of correctional boot camps on offending', *Annals of the American Academy of Political and Social Science*, 578: 126–43.

MCDOUGALL, C., PERRY, A. E., CLARBOUR, J., BOWLES, R., and WORTHY, G. (2009), *Evaluation of HM Prison Service Enhanced Thinking Skills Programme*, Ministry of Justice Research Series 3/09, London: Ministry of Justice.

MCGUIRE J. (ed.) (2002a), *Offender rehabilitation and treatment: Effective programmes and policies to reduce re-offending*, Chichester, UK: Wiley.

—— (2002b), 'Integrating findings from research reviews', in J. McGuire (ed.), *Offender rehabilitation and treatment*, Chichester, UK: Wiley.

MCMURRAN, M. (2002), 'Motivation to change: selection criterion or treatment need?', in M. McMurran (ed.), *Motivating offenders to change*, Chichester, UK: Wiley.

—— and MCGUIRE, J. (eds) (2005), *Social problem solving and offending: Evidence, evaluation and evolution*, Chichester, UK: Wiley.

MCNEILL, F. (2006), 'A desistance paradigm for offender management', *Criminology and Criminal Justice*, 6: 39–62.

MAGUIRE, M. (2004), 'The Crime Reduction Programme: Reflections on the vision and the reality', *Criminology and Criminal Justice*, 4: 213–38.

——, GRUBIN, D., LÖSEL, F., and RAYNOR, P. (2010), '"What works" and the Correctional Services Accreditation Panel: Taking stock from an inside perspective', *Criminology and Criminal Justice*, 10: 37–58.

—— and RAYNOR, P. (2006), 'How the resettlement of prisoners promotes desistance from crime: Or does it?', *Criminology and Criminal Justice*, 6: 19–38.

MARTINSON, R. (1974), 'What works? Questions and answers about prison reform', *The Public Interest*, 35: 22–54.

MARUNA, S. (2001), *Making Good: How ex-convicts reform and rebuilt their lives*, Washington, DC: American Psychological Association.

MILLER, W. and ROLLNICK, S. (2002), *Motivational interviewing: preparing people for change*, 2nd edn, New York: Guilford.

MINISTRY OF JUSTICE (2010), *Breaking the cycle: Effective punishment, rehabilitation and sentencing of offenders*, London: Ministry of Justice.

MITCHELL, O., WILSON D. B., and MACKENZIE, D. L. (2007), 'Does incarceration-based drug treatment reduce reoffending? A meta-analytic synthesis of research', *Journal of Experimental Criminology*, 3: 353–75.

MOFFITT, T. E., CASPI, A., RUTTER, M., and SILVA, P. A. (2001), *Sex differences in antisocial behavior: Conduct disorder, delinquency, and violence in the Dunedin Longitudinal Study*, Cambridge: Cambridge University Press.

MOOS, R. (1975), *Evaluating correctional and community settings*, New York: Wiley.

MORALES, L. A., GARRIDO, V., and SÁNCHEZ-MECA, J. (2010), *Treatment effectiveness in secure corrections of serious (violent or chronic) juvenile offenders*, Stockholm: Swedish National Council for Crime Prevention.

MORGAN, R. (2007), 'Probation, governance and accountability', in L. Gelsthorpe and R. Morgan (eds), *Handbook of probation*, Cullompton, UK: Willan.

—— and OWERS, A. (2001), *Through the prison gate: A joint thematic review by HM Inspectorate of Prisons and Probation*, London: HM Inspectorate of Prisons.

NUGENT, W. R., WILLIAMS, R., and UMBREIT, M. S. (2003), 'Participation in victim-offender mediation and the prevalence of subsequent delinquent behavior: a meta-analysis', *Utah Law Review*, 137: 137–66.

ODGERS, C. L. and MORETTI, M. M. (2002), 'Aggressive and antisocial girls: Research update and challenges', *International Journal of Forensic Mental Health*, 1: 103–19.

OGDEN, T. and HAGEN, K, (2006), 'Multisystemic treatment of serious behavior problems in youth: sustainability of effectiveness two years after intake', *Child and Adolescent Mental Health*, 11: 142–49.

OGLOFF, J. R. P. and DAVIS, M. R. (2004), 'Advances in offender assessment and rehabilitation: Contributions of the risk-needs-responsivity approach', *Psychology, Crime and Law*, 10: 229–42.

ORLINSKY, D. E., GRAWE, K., and PARKS, B. K. (1994), 'Process and outcome in psychotherapy', in A. E. Bergin and S. L. Garfield (eds), *Handbook of psychotherapy and behavior change*, 4th edn., New York: Wiley.

PALMER, T. (1975), 'Martinson revisited', *Journal of Research in Criminology*, 12: 133–52.

—— (1992), *The re-emergence of correctional intervention*, Newbury Park, CA: Sage.

—— (1995), 'Programmatic and non-programmatic aspects of successful interventions: new directions for research', *Crime and Delinquency*, 41: 100–131.

PEARSON, F. S. and LIPTON, D. S., (1999), 'A meta-analytic review of the effectiveness of correction-based treatments for drug abuse', *Prison Journal*, 79: 384–410.

——, LIPTON, D. S., and CLELAND, C. M. (1997), *Rehabilitative programs in adult corrections: CDATE meta-analysis*, Paper presented at the Annual Meeting of the American Society of Criminology, San Diego.

——, ——, ——, and YEE, D. S. (2002), 'The effects of behavioral/cognitive-behavioral programs on recidivism', *Crime and Delinquency*, 48: 476–96.

PETROSINO A. and SOYDAN, H. (2005), 'The impact of program developers as evaluators on criminal recidivism: results from meta-analyses of experimental and quasi-experimental research', *Journal of Experimental Criminology*, 1: 435–50.

——, TURPIN-PETROSINO, C., and BUEHLER, J. (2003), 'Scared straight and other juvenile awareness programs for preventing juvenile delinquency: a systematic review of randomized experimental evidence', *Annals of the American Academy of Social and Political Science*, 589: 41–62.

PORPORINO, F. (2010), 'Bringing sense and sensitivity to corrections: from programmes to "fix" offenders to services to support desistance, in J. Brayford, F. Cowe, and J. Dering (eds), *What else* works? Creative work with offenders, Cullompton, UK: Willan.

PROCHASKA, J. O. and LEVESQUE, D. A. (2002), 'Enhancing motivation of offenders at each stage of change and phase of therapy', in M. McMurran (ed.), Motivating offenders to change, Chichester: Wiley.

RAYNOR, P. and ROBINSON, G. (2005), Rehabilitation, crime and justice, Basingstoke: Palgrave Macmillan.

REDONDO, S., SÁNCHEZ-MECA, J., and GARRIDO, V. (1999), 'The influence of treatment programmes on the recidivism of juvenile and adult offenders: A European meta-analytic review', Psychology, Crime and Law, 5: 251–78.

——, ——, and —— (2002), 'Crime treatment in Europe: A review of outcome studies', in J. McGuire (ed.), Offender rehabilitation and treatment: Effective programmes and policies to reduce re-offending, Chichester: Wiley.

RENZEMA, M. and MAYO-WILSON, E. (2005), 'Can electronic monitoring reduce crime for moderate to high-risk offenders?', Journal of Experimental Criminology, 1: 215–37.

RICE, M. E., HARRIS, G. T., and CORMIER, C. A. (1992), 'An evaluation of a maximum security therapeutic community for psychopaths and other mentally disordered offenders', Law and Human Behavior, 16: 399–412.

ROBERTS, J. (1997), 'History of the therapeutic community', in E. Cullon, L. Jones, and R. Woodward (eds), Therapeutic communities for offenders, Chichester, UK: Wiley.

ROMIG, A. D. (1978), Justice for our children: An examination of juvenile delinquent rehabilitation programs, Lexington, MA: Lexington Books.

ROSS, R. D. and ROSS D. R. (eds) (1995), Thinking straight: The Reasoning and Rehabilitation program for delinquency prevention and offender rehabilitation, Ottawa: Air Training and Publications.

SADLIER, G. (2010), Evaluation of the impact of the HM Prison Service Enhanced Thinking Skills programme on reoffending outcomes of the Surveying Prisoner Crime Reduction (SPCR) sample, Ministry of Justice Research Series 19/10, London: Ministry of Justice.

SALEKIN, R. T., WORLEY, C., and GRIMES, R. D. (2010), 'Treatment of psychopathy: A review and brief introduction to the mental model approach for psychopathy', Behavioral Sciences and the Law, 28: 235–66.

SAMPSON, R. J. and LAUB, J. H. (1993), Crime in the making: Pathways and turning points through life, Cambridge, MA: Harvard University Press.

SCHMUCKER, M. and LÖSEL, F. (2009), 'A systematic review of high-quality evaluations of sexual offender treatment', Paper presented at the 9th Annual Conference of the European Society of Criminology, 9–12 September 2009, Ljubljana, Slovenia.

SECHREST, L. B., WHITE, S. O., and BROWN, E. D. (1979), The rehabilitation of criminal offenders: problems and prospects, Washington, DC: National Academy of Sciences.

SHAFFER, D. K. and PRATT, T. C. (2009), 'Meta-analysis, moderators, and treatment effectiveness: The importance of digging deeper for evidence of program integrity', Journal of Offender Rehabilitation, 48: 101–19.

SHAPLAND, J., ATKINSON, A., ATKINSON, H., DIGNAN, J., EDWARDS, L., HIBBERT, J., HOWES, M., JOHNSTONE, J., ROBINSON, G., and SORSBY, A. (2008), Does restorative justice affect reconviction?, Ministry of Justice Research Series No. 10/08, London: National Offender Management Service.

SHERMAN, L. W. (2009), 'Testing for analysts' bias in crime prevention experiments: can we accept Eisner's one tailed test?', Journal of Experimental Criminology, 5: 185–200.

SHERMAN, L. W., GOTTFREDSON, D. C., MACKENZIE, D. L., ECK, J. E., REUTER, P., and BUSHWAY, S. D. (1997), Preventing crime: What works, what doesn't, what's promising, Washington, DC: U.S. Department of Justice, National Institute of Justice.

—— and STRANG, H. (2007), Restorative justice: The evidence, London: The Smith Institute.

SMITH, M. L., GLASS, G. V., and MILLER, W. R. (1980), The benefits of psychotherapy, Baltimore: John Hopkins Press.

SMITH, P., GOGGIN, C., and GENDREAU, P. (2002), The effects of prison sentences and intermediate sanctions on recidivism: General effects and individual differences, Research Report JS42–103/2002, Ottawa: Public Works and Government Services Canada.

SUNDELL, K., HANSSON, K., LÖFHOLM, C. A., et al, (2008) 'The transportability of multisystemic therapy to Sweden: Short-term results from a randomized trial of conduct disordered youths', Journal of Family Psychology, 22: 550–60.

THEOBALD, D. and FARRINGTON, D. P. (2009), 'Effects of getting married on offending: Results from a prospective longitudinal survey of males', European Journal of Criminology, 6: 496–516.

TOLAN, P., HENRY, D., SCHOENY, M., and BASS, A. (2008), 'Mentoring interventions to affect juvenile delinquency and associated problems', Campbell Collaboration, www.campbellcollaboration.org/reviews_crime_justice/index.php.

TONG, L. S. J. and FARRINGTON, D. P. (2006), 'How effective is the Reasoning and Rehabilitation programme in reducing offending? A meta-analysis of evaluations in four countries', Psychology, Crime and Law, 12: 3–24.

TRAVERS, R., WAKELING, H. C., MANN, R. E., and HOLLIN, C. R. (2010), 'Reconviction following a cognitive skills intervention: An alternative quasi-experimental methodology', Legal and Criminological Psychology (published online 2011).

VISHER, C. A., WINTERFIELD, L., and COGGESHALL, M. B. (2006), 'Systematic review of non-custodial employment programs: Impact on recidivism rates of ex-offenders'. www.campbellcollaboration.org/reviews_crime_justice/index.php.

VON HIRSCH, A. (1976), Doing justice: The choice of punishments, Boston, MA: Northeastern University Press.

Von Liszt, F. (1882/83), *Der Zweckgedanke im Strafrecht* [The purpose of thought in criminal law], Berlin: de Gruyter.

Wakeling, H. C., Mann, R. E., and Travers, R. (2011), *Reconviction following sex offender treatment: An alternative quasi-experimental methodology*, Unpublished paper, London: NOMS.

Walker, N. (1991), *Why punish?*, Oxford, UK: Oxford University Press.

Walmsley, R. (2008), *World prison population list*, 8th edn, London: King's College International Centre of Prison Studies.

Ward, T. and Brown, M. (2004), 'The good lives model and conceptual issues in offender rehabilitation', *Psychology, Crime and Law*, 10: 243–57.

Ward, T. and Maruna, S. (2007), *Rehabilitation: Beyond the risk-paradigm*, London: Routledge.

——, Mann, R. E., and Gannon, T. A. (2007), 'The good lives model of offender rehabilitation: Clinical implications', *Aggression and Violent Behavior*, 12: 87–107.

Ware, J., Mann, R. E., and Wakeling, H. C. (2009), 'Group versus individual treatment: What is the best modality for treating sexual offenders?', *Sexual Abuse in Australia and New Zealand*, 1: 70–8.

Weisburd, D., Lum, C. M., and Petrosino, A. (2001), 'Does research design affect study outcomes in criminal justice?', *The Annals of the American Academy of Political and Social Science*, 578: 50–70.

Welsh, B. C. and Farrington, D. P. (2000), 'Correctional intervention programs and cost benefit analysis', *Criminal Justice and Behavior*, 27: 115–33.

——, Peel, M. E., Farrington, D. P., Elffers, H., and Braga, A. A. (2011), 'Research design influence on study outcomes in crime and justice: a partial replication with public area surveillance', *Journal of Experimental Criminology*, 7 (published online 2010).

Wermink, H., Blokland, A., Nieuwberta, P., Nagin, D., and Tollenaar, N. (2010), 'Comparing the effects of community service and short-term imprisonment on recidivism: a matched samples approach', *Journal of Experimental Criminology*, 6: 325–49.

Werner, E. E. and Smith, R. S. (1992), *Overcoming the odds*, Ithaca, NY: Cornell University Press.

Whitehead, P.R., Ward, T., and Collie, R. M. (2007), 'Time for a change: Applying the Good Lives Model of rehabilitation to a high-risk violent offender', *International Journal of Offender Therapy and Comparative Criminology*, 51: 578–98.

Wilson, D. B., Gallagher, C.A., and Mackenzie, D. L. (2000), 'A meta-analysis of correction-based education, vocation, and work programs for adult offenders', *Journal of Research on Crime and Delinquency*, 37: 347–68.

——, Lipsey, M. W., and Soydan, H. (2003), 'Are mainstream programs for juvenile delinquency less effective with minority youth than majority youth? A meta-analysis of outcomes research', *Research on Social Work Practice*, 13: 3–26.

——, Mitchell, O., and Mackenzie, D. L. (2006), 'A systematic review of drug court effects on recidivism', *Journal of Experimental Criminology*, 2: 459–87.

Windlesham, D. (1998), *Politics, punishment and populism*, New York: Oxford University Press.

Wormith, J. S., Althouse, R., Simpson, M., Reitzel, L. R., Fagan, T. L., and Morgan, R. D. (2007), 'The rehabilitation and reintegration of offenders: The current landscape and some future directions for correctional psychology', *Criminal Justice and Behavior*, 34: 879–92.

Zahn, M. A., Day, J. C., Mihalic, S. F., and Tichavsy, L. (2009), 'Determining what works for girls in the juvenile justice system', *Crime and Delinquency*, 55: 266–93.

# INDEX

# Oxford University Press publishes an impressive range of inspiring criminology titles

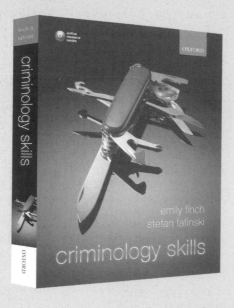

**Criminology Skills**
March 2012

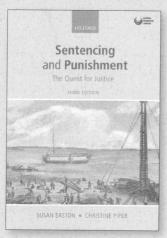

**Sentencing and Punishment**
June 2012

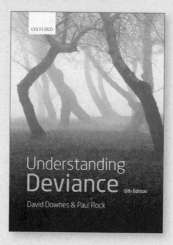

**Understanding Deviance**
March 2011

**The British Journal of Criminology**
www.bjc.oxfordjournals.org